The
Mother
of All
Baby Name
Books

The Mother of All Baby Name Books

Over 94,000 Baby Names Complete with Origins and Meanings

Bruce Lansky

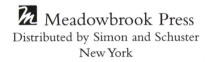 Meadowbrook Press
Distributed by Simon and Schuster
New York

Acknowledgments

The lists of the most popular girls' and boys' names in the United States were compiled by the Social Security Administration. The lists are based on a 100 percent sample of social security card applications through the first nine months of the year noted. The names are not grouped by variant spellings. (For example, Hannah and Hanna are treated as two separate names and ranked based on their individual popularity.)

Library of Congress Cataloging-in-Publication Data

Lansky, Bruce.
   The mother of all baby name books : over 94,000 names complete with origins and meanings / by Bruce Lansky.
       p. cm.
   ISBN 0-88166-451-0 (Meadowbrook)   ISBN 0-684-01870-5 (Simon & Schuster)
   1. Names, Personal—Dictionaries. I. Title
   CS2377 .L373 2003
   929.4'4--dc21

                                                                    2002153553

Editorial Director: Christine Zuchora-Walske
Editors: Megan McGinnis and Angela Wiechmann
Contributing Editor: Liya Lev Oertel
Production Manager: Paul Woods
Art Director: Peggy Bates
Desktop Publishing: Danielle White
Cover Photos: Digital Vision, Corbis Images, Eyewire Images, Hemera,
                MediaFocus International

Published by Meadowbrook Press, 5451 Smetana Drive, Minnetonka, Minnesota 55343

www.meadowbrookpress.com

BOOK TRADE DISTRIBUTION by Simon & Schuster, a division of Simon and Schuster, Inc., 1230 Avenue of the Americas, New York, New York 10020

07 06 05   13 12 11 10 9 8 7 6 5

Printed in the United States of America

Contents

15 Things to Consider When Naming Your Baby

1. Namesakes

Exact reproductions of a person's name, even if it is followed by Jr. or II, are often confusing to everyone involved. Parents frequently vary the middle name of a son who carries his father's first and last names, and then call the son by his middle name to distinguish him from his father; but the potential for confusion still exists. What's worse, the child never gets the satisfaction of having a name and a clear identity of his own.

Namesakes can also lead to unfortunate name choices. Somehow the name Mildred just doesn't seem to fit a little girl comfortably, even though it fits eighty-year-old Aunt Mildred perfectly. Generally, make sure that a namesake's name is one you'd choose on its own merits, quite apart from the good feelings you have for the person you're complimenting this way.

2. Nationality

If you choose a "foreign-sounding" name, be sure it's not unpronounceable or unspellable, or the name will be a burden to your child. Combinations of names from different countries, like Francois Finklebaum or Marco Mazarowski, may provoke smiles. So if you want to combine names with different ethnic roots, try them out on lots of people before making a final decision.

3. Religion

To some parents it is important to follow religious traditions in naming a baby. Roman Catholics have traditionally chosen saints' names, sometimes using Mary as a first name for each daughter and pairing it with different middle names: Mary Rose, Mary Margaret, and so on. Jews traditionally choose Old Testament names, often the name of a deceased relative, while Protestants choose both Old and New Testament names. Muslims turn to the Koran and the names of Mohammed and his family as traditional sources of names.

4. Gender

There are two opposing lines of thought on names that can be given to boys and girls alike, whether they are changeable ones like Carol/Carroll, Leslie/Lesley, and Claire/Clair or the truly unisex names like Robin, Chris, and Terry. Some parents feel that a unisex name allows them to pick a name with certainty before the baby's sex is known and that such names "type" children in gender roles and expectations less than traditional boy names and girl names do. Others argue that it's unfair and psychologically harmful to require a child to explain which sex he or she is. (Remember the song "A Boy Named Sue"?) Finally, boys may feel more threatened or insulted when they are presumed to be girls than girls may when they're taken to be boys.

5. Number of Names

No law requires a person to have three names, though most forms provide spaces for a first name, middle initial or name, and surname. When choosing a name for your child, you have several options: a first and last name; a first and last name and only a middle initial (Harry S. Truman's S is just an S); initials for both first and middle names; or several middle names. Keep your child's lifelong use of the name in mind when you do something unusual—four middle names are going to cause space problems for your child every time he or she fills out a form!

6. Sounds

The combination of letters in a person's name can make saying the name easier or harder. Alliteration, as in Tina Turner or Pat Paulsen, is fine, but such rhymes as Tyrone Cohn or Alice Palace invite teasing. Joke names, punning names, and other displays of your wit may sound funny, but living with such a name is no laughing matter.

7. Rhythms

Most naming specialists agree that unequal numbers of syllables create pleasing rhythms. Such names as Dwight David Eisenhower or Molly Melinda Grooms fit this pattern. When first and last names have equal numbers of syllables, a middle name with a different number creates a nice effect, as in Albert Anthony Cleveland or Gail Canova Pons. Single-syllable names can be especially forceful if each name has a rather long sound, as in Mark Twain or Charles Rath.

8. Pronunciation

Nobody likes having his or her name constantly mispronounced. If you pick an unusual name, such as Jésus or Genviève (hay-soos and zhan-vee-ev), don't expect people to pronounce it correctly. Other names with high mispronunciation potential are names that have more than one common pronunciation, as in Alicia (does the second syllable rhyme with fish or leash?) or Shana (does the name rhyme with Anna or Dana?). And if you choose a unique pronunciation of a name (for example, pronouncing Nina like Dinah), don't expect many people to get it right.

9. Spelling

In his poem *Don Juan,* Lord Byron writes, "Thrice happy he whose name has been well spelt," and it's true that you feel a special kind of irritation when your name gets misspelled.

Ordinary spellings have the force of common sense behind them. On the other hand, a new or unusual spelling can revitalize an old name. If the name Ethel only reminds you of Ethel Mertz in the old *I Love Lucy* show, but your mate is crazy about having a daughter with that name, perhaps Ethelle will be a happy substitute. However, some people think it's silly to vary from "traditional" spellings of names and are prejudiced against any Thom, Dik, or Hari.

10. Popularity

Some names are so popular, you shouldn't be surprised to find more than one child with that name in your child's classroom. A child with a very popular name may feel that he or she must "share" it with others, while a child with a very uncommon name is likely to feel that it is uniquely his or hers. However, a child with a popular name may be accepted by peers more easily than a child with a very uncommon name, which may be perceived as weird.

11. Uniqueness

Did you ever try to look in the phone book for the telephone number of someone called John Smith? You wouldn't be able to find it without also knowing the address. To avoid confusion, many people with common last names choose distinctive first and/or middle names for their children. However, a highly unusual name, such as Teague or Hestia, could be an even greater disservice to your child than Michael or Emily.

12. Stereotypes

Most names call to mind physical or personality traits that often stem from a well-known namesake, real or fictional. Some names—Adolf and Judas, for instance—may never outlive the terrible associations they receive from a single person who bore them. Because the image of a name will affect its owner's self-image as well as the way he or she is perceived by others, consider what associations come to mind as you make your selections.

13. Initials

Folk wisdom has it that a person whose initials spell a word—any word—is destined to be successful in life. But it can be irksome, even embarrassing, to have DUD or HAG stamped on your suitcases and jewelry. So be sure your child's initials spell "happy" words—or none at all—to avoid these problems.

14. Nicknames

Most names have shortened or familiar forms that are used during childhood or at different stages of life. For example, Michael might be called Mikey as a child, Mike as a teenager, and Michael on his college application. So if you don't want your daughter to be called Sam, don't name her Samantha.

If you are thinking of giving your child a nickname as a legal name, remember that Trisha may grow weary of explaining that her full name is not Patricia. And consider the fact that names that sound cute for a child, as in Missy and Timmy, could prove embarrassing later in life. Can you picture Grandma Missy and Grandpa Timmy?

15. Meanings

Most people don't know the meanings of their names—first, middle, or last. But most names do have meanings, and you should at least find out what your favorite choices mean before giving them to your child. A name that means something funny or embarrassing probably won't overshadow your child's life, but if you have to choose between two names that are equally attractive to you, meanings may help tip the balance.

The 100 Most Popular Girls' Names of 2002

1. Emily
2. Madison
3. Hannah
4. Emma
5. Alexis
6. Ashley
7. Abigail
8. Sarah
9. Samantha
10. Olivia
11. Elizabeth
12. Alyssa
13. Lauren
14. Isabella
15. Grace
16. Jessica
17. Brianna
18. Taylor
19. Kayla
20. Anna
21. Victoria
22. Megan
23. Sydney
24. Chloe
25. Rachel
26. Jasmine
27. Sophia
28. Jennifer
29. Morgan
30. Natalie
31. Julia
32. Kaitlyn
33. Hailey
34. Destiny
35. Haley
36. Katherine
37. Nicole
38. Alexandra
39. Maria
40. Savannah
41. Stephanie
42. Mia
43. Mackenzie
44. Allison
45. Amanda
46. Jordan
47. Jenna
48. Faith
49. Paige
50. Makayla
51. Andrea
52. Mary
53. Brooke
54. Katelyn
55. Rebecca
56. Madeline
57. Michelle
58. Kaylee
59. Sara
60. Kimberly
61. Zoe
62. Kylie
63. Aaliyah
64. Sierra
65. Amber
66. Caroline
67. Gabrielle
68. Vanessa
69. Alexa
70. Trinity
71. Danielle
72. Erin
73. Autumn
74. Angelina
75. Shelby
76. Gabriella
77. Riley
78. Jada
79. Lily
80. Melissa
81. Jacqueline
82. Angela
83. Ava
84. Isabel
85. Bailey
86. Ariana
87. Jade
88. Melanie
89. Courtney
90. Leah
91. Maya
92. Ella
93. Jocelyn
94. Leslie
95. Claire
96. Christina
97. Lillian
98. Evelyn
99. Gabriela
100. Catherine

The 100 Most Popular Boys' Names of 2002

1. Jacob
2. Michael
3. Joshua
4. Matthew
5. Ethan
6. Joseph
7. Andrew
8. Christopher
9. Daniel
10. Nicholas
11. William
12. Anthony
13. David
14. Tyler
15. Alexander
16. Ryan
17. John
18. James
19. Zachary
20. Brandon
21. Jonathan
22. Justin
23. Christian
24. Dylan
25. Samuel
26. Austin
27. Jose
28. Benjamin
29. Nathan
30. Logan
31. Kevin
32. Gabriel
33. Robert
34. Noah
35. Caleb
36. Thomas
37. Jordan
38. Hunter
39. Cameron
40. Kyle
41. Elijah
42. Jason
43. Jack
44. Aaron
45. Isaiah
46. Angel
47. Luke
48. Connor
49. Luis
50. Isaac
51. Brian
52. Juan
53. Jackson
54. Eric
55. Mason
56. Adam
57. Evan
58. Carlos
59. Charles
60. Sean
61. Gavin
62. Alex
63. Aidan
64. Bryan
65. Nathaniel
66. Jesus
67. Ian
68. Steven
69. Cole
70. Timothy
71. Cody
72. Adrian
73. Seth
74. Sebastian
75. Devin
76. Lucas
77. Richard
78. Blake
79. Julian
80. Patrick
81. Trevor
82. Jared
83. Miguel
84. Chase
85. Dominic
86. Antonio
87. Xavier
88. Jeremiah
89. Jaden
90. Alejandro
91. Jeremy
92. Jesse
93. Garrett
94. Diego
95. Mark
96. Owen
97. Hayden
98. Victor
99. Bryce
100. Riley

Baby Name Worksheet

Mom's Favorite Names

rating	girls	rating	boys
_____	_____	_____	_____
_____	_____	_____	_____
_____	_____	_____	_____
_____	_____	_____	_____
_____	_____	_____	_____
_____	_____	_____	_____
_____	_____	_____	_____
_____	_____	_____	_____
_____	_____	_____	_____
_____	_____	_____	_____
_____	_____	_____	_____
_____	_____	_____	_____
_____	_____	_____	_____

Dad's Favorite Names

rating	girls	rating	boys
_____	_____	_____	_____
_____	_____	_____	_____
_____	_____	_____	_____
_____	_____	_____	_____
_____	_____	_____	_____
_____	_____	_____	_____
_____	_____	_____	_____
_____	_____	_____	_____
_____	_____	_____	_____
_____	_____	_____	_____
_____	_____	_____	_____

The Mother of All Baby Name Books

Final Choice Worksheet

Girls' Names

rating	first	middle	last
_____	_____	_____	_____
_____	_____	_____	_____
_____	_____	_____	_____
_____	_____	_____	_____
_____	_____	_____	_____
_____	_____	_____	_____
_____	_____	_____	_____
_____	_____	_____	_____
_____	_____	_____	_____

Boys' Names

rating	first	middle	last
_____	_____	_____	_____
_____	_____	_____	_____
_____	_____	_____	_____
_____	_____	_____	_____
_____	_____	_____	_____
_____	_____	_____	_____
_____	_____	_____	_____
_____	_____	_____	_____

The 15 Things to Consider:

namesakes, nationality, religion, gender, number of names, sounds, rhythms, pronunciation, spelling, popularity, uniqueness, stereotypes, initials, nicknames, meanings.

Girls

'Aolani (Hawaiian) heavenly cloud.
Aolanee, Aolaney, Aolania, Aolaniah, Aolanie, Aolany, Aolanya

'Aulani (Hawaiian) royal messenger.
Aulanee, Aulaney, Aulania, Aulanie, Aulany, Aulanya, Aulanyah, Lani, Lanie

A'lexus (American) a form of Alexis.

Aaleyah (Hebrew) a form of Aliya.
Aalayah, Aalayaha, Aalea, Aaleah, Aaleaha, Aaleeyah, Aaleyiah, Aaleyyah

Aaliah (Hebrew) a form of Aliya.
Aaliaya, Aaliayah

Aalisha (Greek) a form of Alisha.
Aaleasha, Aaliesha

Aaliya, Aaliyah (Hebrew) forms of Aliya.
Aahliyah, Aailiyah, Aailyah, Aalaiya, Aalia, Aalieyha, Aaliyaha, Aaliyha, Aalliah, Aalliyah

Aalyiah (Hebrew) a form of Aliya.
Aalyah

Aaron (Hebrew) enlightened. (Arabic) messenger. Bible: the brother of Moses and the first high priest. See also Arin, Erin.

Aarti (Hebrew, Hindi) a form of Arti.

Aasta (Norse) love.
Aastah, Asta, Astah

Aba (Fante, Twi) born on Thursday.

Abagael, Abagail, Abbagail (Hebrew) forms of Abigail.
Abagaile, Abagale, Abagayle, Abageal, Abagil, Abbagael, Abbagale, Abbagayle

Abbey, Abbi, Abbie, Abby (Hebrew) familiar forms of Abigail.
Aabbee, Abbe, Abbea, Abbee, Abbeigh, Abbye, Abea, Abee, Abeey, Abey, Abi, Abia, Abie, Aby

Abbigail, Abbigale, Abbigayle, Abigael, Abigayle (Hebrew) forms of Abigail.
Abbigael, Abbigal, Abbigayl

Abbygail, Abygail (Hebrew) forms of Abigail.
Abbygael, Abbygale, Abbygayl, Abbygayle, Abygael, Abygaile, Abygale, Abygayl, Abygayle

Abeer (Hebrew) a short form of Abira.
Abeir, Abiir, Abir

Abegail (Hebrew) a form of Abigail.
Abegael, Abegaile, Abegale, Abegayle

Abelina (American) a combination of Abbey + Lina.
Abilana, Abilene

Abena (Akan) born on Tuesday.
Abenah, Abeni, Abina, Abinah, Abyna, Abynah

Abia (Arabic) great.
Abbia, Abbiah, Abiah, Abya

Abiann, Abianne (American) combinations of Abbey + Ann.
Abian

Abida (Arabic) worshiper.
Abedah, Abidah

Abigail (Hebrew) father's joy. Bible: one of the wives of King David. See also Gail.
Abaigael, Abaigeal, Abbegaele, Abbegail, Abbegale, Abbegayle, Abbeygale, Abbiegail, Abbiegayle, Abgail, Abgale, Abgayle, Abigaile, Abigaill, Abigal, Abigale, Abigayil, Abigayl, Abigel, Abigial, Abugail, Avigail

Abinaya (American) a form of Abiann.
Abenaa, Abenaya, Abinaa, Abinaiya, Abinayan

Abira (Hebrew) my strength.
Abbira, Abeerah, Abera, Aberah, Abhira, Abirah, Abyra, Abyrah

Abra (Hebrew) mother of many nations.
Abrah, Abree, Abri

Abria (Hebrew) a form of Abra.
Abrea, Abréa, Abreia, Abriah, Abriéa, Abrya, Abryah

Abrial (French) open; secure, protected.
Abrail, Abreal, Abreale, Abriale

Abriana, Abrianna (Italian) forms of Abra.
Abbrienna, Abbryana, Abranna, Abrannah,
Abreana, Abreanna, Abreanne, Abreeana,
Abreona, Abreonia, Abrianah, Abriania,
Abrianiah, Abriann, Abriannah, Abrieana,
Abrien, Abrienna, Abrienne, Abrietta,
Abrion, Abrionée, Abrionne, Abriunna,
Abryan, Abryana, Abryanah, Abryann,
Abryanna, Abryannah, Abryanne, Abryona

Abrielle (French) a form of Abrial.
Aabriella, Abriel, Abriela, Abriell, Abryele,
Abryell, Abryella, Abryelle

Abril (French) a form of Abrial.
Abrilla, Abrille

Acacia (Greek) thorny. Mythology: the
acacia tree symbolizes immortality and
resurrection. See also Casey.
Acaciah, Acacya, Acacyah, Acasha, Acatia,
Accassia, Acey, Acie, Akacia, Cacia, Caciah,
Cacya, Cacyah, Casia, Kasia

Achilla (Greek) a form of Achilles (see
Boys' Names).
Achila, Achilah, Achillah, Achyla, Achylah,
Achylla, Achyllah

Acima (Illyrian) praised by God.
Acimah, Acyma, Acymah

Ada (German) a short form of Adelaide.
(English) prosperous; happy. (Hebrew) a
form of Adah.
Adabelle, Adan, Adaya, Adda, Auda

Adah (Hebrew) ornament. (German,
English) a form of Ada.
Addah

Adair (Greek) a form of Adara.
Adaire, Adare, Adayr, Adayre

Adalene (Spanish) a form of Adalia.
Adalane, Adalena, Adalin, Adalina, Adaline,
Adalinn, Adalyn, Adalynn, Adalynne,
Addalyn, Addalynn

Adalia (German, Spanish) noble.
Adal, Adala, Adalah, Adalea, Adaleah,
Adalee, Adalene, Adali, Adaliah, Adalie,
Adall, Adalla, Adalle, Adallia, Adalliah,
Adallya, Adallyah, Adaly, Adalya, Adalyah,
Addal, Addala, Addaly

Adama (Phoenician, Hebrew) a form of
Adam (see Boys' Names).
Adamah, Adamia, Adamiah, Adamina,
Adaminah, Adamya, Adamyah, Adamyna,
Adamynah, Adamyne

Adamma (Ibo) child of beauty.

Adana (Spanish) a form of Adama.
Adanah, Adania, Adaniah, Adanya

Adanna (Nigerian) her father's daughter.

Adar (Syrian) ruler. (Hebrew) noble;
exalted.
Adare, Adayr

Adara (Greek) beauty. (Arabic) virgin.
Adaira, Adairah, Adaora, Adar, Adarah,
Adare, Adaria, Adarra, Adasha, Adauré,
Adayra, Adayrah

Adawna (Latin) beautiful sunrise.
Adawnah

Adaya (American) a form of Ada.
Adaija, Adaijah, Adaja, Adajah, Adayah,
Adayja, Adayjah, Addiah, Adejah

Addie, Addy (Greek, German) familiar
forms of Adelaide, Adrienne.
Aday, Adde, Addee, Addey, Addi, Addia,
Ade, Adee, Adei, Adey, Adeye, Adi, Adie,
Ady, Atti, Attie, Atty

Addison (English) child of Adam.
Addis, Addisen, Addisson

Addyson, Adyson (English) forms of
Addison.
Adysen

Adela (English) a short form of Adelaide.
Adelae, Adelah, Adelista, Adella, Adelya,
Adelyah

Adelaida (German) a form of Adelaide.
Adelayda, Adelaydah, Adelka

Adelaide (German) noble and serene. See
also Ada, Adela, Adeline, Adele, Ailis,
Delia, Della, Ela, Elke, Heidi.
Adalaid, Adalaide, Adalayd, Adalayde,
Adelade, Adelaid, Adelais, Adelayd, Adelayde,
Adelei, Adelheid, Adeliade, Aley, Edelaid,
Edelaide, Laidey, Laidy

Adelais (French) a form of Adelaide.

Adele, Adelle (English) short forms of Adelaide, Adeline.
Adel, Adell, Adelie, Adile

Adelia (Spanish) a form of Adelaide.
Adeliah

Adelina (English) a form of Adeline.
Adalina, Adeleana, Adelena, Adeliana, Adellena, Adellyna, Adileena, Adlena

Adelinda (Teutonic) noble; serpent.
Adelindah, Adelynda, Adelyndah

Adeline (English) a form of Adelaide.
Adaline, Adelaine, Adeleine, Adelin, Adelind, Adelita, Adeliya, Adelyn, Adelyne, Adelynn, Adelynne, Adlin, Adline, Adlyn, Adlynn

Adelpha (Greek) sister.
Adelfa, Adelfah, Adelfe, Adelfia, Adelphah, Adelphe, Adelphia, Adelphya, Adelphyah

Adena (Hebrew) noble; adorned.
Adeana, Adeanah, Adeane, Adeen, Adeena, Adeenah, Adeene, Aden, Adenah, Adene, Adenia, Adenna

Adia (Swahili) gift.
Addia, Adea, Adéa, Adiah

Adiel (Hebrew) ornament of the Lord.
(African) goat.
Adiela, Adielah, Adiele, Adiell, Adiella, Adielle, Adyel, Adyela, Adyelah, Adyele, Adyell, Adyella, Adyellah, Adyelle

Adila (Arabic) equal.
Adeala, Adeela, Adeola, Adilah, Adileh, Adilia, Adyla

Adilene (English) a form of Adeline.
Adilen, Adileni, Adilenne, Adlen, Adlene

Adina (Hebrew) a form of Adena. See also Dina.
Adeana, Adiana, Adiena, Adinah, Adine, Adinna, Adyna, Adynah, Adyne

Adira (Hebrew) strong.
Ader, Adera, Aderah, Aderra, Adhira, Adirah, Adirana, Adyra, Adyrah

Adison (English) a form of Addison.
Adis, Adisa, Adisen, Adisynne

Aditi (Hindi) unbound. Religion: the mother of the Hindu sun gods.
Aditee, Adithi, Aditie, Aditti, Adity, Adytee, Adytey, Adyti, Adytie, Adyty

Adleigh (Hebrew) my ornament.
Adla, Adleni

Adonia (Spanish) beautiful.
Adoniah, Adonica, Adonis, Adonna, Adonnica, Adonya, Adonyah

Adora (Latin) beloved. See also Dora.
Adorah, Adore, Adoree, Adoria, Adoriah, Adorya, Adoryah

Adra (Arabic) virgin.

Adreana, Adreanna (Latin) forms of Adrienne.
Adrean, Adreanah, Adreane, Adreann, Adreannah, Adreanne, Adreauna, Adreeanna, Adreen, Adreena, Adreenah, Adreene, Adreeyana, Adrena, Adrene, Adrenea, Adréona, Adreonia, Adreonna

Adria (English) a short form of Adriana, Adrienne.
Adrea, Adreah, Adriah, Adriani, Adrya

Adrian, Adriane, Adrianne, Adrien, Adriene (English) forms of Adrienne.
Addrian, Adranne, Adriann

Adriana, Adrianna (Italian) forms of Adrienne.
Addrianna, Addriyanna, Adreiana, Adreinna, Adrianah, Adriannah, Adriannea, Adriannia, Adrionna

Adrielle (Hebrew) member of God's flock.
Adriel, Adrielli, Adryelle

Adrienna (Italian) a form of Adrienne. See also Edrianna.
Adrieanna, Adrieaunna, Adriena, Adrienah, Adrienia, Adriennah, Adrieunna, Adriyanna

Adrienne (Greek) rich. (Latin) dark. See also Hadriane.
Adreinne, Adriayon, Adrie, Adrieanne, Adrien, Adrienn, Adrion

Adrina (English) a short form of Adriana.
Adrinah, Adrine, Adrinne

Adriyanna (American) a form of Adrienne.
Adrieyana, Adriyana, Adryan, Adryana,
Adryanah, Adryane, Adryann, Adryanna,
Adryannah, Adryanne

Adya (Hindi) Sunday.
Adia

Aerial, Aeriel (Hebrew) forms of Ariel.
Aeriale, Aeriela, Aerielah, Aeriell, Aeriella,
Aeriellah, Aerielle, Aeril, Aerile, Aeryal

Aerin (Hebrew, Arabic) a form of Aaron,
Arin.

Aerona (Welsh) berry.
Aeronah, Aeronna, Aeronnah

Afi (African) born on Friday.
Affi, Afia, Efi, Efia

Afina (Hebrew) young doe.
Afinah, Afynah, Aphina, Aphinah, Aphyna,
Aphynah

Afra (Hebrew) young doe. (Arabic) earth
color. See also Aphra.
Affery, Affrah, Affrey, Affrie, Afraa, Afrah,
Afria, Afriah, Afrya, Afryah

Africa (Irish) pleasant. Geography: one of
the seven continents.
Affreeca, Affreecah, Affrica, Affricah, Affricka,
Affryca, Affrycah, Afreeca, Afreecah, Afric,
Africah, Africaya, Africia, Africiana, Afryca,
Afrycah, Afrycka, Afryckah, Aifric

Afrika (Irish) a form of Africa.
Affreeka, Affreekah, Affryka, Affrykah,
Afreeka, Afreekah, Afrikah, Afryka, Afrykah

Afrodite (Greek) a form of Aphrodite.
Afrodita

Afton (English) from Afton, England.
Aftan, Aftine, Aftinn, Aftona, Aftonah,
Aftone, Aftonia, Aftoniah, Aftonie, Aftony,
Aftonya, Aftonyah, Aftonye, Aftyn

Aganetha (Greek) a form of Agnes.

Agate (English) a semiprecious stone.

Agatha (Greek) good, kind. Literature:
Agatha Christie was a British writer of
more than seventy detective novels. See
also Gasha.

Agace, Agacia, Agafa, Agafia, Agaisha,
Agasha, Agata, Agatah, Agathia, Agathiah,
Agathya, Agathyah, Agatka, Agetha, Aggie,
Agota, Agotha, Agueda, Agytha, Atka

Agathe (Greek) a form of Agatha.
Agathi, Agathie, Agathy

Aggie (Greek) a short form of Agatha,
Agnes.
Ag, Aggy, Agi

Aglaia (Greek) beautiful.
Aglae, Aglaiah, Aglaya, Aglayah, Aglaye

Agnella (Greek) a form of Agnes.
Agnela, Agnelah, Agnele, Agnelia, Agneliah,
Agnelie, Agnellah, Agnelle, Agnellia,
Agnelliah, Agnellie, Agnellya, Agnellyah

Agnes (Greek) pure. See also Aneesa,
Anice, Anisha, Ina, Ines, Necha, Nessa,
Nessie, Neza, Nyusha, Una, Ynez.
Agna, Agne, Agneis, Agnés, Agnesa, Agnesca,
Agnese, Agnesina, Agness, Agnessa, Agnesse,
Agneta, Agnete, Agnetha, Agneti, Agnetis,
Agnetta, Agnette, Agnies, Agniya, Agnola,
Agnus, Aignéis, Aneska

Agnieszka (Greek) a form of Agnes.

Agrippina (Latin) born feet first.
Agripa, Agripah, Agripina, Agripinah,
Agripine, Agrippah, Agrippinah, Agrippine,
Agrypina, Agrypinah, Agrypine, Agryppina,
Agryppinah, Agryppine, Agryppyna,
Agryppynah, Agryppyne

Ahava (Hebrew) beloved.
Ahavah, Ahivia, Ahuva, Ahuvah

Ahlam (Arabic) witty; one who has pleasant dreams.

Ahliya (Hebrew) a form of Aliya.
Ahlai, Ahlaia, Ahlaya, Ahleah, Ahleeyah,
Ahley, Ahleya, Ahlia, Ahliah, Ahliyah

Ahulani (Hawaiian) heavenly shrine.
Ahulanee, Ahulaney, Ahulania, Ahulaniah,
Ahulanie, Ahulany, Ahulanya, Ahulanyah

Ai (Japanese) love; indigo blue.

Aida (Latin) helpful. (English) a form of Ada.
Aidah, Aidee, Ayda, Aydah

Aidan, Aiden (Latin) forms of Aida.
Adan, Aden, Adene, Aidana, Aidanah, Aidane, Aidann, Aidanna, Aidannah, Aidanne, Aydan, Aydana, Aydanah, Aydane, Aydann, Aydanna, Aydannah, Aydanne

Aide (Latin, English) a short form of Aida.

Aiesha (Swahili, Arabic) a form of Aisha.
Aieshah, Aieshia

Aiko (Japanese) beloved.

Ailani (Hawaiian) chief.
Aelani, Ailana

Aileen (Scottish) light bearer. (Irish) a form of Helen. See also Eileen.
Ailean, Aileana, Aileanah, Aileane, Aileena, Ailein, Aileina, Ailen, Ailena, Ailenah, Ailene, Aileyn, Aileyna, Aileynah, Ailin, Ailina, Ailinn, Aillen, Ailyn, Ailyna, Alean, Aleana, Aleanah, Aleane, Aylean, Ayleana, Ayleen, Ayleena, Aylein, Ayleina, Ayleyn, Ayleyna, Aylin, Aylina, Aylyn, Aylyna

Aili (Scottish) a form of Alice. (Finnish) a form of Helen.
Aila, Ailee, Ailey, Ailie, Aily

Ailis (Irish) a form of Adelaide.
Ailesh, Ailish, Ailyse, Eilis

Ailsa (Scottish) island dweller. Geography: Ailsa Craig is an island in Scotland.
Ailsah, Ailsha, Aylsa, Aylsah

Ailya (Hebrew) a form of Aliya.
Ailiyah

Aime, Aimie (Latin, French) forms of Aimee.

Aimee (Latin) a form of Amy. (French) loved.
Aimée, Aimey, Aimi, Aimia, Aimy, Aimya

Ainsley (Scottish) my own meadow.
Ainslea, Ainsleah, Ainslee, Ainslei, Ainsleigh, Ainsly, Aynslea, Aynsleah, Aynslee, Aynslei, Aynsleigh, Aynsley, Aynsli, Aynslie, Aynsly

Ainslie (Scottish) a form of Ainsley.
Ainsli

Airiana (English) a form of Ariana.
Airana, Airanna, Aireana, Aireanah, Aireanna, Aireona, Aireonna, Aireyonna, Airianna, Airianne, Airiona, Airriana, Airrion, Airryon, Airyana, Airyanna

Airiél (Hebrew) a form of Ariel.
Aieral, Aierel, Aiiryel, Aire, Aireal, Aireale, Aireel, Airel, Airele, Airelle, Airi, Airial, Airiale, Airrel

Airleas (Irish) promise.
Airlea, Airleah, Airlee, Airlei, Airleigh, Airley, Airli, Airlie, Airly, Ayrlea, Ayrleas, Ayrlee, Ayrlei, Ayrleigh, Ayrley, Ayrli, Aylie, Ayrly

Aisha (Swahili) life. (Arabic) woman. See also Asha, Asia, Iesha, Isha, Keisha, Leisha, Yiesha.
Aaisha, Aaishah, Aeisha, Aeshia, Aesha, Aeshah, Aheesha, Aiasha, Aieysha, Aiiesha, Aisa, Aischa, Aish, Aishah, Aisheh, Aiyesha, Aiysha, Aysa, Ayse, Aytza

Aishia (Swahili, Arabic) a form of Aisha.
Aishiah

Aisling (Irish) a form of Aislinn.

Aislinn, Aislynn (Irish) forms of Ashlyn.
Aishellyn, Aishlinn, Aislee, Aisley, Aislin, Aislyn, Aislynne, Ayslin, Ayslinn, Ayslyn, Ayslynn

Aixa (Latin, German) a form of Axelle.

Aiyana (Native American) forever flowering.
Aiyanah, Aiyhana, Aiyona, Aiyonia

Aiyanna (Native American) a form of Aiyana. (Hindi) a form of Ayanna.
Aianna, Aiyannah, Aiyonna, Aiyunna

Aja (Hindi) goat.
Ahjah, Aija, Aijah, Ajá, Ajada, Ajara, Ajaran, Ajare, Ajaree, Ajha, Ajya, Ajyah

Ajah (Hindi) a form of Aja.

Ajanae (American) a combination of the letter A + Janae.
Ajahnae, Ajahne, Ajana, Ajanaé, Ajane, Ajané, Ajanee, Ajanique, Ajena, Ajenae, Ajené

Ajee, Ajée (Punjabi, American) forms of Ajay (see Boys' Names).

Ajia (Hindi) a form of Aja.
Aijia, Ajhia, Aji, Ajiah, Ajjia

Akasha (American) a form of Akeisha.
Akasia

Akayla (American) a combination of the letter A + Kayla.
Akaela, Akaelia, Akaila, Akailah, Akala, Akaylah, Akaylia

Akeisha (American) a combination of the letter A + Keisha.
Akaesha, Akaisha, Akeecia, Akeesha, Akeishia, Akeshia, Akisha

Akela (Hawaiian) noble.
Ahkayla, Ahkeelah, Akeia, Akeiah, Akelah, Akelia, Akeliah, Akeya, Akeyah

Akeria (American) a form of Akira.
Akera, Akerah, Akeri, Akerra

Akeyla (Hawaiian) a form of Akela.
Akeylah

Aki (Japanese) born in autumn.
Akee, Akeeye, Akei, Akey, Akie, Aky

Akia (American) a combination of the letter A + Kia.
Akaja, Akeia, Akeiah, Akeya, Akeyah, Akiá, Akiah, Akiane, Akiaya, Akiea, Akiya, Akiyah, Akya, Akyan, Akyia, Akyiah

Akiko (Japanese) bright light.
Akyko

Akila (Arabic) a form of Akilah.

Akilah (Arabic) intelligent.
Aikiela, Aikilah, Akeela, Akeelah, Akeila, Akeilah, Akeiyla, Akiela, Akielah, Akilaih, Akilia, Akilka, Akilkah, Akillah, Akkila, Akyla, Akylah

Akili (Tanzanian) wisdom.
Akilea, Akileah, Akilee, Akilei, Akileigh, Akiliah, Akilie, Akily, Akylee, Akyli, Akylie

Akina (Japanese) spring flower.

Akira (American) a combination of the letter A + Kira.
Akiera, Akierra, Akirah, Akire, Akiria, Akirrah, Akyra

Alaa (Arabic) a form of Aladdin (see Boys' Names).
Ala

Alaina (Irish) a form of Alana.
Alain, Alainah, Alaine, Alainna, Alainnah, Allaina, Allainah, Allaine

Alair (French) a form of Hilary.
Alaira, Allaire

Alamea (Hawaiian) ripe; precious.
Alameah, Alameya, Alameyah, Alamia, Alamiah, Almya, Almyah

Alameda (Spanish) poplar tree.
Alamedah

Alana (Irish) attractive; peaceful. (Hawaiian) offering. See also Lana.
Aalaina, Alaana, Alanae, Alane, Alanea, Alania, Alawna, Aleine, Alleyna, Alleynah, Alleyne

Alanah (Irish, Hawaiian) a form of Alana.

Alandra (Spanish) a form of Alexandra, Alexandria.
Alantra, Aleandra

Alandria (Spanish) a form of Alexandra, Alexandria.
Alandrea, Aleandrea

Alani (Hawaiian) orange tree. (Irish) a form of Alana.
Alaini, Alainie, Alanea, Alanee, Alaney, Alania, Alaniah, Alanie, Alaney, Alannie, Alany, Alanya, Alanyah

Alanis (Irish) beautiful; bright.
Alanisa, Alanisah, Alanise, Alaniss, Alanissa, Alanissah, Alanisse, Alannis, Alannisa, Alannisah, Alannise, Alannys, Alannysa, Alannyse, Alanys, Alanysa, Alanysah, Alanyse, Alanyss, Alanyssa, Alanyssah, Alanysse

Alanna, Alannah (Irish) forms of Alana.

Alanza (Spanish) noble and eager.

Alarice (German) ruler of all.
Alarica, Alaricah, Alaricia, Alarisa, Alarisah, Alarise, Allaryca, Allaryce, Alrica, Alricah, Alryca, Alrycah, Alryqua, Alryque

Alastrina (Scottish) defender of humankind.

Alastriana, Alastrianah, Alastriane,
Alastrianna, Alastriannah, Alastrianne,
Alastrinah, Alastrine, Alastryan, Alastryana,
Alastryanah, Alastryane, Alastryann,
Alastryanna, Alastryannah, Alastryanne,
Alastryn, Alastryna, Alastrynah, Alastryne,
Alastrynia, Alastryniah, Alastrynya,
Alastrynyah

Alaura (American) a form of Alora.

Alaya (Hebrew) a form of Aliya.
Alayah

Alayna (Irish) a form of Alana.
Alaynah, Alayne, Alaynna, Alaynnah

Alaysha, Alaysia (American) forms of
Alicia.
Alaysh, Alayshia

Alba (Latin) from Alba Longa, an ancient
city near Rome, Italy.
Albah, Albana, Albani, Albania, Albanie,
Albany, Albeni, Albina, Albinah, Albine,
Albinia, Albinka, Albyna, Albynah, Albyne,
Aubina, Aubinah, Aubine, Aubyna,
Aubynah, Aubyne, Elba

Alberta (German, French) noble and
bright. See also Auberte, Bertha, Elberta.
Albertina, Albertinah, Albertine, Albertyna,
Albertyne, Albirta, Albirtina, Albirtina,
Albirtine, Albirtyna, Albrette, Alburta,
Alburtah, Alburtina, Alburtinah, Alburtine,
Alburtyna, Alburtynah, Alburtyne, Albyrta,
Albyrtah, Albyrtina, Albyrtine, Albyrtyna,
Albyrtynah, Albyrtyne, Alverta, Alvertah,
Alvertina, Alvertine

Albreanna (American) a combination of
Alberta + Breanna (see Breana).
Albré, Albrea, Albreona, Albreonna, Albreyon

Alcina (Greek) strong-minded.
Alceena, Alcie, Alcinah, Alcine, Alcinia,
Alciniah, Alcyna, Alcynah, Alcyne, Alseena,
Alsina, Alsinah, Alsinia, Alsine, Alsyn,
Alsyna, Alsynah, Alsyne, Alzina, Alzinah,
Alzine, Alzyna, Alzynah, Alzyne

Alda (German) old; elder.
Aldah, Aldina, Aldine

Alden (English) old; wise protector.
Aldan, Aldon, Aldyn

Aldina, Aldine (Hebrew) forms of Alda.
Aldeana, Aldene, Aldona, Aldyna, Aldyne

Aldora (English) gift; superior.
Aldorah

Alea, Aleah (Arabic) high, exalted.
(Persian) God's being.
Aileah, Allea, Alleah, Alleea, Alleeah

Aleaha (Arabic, Persian) a form of Alea.

Aleasha (Greek) a form of Alisha.
Aleashae, Aleashea, Aleashia, Aleasia,
Aleassa

Alecia (Greek) a form of Alicia.
Aalecia, Ahlasia, Aleacia, Aleacya, Aleasia,
Alecea, Aleceea, Aleceia, Aleciya, Aleciyah,
Alecy, Alecya, Aleicia, Allecia

Aleea (Arabic, Persian) a form of Alea.
(Hebrew) a form of Aliya.
Aleeah

Aleecia (Greek) a form of Alicia.
Aleeceia, Aleeciah, Aleesia, Aleesiya, Alleecia

Aleela (Swahili) she cries.
Aleala, Alealah, Aleelah, Aleila, Aleilah,
Aleighla, Aleighlah, Aleyla, Aleylah, Alila,
Alile, Alyla, Alylah

Aleena (Dutch) a form of Aleene.
Ahleena, Aleana, Aleanah, Aleeanna,
Aleenah, Aleina, Aleinah, Aleighna,
Aleighnah

Aleene (Dutch) alone. See also Allene.
Aleane, Aleine, Aleighn, Aleighne, Alyn,
Alyne

Aleesa (Greek) a form of Alice, Alyssa.
See also Alisa.
Aleessa

Aleesha (Greek) a form of Alisha.
Aleeshah, Aleeshia, Aleeshia, Aleeshya

Aleeya (Hebrew) a form of Aliya.
Alee, Aleeyah, Aleiya, Aleiyah

Aleeza (Hebrew) a form of Aliza. See also
Leeza.
Aleaza, Aleazah, Aleezah, Aleiza, Aleizah,
Aleyza, Aleyzah

Alegria (Spanish) cheerful.
Aleggra, Alegra

Aleia, Aleigha (Arabic, Persian) forms of
Alea.
Alei, Aleiah

Aleisha (Greek) a form of Alicia, Alisha.
Aleisa

Alejandra (Spanish) a form of Alexandra.
*Aleiandra, Alejanda, Alejandr, Alejandrea,
Alejandria, Alejandro*

Alejandrina (Spanish) a form of
Alejandra.

Aleka (Hawaiian) a form of Alice.
*Aleaka, Aleakah, Aleeka, Aleekah, Aleika,
Aleikah, Alekah, Aleyka, Aleykah*

Aleksa (Greek) a form of Alexa.
Aleksha

Aleksandra (Greek) a form of Alexandra.
*Alecsandra, Alecxandra, Alecxandrah,
Aleczandra, Aleczandrah, Aleksasha,
Aleksandrija, Aleksandriya*

Alena (Russian) a form of Helen.
*Aleana, Aleanah, Aleina, Alenah, Alene,
Alenea, Aleni, Alenia, Alenka, Alenna,
Alennah, Alenya, Aliena*

Aleria (Latin) eagle.
*Alearia, Aleariah, Alearya, Alearyah,
Aleriah, Alerya, Aleryah*

Alesha (Greek) a form of Alicia, Alisha.
Alesa, Alesah

Aleshia (Greek) a form of Alicia, Alisha.
Aleshya

Alesia, Alessia (Greek) forms of Alice,
Alicia, Alisha.
*Alesiah, Alessea, Alessiah, Alesya, Alesyah,
Allesia*

Alessa (Greek) a form of Alice.
Alessi, Allessa

Alessandra (Italian) a form of Alexandra.
*Alesandra, Alesandrea, Alessandria,
Alessandriah, Alessandrie, Alessandryn,
Alessandryna, Alessandryne, Alissandra,
Alissondra, Allesand, Allessandra*

Aleta (Greek) a form of Alida. See also
Leta.

*Aleata, Aleatah, Aleeta, Aleetah, Aleighta,
Aleita, Aleitah, Aletah, Aletta, Alettah,
Alette, Aleyta, Aleytah, Alletta*

Aletha (Greek) a short form of Alethea.

Alethea (Greek) truth.
*Alathea, Alatheah, Alathia, Alathiah,
Aleathia, Aleathiah, Aleathya, Aleathyah,
Aleethea, Aleetheah, Aleethia, Aleethiah,
Aleethya, Aleethyah, Aleithea, Aleitheah,
Aleithia, Aleithiah, Aleithya, Aleithyah,
Aleighthea, Aleighthia, Aleighthya, Aletea,
Aletheah, Aletheia, Aletheiah, Alethia,
Alethiah, Aletia, Alithea, Alitheah, Alithia,
Alithiah, Allethea, Alythea, Alytheah,
Alythia, Alythiah, Alythya, Alythyah*

Alette (Latin) wing.
Aletta, Alettah

Alex (Greek) a short form of Alexander,
Alexandra.
Aleix, Aleks, Alexx, Allex, Allexx

Alex Ann, Alex Anne, Alexane, Alexanne
(American) combinations of Alex + Ann.
*Alex-Ann, Alex-Anne, Alexan, Alexann,
Alexanna, Alexian, Alexiana, Alexina,
Alexinah, Alexine, Alexyna, Alexynah,
Alexyne*

Alexa (Greek) a short form of Alexandra.
*Aleixa, Alekia, Aleksi, Alexah, Alexxa,
Allexa, Alyxa*

Alexander (Greek) defender of mankind.
History: Alexander the Great was the
conqueror of the Greek Empire.
*Al, Alec, Alecander, Alecsandar, Alecsander,
Alecxander, Alejándro, Alek, Alekos,
Aleksandar, Aleksander, Aleksei, Alekzander,
Alessander, Alessandro, Alexandar, Alexandor,
Alexandr, Alexandro, Alexandros, Alexxander,
Alexzander, Alic, Alick, Alisander, Alixander*

Alexanderia (Greek) a form of
Alexandria.

Alexandra (Greek) a form of Alexander.
History: the last czarina of Russia. See
also Lexi, Lexia, Olesia, Ritsa, Sandra,
Sandrine, Sasha, Shura, Sondra, Xandra,
Zandra.

Alaxandra, Alexande, Alexandera, Alexina, Alexine, Alexxandra, Alexxandrah, Alixsandra, Aljexi, Alla, Lexandra

Alexandre (Greek) a form of Alexandra.

Alexandrea (Greek) a form of Alexandria.
Alexanndrea

Alexandria (Greek) a form of Alexandra. See also Xandra, Zandra.
Alaxandria, Alecsandria, Alecxandria, Alecxandriah, Alecxandrya, Alecxandryah, Aleczandria, Aleczandriah, Aleczandrya, Aleczandryah, Alexandreia, Alexandriah, Alexandrie, Alexandriea, Alexandrieah, Alexandrya, Alexandryah, Alexanndria, Alexanndrya, Alexendria, Alexxandria, Alexxandriah, Alexxandrya, Alexxandryah, Alixandrea, Alixzandria

Alexandrine (Greek) a form of Alexandra. See also Drina.
Alecsandrina, Alejandrine, Alejandryn, Alejandryna, Alejandryne, Aleksandrina, Aleksandryne, Alexandreana, Alexandrena, Alexandrina, Alexandrinah, Alexendrine, Alexzandrina, Alexzandrinah, Alexzandrine, Alexzandryna, Alexzandrynah

Alexas, Alexes, Alexiss, Alexsis, Alexus, Alexxis, Alexxus, Alexys, Allexis, Allexus (Greek) forms of Alexis.
Alexess, Alexuss, Alexyss, Allexys

Alexcia (Greek) a form of Alexia.

Alexe (Greek) a form of Alex.

Alexi, Alexie (Greek) short forms of Alexandra.
Aleksey, Aleksi, Alexey, Alexy

Alexia (Greek) a short form of Alexandria. See also Lexia.
Aleksia, Aleksiah, Aleksya, Aleksyah, Aleska, Alexea, Alexiah, Alexsia, Alexsiya, Allexia, Alyxia

Alexis (Greek) a short form of Alexandra.
Aalexis, Aalexus, Aalexxus, Aelexus, Ahlexis, Ahlexus, Alaxis, Alecsis, Alecsus, Alecxis, Aleexis, Aleksis, Aleksys, Alexias, Alexiou, Alexiz, Alexsus, Alexsys, Alexxiz, Alexyes, Alexyis, Alixis, Alixus, Elexis, Elexus, Lexis, Lexus

Alexius (Greek) a form of Alexis.
Allexius

Alexsa (Greek) a form of Alexa.
Alexssa

Alexsandra (Greek) a form of Alexandra.
Alexsandria, Alexsandro

Alexzandra (Greek) a form of Alexandra.
Alexzand, Alexzandrah

Alexzandria (Greek) a form of Alexandria.
Alexzandrea, Alexzandriah, Alexzandrya

Aleya, Aleyah (Hebrew) forms of Aliya.
Aleayah, Aléyah, Aleyia, Aleyiah

Alfie (English) a familiar form of Alfreda.
Alfi, Alfy

Alfonsa (German) noble and eager.
Alfonsia, Alfonsina, Alfonsine, Alfonsyna, Alfonsyne

Alfreda (English) elf counselor; wise counselor. See also Effie, Elfrida, Freda, Frederica.
Alfredah, Alfredda, Alfredia, Alfreeda, Alfreida, Alfrida, Alfridah, Alfrieda, Alfryda, Alfrydah, Alfrydda, Alfryddah

Ali, Alie, Alley, Alli, Allie, Ally, Aly (Greek) familiar forms of Alice, Alicia, Alisha, Alison.
Alee, Alei, Aleigh, Aley, Allea, Allee, Allei, Alleigh

Alia, Aliah, Allia, Alliah (Hebrew) forms of Aliya. See also Aaliya, Alea.
Aelia, Allea, Alleah, Alya

Alice (Greek) truthful. (German) noble. See also Aili, Aleka, Ali, Alisa, Alison, Alyce, Alysa, Elke.
Adelice, Aleece, Aleese, Alicie, Alics, Aliece, Aliese, Alla, Alleece, Alles, Allesse, Allice

Alicen, Alicyn, Alisyn, Allisyn (English) forms of Alison.

Alicia (English) a form of Alice. See also Elicia, Licia.
Aelicia, Adelicia, Aleacia, Aleaciah, Alecea, Aleicia, Aleiciah, Aleisia, Aleisiah, Aleisya, Aleisyah, Aleighcia, Aleighsia, Aleighsya, Alicea, Alicha, Alichia, Aliciah, Alician, Alicija, Aliecia, Allicea, Ilysa

Alicja (English) a form of Alicia.
Alicya

Alida (Latin) small and winged. (Spanish)
noble. See also Aleta, Lida, Oleda.
Adelita, Aleda, Aledah, Aleida, Alidah,
Alidia, Alidiah, Alleda, Alledah, Allida,
Allidah, Alyda, Alydia, Elida, Elidia

Aliesha (Greek) a form of Alisha.
Alieshai, Alieshia, Alliesha

Alika (Hawaiian) truthful. (Swahili) most
beautiful.
Aleka, Alica, Alikah, Alike, Alikee, Aliki,
Aliqua, Aliquah, Alique, Alyka, Alykah,
Alyqua, Alyquah

Alima (Arabic) sea maiden; musical.
Alimah, Alyma, Alymah

Alina (Slavic) bright. (Scottish) fair.
(English) a short form of Adeline. See
also Alena.
Aleana, Aleanah, Aleina, Aleinah, Aliana,
Alianna, Alinah, Alinna

Aline (Scottish) a form of Aileen, Alina.
Alianne, Alline

Alisa, Allisa (Greek) forms of Alice,
Alyssa. See also Elisa, Ilisa.
Aaliysah, Alisah, Alisea, Aliysa

Alissa, Allissa (Greek) forms of Alice,
Alyssa.
Aalissah, Alissah, Alisza, Allisah, Allissah

Alise, Allise (Greek) forms of Alice.
Alis, Aliss, Alisse, Alisse, Allis, Alliss, Allisse

Alisha (Greek) truthful. (German) noble.
(English) a form of Alicia. See also Elisha,
Ilisha, Lisha.
Aliscia, Alisea, Alishah, Alishay, Alishaye,
Alishya, Alissya, Alisyia, Alitsha, Allissia,
Alyssaya

Alishia (English) a form of Alisha.
Alishea, Alisheia, Alishiana

Alisia, Alissia (English) forms of Alisha.

Alison, Allison (English) forms of Alice.
See also Lissie.
Aleason, Aleeson, Aleison, Aleighson, Alisan,
Alisann, Alisanne, Alisen, Alisenne, Alisin,
Alision, Alisonn, Alisson, Alissun, Alissyn,
Alisun, Alysine, Alles, Allesse, Alleyson,
Allisan, Allisen, Allisin, Allisine, Allisone,
Allisson, Allisun, Allsun, Alson, Alsone,
Elisan, Elisen, Elisin, Elison, Elisun, Elisyn

Alita (Spanish) a form of Alida.
Alitah, Allita, Allitah, Allitta, Allittah,
Allyta, Allytah, Alyta, Alytah

Alivia (Latin) a form of Olivia.
Alivah

Alix (Greek) a short form of Alexandra,
Alice.
Alixe, Alixia, Allix, Alyx

Alixandra (Greek) a form of Alexandra.
Alixandrah, Alixzandra, Alixzandrah,
Allixandra

Alixandria (Greek) a form of Alexandria.
Alixandriah, Alixandrina, Alixandrinah,
Alixandrine, Alixandriya, Alixzandria,
Alixzandriah, Alixzandrina, Alixzandryna,
Alixzandrynah, Alixzandryne, Allixandria,
Allixandrya

Aliya (Hebrew) ascender.
Aeliyah, Alieya, Alieyah, Aliyiah, Alliyha,
Alliyia

Aliyah, Alliyah (Hebrew) forms of Aliya.
Aliyyah, Alliya, Alliyyah

Aliye (Arabic) noble.
Aliyeh

Aliza (Hebrew) joyful. See also Aleeza,
Eliza.
Alieza, Aliezah, Alitza, Alitzah, Alizah,
Alizee, Alyza, Alyzah

Alizabeth (Hebrew) a form of Elizabeth.
Alyzabeth

Alize (Greek, German) a form of Alice.
(Hebrew) a short form of Aliza.
Aliz

Allana, Allanah (Irish) forms of Alana.
Allanie, Allanna, Allannah, Allanne, Allauna

Allegra (Latin) cheerful.
Allegrah, Allegria, Legra

Allena (Irish) a form of Alana.
Alleyna, Alleynah

Allene (Dutch) a form of Aleene. (Scottish) a form of Aline.
Alene, Alleen

Allethea (Greek) a form of Alethea.
Allathea, Allatheah, Allathia, Allathiah, Alletheah, Allethia, Allethiah, Allethya, Allethyah, Allythea, Allytheah, Allythia, Allythiah, Allythya, Allythyah

Allicia (English) a form of Alicia.

Allisha (Greek, German, English) a form of Alisha.

Allyn (Scottish) a form of Aileen, Alina. See also Aline.
Allyne, Alyne, Alynne

Allysa, Allyssa (Greek) a form of Alyssa.
Allyisa, Allysah, Allyssah

Allysen, Allyson, Alyson (English) forms of Alison.
Allysonn, Allysson, Allysun, Allysyn, Allysyne, Alysan, Alysen, Alysene, Alysin, Alysine, Alysone, Alysun, Alysyn, Alysyne, Alyzane, Alyzen, Alyzene, Alyzin, Alyzine, Alyzyn, Alyzyne

Allysha, Alycia, Alysha, Alysia (English) forms of Alicia.
Alyssha, Lycia

Alma (Arabic) learned. (Latin) soul.
Almah, Almar, Almarah

Almeda (Arabic) ambitious.
Allmeda, Allmedah, Allmeta, Almea, Almedah, Almeta, Almetah, Almetta, Almettah, Almida, Almidah, Almyda, Almydah

Almira (Arabic) aristocratic, princess; exalted. (Spanish) from Almeíra, Spain. See also Elmira, Mira.
Allmeera, Allmera, Allmerah, Allmeria, Allmira, Allmirah, Almeera, Almeeria, Almeira, Almera, Almeria, Almeriah, Almirah, Almire, Almyra, Almyrah

Almita (Latin) kind.
Allmita, Almitah, Almyta, Almytah

Alodie (English) rich. See also Elodie.
Alodea, Alodee, Alodey, Alodi, Alodia, Alody, Alodya, Alodyah, Alodye

Aloha (Hawaiian) loving, kindhearted, charitable.
Alohah, Alohi

Aloisa (German) famous warrior.
Aloisia, Aloysa, Aloysia

Aloma (Latin) a short form of Paloma.

Alonda (Spanish) a form of Alexandra.

Alondra (Spanish) a form of Alexandra.
Allandra

Alonna (Irish) a form of Alana.
Allona, Allonah, Alona, Alonah, Alonnah, Alonya, Alonyah

Alonza (English) noble and eager.

Alora (American) a combination of the letter A + Lora.
Alorah, Alorha, Alorie, Aloura, Alouria

Alpha (Greek) first-born. Linguistics: the first letter of the Greek alphabet.
Alfa, Alfah, Alfia, Alfiah, Alfya, Alfyah, Alphah, Alphia, Alphiah, Alphya, Alphyah

Alta (Latin) high; tall.
Allta, Altah, Altana, Altanna, Altea, Alto

Altair (Greek) star. (Arabic) flying eagle.
Altaira, Altaire, Altayr, Altayra, Altayrah, Altayre

Althea (Greek) wholesome; healer. History: Althea Gibson was the first African American to win a major tennis title. See also Thea.
Altha, Altheah, Altheda, Althedah, Altheya, Althia, Althiah, Althya, Althyah, Elthea, Eltheya, Elthia

Alva (Latin, Spanish) white; light skinned. See also Elva.
Alvah, Alvana, Alvanna, Alvannah

Alvera (Latin) honest.
Alverah, Alveria, Alveriah, Alverya, Alveryah, Alvira, Alvirah, Alvyra, Alvyrah

Alvina (English) friend to all; noble friend; friend to elves. See also Elva, Vina.
Alveana, Alveanah, Alveane, Alveanea, Alveen, Alveena, Alveenah, Alveene, Alveenia, Alvena, Alvenah, Alvenea, Alvie, Alvinae, Alvinah, Alvincia, Alvine, Alvinea, Alvinesha,

Alvina *(cont.)*
Alvinia, Alvinna, Alvinnah, Alvita, Alvona, Alvyna, Alvynah, Alvyne, Alwin, Alwina, Alwyn

Alyah (Hebrew) a form of Aliya.
Allya, Allyah, Alya, Alyya, Alyyah

Alyce, Alyse, Alysse (Greek) forms of Alice.
Allyce, Allys, Allyse, Allyss, Alys, Alyss

Alyiah (Hebrew) a form of Aliya.
Alyia

Alyna (Dutch) a form of Aleene. (Slavic, Scottish, English) a form of Alina.
Alynah, Alyona

Alysa (Greek) a form of Alyssa.
Alysah

Alyshia (English) a form of Alicia.

Alyssa (Greek) rational. Botany: alyssum is a flowering herb. See also Alice, Alisa, Elissa.
Ahlyssa, Alyesa, Alyessa, Alyissa, Alyssah, Ilyssa, Lyssa, Lyssah

Alyssia (Greek) a form of Alyssa.

Alyx (Greek) a form of Alex.

Alyxandra (Greek) a form of Alexandra.
Alyxandrah, Alyxzandra, Alyxzandrah

Alyxandria (Greek) a form of Alexandria.
Alyxandrea, Alyxandriah, Alyxandrya, Alyxandryah, Alyxzandria, Alyxzandriah, Alyxzandrya, Alyxzandryah

Alyxis (Greek) a form of Alexis.

Alzena (Arabic) woman.
Alsena, Alsenah, Alxena, Alxenah, Alxina, Alxinah, Alxyna, Alxynah, Alzenah, Alzina, Alzinah, Alzyna, Alzynah

Am (Vietnamese) lunar; female.

Ama (African) born on Saturday.
Amah

Amabel (Latin) lovable. See also Bel, Mabel.
Amabela, Amabelah, Amabele, Amabell, Amabella, Amabellah, Amabelle, Ambela, Ambelah, Ambele, Ambell, Ambella,

Ambellah, Amebelle, Amibel, Amibela, Amibelah, Amibele, Amibell, Amibella, Amibellah, Amibelle, Amybel, Amybell, Amybella, Amybelle

Amada (Spanish) beloved.
Amadee, Amadey, Amadi, Amadie, Amadita, Amady, Amata

Amadea (Latin) loves God.
Amadeah, Amadeya, Amadeyah, Amadia, Amadiah, Amadya, Amadyah

Amairani, Amairany (Greek) forms of Amara.
Amairaine, Amairane, Amairanie

Amal (Hebrew) worker. (Arabic) hopeful.
Amala, Amalah, Amalla, Amallah

Amalia (German) a form of Amelia.
Ahmalia, Amalea, Amaleah, Amaleta, Amaliah, Amalija, Amalisa, Amalita, Amalitah, Amaliya, Amalya, Amalyah, Amalyn

Amalie (German) a form of Amelia.
Amalee, Amalei, Amaleigh, Amaley, Amali, Amaly

Amaline (German) a form of Amelia.
Amalean, Amaleana, Amaleane, Amaleen, Amaleena, Amaleene, Amalin, Amalina, Amalyn, Amalyna, Amalyne, Amalynn, Amelina, Ameline, Amilina, Amiline, Amilyn, Amilynn, Amilynna, Amilynne, Ammalyn, Ammalynn, Ammalynne, Ammilina, Ammiline

Aman (Arabic) a short form of Amani.
Amane

Amanada (Latin) a form of Amanda.

Amanda (Latin) lovable. See also Manda, Mandy.
Amandah, Amandalee, Amandalyn, Amande, Amandea, Amandee, Amandey, Amandi, Amandia, Amandiah, Amandie, Amandina, Amandine, Amandy, Amandya, Amandyah

Amandeep (Punjabi) peaceful light.

Amani (Arabic) a form of Imani.
Aamani, Ahmani, Amanee, Amaney, Amanie, Ammanu

Amanjot (Punjabi) a form of Amandeep.

Amanpreet (Punjabi) a form of Amandeep.

Amara (Greek) eternally beautiful. See also Mara.
Amaira, Amar, Amarah, Amaria, Amariah, Amarya, Amaryah

Amaranta (Spanish) a flower that never fades.
Amaranth, Amarantha, Amaranthe

Amari (Greek) a form of Amara.
Amaree, Amarie, Amarii, Amarri

Amarina (Australian) rain.
Amarin, Amarinah, Amarine, Amaryn, Amarynah, Amaryne

Amaris (Hebrew) promised by God.
Amaarisah, Amarisa, Amariss, Amarissa, Amarys, Amarysa, Amarysah, Amaryss, Amaryssa, Amaryssah, Maris

Amaryllis (Greek) fresh; flower.
Amarilis, Amarillis, Amaryl, Amaryla, Amarylah, Amarylis, Amarylla, Amaryllah

Amaui (Hawaiian) thrush.

Amaya (Japanese) night rain.
Amaia, Amaiah, Amayah

Ambar (French) a form of Amber.

Amber (French) amber.
Aamber, Ahmber, Amberia, Amberise, Ambur, Ammber, Ember

Amber-Lynn, Amberlyn, Amberlynn (American) combinations of Amber + Lynn.
Ambarlina, Ambarline, Amber Lynn, Amber Lynne, Amber-Lynne, Amberlin, Amberlina, Amberline, Amberlyne, Amberlynne, Amburlina, Amburline

Amberlee, Amberley, Amberly (American) familiar forms of Amber.
Ambarlea, Ambarlee, Ambarlei, Ambarleigh, Ambarley, Ambarli, Ambarlie, Ambarly, Amberle, Amberlea, Amberlei, Amberleigh, Amberli, Amberlia, Amberliah, Amberlie, Amberlly, Amberlyah, Amberlye, Amburlea, Amburlee, Amburlei, Amburleigh, Amburley,

Amburli, Amburlia, Amburlie, Amburly, Amburlya

Ambra (American) a form of Amber.

Ambria (American) a form of Amber.
Ambrea, Ambriah

Ambrosia (Greek) immortal.
Ambrosa, Ambrosah, Ambrosiah, Ambrosina, Ambrosine, Ambrosyn, Ambrosyna, Ambrosyne, Ambrozin, Ambrozinah, Ambrozine, Ambrozyn, Ambrozyna, Ambrozyne

Ambyr (French) a form of Amber.
Ambyre

Amee, Ami, Amie, Amiee (French) forms of Amy.
Amii, Amiiee, Ammee, Ammie, Ammiee

Ameena (Arabic) a form of Amina.
Ameenah

Ameera (Hebrew, Arabic) a form of Amira.
Ameerah

Amelia (German) hard working. (Latin) a form of Emily. History: Amelia Earhart, an American aviator, was the first woman to fly solo across the Atlantic Ocean. See also Ima, Melia, Millie, Nuela, Yamelia.
Aemilia, Aimilia, Amalie, Amaline, Amaliya, Ameila, Ameilia, Amelisa, Amelita, Amella, Amylia, Amyliah, Amylya, Amylyah

Amelie, Amely (French) forms of Amelia.
Amelee, Ameleigh, Ameley, Amélie

Amelinda (American) a combination of Amelia + Linda.
Amalinda, Amalindah, Amalynda, Amalyndah, Amelindah, Amerlindah, Amilinda, Amilindah, Amilynda, Amilyndah

America (Teutonic) industrious.
Amarica, Amaricah, Amaricka, Amarickah, Amarika, Amarikah, Americah, Americana, Americka, Amerika, Amerikah, Ameriqua, Ameriquah, Amerique, Ameryca, Amerycah, Amerycka, Ameryckah, Ameryka, Amerykah, Ameryqua, Ameryque

Amethyst (Greek) wine; purple-violet gemstone. History: in the ancient world, the amethyst stone was believed to help prevent drunkenness.

Amethyst *(cont.)*
Amathist, Amathista, Amathiste, Amathysta,
Amathyste, Amethist, Amethista, Amethiste,
Amethistia, Amethysta, Amethyste,
Amethystia, Amethystya, Amethystyah

Amia (Hebrew) a form of Amy.
Amio

Amilia (Latin, German) a form of Amelia.
Amiliah, Amilisa, Amilita, Amillia, Amilya

Amilie (Latin, German) a form of Amelia.
Amilee, Amili, Amily

Amina (Arabic) trustworthy, faithful.
History: the mother of the prophet
Muhammad.
Aamena, Aamina, Aminda, Amindah,
Aminta, Amintah

Aminah (Arabic) a form of Amina.
Aaminah

Amira (Hebrew) speech; utterance.
(Arabic) princess. See also Mira.
Amyra, Amyrah

Amirah (Hebrew, Arabic) a form of Amira.

Amissa (Hebrew) truth.
Amisa, Amisah, Amise, Amisia, Amisiah,
Amissah, Amiza, Amizah, Amysa, Amysah,
Amysia, Amysiah, Amysya, Amysyah,
Amyza, Amyzah

Amita (Hebrew) truth.
Ameeta, Ameetah, Amitah, Amitha, Amyta,
Amytah

Amity (Latin) friendship.
Amitee, Amitey, Amiti, Amitie, Amytee,
Amytey, Amyti, Amytie, Amyty

Amlika (Hindi) mother.
Amlikah, Amylka, Amylkah

Amma (Hindi) mother.

Amorette (Latin) beloved; loving.
Amoreta, Amoretah, Amorete, Amorett,
Amoretta, Amorettah, Amorit, Amorita,
Amoritah, Amoritt, Amoritta, Amoritte,
Amoryt, Amoryta, Amorytah, Amoryte,
Amorytt, Amorytta, Amoryttah, Amorytte

Amorie (German) industrious leader.

Amparo (Spanish) protected.

Amrit (Sanskrit) nectar.

Amrita (Spanish) a form of Amorette.
Amritah, Amritta, Amritte, Amryta,
Amrytah, Amryte, Amrytta, Amryttah,
Amrytte

Amy (Latin) beloved. See also Aimee,
Emma, Esmé.
Aami, Amata, Amatah, Ame, Amei, Amey,
Ammy, Amye, Amylyn

An (Chinese) peaceful.

Ana (Hawaiian, Spanish) a form of
Hannah.

Anaba (Native American) she returns
from battle.
Anabah

Anabel, Anabelle, Annabell, Annabelle
(English) forms of Annabel.
Anabela, Anabele, Anabell, Anna-Bell,
Annahbell, Annahbelle, Annebell, Annebelle,
Annibell, Annibelle, Annybell, Annybelle

Anahi, Anahy (Persian) short forms of
Anahita.
Anahai

Anahit (Persian) a short form of Anahita.

Anahita (Persian) the immaculate one.
Mythology: a water goddess.

Anai (Hawaiian, Spanish) a form of Ana.
Anaia

Anais (Hebrew) gracious.
Anaise, Anaïse, Anaiss, Anays, Anayss

Anakaren (English) a combination of
Ana + Karen.
Annakaren

Anala (Hindi) fine.
Analah

Analaura (English) a combination of Ana
+ Laura.
Annalaura

Anali (Hindu, Indian) fire, fiery.

Analicia (English) a form of Analisa.
Analisha, Analisia

Analisa, Annalisa (English) combinations of Anna + Lisa.
Analice, Analissa, Annaliesa, Annalissa, Annalyca, Annalyce, Annalysa

Analise, Annalise (English) forms of Analisa.
Analis, Annalisse, Annalys, Annalyse

Anamaria (English) a combination of Ana + Maria.
Anamarie, Anamary

Ananda (Hindi) blissful.
Anandah

Anastacia, Anastazia, Annastasia (Greek) forms of Anastasia.
Anastace, Anastaciah, Anastacie, Anastacya, Anastacyah, Anastaziah, Anastazya

Anastasia (Greek) resurrection. See also Nastasia, Stacey, Stacia, Stasya.
Anastase, Anastascia, Anastasee, Anastasha, Anastashia, Anastasie, Anastasija, Anastassia, Anastassya, Anastasya, Anastatia, Anastaysia, Anastice, Anestasia, Annastasija, Annastaysia, Annastazia, Annestasia, Annestassia, Annstás, Anstace, Anstice

Anatola (Greek) from the east.
Anatolah, Anatolia, Anatoliah, Anatolya, Anatolyah, Annatola, Annatolah, Annatolia, Annatoliah, Annatolya, Annatolyah

Anci (Hungarian) a form of Hannah.
Annus, Annushka

Andee, Andi, Andie (American) short forms of Andrea, Fernanda.
Ande, Andea, Andy

Andra (Greek, Latin) a short form of Andrea.
Andrah

Andrea (Greek) strong; courageous. See also Ondrea.
Aindrea, Andera, Anderea, Andraia, Andraya, Andreah, Andreaka, Andreea, Andreja, Andreka, Andrel, Andrell, Andrelle, Andreo, Andressa, Andrette, Andriea, Andrieka, Andrietta, Andris, Andrya, Andryah

Andréa (French) a form of Andrea.
Andrée

Andreana, Andreanna (Greek) forms of Andrea.
Ahndrianna, Andreanah, Andreannah, Andreeana, Andreeanah, Andrena, Andreyana, Andreyonna

Andreane, Andreanne, Andree Ann, Andree Anne (Greek) combinations of Andrea + Ann.
Andrean, Andreann, Andreean, Andreeane, Andreeanne, Andrene, Andrian, Andriann, Andrianne, Andrienne, Andryane, Andryann, Andryanne

Andree (Greek) a short form of Andrea.
Andri

Andreia (Greek) a form of Andrea.

Andreina (Greek) a form of Andrea.

Andreya (Greek) a form of Andrea.

Andria (Greek) a form of Andrea.
Andriah

Andriana, Andrianna (Greek) forms of Andrea.
Andrianah, Andriannah, Andrina, Andrinah, Andriona, Andrionna, Andryana, Andryanah, Andryanna, Andryannah

Aneesa (Greek) a form of Agnes.
Anee, Aneesah, Aneese, Aneisa

Aneesha (Greek) a form of Agnes.
Aneeshah, Aneesia, Aneisha

Aneko (Japanese) older sister.

Anel (Hawaiian) a short form of Anela.
Anelle

Anela (Hawaiian) angel.
Anelah, Anella, Anellah

Anesha (Greek) a form of Agnes.
Ahnesha

Aneshia (Greek) a form of Agnes.
Ahnesshia

Anesia (Greek) a form of Agnes.
Ahnesia, Anessia

Anessa, Annessa (Greek) forms of Agnes.

Aneta (Spanish) a form of Anita. (French) a form of Annette.
Anetah

Anetra (American) a form of Annette.
Anetrah

Anezka (Czech) a form of Hannah.

Angel, Angele, Angell, Angelle (Greek) short forms of Angela.
Angéle, Angil, Anjel, Anjelle

Angela (Greek) angel; messenger. See also Engel.
Angala, Anganita, Angelanell, Angelanette, Angelo, Angiola, Anglea, Anjella, Anjellah

Angelea, Angelie (Greek) forms of Angela.
Angelee, Angeleigh, Angeli

Angelena (Russian) a form of Angela.
Angalena, Angalina, Angeleana

Angeles (Spanish) a form of Angela.

Angelia (Greek) a form of Angela.
Angeleah

Angelic (Russian) a short form of Angelica.
Angalic

Angelica, Angelika, Angellica (Greek) forms of Angela. See also Anjelica, Engelica.
Angelici, Angelike, Angeliki, Angilica

Angelicia (Russian) a form of Angelica.

Angelina (Russian) a form of Angela.
Angeliana, Angelinah, Angellina, Angelyna, Anhelina, Anjelina

Angeline, Angelyn (Russian) forms of Angela.
Angeleen, Angelene, Angelin, Angelyne, Angelynn, Angelynne

Angelique (French) a form of Angela.
Angeliqua, Angeliquah, Angélique, Angilique, Anjelique

Angelisa (American) a combination of Angela + Lisa.

Angelita (Spanish) a form of Angela.
Angellita

Angella (Greek) a form of Angela.
Angellah

Angeni (Native American) spirit.
Angeenee, Angeeni, Angeenie, Angeeny, Angenia, Anjeenee, Anjeeney, Anjeeni, Anjeenia, Anjeenie, Anjeeny, Anjenee, Anjeney, Anjenie, Anjeny

Angie (Greek) a familiar form of Angela.
Ange, Angee, Angey, Angi, Angy, Anjee

Anh (Vietnamese) peace; safety.

Ani (Hawaiian) beautiful.
Aany, Aanye, Anee, Aney, Anie, Any

Ania (Polish) a form of Hannah.
Ahnia, Aniah

Anica, Anika (Czech) familiar forms of Anna.
Aanika, Anaka, Aneeky, Aneka, Anekah, Anicah, Anicka, Anikah, Anikka, Aniko, Annaka, Anniki, Annikki, Anyca, Anycah, Anyka, Anykah, Anyqua, Anyquah

Anice, Anise (English) forms of Agnes.
Anesse, Anis, Annes, Annice, Annis, Annise, Anniss, Annisse, Annus, Annys, Annyse, Annyss, Annysse, Anys

Aniela (Polish) a form of Anna.
Anielah, Aniella, Aniellah, Anielle, Anniela, Anlielah, Anniella, Anniellah, Annielle, Anyel, Anyela, Anyele, Anyella, Anyellah, Anyelle

Anik (Czech) a short form of Anica.
Anike, Anikke

Anila (Hindi) Religion: an attendant of the Hindu god Vishnu.
Anilah, Anilla, Anillah, Anyla, Anylah, Anylla, Anyllah

Aniqua (Czech) a form of Anica.
Aniquah

Anisa, Anisah (Arabic) friendly. See also Anissa.

Anisha, Annisha (English) forms of Agnes, Ann.
Aanisha, Aeniesha

Anissa (English) a form of Agnes, Ann. (Arabic) a form of Anisa.
Anissah

Anita (Spanish) a form of Ann, Anna. See also Nita.
Aneeta, Aneetah, Aneethah, Anetha, Anitha, Anithah, Anitia, Anitta, Anittah, Anitte, Annita, Annitah, Annite, Annitta, Annittah, Annitte, Annyta, Annytah, Annytta, Annyttah, Annytte, Anyta, Anytah

Anitra (Spanish) a form of Anita.

Aniya (Russian) a form of Anya.
Aaniyah, Anaya, Aneya, Aneyah, Aniyah

Anja (Russian) a form of Anya.
Anje

Anjali (Hindu) offering with both hands. (Indian) offering with devotion.

Anjela (Greek) a form of Angela.
Anjelah

Anjelica (Greek) a form of Angela. See also Angelica.
Anjelika

Anka (Polish) a familiar form of Hannah.
Anke

Ann, Anne (English) gracious.
Ane, Annchen, Annze, Anouche

Ann Catherine, Anne Catherine (American) combinations of Ann + Catherine.
Ann-Catherine, Anncatherine, Anne-Catherine, Annecatherine

Ann Julie, Anne Julie (American) combinations of Ann + Julie.
Ann-Julie, Annjulie, Anne-Julie, Annejulie

Ann Marie, Ann-Marie, Anne Marie, Anne-Marie, Annemarie, Annmarie, (English) combinations of Ann + Marie.
Anmaree, Anmari, Anmarie, Anmary, Anmarya, Anmaryah, Annmaree, Annmari, Annmary

Ann Sophie, Anne Sophie, Anne-Sophie (American) combinations of Ann + Sophie.
Ann-Sophie

Anna (German, Italian, Czech, Swedish) gracious. Culture: Anna Pavlova was a famous Russian ballerina. See also Anica, Anissa, Nina.

Ahnna, Anah, Aniela, Annice, Annina, Annora, Anona, Anyu, Aska

Anna Maria, Annamaria (English) combinations of Anna + Maria.
Anna-Maria

Anna Marie, Anna-Marie, Annamarie (English) combinations of Anna + Marie.

Annabel (English) a combination of Anna + Bel.
Anabele, Annabal, Annahbel, Annebel, Annebele, Annibel, Annibele, Annybel, Annybele

Annabella (English) a form of Annabel.
Anabela, Anabella, Annabelah, Annabellah, Annahbella, Annebela, Annebelah, Annebella, Annebellah, Annibela, Annibelah, Annibella, Annibellah, Annybela, Annybelah, Annybella, Annybellah

Annah (German, Italian, Czech, Swedish) a form of Anna.

Annalee (Finnish) a form of Annalie.

Annalie (Finnish) a form of Hannah.
Analee, Annalea, Annaleah, Annaleigh, Annaleigha, Annali, Anneli, Annelie

Annaliese (English) a form of Analisa.

Anneka (Swedish) a form of Hannah.
Annaka, Annekah

Anneke (Czech) a form of Anik. (Swedish) a form of Anneka.

Anneliese, Annelise (English) forms of Annelisa.
Analiese, Anelise, Annelyse

Annelisa (English) a combination of Ann + Lisa.
Anelisa, Annelys, Annelysa

Annette (French) a form of Ann. See also Anetra, Nettie.
Anet, Anete, Anett, Anetta, Anette, Annet, Anneta, Annetah, Annete, Anneth, Annett, Annetta, Annettah

Annick, Annik (Russian) short forms of Annika.
Annike

Annie, Anny (English) familiar forms of Ann.
Annee, Anney, Anni

Annie Claude (American) a combination of Annie + Claude.
Annie-Claude

Annie Kim (American) a combination of Annie + Kim.
Annie-Kim

Annie Pier (American) a combination of Annie + Pier.
Annie-Pier

Annika (Russian) a form of Ann. (Swedish) a form of Anneka.
Annicka, Anniki, Annikka, Annikki, Anninka, Annushka, Anouska, Anuska

Annina (Hebrew) graceful.
Anina, Aninah, Anninah, Annyna, Annynah, Anyna, Anynah

Annisa, Annissa (Arabic) a form of Anisa. (English) a form of Anissa.
Annisah, Annissah

Annjanette (American) a combination of Ann + Janette (see Janett).
Angen, Angenett, Angenette, Anjane, Anjanetta, Anjani

Annmaria (American) a combination of Ann + Maria.
Anmaria, Anmariah, Annmariah, Annmarya, Annmaryah

Annora (Latin) honor.
Anora, Anorah, Anoria, Anoriah, Annorah, Annore, Annoria, Annoriah, Annoryah, Anorya, Anoryah

Anona (English) pineapple.
Anonah, Annona, Annonah, Annonia, Annoniah, Annonya, Annonyah

Anouhea (Hawaiian) cool, soft fragrance.

Anouk (Dutch) a familiar form of Anna.

Anselma (German) divine protector.
Anselmah, Anzelma, Anzelmah, Selma, Zelma

Ansleigh, Ansley (Scottish) forms of Ainsley.

Anslea, Ansleah, Anslee, Anslei, Ansleigh, Ansli, Anslie, Ansly

Antania (Greek, Latin) a form of Antonia.

Anthea (Greek) flower.
Antha, Anthe, Antheah, Anthia, Anthiah, Anthya, Anthyah, Thia

Anthony (Latin) praiseworthy. (Greek) flourishing.

Antionette (French) a form of Antonia.
Antionet, Antionett, Anntionett

Antoinette (French) a form of Antonia. See also Nettie, Toinette, Toni.
Anta, Antanette, Antoinella, Antoinet, Antonice, Antonieta, Antonietta

Antonella (French) a form of Antoinette.

Antonette (French) a form of Antoinette.
Antonett, Antonetta

Antonia (Greek) flourishing. (Latin) praiseworthy. See also Toni, Tonya, Tosha.
Ansonia, Ansonya, Antinia, Antona, Antonee, Antoney, Antoni, Antoñía, Antoniah, Antonice, Antonie, Antoniya, Antonnea, Antonnia, Antonniah, Antonya, Antonyah

Antonice (Latin) a form of Antonia.
Antanise, Antonias, Antonica, Antonicah, Antonise

Antonina (Greek, Latin) a form of Antonia.
Antonine

Antonique (French) a form of Antoinette.

Antonisha (Latin) a form of Antonice.
Antanisha, Antonesha, Antoneshia

Anya (Russian) a form of Anna.
Annya, Annyah, Anyah

Anyssa (English) a form of Anissa.
Annysa, Annysah, Annyssa, Anysa, Anysah, Anysha, Anyssah

Aphra (Hebrew) young doe. See also Afra.
Aphrah

Aphrodite (Greek) Mythology: the goddess of love and beauty.
Aphrodita, Aphrodyta, Aphrodytah, Aphrodyte

Apoline (Greek) a form of Appollonia.
Apolina, Apollina, Apollinah, Apolline,
Apollyn, Apollyna, Apollynah, Apollyne,
Appolina, Appolinah, Appoline, Appollina,
Appollinah, Appolline, Appollyn, Appollyna,
Appollynah, Appollyne

Appollonia (Greek) a form of Apollo (see
Boys' Names).
Apollonia, Apolloniah, Apollonya, Apollonyah,
Apolonia, Apoloniah, Apolonie, Apolonya,
Apolonyah, Appolloniah, Appollonya,
Appollonyah

April (Latin) opening. See also Avril.
Aprel, Aprela, Aprele, Aprella, Aprelle,
Apriell, Aprielle, Aprila, Aprilah, Aprile,
Aprilett, Apriletta, Aprilette, Aprili, Aprill,
Aprilla, Aprillah, Aprille

Apryl (Latin) a form of April.
Apryla, Aprylah, Apryle, Aprylla, Aprylle

Aquene (Native American) peaceful.
Aqueen, Aqueena, Aqueene

Aquila (Latin, Spanish) eagle.
Acquilla, Aquil, Aquilas, Aquileo, Aquiles,
Aquilino, Aquill, Aquille, Aquillino, Aquyl,
Aquyla, Aquyll, Aquylla

Aquilla (Latin, Spanish) a form of Aquila.

Ara (Arabic) opinionated.
Ahraya, Aira, Arae, Arah

Arabella (Latin) beautiful altar. See also
Belle, Orabella.
Arabel, Arabela, Arabelah, Arabele, Arabell,
Arabellah, Arabelle

Araceli, Aracely (Latin) heavenly altar.
Aracele, Aracelia, Aracelli

Araseli (Latin) a form of Araceli.
Arasely

Araya (Arabic) a form of Ara.
Arayah

Arcelia (Latin) a form of Araceli.
Arceli

Ardelle (Latin) warm; enthusiastic.
Ardel, Ardela, Ardelah, Ardele, Ardelia,
Ardeliah, Ardelis, Ardell, Ardella, Ardellah

Arden (English) valley of the eagle.
Literature: in Shakespeare, a romantic
place of refuge.
Ardan, Ardana, Ardane, Ardean, Adeana,
Ardeane, Ardeen, Ardeena, Ardeenah,
Ardeene, Ardena, Ardenah, Ardene, Ardenia,
Ardin, Ardina, Ardinah, Ardine, Ardun,
Ardyn, Ardyna, Ardynah, Ardyne

Ardi (Hebrew) a short form of Arden,
Ardice, Ardith.
Ardie

Ardice (Hebrew) a form of Ardith.
Ardis, Ardisa, Ardisah, Ardise, Ardiss, Ardissa,
Ardisse, Ardyce, Ardys, Ardyse, Ardyss, Ardyssa,
Ardysse

Ardith (Hebrew) flowering field.
Ardath, Ardyth, Ardythe

Areil (American) a form of Areli.
Areile

Areli, Arely (American) forms of Oralee.
Arelee, Arelis, Arelli, Arellia, Arelly

Arella (Hebrew) angel; messenger.
Arela, Arelah, Arellah, Arelle, Orella, Orelle

Aretha (Greek) virtuous. See also Oretha,
Retha.
Areata, Areatah, Areatha, Areathah, Areathia,
Areathiah, Areeta, Areetah, Areetha, Areethah,
Areethia, Areta, Aretah, Arethea, Aretheah,
Arethia, Arethiah, Aretina, Aretta, Arettah,
Arette, Arita, Aritha, Arithah, Arytha,
Arythah, Arythia, Arythiah, Arythya,
Arythyah

Ari, Arie (Hebrew) short forms of Ariel.

Aria (Hebrew) a form of Ariel.
Ariea, Arya, Aryah, Aryia

Ariadna (Greek) a form of Ariadne.
Ariadnah, Aryadna, Aryadnah

Ariadne (Greek) holy. Mythology: the
daughter of King Minos of Crete.

Ariah (Hebrew) a form of Aria.

Arial (Hebrew) a form of Ariel.
Ariale

Arian, Ariane (French) forms of Ariana.
Aerian, Aerion, Arianie, Arien, Ariene,
Arieon

Ariana, Arianna (Greek) holy.
Aeriana, Aerianna, Aerionna, Ahreanna,
Ahriana, Ahrianna, Airiana, Arianah,
Ariannah, Ariena, Arienah, Arienna,
Ariennah, Arihana

Arianne (English) a form of Ariana.
Aeriann, Aerionne, Airiann, Ariann,
Ariannie, Arieann, Arienne, Arionne

Arica, Arika (Scandinavian) forms of
Erica.
Aerica, Aericka, Aeryka, Aricah, Aricca,
Ariccah, Aricka, Arickah, Arikah, Arike,
Arikka, Arikkah, Ariqua, Aryca, Arycah,
Arycca, Aryccah, Arycka, Aryckah, Aryka,
Arykah, Arykka, Arykkah, Aryqua

Arieanna (Greek) a form of Ariana.
Arieana

Ariel (Hebrew) lioness of God.
Ahriel, Aire, Aireal, Airial, Arieal, Arrieal

Ariela, Ariella (Hebrew) forms of Ariel.
Arielah, Ariellah, Aryela, Aryelah, Aryella,
Aryellah

Ariele, Ariell, Arielle, Arriel (French)
forms of Ariel.
Arriele, Arriell, Arrielle

Aries (Greek) Mythology: Ares was the
Greek god of war. (Latin) ram.
Arees, Ares, Arie, Ariez, Aryes

Arietta (Italian) short aria, melody.
Ariet, Arieta, Arietah, Ariete, Ariett,
Ariettah, Ariette, Aryet, Aryeta, Aryetah,
Aryete, Aryett, Aryetta, Aryettah, Aryette

Arin (Hebrew, Arabic) a form of Aaron.
See also Erin.
Arinn, Arrin

Ariona, Arionna (Greek) forms of Ariana.

Arissa (Greek) a form of Arista.

Arista (Greek) best.
Aris, Aristana, Aristen

Arla (German) a form of Carla.

Arleen (Irish) a form of Arlene.
Arleene

Arleigh (English) a form of Harley.
Arlea, Arleah, Arlee, Arley, Arlie, Arly

Arlena (Irish) a form of Arlene.
Arlana, Arlanah, Arleena, Arleina, Arlenah,
Arliena, Arlienah, Arlina, Arlinah, Arlinda

Arlene (Irish) pledge. See also Erline,
Lena, Lina.
Airlen, Arlein, Arleine, Arlen, Arlenis,
Arleyne, Arlien, Arliene, Arlin, Arline, Arlis

Arlette (English) a form of Arlene.
Arleta, Arletah, Arlete, Arletta, Arlettah,
Arletty

Arlynn (American) a combination of
Arlene + Lynn.
Arlyn, Arlyne, Arlynna, Arlynne

Armani (Persian) desire, goal.
Armahni, Arman, Armanee, Armanii

Armide (Latin) armed warrior.
Armid, Armidea, Armidee, Armidia,
Armidiah, Armydea, Armydee, Armydia,
Armydiah, Armydya

Armine (Latin) noble. (German) soldier.
(French) a form of Herman (see Boys'
Names).
Armina, Arminah, Arminee, Arminey,
Arminel, Armini, Arminie, Armyn, Armyna,
Armynah, Armyne

Arnelle (German) eagle.
Arnel, Arnela, Arnelah, Arnele, Arnell,
Arnella, Arnellah

Arnette (English) little eagle.
Arnet, Arneta, Arnett, Arnetta, Arnettah

Arnina (Hebrew) enlightened. (Arabic) a
form of Aaron.
Aarnina, Arninah, Arnine, Arnona,
Arnonah, Arnyna, Arnynah

Arriana (Greek) a form of Ariana.
Arrianna

Artemis (Greek) Mythology: the goddess
of the hunt and the moon.
Artema, Artemah, Artemisa, Artemise,
Artemisia, Artemys, Artemysia, Artemysya

Artha (Hindi) wealthy, prosperous.
Arthah, Arthea, Arthi

Arti (Hebrew) a form of Ardi. (Hindi) a
familiar form of Artha.
Artie

Artis (Irish) noble; lofty hill. (Scottish)
bear. (English) rock. (Icelandic) follower
of Thor.
*Arthelia, Arthene, Arthette, Arthurette,
Arthurina, Arthurine, Artina, Artine, Artice,
Artisa, Artise, Artyna, Artynah, Artyne,
Artys, Artysa, Artyse*

Aryana, Aryanna (Italian) forms of Ariana.
*Aryan, Aryanah, Aryane, Aryann,
Aryannah, Aryanne, Aryonna*

Aryel, Aryelle (Hebrew) forms of Ariel.
Aryele, Aryell

Aryn (Hebrew) a form of Aaron.
Aryne, Arynn, Arynne

Aryssa (Greek) a form of Arissa.

Asa (Japanese) born in the morning.
Asah

Asha (Arabic, Swahili) a form of Aisha,
Ashia.

Ashante, Ashanté (Swahili) forms of
Ashanti.

Ashanti (Swahili) from a tribe in West
Africa.
*Achante, Achanti, Asante, Ashanta,
Ashantae, Ashantah, Ashantee, Ashantey,
Ashantia, Ashantie, Ashaunta, Ashauntae,
Ashauntee, Ashaunti, Ashauntia,
Ashauntiah, Ashaunty, Ashauntya,
Ashuntae, Ashunti, Ashuntie*

Asheley, Ashely (English) forms of Ashley.
*Ashelee, Ashelei, Asheleigh, Ashelie,
Ashelley, Ashelly*

Ashia (Arabic) life.
Ayshia

Ashira (Hebrew) rich.
Ashirah, Ashyra, Ashyrah

Ashlan, Ashlen, Ashlin (English) forms
of Ashlyn.
Ashliann, Ashlianne, Ashline

**Ashle, Ashlea, Ashlee, Ashlei, Ashleigh,
Ashli, Ashlie, Ashliegh, Ashly** (English)
forms of Ashley.
Ashleah, Ashleeh, Ashliee, Ashlye

Ashleen (Irish) a form of Ashlyn.
*Ashlean, Ashleann, Ashleene, Ashlena,
Ashlenah, Ashlene, Ashlina, Ashlinah,
Ashlyna*

Ashley (English) ash-tree meadow. See
also Lee.
*Ahslee, Ahsleigh, Aishlee, Ashala, Ashalee,
Ashalei, Ashaley, Ashla, Ashlay, Ashleay,
Ashleigh, Ashleye, Ashlia, Ashliah, Ashlya,
Ashlyah*

Ashlyn, Ashlynn, Ashlynne (English)
ash-tree pool. (Irish) vision, dream.
Ashling, Ashlyne

Ashonti (Swahili) a form of Ashanti.

Ashten, Ashtin, Ashtyn (English) forms
of Ashton.
Ashtine, Ashtynne

Ashton (English) ash-tree settlement.

Ashya (Arabic) a form of Ashia.
Ashyah, Ashyia

Asia (Greek) resurrection. (English) east-
ern sunrise. (Swahili) a form of Aisha.
*Ahsia, Aisia, Aisian, Asian, Asianae, Ayzia,
Esia, Esiah, Esya, Esyah*

Asiah (Greek, English, Swahili) a form of
Asia.

Asiya (Arabic) one who tends to the
weak, one who heals.

Asja (American) a form of Asia.

Asma (Arabic) excellent; precious.

Aspen (English) aspen tree.
Aspin, Aspina, Aspine

Aspyn (English) a form of Aspen.
Aspyna, Aspyne

Aster (English) a form of Astra.
Astar, Astera, Asteria, Astir, Astor, Astyr

Astra (Greek) star.
*Asta, Astara, Astraea, Astrah, Astrea, Astreah,
Astree, Astrey, Astria, Astiah, Astrya, Astryah*

Astrid (Scandinavian) divine strength.
Astrad, Astread, Astred, Astreed, Astri, Astrida,
Astrik, Astrod, Astrud, Astryd, Atti, Estrid

Asya (Greek, English, Swahili) a form of
Asia.
Asyah

Atalanta (Greek) mighty huntress.
Mythology: an athletic young woman
who refused to marry any man who
could not outrun her in a footrace. See
also Lani.
Atalantah, Atalaya, Atlee

Atara (Hebrew) crown.
Atarah, Ataree, Ataria, Atariah, Atarya,
Ataryah, Ateara, Atearah, Atera, Aterah

Athalia (Hebrew) the Lord is mighty.
Atali, Atalie, Athalea, Athaleah, Athalee,
Athalei, Athaleigh, Athaley, Athali, Athaliah,
Athalie, Athaly, Athalya, Athalyah

Athena (Greek) wise. Mythology: the
goddess of wisdom.
Atheana, Atheanah, Athenah, Athenais,
Athene, Athenea

Athina (Greek) a form of Athena.
Atina

Atira (Hebrew) prayer.
Atirah, Atyra, Atyrah

Atiya (Arabic) gift.

Atlanta (Greek) a form of Atalanta.
Atlantah, Atlante, Atlantia, Atlantiah,
Atlantya, Atlantyah

Auberte (French) a form of Alberta.
Auberta, Aubertah, Aubertha, Auberthe,
Aubertina, Aubertine, Aubine, Aubirta,
Aubirtah, Aubirte, Auburta, Auburte,
Aubyrta, Aubyrtah, Aubyrte

Aubree, Aubri, Aubrie, Aubry (French)
forms of Aubrey.
Auberi, Aubre, Aubrei, Aubreigh, Aubria,
Aubriah

Aubrey (German) noble; bearlike.
(French) blond ruler; elf ruler.
Aubary, Aubery, Aubray, Aubrea, Aubreah,
Aubrette, Aubrya, Aubryah, Aubury

Aubriana, Aubrianna (English) combi-
nations of Aubrey + Anna.
Aubreyana, Aubreyanna, Aubreyanne,
Aubreyena, Aubrian, Aubrianah, Aubriane,
Aubriann, Aubriannah, Aubrianne, Aubryan,
Aubryana, Aubryanah, Aubryane, Aubryann,
Aubryanna, Aubryannah, Aubryanne

Aubrielle (French) a form of Aubrey.

Auburn (Latin) reddish brown.
Abern, Aberne, Abirn, Abirne, Aburn,
Aburne, Abyrn, Abyrne, Aubern, Auberne,
Aubin, Aubirn, Aubirne, Aubun, Auburne,
Aubyrn, Aubyrne

Aude, Audey (English) familiar forms of
Audrey.
Audi, Audie

Audra (French) a form of Audrey.
Audrah

Audrea (French) a form of Audrey.
Audria, Audriah, Audriea, Audrya, Audryah

Audreanne, Audrey Ann, Audrey Anne
(English) combinations of Audrey + Ann.
Audreen, Audrianne, Audrienne, Audrey-
Ann, Audrey-Anne

Audree, Audrie, Audry (English) forms
of Audrey.
Audre, Audri

Audrey (English) noble strength.
Adrey, Audey, Audray, Audrin, Audriya,
Audrye

Audrey Maud, Audrey Maude (English)
combinations of Audrey + Maud.
Audrey-Maud, Audrey-Maude,
Audreymaud, Audreymaude

Audriana, Audrianna (English) combi-
nations of Audrey + Anna.
Audreanna, Audrienna, Audryana,
Audryanna

Audrina (English) a form of Audriana.

Audris (German) fortunate, wealthy.
Audrys

August (Latin) born in the eighth month.
A short form of Augustine.
Auguste

Augusta (Latin) a short form of Augustine. See also Gusta.
Agusta, Augustah, Augustia, Augustus, Austina

Augustine (Latin) majestic. Religion: Saint Augustine was the first archbishop of Canterbury. See also Tina.
Agostina, Agostine, Agostyna, Agostyne, Agustina, Augusteen, Augusteena, Augusteene, Augustina, Augustinah, Augustyna, Augustyne

Aundrea (Greek) a form of Andrea.
Aundreah

Aura (Greek) soft breeze. (Latin) golden. See also Ora.
Aurah, Aurea, Aureah, Auri, Auria, Auriah, Aurya, Auryah

Aurelia (Latin) golden. See also Oralia.
Auralea, Auraleah, Auralia, Aurea, Aureah, Aureal, Aurel, Aurela, Aurelah, Aurele, Aurelea, Aureliana, Aurella, Aurellah, Auria, Auriah, Aurie, Aurilia, Auriola, Auriolah, Auriolla, Auriollah, Aurita

Aurelie (Latin) a form of Aurelia.
Auralee, Auralei, Auraleigh, Auraley, Aurali, Auraliah, Auraly, Aurelee, Aurelei, Aureli, Aurell, Aurelle, Auriol, Aurioll, Auriolle

Auriel (Hebrew) a form of Ariel.
Aurielle

Aurora (Latin) dawn. Mythology: the goddess of dawn.
Aurorah, Aurore, Aurure, Ora, Ori, Orie, Rora

Austen, Austin, Austyn (Latin) short forms of Augustine.
Austina, Austinah, Austyna, Austynah, Austyne, Austynn

Autum (American) a form of Autumn.

Autumn (Latin) autumn.
Autom

Ava (Greek) a form of Eva.
Avada, Avae, Avah, Ave, Aveen

Avaline (English) a form of Evelyn.
Avalean, Avaleana, Avaleanah, Avaleen, Avaleena, Avaleenah, Avaleene, Avalina, Avalinah, Avalyn, Avalyna, Avalynah, Avalyne, Avelean, Aveleana, Aveleanah, Aveleen, Aveleena, Aveleenah, Aveleene, Avelina, Avelinah, Avelyn, Avelyna, Avelynah, Avelyne

Avalon (Latin) island.
Avallon, Avalona, Avalonah, Avaloni, Avalonia, Avaloniah, Avalonie, Avalony, Avalonya, Avalonyah

Averi, Averie, Avery (English) forms of Aubrey.
Aivree, Avaree, Avarey, Avari, Avarie, Avary, Averee, Averey, Avry

Aviana (Latin) a form of Avis.
Avianca, Avianna

Avis (Latin) bird.
Avais, Aveis, Aves, Avi, Avia, Aviance, Avice, Avicia, Avise, Avyce, Avys, Avyse

Aviva (Hebrew) springtime. See also Viva.
Aviv, Avivah, Avivi, Avivice, Avivie, Avivit, Avni, Avnit, Avri, Avrit, Avy, Avyva, Avyvah

Avneet (Hebrew) a form of Avner (see Boys' Names).

Avril (French) a form of April.
Avaril, Avarila, Avarile, Avarill, Avarilla, Avarille, Averil, Averila, Averilah, Averill, Averilla, Averille, Averyl, Averyla, Averyle, Averyll, Averylla, Averylle, Avra, Avri, Avrilett, Avriletta, Avrilette, Avrilia, Avrill, Avrille, Avrillia, Avryl, Avryla, Avrylah, Avryle, Avryll, Avrylla, Avryllah, Avrylle, Avryllett, Avrylletta, Avryllette, Avy

Axelle (Latin) axe. (German) small oak tree; source of life.

Aya (Hebrew) bird; fly swiftly.
Aia, Aiah, Aiya, Aiyah

Ayah (Hebrew) a form of Aya.

Ayan (Hindi) a short form of Ayanna.

Ayana (Native American) a form of Aiyana. (Hindi) a form of Ayanna.

Ayanna (Hindi) innocent.
Ahyana, Ayana, Ayania, Ayaniah, Ayannah, Ayannica, Ayna

Ayat (Islamic) sign, revelation.

Ayesha (Persian) a form of Aisha.
Ayasha, Ayeshah, Ayeshia, Ayeshiah, Ayessa, Ayisha, Ayishah, Ayshea, Ayshia, Ayshiah, Ayshya, Ayshyah

Ayita (Cherokee) first in the dance.
Aitah

Ayla (Hebrew) oak tree.
Aylah, Aylana, Aylanah, Aylanna, Aylannah, Aylea, Aylee, Ayleen, Ayleena, Aylena, Aylene, Aylie, Aylin

Aysha (Persian) a form of Aisha.
Ayshah, Ayshe

Aysia (English) a form of Asia. (Persian) a form of Aisha.
Aysiah, Aysian

Aza (Arabic) comfort.
Aiza, Aizha

Azalea (Greek) dry. Botany: a shrub with showy, colorful flowers that grows in dry soil.
Azaleah, Azalee, Azalei, Azaleigh, Azaley, Azali, Azalia, Azaliah, Azalie, Azaly, Azalya, Azalyah, Azelea, Azeleah, Azelia, Azeliah, Azelya, Azelyah

Azaria (Hebrew) a form of Azuriah (see Boys' Names).
Azariah

Azia (Arabic) a form of Aza.
Aizia

Aziza (Swahili) precious.
Azizah, Azize

Azura (Persian) blue semiprecious stone.
Azora, Azorah, Azurah, Azurina, Azurine, Azuryn, Azuryna, Azurynah, Azuryne

Azure (Persian) a form of Azura.

B

Baba (African) born on Thursday.
Aba, Abah, Babah

Babe (Latin) a familiar form of Barbara. (American) a form of Baby.

Babette (French, German) a familiar form of Barbara.
Babet, Babeta, Babetah, Babett, Babetta, Babettah, Babita, Babitta, Babitte, Barbet, Barbett, Barbetta, Barbette, Barbita

Babs (American) a familiar form of Barbara.
Bab

Baby (American) baby.
Babby, Babe, Babea, Babee, Babey, Babi, Babie, Bebe, Bebea, Bebee, Bebey, Bebi, Bebia, Bebie, Beby, Bebya

Badia (Arabic) elegant.
Badiah

Bailee, Baileigh, Baili, Bailie, Baillie, Baily (English) forms of Bailey.
Bailea, Baileah, Bailei, Bailia, Baillee, Bailley, Bailli, Bailly,

Bailey (English) bailiff.
Baelee, Baeleigh, Baeley, Baeli, Bali, Balley

Baka (Hindi) crane.
Bakah

Bakana (Australian) guardian.
Bakanah, Bakanna, Bakannah

Bakari (Swahili) noble promise.
Bakarie, Bakary

Bakarne (Basque) solitude.

Bakula (Hindi) flower.
Bakulah

Balbina (Latin) stammerer.
Balbinah, Balbine, Balbyna, Balbynah, Balbyne

Baleigh (English) a form of Bailey.

Bambi (Italian) child.
Bambea, Bambee, Bambia, Bambiah, Bambie, Bamby, Bambya

Ban (Arabic) has revealed oneself; has appeared.

Bandi (Punjabi) prisoner.
Banda, Bandah, Bandee, Bandey, Bandia, Bandiah, Bandie, Bandy, Bandya, Bandyah

Bao (Chinese) treasure.

Baptista (Latin) baptizer.
Baptisa, Baptissa, Baptisse, Baptiste, Baptysa, Baptysah, Baptyse, Baptyssa, Baptysta, Batista, Battista, Bautista

Bara, Barra (Hebrew) chosen.
Bára, Barah, Barra, Barrah

Barb (Latin) a short form of Barbara.
Barba, Barbe

Barbara (Latin) stranger, foreigner. See also Bebe, Varvara, Wava.
Babara, Babb, Babbie, Babe, Babette, Babina, Babs, Barbara-Ann, Barbarina, Barbarit, Barbarita, Barbary, Barbeeleen, Barbel, Barbera, Barbica, Barbora, Barborah, Barborka, Barbraann, Barbro, Barùska, Basha

Barbie (American) a familiar form of Barbara.
Barbea, Barbee, Barbey, Barbi, Barby, Baubie

Barbra (American) a form of Barbara.
Barbraa, Barbro

Bari (Irish) a form of Barrie.

Barika (Swahili) success.
Barikah, Baryka, Barykah

Barran (Irish) top of a small hill. (Russian) ram.
Baran, Barana, Baranah, Barean, Bareana, Bareane, Bareen, Bareena, Bareenah, Bareene, Barein, Bareina, Bareinah, Bareine, Bareyba, Bareyn, Bareynah, Bareyne, Barin, Barina, Barinah, Barine, Barreen, Barreena, Barreenah, Barreene, Barrin, Barrina, Barrinah, Barrine, Barryn, Barryna, Barrynah, Barryne

Barrett (German) strong as a bear.

Barrie (Irish) spear; markswoman.
Barea, Baree, Barey, Barri, Barria, Barriah, Barrya, Barryah, Barya, Baryah, Berri, Berrie, Berry

Basia (Hebrew) daughter of God.
Bashiah, Bashya, Bashyah, Basiah, Basya, Basyah, Bathia, Batia, Batya, Bithia, Bitya

Basillia (Greek, Latin) royal; queenly.
Basilia, Basiliah, Basilie, Basilla, Basillah, Basillie, Basyla, Basylah, Basyle, Basyll, Basylla, Basyllah, Basylle, Bazila, Bazilah, Bazile, Bazilie, Bazill, Bazilla, Bazillah, Bazille, Bazillia, Bazilliah, Bazillie, Bazyla, Bazylah, Bazyle, Bazyll, Bazylla, Bazyllah, Bazylle

Bathany (Aramaic) a form of Bethany.
Bathanea, Bathaneah, Bathanee, Bathaney, Bathani, Bathania, Bathaniah, Bathanie, Bathannee, Bathanney, Bathanni, Bathannia, Bathanniah, Bathannie, Bathanny, Bathanya, Bathenee, Batheney, Batheni, Bathenia, Batheniah, Bathenie, Batheny

Bathilda (German) warrior.
Bathildah, Bathilde, Bathylda, Bathyldah, Bathylde

Bathsheba (Hebrew) daughter of the oath; seventh daughter. Bible: a wife of King David. See also Sheba.
Bathshua, Batsheva, Batshevah, Bersaba, Bethsabee, Bethsheba

Batini (Swahili) inner thoughts.

Batoul (Arabic) virgin.

Baylea, Baylee, Bayleigh, Bayley, Bayli, Baylie (English) forms of Bailey.
Bayla, Bayle, Bayleah, Baylei, Baylia, Bayliah, Bayliee, Bayliegh, Bayly

Bayo (Yoruba) joy is found.
Baio

Bea (American) a short form of Beatrice.

Beata (Latin) a short form of Beatrice.
Beatah, Beatta, Beeta, Beetah, Beita, Beitah, Beyta, Beytah

Beatrice (Latin) blessed; happy; bringer of joy. See also Trish, Trixie.

Beatrice *(cont.)*
Bea, Beata, Beatrica, Béatrice, Beatricia,
Beatriks, Beatrisa, Beatrise, Beatrissa, Beatrix,
Beatryx, Beattie, Beatty, Bebe, Bee, Beitris,
Trice

Beatris, Beatriz (Latin) forms of Beatrice.
Beatriss, Beatryz

Bebe (Spanish) a form of Barbara, Beatrice.
BB, Beebee, Bibi

Becca (Hebrew) a short form of Rebecca.
Beca, Becah, Beccah, Beka, Bekah, Bekka

Becka (Hebrew) a form of Becca.
Beckah

Becky (American) a familiar form of
Rebecca.
Beckey, Becki, Beckie, Beki, Bekie, Beky

Bedelia (Irish) a form of Bridget.
Bedeelia, Bedeliah, Bedelya, Bedelyah,
Biddy, Bidelia

Bee (American) a short form of Beatrice.

Bel (Hindi) sacred wood of apple trees. A
short form of Amabel, Belinda, Isabel.
See also Belle.
Bell

Bela (Czech) white. (Hungarian) bright.
Belah, Belau, Belia, Beliah, Biela

Belen (Greek) arrow. (Spanish) Bethlehem.
Belina

Belicia (Spanish) dedicated to God.
Beli, Belica, Beliciah, Belicya, Belicyah,
Belysia, Belysia, Belysiah, Belysya, Belysyah

Belinda (Spanish) beautiful. Literature: a
name coined by English poet Alexander
Pope in *The Rape of the Lock*. See also
Blinda, Linda.
Balina, Balinah, Balinda, Balindah,
Balinde, Baline, Ballinda, Ballindah,
Ballinde, Belina, Belinah, Belindah, Belinde,
Belindra, Bellinda, Bellindah, Bellinde,
Bellynda, Bellyndah, Bellynde, Belynda

Bella (Latin) beautiful.
Bellah, Bellau

Belle (French) beautiful. A short form of
Arabella, Belinda, Isabel. See also Bel,
Billie.
Belita, Bell, Belli, Bellina

Belva (Latin) beautiful view.
Belvia, Belviah, Belvya, Belvyah

Bena (Native American) pheasant. See
also Bina.
Benah, Benea, Benna, Bennah

Benecia (Latin) a short form of Benedicta.
Beneciah, Benecya, Benecyah, Beneisha,
Benicia, Benish, Benisha, Benishia, Bennicia,
Benniciah, Bennicie, Bennicya, Bennycia,
Bennyciah, Bennycya, Bennycyah

Benedicta (Latin) blessed.
Bendite, Benedetta, Benedettah, Benedictina,
Benedikta, Benedycta, Benedykta, Bengta,
Benna, Bennicia, Benoîte, Binney

Benedicte (Latin) a form of Benedicta.
Bendite, Benedette, Benedictine

Benita (Spanish) a form of Benedicta.
Beneta, Benetta, Benite, Benitta, Bennita,
Benyta, Benytah, Benyte, Neeta

Bennett (Latin) little blessed one.
Bennet, Bennetta

Benni (Latin) a familiar form of Benedicta.
Bennie, Binni, Binnie, Binny

Bente (Latin) blessed.

Berdine (German) glorious; inner light.
Berdina, Berdinah, Berdyn, Berdyna,
Berdynah, Berdyne, Birdeen, Birdeena,
Birdeene, Birdena, Birdene, Birdenie,
Birdina, Byrdeena, Byrdeenah, Byrdeene,
Byrdina, Byrdinah, Byrdine, Byrdyna,
Byrdynah, Byrdyne

Berenice, Berenise (Greek) forms of
Bernice.
Berenisse, Bereniz, Berenize

Berget (Irish) a form of Bridget.
Bergette, Bergit

Berit (German) glorious.
Beret, Bereta, Berete, Berett, Beretta, Berette,
Biret, Bireta, Birete, Birett, Biretta, Birette,
Byret, Byreta, Byrete, Byrett, Byretta, Byrette

Berkley (Scottish, English) birch-tree meadow.
Berkeley, Berkly

Berlynn (English) a combination of Bertha + Lynn.
Berla, Berlin, Berlinda, Berline, Berling, Berlyn, Berlyne, Berlynne

Bernadette (French) a form of Bernadine. See also Nadette.
Bera, Beradette, Berna, Bernadet, Bernadeta, Bernadetah, Bernadete, Bernadett, Bernadetta, Bernadettah, Bernadit, Bernadita, Bernaditah, Bernadite, Bernadyta, Bernadytah, Bernadyte, Bernarda, Bernardette, Bernedet, Bernedette, Bernessa, Berneta

Bernadine (English, German) brave as a bear.
Bernadeen, Bernadeena, Bernadeenah, Bernadeene, Bernaden, Bernadena, Bernadenah, Bernadene, Bernadin, Bernadina, Bernadinah, Bernadyn, Bernadyna, Bernadynah, Bernadyne, Bernardina, Bernardine, Berni

Berneta (French) a short form of Bernadette.
Bernatta, Bernetah, Bernete, Bernetta, Bernettah, Bernette, Bernit, Bernita, Bernitah, Bernite, Bernyt, Bernyta, Bernytah, Bernyte

Berni (English) a familiar form of Bernadine, Bernice.
Bernie, Berny

Bernice (Greek) bringer of victory. See also Bunny, Vernice.
Berenike, Bernece, Berneece, Berneese, Bernese, Bernessa, Bernica, Bernicah, Bernicia, Bernicka, Bernika, Bernikah, Bernise, Bernyc, Bernyce, Bernyse, Nixie

Berry (English) berry. A short form of Bernice.
Beree, Berey, Beri, Berie, Berree, Berrey, Berri, Berrie, Bery

Berta (German) a form of Berit, Bertha.

Bertha (German) bright; illustrious; brilliant ruler. A short form of Alberta. See also Birdie, Peke.

Barta, Bartha, Berth, Berthe, Bertille, Bertita, Bertrona, Bertus, Birtha, Birthe, Byrth, Byrtha, Byrthah

Berti (German, English) a familiar form of Gilberte, Bertina.
Berte, Bertie, Berty

Bertille (French) a form of Bertha.
Bertilla

Bertina (English) bright, shining.
Berteana, Berteanah, Berteena, Berteenah, Berteene, Bertinah, Bertine, Bertyna, Bertynah, Bertyne, Birteana, Birteanah, Birteena, Birteenah, Birteene, Birtinah, Birtine, Birtyna, Birtynah, Birtyne, Byrteana, Byrteanah, Byrteena, Byrteenah, Byrteene, Byrtinah, Byrtine, Byrtyna, Byrtynah, Byrtyne

Berwyn (Welsh) white head.
Berwin, Berwina, Berwinah, Berwine, Berwyna, Berwynah, Berwyne, Berwynn, Berwynna, Berwynnah, Berwynne

Beryl (Greek) sea green jewel.
Beral, Beril, Berila, Berile, Berill, Berille, Beryle, Berylla, Berylle

Bess (Hebrew) a short form of Bessie.

Bessie (Hebrew) a familiar form of Elizabeth.
Besee, Besey, Besi, Besie, Bessee, Bessey, Bessi, Bessy, Besy

Beth (Hebrew, Aramaic) house of God. A short form of Bethany, Elizabeth.
Betha, Bethe, Bethia

Bethani, Bethanie (Aramaic) forms of Bethany.
Bethanee, Bethania, Bethaniah, Bethannee, Bethannie, Bethenee, Bethenni, Bethennie, Bethni, Bethnie

Bethann (English) a combination of Beth + Ann.
Bathana, Beth-Ann, Beth-Anne, Bethan, Bethanah, Bethane, Bethanna, Bethannah, Bethanne, Bethena, Bethina, Bethinah, Bethine, Bethyn, Bethyna, Bethynah, Bethyne

Bethany (Aramaic) house of figs. Bible: the site of Lazarus's resurrection.
Bathanny, Bethaney, Bethanney, Bethanny, Betheney, Bethenney, Bethenny, Betheny, Bethia, Bethina, Bethney, Bethny, Betthany

Bethel (Hebrew) from God's house.
Bethal, Bethall, Bethell, Bethil, Bethill, Bethol, Betholl, Bethyl, Bethyll

Betsy (American) a familiar form of Elizabeth.
Betsee, Betsey, Betsi, Betsia, Betsie, Betsya, Betsyah, Betsye

Bette (French) a form of Betty.
Beta, Betah, Bete, Betea, Betia, Betka, Bett, Betta, Bettah

Bettina (American) a combination of Beth + Tina.
Betina, Betinah, Betine, Betti, Bettinah, Bettine, Bettyna, Bettynah, Bettyne, Betyna, Betynah, Betyne

Betty (Hebrew) consecrated to God. (English) a familiar form of Elizabeth.
Betee, Betey, Beti, Betie, Bettee, Bettey, Betti, Bettie, Betty-Jean, Betty-Jo, Betty-Lou, Bettye, Bettyjean, Bettyjo, Bettylou, Bety, Boski, Bözsi

Betula (Hebrew) girl, maiden.
Betulah, Betulla, Betullah

Beulah (Hebrew) married. Bible: Beulah is a name for Israel.
Beula, Beulla, Beullah

Bev (English) a short form of Beverly.

Bevanne (Welsh) child of Evan.
Bevan, Bevann, Bevany, Bevin, Bevina, Bevine, Bevinnah, Bevyn, Bevyna, Bevyne

Beverley (English) a form of Beverly.
Beverle, Beverlea, Beverleah, Beverlee, Beverlei, Beverleigh

Beverly (English) beaver field. See also Buffy.
Bevalee, Beverlie, Beverlly, Bevlea, Bevlee, Bevlei, Bevleigh, Bevley, Bevli, Bevlie, Bevly, Bevlyn, Bevlynn, Bevlynne, Bevvy, Verly

Beverlyann (American) a combination of Beverly + Ann.
Beverliann, Beverlianne, Beverlyanne

Bian (Vietnamese) hidden; secretive.
Biane, Biann, Bianne, Byan, Byane, Byann, Byanne

Bianca (Italian) white. See also Blanca, Vianca.
Biancca, Biancha, Biancia, Bianco, Bianey, Bianica, Biannca, Biannqua, Binney, Byanca, Byancah, Byanqua

Bianka (Italian) a form of Bianca.
Beyanka, Biankah, Biannka, Byancka, Byanckah, Byanka, Byankah

Bibi (Latin) a short form of Bibiana. (Arabic) lady. (Spanish) a form of Bebe.
BeBe, Beebee, Byby

Bibiana (Latin) lively.
Bibianah, Bibiane, Bibiann, Bibianna, Bibiannah, Bibianne, Bibyan, Bibyana, Bibyanah, Bibyann, Bibyanna, Bibyannah, Bibyanne, Bybian, Bybiana, Bybianah, Bybiane, Bybiann, Bybianna, Bybiannah, Bybianne, Bybyan, Bybyana, Bybyanah, Bybyane, Bybyann, Bybyanna, Bybyannah, Bybyanne

Biddy (Irish) a familiar form of Bedelia.
Biddie

Billi, Billy (English) forms of Billie.
Biley, Bili, Billey, Billye, Bily, Byley, Byli, Bylli, Bylly, Byly

Billie (English) strong willed. (German, French) a familiar form of Belle, Wilhelmina.
Bilea, Bileah, Bilee, Bilei, Bileigh, Bilie, Billea, Billee, Bylea, Byleah, Bylee, Bylei, Byleigh, Bylie, Byllea, Byllee, Byllei, Bylleigh, Byllie

Billie-Jean (American) a combination of Billie + Jean.
Billiejean, Billy-Jean, Billyjean

Billie-Jo (American) a combination of Billie + Jo.
Billiejo, Billy-Jo, Billyjo

Bina (Hebrew) wise; understanding.
(Swahili) dancer. (Latin) a short form
of Sabina. See also Bena.
Binah, Binney, Binta, Bintah, Byna, Bynah

Binney (English) a familiar form of
Benedicta, Bianca, Bina.
Binnee, Binni, Binnie, Binny

Bionca (Italian) a form of Bianca.
*Beonca, Beyonca, Beyonka, Bioncha,
Bionica, Bionka, Bionnca*

Birdie (English) bird. (German) a familiar
form of Bertha.
*Bird, Birde, Birdea, Birdee, Birdella,
Birdena, Birdey, Birdi, Birdy, Byrd, Byrda,
Byrde, Byrdey, Byrdie, Byrdy*

Birgitte (Swedish) a form of Bridget.
*Berget, Bergeta, Birgit, Birgita, Birgitt,
Birgitta*

Bjorg (Scandinavian) salvation.
Bjorga

Bladina (Latin) friendly.
*Bladea, Bladeana, Bladeanah, Bladeane,
Bladeen, Bladeena, Bladeene, Bladene,
Bladine, Bladyn, Bladyna, Bladyne*

Blaine (Irish) thin.
Blain, Blane

Blair (Scottish) plains dweller.
Blare, Blayr, Blayre

Blaire (Scottish) a form of Blair.

Blaise (French) one who stammers.
*Blais, Blaisia, Blaiz, Blaize, Blasha, Blasia,
Blayse, Blayz, Blayze, Blaza, Blaze,
Blazena, Blazia*

Blake (English) dark.
Blaik, Blaike, Blaque, Blayk, Blayke

Blakely (English) dark meadow.
*Blaiklea, Blaiklee, Blaiklei, Blaikleigh,
Blaikley, Blaikli, Blaiklie, Blaikly, Blakelea,
Blakeleah, Blakelee, Blakelei, Blakeleigh,
Blakeley, Blakeli, Blakelie, Blakelyn,
Blakelynn, Blakesley, Blakley, Blakli,
Blayklea, Blaykleah, Blayklee, Blayklei,
Blaykleigh, Blaykli, Blayklie, Blaykly*

Blanca (Italian) a form of Bianca.
*Belanca, Belancah, Belancka, Belanckah,
Belanka, Belankah, Bellanca, Bellancah,
Bellancka, Bellanckah, Bellanka, Bellankah,
Blancah, Blancka, Blanka, Blankah, Blannca,
Blanncah, Blannka, Blannkah, Blanqua*

Blanche (French) a form of Bianca.
Blanch, Blancha, Blinney

Blayne (Irish) a form of Blaine.
Blayn

Blinda (American) a short form of
Belinda.
Blynda

Bliss (English) blissful, joyful.
*Blis, Blisa, Blissa, Blisse, Blys, Blysa, Blyss,
Blyssa, Blysse*

Blodwyn (Welsh) flower. See also Wynne.
*Blodwen, Blodwin, Blodwina, Blodwinah,
Blodwine, Blodwyna, Blodwynah, Blodwyne,
Blodwynn, Blodwynna, Blodwynnah,
Blodwynne, Blodyn*

Blondelle (French) blond, fair haired.
*Blondel, Blondele, Blondelia, Blondeliah,
Blondell, Blondella, Blondelya, Blondelyah*

Blondie (American) a familiar form of
Blondelle.
*Blondea, Blondee, Blondey, Blondi, Blondia,
Blondiah, Blondy, Blondya*

Blossom (English) flower.

Blum (Yiddish) flower.
Bluma, Blumah

Blythe (English) happy, cheerful.
Blithe, Blyss, Blyth

Bo (Chinese) precious.
Beau, Bow

Boacha (Hebrew) blessed.

Bobbette (American) a familiar form of
Roberta.
Bobbet, Bobbetta, Bobinetta, Bobinette

Bobbi, Bobbie (American) familiar
forms of Barbara, Roberta.
*Baubie, Bobbe, Bobbea, Bobbee, Bobbey,
Bobbie-Jean, Bobbie-Lynn, Bobbie-Sue,*

Bobbi, Bobbie *(cont.)*
Bobbisue, Bobby, Bobbye, Bobea, Bobee,
Bobey, Bobi, Bobie, Bobina, Bobine, Boby

Bobbi-Ann, Bobbie-Ann (American)
combinations of Bobbi + Ann.
Bobbi-Anne, Bobbiann, Bobbianne, Bobbie-
Anne, Bobby-Ann, Bobby-Anne, Bobbyann,
Bobbyanne

Bobbi-Jo, Bobbie-Jo (American) combinations of Bobbi + Jo.
Bobbiejo, Bobbijo, Bobby-Jo, Bobijo

Bobbi-Lee (American) a combination of
Bobbi + Lee.
Bobbie-Lee, Bobbilee, Bobby-Leigh,
Bobbylee, Bobile

Bodil (Norwegian) mighty ruler.
Bodila, Bodilah, Bodyl, Bodyla, Bodylah

Bonita (Spanish) pretty.
Bonesha, Bonetta, Bonitah, Bonitta,
Bonittah, Bonnetta, Bonnita, Bonnitah,
Bonnitta, Bonnyta, Bonnytta, Bonyta,
Bonytta

Bonnie, Bonny (English, Scottish) beauti-
ful, pretty. (Spanish) familiar forms of
Bonita.
Bonea, Bonee, Boney, Boni, Bonia, Boniah,
Bonie, Bonne, Bonnea, Bonnee, Bonnell,
Bonney, Bonni, Bonnia, Bonniah, Bonnin

Bonnie-Bell (American) a combination
of Bonnie + Belle.
Bonnebell, Bonnebelle, Bonnibela,
Bonnibelah, Bonnibele, Bonnibella,
Bonnibellah, Bonnibell, Bonnibelle,
Bonniebell, Bonniebelle, Bonnybell,
Bonnybelle

Bracken (English) fern.
Brackin, Brackyn, Braken, Brakin, Brakyn

Bradley (English) broad meadow.
Bradlea, Bradleah, Bradlee, Bradlei, Bradleigh,
Bradli, Bradlia, Bradliah, Bradlie, Bradly,
Bradlya

Brady (Irish) spirited.
Bradee, Bradey, Bradi, Bradie, Braedi,
Braidee, Braidey, Braidi, Braidie, Braidy,
Braydee

Braeden (English) broad hill.
Bradyn, Bradynn, Braedan, Braedean,
Braedyn, Braidan, Braiden, Braidyn,
Brayden, Braydn, Braydon

Braelyn (American) a combination of
Braeden + Lynn.
Braelee, Braeleigh, Braelin, Braelle, Braelon,
Braelynn, Braelynne, Brailee, Brailenn,
Brailey, Braili, Brailyn, Braylee, Brayley,
Braylin, Braylon, Braylyn, Braylynn

Branda (Hebrew) blessing.

Brande, Brandee, Brandi, Brandie
(Dutch) forms of Brandy.
Brandea, Brandeece, Brandeese, Brandei,
Brandia, Brandice, Brandiee, Brandii,
Brandily, Brandin, Brandina, Brani,
Branndie, Brendee, Brendi

Branden (English) beacon valley.
Brandan, Brandine, Brandyn

Brandis (Dutch) a form of Brandy.
Brandise, Brandiss, Brandisse

Brandon (English) a form of Branden.

Brandy (Dutch) an after-dinner drink
made from distilled wine.
Bradys, Brand, Brandace, Brandaise,
Brandala, Brandeli, Brandell, Brandy-Lee,
Brandy-Leigh, Brandye, Brandylee,
Brandysa, Brandyse, Brandyss, Brandyssa,
Brandysse, Brann, Brantley, Branyell, Brendy

Brandy-Lynn (American) a combination
of Brandy + Lynn.
Brandalyn, Brandalynn, Brandelyn,
Brandelynn, Brandelynne, Brandilyn,
Brandilynn, Brandilynne, Brandlin,
Brandlyn, Brandlynn, Brandlynne,
Brandolyn, Brandolynn, Brandolynne,
Brandy-Lyn, Brandy-Lynne, Brandylyn,
Brandylynne

Braxton (English) Brock's town.
Braxten, Braxtyn

Bre (Irish, English) a form of Bree.

Brea, Breah (Irish) short forms of Breana,
Briana.
Breea, Breeah

Breahna (Irish) a form of Breana, Briana.

Breana, Breanna, Bréana, Bréanna
(Irish) forms of Briana.
Bre-Anna, Breanah, Breanda, Breannah,
Breannea, Breannia, Breasha, Breawna,
Breila

Breann, Breanne (Irish) short forms of
Briana.
Bre-Ann, Bre-Anne, Breane, Breaunne,
Breiann, Breighann, Breyenne, Brieon

Breasha (Russian) a familiar form of
Breana.

Breauna, Breaunna, Breunna, Briauna,
Briaunna (Irish) forms of Briana.
Breeauna, Breuna

Breck (Irish) freckled.
Brec, Breca, Brecah, Brecka, Breckah,
Brecken, Brek, Breka, Brekah

Bree (English) broth. (Irish) a short form
of Breann. See also Brie.
Breay, Brey

Breean (Irish) a short form of Briana.
Breeane, Breeann, Breeanne, Breelyn, Breeon

Breeana, Breeanna (Irish) forms of
Briana.
Breeanah, Breeannah

Breena (Irish) fairy palace. A form of
Brina.
Breenah, Breene, Breenea, Breenia,
Breeniah, Breina, Breinah

Breeze (English) light wind; carefree.
Brease, Breaz, Breaze, Brees, Breese, Breez,
Briez, Brieze, Bryez, Bryeze, Bryze

Breiana, Breianna (Irish) forms of Briana.
Breian, Breianah, Breiane, Breiann,
Breiannah, Breianne

Breigh (Irish) a form of Bree.
Brei

Brena, Brenna (Irish) forms of Brenda.
Bren, Brenah, Brenie, Brenin, Brenn,
Brennah, Brennaugh, Brenne

Brenda (Irish) little raven. (English) sword.
Brandah, Brandea, Brendah, Brendell,
Brendelle, Brendette, Brendie, Brendyl,
Brennda, Brenndah, Brinda, Brindah,

Brinnda, Brinndah, Brynda, Bryndah,
Brynnda, Brynndah

Brenda-Lee (American) a combination
of Brenda + Lee.
Brendalee, Brendaleigh, Brendali, Brendaly,
Brendalys, Brenlee, Brenley

Brennan (English) a form of Brendan
(see Boys' Names).
Brennea, Brennen, Brennon, Brennyn

Breona, Bréona, Breonna, Bréonna
(Irish) forms of Briana.
Breaona, Breaonah, Breeona, Breeonah,
Breiona, Breionah, Breionna, Breonah,
Breonie, Breonne

Breonia (Irish) a form of Breona.

Bret, Brett, Brette (Irish) short forms of
Britany. See also Brita.
Breat, Breatte, Breta, Bretah, Bretta,
Brettah, Brettea, Brettia, Brettin, Bretton

Breyana, Breyann, Breyanna (Irish)
forms of Briana.
Breyan, Breyane, Breyannah, Breyanne,
Breyna, Breynah

Breyona, Breyonna (Irish) forms of
Briana.
Breyonah, Breyonia

Bria, Briah (Irish) short forms of Briana.
See also Brea.
Brya, Bryah

Briahna (Irish) a form of Briana.

Briana, Brianna (Irish) strong; virtuous,
honorable.
Bhrianna, Brana, Brianni, Briannon

Brianca (Irish) a form of Briana.

Brianda (Irish) a form of Briana.
Briand

Briann, Brianne (Irish) short forms of
Briana.
Briane

Briannah (Irish) a form of Briana.
Brianah

Briar (French) heather.
Brear, Brier, Bryar

Brice (Welsh) a form of Bryce.

Bridey (Irish) a familiar form of Bridget.
Bridea, Brideah, Bridee, Bridi, Bridie, Bridy, Brydea, Brydee, Brydey, Brydi, Brydie, Brydy

Bridget (Irish) strong. See also Bedelia, Bryga, Gitta.
Berget, Birgitte, Bride, Bridey, Bridger, Bridgeta, Bridgetah, Bridgete, Bridgid, Bridgit, Bridgita, Bridgitah, Bridgite, Bridgot, Brietta, Brigada, Briget, Brydget, Brydgeta, Brydgetah, Brydgete

Bridgett, Bridgette (Irish) forms of Bridget.
Bridgetta, Bridgettah, Bridggett, Bridgitt, Bridgitta, Bridgittah, Bridgitte, Briggitte, Brigitta, Brydgett, Brydgetta, Brydgettah, Brydgette

Brie (French) a type of cheese. Geography: a region in France known for its cheese. See also Bree.
Bri, Briea, Briena, Brieon, Brietta, Briette, Bry, Brye

Brieana, Brieanna (American) combinations of Brie + Anna. See also Briana.
Brieannah

Brieann, Brieanne (American) combinations of Brie + Ann.
Brie-Ann, Brie-Anne

Briel, Brielle (French) forms of Brie.
Breael, Breaele, Breaell, Breaelle, Breel, Breell, Breelle, Briela, Brielah, Briele, Briell, Briella, Bryel, Bryela, Bryelah, Bryele, Bryell, Bryella, Bryellah, Bryelle

Brienna (Irish) forms of Briana.
Brieon, Brieona

Brienne (French) a short form of Briana.
Briene, Brienn

Brieonna (Irish) a form of Briana.

Brigette (French) a form of Bridget.
Briget, Brigett, Brigetta, Brigettee, Brigget

Brighton (English) bright town.
Breighton, Bright, Brightin, Bryton

Brigid (Irish) a form of Bridget.
Brigida

Brigit, Brigitte (French) forms of Bridget.
Briggitte, Brigita

Brina (Latin) a short form of Sabrina. (Irish) a familiar form of Briana.
Breina, Breinah, Brin, Brinah, Brinan, Brinda, Brindi, Brindy, Briney, Brinia, Brinlee, Brinly, Brinn, Brinna, Brinnah, Brinnan

Briona, Brionna (Irish) forms of Briana.
Brionah, Brione, Brionnah, Brionne, Briony, Briunna, Bryony

Brisa (Spanish) beloved. Mythology: Briseis was the Greek name of Achilles's beloved.
Breza, Brisah, Brisha, Brishia, Brissa, Brysa, Brysah, Bryssa, Bryssah

Bristol (English) the site of the bridge; from Bristol, England.

Brita (Irish) a form of Bridget. (English) a short form of Britany.
Breata, Breatah, Breatta, Breattah, Bretta, Briet, Brieta, Briete, Briett, Brietta, Briette, Brit, Bryt, Bryta, Brytah, Bryte, Brytia

Britaney, Britani, Britanie, Brittanee, Brittaney, Brittani, Brittanie (English) forms of Britany.
Britana, Britanah, Britane, Britanee, Britania, Britanica, Britanii, Britanna, Britanni, Britannia, Britanny, Britatani, Brittanah, Brittane, Brittanni, Brittannia, Brittannie

Britany, Brittany (English) from Britain. See also Bret.
Briteny, Britkney, Britley, Britlyn, Brittainee, Brittainey, Brittainny, Brittainy, Brittamy, Brittana, Brittania, Brittanica, Brittany-Ann, Brittanyne, Brittell, Brittlin, Brittlynn

Britin, Brittin (English) from Britain.
Breatin, Breatina, Breatinah, Breatine, Breattin, Breattina, Breattinah, Breattine, Bretin, Bretina, Bretinah, Bretine, Bretyn, Bretyna, Bretynah, Bretyne, Britan, Britann, Britia, Britina, Britinah, Britine, Briton, Brittin, Brittina, Brittine, Bryttin, Bryttina, Bryttine

British (English) from Britain.

Britnee, Britney, Britni, Britnie, Britny, Brittnay, Brittnee, Brittney, Brittni, Brittnie, Brittny (English) forms of Britany.
Bittney, Bridnee, Bridney, Britnay, Britne, Britnei, Britnye, Brittnaye, Brittne, Brittnea, Brittnei, Brittneigh, Brytnea, Brytni

Briton, Brittin, Britton (English) forms of Britin.

Britt (Swedish, Latin) a short form of Britta.
Briet, Brit, Britte, Brytte

Britta (Swedish) strong. (Latin) a short form of Britany.
Brita, Brittah, Brytta, Bryttah

Brittan, Britten (English) forms of Britin. Short forms of Britany.

Brittanny (English) a form of Britany.

Britteny (English) a form of Britany.
Britenee, Briteney, Briteni, Britenie, Briteny, Brittenay, Brittenee, Britteney, Britteni, Brittenie

Brittiany (English) a form of Britany.
Britianey, Brittiani, Brittianni

Brittini, Brittiny (English) forms of Britany.
Britini, Britinie, Brittinee, Brittiney, Brittinie

Brittony (English) a form of Britany.

Briyana, Briyanna (Irish) forms of Briana.

Brodie (Irish) ditch; canal builder.
Brodee, Brodi, Brody

Brogan (Irish) a heavy work shoe.
Brogen, Broghan, Broghen

Bronnie (Welsh) a familiar form of Bronwyn.
Bron, Broney, Bronia, Broniah, Bronie, Bronnee, Bronney, Bronny, Bronya

Bronte (Greek) thunder. (Gaelic) bestower. Literature: Charlotte, Emily, and Anne Brontë were sister writers from England.
Bronté, Brontë

Bronwen (Welsh) a form of Bronwyn.

Bronwyn (Welsh) white breasted. See also Rhonwyn.
Bronwin, Bronwina, Bronwinah, Bronwine, Bronwynn, Bronwynna, Bronwynne

Brook, Brooke (English) brook, stream.
Bhrooke, Brookee, Brookelle, Brookey, Brookia, Brookie, Brooky

Brooke-Lynn, Brookelyn, Brookelynn (American) forms of Brooklyn.
Brookelina, Brookeline, Brookellen, Brookellin, Brookellina, Brookelline, Brookellyn, Brookellyna, Brookellyne, Brookelyn, Brookelyna, Brookelyne, Brookelynn

Brooklin (American) a form of Brooklyn.
Brooklina, Brookline

Brooklyn, Brooklyne, Brooklynn, Brooklynne (American) combinations of Brook + Lynn.
Brooklen, Brooklyna

Brooks (English) a form of Brook.

Bruna (German) a short form of Brunhilda.
Brona

Brunhilda (German) armored warrior.
Brinhild, Brinhilda, Brinhilde, Bruna, Brunhild, Brunhildah, Brunhilde, Brunnhild, Brunnhilda, Brunnhildah, Brünnhilde, Brynhild, Brynhilda, Brynhildah, Brynhilde, Brynhyld, Brynhylda, Brynhyldah, Brynhylde, Hilda

Bryana, Bryanna (Irish) forms of Briana.
Bryanah, Bryannah, Bryanni

Bryanne (Irish) a short form of Bryana.
Bryane, Bryann

Bryce (Welsh) alert; ambitious.

Bryga (Polish) a form of Bridget.
Brygid, Brygida, Brygitka

Brylee, Brylie (American) a combination of the letter B + Riley.
Brylei, Bryley, Bryli

Bryn, Brynn (Latin) from the boundary line. (Welsh) mound.
Brin, Brinn, Brynee

Bryna (Latin, Irish) a form of Brina.
Brinah, Brinan, Brinna, Brinnah, Brinnan,
Brynah, Brynan, Brynna, Brynnah,
Brynnan

Brynne (Latin, Welsh) a form of Bryn.

Bryona, Bryonna (Irish) forms of Briana.
Brionie, Bryonah, Bryone, Bryonee, Bryoney,
Bryoni, Bryonia, Bryony

Bryttani, Bryttany (English) forms of
Britany.
Brytanee, Brytaney, Brytani, Brytania,
Brytanie, Brytanny, Brytany, Bryttanee,
Bryttaney, Bryttania, Bryttanie, Bryttine

Bryttni (English) a form of Britany.
Brytnee, Brytney, Brytni, Brytnie, Brytny,
Bryttnee, Bryttney, Bryttnie, Bryttny,
Brytton

Buffy (American) buffalo; from the plains.
Bufee, Bufey, Buffee, Buffey, Buffi, Buffie,
Buffye, Bufi, Bufie, Bufy

Bunny (Greek) a familiar form of Bernice.
(English) little rabbit. See also Bonnie.
Bunee, Buney, Buni, Bunie, Bunnea,
Bunnee, Bunney, Bunni, Bunnia, Bunnie,
Buny

Burgundy (French) Geography: a region
of France known for its Burgundy wine.
Burgandee, Burgandey, Burgandi, Burgandie,
Burgandy, Burgunde, Burgundee, Burgundey,
Burgundi, Burgundie

Bushra (Arabic) good omen.

Byanna (Irish) a form of Briana.
Biana, Bianah, Bianna, Byanah, Byannah

Cache, Cachet (French) prestigious;
desirous.
Cachae, Cachea, Cachee, Cachée

Cadence (Latin) rhythm.
Cadena, Cadenah, Cadenza, Kadena,
Kadenah, Kadenza, Kadenzah

Cadie, Cady (English) forms of Kady.
Cade, Cadea, Cadee, Cadey, Cadi, Cadia,
Cadiah, Cadine, Cadya, Cadyah, Cadye

Caecey (Irish) a form of Casey.
Caecea, Caecee, Caeci, Caecia, Caeciah,
Caecie, Caecy, Caesea, Caesee, Caesey,
Caesi, Caesie, Caesy

Caela (Hebrew) a form of Kayla.

Caeley (American) forms of Kaylee, Kelly.
Caelea, Caeleah, Caelee, Caelei, Caeleigh,
Caeli, Caelia, Caelie, Caelly, Caely

Caelin, Caelyn (American) forms of
Kaelyn.
Caelan, Caelean, Caeleana, Caeleanah,
Caeleane, Caeleen, Caeleena, Caeleenah,
Caeleene, Caelen, Caelena, Caelenah,
Caelene, Caelina, Caelinah, Caeline, Caelinn,
Caelyna, Caelynah, Caelyne, Caelynn

Cafleen (Irish) a form of Cathleen.
Cafflean, Caffleana, Caffleanah, Caffleane,
Caffleen, Caffleena, Caffleenah, Caffleene,
Cafflein, Caffleina, Caffleinah, Caffleine,
Cafflin, Cafflina, Cafflinah, Caffline, Cafflyn,
Cafflyna, Cafflynah, Cafflyne, Caflean,
Cafleana, Cafleanah, Cafleane, Cafleena,
Cafleenah, Cafleene, Caflein, Cafleina,
Cafleinah, Cafleine, Caflin, Caflina,
Caflinah, Cafline, Caflyn, Caflyna,
Caflynah, Caflyne

Cai (Vietnamese) feminine.
Cae, Cay, Caye

Caicey (Irish) a form of Casey.
Caicea, Caicee, Caici, Caicia, Caiciah, Caicie,
Caicy, Caisea, Caisee, Caisey, Caisi, Caisia,
Caisiah, Caisie, Caisy

Caila (Hebrew) a form of Kayla.

Cailee, Caileigh, Cailey (American)
forms of Kaylee, Kelly.
Cailea, Caileah, Caili, Cailia, Cailie,
Cailley, Caillie, Caily

Cailida (Spanish) adoring.
Caelida, Caelidah, Cailidah, Cailidora,
Cailidorah, Callidora, Callidorah, Caylida,
Caylidah, Kailida, Kailidah, Kaylida,
Kaylidah

Cailin, Cailyn (American) forms of Caitlin.
Cailan, Caileen, Caileena, Caileenah,
Caileene, Cailena, Cailenah, Cailene,
Cailina, Cailine, Cailyna, Cailyne,
Cailynn, Cailynne, Calen

Caitlan, Caitlen, Caitlyn, Caitlynn,
Caitlynne (Irish) forms of Caitlin,
Kaitlan.
Caitlana, Caitland, Caitlandt, Caitlane,
Caitlena, Caitlene, Caitlenn, Caitlyna,
Caitlyne

Caitlin (Irish) pure. See also Kaitlin,
Katalina.
Caetlan, Caetlana, Caetlane, Caetlen,
Caetlena, Caetlene, Caetlin, Caetlina,
Caetline, Caetlyn, Caetlyna, Caetlyne,
Caitleen, Caitline, Caitlinn, Caitlon

Cala, Calla (Arabic) castle, fortress. See
also Calie, Kala.
Calah, Calan, Calana, Calia, Caliah, Callah

Calala (Spanish) a familiar form of
Chandelaria.

Calandra (Greek) lark.
Calan, Calandre, Calandrea, Calandria,
Calandriah, Caleida, Calendra, Calendrah,
Calendre, Caylandra, Caylandrea,
Caylandria, Caylandriah, Kalandra,
Kalandria

Calantha (Greek) beautiful blossom.
Calanthah, Calanthia, Calanthiah,
Calanthya, Calanthyah

Caledonia (Latin) from Scotland.
Caledona, Caledoniah, Caledonya,
Caledonyah, Caldona, Caldonah, Caldonia,
Caldoniah, Caldonya, Caldonyah

Calee, Caleigh, Caley, Calley
(American) forms of Caeley.
Calea, Caleah, Calei, Calleigh

Cali, Calli (Greek) forms of Calie. See
also Kali.
Calia, Caliah

Calida (Spanish) warm; ardent. See also
Kalida.
Calina, Callida, Callyda, Callydah,
Calyda, Calydah

Calie, Callie, Cally (Greek, Arabic)
familiar forms of Cala, Calista. See also
Kalli.
Cal, Callea, Calleah, Callee, Callei, Calli,
Callia, Calliah, Caly

Calinda (Hindi) a form of Kalinda.
Calindah, Calinde, Callinda, Calynd,
Calynda, Calyndah, Calynde

Calista, Callista (Greek) most beautiful.
See also Kalista.
Calesta, Calestah, Calistah, Callesta,
Callestah, Callistah, Callysta, Callystah,
Calysta

Callan (German) likes to talk, chatter.
Callen, Callin, Callon, Callun, Callyn,
Kallan, Kallen, Kallin, Kallon, Kallun,
Kallyn

Callidora (Greek) gift of beauty.

Calliope (Greek) beautiful voice.
Mythology: Calliope was the Muse of
epic poetry. See also Kalliope.
Calliopee

Callula (Latin) beauty; light.
Calula, Calulah, Callulah, Kallula,
Kallulah, Kalula, Kalulah

Calumina (Irish) dove.
Caluminah, Calumyna, Calumynah

Calvina (Latin) bald.
Calveana, Calveanah, Calveane, Calveania,
Calveaniah, Calveena, Calveenah, Calveenia,
Calveeniah, Calvinah, Calvine, Calvinetta,
Calvinette, Calvyna, Calvynah, Calvyne

Calyca (Greek) a form of Kalyca.
Calica, Calicah, Calicka, Calickah, Calika,
Calikah, Calycah

Calyn (Scottish) a form of Caelan (see
Boys' Names). (American) a form of
Caelin. (German) a form of Callan (see
Boys' Names).
Callyn, Caylan, Caylen, Cayley, Caylin,
Caylon, Caylyn

Calypso (Greek) concealer. Botany: a
pink orchid native to northern regions.
Mythology: the sea nymph who held
Odysseus captive for seven years.
Calipso, Caly, Lypsie, Lypsy

Cam (Vietnamese) sweet citrus.
Kam

Camara (American) a form of Cameron.
Camira, Camry

Camarin (Scottish) a form of Cameron.

Camberly (American) a form of Kimberly.
Camber, Camberlee, Camberleigh

Cambria (Latin) from Wales. See also
Kambria.
*Camberry, Cambrea, Cambree, Cambreia,
Cambriah, Cambrie, Cambrina, Cambry,
Cambrya, Cambryah*

Camden (Scottish) winding valley.
Camdyn

Camelia, Camellia (Italian) Botany: a
camellia is an evergreen tree or shrub
with fragrant roselike flowers. See
also Kamelia.
*Camala, Camalia, Camallia, Camela,
Cameliah, Camelita, Camella, Camellita,
Camelya, Camelyah, Camillia, Camilliah,
Chamelea, Chameleah, Chamelia,
Chameliah, Chamellia, Chamelliah,
Chamelya, Chamelyah, Chamilia,
Chamylia, Chamyliah*

Cameo (Latin) gem or shell on which a
portrait is carved.
*Cami, Camio, Camyo, Kameo, Kamio,
Kamyo*

Camera (American) a form of Cameron.
Cameri, Cameria

Cameron (Scottish) crooked nose. See
also Kameron.
*Cameran, Camerana, Cameren, Cameria,
Cameriah, Camerie, Camerin, Camerya,
Cameryah, Cameryn, Camira, Camiran,
Camiron*

Camesha (American) a form of Camisha.
*Cameasha, Cameesha, Cameisha, Camesa,
Cameshaa, Cameshia, Cameshiah,
Camyeshia, Kamesha, Kameshia*

Cami, Camie, Cammie, Cammy
(French) short forms of Camille. See
also Kami.
*Camee, Camey, Camia, Camiah, Cammi,
Cammye, Camy, Camya, Camyah*

Camila, Camilla (Italian) forms of Camille.
See also Kamila, Mila.
*Camilah, Camilia, Camillah, Camillia,
Camilya, Cammila, Cammilah, Cammilla,
Cammyla, Cammylah, Cammylla,
Cammyllah, Chamika, Chamila, Chamilla,
Chamylla, Chamyllah*

Camille (French) young ceremonial
attendant. See also Millie.
*Cami, Camiel, Camielle, Camil, Camile,
Camill, Cammile, Cammill, Cammille,
Cammillie, Cammilyn, Cammyl, Cammyle,
Cammyll, Cammylle, Chamelee, Chamelei,
Chameley, Chamelie, Chamelle, Chamely,
Chamille, Kamille*

Camisha (American) a combination of
Cami + Aisha.
Camiesha

Campbell (Latin, French) beautiful field.
(Scottish) crooked mouth.
Cambel, Cambell, Camp, Campy, Kampbell

Camri, Camrie, Camry (American) short
forms of Camryn. See also Kamri.
Camrea, Camree, Camrey

Camryn (American) a form of Cameron.
See also Kamryn.
Camri, Camrin, Camron, Camrynn

Camylle (French) a form of Camille.
*Cammyl, Cammyle, Cammyll, Camyle,
Camyll*

Canda (Greek) a form of Candace.
(Spanish) a short form of Chandelaria.

Candace (Greek) glittering white; glowing. History: the title of the queens of
ancient Ethiopia. See also Dacey, Kandace.
*Cace, Canace, Candas, Candece, Candelle,
Candiace, Candyce*

Candelaria (Spanish) a form of
Chandelaria.

Candi (American) a familiar form of
Candace, Candice, Candida. See also
Candie, Kandi. (Spanish) a familiar form
of Chandelaria.

Candice, Candis (Greek) forms of
Candace.
*Candes, Candias, Candies, Candise,
Candiss, Candus*

Candida (Latin) bright white.
Candeea, Candi, Candia, Candide, Candita

Candie, Candy (American) familiar
forms of Candace, Candice, Candida.
See also Candi, Kandi.
*Candea, Candee, Candia, Candiah,
Candya, Candyah*

Candra (Latin) glowing. See also Kandra.
*Candrah, Candrea, Candria, Candriah,
Candrya, Candryah*

Candyce (Greek) a form of Candace.
Candys, Candyse, Cyndyss

Cantara (Arabic) small crossing.
Cantarah

Cantrelle (French) song.
*Cantrel, Cantrela, Cantrelah, Cantrele,
Cantrella, Cantrellah, Kantrel, Kantrella,
Kantrelle*

Capri (Italian) a short form of Caprice.
Geography: an island off the west coast
of Italy. See also Kapri.
*Capree, Caprey, Capria, Capriah, Caprie,
Capry, Caprya, Capryah*

Caprice (Italian) fanciful.
*Cappi, Caprece, Caprecia, Capresha,
Capricia, Capriese, Caprina, Capris,
Caprise, Caprisha, Capritta*

Cara, Carah (Latin) dear. (Irish) friend.
See also Karah.
Caira, Caragh, Caranda, Carrah

Caralee (Irish) a form of Cara.
Caralea, Caraleigh, Caralia, Caralie, Carely

Caralyn (English) a form of Caroline.
*Caralan, Caralana, Caralanah, Caralane,
Caralin, Caralina, Caralinah, Caraline,
Caralynn, Caralynna, Caralynne, Carralean,
Carraleana, Carraleanah, Carraleane,*

Carraleen, Carraleena, Carraleenah,
Carraleene, Carralin, Carralina, Carralinah,
Carraline, Carralyn, Carralyna, Carralynah,
Carralyne

Carelyn (English) a form of Caroline.
*Carrelean, Carreleana, Carreleanah,
Carreleane, Carreleene, Carrelin, Carrelina,
Carrelinah, Carreline, Carrelyn, Carrelyna,
Carrelynah, Carrelyne*

Caren (Welsh) a form of Caron. (Italian)
a form of Carina.

Carenza (Irish) a form of Karenza.
*Caranza, Caranzah, Caranzia, Caranziah,
Carenzah, Carenzia, Carenziah, Carenzya,
Carenzyah*

Caressa (French) a form of Carissa.
*Carass, Carassa, Carassah, Caresa, Carese,
Caresse, Charessa, Charesse, Karessa*

Carey (Welsh) a familiar form of Cara,
Caroline, Karen, Katherine. See also
Carrie, Kari.
Caree, Carrey

Cari, Carie (Welsh) forms of Carey, Kari.
Caria, Cariah

Carilyn (English) a form of Caroline.
*Carilean, Carileana, Carileanah, Carileane,
Carileen, Carileena, Carileenah, Carileene,
Carilene, Carilin, Cariline, Carrileen,
Carrileena, Carrileenah, Carrileene,
Carrilin, Carrilina, Carrilinah, Carriline*

Carina (Italian) dear little one. (Greek) a
familiar form of Cora. (Swedish) a form
of Karen.
*Carana, Caranah, Carena, Carenah,
Carinah, Carinna, Carrina, Carrinah,
Carryna, Carrynah, Caryna, Carynah*

Carine (Italian) a form of Carina.
Carinne, Carrian, Carrine

Carisa, Carrisa, Carrissa (Greek) forms
of Carissa.
*Caris, Carisah, Carise, Carisha, Carisia,
Carysa, Carysah, Charisa*

Carisma (Greek) a form of Karisma.
*Carismah, Carismara, Carysma, Carysmah,
Carysmara*

Carissa (Greek) beloved. See also Karisa.
Caressa, Cariss, Carissah, Carisse, Caryssa, Caryssah

Carita (Latin) charitable.
Caritah, Caritta, Carittah, Caryta, Carytah, Carytta, Caryttah, Karita, Karitah, Karitta, Karittah

Carla (German) farmer. (English) strong. (Latin) a form of Carol, Caroline. See also Karla.
Carila, Carilah, Carilla, Carillah, Carlah, Carleta, Carliqua, Carlique, Carliyle, Carlonda, Carlyjo, Carlyle, Carlysle

Carlee, Carleigh, Carley, Carli, Carlie (English) forms of Carly. See also Karlee, Karley.
Carle, Carlea, Carleah, Carleh, Carlei, Carlia, Carliah

Carleen, Carlene (English) forms of Caroline. See also Karleen.
Carlaen, Carlaena, Carlane, Carlean, Carleana, Carleanah, Carleane, Carleena, Carleenah, Carleene, Carlein, Carleina, Carleine, Carlen, Carlenah, Carlenna, Carleyn, Carleyna, Carleyne, Carline, Carllen, Carlyne

Carlena (English) a form of Caroline.

Carlin (Irish) little champion. (Latin) a short form of Caroline.
Carlan, Carlana, Carlandra, Carlinda, Carlindah, Carline, Carllan, Carllin, Carlyn, Carrlin

Carlina (Latin, Irish) a form of Carlin
Carlinah

Carling (Latin, Irish) a form of Carlin.

Carlisa (American) a form of Carlissa.
Carilis, Carilise, Carilyse, Carletha, Carlethe, Carlis, Carlisah, Carlise, Carlysa, Carlysah, Carlyse

Carlisha (American) a form of Carlissa.
Carleasha, Carleashah, Carleesha, Carleesia, Carleesiah, Carlesia, Carlesiah, Carlicia, Carlisia, Carlisiah

Carlissa (American) a combination of Carla + Lissa.

Carleeza, Carlisa, Carliss, Carlissah, Carlisse, Carlissia, Carlissiah, Carlista, Carlyssa, Carlyssah

Carlita (Italian) a form of Carlotta.
Carlitah

Carlotta (Italian) a form of Charlotte.
Carleta, Carletah, Carlete, Carletta, Carlettah, Carlette, Carlite, Carlot, Carlota, Carlotah, Carlote, Carlott, Carlottah, Carlotte, Carolet, Caroleta, Carolete, Carolett, Caroletta, Carolette

Carly (English) a familiar form of Caroline, Charlotte. See also Karley.
Carli, Carlie, Carlya, Carlyah, Carlye

Carlyle (English) Carla's island.
Carlyse, Carlysle

Carlyn, Carlynn (Irish) forms of Carlin.
Carllyn, Carllyna, Carllynah, Carllyne, Carlyna, Carlynah, Carlynne

Carman (Latin) a form of Carmen.

Carmel (Hebrew) a short form of Carmela.
Carmal, Carmele, Carmelie, Carmell, Carmelle, Carmely, Carmil, Carmile, Carmill, Carmille, Carmyle, Carmylle

Carmela, Carmella (Hebrew) garden; vineyard. Bible: Mount Carmel in Israel is often thought of as paradise. See also Karmel.
Carmala, Carmalah, Carmalina, Carmalinah, Carmaline, Carmalla, Carmarit, Carmelah, Carmeli, Carmelia, Carmeliah, Carmelina, Carmeline, Carmellah, Carmellia, Carmelliah, Carmellina, Carmelya, Carmesa, Carmesha, Carmi, Carmie, Carmiel, Carmila, Carmilla, Carmillia, Carmilliah, Carmillya, Carmillyah, Carmisha, Carmyllia, Carmylliah, Carmyllya, Carmyllyah, Carmyla, Carmylah, Carmylla

Carmelit (Hebrew) a short form of Carmelita.
Carmalit, Carmellit

Carmelita (Hebrew) a form of Carmela.
Carmaletta, Carmalita, Carmelitha, Carmelitia, Carmellita, Carmellitia, Carmellitha, Leeta, Lita

Carmen (Latin) song. Religion: Nuestra Señora del Carmen—Our Lady of Mount Carmel—is one of the titles of the Virgin Mary. See also Karmen.
Carma, Carmain, Carmaina, Carmaine, Carmana, Carmanah, Carmane, Carmena, Carmencita, Carmene, Carmi, Carmia, Carmita, Carmon, Carmona

Carmina (Latin) a form of Carmine.
Carminah, Carmyna, Carmynah, Karmina, Karminah

Carmine (Latin) song; red.
Carmin, Carmyn, Carmyne, Carmynn, Karmine, Karmyne

Carnelian (Latin) clear, reddish stone.
Carnelia, Carneliah, Carnelya, Carnelyah, Carnelyan

Carniela (Greek) a form of Karniela.
Carniela, Carniele, Carniell, Carniella, Carnielle, Carnyel, Carnyela, Carnyella, Carnyelle

Carol (German) farmer. (French) song of joy. (English) strong. See also Charlene, Kalle, Karol.
Caral, Carall, Carel, Carele, Carell, Carelle, Cariel, Caril, Carile, Carill, Caro, Carola, Carolenia, Carolinda, Caroll, Carral, Carrall, Carrel, Carrell, Carrelle, Carril, Carrill, Carrol, Carroll

Carol Ann, Carol Anne, Carolan, Carolane, Carolanne (American) combinations of Carol + Ann. Forms of Caroline.
Carolana, Carolanah, Carolann, Carolanna, Carole-Anne

Carole (English) a form of Carol.
Carolee, Karole, Karrole

Carolina (Italian) a form of Caroline. See also Karolina.
Carilena, Carlena, Caroleana, Caroleanah, Caroleena, Caroleina, Carolena, Carolinah, Carroleena, Carroleenah, Carrolena, Carrolina, Carrolinah

Caroline (French) little and strong. See also Carla, Carleen, Carlin, Karolina.
Caralyn, Carelyn, Carilyn, Carilynn, Carilynne, Caro, Carolean, Caroleane,
Caroleen, Carolin, Carroleen, Carroleene, Carrolene, Carrolin, Carroline

Carolyn, Carolyne, Carolynn (English) forms of Caroline. See also Karolyn.
Carolyna, Carolynah, Carolynne, Carrolyn, Carrolyna, Carrolynah, Carrolyne, Carrolynn, Carrolynna, Carrolynnah, Carrolynne

Caron (Welsh) loving, kindhearted, charitable.
Caaran, Caaren, Caarin, Caaron, Caran, Carane, Carene, Carin, Carinn, Caronne, Carran, Carrin, Carren, Carron, Carrone, Carrun, Carun

Carra (Irish) a form of Cara.
Carrah

Carrie (English) a familiar form of Carol, Caroline. See also Carey, Kari, Karri.
Carree, Carrey, Carri, Carria, Carry, Cary

Carrigan (Irish) a form of Corrigan (see Boys' Names).
Carrigen

Carrington (Welsh) rocky town.

Carson (English) child of Carr.
Carsen, Carsyn

Carter (English) cart driver.

Cary (Welsh) a form of Carey.
Carya, Caryah

Caryl (Latin) a form of Carol.
Carryl, Carryle, Carryll, Carrylle, Caryle, Caryll, Carylle

Caryn (Danish) a form of Karen.
Caaryn, Carryn, Carryna, Carrynah, Carryne, Caryna, Carynah, Caryne, Carynn

Carys (Welsh) love.
Caris, Caryse, Caryss, Carysse, Ceris, Cerys

Casandra (Greek) a form of Cassandra.
Casandera, Casandre, Casandrea, Casandrey, Casandri, Casandria, Casandrina, Casandrine, Casanndra

Casey (Irish) brave. (Greek) a familiar form of Acacia. See also Kasey.
Cacee, Cacy, Caecey, Caicey, Cascy, Casea, Casee, Casy, Cayse, Caysea, Caysee, Caysey, Caysy

Cashmere (Slavic) a form of Casimir (see Boys' Names).
Cash, Cashemere, Cashi, Cashmeire

Casi, Casie (Irish) forms of Casey.
Caci, Cacia, Cacie, Casci, Cascie, Casia, Cayci, Caycia, Cayciah, Caysi, Caysia, Caysiah, Caysie, Cazzi

Casidy, Cassidee, Cassidi, Cassidie (Irish) forms of Cassidy.
Casidee, Casidey, Casidi, Casidia, Casidiah, Casidie

Casimira (Slavic) peacemaker. See also Kasimira.
Casimiera, Casimirah, Casmira, Casmirah, Casmyra, Casmyrah, Cazmira, Cazmirah, Cazmyra, Cazmyrah

Cass (Greek) a short form of Cassandra.
Cas, Cassa, Kas, Kass

Cassady (Irish) a form of Cassidy.
Casadea, Casadee, Casadey, Casadi, Casadia, Casadiah, Casadie, Casady, Cassaday, Cassadea, Cassadee, Cassadey, Cassadi, Cassadia, Cassadiah, Cassadie, Cassadina

Cassandra (Greek) helper of men. Mythology: a prophetess of ancient Greece whose prophesies were not believed. See also Kasandra, Krisandra, Sandra, Sandy, Zandra.
Cassander, Cassandera, Cassandri, Cassandry, Chrisandra, Chrisandrah, Crisandra, Crisandrah, Crysandra, Crysandrah

Cassandre (Greek) a form of Cassandra.

Cassaundra (Greek) a form of Cassandra.
Casaundra, Casaundre, Casaundri, Casaundria, Cassaundre, Cassaundri, Cassundra, Cassundre, Cassundri, Cassundria, Cassundrina, Cazzandra, Cazzandre, Cazzandria

Cassey, Cassi, Cassie, Cassy (Greek) familiar forms of Cassandra, Catherine. See also Kassi.
Casse, Cassee, Cassii, Cassye

Cassia (Greek) a cinnamon-like spice. See also Kasia.

Casia, Casiah, Cass, Cassiah, Cassya, Cassyah, Casya, Cazia, Caziah, Cazya, Cazyah, Cazzia, Cazziah, Cazzya, Cazzyah

Cassidy (Irish) clever. See also Kassidy.
Casseday, Cassiddy, Cassidey, Cassidia, Cassity, Cassydi, Cassydie, Cassydy, Casydi, Casydie, Casydy, Cazidy, Cazzidy

Cassiopeia (Greek) clever. Mythology: the wife of the Ethiopian king Cepheus; the mother of Andromeda.
Cassio

Cassondra (Greek) a form of Cassandra.
Casondra, Casondre, Casondria, Casondriah, Cassondre, Cassondri, Cassondria, Cazzondra, Cazzondre, Cazzondria

Catalina (Spanish) a form of Catherine. See also Katalina.
Cataleen, Catalena, Catalene, Catalin, Catalinah, Cataline, Catalyn, Catalyna, Catana, Catania, Catanya, Cateline, Catelini

Catarina (German) a form of Catherine.
Catarena, Catarin, Catarine, Cattarina, Cattarinah, Cattarine

Catelin, Catelyn, Catelynn (Irish) forms of Caitlin.
Cateline, Catelyne

Caterina (German) a form of Catherine.
Catereana, Catereanah, Catereane, Catereena, Catereenah, Catereene, Caterin, Caterinah, Caterine, Cateryna, Caterynah, Cateryne

Catharine (Greek) a form of Catherine.
Catharen, Catharin, Catharina, Catharinah, Catharyn

Catherine (Greek) pure. (English) a form of Katherine.
Cairena, Cairene, Cairina, Caitrin, Cat, Cate, Cathann, Cathanne, Cathenne, Catheren, Catherene, Catheria, Catherin, Catherina, Catherinah, Catlaina, Catreeka, Catrelle, Catrice, Catricia, Catrika

Catheryn (Greek, English) a form of Catherine.
Catheryne

Cathi (Greek) a form of Cathy.
Cathie

Cathleen (Irish) a form of Catherine. See also Caitlin, Kathleen.
Caithlyn, Cathalean, Cathaleana, Cathaleanah, Cathaleane, Cathaleen, Cathaleena, Cathaleenah, Cathaleene, Cathalen, Cathalena, Cathalenah, Cathalene, Cathalin, Cathalina, Cathalinah, Cathaline, Cathalyn, Cathalyna, Cathalynah, Cathalyne, Catheleen, Catheleena, Catheleenah, Catheleene, Cathelen, Cathelena, Cathelenah, Cathelene, Cathelin, Cathelina, Cathelinah, Catheline, Cathelyn, Cathelyna, Cathelynah, Cathelyne, Cathlean, Cathleana, Cathleanah, Cathleane, Cathleena, Cathleenah, Cathleene, Cathlein, Cathleina, Cathleinah, Cathleine, Cathlen, Cathlena, Cathlenah, Cathlene, Cathleyn, Cathlin, Cathlina, Cathlinah, Cathline, Cathlyn, Cathlyna, Cathlynah, Cathlyne, Cathlynn

Cathrine, Cathryn (Greek) forms of Catherine.
Cathrina, Cathrinah, Cathryna, Cathrynah, Cathryne, Cathrynn, Catryn

Cathy (Greek) a familiar form of Catherine, Cathleen. See also Kathi.
Catha, Cathe, Cathea, Cathee, Cathey

Catia (Russian) a form of Katia.
Cattiah

Catie (English) a form of Katie.

Catina (English) a form of Katina.
Cateana, Cateanah, Cateena, Cateenah, Cateina, Cateinah, Cateyna, Cateynah, Catinah, Catine, Catyn, Catyna, Catynah, Catyne

Catlin (Irish) a form of Caitlin.
Catlee, Catleen, Catleene, Catlina, Catline, Catlyn, Catlyna, Catlyne, Catlynn, Catlynne

Catriel (Hebrew) a form of Katriel.
Catriela, Catrielah, Catriele, Catriell, Catriella, Catriellah, Catrielle

Catrina (Slavic) a form of Catherine, Katrina.
Caetreana, Caetreanah, Caetreena, Caetreenah, Caetreina, Caetreinah, Caetreyna, Caetreynah, Caetrina, Caetrinah, Caetryna, Caetrynah, Caitreana, Caitreanah, Caitreena, Caitreenah, Caitreina, Caitreinah, Caitreyna, Caitreynah, Caitriana, Caitrina, Caitrinah, Caitriona, Caitryna, Caitrynah, Catreana, Catreanah, Catreane, Catreen, Catreena, Catreenah, Catreene, Catren, Catrena, Catrenah, Catrene, Catrenia, Catrin, Catrinah, Catrine, Catrinia, Catryn, Catryna, Catrynah, Catryne, Catrynia, Catrynya, Catya, Catyah, Caytreana, Caytreanah, Caytreena, Caytreenah, Caytreina, Caytreinah, Caytreyna, Caytreynah, Caytrina, Caytrinah, Caytryna, Caytrynah

Catriona (Slavic) a form of Catherine, Katrina.
Catrionah, Catrione, Catroina

Cayce (Greek, Irish) a form of Casey.
Caycea, Caycee, Caycey, Caycy,

Cayla, Caylah (Hebrew) forms of Kayla.
Caylan, Caylana, Caylanah, Caylea, Cayleah, Caylia, Cayliah

Caylee, Cayleigh, Cayley, Cayli, Caylie (American) forms of Kaylee, Kelly.
Cayle, Caylea, Cayleah, Caylei, Caylia, Cayly

Caylen, Caylin (American) forms of Caitlin.
Caylean, Cayleana, Cayleanah, Cayleane, Cayleen, Cayleena, Cayleenah, Cayleene, Caylena, Caylenah, Caylene, Caylina, Cayline, Caylyn, Caylyna, Caylyne, Caylynne

Ceaira (Irish) a form of Ciara.
Ceairah, Ceairra

Ceanna (Italian) a form of Ciana.

Ceara, Cearra (Irish) forms of Ciara.
Cearaa, Cearah, Cearie, Seara, Searah

Cecelia (Latin) a form of Cecilia. See also Sheila.
Cacelea, Caceleah, Cacelia, Cece, Ceceilia, Cecelyn, Cecette, Cescelia, Cescelie

Cecile (Latin) a form of Cecilia.
Cecilla, Cecille

Cecilia (Latin) blind. See also Cicely,
Cissy, Secilia, Selia, Sissy.
*Cacilia, Caciliah, Caecilia, Caeciliah, Cecil,
Cecila, Cecilea, Ceciliah, Cecilija, Cecillia,
Cecilya, Ceclia, Cecylia, Cecyliah, Cecylja,
Cecylya, Cecylyah, Cee, Ceil, Ceila,
Ceilagh, Ceileh, Ceileigh, Ceilena*

Cecily (Latin) a form of Cecilia.
*Cacelee, Cacelei, Caceleigh, Caceley, Caceli,
Cacilie, Caecilie, Ceceli, Cecelie, Cecely,
Cecilee, Ceciley, Cecilie, Cescily, Cilley*

Cedar (Latin) a kind of evergreen
conifer.

Cedrica (English) battle chieftain.
Cadryca, Cadrycah, Cedricah

Ceil (Latin) a short form of Cecilia.
Ceel, Ciel

Ceilidh (Irish) country dance.

Ceira, Ceirra (Irish) forms of Ciara.
Ceire

Celandine (Latin) an herb with yellow
flowers. (Greek) swallow.
*Celandina, Celandinah, Celandrina,
Celandrinah, Celandrine, Celandryna,
Celandrynah, Celandryne*

Celena (Greek) a form of Selena.
*Caleena, Calena, Celeana, Celeanah,
Celeena, Celeenah, Celenia, Cena*

Celene (Greek) a form of Celena.
*Celean, Celeane, Celeen, Celeene, Celyne,
Cylyne*

Celesta (Latin) a form of Celeste.
Celestah

Celeste (Latin) celestial, heavenly.
*Cele, Celeeste, Celense, Celes, Celesia,
Celesley, Celest, Celestar, Celestelle,
Celestia, Celestial, Cellest, Celleste, Seleste*

Celestina (Latin) a form of Celeste.
*Celesteana, Celesteanah, Celesteena,
Celesteenah, Celestinah, Celestinia,
Celestyna, Celestynah, Celestyne, Selestina*

Celestine (Latin) a form of Celeste.
*Celesteane, Celesteen, Celesteene, Celestin,
Celestyn*

Celia (Latin) a short form of Cecilia.
*Ceilia, Celea, Celeah, Celee, Celei, Celeigh,
Celey, Celi, Celiah, Celie, Cellia, Celliah,
Cellya, Cellyah, Cely*

Celina (Greek) a form of Celena. See also
Selina.
*Calina, Celeana, Celeanah, Celeena,
Celeenah, Celinah, Celinda, Celinia,
Celiniah, Celinka, Celinna, Celka, Cellina,
Celyna, Celynah, Cilina, Cilinah, Cillina,
Cillinah, Cylina, Cylinah*

Celine (Greek) a form of Celena.
*Caline, Celeane, Celeene, Celin, Céline,
Cellinn, Celyn, Celyne, Ciline, Cilline*

Celosia (Greek) dry; burning.
*Celosiah, Celosya, Celosyah, Selosia,
Selosiah, Selosya, Selosyah*

Celsey (Scandinavian, Scottish, English) a
form of Kelsey.

Cera (French) a short form of Cerise.
Cerea, Ceri, Ceria, Cerra

Cerella (Latin) springtime.
*Cerela, Cerelah, Cerelia, Cereliah, Cerelisa,
Cerellah, Cerelle, Cerelya, Cerelyah, Serelia,
Sereliah, Serella Serelya, Serelyah*

Ceres (Latin) Mythology: the Roman
goddess of agriculture. Astronomy: the
first asteroid discovered to have an orbit
between Mars and Saturn.
Cerese, Ceress, Ceressa

Cerise (French) cherry; cherry red.
*Carisce, Carise, Carisse, Caryce, Caryse,
Cerice, Cericia, Cerissa, Cerria, Cerrice,
Cerrina, Cerrita, Cerryce, Ceryce, Ceryse,
Sherise, Sheriss, Sherisse*

Cesilia (Latin) a form of Cecilia.
Cesia, Cesya

Chabeli (French) a form of Chablis.
Chabelly, Chabely

Chablis (French) a dry white wine.
Geography: a region in France where
wine grapes are grown.

Chablea, Chableah, Chablee, Chabley,
Chabli, Chablia, Chablie, Chabliss, Chably,
Chablys, Chablyss

Chadee (French) from Chad, a country
in north-central Africa. See also Sade.
Chadae, Chadai, Chaday, Chaddae,
Chaddai, Chadday, Chade, Chadea, Chadey,
Chadi, Chadia, Chadiah, Chadie, Chady

Chahna (Hindu, Indian) love; light, illu-
mination.

Chai (Hebrew) life.
Chae, Chaela, Chaeli, Chaelia, Chaella,
Chaelle, Chaena, Chaia, Chay

Chaka (Sanskrit) a form of Chakra. See
also Shaka.
Chakai, Chakia, Chakiah, Chakka,
Chakkah, Chakya, Chakyah

Chakra (Sanskrit) circle of energy.
Chakara, Chakaria, Chakena, Chakina,
Chakira, Chakrah, Chakria, Chakriya,
Chakyra, Chakyrah, Shakra, Shakrah

Chalice (French) goblet.
Chalace, Chalcia, Chalcie, Chalece, Chalicea,
Chalie, Chaliece, Chaliese, Chalis, Chalisa,
Chalise, Chalisk, Chalissa, Chalisse, Challa,
Challis, Challisa, Challise, Challiss,
Challissa, Challisse, Challyce, Challysa,
Challyse, Challysse, Chalsey, Chalyce,
Chalyn, Chalyse, Chalyssa, Chalysse

Chalina (Spanish) a form of Rose. See
also Shalena.
Chalin, Chalinah, Chaline, Chalini,
Challain, Challaina, Challaine, Chalyn,
Chalyna, Chalynah, Chalyne

Chalonna (American) a combination of
the prefix Cha + Lona.
Chalon, Chalona, Chalonah, Chalonda,
Chalone, Chalonee, Chalonn, Chalonnah,
Chalonne, Chalonnee, Chalonte, Shalon

Chambray (French) a lightweight fabric.
Chambrae, Chambrai, Chambre, Chambree,
Chambrée, Chambrey, Chambria, Chambrie,
Chambry, Shambrae, Shambrai, Shambre,
Shambree, Shambrée, Shambrey, Shambria,
Shambrie, Shambry

Chamique (American) a form of Shamika.

Champagne (French) a province in eastern France; a wine made in this province.

Chan (Cambodian) sweet-smelling tree.

Chana (Hebrew) a form of Hannah.
Chanae, Chanah, Chanai, Chanay,
Chanea, Chanie, Channa, Channah

Chance (English) a short form of Chancey.

Chancey (English) chancellor; church
official.
Chancee, Chancie, Chancy

Chanda (Sanskrit) short tempered.
Religion: the demon defeated by the
Hindu goddess Chamunda. See also
Shanda.
Chandah, Chandea, Chandee, Chandey,
Chandi, Chandia, Chandiah, Chandie,
Chandin, Chandy, Chandya

Chandani (Hindi) moonlight.
Chandanee, Chandaney, Chandania,
Chandaniah, Chandany, Chandanya,
Chandanyah

Chandelaria (Spanish) candle.
Candeleria, Candeleva, Candelona,
Candeloria, Candeluria, Kandelaria.

Chandelle (French) candle.
Chandal, Chandala, Chandalah, Chandale,
Chandel, Chandela, Chandelah, Chandele,
Chandell, Chandella, Chandellah, Shandal,
Shandel, Shandela, Shandelah, Shandele,
Shandell, Shandella, Shandellah, Shandelle

Chandi (Indian) moonlight. (Sanskrit) a
form of Chanda.

Chandler (Hindi) moon. (Old English)
candlemaker.
Chandlar, Chandlier, Chandlor, Chandlyr

Chandra (Sanskrit) moon. Religion: the
Hindu god of the moon. See also
Shandra.
Chandrae, Chandrah, Chandray, Chandre,
Chandrea, Chandrelle, Chandria, Chandrya

Chanel, Channel (English) channel. See
also Shanel.
Chanal, Chanall, Chanalla, Chanalle,
Chaneel, Chaneil, Chanele, Channal

Chanell, Chanelle, Channelle (English)
forms of Chanel.
Chanella, Channell, Shanell

Chaney (French) oak.
*Chaynee, Cheaney, Cheney, Cheyne,
Cheyney*

Chanice, Chanise (American) a form of
Shanice.
Chanisse, Chenice, Chenise

Channa (Hindi) chickpea.
Channah

Channing (English) wise. (French) canon;
church official.
*Chane, Chanin, Chaning, Chann,
Channin, Channyn, Chanyn*

Chantal, Chantale, Chantalle (French)
song.
*Chandal, Chantaal, Chantael, Chantala,
Chantalah, Chantall, Chantasia, Chanteau,
Chantle, Chantoya, Chantrill*

Chantara (American) a form of Chantal.
*Chantarah, Chantarai, Chantarra,
Chantarrah, Chantarria, Chantarriah,
Chantarrya, Chantarryah*

Chante, Chanté (French) short forms of
Chantal.
*Chanta, Chantae, Chantai, Chantay,
Chantaye, Chantéa, Chantee, Chanti,
Chaunte, Chauntea, Chauntéa, Chauntee*

Chantel, Chantele, Chantell, Chantelle
(French) forms of Chantal. See also
Shantel.
*Chanteese, Chantela, Chantelah, Chantella,
Chantellah, Chanter, Chantey, Chantez,
Chantrel, Chantrell, Chantrelle, Chatell,
Chontel, Chontela, Chontelah, Chontele,
Chontell, Chontella, Chontellah, Chontelle*

Chantia (French) a form of Chante.

Chantile (French) a form of Chantal.
*Chantil, Chantila, Chantile, Chantill,
Chantilla, Chantille, Chantril, Chantrill,
Chantrille*

Chantilly (French) fine lace. See also
Shantille.
*Chantiel, Chantielle, Chantil, Chantila,
Chantilea, Chantileah, Chantilée, Chantilei,*
*Chantileigh, Chantiley, Chantili, Chantilia,
Chantilie, Chantill, Chantilla, Chantillea,
Chantilleah, Chantille, Chantillee, Chantillei,
Chantilleigh, Chantilley, Chantilli, Chantillia,
Chantillie, Chantily, Chantyly*

Chantrea (Cambodian) moon; moonbeam.
Chantra, Chantrey, Chantri, Chantria

Chantrice (French) singer. See also
Shantrice.
Chantreese, Chantress

Chardae, Charde (Punjabi) charitable.
(French) short forms of Chardonnay.
See also Shardae.
*Charda, Chardai, Charday, Chardea,
Chardee, Chardée, Chardese, Chardey,
Chardie*

Chardonnay (French) a dry white wine.
*Char, Chardnay, Chardney, Chardon,
Chardona, Chardonae, Chardonai,
Chardonay, Chardonaye, Chardonee,
Chardonna, Chardonnae, Chardonnai,
Chardonnee, Chardonnée, Chardonney,
Shardonae, Shardonai, Shardonay,
Shardonaye, Shardonnay*

Charice (Greek) a form of Charis.

Charis (Greek) grace; kindness.
*Charece, Chareece, Chareeze, Charese,
Chari, Charie, Charise, Charish, Chariss,
Charris, Charriss, Charrys, Charryss,
Charys, Charyse, Charyss, Charysse*

Charisma (Greek) the gift of leadership.

Charissa (Greek) a form of Charity.
*Charesa, Charessa, Charisa, Charisah,
Charisha, Chariss, Charissah, Charista,
Charrisa, Charrisah, Charrissa, Charrissah,
Charrysa, Charrysah, Charryssa, Charryssah,
Charysa, Charysah, Charyssa, Charyssah*

Charisse (Greek) a form of Charity.
*Charese, Charesse, Charise, Charissee,
Charrise, Charrisse, Charryse, Charrysse,
Charysse*

Charity (Latin) charity, kindness.
*Chariety, Charista, Charita, Charitah,
Charitas, Charitea, Charitee, Charitey,
Chariti, Charitia, Charitiah, Charitie,*

Charitina, Charitine, Charityna, Charityne, Charytey, Charytia, Charytiah, Charyty, Charytya, Charytyah, Sharity

Charla (French, English) a short form of Charlene, Charlotte.
Char, Charlae, Chalah, Charlai, Charlea

Charlaine (English) a form of Charlene.
Charlaina, Charlane, Charlanna, Charlayna, Charlayne, Charlein, Charleina, Charleine, Charleyn, Charleyna, Charleyne

Charlee, Charleigh, Charley, Charli, Charly (German, English) forms of Charlie.
Charle, Charlea, Charleah, Charlei, Charlya

Charleen, Charline (English) forms of Charlene.
Charleena, Charleene, Charlin, Charlina

Charlene (English) a form of Caroline. See also Carol, Karla, Sharlene.
Charlaine, Charlean, Charleana, Charleane, Charleesa, Charlein, Charleina, Charleine, Charlena, Charlenae, Charlenah, Charlesena, Charlyn, Charlyna, Charlyne, Charlynn, Charlynne, Charlzina, Charoline

Charlie (German, English) strong.
Charlia, Charliah, Charyl, Chatty, Sharli, Sharlie

Charlisa (French) a form of Charlotte.

Charlotte (French) a form of Caroline. Literature: Charlotte Brontë was a British novelist and poet best known for her novel *Jane Eyre*. See also Karlotte, Lotte, Sharlotte, Tottie.
Chara, Charil, Charl, Charlet, Charleta, Charletah, Charlete, Charlett, Charletta, Charlettah, Charlette, Charlita, Charlot, Charlota, Charlotah, Charlote, Charlott, Charlotta, Charlottah, Charlottie, Charlotty, Charolet, Charolette, Charolot, Charolotte

Charmaine (French) a form of Carmen. See also Karmaine, Sharmaine.
Charamy, Charma, Charmae, Charmagne, Charmaigne, Charmain, Charmaina, Charmainah, Charmalique, Charmar, Charmara, Charmayane, Charmayn,

Charmayna, Charmaynah, Charmayne, Charmeen, Charmeine, Charmene, Charmese, Charmian, Charmin, Charmine, Charmion, Charmisa, Charmon, Charmyn, Charmyne, Charmynne

Charmane (French) a form of Charmaine.
Charman

Charnette (American) a combination of Charo + Annette.
Charnetta, Charnita

Charnika (American) a combination of Charo + Nika.
Charneka, Charniqua, Charnique

Charo (Spanish) a familiar form of Rosa.
Charoe, Charow

Charyanna (American) a combination of Charo + Anna.
Charian, Charyian, Cheryn

Chase (French) hunter.
Chace, Chaise, Chasen, Chason, Chass, Chasse, Chastan, Chasten, Chastin, Chastinn, Chaston, Chayse, Chasyn

Chasidy, Chassidy (Latin) forms of Chastity.
Chasa Dee, Chasadie, Chasady, Chasidee, Chasidey, Chasidie, Chassedi, Chassidi, Chasydi

Chasity (Latin) a form of Chastity.
Chasiti, Chasitie, Chasitty, Chassey, Chassie, Chassiti, Chassity, Chassy

Chastity (Latin) pure.
Chasta, Chastady, Chastidy, Chastitea, Chastitee, Chastitey, Chastiti, Chastitie, Chastney, Chasty

Chauntel (French) a form of Chantal.
Chaunta, Chauntae, Chauntay, Chaunte, Chauntell, Chauntelle, Chawntel, Chawntell, Chawntelle, Chontelle

Chava (Hebrew) life. (Yiddish) bird. Religion: the original name of Eve.
Chabah, Chavae, Chavah, Chavala, Chavalah, Chavarra, Chavarria, Chave, Chavé, Chavetta, Chavette, Chaviva, Chavvis, Hava, Kaÿa

Chavella (Spanish) a form of Isabel.
Chavel, Chavela, Chavelah, Chavele,
Chaveli, Chavelia, Chavelie, Chavell,
Chavellah, Chavelle, Chavely

Chavi (Gypsy) girl.
Chavali, Chavee, Chavey, Chavia, Chaviah,
Chavie, Chavy, Chavya, Chavyah

Chavon (Hebrew) a form of Jane.
Chavaughn, Chavaughna, Chavaughne,
Chavawn, Chavawna, Chavawnah,
Chavawne, Chavona, Chavonah, Chavonda,
Chavondah, Chavondria, Chavondriah,
Chavone, Chavonn, Chevaughn,
Chevaughna, Chevaughne, Chevawn,
Chevawna, Chevawnah, Chevawne,
Chevon, Chevona, Chevonn, Shavon

Chavonne (Hebrew) a form of Chavon.
(American) a combination of the prefix
Cha + Yvonne.
Chavondria, Chavonna, Chavonnah,
Chevonna, Chevonnah, Chevonne

Chaya (Hebrew) life; living.
Chaia, Chaiah, Chaike, Chaye, Chayka,
Chayra

Chayla (English) a form of Chaylea.
Chaylah

Chaylea (English) a combination of
Chaya + Lea.
Chailea, Chaileah, Chailee, Chailei,
Chaileigh, Chailey, Chaili, Chailia,
Chailiah, Chailie, Chaily, Chayleah,
Chaylee, Chayleena, Chayleene, Chaylei,
Chayleigh, Chaylena, Chaylene, Chayley,
Chayli, Chaylie, Chayly

Chelby (English) a form of Shelby.

Chelci, Chelcie, Chelsee, Chelsey,
Chelsi, Chelsie, Chelsy (English) forms
of Chelsea.
Chelcia, Chelciah, Chellsie, Chelssy,
Chelssey, Chelssie, Chelsye

Chelley (English) a form of Shelley.
Chellea, Chelleah, Chellee, Chellei,
Chelleigh, Chelli, Chellie, Chelly

Chelsa (English) a form of Chelsea.
Chelsae, Chelsah

Chelse (English) a form of Chelsea.
Chelce

Chelsea (English) seaport. See also
Kelsey, Shelsea.
Chelcea, Chelcee, Chelcey, Chelcy, Chelese,
Chelesia, Chelli, Chellie, Chellise, Chelsay,
Chelseah, Chelsei, Chelseigh, Chesea,
Cheslee, Chesley, Cheslie, Chessea, Chessie

Chelsia (English) a form of Chelsea.

Chemarin (Hebrew) girl in black.
Chemarina, Chemarine, Chemaryn,
Chemaryna, Chemaryne

Chenelle (English) a form of Chanel.
Chenel, Chenell

Chenetta (French) oak tree.
Chenet, Cheneta, Chenetah, Chenete,
Chenett, Chenettah, Chenette

Chenoa (Native American) white dove.
Chenee, Chenika, Chenita, Chenna,
Chenoah

Cher (French) beloved, dearest. (English)
a short form of Cherilyn.
Chere, Sher, Shere, Sherr

Cherelle, Cherrell, Cherrelle (French)
forms of Cheryl. See also Sherelle.
Charel, Charela, Charelah, Charele, Charell,
Charella, Charellah, Charelle, Cherel, Cherell,
Cherella, Cherille, Cherrel, Cherrela, Cherrila,
Cherrile

Cherese (Greek) a form of Cherish.
Chereese, Cheresa, Cheresse

Cheri, Cherie, Cherri (French) familiar
forms of Cher.
Cheree, Chérie, Cheriee, Cherree, Cherrie

Cherice, Cherise, Cherisse (French)
forms of Cherish. See also Sharice,
Sherice.
Cherece, Chereece, Chereese, Cheriss,
Cherissa, Cherrise, Cherys, Cherysa,
Cherysah, Cheryse

Cherilyn (English) a combination of
Cheryl + Lynn. See also Sherylyn.
Cheralyn, Chereen, Chereena, Cherilin,
Cherilina, Cherilinah, Cheriline, Cherilyna,

Cherilynah, Cherilyne, Cherilynn, Cherlyn, Cherlynn, Cherralyn, Cherrilyn, Cherrylyn, Cheryl-Lyn, Cheryl-Lynn, Cheryl-Lynne, Cherylene, Cherylin, Cheryline, Cherylyn, Cherylynn, Cherylynne

Cherish (English) dearly held, precious.
Charish, Charisha, Charishe, Charysha, Charyshah, Cheerish, Cheerisha, Cherisha, Cherishah, Cherishe, Cherrish, Cherrisha, Cherrishe, Cherysh, Cherysha, Cheryshe, Sherish

Cherita (Latin) a form of Charity.
Chereata, Chereatah, Chereeta, Chereetah, Cherida, Cherita, Cheritah, Cherrita, Cheryta, Cherytah

Cherokee (Native American) a tribal name.
Cherika, Cherikia, Cherkita, Cherokei, Cherokey, Cheroki, Cherokia, Cherokie, Cheroky, Cherrokee, Sherokee

Cherry (Latin) a familiar form of Charity. (French) cherry; cherry red.
Chere, Cherea, Cheree, Cherey, Cherr, Cherrea, Cherree, Cherrey, Cherreye, Cherri, Cherriann, Cherrianna, Cherrianne, Cherrie, Cherry-Ann, Cherry-Anne, Cherrye, Chery, Cherye

Cheryl (French) beloved. See also Sheryl.
Charil, Charyl, Cheral, Cheril, Cherila, Cherrelle, Cherril, Cheryl-Ann, Cheryl-Anne, Cheryl-Lee, Cheryle, Cherylee, Cheryll, Cherylle

Chesarey (American) a form of Desiree.
Chesarae

Chesna (Slavic) peaceful.
Chesnah, Chessna, Chessnah, Chezna, Cheznah, Cheznia, Chezniah, Cheznya, Cheznyah

Chesney (Slavic) a form of Chesna.
Chesnee, Chesnie, Chesny

Chessa (American) a short form of Chesarey.
Chessi, Chessie, Chessy

Chevelle (Spanish) a form of Chavella.
Chevie

Cheyann, Cheyanne (Cheyenne) forms of Cheyenne.
Cheian, Cheiann, Cheianne, Cheyan, Cheyane, Cheyeanne

Cheyanna (Cheyenne) a form of Cheyenne.
Cheyana

Cheyene (Cheyenne) a form of Cheyenne.

Cheyenna (Cheyenne) a form of Cheyenne.
Cheyeana, Cheyeanna, Cheyena

Cheyenne (Cheyenne) a tribal name. See also Shaianne, Sheyanne, Shian, Shyan.
Cheyeene, Cheyenn, Chi-Anna, Chianne, Chie, Chyanne

Cheyla (American) a form of Sheila.
Cheylan, Cheyleigh, Cheylo

Cheyna (American) a short form of Cheyenne.
Chey, Cheye, Cheyne, Cheynee, Cheyney, Cheynna

Chi (Cheyenne) a short form of Cheyenne.

Chiara (Italian) a form of Clara.
Cheara, Chiarra, Chyara

Chika (Japanese) near and dear.
Chikah, Chikaka, Chikako, Chikara, Chikona, Chyka, Chykah

Chiku (Swahili) chatterer.

Chilali (Native American) snowbird.
Chilalea, Chilaleah, Chilalee, Chilalei, Chilaleigh, Chilalie, Chilaly

China (Chinese) fine porcelain. Geography: a country in eastern Asia. See also Ciana, Shina.
Chinaetta, Chinah, Chinasa, Chinda, Chine, Chinea, Chinesia, Chinita, Chinna, Chinwa, Chynna

Chinira (Swahili) God receives.
Chinara, Chinarah, Chinirah, Chynira, Chynirah

Chinue (Ibo) God's own blessing.

Chiquita (Spanish) little one. See also Shiquita.
Chaqueta, Chaquita, Chica, Chickie, Chicky, Chikata, Chikita, Chiqueta, Chiquila, Chiquite, Chiquitha, Chiquithe, Chiquitia, Chiquitta

Chiyo (Japanese) eternal.
Chiya

Chloe (Greek) blooming, verdant. Mythology: another name for Demeter, the goddess of agriculture. See also Kloe.
Chloé, Chlöe, Chloea, Chloee, Chloey, Chloie, Cloe

Chloris (Greek) pale. Mythology: the only daughter of Niobe to escape the vengeful arrows of Apollo and Artemis. See also Kloris, Loris.
Chlorise, Chlorys, Chloryse, Cloris, Clorise, Clorys, Cloryse

Chlorissa (Greek) a form of Chloris.
Chlorisa, Chlorysa, Clorisa, Clorysa

Cho (Korean) beautiful.
Choe

Cholena (Native American) bird.
Choleana, Choleanah, Choleane, Choleena, Choleenah, Choleene, Choleina, Choleinah, Choleine, Cholenah, Cholene, Choleyna, Choleynah, Choleyne, Cholina, Cholinah, Choline, Cholyna, Cholynah, Cholyne

Chriki (Swahili) blessing.

Chris (Greek) a short form of Christopher, Christina. See also Kris.
Chrys, Cris

Chrissa (Greek) a short form of Christina. See also Khrissa.
Chrisea, Chrissea, Chrysa, Chryssa, Crissa, Cryssa

Chrissanth (Greek) gold flower. Botany: chrysanthemums are ornamental, showy flowers.
Chrisanth, Chrisantha, Chrisanthia, Chrisanthiah, Chrisanthya, Chrisanthyah, Chrysantha, Chrysanthe, Chrysanthia, Chrysanthiah, Chryzanta, Chryzante, Chryzanthia, Chryzanthiah, Chryzanthya, Chryzanthyah

Chrissie, Chrissy (English) familiar forms of Christina.
Chrisee, Chrisi, Chrisie, Chrissee, Chrissey, Chrissi, Chrisy, Crissie, Chryssi, Chryssie, Chryssy, Chrysy, Khrissy

Christa (German) a short form of Christina. History: Christa McAuliffe, an American school teacher, was the first civilian on a U.S. space flight. See also Krista.
Christah, Christar, Christara, Crysta

Christabel (Latin, French) beautiful Christian. See also Kristabel.
Christabeel, Christabela, Christabelah, Christabele, Christabell, Christabella, Christabellah, Christabelle, Christable, Christobel, Christobell, Christobella, Christobelle, Chrystabel, Chrystabela, Chrystabelah, Chrystabele, Chrystabell, Chrystabella, Chrystabellah, Chrystabelle, Chrystobel, Chrystobela, Chrystobelah, Chrystobele, Chrystobell, Chrystobella, Chrystobellah, Chrystobelle, Cristabel, Cristabela, Cristabelah, Cristabele, Cristabell, Cristabella, Cristabellah, Cristabelle

Christain (Greek) a form of Christina.
Christaina, Christainah, Christaine, Christane, Christayn, Christayna, Christaynah, Christayne

Christal (Latin) a form of Crystal. (Scottish) a form of Christina.
Christalene, Christalin, Christalina, Christaline, Christall, Christalle, Christalyn, Christle, Chrystal

Christan, Christen, Christin, Christyn (Greek) short forms of Christina. See also Kristen.
Christana, Christanah, Christann, Christanna, Christyne, Chrystan, Chrysten, Chrystin, Chryston, Chrystyn

Christel, Christelle, Chrystel (French) forms of Christal.
Christele, Christell, Chrystelle

Christena (Greek) a form of Christina.
Christeina, Christeinah, Christeinna, Christeinnah

Christene (Greek) a form of Christina.
Christein, Christeine, Christeinn,
Christeinne

Christi, Christie (Greek) short forms of
Christina, Christine. See also Christy,
Cristi, Kristi, Kristy.
Christee, Christia, Chrystee, Chrysti,
Chrystie

Christian, Christiane, Christianne
(Greek) forms of Christina. See also
Kristian, Krystian.
Christi-Ann, Christi-Anne, Christiann,
Christianni, Christiaun, Christiean, Christien,
Christienne, Christinan, Christy-Ann,
Christy-Anne, Chrystian, Chrystiane,
Chrystiann, Chrystianne, Chrystyan,
Chrystyane, Chrystyann, Chrystyanne,
Crestian, Crestiane, Crestiann, Crestianne,
Crestienne, Crestyane, Crestyann, Crestyanne,
Cristyan, Cristyane, Cristyann, Cristyanne,
Crystian, Crystiane, Crystiann, Crystianne,
Crystyan, Crystyane, Crystyann, Crystyanne

Christiana, Christianna (Greek) forms
of Christina.
Christianah, Christiannah, Christiannia,
Christianniah, Christiena, Chrystiana,
Chrystianah, Chrystianna, Chrystiannah,
Chrystyana, Chrystyanah, Chrystyanna,
Chrystyannah, Crestiana, Crestianah,
Crestianna, Crestiannah, Crestyana,
Crestyanah, Crestyanna, Crestyannah,
Cristyana, Cristyanah, Cristyanna,
Cristyannah, Crystiana, Crystianah,
Crystyana, Crystyanah, Crystyanna,
Crystyannah

Christina (Greek) Christian; anointed.
See also Khristina, Kristina, Stina, Tina.
Christeana, Christeanah, Christeena,
Christeenah, Christeina, Christeinah,
Christella, Christinaa, Christinah,
Christinea, Christinia, Christinna,
Christinnah, Christna, Christyna,
Christynah, Christynna, Chrystena,
Chrystina, Chrystyna, Chrystynah,
Cristeena, Cristena

Christine (French, English) a form of
Christina. See also Khristine, Kirsten,
Kristen, Kristine.

Chrisa, Christean, Christeane, Christeen,
Christeene, Christyne, Chrystyne, Cristeen,
Cristene, Crystine

Christophe (Greek) a form of
Christopher.

Christopher (Greek) Christ-bearer.
Religion: the patron saint of travelers
and drivers.
Chrisopherson, Christapher, Christepher,
Christerpher, Christhoper, Christipher,
Christobal, Christofer, Christoff, Christoher,
Christopehr, Christoper, Christophe,
Christopherr, Christophor, Christophoros,
Christophr, Christophre, Christophyer,
Christophyr, Christorpher, Christos,
Christovao, Christpher, Christphere,
Christphor, Christpor, Christrpher,
Chrystopher, Cristobal, Cristoforo

Christy (English) a short form of
Christina, Christine. See also Christi.
Christey, Chrystey, Chrysty, Cristy

Chrys (English) a form of Chris.
Krys

Chrysta (German) a short form of
Christina.
Chrystah, Chrystar, Chrystara

Chrystal (Latin) a form of Christal.
Chrystal-Lynn, Chrystale, Chrystalin,
Chrystalina, Chrystaline, Chrystalla,
Chrystallina, Chrystallynn

Chrystel (French) a form of Christal.
Chrystelle

Chu Hua (Chinese) chrysanthemum.

Chumani (Lakota) dewdrops.
Chumanee, Chumany

Chun (Burmese) nature's renewal.

Chyann, Chyanne (Cheyenne) forms of
Cheyenne.
Chyan, Chyana, Chyane, Chyanna

Chyenne (Cheyenne) a form of
Cheyenne.
Chyeana, Chyen, Chyena, Chyene,
Chyenn, Chyenna, Chyennee

Chyna, Chynna (Chinese) forms of
China.
Chynah, Chynnah

Cian (Irish) ancient.
Ciann, Cien

Ciana, Cianna (Chinese) forms of China.
(Italian) forms of Jane.
Cianah, Ciandra

Ciara, Ciarra (Irish) black. See also Sierra.
*Ceara, Chiairah, Ciaara, Ciaera, Ciaira,
Ciar, Ciarah, Ciaria, Ciarrah, Ciora, Ciorah,
Cioria, Cyara, Cyarah, Cyarra, Cyarrah*

Cicely (English) a form of Cecilia. See
also Sissy.
*Cicelea, Ciceleah, Cicelee, Cicelei, Ciceleigh,
Ciceley, Ciceli, Cicelia, Cicelie, Ciciley,
Cicilia, Cicilie, Cicily, Cile, Cilka, Cilla,
Cilli, Cillie, Cilly, Siselee, Siselei, Siseleigh,
Siseli, Siselie, Sisely*

Cidney (French) a form of Sydney.
Cidnee, Cidni, Cidnie

Ciearra (Irish) a form of Ciara.
Cieara, Ciearria

Cienna (Italian) a form of Ciana.

Ciera, Cierra (Irish) forms of Ciara.
*Cierah, Ciere, Cieria, Cierrah, Cierre,
Cierria, Cierro*

Cinderella (French, English) little cinder
girl. Literature: a fairy-tale heroine.
*Cindella, Cinderel, Cinderela, Cinderelah,
Cinderele, Cinderellah, Cinderelle, Cynderel,
Cynderela, Cynderelah, Cynderele, Cynderell,
Cynderella, Cynderellah, Cynderelle, Sinderel,
Sinderela, Sinderele, Sinderell, Sinderella,
Sinderelle, Synderell, Synderella, Synderelle*

Cindi (Greek) a form of Cindy.
Cindie

Cindy (Greek) moon. (Latin) a familiar
form of Cynthia. See also Sindy.
Cindea, Cindeah, Cindee, Cindey

Cinnamon (Greek) aromatic, reddish-
brown spice.
*Cinamon, Cynamon, Cynnamon, Sinamon,
Sinnamon, Synamon, Synnamon*

Cinnia (Latin) curly haired.
*Cinia, Ciniah, Cinniah, Sinia, Siniah,
Sinnia, Sinniah*

Cinthia, Cinthya (Greek) forms of
Cynthia.
Cinthiah, Cinthiya, Cinthyah,

Cintia (Greek) a form of Cynthia.

Cipriana (Italian) from the island of
Cyprus.
*Cipres, Cipress, Cipriane, Cipriann,
Ciprianna, Ciprianne, Cyprian, Cypriana,
Cypriane, Cyprienne*

Cira (Spanish) a form of Cyrilla.
*Cirah, Ciria, Ciriah, Cyra, Cyrah, Cyria,
Cyriah, Cyrya, Cyryah, Siria, Syria, Syrya*

Cissy (American) a familiar form of
Cecilia, Cicely.
Cissey, Cissi, Cissie

Citlali (Nahuatl) star.
Citlaly

Clair, Claire (French) forms of Clara.
Claare, Klaire, Klarye

Clairissa (Greek) a form of Clarissa.
Clairisa, Clairisse, Claraissa

Clancy (Irish) redheaded fighter.
*Clance, Clancee, Clancey, Clanci, Clancie,
Claney, Clanse, Clansee, Clansey, Clansi,
Clansie, Clansy*

Clara (Latin) clear; bright. Music: Clara
Schumann was a famous nineteenth-
century German composer. See also
Chiara, Klara.
*Claara, Claarah, Claira, Clairah, Clarah,
Claresta, Clarie, Clarina, Clarinda, Clarine*

Clarabelle (Latin) bright and beautiful.
*Clarabel, Clarabela, Clarabelah, Clarabele,
Clarabell, Clarabella, Clarabellah, Clarobel,
Clarobela, Clarobelah, Clarobele, Clarobell,
Clarobella, Clarobellah, Clarobelle, Clarybel,
Clarybela, Clarybelah, Clarybele, Clarybell,
Clarybella, Clarybellah, Clarybelle*

Clare (English) a form of Clara.
Clar

Clarenza (Latin) clear; victorious.
Clarensia, Clarensiah, Clarensya,
Clarensyah, Clarenzia, Clarenziah,
Clarenzya, Clarenzyah

Claribel (Latin) a form of Clarabelle.
Claribela, Claribelah, Claribele, Claribell,
Claribella, Claribellah, Claribelle

Clarice, Clarisse (Italian) forms of Clara.
Clareace, Clarease, Clareece, Clareese,
Claris, Clarise, Clariss, Claryc, Claryce,
Clarys, Claryse, Cleriese, Klarice, Klarise

Clarie (Latin) a familiar form of Clara.
Clarey, Clari, Clary

Clarinda (Latin, Spanish) bright; beautiful.
Clairinda, Clairynda, Clarindah, Clarynda,
Claryndah

Clarisa (Greek) a form of Clarissa.
Claresa, Claris, Clarisah, Clarise, Clarisia,
Clarys, Clarysa, Clarysah, Claryse

Clarissa (Greek) brilliant. (Italian) a form
of Clara. See also Klarissa.
Clarecia, Claressa, Claresta, Clariss,
Clarissah, Clarisse, Clarissia, Claritza,
Clarizza, Clarrisa, Clarrissa, Claryss,
Claryssa, Claryssah, Clarysse, Clerissa

Clarita (Spanish) a form of Clara. See
also Klarita.
Clairette, Clareata, Clareatah, Clareate,
Clareeta, Clareetah, Clareete, Claret, Clareta,
Claretah, Clarete, Clarett, Claretta, Clarettah,
Clarette, Claritah, Clarite, Claritta, Clarittah,
Claritte, Claritza, Claryt, Claryta, Clarytah,
Claryte, Clarytt, Clarytta, Claryttah, Clarytte

Claude (Latin, French) lame.
Claud, Claudio, Claudis, Claudius

Claudel (Latin) a form of Claude, Claudia.
Claudell, Claudelle

Claudette (French) a form of Claudia.
Clauddetta, Claudet, Claudeta, Claudetah,
Claudete, Claudett, Claudetta, Clawdet,
Clawdeta, Clawdetah, Clawdete, Clawdett,
Clawdetta, Clawdettah, Clawdette

Claudia (Latin) a form of Claude. See
also Gladys, Klaudia.
Clauda, Claudah, Claudea, Claudex,
Claudiah, Claudine

Claudie (Latin) a form of Claudia.
Claudee, Claudey, Claudi, Claudy

Claudine (French) a form of Claudia.
Claudan, Claudanus, Claudeen, Claudian,
Claudiana, Claudiane, Claudianus,
Claudie-Anne, Claudien, Claudin,
Claudina, Claudinah, Claudyn, Claudyna,
Claudynah, Claudyne

Clea (Greek) a form of Cleo, Clio.

Clematis (Greek) creeping vine. Botany:
a climbing plant with colorful flowers
or decorative fruit clusters.
Clematisa, Clematise, Clematiss,
Clematissa, Clematisse, Clematys,
Clematysa, Clematyse, Clematyss,
Clematyssa, Clematysse

Clemence (Latin) a form of Clementine.

Clementina (German) a form of
Clementine.
Clementinah, Clementyna, Clementynah

Clementine (Latin) merciful. See also
Klementine.
Clemencia, Clemencie, Clemency, Clemente,
Clementia, Clementiah, Clementina,
Clementyn, Clementyne, Clemenza, Clemette

Cleo (Greek) a short form of Cleopatra.
Chleo, Clea, Kleo

Cleone (Greek) famous.
Cleaona, Cleaonee, Cleaoney, Cleoni,
Cleonie, Cleonna, Cleony, Cliona

Cleopatra (Greek) her father's fame.
History: a great Egyptian queen.
Kleopatra

Cleta (Greek) illustrious.
Cletah

Clio (Greek) proclaimer; glorifier.
Mythology: the Muse of history.
Klio

Cloe (Greek) a form of Chloe.
Clo, Cloea, Cloee, Cloei, Cloey, Cloi, Cloie,
Clowee, Clowey, Clowi, Clowie

Clotilda (German) heroine.
Chlotilda, Chlotilde, Clotilde, Klothilda,
Klothilde

Coco (Spanish) coconut. See also Koko.

Codi, Codie, Cody (English) cushion. See also Kodi.
Coady, Codea, Codee, Codey, Codia

Colbi, Colbie (English) forms of Colby.

Colby (English) coal town. Geography: a region in England known for cheese-making. See also Kolbi.
Colbea, Colbee, Colbey

Coleen (Irish) a form of Colleen.
Colean, Coleane, Coleene, Colene

Colette, Collette (Greek, French) familiar forms of Nicole. See also Kolette.
Coe, Coetta, Colet, Coleta, Colete, Colett, Coletta, Colettah, Collet, Collete, Collett, Colletta

Colleen (Irish) girl. See also Kolina.
Coel, Cole, Coley, Coline, Collean, Colleane, Colleene, Collen, Collene, Collie, Collina, Colline, Colly, Collyn, Collyne, Colyn, Colyne

Collina (Irish) a form of Colleen.
Coleana, Coleena, Coleenah, Colena, Colina, Colinah, Colinda, Colleana, Colleena, Colleenah, Collinah, Collyna, Collynah, Colyna, Colynah

Columba (Latin) dove.
Colombe, Columbe, Columbia, Columbina, Columbinah, Columbine, Columbyna, Columbynah, Columbyne

Concepcion (Spanish) a form of Conchita. Religion: refers to the Immaculate Conception.
Concepta, Conceptia

Concetta (Italian) pure.
Concettina, Conchetta

Conchita (Spanish) conception.
Chita, Concha, Conciana, Concianah, Conciann, Concianna, Conciannah, Concianne

Concordia (Latin) harmonious. Mythology: the goddess governing the peace after war.
Con, Concorda, Concordah, Concordiah, Concordya, Concordyah, Cordae, Cordaye

Conner, Connor (Scottish) wise. (Irish) praised; exalted.
Connar, Connery, Conor

Connie (Latin) a familiar form of Constance.
Con, Conee, Coney, Coni, Conie, Connee, Conney, Conni, Conny, Cony, Konnie, Konny

Constance (Latin) constant; firm. History: Constance Motley was the first African American woman to be appointed as a U.S. federal judge. See also Konstance, Kosta.
Constancia, Constancy, Constanta, Constantia, Constantina, Constantine, Constanza, Constynse

Constanza (Spanish) a form of Constance.
Constanz, Constanze

Consuela (Spanish) a form of Consuelo.
Consuella, Consula

Consuelo (Spanish) consolation. Religion: Nuestra Señora del Consuelo—Our Lady of Consolation—is a name for the Virgin Mary.
Consolata, Conzuelo, Konsuela, Konsuelo

Contessa (Italian) an Italian countess.

Cooper (English) barrel maker.
Coop, Couper, Kooper, Kuepper

Cora (Greek) maiden. Mythology: Kore is another name for Persephone, the goddess of the underworld. See also Kora.
Corah, Corra

Corabelle (American) a combination of Cora + Belle.
Corabel, Corabela, Corabelah, Corabele, Corabell, Corabella, Corabellah, Korabel, Korabela, Korabelah, Korabele, Korabell, Korabella, Korabellah

Coral (Latin) coral. See also Koral.
Coraal, Corel, Corela, Corelah, Corele, Corell, Corella, Corellah, Corelle, Coril, Corila, Corilah, Corill, Corilla, Corillah, Corille, Corral, Coryl, Coryla, Corylah, Coryle, Coryll, Corylla, Coryllah, Corylle

Coralee (American) a combination of Cora + Lee.

Cora-Lee, Coralea, Coraleah, Coralei,
Coraleigh, Coralena, Coralene, Coraley,
Coraline, Coraly, Coralyn, Corella, Corilee,
Koralea, Koraleah, Koralei, Koraleigh,
Korali, Koralie, Koraly

Coralie (American) a form of Coralee.
Corali, Coralia, Coraliah, Coralin, Coralina,
Coralinah, Coraline, Coralynn, Coralynne

Corazon (Spanish) heart.
Corazona

Corbin (Latin) raven.
Corbe, Corbi, Corby, Corbyn, Corbynn

Cordasha (American) a combination of
Cora + Dasha.

Cordelia (Latin) warm-hearted. (Welsh)
sea jewel. See also Delia, Della, Kordelia.
Cordae, Cordelie, Cordellia, Cordellya,
Cordett, Cordette, Cordi, Cordilia, Cordilla,
Cordula, Cordulia

Cordella (French) rope maker.
Cordel, Codela, Cordelah, Cordele, Cordell,
Cordellah, Cordelle

Cordi (Welsh) a short form of Cordelia.
Cordey, Cordia, Cordie, Cordy

Coreen (Greek) a form of Corinne.
Coreene

Coreena (Greek) a form of Corinne.
Coreenah

Coretta (Greek) a familiar form of Cora.
See also Koretta.
Coreta, Coretah, Corete, Corett, Corettah,
Corette, Correta, Corretta, Corrette

Corey, Cory (Irish) from the hollow.
(Greek) familiar forms of Cora. See also
Korey.
Coree, Correy, Correye, Corry

Cori, Corie, Corrie (Irish) forms of
Corey.

Coriann, Corianne (American) combi-
nations of Cori + Ann.
Corean, Coreane, Cori-Ann, Corian,
Coriane, Corri-Ann, Corri-Anne, Corrianne,
Corrie-Ann, Corrie-Anne

Corin (Greek) a form of Corinne.
Corinn

Corina, Corinna, Corrina (Greek) forms
of Corinne. See also Korina.
Coreana, Coreanah, Coriana, Corianna,
Corinah, Corinda, Corinnah, Correana,
Correanah, Correena, Correenah, Correna,
Correnah, Corrinah, Corrinna, Corrinnah,
Corryna, Corrynah, Coryna, Corynah

Corine (Greek) a form of Corinne.

Corinne (Greek) maiden.
Coren, Corinee

Corissa (Greek) a familiar form of Cora.
Coresa, Coressa, Corisa, Corisah, Corissah,
Corysa, Corysah, Coryssa, Coryssah,
Korissa

Corliss (English) cheerful; goodhearted.
Corlis, Corlisa, Corlisah, Corlise, Corlissa,
Corlissah, Corlisse, Corly, Corlys, Corlysa,
Corlysah, Corlyse, Corlyss, Corlyssa,
Corlyssah, Corlysse, Korliss

Cornelia (Latin) horn colored. See also
Kornelia, Nelia, Nellie.
Carna, Carniella, Corneilla, Cornela,
Cornelie, Cornella, Cornelle, Cornelya,
Cornie, Cornilear, Cornisha, Corny

Corona (Latin) crown.
Coronah, Coronna, Coronnah, Korona,
Koronah, Koronna, Koronnah

Corrin, Corrine, Corrinne (Greek)
forms of Corinne.
Correan, Correane, Correen, Correene,
Corren, Correne, Corrinn, Corryn, Corryne

Cortina (American) a form of Kortina.
Cortinah, Cortine, Cortyn, Cortyna,
Cortyne

Cortnee, Cortney, Cortni, Cortnie
(English) forms of Courtney.
Cortnae, Cortnai, Cortnay, Cortne, Cortnea,
Cortneia, Cortny, Cortnye, Corttney

Coryn, Corynn (Greek) a form of
Corinne.
Coryne, Corynne

Cosette (French) a familiar form of
Nicole.

Cosette (cont.)
Coset, Coseta, Cosetah, Cosete, Cosett,
Cosetta, Cosettah, Cossetta, Cossette, Cozette

Cosima (Greek) orderly; harmonious;
universe.
Cosimah, Cosyma, Cosymah

Courtenay, Courteney (English) forms
of Courtney.
Courtaney, Courtany, Courtena, Courtene,
Courteny

Courtline, Courtlyn (English) forms of
Courtney.
Courtlin, Courtlina, Courtlinah, Courtlyna,
Courtlynah, Courtlyne, Courtlynn

**Courtnee, Courtnei, Courtni,
Courtnie, Courtny** (English) forms of
Courtney. See also Kortnee, Kourtnee.
Courtne, Courtnée

Courtney (English) from the court.
Courtnae, Courtnai, Courtnay, Courtneigh,
Courtnii, Courtoni, Courtonie, Courtony

Cree (Algonquin) a Native American
tribe and language of central North
America.

Crisbell (American) a combination of
Crista + Belle.
Crisbel, Cristabel

Crispina (Latin) curly haired.
Crispin, Crispine, Crispyn, Crispyna,
Crispynah, Crispyne

Crista (Italian) a form of Christa.
Cristah

Cristal (Latin) a form of Crystal.
Cristalie, Cristalle, Cristel, Cristela,
Cristelia, Cristell, Cristella, Cristelle,
Cristhie, Cristle

Cristan, Cristen, Cristin (Greek) forms
of Christan. See also Kristin.
Cristana, Cristanah, Cristane, Criston,
Cristyn, Crystan, Crysten, Crystin, Crystyn

Cristi, Cristy (English) familiar forms of
Cristina. Forms of Christy. See also
Christi, Kristi, Kristy.
Cristee, Cristey, Cristia, Cristie, Crystee,
Crystey, Crysti, Crystia, Crystie, Crysty

Cristian (Greek) a form of Christian.
Cristiana, Cristianah, Cristiane, Cristiann,
Cristianna, Cristiannah, Cristianne

Cristina (Greek) a form of Christina. See
also Kristina.
Cristaina, Cristainah, Cristeana,
Cristeanah, Cristeena, Cristeenah,
Cristeina, Cristeinah, Cristena, Cristenah,
Cristinah, Cristiona, Crystyna, Crystynah

Cristine (Greek) a form of Christine.
Cristain, Cristaine, Cristean, Cristeane,
Cristeen, Cristeene, Cristein, Cristeine,
Cristene, Crystyn, Crystyne

Crysta (Italian) a form of Christa.

Crystal (Latin) clear, brilliant glass. See
also Kristal, Krystal.
Crystala, Crystale, Crystalee, Crystall,
Crystalle, Crystaly, Crystela, Crystelia,
Crysthelle, Crystl, Crystle, Crystol,
Crystole, Crystyl

Crystalin (Latin) crystal pool. See also
Krystalyn.
Cristalanna, Cristalin, Cristalina, Cristaline,
Cristallina, Cristalyn, Cristalyna, Cristalyne,
Cristilyn, Crystal-Lynn, Crystalina,
Crystaline, Crystallynn, Crystallynne,
Crystalyn, Crystalyna, Crystalyne,
Crystalynn

Crystel (Latin) a form of Crystal.
Crystell, Crystella, Crystelle

Crystina (Greek) a form of Christina.
Crystin, Crystine, Crystyn, Crystyna,
Crystyne

Curran (Irish) heroine.
Cura, Curin, Curina, Curinna

Cuthberta (English) brilliant.
Cuthbertina, Cuthbirta, Cuthbirtina,
Cuthburta, Cuthburtina, Cuthburtine,
Cuthbyrta, Cuthbyrtina

Cybele (Greek) a form of Sybil.
Cebel, Cebela, Cebele, Cibel, Cibela,
Cibele, Cibell, Cibella, Cibelle, Cybel,
Cybela, Cybell, Cybella, Cybelle, Cybil,
Cybill, Cybille, Cybyl, Cybyla, Cybyle,
Cybyll, Cybylla, Cybylle

Cydnee, Cydney, Cydni (French) forms of Sydney.
Cydne, Cydnei, Cydnie

Cyerra (Irish) a form of Ciara.
Cyera, Cyerah, Cyerrah Cyerria, Cyra, Cyrah

Cynara (Greek) thistle.
Cinara, Cinarah, Cynarah, Sinara, Sinarah, Synara, Synarah

Cyndee, Cyndi (Greek) forms of Cindy.
Cynda, Cyndal, Cyndale, Cyndall, Cyndel, Cyndey, Cyndia, Cyndie, Cyndle, Cyndy

Cynthia (Greek) moon. Mythology: another name for Artemis, the moon goddess. See also Hyacinth, Kynthia, Synthia.
Cyneria, Cynethia, Cynithia, Cynthea, Cynthiah, Cynthiana, Cynthiann, Cynthie, Cynthria, Cynthy, Cynthya, Cynthyah, Cyntreia

Cyntia (Greek) a form of Cynthia.

Cypress (Greek) a coniferous tree.

Cyrena (Greek) a form of Sirena.
Ciren, Cirena, Cirenah, Cirene, Cyren, Cyrenah, Cyrene, Cyrenia, Cyreniah

Cyrilla (Greek) noble.
Cerelia, Cerella, Cira, Cirah, Cirila, Cirilah, Cirilla, Cirylla, Cyrah, Cyrella, Cyrelle, Cyrila, Cyrille, Cyryll, Cyrylla, Cyrylle

Czarina (German) a Russian empress.
Tsarina

D

D'andra (American) a form of Deandra.

D'andrea (American) a form of Deandra.

D'asia (American) a form of Dasia.

D'ericka (American) a form of Derika.
D'erica, D'erika

D'onna (American) a form of Donna.

Da'jah (American) a form of Daja.

Dacey (Irish) southerner. (Greek) a familiar form of Candace.
Dacee, Dacei, Daci, Dacie, Dacy, Daicee, Daici, Daicie, Daicy, Daycee, Daycie, Daycy

Dacia (Irish) a form of Dacey.
Dacea, Daciah, Dacya, Dacyah

Dae (English) day. See also Dai.

Daeja (French) a form of Déja.
Daejah, Daejia

Daelynn (American) a combination of Dae + Lynn.
Daeleen, Daelena, Daelin, Daelyn, Daelynne

Daesha (American) a form of Dasha.

Daeshandra (American) a combination of Dae + Shandra.
Daeshandria, Daeshaundra, Daeshaundria, Daeshawndra, Daeshawndria, Daeshondra, Daeshondria

Daeshawna (American) a combination of Dae + Shawna.
Daeshan, Daeshaun, Daeshauna, Daeshavon, Daeshawn, Daeshawntia, Daeshon, Daeshona, Daiseana, Daiseanah, Daishaughn, Daishaughna, Daishaughnah, Daishaun, Daishauna, Daishaunah, Daishawn, Daishawna, Daishawnah, Daysean, Dayseana, Dayseanah, Dayshaughna, Dayshaughnah, Dayshaun, Dayshauna, Dayshaunah, Dayshawn, Dayshawna

Daeshonda (American) a combination of Dae + Shonda.
Daeshanda, Daeshawnda

Dafny (American) a form of Daphne.
Dafany, Daffany, Daffie, Daffy, Dafna, Dafne, Dafney, Dafnie

Dagmar (German) glorious.
Dagmara, Dagmarah, Dagmaria, Dagmariah, Dagmarya, Dagmaryah

Dagny (Scandinavian) day.
Dagna, Dagnah, Dagnana, Dagnanna, Dagne, Dagnee, Dagney, Dagnia, Dagniah, Dagnie

Dahlia (Scandinavian) valley. Botany: a perennial flower. See also Dalia.
Dahliah, Dahlya, Dahlyah, Dahlye

Dai (Japanese) great. See also Dae.
Day, Daye

Daija, Daijah (French) forms of Déja.
Daijaah, Daijea, Daijha, Daijhah, Dayja

Daina (English) a form of Dana.
Dainah, Dainna

Daisey (English) a form of Daisy.

Daisha (American) a form of Dasha.
Daishae, Daishia, Daishya

Daisia (American) a form of Dasha.

Daisy (English) day's eye. Botany: a white and yellow flower.
Daisee, Daisi, Daisie, Dasee, Dasey, Dasi, Dasie, Dasy

Daiya (Polish) present.
Daia, Daiah, Daiyah, Daya, Dayah

Daja, Dajah (French) forms of Déja.
Dajae, Dajai, Daje, Dajha, Dajia

Dakayla (American) a combination of the prefix Da + Kayla.
Dakala, Dakila

Dakira (American) a combination of the prefix Da + Kira.
Dakara, Dakaria, Dakarra, Dakirah, Dakyra

Dakoda, Dakotah (Dakota) forms of Dakota.

Dakota (Dakota) a tribal name.
Dakkota, Dakotha, Dakotta, Dekoda, Dekodah, Dekota, Dekotah, Dekotha, Takota, Takotah

Dale (English) valley.
Dael, Daela, Dahl, Dail, Daila, Daile, Daleleana, Dalene, Dalina, Daline, Dayl

Dalena (English) a form of Dale.
Daleena, Dalenah, Dalenna, Dalennah

Dalia, Daliah (Hebrew) branch. See also Dahlia.
Daelia, Dailia, Daleah, Daleia, Dalialah, Daliyah

Dalila (Swahili) gentle.
Dalela, Dalida, Dalilah, Dalilia

Dalisha (American) a form of Dallas.
Dalisa, Dalishea, Dalishia, Dalishya, Dalisia, Dalissia, Dalissiah, Dalyssa

Dallas (Irish) wise.
Dallace, Dallus, Dallys, Dalyce, Dalys, Dalyss, Dalysse

Dallis (Irish) a form of Dallas.
Dalis, Dalise, Dalisse, Dallise

Dalton (English) town in the valley.
Dal, Dalaton, Dalltan, Dallten, Dalltin, Dallton, Dalltyn, Dalt, Daltan, Dalten, Daltin, Daltyn, Daulton, Delton

Damara (Greek) a form of Damaris.

Damaris (Greek) gentle girl. See also Maris.
Dama, Damar, Damarius, Damary, Damarylis, Damarys, Damarysa, Damaryss, Damaryssa, Damarysse, Dameress, Dameressa, Dameris, Damiris, Dammaris, Dammeris, Damris, Damriss, Damrissa, Demara, Demaras, Demaris, Demariss, Demarissa, Demarys, Demarysa, Demarysah, Demaryse, Demaryss, Demaryssa, Demaryssah, Demarysse

Damesha (Spanish) a form of Damita.
Dameshia, Damesia, Damesiah

Damia (Greek) a short form of Damiana.
Damiah, Damya, Damyah

Damiana (Greek) tamer, soother.
Daimenia, Daimiona, Damianah, Damiane, Damiann, Damianna, Damiannae, Damiannah, Damianne, Damien, Damienne, Damiona, Damon, Damyana, Damyanah, Damyann, Damyanna, Damyannah, Damyanne, Demion

Damica (French) friendly.
Damee, Dameeca, Dameecah, Dameeka, Dameka, Damekah, Damicah, Damicia, Damicka, Damie, Damieka, Damika, Damikah, Damyka, Demeeca, Demeecah, Demeeka, Demeka, Demekah, Demica, Demicah, Demicka, Demika, Demikah, Demyca, Demycah, Demycka, Demyka, Demykah

Damita (Spanish) small noblewoman.
Dameeta, Dameetah, Dametia, Dametiah,
Dametra, Dametrah, Damitah, Damyta,
Damytah

Damonica (American) a combination of
the prefix Da + Monica.
Damonec, Damoneke, Damonik, Damonika,
Damonique

Damzel (French) lady, maiden.
Damzela, Damzele, Damzell, Damzella,
Damzellah, Damzelle

Dana (English) from Denmark; bright as
day.
Daena, Daenah, Danaia, Danan, Danarra,
Dane, Danean, Daneana

Danae (Greek) Mythology: the mother
of Perseus.
Danaë, Danay, Danayla, Danays, Danai,
Danea, Danee, Dannae, Denee

Danah (English) a form of Dana.

Danalyn (American) a combination of
Dana + Lynn.
Danalee, Donaleen

Danasia (American) a form of Danessa.

Daneil (Hebrew) a form of Danielle.
Daneal, Daneala, Daneale, Daneel,
Daneela, Daneila, Daneille

Daneisha (American) a form of Danessa.

Danella (American) a form of Danielle.
Danala, Danalah, Danayla, Danela,
Danelia, Dannala, Dannalah, Donella,
Donnella

Danelle (Hebrew) a form of Danielle.
Danael, Danale, Danalle, Danel, Danele,
Danell, Donelle, Donnelle

Danesha (American) a form of Danessa.

Daneshia (American) a form of Danessa.

Danessa (American) a combination of
Danielle + Vanessa. See also Donesha.
Danesa, Danesah, Danessah, Danessia,
Daniesa, Danisa, Danisah, Danissa,
Danissah, Danissia, Danissiah, Danysa,
Danysah, Danyssa, Danyssah

Danessia (American) a form of Danessa.
Danesia, Danieshia, Danisia, Danissia

Danette (American) a form of Danielle.
Danetra, Danett, Danetta, Donnita,
Donnite, Donnyta, Donnytta, Donnytte

Dani, Danni (Hebrew) familiar forms of
Danielle.
Danee, Daney, Danie, Danne, Dannee,
Danney, Dannie, Dannii, Danny, Dannye,
Dany

Dania, Danya (Hebrew) short forms of
Danielle.
Daniah, Danja, Dannia, Danyae

Danica, Danika (Slavic) morning star.
(Hebrew) forms of Danielle.
Daneca, Daneeca, Daneecah, Daneeka,
Daneekah, Danicah, Danicka, Danieka,
Danikah, Danikia, Danikiah, Danikla,
Danneeka, Donica, Donika, Donnaica,
Donnica, Donnicka, Donnika, Donnike

Danice (American) a combination of
Danielle + Janice.
Danis, Danisa, Danisah, Danise, Daniss,
Danissa, Danissah, Danisse, Danyce,
Danys, Danysa, Danysah, Danyse, Donice

Daniel, Daniele, Daniell, Dannielle
(Hebrew, French) forms of Danielle.
Danniel, Danniele, Danniell

Daniela (Italian) a form of Danielle.
Daniala, Danialla, Daniellah, Danijela,
Dannilla, Danyela

Danielan (Spanish) a form of Danielle.

Daniella (English) a form of Dana,
Danielle.
Danka, Danniella, Danyella

Danielle (Hebrew, French) God is my
judge.
Daneen, Daneil, Daneille, Danial, Danialle,
Danielan, Danielka, Danilka, Danille,
Danniele, Donniella

Daniesha (American) a form of Danessa.

Danille (American) a form of Danielle.
Danila, Danile, Danilla, Dannille

Daniqua (Hebrew, Slavic) a form of Danica.
Daniquah

Danisha (American) a form of Danessa.
Danishia

Danit (Hebrew) a form of Danielle.
Danett, Danis, Daniss, Danitra, Danitrea, Danitria, Danitza, Daniz

Danita (Hebrew) a form of Danielle.

Danna, Dannah (American) short forms of Danella. (Hebrew) forms of Dana.

Dannica (Hebrew, Slavic) a form of Danica.
Dannika, Dannikah

Danyale, Danyel, Danyell, Danyelle (American) forms of Danielle.
Daniyel, Danyae, Danyail, Danyaile, Danyal, Danyea, Danyele, Danyiel, Danyielle, Danyle, Donnyale, Donnyell, Donyale, Donyell

Danyka (American) a form of Danica.
Danyca, Danycah, Danycka, Danykah, Danyqua, Danyquah

Daphne (Greek) laurel tree.
Dafnee, Dafney, Dafni, Dafnie, Dafny, Daphane, Daphaney, Daphanie, Daphany, Dapheney, Daphna, Daphni, Daphnie, Daphnique, Daphnit, Daphny

Daphnee, Daphney (Greek) forms of Daphne.

Dara (Hebrew) compassionate.
Dahra, Dahrah, Daira, Dairah, Daraka, Daralea, Daralee, Daraleigh, Daraley, Daralie, Daravie, Darda, Darja, Darra

Darah, Darrah (Hebrew) forms of Dara.

Daralis (English) beloved.
Daralisa, Daralisah, Daralise, Daralysa, Daralyse

Darbi (Irish, Scandinavian) a form of Darby.
Darbia, Darbiah, Darbie

Darby (Irish) free. (Scandinavian) deer estate.
Darb, Darbe, Darbea, Darbee, Darbra, Darbye

Darcelle (French) a form of Darcy.
Darcel, Darcela, Darcelah, Darcele, Darcell, Darcella, Darcellah, Darselle

Darci, Darcie (Irish, French) forms of Darcy.
Darcia, Darciah

Darcy (Irish) dark. (French) fortress.
Darcea, Darcee, Darcey, Darsea, Darsee, Darsey, Darsi, Darsie, Darsy

Daria (Greek) wealthy.
Dari, Dariya, Darria, Darriah

Darian, Dariane, Darianne, Darrian (Greek) forms of Daron.
Dariann, Dariyan, Dariyanne, Darriane, Darriann, Darrianne

Darianna (Greek) a form of Daron.
Dariana, Darriana, Darrianna, Driana

Darice (Persian) queen, ruler.
Dareece, Darees, Dareese, Daricia, Dariciah, Darisa, Darissa, Darycia, Darys, Darysa, Darysah, Daryse, Darysia, Darysiah, Darysya, Darysyah

Dariel, Darielle, Darrielle (French) forms of Daryl.
Dariela, Darielah, Dariele, Dariell, Dariella, Dariellah, Darriel, Daryel, Daryelah, Daryele, Daryell, Daryella, Daryellah, Daryelle

Darien, Darienne, Darrien (Greek) forms of Daron.
Dariene, Darriene

Darilynn (American) a form of Darlene.
Daralin, Daralina, Daralinah, Daraline, Daralyn, Daralyna, Daralyne, Daralynn, Daralynne, Darelin, Darileana, Darileanah, Darileen, Darileena, Darileenah, Darilin, Darilina, Darilinah, Dariline, Darilyn, Darilyna, Darilynah, Darilyne, Darilynne, Darylin, Darylina, Darylinah, Daryline, Darylyn, Darylyna, Darylynah, Darylyne, Darylynn, Darylynne

Darion, Darrion (Irish) forms of Daron.
Dariona, Darione, Darionna, Darionne, Darriona, Darrionna

Darla (English) a short form of Darlene.
Darlah, Darlecia, Darli, Darlice, Darlie, Darlis, Darly, Darlys

Darlene (French) little darling. See also Daryl.
Darlean, Darlee, Darleen, Darleena, Darleenah, Darleene, Darlen, Darlena, Darlenah, Darlenia, Darlenne, Darletha

Darlin, Darlyn (French) forms of Darlene.
Darlina, Darlinah, Darline, Darling, Darlyna, Darlynah, Darlyne, Darlynn, Darlynne

Darnee (Irish) a familiar form of Darnelle.

Darneisha (American) a form of Darnelle.
Darneishia, Darniesha, Darrenisha

Darnelle (English) hidden place.
Darnel, Darnela, Darnelah, Darnele, Darnell, Darnella, Darnellah, Darnetta, Darnette, Darnice, Darniece, Darnita, Darnyell, Darnyella, Darnyelle

Darnesha (American) a form of Darnelle.
Darneshea, Darneshia, Darnesia

Darnisha (American) a form of Darnelle.
Darnishia, Darnisia

Daron (Irish) a form of Daryn.
Darona, Daronah, Darron

Daronica (American) a form of Daron.
Daronicah, Daronice, Daronicka, Daronickah, Daronik, Daronika, Daronikah, Daroniqua, Daronique, Daronyca, Daronycah, Daronycka, Daronyckah, Daronyka, Daronykah, Daronyqua

Darselle (French) a form of Darcelle.
Darsel, Darsell, Darsella

Daru (Hindi) pine tree.
Darua, Darue, Daroo

Darya (Greek) a form of Daria.
Darrya, Darryah, Daryah, Daryia

Daryan (Greek, Irish) a form of Daryn.

Daryl (English) beloved. (French) a short form of Darlene.
Darel, Darela, Darelah, Darell, Darellah, Darelle, Daril, Darila, Darile, Darill, Darilla, Darillah, Darille, Darilynn, Darrel, Darrell, Darrelle, Darreshia, Darril, Darrila, Darrilah, Darrile, Darrill, Darrilla, Darrille, Darryl, Darryla, Darryle, Darryll, Darrylla, Darrylle, Daryla, Daryle, Daryll, Darylla, Daryllah, Darylle

Daryn (Greek) gifts. (Irish) great.
Darin, Darina, Darinah, Daryna, Darynah, Daryne, Darynn, Darynne

Dasha (Russian) a form of Dorothy.
Dashae, Dashah, Dashenka

Dashawn (American) a short form of Dashawna.
Dasean, Dashaughn, Dashaun

Dashawna (American) a combination of the prefix Da + Shawna.
Daseana, Daseanah, Dashaughna, Dashaughnah, Dashauna, Dashaunah, Dashawnah, Dashawnna, Dashell, Dayshana, Dayshawnna, Dayshona

Dashay (American) a familiar form of Dashawna.

Dashia (Russian) a form of Dorothy.
Dashiah

Dashiki (Swahili) loose-fitting shirt worn in Africa.
Dasheka, Dashi, Dashika, Dashka, Desheka, Deshiki

Dashonda (American) a combination of the prefix Da + Shonda.
Dashawnda, Dishante

Dasia (Russian) a form of Dasha.
Dasiah, Daysha

Davalinda (American) a combination of Davida + Linda.
Davalindah, Davalinde, Davelinda, Davilinda, Davylinda

Davalynda (American) a form of Davalinda.
Davelynda, Davilynda, Davylinda, Davylindah, Davylynda

Davalynn (American) a combination of
Davida + Lynn.
Davalin, Davalyn, Davalynne, Davelin,
Davelyn, Davelynn, Davelynne, Davilin,
Davilyn, Davilynn, Davilynne, Dayleen,
Devlyn

David (Hebrew) beloved. Bible: the second king of Israel.

Davida (Hebrew) a form of David. See
also Vida.
Daveda, Daveta, Davetta, Davette, Davika

Davina (Scottish) a form of Davida. See
also Vina.
Dava, Davannah, Davean, Davee, Daveen,
Daveena, Davene, Daveon, Davey, Davi,
Daviana, Davie, Davin, Davinder, Davine,
Davineen, Davinia, Davinna, Davria,
Devean, Deveen, Devene

Davisha (American) a combination of the
prefix Da + Aisha.
Daveisha, Davesia, Davis, Davisa

Davita (Scottish) a form of Davina.

Davon (Scottish, English) a short form of
Davonna.
Davonne

Davonna (Scottish, English) a form of
Davina, Devonna.
Davion, Daviona, Davionna, Davona,
Davonah, Davonda, Davondah, Davone,
Davonia, Davonnah, Davonnia

Dawn (English) sunrise, dawn.
Dawin, Dawina, Dawne, Dawnee, Dawnetta,
Dawnisha, Dawnlin, Dawnlina, Dawnline,
Dawnlyna, Dawnlyne, Dawnlynn, Dawnn,
Dawnrae

Dawna (English) a form of Dawn.
Dawana, Dawanah, Dawandra, Dawandrea,
Dawanna, Dawannah, Dawnah, Dawnna,
Dawnnah, Dawnya

Dawnetta (American) a form of Dawn.
Dawnet, Dawneta, Dawnete, Dawnett,
Dawnette

Dawnisha (American) a form of Dawn.
Dawnesha, Dawni, Dawniell, Dawnielle,
Dawnishia, Dawnisia, Dawniss, Dawnita,
Dawnnisha, Dawnysha, Dawnysia

Dawnyelle (American) a combination of
Dawn + Danielle.
Dawnele, Dawnell, Dawnella, Dawnelle,
Dawnyel, Dawnyell, Dawnyella

Dayana, Dayanna (Latin) forms of
Diana.
Dayanara, Dayani, Dayanne, Dayanni,
Deyanaira, Dyani, Dyia

Dayla (English) a form of Dale.
Daylea, Daylee

Daylan, Daylin (English) forms of Dale.
Daylen, Daylon

Dayle (English) a form of Dale.

Dayna (Scandinavian) a form of Dana.
Daynah, Dayne, Daynna, Deyna

Daysha (American) a form of Dasha.
Daysa, Dayshalie, Daysia, Deisha

Daysi (English) a form of Daisy.
Daysee, Daysey, Daysia, Daysie, Daysy

Dayton, Daytona (English) day town;
bright, sunny town.
Daytonia

De'ja, Deja, Dejá, Dejah, Déjah (French)
forms of Déja.
Deejay, Dejae, Dejai, Dejay, Dejaya

Deana (Latin) divine. (English) valley.
Deahana, Deahanah, Deanah, Deane,
Deaniel, Deaniela, Deanielah, Deaniele,
Deaniell, Deaniellah, Deanielle, Deanisha,
Deeana

Deandra (American) a combination of
Dee + Andrea.
Dandrea, Deandrah, Deandre, Deandré,
Deandree, Deanndra, Deeandra, Deyaneira,
Diondria, Dyandra

Deandrea (American) a form of Deandra.
Deandreia, Deandria, Deandriah,
Deandrya, Deandryah

Deangela (Italian) a combination of the
prefix De + Angela.
Deangala, Deangalique, Deangle

Deann, Deanne (Latin) forms of Diane.
Deahanne, Deane, Déanne, Dee-Ann,
Deeann, Deeanne

Deanna, Déanna (Latin) forms of Deana, Diana.
Deaana, Deahanna, Deahannah, Deannah, Deannia

Deasia, Déasia (American) forms of Dasia.

Deaundra (American) a form of Deandra.
Deaundria

Debbie, Debby (Hebrew) familiar forms of Deborah.
Debbea, Debbee, Debbey, Debbi, Debea, Debee, Debey, Debi, Debie, Deby

Debora (Hebrew) a form of Deborah.
Debbora

Deborah (Hebrew) bee. Bible: a great Hebrew prophetess.
Deb, Debbera, Debberah, Debborah, Debera, Deberah, Debor, Deboran, Deborha, Deborrah, Debrena, Debrina, Debroah, Dobra

Debra (American) a form of Deborah.
Debbra, Debbrah, Debrah, Debrea, Debria

December (Latin) born in the twelfth month.

Dedra (American) a form of Deirdre.
Deadra, Deadrah, Dedrah

Dedriana (American) a combination of Dedra + Adriana.
Dedranae

Dee (Welsh) black, dark.
De, Dea, Deah, Dede, Dedie, Dee Dee, Deea, Deedee, Didi

Deeanna (Latin) a form of Deana, Diana.

Deedra (American) a form of Deirdre.
Deeddra, Deedrah, Deedrea, Deedri, Deedrie

Deena (American) a form of Deana, Dena, Dinah.
Deenah, Deenna, Deennah

Deianeira (Greek) Mythology: Deianira was the wife of the Greek hero Heracles.
Daeanaira, Daeanairah, Daeianeira, Daeianeirah, Daianaira, Daianairah, Dayanaira, Dayanairah, Deianaira, Deianairah, Deianeirah

Deidra, Deidre (Irish) forms of Deirdre.
Deidrah, Deidrea, Deidrie, Diedre, Dydree, Dydri, Dydrie, Dydry

Deirdre (Irish) sorrowful; wanderer.
Deerdra, Deerdrah, Deerdre, Deirdree, Didi, Dierdra, Dierdre, Diérdre, Dierdrie, Dyerdre

Deisy (English) a form of Daisy.
Deisi, Deissy

Deitra (Greek) a short form of Demetria.
Deatra, Deatrah, Deetra, Deetrah, Deitrah, Detria, Deytra, Deytrah

Déja (French) before.

Dejanae (French) a form of Déja.
Dajahnae, Dajona, Dejana, Dejanah, Dejanai, Dejanay, Dejane, Dejanea, Dejanee, Dejanna, Dejannaye, Dejena, Dejonae

Dejanelle (French) a form of Déja.
Dejanel, Dejanela, Dejanelah, Dejanele, Dejanell, Dejanella, Dejanellah, Dejonelle

Dejon (French) a form of Déja.
Daijon, Dajan, Dejone, Dejonee, Dejonna

Deka (Somali) pleasing.
Dekah

Delacey, Delacy (American) combinations of the prefix De + Lacey.
Delaceya

Delaina (German) a form of Delana.
Delainah

Delaine (Irish) a short form of Delainey.

Delainey (Irish) a form of Delaney.
Delainee, Delaini, Delainie, Delainy

Delana (German) noble protector.
Dalaina, Dalainah, Dalaine, Dalanah, Dalanna, Dalannah, Dalayna, Dalaynah, Dalina, Dalinah, Dalinda, Dalinna, Delanah, Delania, Delanna, Delannah, Delanya, Deleina, Deleinah, Delena, Delenya, Deleyna, Deleynah, Dellaina

Delaney (Irish) descendant of the challenger. (English) a form of Adeline.
Dalanee, Dalaney, Dalania, Dalene, Daleney, Daline, Del, Delane, Delanee,

Delaney *(cont.)*
Delany, Delayne, Delayney, Deleine,
Deleyne, Dellanee, Dellaney, Dellany

Delanie (Irish) a form of Delaney.
Delani, Delaynie, Deleani, Dellani, Dellanie

Delayna (German) a form of Delana.
Delaynah

Deleena (French) dear; small.
Deleana, Deleanah, Deleane, Deleenah,
Deleene, Delyna, Delynah, Delyne

Delfina (Spanish) dolphin. (Greek) a
form of Delphine.
Delfeena, Delfi, Delfie, Delfin, Delfinah,
Delfine, Delfyn, Delfyna, Delfynah, Delfyne

Delia (Greek) visible; from Delos, Greece.
(German, Welsh) a short form of
Adelaide, Cordelia. Mythology: a festival
of Apollo held in ancient Greece.
Dehlia, Delea, Deleah, Deli, Deliah, Deliana,
Delianne, Delinda, Dellia, Delliah, Dellya,
Dellyah, Delya, Delyah

Delicia (English) delightful.
Delecia, Delesha, Delica, Delice, Delight,
Delighta, Delisia, Delisiah, Deliz, Deliza,
Delizah, Delize, Delizia, Delya, Delys,
Delyse, Delysia, Delysiah, Delysya,
Delysyah, Doleesha

Delilah (Hebrew) brooder. Bible: the
companion of Samson. See also Lila.
Dalialah, Daliliah, Delila, Delilia, Delilla,
Delyla, Delylla

Delina (French) a form of Deleena.
Delinah, Deline

Delisa (English) a form of Delicia.
Delisah, Delise

Delisha (English) a form of Delicia.
Delishia

Della (English) a short form of Adelaide,
Cordelia, Delaney.
Del, Dela, Dell, Delle, Delli, Dellie, Dells

Delmar (Latin) sea.
Delma, Delmah, Delmara, Delmarah,
Delmare, Delmaria, Delmariah, Delmarya,
Delmaryah

Delores, Deloris (Spanish) forms of
Dolores.
Delora, Delorah, Delore, Deloree, Delorey,
Deloria, Deloriah, Delories, Deloriesa,
Delorise, Deloriss, Delorissa, Delorissah,
Delorisse, Delorita, Delorite, Deloritta,
Delorys, Deloryse, Deloryss, Deloryta,
Delorytta, Deloryttah, Delsie

Delphine (Greek) from Delphi, Greece.
See also Delfina.
Delpha, Delphe, Delphi, Delphia, Delphiah,
Delphie, Delphina, Delphinah, Delphinia,
Delphiniah, Delphinie, Delphy, Delphyna,
Delphynah, Delphyne, Delvina, Delvinah,
Delvine, Delvinia, Delviniah, Delvyna,
Delvynah, Delvyne, Delvynia, Delvyniah,
Delvynya, Delvynyah, Dolphina,
Dolphinah, Dolphine, Dolphyn, Dolphyna,
Dolphynah, Dolphyne

Delsie (English) a familiar form of
Delores.
Delcea, Delcee, Delsa, Delsea, Delsee,
Delsey, Delsi, Delsia, Delsy, Delza

Delta (Greek) door. Linguistics: the
fourth letter in the Greek alphabet.
Geography: a triangular land mass at the
mouth of a river.
Deltah, Deltar, Deltare, Deltaria, Deltarya,
Deltaryah, Delte, Deltora, Deltoria, Deltra

Delwyn (English) proud friend; friend
from the valley.
Delwin

Demetra (Greek) a short form of
Demetria.
Demetrah

Demetria (Greek) cover of the earth.
Mythology: Demeter was the Greek
goddess of the harvest.
Deitra, Demeetra, Demeetrah, Demeta,
Demeteria, Demetriana, Demetrianna,
Demetrias, Demetrice, Demetriona, Demetris,
Demetrish, Demetrius, Dymeetra, Dymeetrah,
Dymetra, Dymetrah, Dymitra, Dymitrah,
Dymitria, Dymitriah, Dymytria, Dymytriah,
Dymytrya, Dymytryah

Demi (French) half. (Greek) a short form
of Demetria.

Demee, Demey, Demia, Demiah, Demie, Demii, Demmee, Demmey, Demmi, Demmie, Demmy, Demy

Demitria (Greek) a form of Demetria.
Demita, Demitah, Demitra, Demitrah

Dena (English, Native American) valley. (Hebrew) a form of Dinah. See also Deana.
Deane, Deeyn, Denah, Dene, Denea, Deney, Denna

Denae (Hebrew) a form of Dena.
Denaé, Denai, Denay, Denee, Deneé

Deneisha (American) a form of Denisha.
Deneichia, Deneishea

Denesha (American) a form of Denisha.
Deneshia

Deni (French) a short form of Denise.
Denee, Deney, Denie, Dennee, Denney, Denni, Dennie, Denny, Deny, Dinnie, Dinny

Denica, Denika (Slavic) forms of Danica.
Denicah, Denikah, Denikia

Denice (French) a form of Denise.
Denicy

Denis (French) a form of Denise.

Denise (French) Mythology: follower of Dionysus, the god of wine.
Danice, Danise, Denece, Denese, Deni, Deniece, Deniese, Denize, Denyce, Denys, Denyse, Dineece, Dineese, Dinice, Dinise, Dinyce, Dinyse, Dynice, Dynise, Dynyce, Dynyse

Denisha (American) a form of Denise.
Deneesha, Deniesha, Denishia

Denisse (French) a form of Denise.
Denesse, Deniss, Denissa, Denyss

Denita (Hebrew) a form of Danita.

Denver (English) green valley. Geography: the capital of Colorado.
Denvor

Deon (English) a short form of Deona.

Deona, Deonna (English) a form of Dena.
Deonah, Deonne

Deondra (American, Greek, English) a form of Deandra, Deona, Diona.

Derian (Greek) a form of Daryn.
Derrian

Derica, Derrica, Derricka (German) forms of Derika.
Dericah, Dericka, Derricah

Derika (German) ruler of the people.
Dereka, Derekah, Derekia, Derekiah, Derekya, Derekyah, Derikah, Deriqua, Deriquah, Derique, Derrika, Derrikah, Derriqua, Derryca, Derrycah, Derrycka, Derryka, Derryqua

Derry (Irish) redhead.
Deree, Derey, Deri, Derie, Derree, Derrey, Derri, Derrie, Dery

Deryn (Welsh) bird.
Deran, Derana, Deranah, Derane, Deren, Derena, Derenah, Derene, Derien, Derienne, Derin, Derina, Derinah, Derine, Derion, Deron, Derona, Deronah, Derone, Derran, Derrana, Derranah, Derrane, Derren, Derrin, Derrina, Derrinah, Derrine, Derrion, Derriona, Derryn, Derryna, Derrynah, Derryne, Deryna, Derynah, Deryne

Desarae, Desaray (French) forms of Desiree.
Desara, Desarah, Desarai, Desaraie, Desare, Desaré, Desarea, Desaree, Desarey, Desaria, Desarie, Desary

Deserae, Deseray, Deseree (French) forms of Desiree.
Desera, Deserah, Deserai, Deseraia, Deseraie, Desere, Deseret, Deserey, Deseri, Deseria, Deserie, Deserrae, Deserrai, Deserray, Deserré, Dessirae

Deshawn (American) a short form of Deshawna.
Deshan, Deshane, Deshaun

Deshawna (American) a combination of the prefix De + Shawna.
Desheania, Deshona, Deshonna

Deshawnda (American) a combination of the prefix De + Shawnda.
Deshanda, Deshandra, Deshaundra, Deshawndra, Deshonda

Deshay (American) a familiar form of Deshawna.

Desi (French) a short form of Desiree.
Desea, Desee, Desey, Desie, Désir, Desira, Desy, Dezi, Dezia, Dezzia, Dezzie

Desirae, Desiray, Desirea, Desireé, Desirée, Desiree' (French) forms of Desiree.

Desire (French) a form of Desiree.

Desiree (French) desired, longed for.
Desira, Desirah, Desirai, Desireah, Désirée, Desirey, Desiri, Desray, Desree, Dessie, Dessirae, Dessire, Dessiree, Desyrae, Desyrai, Desyray

Despina (Greek) a form of Despoina.

Despoina (Greek) mistress, lady.

Dessa (Greek) wanderer. (French) a form of Desiree.
Desa, Desah, Dessah

Desta (Ethiopian) happy. (French) a short form of Destiny.
Destah, Desti, Destie, Desty

Destanee, Destaney, Destani, Destanie, Destany (French) forms of Destiny.
Destania, Destannee, Destanney, Destanni, Destannia, Destannie, Destanny

Desteny (French) a form of Destiny.
Destenee, Desteni, Destenia, Destenie

Destin (French) a short form of Destiny.

Destine, Destinee, Destinée, Destiney, Destini, Destinie (French) forms of Destiny.
Destiana, Destinnee, Destinni, Destinnia, Destinnie, Destnie

Destiny (French) fate.
Desnine, Desta, Desteney, Destinia, Destiniah, Destinny, Destonie, Dezstany

Destyne, Destynee, Destyni (French) forms of Destiny.
Desty, Destyn, Destynia, Destyniah, Destynie, Destyny, Destynya, Destynyah

Deva (Hindi) divine.
Deava, Deavah, Deeva, Deevah, Devah, Diva, Divah, Dyva, Dyvah

Devan (Irish) a form of Devin.
Devana, Devane, Devanee, Devaney, Devani, Devania, Devanie, Devann, Devanna, Devannae, Devanne, Devany

Devi (Hindi) goddess. Religion: the Hindu goddess of power and destruction.

Devika (Sanskrit) little goddess.

Devin (Irish) poet.
Deaven, Deven, Devena, Devene, Devenja, Devenje, Deveny, Deveyn, Deveyna, Deveyne, Devyna, Devyne, Devynee, Devyney, Devyni, Devynia, Devyniah, Devyny, Devynya, Devynyah

Devina (Scottish, Irish, Latin) a form of Davina, Devin, Divina.
Deveena, Devinae, Devinah, Devinia, Deviniah, Devinie, Devinna

Devinne (Irish) a form of Devin.
Devine, Devinn, Devinna

Devon (English) a short form of Devonna. (Irish) a form of Devin.
Devion, Devione, Devionne, Devone, Devoni, Devonn, Devonne

Devona (English) a form of Devonna.
Devonah, Devonda

Devonna (English) from Devonshire.
Devondra, Devonia, Devonnah, Divona, Divonah, Divonna, Divonnah, Dyvona, Dyvonah, Dyvonna, Dyvonnah

Devora (Hebrew) a form of Deborah.
Deva, Devorah, Devra, Devrah, Dyvora, Dyvorah

Devyn, Devynn (Irish) forms of Devin.
Deveyn, Devyne, Devynne

Dextra (Latin) adroit, skillful.
Dekstra, Dextrah, Dextria

Deysi (English) a form of Daisy.
Deysia, Deysy

Dezarae, Dezaray, Dezaree (French) forms of Desiree.
Dezaraee, Dezarai, Dezare, Dezarey, Dezerai, Dezeray, Dezere, Dezerea, Dezeree, Dezerie, Dezorae, Dezorai, Dezoray, Dezzirae, Dezra, Dezrae, Dezrai, Dezray, Dezyrae, Dezzrae, Dezzrai, Dezzray

Dezirae, Deziray, Deziree (French) forms of Desiree.
Dezirea, Deziree

Dhara (Indian) earth.

Di (Latin) a short form of Diana, Diane.
Dy

Dia (Latin) a short form of Diana, Diane.

Diamon (Latin) a short form of Diamond.

Diamond (Latin) precious gem.
Diamantina, Diamantra, Diamonda, Diamondah, Diamonde, Diamonia, Diamonte, Diamontina, Dimond, Dimonda, Dimondah, Dimonde

Diamonique (American, Latin) a form of Damonica, Diamond
Diamoniqua

Diana (Latin) divine. Mythology: the goddess of the hunt, the moon, and fertility. See also Deann, Deanna, Dyana.
Daiana, Daianna, Diaana, Diaanah, Dianah, Dianalyn, Dianarose, Dianatris, Dianca, Dianelis, Diania, Dianiah, Dianiella, Dianielle, Dianita, Dianya, Dianyah, Dianys, Didi, Dihana, Dihanah, Dihanna

Diandra (American, Latin) a form of Deandra, Diana.
Diandre, Diandrea

Diane, Dianne (Latin) short forms of Diana.
Deane, Deeane, Deeanne, Diaan, Diaane, Diahann, Dian, Diani, Dianie, Diann, Dihan, Dihane, Dihann, Dihanne

Dianna (Latin) a form of Diana.
Diahanna, Diannah

Diantha (Greek) divine flower.
Diandre, Dianthah, Dianthe, Dyantha, Dyanthah, Dyanthe, Dyanthia, Dyanthiah, Dyanthya, Dyanthyah

Diedra (Irish) a form of Deirdre.
Didra, Diedre

Dillan (Irish) loyal, faithful.
Dillon, Dillyn

Dillian (Latin) worshipped.
Dilliana, Dillianna, Dilliannah, Dilliane, Dillianne, Dylian, Dyliana, Dylianah, Dyliane, Dyllian, Dylliana, Dylliane, Dylliann, Dyllianna, Dylliannah, Dyllianne, Dylyan, Dylyana, Dylyanah, Dylyane, Dylyann, Dylyanna, Dylyannah, Dylyanne

Dilys (Welsh) perfect; true. See also Dyllis.
Dilis, Dilisa, Dilisah, Dilise, Dillis, Dillisa, Dillisah, Dillise, Dillys, Dilysa, Dilysah, Dilyse, Dylys

Dina (Hebrew) a form of Dinah.
Dinna

Dinah (Hebrew) vindicated. Bible: a daughter of Jacob and Leah.
Dinnah, Dyna, Dynah, Dynna, Dynnah

Dinesha (American) a form of Danessa.

Dinka (Swahili) people.
Dinkah, Dynka, Dynkah

Diona, Dionna (Greek) forms of Dionne.
Deonia, Deonyia, Dionah, Dyona, Dyonah

Diondra (Greek) a form of Dionne.
Diondrea

Dionne (Greek) divine queen. Mythology: Dione was the mother of Aphrodite, the goddess of love.
Deonne, Dion, Dione, Dionee, Dioney, Dioni, Dionie, Dionis, Dionte, Diony, Dyon, Dyone, Dyonee, Dyoney, Dyoni, Dyonie, Dyony

Dior (French) golden.
Diora, Diorah, Diore, Diorra, Diorrah, Diorre, Dyor, Dyora, Dyorah, Dyorra, Dyorrah, Dyorre

Dita (Spanish) a form of Edith.
Ditah, Ditka, Ditta, Dyta, Dytah

Divinia (Latin) divine.
Diveena, Divina, Divinah, Divine, Diviniah, Diviniea, Dyveena, Dyvina, Dyvinah, Dyvinia, Dyvyniah, Dyvyna, Dyvynah, Dyvynia, Dyvyniah, Dyvynya

Divya (Latin) a form of Divinia.

Dixie (French) tenth. (English) wall; dike. Geography: a nickname for the American South.

Dixie *(cont.)*
Dix, Dixee, Dixey, Dixi, Dixy, Dyxee, Dyxey, Dyxi, Dyxie, Dyxy

Diza (Hebrew) joyful.
Ditza, Ditzah, Dizah, Dyza, Dyzah

Doanne (English) low, rolling hills.
Doan, Doana, Doanah, Doann, Doanna, Doannah, Doean, Doeana, Doeanah, Doeane, Doeann, Doeanna, Doeannah, Doeanne

Docila (Latin) gentle; docile.
Docilah, Docile, Docilla, Docillah, Docille, Docyl, Docyla, Docylah, Docyle, Docyll, Docylla, Docyllah, Docylle

Dodie (Hebrew) beloved. (Greek) a familiar form of Dorothy.
Doda, Dode, Dodea, Dodee, Dodey, Dodi, Dodia, Dodiah, Dody, Dodya, Dodyah

Dolly (American) a short form of Dolores, Dorothy.
Dol, Dolea, Doleah, Dolee, Dolei, Doleigh, Doley, Doli, Dolia, Doliah, Dolie, Doll, Dollea, Dolleah, Dollee, Dollei, Dolleigh, Dolley, Dolli, Dollie, Dollina, Doly

Dolores (Spanish) sorrowful. Religion: Nuestra Señora de los Dolores—Our Lady of Sorrows—is a name for the Virgin Mary. See also Lola.
Deloria, Dolorcitas, Dolorita, Doloritas

Domanique (French) a form of Dominica.

Domenica (Latin) a form of Dominica.
Domeneka, Domenicah, Domenicka, Domenika

Domenique (French) a form of Dominica.
Domeneque, Domeniqua, Domeniquah

Dominica, Dominika (Latin) belonging to the Lord. See also Mika.
Domineca, Domineka, Dominga, Domini, Dominia, Dominiah, Dominicah, Dominick, Dominicka, Dominikah, Dominixe, Domino, Dominyika, Domka, Domnica, Domnicah, Domnicka, Domnika, Domonica, Domonice, Domonika

Dominique (French) a form of Dominica.

Domineque, Dominiqua, Dominiquah, Domino, Dominoque, Dominuque, Domique

Domino (English) a short form of Dominica.
Domina, Dominah, Domyna, Domynah, Domyno

Dominque (French) a short form of Dominique.

Domonique (French) a form of Dominique.
Domminique, Domoniqua, Domoniquah

Dona (English) world leader; proud ruler. (Italian) a form of Donna.
Donae, Donah, Donalda, Donaldina, Donelda, Donellia, Doni

Doña (Italian) a form of Donna.
Donail, Donalea, Donalisa, Donay

Donata (Latin) gift.
Donatha, Donathia, Donathiah, Donathya, Donathyah, Donato, Donatta, Donetta, Donette, Donita, Donnette, Donnita, Donte

Dondi (American) a familiar form of Donna.
Dondra, Dondrea, Dondria

Doneisha (American) a form of Danessa.
Donasha, Donashay, Doneishia

Donesha (American) a form of Danessa.

Doneshia (American) a form of Danessa.
Donneshia

Donia (Italian) a form of Donna.
Doni, Donie, Donise, Donitrae

Donielle (American) a form of Danielle.
Doniel, Doniele, Doniell, Donniel, Donniela, Donniele, Donniell, Donnielle, Donnyel, Donnyele, Donnyell, Donnyelle, Donyel, Donyele, Donyell, Donyelle

Donisha, Donnisha (American) a form of Danessa.
Donisa, Donishia, Donnisa, Donnise, Donnissa, Donnisse.

Donna (Italian) lady.
Dondi, Donnae, Donnah, Donnai, Donnalee, Donnalen, Donnay, Donnaya, Donne, Donnell, Donni, Donnie, Donny, Dontia

Donniella (American) a form of Danielle.
Donella, Doniela, Doniella, Donnella, Donniellah, Donnyela, Donnyella, Donyela, Donyelah, Donyella, Donyellah

Donya (Italian) a form of Donna.

Dora (Greek) gift. A short form of Adora, Eudora, Pandora, Theodora.
Dorah, Doralia, Doraliah, Doralie, Doralisa, Doraly, Doralynn, Doran, Dorana, Dorchen, Dorece, Doreece, Dorelia, Dorella, Dorelle, Doresha, Doressa, Doretta, Dorielle, Dorika, Doriley, Dorilis, Dorion, Dorita, Doro

Dorabella (English) a combination of Dora + Bella.
Dorabel, Dorabela, Dorabelah, Dorabele, Dorabell, Dorabellah, Dorabelle

Doralynn (English) a combination of Dora + Lynn.
Doralin, Doralina, Doraline, Doralyn, Doralyna, Doralynah, Doralyne, Doralynne, Dorlin

Dorcas (Greek) gazelle. Bible: New Testament translation of the name Tabitha.

Doreen (Irish) moody, sullen. (French) golden. (Greek) a form of Dora.
Doreana, Doreanah, Doreena, Doreenah, Doreene, Dorena, Dorenah, Dorene, Dorin, Dorine, Doryn, Doryna, Dorynah, Doryne

Doretta (American) a form of Dora, Dorothy.
Doret, Doreta, Doretah, Dorete, Doretha, Dorett, Dorettah, Dorette, Dorettie, Dorita, Doritah, Doritta, Dorittah, Doryta, Dorytah, Dorytta, Doryttah

Dori, Dory (American) familiar forms of Dora, Doria, Doris, Dorothy.
Dore, Dorey, Dorie, Dorree, Dorri, Dorrie, Dorry

Doria (Greek) a form of Dorian.
Doriah, Dorria, Dorrya, Dorryah, Dorya, Doryah

Dorian, Doriane, Dorianne (Greek) from Doris, Greece.
Dorean, Doreane, Doriana, Doriann, Dorianna, Dorina, Dorinah, Dorriane

Dorinda (Spanish) a form of Dora.
Dorindah, Dorynda, Doryndah

Doris (Greek) sea. Mythology: wife of Nereus and mother of the Nereids or sea nymphs.
Doreece, Doreese, Dorice, Dorisa, Dorise, Dorreece, Dorreese, Dorris, Dorrise, Dorrys, Dorryse, Dorys

Dorothea (Greek) a form of Dorothy. See also Thea.
Dorathia, Dorathya, Dorethea, Dorofia, Dorotea, Doroteya, Dorotha, Dorothia, Dorotthea, Dorottia, Dorottya, Dorthea, Dorthia, Doryfia, Doryfya

Dorothee (Greek) a form of Dorothy.

Dorothy (Greek) gift of God. See also Dasha, Dodie, Lolotea, Theodora.
Dasya, Do, Doa, Doe, Doortje, Dorathee, Dorathey, Dorathi, Dorathie, Dorathy, Dordei, Dordi, Dorefee, Dorethie, Doretta, Dorifey, Dorika, Doritha, Dorka, Dorle, Dorlisa, Doro, Dorofey, Dorolice, Dorosia, Dorota, Dorothey, Dorothi, Dorothie, Dorottya, Dorte, Dortha, Dorthy, Doryfey, Dosi, Dossie, Dosya

Dorrit (Greek) dwelling. (Hebrew) generation.
Dorit, Dorita, Dorite, Doritt, Doritte, Dorrite, Doryt, Doryte, Dorytt, Dorytte

Dottie, Dotty (Greek) familiar forms of Dorothy.
Dot, Dotea, Dotee, Dotey, Doti, Dotie, Dott, Dottea, Dottee, Dottey, Dotti, Doty

Dreama (English) dreamer.
Dreamah, Dreamar, Dreamara, Dreamare, Dreamaria, Dreamariah, Dreamarya, Dreamaryah, Dreema, Dreemah, Dreemar, Dreemara, Dreemarah, Dreemare, Dreemaria, Dreemariah, Dreemarya, Dreemaryah

Drew (Greek) courageous; strong. (Latin) a short form of Drusilla.
Drewa, Drewee, Drewia, Drewie, Drewy

Drina (Spanish) a form of Alexandrine.
Dreena, Drena, Drinah, Drinka, Dryna,
Drynah

Drucilla (Latin) a form of Drusilla.
Drucela, Drucella, Drucill, Drucillah,
Drucyla, Drucylah, Drucyle, Drucylla,
Drucyllah, Drucylle, Druscila

Drue (Greek) a form of Drew.
Dru

Drusi (Latin) a short form of Drusilla.
Drucey, Druci, Drucie, Drucy, Drusey,
Drusie, Drusy

Drusilla (Latin) descendant of Drusus, the
strong one. See also Drew.
Drewcela, Drewcella, Drewcila, Drewcilla,
Drewcyla, Drewcylah, Drewcylla, Drewcyllah,
Drewsila, Drewsilah, Drewsilla, Drewsillah,
Drewsyla, Drewsylah, Drewsylla, Drewsyllah,
Druscilla, Druscille, Drusila, Drusilah,
Drusillah, Drusille, Drusyla, Drusylah,
Drusyle, Drusylla, Drusyllah, Drusylle

Duena (Spanish) chaperon.
Duenah, Duenna, Duennah

Dulce (Latin) sweet.
Delcina, Delcine, Douce, Douci, Doucie,
Dulcea, Dulcee, Dulcey, Dulci, Dulcia,
Dulciana, Dulciane, Dulciann, Dulcianna,
Dulcianne, Dulcibel, Dulcibela, Dulcibell,
Dulcibella, Dulcibelle, Dulcie, Dulcy, Dulse,
Dulsea, Dulsee, Dulsey, Dulsi, Dulsie, Dulsy

Dulcinea (Spanish) sweet. Literature: Don
Quixote's love interest.
Dulcine, Dulcinea

Durene (Latin) enduring.
Durean, Dureana, Dureanah, Dureane,
Dureen, Dureena, Dureenah, Dureene,
Durena, Durenah, Durin, Durina, Durinah,
Durine, Duryn, Duryna, Durynah, Duryne

Duscha (Russian) soul; sweetheart; term
of endearment.
Duschah, Dusha, Dushenka

Dusti, Dusty (English) familiar forms of
Dustin.
Dustea, Dustee, Dustey, Dustie

Dustin (German) valiant fighter. (English)
brown rock quarry.
Dust, Dustain, Dustan, Dusten, Dustion,
Duston, Dustyn, Dustynn

Dustine (German) a form of Dustin.
Dustean, Dusteana, Dusteanah, Dusteane,
Dusteena, Dusteenah, Dusteene, Dustina,
Dustinah, Dustyna, Dustynah, Dustyne

Dyamond (Latin) a form of Diamond.
Dyamin, Dyamon, Dyamonda,
Dyamondah, Dyamonde, Dyamone

Dyana, Dyanna (Latin) forms of Diana.
Dyaan, Dyaana, Dyaanah, Dyan, Dyanah,
Dyane, Dyann, Dyanne, Dyhan, Dyhana,
Dyhane, Dyhann, Dyhanna, Dyhanne

Dyani (Native American) deer.
Dianee, Dianey, Diani, Dianie, Diany,
Dyanee, Dyaney, Dyanie, Dyany

Dylan (Welsh) sea.
Dylaan, Dylane, Dylanee, Dylanie,
Dylann, Dylen, Dylin, Dyllan, Dylynn

Dylana (Welsh) a form of Dylan.
Dylaina, Dylanna

Dyllis (Welsh) sincere. See also Dilys.
Dylis, Dylissa, Dylissah, Dyllys, Dyllysa,
Dyllyse, Dylys, Dylysa, Dylysah, Dylyse,
Dylyss, Dylyssa, Dylyssah

Dymond (Latin) a form of Diamond.
Dymin, Dymon, Dymonda, Dymondah,
Dymonde, Dymone, Dymonn, Dymont,
Dymonte

Dynasty (Latin) powerful ruler.
Dynastee, Dynasti, Dynastie

Dyshawna (American) a combination of
the prefix Dy + Shawna.
Dyshanta, Dyshawn, Dyshonda, Dyshonna

E

Eadda (English) wealthy; successful.
Eada, Eadah, Eaddah

Earlene (Irish) pledge. (English) noble-
woman.
Earla, Earlean, Earlecia, Earleen, Earleena,
Earlena, Earlina, Earlinah, Earlinda,
Earline, Earlyn, Earlyna, Earlynah, Earlyne

Eartha (English) earthy.
Earthah, Earthia, Earthiah, Earthya, Earthyah, Erta, Erthah

Easter (English) Easter time. History: a name for a child born on Easter.
Eastan, Eastera, Easterina, Easterine, Easteryn, Easteryna, Easteryne, Eastlyn, Easton

Eavan (Irish) fair.
Eavana, Eavanah, Eavane

Ebone, Eboné, Ebonee, Eboney, Eboni, Ebonie (Greek) forms of Ebony.
Ebonne, Ebonnee, Ebonni, Ebonnie

Ebony (Greek) a hard, dark wood.
Abonee, Abony, Eban, Ebanee, Ebanie, Ebany, Ebbony, Ebeni, Ebonea, Ebonique, Ebonisha, Ebonye, Ebonyi

Echo (Greek) repeated sound. Mythology: the nymph who pined for the love of Narcissus until only her voice remained.
Echoe, Ecko, Eco, Ekko, Ekkoe

Eda (Irish, English) a short form of Edana, Edith.
Edah

Edana (Irish) ardent; flame.
Edan, Edanah, Edanna

Edda (German) a form of Hedda.
Eddah

Eddy (American) a familiar form of Edwina.
Eady, Eddee, Eddey, Eddi, Eddie, Edee, Edey, Edi, Edie, Edy

Edeline (English) noble; kind.
Adeline, Edelin, Edelina, Edelinah, Edelyn, Edelyna, Edelynah, Edelyne, Ediline, Edilyne, Edolina, Edoline

Eden (Babylonian) a plain. (Hebrew) delightful. Bible: the earthly paradise.
Eaden, Edan, Ede, Edena, Edene, Edenia, Edin, Edine, Edon, Edona, Edonah, Edone, Edyn, Edyne

Edeva (English) expensive present.
Eddeva, Eddevah, Eddeve, Edevah

Edian (Hebrew) decoration for God.
Edia, Edya, Edyah, Edyan

Edie (English) a familiar form of Edith.
Eadie, Edi, Edy, Edye, Eyde, Eydie

Edina (English) prosperous fort.
Edena, Edenah, Edinah, Edyna, Edynah

Edith (English) rich gift. See also Dita.
Eadith, Eda, Ede, Edetta, Edette, Edie, Edit, Edita, Edite, Editha, Edithe, Editta, Ediva, Edyta, Edyth, Edytha, Edythe

Edlyn (English) prosperous; noble.
Edlin, Edlina, Edline, Edlyna, Edlyne

Edmunda (English) prosperous protector.
Edmona, Edmonah, Edmonda, Edmondah, Edmondea, Edmondee, Edmondey, Edmuna, Edmunah, Edmundea, Edmundey

Edna (Hebrew) rejuvenation. Religion: the wife of Enoch, according to the Book of Enoch.
Adna, Adnisha, Ednah, Edneisha, Edneshia, Ednisha, Ednita, Edona

Edrea (English) a short form of Edrice, Edrianna.
Edreah, Edria, Edriah, Edra, Edrah, Edrya, Edryah

Edrianna (Greek) a form of Adrienne.
Edrena, Edriana, Edrina

Edrice (English) prosperous ruler.
Edrica, Edricah, Edricia, Edriciah, Edris, Edriss, Edrissa, Edrisse, Edryca, Edrycah, Edrycia, Edryciah, Edrycya, Edrycyah, Edrys, Edryss, Edryssa, Edrysse

Edwardina (English) prosperous guardian.
Edwardinah, Edwardine, Edwardyna, Edwardynah, Edwardyne

Edwina (English) prosperous friend. See also Winnie.
Eddwina, Eddwinah, Eddwine, Eddwyn, Eddwyna, Eddwynah, Eddwyne, Eddy, Edween, Edweena, Edweenah, Edweene, Edwena, Edwinah, Edwine, Edwinna, Edwinnah, Edwinne, Edwyn, Edwyna, Edwynah, Edwyne, Edwynn

Effia (Ghanaian) born on Friday.

Effie (Greek) spoken well of. (English) a short form of Alfreda, Euphemia.
Efea, Efee, Effea, Effee, Effi, Effia, Effy, Efi, Efie, Efy, Ephie

Efrata (Hebrew) honored.
Efratah

Efrona (Hebrew) songbird.
Efronah, Efronna, Efronnah

Egberta (English) bright sword.
Egbertah, Egberte, Egbirt, Egbirte, Egburt, Egburte, Egbyrt, Egbyrte

Eileen (Irish) a form of Helen. See also Aileen, Ilene.
Eilean, Eileana, Eileane, Eileena, Eileenah, Eileene, Eilena, Eilene, Eiley, Eilie, Eilieh, Eilina, Eiline, Eilleen, Eillen, Eilyn, Eleane, Eleen, Eleene, Elene, Elin, Elyn, Elyna, Eylean, Eyleana, Eyleen, Eyleena, Eylein, Eyleina, Eyleyn, Eyleyna, Eylin, Eylina, Eylyn, Eylyna

Eira (Welsh) snow.
Eir, Eirah, Eyr, Eyra, Eyrah

Eirene (Greek) a form of Irene.
Eereen, Eereena, Eereene, Eireen, Eireena, Eirena, Ereen, Ereena, Ereene, Erena, Eyren, Eyrena, Eyrene

Eirween (Welsh) white snow.
Eirwena, Eirwenah, Eirwene, Eyrwen, Irwen, Irwena, Irwenah, Irwene

Ekaterina (Russian) a form of Katherine.
Ekaterine, Ekaterini

Ela (Polish) a form of Adelaide.
Elah, Ellah

Elaina (French) a form of Helen.
Elainah, Elainea, Elainia, Elainna

Elaine (French) a form of Helen. See also Laine, Lainey.
Eilane, Elain, Elaini, Elane, Elani, Elanie, Elanit, Elauna, Elayn, Elayne, Ellaine

Elana (Greek) a short form of Eleanor. See also Ilana, Lana.
Elan, Elanah, Elanee, Elaney, Elania, Elanie, Elanna, Elannah, Elanne, Elanni, Ellana, Ellanah, Ellann, Ellanna, Ellannah

Elanora (Australian) from the shore.
Elanorah, Elanore, Ellanora, Ellanorah, Ellanore, Ellanorra, Ellanorrah, Ellanorre

Elayna (French) a form of Elaina.
Elaynah, Elayne, Elayni

Elberta (English) a form of Alberta.
Elbertah, Elberte, Elbertha, Elberthina, Elberthine, Elbertina, Elbertine, Elbirta, Elbirtah, Elburta, Elburtah, Elbyrta, Elbyrtah, Ellberta, Ellbertah, Ellberte, Ellbirta, Ellbirtah, Ellburta, Ellburtah, Ellbyrta, Ellbyrtah

Eldora (Spanish) golden, gilded.
Eldorah, Eldoree, Eldorey, Eldori, Eldoria, Eldorie, Eldory, Elldora, Elldorah

Eldrida (English) wise counselor.
Eldridah, Eldryda, Eldrydah, Eldryde

Eleanor (Greek) light. History: Anna Eleanor Roosevelt was a U.S. delegate to the United Nations, a writer, and the thirty-second First Lady of the United States. See also Elana, Ella, Ellen, Helen, Leanore, Lena, Lenore, Leonor, Leora, Nellie, Nora, Noreen.
Alienor, Elanor, Elenor, Elenore, Eleonor, Eleonore, Elianore, Elladine, Elleanor, Elleanore, Ellenor, Elliner, Ellynor, Ellynore, Elna, Elnore, Elynor, Elynore

Eleanora (Greek) a form of Eleanor. See also Lena.
Alienora, Elenora, Elenorah, Eleonora, Elianora, Elinora, Elleanora, Ellenora, Ellenorah, Ellynora, Elyenora, Elynora, Elynorah

Eleanore (Greek) a form of Eleanor.

Electra (Greek) shining; brilliant. Mythology: the daughter of Agamemnon, leader of the Greeks in the Trojan War.
Electrah, Elektra, Elektrah

Eleebana (Australian) beautiful.
Elebana, Elebanah, Elebanna, Elebannah, Eleebanna, Eleebannah

Elena (Greek) a form of Eleanor. (Italian) a form of Helen.
Eleana, Eleen, Eleena, Elen, Elenah, Elene, Elenitsa, Elenka, Elenna, Elenoa, Elenola, Lena

Eleni (Greek) a familiar form of Eleanor.
Elenee, Elenie, Eleny

Eleora (Hebrew) the Lord is my light.
*Eleorah, Eliora, Eliorah, Elioria, Elioriah,
Eliorya, Elioryah, Elira, Elora*

Elesha (Greek, Hebrew) a form of Elisha.
Eleshia, Ellesha

Eletta (English) elf; mischievous.
*Eleta, Eletah, Elete, Elett, Elettah, Elette,
Elletta, Ellette*

Elexis, Elexus (Greek) forms of Alexis.
*Elexas, Elexes, Elexess, Elexeya, Elexia,
Elexiah, Elexius, Elexsus, Elexxus, Elexys*

Elfrida (German) peaceful. See also Freda.
*Elfrea, Elfreda, Elfredah, Elfredda, Elfrede,
Elfreeda, Elfreyda, Elfride, Elfrieda, Elfriede,
Elfryda, Elfrydah*

Elga (Norwegian) pious. (German) a
form of Helga.
Elgah, Elgar, Elgara, Elgiva

Eli (Hebrew) uplifted. See also Elli.
Ele, Elee, Elei, Eleigh, Eley, Elie, Ely

Elia (Hebrew) a short form of Eliana.
Eliah

Eliana (Hebrew) my God has answered
me. See also Iliana.
*Elianah, Elianna, Eliannah, Elliana,
Ellianah, Ellianna, Elliannah, Ellyana,
Ellyanah, Elyana, Elyanah, Elyanna,
Elyannah, Liana, Liane*

Eliane, Elianne (Hebrew) forms of Eliana.
Elliane, Ellianne, Ellyane, Ellyanne, Elyanne

Elicia (Hebrew) a form of Elisha. See also
Alicia.
*Elecia, Eleecia, Eleesia, Elica, Elicea, Eliceah,
Elicet, Elichia, Eliciah, Eliscia, Ellecia,
Elleecia, Elleeciah, Ellesia, Ellicia, Elliciah*

Elida (Latin) a form of Alida.
Elidee, Elidia, Elidy

Elide (Latin) a form of Elida.

Elijah (Hebrew) the Lord is my God.
Bible: a great Hebrew prophet.
*Elia, Elian, Elija, Elijha, Elijiah, Elijio,
Elijuah, Elijuo, Elijsha, Eliya, Eliyah,
Ellija, Ellijah, Ellyjah*

Elina (Greek, Italian) a form of Elena.
(English) a form of Ellen.
Elinah, Elinda

Elili (Tamil) beautiful.

Elinor (Greek) a form of Eleanor.
Elinore, Ellinor, Ellinore

Elisa, Ellisa (Spanish, Italian, English)
short forms of Elizabeth. See also Alisa,
Ilisa, Lisa.
*Elecea, Eleesa, Elesa, Elesia, Elisah, Elisya,
Elleesa, Ellisia, Ellissa, Ellissia, Ellissya,
Ellisya*

Elisabet (Hebrew) a form of Elizabeth.
*Elisabeta, Elisabete, Elisabetta, Elisabette,
Elisebet, Elisebeta, Elisebete, Elisebett,
Elisebetta, Elisebette*

Elisabeth (Hebrew) a form of Elizabeth.
*Elisabethe, Elisabith, Elisebeth, Elisheba,
Elishebah, Ellisabeth, Elsabeth, Elysabeth*

Elise (French, English) a short form of
Elizabeth, Elysia. See also Ilise, Liese,
Liset, Lissie.
*Eilis, Eilise, Eleese, Elese, Elice, Elis, Élise,
Elisee, Elisie, Elisse, Elizé, Elleece, Elleese,
Ellice, Ellise, Ellyce, Ellyse, Ellyze, Elyce,
Elyci, Elyze*

Elisha (Hebrew) consecrated to God.
(Greek) a form of Alisha. See also
Ilisha, Lisha.
*Eleacia, Eleasha, Eleesha, Eleeshia, Eleisha,
Eleticia, Elishah, Elishia, Elishiah, Elishua,
Eliska, Ellisha, Ellishah, Ellishia, Ellishiah,
Elsha*

Elisheva (Hebrew) a form of Elisabeth.
Elishevah

Elisia (Hebrew) a form of Elisha.
Elissia

Elissa (Greek, English) a form of Elizabeth.
A short form of Melissa. See also Alissa,
Alyssa, Lissa.
Elissah, Ellissa, Ilissa, Ilyssa

Elita (Latin, French) chosen. See also
Lida, Lita.
*Eleata, Eleatah, Eleeta, Eleetah, Eleita,
Eleitah, Elitah, Elitia, Elitie, Ellita, Ellitia,
Ellitie, Ellyt, Ellyta, Ellytah, Ellyte, Elyt,
Elyta, Elytah, Elyte, Ilida, Ilita, Litia*

Eliza (Hebrew) a short form of Elizabeth. See also Aliza.
Eliz, Elizah, Elizaida, Elizalina, Elize, Elizea, Elizeah, Elizza, Elizzah, Elliza, Ellizah, Ellizza, Ellizzah, Ellyza, Ellyzah, Elyza, Elyzah, Elyzza, Elyzzah

Elizabet (Hebrew) a form of Elizabeth.
Elizabeta, Elizabete, Elizabett, Elizabetta, Elizabette, Elizebet, Elizebeta, Elizebete, Elizebett, Ellizebet, Ellizebeta, Ellizebete, Ellysabet, Ellysabeta, Ellysabete, Ellysabett, Ellysabetta, Ellysabette, Ellysebet, Ellysebeta, Ellysebete, Ellysebett, Ellysebetta, Ellysebette, Elsabet, Elsabete, Elsabett, Elysabet, Elysabeta, Elysabete, Elysabett

Elizabeth (Hebrew) consecrated to God. Bible: the mother of John the Baptist. See also Bess, Beth, Betsy, Betty, Elsa, Ilse, Libby, Liese, Liesel, Lisa, Lisbeth, Liset, Lissa, Lissie, Liz, Liza, Lizabeta, Lizabeth, Lizbeth, Lizina, Lizzie, Veta, Yelisabeta, Zizi.
Alizabeth, Eliabeth, Elizabea, Elizabee, Ellizabeth, Elschen, Elysabeth, Elzbieta, Elzsébet, Helsa, Ilizzabet, Lusa

Elizaveta (Polish, English) a form of Elizabeth.
Elisavet, Elisaveta, Elisavetta, Elisveta, Elizavet, Elizavetta, Elizveta, Elsveta, Elzveta

Elizebeth (Hebrew) a form of Elizabeth.
Ellizebeth

Elka (Polish) a form of Elizabeth.
Elkah, Ilka, Ilkah

Elke (German) a form of Adelaide, Alice.
Elkee, Elkey, Elki, Elkie, Elky, Ilki

Ella (English) elfin; beautiful fairy-woman. (Greek) a short form of Eleanor.
Ela, Elah, Ellah, Ellamae, Ellia

Elle (Greek) a short form of Eleanor. (French) she.
El, Ele, Ell

Ellen (English) a form of Eleanor, Helen.
Elen, Elene, Elenee, Elenie, Eleny, Elin, Eline, Ellan, Ellene, Ellin, Ellon

Ellena (Greek, Italian) a form of Elena. (English) a form of Ellen.
Ellenah

Ellery (English) elder-tree island.
Elari, Elarie, Elery, Ellari, Ellarie, Ellary, Ellerey, Elleri, Ellerie

Elli, Ellie, Elly (English) short forms of Eleanor, Ella, Ellen. See also Eli.
Ellea, Elleah, Ellee, Ellei, Elleigh, Elley, Ellia, Elliah, Ellya

Ellice (English) a form of Elise.
Ellecia, Ellyce, Elyce

Ellis (English) a form of Elias (see Boys' Names).
Elis, Ellys, Elys

Ellison (English) child of Ellis.
Elison, Ellson, Ellyson, Elson, Elyson

Ellyn (English) a form of Ellen.
Ellyna, Ellynah, Ellyne, Ellynn, Ellynne, Elyn

Elma (Turkish) sweet fruit.
Ellma, Ellmah, Ellmar, Elmah, Elmar

Elmina (English) noble.
Almina, Alminah, Almyna, Almynah, Elminah, Elmyna, Elmynah

Elmira (Arabic, Spanish) a form of Almira.
Ellmara, Ellmarah, Elmara, Elmarah, Elmear, Elmeara, Elmearah, Elmeera, Elmeerah, Elmeira, Elmeirah, Elmera, Elmerah, Elmeria, Elmirah, Elmiria, Elmiriah, Elmyra, Elmyrah, Elmyria, Elmyriah, Elmyrya, Elmyryah

Elnora (American) a combination of Ella + Nora.

Elodie (English) a form of Alodie.
Elodea, Elodee, Elodey, Elodi, Elodia, Elodiah, Elody, Elodya, Elodyah, Elodye

Eloisa (French) a form of Eloise.
Eloisia, Elouisa, Elouisah, Eloysa

Eloise (French) a form of Louise.
Elois, Elouise

Elora (American) a short form of Elnora.
Ellora, Elloree, Elorah, Elorie

Elsa (German) noble. (Hebrew) a short form of Elizabeth. See also Ilse.

Elcea, Ellsa, Ellsah, Ellse, Ellsea, Ellsia, Elsah, Else, Elsia, Elsje

Elsbeth (German) a form of Elizabeth.
Elsbet, Elsbeth, Elzbet, Elzbieta

Elsie (German) a familiar form of Elsa, Helsa.
Elcee, Elcey, Ellcee, Ellcey, Ellci, Ellcia, Ellcie, Ellcy, Ellsee, Ellsey, Ellsi, Ellsia, Ellsie, Ellsy, Elsey, Elsi, Elsy

Elspeth (Scottish) a form of Elizabeth.
Elspet, Elspie

Elva (English) elfin. See also Alva, Alvina.
Elvah, Elvie

Elvera (Latin, Spanish, German) a form of Elvira.
Elverah

Elvia (English) a form of Elva.
Elviah, Elvya, Elvyah

Elvie (English) a form of Elva.
Elvea, Elvee, Elvey, Elvi, Elvy

Elvina (English) a form of Alvina.
Elveana, Elveanah, Elvena, Elvenah, Elvenea, Elvinah, Elvine, Elvinea, Elvinia, Elvinna, Elvinnia, Elvyna, Elvynah, Elvyne, Elvynia, Elvyniah, Elvynie, Elvynna, Elvynnah, Elvyny, Elvynya, Elvynyah, Elvynye

Elvira (Latin) white; blond. (German) closed up. (Spanish) elfin. Geography: the town in Spain that hosted a Catholic synod in 300 A.D.
Elvara, Elvarah, Elvirah, Elvire, Elvyra, Elvyrah, Elwira, Elwirah, Elwyra, Elwyrah, Vira

Elycia (Hebrew) a form of Elisha.
Ellycia

Elysa (Spanish, Italian, English) a form of Elisa.
Ellysa, Elyssia, Elyssya, Elysya

Elyse (French, English) a form of Elise. (Latin) a form of Elysia.
Ellyse, Elyce, Elys, Elysee, Elysse

Elysha (Hebrew) a form of Elisha.
Ellysha, Ellyshah, Ellyshia, Ellyshiah, Ellyshya, Ellyshyah, Elyshia

Elysia (Greek) sweet; blissful. Mythology: Elysium was the dwelling place of happy souls.
Elishia, Ellysia, Ellysiah, Elysiah, Elysya, Elysyah, Ilysha, Ilysia

Elyssa (Greek, English) a form of Elissa. (Latin) a form of Elysia.
Ellyssa, Elyssah

Ema (German) a form of Emma.
Emah

Emalee, Emaleigh, Emalie, Emaly (American) forms of Emily.
Emaili, Emaily, Emalea, Emali, Emalia

Eman (Arabic) a short form of Emani.

Emani (Arabic) a form of Iman.
Emane, Emaneé, Emanie, Emann

Emanuelle (Hebrew) a form of Emmanuelle.
Emanual, Emanuel, Emanuela, Emanuele, Emanuell, Emanuella, Emanuellah

Emari (German) a form of Emery.
Emarri

Ember (French) a form of Amber.
Emberlee, Emberly

Emelia (Latin) a form of Amelia.

Emelie, Emely (Latin) forms of Emily.
Emeli, Emelita, Emellie, Emelly

Emeline (French) a form of Emily.
Emelin, Emelina

Emerald (French) bright green gemstone.
Emelda, Emeldah, Emmarald, Emmerald

Emery (German) industrious leader.
Emeri, Emerie, Emerre

Emie, Emmie (German) forms of Emmy.
Emi, Emiy, Emmi

Emile, Emilee, Emileigh, Emiley, Emili, Emilie, Emilly, Emmily (English) forms of Emily.
Emilea, Emilei, Émilie, Emiliee, Emillee, Emillie, Emmélie, Emmilee, Emmilei, Emmileigh, Emmiley, Emmili, Emmilie, Emmilly, Emmilye

Emilia (Italian) a form of Amelia, Emily.
Emila, Emilea, Emileah, Emiliah, Emilya,
Emilyah, Emmilea, Emmileah, Emmilia,
Emmilya

Emily (Latin) flatterer. (German) industri-
ous. See also Amelia, Emma, Millie.
Eimile, Émilie, Emilis, Emilye, Emmaley,
Emmaly, Emmélie, Emyle

Emilyann (American) a combination of
Emily + Ann.
Emileane, Emileann, Emileanna, Emileanne,
Emiliana, Emiliann, Emilianna, Emilianne,
Emillyane, Emillyann, Emillyanna,
Emillyanne, Emliana, Emliann, Emlianna,
Emlianne

Emilyn (American) a form of Emmalynn.
Emilynn, Emilynne

Emma (German) a short form of Emily.
See also Amy.
Em, Emmah

Emmalee, Emmalie (American) combi-
nations of Emma + Lee. Forms of Emily.
Emalea, Emalee, Emilee, Emmalea,
Emmaleah, Emmalei, Emmaleigh, Emmaley,
Emmali, Emmalia, Emmaliah, Emmaliese,
Emmaly, Emmalya, Emmalye, Emmalyse

Emmaline (French) a form of Emily.
Emalin, Emalina, Emaline, Emilienne,
Emilina, Emiline, Emillin, Emillina, Emilline,
Emmalene, Emmalin, Emmalina, Emmelin,
Emmilin, Emmilina, Emmiline, Emmilyn,
Emmilyna, Emmilyne, Emmylin, Emmylina,
Emmyline, Emylin, Emylina, Emyline

Emmalynn (American) a combination of
Emma + Lynn.
Emalyn, Emalyna, Emalyne, Emelyn,
Emelyna, Emelyne, Emelynne, Emlyn,
Emlynn, Emlynne, Emmalyn, Emmalynne,
Emylyn, Emylyna, Emylyne

Emmanuelle (Hebrew) God is with us.
Emmanuela, Emmanuele, Emmanuell,
Emmanuella, Emmanuellah

Emmeline (French) a form of Emmaline.
Emmelina

Emmy, Emy (German) familiar forms of
Emma.
Emmey, Emmye

Emmylou (American) a combination of
Emmy + Lou.
Emiloo, Emilou, Emilu, Emlou, Emmalou,
Emmelou, Emmiloo, Emmilou, Emmilu,
Emmyloo, Emmylu, Emylou, Emylu

Emory (German) a form of Emery.
Amory, Emmo, Emmori, Emmorie, Emmory,
Emorye

Emylee (American) a form of Emily.

Ena, Enna (Irish) forms of Helen.
Enah

Enchantra (English) enchanting.
Enchantrah, Enchantria, Enchantrya,
Enchantryah

Endora (Hebrew) fountain.
Endorah, Endorra, Endorrah

Engel (Greek) a form of Angel.
Engele, Engell, Engelle, Enjel, Enjele,
Enjell, Enjelle

Engela (Greek) a form of Angela.
Engelah, Engella, Engellah, Enjela, Enjelah,
Enjella

Engelica (Greek) a form of Angelica.
Engelika, Engeliqua, Engeliquah, Engelique,
Engelyca, Engelycka, Enjelliqua, Enjellique,
Enjellyca, Enjellycah, Enjellycka, Enjellyka,
Enjellykah, Enjellyqua, Enjellyquah,
Enjellyque

Engracia (Spanish) graceful.
Engrace, Engracee, Engraciah, Engracya,
Engrasia, Engrasiah, Engrasya

Enid (Welsh) life; spirit.
Enida, Ennid, Ennida, Ennyd, Ennyda,
Enyd, Enyda, Enydah

Enrica (Spanish) a form of Henrietta. See
also Rica.
Enricah, Enrichetta, Enricka, Enrickah,
Enrieta, Enrietta, Enriette, Enrika, Enrikah,
Enrikka, Enrikkah, Enrikke, Enriqua,
Enrique, Enriqueta, Enriquetta, Enriquette,
Enryca, Enrycah, Enryka, Enrykah

Enya (Scottish) jewel; blazing.
Enia, Eniah, Enyah

Enye (Hebrew) grace.

Epiphany (Greek) manifestation.
Religion: A Christian feast on January 6
celebrating the manifestation of Jesus'
divine nature to the Magi. See also
Theophania.
*Ephana, Epifanee, Epifaney, Epifani,
Epifania, Epifanie, Epiphanee, Epiphaney,
Epiphani, Epiphania, Epiphanie, Epyfanee,
Epyfaney, Epyfani, Epyfania, Epyfanie,
Epyfany, Epyphanee, Epyphaney, Epyphani,
Epyphania, Epyphanie, Epyphany*

Eppie (English) a familiar form of
Euphemia.
Eppy

Erasma (Greek) lovable.
Erasmah

Erela (Hebrew) angel.
Elelah, Erell, Erella, Erellah

Erica (Scandinavian) ruler of all. (English)
brave ruler. See also Arica, Rica, Ricki.
*Ericah, Ericca, Ericha, Eriqua, Erique,
Errica, Eryca, Erycah*

Ericka (Scandinavian) a form of Erica.
Erickah, Erricka

Erika, Erikka (Scandinavian) a form of
Erica.
*Erikaa, Erikah, Errika, Eryka, Erykah,
Erykka, Eyrika*

Erin (Irish) peace. History: another name
for Ireland. See also Arin.
*Earin, Earrin, Eran, Erana, Eren, Erena,
Erenah, Erene, Ereni, Erenia, Ereniah, Eri,
Erian, Erina, Erine, Erinete, Erinett,
Erinetta*

Erinn, Errin (Irish) forms of Erin.
Erinna, Erinnah, Erinne

Erline (Irish) a form of Arlene.
*Erla, Erlana, Erlean, Erleana, Erleanah,
Erleane, Erleen, Erleena, Erleene, Erlene,
Erlenne, Erlin, Erlina, Erlinda, Erlisha,
Erlyn, Erlyna, Erlynah, Erlyne*

Erma (Latin) a short form of Ermine,
Hermina. See also Irma.
Ermelinda

Ermine (Latin) a form of Hermina.
Ermin, Ermina, Erminda, Erminia, Erminie

Erna (English) a short form of Ernestine.

Ernestina (English) a form of Ernestine.
Ernesta, Ernesztina

Ernestine (English) earnest, sincere.
Erna, Ernaline, Ernesia

Eryn, Erynn (Irish) a form of Erin.
*Eiryn, Eryna, Eryne, Erynna, Erynnah,
Erynne*

Eshe (Swahili) life.
Eisha, Esha, Eshah

Esmé (French) a familiar form of
Esmeralda. A form of Amy.
*Esma, Esmae, Esmah, Esmai, Esmay, Esme,
Esmëe, Esmei, Esmey*

Esmeralda (Greek, Spanish) a form of
Emerald.
*Esmaralda, Esmerelda, Esmerilda,
Esmiralda, Ezmerelda, Ezmirilda*

Esperanza (Spanish) hope. See also
Speranza.
*Esparanza, Espe, Esperance, Esperans,
Esperansa, Esperanta, Esperanz, Esperenza*

Essence (Latin) life; existence.
*Essa, Essenc, Essencee, Essences, Essenes,
Essense, Essynce*

Essie (English) a short form of Estelle,
Esther.
Essa, Essey, Essy

Estee (English) a short form of Estelle,
Esther.
Esta, Estée, Estey, Esti, Estie, Esty

Estefani, Estefany (Spanish) forms of
Stephanie.
Estefane, Estefanie

Estefania (Spanish) a form of Stephanie.
Estafania, Estefana

Estela, Estella (French) a form of Estelle.
*Estelah, Esteleta, Estelita, Estellah, Estellita,
Esthella*

Estelle (French) a form of Esther. See also Stella, Trella.
Estel, Estele, Esteley, Estelin, Estelina, Esteline, Estell, Estellin, Estellina, Estelline, Esthel, Esthela, Esthele, Esthell, Esthelle

Estephanie, Estephany (Spanish) forms of Stephanie.
Estephania, Estephani

Ester (Persian) a form of Esther.
Estera, Esterre

Esther (Persian) star. Bible: the Jewish captive whom Ahasuerus made his queen. See also Hester.
Estar, Esthur, Eszter, Eszti

Estrella (French) star.
Estrela, Estrelah, Estrele, Estrelinha, Estrell, Estrelle, Estrelleta, Estrellita, Estrelyta, Estrelytah, Estrilita, Estrilyta, Estrylita, Estrylyta

Eternity (Latin) eternity.

Ethana (Hebrew) strong; firm.
Ethanah, Ethena, Ethenah

Ethel (English) noble.
Ethela, Ethelah, Ethelda, Ethelin, Ethelina, Etheline, Ethella, Ethelle, Ethelyn, Ethelyna, Ethelyne, Ethelynn, Ethelynna, Ethelynne, Ethyl

Etienne (French) a form of Stephan (see Boys' Names.)
Ètienne

Étoile (French) star.
Etoila, Etoilah, Etoyla, Etoylah, Etoyle

Etta (German) little. (English) a short form of Henrietta.
Etka, Etke, Ettah, Etti, Ettie, Etty, Ety, Itke, Itta

Eudora (Greek) honored gift. See also Dora.
Eudorah, Eudore

Eugena (Greek) a form of Eugenia.

Eugenia (Greek) born to nobility. See also Gina, Yevgenia.
Eugeena, Eugeenah, Eugeenia, Eugeeniah, Eugeniah, Eugenina, Eugina, Eugyna, Eugynah, Eugynia, Eugyniah, Eujania,

Eujaniah, Eujanya, Eujanyah, Evgenia, Evgeniah, Evgenya, Evgenyah

Eugenie (Greek) a form of Eugenia.
Eugeenee, Eugeeney, Eugeeni, Eugeenie, Eugenee, Eugeney, Eugeni, Eugénie, Eugine, Eugynie, Eugyny, Eujanee, Eujaney, Eujani, Eujanie, Eujany

Eulalia (Greek) well-spoken. See also Ula.
Eula, Eulah, Eulalea, Eulalee, Eulalie, Eulalya, Eulalyah, Eulia, Euliah, Eulya, Eulyah

Eun (Korean) silver.
Euna, Eunah

Eunice (Greek) happy; victorious. Bible: the mother of Saint Timothy. See also Unice.
Euna, Eunique, Eunise, Euniss, Eunisse, Eunys, Eunysa, Eunysah, Eunyse

Euphemia (Greek) spoken well of, in good repute. History: a fourth-century Christian martyr. See also Phemie.
Effam, Eppie, Eufemia, Eufemiah, Euphan, Euphemie, Euphemy, Euphemya, Euphemyah, Euphie

Eurydice (Greek) wide, broad. Mythology: the wife of Orpheus.
Euridice, Euridyce, Eurydyce

Eustacia (Greek) productive. (Latin) stable; calm. See also Stacey.
Eustaciah, Eustacya, Eustasia, Eustasiah, Eustasya, Eustasyah

Eva (Greek) a short form of Evangelina. (Hebrew) a form of Eve. See also Ava, Chava.
Éva, Evah, Evalea, Evaleah, Evalee, Evalei, Evaleigh, Evaley, Evali, Evalia, Evalie, Evaly, Evike, Evva, Ewa, Ewah

Evaline (French) a form of Evelyn.
Evalean, Evaleana, Evaleanah, Evaleane, Evaleen, Evaleena, Evaleenah, Evaleene, Evalene, Evalin, Evalina, Evalyn, Evalyna, Evalynah, Evalyne, Evalynn, Evalynne

Evan (Irish) young warrior. (English) a form of John (see Boys' Names).
Eoin, Ev, Evaine, Evann, Evans, Even, Evens, Evin, Evon, Evun, Ewan, Ewen

Evangelina (Greek) bearer of good news.
Evangeleana, Evangeleanah, Evangeleena,
Evangelia, Evangelica, Evangeliqua,
Evangelique, Evangelista, Evangelyna,
Evangelynah

Evangeline (Greek) a form of Evangelina.
Evangeleane, Evangeleene, Evangelene,
Evangelyn, Evangelyne, Evangelynn

Evania (Greek, Irish) a form of Evan.
Evana, Evanah, Evania, Evaniah, Evanja,
Evanjah, Evanka, Evanna, Evannah,
Evanne, Evannja, Evannjah, Evanny,
Evannya, Evany, Evanya, Evanyah,
Eveania, Evvanne, Evvunea, Evyan

Evanthe (Greek) flower.
Evantha

Eve (Hebrew) life. Bible: the first woman
created by God. (French) a short form
of Evonne. See also Hava, Naeva, Vica,
Yeva.
Eav, Eave, Evita, Evuska, Evyn

Eve Marie (English) a combination of
Eve + Marie.
Eve-Marie

Evelin, Eveline, Evelyne (English) forms
of Evelyn.
Evelean, Eveleane, Eveleen, Eveleene,
Evelen, Evelene

Evelina (English) a form of Evelyn.
Eveleanah, Eveleeana, Eveleena, Eveleenah,
Evelena, Evelenah, Evelinah, Evelyna,
Evelynah, Ewalina

Evelyn (English) hazelnut. See also Avaline.
Evaline, Eveleen, Evelene, Evelynn, Evelynne,
Evline

Everett (German) courageous as a boar.

Evette (French) a form of Yvette. A
familiar form of Evonne. See also Ivette.
Evet, Evete, Evett

Evie (Hungarian) a form of Eve.
Evee, Evey, Evi, Evicka, Evike, Evka,
Evuska, Evvee, Evvey, Evvi, Evvia, Evvie,
Evvy, Evvya, Evy, Ewa

Evita (Spanish) a form of Eve.
Eveta, Evetah, Evetta, Evettah, Evitta,
Evyta, Evytta

Evline (English) a form of Evelyn.
Evleen, Evlene, Evlin, Evlina, Evlyn,
Evlynn, Evlynne

Evonne (French) a form of Yvonne. See
also Ivonne.
Evanne, Evenie, Evenne, Eveny, Evona,
Evonah, Evone, Evoni, Evonn, Evonna,
Evonnie, Evonny, Evony, Evyn, Evynn,
Eyona, Eyvone

Eyota (Native American) great.
Eyotah

Ezrela (Hebrew) reaffirming faith.
Esrela, Esrelah, Esrele, Esrell, Esrella,
Esrellah, Esrelle, Ezrelah, Ezrele, Ezrella,
Ezrellah, Ezrelle

Ezri (Hebrew) helper; strong.
Ezra, Ezrah, Ezria, Ezriah, Ezrya, Ezryah

Fabia (Latin) bean grower.
Fabiah, Fabra, Fabria, Fabya, Fabyah

Fabiana (Latin) a form of Fabia.
Fabianah, Fabianna, Fabiannah, Fabienna,
Fabiennah, Fabyana, Fabyanah, Fabyanna,
Fabyannah

Fabienne (Latin) a form of Fabia.
Fabian, Fabiann, Fabianne, Fabiene, Fabienn,
Fabyan, Fabyane, Fabyann, Fabyanne

Fabiola (Latin) a form of Fabia.
Fabiolah, Fabiole, Fabyola

Fabrienne (French) little blacksmith;
apprentice.
Fabreanne, Fabrian, Fabriana, Fabrianah,
Fabriann, Fabrianna, Fabriannah, Fabrianne,
Fabrien, Fabriena, Fabrienah, Fabrienn,
Fabrienna, Fabriennah, Fabryan, Fabryana,
Fabryanah, Fabryane, Fabryann, Fabryanna,
Fabryannah, Fabryanne, Fabryen, Fabryena,
Fabryenah, Fabryene, Fabryenn, Fabryenna,
Fabryennah, Fabryenne

Fabrizia (Italian) craftswoman.
Fabriziah, Fabrizya, Fabrizyah, Fabryzia, Fabryziah, Fabryzya, Fabryzyah

Fadila (Arabic) generous.
Fadilah, Fadyla, Fadylah

Faina (English) happy.
Fainah, Faine, Fayin, Fayina, Fayinah, Fayine, Fayna, Faynah, Fayne, Feana, Feanah, Fenna

Fairlee (English) from a yellow meadow.
Fairlea, Faileah, Fairlei, Fairleigh, Fairley, Fairli, Fairlia, Fairliah, Fairlie, Fairly, Fairlya, Fayrlea, Fayrleah, Fayrlee, Fayrlei, Fayrleigh, Fayrley, Fayrli, Fayrlia, Fayrliah, Fayrlie, Fayrly, Fayrlya

Faith (English) faithful; fidelity. See also Faye, Fidelity.
Faeth, Faethe, Faithe

Faiza, Faizah (Arabic) victorious.
Fayza, Fayzah

Falda (Icelandic) folded wings.
Faida, Faldah, Fayda, Faydah

Falicia (Latin) a form of Felicia.
Falecia, Faleshia

Faline (Latin) catlike.
Falean, Faleana, Faleanah, Faleane, Faleen, Faleena, Faleenah, Faleene, Falena, Falene, Falin, Falina, Falinah, Falinia, Faliniah, Fallin, Fallina, Fallinah, Falline, Faylina, Fayline, Faylyn, Faylynn, Faylynne, Felenia, Felina, Felinah, Feline, Felinia, Feliniah, Felyn, Felyna, Felynah, Felyne

Falisha (Latin) a form of Felicia.
Faleisha, Falesha, Falleshia

Fallon (Irish) grandchild of the ruler.
Fallan, Fallann, Fallanna, Fallannah, Fallanne, Fallen, Fallenn, Fallenna, Fallennah, Fallenne, Fallona, Fallonah, Fallone, Fallonia, Falloniah, Fallonne, Fallonya, Fallonyah

Falon (Irish) a form of Fallon.
Falan, Falen, Phalon

Falyn (Irish) a form of Fallon.
Fallyn, Fallyne, Falyna, Falynah, Falyne, Falynn, Falynne

Fanchone (French) freedom.
Fanchon, Fanchona, Fanchonah

Fancy (French) betrothed. (English) whimsical; decorative.
Fancee, Fanchette, Fanci, Fancia, Fancie

Fannie, Fanny (American) familiar forms of Frances.
Fan, Fanette, Fani, Fania, Fannee, Fanney, Fanni, Fannia

Fantasia (Greek) imagination.
Fantasy, Fantasya, Fantaysia, Fantazia, Fiantasi

Fany (American) a form of Fannie.
Fanya

Farah, Farrah (English) beautiful; pleasant.
Fara, Faria, Fariah, Farra, Farria, Farriah, Farrya, Farryah, Farya, Faryah, Fayre

Faren, Farren (English) wanderer.
Faran, Farana, Farane, Fare, Farin, Farine, Faron, Faronah, Farrahn, Farran, Farrand, Farrin, Farron, Farryn, Faryn, Feran, Ferin, Feron, Ferran, Ferren, Ferrin, Ferron, Ferryn

Farica (German) peaceful ruler.
Faricah, Faricka, Farika, Farikah, Fariqua, Fariquah, Farique, Faryca, Farycah, Farycka, Faryka, Faryqua, Faryquah, Faryque

Fariha (Muslim, Arabic) happy, joyful, cheerful, glad.
Farihah

Fatema (Arabic) a form of Fatima.

Fatima (Arabic) daughter of the Prophet. History: the daughter of Muhammad.
Fathma, Fatime, Fattim, Fatyma, Fatymah

Fatimah (Arabic) a form of Fatima.

Fatma, Fatme (Arabic) short forms of Fatima.
Fatmah

Faustine (Latin) lucky, fortunate.
Fausta, Faustah, Faustean, Fausteana, Fausteanah, Fausteane, Fausteen, Fausteena, Fausteenah, Fausteene, Faustin, Faustina, Faustinah, Faustyn, Faustyna, Faustynah, Faustyne

Faviola (Latin) a form of Fabia.
Faviana, Faviolha

Fawn (French) young deer.
Faun, Faune, Fawne

Fawna (French) a form of Fawn.
Fauna, Faunah, Faunia, Fauniah, Fauny,
Faunya, Faunyah, Fawnah, Fawnia,
Fawniah, Fawnna, Fawny, Fawnya, Fawnyah

Faxon (German) long-haired.
Faxan, Faxana, Faxanah, Faxane, Faxann,
Faxanna, Faxannah, Faxanne, Faxen,
Faxin, Faxina, Faxinah, Faxine, Faxyn,
Faxyna, Faxynah, Faxyne

Fay (French, English) a form of Faye.

Fayana (French) a form of Faye.
Fayanah, Fayann, Fayanna, Fayannah,
Fayanne

Faye (French) fairy; elf. (English) a form
of Faith.
Fae, Fai, Faie, Faya, Fayah, Fayana,
Fayette, Fei, Fey, Feya, Feyah, Feye

Fayette (French) a form of Faye.
Fayet, Fayett, Fayetta, Fayettah

Fayola (Nigerian) lucky.
Faiola, Faiolah, Fayla, Fayolah, Feyla

Fayre (English) fair; light haired.
Fair, Faira, Faire, Fairey, Fairy, Faree, Farey,
Fari, Farie, Fary, Farye, Fayree, Fayrey,
Fayri, Fayrie, Fayry

Faythe (English) a form of Faith.
Fayeth, Fayethe, Fayth

Febe (Greek) a form of Phoebe.
Feba, Febo, Feebe, Feebea, Feebee, Fibee

Feena (Irish) small fawn.
Feana, Feanah, Feenah

Felecia (Latin) a form of Felicia.
Flecia

Felica (Spanish) a short form of Felicia.
Falica, Falisa, Felisca, Felissa, Feliza

Felice (Latin) a short form of Felicia.
Felece, Felicie, Felis, Felise, Felize, Felyc,
Felyce, Felycie, Felycye, Felys, Felyse, Felysie,
Felysse, Felysye

Felicia (Latin) fortunate; happy. See also
Lecia, Phylicia.
Fela, Feliciah, Feliciana, Felicidad, Felicija,
Felicitas, Felicya, Felisea, Felisia, Felisiah,
Felissya, Felita, Felixia, Felizia, Felka, Fellcia,
Felycia, Felyciah, Felycya, Felycyah, Felysia,
Felysiah, Felyssia, Felysya, Felysyah, Filicia,
Filiciah, Fleasia, Fleichia, Fleishia, Flichia

Feliciana (Italian, Spanish) a form of
Felicia.
Felicianna, Felicijanna, Feliciona,
Felicyanna, Felicyanne, Felisiana

Felicitas (Italian) a form of Felicia.
Felicita, Felicitah, Felicyta, Felicytah,
Felicytas, Felisita, Felycita, Felycitah,
Felycyta, Felycytah, Felycytas

Felicity (English) a form of Felicia.
Falicitee, Falicitey, Faliciti, Falicitia, Falicitie,
Falicity, Félicité, Felicitee, Felicitey, Feliciti,
Felicitia, Felicitie, Felisity, Felycytee, Felycytey,
Felycyti, Felycytie, Felycyty

Felisa (Latin) a form of Felicia.

Felisha (Latin) a form of Felicia.
Feleasha, Feleisha, Felesha, Felishia,
Fellishia, Felysha, Flisha

Femi (French) woman. (Nigerian) love me.
Femia, Femiah, Femie, Femmi, Femmie,
Femy, Femya, Femyah

Fenella (Irish) a form of Fionnula.
Fenel, Fenell, Fenellah, Fenelle, Fennal,
Fennall, Fennalla, Fennallah, Fennella,
Fennelle, Finel, Finell, Finella, Finellah,
Finelle, Finnal, Finnala, Finnall, Finnalla,
Finnallah, Finnalle, Fynela, Fynelah, Fynele,
Fynell, Fynella, Fynelle, Fynnela, Fynnelah,
Fynnele, Fynnell, Fynnella, Fynnellah,
Fynnelle

Fenna (Irish) fair-haired.
Fena, Fenah, Fennah, Fina, Finah, Finna,
Finnah, Fyna, Fynah, Fynna, Fynnah

Feodora (Greek) gift of God.
Fedora, Fedorah, Fedoria, Fedorra, Fedorrah

Fern (English) fern. (German) a short
form of Fernanda.
Ferna, Fernah, Ferne, Ferni, Firn, Firne,
Furn, Furne, Fyrn, Fyrne

Fernanda (German) daring, adventurous.
See also Andee, Nan.
Ferdie, Ferdinanda, Ferdinandah,
Ferdinande, Fernandah, Fernande,
Fernandette, Fernandina, Fernandinah,
Fernandine, Fernandyn, Fernandyna,
Fernandyne, Nanda

Fernley (English) from the fern meadow.
Ferlea, Fernleah, Fernlee, Fernlei, Fernleigh,
Fernli, Fernlie, Fernly

Fiala (Czech) violet flower.
Fialah, Fyala, Fyalah

Fidelia (Latin) a form of Fidelity.
Fidea, Fideah, Fidel, Fidela, Fidelah, Fidele,
Fideliah, Fidelina, Fidell, Fidella, Fidellah,
Fidelle, Fydea, Fydeah, Fydel, Fydela,
Fydelah, Fydele, Fydell, Fydella, Fydellah,
Fydelle

Fidelity (Latin) faithful, true. See also Faith.
Fidelia, Fidelita, Fidelitee, Fidelitey, Fideliti,
Fidelitie, Fydelitee, Fydelitey, Fydeliti,
Fydelitie, Fydelity

Fifi (French) a familiar form of Josephine.
Fe-Fe, Fee-Fee, Feef, Feefee, Fefe, Fefi,
Fefie, Fefy, Fiffi, Fiffy, Fifina, Fifinah,
Fifine, Fy-Fy, Fyfy, Phiphi, Phyphy

Filia (Greek) friend.
Filiah, Filya, Fylia, Fyliah, Fylya, Fylyah

Filippa (Italian) a form of Philippa.
Felipa, Felipe, Felippa, Filipa, Filipina,
Filippina, Filpina

Filma (German) veiled.
Filmah, Filmar, Filmaria, Filmarya, Fylma,
Fylmah, Fylmara, Fylmaria, Fylmarya

Filomena (Italian) a form of Philomena.
Fila, Filah, Filemon, Filomenah, Filomene,
Filomina, Filominah, Filomyna, Filomyne,
Fylomena, Fylomenah, Fylomina, Fylomine,
Fylomyna, Fylomyne

Fiona (Irish) fair, white.
Feeona, Feeonah, Feeoni, Feeonie, Feeony,
Feona, Feonah, Feonia, Feoniah, Fionah,
Fionna, Fionnah, Fionni, Fionnia, Fionniah,
Fionne, Fionnea, Fionneah, Fionnee, Fyona,
Fyonah, Fyoni, Fyonia, Fyoniah, Fyonie,

Fyony, Fyonya, Fyonyah, Phiona, Phionah,
Phyona, Phyonah

Fionnula (Irish) white shouldered. See
also Nola, Nuala.
Fenella, Fenula, Finnula, Finnulah,
Finnule, Finola, Finolah, Finonnula,
Finula, Fionnuala, Fionnualah, Fionnulah,
Fionula, Fynola, Fynolah

Fiorella (Italian) little flower.
Fiorelle

Fira (English) fiery.
Firah, Fyra, Fyrah

Flair (English) style; verve.
Flaira, Flaire, Flare, Flayr, Flayra, Flayre

Flanna (Irish) a short form of Flannery.
Flan, Flana, Flanah, Flann, Flannah

Flannery (Irish) redhead. Literature:
Flannery O'Connor was a renowned
American writer.
Flanneree, Flannerey, Flanneri, Flannerie

Flavia (Latin) blond, golden haired.
Flavere, Flaviah, Flavianna, Flavianne,
Flaviar, Flavien, Flavienne, Flaviere, Flavio,
Flavya, Flavyah, Flavyere, Flawia, Flawya,
Flawyah, Fulvia

Flavie (Latin) a form of Flavia.
Flavi

Fleta (English) swift, fast.
Fleata, Fleatah, Fleeta, Fleetah, Fletah,
Flita, Flitah, Flyta, Flytah

Fleur (French) flower.
Fleure, Fleuree

Fleurette (French) a form of Fleur.
Fleuret, Fleurett, Fleuretta, Fleurettah,
Floretta, Florettah, Florette, Flouretta,
Flourette

Fliora (Irish) a form of Flora.
Fliorah

Flo (American) a short form of Florence.
Flow

Flor (Latin) a short form of Florence.
Flore

Flora (Latin) flower. A short form of
Florence. See also Lore.

*Fiora, Fiore, Fiorenza, Flaura, Flaurah,
Flauria, Flauriah, Flaury, Flaurya, Flauryah,
Fliora, Florah, Florelle, Florey, Floria, Florica*

Florelle (Latin) a form of Flora.
Florel, Florell, Florella, Florellah

Florence (Latin) blooming; flowery; prosperous. History: Florence Nightingale, a British nurse, is considered the founder of modern nursing. See also Florida.
*Fiorenza, Fiorenze, Flarance, Flarence,
Florance, Florancia, Floranciah, Florancie,
Floren, Florena, Florencia, Florenciah,
Florencija, Florency, Florencya, Florendra,
Florene, Florentia, Florentina, Florentyna,
Florenza, Florina, Florine*

Floria (Basque) a form of Flora.
Floriah, Florria, Florya, Floryah

Florian (Latin) flowering, blooming.
*Florann, Floren, Floriana, Florianna,
Florianne, Florin, Florinah, Florine, Floryn,
Floryna, Florynah, Floryne*

Florida (Spanish) a form of Florence.
*Floridah, Floridia, Floridiah, Florind,
Florinda, Florindah, Florinde, Florita,
Floryda, Florydah, Florynd, Florynda,
Floryndah, Florynde*

Florie (English) a familiar form of Florence.
*Flore, Floree, Florey, Flori, Florri, Florrie,
Florry, Flory*

Florimel (Greek) sweet nectar.
*Florimela, Florimele, Florimell, Florimella,
Florimelle, Florymel, Florymela, Florymele,
Florymell, Florymella, Florymelle*

Floris (English) a form of Florence.
*Florisa, Florisah, Florise, Floriss, Florissa,
Florissah, Florisse, Florys, Florysa, Florysah,
Floryse, Floryss, Floryssa, Floryssah, Florysse*

Flossie (English) a familiar form of Florence.
Floss, Flossi, Flossy

Fola (Yoruba) honorable.
Floah

Foluke (Yoruba) given to God.
Foluc, Foluck, Foluk

Fonda (Latin) foundation. (Spanish) inn.
Fondah, Fondea, Fonta, Fontah

Fontanna (French) fountain.
*Fontain, Fontaina, Fontainah, Fontaine,
Fontana, Fontanah, Fontane, Fontannah,
Fontanne, Fontayn, Fontayna, Fontaynah,
Fontayne*

Forrest (French) forest; forester.
Forest, Forreste, Forrestt, Forrie

Fortuna (Latin) fortune; fortunate.
*Fortoona, Fortunah, Fortunata, Fortunate,
Fortune, Fortunia, Fortuniah, Fortunya,
Fortunyah*

Fosette (French) dimpled.
Foset, Foseta, Fosetah, Fosete, Fosett, Fosetta

Fotina (Greek) light. See also Photina.
*Fotin, Fotine, Fotinia, Fotiniah, Fotinya,
Fotinyah, Fotyna, Fotyne, Fotynia,
Fotyniah, Fotynya, Fotynyah*

Fran (Latin) a short form of Frances.
Frain, Frann, Frayn

Frances (Latin) free; from France. See also Paquita.
France, Francena, Francess, Francesta

Francesca, Franceska (Italian) forms of Frances.
Francessca, Francesta

Franchesca, Francheska (Italian) forms of Francesca.
*Cheka, Chekka, Chesca, Cheska,
Francheca, Francheka, Franchelle, Franchesa,
Franchessca, Franchesska*

Franchette (French) a form of Frances.
*Franceta, Francetta, Francette, Francheta,
Franchetah, Franchete, Franchett, Franchetta,
Franchettah, Franzet, Franzeta, Franzetah,
Franzete, Franzett, Franzetta, Franzettah,
Franzette*

Franci (Hungarian) a familiar form of Francine.
*Francee, Francey, Francia, Francie, Francy,
Francya, Francye*

Francine (French) a form of Frances.
*Franceen, Franceine, Franceline, Francene,
Francenia, Francin, Francina, Francyn,*

Francine *(cont.)*
*Francyna, Francyne, Fransin, Fransina,
Fransinah, Fransine, Fransyn, Fransyna,
Fransynah, Fransyne, Franzin, Franzina,
Franzinah, Franzine, Franzyn, Franzyna,
Franzynah, Franzyne*

Francis (Latin) a form of Frances.
*Francise, Franis, Franise, Franiss, Franisse,
Franncia, Francys, Frantis, Frantisa, Frantise,
Frantiss, Frantissa, Frantisse*

Francisca (Italian) a form of Frances.
*Franciska, Franciszka, Frantiska, Franziska,
Franzyska*

Francoise, Françoise (French) forms of
Frances.

Franki, Frankie (American) familiar
forms of Frances.
*Franca, Francah, Francka, Francki, Franka,
Frankah, Franke, Frankee, Frankey, Frankia,
Frankiah, Franky, Frankyah, Frankye*

Frannie, Franny (English) familiar forms
of Frances.
Frani, Frania, Franney, Franni, Frany

Franzea (Spanish) a form of Frances.
*Frazea, Franzia, Franziah, Franzya,
Franzyah*

Freda (German) a short form of Alfreda,
Elfrida, Frederica, Sigfreda.
*Fraida, Fraidah, Frayda, Frayde, Fraydina,
Fraydine, Fraydyna, Fraydyne, Fredah,
Fredda, Fredra, Freeda, Freedah, Freeha*

Freddi, Freddie (English) familiar forms
of Frederica, Winifred.
*Fredda, Freddah, Freddee, Freddey, Freddia,
Freddy, Fredee, Fredey, Fredi, Fredia,
Frediah, Fredie, Fredy, Fredya, Fredyah, Frici*

Fredella (English) a form of Frederica.
*Fredel, Fredela, Fredelah, Fredele, Fredell,
Fredellah, Fredelle*

Frederica (German) peaceful ruler. See
also Alfreda, Rica, Ricki.
*Federica, Feriga, Fredalena, Fredaline,
Frederina, Frederine, Fredith, Fredora,
Fredreca, Fredrica, Fredricah, Fredricia,
Fryderica*

Frederika (German) a form of Frederica.
*Fredericka, Frederickina, Fredreka, Fredrika,
Fryderika, Fryderikah, Fryderyka*

Frederike (German) a form of Frederica.
*Fredericke, Frederyc, Frederyck, Frederyk,
Fridrike, Friederike*

Frederique (French) a form of Frederica.
*Frederiqua, Frederiquah, Frédérique,
Fredriqua, Fredriquah, Fredrique, Frideryqua,
Frideryquah, Frideryque, Fryderiqua,
Fryderiquah, Fryderique, Rike*

Fredricka (German) a short form of
Frederika.

Freedom (English) freedom.

Freida (German) a form of Frida.
*Freia, Freiah, Freidah, Freide, Freyda,
Freydah*

Freja (Scandinavian) a form of Freya.
*Fraja, Fray, Fraya, Frayah, Freia, Freiah,
Frehah*

Freya (Scandinavian) noblewoman.
Mythology: the Norse goddess of love.
Frey, Freyah

Frida (German) a short form of Alfreda,
Elfrida, Frederica, Sigfreda.
*Fridah, Frideborg, Frieda, Friedah, Fryda,
Frydah, Frydda, Fryddah*

Fritzi (German) a familiar form of
Frederica.
*Friezi, Fritze, Fritzee, Fritzey, Fritzie,
Fritzinn, Fritzline, Fritzy, Frytzee, Frytzey,
Frytzi, Frytzie, Frytzy*

Frodina (German) wise friend.
*Frodinah, Frodine, Frodyn, Frodyna,
Frodynah, Frodyne*

Fronde (Latin) leafy branch.

Fronya (Latin) forehead.
Fronia, Froniah, Fronyah

Fulla (German) full.
Fula, Fulah, Fullah

Futura (Latin) future.
*Futurah, Future, Futuria, Futuriah, Futurya,
Futuryah*

Fynballa (Irish) fair.
*Finabala, Finbalah, Finballa, Finballah,
Fynbala, Fynbalah, Fynballah*

G

Gabele (French) a short form of
Gabrielle.
*Gabal, Gabala, Gabalah, Gabale, Gaball,
Gaballa, Gaballah, Gaballe, Gabel, Gabela,
Gabelah, Gabell, Gabella, Gabellah,
Gabelle, Gable*

Gabor (Hungarian) God is my strength.
Gabora, Gaborah, Gabore

Gabriel, Gabriele, Gabriell (French)
forms of Gabrielle.
*Gabbriel, Gabbryel, Gabreal, Gabreale,
Gabreil, Gabrial, Gabryel*

Gabriela, Gabriella (Italian) forms of
Gabrielle.
*Gabriala, Gabrialla, Gabrielah, Gabrielia,
Gabriellah, Gabriellia, Gabriello, Gabrila,
Gabrilla, Gabryela, Gabryella, Gabryiela*

Gabrielle (French) devoted to God.
*Gabbrielle, Gabielle, Gabrealle, Gabriana,
Gabrille, Gabrina, Gabriolett, Gabrioletta,
Gabriolette, Gabriylle, Gabryell, Gabryelle,
Gavriella*

Gaby (French) a familiar form of
Gabrielle.
*Gabb, Gabbea, Gabbee, Gabbey, Gabbi,
Gabbie, Gabby, Gabey, Gabi, Gabie,
Gavi, Gavy*

Gada (Hebrew) lucky.
Gadah

Gaea (Greek) planet Earth. Mythology:
the Greek goddess of Earth.
Gaeah, Gaia, Gaiah, Gaiea, Gaya, Gayah

Gaetana (Italian) from Gaeta. Geography:
a city in southern Italy.
*Gaetan, Gaetanah, Gaétane, Gaetanna,
Gaetanne, Gaitana, Gaitanah, Gaitann,
Gaitanna, Gaitanne, Gaytana, Gaytane,
Gaytanna, Gaytanne*

Gagandeep (Sikh) sky's light.
Gagandip, Gagnadeep, Gagndeep

Gage (French) promise.
Gaeg, Gaege, Gaig, Gaige, Gayg, Gayge

Gail (English) merry, lively. (Hebrew) a
short form of Abigail.
*Gael, Gaela, Gaell, Gaella, Gaelle, Gaila,
Gaile, Gale, Gaylia*

Gailine (English) a form of Gail.
*Gailean, Gaileana, Gaileane, Gaileena,
Gailina, Gailyn, Gailyna, Gailyne,
Gayleen, Gayleena, Gaylina, Gayline,
Gaylyn, Gaylyna, Gaylynah, Gaylyne*

Gala (Norwegian) singer.
Galah, Galla, Gallah

Galatea (Greek) Mythology: Galatea was
a statue of a beautiful woman carved by
Pygmalion, who fell in love with her
and persuaded the goddess Aphrodite to
bring the statue to life.
*Galanthe, Galanthea, Galatee, Galatey,
Galati, Galatia, Galatiah, Galatie, Galaty,
Galatya, Galatyah*

Galaxy (Latin) universe; the Milky Way.
*Galaxee, Galaxey, Galaxi, Galaxia,
Galaxiah*

Galen (Greek) healer; calm. (Irish) little
and lively.
*Gaelen, Gaellen, Galane, Galean, Galeane,
Galeene, Galene, Gallane, Galleene, Gallen,
Gallene, Galyn, Galyne, Gaylaine,
Gayleen, Gaylen, Gaylene, Gaylyn*

Galena (Greek) healer; calm.
*Galana, Galanah, Galenah, Gallana,
Gallanah, Gallena, Gallenah*

Gali (Hebrew) hill; fountain; spring.
*Gailee, Galea, Galeah, Galee, Galei,
Galeigh, Galey, Galice, Galie, Gallea,
Galleah, Gallee, Gallei, Galleigh, Galley,
Galli, Gallie, Gally, Galy*

Galina (Russian) a form of Helen.
*Gailya, Galaina, Galainah, Galaine,
Galayna, Galaynah, Galayne, Galeana,
Galeena, Galeenah, Galenka, Galia, Galiah,
Galiana, Galianah, Galiane, Galiena,
Galinah, Galine, Galinka, Gallin, Gallina,*

Galina *(cont.)*
Gallinah, Galline, Gallyn, Gallyna, Gallynah, Gallyne, Galochka, Galya, Galyah, Galyna, Galynah

Gamela (Scandinavian) elder.
Gamala, Gamalah, Gamale, Gamelah, Gamele

Gamila (Arabic) beautiful.

Ganesa (Hindi) fortunate. Religion: Ganesha was the Hindu god of wisdom.
Ganesah, Ganessa, Ganessah

Ganya (Hebrew) garden of the Lord. (Zulu) clever.
Gana, Gani, Gania, Ganiah, Ganice, Ganit, Ganyah

Gardenia (English) Botany: a sweet-smelling flower.
Deeni, Denia, Gardeen, Gardeena, Gardeene, Garden, Gardena, Gardene, Gardin, Gardina, Gardine, Gardinia, Gardyn, Gardyna, Gardyne

Garland (French) wreath of flowers.
Garlan, Garlana, Garlanah, Garlane, Garleen, Garleena, Garleenah, Garleene, Garlena, Garlenah, Garlene, Garlind, Garlinda, Garlindah, Garlinde, Garlyn, Garlynd, Garlynda, Garlyndah, Garlynde

Garnet (English) dark red gem.
Garneta, Garnetah, Garnete, Garnett, Garnetta, Garnettah, Garnette

Garyn (English) spear carrier.
Garan, Garana, Garane, Garen, Garin, Garina, Garine, Garra, Garran, Garrana, Garrane, Garrin, Garrina, Garrine, Garryn, Garyna, Garyne, Garynna, Garynne

Gasha (Russian) a familiar form of Agatha.
Gashah, Gashka

Gavriella (Hebrew) a form of Gabrielle.
Gavila, Gavilla, Gavra, Gavrel, Gavrela, Gavrelah, Gavrelia, Gavreliah, Gavrell, Gavrella, Gavrellah, Gavrelle, Gavrid, Gavrieela, Gavriela, Gavrielle, Gavrila, Gavrilla, Gavrille, Gavryl, Gavryla, Gavryle, Gavryll, Gavrylla, Gavrylle

Gay (French) merry.
Gae, Gai, Gaie, Gaye

Gayla (English) a form of Gail.

Gayle (English) a form of Gail.
Gayel, Gayell, Gayella, Gayelle, Gayl

Gaylia (English) a form of Gail.
Gaelia, Gaeliah, Gailia, Gailiah, Gayliah

Gayna (English) a familiar form of Guinevere.
Gaena, Gaenah, Gaina, Gainah, Gaynah, Gayner, Gaynor

Geanna (Italian) a form of Giana.
Geannah, Geona, Geonna

Geela (Hebrew) joyful.
Gela, Gila

Geena (American) a form of Gena.
Geana, Geanah, Geania, Geeana, Geeanna, Geenia

Gelya (Russian) angelic.

Gema, Gemma (Latin, Italian) jewel, precious stone. See also Jemma.
Gem, Gemah, Gemee, Gemey, Gemia, Gemiah, Gemie, Gemmah, Gemmee, Gemmey, Gemmi, Gemmia, Gemmiah, Gemmie, Gemmy, Gemy

Gemini (Greek) twin.
Gemelle, Gemina, Geminia, Geminine, Gemmina

Gen (Japanese) spring. A short form of names beginning with "Gen."
Genn

Gena (French) a form of Gina. A short form of Geneva, Genevieve, Iphigenia.
Genae, Genah, Genai, Genea, Geneja

Geneen (Scottish) a form of Jeanine.
Geanine, Geannine, Genene, Genine, Gineen, Ginene

Genell (American) a form of Jenell.

Genesis (Latin) origin; birth.
Genes, Genese, Genesha, Genesia, Genesiss, Genessa, Genesse, Genessie, Genicis, Genises, Genysis, Yenesis

Genessis (Latin) a form of Genesis.

Geneva (French) juniper tree. A short form of Genevieve. Geography: a city in Switzerland. See also Jeneva.
Geneeva, Geneevah, Geneieve, Geneiva, Geneive, Genevah, Geneve, Genevia, Geneviah, Genneeva, Genneevah, Ginneeva, Ginneevah, Ginneva, Ginnevah, Gyniva, Gynniva, Gynnivah, Gynnyva, Gynnyvah

Genevieve (German, French) a form of Guinevere. See also Gwendolyn.
Genaveeve, Genaveve, Genavie, Genavieve, Genavive, Geneveve, Genevie, Genéviéve, Genevievre, Genevive, Genivive, Genvieve, Gineveve, Ginevieve, Ginevive, Guinevieve, Guinivive, Guynieve, Guyniviv, Guynivive, Gwenevieve, Gwenivive, Gwiniviev, Gwinivieve, Gwynivive, Gynevieve, Janavieve, Jenevieve, Jennavieve

Genevra (French, Welsh) a form of Guinevere.
Genever, Genevera, Genevrah, Genovera, Ginevra, Ginevrah

Genice (American) a form of Janice.
Genece, Geneice, Genesa, Genesee, Genessia, Genis, Genise

Genie (French) a familiar form of Gena.
Geni, Genia

Genita (American) a form of Janita.
Genet, Geneta

Genna (English) a form of Jenna.
Gennae, Gennai, Gennay, Genni, Gennie, Genny

Gennifer (American) a form of Jennifer.
Genifer

Genovieve (French) a form of Genevieve.
Genoveva, Genoveve, Genovive, Genowica

Gentry (English) a form of Gent (see Boys' Names).

Georgeann, Georgeanne (English) combinations of Georgia + Ann.
Georgann, Georganne, Georgean, Georgiann, Georgianne, Georgieann, Georgyan, Georgyann, Georgyanne

Georgeanna (English) a combination of Georgia + Anna.
Georgana, Georganna, Georgeana, Georgeannah, Georgeannia, Georgyana, Georgyanah, Georgyanna, Georgyannah, Giorgianna

Georgene (English) a familiar form of Georgia.
Georgeene, Georgienne, Georgine, Georgyn, Georgyne, Jeorgine, Jeorjine, Jeorjyne

Georgette (French) a form of Georgia.
Georget, Georgeta, Georgete, Georgett, Georgetta, Georjetta

Georgia (Greek) farmer. Art: Georgia O'Keeffe was an American painter known especially for her paintings of flowers. Geography: a southern American state; a country in Eastern Europe. See also Jirina, Jorja.
Giorgia

Georgiana, Georgianna (English) forms of Georgeanna.
Georgiannah, Georgionna

Georgie (English) a familiar form of Georgeanne, Georgia, Georgiana.
Georgi, Georgy, Giorgi

Georgina (English) a form of Georgia.
Georgeena, Georgeenah, Georgeina, Georgena, Georgenah, Georgenia, Georgiena, Georgienna, Georginah, Georgine, Georgyna, Georgynah, Giorgina, Jeorgina, Jeorginah, Jeorjina, Jeorjinah, Jeorjyna, Jorgina

Geovanna (Italian) a form of Giovanna.
Geovana, Geovonna

Geralda (German) a short form of Geraldine.
Giralda, Giraldah, Gyralda, Gyraldah

Geraldine (German) mighty with a spear. See also Dena, Jeraldine.
Geralda, Geraldeen, Geraldeena, Geraldeenah, Geraldeene, Geraldina, Geraldyna, Geraldyne, Gerhardine, Gerianna, Gerianne, Gerlina, Gerlinda, Gerrianne, Gerrilee

Geralyn (American) a combination of Geraldine + Lynn.
Geralin, Geralina, Geraline, Geralisha, Geralyna, Geralyne, Geralynn, Gerilyn, Gerrilyn

Gerarda (English) brave spearwoman.
Gerardine, Gerardo

Gerda (Norwegian) protector. (German) a familiar form of Gertrude.
Gerdah, Gerta

Geri, Gerri (American) familiar forms of Geraldine. See also Jeri.
Geree, Gerey, Gerie, Gerree, Gerrey, Gerrie, Gerry, Gery

Germaine (French) from Germany. See also Jermaine.
Germain, Germaina, Germainah, Germana, Germane, Germanee, Germani, Germanie, Germaya, Germayn, Germayna, Germaynah, Germayne, Germine, Germini, Germinie, Germyn, Germyna, Germyne

Gertie (German) a familiar form of Gertrude.
Gert, Gertey, Gerti, Gerty

Gertrude (German) beloved warrior. See also Trudy.
Geertrud, Geertruda, Geertrude, Geertrudi, Geertrudie, Geertrudy, Geitruda, Gerruda, Gerrudah, Gertina, Gertraud, Gertraude, Gertrud, Gertruda, Gertrudah, Gertrudia, Gertrudis, Gertruide, Gertruyd, Gertruyde, Girtrud, Girtruda, Girtrude, Gyrtrud, Gyrtruda, Gyrtrude

Gervaise (French) skilled with a spear.
Gervayse, Gervis

Gessica (Italian) a form of Jessica.
Gesica, Gesika, Gesikah, Gess, Gesse, Gessika, Gessikah, Gessy, Gessyca, Gessyka, Gesyca, Gesyka

Geva (Hebrew) hill.
Gevah

Ghada (Arabic) young; tender.
Gada, Gadah, Ghadah

Ghita (Italian) pearly.
Ghyta, Gyta

Gia (Italian) a short form of Giana.
Giah, Gya, Gyah

Giacinta (Italian) a form of Hyacinth.
Giacynta, Giacyntah, Gyacinta, Gyacynta

Giacobba (Hebrew) supplanter, substitute.
Giacoba, Giacobah, Giacobbah, Gyacoba, Gyacobba, Gyacobbah

Giana, Gianna (Italian) a short form of Giovanna. See also Jianna, Johana.
Gian, Gianah, Gianel, Gianela, Gianele, Gianell, Gianella, Gianelle, Gianet, Gianeta, Gianete, Gianett, Gianetta, Gianette, Gianina, Gianinna, Giannah, Gianne, Giannee, Giannella, Giannetta, Gianni, Giannie, Giannina, Gianny, Gianoula, Gyan, Gyana, Gyanah, Gyann, Gyanna, Gyannah

Gidget (English) giddy.
Gydget

Gigi (French) a familiar form of Gilberte.
G.G., Geegee, Geygey, Giggi, Gygy, Jeejee, Jeyjey, Jiji

Gilana (Hebrew) joyful.
Gila, Gilah, Gilanah, Gilane, Gilania, Gilanie, Gilena, Gilenia, Gyla, Gylah, Gylan, Gylana, Gylanah, Gylane

Gilberte (German) brilliant; pledge; trustworthy. See also Berti.
Gilberta, Gilbertia, Gilbertina, Gilbertine, Gilbertyna, Gilbertyne, Gilbirt, Gilbirta, Gilbirte, Gilbirtia, Gilbirtina, Gilbirtine, Gilburta, Gilburte, Gilburtia, Gilburtina, Gilburtine, Gilburtyna, Gilbyrta, Gilbyrte, Gilbyrtia, Gilbyrtina, Gilbyrtyna, Gylberta, Gylbertah, Gylberte, Gylbertina, Gylbertyna, Gylbirta, Gylbirte, Gylbirtia, Gylbirtina, Gylbirtine, Gylbirtyna, Gylburta, Gylburte, Gylburtia, Gylburtina, Gylburtyna, Gylbyrta, Gylbyrte, Gylbyrtia, Gylbyrtina, Gylbyrtyna

Gilda (English) covered with gold.
Gildah, Gilde, Gildi, Gildie, Gildy, Guilda, Guildah, Guylda, Guyldah, Gylda, Gyldah

Gill (Latin, German) a short form of Gilberte, Gillian.
Gili, Gilli, Gillie, Gilly, Gyl, Gyll

Gillian (Latin) a form of Jillian.
Gilian, Giliana, Gilianah, Giliane, Gilleann, Gilleanna, Gilleanne, Gilliana, Gillianah, Gilliane, Gilliann, Gillianna, Gillianne, Gillien, Gillyan, Gillyana, Gillyanah, Gillyane, Gillyann, Gillyanna, Gillyannah,

Gillyanne, Gylian, Gyliana, Gylianah, Gyliane, Gyliann, Gylianna, Gyliannah, Gylianne, Gyllian, Gylliana, Gyllianah, Gylliane, Gylliann, Gyllianna, Gylliannah, Gyllianne, Gyllyan, Gyllyana, Gyllyanah, Gyllyane, Lian

Gin (Japanese) silver. A short form of names beginning with "Gin."
Gean, Geane, Geen, Gyn, Gynn

Gina (Italian) a short form of Angelina, Eugenia, Regina, Virginia. See also Jina.
Geenah, Ginah, Ginai, Ginna, Gyna, Gynah

Ginette (English) a form of Genevieve.
Ginata, Ginatah, Ginett, Ginetta, Ginnetta, Ginnette

Ginger (Latin) flower; spice. A familiar form of Virginia.
Ginja, Ginjah, Ginjar, Ginjer, Gynger, Gynjer

Ginia (Latin) a familiar form of Virginia.
Ginea, Gineah, Giniah, Gynia, Gyniah, Gynya, Gynyah

Ginnifer (English) white; smooth; soft. (Welsh) a form of Jennifer.
Ginifer, Gynifer, Gyniffer

Ginny (English) a familiar form of Ginger, Virginia. See also Jin, Jinny.
Gini, Ginnee, Ginney, Ginni, Ginnie, Giny, Gionni, Gionny, Gyni, Gynie, Gynni, Gynnie, Gynny

Giordana (Italian) a form of Jordana.
Giadana, Giadanah, Giadanna, Giadannah, Giodana, Giodanah, Giodanna, Giodannah, Giordanah, Giordanna, Giordannah, Gyodana, Gyodanah, Gyodanna, Gyodannah, Gyordana, Gyordanah, Gyordanna, Gyordannah

Giorgianna (English) a form of Georgeanna.

Giorsala (Scottish) graceful.
Giorsal, Giorsalah, Gyorsal, Gyorsala, Gyorsalah

Giovanna (Italian) a form of Jane.
Giavana, Giavanah, Giavanna, Giavannah, Giavonna, Giovana, Giovanah, Giovannah,

Giovanne, Giovannica, Giovona, Giovonah, Giovonna, Giovonnah, Givonnie, Gyovana, Gyovanah, Gyovanna, Gyovannah, Jeveny

Giovanni (Italian) a form of Giovanna.

Gisa (Hebrew) carved stone.
Gazit, Gisah, Gissa, Gysa, Gysah

Gisel, Gisell, Gissel, Gisselle (German) forms of Giselle.
Gisele, Gissele, Gissell

Gisela (German) a form of Giselle.
Giselah, Giselda, Giselia, Gisella, Gisellah, Gissela, Gissella, Gysela, Gysella

Giselle (German) pledge; hostage. See also Jizelle.
Ghisele, Geséle, Giseli, Gizela, Gysel, Gysele, Gysell, Gyselle

Gita (Yiddish) good. (Polish) a short form of Margaret.
Gitah, Gitka, Gyta, Gytah

Gitana (Spanish) gypsy; wanderer.
Gitanna, Gytana, Gytanna

Gitel (Hebrew) good.
Gitela, Gitelah, Gitele, Gitell, Gitella, Gitelle, Gytel, Gytell, Gytella, Gytellah, Gytelle

Githa (Greek) good. (English) gift.
Githah, Gytha, Gythah

Gitta (Irish) a short form of Bridget.
Getta, Gittah

Giulana (Italian) a form of Guilia.
Giulianna, Giulliana

Giulia (Italian) a form of Julia.
Guila, Guiliana, Guilietta, Guiliette

Giuseppina (Italian) a form of Josephine.

Giustina (Italian) a form of Justine.
Giustine, Gustina, Gustinah, Gustine, Gustyn, Gustyna, Gustynah, Gustyne

Gizela (Czech) a form of Giselle.
Gizella, Gizi, Giziki, Gizus, Gyzela, Gyzelah, Gyzella

Gizelle (Czech) a form of Giselle.
Gizel, Gizele, Gizell, Gyzel, Gyzele, Gyzell, Gyzelle

Gladis (Irish) a form of Gladys.
Gladi, Gladiz

Gladys (Latin) small sword. (Irish)
princess. (Welsh) a form of Claudia.
Glad, Gladdys, Gladness, Gladuse, Gladwys,
Glady, Gladyss, Gleddis, Gleddys

Glenda (Welsh) a form of Glenna.
Glanda, Glendah, Glennda, Glenndah,
Glynda

Glenna (Irish) valley, glen. See also
Glynnis.
Glenetta, Glenina, Glenine, Glenn, Glenne,
Glennesha, Glennia, Glennie, Glenora,
Gleny, Glyn, Glynna

Glennesha (American) a form of Glenna.
Gleneesha, Gleneisha, Glenesha, Glenicia,
Glenisha, Glenneesha, Glennisha,
Glennishia, Glynesha, Glynisha

Gloria (Latin) glory. History: Gloria
Steinem, a leading American feminist,
founded *Ms.* magazine.
Glorea, Gloresha, Gloriah, Gloribel,
Gloriela, Gloriella, Glorielle, Gloris,
Glorisha, Glorvina, Glorya, Gloryah

Gloriann, Glorianne (American) combi-
nations of Gloria + Ann.
Glorian, Gloriana, Gloriane, Glorianna,
Glorien, Gloriena, Gloriene, Glorienn,
Glorienna, Glorienne, Gloryan, Gloryana,
Gloryane, Gloryann, Gloryanna, Gloryanne,
Gloryen, Gloryena, Gloryene, Gloryenn,
Gloryenna, Gloryenne

Glory (Latin) a form of Gloria.
Glore, Gloree, Glorey, Glori, Glorie, Glorye

Glynnis (Welsh) a form of Glenna.
Glenice, Glenis, Glenise, Glennis, Glennys,
Glenwys, Glenys, Glenyse, Glenyss, Glinnis,
Glinys, Glynice, Glynis, Glyniss, Glynitra,
Glynnys, Glynys, Glynyss

Godiva (English) God's present.
Godivah, Godyva, Godyvah

Golda (English) gold. History: Golda
Meir was a Russian-born politician who
served as prime minister of Israel.
Goldah, Goldarina, Goldia, Goldiah,
Goldine, Goldya, Goldyah

Goldie (English) a familiar form of Golda.
Goldea, Goldee, Goldey, Goldi, Goldy

Goldine (English) a form of Golda.
Goldeena, Goldeene, Golden, Goldena,
Goldene, Goldina, Goldinah, Goldyn,
Goldyna, Goldynah, Goldyne

Goma (Swahili) joyful dance.
Gomah

Grace (Latin) graceful.
Engracia, Graca, Gracelia, Gracella, Gracia,
Gracinha, Graciosa, Graice, Graise, Grase,
Gratia, Greice, Greyce, Greyse

Graceann, Graceanne (English) combinations of Grace + Ann.
Graceanna, Graciana, Gracianna

Gracelyn, Gracelynn, Gracelynne
(English) combinations of Grace + Lynn.
Gracelin, Gracelinn, Gracelinne, Gracelyne

Gracen, Gracyn (English) short forms of
Graceanne.
Gracin

Gracia (Spanish) a form of Grace.
Gracea, Graciah, Graicia, Graiciah, Graisia,
Graisiah, Grasia, Grasiah, Graycia, Grayciah,
Graysia, Graysiah, Grazia, Graziah

Gracie (English) a familiar form of Grace.
Gracee, Gracey, Graci, Gracy, Graecie, Graysie

Graciela (Spanish) a form of Grace.
Graciella, Gracielle

Grant (English) great; giving.

Gratiana (Hebrew) graceful.
Gratian, Gratiane, Gratiann, Gratianna,
Gratianne, Gratyan, Gratyana, Gratyane,
Gratyann, Gratyanna, Gratyanne

Grayce (Latin) a form of Grace.

Grayson (English) bailiff's child.
Graison, Graisyn, Grasien, Grasyn, Gray,
Graysen

Graziella (Italian) a form of Grace.
Graziel, Graziela, Graziele, Graziell,
Grazielle, Graziosa, Grazyna

Grecia (Latin) a form of Grace.

Greer (Scottish) vigilant.
Grear, Grier, Gryer

Greta, Gretta (German) short forms of Gretchen, Margaret.
Grata, Gratah, Greata, Greatah, Greeta, Greetah, Gretah, Grete, Gretha, Grethe, Grette, Grieta, Gryta, Grytta

Gretchen (German) a form of Margaret.
Gretchan, Gretchin, Gretchon, Gretchun, Gretchyn

Gretel (German) a form of Margaret.
Greatal, Greatel, Gretal, Gretall, Gretell, Grethal, Grethel, Gretil, Gretill, Grettal, Gretyl, Gretyll

Gricelda (German) a form of Griselda.
Gricelle

Grisel (German) a short form of Griselda.
Grisell, Griselle, Grissel, Grissele, Grissell, Grizel, Grizella, Grizelle

Griselda (German) gray woman warrior. See also Selda, Zelda.
Griseldis, Griseldys, Griselys, Grishild, Grishilda, Grishilde, Grisselda, Grissely, Grizelda, Gryselda, Gryzelda

Guadalupe (Arabic) river of black stones. See also Lupe.
Guadalup, Guadelupe, Guadlupe, Guadulupe, Gudalupe

Gudrun (Scandinavian) battler. See also Runa.
Gudren, Gudrin, Gudrina, Gudrine, Gudrinn, Gudrinna, Gudrinne, Gudruna

Guillerma (Spanish) a short form of Guillermina.
Guilla

Guillermina (Spanish) a form of Wilhelmina.

Guinevere (French, Welsh) white wave; white phantom. Literature: the wife of King Arthur. See also Gayna, Genevra, Jennifer, Winifred, Wynne.
Guenevere, Guenna, Guinievre, Guinivere, Guinna, Gwenevere, Gwenivere, Gwenora, Gwenore, Gwynivere, Gwynnevere

Gunda (Norwegian) female warrior.
Gundah, Gundala, Gunta

Gurit (Hebrew) innocent baby.
Gurita, Gurite, Guryta, Guryte

Gurleen (Sikh) follower of the guru.

Gurley (Australian) willow.
Gurlea, Gurleah, Gurlee, Gurlei, Gurleigh, Gurli, Gurlie, Gurly

Gurpreet (Punjabi) religion.
Gurprit

Gusta (Latin) a short form of Augusta.
Gus, Gussi, Gussie, Gussy

Gustey (English) windy.
Gustea, Gustee, Gusti, Gustie, Gusty

Gwen (Welsh) a short form of Guinevere, Gwendolyn.
Gwenesha, Gweness, Gwenessa, Gweneta, Gwenetta, Gwenette, Gweni, Gwenisha, Gwenishia, Gwenita, Gwenite, Gwenitta, Gwenitte, Gwenn, Gwenna, Gwenneta, Gwennete, Gwennetta, Gwennette, Gwennie, Gwenny

Gwenda (Welsh) a familiar form of Gwendolyn.
Gwinda, Gwynda, Gwynedd

Gwendolyn (Welsh) white wave; white browed; new moon. Literature: Gwendoloena was the wife of Merlin, the magician. See also Genevieve, Gwyneth, Wendy.
Guendolen, Gwendalee, Gwendalin, Gwendaline, Gwendalyn, Gwendalynn, Gwendela, Gwendelyn, Gwendelynn, Gwendilyn, Gwendolen, Gwendolene, Gwendolin, Gwendolina, Gwendoline, Gwendolyne, Gwendolynn, Gwendolynne, Gwendylan, Gwindolin, Gwindolina, Gwindoline, Gwindolyn, Gwindolyna, Gwindolyne, Gwyndolin, Gwyndolina, Gwyndoline, Gwyndolyn, Gwyndolyna, Gwyndolyne, Gwynndolen

Gwyn (Welsh) a short form of Gwyneth.
Gwin, Gwine, Gwineta, Gwinete, Gwinisha, Gwinita, Gwinite, Gwinitta, Gwinitte, Gwinn, Gwinne, Gwynn, Gwynne

Gwyneth (Welsh) a form of Gwendolyn. See also Winnie, Wynne.

Gwyneth *(cont.)*
*Gweneth, Gwenetta, Gwenette, Gwenith,
Gwenneth, Gwennyth, Gwenyth, Gwineth,
Gwinneth, Gwynaeth, Gwynneth*

Gypsy (English) wanderer.
*Gipsea, Gipsee, Gipsey, Gipsi, Gipsie, Gipsy,
Gypsea, Gypsee, Gypsey, Gypsi, Gypsie, Jipsi*

Habiba (Arabic) beloved.
Habibah, Habibeh

Hachi (Japanese) eight; good luck. (Native
American) river.
Hachee, Hachie, Hachiko, Hachiyo, Hachy

Hadara (Hebrew) adorned with beauty.
*Hadarah, Hadaria, Hadariah, Hadarya,
Hadaryah*

Hadassah (Hebrew) myrtle tree.
*Hadas, Hadasah, Hadassa, Haddasa,
Haddasah*

Hadeel (Arabic) a form of Hadil.

Hadil (Arabic) cooing of pigeons.

Hadiya (Swahili) gift.
*Hadaya, Hadia, Hadiyah, Hadiyyah, Hadya,
Hadyea*

Hadley (English) field of heather.
*Hadlea, Hadleah, Hadlee, Hadlei, Hadleigh,
Hadli, Hadlie, Hadly*

Hadriane (Greek, Latin) a form of
Adrienne.
*Hadriana, Hadrianna, Hadrianne, Hadriene,
Hadrienne*

Hae (Korean) ocean.

Haeley (English) a form of Hayley.
*Haelee, Haeleigh, Haeli, Haelie, Haelleigh,
Haelli, Haellie, Haely*

Hafsa (Muslim) cub; young lioness.
Hafsah, Hafza

Hafwen (Welsh) pleasant summer.
*Hafwena, Hafwenah, Hafwene, Hafwin,
Hafwina, Hafwinah, Hafwine, Hafwyn,
Hafwyna, Hafwynah, Hafwyne*

Hagar (Hebrew) forsaken; stranger. Bible:
Sarah's handmaiden, the mother of
Ishmael.
*Hagara, Hagarah, Hagaria, Hagariah,
Hagarya, Hagaryah, Haggar*

Haidee (Greek) modest.
*Hady, Hadyee, Haide, Haidea, Haideah,
Haidey, Haidi, Haidia, Haidy, Haydee,
Haydey, Haydy*

Haiden (English) heather-covered hill.
Haden, Hadyn, Haeden, Haidn, Haidyn

**Haile, Hailee, Haileigh, Hailey, Haili,
Hailie, Haily** (English) forms of Hayley.
*Haiely, Hailea, Haileah, Hailei, Hailia,
Haille, Haillee, Hailley, Hailli, Haillie, Hailly*

Hajar (Hebrew) a form of Hagar.
*Hajara, Hajarah, Hajaria, Hajariah, Hajarya,
Hajaryah*

Hala (African) a form of Halla.
Halah, Halya, Halyah

Haldana (Norwegian) half Danish.
*Haldanah, Haldania, Haldaniah, Haldanna,
Haldannah, Haldannya, Haldannyah,
Haldanya, Haldanyah*

**Halee, Haleigh, Hali, Halie, Hallee,
Halley, Halli, Hallie** (Scandinavian)
forms of Haley.
*Hale, Haleh, Halei, Haliegh, Hallea, Halleah,
Hallei, Halleigh, Hallia, Halliah, Hally,
Hallya, Hallyah, Hallye, Haly, Halye*

Haley (Scandinavian) heroine. See also
Hayley.

Halia (Hawaiian) in loving memory.
*Halea, Haleaah, Haleah, Haleea, Haleeah,
Haleia, Haleiah, Haliah, Halya, Halyah*

Haliaka (Hawaiian) leader.
Haliakah, Halyaka, Halyakah

Halima (Arabic) a form of Halimah.
Halime

Halimah (Arabic) gentle; patient.
Haleema, Haleemah, Halyma, Halymah

Halimeda (Greek) loves the sea.
Halimedah, Halymeda, Halymedah

Halina (Hawaiian) likeness. (Russian) a form of Helen.
Haleen, Haleena, Halena, Halinah, Haline, Halinka, Halyn, Halyna, Halynah, Halyne

Halla (African) unexpected gift.
Hallah, Hallia, Halliah, Hallya, Hallyah

Halle (African) a form of Halla. (Scandinavian) a form of Haley.

Halona (Native American) fortunate.
Hallona, Hallonah, Halonah, Haloona, Haona

Halsey (English) Hall's island.
Halsea, Halsie

Hama (Japanese) shore.

Hana, Hanah (Japanese) flower. (Arabic) happiness. (Slavic) forms of Hannah.
Hanae, Hanicka, Hanka

Hanako (Japanese) flower child.

Hanan (Japanese, Arabic, Slavic) a form of Hana.
Hanin

Haneen (Japanese, Arabic, Slavic) a form of Hana.

Hanele (Hebrew) compassionate.
Hanal, Hanall, Hanalla, Hanalle, Hanel, Hanela, Hanelah, Hanell, Hanella, Hanelle, Hannel, Hannell, Hannella, Hannelle

Hania (Hebrew) resting place.
Haniah, Haniya, Hanja, Hannia, Hanniah, Hanya, Hanyah

Hanifa (Arabic) true believer.
Haneefa, Hanifa, Hanyfa, Hanyfah

Hanna (Hebrew) a form of Hannah.
Honna

Hannah (Hebrew) gracious. Bible: the mother of Samuel. See also Anci, Anezka, Ania, Anka, Ann, Anna, Annalie, Anneka, Chana, Nina, Nusi.
Hanneke, Hannele, Hannon, Honnah

Hanni (Hebrew) a familiar form of Hannah.
Hani, Hanita, Hanitah, Hanne, Hannie, Hanny

Happy (English) happy.
Happea, Happee, Happey, Happi, Happie

Hara (Hindi) tawny. Religion: another name for the Hindu god Shiva, the destroyer.
Harah

Haralda (Scandinavian) army ruler.
Harelda, Hareldah, Heralda, Heraldah

Harjot (Sikh) God's light.

Harlee, Harleigh, Harli, Harlie (English) forms of Harley.
Harlea, Harleah, Harlei

Harleen, Harlene (English) forms of Harley.
Harlean, Harleana, Harleanah, Harleane, Harleena, Harleenah, Harleene, Harlein, Harleina, Harleinah, Harleine, Harlena, Harlenah, Harleyn, Harleyna, Harleynah, Harleyne, Harlin, Harlina, Harlinah, Harline, Harlyn, Harlyna, Harlynah, Harlyne

Harley (English) meadow of the hare. See also Arleigh.
Harleey, Harlene, Harly

Harleyann (English) a combination of Harley + Ann.
Harlann, Harlanna, Harlanne, Harleyanna, Harleyanne, Harliann, Harlianna, Harlianne

Harmony (Latin) harmonious.
Harmene, Harmeni, Harmon, Harmone, Harmonee, Harmonei, Harmoney, Harmoni, Harmonia, Harmoniah, Harmonie, Harmonya, Harmonyah

Harper (English) harp player.
Harp, Harpo

Harpreet (Punjabi) devoted to God.
Harprit

Harriet (French) ruler of the household. (English) a form of Henrietta. Literature: Harriet Beecher Stowe was an American writer noted for her novel *Uncle Tom's Cabin*.
Harietta, Hariette, Hariot, Hariott, Harri, Harrie, Harriett, Harrietta, Harriette, Harriot, Harriott, Harryet, Harryeta, Harryetah, Harryete, Harryett, Harryetta, Harryettah, Harryette, Haryet, Haryeta,

Harriet *(cont.)*
  Haryetah, Haryete, Haryett, Haryetta,
  Haryettah, Haryette

Haru (Japanese) spring.

Hasana (Swahili) she arrived first.
  Culture: a name used for the first-born
  female twin. See also Huseina.
  Hasanna, Hasna, Hassana, Hassna, Hassona

Hasia (Hebrew) protected by God.
  Hasiah, Hasya, Hasyah

Hasina (Swahili) good.
  Haseena, Hasena, Hasinah, Hassina,
  Hasyn, Hasyna, Hasynah, Hasyne

Hateya (Moquelumnan) footprints.
  Hateia, Hateiah, Hateyah

Hathor (Egyptian) goddess of the sky.
  Hathora, Hathorah, Hathore

Hattie (English) familiar forms of
  Harriet, Henrietta.
  Hatti, Hatty, Hetti, Hettie, Hetty

Haukea (Hawaiian) snow.
  Haukia, Haukiah, Haukya, Haukyah

Hausu (Moquelumnan) like a bear yawn-
  ing upon awakening.

Hava (Hebrew) a form of Chava. See
  also Eve.
  Havah, Havvah

Haven (English) a form of Heaven.
  Havan, Havana, Havanna, Havannah,
  Havyn

Haviva (Hebrew) beloved.
  Havalee, Havelah, Havi

Haya (Arabic) humble, modest.
  Haia, Haiah, Hayah

Hayat (Arabic) life.

Hayden (English) a form of Haiden.
  Hayde, Haydin, Haydn, Haydon

Hayfa (Arabic) shapely.
  Haifa, Haifah, Hayfah

**Hayle, Haylea, Haylee, Hayleigh, Hayli,
Haylie** (English) forms of Hayley.
  Hayleah, Haylei, Haylia, Hayliah, Haylle,
  Hayllie

Hayley (English) hay meadow. See also
  Haley.
  Hayly

Hazel (English) hazelnut tree; command-
  ing authority.
  Haize, Haizela, Haizelah, Haizell, Haizella,
  Haizellah, Haizelle, Hayzal, Hayzala,
  Hayzalah, Hayzale, Hayzall, Hayzalla,
  Hayzallah, Hayzalle, Hazal, Hazaline,
  Hazall, Hazalla, Hazallah, Hazalle, Haze,
  Hazeline, Hazell, Hazella, Hazelle, Hazen,
  Hazyl, Hazzal, Hazzel, Hazzell, Hazzella,
  Hazzellah, Hazzelle, Heyzal, Heyzel

Heather (English) flowering heather.
  Heath, Heathar, Heatherlee, Heatherly,
  Hethar, Hether

Heaven (English) place of beauty and
  happiness. Bible: where God and angels
  are said to dwell.
  Heavan, Heavin, Heavon, Heavyn, Hevean,
  Heven, Hevin

Heavenly (English) a form of Heaven.
  Heavenlea, Heavenleah, Heavenlee,
  Heavenlei, Heavenleigh, Heavenley,
  Heavenli, Heavenlie

Heba (Greek) a form of Hebe.
  Hebah

Hebe (Greek) Mythology: the Greek
  goddess of youth and spring.
  Hebee, Hebey, Hebi, Hebia, Hebie, Heby

Hedda (German) battler. See also Edda,
  Hedy.
  Heda, Hedah, Hedaya, Heddah, Hedia, Hedu

Hedwig (German) warrior.
  Hedvick, Hedvig, Hedvige, Hedvika,
  Hedwiga, Hedwyg, Hedwyga, Hendvig,
  Hendvyg, Jadviga

Hedy (Greek) delightful; sweet. (German)
  a familiar form of Hedda.
  Heddee, Heddey, Heddi, Heddie, Heddy,
  Hede, Hedee, Hedey, Hedi, Hedie

Heidi, Heidy (German) short forms of
  Adelaide.
  Heida, Heide, Heidea, Heidee, Heidey,
  Heidie, Heydy, Hidea, Hidee, Hidey, Hidi,
  Hidie, Hidy, Hiede, Hiedi, Hydi

Helaina (Greek) a form of Helena.
Halaina, Halainah, Helainah

Helaku (Native American) sunny day.
Helakoo

Helana (Greek) a form of Helena.
Helanah, Helania

Helen (Greek) light. See also Aileen, Aili, Alena, Eileen, Elaina, Elaine, Eleanor, Ellen, Galina, Ila, Ilene, Ilona, Jelena, Leanore, Leena, Lelya, Lenci, Lene, Liolya, Nellie, Nitsa, Olena, Onella, Yalena, Yelena.
Elana, Ena, Halina, Hela, Helan, Hele, Helean, Heleen, Helin, Helon, Helyn, Holain

Helena (Greek) a form of Helen. See also Ilena.
Halayna, Halaynah, Halena, Halina, Helayna, Helaynah, Heleana, Heleanah, Heleena, Heleenah, Helenah, Helenia, Helenka, Helenna, Helina, Helinah, Hellaina, Hellana, Hellanah, Hellanna, Hellena, Hellenna, Helona, Helonna, Helyna, Helynah

Helene (French) a form of Helen.
Halaine, Halayn, Halayne, Helain, Helaine, Helane, Helanie, Helayn, Helayne, Heleen, Heleine, Héléne, Helenor, Heline, Hellain, Hellaine, Hellenor

Helga (German) pious. (Scandinavian) a form of Olga. See also Elga.
Helgah

Helice (Greek) spiral.
Helicia, Heliciah, Helyce, Helycia, Helyciah, Helycya, Helycyah

Helki (Native American) touched.
Helkee, Helkey, Helkie, Helky

Hellen (Greek) a form of Helen.
Hellan, Helle, Helli, Hellin, Hellon, Hellyn

Helma (German) a short form of Wilhelmina.
Halma, Halmah, Helmah, Helme, Helmi, Helmine, Hilma, Hilmah, Hylma, Hylmah

Heloise (French) a form of Louise.
Heloisa, Heloisah, Héloïse, Heloysa, Heloysah, Heloyse, Hlois

Helsa (Danish) a form of Elizabeth.
Helsah, Helse, Helsey, Helsi, Helsia, Helsiah, Helsie, Helsy, Helsya, Helsyah

Heltu (Moquelumnan) like a bear reaching out.
Heltoo

Hendrika (Dutch) a form of Henrietta.
Hendrica, Hendrinka, Hendrinkah, Henrica, Henrika, Henryka, Henrykah

Henna (English) a familiar form of Henrietta.
Hena, Henaa, Henah, Heni, Henia, Henka, Hennah, Henny, Henya

Henrietta (English) ruler of the household. See also Enrica, Etta, Yetta.
Heneretta, Hennrietta, Henretta, Henrie, Henrieta, Henrique, Henriquetta, Henriquette, Henriquieta, Henriquiette, Henryet, Henryeta, Henryetah, Henryete, Henryett, Henryetta, Henryettah

Henriette (French) a form of Henrietta.
Hennriette, Henriete, Henryette

Hera (Greek) queen; jealous. Mythology: the queen of heaven and the wife of Zeus.
Herah, Heria, Heriah, Herya, Heryah

Herberta (German) glorious soldier.
Herbertah, Herbertia, Herbertiah, Herbirta, Herbirtah, Herbirtia, Herburta, Herburtah, Herburtia, Herbyrta, Herbyrtah

Hermia (Greek) messenger.

Hermina (Latin) noble. (German) soldier. See also Erma, Ermine, Irma.
Herma, Hermalina, Hermia, Herminah, Hermine, Herminna

Herminia (Latin, German) a form of Hermina.
Hermenia, Herminiah

Hermione (Greek) earthy.
Hermion, Hermiona, Hermoine, Hermyon, Hermyona, Hermyonah, Hermyone

Hermosa (Spanish) beautiful.
Hermosah

Hertha (English) child of the earth.
Heartha, Hearthah, Hearthea, Heartheah,
Hearthia, Hearthiah, Hearthya, Hearthyah,
Herta, Hertah, Herthah, Herthia, Herthiah,
Herthya, Herthyah, Hirtha

Hester (Dutch) a form of Esther.
Hessi, Hessie, Hessye, Hestar, Hestarr,
Hesther

Hestia (Persian) star. Mythology: the
Greek goddess of the hearth and home.
Hestea, Hesti, Hestiah, Hestie, Hesty,
Hestya, Hestyah

Heta (Native American) racer.
Hetah

Hetta (German) a form of Hedda.
(English) a familiar form of Henrietta.

Hettie (German) a familiar form of
Henrietta, Hester.
Hetti, Hetty

Hialeah (Cherokee) lovely meadow.
Hialea, Hialee, Hialei, Hialeigh, Hiali,
Hialie, Hialy, Hyalea, Hyaleah, Hyalee,
Hyalei, Hyaleigh, Hyali, Hyalie, Hyaly

Hiawatha (Iroquois) creator of rivers.
History: the Onondagan leader who
organized the Iroquois confederacy.
Hiawathah, Hyawatha, Hyawathah

Hiba (Arabic) a form of Hibah.

Hibah (Arabic) gift.
Hyba, Hybah

Hibernia (Latin) comes from Ireland.
Hibernina, Hiberninah, Hibernine,
Hibernya, Hibernyah, Hibernyna,
Hybernyah, Hybernyne

Hibiscus (Latin) Botany: tropical trees or
shrubs with large, showy, colorful flowers.
Hibyscus, Hybyscus

Hilary, Hillary (Greek) cheerful, merry.
See also Alair.
Hilaire, Hilarea, Hilaree, Hilarey, Hilari,
Hilaria, Hilarie, Hilery, Hiliary, Hillarea,
Hillaree, Hillarey, Hillari, Hillarie, Hilleary,
Hilleree, Hilleri, Hillerie, Hillery, Hillianne,
Hilliary, Hillory, Hylarea, Hylaree, Hylarey,

Hylari, Hylarie, Hylary, Hyllarea, Hyllaree,
Hyllarey, Hyllari, Hyllarie, Hyllary

Hilda (German) a short form of
Brunhilda, Hildegarde.
Hildah, Hilde, Hildee, Hildey, Hildi, Hildia,
Hildie, Hildur, Hildy, Hillda, Hilldah, Hilldee,
Hilldey, Hilldi, Hilldia, Hilldie, Hilldy,
Hulda, Hylda, Hyldah, Hyldea, Hyldee,
Hyldey, Hyldi, Hyldie, Hyldy, Hylldea,
Hylldee, Hylldey, Hylldi, Hylldie, Hylldy

Hildegarde (German) fortress.
Hildaagard, Hildaagarde, Hildagard,
Hildagarde, Hildegard, Hildegaurd,
Hildegaurda, Hildegaurde, Hildred,
Hyldaagard, Hyldaagarde, Hyldaaguard,
Hyldaaguarde, Hyldagard, Hyldagarde,
Hyldegard, Hyldegarde, Hyldeguard,
Hyldeguarde

Hildemare (German) splendid.
Hildemar, Hildemara, Hyldemar,
Hyldemara, Hyldemare

Hilma (German) protected.
Hilmah, Hylma, Hylmah

Hinda (Hebrew) hind; doe.
Hindah, Hindey, Hindie, Hindy, Hynda,
Hyndah

Hiriko (Japanese) generous.
Hiroko, Hiryko, Hyriko, Hyroko, Hyryko

Hisa (Japanese) long lasting.
Hisae, Hisah, Hisako, Hisay, Hisayo, Hysa,
Hysah

Hiti (Eskimo) hyena.
Hitty

Hoa (Vietnamese) flower; peace.
Ho, Hoah, Hoai

Hoda (Muslim, Arabic) a form of Huda.

Hola (Hopi) seed-filled club.
Holah, Holla, Hollah

Holain (Greek) a form of Helen.
Holaina, Holainah, Holaine, Holana,
Holanah, Holane, Holayn, Holayna,
Holaynah, Holayne

Holland (French) Geography: A popular
name for the Netherlands.
Holand, Hollan

Hollee, Holley, Holli, Hollie (English)
forms of Holly.
Holle

Hollis (English) near the holly bushes.
Holice, Holisa, Holisah, Holise, Holiss,
Holissa, Holissah, Holisse, Hollice, Hollise,
Hollyce, Hollys, Hollysa, Hollysah, Hollyse,
Hollyss, Hollyssa, Hollyssah, Hollysse,
Holyce, Holys, Holysa, Holysah, Holyse,
Holyss, Holyssa, Holyssah, Holysse

Holly (English) holly tree.
Holea, Holeah, Holee, Holei, Holeigh, Holey,
Holi, Holie, Hollea, Holleah, Hollei, Holleigh,
Hollye, Holy

Hollyann (English) a combination of
Holly + Ann.
Holliann, Hollianna, Hollianne, Hollyanne

Hollyn (English) a short form of Hollyann.
Holeena, Holin, Hollina, Hollynn

Honesta (Latin) honest.
Honest, Honestah, Honestia,

Honesty (Latin) honesty.
Honestee, Honestey, Honesti, Honestie

Honey (English) sweet. (Latin) a familiar
form of Honora.
Honalee, Honea, Honeah, Honee, Honi,
Honia, Honiah, Honie, Honnea, Honnee,
Honney, Honni, Honnie, Honny, Hony,
Hunea, Hunee, Huney, Huni, Hunie,
Hunnee, Hunney, Hunni, Hunnie, Hunny

Hong (Vietnamese) pink.
Hoong

Honora (Latin) honorable. See also Nora,
Onora.
Honner, Honnor, Honnour, Honor, Honorah,
Honorata, Honore, Honoree, Honori, Honoria,
Honoriah, Honorie, Honorina, Honorine,
Honour, Honoura, Honourah, Honoure,
Honouria, Honouriah, Honoury, Honourya,
Honouryah

Honovi (Native American) strong.
Honovee, Honovey, Honovie, Honovy

Hope (English) hope.

Hopi (Hopi) peaceful.
Hopee, Hopey, Hopie, Hopy

Horatia (Latin) keeper of the hours.
Horacia, Horaciah, Horacya, Horacyah,
Horatya, Horatyah

Hortense (Latin) gardener. See also
Ortensia.
Hortencia, Hortensia, Hortensiah, Hortensya,
Hortensyah

Hosanna (Latin) a shout of praise or
adoration derived from the Hebrew
phrase "Save now!"

Hoshi (Japanese) star.
Hoshee, Hoshey, Hoshie, Hoshiko, Hoshiyo,
Hoshy

Howi (Moquelumnan) turtledove.
Howee, Howey, Howie, Howy

Hua (Chinese) flower.

Huata (Moquelumnan) basket carrier.
Huatah

Huberta (German) bright mind; bright
spirit.
Hubertah, Hubertia, Hubertiah, Hubertya,
Hubertyah, Hughbirta, Hughbirtah,
Hughbirtia, Hughbirtiah, Hughbirtya,
Hughbirtyah, Hughburta, Hughburtah,
Hughburtia, Hughburtiah, Hughburtya,
Hughburtyah, Hughbyrta, Hughbyrtah,
Hughbyrtia, Hughbyrtiah, Hughbyrtya,
Hughbyrtyah

Huda (Muslim, Arabic) to lead upon the
right path.

Huette (German) bright mind; bright
spirit.
Huet, Hueta, Huetah, Huete, Huett,
Huetta, Huettah, Huit, Huita, Huitah,
Huitt, Huitta, Huittah, Huitte, Hugeta,
Hugetah, Hugetta, Hughet, Hugheta,
Hughetah, Hughete, Hughett, Hughetta,
Hughettah, Hughette, Huguette, Huyet,
Huyeta, Huyetah, Huyete, Huyett, Huyetta,
Huyetta, Huyette

Humilia (Polish) humble.
Humiliah, Humillia, Humilliah, Humylia,
Humyliah, Humylya, Humylyah

Hunter (English) hunter.
Hunta, Huntah, Huntar, Huntter

Huong (Vietnamese) flower.

Huseina (Swahili) a form of Hasana.

Hyacinth (Greek) Botany: a plant with colorful, fragrant flowers. See also Cynthia, Giacinta, Jacinda.
Hyacintha, Hyacinthe, Hyacinthia, Hyacinthie, Hycinth, Hycynth

Hydi, Hydeia (German) forms of Heidi.
Hyde, Hydea, Hydee, Hydey, Hydia, Hydie, Hydiea, Hydy

Hye (Korean) graceful.

I

Ian (Hebrew) God is gracious.
Iaian, Iain, Iana, Iann, Ianna, Iannel, Iyana

Ianira (Greek) enchantress.
Ianirah, Ianyra, Ianyrah

Ianthe (Greek) violet flower.
Iantha, Ianthia, Ianthina, Ianthine, Ianthya, Ianthyah, Ianthyna

Icess (Egyptian) a form of Isis.
Ices, Icesis, Icesse, Icey, Icia, Icis, Icy

Ida (German) hard working. (English) prosperous.
Idah, Idaia, Idaly, Idamae, Idania, Idarina, Idarine, Idaya, Idda, Ide, Idelle, Idetta, Idette, Idys, Iida, Iidda, Yda, Ydah

Idabelle (English) a combination of Ida + Belle.
Idabel, Idabela, Idabelah, Idabele, Idabell, Idabella, Idabellah

Idalia (Greek) sun.
Idaliah, Idalya, Idalyah

Idalina (English) a combination of Ida + Lina.
Idaleen, Idaleena, Idaleene, Idalena, Idalene, Idaline

Idalis (English) a form of Ida.
Idalesse, Idalise, Idaliz, Idallas, Idallis, Idelis, Idelys, Idialis

Ideashia (American) a combination of Ida + Iesha.
Idasha, Idaysha, Ideesha, Idesha

Idelia (German) noble.
Ideliah, Idelya, Idelyah

Idelle (Welsh) a form of Ida.
Idela, Idelah, Idele, Idell, Idella, Idellah

Idil (Welsh) a form of Ida.
Idal

Ieasha (American) a form of Iesha.
Ieachia, Ieachya, Ieashe

Ieisha (American) a form of Iesha.
Ieishia

Iesha (American) a form of Aisha.
Iaisha, Ieaisha, Ieesha, Iescha, Ieshah, Ieshya, Ieshyah, Ieysha, Ieyshah, Iiesha, Iisha

Ieshia (American) a form of Iesha.
Ieeshia, Ieshea, Iesheia

Ignacia (Latin) fiery, ardent.
Ignaci, Ignaciah, Ignacie, Ignacya, Ignacyah, Ignasha, Ignashah, Ignashia, Ignashya, Ignashyah, Ignatia, Ignatya, Ignatyah, Ignatzia, Ignazia, Ignazya, Ignazyah, Ignezia, Ignezya, Ignezyah, Inignatia, Inignatiah, Inignatya, Inignatyah

Ignia (Latin) a short form of Ignacia.
Igniah, Ignya, Ignyah

Igraine (Irish) graceful.
Igraina, Igrainah, Igrayn, Igrayna, Igraynah, Igrayne

Ikia (Hebrew) God is my salvation. (Hawaiian) a form of Isaiah (see Boys' Names).
Ikaisha, Ikea, Ikeea, Ikeesha, Ikeeshia, Ikeia, Ikeisha, Ikeishi, Ikeishia, Ikesha, Ikeshia, Ikeya, Ikeyia, Ikiah, Ikiea, Ikiia, Ikya, Ikyah

Ila (Hungarian) a form of Helen.
Ilah

Ilaina (Hebrew) a form of Ilana.
Ilainah, Ilaine, Ilainee, Ilainey, Ilaini, Ilainia, Ilainie, Ileina, Ileinah, Ileinee, Ileiney, Ileini, Ileinie, Ileiny, Ileyna, Ileynah, Ileynee, Ileyney, Ileyni, Ileynie, Ileyny

Ilana (Hebrew) tree.
Ilanah, Ilane, Ilanee, Ilaney, Ilani, Ilania, Ilanie, Illana, Illanah, Illane, Illanee, Illaney, Illani, Ilania, Illanie, Ilanit, Illanna, Illannah, Illanne

Ileana (Hebrew) a form of Iliana.
Ilea, Ileah, Ileanah, Ileanee, Ileaney, Ileani, Ileanie, Ileanna, Ileannah, Ileanne, Ileany, Illeana, Illeanah

Ilena (Greek) a form of Helena.
Ileena, Ileenah, Ileina, Ilina, Ilinah, Ilinee, Iliney, Ilini, Ilinie, Iliny, Ilyna, Ilynah, Ilynee, Ilyney, Ilyni, Ilynie, Ilyny

Ilene (Irish) a form of Helen. See also Aileen, Eileen.
Ilean, Ileane, Ileanne, Ileen, Ileene, Ileine, Ileyne, Iline, Illeane, Ilyne

Iliana (Greek) from Troy.
Ili, Ilia, Ilian, Iliani, Iliania, Ilina, Ilinah, Illian, Illiana, Illianah, Illiane, Illiani, Illianna, Illiannah, Illianne, Illyana, Illyane, Illyanna, Illyanne

Ilima (Hawaiian) flower of Oahu.
Ilimah, Ilyma, Ilymah

Ilisa (Scottish, English) a form of Alisa, Elisa.
Ilicia, Ilisah, Ilissa, Ilissah, Iliza, Illisa, Illisah, Illissa, Illissah

Ilise (German) a form of Elise.
Ilese, Ilisse, Illyse, Illysse, Ilyce, Ilyse, Ilysse

Ilisha (Hebrew) a form of Alisha, Elisha. See also Lisha.
Ileshia, Ilishia, Ilysha, Ilyshia

Ilka (Hungarian) a familiar form of Ilona.
Ilke, Ilki, Ilkie, Ilky, Milka, Milke

Ilona (Hungarian) a form of Helen.
Illona, Illonia, Illonya, Ilone, Iloni, Ilonie, Ilonka, Ilyona

Ilsa (German) a form of Ilse.

Ilse (German) a form of Elizabeth. See also Elsa.
Ilsey, Ilsie, Ilsy

Iluminada (Spanish) shining.
Ilumina, Iluminah, Ilumine, Ilumyna, Ilumynah, Ilumyne

Ilyssa (Scottish, English) a form of Ilisa.
Illysa, Illysah, Illyssa, Illyssah, Ilycia, Ilysa, Ilysah, Ilysia, Ilyssah, Ilyza

Ima (Japanese) presently. (German) a familiar form of Amelia.
Imah

Imala (Native American) strong-minded.
Imalah

Iman (Arabic) believer.
Aman, Imana, Imanah, Imane

Imani (Arabic) a form of Iman.
Imahni, Imanee, Imania, Imaniah, Imanie, Imanii, Imany

Imber (Polish) ginger.
Imbera, Imberah, Imbere

Imelda (German) warrior.
Imalda, Imeldah, Irmhilde, Melda

Imena (African) dream.
Imee, Imenah, Imene

Imogene (Latin) image, likeness.
Emogen, Emogena, Emogene, Emojean, Emojeana, Imagena, Imagene, Imagina, Imajean, Imogeen, Imogeene, Imogen, Imogena, Imogene, Imogenia, Imogina, Imogine, Imogyn, Imogyne, Imojean, Imojeen

Imoni (Arabic) a form of Iman.
Imonee

Ina (Irish) a form of Agnes.
Ena, Inanna, Inanne

Inari (Finnish) lake.
Inaree, Inarey, Inarie, Inary

Inca (Spanish) ruler. History: a Quechuan people from highland Peru who established an empire from northern Ecuador to central Chile before being conquered by the Spanish.
Incah, Incan, Incana, Inka, Inkah

India (Sanskrit) river. Geography: a country of southern Asia.
Indea, Indeah, Indee, Indeia, Indeya, Indi, Indiah, Indie, Indy

Indiana (American) Geography: a state in the north-central United States.
Indeana, Indeanah, Indeanna, Indeannah, Indian, Indianah, Indiane, Indianna,

Indiana *(cont.)*
Indiannah, Indianne, Indyana, Indyanah,
Indyann, Indyanna, Indyannah, Indyanne

Indigo (Latin) dark blue color.
Indego, Indiga, Indygo

Indira (Hindi) splendid. History: Indira
Nehru Gandi was an Indian politician
and prime minister.
Indiara, Indirah, Indra, Indre, Indria, Indyra,
Indyrah

Indya (Sanskrit) a form of India.
Indieya, Indiya

Ines, Inez (Spanish) forms of Agnes. See
also Ynez.
Inés, Inesa, Inesita, Inésita, Inessa

Infiniti (Latin) a form of Infinity.

Infinity (Latin) infinity.

Inga (Scandinavian) a short form of
Ingrid.
Ingaberg, Ingaborg, Ingah, Inge, Ingeberg,
Ingeborg, Ingela

Ingrid (Scandinavian) hero's daughter;
beautiful daughter.
Inger, Ingrede

Iniga (Latin) fiery, ardent.
Ingatia, Inigah, Inyga, Inygah

Inoa (Hawaiian) name.
Inoah

Inocencia (Spanish) innocent.
Innocencia, Innocenciah, Innocencya,
Innocencyah, Innocentia, Innocenzia,
Innocenziah, Innocenzya, Innocenzyah,
Inocenciah, Inocencya, Inocenzia, Inocenzya

Ioana (Romanian) a form of Joan.
Ioanah, Ioani, Ioanna, Ioannah, Ioanne

Iola (Greek) dawn; violet colored. (Welsh)
worthy of the Lord.
Iolah, Iole, Iolee, Iolia

Iolana (Hawaiian) soaring like a hawk.
Iolanah, Iolane, Iolann, Iolanna, Iolannah,
Iolanne

Iolanthe (English) a form of Yolanda. See
also Jolanda.
Iolanda, Iolande, Iolantha

Iona (Greek) violet flower.
Ione, Ionee, Ioney, Ioni, Ionia, Ioniah, Ionie,
Iony, Iyona, Iyonna

Iphigenia (Greek) sacrifice. Mythology:
the daughter of the Greek leader
Agamemnon. See also Gena.
Iphgena, Iphigeniah, Iphigenya, Iphigenyah

Ira (Hebrew) watchful. (Russian) a short
form of Irina.
Irah

Irena (Russian) a form of Irene.
Ireana, Ireanah, Ireena, Ireenah, Irenah,
Irenea, Irenka

Irene (Greek) peaceful. Mythology: the
goddess of peace. See also Eirene, Orina,
Rena, Rene, Yarina.
Irean, Ireane, Ireen, Ireene, Irén, Irien, Irine,
Iryn, Iryne, Jereni

Ireny (Greek) a familiar form of Irene.
Irenee, Ireney, Ireni, Irenie, Iryni, Irynie, Iryny

Irina (Russian) a form of Irene.
Eirena, Erena, Ira, Irana, Iranda, Iranna,
Iriana, Irin, Irinah, Irinia, Irona, Iryna,
Irynah, Rina

Iris (Greek) rainbow. Mythology: the
goddess of the rainbow and messenger
of the gods.
Irisa, Irisha, Iriss, Irissa, Irisse, Irita, Irys,
Irysa, Irysah, Iryse, Iryssa, Iryssah, Irysse

Irma (Latin) a form of Erma. (German) a
short form of Irmgaard.
Irmah

Irmgaard (German) noble.
Irmguard, Irmi

Irmine (Latin) noble.
Irmina, Irminah, Irminia, Irmyn, Irmynah,
Irmyne

Irvette (Irish) attractive. (Welsh) white
river. (English) sea friend.
Irvet, Irveta, Irvetah, Irvete, Irvett, Irvetta,
Irvettah

Isa (Spanish) a short form of Isabel.
Isah, Issa, Issah

Isabeau (French) a form of Isabel.

Isabel (Spanish) consecrated to God. See also Bel, Belle, Chavella, Ysabel.
Isabal, Isabeal, Isabele, Isabeli, Isabelia, Isabelita, Isabello, Isbel, Iseabal, Ishbel, Issabel, Issie, Izabel, Izabele

Isabela, Isabella (Italian) forms of Isabel.
Issabella

Isabell, Isabelle (French) forms of Isabel.
Issabell, Issabelle

Isadora (Latin) gift of Isis.
Isadoria, Isadoriah, Isadorya, Isadoryah, Isidora, Izadora, Izadorah, Izadore

Isamar (Hebrew) a form of Itamar.
Isamari, Isamaria

Isel (Scottish) a short form of Isela.

Isela (Scottish) a form of Isla.

Isha (American) a form of Aisha.
Ishae, Ishah, Ishana, Ishanaa, Ishanda, Ishanee, Ishaney, Ishani, Ishanna, Ishaun, Ishawna, Ishaya, Ishenda, Ishia, Iysha

Ishi (Japanese) rock.
Ishiko, Ishiyo, Shiko, Shiyo

Isis (Egyptian) supreme goddess. Mythology: the goddess of nature and fertility.
Ices, Icess, Isiss, Issis, Issisa, Issise, Issys, Isys

Isla (Scottish) Geography: the River Isla in Scotland.
Islah

Ismaela (Hebrew) God will hear.
Ismaila, Ismayla

Ismena (Greek) wise.
Ismenah, Ismenia, Ismeniah, Ismenya, Ismenyah

Isobel (Spanish) a form of Isabel.
Isobell, Isobella, Isobelle, Isopel

Isoka (Benin) gift from God.
Isokah, Soka

Isolde (Welsh) fair lady. Literature: a princess in the Arthurian legends; a heroine in the medieval romance *Tristan and Isolde*. See also Yseult.
Isault, Isolad, Isolda, Isolt, Izolde, Izolt

Isra (Iranian) rainbow.

Issie (Spanish) a familiar form of Isabel.
Issi, Issy, Iza

Ita (Irish) thirsty.
Itah

Italia (Italian) from Italy.
Italea, Italeah, Italee, Italei, Italeigh, Itali, Italiah, Italie, Italy, Italya, Italyah

Itamar (Hebrew) palm island.
Ithamar, Ittamar

Itsel (Spanish) a form of Itzel.
Itesel, Itssel

Itzayana (Spanish) a form of Itzel.

Itzel (Spanish) protected.
Itcel, Itchel, Itza, Itzallana, Itzell, Ixchel

Iva (Slavic) a short form of Ivana.
Ivah

Ivana (Slavic) God is gracious. See also Yvanna.
Ivanah, Ivania, Ivaniah, Ivanka, Ivany, Ivanya, Ivanyah

Ivanna (Slavic) a form of Ivana.
Ivannah, Ivannia, Ivanniah, Ivannya, Ivannyah

Iverem (Tiv) good fortune; blessing.

Iverna (Latin) from Ireland.
Ivernah

Ivette (French) a form of Yvette. See also Evette.
Ivet, Ivete, Iveth, Ivetha, Ivett, Ivetta

Ivey (English) a form of Ivy.
Ivee

Ivon (French) a form of Ivonne.
Ivona, Ivone

Ivonne (French) a form of Yvonne. See also Evonne.
Ivonna, Iwona, Iwonka, Iwonna, Iwonne

Ivory (Latin) made of ivory.
Ivoory, Ivoree, Ivorey, Ivori, Ivorie, Ivorine, Ivree

Ivria (Hebrew) from the land of Abraham.
Ivriah, Ivrit

Ivy (English) ivy tree.
Ivi, Ivia, Iviann, Ivianna, Ivianne, Ivie, Ivye

Iyabo (Yoruba) mother has returned.

Iyana, Iyanna (Hebrew) forms of Ian.
Iyanah, Iyannah, Iyannia

Iyesha (American) a form of Iesha.

Izabella (Spanish) a form of Isabel.
Izabela, Izabell, Izabellah, Izabelle, Izobella

Izusa (Native American) white stone.
Izusah

J

Ja (Korean) attractive. (Hawaiian) fiery.
Jah

Ja'lisa (American) a form of Jalisa.

Ja'nae (American) a form of Janae.

Jaafar (Arabic) small stream.

Jaamini (Hindi) evening.
Jaaminee, Jaaminey, Jaaminie, Jaaminy

Jabrea, Jabria (American) combinations of the prefix Ja + Brea.
Jabreal, Jabree, Jabreea, Jabreena, Jabrelle, Jabreona, Jabri, Jabriah, Jabriana, Jabrie, Jabriel, Jabrielle, Jabrienna, Jabrina

Jacalyn (American) a form of Jacqueline.
Jacalean, Jacaleana, Jacaleanah, Jacaleane, Jacaleen, Jacaleena, Jacaleenah, Jacaleene, Jacalein, Jacaleina, Jacaleinah, Jacaleine, Jacaleyn, Jacaleyna, Jacaleynah, Jacaleyne, Jacalin, Jacalina, Jacalinah, Jacaline, Jacalyna, Jacalynah, Jacalyne, Jacalynn

Jacee, Jaci, Jacie (Greek) forms of Jacey.
Jacci, Jacia, Jaciah, Jaciel, Jaciela, Jaciele

Jacelyn (American) a form of Jocelyn.
Jacelean, Jaceleana, Jaceleanah, Jaceleane, Jaceleen, Jaceleena, Jaceleenah, Jaceleene, Jacelein, Jaceleina, Jaceleinah, Jaceleine, Jaceleyn, Jaceleyna, Jaceleynah, Jaceleyne, Jacelin, Jacelina, Jacelinah, Jaceline, Jacelyna, Jacelynah, Jacelyne, Jacelynn, Jacelynna, Jacelynnah, Jacelynne, Jacilin, Jacilina, Jacilinah, Jaciline, Jacilyn, Jacilyne, Jacilynn, Jacylin, Jacylina, Jacylinah, Jacyline, Jacylyn, Jacylyna, Jacylynah, Jacylyne, Jacylynn

Jacey, Jacy (American) combinations of the initials J. + C. (Greek) familiar forms of Jacinda.
Jac-E, Jace, Jacea, Jacya, Jacyah, Jaice, Jaicee, Jaici, Jaicie

Jacinda (Greek) beautiful, attractive. (Spanish) a form of Hyacinth.
Jacenda, Jacindah, Jacinde, Jacindea, Jacindee, Jacindey, Jacindi, Jacindia, Jacindie, Jacindy, Jacinna, Jacinnia, Jacyn, Jacynda, Jacyndah, Jacyndea, Jacyndee, Jacyndi, Jacyndia, Jacyndy, Jakinda, Jasinda, Jasindah, Jasinde, Jasindea, Jasindey, Jasindi, Jasindia, Jasindy, Jasynda, Jasyndah, Jasyndea, Jasyndee, Jasyndey, Jasyndi, Jasyndia, Jasyndie, Jasyndy, Jaxina, Jaxine, Jaxyn, Jaxyna, Jaxynah, Jaxyne, Jazinda, Jazindah, Jazindea, Jazindee, Jazindia, Jazindie, Jazindy

Jacinta (Greek) a form of Jacinda.
Jacanta, Jacent, Jacenta, Jacentah, Jacente, Jacintah, Jacintia, Jacynta, Jacyntah, Jasinta, Jasintah, Jasinte, Jaxinta, Jaxintah, Jaxinte, Jazinta, Jazintah, Jazynte

Jacinthe (Spanish) a form of Jacinda.
Jacinte, Jacinth, Jacintha, Jacinthia, Jacinthy

Jackalyn (American) a form of Jacqueline.
Jackalean, Jackaleana, Jackaleanah, Jackaleane, Jackaleen, Jackaleena, Jackaleenah, Jackaleene, Jackalein, Jackaleina, Jackaleinah, Jackaleine, Jackalene, Jackaleyn, Jackaleyna, Jackaleynah, Jackaleyne, Jackalin, Jackalina, Jackalinah, Jackaline, Jackalyna, Jackalynah, Jackalyne, Jackalynn, Jackalynne

Jackeline, Jackelyn (American) forms of Jacqueline.
Jackelin, Jackelline, Jackellyn, Jackelynn, Jackelynne, Jockeline

Jacki, Jackie (American) familiar forms of Jacqueline. See also Jacqui.
Jackea, Jackee, Jackey, Jackia, Jackiah, Jackielee, Jacky, Jackye

Jackilyn (American) a form of Jacqueline.
Jackilean, Jackileana, Jackileanah, Jackileane, Jackileen, Jackileena, Jackileenah, Jackileene, Jackilein, Jackileina, Jackileinah, Jackileine, Jackileyn, Jackileyna, Jackileynah, Jackileyne, Jackilin, Jackilynn, Jackilynne

Jacklyn, Jacklynn (American) short forms of Jacqueline.
Jacklin, Jackline, Jacklyne, Jacklynne

Jackolyn (American) a form of Jacqueline.
Jackolin, Jackoline, Jackolynn, Jackolynne

Jackquel (French) a short form of Jacqueline.

Jackquelyn (French) a form of Jacqueline.
Jackqueline, Jackquelyna, Jackquelynah, Jackquelyne, Jackquelynn, Jackquelynna, Jackquelynnah, Jackquelynne, Jackquetta, Jackquilin, Jackquiline, Jackquilyn, Jackquilynn, Jackquilynne

Jackson (English) child of Jack.
Jacksen, Jacksin, Jacson, Jakson, Jaxon

Jaclyn, Jaclynn (American) short forms of Jacqueline.
Jacleen, Jaclin, Jacline, Jaclyne

Jacob (Hebrew) supplanter, substitute. Bible: son of Isaac, brother of Esau.

Jacobella (Italian) a form of Jacobi.
Jacobela, Jacobell

Jacobi (Hebrew) a form of Jacob.
Coby, Jacoba, Jacobah, Jacobea, Jacobee, Jacobella, Jacobette, Jacobia, Jacobiah, Jacobie, Jacobina, Jacobinah, Jacobine, Jacoby, Jacobya, Jacobyah, Jacobye, Jacolbi, Jacolbia, Jacolby, Jacovina, Jacovinah, Jacovine, Jacuba, Jakoba, Jakobea, Jakobee, Jakobey, Jakobi, Jakobia, Jakobiah, Jakobie, Jakoby, Jakobya, Jakubah, Jocoby, Jocolby, Jocovyn, Jocovyna, Jocovynah, Jocovyne

Jacolyn (American) a form of Jacqueline.
Jacolean, Jacoleana, Jacoleanah, Jacoleane, Jacoleen, Jacoleena, Jacoleenah, Jacoleene, Jacolein, Jacoleina, Jacoleinah, Jacoleine,

Jacolin, Jacolina, Jacolinah, Jacoline, Jacolyna, Jacolynah, Jacolyne, Jacolynn, Jacolynna, Jacolynnah, Jacolynne

Jacqualine (French) a form of Jacqueline.
Jacqualin, Jacqualine, Jacqualyn, Jacqualyne, Jacqualynn

Jacqueena (French) a form of Jacqueline.
Jacqueen, Jacqueenah, Jacqueene, Jacqueenia, Jacqueeniah, Jacqueenie, Jacqueine, Jacquine, Jaqueen, Jaqueena, Jaqueenah, Jaqueene, Jaqueenia, Jaqueeniah, Jaqueenie, Jaqueeny, Jaqueenya, Jaqueenyah

Jacquelin, Jacquelyn, Jacquelyne, Jacquelynn (French) forms of Jacqueline.
Jacquelynne

Jacqueline (French) supplanter, substitute; little Jacqui.
Jacquel, Jacquelean, Jacqueleana, Jacqueleanah, Jacqueleane, Jacqueleen, Jacqueleena, Jacqueleenah, Jacqueleene, Jacquelein, Jacqueleina, Jacqueleinah, Jacqueleine, Jacquelene, Jacqueleyn, Jacqueleyna, Jacqueleynah, Jacqueleyne, Jacquelina, Jacquelinah, Jacquena, Jacquene, Jacquenetta, Jacquenette, Jacquiline, Jocqueline

Jacquetta (French) a form of Jacqueline.
Jacquette

Jacqui (French) a short form of Jacqueline. See also Jacki.
Jacquai, Jacquay, Jacqué, Jacquee, Jacqueta, Jacquete, Jacquey, Jacquie, Jacquise, Jacquita, Jakquee, Jakquei, Jakquey, Jakqui, Jakquie, Jakquy, Jaquai, Jaquay, Jaquee, Jaquei, Jaquey, Jaqui, Jaquie, Jaquiese, Jaquina, Jaquy

Jacquiline (French) a form of Jacqueline.
Jacquil, Jacquilin, Jacquilyn, Jacquilyne, Jacquilynn

Jacqulin, Jacquline, Jacqulyn (American) forms of Jacqueline.
Jacqul, Jacqulyne, Jacqulynn, Jacqulynne, Jacquoline

Jacyline (French) a form of Jacqueline.
Jacylean, Jacyleana, Jacyleanah, Jacyleane, Jacyleen, Jacyleena, Jacyleenah, Jacyleene, Jacylein, Jacyleina, Jacyleinah, Jacyleine, Jacyleyn, Jacyleyna, Jacyleynah, Jacyleyne, Jacylin, Jacylina, Jacylinah, Jacylyn, Jacylyna,

Jacyline *(cont.)*
Jacylynah, Jacylyne, Jacylynn, Jacylynna,
Jacylynnah, Jacylynne

Jacynthe (Spanish) a form of Jacinda.
Jacynta, Jacynth, Jacyntha, Jacyntheia,
Jacynthia, Jacynthy

Jada (Hebrew) wise. (Spanish) a form of
Jade.
Jadae, Jadah, Jadda, Jaddah, Jadea, Jadeah

Jade (Spanish) jade.
Jadeann, Jadee, Jadera, Jadienne, Jaed

Jadelyn (American) a combination of
Jade + Lynn.
Jadalyn, Jadelaine, Jadeline, Jadelyne,
Jadelynn, Jadielin, Jadielyn

Jaden, Jadyn (Spanish) forms of Jade.
Jadeen, Jadeena, Jadena, Jadene, Jadeyn,
Jadienna, Jadienne, Jadin, Jadine, Jadynn,
Jaeden, Jaedine

Jadie (Spanish) a familiar form of Jade.
Jadi

Jadzia (Spanish) a form of Jade.
Jadziah

Jae (Latin) jaybird. (French) a familiar
form of Jacqueline.
Jaea, Jaey, Jaya

Jaeda (Spanish) a form of Jada.
Jaedah, Jaedra

Jaedyn (Spanish) a form of Jade.
Jaedynn

Jael (Hebrew) mountain goat; climber.
See also Yael.
Jaele, Jaelea, Jaeleah, Jaelee, Jaelei, Jaeleigh,
Jaeley, Jaeli, Jaelia, Jaeliah, Jaelie, Jaell, Jaelle,
Jaelly, Jaely, Jahla, Jahlea, Jahlee, Jahlei,
Jahleigh, Jahley, Jahli, Jahlia, Jahliah, Jahlie,
Jahly, Jahlya, Jahlyah, Jailea, Jaileah, Jailee,
Jailei, Jaileigh, Jailey, Jaili, Jailia, Jailiah,
Jailie, Jaily

Jaela (Hebrew) a form of Jael.
Jaelah, Jaella, Jaellah, Jaelya, Jaelyah

Jaelyn, Jaelynn (American) combinations
of Jae + Lynn.

Jaeleen, Jaeleena, Jaeleenah, Jaeleene, Jaelen,
Jaelena, Jaelenah, Jaelene, Jaelin, Jaeline,
Jaelinn, Jaelyna, Jaelynah, Jaelyne

Jaffa (Hebrew) a form of Yaffa.
Jaffice, Jaffit, Jafit, Jafra

Jaha (Swahili) dignified.
Jahaida, Jahida, Jahira, Jahitza

Jahaira (Swahili) a form of Jaha.
Jaharra, Jahayra

Jahna (American) a form of Johna.
Jahnaia, Jahnaya

Jai (Tai) heart. (Latin) a form of Jaye.

Jaid, Jaide (Spanish) forms of Jade.

Jaida (Hebrew, Spanish) a form of Jada.
Jaidah

Jaiden, Jaidyn (Spanish) forms of Jade.
Jaidan, Jaidey, Jaidi, Jaidin, Jaidon

Jaila (Hebrew) a form of Jael.
Jailya, Jailyah

Jailene (American) a form of Jaelyn.
Jaileen, Jaileena, Jaileenah, Jaileene, Jailen,
Jailena, Jailenah

Jailyn (American) a form of Jaelyn.
Jailin, Jailine, Jailyna, Jailynah, Jailyne

Jaime (French) I love.
Jaema, Jaemah, Jaemea, Jaemeah, Jahmea,
Jaima, Jaimah, Jaimini, Jaimme, Jaimy, Jamee

Jaimee, Jaimi, Jaimie (French) forms of
Jaime.
Jaemee, Jaemey, Jaemi, Jaemia, Jaemiah,
Jaemie, Jaemy, Jaemya, Jaemyah, Jahmee,
Jahmey, Jahmi, Jahmie, Jahmy, Jaimea,
Jaimeah, Jaimey, Jaimia, Jaimiah, Jaimmie,
Jaimy, Jaimya, Jaimyah

Jaimilynn (English) a combination of
Jaime + Lynn.
Jaimielin, Jaimielina, Jaimielinah, Jaimieline,
Jaimielyn, Jaimielyna, Jaimielyne, Jaimielynn,
Jaimielynne, Jaimilin, Jaimilina, Jaimilinah,
Jaimiline, Jaimilyn, Jaimilyna, Jaimilyne,
Jaimilynn, Jaimilynna, Jaimilynne, Jaymielin,
Jaymielina, Jaymielinah, Jaymieline, Jaymielyn,
Jaymielyna, Jaymielyne, Jaymielynn,
Jaymielynne, Jaymilin, Jaymilina, Jaymilinah,

Jaymiline, Jaymilyn, Jaymilyna, Jaymilyne, Jaymilynn, Jaymilynna, Jaymilynne

Jaina (Hebrew, American) a form of Janae.
Jainah

Jaira (Spanish) Jehovah teaches.
Jahra, Jahrah, Jairah, Jairy, Jayra, Jayrah

Jakalyn (American) a form of Jacqueline.
Jakalean, Jakaleana, Jakaleanah, Jakaleane, Jakaleen, Jakaleena, Jakaleenah, Jakaleene, Jakalein, Jakaleina, Jakaleinah, Jakaleine, Jakaleyn, Jakaleyna, Jakaleynah, Jakaleyne, Jakalin, Jakalina, Jakalinah, Jakaline, Jakalyna, Jakalynah, Jakalyne, Jakalynn, Jakalynna, Jakalynnah, Jakalynne

Jakeisha (American) a combination of Jakki + Aisha.
Jacqeesha, Jacqueisha, Jacqueysha, Jakeesha, Jakeeshia, Jakeishia, Jakeishiah, Jakeisia, Jakesha, Jakeshia, Jakeshiah, Jakeysha, Jakeyshia, Jakeyshiah, Jakisha, Jakishia, Jakishiah, Jaqueisha, Jaqueishia, Jaqueishiah, Jaqueysha, Jaquisha, Jaquysha

Jakelin (American) a form of Jacqueline.
Jakeline, Jakelyn, Jakelynn, Jakelynne

Jakeria (American) a form of Jacki.

Jakia (American) a form of Jacki.
Jakiah, Jakiya, Jakiyah, Jakkea, Jakkia, Jakkiah, Jakkya, Jakkyah

Jakinda (Spanish) a form of Jacinda.
Jackinda, Jackindra, Jakindah, Jakynda, Jakyndah, Jakyndra, Jakyndrah

Jakki (American) a form of Jacki.
Jakala, Jakea, Jakee, Jakeela, Jakeida, Jakeita, Jakel, Jakela, Jakelah, Jakelia, Jakeliah, Jakell, Jakella, Jakelle, Jakena, Jakenah, Jaket, Jaketa, Jaketah, Jakete, Jaketta, Jakettah, Jakette, Jakeva, Jakevah, Jakevia, Jaki, Jakie, Jakita, Jakke, Jakkee, Jakkie, Jakky, Jaky

Jakolyn (American) a form of Jacqueline.
Jakolean, Jakoleana, Jakoleanah, Jakoleane, Jakoleen, Jakoleena, Jakoleenah, Jakoleene, Jakolein, Jakoleina, Jakoleinah, Jakoleine, Jakoleyn, Jakoleyna, Jakoleynah, Jakoleyne, Jakolin, Jakolina, Jakolinah, Jakoline, Jakolyna, Jakolynah, Jakolyne, Jakolynn, Jakolynna, Jakolynnah, Jakolynne

Jakqueline (French) a form of Jacqueline.
Jakquelean, Jakqueleana, Jakqueleanah, Jakqueleane, Jakqueleen, Jakqueleena, Jakqueleenah, Jakqueleene, Jakquelein, Jakqueleina, Jakqueleinah, Jakqueleine, Jakqueleyn, Jakqueleyna, Jakqueleynah, Jakqueleyne, Jakquelin, Jakquelina, Jakquelinah, Jakquelyn, Jakquelyna, Jakquelynah, Jakquelyne, Jakquelynn, Jakquelynnah, Jakquelynne

Jakyra (American) a form of Jacki.
Jakira

Jala (Iranian) brightness. (Arabic) clarity, elucidation.

Jalea, Jalia (American) combinations of Jae + Leah.
Jaleah, Jalee, Jaleea, Jaleeya, Jaleia, Jalitza

Jalecia (American) a form of Jalisa.

Jaleesa (American) a form of Jalisa.
Jaleasa, Jalece, Jalecea, Jaleesah, Jaleese, Jaleesia, Jaleisa, Jaleisha, Jaleisya

Jalen (American) a short form of Jalena.

Jalena (American) a combination of Jane + Lena.
Jalaina, Jalainah, Jalaine, Jalana, Jalanah, Jalane, Jalani, Jalanie, Jalanna, Jalanne, Jalayna, Jalaynah, Jalayne, Jaleana, Jaleanah, Jaleena, Jaleenah, Jalenah, Jallena

Jalene (American) a form of Jalena.
Jalean, Jaleane, Jaleen, Jaleene

Jalesa, Jalessa (American) forms of Jalisa.
Jalese, Jalesha, Jaleshia, Jalesia

Jalicia, Jalisha (American) forms of Jalisa.
Jalisia

Jalila (Arabic) great.
Jalilah, Jalile, Jallila, Jallilah, Jallile, Jallyl, Jallyla, Jallyle

Jalinda (American) a combination of Jae + Linda.
Jaelinda, Jaelindah, Jaelynda, Jaelyndah, Jailinda, Jailindah, Jailynda, Jailyndah, Jaylinda, Jaylindah, Jaylynda, Jaylyndah

Jalini (Hindi) lives next to the ocean.
Jalinee, Jaliney, Jalinie, Jaliny

Jalisa, Jalissa (American) combinations of Jae + Lisa.
Jalise

Jaliya (American) a form of Jalea.

Jalyn, Jalynn (American) combinations of Jae + Lynn. See also Jaylyn.
Jalin, Jalina, Jalinah, Jaline, Jalyna, Jalynah, Jalyne, Jalynne

Jalysa (American) a form of Jalisa.
Jalyse, Jalyssa, Jalyssia

Jama (Sanskrit) daughter.
Jamah

Jamaica (Spanish) Geography: an island in the Caribbean.
Jamacia, Jameca, Jameica, Jamoka, Jemaica

Jamani (American) a form of Jami.
Jamana

Jamara (American) a form of Jamaria.

Jamaria (American) combinations of Jae + Maria.
Jamar, Jamarea, Jamaree, Jamari, Jamarie, Jameira, Jamerial

Jamecia (Spanish) a form of Jamaica.

Jamee (French) a form of Jaime.
Jamea, Jameah, Jamei, Jammee

Jameela (Arabic) a form of Jamila.
Jameelah, Jameele

Jameika (Spanish) a form of Jamaica.
Jamaika, Jamaka

Jameisha (American) a form of Jami.
Jamiesha

Jameka (Spanish) a form of Jamaica.
Jamecka, Jamekka

Jamekia (Spanish) a form of Jamaica.

Jamelia (Arabic) a form of Jamila.
Jahmelia, Jameelia, Jameeliah, Jameliah, Jamelya, Jamilya, Jamilyah

James (Hebrew) supplanter, substitute. (English) a form of Jacob. Bible: James the Great and James the Less were two of the Twelve Apostles.

Jamese (American) a form of Jami.
Jamesse, Jamis, Jamise

Jamesha (American) a form of Jami.
Jamesa, Jamesah, Jameshya, Jamesica, Jamesika, Jamesina, Jamesinah, Jamesine, Jamessa, Jameta, Jametta, Jamette, Jameysha, Jameyshya, Jameysina, Jameysinah, Jameysine, Jameysyna, Jameysynah, Jameysyne, Jammysha, Jamysha

Jameshia (American) a form of Jami.
Jameshyia, Jameyshia, Jameyshiah, Jameyshyah

Jamesia (American) a form of Jami.

Jamey (English) a form of Jami.
Jammey

Jami, Jamie (Hebrew, English) forms of James.
Jamani, Jamay, Jamii, Jamy, Jamye, Jamyee, Jaymie

Jamia (English) a form of Jami.
Jamea, Jamiah, Jamiea, Jamiia, Jammea, Jammia, Jammiah, Jammiia, Jammiiah, Jaymea, Jaymeah, Jaymia, Jaymmea, Jaymmeah, Jaymmia, Jaymmiah, Jaymmya, Jaymya, Jaymyea

Jamica, Jamika (Spanish) forms of Jamaica.
Jamikah, Jamyka, Jamykah, Jemika, Jemyka

Jamie-Lee (American) a form of Jamilee.
Jamielee

Jamie-Lynn (American) a form of Jamilynn.
Jami-Lyn, Jami-Lynn, Jami-Lynne, Jamie-Lyn, Jamie-Lynne

Jamila (Arabic) beautiful. See also Yamila.
Jahmeala, Jahmealah, Jahmeale, Jahmela, Jahmil, Jahmila, Jahmilah, Jahmill, Jahmilla, Jahmille, Jahmyla, Jahmylah, Jahmylla, Jahmyllah, Jahmylle, Jaimeala, Jaimealah, Jaimeale, Jaimila, Jaimilah, Jaimile, Jaimilla, Jaimillah, Jaimille, Jaimyla, Jaimylah, Jaimyle, Jaimylla, Jaimyllah, Jaimylle, Jameala, Jamealah, Jameale, Jameall, Jamealla, Jamealle, Jamela, Jamelah, Jamell, Jamella, Jamellah, Jamelle, Jamely, Jamiela, Jamyla, Jemila

Jamilah, Jamilla, Jamillah (Arabic) forms of Jamila.
Jamille

Jamilee (English) a combination of Jami + Lee.
Jahmilea, Jahmileah, Jahmilee, Jahmilei, Jahmileigh, Jahmili, Jahmilia, Jahmiliah, Jahmilie, Jahmily, Jaimilea, Jaimileah, Jaimilee, Jaimilei, Jaimileigh, Jaimiley, Jaimili, Jaimilia, Jaimiliah, Jaimilie, Jaimily, Jamilea, Jamileah, Jamilei, Jamileigh, Jamiley, Jamili, Jamilie, Jamily, Jaymilea, Jaymileah, Jaymilee, Jaymilei, Jaymileigh, Jaymiley, Jaymili, Jaymilia, Jaymiliah, Jaymilie, Jaymily, Jaymyly

Jamilia (Arabic) a form of Jamila.
Jamiliah, Jamillia, Jamilliah

Jamilynn (English) a combination of Jami + Lynn.
Jahmielin, Jahmielina, Jahmielinah, Jahmieline, Jahmielyn, Jahmielyna, Jahmielynah, Jahmielyne, Jahmielynn, Jahmielynne, Jahmilin, Jahmilina, Jahmilinah, Jahmiline, Jahmilyn, Jahmilyna, Jahmilyne, Jahmilynn, Jahmilynna, Jahmilynne, Jamielin, Jamielina, Jamielinah, Jamieline, Jamielyn, Jamielyna, Jamielyne, Jamielynn, Jamielynne, Jamilean, Jamileana, Jamileanah, Jamileane, Jamileen, Jamileena, Jamileenah, Jamileene, Jamilin, Jamilina, Jamilinah, Jamiline, Jamilyn, Jamilyna, Jamilynah, Jamilyne, Jamilynna, Jamilynne

Jamira (American) a form of Jamaria.

Jamisha (American) a form of Jami.
Jamisa, Jamisah, Jammesha, Jammisha

Jamison (English) child of James.
Jaemison, Jaemyson, Jaimison, Jaimyson, Jamiesen, Jamieson, Jamisen, Jamyson, Jaymison, Jaymyson

Jamiya (English) a form of Jami.
Jamiyah

Jammie (American) a form of Jami.
Jammi, Jammice, Jammii, Jammiie, Jammise

Jamonica (American) a combination of Jami + Monica.
Jamoni

Jamya (English) a form of Jami.
Jamyah

Jamylin (American) a form of Jamilynn.
Jamylin, Jamyline, Jamylyn, Jamylyne, Jamylynn, Jamylynne, Jaymylin, Jaymyline, Jaymylyn, Jaymylyne, Jaymylynn, Jaymylynne

Jan (English) a short form of Jane, Janet, Janice.
Jaan, Jandy, Jann, Janne

Jana (Hebrew) gracious, merciful. (Slavic) a form of Jane. See also Yana.
Jaana, Jaanah, Janah, Janalee, Janalisa, Janya, Janyah

Janae (American) a form of Jane. (Hebrew) a form of Jana.
Jaena, Jaeena, Janaea, Janaeh, Janah, Jannae

Janaé (American, Hebrew) a form of Janae.

Janai (American) a form of Janae.
Janaia, Janaiah, Janaira, Janaiya, Jannai, Jenai, Jenaia, Jennai

Janaki (Hindi) mother.
Janakee, Janakey, Janakie, Janaky

Janalee (American) a combination of Jana + Lee.
Janalea, Janaleah, Janalei, Janaleigh, Janaley, Janaly

Janalynn (American) a combination of Jana + Lynn.
Janalin, Janalina, Janaline, Janalyn, Janalyna, Janalyne, Janalynna, Janalynne

Janan (Arabic) heart; soul.
Jananee, Jananey, Janani, Janania, Jananiah, Jananie, Janann, Jananni, Janany

Janay, Janaye (American) a form of Jane. (Hebrew, Arabic) a form of Janna.
Jannay

Janaya (American) a form of Jane. (Hebrew, Arabic) a form of Janna.
Jananyah

Jane (Hebrew) God is gracious. See also Chavon, Jean, Joan, Juanita, Seana, Shana, Shawna, Sheena, Shona, Shunta, Sinead, Zaneta, Zanna, Zhana.

Jane (cont.)
Jaane, Jaeen, Jaeene, Jaen, Jaene, Jahne, Jain, Jaine, Janka, Jasia

Janea, Janee (American) a form of Janae.
Janée

Janecia (Hebrew, English) a form of Janice.
Janeciah

Janeen (French) a form of Janine.
Janeena, Janeene

Janeisha (American) a form of Janessa.
Janiesha

Janel, Janell, Jannell, Jannelle (French) forms of Janelle.
Jaenel, Jaenela, Jaenelah, Jaenell, Jainel, Jainela, Jainelah, Jainell, Janela, Janiel, Jannel, Janyll, Jaynel, Jaynela, Jaynelah, Jaynell

Janelle (French) a form of Jane.
Jaenele, Jaenella, Jaenellah, Jaenelle, Jainele, Jainella, Jainelle, Janele, Janelis, Janella, Janellah, Janelys, Janielle, Janille, Jannella, Jannellah, Jannellies, Jaynele, Jaynella, Jaynelle

Janelly, Janely (French) forms of Janelle.
Janelli, Janellie

Janese (Hebrew) a form of Janis. (English) a form of Jane.
Janesey, Janess, Janesse

Janesha (American) a form of Janessa.
Janeshia, Janishia, Jannesha, Jannisha, Janysha, Jenesha, Jenisha, Jennisha

Janessa (American) a form of Jane.
Janeesa, Janesa, Janesea, Janesia, Janeska, Janessi, Janessia, Janiesa, Janisa, Janisah, Janissa, Jannesa, Jannessa, Jannisa, Jannisah, Jannissa, Jannysa, Jannysah, Janysa, Janysah, Janyssa, Janyssah, Jenesa, Jenissa, Jennisa, Jennissa

Janet (English) a form of Jane. See also Jessie, Yanet.
Janata, Janeat, Janeata, Janeatah, Janeate, Janeet, Janeeta, Janeetah, Janeete, Janeta, Janetah, Janete, Janneta, Jannite, Janot, Janota, Janote, Janta, Jante, Janyt, Janyte, Jenet, Jenete

Janeth (English) a form of Janet.
Janetha, Janith, Janithe, Janneth

Janett, Janette, Jannet, Jannette (French) forms of Janet.
Janeatt, Janeatte, Jannett, Jannitte, Janytte

Janetta (French) a form of Janet.
Janeattah, Janettah, Jannetta

Janey, Jani, Janie, Jany (English) familiar forms of Jane.
Janiyh, Jaynee

Jania (Hebrew) a form of Jana. (Slavic) a form of Jane.
Janiah

Janica (Hebrew) a form of Jane.
Janicka

Janice (Hebrew) God is gracious. (English) a familiar form of Jane. See also Genice.
Janece, Janizzette, Jannice, Jannyc, Jannyce, Janyce, Jhanice, Jynice

Janick (Slavic) a short form of Janica.
Janyck

Janiece (Hebrew, English) a form of Janice.
Janeace, Janeece, Janeice, Janneece, Janneice, Janniece

Janik (Slavic) a short form of Janika.
Janike, Janikke, Jannik, Jannike, Janyk

Janika (Slavic) a form of Jane.
Janaca, Janeca, Janecka, Janeeca, Janeeka, Janeica, Janeika, Janeka, Janieka, Janikka, Janka, Jankia, Jannica, Jannika, Jannyca, Janyca, Janycah, Janycka, Janyka, Jonika

Janina (French) a form of Jane.
Janeana, Janena, Janinah, Jannina, Jannyna, Janyna, Janynah, Jenina, Jenyna, Jenynah

Janine (French) a form of Jane.
Janean, Janeane, Janeann, Janeanne, Janene, Jannen, Jannene, Jannine, Jannyne, Janyne, Jeneen, Jenyne

Janiqua (French) a form of Jane.
Janicqua, Janicquah, Janiquah, Janyqua, Janyquah, Jeniqua, Jeniquah, Jenyqua, Jenyquah

Janique (French) a form of Jane.
Janic, Janicque, Jannique, Janyque, Jenique, Jenyque

Janis, Janise (Hebrew, English) forms of Janice.
Janease, Janees, Janeese, Janeise, Janiese, Janisse, Jannis, Jannise, Jannisse, Jannys, Jannyse, Janys, Janyse, Janyss, Janysse, Jenesse, Jenis, Jennise, Jennisse

Janisha (American) a form of Janessa.

Janita (American) a form of Juanita. See also Genita.
Janeata, Janeatah, Janeeta, Janeetah, Janeita, Janeitah, Janitah, Janitra, Janitza, Janneta, Jannita, Jannitah, Jannitta, Jannittah, Janyta, Janytah, Janytta, Janyttah, Jaynita, Jaynite, Jaynitta, Jaynitte, Jeneata, Jeneatah, Jeneeta, Jeneetah, Jenita, Jenitah, Jennita, Jennitah, Jennyta, Jenyta, Jenytah

Janna (Arabic) harvest of fruit. (Hebrew) a short form of Johana.
Jannae, Jannai, Jannia, Janniah, Jannya, Jannyah

Jannah (Hebrew, English) a form of Janna.

Jannali (Australian) moon.
Janali, Janalia, Janaliah, Janalie, Jannalea, Jannaleah, Jannalee, Jannalei, Jannaleigh, Jannaley, Jannalia, Jannaliah, Jannalie, Jannaly, Jannalya, Jannalyah

Jannick (Slavic) a form of Janick.

Jannie (English) a familiar form of Jan, Jane.
Janney, Janni, Janny

Japonica (Latin) from Japan. Botany: an ornamental shrub with red flowers native to Japan.
Japonicah, Japonicka, Japonika, Japonikah, Japonyca, Japonycah, Japonycka, Japonyka, Japonykah

Jaquana (American) a combination of Jacqueline + Anna.
Jaqua, Jaquai, Jaquanda, Jaquania, Jaquanna

Jaquelen, Jaquelin, Jaqueline, Jaquelyn (French) forms of Jacqueline.
Jaquala, Jaqualin, Jaqualine, Jaquelean, Jaqueleana, Jaqueleanah, Jaqueleane, Jaqueleen, Jaqueleena, Jaqueleenah, Jaqueleene, Jaquelein, Jaqueleina, Jaqueleinah, Jaqueleine, Jaqueleyn, Jaqueleyna, Jaqueleynah,

Jaqueleyne, Jaquelina, Jaquelinah, Jaquella, Jaquelyna, Jaquelynah, Jaquelyne, Jaquelynn, Jaquelynna, Jaquelynnah, Jaquelynne, Jaquera, Jaqulene, Jaquonna

Jaquetta (French) a form of Jacqui.

Jaquiline (French) a form of Jacqueline.
Jaquilean, Jaquileana, Jaquileanah, Jaquileane, Jaquileen, Jaquileena, Jaquileenah, Jaquileene, Jaquilein, Jaquileina, Jaquileinah, Jaquileine, Jaquileyn, Jaquileyna, Jaquileynah, Jaquileyne, Jaquilin, Jaquilina, Jaquilinah, Jaquilyn, Jaquilyna, Jaquilynah, Jaquilyne, Jaquilynn, Jaquilynna, Jaquilynnah, Jaquilynne

Jaquita (French) a form of Jacqui.

Jardena (French, Spanish) garden. (Hebrew) a form of Jordan.
Jardan, Jardana, Jardanah, Jardane, Jardania, Jarden, Jardene, Jardenia, Jardin, Jardina, Jardinah, Jardine, Jardyn, Jardyna, Jardyne, Jardynia

Jarian (American) a combination of Jane + Marian.

Jarita (Arabic) earthen water jug.
Jara, Jareata, Jareatah, Jareet, Jareeta, Jareetah, Jareita, Jareitah, Jaretta, Jari, Jaria, Jariah, Jarica, Jarida, Jarietta, Jariette, Jarika, Jarina, Jarinah, Jaritta, Jaritte, Jaritza, Jarixa, Jarnita, Jarnite, Jarrika, Jarrike, Jarrina, Jarrine, Jaryta, Jarytah, Jaryte, Jarytta, Jarytte

Jarmilla (Slavic) a form of Yarmilla.
Jarmila, Jarmilah, Jarmile, Jarmill, Jarmille, Jarmyla, Jarmylah, Jarmyle, Jarmyll, Jarmylla, Jarmyllah, Jarmylle

Jarnila (Arabic) beautiful.
Jarnilah, Jarnile, Jarnill, Jarnilla, Jarnillah, Jarnille, Jarnyl, Jarnyla, Jarnylah, Jarnyle, Jarnyll, Jarnylla, Jarnyllah, Jarnylle

Jarvia (German) skilled with a spear.
Jarviah, Jarvya, Jarvyah

Jarvinia (German) intelligent; keen as a spear.
Jarviniah, Jarvinya, Jarvinyah, Jarvynya, Jarvynyah

Jas (American) a short form of Jasmine.
Jase, Jass, Jaz, Jazz, Jazze

Jasa (Polish) a form of Jane.
Jaysa, Jasyah

Jasey (Polish) a form of Jane.
Jasea

Jasia (Polish) a form of Jane.
Jaisha, Jasha, Jashae, Jashala, Jashona, Jashonte, Jazia, Jaziah, Jazya, Jazyah, Jazzia, Jazziah, Jazzya, Jazzyah

Jaskiran (Sikh) a form of Jaskaran (see Boys' Names).

Jasleen (Latin) a form of Jocelyn.
Jaslene, Jaslien, Jasline

Jaslyn (Latin) a form of Jocelyn.
Jaslin, Jaslynn, Jaslynne

Jasma (Persian) a short form of Jasmine.

Jasmain, Jasmaine (Persian) forms of Jasmine.
Jasmane, Jassmain, Jassmaine

Jasman (Persian) a form of Jasmine.

Jasmarie (American) a combination of Jasmine + Marie.
Jasmari

Jasmeen (Persian) a form of Jasmine.

Jasmeet (Persian) a form of Jasmine.
Jasmit, Jassmit

Jasmin, Jasmyn, Jasmyne, Jassmine (Persian) forms of Jasmine.
Jasmynn, Jasmynne, Jassmin, Jassminn, Jassmyn

Jasmina (Persian) a form of Jasmine.
Jasminah, Jasmyna, Jasmynah, Jassma, Jazmina, Jazminah, Jazmyna, Jazmynah, Jazzmina, Jazzminah, Jazzmyna, Jazzmynah, Jesmina, Jesminah, Jesmyna, Jesmynah, Jessmina, Jessminah, Jessmyna, Jessmynah, Jezmina, Jezminah, Jezzmina, Jezzminah, Jezzmyna, Jezzmynah

Jasmine (Persian) jasmine flower. See also Jessamine, Yasmin.
Jasimin, Jasmain, Jasme, Jasmen, Jasmene, Jasminne, Jasmira, Jasmon, Jassmon, Jesmin, Jesmine, Jesmyn, Jesmyne, Jessmin, Jessmine, Jessmyn, Jessmyne

Jasper (French) red, yellow, or brown ornamental stone.
Jaspa, Jaspah, Jaspar, Jaspera, Jaspere

Jaspreet (Punjabi) virtuous.
Jasparit, Jasparita, Jasparite, Jasprit, Jasprita, Jasprite, Jaspryta, Jasprytah, Jaspryte

Jassi (Persian) a familiar form of Jasmine.
Jasee, Jasi, Jasie, Jassee, Jassey, Jassie, Jassy

Jatara (American) a combination of Jane + Tara.
Jatarah, Jataria, Jatariah, Jatarra, Jatarrah, Jatarria, Jatori, Jatoria, Jatoriah, Jatorie, Jatory, Jatorya, Jatoryah

Javana (Malayan) from Java.
Javanah, Javanna, Javannah, Javanne, Javannia, Jawana, Jawanna, Jawn

Javiera (Spanish) owner of a new house. See also Xaviera.
Javeera, Javeerah, Javierah, Javyra, Javyrah, Viera

Javon (Malayan) a short form of Javana.

Javona, Javonna (Malayan) forms of Javana.
Javonah, Javonda, Javone, Javoni, Javonia, Javonn, Javonnah, Javonne, Javonni, Javonnia, Javonniah, Javonya, Javonyah

Jaya (Hindi) victory.
Jaea, Jaia, Jaiah, Jayah

Jayanna (American) a combination of Jaye + Anna.
Jay-Anna, Jaye-Anna, Jayeanna

Jayce, Jaycee, Jayci, Jaycie (American) forms of Jacey.
Jaycey, Jaycy

Jayda (Spanish) a form of Jada.
Jaydah, Jeyda

Jayde (Spanish) a form of Jade.
Jayd

Jaydee (American) a combination of the initials J. + D.
Jadee, Jadey, Jady, Jaydey, Jaydi, Jaydie, Jaydy

Jayden (Spanish) a form of Jade.
Jaydeen, Jaydene, Jaydin, Jaydn, Jaydon

Jaye (Latin) jaybird.
Jae, Jah, Jay

Jayla (American) a short form of Jayleen.
Jaylaa, Jaylah, Jaylea, Jayleah, Jaylei, Jayleigh, Jayley, Jayli, Jaylia, Jayliah, Jaylie, Jayly

Jaylee (American) a familiar form of Jaylyn.

Jayleen, Jaylene (American) forms of Jaylyn.
Jayelene, Jayleana, Jayleena, Jayleenah, Jayleene, Jaylena, Jaylenne, Jayline

Jaylen, Jaylin (American) forms of Jaylyn.
Jaylan, Jaylinn

Jaylyn, Jaylynn (American) combinations of Jaye + Lynn. See also Jalyn.
Jaylyna, Jaylynah, Jaylyne, Jaylynne

Jayme, Jaymee, Jaymi, Jaymie (English) forms of Jami.
Jayma, Jaymey, Jaymine, Jaymini, Jaymma, Jaymmi, Jaymmie, Jaymmy, Jaymy, Jaymye, Jaymyee

Jayna (Hebrew) a form of Jane.
Jaena, Jaenah, Jaina, Jainah, Jaynae, Jaynah, Jaynna, Jaynnah

Jayne (Hindi) victorious. (English) a form of Jane.
Jayn, Jaynn, Jaynne

Jaynee, Jaynie (English) familiar forms of Jayne.
Jaynay, Jayni

Jazlyn, Jazlynn, Jazzlyn (American) a combinations of Jazman + Lynn.
Jazaline, Jazalyn, Jazlean, Jazleana, Jazleanah, Jazleane, Jazleen, Jazleena, Jazleenah, Jazleene, Jazlene, Jazlin, Jazlina, Jazlinah, Jazline, Jazlon, Jazlyna, Jazlynah, Jazlyne, Jazlynna, Jazlynnah, Jazlynne, Jazzalyn, Jazzleen, Jazzleena, Jazzleenah, Jazzleene, Jazzlene, Jazzlin, Jazzlina, Jazzlinah, Jazzline, Jazzlyna, Jazzlynah, Jazzlyne, Jazzlynn, Jazzlynna, Jazzlynnah, Jazzlynne

Jazman, Jazmen, Jazmin, Jazmine, Jazmyn, Jazmyne, Jazzmen, Jazzmin, Jazzmine, Jazzmyn, Jazzmyne (Persian) forms of Jasmine.
Jazmaine, Jazminn, Jazmon, Jazmynn, Jazmynne, Jazzman, Jazzmeen, Jazzmene,

Jazzmenn, Jazzmon, Jezmin, Jezmine, Jezzmin, Jezzmine, Jezzmyn, Jezzmyne

Jazz (American) jazz.
Jaz, Jazee, Jazey, Jazi, Jazie, Jazy, Jazzee, Jazzey, Jazzi, Jazzie, Jazzy

Jean (Scottish) God is gracious. See also Kini.
Jeanann, Jeancie, Jeane, Jeaneia, Jeaneva, Jeanice, Jeanmaria, Jeanmarie, Jeann, Jeanné, Jeantelle, Jeen, Jeene

Jeana, Jeanna (Scottish) forms of Jean.
Jeanae, Jeannae, Jeannah, Jeannia, Jeena, Jeenia

Jeanelle (American) a form of Jenell.
Jeanell

Jeanetta (French) a form of Jean.
Jeanettah

Jeanette, Jeannett, Jeannette (French) forms of Jean.
Jeanet, Jeaneta, Jeanetah, Jeanete, Jeanett, Jeanetton, Jeanita, Jeannete, Jeannetta, Jeannita, Jeannot, Jinet, Jineta, Jinetah, Jinete, Jinett, Jinetta, Jinettah, Jinette, Jonet, Joneta, Jonetah, Jonete, Jonett, Jonetta, Jonettah, Jonette, Jynet, Jyneta, Jynetah, Jynete, Jynett, Jynetta, Jynettah, Jynette

Jeanie, Jeannie (Scottish) familiar forms of Jean.
Jeanee, Jeani, Jeannee, Jeanney, Jeanny, Jeany

Jeanine, Jeannine, Jenine (Scottish) forms of Jean. See also Geneen.
Jeaneane, Jeaneen, Jeanene, Jeanina, Jeannina, Jennine

Jeanne (Scottish) a form of Jean.

Jelani (Russian) a form of Jelena.
Jelanni

Jelena (Russian) a form of Helen. See also Yelena.
Jelaina, Jelainah, Jelaine, Jelana, Jelanah, Jelane, Jelayna, Jelaynah, Jelayne, Jelean, Jeleana, Jeleanah, Jeleane, Jeleen, Jeleena, Jeleenah, Jeleene, Jelenah, Jelene, Jelin, Jelina, Jelinah, Jeline, Jelyn, Jelyna, Jelynah, Jelyne

Jelisa (American) a combination of Jean + Lisa.
Jelesha, Jelise, Jellese, Jellice, Jelysa, Jillisa

Jelissa (American) a form of Jelisa.
Jelessa, Jelyssa, Jillissa

Jem (Hebrew) a short form of Jemima.
Gem, Jemee, Jemey, Jemi, Jemie, Jemm, Jemy

Jemila (Arabic) a form of Jamila.
Jemeala, Jemealah, Jemeela, Jemeelah, Jemeelia, Jemeeliah, Jemela, Jemelah, Jemelia, Jemeliah, Jemila, Jemilla, Jemillah, Jemille, Jemyl, Jemyla, Jemylah, Jemyle, Jemyll, Jemylla, Jemyllah, Jemylle

Jemima (Hebrew) dove.
Gemima, Gemimah, Jamim, Jamima, Jemimah, Jemyma, Jemymah

Jemma (Hebrew) a short form of Jemima. (English) a form of Gema.
Jema, Jemah, Jemia, Jemiah, Jemmah, Jemmee, Jemmey, Jemmi, Jemmia, Jemmiah, Jemmie, Jemmy, Jemmya, Jemmyah

Jena, Jennah (Arabic) forms of Jenna.
Jenah, Jenal, Jenya, Jenyah

Jenae, Jenay (American, Hebrew) forms of Janae. (Arabic) forms of Jenna.
Jenai, Jenea, Jennae, Jennay, Jennaye

Jenaya (American, Hebrew) a form of Janae. (Arabic) a form of Jenna.
Jenia, Jeniah, Jennaya

Jendaya (Zimbabwean) thankful.
Daya, Jenda, Jendaia, Jandaiah, Jendayah

Jeneleah (American) a combination of Jenny + Leah.
Jenalea, Jenaleah, Jenalia, Jenaliah, Jenelea, Jenelia, Jeneliah, Jenilea, Jenileah, Jenilia, Jeniliah, Jennalea, Jennaleah, Jennalia, Jennaliah, Jennelea, Jenneleah, Jennelia, Jenneliah, Jennilea, Jennileah, Jennilia, Jenniliah, Jennylea, Jennyleah, Jennylia, Jennyliah, Jenylea, Jenyleah, Jenylia, Jenyliah

Jenell, Jenelle, Jennelle (American) combinations of Jenny + Nell.
Genell, Jenall, Jenalle, Jenel, Jenela, Jenelah, Jenele, Jenella, Jenellah, Jenille, Jennel, Jennele, Jennell, Jennella, Jennielle, Jennille, Jinelle, Jinnell

Jenessa (American) a form of Jenisa.
Jenesa, Jenese, Jenesia, Jenessia, Jennesa, Jennese, Jennessa, Jinessa

Jenette (French) a form of Jean.
Jeneta, Jenetah, Jenett, Jenetta, Jenettah, Jennet, Jennett, Jennetta, Jennette, Jennita

Jeneva (French) a form of Geneva.
Janeva, Jeaneva, Jenava, Jenavah, Jenevah, Jenevia, Jeneviah, Jenniva, Jennivah

Jeni, Jenni, Jennie (Welsh) familiar forms of Jennifer. See also Jenny.
Jenee, Jenie, Jenne, Jenné, Jennee, Jenney, Jennia, Jenniah, Jennier, Jennita, Jennora

Jenica, Jenika, Jennica, Jennicah (Romanian) forms of Jane.
Jeneca, Jenicah, Jenicka, Jenickah, Jenikah, Jenikka, Jeniqua, Jeniquah, Jenique, Jennicka, Jennickah, Jennika, Jennikah, Jenniqua, Jenniquah, Jennique, Jennyca, Jennycah, Jennycka, Jennyckah, Jennyka, Jennykah, Jennyqua, Jennyquah, Jenyca, Jenycah, Jenyka

Jenice, Jenise (Hebrew) forms of Janice.
Jenicee, Jenicy, Jennise, Jennyce, Jennyse

Jenifer, Jeniffer, Jenniffer (Welsh) forms of Jennifer.
Jenifar, Jenipher

Jenilee, Jennilee (American) combinations of Jeni + Lee. See also Jenny Lee.
Jenelee, Jenelei, Jeneleigh, Jeneley, Jeneli, Jenelie, Jenelly, Jenely, Jenilei, Jenileigh, Jeniley, Jenili, Jenilie, Jenily, Jennelee, Jennelei, Jenneleigh, Jennely, Jennielee, Jennilee, Jennilei, Jennileigh, Jenniley, Jennili, Jennilie, Jennily, Jinnalee

Jenisa (American) a combination of Jennifer + Nisa.
Jenisha, Jenissa, Jenisse, Jennisa, Jennise, Jennisha, Jennissa, Jennisse, Jennysa, Jennyssa, Jenysa, Jenyse, Jenyssa, Jenysse

Jenka (Czech) a form of Jane.

Jenna (Arabic) small bird. (Welsh) a short form of Jennifer. See also Gen.
Janah, Jennae, Jennai, Jennat, Jennay, Jennaya, Jennaye, Jhenna

Jenna-Lee, Jennalee (American) combinations of Jenna + Lee.

Jenalee, Jenalei, Jenaleigh, Jenaley, Jenali, Jenalie, Jenaly, Jenna-Leigh, Jennalei, Jennaleigh

Jennafer (Welsh) a form of Jennifer.
Jenafar, Jenafer, Jennafar

Jennifer (Welsh) white wave; white phantom. A form of Guinevere. See also Gennifer, Ginnifer, Yenifer.
Jen, Jenefar, Jenefer, Jeneffar, Jeneffer, Jennefar, Jennefer, Jennifar, Jenniferanne, Jenniferlee, Jenniffe, Jenniffier, Jennifier, Jenniphe, Jennipher

Jennilyn, Jennilynn (American) a combination of Jeni + Lynn.
Jenalin, Jenalyn, Jenelyn, Jenilyn, Jennalin, Jennaline, Jennalyn, Jennalyne, Jennalynn, Jennalynne, Jennilin, Jenniline, Jennilyne, Jennilynne

Jenny (Welsh) a familiar form of Jennifer. See also Jeni.
Jenney, Jennya, Jennyah, Jeny, Jenya, Jenyah

Jenny Lee (American) a combination of Jenny + Lee. See also Jenilee.
Jennylee, Jennylei, Jennyleigh, Jennyley, Jennyli, Jennylie, Jennyly, Jenylee, Jenylei, Jenyleigh, Jenyley, Jenyli, Jenylie, Jenyly

Jennyfer (Welsh) a form of Jennifer.
Jennyfar, Jenyfar, Jenyfer

Jensen (Scandinavian) a form of Janson (see Boys' Names).
Jensan, Jensin, Jenson, Jensyn

Jensine (Welsh) a form of Jeni.

Jeraldine (English) a form of Geraldine.
Jeraldeen, Jeraldeena, Jeraldena, Jeraldene, Jeraldin, Jeraldina, Jeraldinah, Jeraldyn, Jeraldyna, Jeraldynah, Jeraldyne, Jeralee

Jeremia (Hebrew) God will uplift.
Jeramia, Jeramiah, Jeramya, Jeramyah, Jeremiah, Jeremya, Jeremyah

Jereni (Russian) a form of Irene.
Jerena, Jerenae, Jerenee, Jerenia, Jereniah, Jerenie, Jereny, Jerenya, Jerenyah, Jerina

Jeri, Jerri, Jerrie (American) short forms of Jeraldine. See also Geri.
Jera, JeRae, Jerae, Jeree, Jerey, Jerie, Jeriel, Jerilee, Jerinda, Jerra, Jerrah, Jerrece, Jerree,

Jerrey, Jerriann, Jerrilee, Jerrine, Jerry, Jerrylea, Jerrylee, Jerryne, Jery, Jerzy

Jerica, Jericka, Jerika, Jerrica, Jerrika (American) combinations of Jeri + Erica.
Jereca, Jerecka, Jericah, Jerice, Jerikah, Jeriqua, Jeriquah, Jerreka, Jerricah, Jerricca, Jerrice, Jerricha, Jerricka, Jerrieka, Jeryca, Jerycah, Jerycka, Jeryka, Jerykah, Jeryqua, Jeryquah

Jerilyn (American) a combination of Jeri + Lynn.
Jeralin, Jeralina, Jeralinah, Jeraline, Jeralyn, Jeralyna, Jeralynah, Jeralyne, Jeralynn, Jeralynne, Jerelin, Jereline, Jerelyn, Jerelyne, Jerelynn, Jerelynne, Jerilin, Jerilina, Jerilinah, Jeriline, Jerilyna, Jerilynah, Jerilyne, Jerilynn, Jerilynna, Jerilynnah, Jerilynne, Jerrilin, Jerriline, Jerrilyn, Jerrilyne, Jerrilynn, Jerrilynne, Jerylin, Jerylina, Jerylinah, Jeryline, Jerylyn, Jerylyna, Jerylynah, Jerylyne

Jermaine (French) a form of Germaine.
Jerma, Jermain, Jermaina, Jermainah, Jerman, Jermanay, Jermanaye, Jermane, Jermanee, Jermani, Jermanique, Jermany, Jermayn, Jermayna, Jermaynah, Jermayne, Jermecia, Jermia, Jermice, Jermicia, Jermila

Jermeka (French) a form of Jermaine.
Jermika

Jeroma (Latin) holy.
Geroma, Geromah, Jeromah, Jerometta, Jeromette, Jeromima, Jeromyma

Jerusha (Hebrew) inheritance.
Jerushah, Yerusha

Jesenia, Jessenia (Arabic) flower.
Jescenia, Jesceniah, Jescenya, Jescenyah, Jeseniah, Jesenya, Jesenyah, Jessennia, Jessenya

Jesi, Jesse, Jessi, Jessye (Hebrew) forms of Jessie.
Jese, Jessee

Jesica, Jesika, Jessicca, Jessika (Hebrew) forms of Jessica.
Jesicah, Jesicca, Jesikah, Jesikkah, Jessikah

Jessa (American) a short form of Jessalyn, Jessamine, Jessica.
Jesa, Jesha, Jessah

Jessalyn (American) a combination of Jessica + Lynn.

Jessalyn *(cont.)*
Jesalin, Jesaline, Jesalyn, Jesalyne, Jesalynn, Jesalynne, Jessalin, Jessalina, Jessalinah, Jessaline, Jessalyna, Jessalynah, Jessalyne, Jessalynn, Jessalynne, Jesselin, Jesseline, Jesselyn, Jesselyne, Jesselynn, Jesselynne

Jessamine (French) a form of Jasmine.
Jesamin, Jesamina, Jesaminah, Jesamine, Jesamon, Jesamona, Jesamone, Jesamyn, Jesamyna, Jesamynah, Jesamyne, Jessamin, Jessamina, Jessaminah, Jessamon, Jessamona, Jessamonah, Jessamone, Jessamy, Jessamya, Jessamyah, Jessamyn, Jessamyna, Jessamynah, Jessamyne, Jessemin, Jessemina, Jesseminah, Jessemine, Jessimin, Jessimine, Jessmin, Jessmina, Jessminah, Jessmine, Jessmon, Jessmona, Jessmonah, Jessmone, Jessmy, Jessmyn, Jessmyna, Jessmynah, Jessmyne

Jesseca (Hebrew) a form of Jessica.
Jessecah, Jesseeca, Jesseeka, Jesseka, Jessekah

Jessica (Hebrew) wealthy. Literature: a name perhaps invented by Shakespeare for a character in his play *The Merchant of Venice*. See also Gessica, Yesica.
Jesicka, Jessaca, Jessca, Jesscia, Jessia, Jessicah, Jessicia, Jessicka, Jessieka, Jessiqua, Jessiquah, Jessique, Jezeca, Jezecah, Jezecka, Jezeka, Jezekah, Jezica, Jezicah, Jezicka, Jezika, Jezikah, Jeziqua, Jeziquah, Jezyca, Jezycah, Jezycka, Jezyka, Jisica, Jisicah, Jisicka, Jisika, Jisikah, Jisiqua, Jisiquah, Jysica, Jysicah, Jysicka, Jysika, Jyssica, Jyssicah, Jyssicka, Jyssika, Jyssikah, Jyssiqua, Jyssiquah, Jyssyca, Jyssycka, Jyssyka, Jyssykah, Jysyka, Jysykah, Jysyqua, Jysyquah

Jessica-Lynn (American) a combination of Jessica + Lynn.
Jessica-Lyn, Jessica-Lynne, Jessicalyn, Jessicalynn, Jessicalynne

Jessie, Jessy (Hebrew) short forms of Jessica. (Scottish) forms of Janet.
Jescie, Jesea, Jesee, Jesey, Jesie, Jess, Jessé, Jessea, Jessee, Jessey, Jessia, Jessiah, Jessiya, Jesy

Jessilyn (American) a form of Jessalyn.
Jesilin, Jesiline, Jesilyn, Jesilyne, Jesilynn, Jesilynne, Jessilynn

Jesslyn (American) a short form of Jessalyn.
Jesslin, Jesslynn, Jesslynne

Jessyca, Jessyka (Hebrew) forms of Jessica.
Jessycka, Jessyqua, Jessyquah

Jesus (Hebrew) God is my salvation. A form of Joshua. Bible: son of Mary and Joseph, believed by Christians to be the Son of God.

Jésusa (Hebrew, Spanish) a form of Jesus.
Jesusita, Jesusyta

Jetta (English) jet black mineral. (American) a familiar form of Jevette.
Jeta, Jetah, Jetia, Jetiah, Jetje, Jett, Jettah, Jette, Jetti, Jettia, Jettiah, Jettie, Jetty, Jettya, Jettyah

Jevette (American) a combination of Jean + Yvette.
Jeva, Jeveta, Jevetta

Jewel (French) precious gem.
Jewal, Jewele, Jewelei, Jeweleigh, Jeweli, Jewelie, Jewely, Juel, Juela, Juele

Jewelana (American) a combination of Jewel + Anna.
Jewelanah, Jewelann, Jeweliana, Jeweliann, Juelana, Juelanah, Julana, Julanah

Jewell (French) a form of Jewel.
Jewella, Jewelle, Jewellea, Jewelleah, Jewellee, Jewellene, Jewellie

Jezabel (Hebrew) a form of Jezebel.
Jesabel, Jesabela, Jesabelah, Jesabele, Jesabell, Jesabella, Jesabellah, Jesabelle, Jessabel, Jessabela, Jessabelah, Jessabele, Jessabell, Jessabella, Jessabellah, Jessabelle, Jezabela, Jezabelah, Jezabele, Jezabell, Jezabella, Jezabellah, Jezabelle

Jezebel (Hebrew) unexalted; impure. Bible: the wife of King Ahab.
Jesibel, Jessebel, Jessebela, Jessebelah, Jessebele, Jessebell, Jessebella, Jessebellah, Jessebelle, Jez, Jezebela, Jezebelah, Jezebele, Jezebell, Jezebella, Jezebellah, Jezebelle

Jianna (Italian) a form of Giana.
Jiana, Jianah, Jianina, Jianine, Jiannah, Jianni, Jiannini, Jyana, Jyanah, Jyanna, Jyannah

Jibon (Hindi) life.
Jibona, Jibonah, Jibone, Jybon, Jybona, Jybonah, Jybone

Jill (English) a short form of Jillian.
Jil, Jyl, Jyll

Jillaine (Latin) a form of Jillian.
Jilain, Jilaina, Jilaine, Jilane, Jilayne, Jillain, Jillaina, Jillane, Jillayn, Jillayna, Jillayne, Jylain, Jylaina, Jylaine, Jylan, Jylane, Jyllain, Jyllaina, Jyllaine, Jyllane, Jyllanne, Jyllayn, Jyllayna, Jyllayne

Jillanna (Latin) a form of Jillian.
Jilan, Jilana, Jillana, Jillann, Jillannah, Jillanne, Jylana, Jyllana, Jyllanah, Jyllann, Jyllanna, Jyllannah

Jilleen (Irish) a form of Jillian.
Jileen, Jilene, Jiline, Jillene, Jillenne, Jilline, Jillyn

Jilli (Australian) today.
Jilea, Jileah, Jilee, Jilei, Jileigh, Jili, Jilie, Jillea, Jilleah, Jillee, Jillei, Jilleigh, Jilley, Jillie, Jilly, Jily, Jylea, Jyleah, Jylee, Jylei, Jyleigh, Jyley, Jyli, Jylie, Jyllea, Jylleah, Jyllee, Jyllei, Jylleigh, Jylli, Jyllie, Jylly, Jyly

Jillian (Latin) youthful. See also Gillian.
Jilian, Jiliana, Jilianah, Jiliane, Jiliann, Jilianna, Jiliannah, Jilianne, Jilienna, Jilienne, Jillaine, Jillanna, Jilleen, Jilliana, Jillianah, Jilliane, Jilliann, Jillianna, Jilliannah, Jillianne, Jillien, Jillienne, Jillion, Jilliyn, Jillyan, Jillyana, Jillyanah, Jillyane, Jillyann, Jillyanna, Jillyannah, Jillyanne, Jilyan, Jilyana, Jilyanah, Jilyane, Jilyann, Jilyanna, Jilyannah, Jilyanne, Jyllian

Jimena (Hebrew, American) a form of Jimi.

Jimi (Hebrew) supplanter, substitute.
Jimae, Jimaria, Jimee, Jimella, Jimey, Jimia, Jimiah, Jimie, Jimiyah, Jimmee, Jimmeka, Jimmet, Jimmey, Jimmi, Jimmia, Jimmie, Jimmy, Jimy, Jymee, Jymey, Jymi, Jymie, Jymmee, Jymmey, Jymmi, Jymmie, Jymmy, Jymy

Jimisha (American) a combination of Jimi + Aisha.
Jimica, Jimicia, Jimmicia, Jimysha

Jin (Japanese) tender. (American) a short form of Ginny, Jinny.
Jyn

Jina (Swahili) baby with a name. (Italian) a form of Gina.
Jinae, Jinah, Jinan, Jinda, Jinna, Jinnae, Jinnah, Jyna, Jynah, Jynna, Jynnah

Jinny (Scottish) a familiar form of Jenny. (American) a familiar form of Virginia. See also Ginny.
Jinee, Jiney, Jini, Jinie, Jinnee, Jinney, Jinni, Jinnie, Jiny, Jynee, Jyney, Jyni, Jynie, Jynnee, Jynney, Jynni, Jynnie, Jynny, Jyny

Jira (African) related by blood.

Jirakee (Australian) waterfall, cascade.
Jirakei, Jirakey, Jiraki, Jirakie, Jiraky, Jyrakee, Jyrakei, Jyrakey, Jyraki, Jyrakie, Jyraky

Jirina (Czech) a form of Georgia.
Jirah, Jireana, Jireanah, Jireena, Jireenah, Jireh, Jirinah, Jiryna, Jirynah, Jyreana, Jyreanah, Jyreena, Jyreenah, Jyrina, Jyrinah, Jyryna, Jyrynah

Jizelle (American) a form of Giselle.
Jessel, Jezel, Jezela, Jezelah, Jezele, Jezell, Jezella, Jezellah, Jezelle, Jisel, Jisela, Jisele, Jisell, Jisella, Jiselle, Jissel, Jissell, Jissella, Jisselle, Jizel, Jizela, Jizele, Jizell, Jizella, Joselle, Jyzel, Jyzela, Jyzele, Jyzell, Jyzella, Jyzelle

Jo (American) a short form of Joana, Jolene, Josephine.
Joangie, Joe, Joee, Joetta, Joette, Joh

Joan (Hebrew) God is gracious. History: Joan of Arc was a fifteenth-century heroine and resistance fighter. See also Ioana, Jane, Jean, Juanita, Siobhan.
Joaneil, Joanmarie, Joannanette, Joayn, Joen, Joenn, Jonni

Joana, Joanna (English) a form of Joan. See also Yoana.
Janka, Jhoana, Jo-Ana, Jo-Anie, Jo-Anna, Jo-Annie, Joahna, Joanah, Joandra, Joanka, Joananna, Joanka, Joannah, Joayna, Joeana, Joeanah, Joeanna, Joeannah, Joena, Joenah, Joenna, Joennah

Joanie, Joannie, Joanny, Joany (Hebrew) familiar forms of Joan.
Joanee, Joaney, Joani, Joanney, Joanni, Joenie

Joann, Joanne (English) forms of Joan.
Jo-Ann, Jo-Anne, Joanann, Joananne, Joane, Joayne, Joeane, Joeann, Joeanne, Joenn, Joenne

Joaquina (Hebrew) God will establish.
Joaquinah, Joaquine, Joaquyn, Joaquyna, Joaquynah, Joaquyne

Jobeth (English) a combination of Jo + Beth.
Jobetha, Jobethe, Joebeth, Joebetha, Joebethe, Johbeth, Johbetha, Johbethe

Jobina (Hebrew) a form of Joby.
Jobeana, Jobeanah, Jobeena, Jobeenah, Jobin, Jobinah, Jobine, Jobyna, Jobynah, Jobyne

Joby (Hebrew) afflicted. (English) a familiar form of Jobeth.
Jobea, Jobee, Jobey, Jobi, Jobie, Jobina, Jobita, Jobitt, Jobitta, Jobitte, Jobrina, Jobya, Jobye

Jocacia (American) a combination of Joy + Acacia.

Jocelin, Joceline, Jocelyne, Jocelynn (Latin) forms of Jocelyn.
Jocelina, Jocelinah, Jocelinn, Jocelynne

Jocelyn (Latin) joyous. See also Yocelin, Yoselin.
Jocalin, Jocalina, Jocaline, Jocalyn, Jocelle, Joci, Jocia, Jocilyn, Jocilynn, Jocinta, Joscelin, Josilin, Jossalin

Joclyn (Latin) a short form of Jocelyn.
Joclynn, Joclynne

Jodee, Jodi, Jodie, Jody (American) familiar forms of Judith.
Jode, Jodea, Jodele, Jodell, Jodelle, Jodevea, Jodey, Jodi-Lee, Jodi-Lynn, Jodia, Jodiee, Jodilee, Jodilynn, Joedee, Joedey, Joedi, Joedie, Joedy, Johdea, Johdee, Johdey, Johdi, Johdie, Johdy, Jowdee, Jowdey, Jowdi, Jowdie, Jowdy

Jodiann (American) a combination of Jodi (see Jodee) + Ann.
Jodene, Jodi-Ann, Jodi-Anna, Jodi-Anne, Jodianna, Jodianne, Jodine, Jody-Ann, Jody-Anna, Jody-Anne, Jodyann, Jodyanna, Jodyanne, Jodyne

Joelle (Hebrew) God is willing.
Joela, Joelah, Joele, Joelee, Joeli, Joelia, Joelie, Joell, Joella, Joellah, Joëlle, Joelli, Joelly, Joely,

Jowel, Jowela, Jowelah, Jowele, Jowell, Jowella, Jowellah, Jowelle, Joyelle

Joelynn (American) a combination of Joelle + Lynn.
Joelean, Joeleana, Joeleanah, Joeleane, Joeleen, Joeleena, Joeleenah, Joeleene, Joelena, Joelenah, Joelene, Joelin, Joelina, Joelinah, Joeline, Joellen, Joellena, Joellenah, Joellene, Joellyn, Joelyn, Joelyne

Joey (American) a familiar form of Jo.

Johana, Johanna, Johannah (German) forms of Joana. See also Giana.
Johan, Johanah, Johanka, Johann, Johonna, Joyhanna, Joyhannah

Johanie, Johannie, Johanny (Hebrew) forms of Joanie.
Johane, Johani, Johanni, Johany

Johanne (German) a short form of Johana. A form of Joann.

Johna, Johnna (American) forms of Joana, Johana.
Jhona, Jhonna, Johnda, Joncie, Jonda, Jondrea, Jutta

Johnae (American) a form of Janae.

Johnesha (American) a form of Johnnessa.
Johnecia

Johnetta (American) a form of Jonita.
Johnette, Jonetta, Jonette

Johnisha (American) a form of Johnnessa.

Johnnessa (American) a combination of Johna + Nessa.
Jahnessa, Johneatha, Johnetra, Johnishi, Johnnise, Jonyssa

Johnnie (Hebrew) a form of Joanie.
Johni, Johnie, Johnni, Johnnie-Lynn, Johnnielynn, Johnny

Joi, Joie (Latin) forms of Joy.
Joia, Joiah

Jokia (Swahili) beautiful robe.
Jokiah, Jokya, Jokyah

Jolan (Hungarian) violet blossom.
Jola, Jolán, Jolana, Jolanah, Jolane, Jolanee, Jolaney, Jolani, Jolania, Jolaniah, Jolanie, Jolany, Jolanya, Jolanyah

Jolanda (Greek) a form of Yolanda. See also Iolanthe.
Joland, Jolande, Jolander, Jolanka, Jolánta, Jolante, Jolantha, Jolanthe

Jolee (French) a form of Jolie.
Jole, Jolea, Joleah, Jolei, Joleigh, Joley, Jollea, Jolleah, Jollee, Jollei, Jolleigh

Joleen, Joline (English) forms of Jolene.
Jolean, Joleane, Joleene, Jolin, Jolinn, Jolleen, Jolleene, Jollene, Jollin, Jolline

Jolena (Hebrew) a form of Jolene.
Jolaina, Jolana, Jolanna, Jolanta, Joleana, Joleanah, Joleena, Joleenah, Jolenna, Jolina, Jolinah, Jolinda, Jolinna, Jolleena, Jollina, Jollinah, Jollyna, Jollynah, Jolyana, Jolyanna, Jolyannah, Jolyna, Jolynah

Jolene (Hebrew) God will add, God will increase. (English) a form of Josephine.
Jolaine, Jolane, Jolanne, Jolayne, Jole, Joléne, Jolenne, Jolleane, Jollyn, Jollyne, Jolyne

Jolie (French) pretty.
Joli, Jolibeth, Jolli, Jollie, Jolly, Joly, Jolye

Jolisa (American) a combination of Jo + Lisa.
Joleesa, Joleisha, Joleishia, Jolieasa, Jolise, Jolisha, Jolisia, Jolissa, Jolysa, Jolyssa

Jolyane (English) a form of Jolene.
Jolyanne

Jolyn, Jolynn (American) combinations of Jo + Lynn.
Jolyna, Jolynah, Jolyne, Jolynne

Jona (Hebrew) a short form of Jonina.
Jonah, Jonai, Jonia, Joniah, Jonnah

Jonae (American, Hebrew) a form of Janae. A form of Jona.

Jonatha (Hebrew) a form of Jonathan.
Johnasha, Johnasia

Jonathan (Hebrew) gift of God. Bible: the son of King Saul who became a loyal friend of David.

Jonell, Jonelle (American) combinations of Joan + Elle.
Jahnel, Jahnell, Jahnelle, Joanel, Joanela, Joanele, Joanelle, Joannel, Johnel, Johnela, Johnele, Johnell, Johnella, Johnelle, Jonel,

Jonela, Jonelah, Jonele, Jonella, Jonilla, Jonille, Jonyelle, Jynell, Jynelle

Jonesha (American) a form of Jonatha.
Joneisha, Jonesa, Joneshia, Jonessa, Jonneisha, Jonnesha, Jonnessia

Joni (American) a familiar form of Joan.
Jonann, Joncee, Joncey, Jonci, Joncie, Jone, Jonee, Joney, Joni-Lee, Jonice, Jonie, Jonilee, Jony

Jonika (American) a form of Janika.
Johnica, Johnique, Johnnica, Johnnika, Johnquia, Joneeka, Joneika, Jonica, Jonicah, Joniqua, Jonique

Jonina (Hebrew) dove. See also Yonina.
Jona, Joneen, Joneena, Joneene, Joninah, Jonine, Jonnina, Jonyna, Jonynah

Jonisha (American) a form of Jonatha.
Jonis, Jonisa, Jonise, Jonishah, Jonishia

Jonita (Hebrew) a form of Jonina. See also Yonita.
Johnita, Johnittia, Jonatee, Jonatey, Jonati, Jonatia, Jonatie, Joneata, Joneatah, Joneeta, Joneetah, Jonit, Jonitae, Jonitah, Jonite, Jonnita, Jonyta, Jonytah

Jonna (American) a form of Joana, Johana.

Jonni, Jonnie (American) familiar forms of Joan.
Jonny

Jonquil (Latin, English) Botany: an ornamental plant with fragrant yellow flowers.
Jonquelle, Jonquie, Jonquila, Jonquile, Jonquill, Jonquilla, Jonquille, Jonquyl, Jonquyla, Jonquylah, Jonquyle, Jonquyll, Jonquylla, Jonquyllah, Jonquylle

Jontel (American) a form of Johna.
Jonta, Jontae, Jontaé, Jontai, Jontaia, Jontaya, Jontaye, Jontela, Jontele, Jontell, Jontella, Jontelle, Jontia, Jontiah, Jontila, Jontrice

Jora (Hebrew) autumn rain.
Jorah, Jorai, Joria, Joriah

Jordain, Jordane (Hebrew) forms of Jordan.
Jordaine, Jordayn, Jordayne

Jordan (Hebrew) descending. See also Jardena.
Jordea, Jordee, Jordi, Jordian, Jordie

Jordana, Jordanna (Hebrew) forms of
Jordan. See also Giordana, Yordana.
Jorda, Jordah, Jordaina, Jordannah, Jordayna,
Jordena, Jordenna, Jordina, Jordinna, Jordona,
Jordonna, Jordyna, Jordynna, Jourdana,
Jourdanna

Jordann, Jordanne, Jorden, Jordin,
Jordon, Jordyn, Jordyne, Jordynn
(Hebrew) forms of Jordan.
Jordene, Jordenn, Jordenne, Jordine, Jordinn,
Jordinne, Jordone, Jordonne, Jordynne

Jori, Jorie, Jory (Hebrew) familiar forms
of Jordan.
Jorea, Joree, Jorée, Jorey, Jorin, Jorina, Jorine,
Jorita, Jorre, Jorrey, Jorri, Jorrian, Jorrie, Jorry

Joriann (American) a combination of Jori
+ Ann.
Jori-Ann, Jori-Anna, Jori-Anne, Jorian,
Joriana, Jorianah, Joriane, Jorianna,
Joriannah, Jorianne, Jorriann, Jorrianna,
Jorrianne, Jorryann, Jorryanna, Jorryanne,
Joryana, Joryanah, Joryane, Joryann,
Joryanna, Joryanne

Jorja (American) a form of Georgia.
Jeorgi, Jeorgia, Jorga, Jorgah, Jorgan, Jorgana,
Jorgane, Jorgi, Jorgia, Jorgiah, Jorgie, Jorgina,
Jorgine, Jorjan, Jorjana, Jorjanah, Jorjane,
Jorji, Jorjia, Jorjiah, Jorjina, Jorjiya, Jorjiyah

Josalyn, Jossalin (Latin) forms of Jocelyn.
Josalene, Josalin, Josalina, Josalinah, Josalind,
Josaline, Josalynn, Joshalyne Jossalina,
Jossalinah, Jossaline, Jossalyn, Jossalynn,
Jossalynne

Joscelin, Joscelyn (Latin) forms of
Jocelyn.
Josceline, Joscelyne, Joscelynn, Joscelynne

Jose (Spanish) a form of Joseph.

Josee, Josée (American) familiar forms
of Josephine.
Joesee, Josse, Jossee, Jozee

Josefina (Spanish) a form of Josephine.
Josaffina, Josaffine, Josefa, Josefena, Joseffa,
Josefine, Jozafin, Jozafina, Jozafine, Jozefa,
Jozefin, Jozefina, Jozefinah, Jozefine

Joselin, Joseline, Joselyn, Joselyne,
Josselyn (Latin) forms of Jocelyn.

Joselina, Joselinah, Joselinne, Joselynn,
Joselynne, Joshely, Josselen, Josselin, Josseline,
Jossellen, Jossellin, Jossellyn, Josselyne,
Josselynn, Josselynne

Joselle (American) a form of Jizelle.
Joesell, Joesella, Joeselle, Josel, Josela, Josele,
Josell, Josella, Jozelle

Joseph (Hebrew) God will add, God will
increase. Bible: in the Old Testament, the
son of Jacob who came to rule Egypt; in
the New Testament, the husband of Mary.

Josepha (German) a form of Josephine.
Josephah, Jozepha

Josephina (French) a form of Josephine.
Fina, Josaphina, Josephena, Josephyna

Josephine (French) a form of Joseph. See
also Fifi, Giuseppina, Pepita, Yosepha.
Josaphine, Josephene, Josephin, Josephiney,
Josephyn, Josephyne, Jozephine, Sefa

Josette (French) a familiar form of
Josephine.
Joesetta, Joesette, Joset, Joseta, Josetah, Josete,
Josett, Josetta, Josettah, Joshet, Josheta,
Joshetah, Joshete, Joshett, Joshetta, Joshettah,
Joshette, Josit, Josita, Jositah, Josite, Jositt,
Jositta, Josittah, Jositte, Josyt, Josyta, Josytah,
Josyte, Josytt, Josytta, Josyttah, Josytte, Jozet,
Jozeta, Jozetah, Jozete, Jozett, Jozetta,
Jozettah, Jozette

Josey, Josi, Josie, Jossie (Hebrew) familiar forms of Josephine.
Joesey, Josia, Josiah, Josy, Josye

Joshann (American) a combination of
Joshlyn + Ann.
Joshan, Joshana, Joshanah, Joshanna,
Joshannah, Joshanne

Joshelle (American) a combination of
Joshlyn + Elle.
Joshel, Joshela, Joshelah, Joshele, Joshell,
Joshella, Joshellah

Joshlyn (Latin) a form of Jocelyn.
(Hebrew) a form of Joshua.
Joshalin, Joshalina, Joshalinah, Joshaline,
Joshalyn, Joshalynn, Joshalynne, Joshlean,
Joshleana, Joshleanah, Joshleane, Joshleen,
Joshleena, Joshleenah, Joshleene, Joshlene,

Joshlin, Joshlina, Joshlinah, Joshline,
Joshlyna, Joshlynah, Joshlyne, Joshlynn,
Joshlynna, Joshlynnah, Joshlynne

Joshua (Hebrew) God is my salvation.
Bible: led the Israelites into the
Promised Land.

Josiane, Josiann, Josianne (American)
combinations of Josie (see Josey) + Ann.
Josian, Josiana, Josianna, Josie-Ann,
Josieann, Josina, Josinah, Josine, Josinee,
Josyn, Josyna, Josyne, Jozan, Jozana, Jozane,
Jozian, Joziana, Joziane, Joziann, Jozianna,
Jozianne, Jozyn, Jozyna, Jozyne

Josilin, Josilyn (Latin) forms of Jocelyn.
Josielin, Josielina, Josieline, Josiline, Josilyne,
Josilynn, Josilynne

Joslin, Joslyn, Joslynn (Latin) short forms
of Jocelyn.
Joslina, Joslinah, Josline, Joslyne, Joslynne,
Josslyn, Josslyne, Josslynn, Josslynne

Jossline (Latin) a form of Jocelyn.
Josslin

Jourdan (Hebrew) a form of Jordan.
Jourdain, Jourdann, Jourdanne, Jourden,
Jourdian, Jourdon, Jourdyn

Journey (English) journey.

Jovana (Latin) a form of Jovanna.
Jovanah, Jovane, Jovania, Jovaniah

Jovanna (Latin) majestic. (Italian) a form
of Giovanna. Mythology: Jove, also
known as Jupiter, was the supreme
Roman god.
Jeovana, Jeovanna, Jouvan, Jovado, Joval,
Jovan, Jovann, Jovannah, Jovannia,
Jovanniah, Jovannie, Jovena, Jovenah,
Jovenia, Joveniah, Joviana, Jovina, Jovon,
Jovona, Jovonah, Jovonda, Jovone, Jovonia,
Jovonn, Jovonna, Jovonnah, Jovonne, Jowan,
Jowana, Jowanna

Jovannie (Italian) a familiar form of
Jovanna.
Jovanee, Jovaney, Jovani, Jovanie, Jovanne,
Jovannee, Jovanni, Jovanny, Jovany, Jovonnie

Jovi (Latin) a short form of Jovita.
Jovee, Jovey, Jovia, Joviah, Jovie, Jovy, Jovya,
Jovyah

Joviana (Latin) a form of Jovanna.
Jovian, Jovianah, Joviane, Joviann, Jovianna,
Joviannah, Jovianne, Jovyan, Jovyana,
Jovyanah, Jovyane, Jovyann, Jovyanna,
Jovyannah, Jovyanne

Jovina (Latin) a form of Jovanna.
Jovinah, Jovine, Jovyn, Jovyna, Jovynah,
Jovyne

Jovita (Latin) jovial.
Joveda, Jovet, Joveta, Jovete, Jovett, Jovetta,
Jovette, Jovi, Jovida, Jovidah, Jovit, Jovitah,
Jovite, Jovitt, Jovitta, Jovitte, Jovyta, Jovytah,
Jovyte, Jovytt, Jovytta, Jovyttah, Jovytte

Joy (Latin) joyous.
Joye, Joyeeta, Joyella, Joyous, Joyvina

Joya (Latin) a form of Joy.
Joyah, Joyia

Joyann, Joyanne (American) combina-
tions of Joy + Ann.
Joian, Joiana, Joianah, Joiane, Joiann,
Joianna, Joiannah, Joianne, Joyan, Joyana,
Joyanah, Joyane, Joyanna, Joyannah

Joyce (Latin) joyous. A short form of
Joycelyn.
Joice, Joise, Joycee, Joycey, Joycia, Joyciah,
Joycie, Joyse, Joysel

Joycelyn (American) a form of Jocelyn.
Joycalin, Joycalina, Joycalinah, Joycaline,
Joycalyn, Joycalyna, Joycalynah, Joycalyne,
Joycelin, Joycelina, Joycelinah, Joyceline,
Joycelyna, Joycelynah, Joycelyne, Joycelynn,
Joycelynne, Joysalin, Joysalina, Joysalinah,
Joysaline, Joysalyn

Joylyn (American) a combination of Joy
+ Lynn.
Joialin, Joialine, Joialyn, Joialyna, Joialyne,
Joilin, Joilina, Joilinah, Joiline, Joilyn,
Joilyna, Joilynah, Joilyne, Joy-Lynn, Joyleen,
Joylene, Joylin, Joylina, Joylinah, Joyline,
Joylyna, Joylynah, Joylyne, Joylynn, Joylynne

Jozephine (French) a form of Josephine.
Jozaphin, Jozaphina, Jozaphinah,
Jozaphine, Jozaphyn, Jozaphyna,
Jozaphynah, Jozaphyne, Jozephin,
Jozephina, Jozephinah, Jozephyn,
Jozephyna, Jozephynah, Jozephyne

Jozie (Hebrew) a familiar form of Josephine.
Joze, Jozee, Jozée, Jozey, Jozi, Jozy, Jozze, Jozzee, Jozzey, Jozzi, Jozzie, Jozzy

Juana (Spanish) a short form of Juanita.
Juanah, Juanell, Juaney, Juanika, Juanit, Juanna, Juannah, Juannia

Juandalyn (Spanish) a form of Juanita.
Jualinn, Juandalin, Juandalina, Juandaline, Juandalyna, Juandalyne, Juandalynn, Juandalynne

Juanita (Spanish) a form of Jane, Joan. See also Kwanita, Nita, Waneta, Wanika.
Juaneice, Juanequa, Juanesha, Juanice, Juanicia, Juaniqua, Juanisha, Juanishia

Jubilee (Latin) joyful celebration.
Jubilea, Jubileah, Jubilei, Jubileigh, Jubili, Jubilia, Jubiliah, Jubilie, Jubily, Jubilya, Jubilyah, Jubylea, Jubyleah, Jubylee, Jubylei, Jubyleigh, Jubyley, Jubyli, Jubylia, Jubyliah, Jubylie, Jubyly

Juci (Hungarian) a form of Judy.
Jucee, Jucey, Jucia, Juciah, Jucie, Jucika, Jucy, Jucya, Jucyah

Judine (Hebrew) a form of Judith.
Judeen, Judeena, Judeenah, Judena, Judene, Judin, Judina, Judinah, Judyn, Judyna, Judynah, Judyne

Judith (Hebrew) praised. Mythology: the slayer of Holofernes, according to ancient Jewish legend. See also Yehudit, Yudita.
Giuditta, Ioudith, Jude, Judett, Judetta, Judette, Judine, Judit, Judita, Judite, Juditha, Judithe, Juditt, Juditta, Juditte, Judyta, Judytt, Judytta, Judytte, Jutka

Judy (Hebrew) a familiar form of Judith.
Judea, Judee, Judey, Judi, Judie, Judye

Judyann (American) a combination of Judy + Ann.
Judana, Judane, Judiana, Judiane, Judiann, Judianna, Judiannah, Judianne, Judyanna, Judyanne

Jula (Polish) a form of Julia.
Jewlah, Juela, Juelah, Julah, Julca, Julcia, Julea, Juleah, Juliska, Julka

Julee (English) a form of Julie.

Julene (Basque) a form of Julia. See also Yulene.
Julean, Juleana, Juleanah, Juleane, Juleen, Juleena, Juleenah, Juleene, Julena, Julenah, Julenia, Juleniah, Julina, Juline, Julinka, Juliska, Jullean, Julleana, Julleanah, Julleane, Julleen, Julleena, Julleenah, Julleene, Jullena, Jullene, Jullin, Jullina, Jullinah, Julline, Jullyna, Jullynah, Jullyne, Julyna, Julynah, Julyne

Julia (Latin) youthful. See also Giulia, Jill, Jillian, Sulia, Yulia.
Iulia, Jewelea, Jeweleah, Jewelia, Jeweliah, Jewelya, Jewlya, Jewlyah, Juelea, Jueleah, Jula, Julea, Juleah, Juliah, Julica, Juliea, Julija, Julita, Juliya, Julka, Julya

Julian, Juliane, Juliann, Julianne, Jullian (English) forms of Julia. See also Julie Ann.
Jewelian, Jeweliane, Jeweliann, Jewelianne, Jewliane, Jewliann, Jewlianne, Julean, Juleann, Julijanne, Juline, Julyan, Julyane, Julyann, Julyanne

Juliana (Czech, Spanish) a form of Julia.
Jeweliana, Jewelianah, Jewelianna, Jeweliannah, Jewliana, Jewlianah, Jewlianna, Jewliannah, Julianah, Julianna, Julieana, Julieanah, Juliena, Julienna, Juliennah, Julijana, Julijanah, Julijanna, Julijannah, Julina, Julinah, Julliana, Jullianna, Julyana, Julyanah, Julyanna, Julyannah, Yuliana

Julianna (Hungarian) a form of Julia. See also Juliana.

Julie (English) a form of Julia.
Jewelee, Jewelei, Jeweleigh, Jeweli, Jewelie, Jewlie, Juel, Juelee, Juelei, Jueleigh, Jueli, Juelie, Juely, Jule, Julei, Juleigh, Julene, Juli, Julie-Lynn, Julie-Mae, Julle, Jullee, Julli, Jullie, Jully, July

Julie Ann, Julie Anne, Julieann (American) combinations of Julie + Ann. See also Julian.
Julie-Ann, Julie-Anne, Juliean, Julieane, Julieanne

Julieanna (American) a form of Juliana.
Julie Anna, Julie-Anna

Julienne (English) a form of Julia.
Julien, Juliene, Julienn

Juliet, Juliette (French) forms of Julia.
*Jewelett, Jeweletta, Jewelette, Jeweliet,
Jeweliete, Jeweliett, Jeweliette, Jewelyet,
Jewelyete, Jewelyett, Jewelyette, Jolet, Jolete,
Juelet, Juelete, Juelett, Juelette, Juleate,
Juliete, Juliett, Jullet, Julliet, Julliete, Julliett,
Julliette, Julyet, Julyete, Julyett, Julyette*

Julieta (French) a form of Julia.
*Guilietta, Jewelieta, Jewelietta, Jewelyeta,
Jewelyetta, Juleata, Juleatah, Julietah,
Julietta, Juliettah, Jullieta, Jullietah, Jullietta,
Julyeta, Julyetah, Julyetta, Julyettah*

Julisa, Julissa (Latin) forms of Julia.
Julis, Julisha, Julysa, Julyssa

Julita (Spanish) a form of Julia.
*Joleta, Joletah, Jueleta, Jueletah, Jueletta,
Juelettah, Juleet, Juleeta, Juleetah, Juleete,
Julet, Juleta, Juletah, Julett, Juletta, Julette,
Julit, Julitah, Julite, Julitt, Julitta, Julittah,
Julitte, Julyta*

Jumaris (American) a combination of
Julie + Maris.

Jun (Chinese) truthful.

June (Latin) born in the sixth month.
*Juin, Juine, Juna, Junel, Junell, Junella,
Junelle, Junett, Junetta, Junette, Juney, Juniet,
Junieta, Juniett, Junietta, Juniette, Junill,
Junilla, Junille, Junina, Junine, Junita, Junn,
Junula*

Junee (Latin) a familiar form of June.
Junea, Juney, Juni, Junia, Juniah, Junie, Juny

Juno (Latin) queen. Mythology: the
supreme Roman goddess.

Jupita (Latin) Mythology: Jupiter is the
supreme Roman god and the husband
of Juno. Astronomy: Jupiter is the largest
planet in the solar system and the fifth
planet from the sun.
*Jupitah, Jupitor, Jupyta, Jupytah, Jupyter,
Jupytor*

Jurisa (Slavic) storm.
*Jurisah, Jurissa, Jurissah, Jurysa, Jurysah,
Juryssa, Juryssah*

Jurnee (American) a form of Journey.

Justa (Latin) a short form of Justina,
Justine.
Justah, Juste, Justea, Justi, Justie, Justy

Justice (Latin) a form of Justin.
Justys, Justyse

Justin (Latin) just, righteous.

Justina (Italian) a form of Justine. See also
Giustina.
*Justeana, Justeanah, Justeena, Justeenah,
Justeina, Justeinah, Jestena, Justeyna,
Justeynah, Justinah, Justinna*

Justine (Latin) a form of Justin.
*Jestine, Justean, Justeane, Justeen, Justeene,
Justein, Justeine, Justeyn, Justeyne*

Justis, Justise, Justus, Justyce (Latin)
forms of Justice.
Justiss, Justisse

Justyna (Italian) a form of Justine.
Justynah

Justyne (Latin) a form of Justine.
Justyn, Justynn, Justynne

Jyllian (Latin) a form of Jillian.
*Jylian, Jyliana, Jylianah, Jyliane, Jyliann,
Jylianna, Jyliannah, Jylianne, Jylliana,
Jyllianah, Jylliane, Jylliann, Jyllianna,
Jylliannah, Jyllianne, Jyllyan, Jyllyana,
Jyllyanah, Jyllyane, Jyllyann, Jyllyanna,
Jyllyannah, Jyllyanne*

K

Ka'la (Arabic) a form of Kala.

Kacee, Kaci, Kacie (Irish, American)
forms of Kacey.

Kacey, Kacy (Irish) brave. (American)
forms of Casey. A combination of the
initials K. + C.
*Kace, Kaecee, Kaecey, Kaeci, Kaecie, Kaecy,
Kaicee, Kaicey, Kaici, Kaicie, Kaicy, Kasci*

Kachina (Native American) sacred dancer.
Kachin, Kachinah, Kachine, Kachinee,
Kachiney, Kachyn, Kachyna, Kachynah,
Kachyne

Kacia (Greek) a short form of Acacia.
Kacya, Kaecea, Kaecia, Kaeciah, Kaesea,
Kaesia, Kaesiah, Kaicea, Kaicia, Kaiciah,
Kaisea, Kaisia, Kaisiah, Kasea, Kasya,
Kaycia, Kaysea, Kaysia

Kadedra (American) a combination of
Kady + Dedra.
Kadeadra, Kadedrah, Kadedria

Kadee, Kadi, Kadie (English) forms of
Kady.
Kaddia, Kaddiah, Kaddie, Kadia, Kadiah

Kadeejah (Arabic) a form of Kadijah.
Kadeeja

Kadeesha (American) a form of Kadesha.
Kadeeshia, Kadeesia, Kadeesiah, Kadeezia

Kadeidra (American) a form of Kadedra.
Kadeedra, Kadeidre, Kadeidria

Kadeija (Arabic) a form of Kadijah.
Kadeijah

Kadeisha (American) a form of Kadesha.

Kadeja, Kadejah (Arabic) forms of
Kadijah.
Kadejá, Kadejia

Kadelyn (American) a combination of
Kady + Lynn.

Kadesha (American) a combination of
Kady + Aisha.
Kadesa, Kadessa, Kadiesha, Kadieshia,
Kadysha, Kadyshia

Kadeshia (American) a form of Kadesha.
Kadesheia

Kadesia (American) a form of Kadesha.
Kadezia

Kadija (Arabic) a form of Kadijah.

Kadijah (Arabic) trustworthy.
Kadajah

Kadisha (American) a form of Kadesha.
Kadishia, Kadisia

Kady (English) a form of Katy. A combi-
nation of the initials K. + D. See also
Cadie.
K. D., Kaddy, Kade, Kadea, Kadey, Kadya,
Kadyn, Kaidi, Kaidy

Kae (Greek, Teutonic, Latin) a form of Kay.

Kaedé (Japanese) maple leaf.

Kaela (Hebrew, Arabic) beloved, sweetheart. A short form of Kalila, Kelila.
Kaelah, Kaelea, Kaeleah

Kaelee, Kaeleigh, Kaeley, Kaeli, Kaelie,
Kaely (American) forms of Kaela.
Kaelei, Kaelia, Kaeliah, Kaelii, Kaelly, Kaelye

Kaelen, Kaelin, Kaelynn (American)
forms of Kaelyn.
Kaelean, Kaeleana, Kaeleane, Kaeleen,
Kaeleena, Kaeleene, Kaelein, Kaeleina,
Kaeleine, Kaelene, Kaelina, Kaeline,
Kaelinn, Kaelynne

Kaelyn (American) a combination of Kae
+ Lynn. See also Caelin, Kaylyn.
Kaelan, Kaeleyn, Kaeleyna, Kaeleyne,
Kaelyna, Kaelyne

Kaetlyn (Irish) a form of Kaitlin.
Kaetlin, Kaetlynn, Kaetlynne

Kaferine (Greek) a form of Katherine.
Kaferin, Kaferina, Kaferinah, Kaferyn,
Kaferyna, Kaferynah, Kaferyne, Kafferin,
Kafferina, Kafferinah, Kafferine, Kafferyn,
Kafferyna, Kafferynah, Kafferyne

Kafleen (Irish) a form of Kathleen.
Kafflean, Kaffleana, Kaffleanah, Kaffleane,
Kaffleen, Kaffleena, Kaffleenah, Kaffleene,
Kafflein, Kaffleina, Kaffleinah, Kaffleine,
Kafflin, Kafflina, Kafflinah, Kaffline, Kafflyn,
Kafflyna, Kafflynah, Kafflyne, Kaflean,
Kafleana, Kafleanah, Kafleane, Kafleena,
Kafleenah, Kafleene, Kaflein, Kafleina,
Kafleinah, Kafleine, Kaflin, Kaflina,
Kaflinah, Kafline, Kaflyn, Kaflyna,
Kaflynah, Kaflyne

Kagami (Japanese) mirror.
Kagamee

Kahla (Arabic) a form of Kala.
Kahlah, Kahlea, Kahleah

Kahli (American) a form of Kalee.
Kahlee, Kahlei, Kahleigh, Kahley, Kahlie, Kahly

Kahsha (Native American) fur robe.
Kashae, Kashia

Kai (Hawaiian) sea. (Hopi, Navajo) willow tree.
Kae, Kaie

Kaia (Greek) earth. Mythology: Gaea was the earth goddess.
Kaiah

Kaija (Greek) a form of Kaia.

Kaila (Hebrew) laurel; crown.
Kailea, Kaileah, Kailia, Kailiah

Kailah (Hebrew) a form of Kaila.

Kailani (Hawaiian) sky. See also Kalani.
Kaelana, Kaelanah, Kaelanea, Kaelanee, Kaelaney, Kaelani, Kaelania, Kaelaniah, Kaelanie, Kaelany, Kaelanya, Kailana, Kailanah, Kailanea, Kailanee, Kailaney, Kailania, Kailaniah, Kailanie, Kailany, Kailanya

Kaile, Kailee, Kaileigh, Kailey, Kaili, Kailie, Kaily (American) familiar forms of Kaila. Forms of Kaylee.
Kaileh, Kailei, Kailia, Kailiah, Kailli, Kaillie, Kailya

Kaileen (American) a form of Kaitlin.
Kaileena, Kaileene

Kailen, Kailin, Kailyn, Kailynn (American) forms of Kaitlin.
Kailan, Kailean, Kaileana, Kaileane, Kailein, Kaileina, Kaileine, Kailena, Kailene, Kaileyne, Kailina, Kailine, Kailon, Kailyna, Kailyne, Kailynne

Kaimana (Hawaiian) diamond.
Kaemana, Kaemanah, Kaemane, Kaiman, Kaimanah, Kaimane, Kayman, Kaymana, Kaymanah, Kaymane

Kaimi (Hawaiian) seeker.

Kaira (Greek) a form of Kairos. (Greek, Danish) a form of Kara.
Kairra

Kairos (Greek) opportunity.

Kaisa (Swedish) pure.
Kaisah, Kaysa, Kaysah

Kaisha (American) a short form of Kaishawn.

Kaishawn (American) a combination of Kai + Shawna.
Kaeshun, Kaishala, Kaishon

Kaitlan, Kaitlen, Kaitlinn, Kaitlyn, Kaitlyne, Kaitlynn, Kaitlynne (Irish) forms of Kaitlin.
Kaitlinne, Kaitlyna, Kaitlynah

Kaitland (Irish) a form of Caitlin.
Kaitlind

Kaitlin (Irish) pure. See also Caitlin, Katelin.
Kaitelynne, Kaitleen, Kaitlina, Kaitlinah, Kaitline, Kaitlon

Kaiya (Japanese) forgiveness. (Aboriginal) a type of spear.
Kaiyah, Kaiyia

Kala (Arabic) a short form of Kalila. A form of Cala.

Kalah, Kalla (Arabic) forms of Kala.
Kallah

Kalama (Hawaiian) torch.

Kalan (American) a form of Kaelyn, Kaylyn. (Hawaiian) a short form of Kalani. (Slavic) a form of Kallan.

Kalani (Hawaiian) chieftain; sky. See also Kailani.
Kalana, Kalanah, Kalanea, Kalanee, Kalaney, Kalania, Kalaniah, Kalanie, Kalona, Kalonah, Kalonea, Kalonee, Kaloney, Kaloni, Kalonia, Kaloniah, Kalonie, Kalony

Kalare (Latin, Basque) bright; clear.

Kalasia (Tongan) graceful.
Kalasiah, Kalasya, Kalasyah

Kalauni (Tongan) crown.
Kalaunea, Kalaunee, Kalauney, Kalaunia, Kalauniah, Kalaunie, Kalauny, Kalaunya

Kalea (Hawaiian) bright; clear.
Kahlea, Kahleah, Kailea, Kaileah, Kaleah, Kaleeia, Kaleia, Kallea, Kalleah, Khalea, Khaleah

Kalee, Kalei, Kaleigh, Kaley, Kalie, Kalley, Kally, Kaly (American) forms of Calee, Kaylee. (Sanskrit, Hawaiian) forms of Kali. (Greek) forms of Kalli. (Arabic) familiar forms of Kalila.
Kallee, Kalleigh, Kallye

Kaleen, Kalene (Hawaiian) short forms of Kalena.

Kaleena (Hawaiian) a form of Kalena. (Slavic) a form of Kalina.

Kalei (Hawaiian) flower wreath.
Kahlei, Kailei, Kallei, Kaylei, Khalei

Kalen (Slavic) a form of Kallan.
Kallen

Kalena (Hawaiian) pure. See also Kalina.
Kalenea, Kalenna

Kalere (Swahili) short woman.
Kaleer

Kali (Hindi) the black one. (Hawaiian) hesitating. Religion: a form of the Hindu goddess Devi. See also Cali.

Kalia, Kaliah (Hawaiian) forms of Kalea.
Kaliea, Kalieya, Kalya

Kalida (Spanish) a form of Calida.
Kalidah, Kallida, Kallidah, Kallyda, Kallydah, Kalyda, Kalydah

Kalifa (Somali) chaste; holy.
Califa, Califah, Kalifah

Kalila (Arabic) beloved, sweetheart. See also Kaela.
Calila, Calilah, Kahlila, Kaleela, Kalilla, Kallila, Kaylil, Kaylila, Kylila, Kylilah, Kylillah

Kalin (Slavic, Hawaiian) a short form of Kalina. (American) a form of Kaelyn, Kaylyn.

Kalina (Slavic) flower. (Hawaiian) a form of Karen. See also Kalena.

Kalinah, Kaline, Kalinna, Kalyna, Kalynah, Kalynna

Kalinda (Hindi) sun. See also Calinda.
Kaleenda, Kalindah, Kalindi, Kalindie, Kalindy, Kalynd, Kalynda, Kalynde, Kalyndi

Kalisa (American) a combination of Kate + Lisa.
Kalise, Kalysa, Kalyssa

Kalisha (American) a combination of Kate + Aisha.
Kaleesha, Kaleisha, Kalishia

Kaliska (Moquelumnan) coyote chasing deer.
Kaliskah, Kalyska, Kalyskah

Kalissa (American) a form of Kalisa.

Kalista, Kallista (Greek) forms of Calista.
Kalesta, Kalistah, Kallesta, Kallistar, Kallistara, Kallistarah, Kallistarr, Kallistarra, Kallistarrah, Kallysta, Kaysta

Kallan (Slavic) stream, river.
Kalahn, Kalan, Kallin, Kallon, Kallyn, Kalon

Kalle (Finnish) a form of Carol.
Kaille, Kaylle

Kalli, Kallie (Greek) forms of Calie. Familiar forms of Kalista, Kalliope, Kalliyan.
Kalle, Kallee, Kallita, Kally

Kalliope (Greek) a form of Calliope.
Kalliopee, Kallyope

Kalliyan (Cambodian) best.

Kallolee (Hindi) happy.
Kallolea, Kalloleah, Kallolei, Kalloleigh, Kalloley, Kalloli, Kallolie, Kalloly

Kaloni (Tongan) fragrant; perfume.
Kalona, Kalonah, Kalonee, Kaloney, Kalonia, Kaloniah, Kalonie, Kalony, Kalonya, Kalonyah

Kalonice (Greek) beauty's victory.

Kaltha (English) marigold, yellow flower.

Kaluwa (Swahili) forgotten one.
Kalua

Kalyca (Greek) rosebud. See also Calyca.
Kalica, Kalicah, Kalika, Kaly, Kalycah, Kalyka, Kalykah

Kalyn, Kalynn (American) forms of Kaylyn.
Kalin, Kallen, Kallin, Kallon, Kallyn, Kalyne, Kalynne

Kama (Sanskrit) loved one. Religion: the Hindu god of love.
Kamah, Kamma, Kammah

Kamala (Hindi) lotus.
Kamalah, Kammala

Kamalei (Hawaiian) beloved child.
Kamalea, Kamaleah, Kamaleigh

Kamali (Mahona) spirit guide; protector.
Kamaley, Kamalie, Kamaly

Kamalynn, Kamalynne (American) combinations of Kama + Lynn.
Kamlean, Kamleana, Kamleanah, Kamleane, Kamleen, Kamleena, Kamleenah, Kamleene, Kamlin, Kamlina, Kamlinah, Kamline, Kamlyn, Kamlyna, Kamlynah, Kamlyne, Kammalean, Kammaleana, Kammaleanah, Kammaleane, Kammaleen, Kammaleena, Kammaleenah, Kammaleene, Kammalin, Kammalina, Kammalinah, Kammaline, Kammalyn, Kammalyna, Kammalynah, Kammalyne, Kammalynn

Kamara (Swahili) a short form of Kamaria.

Kamari (Swahili) a short form of Kamaria.
Kamaree, Kamarie

Kamaria (Swahili) moonlight.
Kamar, Kamarae, Kamariah, Kamariya, Kamariyah, Kamarya, Kamaryah

Kamata (Moquelumnan) gambler.

Kamballa (Australian) young woman.
Kambala, Kambalah, Kamballah

Kambria (Latin) a form of Cambria.
Kambra, Kambrie, Kambriea, Kambry

Kamea (Hawaiian) one and only; precious.
Camea, Cameah, Kameah, Kamee, Kameo, Kammia, Kammiah, Kamya, Kamyah

Kameke (Swahili) blind.

Kameko (Japanese) turtle child. Mythology: the turtle symbolizes longevity.
Kameeko, Kamiko, Kamyko

Kameli (Hawaiian) honey.
Kamely

Kamelia (Italian) a form of Camelia.
Kameliah, Kamellia, Kamelya, Kamelyah, Kamilia, Kamillia, Kamilliah, Kamillya, Kamilya, Kamylia, Kamyliah

Kameron, Kameryn (American) forms of Cameron.
Kameran, Kamerona, Kameronia

Kami (Japanese) divine aura. (Italian, North African) a short form of Kamila, Kamilah. See also Cami.
Kamey, Kammi, Kammie, Kammy, Kammye, Kamy

Kamie (Italian, North African, Japanese) a form of Kami.

Kamila (Slavic) a form of Camila. See also Millie.
Kameela, Kamela, Kamella, Kamilka, Kamilla, Kamillah, Kamma, Kammilla, Kamyla, Kamylla, Kamylle

Kamilah (North African) perfect.
Kameela, Kameelah, Kamillah, Kammilah, Kamylah, Kamyllah

Kamille (Slavic) a short form of Kamila.
Kamil, Kamile, Kamyl, Kamyle, Kamyll

Kamiya (Hawaiian) a form of Kamea.
Kamia, Kamiah, Kamiyah

Kamri (American) a short form of Kameron. See also Camri.
Kamree, Kamrey, Kamrie

Kamry (American) a form of Kamri.
Kamrye

Kamryn (American) a short form of Kameron. See also Camryn.
Kamren, Kamrin, Kamron, Kamrynn

Kanani (Hawaiian) beautiful.
Kana, Kanae, Kanan, Kanana, Kananah, Kananea, Kananee, Kanania, Kananiah, Kananie, Kanany, Kananya, Kananyah

Kanda (Native American) magical power.

Kandace, Kandice (Greek) glittering white; glowing. (American) forms of Candace, Candice.
Kandas, Kandess, Kandus

Kandi (American) a familiar form of Kandace. See also Candi.
Kandea, Kandee, Kandey, Kandhi, Kandia, Kandiah, Kandie, Kandy, Kandya, Kandyah, Kendi, Kendie, Kendy, Kenndi, Kenndie, Kenndy

Kandis, Kandyce (Greek, American) forms of Kandace.
Kandise, Kandiss, Kandys, Kandyse

Kandra (American) a form of Kendra. See also Candra.
Kandrah, Kandrea, Kandree, Kandria, Kandriah, Kandrya, Kandryah

Kane (Japanese) two right hands.

Kaneesha (American) a form of Keneisha.

Kaneisha (American) a form of Keneisha.
Kaneasha, Kanecia, Kaneysha, Kaniece

Kaneli (Tongan) canary yellow.
Kanelea, Kaneleah, Kanelee, Kanelei, Kaneleigh, Kanelia, Kaneliah, Kanelie, Kanely, Kanelya

Kanene (Swahili) a little important thing.

Kanesha (American) a form of Keneisha.
Kanesah, Kaneshea, Kaneshia, Kanessa

Kani (Hawaiian) sound.
Canee, Caney, Cani, Canie, Cany, Kanee, Kanie, Kany

Kanika (Mwera) black cloth.
Kanica, Kanicka

Kanisha (American) a form of Keneisha.
Kanishia

Kaniva (Tongan) Milky Way, universe, galaxy.
Kanivah, Kanyva, Kanyvah

Kaniya (Hindi, Tai) a form of Kanya.
Kanea, Kania, Kaniah

Kannitha (Cambodian) angel.

Kanoa (Hawaiian) free.

Kanya (Hindi) virgin. (Tai) young lady. Religion: a form of the Hindu goddess Devi.
Kanja, Kanjah, Kanyah, Kanyia

Kapri (American) a form of Capri.
Kapre, Kapree, Kapria, Kaprice, Kapricia, Kaprisha, Kaprisia

Kapua (Hawaiian) blossom.

Kapuki (Swahili) first-born daughter.

Kara (Greek, Danish) pure.

Karah (Greek, Danish) a form of Kara. (Irish, Italian) a form of Cara.

Karalana (English) a combination of Kara + Lana.
Karalain, Karalaina, Karalainah, Karalaine, Karalanah, Karalane, Karalayn, Karalayna, Karalaynah, Karalayne

Karalee (English) a combination of Kara + Lee.
Karalea, Karaleah, Karalei, Karaleigh, Karaley, Karali, Karalia, Karaliah, Karalie, Karaly, Karralea, Karraleah, Karralee, Karralei, Karraleigh, Karraley, Karrali, Karralie, Karraly

Karalyn (English) a form of Karalynn. (American) a form of Karolyn.
Karalyna

Karalynn (English) a combination of Kara + Lynn.
Karalin, Karaline, Karalyne, Karalynne

Kareela (Australian) southern wind.
Kareala, Karealah, Karealla, Kareallah, Karela, Karelah, Karella, Karellah

Kareema (Arabic) a form of Karimah.
Kareemah

Kareen (Scandinavian) a short form of Karena. A form of Karin.
Karean, Kareane, Kareene, Karene, Karrane, Karreen, Karrene

Kareena (Scandinavian) a form of Karena.
Kareenah, Karreena

Karel, Karelle (American) forms of Carol.
Karell

Karely (American) a familiar form of Karel.
Kareli

Karen (Greek) pure. See also Carey, Carina, Caryn.
Kaaran, Kaaren, Kaarun, Karaina, Karan, Karna, Karon, Karran, Karren, Karrun

Karena (Scandinavian) a form of Karen.
Kareana, Kareina, Karenah, Karrana, Karranah, Karrena, Karrenah

Karenza (Cornish) loving, affectionate. See also Carenza.
Karansa, Karansah, Karansia, Karansiah, Karanza, Karanzah, Karanzia, Karanziah, Karanzya, Karanzyah, Karensa, Karensah, Karensia, Karensiah, Karenzah, Karenzia, Karenziah, Karenzya, Karenzyah, Kerensa

Karessa (French) a form of Caressa.

Karey, Karie, Kary (Greek, Danish) forms of Kari.

Kari (Greek) pure. (Danish) a form of Caroline, Katherine. See also Carey, Cari, Carrie, Karri.
Karee

Karia (Greek, Danish) a form of Kari.
Kariah

Kariane, Kariann, Karianne (American) combinations of Kari + Ann.
Karian, Kariana, Karianna

Karida (Arabic) untouched, pure.
Kareeda, Karidah, Karinda, Karita, Karyda, Karydah, Karynda, Karyndah

Karilyn, Karilynn (American) combinations of Kari + Lynn.
Kareelin, Kareeline, Kareelinn, Kareelyn, Kareelyne, Kareelynn, Kareelynne, Karilin, Kariline, Karilinn, Karilyne, Karilynne, Karylin, Karyline, Karylinn, Karylyn, Karylyne, Karylynn, Karylynne

Karima (Arabic) a form of Karimah.

Karimah (Arabic) generous.
Karim, Karime, Karyma, Karymah

Karin (Scandinavian) a form of Karen.
Kaarin, Karinne, Karrin, Karrine

Karina (Russian) a form of Karen.
Kaarina, Karinna, Karrina, Karrinah

Karine (Russian) a form of Karen.
Karrine, Karryne, Karyne

Karis (Greek) graceful.
Kares, Karese, Karess, Karesse, Karice, Karise, Kariss, Karisse, Karris, Karys, Karyse, Karyss, Karysse

Karisa, Karissa, Karrisa (Greek) forms of Carissa.
Karesa, Karesah, Karessa, Karessah, Karisah, Karisha, Karissah, Karissimia, Kariza, Karrissa, Kerisa

Karishma (American) a form of Karisma.

Karisma (Greek) divinely favored. See also Carisma.
Karismah, Karismara, Karysma, Karysmah, Karysmara

Karla (German) a form of Carla. (Slavic) a short form of Karoline.
Karila, Karilla, Karle, Karlea, Karleah, Karlicka, Karlinka, Karlisha, Karlisia, Karlitha, Karlla, Karlon

Karlee, Karleigh, Karli, Karlie (American) forms of Karley. See also Carli.
Karlia, Karliah

Karleen, Karlene (American) forms of Karla. See also Carleen.
Karlean, Karleane, Karleene, Karlein, Karleine, Karlen, Karleyn, Karleyne, Karlign, Karlin, Karline, Karlyan

Karlena (American) a form of Karleen.
Karleana, Karleanah, Karleena, Karleenah, Karleina, Karleinah, Karlenah, Karleyna, Karleynah, Karlina, Karlinah, Karlinna, Karlyna, Karlynah

Karley, Karly (Latin) little and strong. (American) forms of Carly.
Karlea, Karleah, Karlei, Karlya, Karlyah, Karlye

Karlotte (American) a form of Charlotte.
Karletta, Karlette, Karlita, Karlotta

Karlyn (American) a form of Karla.
Karlyne, Karlynn, Karlynne

Karma (Hindi) fate, destiny; action.
Carma, Carmah, Karmah, Karmana

Karmaine (French) a form of Charmaine.
*Karmain, Karmaina, Karmane, Karmayn,
Karmayna, Karmayne, Karmein, Karmeina,
Karmeine, Karmeyn, Karmeyna, Karmeyne,
Kharmain, Kharmaina, Kharmaine,
Kharmayn, Kharmayna, Kharmayne,
Kharmein, Kharmeina, Kharmeine,
Kharmeyn, Kharmeyna, Kharmeyne*

Karmel (Hebrew) a form of Carmela.
*Karmeita, Karmela, Karmelah, Karmele,
Karmelina, Karmell, Karmella, Karmellah,
Karmelle, Karmellia, Karmelliah, Karmellya,
Karmellyah, Karmiella, Karmielle, Karmyla*

Karmen (Latin) song.
*Karman, Karmencita, Karmin, Karmita,
Karmon, Karmyn, Karmyna, Karmynah*

Karmiti (Bantu) tree.
*Karmitee, Karmitey, Karmitie, Karmity,
Karmytee, Karmytey, Karmyti, Karmytie,
Karmyty*

Karniela (Greek) cornel tree. (Latin)
horn colored. See also Carniela.
*Karniel, Karnielah, Karniele, Karniella,
Karnielle, Karnis, Karnyel, Karnyela,
Karnyele, Karnyell, Karnyella, Karnyelle*

Karol, Karoll (Slavic) forms of Carol.
*Karilla, Karily, Karola, Karole, Karoly,
Karrol, Karyl, Karyla, Karyle, Karyll,
Karylle, Kerril*

**Karol Ann, Karolane, Karolann,
Karolanne** (American) combinations of
Karol + Ann.
Karol-Anne, Karolan

Karolina (Slavic) a form of Carolina.
*Karalena, Karilena, Karilina, Karolainah,
Karolayna, Karolaynah, Karoleena, Karolena,
Karolinah, Karolinka, Karrolena*

Karoline (Slavic) a form of Caroline.
*Karaleen, Karalene, Karalin, Karaline,
Karileen, Karilene, Karilin, Kariline,
Karlen, Karling, Karolin, Karroleen,
Karrolene, Karrolin, Karroline*

Karolyn (American) a form of Carolyn.
*Karilyn, Karilyna, Karilynn, Karilynne,
Karolyna, Karolynah, Karolyne, Karolynn,
Karolynne, Karrolyn, Karrolyna,
Karrolynn, Karrolynne*

Karon (American) a form of Karen.
*Kaaron, Karona, Karonah, Karone,
Karonia, Karoniah, Karonie, Karony,
Karonya, Karonyah, Karron, Kerron*

Karra (Greek, Danish) a form of Kara.

Karrah (Greek, Danish, Irish, Italian) a
form of Karah.

Karri, Karrie (American) forms of
Carrie. See also Kari.
Karree, Karrey, Karry

Karsen, Karson, Karsyn (English) child
of Kar. Forms of Carson.

Karuna (Hindi) merciful.

Karyn (American) a form of Karen.
*Kaaryn, Karryn, Karryne, Karyne, Karynn,
Kerrynn, Kerrynne*

Karyna (American) a form of Karina.
Karryna, Karrynah, Karynah, Karynna

Karyssa (Greek) a form of Carissa.
Karysa, Karysah, Karyssah

Kasa (Hopi) fur robe.

Kasandra, Kassandra, Kassandre
(Greek) forms of Cassandra.
*Kasander, Kasandrah, Kasandre, Kasandria,
Kasandrina, Kasandrine, Kasoundra,
Kassandr, Kassandrah, Kassandré,
Kassandria, Kassandriah, Kassundra,
Kassundre, Kassundria, Kassundriah,
Kazandra, Kazandrah, Kazandria,
Kazandriah, Kazzandra, Kazzandrah,
Kazzandre, Kazzandria, Kazzandriah,
Kazzandrya, Kazzandryah*

Kasaundra, Kassaundra (Greek) forms
of Kasandra.
*Kasaundrah, Kassaundre, Kassaundria,
Kassaundriah*

Kasen (Danish) a form of Katherine.
Kasena, Kasenah, Kasene, Kasin

Kasey (Irish) brave. (American) a form of Casey, Kacey.
Kaesee, Kaesey, Kaesi, Kaesie, Kaesy, Kaisee, Kaisey, Kaisi, Kaisie, Kaisy, Kasci, Kascy, Kasee, Kassee, Kasy

Kasha (Native American) a form of Kahsha. (American) a form of Kashawna.
Kashae

Kashawna (American) a combination of Kate + Shawna.
Kashana, Kashanna, Kashauna, Kashawn, Kasheana, Kasheanna, Kasheena, Kashena, Kashonda, Kashonna

Kashmere (Sanskrit) a form of Kashmir.

Kashmir (Sanskrit) Geography: a region located between India and Pakistan.
Cashmere, Kashmear, Kashmia, Kashmira, Kasmir, Kasmira, Kazmir, Kazmira

Kasi (Hindi) from the holy city.

Kasia (Polish) a form of Katherine. See also Cassia.
Kashia, Kasiah, Kasian, Kasienka, Kasja, Kaska, Kassa, Kassya, Kassyah, Kasya, Kasyah, Kazia, Kaziah, Kazya, Kazyah, Kazzia, Kazziah, Kazzya, Kazzyah

Kasidy (Irish) a form of Kassidy.

Kasie (Irish, American) a form of Kasey. (Hindi) a form of Kasi.

Kasimira (Slavic) a form of Casimira.
Kasimera, Kasimerah, Kasimiera, Kasimirah, Kasmira, Kasmirah, Kasmiria, Kasmiriah, Kasmirya, Kasmiryah, Kasmyra, Kasmyrah, Kazmira, Kazmirah, Kazmiria, Kazmiriah, Kazmyra, Kazmyrah, Kazmyria, Kazmyriah, Kazmyrya, Kazmyryah, Kazzmira, Kazzmirah, Kazzmiria, Kazzmiriah, Kazzmirya, Kazzmiryah, Kazzmyra, Kazzmyrah, Kazzmyrya, Kazzmyryah

Kasinda (Umbundu) our last baby.

Kasondra, Kassondra (Greek) forms of Cassandra.
Kassondrah, Kassondria

Kassey (American) a form of Kassi. (Irish, American) a form of Kasey.

Kassi, Kassie, Kassy (American) familiar forms of Kasandra, Kassidy. See also Cassey.
Kassee, Kasy, Kazi, Kazie, Kazy, Kazzi, Kazzie, Kazzy

Kassia (Polish) a form of Kasia. (American) a form of Kassi.
Kassiah

Kassidee, Kassidi (Irish, American) forms of Kassidy.
Kasidee

Kassidy (Irish) clever. (American) a form of Cassidy.
Kasadee, Kasadey, Kasadi, Kasadia, Kasadie, Kasady, Kasidey, Kasidi, Kasidia, Kasidie, Kassadea, Kassadee, Kassadey, Kassadi, Kassadia, Kassadiah, Kassadie, Kassadina, Kassady, Kassadya, Kasseday, Kassedee, Kassiddy, Kassidea, Kassidey, Kassidia, Kassidiah, Kassidie, Kassity, Kassydee, Kassydi, Kassydia, Kassydie, Kassydy, Kasydee, Kasydey, Kasydi, Kasydie, Kasydy, Kazadea, Kazadee, Kazadey, Kazadi, Kazadia, Kazadiah, Kazadie, Kazady, Kazadya, Kazidy, Kazydy, Kazzadea, Kazzadee, Kazzadey, Kazzadi, Kazzadia, Kazzadiah, Kazzadie, Kazzady

Katalina (Irish) a form of Caitlin. See also Catalina.
Kataleen, Kataleena, Katalena, Katalin, Katalinah, Kataline, Katalyn, Katalynn

Katarina (Czech) a form of Katherine.
Kata, Katarain, Kataraina, Katarainah, Kataraine, Katareena, Katarena, Katarin, Katarinah, Katarine, Katarinna, Katarinne, Katarrina, Kataryn, Kataryna, Katarynah, Kataryne, Katinka, Katrika, Katrinka

Katarzyna (Czech) a form of Katherine.

Kate (Greek) pure. (English) a short form of Katherine.
Kait, Kata, Katica, Katka, Kayt

Kate-Lynn (American) a combination of Kate + Lynn.
Kate Lyn, Kate Lynn, Kate Lynne, Kate-Lyn, Kate-Lynne

Katee, Katey (English) familiar forms of Kate, Katherine. See also Katie.

Kateland (Irish) a form of Caitlin.
Katelind

Katelee (American) a combination of
Kate + Lee.
*Katelea, Kateleah, Katelei, Kateleigh, Kateley,
Kateli, Katelia, Kateliah, Katelie, Kately*

**Katelin, Katelyn, Katelyne, Katelynn,
Katelynne** (Irish) forms of Caitlin. See
also Kaitlin.
*Kaetlin, Katalin, Katelan, Kateleen,
Katelen, Katelene, Kateline, Katelinn,
Katelun, Katelyna, Katelynah, Katewin,
Katewina, Katewinah, Katewine, Katewyn,
Katewyna, Katewynah, Katewyne*

Katerina (Slavic) a form of Katherine.
*Katenka, Katereana, Katereanah, Katereena,
Katereenah, Katerinah, Katerini, Katerinia,
Kateriniah, Kateriny, Katerinka*

Katerine (Slavic) a form of Katherine.
Kateren

Katharina (Greek) a form of Katharine.
Katharinah, Katharyna, Katharynah

Katharine, Katharyn (Greek) forms of
Katherine.
Katharaine, Katharin, Katharyne

Katherin, Katheryn, Katheryne (Greek)
forms of Katherine.

Katherina (Greek) a form of Katherine.
Katherinah, Katheryna, Katherynah

Katherine (Greek) pure. See also Carey,
Catherine, Ekaterina, Kara, Karen, Kari,
Kasia, Katerina, Yekaterina.
*Ekaterina, Ekatrinna, Kasen, Kat, Katchen,
Kathann, Kathanne, Kathereen, Katheren,
Katherene, Katherenne, Kathyrine, Katlaina,
Katoka, Katreeka, Katreen*

Kathi, Kathy (English) familiar forms of
Katherine, Kathleen. See also Cathi,
Cathy.
*Kaethe, Katha, Kathe, Kathee, Kathey,
Kathie, Katka, Katla, Kató*

Kathia, Kathya (English) forms of Kathi.
Kathiah, Kathye

Kathleen (Irish) a form of Katherine. See
also Cathleen.
*Katheleen, Kathelene, Kathileen, Kathlean,
Kathleena, Kathleenah, Kathleene, Kathlein,
Kathleina, Kathleinah, Kathleine, Kathlene,
Kathlina, Kathlinah, Kathline, Katleen*

Kathlyn (Irish) a form of Kathleen.
*Kathlin, Kathlyna, Kathlynah, Kathlyne,
Kathlynn*

Kathrin, Kathrine (Greek) forms of
Katherine.
*Kathran, Kathreen, Kathren, Kathrene,
Kathron, Kathrun, Kathryn*

Kathrina (Danish) a form of Katherine.
Kathreena, Kathrinah, Kathryna, Kathrynah

Kathryn, Kathryne, Kathrynn (English)
forms of Katherine.
Kathren, Kathrynne

Kati (Estonian) a familiar form of Kate.

Katia, Katya (Russian) forms of
Katherine.
*Cattiah, Kãtia, Katiah, Katinka, Katiya,
Kattia, Kattiah, Katyah*

Katie (English) a familiar form of Kate.
See also Katy.
Kaaitea, Kaitee, Kaitie, Kaitey

Katie-Lynn (American) a combination of
Katie + Lynn.
*Katie Lyn, Katie Lynn, Katie Lynne,
Katie-Lyn, Katie-Lynne, Katy Lyn, Katy
Lynn, Katy Lynne, Katy-Lyn, Katy-Lynn,
Katy-Lynne*

Katilyn (Irish) a form of Katlyn.
Katilin, Katilynn

Katina (English, Russian) a form of
Katherine.
*Kateana, Kateanah, Kateena, Kateenah,
Kateina, Kateinah, Kateyna, Kateynah,
Katinah, Katine, Katyn, Katyna, Katynah,
Katyne*

Katja (Estonian) a form of Kate.
Kaatje, Katye

Katlin, Katlyne, Katlynn (Greek, Irish)
forms of Katlyn.
*Katlina, Katline, Katlyna, Katlynd,
Katlynne*

Katlyn (Greek) pure. (Irish) a form of Katelin.
Kaatlain, Katland

Katreen, Katrin, Katrine (English) forms of Katherine.
Katreene, Katren, Katrene, Katrian, Katriane, Katriann, Katrianne, Katrien, Katrinne, Katryn, Katryne

Katrena (German) a form of Katrina.
Katrenah

Katrice (German) a form of Katrina.
Katricia

Katriel (Hebrew) God is my crown. See also Catriel.
Katrelle, Katri, Katrie, Katriela, Katrielah, Katriele, Katriell, Katriella, Katriellah, Katrielle, Katry, Katryel, Katryela, Katryelah, Katryele, Katryell, Katryella, Katryellah, Katryelle

Katrina (German) a form of Katherine. See also Catrina, Trina.
Kaetreana, Kaetreanah, Kaetreena, Kaetreenah, Kaetreina, Kaetreinah, Kaetreyna, Kaetreynah, Kaetrina, Kaetrinah, Kaetryna, Kaetrynah, Kaitreana, Kaitreanah, Kaitreena, Kaitreenah, Kaitreina, Kaitreinah, Kaitreyna, Kaitreynah, Kaitrina, Kaitrinah, Kaitryna, Kaitrynah, Katreana, Katreanah, Katreena, Katreenah, Katreina, Katreinah, Katreyna, Katreynah, Katri, Katriana, Katrianah, Katrianna, Katriannah, Katrien, Katriena, Katrienah, Katrinah, Katrinia, Katrinna, Katrinnah, Katriona, Kattrina, Kattryna, Katus, Kaytreana, Kaytreanah, Kaytreena, Kaytreenah, Kaytreina, Kaytreinah, Kaytreyna, Kaytreynah, Kaytrina, Kaytrinah, Kaytryna, Kaytrynah

Katrinelle (American) a combination of Katrina + Elle.
Katrinal, Katrinel, Katrinela, Katrinele, Katrinell, Katrinella, Katrynel, Katrynela, Katrynele, Katrynell, Katrynella, Katrynelle

Katryna (German) a form of Katrina.
Katrynah

Kattie, Katty (English) familiar forms of Kate.
Katti

Katy (English) a familiar form of Kate. See also Cadie, Katie.

Kaulana (Hawaiian) famous.
Kahuna, Kaula, Kauna

Kaveri (Hindi) Geography: a sacred river in India.

Kavindra (Hindi) poet.

Kavita (Indian) a poem.

Kawena (Hawaiian) glow.
Kawana, Kawona

Kay (Greek) rejoicer. (Teutonic) a fortified place. (Latin) merry. A short form of Katherine.
Caye, Kaye

Kaya (Hopi) wise child. (Japanese) resting place.
Kaea, Kaja, Kayah, Kayia

Kayanna (American) a combination of Kay + Anna.
Kay Anna

Kayce, Kaycee, Kayci, Kaycie, Kaysie (American) combinations of the initials K. + C.
Kaycey, Kaycy, Kaysci, Kaysee, Kaysey, Kaysi, Kaysii, Kaysy

Kaydee (American) a combination of the initials K. + D. See also Katie.
Kayda, Kayde, Kaydey, Kaydi, Kaydie, Kaydy

Kayden (American) a form of Kaydee.

Kayla (Arabic, Hebrew) laurel; crown. A form of Kaela, Kaila. See also Cayla.
Kaelea, Kaylea

Kaylah (Arabic, Hebrew) a form of Kayla.

Kaylan, Kaylen (Hebrew) forms of Kayleen.
Kayland, Kaylann, Kaylean, Kayleana, Kayleanna, Kaylenn

Kaylani (Hawaiian) a form of Kailani, Keilana.
Kaylana, Kaylanah, Kaylanea, Kaylanee, Kaylaney, Kaylania, Kaylaniah, Kaylanie, Kaylany, Kaylanya

Kayle, Kayleigh, Kayley, Kayli, Kaylie
(American) forms of Kaylee.

Kaylea (Hawaiian) a form of Kalea.
(Arabic, Hebrew) a form of Kayla.
Kayleah

Kaylee (American) a form of Kayla. See
also Caeley, Kalee.
*Kaylei, Kayly, Kaylya, Keylea, Keyleah,
Keylee, Keylei, Keyleigh, Keyley, Keyli,
Keylia, Keyliah, Keylie, Keyly*

Kayleen, Kaylene (Hebrew) beloved,
sweetheart. Forms of Kayla.
*Kaylean, Kayleane, Kayleene, Kaylein,
Kayleine*

Kaylena (Hebrew) a form of Kayleen.
Kayleana, Kayleena, Kayleina

Kaylia (Arabic, Hebrew) a form of Kayla.
(American) a form of Kaylee.
Kayliah

Kaylin, Kaylon (American) forms of
Kaylyn.
Kaylina, Kayline

Kaylyn, Kaylynn, Kaylynne (American)
combinations of Kay + Lynn. See also
Kaelyn.
Kaylyna, Kaylyne

Kayte, Kaytie (English) forms of Katy.
Kaytee

Kaytlin, Kaytlyn (Irish) forms of Kaitlin.
*Kaytlan, Kaytlann, Kaytlen, Kaytlyne,
Kaytlynn, Kaytlynne*

Kc (American) a combination of the initials K. + C.
K. C.

Keagan (Irish) a form of Keegan.
Keagean, Keagen, Keaghan, Keagyn

Keaira, Keairra (Irish) forms of Keara.
Keair, Keairah, Keairre, Keairrea

Keala (Hawaiian) path.
*Kealah, Kealea, Kealeah, Kealee, Kealei,
Kealeigh, Keali, Kealia, Kealiah, Kealie,
Kealy, Kealya*

Keana, Keanna (German) bold; sharp.
(Irish) beautiful.
*Keanah, Keanne, Keenan, Keeyana,
Keeyanah, Keeyanna*

Keandra (American) a form of Kenda.
*Keandrah, Keandre, Keandrea, Keandria,
Kedeana, Kedia*

Keanu (German, Irish) a form of Keana.

Keara (Irish) dark; black.
Kearah, Kearia

Kearra (Irish) a form of Keara.

Kearsten, Kearstin, Kearston (Greek)
forms of Kirsten.
Kearstyn

Keasha (African) a form of Keisha.
Keashia

Keaton (English) where hawks fly.
*Keatan, Keaten, Keatin, Keatton, Keatun,
Keatyn, Keetan, Keeten, Keetin, Keeton,
Keetun, Keetyn, Keitan, Keiten, Keiton,
Keitun, Keityn, Keytan, Keyten, Keytin,
Keyton, Keytun, Keytyn*

Kecia (American) a form of Keshia.

Keegan (Irish) little; fiery.
*Kaegan, Kagan, Keegen, Keeghan, Keegin,
Keegon, Keegun, Kegan, Keigan*

Keeley, Keely (Irish) forms of Kelly.
*Kealee, Kealey, Keali, Kealie, Keallie,
Kealy, Keela, Keelah, Keelan, Keele, Keelea,
Keeleah, Keelee, Keelei, Keeleigh, Keeli,
Keelia, Keeliah, Keelie, Keellie, Keelya,
Keelyah, Keelye, Kiela, Kiele, Kieley, Kielly,
Kiely*

Keelin, Keelyn (Irish) forms of Kellyn.
Kealyn, Keilan, Kielyn

Keena (Irish) brave.
*Keenah, Keenya, Keina, Keinah, Keyna,
Keynah, Kina*

Keera (Irish) a form of Keara. (Persian,
Latin) a form of Kira. (Greek) a form
of Kyra.
Keerra

Keesha (American) a form of Keisha.
*Keesa, Keeshae, Keeshana, Keeshanne,
Keeshawna, Keeshia, Keeshiah, Keeshonna,
Keeshy, Keeshya, Keeshyah*

Kei (Japanese) reverent.

Keiana, Keianna (Irish) forms of Keana.
(American) forms of Kiana.
Keiann, Keiannah

Keiara, Keiarra (Irish) forms of Keara.
Keiarah

Keiki (Hawaiian) child.
*Keikana, Keikann, Keikanna, Keikanne,
Keyki, Kiki*

Keiko (Japanese) happy child.
Keyko

Keila, Keilah (Arabic, Hebrew) forms of
Kayla.

Keilana (Hawaiian) gloriously calm.
*Kealaina, Kealainah, Kealana, Kealanah,
Kealanna, Kealannah, Keelaina, Keelainah,
Keelana, Keelanah, Keelayna, Keelaynah,
Keilaina, Keilainah, Keilanah, Keilanna,
Keilannah, Keilayna, Keilaynah, Keylaina,
Keylainah, Keylana, Keylanah, Keylayna,
Keylaynah*

Keilani (Hawaiian) glorious chief.
*Kealaine, Kealainee, Kealane, Kealanee,
Kealanne, Kealannee, Keelane, Keelanee,
Keelayn, Keelayne, Keelaynee, Keilaine,
Keilainee, Keilan, Keilane, Keilanee,
Keilanne, Keilannee, Keilany, Keilayn,
Keilayne, Keilaynee, Kelana, Kelanah,
Kelane, Kelani, Kelanie, Keylaine,
Keylainee, Keylane, Keylanee, Keylayn,
Keylayne, Keylaynee*

Keily (Irish) a form of Keeley, Kiley.
*Keighla, Keighlea, Keighlee, Keighlei,
Keighleigh, Keighley, Keighli, Keighlia,
Keighliah, Keighlie, Keighly, Keilea, Keileah,
Keilee, Keilei, Keileigh, Keiley, Keili, Keilia,
Keiliah, Keilie, Keilley, Keilly, Keilya*

Keiona, Keionna (Irish) forms of Keana.

Keiosha (American) a form of Keesha.

Keira, Keirra (Irish) forms of Keara.
Keirrah

Keirsten, Keirstin, Keirstyn (Greek)
forms of Kirsten.
Keirstan, Keirstein, Keirston, Keirstynne

Keisha (African) favorite.
*Keishah, Keishaun, Keishauna, Keishawn,
Keishia, Keishiah, Keishya, Keishyah,
Keschia*

Keita (Scottish) woods; enclosed place.
Keiti

Kekona (Hawaiian) second-born child.

Kela (Arabic, Hebrew) a form of Kayla.
Kelah

Kelby (German) farm by the spring.
Kelbea, Kelbee, Kelbey, Kelbi, Kelbie

Kelcee, Kelcey, Kelci, Kelcie, Kelcy
(Scottish) forms of Kelsey.
*Kelce, Kelcea, Kelcia, Kellcea, Kellcee, Kellcey,
Kellci, Kellcia, Kellciah, Kellcie, Kellcy*

Kele (Hopi) sparrow hawk.
Kelea, Keleah

**Keli, Kellee, Kelleigh, Kelley, Kelli,
Kellie** (Irish) familiar forms of Kelly.
*Kelee, Kelei, Keleigh, Keley, Kelie, Kellei,
Kellisa*

Kelia (Irish) a form of Kelly.
Keliah, Kellea, Kelleah, Kellia, Kelliah

Kelila (Hebrew) crown, laurel. See also
Kaela, Kayla, Kalila.
Kelilah, Kelula, Kelulah

Kellan, Kellen (Irish) forms of Kellyn.
Kelleen, Kellene

**Kellsey, Kellsie, Kelsea, Kelsee, Kelsei,
Kelsi, Kelsie, Kelsy** (Scandinavian,
Scottish, English) forms of Kelsey.
*Kellsea, Kellsee, Kellsei, Kellsia, Kellsiah,
Kellsy, Kelsae, Kelsay, Kelsye*

Kelly (Irish) brave warrior. See also Caeley.
Kellye, Kely, Kelya

Kelly Ann, Kelly Anne, Kellyanne (Irish)
combinations of Kelly + Ann.
Kelliann, Kellianne, Kellyann

Kellyn, Kellynn (Irish) combinations of
Kelly + Lynn.
Kellina, Kellinah, Kelline, Kellynne

Kelsa (Scandinavian, Scottish, English) a short form of Kelsey.
Kelse

Kelsey (Scandinavian, Scottish) ship island. (English) a form of Chelsea.
Kelda

Kemberly (English) a form of Kimberly.
Kemberlea, Kemberleah, Kemberlee, Kemberlei, Kemberleigh, Kemberli, Kemberlia, Kemberliah, Kemberlie, Kemberly

Kena, Kenna (Irish) short forms of Kennice.
Kenah, Kennah

Kenadee, Kenadi, Kennadi, Kennady (Irish) forms of Kennedy.
Kennadee, Kennadie

Kenda (English) water baby. (Dakota) magical power.
Kendah, Kennda

Kendahl, Kendal, Kendel, Kendell (English) forms of Kendall.
Kendala, Kendalah, Kendale, Kendalie, Kendalla, Kendallah, Kendalle, Kendela, Kendelah, Kendele, Kendella, Kendellah, Kendelle

Kendall (English) ruler of the valley.
Kendera, Kendia, Kendil, Kinda, Kindal, Kindall, Kindi, Kindle, Kynda, Kyndel

Kendalyn (American) a form of Kendellyn.
Kendalin, Kendalynn

Kendellyn (American) a combination of Kendall + Lynn.
Kendelan, Kendelana, Kendelanah, Kendelane, Kendellan, Kendellana, Kendellanah, Kendellane, Kendelin, Kendelina, Kendelinah, Kendeline, Kendellyna, Kendellynah, Kendellyne, Kendelyn, Kendelyna, Kendelynah, Kendelyne

Kendra (English) a form of Kenda.
Kendrah, Kendre, Kenndra, Kentra, Kentrae

Kendria (English) a form of Kenda.
Kendrea, Kendreah, Kendriah, Kendrya, Kendryah

Kendyl, Kendyll (English) forms of Kendall.
Kendyle

Kenedi, Kennedi, Kennedie (Irish) forms of Kennedy.
Kenedee, Kenedey, Kenedie, Kenedy

Keneisha (American) a combination of the prefix Ken + Aisha.
Keneesha, Kenneisha, Kennysha, Kenysha, Kenyshah, Kineisha

Kenenza (English) a form of Kennice.
Kenza

Kenesha (American) a form of Keneisha.
Keneshia, Kennesha, Kenneshia

Kenia, Kennia (Hebrew) forms of Kenya.
Keniah, Keniya, Kenja, Kenjah

Kenise (English) a form of Kennice.
Kenisa, Kenissa, Kenissah, Kennis, Kennisa, Kennisah, Kennise, Kenniss, Kennissa, Kennissah, Kennisse, Kenys, Kenysa, Kenysah, Kenyse, Kenyss, Kenyssa, Kenyssah, Kenysse

Kenisha, Kennisha (American) forms of Keneisha.
Kenishah, Kenishia

Kenley (English) royal meadow.
Kenlea, Kenlee, Kenleigh, Kenli, Kenlie, Kennlea, Kennlee, Kennleigh, Kennley, Kennli, Kennlie, Kennly, Kenly

Kennedy (Irish) helmeted chief. History: John F. Kennedy was the thirty-fifth U.S. president.
Kenidee, Kenidi, Kenidie, Kenidy, Kennedee, Kennedey, Kennedie, Kennidi, Kennidy, Kynnedi

Kenni (English) a familiar form of Kennice.
Kenee, Keni, Kenne, Kennee, Kenney, Kennie, Kenny, Kennye

Kennice (English) beautiful.
Kanice, Keneese, Kenenza, Kenese

Kenya (Hebrew) animal horn. Geography: a country in Africa.
Keenya, Kenyah, Kenyia

Kenyana (Hebrew) a form of Kenya.

Kenyata, Kenyatta (American) forms of Kenya.
Kenyatah, Kenyatte, Kenyattia

Kenyetta (American) a form of Kenya.
Kenyette

Kenzi (Scottish, Irish) a form of Kenzie.

Kenzie (Scottish) light skinned. (Irish) a short form of Mackenzie.
Kenzea, Kenzee, Kenzey, Kenzia, Kenzy

Keona, Keonna (Irish) forms of Keana.
Keeyona, Keeyonna, Keoana, Keonnah

Keondra (American) a form of Kenda.
Keonda, Keondre, Keondria

Keoni (Irish) a form of Keana.
Keonia, Keonni, Keonnia

Keosha (American) a short form of Keneisha.
Keoshae, Keoshi, Keoshia, Keosia

Kera, Kerra (Hindi) short forms of Kerani.
Kerah

Kerani (Hindi) sacred bells. See also Rani.
Kerana, Keranee, Keraney, Kerania, Keraniah, Keranie, Kerany, Keranya, Keranyah

Keren (Hebrew) animal's horn.
Keran, Keron, Kerran, Kerre, Kerren, Kerron, Keryn, Kieren, Kierin, Kieron, Kieryn

Kerensa (Cornish) a form of Karenza.
Kerensah, Kerenza, Kerenzah

Keri, Kerri, Kerrie (Irish) forms of Kerry.

Keriann, Kerrianne (Irish) combinations of Keri + Ann.
Kerian, Keriana, Kerianah, Keriane, Kerianna, Keriannah, Kerriane, Kerriann, Kerrianne, Kerryann, Kerryanna, Kerryannah, Kerryanne, Keryan, Keryana, Keryanah, Keryane, Keryann, Keryanna, Keryannah, Keryanne

Kerielle, Kerrielle (American) combinations of Keri + Elle.
Keriel, Keriela, Kerielah, Keriele, Keriell, Keriella, Keriellah, Kerriel, Kerriela, Kerrielah, Kerriele, Kerriell, Kerriella, Kerriellah, Kerryell, Kerryella, Kerryellah,

Kerryelle, Keryel, Keryela, Keryelah, Keryele, Keryell, Keryella, Keryellah, Keryelle

Kerrin (Hebrew) a form of Keren.
Kerin

Kerry (Irish) dark haired. Geography: a county in Ireland.
Keary, Keiry, Keree, Kerey, Kery

Kersten, Kerstin, Kerstyn (Scandinavian) forms of Kirsten.
Kerstain, Kerstaine, Kerstan, Kerstane, Kerste, Kerstean, Kersteane, Kersteen, Kersteene, Kerstein, Kerstene, Kerstie, Kerstien, Kerstine, Kerston, Kerstyne, Kerstynn

Kerstina (Scandinavian) a form of Kristina.
Kerstaina, Kerstainah, Kerstana, Kerstanah, Kersteana, Kersteanah, Kersteena, Kersteenah, Kerstena, Kerstenah, Kerstinah, Kerstyna, Kerstynah, Kurstaina, Kurstainah, Kursteana, Kursteanah, Kursteena, Kursteenah, Kurstina, Kurstinah, Kurstyna, Kurstynah

Kesare (Latin) long haired. (Russian) a form of Caesar (see Boys' Names).

Kesha (American) a form of Keisha.
Keshah, Keshal, Keshala

Keshara (American) a form of Keisha.

Keshawna (American) a form of Keisha.
Keshan, Keshana, Keshawn, Keshawnna

Keshet (Hebrew) rainbow.
Kesetta, Kesettah, Kesette, Kesheta, Keshetah, Keshete, Keshett, Keshetta, Keshettah, Keshette

Keshia (American) a form of Keisha. A short form of Keneisha.
Keshea

Kesi (Swahili) born during difficult times.
Kesee, Kesey, Kesie, Kesy

Kesia (African) favorite.
Kesiah, Kessia, Kessiah, Kessya, Kessyah

Kesley (Scandinavian, Scottish) a form of Kelsey.
Kesly

Kessie (Ashanti) chubby baby.
Kess, Kessa, Kesse, Kessey, Kessi

Ketifa (Arabic) flower.
Ketifah, Kettifa, Kettifah, Kettyfa, Kettyfah, Ketyfa, Ketyfah

Ketina (Hebrew) girl.
Keteena, Keteenah, Ketinah, Ketyna, Ketynah

Kevina (Irish) a form of Kevyn.
Kevinah

Kevyn (Irish) beautiful.
Keva, Kevan, Keven, Kevern, Keverna, Kevernah, Kevia, Keviana, Kevine, Kevinna, Kevion, Kevionna, Kevirn, Kevirna, Kevirnah, Kevirne, Kevon, Kevona, Kevone, Kevonia, Kevonna, Kevonne, Kevonya, Kevynn, Kevyrn, Kevyrna, Kevyrnah, Kevyrne

Keyana, Keyanna (American) forms of Kiana.
Keya, Keyanah, Keyanda, Keyannah

Keyandra (American) a form of Kiana.

Keyara, Keyarra (Irish) forms of Kiara.
Keyarah, Keyari

Keyera, Keyerra (Irish) forms of Kiara.
Keyeira, Keyerah

Keyla (Arabic, Hebrew) a form of Kayla.
Keylah

Keyona, Keyonna (American) forms of Kiana.
Keyonnie

Keyonda (American) a form of Kiana.

Keyondra (American) a form of Kiana.

Keyonia (American) a form of Kiana.
Keyonnia

Keyosha (American) a form of Keisha.
Keyoshia

Keysha (American) a form of Keisha.
Keyshah, Keyshana, Keyshanna, Keyshawn, Keyshawna, Keyshia, Keyshiah, Keyshla, Keyshona, Keyshonna, Keyshya, Keyshyah

Kezia (Hebrew) a form of Keziah.
Kezzia

Keziah (Hebrew) cinnamon-like spice. Bible: one of the daughters of Job.
Kazia, Kaziah, Ketzi, Ketzia, Ketziah, Ketzya, Ketzyah, Kezi, Kezya, Kezyah, Kezziah, Kizia, Kiziah, Kizzia, Kizziah, Kyzia, Kyziah, Kyzzia, Kyzziah, Kyzzya, Kyzzyah

Khadeeja (Arabic) a form of Khadijah.
Khadeejah

Khadeja, Khadejah (Arabic) a form of Khadijah.
Khadejha

Khadija (Arabic) a form of Khadijah.

Khadijah (Arabic) trustworthy. History: Muhammed's first wife.
Khadaja, Khadajah, Khadije, Khadijia, Khadijiah

Khalia, Khaliah (Arabic) forms of Khalida.

Khalida (Arabic) immortal, everlasting.
Khali, Khalidda, Khalita

Khalilah (Arabic) a form of Kalila.
Khalila, Khalillah

Khaliyah (Arabic) a form of Khalida.

Khayla (Arabic, Hebrew) a form of Kayla.

Khiana (American) a form of Kiana.
Khianah, Khianna

Khimberly (English) a form of Kimberly.
Khimberlea, Khimberleah, Khimberlee, Khimberlei, Khimberleigh, Khimberley, Khimberli, Khimberlia, Khimberliah, Khimberlie, Khymberlea, Khymberleah, Khymberlee, Khymberlei, Khymberleigh, Khymberley, Khymberli, Khymberlia, Khymberliah, Khymberlie, Khymberly

Khrisha (American, Czech) a form of Khrissa.
Krisia, Krysha

Khrissa (American) a form of Chrissa. (Czech) a form of Krista.
Khrishia, Khryssa, Kryssa

Khristina (Russian, Scandinavian) a form of Kristina, Christina.
Khristeana, Khristeanah, Khristeena, Khristeenah, Khristeina, Khristeinah,

Khristinah, Khristya, Khristyana, Khristyna, Khristynah, Khrystyna, Khrystynah

Khristine (Scandinavian) a form of Christine.
Khristean, Khristeane, Khristeen, Khristeene, Khristein, Khristeine, Khristeyn, Khristeyne, Khristyne, Khrystean, Khrysteane, Khrysteen, Khrysteene, Khrystein, Khrysteine, Khrysteyn, Khrysteyne, Khrystyne, Khrystynne

Ki (Korean) arisen.

Kia (African) season's beginning. (American) a short form of Kiana.

Kiah (African, American) a form of Kia.

Kiahna (American) a form of Kiana.

Kiaira (Irish) a form of Kiara.

Kiana (American) a combination of the prefix Ki + Ana.
Kianah, Kiandria, Kiane, Kianne

Kiandra (American) a form of Kiana.

Kiani (American) a form of Kiana.
Kiania, Kianni

Kianna (American) a form of Kiana.
Kiannah

Kiara (Irish) little and dark.

Kiaria (Japanese) fortunate.
Kichi

Kiarra (Irish) a form of Kiara. (Japanese) a form of Kiaria.

Kiauna (American) a form of Kiana.
Kiaundra

Kieanna (American) a form of Kiana.

Kieara (Irish) a form of Kiara.
Kiearah, Kiearra

Kiele (Hawaiian) gardenia; fragrant blossom.
Kiela, Kielea, Kieleah, Kielee, Kielei, Kieleigh, Kieley, Kieli, Kielia, Kieliah, Kielie, Kielli, Kielly, Kiely

Kiera, Kierra (Irish) forms of Kerry.
Kierea

Kieran (Irish) little and dark; little Keir. A form of Kerry. (Hindi) a form of Kiran.
Kierana, Kieranah, Kierane, Kieranna, Kieren, Kieron

Kiersten, Kierstin, Kierston, Kierstyn (Scandinavian) forms of Kirsten.
Kierstan, Kierstynn

Kiesha (American) a form of Keisha.

Kiki (Spanish) a familiar form of names ending in "queta."
Kikee, Kikey, Kikie, Kiky

Kiku (Japanese) chrysanthemum.
Kiko

Kilee (Irish) a form of Kiley.
Killee

Kiley (Irish) attractive; from the straits. See also Kylie.
Kielea, Kieleah, Kielee, Kielei, Kieleigh, Kieley, Kieli, Kielia, Kieliah, Kielie, Kiely, Kilea, Kileah, Kilei, Kileigh, Kili, Kilie, Killey, Killi, Killie, Killy, Kily

Kilia (Hawaiian) heaven.
Kiliah, Killea, Killeah, Killia, Killiah, Kylia, Kyliah, Kylya, Kylyah

Kim (Vietnamese) needle. (English) a short form of Kimberly.
Kem, Khim, Khime, Khimm, Khym, Khyme, Khymm, Kima, Kimette, Kimm

Kimalina (American) a combination of Kim + Lina.
Kimalinah, Kimaline, Kimalyn, Kimalyna, Kimalynah, Kimalyne, Kymalyn, Kymalyna, Kymalynah, Kymalyne

Kimana (Shoshone) butterfly.
Kiman, Kimanah, Kimane, Kimann, Kimanna, Kimannah, Kimanne, Kymana, Kymanah, Kymane, Kymanna, Kymannah, Kymanne

Kimani (Shoshone) a form of Kimana.

Kimbalee (English) a form of Kimberly.
Kimbalea, Kimbaleah, Kimbalei, Kimbaleigh, Kymbalea, Kymbaleah, Kymbalee, Kymbalei, Kymbaleigh, Kymbali, Kymbalia, Kymbaliah, Kymbalie,

Kimbalee *(cont.)*
Kymballea, Kymballeah, Kymballee,
Kymballei, Kymballeigh, Kymballie

Kimber (English) a short form of
Kimberly.
Kimbra

Kimberlee, Kimberley, Kimberli,
Kimberlie (English) forms of Kimberly.
Kimberlea, Kimberleah, Kimberlei,
Kimberleigh, Kimberlia, Kimberliah, Kimbley

Kimberlin, Kimberlyn, Kimberlynn
(English) forms of Kimberly.
Kemberlin, Kemberlina, Kemberlinah,
Kemberline, Kemberlyn, Kemberlyna,
Kemberlynah, Kemberlyne, Khimberlin,
Khimberlina, Khimberlinah, Khimberline,
Khimberlyn, Khimberlyna, Khimberlynah,
Khimberlyne, Kimbalina, Kimbalinah,
Kimbaline, Kimbalyn, Kimbalyna,
Kimbalynah, Kimbalyne, Kimberlina,
Kimberlinah, Kimberline, Kimberlyna,
Kimberlynah, Kimberlyne, Kymbalin,
Kymbalina, Kymbalinah, Kymbaline

Kimberly (English) chief, ruler.
Cymberly, Cymbre, Kimba, Kimbalee,
Kimbely, Kimberely, Kimbery, Kimbria,
Kimbrie, Kimbry

Kimi (Japanese) righteous.
Kimee, Kimey, Kimia, Kimie, Kimiyo,
Kimmi, Kimy

Kimiko (Japanese) righteous child.
Kimik, Kimika, Kimyko, Kymyko

Kimmie, Kimmy (English) familiar forms
of Kimberly.
Kimme, Kimmee, Kimmey, Kimmi

Kina (Hawaiian) from China. (Irish) wise.
Kinah, Kyna, Kynah

Kindra (English) a form of Kendra.

Kineisha (American) a form of Keneisha.
Kineesha, Kinesha, Kineshia, Kinisha,
Kinishia

Kineta (Greek) energetic.
Kinet, Kinetah, Kinete, Kinett, Kinetta,
Kinettah, Kinette, Kynet, Kyneta, Kynetah,
Kynete, Kynett, Kynetta, Kynettah, Kynette

Kini (Hawaiian) a form of Jean.
Kina

Kinsey (English) offspring; relative.
Kinsee

Kinsley (American) a form of Kinsey.
Kinslee, Kinslie, Kinslyn

Kinza (American) a form of Kinsey.

Kinzie (Scottish, Irish) a form of Kenzie.
(English) a form of Kinsey.
Kinze, Kinzee, Kinzey, Kinzi, Kinzie,
Kinzy

Kioko (Japanese) happy child.
Kioka, Kiyo, Kiyoko

Kiona (Native American) brown hills.
Kionah, Kioni, Kiowa, Kiowah, Kyona,
Kyonah, Kyowa, Kyowah

Kionna (Native American) a form of
Kiona.

Kip (English) pointed hill.
Kipp, Kyp, Kypp

Kira (Persian) sun. (Latin) light. See also
Kyra.
Kirah, Kiria, Kiro, Kirra, Kirrah, Kirri,
Kirrie

Kiran (Hindi) ray of light.
Kearan, Kearen, Kearin, Kearon, Keeran,
Keerana, Keeranah, Keerane, Keeren,
Keerin, Keeron, Keiran, Keiren, Keirin,
Keiron, Keiryn, Kirana, Kiranah, Kirane,
Kirran, Kirrana, Kirranah, Kirrane, Kyran,
Kyrana, Kyranah, Kyrane, Kyren, Kyrin,
Kyron, Kyryn

Kiranjit (Hindi) a form of Kiran.

Kiranjot (Hindi) a form of Kiran.

Kirby (Scandinavian) church village.
(English) cottage by the water.
Kerbea, Kerbee, Kerbey, Kerbi, Kerbie, Kerby,
Kirbea, Kirbee, Kirbey, Kirbi, Kirbie, Kyrbea,
Kyrbee, Kyrbey, Kyrbi, Kyrbie, Kyrby

Kiri (Cambodian) mountain. (Maori)
tree bark.
Kirea, Kiree, Kirey, Kirie, Kiry

Kiriann, Kirianne (American) combinations of Kiri + Ann.

Kirian, Kiriana, Kirianah, Kiriane,
Kirianna, Kiriannah, Kyrian, Kyriana,
Kyrianah, Kyriane, Kyriann, Kyrianna,
Kyriannah, Kyrianne, Kyryan, Kyryana,
Kyryanah, Kyryane, Kyryann, Kyryanna,
Kyryannah, Kyryanne

Kirilina (American) a combination of
Kiri + Lina.
Kirilin, Kirilinah, Kiriline, Kirilyn,
Kirilyna, Kirilynah, Kirilyne, Kyrilin,
Kyrilina, Kyrilinah, Kyriline, Kyrilyn,
Kyrilyna, Kyrilynah, Kyrilyne, Kyrylin,
Kyrylina, Kyrylinah, Kyryline, Kyrylyn,
Kyrylyna, Kyrylynah, Kyrylyne

Kirima (Eskimo) hill.

Kirsi (Hindi) amaranth blossoms.
Kirsie

Kirsta (Scandinavian) a form of Kirsten.
Kirstai, Kirste

Kirstan, Kirstin, Kirstyn (Greek,
Scandinavian) forms of Kirsten.
Kirstine, Kirstyne, Kirstynn

Kirsten (Greek) Christian; annointed.
(Scandinavian) a form of Christine.
Karsten, Karstin, Karstina, Karstinah,
Karstine, Kirstain, Kirstaine, Kirstane,
Kirsteen, Kirstene, Kirsteni, Kirstien,
Kirston, Kirstone, Kjersten, Kurstain,
Kurstaine, Kurstean, Kursteane, Kursteen,
Kursteene, Kursten, Kurstin, Kurstine,
Kurstyn, Kurstyne

Kirsti, Kirstie, Kirsty (Greek,
Scandinavian) familiar forms of Kirsten.
Kerstea, Kerstee, Kerstey, Kersti, Kerstia,
Kerstiah, Kerstie, Kersty, Kirstea, Kirstee,
Kirstey, Kirstia, Kirstiah, Kirstya, Kirstye,
Kjersti, Kurstea, Kurstee, Kurstey, Kursti,
Kurstia, Kurstiah, Kurstie, Kursty, Kyrstea,
Kyrstee, Kyrstey, Kyrsti, Kyrstie, Kyrsty

Kirstina (Scandinavian) a form of Kristina.
Kirstaina, Kirstainah, Kirstana, Kirstanah,
Kirstinah, Kirstona, Kirstonah, Kirstyna,
Kirstynah

Kisa (Russian) kitten.
Kisah, Kiska, Kiza, Kysa, Kysah, Kyssa,
Kyssah

Kisha (African) a form of Keisha.
(Russian) a form of Kisa.
Kishanda

Kishi (Japanese) long and happy life.
Kishee, Kishey, Kishie, Kishy

Kismet (Arabic) lot, fate; fortune.
Kismeta, Kismetah, Kismete, Kismett,
Kismetta, Kismettah, Kismette, Kissmet,
Kissmeta, Kissmetah, Kissmete, Kissmett,
Kissmetta, Kissmettah, Kissmette, Kysmet,
Kysmeta, Kysmetah, Kysmete, Kysmett,
Kysmetta, Kysmettah, Kysmette, Kyssmet,
Kyssmeta, Kyssmetah, Kyssmete, Kyssmett,
Kyssmetta, Kyssmettah, Kyssmette

Kissa (Ugandan) born after twins.
Kissah, Kysa, Kysah, Kyssa, Kyssah

Kita (Japanese) north.

Kitra (Hebrew) crowned.
Kitrah

Kitty (Greek) a familiar form of
Katherine.
Ketter, Ketti, Ketty, Kit, Kittee, Kitteen,
Kittey, Kitti, Kittie

Kiwa (Japanese) borderline.

Kiya, Kiyah (American) short forms of
Kiyana.

Kiyana, Kiyanna (American) forms of
Kiana.
Kiyan, Kiyani, Kiyenna

Kizzy (American) a familiar form of
Keziah.
Kezi, Kezie, Kezy, Kezzee, Kezzey, Kezzi,
Kezzie, Kezzy, Kissie, Kizee, Kizey, Kizi,
Kizie, Kizy, Kizzee, Kizzey, Kizzi, Kizzie,
Kyzee, Kyzey, Kyzi, Kyzie, Kyzy, Kyzzee,
Kyzzey, Kyzzi, Kyzzie, Kyzzy

Klaire (French) a form of Clair.
Klair

Klara (Hungarian) a form of Clara.
Klaara, Klaarah, Klaare, Klára, Klarah,
Klari, Klarika

Klarise (German) a form of Klarissa.
Klarice, Kláris, Klarisse, Klaryce, Klaryse,
Klaryss

Klarissa (German) clear, bright. (Italian) a form of Clarissa.
Klarisa, Klarisah, Klarissah, Klarisza, Klarrisa, Klarrissa, Klarrissia, Klarysa, Klarysah, Klaryssa, Klaryssah, Klarysse, Kleresa

Klarita (Spanish) a form of Clarita.
Klareata, Klareatah, Klareate, Klareeta, Klareetah, Klareete, Klaret, Klareta, Klaretah, Klarete, Klarett, Klaretta, Klarettah, Klarette, Klaritah, Klarite, Klaritta, Klarittah, Klaritte, Klaryta, Klarytah, Klaryte, Klarytta, Klaryttah, Klarytte

Klaudia (American) a form of Claudia.
Klaudiah, Klaudija, Klaudja, Klaudya, Klaudyah

Klementine (Latin) a form of Clementine.
Klementina, Klementinah, Klementyn, Klementyna, Klementynah, Klementyne

Kloe (American) a form of Chloe.
Khloe, Khloea, Khloee, Khloey, Khloi, Khloie, Khloy, Kloea, Kloee, Kloey, Klohe, Kloi, Kloie, Klowee, Klowey, Klowi, Klowie, Klowy

Kloris (Greek) a form of Chloris.
Khloris, Khlorisa, Khlorise, Khlorys, Khlorysa, Khloryse, Klorisa, Klorise, Klorys, Klorysa, Kloryse

Kodi, Kodie, Kody (American) forms of Codi.
Kodea, Kodee, Kodey, Kodye, Koedi

Koemi (Japanese) smiling.
Koemee, Koemey, Koemie, Koemy

Koffi (Swahili) born on Friday.
Kaffe, Kaffi, Koffe, Koffie

Koko (Japanese) stork. See also Coco.

Kolbi, Kolby (American) forms of Colby.
Kobie, Koby, Kolbee, Kolbey, Kolbie

Kolette (Greek, French) a form of Colette.
Kolet, Koleta, Koletah, Kolete, Kolett, Koletta, Kolettah, Kollette

Koleyn (Australian) winter.
Kolein, Koleina, Koleine, Koleyna, Koleynah, Koleyne

Kolfinnia (Scandinavian) white.
Kolfinia, Kolfiniah, Kolfinna, Kolfinnah, Kolfinniah

Kolina (Swedish) a form of Katherine. See also Colleen.
Koleena, Kolena, Koli, Kolinah, Kollena, Kolyna, Kolynah

Kolleen (Swedish) a form of Kolina. (Irish) a form of Colleen.
Koleen, Kolene, Kollene, Kolyn, Kolyne

Kolora (Australian) lake.
Kolorah, Kolori, Kolorie, Kolory

Komal (Hindi, Indian) delicate.
Komala

Kona (Hawaiian) lady. (Hindi) angular.
Koni, Konia

Konrada (German) brave counselor.
Conrada

Konstance (Latin) a form of Constance.
Konstancia, Konstancja, Konstancy, Konstancyna, Konstantina, Konstantine, Konstanza, Konstanze

Kora (Greek) a form of Cora.
Korah, Kore, Koressa, Korra

Koral (American) a form of Coral.
Korel, Korele, Korella, Korilla, Korral, Korrel, Korrell, Korrelle

Kordelia (Latin, Welsh) a form of Cordelia.
Kordel, Kordellia, Kordellya, Kordellyah, Kordelya, Kordelyah, Kordula

Koren (Greek) a form of Karen, Kora, Korin.

Koretta (Greek) a familiar form of Kora. See also Coretta.
Koret, Koreta, Koretah, Korete, Korett, Korette, Korretta

Korey, Kori, Korie, Korri, Kory (American) familiar forms of Korina. See also Corey, Cori.
Koree, Koria, Korrie, Korry

Korin, Korine, Korinne, Korrin, Koryn (Greek) short forms of Korina.

Korane, Koranne, Korean, Koreane, Koreen, Koreene, Koreine, Korene, Koreyne, Koriane, Korianne, Korinn, Korrine, Korrinne, Korryn, Korrynne, Koryne, Korynn, Korynne

Korina (Greek) a form of Corina.
Korana, Koranah, Koranna, Korannah, Koreana, Koreanah, Koreena, Koreenah, Koreina, Koreinah, Korena, Korenah, Koreyna, Koreynah, Koriana, Korianna, Korinah, Korine, Korinna, Korinnah, Korreena, Korrina, Korrinna, Koryna, Korynah, Korynna, Korynnah

Kornelia (Latin) a form of Cornelia.
Korneliah, Kornelija, Kornelis, Kornelya, Kornelyah, Korny

Kortina (American) a combination of Kora + Tina. See also Cortina.
Kortinah, Kortine, Kortyn, Kortyna, Kortyne

Kortnee, Kortney, Kortni, Kortnie (English) forms of Courtney.
Kortnay, Kortny

Kosma (Greek) order; universe.
Cosma

Kosta (Latin) a short form of Constance.
Kostia, Kostiah, Kostya, Kostyah

Koto (Japanese) harp.

Kourtnee, Kourtnei, Kourtney, Kourtni, Kourtnie (American) forms of Courtney.
Kourtnay, Kourtne, Kourtneigh, Kourtny, Kourtynie

Kris (American) a short form of Kristine. A form of Chris.
Khris, Khriss, Khrys, Khryss, Kriss, Krys, Kryss

Krisandra (Greek) a form of Cassandra.
Khrisandra, Khrisandrah, Khrysandra, Khrysandrah, Krisanda, Krissandra, Krizandra, Krizandrah, Krysandra, Krysandrah, Kryzandra, Kryzandrah

Krishna (Hindi) delightful, pleasurable. Religion: one of the human incarnations of the Hindu god Vishnu.
Kistna, Kistnah, Krishnah, Kryshna, Kryshnah

Krissa (American, Czech) a form of Khrissa.
Kryssa

Krissy (American) a familiar form of Kris.
Krissey, Krissi, Krissie

Krista (Czech) a form of Christina. See also Christa.
Khrista, Khrysta, Krysta

Kristabel (Latin, French) a form of Christabel.
Kristabela, Kristabelah, Kristabele, Kristabell, Kristabella, Kristabellah, Kristabelle, Krystabel, Krystabele, Krystabell, Krystabella, Krystabelle

Kristain (Greek) a form of Kristen.
Khristein, Kristaina, Kristainah, Kristaine, Kristayn, Kristayna, Kristaynah, Kristayne, Kristein, Kristeine, Kristeyn, Kristeyne, Krystein, Krysteine

Kristal, Kristel, Kristelle (Latin) forms of Crystal. See also Krystal.
Kristale, Kristall, Kristalle, Kristele, Kristell, Kristella, Kristill, Kristl, Kristle

Kristalyn (American) a form of Krystalyn.
Kristalina, Kristaline, Kristalyna, Kristalyne, Kristalynn

Kristan, Kriston (Greek) forms of Kristen.
Kristana, Kristanah, Kristane, Kristanna, Kristanne

Kristen (Greek) Christian; annointed. (Scandinavian) a form of Christine.
Christen, Khristen, Khristin, Khristyn, Khrystin, Kristene, Kristiin

Kristena (Greek, Scandinavian) a form of Kristina.

Kristi, Kristie (Scandinavian) short forms of Kristine.
Christi, Khristee, Khristi, Khristie, Khrystee, Khrysti, Khrystie, Kristia, Krysti, Krystie

Kristian (Greek) Christian; annointed. A form of Christian.
Khristian, Khristiane, Khristiann, Khristianne, Khristien, Krestian, Krestiane, Krestiann, Krestianne, Kristi-Ann, Kristi-Anne, Kristiane, Kristiann, Kristianne,

Kristian (cont.)
Kristien, Kristienne, Kristy-Ann, Kristy-
Anne, Kristyan, Kristyane, Kristyann,
Kristyanne

Kristiana, Kristianna (Greek) forms of
Kristian.
Khristeana, Khristeanah, Khristiana,
Khristianah, Khristianna, Khristiannah,
Krestiana, Krestianah, Krestianna,
Krestiannah, Kristianah, Kristiannah,
Kristyana, Kristyanah, Kristyanna,
Kristyannah

Kristin (Scandinavian) a form of Kristen.
See also Cristan.
Kristinn

Kristina (Greek) Christian; annointed.
(Scandinavian) a form of Christina. See
also Cristina.
Khristina, Kristeena, Kristeenah, Kristeina,
Kristeinah, Kristinah

Kristine (Scandinavian) a form of
Christine.
Khristean, Khristeane, Kristeen, Kristeene,
Kristein, Kristeine, Kristene, Kristyne,
Kristynn, Kristynne

Kristy (American) a familiar form of
Kristine, Krystal. See also Cristi, Kristi.
Khristey, Khristy, Khrystey, Khrysty, Kristey

Kristyn (Greek) a form of Kristen.
Khristyn, Khrystyn, Kristyne, Kristynn,
Kristynne

Kristyna (Greek, Scandinavian) a form of
Kristina.
Kristynah, Kristynna, Kristynnah

Krysta (Polish) a form of Krista.
Krystah, Krystka

Krystal (American) clear, brilliant glass.
Krystalann, Krystalanne, Krystale, Krystall,
Krystalle, Krystil, Krystol, Krystyl, Krystyle,
Krystyll, Krystylle

Krystalee (American) a combination of
Krystal + Lee.
Kristalea, Kristaleah, Kristalee, Krystalea,
Krystaleah, Krystlea, Krystleah, Krystlee,
Krystlelea, Krystleleah, Krystlelee

Krystalyn, Krystalynn (American) com-
binations of Krystal + Lynn. See also
Crystalin.
Khristalin, Khristalina, Khristaline,
Khrystalin, Khrystalina, Khrystaline,
Kristelina, Kristeline, Kristilyn, Kristilynn,
Kristlyn, Krystaleen, Krystalene, Krystalin,
Krystalina, Krystaline, Krystallyn,
Krystalyna, Krystalyne, Krystalynne,
Krystelina, Krysteline

Krystan, Krysten (Greek) forms of
Kristen.
Krystana, Krystanah, Krystane, Krystena,
Krystenah, Krystene, Krystenia, Kryston

Krystel, Krystelle (Latin) forms of Krystal.
Krystele, Krystell, Krystella

Krystian (Greek) a form of Christian.
Krystiann, Krystianne, Krysty-Ann, Krysty-
Anne, Krystyan, Krystyane, Krystyann,
Krystyanne, Krystyen

Krystiana (Greek) a form of Krystian.
Krysteana, Krysteanah, Krystianah,
Krystianna, Krystiannah, Krystyana,
Krystyanah, Krystyanna, Krystyannah

Krystin, Krystyn (Czech) forms of Kristin.
Krystyne, Krystynn, Krystynne

Krystina (Greek) a form of Kristina.
Krysteana, Krysteanah, Krysteena,
Krysteenah, Krysteina, Krysteinah,
Krystena, Krystinah

Krystine (Scandinavian) a form of
Kristina. (Czech) a form of Krystin.
Krystean, Krysteane, Krysteen, Krysteene,
Krystein, Krysteine, Krysteyn, Krysteyne,
Kryston

Krystle (American) a form of Krystal.
Krystl, Krystyl, Krystyle, Krystyll, Krystylle

Krystyna (Greek) a form of Kristina.
Krystynah, Krystynna, Krystynnah

Kudio (Swahili) born on Monday.

Kuma (Japanese) bear. (Tongan) mouse.
Kumah

Kumari (Sanskrit) woman.
Kumaree, Kumarey, Kumaria, Kumariah,
Kumarie, Kumary, Kumarya, Kumaryah

Kumberlin (Australian) sweet.
Cumberlin, Cumberlina, Cumberline,
Cumberlyn, Cumberlyne, Kumberlina,
Kumberline, Kumberlyn, Kumberlyne

Kumi (Japanese) braid.
Kumee, Kumie, Kumy

Kumiko (Japanese) girl with braids.

Kumuda (Sanskrit) lotus flower.

Kunani (Hawaiian) beautiful.
Kunanee, Kunaney, Kunanie, Kunany

Kuniko (Japanese) child from the country.

Kunto (Twi) third-born.

Kuri (Japanese) chestnut.
Curee, Curey, Curi, Curie, Cury, Kuree,
Kurey, Kurie, Kury

Kusa (Hindi) God's grass.

Kwanita (Zuni) a form of Juanita.

Kwashi (Swahili) born on Sunday.

Kwau (Swahili) born on Thursday.

Kya (African) diamond in the sky.
(American) a form of Kia.

Kyah (African, American) a form of Kya.

Kyana, Kyanna (American) forms of
Kiana.
Kyanah, Kyani, Kyann, Kyannah, Kyanne,
Kyanni, Kyeana, Kyeanna

Kyara (Irish) a form of Kiara.
Kiyara, Kiyera, Kiyerra, Kyarah, Kyaria,
Kyarie, Kyarra

Kyera, Kyerra (Irish) forms of Kiara.

Kyla (Irish) lovely. (Yiddish) crown; laurel.
Khyla, Kyela, Kyella, Kylia

Kylah (Irish, Yiddish) a form of Kyla.

Kyle (Irish) attractive.
Kial, Kiele, Kiell, Kielle, Kile, Kyel, Kyele,
Kyell, Kyelle

Kylea, Kylee, Kyleigh, Kyley, Kyli
(West Australian Aboriginal, Irish) forms
of Kylie.
Kyleah, Kyllea, Kylleah, Kyllee, Kylleigh,
Kylley, Kylli

Kyleen, Kylene (Irish) forms of Kyle.

Kyler (English) a form of Kyle.
Kylar, Kylor

Kylie (West Australian Aboriginal) curled
stick; boomerang. (Irish) a familiar form
of Kyle. See also Kiley.
Kye, Kylei, Kylia, Kyliah, Kyliee, Kyliegh,
Kyllei, Kyllia, Kylliah, Kyllie, Kylly, Kyly,
Kylya, Kylyah

Kylynn (Irish) a form of Kyle.
Kylenn, Kylynne

Kym (Vietnamese, English) a form of Kim.
Kymm

Kymber (English) a form of Kimber.

Kymberlee, Kymberli, Kymberly
(English) forms of Kimberly.
Kymberlea, Kymberleah, Kymberlei,
Kymberleigh, Kymberley, Kymberlia,
Kymberliah, Kymberlie

Kymberlyn (English) a form of Kimberlin.
Kymberlynn, Kymberlynne

Kyndal, Kyndall (English) forms of
Kendall.
Kyndahl, Kyndalle, Kyndel, Kyndell,
Kyndelle, Kyndle, Kyndol

Kyndra (English) a form of Kendra.

Kynthia (Greek) a form of Cynthia.
Kyndi

Kyoko (Japanese) mirror.
Kyoka, Kyokah

Kyra (Greek) noble. A form of Cyrilla.
See also Kira.
Kyrah, Kyria, Kyriah, Kyriann, Kyrra,
Kyrrah

Kyrene (Greek) noble.
Kirena, Kirenah, Kirene, Kyrena, Kyrenah

Kyrie (Cambodian, Maori) a form of
Kiri. (Greek) a familiar form of Kyra.
Kyrea, Kyree, Kyrey, Kyri, Kyry

Kyrsten, Kyrstin, Kyrstyn (Greek,
Scandinavian) forms of Kirsten.
Kyersten

L

Labreana (American) a combination of the prefix La + Breana.
Labreanah, Labreann, Labreanna, Labreannah, Labreanne, Labrenna, Labrennah

Labrenda (American) a combination of the prefix La + Brenda.
Labrinda, Labrindah, Labrynda, Labryndah

Lace, Lacee, Laci, Lacie (Greek, Latin) forms of Lacey.

Lacey, Lacy (Latin) cheerful. (Greek) familiar forms of Larissa.
Lacea, Lacia, Laciah, Laciann, Lacianne, Lacye, Laicee, Laicey, Laici, Laicia, Laiciah, Laicie, Laicy, Layce, Lece

Lachandra (American) a combination of the prefix La + Chandra.
Lachanda, Lachandah, Lachander, Lachandice, Lachandrah, Lachandrica, Lachandrice, Lachandryce

Lachlanina (Scottish) land of lakes.
Lachianina, Lachianinah, Lachlanee, Lachlani, Lachlania, Lachlanie, Lachlany, Lachyanina, Lachyaninah, Lochlanee, Lochlaney, Lochlani, Lochlanie, Lochlany

Lacole (Italian) a form of Nicole.
Lacola, Lacollah, Lacolle, Lecola, Lecole, Lecolla, Lecolle

Lacrecia (Latin) a form of Lucretia.
Lacrasha, Lacreash, Lacreasha, Lacreashia, Lacreisha, Lacresha, Lacreshah, Lacreshia, Lacreshiah, Lacresia, Lacretia, Lacretiah, Lacretya, Lacretyah, Lacricia, Lacriciah, Lacriesha, Lacrisah, Lacrisha, Lacrishia, Lacrishiah, Lacrissa, Lacrycia, Lacryciah, Lacrycya, Lacrycyah

Lada (Russian) Mythology: the Slavic goddess of beauty.
Ladah, Ladia, Ladiah, Ladya, Ladyah

Ladaisha (American) a form of Ladasha.
Ladaisa, Ladaishea, Ladaishia

Ladan (American) a short form of Ladana.
Ladann, Ladanne

Ladana (American) a combination of the prefix La + Dana.
Ladanah, Ladanna, Ladannah

Ladanica (American) a combination of the prefix La + Danica.
Ladanicah, Ladanicka, Ladanika, Ladanikah, Ladanyca, Ladanycah, Ladanycka, Ladanyka, Ladanykah

Ladasha (American) a combination of the prefix La + Dasha.
Ladaesha, Ladaseha, Ladashah, Ladashiah, Ladashia, Ladasia, Ladassa, Ladaysha, Ladesha, Ladisha, Ladosha

Ladawna (American) a combination of the prefix La + Dawna.
Ladawn, Ladawnah, Ladawne, Ladawnee, Ladawni, Ladawnia, Ladawniah, Ladawnie, Ladawny

Ladeidra (American) a combination of the prefix La + Deidra.
Ladedra, Ladiedra

Ladivina (American) a combination of the prefix La + Divinia.
Ladivinah, Ladivine, Ladivyna, Ladivynah, Ladivyne, Ladyvyna, Ladyvynah, Ladyvyne

Ladonna (American) a combination of the prefix La + Donna.
Ladon, Ladona, Ladonah, Ladonia, Ladoniah, Ladonnah, Ladonne, Ladonnia, Ladonniah, Ladonnya, Ladonnyah, Ladonya, Ladonyah

Laela (Arabic, Hebrew) a form of Leila.
Lael, Laele, Laelea, Laeleah, Laelee, Laelei, Laeleigh, Laeley, Laeli, Laelia, Laeliah, Laelie, Laell, Laella, Laellah, Laelle, Laely, Laelya, Laelyah

Laeticia, Laetitia (Latin) forms of Leticia.
Laeticha, Laetichah, Laetichya, Laetichyah, Laeticiah, Laeticya, Laeticyah, Laetita, Laetitiah, Laetizia, Laetiziah, Laetizya, Laetycia, Laetyciah, Laetycya, Laetycyah, Laetyta, Laetytah, Laetyte, Laetytia, Laetytiah, Laitichya, Laitichyah, Laiticia, Laiticiah, Laitita, Laititah, Laititia,

Laititiah, Laytitia, Laytitiah, Laytytia, Laytytiah, Laytytya, Laytytyah

Laflora (American) a combination of the prefix La + Flora.
Laflorah, Leflora, Leflorah

Lahela (Hawaiian) a form of Rachel.
Lahelah

Laila (Arabic) a form of Leila.
Lailah, Laile, Lailea, Laileah, Lailee, Lailei, Laileigh, Lailey, Laili, Lailia, Lailiah, Lailie, Lailla, Laillah, Laille, Laily, Lailya, Lailyah

Lailaka (Tongan) lilac.
Laelaka, Laelakah, Lailakah, Laylaka, Laylakah

Laina (French) a form of Laine. (English) a form of Lane.
Laena, Laenah, Lainah, Lainna, Layna, Laynah

Laine (French) a short form of Elaine. See also Lane.
Laen, Laene, Laenia, Laeniah, Lain, Lainia, Lainiah

Lainey (French) a familiar form of Elaine.
Laenee, Laeney, Laeni, Laenie, Laeny, Laenya, Laenyah, Lainee, Laini, Lainie, Lainy, Lainya, Lainyah

Laione (Tongan) lion.
Laeona, Laeonah, Laeone, Laiona, Laionah, Layona, Layonah, Layone

Lajessica (American) a combination of the prefix La + Jessica.
Lajesica, Lajesicah, Lajesika, Lajesikah, Lajessicah, Lajessika, Lajessikah, Lajessyca, Lajessycah, Lajessycka, Lajessyckah, Lajessyka, Lajessykah

Lajila (Hindi) shy; coy.
Lajilah, Lajilla, Lajillah

Lajuana (American) a combination of the prefix La + Juana.
Lajuanah, Lajuanna, Lajuannah, Lajunna, Lajunnah, Lawana, Lawanah, Lawanna, Lawannah, Lawanne, Lawanza, Lawanze, Laweania

Lajuliet, Lajuliette (American) a combination of the prefix La + Juliet.

Lajulieta, Lajulietah, Lajuliete, Lajuliett, Lajulietta, Lajuliettah, Lajulyet, Lajulyeta, Lajulyetah, Lajulyete, Lajulyett, Lajulyetta, Lajulyettah, Lajulyette

Laka (Hawaiian) attractive; seductive; tame. Mythology: the goddess of the hula.
Lakah

Lakaya (American) a form of Lakayla.

Lakayla (American) a combination of the prefix La + Kayla.
Lakala, Lakeila, Lakela, Lakella

Lakeisha (American) a combination of the prefix La + Keisha. See also Lekasha.
Lakaiesha, Lakaisha, Lakaysha, Lakaysia, Lakeasha, Lakeysha, Lakeyshah

Laken, Lakin, Lakyn (American) short forms of Lakendra.
Lakena, Lakine, Lakyna, Lakynn

Lakendra (American) a combination of the prefix La + Kendra.
Lakanda, Lakandah, Lakande, Lakandra, Lakedra, Laken, Lakenda, Lakendrah, Lakendrya, Lakendryah

Lakenya (American) a combination of the prefix La + Kenya.
Lakeena, Lakeenna, Lakeenya, Lakena, Lakenah, Lakenia, Lakeniah, Lakenja, Lakenyah, Lakina, Lakinja, Lakinya, Lakinyah, Lakwanya, Lekenia, Lekeniah, Lekenya, Lekenyah

Lakesha (American) a form of Lakeisha.
Lakasha, Lakeesh, Lakeesha, Lakesa

Lakeshia (American) a form of Lakeisha.
Lakashia, Lakeashia, Lakeashiah, Lakeashya, Lakeashyah, Lakecia, Lakeciah, Lakeeshia, Lakeeshiah, Lakeeshya, Lakeeshyah, Lakeishia, Lakeishiah, Lakese, Lakeseia, Lakeshiah, Lakeshya, Lakeshyah, Lakesi, Lakesia, Lakesiah, Lakeyshia, Lakezia, Lakicia, Lakieshia

Laketa (American) a combination of the prefix La + Keita.
Lakeet, Lakeeta, Lakeetah, Lakeita, Lakeitha, Lakeithia, Laketha, Laketia, Laketiah, Lakett, Laketta, Lakette, Lakieta, Lakietha, Lakyta, Lakytah, Lakyte,

Laketa *(cont.)*
Lakytia, Lakytiah, Lakytta, Lakyttah,
Lakytte, Lakytya, Lakytyah

Lakeya (Hindi) a form of Lakya.
Lakeyah

Lakia (Arabic) found treasure.
Lakiah, Lakiea, Lakkia

Lakiesha (American) a form of Lakeisha.

Lakisha (American) a form of Lakeisha.

Lakita (American) a form of Laketa.
Lakitia, Lakitiah, Lakitra, Lakitri, Lakitt,
Lakitta, Lakitte

Lakiya (Hindi) a form of Lakya.
Lakieya

Lakkari (Australian) honeysuckle tree.
Lakaree, Lakarey, Lakari, Lakaria, Lakariah,
Lakarie, Lakary, Lakkaree, Lakkarey,
Lakkarie, Lakkary, Lakkarya, Lakkaryah

Lakota (Dakota) a tribal name.
Lakoda, Lakohta, Lakotah

Lakresha (American) a form of Lucretia.
Lacresha, Lacreshia, Lacreshiah, Lacresia,
Lacresiah, Lacretia, Lacretiah, Lacrisha,
Lakreshia, Lakreshiah, Lakrisha, Lakrysha,
Lakryshah, Lekresha, Lekreshia, Lekreshiah,
Lekreshya, Lekreshyah, Lekresia

Lakya (Hindi) born on Thursday.
Lakyah, Lakyia

Lala (Slavic) tulip.
Lalah, Lalla, Lallah

Lalasa (Hindi) love.
Lalassa, Lallasa

Laleh (Persian) tulip.
Lalah

Lali (Spanish) a form of Lulani.
Lalea, Laleah, Lalee, Lalei, Laleigh, Laley,
Lalia, Laliah, Lalie, Laly, Lalya, Lalyah

Lalirra (Australian) chatty.
Lalira, Lalirah, Lalirrah, Lalyra, Lalyrah,
Lalyrra, Lalyrrah, Lira, Lirra, Lirrah, Lyra,
Lyrah, Lyrra, Lyrrah

Lalita (Greek) talkative. (Sanskrit) charm-
ing; candid.
Laleata, Laleatah, Laleate, Laleeta, Laleetah,
Laleete, Laleita, Laleitah, Laleite, Lalitah,
Lalite, Lalitt, Lalitta, Lalitte, Lalyta, Lalytah,
Lalyte, Lalytta, Lalyttah, Lalytte

Lallie (English) babbler.
Lallea, Lalleah, Lallee, Lallei, Lalleigh,
Lalley, Lalli, Lallia, Lalliah, Lally, Lallya,
Lallyah

Lama (German) a short form of Lamberta.
Lamah

Lamani (Tongan) lemon.
Lamanee, Lamaney, Lamania, Lamaniah,
Lamanie, Lamany, Lamanya, Lamanyah

Lamberta (German) bright land.
Lamberlina, Lamberline, Lamberlynn,
Lamberlynne, Lambirta, Lambirtah,
Lambirte, Lamburta, Lamburtah, Lamburte,
Lambyrta, Lambyrtah, Lambyrte

Lamesha (American) a combination of
the prefix La + Mesha.
Lamees, Lameesa, Lameesha, Lameise,
Lameisha, Lameshia, Lameshiah, Lamisha,
Lamishia, Lamysha, Lemesha, Lemisha,
Lemysha

Lamia (German) a short form of Lamberta.
Lamiah, Lamya, Lamyah

Lamis (Arabic) soft to the touch.
Lamese, Lamisa, Lamisah, Lamise, Lamiss,
Lamissa, Lamissah, Lamisse, Lamys,
Lamysa, Lamyss, Lamyssa

Lamonica (American) a combination of
the prefix La + Monica.
Lamoni, Lamonika

Lamya (Arabic) dark lipped.
Lama

Lan (Vietnamese) flower.
Lann, Lanne

Lana (Latin) woolly. (Irish) attractive,
peaceful. A short form of Alana, Elana.
(Hawaiian) floating; bouyant.
Lanah, Lanai, Lanaia, Lanata, Lanay,
Lanaya, Lanayah, Laneah, Laneetra

Lanae (Latin, Irish, Hawaiian) a form of Lana.

Landon (English) open, grassy meadow.
Landan, Landen, Landin

Landra (German, Spanish) counselor.
Landrah, Landrea, Landreah, Landria,
Landriah, Landrya, Landryah

Landyn (English) a form of Landon,
London.
Landynne

Lane (English) narrow road. See also
Laine, Layne.
Lanee

Laneisha (American) a combination of
the prefix La + Keneisha.
Laneasha, Lanecia, Laneciah, Laneesha,
Laneise, Laneishia, Laneysha, Lanysha

Lanelle (French) a combination of Lane
+ Elle.
Lanel, Lanela, Lanelah, Lanele, Lanell,
Lanella, Lanellah

Lanesha (American) a form of Laneisha.
Laneshe, Laneshea, Laneshia, Lanesia,
Laness, Lanessa, Lanesse

Lanette (Welsh, French) a form of Linette.

Laney (English) a familiar form of Lane.
Lannee, Lanni, Lannia, Lanniah, Lannie,
Lanny, Lany

Langley (English) long meadow.
Lainglea, Lainglee, Laingleigh, Laingley,
Laingli, Lainglie, Laingly, Langlea, Langlee,
Langleigh, Langli, Langlie, Langly

Lani (Hawaiian) sky; heaven. A short form
of 'Aulani, Atlanta, Laulani, Leilani,
Lulani.
Lanee, Lanei, Lania, Lanita, Lanney, Lanni,
Lannie, Lanny, Lany

Lanie (English) a form of Laney.
(Hawaiian) a form of Lani.

Lanisha (American) a form of Laneisha.
Lanishia

Lanna (Latin, Irish, Hawaiian) a form of
Lana.
Lannah, Lannaia, Lannaya

Lantha (Greek) purple flower.
Lanthia, Lanthiah, Lanthya, Lanthyah

Laporsha (American) a combination of
the prefix La + Porsha.
Laporcha, Laporche, Laporscha, Laporsche,
Laporschia, Laporshe, Laporshia, Laportia

Laqueena (American) a combination of
the prefix La + Queenie.
Laqueen, Laqueene, Laquena, Laquenah,
Laquene, Laquenetta, Laquinna

Laquesha (American) a form of Laquisha.

Laquinta (American) a combination of
the prefix La + Quintana.
Laquanta, Laqueinta, Laquenda, Laqueneta,
Laquenete, Laquenett, Laquenetta, Laquenette,
Laquenta, Laquinda, Laquintah, Laquynta,
Laquyntah

Laquisha (American) a combination of
the prefix La + Queisha.
Laquasha, Laquaysha, Laqueisha, Laquiesha

Laquita (American) a combination of the
prefix La + Queta.
Laqeita, Laqueta, Laquetta, Laquia,
Laquiata, Laquieta, Laquitta, Lequita

Lara (Greek) cheerful. (Latin) shining;
famous. Mythology: a Roman nymph. A
short form of Laraine, Larissa, Laura.
Larah, Laretta, Larette, Laria, Lariah, Larra,
Larrah, Larrya, Larryah, Larya, Laryah

Larae (Greek, Latin) a form of Lara.

Laraina (Latin) a form of Lorraine.
Laraena, Laraenah, Larainah, Larana,
Laranah, Laranna, Larannah, Larayna,
Laraynah, Laraynna, Lareina, Lareinah,
Larena, Larenah, Lareyna, Lareynah,
Larraina, Larrainah, Larrayna, Larraynah,
Larreina, Larreinah, Larreyna, Larreynah,
Lauraina, Laurainah, Laurayna, Lauraynah,
Lawraina, Lawrainah, Lawrayna, Lawraynah

Laraine (Latin) a form of Lorraine.
Laraen, Laraene, Larain, Larainee, Larane,
Larann, Laranne, Larayn, Larayne, Larein,
Lareine, Larene, Lareyn, Lareyne, Larrain,

Laraine *(cont.)*
　*Larraine, Larrayn, Larrayne, Larrein, Larreine,
　Larreyn, Larreyne, Laurain, Lauraine,
　Laurainne, Laurayn, Laurayne, Laurraine,
　Lawrain, Lawraine, Lawrayn, Lawrayne*

Laramie (French) tears of love. Geography:
a town in Wyoming on the Overland
Trail.
　Laramee, Laramey, Larami, Laramy, Laremy

Laren (Latin) a form of Laraine. (Greek) a
short form of Larina.
　Larenn, Larrine, Laryn, Laryne

Lari (Latin) a familiar form of Lara. A
short form of names starting with "Lari."
　Laree, Larey, Larie, Larilia, Larrie

Larianna (American) a combination of
Lari + Anna.
　*Larian, Lariana, Larianah, Lariane,
　Lariann, Lariannah, Larianne, Larrian,
　Larriana, Larrianah, Larriane, Larriann,
　Larrianna, Larriannah, Larrianne, Larryan,
　Larryana, Larryanah, Larryane, Larryann,
　Larryanna, Larryannah, Larryanne*

Laricia (Latin) a form of Laura.
　*Lariciah, Laricya, Laricyah, Larikia, Larycia,
　Laryciah, Larycya, Larycyah, Larykia,
　Lauricia*

Lariel (Hebrew) God's lioness.
　*Lariela, Larielah, Lariele, Lariell, Lariella,
　Lariellah, Larielle, Laryel, Laryela,
　Laryelah, Laryele, Laryell, Laryella,
　Laryellah, Laryelle*

Larina (Greek) sea gull.
　*Larena, Larenah, Larenee, Larinah, Larine,
　Larrina, Larrinah, Laryna, Larynah*

Larisa, Larrisa, Larrissa (Greek) forms of
Larissa.
　*Lareesa, Lareese, Laresa, Laris, Larise,
　Larysa, Laurisa, Lorysa, Lorysah*

Larisha (Greek) a form of Larissa.

Larissa (Greek) cheerful. See also Lacey.
　Laressa, Larissah, Larisse

Lark (English) skylark.
　Larke, Larkee, Larkey

Larlene (Irish) promise.
　*Larlean, Larleana, Larleanah, Larleane,
　Larleen, Larleena, Larleenah, Larleene,
　Larlin, Larlina, Larlinah, Larline, Larlyn,
　Larlyna, Larlynah, Larlyne*

Larmina (Persian) blue sky.
　*Larminah, Larmine, Larmyn, Larmyna,
　Larmynah, Larmyne*

Larnelle (Latin) high degree.
　*Larnel, Larnela, Larnelah, Larnele, Larnell,
　Larnella, Larnellah*

Laryssa (Greek) a form of Larissa.
　Larryssa, Larysse, Laryssia

Lasha (American) a form of Lashae.

Lashae, Lashai, Lashay, Lashea
(American) combinations of the prefix
La + Shay.
　Lashaye

Lashana (American) a combination of
the prefix La + Shana.
　*Lashan, Lashanay, Lashane, Lashanee,
　Lashann, Lashanna, Lashanne, Lashannon,
　Lashona, Lashonna*

Lashanda (American) a combination of
the prefix La + Shanda.
　Lashandra, Lashanta, Lashante

Lashaun, Lashawn, Lashon (American)
short forms of Lashawna.
　*Lasean, Laseane, Lashaughn, Lashaughne,
　Lashaune, Lashaunne, Lashawne, Lesean,
　Leseane, Leshaun, Leshaune, Leshawn,
　Leshawne*

Lashawna (American) a combination of
the prefix La + Shawna.
　*Laseana, Laseanah, Lashaughna,
　Lashaughnah, Lashauna, Lashaunna,
　Lashaunnah, Lashaunta, Lashawni,
　Lashawnia, Lashawnie, Lashawny, Lashona,
　Lashonna, Leseana, Leseanah, Leshauna,
　Leshaunah, Leshawna, Leshawnah*

Lashawnda (American) a form of
Lashonda.
　Lashawnd, Lashawndra

Lashaya (American) a form of Lasha.
　Lashaia

Lashonda (American) a combination of the prefix La + Shonda.
Lachonda, Lashaunda, Lashaundra, Lashond, Lashonde, Lashondia, Lashonta, Lashunda, Lashundra, Lashunta, Lashunte, Leshande, Leshandra, Leshondra, Leshundra

Lashondra (American) a form of Lashonda.

Lassie (Irish) young girl.
Lasee, Lasey, Lasi, Lasie, Lass, Lasse, Lassee, Lassey, Lassi, Lassy, Lasy

Latanya (American) a combination of the prefix La + Tanya.
Latana, Latanah, Latandra, Latania, Lataniah, Latanja, Latanna, Latanua, Latonshia

Latara (American) a combination of the prefix La + Tara.
Latarah, Lataria, Latariah, Latarya, Lotara, Lotarah, Lotaria, Lotarya

Lataree (Japanese) bent branch.
Latarea, Latarey, Latari, Latarie, Latary

Latasha (American) a combination of the prefix La + Tasha.
Latacha, Latai, Lataisha, Latashah, Lataysha, Letasha

Latashia (American) a form of Latasha.
Latacia, Latasia

Latavia (American) a combination of the prefix La + Tavia.

Lateasha (American) a form of Leticia, Latisha.
Lateashya, Lateashyah

Lateefah (Arabic) pleasant. (Hebrew) pat, caress.
Lateefa, Lateifa, Lateyfa, Lateyfah, Letifa

Lateesha (American) a form of Leticia, Latisha.

Lateisha (American) a form of Leticia, Latisha.
Lateicia, Letashia, Letasiah

Latesha (American) a form of Leticia.
Lataeasha, Latecia, Latesa, Latessa, Lateysha, Latisa, Latissa, Latytia, Latytiah, Latytya, Latytyah, Leteisha, Leteshia

Lateshia (American) a form of Leticia.
Lateashia, Lateashiah

Latia (American) a combination of the prefix La + Tia.
Latea, Lateia, Lateka, Latiah, Latja, Latya, Latyah

Laticia (Latin) a form of Leticia.
Laticiah

Latifah (Arabic, Hebrew) a form of Lateefah.
Latifa, Latipha

Latika (Hindi) elegant.
Lateeka, Lateka, Latik, Latikah, Latyka, Latykah

Latina (American) a combination of the prefix La + Tina.
Latean, Lateana, Lateanah, Lateane, Lateen, Lateena, Lateenah, Lateene, Latinah, Latine, Latyna, Latynah, Latyne

Latisha (Latin) joy. (American) a combination of the prefix La + Tisha.
Laetisha, Laetysha, Latecia, Latice, Latiesha, Latishah, Latishia, Latishya, Latissha, Latitia, Latysha, Latyshia, Latyshiah, Latysya, Latysyah

Latona (Latin) Mythology: the powerful goddess who bore Apollo and Diana.
Latonah, Latonna, Latonnah, Latonne

Latonia (Latin, American) a form of Latonya.
Latoni, Latoniah, Latonie

Latonya (American) a combination of the prefix La + Tonya. (Latin) a form of Latona.
Latonee, Latonyah

Latoria (American) a combination of the prefix La + Tori.
Latoira, Latorea, Latoreah, Latoree, Latorey, Latori, Latorio, Latorja, Latorray, Latorreia, Latory, Latorya, Latoyra, Latoyria, Latoyrya

Latosha (American) a combination of the prefix La + Tosha.
Latoshia, Latoshya, Latosia

Latoya (American) a combination of the prefix La + Toya.

Latoya *(cont.)*
Latoia, Latoiya, Latoiyah, LaToya, Latoyia, Latoye, Latoyia, Latoyita, Latoyo

Latrice (American) a combination of the prefix La + Trice.
Latrece, Latreece, Latreese, Latresa, Latrese, Latressa, Letreece, Letrice

Latricia, Latrisha (American) combinations of the prefix La + Tricia.
Latrecia, Latreciah, Latresh, Latresha, Latreshia, Latreshiah, Latreshya, Latrica, Latricah, Latriciah, Latrishia, Latrishiah, Latrysha, Latryshia, Latryshiah, Latryshya

Laulani (Hawaiian) heavenly tree branch.
Laulanea, Laulanee, Laulaney, Laulania, Laulaniah, Laulanie, Laulany, Laulanya, Laulanyah

Laumalie (Tongan) lively, full of spirit.
Laumalea, Laumaleah, Laumalee, Laumalei, Laumaleigh, Laumali, Laumalia, Laumaliah, Laumaly

Laura (Latin) crowned with laurel.
Laurah, Laure, Laurella, Laurka, Lavra, Lawra, Lawrah, Lawrea, Loura

Lauralee (American) a combination of Laura + Lee. (German) a form of Lorelei.
Lauralea, Lauraleah, Lauralei, Lauraleigh, Lauraley, Laurali, Lauralia, Lauraliah, Lauralie, Lauraly, Lauralya

Lauralyn (American) a combination of Laura + Lynn.
Lauralin, Lauralina, Lauralinah, Lauraline, Lauralyna, Lauralyne, Lauralynn, Lauralynna, Lauralynne, Laurelen

Lauran, Laurin (English) forms of Lauren.
Laurine

Laure (Italian) a form of Laura.
Lauré, Lawre

Laureanne (English) a short form of Laurianna. (American) a form of Laurie Ann.

Laurel (Latin) laurel tree.
Laural, Laurala, Lauralah, Laurale, Laurela, Laurelah, Laurele, Laurell, Laurella, Laurellah, Laurelle, Lawrel, Lawrela, Lawrelah, Lawrele, Lawrell, Lawrella, Lawrellah, Lawrelle, Lorel, Lorelle

Laurelei (German) a form of Lorelei. (American) a form of Lauralee.
Laurelea, Laurelee, Laureleigh

Lauren (English) a form of Laura.
Laureen, Laureene, Laurena, Laurenah, Laurene, Laurenne, Laurien

Laurence (Latin) crowned with laurel.
Laurencia, Laurenciah, Laurens, Laurent, Laurentana, Laurentia, Laurentiah, Laurentina, Laurentya, Lawrencia

Lauretta (English) a form of Loretta.
Lauret, Laureta, Lauretah, Laurete, Laurett, Laurettah, Laurette

Lauriane, Laurianne (English) short forms of Laurianna. (American) forms of Laurie Ann.
Laurian

Laurianna (English) a combination of Laurie + Anna.
Laurana, Lauranah, Laurane, Laurann, Lauranna, Laurannah, Lauranne, Laureana, Laureena, Laureenah, Laurenna, Laurennah, Lauriana, Laurina, Lauryna, Laurynah, Lawrana, Lawranah, Lawrena, Lawrenah, Lawrina, Lawrinah, Lawryna, Lawrynah

Laurie (English) a familiar form of Laura.
Lauree, Lauri, Lawree, Lawri, Lawria, Lawriah, Lawrie

Laurie Ann, Laurie Anne (American) combinations of Laurie + Ann.
Laurie-Ann, Laurie-Anne

Laurissa (Greek) a form of Larissa.
Laurissah

Laury (English) a familiar form of Laura.
Lawrey, Lawry, Lawrya, Lawryah

Lauryn (English) a familiar form of Laura.
Lauryna, Laurynah, Lauryne, Laurynn, Laurynna, Laurynnah, Laurynne

Lavani (Tongan) necklace.
Lavanea, Lavaneah, Lavanee, Lavaney, Lavania, Lavaniah, Lavany, Lavanya

Lave (Italian) lava. (English) lady. (Tongan) touch.
Lav

Laveda (Latin) cleansed, purified.
Lavare, Lavedah, Laveta, Lavetah, Lavete, Lavett, Lavetta, Lavette

Lavelle (Latin) cleansing.
Lavel, Lavela, Lavelah, Lavele, Lavell, Lavella, Lavellah

Lavena (Irish, French) joy. (Latin) a form of Lavina.
Lavana, Lavania, Lavenah, Lavenia, Laveniah, Lavenya, Lavenyah

Lavender (Latin) bluish violet, purple. Botany: a plant with clusters of pale purple flowers.
Lavenda, Lavende

Laveni (Tongan) lavender; light purple.
Lavenee, Laveney, Lavenie, Laveny

Lavenita (Tongan) lavender fragrance.
Lavenit, Lavenitah, Lavenyt, Lavenyta, Lavenytah, Lavenyte

Laverne (Latin) springtime. (French) grove of alder trees. See also Verna.
La Verne, Laverine, Lavern, Laverna, Lavernia, Laverniah, Lavernya, Lavernyah, Laveryne

Lavina (Latin) purified; woman of Rome. See also Vina.
Lavena, Lavinah, Lavyna, Lavynah, Lavyne

Lavinia (Latin) a form of Lavina.
Laviniah, Lavinie, Laviniya, Laviniyah, Lavyni, Lavynia, Lavyniah, Lavyny, Lavynya, Lavynyah, Levenia, Leveniah, Levinia, Leviniah, Leviniya, Leviniyah, Levynia, Levyniah, Levynya, Levynyah, Livinia, Liviniah, Lovinia, Lyvinia, Lyviniah, Lyvinya, Lyvinyah

Lavonna (American) a combination of the prefix La + Yvonne.
Lavona, Lavonah, Lavonda, Lavonde, Lavonder, Lavondria, Lavonee, Lavoney, Lavonia, Lavoniah, Lavonica, Lavonie, Lavonnah, Lavonnee, Lavonney, Lavonni, Lavonnie, Lavonny, Lavonnya, Lavonya, Lovona, Lovonah, Lovoni, Lovonia, Lovoniah, Lovonie, Lovonna, Lovonnah, Lovony, Lovonya, Lovonyah

Lavonne (American) a short form of Lavonna.
Lavon, Lavone, Lavonn, Lovon, Lovone, Lovonne

Lawan (Tai) pretty.
Lawana, Lawane, Lawanne

Lawanda (American) a combination of the prefix La + Wanda.
Lawandah, Lawinda, Lawindah, Lawonda, Lawynda, Lawyndah

Lawren (American) a form of Lauren.
Lawran, Lawrane, Lawrene, Lawrin, Lawrine, Lawryn, Lawryne

Layan (Iranian) bright; shining.

Layce (American) a form of Lacey.
Laycee, Laycey, Layci, Laycia, Laycie, Laycy, Laysa, Laysea, Laysie

Layla (Hebrew, Arabic) a form of Leila.
Laylah, Laylea, Layleah, Laylee, Laylei, Layleigh, Layli, Laylia, Layliah, Laylie, Laylla, Laylle, Layly, Laylya, Laylyah

Layne (French) a form of Laine. See also Laine.
Layn

Layney (French) a familiar form of Elaine.
Laynee, Layni, Laynia, Layniah, Laynie, Layny

Lazalea (Greek) eagle ruler.
Lazaleah, Lazalee, Lazalei, Lazaleigh, Lazaley, Lazali, Lazalia, Lazaliah, Lazalie, Lazaly, Lazalya

Le (Vietnamese) pearl.

Lea (Hawaiian) Mythology: the goddess of canoe makers. (Hebrew) a form of Leah.

Lea Marie (American) a combination of Lea + Marie.
Lea-Marie, Leah Marie, Leah-Marie

Leah (Hebrew) weary. Bible: the first wife of Jacob. See also Lia.
Léa

Leala (French) faithful, loyal.
Leal, Lealia, Lealiah, Lealie, Leela, Leelah, Leial

Lean, Leann, Leanne (English) forms of Leeann, Lian.

Leana, Leanna, Leeanna (English) forms of Liana.
Leeana, Leiana, Leianah, Leianna, Leiannah, Leyana, Leyanah, Leyanna, Leyannah

Leandra (Latin) like a lioness.
Leanda, Leandrah, Leandre, Leandrea, Leandria, Leeanda, Leeandra, Leeandrah, Leianda, Leiandah, Leiandra, Leiandrah, Leighandra, Leighandrah, Leyandra, Leyandrah

Leanore (Greek) a form of Eleanor. (English) a form of Helen.
Lanore, Lanoree, Lanorey, Lanori, Lanoriah, Lanorie, Lanory, Lanorya, Lanoryah, Leanor, Leanora, Leanorah

Lece (Latin) a form of Lacey.
Lecee, Lecey, Leci, Lecie, Lecy

Lecia (Latin) a short form of Felecia.
Leacia, Leaciah, Leacya, Leacyah, Leasia, Leasiah, Leasie, Leasy, Leasya, Leasyah, Leasye, Lesha, Leshia, Lesia, Lesiah, Lesya, Lesyah

Leda (Greek) lady. Mythology: the queen of Sparta and the mother of Helen of Troy.
Leada, Leadah, Ledah, Leeda, Leedah, Leida, Leidah, Leighda, Leighdah, Leyda, Lyda, Lydah

Lee (Chinese) plum. (Irish) poetic. (English) meadow. A short form of Ashley, Leah.
Ly

Leea (American) a form of Leah.
Leeah

Leeann, Leeanne (English) a combination of Lee + Ann. A form of Lian.
Leane, Leean, Leian, Leiane, Leiann, Leianne, Leyan, Leyane, Leyann, Leyanne

Leeba (Yiddish) beloved.
Leaba, Leabah, Leebah, Leiba, Leibah, Leighba, Leighbah, Leyba, Leybah, Liba, Libah, Lyba, Lybah

Leena (Estonian) a form of Helen. (Greek, Latin, Arabic) a form of Lina.
Leenah, Leina, Leinah

Leesa (Hebrew, English) a form of Leeza, Lisa.

Leesha (American) a form of Lecia.
Leecia, Leeciah, Leecy, Leecya, Leecyah, Leesia, Leesiah

Leewan (Australian) wind.
Leawan, Leawana, Leawanah, Leewana, Leewanah, Leiwan, Leiwana, Leiwanah, Leighwan, Leighwana, Leighwanah, Leywan, Leywana, Leywanah, Liwan, Liwana, Liwanah, Lywan, Lywana, Lywanah

Leeza (Hebrew) a short form of Aleeza. (English) a form of Lisa, Liza.
Leaza, Leazah, Leezah, Leiza, Leizah, Leighza, Leighzah, Leyza, Leyzah

Lei (Hawaiian) a familiar form of Leilani.

Leia (Hebrew) a form of Leah. (Spanish, Tamil) a form of Leya.
Leiah

Leif (Scandinavian) beloved.
Leaf, Leaff, Leiff, Leyf, Leyff

Leigh (English) a form of Lee.

Leigha (English) a form of Leah.

Leighann, Leighanne (English) forms of Leeann.
Leigh Ann, Leigh Anne, Leigh-Ann, Leigh-Anne, Leighane

Leighanna (English) a form of Liana.
Leigh Anna, Leigh-Anna, Leighana, Leighanah

Leiko (Japanese) arrogant.
Leako, Leeko, Leyko

Leila (Hebrew) dark beauty; night. (Arabic) born at night. See also Laela, Layla, Lila.
Leela, Leelah, Leilia, Leland

Leilah (Hebrew, Arabic) a form of Leila.

Leilani (Hawaiian) heavenly flower; heavenly child.

Lailanee, Lailani, Lailanie, Lailany, Lailoni, Lealanea, Lealaneah, Lealanee, Lealaney, Lealani, Lealania, Lealaniah, Lealanie, Lealany, Leelanea, Leelaneah, Leelanee, Leelaney, Leelani, Leelania, Leelaniah, Leelanie, Leelany, Lei, Leighlanea, Leighlaneah, Leighlanee, Leighlaney, Leighlani, Leighlania, Leighlaniah, Leighlanie, Leighlany, Leilanea, Leilaneah, Leilanee, Leilaney, Leilania, Leilaniah, Leilanie, Leilany, Leiloni, Leilony, Lelanea, Lelaneah, Lelanee, Lelaney, Lelani, Lelania, Lelanie, Lelany, Leylanea, Leylaneah, Leylanee, Leylaney, Leylani, Leylania, Leylaniah, Leylanie, Leylany

Leisa (Hebrew, English) a form of Lisa.
Leisah

Leisha (American) a form of Leticia.

Lekasha (American) a form of Lakeisha.
Lekeesha, Lekesha, Lekeshia, Lekeshiah, Lekeshya, Lekesia, Lekesiah, Lekesya, Lekicia, Lekiciah, Lekisha, Lekishah, Lekysha, Lekyshia, Lekysya

Lekeisha (American) a form of Lakeisha.

Lela (French) a form of Leala. (Hebrew, Arabic) a form of Leila.
Lelah

Leli (Swiss) a form of Magdalen.
Lelee, Lelie, Lely

Lelia (Greek) fair speech. (Hebrew, Arabic) a form of Leila.
Leliah, Lelika, Lelita, Lellia, Lelliah

Lelya (Russian) a form of Helen.
Lellya, Lellyah, Lelyah

Lemana (Australian) oak tree.
Leaman, Leamana, Leamanah, Leemana, Leemanah, Leimana, Leimanah, Lemanah, Leymana, Leymanah

Lena (Hebrew) dwelling or lodging. (Latin) temptress. (Norwegian) illustrious.
(Greek) a short form of Eleanor. Music: Lena Horne, a well-known African American singer and actress.
Lenah, Lenee, Lenka, Lenna, Lennah

Lenci (Hungarian) a form of Helen.
Lencea, Lencee, Lencey, Lencia, Lencie, Lency

Lene (German) a form of Helen.
Leni, Line

Leneisha (American) a combination of the prefix Le + Keneisha.
Lenease, Lenece, Leneece, Leneese, Lenesha, Leniesha, Lenieshia, Leniesia, Leniessia, Lenisa, Lenisah, Lenise, Lenisha, Leniss, Lenissa, Lenissah, Lenisse, Lennise, Lennisha, Lenysa, Lenysah, Lenyse, Lenysha, Lenyss, Lenyssa, Lenyssah, Lenysse, Lynesha

Lenia (German) a form of Leona.
Lenayah, Lenda, Lenea, Leneen, Leney, Lenie, Lenna, Lennah, Lennea, Lennee, Lenney, Lenni, Lennie, Lenny, Leny, Lenya, Lenyah

Lenita (Latin) gentle.
Leneta, Lenett, Lenetta, Lenette, Lenitah, Lenite, Lennett, Lennetta, Lennette

Lenora (Greek, Russian) a form of Eleanor.
Lenorah

Lenore (Greek, Russian) a form of Eleanor.
Lenor, Lenoree

Leola (Latin) lioness.
Leolah

Leolina (Welsh) a form of Leola.
Leolinah, Leoline, Leolyn, Leolyna, Leolynah, Leolyne

Leona (German) brave as a lioness. See also Lona.
Leoine, Leonae, Leonah, Leone, Leonel, Leonela, Leonelah, Leonella, Leonelle, Leonia, Leonice, Leonicia, Leonissa, Liona

Leonarda (German) brave as a lioness.
*Leonardina, Leonardine, Leonardyn,
Leonardyna, Leonardyne*

Leondra (German) a form of Leonarda.
Leondrea, Leondria

Leonie (German) a familiar form of
Leona.
*Leonee, Leoney, Leoni, Léonie, Leonni,
Leonnie, Leony*

Leonna (German) a form of Leona.
Leonne

Leonor, Leonore (Greek) forms of
Eleanor. See also Nora.
Leonora, Leonorah, Léonore

Leontine (Latin) like a lioness.
*Leonina, Leonine, Leontina, Leontyn,
Leontyna, Leontyne, Léontyne, Liontin,
Liontina, Liontine, Liontyna, Liontyne,
Lyontina, Lyontine, Lyontyna, Lyontyne*

Leora (Hebrew) light. (Greek) a familiar
form of Eleanor. See also Liora.
Leeora, Leorah, Leorit

Leotie (Native American) prairie flower.
Leotee, Leoti, Leoty

Lepati (Tongan) leopard.
*Leapati, Leapatie, Leapaty, Leipati, Leipatie,
Leipaty, Lepatie, Lepaty, Leypati, Leypatie,
Leypaty*

Lera (Russian) a short form of Valera.
Lerah, Leria, Leriah, Lerra, Lerrah

**Leslee, Lesleigh, Lesli, Leslie, Lesly,
Leslye** (Scottish) forms of Lesley.
Lesslie, Lessly

Lesley (Scottish) gray fortress.
*Leslea, Lesleah, Leslei, Lezlea, Lezleah,
Lezlee, Lezlei, Lezleigh, Lezley, Lezli,
Lezlie, Lezly*

Leta (Latin) glad. (Swahili) bringer.
(Greek) a short form of Aleta.
*Leata, Leatah, Leighta, Leightah, Leita,
Leitah, Leyta, Leytah*

Letha (Greek) forgetful; oblivion.
*Leitha, Leithia, Lethia, Leythia, Leythiah,
Leythya, Leythyah*

Leticia (Latin) joy. See also Laeticia,
Latisha, Tisha.
*Lateacia, Lateaciah, Lateacya, Lateacyah,
Latycia, Latyciah, Latycya, Latycyah, Let,
Letesa, Letice, Letichia, Leticya, Letisia,
Letisiah, Letissa, Letiza, Letizah, Letizia,
Letiziah, Letizya, Letizyah, Letty, Letycia,
Letyciah, Letycya, Letycyah, Letysya, Letyza,
Letyzia, Letyziah, Letyzya, Letyzyah*

Letifa (Arabic) a form of Lateefah.
*Leitifa, Leitifah, Leitipha, Leitiphah, Letifah,
Letipha, Letiphah, Letyfa, Letyfah, Letypha,
Letyphah*

Letisha (Latin) a form of Leticia.
*Leshia, Letesha, Leteshia, Letish, Letishah,
Letishia, Letishya, Letysha, Letyshya*

Letitia (Latin) a form of Leticia.
*Letita, Letitah, Letiticia, Loutitia, Loutitiah,
Loutitya, Loutytia, Loutytiah, Loutytya,
Loutytyah*

Letty (English) a familiar form of Leticia.
*Letee, Letey, Leti, Letie, Letta, Lettah,
Lettee, Lettey, Letti, Lettie, Lety*

Levana (Hebrew) moon; white. (Latin)
risen. Mythology: the goddess of newborn babies.
*Lévana, Levanah, Levanna, Levannah,
Levenia, Lewana, Livana*

Levani (Fijian) anointed with oil.
Levanee, Levaney, Levanie, Levany

Levania (Latin) rising sun.
*Leavania, Leevania, Leivania, Levannia,
Levanya, Leyvania*

Levia (Hebrew) joined, attached.
Leevya, Levi, Leviah, Levie, Levya, Levyah

Levina (Latin) flash of lightning.
*Levene, Levinah, Livina, Livinna, Lyvina,
Lyvinah, Lyvyna, Lyvynah*

Levona (Hebrew) spice; incense.
*Leavona, Leavonah, Leavonia, Leavoniah,
Leavonna, Leavonnah, Leavonnia,
Leavonniah, Leevona, Leevonah, Leevonia,
Leevoniah, Leevonna, Leevonnia,
Leevonniah, Leighvona, Leighvonah,
Leighvonna, Leighvonnah, Leighvonne,
Leivona, Leivonia, Leivoniah, Leivonna,*

Leivonnah, Leivonnia, Leivonnya, Levon, Levonah, Levonat, Levone, Levonee, Levoni, Levonia, Levoniah, Levonna, Levonnah, Levonne, Levony, Levonya, Levonyah, Leyvona, Leyvonah, Leyvone, Leyvonn, Leyvonna, Leyvonnah, Leyvonne, Livona

Lewana (Hebrew) a form of Levana.
Leawana, Leawanah, Leawanna, Leawannah, Lebhanah, Leewana, Leewanah, Leewanna, Leewannah, Leiwana, Leiwanah, Leiwanna, Leiwannah, Lewanah, Lewanna, Lewannah

Lexandra (Greek) a short form of Alexandra.
Lexa, Lexah, Lexandrah, Lexandria, Lexandriah, Lexandrya, Lexandryah, Lezandra, Lezandrah, Lezandria, Lezandriah, Lixandra, Lixandrah, Lyxandra, Lyxandrah

Lexi, Lexie, Lexy (Greek) familiar forms of Alexandra.
Leksi, Lexey

Lexia (Greek) a familiar form of Alexandra.
Leska, Lesya, Lexane, Lexiah, Lexina, Lexine

Lexis, Lexus, Lexxus (Greek) short forms of Alexius, Alexis.
Laexis, Lexius, Lexsis, Lexuss, Lexxis, Lexyss

Leya (Spanish) loyal. (Tamil) the constellation Leo.

Leyla (Hebrew, Arabic) a form of Leila. (Spanish, Tamil) a form of Leya.
Leylah

Leyna (Estonian, Greek, Latin, Arabic) a form of Leena.
Leynah

Lia (Greek) bringer of good news. (Hebrew, Dutch, Italian) dependent. See also Leah.
Liah, Lya, Lyah

Liama (English) determined guardian.
Liamah, Lyama, Lyamah

Lian (Chinese) graceful willow. (Latin) a short form of Gillian, Lillian.
Lean, Liann, Lyan, Lyann

Liana, Lianna (Latin) youth. (French) bound, wrapped up; tree covered with vines. (English) meadow. (Hebrew) short forms of Eliana.
Lianah, Liannah, Lyana, Lyanah, Lyanna, Lyannah

Liane, Lianne (Hebrew) short forms of Eliane. (English) forms of Lian.
Lyane, Lyanne

Libby (Hebrew) a familiar form of Elizabeth.
Ibby, Lib, Libbea, Libbee, Libbey, Libbi, Libbie, Libea, Libee, Libey, Libi, Libie, Liby, Lyb, Lybbea, Lybbee, Lybbey, Lybbi, Lybbie, Lybby, Lybea, Lybee, Lybey, Lybi, Lybie, Lyby

Liberty (Latin) free.
Libertee, Liberti, Libertie, Libirtee, Libirtey, Libirti, Libirtie, Libirty, Librada, Liburtee, Liburtey, Liburti, Liburtie, Liburty, Libyrtee, Libyrtey, Libyrti, Libyrtie, Libyrty, Lybertee, Lybertey, Lyberti, Lybertia, Lyberty, Lybertya, Lybirtee, Lybirtey, Lybirti, Lybirtie, Lybirty, Lyburtee, Lyburtey, Lyburti, Lyburtie, Lyburty, Lybyrtee, Lybyrtey, Lybyrti, Lybyrtie, Lybyrty

Licia (Greek) a short form of Alicia.
Licha, Liciah, Licya, Licyah, Lishia, Lisia, Lycha, Lycia, Lycya, Lycyah

Lida (Greek) happy. (Slavic) loved by people. (Latin) a short form of Alida, Elita.
Leeda, Lidah, Lidochka, Lyda, Lydah

Lide (Latin, Basque) life.
Lidee, Lyde, Lydee

Lidia (Greek) a form of Lydia.
Lidea, Lidi, Lidiah, Lidija, Lidiya, Lidka, Lidya

Lien (Chinese) lotus.
Liena, Lienn, Lienna, Lienne, Lyen, Lyena, Lyenn, Lyenna, Lyenne

Liesabet (German) a short form of Elizabeth.
Liesbeth, Lyesabet, Lyesabeth

Liese (German) a familiar form of Elise, Elizabeth.
Liesa, Liesah, Lieschen, Lise

Liesel (German) a familiar form of
Elizabeth.
Leasel, Leasela, Leaselah, Leasele, Leasle,
Leesel, Leesela, Leeselah, Leesele, Leesl,
Leesle, Leezel, Leezl, Leisel, Leisela,
Leiselah, Leisele, Leisle, Leysel, Liesl,
Liezel, Liezl, Lisel, Lisela, Liselah, Lisele,
Lysel, Lysela, Lyselah, Lysele

Liesha (Arabic) a form of Aisha.
Liasha, Liashah, Lieshah, Lyaisha,
Lyaishah, Lyasha, Lyashah, Lyeisha,
Lyeishah, Lyesha, Lyeshah

Lila (Arabic) night. (Hindi) free will of
God. (Persian) lilac. A short form of
Dalila, Delilah, Lillian.
Lilla, Lillah

Lilac (Sanskrit) lilac; blue purple.
Lilack, Lilak, Lylac, Lylack, Lylak

Lilah (Arabic, Hindi, Persian) a form of
Lila.

Lili, Lillie (Latin, Arabic) forms of Lilly.
Lilie, Lilli

Lilia (Persian) a form of Lila.
Lilea, Liliah, Lillea, Lilleah, Lilya, Lilyah,
Lylea, Lyleah, Lylia, Lyliah, Lyllea,
Lylleah, Lylya, Lylyah

Lilian, Liliane (Latin) forms of Lillian.
Liliann, Lilianne, Lilion, Lilyan, Lylian,
Lyliane, Lyliann, Lylianne, Lylion, Lylyon

Liliana, Lilliana, Lillianna (Latin) forms
of Lillian.
Lileana, Lilianah, Lilianna, Lilliana,
Lillianah, Lilliannah, Lyliana, Lylianah,
Lylianna, Lyliannah

Lilibeth (English) a combination of Lilly
+ Beth.
Lillibeth, Lillybeth, Lilybeth, Lylibeth,
Lyllibeth, Lyllybeth, Lylybeth

Lilis (Hebrew) a form of Lilith.
Lilisa, Lilise, Liliss, Lilissa, Lilisse, Lillis,
Lylis, Lylisa, Lylise, Lyliss, Lylissa, Lylisse,
Lylys, Lylysa, Lylyse, Lylyss, Lylyssa,
Lylysse

Lilith (Arabic) of the night; night demon.
Mythology: the first wife of Adam,
according to ancient Jewish legends.
Lillith, Lilyth, Lyllyth, Lylyth

Lillian (Latin) lily flower.
Lil, Lilas, Lileane, Lilias, Liliha, Lilja, Lilla,
Lilli, Lillia, Lilliane, Lilliann, Lillianne,
Liuka

Lilly, Lily (Latin, Arabic) familiar forms of
Lilith, Lillian, Lillyann.
Líle, Lilea, Lilee, Lilei, Lileigh, Liley,
Lilijana, Lilika, Lilike, Liliosa, Lilium,
Lilka, Lille, Lillee, Lillei, Lilleigh, Lilley,
Lylee, Lylei, Lyleigh, Lyley, Lyli, Lylie,
Lyllee, Lyllei, Lylleigh, Lylly, Lyly

Lillyann (English) a combination of Lilly
+ Ann. (Latin) a form of Lillian.
Lillyan, Lillyanna, Lillyanne, Lilyan,
Lilyana, Lilyann, Lilyanna, Lilyanne

Lillybelle, Lilybelle (English) combina-
tions of Lilly + Belle.
Lilibel, Lilibela, Lilibelah, Lilibele, Lilibell,
Lilibella, Lilibellah, Lillibel, Lillibela,
Lillibelah, Lillibele, Lillibell, Lillibella,
Lillibellah, Lillibelle, Lilybel, Lilybela,
Lilybelah, Lilybele, Lilybell, Lilybella,
Lilybellah, Lilybelle, Lylibel, Lylibela,
Lylibelah, Lylibele, Lylibell, Lylibella,
Lylibellah, Lylibelle, Lyllibel, Lyllibela,
Lyllibelah, Lyllibele, Lyllibell, Lyllibella,
Lyllibellah, Lyllibelle, Lyllybel, Lyllybela,
Lyllybelah, Lyllybele, Lyllybell, Lyllybella,
Lyllybellah, Lyllybelle, Lylybel, Lylybela,
Lylybelah, Lylybele, Lylybell, Lylybella,
Lylybellah, Lylybelle

Lillybet, Lilybet (English) combinations
of Lilly + Elizabeth.
Lilibet, Lilibeta, Lilibetah, Lilibete, Lillibet,
Lillibeta, Lillibete, Lillybeta, Lillybete,
Lillybett, Lillybetta, Lillybette, Lilybet,
Lilybeta, Lilybete, Lilybett, Lilybetta,
Lilybette, Lylibet, Lylibeta, Lylibetah,
Lylibete, Lyllibet, Lyllibeta, Lyllibete,
Lyllibett, Lyllibetta, Lyllibette, Lyllybet,
Lyllybeta, Lyllybete, Lyllybett, Lyllybetta,
Lyllybette, Lylybet, Lylybeta, Lylybete,
Lylybett, Lylybetta, Lylybette

Limber (Tiv) joyful.
Limba, Limbah, Limbera, Lymba, Lymbah,
Lymber, Lymbera

Lin (Chinese) beautiful jade. (English) a
form of Lynn.
Linley, Linn, Linne

Lina (Greek) light. (Arabic) tender. (Latin)
a form of Lena.
Linah, Linna, Linnah

Linda (Spanish) pretty. See also Lynda.
Lind, Lindah, Linita

Linden (English) linden-tree hill.
Lindan, Lindin, Lindon, Lyndan, Lynden,
Lyndin, Lyndon, Lyndyn

Lindsay, Lindsee, Lindsi, Lindsie, Lindsy
(English) forms of Lindsey.
Lindze, Lindzee, Lindzey, Lindzy

Lindsey (English) linden-tree island; camp
near the stream.
Lind, Lindsea, Lindsei, Lindsi

Lindy (Spanish) a familiar form of Linda.
Linde, Lindea, Lindee, Lindey, Lindi, Lindie

Linette (Welsh) idol. (French) bird.
Linet, Lineta, Linetah, Linete, Linett,
Linetta, Linettah, Linnet, Linneta,
Linnetah, Linnete, Linnett, Linnetta,
Linnettah, Linnette

Ling (Chinese) delicate, dainty.

Linh (Chinese, English) a form of Lin.

Linley (English) flax meadow.
Linlea, Linleah, Linlee, Linlei, Linleigh,
Linli, Linlia, Linliah, Linlie, Linly, Lynlea,
Lynleah, Lynlee, Lynlei, Lynleigh, Lynley,
Lynli, Lynlia, Lynliah, Lynlie, Lynly

Linnea (Scandinavian) lime tree. Botany:
the national flower of Sweden.
Linae, Linea, Lineah, Linnae, Linnaea,
Linneah

Linsey, Linzee, Linzy (English) forms of
Lindsey.
Linsay, Linsea, Linsee, Linsi, Linsie, Linsy,
Linzey, Linzi, Linzie, Linzzi

Liolya (Russian) a form of Helen.
Liolia, Lioliah, Liolyah, Lyolya, Lyolyah

Liona (German) a form of Leona.
Lionah, Lione, Lionee, Lioney, Lioni, Lionia,
Lioniah, Lionie, Liony, Lyona, Lyonah,
Lyone, Lyonee, Lyoney, Lyoni, Lyonia,
Lyoniah, Lyonie, Lyony, Lyonya, Lyonyah

Lionetta (Latin) small lioness.
Lionet, Lioneta, Lionetah, Lionete, Lionett,
Lionettah, Lionette, Lyonet, Lyoneta,
Lyonetah, Lyonete, Lyonett, Lyonetta,
Lyonettah, Lyonette

Liora (Hebrew) light. See also Leora.
Liorah, Lyora, Lyorah

Lirit (Hebrew) poetic; lyrical, musical.
Lirita, Lirite, Lyrit, Lyrita, Lyrite

Liron (Hebrew) my song.
Leron, Lerone, Lirona, Lironah, Lirone,
Lyron, Lyrona, Lyronah, Lyrone

Lis (French) lily.
Lys

Lisa (Hebrew) consecrated to God.
(English) a short form of Elizabeth.
Leasa, Leasah, Leassa, Leassah, Liisa,
Lisah, Lisenka, Liszka, Litsa

Lisa Marie (American) a combination of
Lisa + Marie.
Lisa-Marie

Lisandra (Greek) a form of Lysandra.
Lisandrah, Lisandria, Lisandriah, Lissandra,
Lissandrah, Lissandria, Lissandriah

Lisann, Lisanne (American)
combinations of Lisa + Ann.
Lisanna, Lisannah, Lizanne

Lisbet (English) a short form of Elizabeth.
Lisbeta, Lisbete, Lisbett, Lisbetta, Lisbette,
Lysbet, Lysbeta, Lysbete, Lysbett, Lysbetta,
Lysbette

Lisbeth (English) a short form of
Elizabeth.
Lysbeth

Lise (German) a form of Lisa.

Liset, Lisette, Lisset, Lissette (French)
forms of Lisa. (English) familiar forms of
Elise, Elizabeth.
Liseta, Lisete, Lisett, Lisetta, Lisettina,
Lissete, Lissett

Liseth (French, English) a form of Liset.

Lisha (Arabic) darkness before midnight. (Hebrew) a short form of Alisha, Elisha, Ilisha.
Lishah, Lishe, Lysha, Lyshah, Lyshe

Lissa (Greek) honey bee. A short form of Elissa, Elizabeth, Melissa, Millicent.
Lissah

Lissie (American) a familiar form of Alison, Elise, Elizabeth.
Lissee, Lissey, Lissi, Lissy, Lissye

Lita (Latin) a familiar form of names ending in "lita."
Leata, Leatah, Leet, Leeta, Leetah, Litah, Litia, Litiah, Litta, Lyta, Lytah, Lytia, Lytya

Litonya (Moquelumnan) darting hummingbird.
Litania, Litaniah, Litanya, Litanyah, Litonia, Litoniah, Lytania, Lytaniah, Lytanya, Lytanyah, Lytonia, Lytoniah, Lytonya, Lytonyah

Liv (Latin) a short form of Livia, Olivia.
Lyv

Livana (Hebrew) a form of Levana.
Livanah, Livane, Livanna, Livannah, Livanne, Livna, Livnat, Lyvan, Lyvana, Lyvanah, Lyvane, Lyvanna, Lyvannah, Lyvanne

Livia (Hebrew) crown. A familiar form of Olivia. (Latin) olive.
Levia, Livi, Liviah, Livie, Livy, Livye, Lyvi, Lyvia, Lyviah, Lyvie, Lyvy

Liviya (Hebrew) brave lioness; royal crown.
Leviya, Levya, Liviyah, Livya, Lyvya, Lyvyah

Livona (Hebrew) a form of Levona.
Livonah, Livone, Livonna, Livonnah, Livonne, Lyvona, Lyvonah, Lyvone, Lyvonna, Lyvonnah, Lyvonne

Liyah (Hebrew) a form of Leah.
Liya

Liz (English) a short form of Elizabeth.
Lizz, Lyz, Lyzz

Liza (American) a short form of Elizabeth.
Lizah, Lizela, Lizka, Lizza, Lizzah, Lyza, Lyzah, Lyzza, Lyzzah

Lizabeta (Russian) a form of Elizabeth.
Lisabeta, Lisabetah, Lisabetta, Lisabettah, Lizabetah, Lizabetta, Lizaveta, Lizonka, Lysabetta, Lysabettah, Lyzabeta, Lyzabetah, Lyzabetta, Lyzabettah

Lizabeth (English) a short form of Elizabeth. See also Lyzabeth.
Lisabet, Lisabete, Lisabeth, Lisabett, Lisabette, Lizabet, Lizabete, Lizabett, Lizabette

Lizbet (English) a short form of Elizabeth.
Lizbeta, Lizbete, Lizbett, Lizbetta, Lizbette, Lyzbet, Lyzbeta, Lyzbete

Lizbeth (English) a short form of Elizabeth.
Lyzbeth

Lizet, Lizett, Lizette, Lizzet, Lizzette (French) forms of Liset.
Lizete

Lizeth (French) a form of Liset.
Lizzeth

Lizina (Latvian) a familiar form of Elizabeth.
Lixena, Lixenah, Lixina, Lixinah, Lixyna, Lixynah, Lizinah, Lizine, Lizyna, Lizynah, Lizyne, Lyxina, Lyxinah, Lyxine, Lyxyna, Lyxynah, Lyxyne, Lyzina, Lyzinah, Lyzine, Lyzyna, Lyzynah, Lyzyne

Lizzie, Lizzy (American) familiar forms of Elizabeth.
Lizy

Llian (Welsh) linen.
Lliana, Llianah, Lliane, Lliann, Llianna, Lliannah, Llianne, Llyan, Llyana, Llyanah, Llyane, Llyann, Llyanna, Llyannah, Llyanne

Logan (Irish) meadow.
Logann, Loganne, Logen, Loghan, Logun, Logyn, Logynn

Loila (Australian) sky.
Loilah, Loyla, Loylah

Lois (German) famous warrior.
Loease, Loise, Loiss, Loissa, Loisse, Loyce,
Loys, Loyss, Loyssa, Loysse

Lokalia (Hawaiian) garland of roses.
Lokaliah, Lokalya, Lokalyah

Lola (Spanish) a familiar form of Carlotta,
Dolores, Louise.
Lolah

Lolita (Spanish) sorrowful. A familiar
form of Lola.
Loleata, Loleatah, Loleate, Loleeta, Loleetah,
Loleete, Loleighta, Loleita, Loleitah, Loleta,
Loletah, Lolit, Lolitah, Lolyta, Lolytah,
Lolyte, Lulita

Lolly (English) sweet; candy. A familiar
form of Laura.
Lolea, Loleah, Lolee, Lolei, Loleigh, Loli,
Lolia, Loliah, Lolie, Lollea, Lolleah, Lollee,
Lollei, Lolleigh, Lolley, Lolli, Lollie, Loly

Lolotea (Zuni) a form of Dorothy.
Lolotee, Loloti, Lolotia, Lolotie, Loloty

Lomasi (Native American) pretty flower.
Lomasee, Lomasey, Lomasie, Lomasy

Lona (Latin) lioness. (English) solitary.
(German) a short form of Leona.

London (English) fortress of the moon.
Geography: the capital of the United
Kingdom.
Londen, Londun, Londyn

Loni (American) a form of Lona.
Lonea, Loneah, Lonee, Loney, Lonia,
Loniah, Lonie, Lonnea, Lonnee, Lonney,
Lonni, Lonnia, Lonniah, Lonnie, Lonny,
Lonnya, Lony, Lonya, Lonyah

Lonlee (English) a form of Lona.
Lonlea, Lonleah, Lonlei, Lonleigh, Lonley,
Lonli, Lonlia, Lonliah, Lonlie, Lonly

Lonna (Latin, German, English) a form of
Lona.

Lora (Latin) crowned with laurel.
(American) a form of Laura.
Lorae, Lorah, Lorra, Lorrah

Loraine (Latin) a form of Lorraine.
Loraen, Loraena, Loraenah, Loraene, Lorain,
Loraina, Lorainah, Lorane, Lorann, Lorayn,

Lorayna, Loraynah, Lorayne, Lorein,
Loreina, Loreinah, Loreine, Loreyn,
Loreyna, Loreynah, Loreyne

Lore (Basque) flower. (Latin) a short form
of Flora.
Lor, Lorre

Loreal (German) a form of Lorelei.

Lorelei (German) alluring. Mythology:
the siren of the Rhine River who lured
sailors to their deaths. See also Lurleen.
Loralea, Loraleah, Loralee, Loralei, Loraleigh,
Loraley, Lorali, Loralie, Loralyn, Lorelea,
Loreleah, Lorelee, Loreleigh, Loreli, Lorilea,
Lorileah, Lorilee, Lorilei, Lorileigh, Loriley,
Lorili, Lorilia, Loriliah, Lorilie, Lorily,
Lorilyn, Lorylea, Loryleah, Lorylee, Lorylei,
Loryleigh, Loryley, Loryli, Lorylie, Loryly

Lorelle (American) a form of Laurel.
Loral, Lorala, Lorel, Lorela, Lorelah, Lorele,
Lorell, Lorella, Lorellah, Loriel, Loriela,
Lorielah, Loriele, Loriell, Loriella, Loriellah,
Lorielle, Lorrel, Lorrela, Lorrelah, Lorrele,
Lorrell, Lorrella, Lorrelle, Loryal, Loryala,
Loryalah, Loryale, Loryall, Loryalla,
Loryallah, Loryalle, Loryel, Loryela,
Loryelah, Loryele, Loryell, Loryella,
Loryellah, Loryelle

Loren, Lorin, Loryn (American) forms of
Lauren.
Loran, Lorren, Lorrene, Lorrin, Lorrine,
Lorryn, Lorryne, Loryne, Lorynn, Lorynne

Lorena (English) a form of Lauren.
Lorana, Loranah, Lorenah, Lorenea, Lorenia,
Lorenna, Lorina, Lorinah, Lorrena, Lorrenah,
Lorrina, Lorrinah, Lorryna, Lorrynah,
Loryna, Lorynah, Lorynna, Lorynnah

Lorene (American) a form of Lauren.
Loreen, Lorine

Lorenza (Latin) a form of Laura.
Laurencia, Laurensa, Laurensah, Laurentia,
Laurentina, Laurenza, Laurenzah,
Lawrensa, Lawrensah, Lawrenza,
Lawrenzah, Lorensa, Lorensah, Lorenzah,
Lorinsa, Lorinsah, Lorinza, Lorinzah,
Lorynsa, Lorynsah, Lorynza, Lorynzah

Loretta (English) a familiar form of
Laura.

Loretta *(cont.)*
Larretta, Lawret, Lawreta, Lawretah,
Lawrete, Lawrett, Lawretta, Lawrettah,
Lawrette, Loret, Loreta, Loretah, Lorete,
Lorett, Lorettah, Lorette, Lorit, Lorita,
Loritah, Lorite, Loritta, Lorittah, Loritte,
Lorreta, Lorretah, Lorrete, Lorretta, Lorrette,
Lorrit, Lorrita, Lorritah, Lorritta, Lorritte,
Loryt, Loryta, Lorytah, Loryte, Lorytt,
Lorytta, Loryttah, Lorytte

Lori (Latin) crowned with laurel. (French)
a short form of Lorraine. (American) a
familiar form of Laura.
Loree, Lorey, Loria, Loriah, Lorree, Lorrey,
Lorri, Lorria, Lorriah, Lorrya, Lorrye,
Lorya, Loryah

Loriann, Lorianne (American) combina-
tions of Lori + Ann.
Loreean, Loreeana, Loreeanah, Loreeane,
Loreeann, Loreeanna, Loreeannah,
Loreeanne, Lorian, Loriana, Lorianah,
Loriane, Lorianna, Loriannah, Lorrian,
Lorriana, Lorrianah, Lorriane, Lorriann,
Lorrianna, Lorriannah, Lorrianne, Lorryan,
Lorryana, Lorryanah, Lorryane, Lorryann,
Lorryanna, Lorryannah, Lorryanne, Loryan,
Loryana, Loryanah, Loryane, Loryann,
Loryanna, Loryannah, Loryanne

Loric (Latin) armor.
Lorick, Lorik, Loriq, Loriqua, Lorique,
Loryc, Loryck, Loryk, Loryque

Lorie, Lorrie, Lory (Latin, French,
American) forms of Lori.
Lorry

Lorielle (American) a combination of
Lori + Elle.
Loreel, Loriel, Loriela, Lorielah, Loriele,
Loriell, Loriella, Loryel, Loryela, Loryelah,
Loryele, Loryell, Loryella, Loryellah, Loryelle

Lorikeet (Australian) beautiful, colorful
bird.
Lorikeat, Lorikeata, Lorikeatah, Lorikeate,
Lorikeeta, Lorikeetah, Lorikeete, Loriket,
Loriketa, Loriketah, Lorikete, Lorikett,
Loriketta, Lorikette, Lorykeet

Lorinda (Spanish) a form of Laura.
Lorind, Lorindah, Lorinde, Lorynd,
Lorynda, Loryndah, Lorynde

Loris (Latin) thong. (Dutch) clown.
(Greek) a short form of Chloris.
Laurice, Laurys, Loreace, Lorease, Loreece,
Loreese, Lorice, Lorise, Loriss, Lorisse,
Loryce, Lorys, Loryse, Loryss, Lorysse

Lorissa (Greek, Latin, Dutch) a form of
Loris. A form of Larissa.
Lorisa, Lorisah, Lorissah, Lorysa, Lorysah,
Loryssa, Loryssah

Lorna (Latin) crowned with laurel.
Literature: probably coined by Richard
Blackmore in his novel *Lorna Doone*.
Lornah, Lorne, Lornee, Lorney, Lorrna

Lorraine (Latin) sorrowful. (French) from
Lorraine, a former province of France.
See also Rayna.
Loraine, Lorine, Lorraen, Lorraena,
Lorraenah, Lorraene, Lorrain, Lorraina,
Lorrainah, Lorrane, Lorrayn, Lorrayna,
Lorraynah, Lorrayne, Lorrein, Lorreina,
Lorreinah, Lorreine, Lorreyn, Lorreyna,
Lorreynah, Lorreyne

Lotte (German) a short form of Charlotte.
Lota, Lotah, Lotta, Lottah, Lottchen

Lottie (German) a familiar form of
Charlotte.
Lote, Lotea, Lotee, Lotey, Loti, Lotie, Lottea,
Lottee, Lottey, Lotti, Lotty, Loty

Lotus (Greek) lotus.
Lottus

Lou (American) a short form of Louise,
Luella.
Lu

Louam (Ethiopian) sleep well.
Louama

Louisa (English) a familiar form of
Louise. Literature: Louisa May Alcott
was an American writer and reformer
best known for her novel *Little Women*.
Aloisa, Eloisa, Heloisa, Lawisa, Lawisah,
Loeasa, Loeasah, Loeaza, Loeazah, Loisa,
Loisah, Looesa, Looesah, Louisah, Louisetta,
Louisian, Louisina, Louiza, Louizah,
Louyza, Louyzah, Lovisa

Louise (German) famous warrior. See also Alison, Eloise, Heloise, Lois, Lola, Ludovica, Luella, Lulu.
Lawis, Lawise, Leweese, Leweez, Loeaze, Loise, Looise, Louisane, Louisette, Louisiane, Louisine, Louiz, Louize, Louyz, Louyze, Lowise, Loyce, Loyise, Luis, Luise, Luiz, Luize, Luys, Luyse, Luyz, Luyze

Lourdes (French) from Lourdes, France. Religion: a place where the Virgin Mary was said to have appeared.

Louvaine (English) Louise's vanity.
Louvain, Louvaina, Louvayn, Louvayna, Louvaynah, Louvayne, Lovanne, Luvain, Luvaina, Luvainah, Luvaine, Luvayn, Luvayna, Luvaynah, Luvayne

Love (English) love, kindness, charity.
Lovee, Lovewell, Lovey, Lovi, Lovia, Loviah, Lovie, Lovy, Lovya, Lovyah, Luv, Luvi, Luvia, Luviah, Luvvy, Luvya, Luvyah

Lovely (English) lovely.

Lovinia (Latin) a form of Lavina.
Louvinia, Louviniah, Lovena, Lovenah, Lovenia, Loveniah, Lovina, Lovinah, Loviniah, Lovinya, Lovinyah, Lovynia, Lovyniah, Lovynya, Lovynyah

Lovisa (German) a form of Louisa.
Lovesah, Lovese, Lovessa, Lovessah, Lovesse, Lovisah, Lovissa, Lovissah, Lovisse, Lovys, Lovysa, Lovysah, Lovyse, Lovyss, Lovyssa, Lovyssah, Lovysse

Luann (Hebrew, German) graceful woman warrior. (Hawaiian) happy; relaxed. (American) a combination of Louise + Ann.
Louann, Louanne, Lu, Lua, Luan, Luane, Luanne, Luanni, Luannie, Luanny

Luanna (German) a form of Luann.
Lewana, Lewanna, Louana, Louanah, Louanna, Louannah, Luana, Luwana, Luwanna

Lubov (Russian) love.
Luba, Lubna, Lubochka, Lyuba, Lyubov

Luca (Italian) a form of Lucy.
Lucah, Lucka, Luckah, Luka, Lukah

Lucerne (Latin) lamp; circle of light. Geography: the Lake of Lucerne is in Switzerland.
Lucerina, Lucerinah, Lucerine, Lucerna, Luceryn, Luceryna, Lucerynah, Luceryne

Lucero (Latin) a form of Lucerne.

Lucetta (English) a familiar form of Lucy.
Luceta, Lucetah, Lucettah

Lucette (French) a form of Lucy.
Lucet, Lucete, Lucett

Luci, Lucie (French) familiar forms of Lucy.
Loucee, Louci, Loucie, Lucee

Lucia (Italian, Spanish) a form of Lucy.
Loucea, Loucia, Louciah, Lucea, Lucija, Luciya, Lucya, Lucyah, Luzia, Luziah, Luzya, Luzyah

Luciana (Italian, Spanish) a form of Lucy.
Lucianah, Luciann, Lucianna, Luciannah, Lucianne

Lucienne (French) a form of Lucy.
Lucien, Luciena, Lucienah, Luciene, Lucienna, Luciennah, Lucyan, Lucyana, Lucyanah, Lucyane, Lucyann, Lucyanna, Lucyannah, Lucyanne

Lucila (English) a form of Lucille.
Loucila, Loucilah, Loucilla, Loucillah, Lucilah, Lucilla, Lucillah, Lucyla, Lucylah, Lucylla, Lucyllah, Lusila, Lusilah, Lusilla, Lusillah, Lusyla, Lusylah, Lusylla, Lusyllah, Luzela, Luzelah, Luzella, Luzellah

Lucille (English) a familiar form of Lucy.
Loucil, Loucile, Loucill, Loucille, Lucile, Lucill, Lucyl, Lucyle, Lucyll, Lucylle, Lusil, Lusile, Lusill, Lusille, Lusyl, Lusyle, Lusyll, Lusylle, Luzel, Luzele, Luzell, Luzelle

Lucinda (Latin) a form of Lucy. See also Cindy.
Loucind, Loucinda, Loucindah, Loucinde, Loucint, Loucinta, Loucintah, Loucinte, Loucynd, Loucynda, Loucyndah, Loucynde, Loucynta, Loucyntah, Loucynte, Lousind, Lousinda, Lousindah, Lousinde, Lousynd, Lousynda, Lousyndah, Lousynde, Lousynta, Lousyntah, Lousynte, Lucida, Lucind, Lucindah, Lucinde, Lucindea, Lucinta,

Lucinda *(cont.)*
Lucintah, Lucintea, Lucynd, Lucynda,
Lucyndah, Lucynde, Lucynta, Lucyntah,
Lucynte, Lusind, Lusinda, Lusindah,
Lusinde, Lusinta, Lusintah, Lusinte,
Lusintea, Lusynda, Lusyndah, Lusynde,
Luzinda, Luzindah, Luzinde, Luzinta,
Luzintah, Luzinte, Luzintea, Luzynda,
Luzyndah, Luzynde, Luzynta, Luzyntah,
Luzynte, Luzyntea

Lucindee (Latin) a familiar form of
Lucinda.
Lucindey, Lucindi, Lucindia, Lucindiah,
Lucindie, Lucindy, Lucintee, Lucinti,
Lucintia, Lucintiah, Lucintie, Lucinty,
Lusintee, Lusintey, Lusinti, Lusintia,
Lusintiah, Lusintie, Lusinty, Luzintee,
Luzintey, Luzinti, Luzintia, Luzintiah,
Luzintie, Luzyntee, Luzyntey, Luzynti,
Luzyntia, Luzyntiah, Luzyntie, Luzynty

Lucine (Arabic) moon. (Basque) a form
of Lucy.
Lucin, Lucina, Lucinah, Lucyn, Lucyna,
Lucynah, Lucyne, Lukena, Lukene, Lusin,
Lusina, Lusinah, Lusine, Lusyn, Lusyna,
Lusynah, Lusyne, Luzin, Luzina, Luzinah,
Luzine, Luzyn, Luzyna, Luzynah, Luzyne

Lucita (Spanish) a form of Lucy.
Luceata, Luceatah, Luceeta, Luceetah,
Lucyta, Lucytah, Lusita

Lucky (American) fortunate.
Luckee, Luckey, Lucki, Luckia, Luckiah,
Luckie, Luckya, Lukee, Lukey, Luki, Lukia,
Lukiah, Lukie, Luky

Lucretia (Latin) rich; rewarded.
Lacrecia, Lucrece, Lucréce, Lucrecia, Lucreciah,
Lucreecia, Lucreeciah, Lucresha, Lucreshia,
Lucreshiah, Lucreshya, Lucreshyah, Lucrezia,
Lucrisha, Lucrishah, Lucrishia, Lucrishiah

Lucrezia (Italian) a form of Lucretia.
History: Lucrezia Borgia was the
Duchess of Ferrara and a patron of
learning and the arts.
Lucreziah, Lucrezya, Lucrezyah

Lucy (Latin) light; bringer of light.
Loucey, Loucy, Luca, Luce, Lucette, Lucetta,
Lucika, Lucine, Lucita, Lucye, Lucyee,
Luzca, Luzi, Luzy

Ludmilla (Slavic) loved by the people. See
also Mila.
Ludie, Ludka, Ludmila, Ludmilah, Ludmile,
Ludmyla, Ludmylah, Ludmylla, Ludmyllah,
Ludmylle, Lyuda, Lyudmila

Ludovica (German) a form of Louise.
Liudvika, Ludovika, Ludwiga

Luella (English) elf. (German) a familiar
form of Louise.
Loella, Loellah, Loelle, Looela, Looelah,
Looele, Looella, Looellah, Looelle, Louela,
Louelah, Louele, Louella, Louellah, Louelle,
Ludel, Ludela, Ludelah, Ludele, Ludella,
Ludellah, Ludelle, Luela, Luelah, Luele,
Luell, Luellah, Luelle

Luisa (Spanish) a form of Louisa.
Luisah, Luiza, Luizah, Lujza, Lujzika,
Luysa, Luysah, Luyza, Luyzah

Lulani (Polynesian) highest point of heaven.
Lali, Loulanee, Loulaney, Loulani, Loulanie,
Loulany, Lulanea, Lulanee, Lulaney,
Lulanie, Lulany, Lulanya, Lulanyah

Lulie (English) sleepy.
Lulea, Luleah, Lulee, Lulei, Luleigh, Luley,
Luli, Lulia, Luliah, Luly

Lulu (Arabic) pearl. (English) soothing,
comforting. (Native American) hare.
(German) a familiar form of Louise,
Luella.
Lolo, Looloo, Loulou, Lula

Luna (Latin) moon.
Lunah, Lune, Lunet, Luneta, Lunetah,
Lunete, Lunetta, Lunettah, Lunette,
Lunneta, Lunnete, Lunnett, Lunnetta,
Lunnettah, Lunnette

Lundy (Scottish) grove by the island.
Lundea, Lundee, Lundeyn, Lundi, Lundie

Lupe (Latin) wolf. (Spanish) a short form
of Guadalupe.
Lupee, Lupi, Luppi, Lupy

Lupine (Latin) like a wolf.
Lupina, Lupinah, Lupyna, Lupynah, Lupyne

Lupita (Latin) a form of Lupe.
Lupeata, Lupeatah, Lupeeta, Lupeetah,
Lupet, Lupeta, Lupete, Lupett, Lupetta,
Lupette, Lupyta, Lupytah, Lupyte

Lurleen, Lurlene (Scandinavian) war horn. (German) forms of Lorelei.
Lura, Luralin, Luralina, Luralinah, Luralyn, Luralyna, Luralynah, Luralyne, Lurana, Lurette, Lurlina, Lurlinah, Lurline, Lurlyn, Lurlyna, Lurlynah, Lurlyne

Lusa (Finnish) a form of Elizabeth.
Lusah, Lussa, Lussah

Lusela (Moquelumnan) like a bear swinging its foot when licking it.
Luselah, Lusella, Lusellah, Luselle

Lutana (Australian) moon.
Lutanah, Lutane, Lutania, Lutaniah, Lutanna, Lutannah, Lutanne, Lutannia, Lutannya, Lutanya

Luvena (Latin, English) little; beloved.
Louvena, Louvenah, Lovena, Lovina, Luvenah, Luvenia, Luvenna, Luvennah, Luvina

Luyu (Moquelumnan) like a pecking bird.

Luz (Spanish) light. Religion: Nuestra Señora de Luz—Our Lady of the Light —is another name for the Virgin Mary.
Luzee, Luzi, Luzie, Luzija, Luzy

Luzmaria (Spanish) a combination of Luz + Maria.

Ly (French) a short form of Lyla.

Lycoris (Greek) twilight.
Licoris

Lyda (Greek) a short form of Lydia.

Lydia (Greek) from Lydia, an ancient land in Asia. (Arabic) strife.
Lydie, Lydië, Lydya, Lydyah

Lyla (French) island. (English) a form of Lyle (see Boys' Names). (Arabic, Hindi, Persian) a form of Lila.
Lylah, Lylla, Lyllah

Lynae, Lynnae (English) forms of Lynn.

Lynda (Spanish) pretty. (American) a form of Linda.
Lyndah, Lynde, Lynnda, Lynndah

Lyndee, Lyndi, Lyndie (Spanish) familiar forms of Lynda.
Lyndea, Lyndey, Lyndy, Lynndie, Lynndy

Lyndell (English) a form of Lynelle.
Lindal, Lindall, Lindel, Lindil, Lyndal, Lyndall, Lyndel, Lyndella, Lyndelle, Lyndil

Lyndsay, Lyndsee, Lyndsey, Lyndsie, Lyndsy (American) forms of Lindsey.
Lyndsaye, Lyndsea, Lyndsi, Lyndzee, Lyndzey, Lyndzi, Lyndzie, Lyndzy, Lynndsie

Lynelle (English) pretty.
Linel, Linell, Linnell, Lynel, Lynell, Lynella, Lynnell

Lynette (Welsh) idol. (English) a form of Linette.
Lynet, Lyneta, Lynetah, Lynete, Lynett, Lynetta, Lynettah

Lynlee (English) a form of Lynn.
Lynlea, Lynleah, Lynlei, Lynleigh, Lynley, Lynli, Lynlia, Lynliah, Lynlie, Lynly

Lynn, Lynne (English) waterfall; pool below a waterfall. See also Lin.
Lyn, Lynlee

Lynna (Greek, Latin, Arabic) a form of Lina.
Lyna, Lynah, Lynnah

Lynnea (Scandinavian) a form of Linnea.
Lynea, Lyneah, Lynneah

Lynnell (English) a form of Lynelle.
Lynnella, Lynnelle

Lynnette (Welsh, English) a form of Lynette.
Lyannette, Lynnet, Lynnett, Lynnetta, Lynnettah

Lynsey, Lynsie, Lynzee, Lynzie (American) forms of Lindsey.
Lynnsey, Lynnzey, Lynsy, Lynzey, Lynzi, Lynzy

Lyonella (French) lion cub.
Lionel, Lionela, Lionell, Lionella, Lyonela, Lyonele, Lyonelle

Lyra (Greek) lyre player.
Lira, Lirah, Lirra, Lirrah, Lyrah, Lyre, Lyrie, Lyris, Lyrra, Lyrrah

Lyric (Greek) songlike; words of a song.
Liric, Lirick, Lirik, Lirique, Lyrica, Lyrick, Lyrik, Lyrique, Lyryk, Lyryque

Lyris (Greek) lyre player.
Liris, Lirisa, Lirise, Liriss, Lirissa, Lirisse, Lyrisa, Lyrisah, Lyrise, Lyriss, Lyrissa, Lyrisse, Lyrysa, Lyrysah, Lyryssa, Lyryssah

Lysa (Hebrew, English) a form of Lisa.
Lyesa, Lyesah, Lysah

Lysandra (Greek) liberator.
Lysandrah, Lyssandra, Lyssandrah, Lytle

Lysandre (Greek) a form of Lysandra.

Lysann, Lysanne (American) combinations of Lysandra + Ann.
Lysanna, Lysannah

Lysette (French, English) a form of Liset.

Lyssa (Greek) a form of Lissa.
Lyssah

Lyzabeth (English) a short form of Elizabeth. See also Lizabeth.
Lysabet, Lysabete, Lysabeth, Lysabett, Lysabette, Lyzabet, Lyzabete, Lyzabett, Lyzabette

Ma Kayla (American) a form of Michaela.

Mab (Irish) joyous. (Welsh) baby. Literature: queen of the fairies.
Mabb, Mabry

Mabbina (Irish) a form of Mabel.
Mabine

Mabel (Latin) lovable. A short form of Amabel.
Mabbina, Mabella, Mabelle, Mabil, Mabill, Mable, Mabyn, Maebell, Maibel, Maibele, Maibell, Maible, Maiebell, Maybeline, Maybell, Moibeal

Mabella (English) a form of Mabel.
Mabela, Mabilla, Maebella, Maibela, Maibella, Maiebella

Mabelle (French) a form of Mabel.
Mabele, Mabell, Mabille, Maibelle, Maiebelle

Mac Kenzie (Irish) a form of Mackenzie.

Macaela (Hebrew) a form of Michaela.

Macaria (Greek) happy.
Macariah, Macarya, Macaryah

Macawi (Dakota) generous; motherly.
Macawee, Macawia, Macawie, Macawy

Macayla (American) a form of Michaela.
Macaila, Macala, Macalah, Macaylah, Macayle, Macayli

Macee, Macey, Maci, Macie, Macy (Polish) familiar forms of Macia.
Macye

Machaela (Hebrew) a form of Michaela.
Machael, Machaelah, Machaelie, Machaila, Machala, Macheala

Machiko (Japanese) fortunate child.
Machi, Machika, Machikah, Machyka, Machyko

Macia (Polish) a form of Miriam.
Macelia, Machia, Maciah, Macya, Macyah, Masha, Mashia, Mashiah

Mackayla (American) a form of Michaela.

Mackenna (American) a form of Mackenzie.
Mackena, Mackenah, Mykena, Mykenah, Mykenna, Mykennah

Mackensie, Mackenzi, Mackenzy (American) forms of Mackenzie.
Mackensi, Mackenze, Mackenzye

Mackenzie (Irish) child of the wise leader. See also Kenzie.
Macenzie, Mackenzee, Mackenzey, Mackenzia, Mackinsey, Mackynze, Mykenzie

Mackinsey (Irish) a form of Mackenzie.
Mackinsie, Mackinze, Mackinzee, Mackinzey, Mackinzi, Mackinzie

Mada (English) a short form of Madaline, Magdalen.
Madah, Madda, Maddah, Mahda

Madalaine (English) a form of Madeline.
Madalain, Madalaina, Madalane, Madalayn, Madalayna, Madalayne, Madaleine

Madaline (English) a form of Madeline.
Madaleen, Madalene, Madalin

Madalyn, Madalynn (Greek) forms of
Madeline.
Madalyne, Madalynne

Maddie (English) a familiar form of
Madeline.
*Maddea, Maddee, Maddey, Maddi, Maddy,
Madea, Madee, Madey, Madi, Madie, Mady,
Maidie, Maydey*

**Maddisen, Maddison, Madisen,
Madisson, Madisyn** (English) forms of
Madison.
*Maddisson, Maddisyn, Madissen, Madissyn,
Madisynn, Madisynne*

Maddox (Welsh, English) benefactor's
child.
Madox

Madelaine, Madeleine, Madeliene
(French) forms of Madeline.
*Madelain, Madelane, Madelayne, Madelein,
Madeleyn, Madeleyne*

Madelena (English) a form of Madeline.
*Madalana, Madalena, Madalina,
Maddalena, Maddelena, Maddelina,
Madelaina, Madeleina, Madeleyna,
Madelina, Madelinah, Madelyna*

Madelene, Madelin, Madelyn (Greek,
English) forms of Madeline.
Maddelene, Madelyne, Madelynn, Madelynne

Madeline (Greek) high tower. See also
Lena, Lina, Maud.
*Madailéin, Maddeline, Madel, Madelia,
Madella, Madelle, Madelon, Maighdlin*

Madge (Greek) a familiar form of
Madeline, Margaret.
*Madgee, Madgey, Madgi, Madgie, Madgy,
Mage*

Madilyn, Madilynn (Greek) forms of
Madeline.
Madilen, Madiline, Madilyne

Madison (English) good; child of Maud.
*Maddisan, Maddisin, Maddisun, Maddyson,
Maddysyn, Madisan, Madisin, Madissan,
Madissin, Madisun*

Madlyn (Greek, English) a form of
Madeline.
Madlen, Madlin, Madline

Madolyn (Greek) a form of Madeline.
Madoline, Madolyne, Madolynn, Madolynne

Madonna (Latin) my lady.
Maddona, Maddonah, Madona, Madonnah

Madrona (Spanish) mother.
Madre, Madrena

Madysen, Madyson (English) forms of
Madison.
Madysan, Madysin, Madysun, Madysyn

Mae (English) a form of May. History:
Mae Jemison was the first African
American woman in space.
Maelea, Maeleah, Maelen, Maelle, Maeona

Maegan, Maegen, Maeghan (Irish)
forms of Megan.
*Maeghen, Maeghin, Maeghon, Maeghyn,
Maegin, Maegon, Maegyn*

Maeko (Japanese) honest child.
Maemi

Maeve (Irish) joyous. Mythology: a legendary Celtic queen. See also Mavis.
Maevi, Maevy, Maive, Mayve

Magali, Magalie, Magaly (Hebrew) from
the high tower.
Magally

Magan, Magen, Maghan (Greek) forms
of Megan.
Maggen, Maggin

Magda (Czech, Polish, Russian) a form of
Magdalen.
Magdah, Mahda, Makda

Magdalen (Greek) high tower. Bible:
Magdala was the home of Saint Mary
Magdalen. See also Madeline, Malena,
Marlene.
*Magdala, Magdalane, Magdaleen,
Magdaline, Magdalyn, Magdalyne,
Magdalynn, Magdelan, Magdelane,
Magdelen, Magdelene, Magdelin, Magdeline,
Magdelon, Magdelone, Magdelyn, Magdelyne,
Magdlen, Magola, Maighdlin, Mala, Malaine*

Magdalena (Greek) a form of Magdalen.
*Magdalana, Magdaleny, Magdalina,
Magdalona, Magdalonia, Magdalyna,
Magdelana, Magdelena, Magdelina,
Magdelona, Magdelonia, Magdelyna,
Magdolna*

Magdalene (Greek) a form of Magdalen.

Magena (Native American) coming moon.
Magenna

Maggi, Maggy (English) forms of Maggie.
Magy

Maggie (Greek) pearl. (English) a familiar
form of Magdalen, Margaret.
*Mag, Magee, Magey, Maggey, Magi, Magie,
Magge, Maggee, Maggia, Maggiemae, Magi,
Magie, Mags*

Magnolia (Latin) flowering tree. See also
Nollie.
*Magnolea, Magnoleah, Magnoliah, Magnolya,
Nola*

Maha (Iranian) crystal. (Arabic) wild cow;
cow's eyes.

Mahal (Filipino) love.

Mahala (Arabic) fat, marrow; tender.
(Native American) powerful woman.
*Mahalah, Mahalar, Mahalla, Mahela,
Mahila, Mahlah, Mahlaha, Mehala,
Mehalah*

Mahalia (American) a form of Mahala.
*Mahaley, Mahaliah, Mahalie, Mahaylia,
Mahelea, Maheleah, Mahelia, Mahilia,
Mehalia, Mehaliah, Mehalya, Mehalyah*

Maharene (Ethiopian) forgive us.

Mahayla (American) a form of Mahala.
Mahaylah

Mahesa (Hindi) great lord. Religion: a
name for the Hindu god Shiva.
*Maheesa, Mahisa, Mahissa, Mahysa,
Mahyssa*

Mahila (Sanskrit) woman.
Mahilah, Mahyla, Mahylah

Mahina (Hawaiian) moon glow.
Mahinah, Mahyna, Mahynah

Mahira (Hebrew) energetic.
Mahirah, Mahyra, Mahyrah, Mahri

Mahogany (Spanish) rich; strong.
*Mahoganee, Mahoganey, Mahogani,
Mahogania, Mahoganie*

Mahogony (Spanish) a form of Mahogany.
*Mahagony, Mahogney, Mahogny,
Mahogonee, Mahogoney, Mahogoni,
Mahogonia, Mahogonie, Mahogonya,
Mohogany, Mohogony*

Mai (Japanese) brightness. (Vietnamese)
flower. (Navajo) coyote.
Maie

Maia (Greek) mother; nurse. (English)
kinswoman; maiden. Mythology: the
loveliest of the Pleiades, the seven
daughters of Atlas, and the mother of
Hermes. See also Maya.
Maea

Maiah (Greek, English) a form of Maia.

Maida (English) maiden. (Greek) a short
form of Madeline.
*Maeda, Maidah, Maidel, Maieda, Mayda,
Maydah, Maydena, Mayeda*

Maigan (American) a form of Megan.

Maija (Finnish) a form of Mary.
Maiji, Maikki

Maika (Hebrew) a familiar form of
Michaela.
Maikala, Maikka, Maiko

Maili (Polynesian) gentle breeze.

Maimi (Japanese) smiling truth. See also
Mamie.
*Maemee, Maimee, Maimey, Maimi, Maimie,
Maimy*

Maira (Irish) a form of Mary.
*Maairah, Maera, Maerah, Mairah, Mairia,
Mairiah, Mairim, Mairin, Mairona,
Mairwen, Mairwin, Mairwyn*

Maire (Irish) a form of Mary.
Mair, Mayr, Mayre

Mairghread (Irish, Scottish) a form of
Margaret.
Maergrethe, Maigret, Mairgret

Mairi (Irish) a form of Mary.
Mairee, Mairey, Mairie, Mairy

Maisey, Maisie (Scottish) familiar forms
of Margaret.
*Maesee, Maesey, Maesi, Maesie, Maesy,
Maisa, Maise, Maisee, Maisi, Maizie, Mazey,
Mazie, Mazy, Mazzy, Mysie, Myzie*

Maisha (Arabic) walking with a proud,
swinging gait.
Maisaha

Maison (Arabic) a form of Maysun.

Maita (Spanish) a form of Martha.
*Maeta, Maetah, Maitia, Maitya, Maityah,
Mayta, Maytya, Maytyah*

Maite (Spanish) lovable. A combination of
Maria and Teresa. A form of Maita.

Maitland (American) a form of Maitlyn.

Maitlyn (American) a combination of
Maita + Lynn.
Maitlan, Maitlynn, Mattilyn

Maiya (Greek) a form of Maia.
Maiyah

Maja (Arabic) a short form of Majidah.
*Majah, Majal, Majalisa, Majalyn,
Majalyna, Majalyne, Majalynn, Majalynne*

Majesta (Latin) majestic.
*Magestic, Magestica, Magesticah, Magestiqua,
Magestique, Majestah, Majestic, Majestiqua,
Majestique*

Majidah (Arabic) splendid.
Majid, Majida, Majyd, Majyda, Majydah

Majorie (Greek, Scottish) a form of
Marjorie.

Makaela (American) a form of Michaela.
*Makaelah, Makaelee, Makaella, Makaely,
Makealah*

Makaila (American) a form of Michaela.
*Makail, Makailah, Makailea, Makaileah,
Makailee, Makailei, Makaileigh, Makailey,
Makaili, Makailla, Makaillah, Makaily*

Makala (Hawaiian) myrtle. (Hebrew) a
form of Michaela.
*Makalae, Makalah, Makalai, Makalea,
Makaleah, Makalee, Makalei, Makaleigh,
Makaley, Makali, Makalia, Makaliah,
Makalie, Makaly, Makalya*

Makana (Hawaiian) gift, present.
Makanah, Makanna, Makannah

Makani (Hawaiian) wind.
*Makanee, Makania, Makaniah, Makanie,
Makany, Makanya, Makanyah*

Makara (Hindi) Astrology: another name
for the zodiac sign Capricorn.
Makarah, Makarra, Makarrah

Makayla (American) a form of Michaela.
Makaylah, Makaylla

Makaylee (American) a form of Michaela.
*Makaylea, Makayleah, Makaylei,
Makayleigh, Makayley, Makayli, Makaylia,
Makayliah, Makaylie, Makayly*

Makeda (Ethiopian) beautiful.

Makell (American) a short form of
Makaela, Makala, Makayla.
*Makela, Makelah, Makele, Makella,
Makelle, Mekel*

Makena, Makenna (American) forms of
Mackenna.
Makenah, Makennah

Makensie, Makenzee, Makenzi, Makenzie
(American) forms of Mackenzie.
*Makense, Makensey, Makenze, Makenzey,
Makenzy, Makenzye, Makinzey,
Makynzey, Mykenzie*

Makia, Makiah (Hopi) forms of Makyah
(see Boys' Names).

Makyla (American) a form of Michaela.
Makylah

Mala (Greek) a short form of Magdalen.
Malee, Mali

Malachie (Hebrew) angel of God.
Malachee, Malachey, Malachi, Malachy

Malaika (African) angel.

Malaina (French) a form of Malena.
Malainah

Malak (Hungarian) a form of Malika.

Malana (Hawaiian) bouyant, light.
Malanah, Malanna, Malannah

Malanie (Greek) a form of Melanie.
Malanee, Malaney, Malani, Malania, Malaniah, Malany

Malaya (Filipino) free.
Malaia, Malaiah, Malayaa, Malayah, Malayna

Malea, Maleah (Filipino) forms of Malaya. (Hawaiian, Zuni, Spanish) forms of Malia.

Maleeka (Hungarian) a form of Malika.

Maleena (Hebrew, English, Native American, Russian) a form of Malina.

Maleka (Hungarian) a form of Malika.

Malena (Swedish) a familiar form of Magdalen.
Malayna, Malen, Malenna, Malin, Maline, Malini, Malinna

Malerie (French) a form of Mallory.
Mallerie

Malfreda (German) peaceful worker.
Malfredah, Malfredda, Malfrida, Malfryda, Malfrydda

Malha (Hebrew) queen.

Mali (Tai) jasmine flower. (Tongan) sweet. (Hungarian) a short form of Malika.
Malee, Malei, Maleigh, Maley, Malie, Mallee, Mallei, Malleigh, Malley, Malli, Mallie, Mally, Maly

Malia (Hawaiian, Zuni) a form of Mary. (Spanish) a form of Maria.
Maleeya, Maleeyah, Maleia, Maleiah, Maleigha, Maliaka, Maliasha, Malie, Maliea, Mallea, Malleah, Malleia, Malleiah, Malleigha, Malleya, Mallia, Malliah, Mallya, Malya, Malyah

Maliah (Hawaiian, Zuni, Spanish) a form of Malia.

Malika (Hungarian) industrious. (Arabic) queen.
Malik, Malikee, Maliki, Malikia, Malky, Malyka, Malykah

Malikah (Hungarian) a form of Malika.

Malina (Hebrew) tower. (Native American) soothing. (Russian) raspberry.
Malin, Malinah, Maline, Malinna, Mallie, Malyn, Malyna, Malynah, Malyne

Malinda (Greek) a form of Melinda.
Malindah, Malinde, Malindea, Malindee, Malindia, Malinna, Malynda, Malyndah

Malini (Hindi) gardener.
Malinee, Malinia, Malinie, Maliny, Malyni, Malynia, Malynie, Malyny, Malynya

Malisa, Malissa (Greek) forms of Melissa.
Malisah, Mallissa

Maliyah (Hawaiian, Zuni, Spanish) a form of Malia.
Maliya

Malka (Hebrew) queen.
Malkah, Malki, Malkia, Malkiah, Malkya, Malkyah

Malki (Hebrew) a form of Malka.
Malkee, Malkeh, Malkey, Malkie, Malkiya, Malkiyah

Mallalai (Pashto) beautiful.

Malley (American) a familiar form of Mallory.
Mallee, Malli, Mallie, Mally, Maly

Mallori, Mallorie, Malori, Malorie, Malory (French) forms of Mallory.
Malloree, Malloreigh, Mallorree, Mallorri, Mallorrie, Maloree, Malorey, Melorie, Melory

Mallory (German) army counselor. (French) unlucky.
Malarie, Maliri, Mallari, Mallary, Mallauri, Mallery, Malley, Mallorey, Mallorrey, Mallorry, Malorym, Malree, Malrie, Mellory

Maluhia (Hawaiian) peaceful.

Malulani (Hawaiian) under a peaceful sky.
Malulanea, Malulanee, Malulaney, Malulania, Malulanie, Malulany

Malva (English) a form of Melba.
Malvah, Malvi, Malvy

Malvina (Scottish) a form of Melvina.
Literature: a name created by the eigh-
teenth-century romantic poet James
Macpherson.
Malvane, Malveen, Malveena, Malveenah,
Malvinah, Malvine, Malvinia, Malviniah,
Malvyna, Malvynah, Malvyne, Malvynia,
Malvyniah, Malvynya, Malvynyah

Malyssa (Greek) a form of Melissa.

Mamie (American) a familiar form of
Margaret. See also Maimi.
Maeme, Maemey, Maemi, Maemie, Maemy,
Mame, Mamee, Mami, Mammie, Mamy,
Mamye, Maymee, Maymey, Maymi,
Maymie, Maymy

Mamo (Hawaiian) saffron flower; yellow
bird.

Mana (Hawaiian) psychic; sensitive.
Manah, Manna, Mannah

Manal (Hawaiian) a form of Mana.
Manali, Manalia

Manar (Arabic) guiding light.
Manara, Manayra

Manda (Spanish) woman warrior. (Latin)
a short form of Amanda.
Mandah, Mandea

Mandara (Hindi) calm.
Mandarah

Mandee, Mandi, Mandie (Latin) forms
of Mandy.

Mandeep (Punjabi) enlightened.
Manddep

Mandisa (Xhosa) sweet.
Mandisa, Mandissa, Mandissah, Mandysa,
Mandysah, Mandyssa, Mandyssah

Mandy (Latin) lovable. A familiar form of
Amanda, Manda, Melinda.
Mandey

Manette (French) a form of Mary.
Manet, Maneta, Manete, Manett, Manetta

Mangena (Hebrew) song, melody.
Mangina, Mangyna

Mani (Chinese) a mantra repeated in
Tibetan Buddhist prayer to impart
understanding.
Manee, Maney, Manie, Many

Manilla (Australian) meandering, winding
river.
Manila, Manilah, Manillah, Manille,
Manyla, Manylah, Manylla, Manyllah

Manisha (Indian) intellect.
Mohisha

Manjot (Indian) light of the mind.
Manjyot

Manka (Polish, Russian) a form of Mary.
Mankah

Manon (French) a familiar form of Marie.
Manona, Manone, Mannon, Manyn,
Manyne

Manpreet (Punjabi) mind full of love.
Manpret, Manprit

Mansi (Hopi) plucked flower.
Mancee, Mancey, Manci, Mancie, Mancy,
Mansee, Mansey, Mansie, Mansy

Manuela (Spanish) a form of Emmanuelle.
Manuala, Manuel, Manuele, Manuelita,
Manuell, Manuella, Manuelle

Manya (Russian) a form of Mary.
Mania, Maniah, Manyah

Mara (Hebrew) melody. (Greek) a short
form of Amara. (Slavic) a form
of Mary.
Mahra, Marae, Maralina, Maraline, Marra,
Marrah

Marabel (English) a form of Maribel.
Marabela, Marabelah, Marabele, Marabell,
Marabella, Marabellah, Marabelle

Marah (Greek, Hebrew, Slavic) a form
of Mara.

Maranda (Latin) a form of Miranda.
Marandah

Maraya (Hebrew) a form of Mariah.
Marayah, Mareya

Marcedes (American) a form of
Mercedes.

Marcela (Latin) a form of Marcella.
Marcele, Marcelia

Marcelen (English) a form of Marcella.
Marcelin, Marceline, Marcellin, Marcellina, Marcelline, Marcelyn, Marcilen

Marcelina (English) a form of Marcella.

Marcella (Latin) martial, warlike.
Mythology: Mars was the god of war.
Mairsil, Marca, Marce, Marceil, Marcello, Marcena, Marciella, Marcile, Marcilla, Marella, Marsella, Marshella, Marsial, Marsiala, Marsiale, Marsiella

Marcelle (French) a form of Marcella.
Marcell, Marcile, Marcille, Marselle, Marsielle

Marcena (Latin) a form of Marcella, Marcia.
Maracena, Marceen, Marceena, Marceenah, Marceene, Marcenah, Marcene, Marcenia, Marceyne, Marcina, Marseena, Marseenah, Marseene

Marchelle (American) a form of Marcelle.
Marchella

Marci, Marcie, Marcy (English) familiar forms of Marcella, Marcia.
Marca, Marcee, Marcey, Marcita, Marcye, Marsey, Marsi, Marsie, Marsy

Marcia (Latin) martial, warlike. See also Marquita.
Marcea, Marcena, Marchia, Marchiah, Marciale, Marcsa, Marcya, Marcyah, Marsia

Marciann (American) a combination of Marci + Ann.
Marciana, Marciane, Marcianna, Marcianne, Marcyane, Marcyanna, Marcyanne

Marcilynn (American) a combination of Marci + Lynn.
Marcelyn, Marcilin, Marciline, Marcilyn, Marcilyne, Marcilynne, Marcylen, Marcylin, Marcyline, Marcylyn, Marcylyne, Marcylynn, Marcylynne

Mardella (English) meadow near a lake.
Mardela, Mardelah, Mardele, Mardell, Mardellah, Mardelle

Marden (English) from the meadow with a pool.

Mardana, Mardanah, Mardane, Mardena, Mardenah, Mardene

Mardi (French) born on Tuesday.
(Aramaic) a familiar form of Martha.
Mardea, Mardee, Mardey, Mardie, Mardy

Mare (Irish) a form of Mary.

Mareena (Latin) a form of Marina.
Mareenah, Mareenia

Marelda (German) renowned warrior.
Mareldah, Marella, Marilda, Marildah, Marylda, Maryldah

Maren (Latin) sea. (Aramaic) a form of Mary. See also Marina.
Mareane, Marene, Miren, Mirene, Myren, Myrene

Marena (Latin) a form of Marina.
Marenah, Marenka

Maresa, Maressa (Latin) forms of Marisa.
Maresha, Meresa

Maretta (English) a familiar form of Margaret.
Maret, Mareta, Maretah, Marete, Marett, Marettah, Marette

Margaret (Greek) pearl. History:
Margaret Hilda Thatcher served as British prime minister. See also Gita, Greta, Gretchen, Gretel, Marjorie, Markita, Meg, Megan, Peggy, Reet, Rita.
Marga, Margalo, Marganit, Margara, Margarett, Margarette, Margaro, Margarta, Margat, Margeret, Margeretta, Margerette, Margetha, Margetta, Margiad, Margisia

Margarete (German) a form of Margaret.
Margen, Marghet

Margaretha (German) a form of Margaret.
Margareth, Margarethe

Margarit (Greek) a form of Margaret.
Margalide, Margalit, Margalith, Margarid, Margarite, Margaritt, Margerit

Margarita (Italian, Spanish) a form of Margaret.
Malgerita, Malgherita, Margareta, Margaretta, Margarida, Margaritis, Margaritta, Margeretta, Margharita,

Margherita, Margrieta, Margrita, Margurita,
Marguryta, Marjarita

Margaux (French) a form of Margaret.
Margeaux

Marge (English) a short form of Margaret,
Marjorie.

Margery (English) a form of Margaret.
See also Marjorie.
Margeree, Margerey, Margeri, Margerie,
Margori, Margorie, Margory

Margie (English) a familiar form of Marge,
Margaret.
Margey, Margi, Margy

Margit (Hungarian) a form of Margaret.
Marget, Margette, Margita

Margo, Margot (French) forms of
Margaret.
Mago, Margaro, Margolis, Margote

Margret (German) a form of Margaret.
Margreta, Margrete, Margreth, Margrethe,
Margrett, Margretta, Margrette, Margriet,
Margrieta

Margryta (Lithuanian) a form of Margaret.
Margrita, Margruta, Marguta

Marguerite (French) a form of Margaret.
Margarete, Margarite, Margerite, Marguareta,
Marguarete, Marguaretta, Marguarette,
Marguarita, Marguarite, Marguaritta,
Marguerette, Marguerita, Margurite,
Margueritta, Margueritte, Marguritte,
Marguryt, Marguryte

Mari (Japanese) ball. (Spanish) a form of
Mary.
Maree, Marree, Marri

Maria (Hebrew) bitter; sea of bitterness.
(Italian, Spanish) a form of Mary.
Maie, Marea, Mareah, Mariabella, Mariae,
Mariesa, Mariessa, Marrea, Marria

Mariaelena (Italian) a combination of
Maria + Elena.
Maria Elena

Mariah, Marriah (Hebrew) forms of
Mary. See also Moriah.
Maraia, Marrya, Marryah

Mariam (Hebrew) a form of Miriam.
Mariame, Mariem, Meriame, Meryam

Mariama (Hebrew) a form of Mariam.

Marian, Mariane, Mariann, Marianne
(English) forms of Mary Ann.
Marien, Mariene, Marienn, Marienne,
Marrian, Marriane, Marriann, Marrianne

Mariana, Marianna (Spanish) forms of
Marian.
Marianah, Mariena, Marienah, Marienna,
Mariennah, Marriana, Marrianna,
Maryana, Maryanna, Maryannah

Maribel (French) beautiful. (English) a
combination of Maria + Bel.
Marbelle, Mareabel, Mareabela, Mareabele,
Mareabell, Mareabella, Mareabelle, Mareebel,
Mareebela, Mareebelah, Mareebele, Mareebell,
Mareebella, Mareebellah, Mareebelle,
Mariabella, Maribela, Maribelah, Maribele,
Maribell, Maribella, Maribellah, Maribelle,
Maridel, Marybel, Marybela, Marybelah,
Marybele, Marybell, Marybella, Marybellah,
Marybelle

Maribeth (American) a form of Mary
Beth.
Maribette, Mariebeth

Marica (Italian) a form of Marice.
(Dutch, Slavic) a form of Marika.
Maricah

Maricarmen (American) a form of
Marycarmen.

Marice (Italian) a form of Mary. See also
Maris.
Maryce

Maricela (Latin) a form of Marcella.
Maricel, Mariceli, Maricelia, Maricella,
Maricely

Maridel (English) a form of Maribel.

Marie (French) a form of Mary.
Maree, Marrie

Marie Andree (French) a combination of
Marie + Andree.

Marie Ann, Marie Anne (American)
combinations of Marie + Ann.
Marie-Ann, Marie-Anne

Marie Chantal (French) a combination of Marie + Chantal.
Marie-Chantal

Marie Christi (American) a combination of Marie + Christi.
Marie Christie, Marie Christy, Marie-Christi, Marie-Christie, Marie-Christy

Marie Clair, Marie Claire (American) combinations of Marie + Clair.
Marie Clare, Marie-Clair, Marie-Claire, Marie-Clare

Marie Claude (French) a combination of Marie + Claude.
Marie-Claude

Marie Elaine (American) a combination of Marie + Elaine.
Marie-Elaine

Marie Eve, Marie-Eve (American) combinations of Marie + Eve.

Marie Frances (French) a combination of Marie + Frances.
Marie-Frances

Marie Helene (American) a combination of Marie + Helene.
Marie-Helene

Marie Jeanne (American) a combination of Marie + Jeanne.
Marie Jean, Marie-Jean, Marie-Jeanne

Marie Joelle (French) a combination of Marie + Joelle.
Marie-Joelle

Marie Josee (French) a combination of Marie + Josee.
Marie Josie, Marie-Josee, Marie-Josie

Marie Kim (American) a combination of Marie + Kim.
Marie-Kim

Marie Laurence (French) a combination of Marie + Laurence.
Marie-Laurence

Marie Lou (American) a combination of Marie + Lou.
Marie-Lou

Marie Louise (American) a combination of Marie + Louise.
Marie-Louise

Marie Maud, Marie Maude (American) combinations of Marie + Maud.
Marie-Maud, Marie-Maude

Marie Michele, Marie Michell (American) combinations of Marie + Michele.
Marie Michelle, Marie-Michele, Marie-Michell, Marie-Michelle

Marie Noelle (American) a combination of Marie + Noelle.
Marie Noel, Marie Noele, Marie-Noel, Marie-Noele, Marie-Noelle

Marie Pascale (French) a combination of Marie + Pascale.
Marie Pascal, Marie-Pascal, Marie-Pascale

Marie Philippa (French) a combination of Marie + Philippa.
Marie Philipa, Marie-Philipa, Marie-Philippa

Marie Pier, Marie-Pier, Marie Pierre (French) combinations of Marie + Pier.
Marie-Pierre

Marie Soleil (Spanish) a combination of Marie + Soleil (see Solana).
Marie-Soleil

Marie Sophie (French) a combination of Marie + Sophie.
Marie-Sophie

Mariel, Marielle (German, Dutch) forms of Mary.
Marial, Mariale, Mariall, Marialle, Marieke, Marielana, Mariele, Marieli, Marielie, Mariell, Marielsie, Mariely, Marielys, Maryal, Maryel, Maryil, Maryile, Maryille

Mariela, Mariella (German, Dutch) forms of Mary.
Mariala, Marialah, Marialla, Maryila, Maryilla

Marielena (German, Dutch) a form of Mary.

Marietta (Italian) a familiar form of Marie.

Maretta, Marette, Mariet, Marieta, Mariett, Mariette, Marriet, Marrieta, Marriete, Marrietta, Marriette

Marieve (American) a combination of Mary + Eve.

Marigold (English) Mary's gold. Botany: a plant with yellow or orange flowers.
Mareagold, Mareegold, Mariegold, Marygold

Mariha (Hebrew, Italian, Spanish) a form of Maria.

Marija (Hebrew, Italian, Spanish) a form of Maria.

Marika (Dutch, Slavic) a form of Mary.
Mareeca, Mareecah, Mareeka, Maricka, Marieka, Marieke, Marijke, Marikah, Marike, Marikia, Marikka, Mariqua, Marique, Mariska, Mariske, Marrica, Marricah, Marrika, Marrike, Maryca, Marycah, Marycka, Maryk, Maryka, Maryke, Merica, Mericah, Merika, Merikah, Meriqua, Merique

Mariko (Japanese) circle.
Mareako, Mareecko, Mareeco, Mareeko, Maricko, Marico, Marycko, Maryco, Maryko

Marilee, Marilie, Marily (American) combinations of Mary + Lee. See also Merrilee.
Marilea, Marileah, Marilei, Marileigh, Mariley, Marili, Marilia, Marrilee, Marylea, Maryleah, Marylee, Marylei, Maryleigh, Maryley, Maryli, Marylie, Maryly

Marilla (Hebrew, German) a form of Mary.
Marella, Marelle, Marila, Marilah, Marillah, Maryla, Marylah, Marylla

Marilou, Marilu (American) forms of Marylou.
Mariluz

Marilyn (Hebrew) Mary's line or descendants. See also Merilyn.
Maralin, Maralyn, Maralyne, Maralynn, Maralynne, Marelyn, Marielin, Marielina, Marieline, Marilena, Marilene, Marilin, Marilina, Mariline, Marillyn, Marolyn, Marralynn, Marrilin, Marrilyn, Merrilyn

Marilyne, Marilynn (Hebrew) forms of Marilyn.
Marilynne, Marrilynn, Marrilynne

Marin, Marine, Maryn (Latin, Aramaic) forms of Maren.
Marinn, Maryne

Marina (Latin) sea. See also Maren.
Mareana, Mareanah, Marinae, Marinah, Marinka, Marrina, Marrinah, Marrinia, Maryna, Marynah, Mayne, Marynna, Marynnah, Marynne, Mirena, Myrena, Myrenah

Marinda (Latin) a form of Marina.
Marindi

Marini (Swahili) healthy; pretty.
Marinee, Mariney, Marinie, Marynee, Maryney, Maryni, Marynie, Maryny

Marinna (Latin) a form of Marina.

Marion (French) a form of Mary.
Mariun, Marrian, Marrion, Maryon, Maryonn

Maris (Latin) sea. (Greek) a short form of Amaris, Damaris. See also Marice.
Maries, Marise, Mariss, Marisse, Marris, Marys, Meris, Merris

Marisa (Latin) sea.
Mariesa, Marisah

Marisela (Latin) a form of Marisa.
Mariseli, Marisella, Marishelle, Marissela

Marisha (Russian) a familiar form of Mary.
Mareshah, Marishah, Marishenka, Marishka, Mariska, Marrisha, Marrishah

Marisol (Spanish) sunny sea.
Marise, Marizol, Marysol, Marysola, Maryzol, Maryzola

Marissa (Latin) a form of Maris, Marisa.
Mariessa, Marissah, Marisse, Marizza, Morissa

Marit (Aramaic) lady.
Marite, Maryt, Maryte

Marita (Spanish) a form of Marisa. (Aramaic) a form of Marit.
Maritah, Marité, Maritha, Maryta

Maritsa (Arabic) a form of Maritza.
Maritsah, Marittssa

Maritza (Arabic) blessed.
Maritzah, Marytsa, Marytsah, Marytza, Marytzah

Mariya, Mariyah (Hebrew, Italian, Spanish) a form of Maria. (Arabic) a form of Mariyan.

Mariyan (Arabic) purity.
Mariyana, Mariyanna

Mariza (Latin) a form of Marisa.

Marja (Finnish) a form of Maria.
Marjae, Marjah, Marjatta, Marjatte, Marjie

Marjan (Persian) coral. (Polish) a form of Mary.
Marjana, Marjanah, Marjane, Marjaneh, Marjanna

Marjie (Scottish) a familiar form of Marjorie.
Marje, Marjey, Marji, Marjy

Marjolaine (French) marjoram.
Marjolain, Marjolaina, Marjolayn, Marjolayna, Marjolayne

Marjorie (Greek) a familiar form of Margaret. (Scottish) a form of Mary. See also Margery.
Marjarie, Marjary, Marjerie, Marjery, Marjie, Marjoree, Marjorey, Marjori, Marjory

Markayla (American) a combination or Mary + Kayla.
Marka, Markaiah, Markaya, Markayel, Markeela

Markeisha (English) a combination of Mary + Keisha.
Markasha, Markeesha, Markeisa, Markeisia, Markeysha, Markeyshia, Markeysia, Markiesha, Markieshia, Markiesia, Markysia, Markysiah, Markysya, Markysyah

Markell, Markelle (Latin) forms of Mark (see Boys' Names).
Markel

Markesha (English) a form of Markeisha.

Markeshia (English) a form of Markeisha.
Markesia, Markesiah

Marketa (Czech) a form of Markita.
Markete, Marketta, Markette

Marki (Latin) a form of Markie.

Markia (Latin) a form of Markie.

Markie (Latin) martial, warlike.
Marka, Marke, Markeah, Markee, Markey, Marky, Marquee, Marquey, Marqui, Marquie, Marquy

Markisha (English) a form of Markeisha.
Markishia, Markisia

Markita (Czech) a form of Margaret.
Markeata, Markeatah, Markeda, Markeeda, Markeeta, Markieta, Markitah, Markitha, Markketta, Markkette, Markkyt, Markkyta, Markyttah, Merkate

Marla (English) a short form of Marlena, Marlene.
Marlah

Marlaina (English) a form of Marlena.
Marlainna

Marlana (English) a form of Marlena.
Marlanah, Marlania, Marlanna

Marlayna (English) a form of Marlena.

Marlee, Marleigh, Marley, Marlie, Marly (English) forms of Marlene.
Marlea, Marleah, Marli

Marleen (Greek, Slavic) a form of Marlene.
Marleene

Marlen, Marlin (Greek, Slavic) a form of Marlene. See also Marlyn.
Marlenne, Marline

Marlena (German) a form of Marlene.
Marlaena, Marleana, Marleanah, Marleena, Marleenah, Marleina, Marlyna, Marlynah

Marlene (Greek) high tower. (Slavic) a form of Magdalen.
Marlaine, Marlane, Marlayne, Marlean, Marlein, Marleine

Marleny (Greek, Slavic) a familiar form of Marlene.
Marleni, Marlenie

Marlina (Greek, Slavic) a form of Marlena.
Marlinah, Marlinda

Marlis (English) a short form of Marlisa.
Marles, Marlise, Marliss, Marlisse, Marlys, Marlyse, Marlyss, Marlysse

Marlisa (English) a combination of Maria + Lisa.
Marlissa, Marlysa, Marlyssa

Marlo (English) a form of Mary.
Marlon, Marlona, Marlonah, Marlone, Marlow, Marlowe

Marlyn (Hebrew) a short form of Marilyn. (Greek, Slavic) a form of Marlene. See also Marlen.
Marlyne, Marlynn, Marlynne

Marmara (Greek) sparkling, shining.
Marmarah, Marmee

Marni, Marnie (Hebrew) short forms of Marnina.
Marna, Marnah, Marnay, Marne, Marnea, Marnee, Marney, Marnia, Marniah, Marnique, Marnja, Marny, Marnya, Marnyah, Marnye

Marnina (Hebrew) rejoice.
Marneena, Marneenah, Marninah, Marnyna

Marnisha (Hebrew) a form of Marnina.

Maroula (Greek) a form of Mary.
Maroulah, Maroulla, Maroullah

Marquesha (American) a form of Markeisha.

Marquetta (Spanish) a form of Marcia.
Marquet, Marqueta, Marquete, Marquette

Marquis (French) a form of Marquise.

Marquise (French) noblewoman.
Makeese, Markese, Marquees, Marquese, Marquice, Marquies, Marquiese, Marquisa, Marquisee, Marquisse, Marquiste, Marquyse

Marquisha (American) a form of Marquise.
Marquiesha, Marquisia

Marquita, Marquitta (Spanish) forms of Marcia.
Marquatte, Marqueda, Marquedia, Marquee, Marqueeda, Marqueita, Marqueite, Marquia,

Marquida, Marquietta, Marquiette, Marquite, Marquitia, Marquitra, Marquyta, Marquytah, Marquyte, Marquytta, Marquyttah, Marquytte

Marrisa, Marrissa (Latin) forms of Marisa.
Marrisah, Marrissia

Marsala (Italian) from Marseilles, France.
Marsal, Marsali, Marsalla, Marsallah, Marseilles, Marsela, Marselah, Marsella, Marsellah, Marselle

Marsha (English) a form of Marcia.
Marcha, Marchah, Marchia, Marchya, Marchyah, Marshah, Marshel, Marshele, Marshell, Marshelle, Marshia, Marshiah, Marshiela, Marshya, Marshyah

Marshae, Marshay (English) forms of Marsha.

Marta (English) a short form of Martha, Martina.
Martá, Martä, Martah, Marte, Marttaha, Merta, Merte

Martha (Aramaic) lady; sorrowful. Bible: a friend of Jesus. See also Mardi.
Martaha, Marth, Marthan, Marthe, Marthy, Marticka, Martita, Martus, Martuska, Masia

Marti, Marty (English) familiar forms of Martha, Martina.
Martie

Martia (Latin) a form of Marcia.
Martiah

Martina (Latin) martial, warlike. See also Tina.
Martaina, Martainah, Martana, Martanah, Martanna, Martannah, Martayna, Martaynah, Marteana, Marteanah, Marteena, Marteenah, Martella, Marthena, Marthina, Martinah, Martinia, Martino, Martosia, Martoya, Martricia, Martrina, Martyna, Martynah

Martine (Latin) a form of Martina.
Martain, Martaine, Martane, Martanne, Martayn, Martayne, Martean, Marteane, Marteen, Marteene, Martel, Martelle, Martene, Marthine, Martyn, Martyne, Martynne

Martisha (Latin) a form of Martina.

Martiza (Arabic) blessed.
Martisa, Martisah, Martizah, Martysa, Martysah, Martyza, Martyzah

Maru (Japanese) round.
Maroo

Maruca (Spanish) a form of Mary.
Mariucca, Maruja, Maruka

Marva (Hebrew) sweet sage.
Marvah

Marvella (French) marvelous.
Marvel, Marvela, Marvele, Marvell, Marvellah, Marvelle, Marvely, Marvetta, Marvette, Marvia, Marvil, Marvila, Marvile, Marvill, Marvilla, Marville, Marvyl, Marvyla, Marvyle, Marvyll, Marvylla, Marvylle

Marvina (English) lover of the sea.
Marvinah, Marvinia, Marviniah, Marvyna, Marvynah, Marvynia, Marvyniah, Marvynya, Marvynyah

Mary (Hebrew) bitter; sea of bitterness. Bible: the mother of Jesus. See also Maija, Malia, Maren, Mariah, Marjorie, Maura, Maureen, Miriam, Mitzi, Moira, Molly, Muriel.
Maeree, Maerey, Maeri, Maerie, Maery, Maree, Marella, Marelle, Maricara, Mariquilla, Mariquita, Marrey, Marry, Marye, Maryla, Marynia, Mavra, Meridel, Mirja, Morag, Moya

Mary Ann, Maryan, Maryann, Maryanne (English) combinations of Mary + Ann.
Mary Anne, Mary-Ann, Mary-Anne, Marryann, Maryane, Maryen, Maryena, Maryene, Maryenn, Maryenna, Maryenne, Meryen

Mary Beth, Marybeth (American) combinations of Mary + Beth.
Mareabeth, Mareebeth

Mary Kate, Mary-Kate, Marykate (American) combinations of Mary + Kate.

Mary Katherine (American) a combination of Mary + Katherine.

Mary Catherine, Mary-Catherine, Mary Kathryn, Mary-Katherine, Mary-Kathryn

Mary Margaret, Mary-Margaret (American) combinations of Mary + Margaret.

Marya (Arabic) purity; bright whiteness.

Maryah (Arabic) a form of Marya.

Maryam (Hebrew) a form of Miriam.
Maryama

Marycarmen (American) a combination of Mary + Carmen.

Maryellen (American) a combination of Mary + Ellen.
Marielen, Mariellen, Mary Ellen, Mary-Ellen, Maryelen

Maryjane (American) a combination of Mary + Jane.
Mary Jane, Mary-Jane

Maryjo (American) a combination of Mary + Jo.
Mary Jo, Mary-Jo, Mareajo, Mareejo, Marijo, Marijoe, Marijoh, Maryjoe, Maryjoh

Marylene (Hebrew) a form of Marylin.
Marylina, Maryline

Marylin (Hebrew) a form of Marilyn.
Marylinn, Marylyn, Marylyna, Marylyne, Marylynn, Marylynne

Marylou (American) a combination of Mary + Lou.
Mareelou, Mareelu, Mary Lou, Marylu

Marysa, Maryse, Maryssa (Latin) forms of Marisa.
Marrysa, Marrysah, Marryssa, Marryssah, Marysia

Masada (Hebrew) strong foundation, support.
Masadah, Massada, Massadah

Masago (Japanese) sands of time.
Massago

Masani (Luganda) gap toothed.
Masanee, Masaney, Masania, Masaniah, Masanie, Masany, Masanya, Masanyah

Masha (Russian) a form of Mary.
Mascha, Mashah, Mashenka, Mashka

Mashika (Swahili) born during the rainy season.
Mashyka, Mashykah, Masika

Mason (Arabic) a form of Maysun.

Matana (Hebrew) gift.
Matanah, Matania, Mataniah, Matanna, Matannah, Matannia, Matanniah, Matanya, Matanyah, Matat

Mathena (Hebrew) gift of God.
Mathenah

Mathieu (French) a form of Matthew.
Mathieux, Matthieu

Mathilde (German) a form of Matilda.
Mathild, Mathilda, Mathildis

Matilda (German) powerful battler. See also Maud, Tilda, Tillie.
Máda, Mafalda, Mahaut, Maitilde, Malkin, Mat, Matelda, Matilde, Matilly, Mattilda, Mattylda, Matusha, Matyld, Matylda, Matyldah, Matylde, Metild, Metilda, Metildah, Metilde, Metyld, Metylda, Metyldah, Metylde

Matrika (Hindi) mother. Religion: a name for the Hindu goddess Shakti in the form of the letters of the alphabet.
Matrica, Matricah, Matricka, Matrickah, Matryca, Matrycah, Matrycka, Matryckah, Matryka, Matrykah

Matsuko (Japanese) pine tree.

Mattea (Hebrew) gift of God.
Matea, Mateah, Mathea, Matheah, Mathia, Mathiah, Matia, Matteah, Matthea, Matthia, Matthiah, Mattia, Mattya, Mattyah, Matya

Matthew (Hebrew) gift of God. Bible: author of the Gospel of Matthew.
Mathie, Mathiew, Matthiew, Mattieu, Mattieux

Mattie, Matty (English) familiar forms of Martha, Matilda.
Matte, Mattey, Matti, Mattye

Mattison (English) a form of Madison.

Matusha (Spanish) a form of Matilda.
Matuja, Matuxa

Maud, Maude (English) short forms of Madeline, Matilda. See also Madison.
Maudea, Maudee, Maudey, Maudi, Maudie, Maudine, Maudlin, Maudy

Mauli (Tongan) a New Zealander of Pacific Island descent, also known as a Maori.
Maulea, Mauleah, Maulee, Maulei, Mauleigh, Maulia, Mauliah, Maulie, Mauly

Maura (Irish) dark. A form of Mary, Maureen. See also Moira.
Maurah, Maure, Mauree, Maurette, Mauri, Mauricette, Maurie, Maurita, Mauritia, Maury, Maurya

Maureen (French) dark. (Irish) a form of Mary. See also Morena.
Maireen, Maireena, Maireene, Mairin, Mairina, Mairine, Maurena, Maurene, Maurina, Maurine, Mauritzia, Moureen

Maurelle (French) dark; elfin.
Mauriel, Mauriell, Maurielle

Maurise (French) dark skinned; moor; marshland.
Maurisse, Maurita, Maurizia, Mauriziah, Maurizya, Maurizyah, Mauryzya, Mauryzyah

Maurissa (French) a form of Maurise.
Maurisa, Maurisah, Maurisia, Maurisiah, Maurissah

Mausi (Native American) plucked flower.
Mausee, Mausie, Mausy

Mauve (French) violet colored.
Mauv

Maverick (American) independent.
Maveric, Maverik, Maveryc, Maveryck, Maveryk

Mavia (Irish) happy.
Maviah, Mavie, Mavya, Mavyah

Mavis (French) thrush, songbird. See also Maeve.
Mavas, Mavies, Mavin, Mavine, Maviss, Mavon, Mavos, Mavra, Mavus, Mavys

Maxie (English) a familiar form of Maxine.
Maxi, Maxy

Maxime (Latin) a form of Maxine.
Maxima, Maximiliane

Maxine (Latin) greatest.
*Max, Maxa, Maxeen, Maxeena, Maxeene,
Maxena, Maxene, Maxina, Maxna,
Maxyn, Maxyna, Maxyne, Mazeen,
Mazeena, Mazeene, Mazin, Mazina,
Mazine, Mazyn, Mazyna, Mazyne*

May (Latin) great. (Arabic) discerning.
(English) flower; month of May. See also
Mae, Maia.
*Maj, Mayberry, Maybeth, Mayday, Maydee,
Maydena, Maye, Mayela, Mayella, Mayetta,
Mayrene*

Maya (Hindi) God's creative power.
(Greek) mother; grandmother. (Latin)
great. A form of Maia.
Mayam, Mya

Mayah (Hindi, Greek, Latin) a form of
Maya.

Maybeline (Latin) a familiar form of
Mabel.
*Maebelina, Maebeline, Maibelina,
Maibeline, Maibelyna, Maibelyne,
Maybelina, Maybelyna, Maybelyne*

Maybell (Latin) a form of Mabel.
*Maybel, Maybela, Maybele, Maybella,
Maybelle, Maybull, Mayebell, Mayebella,
Mayebelle*

Maycee (Scottish) a form of Maisey.
*Maysee, Maysey, Maysi, Maysie, Maysy,
Mayzie*

Maygan, Maygen (Irish) forms of Megan.
Mayghan, Maygon

Maylyn (American) a combination of
May + Lynn.
*Mayelene, Mayleen, Maylen, Maylene,
Maylin, Maylon, Maylynn, Maylynne*

Mayoree (Tai) beautiful.
*Mayaria, Mayariah, Mayariya, Mayarya,
Mayaryah, Mayree*

Mayra (Australian) spring wind. (Tai) a
form of Mayoree.
Mayrah

Maysa (Arabic) walks with a proud stride.

Maysun (Arabic) beautiful.
Maesun, Maisun, Mayson

Mayte (Spanish) a form of Maite.

Mazel (Hebrew) lucky.
*Mazal, Mazala, Mazalah, Mazela,
Mazella, Mazelle*

Mc Kenna, Mckena, Mckenna
(American) forms of Mackenna.
Mckennah, Mckinna, Mckinnah

**Mc Kenzie, Mckensey, Mckensie,
Mckenzee, Mckenzi, Mckenzie,
Mckenzy** (Irish) forms of Mackenzie.
*Mckennzie, Mckensee, McKensi, Mckensi,
Mckensy, Mckenze, McKenzee, McKenzey,
Mckenzey, McKenzi, McKenzie, McKenzy,
Mckenzye*

Mckaela (American) a form of Michaela.

Mckaila (American) a form of Michaela.

Mckala (American) a form of Michaela.

Mckayla (American) a form of Michaela.
Mckaylah, Mckayle, Mckayleh

Mckaylee (American) a form of Michaela.
Mckayleigh, Mckayli, Mckaylia, Mckaylie

Mckell (American) a form of Makell.
Mckelle

Mckinley (Scottish) child of the learned
ruler.
Mckinlee, Mckinleigh, Mckinlie, Mckinnley

Mckinzie (American) a form of
Mackenzie.
*Mckinsey, Mckinze, Mckinzea, Mckinzee,
Mckinzi, Mckinzy, Mckynze, Mckynzie*

Mead, Meade (Greek) honey wine.
Meada, Meadah, Meed, Meede

Meadow (English) meadow.

Meagan, Meagen (Irish) forms of Megan.
*Meagain, Meagann, Meagin, Meagnah,
Meagon*

Meaghan (Welsh) a form of Megan.
*Meaghann, Meaghen, Meaghin, Meaghon,
Meaghyn, Meahgan*

Meara (Irish) mirthful.
Mearah, Mearia, Meariah, Mearya, Mearyah

Mechelle (French) a form of Michelle.

Meda (Native American) prophet; priestess.
Medah

Medea (Greek) ruling. (Latin) middle. Mythology: a sorceress who helped Jason get the Golden Fleece.
Medeah, Medeia, Media, Mediah, Medya, Medyah

Medina (Arabic) History: the site of Muhammad's tomb.
Medeana, Medeanah, Medeena, Medeenah, Medinah, Medyna, Medynah

Medora (Greek) mother's gift. Literature: a character in Lord Byron's poem *The Corsair.*
Medorah

Meena (Hindi) blue semiprecious stone; bird. (Greek, German, Dutch) a form of Mena.
Meenah

Meera (Hebrew) a form of Meira.
Meerah

Meg (English) a short form of Margaret, Megan.
Megg

Megan (Greek) pearl; great. (Irish) a form of Margaret.
Magana, Meegen, Meeghan, Meeghen, Meeghin, Meeghon, Meeghyn, Meegin, Meegon, Meegyn, Meganna, Megin, Megon, Megyn, Meigan, Meigen, Meigin, Meigon, Meigyn, Meygan, Meygen, Meygin, Meygon, Meygyn

Megane, Megann, Meganne, Megen, Meggan (Irish) forms of Megan.
Meggen

Megara (Greek) first. Mythology: Heracles's first wife.

Megean (American) a form of Megan.

Meggie, Meggy (English) familiar forms of Margaret, Megan.
Meggi

Megha (Welsh) a short form of Meghan.

Meghan, Meghann (Welsh) forms of Megan.
Meehan, Meghana, Meghane, Meghanne, Meghean, Meghen, Meghon, Meghyn, Mehgan, Mehgen

Mehadi (Hindi) flower.
Mehadee, Mehadie, Mehady

Mehira (Hebrew) speedy; energetic.
Mahira, Mahirah, Mehirah, Mehyra, Mehyrah

Mehitabel (Hebrew) benefited by trusting God.
Mehetabel, Mehitabelle, Hetty, Hitty

Mehri (Persian) kind; lovable; sunny.
Mehree, Mehrie, Mehry

Mei (Hawaiian) great. (Chinese) a short form of Meiying.
Meiko

Meira (Hebrew) light.
Meirah, Mera, Meyra, Meyrah

Meit (Burmese) affectionate.
Meita, Meyt, Meytah

Meiying (Chinese) beautiful flower.
Mei

Mejorana (Spanish) marjoram.
Mejoranah, Mejoranna, Mejorannah

Meka (Hebrew) a familiar form of Michaela.
Mekah

Mekayla (American) a form of Michaela.
Mekaela, Mekaila, Mekala, Mekayela, Mekaylia

Mekenzie (American) a form of Mackenzie.
Mekensie, Mekenzi

Mel (Portuguese, Spanish) sweet as honey.
Mell

Mela (Hindi) religious service. (Polish) a form of Melanie.
Melah, Mella, Mellah

Melaina (Latin, Greek) a form of Melina.
Melainah

Melana (Russian) a form of Melanie.
Melanna, Melena, Melenah

Melaney, Melani, Melannie, Melany
(Greek) forms of Melanie.
Melanney, Melanya

Melanie (Greek) dark skinned.
Meila, Meilani, Meilin, Melaine, Melainie,
Melane, Melanee, Melania, Mélanie,
Melanka, Melasya, Melayne, Melenee,
Meleney, Meleni, Melenia, Melenie, Meleny,
Mellanee, Mellaney, Mellani, Mellanie,
Mellany, Mellenee, Melleney, Melleni,
Mellenie, Melleny, Melya, Milya

Melantha (Greek) dark flower.
Melanthe

Melba (Greek) soft; slender. (Latin)
mallow flower.
Malba, Malbah, Melbah, Melva, Melvah

Mele (Hawaiian) song; poem.
Melle

Melea, Meleah (German) forms of Melia.

Melecent (English) a form of Millicent.
Melacent, Melacenta, Melacente, Melacint,
Melacinte, Melecenta, Melecente, Melecint,
Melecinta, Melecinte

Meleni (Tongan) melon.
Melenee, Meleney, Melenia, Meleniah,
Meleny, Melenya, Melenyah

Melesse (Ethiopian) eternal.
Mellesse

Melia (German) a short form of Amelia.
Melcia, Meleia, Meleisha, Meli, Meliah,
Melida, Melika, Melya, Melyah, Mema,
Mylia, Myliah, Mylya, Mylyah

Melicent (English) a form of Millicent.
Meliscent, Melisent, Melissent, Mellicent,
Mellisent, Melycent, Melycente, Melycint,
Melycinta, Melycinte, Melycynt, Melycynta,
Melycynte

Melina (Latin) canary yellow. (Greek) a
short form of Melinda.
Meleana, Meleanah, Meleane, Meleena,
Melena, Melenah, Meline, Melinia, Meliniah,
Melinna, Melinnah, Melinne

Melinda (Greek) honey. See also Linda,
Melina, Mindi.
Maillie, Melindah, Melinde, Melindee,
Melinder, Melindia, Melindiah, Mellinda,
Milinda, Milynda, Mylenda, Mylinda,
Mylynda

Meliora (Latin) better.
Melior, Meliori, Melioria, Meliorie, Mellear,
Mellor, Mellora, Mellorah, Melyor, Melyora,
Melyorah

Melisa, Mellisa, Mellissa (Greek) forms
of Melissa.
Melisah, Mellissah

Melisande (French) a form of Melissa,
Millicent.
Lisandra, Malisande, Malissande,
Malyssandre, Melesande, Melicend,
Melisanda, Melisandra, Melisandre,
Mélisandré, Melisenda, Melisende,
Melissande, Melissandre, Mellisande,
Melond, Melysanda, Melysande,
Melyssandre

Melissa (Greek) honey bee. See also
Elissa, Lissa, Melisande, Millicent.
Malessa, Melesa, Melessa, Melessah, Mélisa,
Melise, Melisha, Melishia, Melisia, Mélissa,
Melissah, Melisse, Melissia, Meliza,
Melizah, Milissa, Molissia, Mollissa

Melita (Greek) a form of Melissa.
(Spanish) a short form of Carmelita.
Malita, Meleata, Meleatah, Meleatta,
Meleattah, Meleeta, Meleetah, Meleetta,
Meleettah, Meleta, Melitah, Melitta,
Melittah, Melitza, Melletta, Melyta,
Melytah, Melytta, Melyttah, Molita

Melly (American) a familiar form of
names beginning with "Mel." See also
Millie.
Meli, Melie, Melli, Mellie

Melodie (Greek) a form of Melody.

Melody (Greek) melody. See also Elodie.
Meladia, Meloda, Melodah, Melodea,
Melodee, Melodey, Melodi, Melodia,
Melodiah, Melodya, Melodyah, Melodyann,
Melodye

Melonie (American) a form of Melanie.
Melloney, Mellonie, Mellony, Melona,
Melonah, Melone, Melonee, Meloney,
Meloni, Melonia, Meloniah, Melonnie,
Melony, Melonya, Melonyah

Melosa (Spanish) sweet; tender.
Malosa, Malosah, Malossa, Malossah,
Mellosa, Mellosah, Melosah, Melossa,
Melossah

Melrose (American) a combination of
Melanie + Rose.
Melrosa, Melrosah

Melvina (Irish) armored chief. See also
Malvina.
Melevine, Melva, Melveen, Melveena,
Melveenah, Melveene, Melveenia, Melvena,
Melvene, Melvinda, Melvine, Melvinia,
Melviniah, Melvonna, Melvyna, Melvynah,
Melvyne, Melvynia, Melvyniah, Melvynya,
Melvynyah

Melyna (Latin, Greek) a form of Melina.
Melynah, Melynna, Melynnah

Melynda (Greek) a form of Melinda.
Melyndah, Melyne

Melyne (Greek) a short form of Melinda.
Melyn, Melynn, Melynne

Melyssa (Greek) a form of Melissa.
Melysa, Melysah, Melyssah, Melysse

Mena (German, Dutch) strong. (Greek) a
short form of Philomena. History:
Menes is believed to be the first king of
Egypt. See also Mina.
Meana, Meanah, Meina, Meinah, Menah,
Meyna, Meynah

Mendi (Basque) a form of Mary.
Menda, Mendy

Menora (Hebrew) candleholder. Religion:
a menorah is a special nine-branched
candleholder used during the holiday of
Hanukkah.
Menorah, Minora, Minorah, Mynora,
Mynorah

Meranda, Merranda (Latin) forms of
Miranda.
Merana, Merandah, Merandia, Merannda

Mérane (French) a form of Mary.
Meraine, Merrane

Mercades (Latin, Spanish) a form of
Mercedes.
Mercadez, Mercadie

Mercede (Latin, Spanish) a form of
Mercedes.
Merced, Merceda, Mersade

Mercedes (Latin) reward, payment.
(Spanish) merciful.
Meceades, Mercedeas, Mercedees, Mercedies,
Mercedis, Mersades

Mercedez (Latin, Spanish) a form of
Mercedes.
Mercedeez

Mercia (English) a form of Marcia.
History: an ancient British kingdom.

Mercilla (English) a form of Mercy.
Mercillah, Mercille, Mersilla, Mersillah,
Mersille

Mercy (English) compassionate, merciful.
See also Merry.
Merce, Mercee, Mercey, Merci, Mercia,
Merciah, Mercie, Mercina, Mercinah, Mercya,
Mercyah, Mersee, Mersey, Mersi, Mersie,
Mersina, Mersinah, Mersy

Meredith (Welsh) protector of the sea.
Meredeth, Meredif, Merediff, Meredithe,
Meredy, Meredyth, Meredythe, Merrydith,
Merrydithe, Merrydyth

Meri (Finnish) sea. (Irish) a short form of
Meriel.
Meree, Merey, Merie, Mery

Meria (African) rebellious.

Meriah (Hebrew) a form of Mariah.
(African) a form of Meria.

Meridith (Welsh) a form of Meredith.
Meridath, Merideth, Meridie, Meridithe,
Meridyth, Merridie, Merridith, Merridithe,
Merridyth

Meriel (Irish) shining sea.
Merial, Meriele, Meriella, Merielle, Meriol,
Merrial, Merriel, Meryel, Meryela, Meryelah,
Meryell, Meryella, Meryellah, Meryelle

Merilyn (English) a combination of Merry + Lynn. See also Marilyn.
Meralin, Meralina, Meraline, Meralyn, Meralyna, Meralyne, Merelan, Merelen, Merelin, Merelina, Mereline, Merelyn, Merelyna, Merelyne, Merilan, Merilen, Merilin, Merilina, Meriline, Merilyna, Merilyne, Merlyn, Merralin, Merralyn, Merrelina, Merreline, Merrelyn, Merrelynn, Merrillin, Merrillina, Merrilline, Merrilyn, Merrilynn, Merrylyn, Merrylyna, Merrylyne, Merylin, Merylina, Meryline, Merylyn, Merylyna, Merylyne

Merina (Latin) a form of Marina. (Australian) a form of Merrina.
Merinah

Merinda (Australian) beautiful.
Merindah, Merynda, Meryndah

Merisa, Merissa (Latin) forms of Marisa.
Merisah, Merisha, Merissah, Merrisa, Merrisah, Merrissa, Merrissah, Merrysa, Merrysah, Merryssa, Merryssah

Merite (Latin) deserving.
Merita, Meritah, Meritta, Merittah, Meritte, Merrita, Meryta, Merytah, Merytta

Merle (Latin, French) blackbird.
Mearl, Mearla, Mearle, Merl, Merla, Merlina, Merline, Merola, Murle, Myrl, Myrle, Myrleen, Myrlene, Myrline

Merpati (Indonesian) dove.
Merpatee, Merpatie, Merpaty

Merrilee (American) a combination of Merry + Lee. See also Marilee.
Merrilei, Merrileigh, Merriley, Merrili, Merrily, Merrylea, Merryleah, Merrylee, Merrylei, Merryleigh, Merryley, Merryli, Merrylia, Merrylie, Merryly, Merylea, Meryleah, Merylee, Merylei, Meryleigh, Meryley, Meryli, Merylie, Meryly

Merrina (Australian) grass seed.
Meriwa, Meriwah, Merrinah, Merriwa, Merriwah, Merryna, Merrynah, Merrywa, Merrywah, Meryn, Meryna, Merynah

Merritt (Latin) a form of Merite.
Merit, Meritt, Meryt, Meryte, Merytt, Merytte

Merry (English) cheerful, happy. A familiar form of Mercy, Meredith.
Merree, Merri, Merrie, Merrielle, Mery

Meryl (German) famous. (Irish) shining sea. A form of Meriel, Muriel.
Maral, Marel, Meral, Merel, Merelle, Merill, Merrall, Merrel, Merrell, Merrelle, Merril, Merrile, Merrill, Merryl, Meryle, Meryll, Mirel, Mirell, Mirelle, Mirle, Myral, Myrel, Myrelle, Myril, Myrila, Myrile, Myryl, Myryla, Myryle

Mesha (Hindi) another name for the zodiac sign Aries.
Meshah, Meshai, Meshal

Messina (Latin) middle child. (African) spoiler.
Mesina, Mesinah, Messinah, Messyna, Messynah, Mesyna, Mesynah

Meta (German) a short form of Margaret.
Metah, Metta, Mettah, Mette, Metti

Mhairie (Scottish) a form of Mary.
Mhaire, Mhairee, Mhairey, Mhairi, Mhairy, Mhari, Mhary

Mia (Italian) mine. A familiar form of Michaela, Michelle.
Mea, Meah

Miah (Italian) a form of Mia.

Mica, Micha (Hebrew) forms of Micah.

Micaela (Hebrew) a form of Michaela.
Micaelah, Micaele, Micaella, Miceala, Mycael, Mycaela, Mycaelah, Mycaele, Mycala, Mycalah, Mycale

Micah (Hebrew) a form of Michael. Bible: one of the Old Testament prophets.
Meecah

Micaiah (Hebrew) a form of Micah.

Micaila (Hebrew) a form of Michaela.

Micala (Hebrew) a form of Michaela.
Micalah

Micayla (Hebrew) a form of Michaela.
Micayle, Micaylee

Michael (Hebrew) who is like God?
Michaelann, Michaell, Michaelle, Michaelyn

Michaela, Michaella (Hebrew) forms of Michael.

Michaila (Hebrew) a form of Michaela.

Michal (Hebrew) a form of Michael. (Italian) a form of Michele.

Michala, Michalla (Hebrew) forms of Michaela.
Michalah, Michalann, Michale, Michalene, Michalin, Michalina, Michalisha, Michalle

Michayla (Hebrew) a form of Michaela.
Michaylah, Michayle. Micheyla

Micheala (Hebrew) a form of Michaela.
Michealia

Michel (Italian) a form of Michele. (French) a form of Michelle.

Michela (Hebrew) a form of Michala. (Italian) a form of Michele.
Michelia, Michely, Michelyn

Michele, Michell (Italian) forms of Michelle.

Michelina (Italian) a form of Michaela.
Michaelina, Michalina, Mychelina

Micheline (Italian) a form of Michelina.
Michaeline, Michaline, Michellene, Mycheline

Michelle (French) who is like God? See also Shelley.
Machealle, Machele, Machell, Machella, Machelle, Meichelle, Meschell, Meshell, Meshelle, Michaelle, Michéle, Michella, Michellah, Michellyn, Mischel, Mischelle, Mishael, Mishaela, Mishayla, Mishel, Mishele, Mishell, Mishella, Mishellah, Mishelle, Mitchele, Mitchelle, Mychel, Mychele, Mychell, Mychella, Mychelle, Myshel, Myshele, Myshell, Myshella, Myshellah, Myshelle

Michi (Japanese) righteous way.
Miche, Michee, Michey, Michie, Michy

Michiko (Japanese) righteous child.

Mickaela (Hebrew) a form of Michaela.
Mickael

Mickala (Hebrew) a form of Michaela.
Mickalla

Mickayla (Hebrew) a form of Michaela.
Mickeel, Mickell, Mickelle

Mickenzie (American) a form of Mackenzie.
Mickensie, Mickenzee, Mickenzi, Mickenzy

Micki (American) a familiar form of Michaela.
Mickee, Mickeeya, Mickia, Mickie, Micky, Mickya, Miquia

Midori (Japanese) green.
Madorea, Madoree, Madorey, Madori, Madorie, Madory, Midorea, Midoree, Midorey, Midorie, Midory, Mydorea, Mydoree, Mydorey, Mydori, Mydorie, Mydory

Mieko (Japanese) prosperous.
Mieke, Myeko

Mielikki (Finnish) pleasing.

Miette (French) small; sweet.
Mieta, Mietah, Mietta, Miettah, Myeta, Myetah, Myett, Myetta, Myettah, Myette

Migdana (Hebrew) present.
Migdanna, Migdannah, Mygdana, Mygdanah

Migina (Omaha) new moon.
Migeana, Migeanah, Migeena, Migeenah, Miginah, Migyna, Migynah, Mygeana, Mygeanah, Mygeena, Mygeenah, Mygina, Myginah, Mygyna, Mygynah

Mignon (French) dainty, petite; graceful.
Mignona, Mignone, Minyonne, Mygnona, Mygnonah, Mygnone

Mignonette (French) flower.
Mignonetta, Mignonettah, Minnionette, Minnonette, Minyonette, Mygnonetta, Mygnonette

Miguela (Spanish) a form of Michaela.
Micquel, Miguelina, Miguelita

Mika (Japanese) new moon. (Russian) God's child. (Native American) wise racoon. (Hebrew) a form of Micah. (Latin) a form of Dominica.

Mikaela (Hebrew) a form of Michaela.
Mikael, Mikaelah, Mikail, Mikalene, Mikalovna, Mikalyn, Mikea, Mikeisha, Mikeita, Mikeya, Mikiala, Mikiela, Mikkel

Mikah, Mikka (Hebrew, Japanese, Russian, Native American) forms of Mika.

Mikaila (American) a form of Michaela.

Mikal, Mikel, Mikelle (Hebrew) short forms of Michael, Michaela.

Mikala, Mikalah (Hebrew) forms of Michaela.
Mikale, Mikalea, Mikalee, Mikaleh

Mikayla (American) a form of Michaela.
Mikayle

Mikela (Hebrew) a form of Michaela.
Mikele, Mikell, Mikella

Mikelena (Danish) a form of Michaela.
Mykelena

Mikenna (American) a form of Mackenna.
Mikena, Mikenah, Mikennah

Mikenzie (American) a form of Mackenzie.
Mikenzee, Mikenzi, Mikenzy

Mikesha (American) a form of Michaela.

Mikhaela (American) a form of Michaela.
Mikhalea, Mikhelle

Mikhaila (American) a form of Michaela.
Mikhail

Mikhala (American) a form of Michaela.

Mikhayla (American) a form of Michaela.

Miki (Japanese) flower stem.
Mikee, Mikey, Mikie, Mikita, Mikiyo, Mikko, Miko, Miky

Mikia (Japanese) a form of Miki.
Mikkia, Mikkiya

Mikki (Japanese) a form of Miki.
Mikkie

Mikyla (American) a form of Michaela.

Mila (Russian) dear one. (Italian, Slavic) a short form of Camila, Ludmilla.
Milah, Milla, Millah, Myla

Milada (Czech) my love.
Miladah, Miladi, Miladie, Milady, Mylada, Myladah, Myladi, Myladie, Mylady

Milagros (Spanish) miracle.
Milagritos, Milagro, Milagrosa, Milrari, Milrarie

Milan (Italian) from Milan, Italy.
Milane, Milanne

Milana (Italian) from Milan, Italy. (Russian) a form of Melana.
Milani, Milania, Milanie, Milanka, Milanna

Mildred (English) gentle counselor.
Mil, Milda, Mildrene, Mildrid, Mylda, Myldred, Myldreda

Milena (Greek, Hebrew, Russian) a form of Ludmilla, Magdalen, Melanie.
Milenah, Milène, Milenia, Milenny, Milini, Millini, Mylena, Mylenah

Mileta (German) generous, merciful.
Miletah, Milett, Miletta, Milette, Milita, Militah, Myleta, Myletah, Mylita, Mylitah, Mylyta, Mylytah

Milia (German) industrious. A short form of Amelia, Emily.
Milea, Mileah, Miliah, Millea, Milleah, Millia, Milliah, Millya, Milya, Milyah, Mylea, Myleah, Mylia, Myliah, Myllia, Mylliah, Myllya, Myllyah, Mylya, Mylyah

Miliani (Hawaiian) caress.
Milanni, Miliany, Milliani

Mililani (Hawaiian) heavenly caress.
Mililanee, Mililaney, Mililanie, Mililany, Millilani, Mylilanee, Mylilaney, Mylilani, Mylilania, Mylilaniah, Mylilanie, Mylilany, Mylylanee, Mylylaney, Mylylani, Mylylania, Mylylanie

Milissa (Greek) a form of Melissa.
Milessa, Milisa, Milisah, Milissah, Millisa, Millissa, Mylisa, Mylisah, Mylisia, Mylissa, Mylissah, Mylissia, Mylysa, Mylysah, Mylyssa, Mylyssah

Milka (Czech) a form of Amelia.
Milica, Milicah, Milika, Milikah, Milkah, Mylka, Mylkah

Millicent (English) industrious. (Greek) a form of Melissa. See also Lissa, Melisande.
Milicent, Milicenta, Milisent, Milissent, Milliestone, Millisent, Millisenta, Milzie,

Myllicent, Myllicenta, Myllicente, Myllycent,
Myllycenta, Myllycente, Myllysent,
Myllysenta, Myllysente, Mylycent, Mylycenta,
Mylycente, Mylysent, Mylysenta, Mylysente

Millie, Milly (English) familiar forms of
Amelia, Camille, Emily, Kamila, Melissa,
Mildred, Millicent.
Milee, Milei, Mileigh, Miley, Mili, Milie,
Millee, Millei, Milleigh, Milley, Milli,
Mylee, Mylei, Myleigh, Myli, Mylie,
Myllee, Myllei, Mylleigh, Mylley, Mylli,
Myllie, Mylly, Myly

Mima (Burmese) woman.
Mimah, Mimma, Mimmah, Myma,
Mymah, Mymma, Mymmah

Mimi (French) a familiar form of Miriam.
Mimea, Mimee, Mimey, Mimie, Mimmea,
Mimmee, Mimmey, Mimmi, Mimmie,
Mimmy, Mimy, Mymea, Mymee, Mymey,
Mymi, Mymie, Mymmea, Mymmee,
Mymmey, Mymmi, Mymmie, Mymmy,
Mymy

Mina (German) love. (Persian) blue sky.
(Arabic) harbor. (Japanese) south. A
short form of names ending in "mina."
Min, Minah, Myna, Mynah

Minal (Native American) fruit.
Minala, Minalah, Mynala, Mynalah

Minda (Hindi) knowledge.
Mindah, Mynda, Myndah

Mindi, Mindy (Greek) familiar forms of
Melinda.
Mindea, Mindee, Mindey, Mindie,
Mindyanne, Mindylee, Myndea, Myndee,
Myndey, Myndi, Myndie, Myndy

Mine (Japanese) peak; mountain range.
Minee, Mineko, Miney, Mini, Myne, Mynee

Minerva (Latin) wise. Mythology: the
goddess of wisdom.
Merva, Minervah, Minivera, Mynerva,
Mynervah

Minette (French) faithful defender.
Minetta, Minitta, Minitte, Minnette,
Minnita, Mynetta, Mynette, Mynnetta,
Mynnette

Minikin (Dutch) dear, darling.
Minikina, Minikinah, Minikine, Minikyna,
Minikynah, Minikyne, Mynikin, Mynikina,
Mynikinah, Mynikine

Minka (Polish) a short form of
Wilhelmina.
Minkah, Mynka, Mynkah

Minkie (Australian) daylight.
Minkee, Minkey, Minki, Minky, Mynkee,
Mynkey, Mynki, Mynkie, Mynky

Minna (German) a short form of
Wilhelmina.
Minnah, Minta, Mynna, Mynnah

Minnehaha (Native American) laughing
water; waterfall.
Minehaha, Mynehaha, Mynnehaha

Minnie (American) a familiar form of
Mina, Minerva, Minna, Wilhelmina.
Mini, Minie, Minne, Minnee, Minney,
Minni, Minny, Myni, Mynie, Mynnee,
Mynney, Mynni, Mynnie, Mynny, Myny

Minore (Australian) white blossom.
Minora, Minoree, Mynora, Mynorah,
Mynoree

Minowa (Native American) singer.
Minowah, Mynowa, Mynowah

Minta (Latin) mint, minty.
Mintah, Minnta, Minntah, Minty, Mynnta,
Mynntah, Mynta, Myntah

Minya (Osage) older sister.

Mio (Japanese) three times as strong.
Myo

Miquela (Spanish) a form of Michaela.
Miquel, Miquelah, Miquella, Miquelle

Mira (Latin) wonderful. (Spanish) look,
gaze. A short form of Almira, Amira,
Marabel, Mirabel, Miranda.
Mirae, Mirra

Mirabel (Latin) beautiful.
Mirabela, Mirabele, Mirabell, Mirabella,
Mirabellah, Mirabelle, Mirable, Myrabell,
Myrabella, Myrabellah, Myrabelle

Miracle (Latin) wonder, marvel.
Mirica, Miricah

Mirah (Latin, Spanish) a form of Mira.
Mirrah

Miranda (Latin) strange; wonderful; admirable. Literature: the heroine of Shakespeare's *The Tempest*. See also Randee.
Marenda, Miran, Miranada, Mirandah, Mirandia, Mirinda, Mirindé, Mironda, Muranda

Mireille (Hebrew) God spoke. (Latin) wonderful.
Mireil, Mirel, Mirela, Mirele, Mirelle, Mirelys, Miriell, Miriella, Mirielle, Mirilla, Mirille, Myrella, Myrelle, Myrilla, Myrille

Mirella (German, Irish) a form of Meryl. (Hebrew, Latin) a form of Mireille.

Miren (Hebrew) bitter.

Mirena (Hawaiian) beloved.
Mirenah, Myrena, Myrenah

Mireya (Hebrew) a form of Mireille.
Mireea, Mireyda, Miryah

Miri (Gypsy) a short form of Miriam.
Myri, Myry

Miriah (Hebrew) a form of Mireille. (Gypsy) a form of Miriam.
Miria

Miriam (Hebrew) bitter; sea of bitterness. Bible: the original form of Mary. See also Macia, Mimi, Mitzi.
Mairwen, Meriame, Miram, Mirham, Miriama, Miriame, Mirit, Mirjam, Mirriam

Mirian (Hebrew) a form of Miriam.
Miriain, Mirjana, Mirrian, Miryan

Mirna (Irish) polite. (Slavic) peaceful.
Merna, Mernah, Mirnah

Mirranda (Latin) a form of Miranda.

Mirrin (Australian) cloud.
Mirrina, Mirrine, Mirryn, Mirryna, Myrrina, Myrrinah, Myrrine, Myrryn, Myrryna, Myrrynah, Myrryne, Myryna, Myrynah, Myryne

Miryam (Hebrew) a form of Miriam.

Misha (Russian) a form of Michaela.
Mischa, Mishae, Mishela

Missy (English) a familiar form of Melissa, Millicent.
Mise, Misey, Misi, Misie, Missee, Missey, Missi, Missie, Mysea, Mysee, Mysey, Mysi, Mysie, Myssea, Myssee, Myssi, Myssie, Myssy, Mysy

Misti, Mistie (English) forms of Misty.

Misty (English) shrouded by mist.
Missty, Mistea, Mistee, Mistey, Mistin, Mistina, Mistral, Mistylynn, Mystea, Mystee, Mystey, Mysti, Mystie, Mysty

Mitra (Hindi) Religion: god of daylight. (Persian) angel.
Mita

Mituna (Moquelumnan) like a fish wrapped up in leaves.

Mitzi, Mitzy (German) forms of Mary, Miriam.
Mieze, Mitzee, Mitzey, Mitzie, Mytzee, Mytzey, Mytzi, Mytzie, Mytzy

Miwa (Japanese) wise eyes.
Miwah, Miwako, Mywa, Mywah, Mywako

Miya (Japanese) temple.
Miyana, Miyanna

Miyah (Japanese) a form of Miya.

Miyo (Japanese) beautiful generation.
Myo

Miyoko (Japanese) beautiful generation's child.
Miyuko, Myyoko

Miyuki (Japanese) snow.
Miyukee, Myyukee, Myyuki

Moana (Hawaiian) ocean; fragrance.
Moanah, Moane, Moann, Moanna, Moannah, Moanne

Mocha (Arabic) chocolate-flavored coffee.
Mochah, Moka, Mokah

Modesta (Italian, Spanish) a form of Modesty.
Modestah, Modestia

Modestine (French) a form of Modesty.
Modesteen, Modesteena, Modesteene,
Modestina, Modestyn, Modestyna,
Modestyne

Modesty (Latin) modest.
Modesta, Modeste, Modestee, Modestey,
Modestie, Modestine, Modestus

Moesha (American) a short form of
Monisha.
Moeisha, Moeysha

Mohala (Hawaiian) flowers in bloom.
Moala, Mohalah

Mohini (Sanskrit) enchantress.
Mohinee, Mohiney, Mohinie, Mohiny,
Mohynee, Mohyney, Mohyni, Mohynie,
Mohyny

Moira (Irish) great. A form of Mary. See
also Maura.
Moirae, Moirah, Moire, Mouira, Moya,
Moyra, Moyrah

Molara (Basque) a form of Mary.
Molarah, Molarra, Molarrah

Moledina (Australian) creek.
Moledin, Moledinah, Moledine, Moledyn,
Moledyna, Moledynah, Moledyne

Moli (Tongan) orange.
Molea, Molee, Molei, Moleigh, Moley,
Molie, Moly

Molli, Mollie (Irish) forms of Molly.

Molly (Irish) a familiar form of Mary.
Moll, Mollea, Mollee, Mollei, Molleigh,
Molley

Mona (Irish) noble. (Greek) a short form
of Monica, Ramona, Rimona.
Moina, Moinah, Monah, Mone, Monea,
Monna, Monnah, Moyna, Moynah

Monae (American) a form of Monet.

Moneisha (American) a form of
Monisha.

Monet (French) Art: Claude Monet was a
leading French impressionist remembered
for his paintings of water lilies.
Monay, Monaye, Monee

Monica (Greek) solitary. (Latin) advisor.
Monca, Moneeca, Moneecah, Monia, Monic,
Monicah, Monice, Monicia, Monicka,
Monise, Monn, Monnica, Monnicah,
Monnicka, Monnie, Monnyca, Monya,
Monyca, Monycah, Monycka

Monifa (Yoruba) I have my luck.
Monifah, Monyfa, Monyfah

Monika (German) a form of Monica.
Moneeka, Moneekah, Moneeke, Moneik,
Moneka, Monieka, Monikah, Monike,
Monnika, Monnikah, Monnyka, Monyka,
Monykah

Moniqua (French) a form of Monica.
Moniquea, Monniqua

Monique (French) a form of Monica.
Moniquie, Monnique, Monyque, Munique

Monisha (American) a combination of
Monica + Aisha.
Monesha, Monishia

Montana (Spanish) mountain. Geography:
a U.S. state.
Montanah, Montania, Montaniah, Montanna,
Montannah, Monteen, Monteena, Monteenah,
Montina, Montinah, Montyna, Montynah

Monteen (French) a form of Montana.
Monteene, Montine, Montyn, Montyne

Montgomery (English) rich man's
mountain.
Montgomerie, Mountgomery

Monti (Spanish) a familiar form of
Montana. (English) a short form of
Montgomery.
Monte, Montea, Montey, Montia, Montie,
Monty

Moona (English) moon. (Australian)
plenty.
Moonah, Moone, Moonee, Mooney, Mooni,
Moonia, Mooniah, Moonie, Moony,
Moonya, Moonyah

Mora (Spanish) blueberry.
Morae, Morah, Morea, Moreah, Moria,
Morita, Morite, Moryta, Morytah, Moryte

Moree (Australian) water.
Morey, Mori, Morie, Mory

Morela (Polish) apricot.
Morelah, Morelia, Morell, Morella, Morellah, Morelle

Morena (Irish) a form of Maureen.
Mo, Mooreen, Mooreena, Mooreenah, Mooreene, Morain, Moraina, Morainah, Moraine, Morayn, Morayna, Moraynah, Morayne, Moreen, Moreena, Moreenah, Moreene, Morein, Moreina, Moreinah, Moreine, Moren, Morenah, Morene, Morin, Morina, Morinah, Morine, Morreen, Moryn, Moryna, Morynah, Moryne

Morgan (Welsh) seashore. Literature: Morgan le Fay was the half-sister of King Arthur.
Morgain, Morgaina, Morgainah, Morgana, Morganah, Morgance, Morganetta, Morganette, Morganica, Morganna, Morgayn, Morgayna, Morgaynah, Morgayne, Morghen, Morghin, Morghyn, Morgin, Morgon, Morrigan

Morgane, Morgann, Morganne, Morgen, Morghan, Morgyn (Welsh) forms of Morgan.

Moriah (Hebrew) God is my teacher. (French) dark skinned. Bible: the mountain on which the Temple of Solomon was built. See also Mariah.
Moria, Moriel, Morria, Morriah, Morya, Moryah

Morie (Japanese) bay.
Morea, Moree, Morey, Mori, Mory

Morina (Irish) mermaid.
Morinah, Morinna, Morinnah, Moryna, Morynah, Morynna, Morynnah

Morit (Hebrew) teacher.
Moritt, Moritta, Morittah, Morryt, Morryta, Morrytah, Morryte, Moryt, Moryta, Moryte, Morytt, Morytta, Moryttah, Morytte

Morowa (Akan) queen.
Morowah

Morrin (Irish) long-haired.
Morin, Morine, Moryn, Moryne

Morrisa (Latin) dark skinned; moor; marshland.

Morisa, Morisah, Moriset, Morisett, Morisetta, Morisette, Morissa, Morissah, Morrisah, Morrissa, Morrissah, Morysa, Morysah, Moryssa, Moryssah, Morysse

Moselle (Hebrew) drawn from the water. (French) a white wine.
Mosel, Mosela, Moselah, Mosele, Mosella, Mosellah, Mosina, Mozel, Mozela, Mozelah, Mozele, Mozella, Mozellah, Mozelle

Mosi (Swahili) first-born.
Mosea, Mosee, Mosey, Mosie, Mosy

Mosina (Hebrew) a form of Moselle.
Mosinah, Mosine, Mozina, Mozinah, Mozine, Mozyna, Mozynah, Mozyne

Moswen (Tswana) white.
Moswena, Moswenah, Moswin, Moswina, Moswinah, Moswine, Moswyn, Moswyna, Moswynah, Moswyne

Mouna (Arabic) wish, desire.
Mounah, Mounia

Mrena (Slavic) white eyes.
Mren, Mrenah

Mumtaz (Arabic) distinguished.

Muna (Greek, Irish) a form of Mona. (Arabic) a form of Mouna.
Munah, Munia

Mura (Japanese) village.
Murah

Muriel (Arabic) myrrh. (Irish) shining sea. A form of Mary. See also Meryl.
Muire, Murial, Muriell, Muriella, Murielle, Muryel, Muryela, Muryele, Muryell, Muryella, Muryelle

Murphy (Irish) sea warrior.
Merffee, Merffey, Merffi, Merffie, Merffy, Murffee, Murffey, Murffi, Murffie, Murffy, Murphee, Murphey, Murphi, Murphie

Muse (Greek) inspiration. Mythology: the Muses were nine Greek goddesses of the arts and sciences.

Musetta (French) little bagpipe.
Muset, Museta, Musetah, Musete, Musettah, Musette

Mushira (Arabic) counselor.

Musidora (Greek) beautiful muse.
Musidorah, Musidore, Musydor, Musydora, Musydorah, Musydore

Musika (Tongan) music.
Musica, Musicah, Musicka, Musyca, Musycah, Musycka, Musyckah, Musyka, Musykah

Muslimah (Arabic) devout believer.

My (Burmese) a short form of Mya.

Mya (Burmese) emerald. (Italian) a form of Mia.
Meia, Meiah

Myah (Burmese, Italian) a form of Mya.

Mycah (Hebrew) a form of Micah.
Myca

Mychaela (American) a form of Michaela.
Mychael, Mychal, Mychala, Mychall, Mychela, Mychelah, Myshela, Myshelah

Myeisha (American) a form of Moesha.

Myesha (American) a form of Moesha.

Myeshia (American) a form of Moesha.

Myia (Burmese, Italian) a form of Mya.
Myiah

Myiesha (American) a form of Moesha.

Myisha (American) a form of Moesha.

Myka (Hebrew, Japanese, Russian, Native American) a form of Mika.
Mykah

Mykaela (American) a form of Michaela.
Mykael, Mykaelah, Mykyla

Mykaila (American) a form of Michaela.
Mykailah

Mykala (American) a form of Michaela.
Mykal, Mykaleen

Mykayla (American) a form of Michaela.
Mykaylah

Mykel (American) a form of Michael.
Mykela, Mykelah

Myla (English) merciful.
Mylah, Mylla, Myllah

Mylene (Greek) dark.
Mylaine, Mylana, Mylee, Myleen

Myra (Latin) fragrant ointment.
Myrah, Myrena, Myria, Myrra, Myrrah, Myrrha

Myranda (Latin) a form of Miranda.
Myrandah, Myrandia, Myrannda

Myriah (Hebrew, Gypsy) a form of Miriah.
Myria, Myrya, Myryah

Myriam (American) a form of Miriam.
Myriame, Myryam, Myryame

Myrissa (American) a form of Marisa.
Myrisa, Myrisah, Myrissah

Myrna (Irish) beloved.
Merna, Morna, Muirna, Murna, Murnah, Myrnah

Myrtle (Greek) evergreen shrub.
Mertal, Mertel, Mertell, Mertella, Mertelle, Mertis, Mertle, Mirtal, Mirtel, Mirtil, Mirtle, Mirtyl, Murtal, Murtel, Murtella, Murtelle, Myrta, Myrtia, Myrtias, Myrtice, Myrtie, Myrtilla, Myrtis

Myune (Australian) clear water.
Miuna, Miunah, Myuna, Myunah

Nabila (Arabic) born to nobility.
Nabeela, Nabiha, Nabilah, Nabyla, Nabylah

Nachine (Spanish) hot, fiery.
Nachina, Nachinah, Nachyna, Nachynah, Nachyne

Nada (Arabic) a form of Nadda.
Nadah

Nadda (Arabic) generous; dewy.
Naddah

Nadeen, Nadine (French, Slavic) forms of Nadia.
Nadean, Nadeana, Nadeanah, Nadeane, Nadeena, Nadeenah, Nadeene, Nadena, Nadene, Nadien, Nadin, Nadina, Nadyn,

Nadeen, Nadine *(cont.)*
Nadyna, Nadynah, Nadyne, Naidene, Naidine

Nadette (French) a short form of Bernadette.

Nadia (French, Slavic) hopeful.
Nadea, Nadenka, Nadezhda, Nadiah, Nadie, Nadija, Nadijah, Nadka, Nadusha

Nadira (Arabic) rare, precious.
Naadirah, Nadirah, Nadyra, Nadyrah

Nadiyah (French, Slavic) a form of Nadia.
Nadiya

Nadja, Nadya (French, Slavic) forms of Nadia.
Nadjae, Nadjah, Nady, Nadyah

Naeva (French) a form of Eve.
Naeve, Nahvon

Nafisa (Arabic) a form of Nafisah.

Nafisah (Arabic) precious thing; gem.
Nafeesa

Nafuna (Luganda) born feet first.
Nafunah

Nagida (Hebrew) noble; prosperous.
Nagda, Nagdah, Nageeda, Nagyda

Nahid (Persian) Mythology: another name for Venus, the goddess of love and beauty.
Nahyd

Nahimana (Dakota) mystic.

Naida (Greek) water nymph.
Naiad, Nayad, Nyad

Naila (Arabic) successful.
Nayla, Naylah

Nailah (Arabic) a form of Naila.

Naima (Arabic) comfort; peace. (Indian) belonging to one.
Na'ima, Na'imah

Nairi (Armenian) land of rivers. History: a name for ancient Armenia.
Naira, Naire, Nairee, Nairey, Nairia, Nairiah, Nairie, Nairy, Nayra

Naiya (Greek) a form of Naida.
Naia, Naiyana, Naya

Naja, Najah (Greek) forms of Naida. (Arabic) short forms of Najam, Najila.

Najam (Arabic) star.

Najee (Arabic) a form of Naji (see Boys' Names).
Najae, Najée, Najei, Najiee

Najila (Arabic) brilliant eyes.
Najia, Najilah, Najja

Najla (Arabic) a short form of Najila.

Najma (Arabic) a form of Najam.

Nakayla (American) a form of Nicole.
Nakaylah

Nakea (Arabic) a form of Nakia.
Nakeea, Nakeeah

Nakeia (Arabic) a form of Nakia.

Nakeisha (American) a combination of the prefix Na + Keisha.
Nakeasha, Nakeesha, Nakeysha, Nakysha, Nakyshah, Nekeisha

Nakeita (American) a form of Nikita.
Nakeata, Nakeatah, Nakeeta, Nakeitah, Nakeitha, Nakeithia, Nakeithiah, Nakeithra, Nakeitra, Nakeitress, Nakeitta, Nakeitte, Nakeittia, Naketta, Nakette, Nakieta

Nakesha (American) a form of Nakeisha.
Nakeshea, Nakeshia

Nakeya (Arabic) a form of Nakia.
Nakeyah, Nakeyia

Nakia (Arabic) pure.
Nakiaya, Nakiea

Nakiah (Arabic) a form of Nakia.

Nakiesha (American) a form of Nakeisha.

Nakisha (American) a form of Nakeisha.
Nakishia, Nakishiah, Nakishya, Nakishyah

Nakita (American) a form of Nikita.
Nakitha, Nakitia, Nakitta, Nakitte, Nakkita, Naquita, Nakyta, Nakytta, Nakytte

Nakiya (Arabic) a form of Nakia.
Nakiyah

Nala (Tanzanian) queen.

Nalani (Hawaiian) calm as the heavens.
Nalanea, Nalaneah, Nalanee, Nalaney,
Nalania, Nalaniah, Nalanie, Nalany,
Nalanya, Nalanyah

Nami (Japanese) wave.
Namee, Namey, Namie, Namika, Namiko,
Namy

Nan (German) a short form of Fernanda.
(English) a form of Ann.
Nanice, Nanine, Nann, Nanon

Nana (Hawaiian) spring.
Nanah, Nanna, Nannah

Nanci (English) a form of Nancy.
Nancia, Nanciah, Nancie

Nancy (English) gracious. A familiar form
of Nan.
Nainsi, Nance, Nancea, Nancee, Nancey,
Nancine, Nancsi, Nancya, Nancyah, Nancye,
Nanice, Nanncey, Nanncy, Nanouk, Nansee,
Nansey, Nansi, Nanuk

Nandalia (Australian) fire.
Nandalea, Nandaleah, Nandalee, Nandalei,
Nandaleigh, Nandaley, Nandali, Nandaliah,
Nandaly, Nandalya, Nandalyah

Nanette (French) a form of Nancy.
Nanet, Naneta, Nanetah, Nanete, Nanett,
Nanetta, Nanettah, Nannet, Nanneta,
Nannetah, Nannete, Nannett, Nannetta,
Nannettah, Nannette, Nineta, Ninete,
Ninetta, Ninette, Nini, Ninita, Ninnetta,
Ninnette, Nynette

Nani (Greek) charming. (Hawaiian)
beautiful.
Nanee, Naney, Nania, Naniah, Nanie,
Nannee, Nanney, Nanni, Nannie, Nanny,
Nany, Nanya, Nanyah

Nanon (French) a form of Ann.
Nanona, Nanonah, Nanone, Nanonia,
Nanoniah, Nanonya, Nanonyah

Naomi (Hebrew) pleasant, beautiful.
Bible: Ruth's mother-in-law.
Naoma, Naomah, Naome, Naomee,
Naomey, Naomia, Naomiah, Neomie,
Neoma, Neomah, Neomee, Neomi, Neomy

Naomie, Naomy (Hebrew) forms of
Naomi.

Nara (Greek) happy. (English) north.
(Japanese) oak.
Naara, Naarah, Narah, Narra, Narrah

Narcissa (Greek) daffodil. Mythology:
Narcissus was the youth who fell in love
with his own reflection.
Narcessa, Narcisa, Narcissah, Narcisse,
Narcissus, Narcyssa, Narkissa

Narelle (Australian) woman from the sea.
Narel, Narela, Narelah, Narele, Narell,
Narella, Narellah

Nari (Japanese) thunder.
Narea, Naree, Narey, Naria, Nariah, Narie,
Nariko, Nary, Narya, Naryah

Narissa (Greek) a form of Narcissa,
Nerissa.

Narmada (Hindi) pleasure giver.
Narmadah

Nashawna (American) a combination of
the prefix Na + Shawna.
Nashan, Nashana, Nashanda, Nashaun,
Nashauna, Nashaunda, Nashawn,
Nashawnda, Nasheena, Nashounda,
Nashuana

Nashota (Native American) double;
second-born twin.

Nasrin (Muslim, Arabic) wild rose.

Nastasia (Greek) a form of Anastasia.
Nastasha, Nastashia, Nastasja, Nastassa,
Nastassia, Nastassiya, Nastazia, Nastisija,
Naztasia, Naztasiah

Nastassja (Greek) a form of Nastasia.
Nastassya, Nastasya, Nastasyah, Nastya

Nasya (Hebrew) miracle.
Nasia, Nasiah, Nasyah

Nata (Sanskrit) dancer. (Latin) swimmer.
(Native American) speaker; creator.
(Polish, Russian) a form of Natalie.
See also Nadia.
Natah, Natia, Natiah, Natka, Natya,
Natyah

Natacha (Russian) a form of Natasha.
Natachia, Natacia, Naticha

Natalee, Natali, Nataly (Latin) forms of Natalie.
Natally, Natallye, Nattalee, Nattali, Nattaly

Natalia (Russian) a form of Natalie. See also Talia.
Nacia, Natala, Natalah, Natalea, Nataleah, Nataliah, Nataliia, Natalija, Nataliya, Nataliyah, Natalja, Natalka, Natalla, Natallah, Natallea, Natallia, Natelea, Nateleah, Natelia, Nateliah, Natilea, Natileah, Natilia, Natiliah, Natlea, Natleah, Natlia, Natliah, Nattalea, Nattaleah, Nattaleya, Nattaleyah, Nattalia, Nattaliah, Nattlea, Nattleah, Nattlia, Nattliah, Natylea, Natyleah, Natylia, Natyliah

Natalie (Latin) born on Christmas day. See also Nata, Natasha, Noel, Talia.
Nat, Nataleh, Natalei, Nataleigh, Nataley, Nataliee, Natallie, Natelee, Natelei, Nateleigh, Nateley, Nateli, Natelie, Nately, Natilee, Natilei, Natileigh, Natili, Natilie, Natily, Natlee, Natlei, Natleigh, Natley, Natli, Natlie, Natly, Nattalei, Nattaleigh, Nattaley, Nattalie, Nattilie, Nattlee, Nattlei, Nattleigh, Nattley, Nattli, Nattlie, Nattly, Natylee, Natylei, Natyleigh, Natyley, Natyli, Natylie, Natyly

Nataline (Latin) a form of Natalie.
Natalean, Nataleana, Nataleanah, Nataleane, Nataleena, Nataleenah, Nataleene, Natalena, Natalenah, Natalene, Nataléne, Natalina, Natalinah, Natalyn, Natalyna, Natalynah, Natalyne

Natalle (French) a form of Natalie.
Natale

Natalya (Russian) a form of Natalia.
Natalyah, Natelya, Natelyah, Natilya, Natilyah, Nattalya, Nattalyah, Nattlya, Nattlyah, Natylya, Natylyah

Natane (Arapaho) daughter.
Natana, Natanah, Natanna, Natannah, Natanne

Natania (Hebrew) gift of God.
Nataniah, Nataniela, Nataniele, Nataniell, Nataniella, Natanielle, Natanja, Natanjah, Natanya, Natanyah, Natée, Nathania, Nathaniah, Nathanya, Nathanyah,

Nathenia, Natonia, Natoniah, Natonya, Natonyah, Netania, Nethania

Natara (Arabic) sacrifice.
Natarah, Nataria, Natariah, Natarya, Nataryah

Natascha (Russian) a form of Natasha.

Natasha (Russian) a form of Natalie. See also Stacey, Tasha.
Nahtasha, Nastenka, Nastia, Nastja, Natasa, Natashah, Natashea, Natashenka, Natashy, Natasza, Natausha, Natawsha, Nathasha, Nathassha, Netasha

Natashia (Russian) a form of Natasha.
Natashiea, Natashja, Natashya, Natashyah

Natasia, Natassia (Greek) forms of Nastasia.
Natasiah, Natasie

Natassja (Greek) a form of Nastasia.
Natassija, Natasya

Natesa (Hindi) cosmic dancer. Religion: another name for the Hindu god Shiva.
Natisa, Natissa

Natesha (Russian) a form of Natasha.
Nateshia

Nathalia (Latin) a form of Natalie.
Nathalea, Nathaleah, Nathaliah, Nathalya, Nathalyah

Nathalie, Nathaly (Latin) forms of Natalie.
Nathalee, Nathalei, Nathaleigh, Nathaley, Nathali, Nathaly

Natie (English) a familiar form of Natalie.
Nati, Natti, Nattie, Natty

Natisha (Russian) a form of Natasha.
Natishia

Natori (Arabic) a form of Natara.
Natoria

Natosha (Russian) a form of Natasha.
Natoshia, Natoshya, Netosha, Notosha

Nature (Latin) nature; essence; life.
Natural, Naturee, Naturey, Naturia, Naturiah, Naturie, Natury, Naturya, Naturyah

Naudia (French, Slavic) a form of Nadia.
Naudiah

Nava (Hebrew) beautiful; pleasant. See also Naomi.
Navah, Naveh, Navit

Navdeep (Sikh) new light.
Navdip

Naveen (Hindi) a form of Navin (see Boys' Names).

Naveena (Indian) new.

Navit (Hebrew) a form of Nava.
Navita, Navitah, Navyt, Navyta, Navytah

Nayeli, Nayelly, Nayely (Irish) forms of Neila.
Naeyli, Nayela, Nayelia, Nayelli, Nayla, Naylea, Naylia

Neala (Irish) a form of Neila.
Nealah, Nealee, Nealia, Nealie, Nealy

Necha (Spanish) a form of Agnes.
Necho

Neci (Hungarian) fiery, intense.
Necee, Necey, Necia, Neciah, Necie, Necy

Necole (French) a form of Nicole.
Nechola, Necholah, Nechole, Necol, Necola, Necolah, Necoll, Necolle

Neda (Slavic) born on Sunday.
Nedah, Nedi, Nedia, Nedya, Nedyah

Nedda (English) prosperous guardian.
Neddah, Neddi, Neddie, Neddy

Neelam (Indian) sapphire.

Neely (Irish) a familiar form of Nelia.
Neela, Neelee, Neeley, Neeli, Neelia, Neelie, Neelya

Neema (Swahili) born during prosperous times.
Neemah

Neena (Spanish) a form of Nina.
Neana, Neanah, Neenah

Neha (Indian) rain.

Neida (Slavic) a form of Neda.

Neila (Irish) champion. See also Neala, Neely.
Neilah, Neile, Neili, Neilia, Neilie, Neilla, Neille

Neisha (Scandinavian, American) a form of Niesha.
Neishia, Neissia

Nekeisha (American) a form of Nakeisha.
Nechesa, Neikeishia, Nekeasha, Nekeashia, Nekeashiah, Nekeesha, Nekeeshia, Nekeeshiah, Nekesha, Nekeshia, Nekeysha, Nekeyshah, Nekeyshia, Nekeyshya, Nekeyshyah, Nekiesha, Nekisha, Nekysha

Nekia (Arabic) a form of Nakia.
Nekeya, Nekiya, Nekiyah, Nekya, Nekyah

Nelia (Spanish) yellow. (Latin) a familiar form of Cornelia.
Nela, Nelah, Nelea, Neleah, Neliah, Nelka, Nella, Nellah, Nellea, Nelleah, Nellia, Nelliah, Nellya, Nellyah, Nelya, Nelyah

Nell (Greek) a form of Nelle. (English) a short form of Nellie.
Nel

Nelle (Greek) stone.
Nele

Nellie, Nelly (English) familiar forms of Cornelia, Eleanor, Helen, Prunella.
Nelee, Nelei, Neleigh, Neley, Neli, Nellee, Nellei, Nelleigh, Nelley, Nelli, Nellianne, Nellice, Nellis, Nelma

Nellwyn (English) Nellie's friend.
Nellwin, Nellwina, Nellwinah, Nellwine, Nellwinn, Nellwinna, Nellwinnah, Nellwinne, Nellwyna, Nellwynah, Nellwyne, Nellwynn, Nellwynna, Nellwynnah, Nellwynne, Nelwin, Nelwina, Nelwinah, Nelwine, Nelwinn, Nelwinna, Nelwinnah, Nelwinne, Nelwyn, Nelwyna, Nelwynah, Nelwyne, Nelwynn, Nelwynna, Nelwynnah, Nelwynne

Nena (Spanish) a form of Nina.

Nenet (Egyptian) born near the sea. Mythology: Nunet was the goddess of the sea.
Neneta, Nenetah, Nenete, Nennet, Nenneta, Nennetah, Nennete, Nennett, Nennetta, Nennettah, Nennette

Neola (Greek) youthful.
Neolah, Neolla

Neoma (Greek) new moon.
Neomah

Nereida (Greek) a form of Nerine.
Nerida, Neridah

Nereyda (Greek) a form of Nerine.
Nereyida, Neryda, Nerydah

Nerine (Greek) sea nymph.
*Nerina, Nerinah, Nerita, Nerline, Neryn,
Neryna, Nerynah, Neryne*

Nerissa (Greek) sea nymph. See also
Rissa.
Nerisa, Nerrisa, Neryssa

Nerys (Welsh) lady.
*Narice, Nereace, Nerease, Nereece, Nereese,
Nereice, Nereise, Nereyce, Nereyse, Nerice,
Nerise, Nerisse, Neryce, Neryse*

Nesha (Greek) a form of Nessa.
Neshia

Nessa (Scandinavian) promontory.
(Greek) a short form of Agnes. See
also Nessie.
*Neisa, Neisah, Nesa, Nesia, Nesiah,
Nessah, Nessia, Nessiah, Nessya, Nessyah,
Nesta, Nevsa*

Nessie (Greek) a familiar form of Agnes,
Nessa, Vanessa.
*Nese, Nesee, Nesey, Neshie, Nesho, Nesi,
Nesie, Ness, Nessee, Nessey, Nessi, Nessy,
Nest, Nesy*

Neta (Hebrew) plant, shrub. See also
Nettie.
*Netah, Netai, Netia, Netiah, Netta, Nettah,
Nettia, Nettiah, Nettya, Nettyah, Netya,
Netyah*

Netanya (Hebrew) a form of Nathaniel
(see Boys' Names).

Netis (Native American) trustworthy.
*Netisa, Netisah, Netise, Netissa, Netissah,
Netisse, Nettys, Nettysa, Nettysah, Nettyse,
Netys, Netysa, Netysah, Netyse, Netyssa,
Netyssah, Netysse*

Nettie (French) a familiar form of
Annette, Antoinette, Nanette.

*Netee, Netey, Neti, Netie, Nette, Nettee,
Nettey, Netti, Netty, Nety*

Neva (Spanish) snow. (English) new.
Geography: a river in Russia.
*Neiva, Nevah, Neve, Nevia, Neyva, Nieve,
Niva, Nivea, Nivia*

Nevada (Spanish) snow. Geography: a
western U.S. state.
Nevadah

Neve (Hebrew) life.
*Neiv, Neive, Nevee, Nevia, Neviah, Neyva,
Neyve, Nieve, Nyev, Nyeva, Nyevah, Nyeve*

Nevina (Irish) worshipper of the saint.
*Neveen, Neveena, Neveenah, Neveene,
Nevein, Nevena, Nevenah, Nevene,
Neveyan, Nevin, Nevinah, Nevine, Nivena,
Nivenah, Nivina, Nivinah, Nivine, Nyvina,
Nyvinah, Nyvine, Nyvyn, Nyvyna,
Nyvynah, Nyvyne*

Neylan (Turkish) fulfilled wish.
*Nealana, Nealanah, Nealanee, Nealaney,
Nealani, Nealania, Nealaniah, Nealanya,
Nealanyah, Neilana, Neilanah, Neilane,
Neilanee, Neilaney, Neilani, Neilania,
Neilaniah, Neilany, Neilanya, Neilanyah,
Nelana, Nelanah, Nelane, Nelanee,
Nelaney, Nelani, Nelania, Nelaniah,
Nelanie, Nelany, Nelanya, Nelanyah,
Neyla, Neylanah, Neylane, Neylanee,
Neylaney*

Neysa (Greek, Scandinavian) a form of
Nessa.
Neysah, Neysha, Neyshia

Neza (Slavic) a form of Agnes.
Nezah, Nezza, Nezzah

Ngoc (Vietnamese) jade.

Nguyen (Vietnamese) a form of Ngu (see
Boys' Names).

Nia (Irish) a familiar form of Neila.
Mythology: Nia Ben Aur was a
legendary Welsh woman.
Neya, Neyah, Niah, Niajia

Niabi (Osage) fawn.
*Niabia, Niabiah, Niabie, Niaby, Nyabya,
Nyabyah*

Niam (Irish) bright.
Niama, Niamah, Nyam, Nyama, Nyamah

Niamh (Irish) a form of Niam.

Nichelle (American) a combination of Nicole + Michelle. Culture: Nichelle Nichols was the first African American woman featured in a television drama *(Star Trek)*.
Nechel, Nechela, Nechelah, Nechele, Nechell, Nechella, Nechellah, Nechelle, Nichela, Nichelah, Nichele, Nichell, Nichella, Nichellah, Nishell, Nishella, Nishellah, Nishelle, Nychel, Nychela, Nychelah, Nychele, Nychell, Nychella, Nychellah, Nychelle

Nichol, Nichole, Nicholle (French) forms of Nicole.

Nicholas (French) victorious people.

Nicholette (French) a form of Nicole.

Nicki, Nickie, Nicky (French) familiar forms of Nicole. See also Nikki.
Nicci, Nickee, Nickey, Nickeya, Nickia, Nickiya, Nyc, Nyck, Nyckee, Nyckey, Nycki, Nyckie, Nycky

Nickole (French) a form of Nicole.
Nickol

Nicola (Italian) a form of Nicole.
Nacola, Nacolah, Necola, Necolah, Necolla, Necollah, Nicala, Nicalah, Nichala, Nichalah, Nichola, Nicholah, Nickala, Nickalah, Nickola, Nickolah, Nicolah, Nicolea, Nicolla, Nikkola, Nikola, Nikolia, Nycala, Nycalah, Nychala, Nychalah, Nychola, Nycholah, Nyckala, Nyckalah, Nyckola, Nyckolah, Nycola, Nycolah, Nykola, Nykolah

Nicolas (French) a form of Nicholas.

Nicole (French) a form of Nicholas. See also Colette, Cosette, Lacole, Nikita.
Nacole, Nica, Nicia, Nicol, Nicoli, Nicolia, Nicolie, Niquole, Nocole

Nicolette, Nicollette (French) forms of Nicole.

Necholet, Necholeta, Necholetah, Necholete, Necholett, Necholetta, Necholettah, Necholette, Necolet, Necoleta, Necoletah, Necolete, Necolett, Necoletta, Necolettah, Necolette, Nickolet, Nickoleta, Nickoletah, Nickolete, Nickolett, Nickoletta, Nickolettah, Nickolette, Nicolet, Nicoleta, Nicoletah, Nicolete, Nicolett, Nicoletta, Nicolettah, Nicollete, Nyckolet, Nyckoleta, Nyckoletah, Nyckolete, Nyckolett, Nyckoletta, Nyckolettah, Nyckolette, Nycolet, Nycoleta, Nycoletah, Nycolete, Nycolett, Nycoletta, Nycolettah, Nycolette, Nykolet, Nykoleta, Nykoletah, Nykolete, Nykolett, Nykoletta, Nykolettah, Nykolette

Nicolina (French) a form of Nicoline.

Nicoline (French) a familiar form of Nicole.
Nicholine, Nicholyn, Nicoleen, Nicolene, Nicolyn, Nicolyne, Nicolynn, Nicolynne, Nikolene, Nikoline

Nicolle (French) a form of Nicole.

Nidia (Latin) nest.
Nidi, Nidiah, Nidya

Niesha (American) pure. (Scandinavian) a form of Nissa.
Neesha, Nesha, Neshia, Nesia, Nessia, Neysha, Niessia

Nige (Latin) dark night.
Nigea, Nigela, Nigelah, Nigele, Nigell, Nigella, Nigellah, Nigelle, Nygel, Nygela, Nygelah, Nygele, Nygell, Nygella, Nygelle

Nija, Nijah (Latin) a form of Nige.
Nijae

Nika (Russian) belonging to God.
Nikah, Nikka, Nyka, Nykah

Nikayla (American) a form of Nicole.
Nykala, Nykalah

Nike (Greek) victorious. Mythology: the goddess of victory.

Nikelle (American) a form of Nicole.
Nikeille, Nikel, Nikela, Nikelie

Niki (Russian) a short form of Nikita. (American) a familiar form of Nicole.

Niki (cont.)
Nikee, Nikey, Nikie, Niky, Nykee, Nykey, Nyki, Nykie, Nyky

Nikia, Nikkia (Arabic) forms of Nakia. (Russian, American) forms of Niki, Nikki.
Nikiah, Nikkea, Nikkiah

Nikita (Russian) victorious people.
Nakeita, Nicheata, Nicheatah, Nicheeta, Nicheetah, Nickeata, Nickeatah, Nickeeta, Nickeetah, Nikeata, Nikeatah, Nikeeta, Nikeetah, Nikeita, Nikeitah, Nikitah, Nikitia, Nikitta, Nikitte, Niquita, Niquitah, Niquite, Niquitta, Nykeata, Nykeatah, Nykeeta, Nykeetah, Nykeita, Nykeitah, Nykeyta, Nykeytah, Nykita, Nykitah, Nykytah

Nikki (American) a familiar form of Nicole. See also Nicki.
Nikkee, Nikkey, Nikkie, Nikko, Nikky, Niquee, Niquey, Niqui, Niquie, Niquy, Nyk, Nykee, Nykey, Nyki, Nykie, Nykkee, Nykkey, Nykki, Nykkie, Nykky, Nyky, Nyquee, Nyquey, Nyqui, Nyquie, Nyqy

Nikkita (Russian) a form of Nikita.
Nikkitah

Nikkole, Nikole (French) forms of Nicole.
Nikkolie, Nikola, Nikolah, Nikolle

Nikolette (French) a form of Nicole.
Nikkolette, Nikolet, Nikoleta, Nikoletah, Nikolete, Nikolett, Nikoletta, Nikolettah

Nikolina (French) a form of Nicole.
Nikolena

Nila (Latin) Geography: the Nile River in Africa. (Irish) a form of Neila.
Nilah, Nile, Nilea, Nileah, Nilesia, Nilla, Nillah, Nillea, Nilleah

Nima (Hebrew) thread. (Arabic) blessing.
Neema, Nema, Nemah, Niama, Nimah, Nimali, Nimalie, Nimaly, Nyma, Nymah

Nina (Spanish) girl. (Native American) mighty. (Hebrew) a familiar form of Hannah.

Ninah, Ninacska, Ninja, Ninna, Ninosca, Ninoshka, Nyna, Nynah

Ninette (French) small.
Ninet, Nineta, Ninetah, Ninete, Ninett, Ninetta, Ninettah, Nynet, Nyneta, Nynetah, Nynete, Nynett, Nynetta, Nynettah, Nynette

Ninon (French) a form of Nina.
Ninona, Ninonah, Ninone

Nirali (Hebrew) a form of Nirel.

Nirel (Hebrew) light of God.
Nirela, Nirelah, Nirele, Nirell, Nirella, Nirellah, Nirelle, Nyrel, Nyrela, Nyrelah, Nyrele, Nyrell, Nyrella, Nyrellah, Nyrelle

Nirveli (Hindi) water child.
Nirvelea, Nirveleah, Nirvelee, Nirvelei, Nirveleigh, Nirveley, Nirvelie, Nirvely, Nyrvelea, Nyrveleah, Nyrvelee, Nyrvelei, Nyrveleigh, Nyrveley, Nyrvelie, Nyrvely

Nisa (Arabic) woman.
Nisah, Nysa, Nysah

Nisha (American) a form of Niesha, Nissa.
Niasha, Nishay

Nishi (Japanese) west.
Nishee, Nishey, Nishie, Nishy

Nissa (Hebrew) sign, emblem. (Scandinavian) friendly elf; brownie. See also Nyssa.
Nissah, Nisse, Nissi, Nissie, Nissy

Nita (Hebrew) planter. (Choctaw) bear. (Spanish) a short form of Anita, Juanita.
Nitah, Nitai, Nitha, Nithai, Nitika, Nyta, Nytah

Nitara (Hindi) deeply rooted.
Nitarah, Nitarra, Nitarrah, Nytara, Nytarah, Nytarra, Nytarrah

Nitasha (American) a form of Natasha.
Nitashah, Nitasia, Niteisha, Nitisha, Nitishah, Nitishia, Nitishiah, Nytasha, Nytashia, Nytashiah, Nytashya, Nytashyah

Nitsa (Greek) a form of Helen.
Nitsah, Nytsa, Nytsah

Nituna (Native American) daughter.
Nitunah, Nytuna, Nytunah

Nitza (Hebrew) flower bud.
Nitzah, Nitzana, Niza, Nizah, Nytza, Nytzah

Nixie (German) water sprite.
Nixee, Nixey, Nixi, Nixy, Nyxee, Nyxey, Nyxi, Nyxie, Nyxy

Niya, Niyah (Irish) forms of Nia.
Niyana, Niyia

Nizana (Hebrew) a form of Nitza.
Nitzana, Nitzania, Nitzanit, Nitzanita, Zana

Noah (Hebrew) peaceful, restful. Bible: the patriarch who built the ark to survive the Flood.

Noel (Latin) Christmas. See also Natalie, Noelle.
Noël, Noele, Novelenn, Novelia, Nowel, Nowele

Noelani (Hawaiian) beautiful one from heaven. (Latin) a form of Noel.
Noelanee, Noelaney, Noelania, Noelaniah, Noelanie, Noelannee, Noelanney, Noelanni, Noelannie, Noelanny, Noelany, Noelanya, Noelanyah

Noelia (Latin) a form of Noel.

Noeline (Latin) a form of Noel.
Noelean, Noeleana, Noeleanah, Noeleane, Noeleen, Noeleena, Noeleenah, Noeleene, Noelene, Noelin, Noelina, Noelinah, Noelleen, Noellin, Noellina, Noellinah, Noelline, Noellyn, Noellyna, Noellynah, Noellyne, Noelyn, Noelynn, Noleen, Nolein, Noleina, Noleinah, Noleine, Noleyn, Noleyna, Noleynah, Noleyne, Noweleen

Noella (French) a form of Noelle.
Noela, Noelah, Noellah, Nowela, Nowelah, Nowella, Nowellah

Noelle (French) Christmas.
Noell, Nowell, Nowelle

Noely (Latin) a form of Noel.
Noeli, Noelie, Noelly

Noemi, Noemie, Noemy (Hebrew) forms of Naomi.
Noam, Noami, Noamy, Nomee, Nomey, Nomi, Nomie, Nomia, Nomiah

Noga (Hebrew) morning light.
Nogah

Noheli, Nohely (Latin) forms of Noel.
Nohal

Nohemi (Hebrew) a form of Naomi.

Nokomis (Dakota) moon daughter.
Nokoma, Nokomas, Nokomys

Nola (Latin) small bell. (Irish) famous; noble. A short form of Fionnula.

Nolana (Irish) a form of Nola.
Noelan, Noelana, Noelanah, Noelanna, Noelannah, Noelannia, Noelanniah, Noelannya, Noelannyah, Nolanah, Nolanee, Nolaney, Nolani, Nolania, Nolaniah, Nolanie, Nolany, Nolanya, Nolanyah

Noleta (Latin) unwilling.
Noleata, Noleatah, Noleeta, Noleetah, Nolita, Nolitah, Nolyta, Nolytah

Nollie (English) a familiar form of Magnolia.
Nolia, Nolle, Nolley, Nolli, Nolly

Noma (Hawaiian) a form of Norma.
Nomah

Nona (Latin) ninth.
Nonah, Nonee, Noney, Noni, Nonia, Noniah, Nonie, Nonna, Nonnah, Nony, Nonya, Nonyah

Noor (Aramaic) a form of Nura.
Noora, Noorah, Noorie, Nour, Nur

Nora (Greek) light. A familiar form of Eleanor, Honora, Leonor.
Norra

Norah (Greek) a form of Nora.
Norrah

Norberta (Scandinavian) brilliant hero.
Norbertah, Norbirta, Norbirtah, Norburta,
Norburtah, Norbyrta, Norbyrtah

Nordica (Scandinavian) from the north.
Nordic, Nordicah, Nordik, Nordika,
Nordikah, Nordiqua, Nordiquah, Nordyca,
Nordycah, Nordycka, Nordyckah, Nordyka,
Nordykah, Nordyqua, Nordyquah

Noreen (Irish) a form of Eleanor, Nora.
(Latin) a familiar form of Norma.
Noorin, Noreena, Noreene, Noren, Norena,
Norene, Norina, Norine, Nureen

Norell (Scandinavian) from the north.
Narel, Narell, Narelle, Norel, Norela,
Norele, Norella, Norellah, Norelle, Norely

Nori (Japanese) law, tradition.
Noree, Norey, Noria, Noriah, Norico, Norie,
Noriko, Norita, Nory, Norya, Noryah

Norleen (Irish) honest.
Norlan, Norlana, Norlanah, Norlane,
Norlean, Norleana, Norleanah, Norleane,
Norleena, Norleenah, Norleene, Norlein,
Norleina, Norleinah, Norleine, Norleyn,
Norleyna, Norleynah, Norleyne, Norlin,
Norlina, Norlinah, Norline, Norlyn,
Norlyna, Norlynah, Norlyne

Norma (Latin) rule, precept.
Noma, Normi, Normie

Nour (Aramaic) a short form of Nura.
Noura

Nova (Latin) new. A short form of
Novella, Novia. (Hopi) butterfly chaser.
Astronomy: a star that releases bright
bursts of energy.
Novah

Novella (Latin) newcomer.
Novel, Novela, Novelah, Novele, Novell,
Novellah, Novelle

Novia (Spanish) sweetheart.
Noviah, Novka, Novya, Novyah, Nuvia

Nu (Burmese) tender. (Vietnamese) girl.
Nue

Nuala (Irish) a short form of Fionnula.
Nualah, Nula

Nubia (Egyptian) mother of a nation.

Nuela (Spanish) a form of Amelia.

Numilla (Australian) scout, lookout.
Numil, Numila, Numilah, Numile, Numill,
Numillah, Numille, Numyl, Numyla,
Numylah, Numyle, Numyll, Numylla,
Numyllah, Numylle

Nuna (Native American) land.
Nunah

Nunciata (Latin) messenger.
Nunzia, Nunziata, Nunziatah

Nur (Aramaic) a short form of Nura.

Nura (Aramaic) light.
Nurah

Nuria (Aramaic) the Lord's light.
Nuri, Nuriah, Nuriel, Nurin, Nurya,
Nuryah

Nuru (Swahili) daylight.

Nusi (Hungarian) a form of Hannah.
Nusie, Nusy

Nuwa (Chinese) mother goddess.
Mythology: another name for Nü-gua,
the creator of mankind.

Nya, Nyah (Irish) forms of Nia.
Nyaa, Nyia

Nyasia (Greek) a form of Nyssa.

Nycole (French) a form of Nicole.
Nycol, Nycole, Nycolle

Nydia (Latin) nest.
Nyda, Nydiah, Nydya, Nydyah

Nyeisha (American) a form of Niesha.

Nyesha (American) a form of Niesha.
Nyeshia

Nyia (Irish) a form of Nia.

Nykia (Arabic) a form of Nakia.
Nykiah

Nyla (Latin, Irish) a form of Nila.
Nylah, Nyle, Nylea, Nyleah, Nylla,
Nyllah, Nylle, Nyllea, Nylleah

Nyoko (Japanese) gem, treasure.
Nioko

Nyomi (Hebrew) a form of Naomi.
Nyoma, Nyome, Nyomee, Nyomey,
Nyomia, Nyomiah, Nyomie, Nyomy,
Nyomya, Nyomyah

Nyree (Maori) sea.
Niree, Nyra, Nyrie

Nyssa (Greek) beginning. See also Nissa.
Nysa, Nysah, Nyssah

Nyusha (Russian) a form of Agnes.
Nyushenka, Nyushka

Nyx (Greek) night.

Oba (Yoruba) chief, ruler.
Obah

Obelia (Greek) needle.
Obeliah, Obelya, Obelyah

Ocean (Greek) ocean.
Oceanne, Oceon

Oceana (Greek) ocean. Mythology:
Oceanus was the god of the ocean.
Oceanah, Oceananna, Oceania, Oceanna,
Oceaonna

Oceane (Greek) a form of Ocean.

Octavia (Latin) eighth. See also Tavia.
Actavia, Octabia, Octaviah, Octaviais,
Octavian, Octavice, Octavie, Octavienne,
Octavio, Octavious, Octavise, Octavya,
Octawia, Octivia, Oktavia, Oktavija,
Otavia

Odda (Scandinavian) rich.
Oda, Odah, Oddah, Oddia, Oddiah

Ode (Nigerian) born during travels.
Odee, Odey, Odi, Ody, Odya, Odyah

Odeda (Hebrew) strong; courageous.
Odeada, Odeadah, Odedah

Odele (Greek) melody, song.
Odel, Odell, Odelle

Odelette (French) a form of Odele.
Odelat, Odelatt, Odelatta, Odelattah,
Odelatte, Odelet, Odeleta, Odeletah,
Odelete, Odelett, Odeletta

Odelia (Greek) ode; melodic. (Hebrew)
I will praise God. (French) wealthy.
See also Odetta.
Odeelia, Odeleya, Odeliah, Odelina,
Odelinah, Odelinda, Odeline, Odellah,
Odelyn, Odila, Odilah, Odile, Odilia,
Odille, Odyla, Odylah, Odyle, Odyll,
Odylla, Odyllah, Odylle

Odella (English) wood hill.
Odela, Odelah, Odelle, Odelyn

Odera (Hebrew) plough.

Odessa (Greek) odyssey, long voyage.
Adesha, Adeshia, Adessa, Adessia, Odesa,
Odesah, Odessah, Odessia, Odissa,
Odissah, Odysa, Odysah, Odyssa, Odyssah

Odetta (German, French) a form of
Odelia.
Oddeta, Oddetta, Odeta, Odetah, Odettah

Odette (German, French) a form of
Odelia.
Oddet, Oddete, Oddett, Odet, Odete, Odett

Odina (Algonquin) mountain.
Odeana, Odeanah, Odeane, Odeen,
Odeena, Odeenah, Odeene, Odinah, Odyn,
Odyna, Odynah, Odyne

Ofelia (Greek) a form of Ophelia.
Ofeelia, Ofellia, Ofilia

Ofira (Hebrew) gold.
Ofara, Ofarra, Ofarrah, Ophira, Ophirah,
Ophyra, Ophyrah

Ofra (Hebrew) a form of Aphra.
Ofrah, Ofrat, Ophra, Ophrah

Ogin (Native American) wild rose.
Ogina, Ogyn, Ogyna, Ogynah

Ohanna (Hebrew) God's gracious gift.
Ohana, Ohanah, Ohannah

Okalani (Hawaiian) heaven.
Okalana, Okalanah, Okalanea, Okalanee,
Okalaney, Okalania, Okalaniah, Okalanie,
Okalany, Okalanya, Okalanyah, Okiilanee,

Okalani (cont.)
Okiilaney, Okiilani, Okiilanie, Okiilany,
Okilani

Oki (Japanese) middle of the ocean.
Okie

Oksana (Latin) a form of Osanna.
Oksanna

Ola (Scandinavian) ancestor. (Greek) a
short form of Olesia.
Olah

Olalla (Greek) sweetly spoken.
Olallah

Olathe (Native American) beautiful.
Olanth, Olantha, Olanthah, Olanthye,
Olathia

Oldina (Australian) snow.
Oldeena, Oldeenah, Oldenia, Oldeniah,
Oldinah, Oldine, Oldyn, Oldyna, Oldynah,
Oldyne

Oleander (Latin) Botany: a poisonous
evergreen shrub with fragrant white,
rose, or purple flowers.
Oleanda, Oleandah, Oleeanda, Oleeandah,
Oliannda, Olianndah, Oliannde

Oleda (Spanish) a form of Alida. See also
Leda.
Oleta, Olida, Olita

Olen (Russian) deer.
Olian, Olien, Olienah, Oliene, Olyan,
Olyen, Olyene

Olena (Russian) a form of Helen.
Alena, Alyona, Oleena, Olenah, Olenia,
Oleniah, Olenka, Olenna, Olenya, Olya,
Olyena, Olyenah, Olyona

Olesia (Greek) a form of Alexandra.
Cesya, Olecia, Oleesha, Oleishia, Olesha,
Olesiah, Olesya, Olesyah, Olexa, Olice,
Olicia, Olisha, Olishia, Ollicia

Oletha (Scandinavian) nimble.
Oleta, Oletah, Yaletha

Olethea (Latin) truthful. See also Alethea.
Oleathea, Oleatheah, Oleathya, Oleathyah,
Oleta

Olga (Scandinavian) holy. See also Helga,
Olivia.
Olgah, Olgy, Olia, Olva

Olia (Russian) a form of Olga.
Olja, Ollya, Olya, Olyah

Oliana (Polynesian) oleander.
Olianah, Oliane, Oliann, Olianna,
Oliannah, Olianne, Olyan, Olyana,
Olyanah, Olyane, Olyann, Olyanna,
Olyannah, Olyanne

Olimpe (French) a form of Olympia.
Olympe

Olina (Hawaiian) filled with happiness.
Olinah, Olyna, Olynah

Olinda (Latin) scented. (Spanish) protec-
tor of property. (Greek) a form of
Yolanda.
Olindah, Olynda, Olyndah

Olisa (Ibo) God.
Olisah, Olysa, Olysah, Olyssa, Olyssah

Olive (Latin) olive tree.
Oliff, Oliffe, Oliv, Olivet, Olivette, Olliv,
Ollive, Ollyv, Ollyve, Olyv, Olyve

Olivia (Latin) a form of Olive. (English) a
form of Olga. See also Liv, Livia.
Alivia, Alyvia, Olevia, Oliva, Olivea,
Oliveia, Olivetta, Olivette, Olivi, Oliviah,
Olivianne, Olivya, Olivyah, Oliwia, Olva

Ollie (English) a familiar form of Olivia.
Olla, Olly, Ollye

Olwen (Welsh) white footprint.
Olwena, Olwenah, Olwene, Olwenn,
Olwenna, Olwennah, Olwenne, Olwin,
Olwina, Olwinah, Olwine, Olwinn,
Olwinna, Olwinnah, Olwinne, Olwyn,
Olwyna, Olwynah, Olwyne, Olwynn,
Olwynna, Olwynnah, Olwynne

Olympia (Greek) heavenly.
Olimpe, Olimpia, Olimpiah, Olimpias,
Olympiah, Olympias, Olympie, Olympya,
Olympyah

Olympie (German) a form of Olympia.
Olympy

Olyvia (Latin) a form of Olivia.
Olyviah, Olyvya, Olyvyah

Oma (Hebrew) reverent. (German) grandmother. (Arabic) highest.
Omah

Omaira (Arabic) red.
Omar, Omara, Omarah, Omari, Omaria, Omariah, Omarra, Omarya, Omaryah

Omega (Greek) last, final, end. Linguistics: the last letter in the Greek alphabet.
Omegah

Ona (Latin, Irish) a form of Oona. (English) river.
Onah, Onna

Onatah (Iroquois) daughter of the earth and the corn spirit.
Onata

Onawa (Native American) wide awake.
Onaiwa, Onaiwah, Onaja, Onajah, Onawah, Onowa, Onowah

Ondine (Latin) a form of Undine.
Ondene, Ondin, Ondina, Ondinah, Ondyn, Ondyna, Ondynah, Ondyne

Ondrea (Czech) a form of Andrea.
Ohndrea, Ohndreea, Ohndreya, Ohndria, Ondra, Ondrah, Ondraya, Ondreana, Ondreea, Ondreya, Ondri, Ondria, Ondrianna, Ondrie, Ondriea, Ondry, Ondrya, Ondryah

Oneida (Native American) eagerly awaited.
Oneidah, Oneyda, Oneydah, Onida, Onidah, Onyda, Onydah

Oneisha (American) a form of Onesha.

Onella (Hungarian) a form of Helen.
Onela, Onelah, Onellah

Onesha (American) a combination of Ondrea + Aisha.
Oneshia, Onesia, Onessa, Onessia, Onethia, Oniesha, Onisha

Oni (Yoruba) born on holy ground.
Onee, Oney, Onie, Onnie, Ony

Onike (Tongan) onyx.
Onika, Onikah, Onikee

Onora (Latin) a form of Honora.
Onorah, Onoria, Onoriah, Onorina, Onorine, Onoryn, Onoryna, Onorynah, Ornora

Ontario (Native American) beautiful lake. Geography: a province and a lake in Canada.
Oniatario, Ontaryo

Onyx (Greek) onyx.
Onix

Oona (Latin, Irish) a form of Una.
Onnie, Oonagh, Oonie

Opa (Choctaw) owl. (German) grandfather.
Opah

Opal (Hindi) precious stone.
Opala, Opalah, Opale, Opalia, Opalina, Opell, Opella, Opelle

Opalina (Hindi) a form of Opal.
Opaleana, Opaleena, Opalin, Opalinah, Opaline, Opalyn, Opalyna, Opalynah, Opalyne

Opeli (Tongan) opal.
Opelea, Opeleah, Opelee, Opelei, Opeleigh, Opelia, Opeliah, Opelie, Opely, Opelya, Opelyah

Ophelia (Greek) helper. Literature: Hamlet's love interest in the Shakespearean play Hamlet.
Filia, Opheliah, Ophélie, Ophellia, Ophellya, Ophilia, Ophillia, Ophylla, Ophyllia, Ophylliah, Ophyllya, Ophyllyah, Phelia, Pheliah, Phelya, Phelyah

Ophelie (Greek) a form of Ophelia.
Ophellie, Ophelly, Ophely

Oprah (Hebrew) a form of Orpah.
Ophra, Ophrah, Opra

Ora (Latin) prayer. (Spanish) gold. (English) seacoast. (Greek) a form of Aura.
Ohra, Orah, Orlice, Orra

Orabella (Latin) a form of Arabella.
Orabel, Orabela, Orabele, Orabell, Orabelle, Oribel, Oribela, Oribele, Oribell, Oribella, Oribelle, Orybel, Orybela, Orybele, Orybell, Orybella, Orybelle

Oralee (Hebrew) the Lord is my light. See also Yareli.
Areli, Oralea, Oraleah, Oralei, Oraleigh, Oraley, Orali, Oralie, Oralit, Oraly, Oralye, Orelee, Orelie

Oralia (French) a form of Aurelia. See also Oriana.
Oraliah, Oralis, Oralya, Oralyah, Orelia, Oreliah, Oriel, Orielda, Orielle, Oriena, Orla, Orlah, Orlena, Orlene

Oran (Irish) queen.

Orana (Australian) welcome.
Oranah, Oranna, Orannah

Orane (French) rising.

Orazia (Italian) keeper of time.
Orazya, Orazyah, Orzaiah, Orzaya, Orzayah

Orea (Greek) mountains.
Oreah, Oreal, Oria, Oriah

Orela (Latin) announcement from the gods; oracle.
Oreal, Orel, Orelah, Orell, Orella, Orelle

Orenda (Iroquois) magical power.
Orendah

Oretha (Greek) a form of Aretha.
Oreta, Oretah, Oretta, Orettah, Orette

Oriana (Latin) dawn, sunrise. (Irish) golden.
Orane, Orania, Orelda, Ori, Oria, Orian, Oriane, Orianna, Oriannah, Orieana, Oryan, Oryana, Oryanah, Oryane, Oryann, Oryanna, Oryannah, Oryanne

Oriel (Latin) fire. (French) golden; angel of destiny.
Orial, Oriale, Oriall, Orialle, Oriele, Oriell, Orielle, Oryal, Oryale, Oryall, Oryalle, Oryel, Oryell, Oryelle

Oriella (Irish) fair; white skinned.
Oriala, Orialah, Orialla, Oriallah, Oriela, Orielah, Oriellah, Oryala, Oryalah, Oryalla, Oryallah, Oryela, Oryelah, Oryella, Oryellah

Orina (Russian) a form of Irene.
Orinah, Orya, Oryna, Orynah

Orinda (Hebrew) pine tree. (Irish) light skinned, white.
Orenda, Orendah, Orindah, Orynda, Oryndah

Orino (Japanese) worker's field.
Oryno

Oriole (Latin) golden; black-and-orange bird.
Auriel, Oriol, Oriola, Oriolah, Orioll, Oriolla, Oriollah, Oriolle, Oryel, Oryela, Oryelah, Oryele, Oryell, Oryella, Oryellah, Oryelle, Oryol, Oryola, Oryolah, Oryole, Oryoll, Oryolla, Oryollah, Oryolle

Orla (Irish) golden woman.
Orlagh, Orlah

Orlanda (German) famous throughout the land.
Orlandah, Orlandia, Orlantha, Orlinda

Orlena (Latin) golden.
Orlana, Orlanah, Orleana, Orleanah, Orleena, Orleenah, Orleene, Orlenah, Orlene, Orlina, Orlinah, Orline, Orlyn, Orlyna, Orlynah, Orlyne

Orlenda (Russian) eagle.
Orlendah

Orli (Hebrew) light.
Orelea, Oreleah, Orlee, Orlei, Orleigh, Orley, Orlia, Orliah, Orlie, Orly, Orlya, Orlyah

Ormanda (Latin) noble. (German) mariner.
Orma, Ormandah, Ormandia, Ormandiah, Ormandya, Ormandyah

Ornat (Irish) green.
Ornait, Ornaita, Ornaitah, Ornata, Ornatah, Ornate, Ornete, Ornetta, Ornette, Ornit, Ornita, Ornitah, Ornite, Ornitt, Ornitta, Ornittah, Ornitte, Ornyt, Ornyta, Ornytah, Ornyte, Ornytt, Ornytta, Ornyttah, Ornytte

Ornice (Hebrew) cedar tree. (Irish) pale; olive colored.
Orna, Ornah

Orpah (Hebrew) runaway. See also Oprah.
Orpa, Orpha, Orphie

Orquidea (Spanish) orchid.
Orquidia

Orsa (Latin) a short form of Orseline. See also Ursa.
Orsah, Orse

Orseline (Latin) bearlike. (Greek) a form of Ursula.
Orsalin, Orsalina, Orsalinah, Orsaline, Orsalyn, Orsalyna, Orsalynah, Orsalyne, Orsel, Orselina, Orselinah, Orselyn, Orselyna, Orselynah, Orselyne, Orsola, Orsolah

Ortensia (Italian) a form of Hortense.

Orva (French) golden; worthy. (English) brave friend.
Orvah

Orwina (Hebrew) boar friend.
Orwin, Orwinah, Orwine, Orwyn, Orwyna, Orwynah, Orwyne

Osanna (Latin) praise the Lord.
Osana, Osanah, Osannah

Osen (Japanese) one thousand.
Osena, Osenah

Oseye (Benin) merry.
Osey

Osita (Spanish) divinely strong.
Ositah, Osith, Ositha, Osithah, Osithe, Osyta, Osytah, Osyte, Osyth, Osytha, Osythah

Osma (English) divine protector.
Osmah, Ozma, Ozmah

Oswalda (English) God's power; God's crest.
Osvalda, Osvaldah, Oswaldah

Otavia (Italian) a form of Octavia.
Otaviah, Otavya, Otavyah, Ottavia, Ottaviah, Ottavya, Ottavyah

Othelia (Spanish) rich.
Othilia

Otilie (Czech) lucky heroine.
Otila, Otilah, Otka, Ottili, Ottyli, Otyla, Otylah

Otylia (Polish) rich.
Otilia, Ottylia, Ottyliah, Ottyllia, Ottylliah, Ottylya, Ottylyah, Otyliah, Otylya, Otylyah

Ovia (Latin, Danish) egg.
Ova, Ovah, Oviah, Ovya, Ovyah

Owena (Welsh) born to nobility; young warrior.
Owenah, Owina, Owinah, Owyna, Owynah

Oya (Moquelumnan) called forth.
Oia, Oiah, Oyah

Oz (Hebrew) strength.
Ozz

Ozara (Hebrew) treasure, wealth.
Ozarah, Ozarra, Ozarrah

Ozera (Hebrew) helpful. (Russian) lake.
Ozerah, Ozira, Ozirah, Ozyra, Ozyrah

P

Paca (Spanish) a short form of Pancha. See also Paka.

Padget (French) a form of Page.
Padgett, Paget, Pagett

Padma (Hindi) lotus.
Padmah, Padmar

Padmani (Sri Lankan) blossom, flower.
Padmanee, Padmaney, Padmania, Padmaniah, Padmanie, Padmany

Pagan (Latin) from the country.
Pagen, Pagin, Pagon, Pagun, Pagyn

Page (French) young assistant.
Pagi

Paige (English) young child.

Paisley (Scottish) patterned fabric first made in Paisley, Scotland.
Paislay, Paislee, Paisleyann, Paisleyanne, Paizlei, Paizleigh, Paizley, Pasley, Pazley

Paiton (English) warrior's town.
Paitan, Paiten, Paitin, Paityn, Paityne, Paiyton, Paten, Patton, Peita, Peiten, Peitin, Peiton, Peityn, Petan

Paka (Swahili) kitten. See also Paca.
Pakah

Pakuna (Moquelumnan) deer bounding while running downhill.

Pala (Native American) water.
Palah, Palla, Pallah

Palila (Polynesian) bird.
Palilah, Palyla, Palylah

Pallas (Greek) wise. Mythology: another name for Athena, the goddess of wisdom.
Palace, Pallass, Pallassa

Palma (Latin) palm tree.
Pallma, Pamar

Palmela (Greek) a form of Pamela.
Palmelah, Palmelia, Palmeliah, Palmelina, Palmeline, Palmelyn, Palmelyna, Palmelyne

Palmer (Spanish) a short form of Palmira.
Palmir

Palmira (Spanish) a form of Palma.
Pallmirah, Pallmyra, Palmara, Palmarah, Palmaria, Palmariah, Palmarya, Palmaryah, Palmirah, Palmyra, Palmyrah

Paloma (Spanish) dove. See also Aloma.
Palloma, Palomah, Palomar, Palomara, Palomarah, Palomaria, Palomariah, Palomarya, Palomaryah, Palometa, Palomita, Paluma, Peloma

Pamela (Greek) honey.
Palmela, Pam, Pama, Pamala, Pamalah, Pamalia, Pamaliah, Pamalla, Pamalya, Pamalyah, Pamelia, Pameliah, Pamelina, Pamella, Pamelya, Pamelyah, Pami, Pamie, Pamila, Pamilla, Pamm, Pammela, Pammi, Pammie, Pammy, Pamula, Pamy

Pana (Native American) partridge.
Panah, Panna, Pannah

Pancha (Spanish) free; from France.
Paca, Panchah, Panchita

Panchali (Sanskrit) princess from Panchala, a former country in what is now India.
Panchalea, Panchaleah, Panchalee, Panchalei, Panchaleigh, Panchaley, Panchalie, Panchaly

Pandita (Hindi) scholar.

Pandora (Greek) all-gifted. Mythology: a woman who opened a box out of curiosity and released evil into the world. See also Dora.
Pandi, Pandorah, Pandorra, Pandorrah, Pandy, Panndora, Panndorah, Panndorra, Panndorrah

Pansofia (Greek) wise, knowledgeable.
Pansofee, Pansofey, Pansoffee, Pansoffey, Pansoffi, Pansoffia, Pansofi, Pansofiah, Pansofie, Pansophee, Pansophey, Pansophi, Pansophia, Pansophiah, Pansophie, Pansophy, Pansophya, Pansophyah

Pansy (Greek) flower; fragrant. (French) thoughtful.
Pansea, Panseah, Pansee, Pansey, Pansi, Pansia, Pansiah, Pansie, Pansya, Pansyah

Panthea (Greek) all the gods.
Panfia, Panfiah, Pantheah, Pantheia, Pantheya, Panthia, Panthiah, Panthya, Panthyah

Panya (Swahili) mouse; tiny baby. (Russian) a familiar form of Stephanie.
Pania, Paniah, Panyah, Panyia

Panyin (Fante) older twin.

Paola (Italian) a form of Paula.
Paoli, Paolina, Paoline

Papina (Moquelumnan) vine growing on an oak tree.
Papinah, Papyna, Papynah

Paquita (Spanish) a form of Frances.
Paqua

Paradise (Persian) the garden of Eden.

Paramita (Sanskrit) virtuous; perfect.
Paramitah, Paramyta, Paramytah

Pari (Persian) fairy eagle.

Paris (French) Geography: the capital of France. Mythology: the Trojan prince who started the Trojan War by abducting Helen.
Parice, Paries, Parise, Parish, Pariss, Parisse, Parys, Paryse, Paryss, Parysse

Parisa (French) a form of Paris.
Parisha, Parissa, Parrisha, Parysa, Paryssa

Parker (English) park keeper.
Park, Parke

Parnel (French) a form of Pernella.
Parnela, Parnelah, Parnele, Parnell, Parnella, Parnellah, Parnelle

Parris (French) a form of Paris.
Parrise, Parrish, Parrys, Parrysh

Parthenia (Greek) virginal.
Partheenia, Parthena, Parthene, Partheniah, Parthenie, Parthenya, Parthenyah, Parthinia, Pathina

Parvati (Sanskrit) mountain climber.
Parvatee, Parvatey, Parvatia, Parvatiah, Parvatie, Parvaty, Parvatya, Parvatyah

Parveen (Indian) star.

Parveneh (Persian) butterfly.

Pascale (French) born on Easter or Passover.
Pascala, Pascalette, Pascalina, Pascaline, Pascalle, Pascalyn, Pascalyna, Pascalyne, Paschal, Paschale, Paskel, Pasqua, Pasquah

Pasha (Greek) sea.
Palasha, Pascha, Paschah, Pasche, Pashae, Pashe, Pashel, Pashela, Pashelah, Pashele, Pashell, Pashelle, Pashka, Pasia, Passia

Pasifiki (Tongan) Pacific Ocean.
Pacific, Pacifica, Pacificah, Pacificka, Pacifiqua, Pacifiquah, Pacifique, Pacifyca, Pacifycah, Pacifyqua, Pacifyquah, Pacifyque, Pacyfica, Pacyficah, Pacyficka, Pacyfickah, Pacyfiqua, Pacyfiquah, Pacyfique, Pacyfyca, Pacyfycah, Pacyfycka, Pacyfyka, Pacyfyqua, Pacyfyquah, Pacyfyque

Passion (Latin) passion.
Pashion, Pashonne, Pasion, Passionaé, Passionate, Passionette

Pasua (Swahili) born by cesarean section.

Pat (Latin) a short form of Patricia, Patsy.
Patt

Patam (Sanskrit) city.
Patem, Patim, Patom, Pattam, Pattem, Pattim, Pattom, Pattym, Patym

Patamon (Native American) raging.

Pati (Moquelumnan) fish baskets made of willow branches.
Patee, Patey, Patie

Patia (Gypsy, Spanish) leaf. (Latin, English) a familiar form of Patience, Patricia.
Patiah, Patya, Patyah

Patience (English) patient.
Paciencia, Patiance, Patient, Patince, Patishia

Patra (Greek, Latin) a form of Petra.
Patria, Patriah

Patrice (French) a form of Patricia.
Patrease, Patrece, Patreece, Patreese, Patreice, Patriece, Patryce, Patryse, Pattrice

Patricia (Latin) noblewoman. See also Payten, Peyton, Tricia, Trisha, Trissa.
Patresa, Patrica, Patricah, Patricea, Patriceia, Patrichea, Patriciah, Patriciana, Patricianna, Patricja, Patricka, Patrickia, Patrisia, Patrissa

Patrisha (Latin) a form of Patricia.
Patrishah, Patrishia

Patrizia (Italian) a form of Patricia.
Patreeza, Patriza, Patrizah, Patrizzia

Patrycja (American) a form of Patricia.
Patrycia, Patrycya, Patrycyah

Patsy (Latin) a familiar form of Patricia.
Patsee, Patsey, Patsi, Patsie

Patty (English) a familiar form of Patricia.
Patte, Pattee, Pattey, Patti, Pattie, Paty

Paula (Latin) small. See also Pavla, Polly.
Paliki, Paulane, Paulann, Paulla, Pavia

Paulette (Latin) a familiar form of Paula.
Paoleta, Paulet, Pauleta, Pauletah, Paulete, Paulett, Pauletta, Paulettah, Paulita, Paullett, Paulletta, Paullette

Paulie (Latin) a familiar form of Paula.
Paili, Pali, Pauli, Pauly

Paulina (Slavic) a form of Paula.
Paulena, Paulenia, Paulia, Pauliah, Pauliana, Paulianne, Paullena, Paulya, Paulyah, Paulyna, Paulynah, Pawlina, Polena, Polina, Polinia

Pauline (French) a form of Paula.
Paule, Pauleen, Paulene, Paulien, Paulin, Paulyn, Paulyne, Paulynn, Pouline

Pavla (Czech, Russian) a form of Paula.
Pavlina, Pavlinka

Paxton (Latin) peaceful town.
Paxtin, Paxtynn

Payal (Indian) anklet, foot ornament.

Payge (English) a form of Paige.
Payg

Payten, Payton (Irish) forms of Patricia.
Paydon, Paytan, Paytin, Paytn, Paytton, Paytyn

Paz (Spanish) peace.
Pazz

Pazi (Ponca) yellow bird.

Pazia (Hebrew) golden.
Paza, Pazice, Pazise, Pazit, Pazya, Pazyah, Pazyce, Pazyse

Peace (English) peaceful.
Peece

Pearl (Latin) jewel.
Pearle, Pearleen, Pearlena, Pearlene, Pearlette, Pearlina, Pearline, Pearlisha, Pearlyn, Perl, Perle, Perlette, Perlie, Perline, Perlline

Peata (Maori) bringer of joy.
Peatah, Peita, Peitah, Peyta, Peytah

Peggy (Greek) a familiar form of Margaret.
Peg, Pegee, Pegeen, Pegey, Pegg, Peggee, Peggey, Peggi, Peggie, Pegi, Pegie, Pegy

Peighton (Irish) a form of Patricia.

Peke (Hawaiian) a form of Bertha.

Pela (Polish) a short form of Penelope.
Pele

Pelagia (Greek) sea.
Pelage, Pelageia, Pelagiah, Pelagie, Pelagya, Pelagyah, Pelga, Pelgia, Pellagia

Pelipa (Zuni) a form of Philippa.

Pemba (Bambara) the power that controls all life.

Penda (Swahili) loved.
Pandah, Pendah, Pendana

Penelope (Greek) weaver. Mythology: the clever and loyal wife of Odysseus, a Greek hero.
Pen, Peneli, Penelia, Peneliah, Penelie, Penelopa, Penelopea, Penelopee, Penelopey, Penelopi, Penelopia, Penelopiah, Penelopie, Penelopy, Penna, Pennelope, Pennelopea, Pennelopee, Pennelopey, Pennelopi, Pennelopia, Pennelopiah, Pennelopie, Pennelopy, Pinelopi

Peni (Carrier) mind.

Peninah (Hebrew) pearl.
Paninah, Panine, Penina, Penine, Peninit, Peninnah, Penyna, Penynah, Penyne

Pennie, Penny (Greek) familiar forms of Penelope, Peninah.
Penee, Peney, Peni, Penie, Pennee, Penney, Penni, Pennia, Penniah, Peny

Penthea (Greek) fifth-born; mourner.
Pentheah, Penthia, Penthiah, Penthya, Penthyah

Peony (Greek) flower.
Peonee, Peoney, Peoni, Peonie

Pepita (Spanish) a familiar form of Josephine.
Pepa, Pepee, Pepi, Pepie, Pepitah, Pepite, Pepitta, Pepitte, Peppy, Pepy, Pepyta, Pepytah, Pepyte, Peta

Pepper (Latin) condiment from the pepper plant.

Perah (Hebrew) flower.

Perdita (Latin) lost. Literature: a character in Shakespeare's play *The Winter's Tale*.
Perdida, Perditah, Perdy, Perdyta, Perdytah

Perfecta (Spanish) flawless.
Perfect, Perfection

Peri (Greek) mountain dweller. (Persian) fairy or elf.
Perea, Peree, Perey, Peria, Periah, Perie, Perita, Pery

Peridot (French) yellow-green gem.
Peridota, Peridotah, Perydot, Perydota, Perydotah

Perilla (Latin) Botany: an ornamental plant with leaves often used in cooking.
Perila, Perilah, Perillah, Peryla, Perylah, Peryll, Perylla, Peryllah

Perla (Latin) a form of Pearl.
Pearla, Pearlea, Pearleah, Perlah

Perlie (Latin) a familiar form of Pearl.
Pearlee, Pearlei, Pearleigh, Pearley, Pearli, Pearlie, Pearly, Perley, Perli, Perly, Purley, Purly

Perlita (Italian) pearl.
Perleta, Perletta, Perlitta, Perlyta, Perlytta

Pernella (Greek, French) rock. (Latin) a short form of Petronella.
Parnel, Pernel, Pernela, Pernelah, Pernele, Pernell, Pernellah, Pernelle

Perri (Greek, Latin) small rock; traveler. (French) pear tree. (Welsh) child of Harry. (English) a form of Perry.
Peree, Peri, Perie, Perre, Perree, Perriann, Perrie, Perrin, Perrine, Perya, Peryah

Perry (English) a familiar form of Peregrine, Peter (see Boys' Names). See also Perri.
Parry, Perey, Perrey, Perrye, Pery

Persephone (Greek) Mythology: the goddess of the underworld.
Persephanie, Persephany, Persephonie

Persis (Latin) from Persia.
Persia, Persiah, Perssis, Persy, Persys, Persysa, Persysah

Peta (Blackfoot) golden eagle.

Petra (Greek, Latin) small rock. A short form of Petronella.
Pet, Peta, Petraann, Petrah, Petrea, Petrova, Petrovna, Peytra, Pietra

Petrina (Greek) a form of Petronella.
Perinna, Perinnah, Perrine, Petena, Peterina, Petrin, Petrinah, Petrine, Petrona, Petroni, Petronia, Petronie, Petronija, Petrony, Petryn, Petryna, Petryne

Petrisse (German) a form of Petronella.
Petrice, Petriss, Petrissa

Petronella (Greek) small rock. (Latin) of the Roman clan Petronius.

Peronel, Peronella, Peronelle, Peternella, Petrenela, Petrina, Petrisse, Petronela, Petronelle, Petronilla, Petronille

Petula (Latin) seeker.
Petulah

Petunia (Native American) flower.
Petuniah, Petunya, Petunyah

Peyton (Irish) a form of Patricia.
Peyden, Peydon, Peyten, Peytin, Peytyn

Phaedra (Greek) bright.
Faydra, Phadra, Phadrah, Phae, Phaedrah, Phaidra, Phe, Phedra, Phedre

Phallon (Irish) a form of Fallon.
Phalaine, Phalen, Phallan, Phallie, Phalon, Phalyn

Phebe (Greek) a form of Phoebe.
Pheba, Pheby

Phelia (Greek) immortal and wise.
Felia, Feliah, Felya, Felyah, Pheliah, Phelya, Phelyah

Phemie (Scottish) a short form of Euphemia.
Phemea, Phemee, Phemey, Phemi, Phemia, Phemiah, Phemy, Phemya, Phemyah

Pheodora (Greek, Russian) a form of Feodora.
Phedora, Phedorah, Pheodorah, Pheydora, Pheydorah

Philana (Greek) lover of mankind.
Filana, Phila, Philanna, Phileen, Phileene, Philene, Philiane, Philina, Philine, Phillane, Phylana, Phylanah, Phylane, Phyllan, Phyllana, Phyllanah, Phyllane

Philantha (Greek) lover of flowers.
Philanthe, Phylantha, Phylanthe

Philberta (English) brilliant.
Filberta, Filbertah, Filberte, Philbertah, Philberte, Phylbert, Phylberta, Phylbertah, Phylberte, Phyllberta, Phyllbertah, Phyllberte

Philicia (Latin) a form of Phylicia.
Philecia, Philesha, Philica, Philicha, Philiciah, Philycia

Philippa (Greek) lover of horses. See also Filippa.

Philippa *(cont.)*
Phil, Philipa, Philipine, Philippe, Philippina,
Phillie, Phillipa, Phillipe, Phillipina,
Phillippine, Philly, Phylipa, Phylipah,
Phyllipa, Phyllipah, Phyllypa, Phyllypah

Philomela (Greek) lover of songs.
Filomela, Filomelah, Philomelah, Phylomela,
Phylomelah

Philomena (Greek) love song; loved one.
Bible: a first-century saint. See also
Filomena, Mena.
Philoméne, Philomina, Philomine, Phylomina,
Phylomine, Phylomyna, Phylomyne

Philyra (Greek) lover of music.
Philira, Philirah, Phylyra, Phylyrah

Phoebe (Greek) shining. See also Febe.
Phaebe, Phebea, Pheebea, Pheebee, Pheibee,
Pheibey, Pheobe, Pheybee, Pheybey, Phoebey

Phoenix (Latin) phoenix, a legendary bird.
Phenix, Pheonix, Phynix

Photina (Greek) a form of Fotina.
Photine, Photyna, Photyne

Phoung (Vietnamese) phoenix.

Phylicia (Latin) fortunate; happy. (Greek)
a form of Felicia.
Phylecia, Phylesha, Phylesia, Phylica,
Phyliciah, Phylisha, Phylisia, Phylissa,
Phyllecia, Phyllicia, Phylliciah, Phyllisha,
Phyllisia, Phyllissa, Phyllyza

Phyllida (Greek) a form of Phyllis.
Fillida, Philida, Philidah, Phillida,
Phillidah, Phillyda, Phillydah, Phylida,
Phylidah, Phyllidah, Phyllyda, Phyllydah,
Phylyda, Phylydah

Phyllis (Greek) green bough.
Filise, Fillis, Fillys, Fyllis, Philis, Phillis,
Phillisia, Philliss, Philys, Philyss, Phylis,
Phylliss, Phyllys

Pia (Italian) devout.
Piah, Pya, Pyah

Piedad (Spanish) devoted; pious.
Piedada

Pier (French) a form of Petra.
Peret, Peretta, Perette, Pieret, Pierett,
Pieretta, Pierette, Pierra, Pierre, Pierrette,
Pieryn, Pieryna, Pieryne

Pier Ann (American) a combination of
Pier + Ann.
Pier-Ann, Pier Anne, Pier-Anne

Pierce (English) a form of Petra.

Pilar (Spanish) pillar, column.
Peelar, Peeler, Pilár, Pilla, Pillar, Pylar, Pyllar

Pililani (Hawaiian) close to heaven.
Pililanee, Pililaney, Pililanie, Pililany

Ping (Chinese) duckweed. (Vietnamese)
peaceful.

Pinga (Eskimo) Mythology: the goddess
of game and the hunt.
Pingah

Pink (American) the color pink.

Pinterry (Australian) star.
Pinterree, Pinterrey, Pinterri, Pinterrie

Piper (English) pipe player.
Pipper, Pyper

Pippa (English) a short form of Philippa.
Pipa, Pipah, Pippah, Pypa, Pypah, Pyppa,
Pyppah

Pippi (French) rosy cheeked.
Pipee, Pipey, Pipi, Pipie, Pippee, Pippen,
Pippey, Pippie, Pippin, Pippy, Pipy

Piscina (Italian) water.
Pischina, Pishina, Pishinah, Pychina,
Pychinah, Pychyna, Pychynah, Pycina,
Pycinah, Pyshina, Pyshinah, Pyshyna,
Pyshynah

Pita (African) fourth daughter.
Peeta, Peetah, Pitah, Pyta, Pytah

Pixie (English) mischievous fairy.
Pixee, Pixey, Pixi, Pixy, Pyxee, Pyxey,
Pyxi, Pyxie, Pyxy

Placidia (Latin) serene.
Placida, Placide, Placinda, Placyda,
Placydah, Placynda

Platona (Greek) broad shouldered.
Platonah, Platonia, Platoniah, Platonya,
Platonyah

Pleasance (French) pleasant.
Pleasence

Pocahontas (Native American) playful.
Pocohonta

Poeta (Italian) poetry.
Poetah, Poetree, Poetrey, Poetri, Poetrie,
Poetry, Poett, Poetta, Poette

Polla (Arabic) poppy.
Pola, Polah, Pollah

Polly (Latin) a familiar form of Paula,
Pauline.
Polea, Poleah, Polee, Polei, Poleigh, Poley,
Poli, Polie, Poll, Pollea, Polleah, Pollee,
Polleigh, Polley, Polli, Pollie, Poly

Pollyanna (English) a combination of
Polly + Anna. Literature: an overly opti-
mistic heroine created by Eleanor
Porter.
Polian, Poliana, Polianah, Poliane, Poliann,
Polianna, Poliannah, Polianne, Polliann,
Pollianna, Polliannah, Pollianne, Pollyana,
Pollyanah, Pollyane, Pollyann, Pollyannah,
Pollyanne, Polyan, Polyana, Polyanah,
Polyane, Polyann, Polyanna, Polyannah,
Polyanne

Poloma (Choctaw) bow.
Polomah, Polome

Polyxena (Greek) welcoming.
Polyxeena, Polyxeenah, Polyxenah,
Polyxina, Polyxinah, Polyxyna, Polyxynah,
Polyzeena, Polyzeenah, Polyzena, Polyzenah,
Polyzina, Polyzinah, Polyzyna, Polyzynah

Pomona (Latin) apple. Mythology: the
goddess of fruit and fruit trees.
Pomma, Pommah, Pomme, Pomonah

Poni (African) second daughter.
Ponee, Poney, Ponie, Pony

Pooja (Indian) worship.

Poonam (Indian) merit; full moon.
Punam

Poppy (Latin) poppy flower.
Popea, Popeah, Popee, Popey, Popi, Popie,
Poppea, Poppee, Poppey, Poppi, Poppie

Pora, Poria (Hebrew) fruitful.
Porah, Poriah, Porya, Poryah

Porcha (Latin) a form of Portia.
Porchae, Porchai

Porche (Latin) a form of Portia.

Porchia (Latin) a form of Portia.
Porcia

Porscha (German) a form of Portia.
Porcsha, Porschah, Porsché, Porschea,
Porschia

Porsche (German) a form of Portia.
Porcshe, Pourche

Porsha (Latin) a form of Portia.
Porshai, Porshay, Porshe, Porshea, Porshia

Porter (Latin) gatekeeper.
Port, Portie, Porty

Portia (Latin) offering. Literature: the
heroine of Shakespeare's play *The*
Merchant of Venice.
Porta, Portah, Portiah, Portiea, Portya,
Portyah

Posy (English) flower, small bunch of
flowers.
Posee, Posey, Posi, Posia, Posiah, Posie,
Posya, Posyah

Prairie (French) prairie.

Precious (French) precious; dear.
Pracious, Preciouse, Precisha, Prescious,
Preshious, Presious

Premilla (Sanskrit) loving girl.
Premila, Premilah, Premillah, Premyla,
Premylah, Premylla, Premyllah

Presley (English) priest's meadow.
Preslea, Preslee, Preslei, Presli, Preslie, Presly,
Preslye, Pressley, Presslie, Pressly

Pricilla (Latin) a form of Priscilla.
Pricila, Pricilia

Prima (Latin) first, beginning; first child.
Prema, Primah, Primalia, Primara,
Primaria, Primariah, Primetta, Primina,

Prima *(cont.)*
Priminia, Pryma, Prymah, Prymaria,
Prymariah, Prymarya, Prymaryah

Primavera (Italian, Spanish) spring.
Primaverah, Prymavera, Prymaverah

Primrose (English) primrose flower.
Primrosa, Primula, Prymrosa, Prymrose

Princess (English) daughter of royalty.
Princcess, Princes, Princesa, Princessa,
Princetta, Princie, Princilla, Pryncess,
Pryncessa, Pryncessah

Prisca (Latin) a short form of Priscilla.

Priscila (Latin) a form of Priscilla.
Priscilia

Priscilla (Latin) ancient.
Cilla, Piri, Precila, Precilla, Prescilla,
Presilla, Pressilia, Priscela, Priscella, Priscill,
Priscille, Priscillia, Priscillie, Prisella, Prisila,
Prisilla, Prissila, Prissilla, Prycyla, Prycylah,
Pryscylla, Prysilla, Prysillah, Prysylla,
Prysyllah

Prissy (Latin) a familiar form of Priscilla.
Pris, Prisi, Priss, Prissi, Prissie

Priya (Hindi) beloved; sweet natured.
Pria, Priyah

Priyanka (Indian) dear one.
Priyasha

Procopia (Latin) declared leader.

Promise (Latin) promise, pledge.
Promis, Promisea, Promisee, Promisey,
Promisi, Promisie, Promiss, Promissa,
Promisse, Promissee, Promissey, Promissi,
Promissie, Promissy, Promisy, Promys,
Promyse

Prospera (Latin) prosperous.
Prosperitee, Prosperitey, Prosperiti,
Prosperitie, Prosperity

Pru (Latin) a short form of Prudence.
Prue

Prudence (Latin) cautious; discreet.
Prudance, Prudencia, Prudens

Prudy (Latin) a familiar form of Prudence.
Prudee, Prudi, Prudie

Prunella (Latin) brown; little plum. See
also Nellie.
Prunel, Prunela, Prunelah, Prunele, Prunell,
Prunellah, Prunelle

Psyche (Greek) soul. Mythology: a beautiful mortal loved by Eros, the Greek
god of love.
Psyke, Syche, Syke

Pua (Hawaiian) flower.
Puah

Puakea (Hawaiian) white flower.
Puakeah, Puakia, Puakiah, Puakya,
Puakyah

Pualani (Hawaiian) heavenly flower.
Pualanee, Pualaney, Pualania, Pualaniah,
Pualanie, Pualany, Puni

Puja (Indian) worship.

Purity (English) purity.
Pura, Purah, Pure, Pureza, Purisima,
Puritee, Puritey, Puriti, Puritia, Puritiah,
Puritie, Puritya

Pyralis (Greek) fire.
Piralis, Piralissa, Pyralissa

Pyrena (Greek) fiery.
Pirena, Pirenah, Pyrenah, Pyrene

Pythia (Greek) prophet.
Pithea, Pitheah, Pithia, Pithiah, Pythea,
Pytheah, Pythiah, Pythis, Pythya, Pythyah

Q

Qadesh (Egyptian) Mythology: an
Egyptian goddess.
Qadesha, Qadeshah, Quedesh, Quedesha

Qadira (Arabic) powerful.
Kadira, Kadirah, Qadirah, Qadyra

Qamra (Arabic) moon.
Kamra, Qamrah

Qiana (American) a form of Quiana.

Qitarah (Arabic) fragrant.
Qitara, Qytara, Qytarah

Quaashie (Ewe) born on Sunday.
Quashi, Quashie, Quashy

Quadeisha (American) a combination of Qadira + Aisha.
Qudaisha, Quadaishia, Quadajah, Quadasha, Quadasia, Quadayshia, Quadaza, Quadejah, Quadesha, Quadeshia, Quadiasha, Quaesha

Quaneisha (American) a combination of the prefix Qu + Niesha.
Quaneasa, Quanece, Quanecia, Quaneesha, Quaneice, Quansha, Quneasha, Quynecia, Qwanisha, Qynecia, Qynisha

Quanesha (American) a form of Quaneisha.
Quamesha, Quaneshia, Quanesia, Quanessa, Quanessia, Quannesha, Quanneshia, Quannezia, Quayneshia, Quonesha, Quynesha, Quynesia

Quanika (American) a combination of the prefix Qu + Nika.
Quanikka, Quanikki, Quaniqua, Quanique, Quantenique, Quanyka, Quanykka, Quanykki, Quanyque, Quawanica, Quawanyca, Queenika, Queenique

Quanisha (American) a form of Quaneisha.
Quaniesha, Quanishia, Quarnisha, Quaynisha, Queenisha, Quynisha, Quynishia, Quynsha, Qynisha, Qynysha

Quarralia (Australian) star.
Quaralia, Quaraliah, Quaralya, Quaralyah, Quarraliah, Quarralya, Quarralyah

Quartilla (Latin) fourth.
Quantilla, Quartila, Quartilah, Quartile, Quartillah, Quartille, Quartyla, Quartylah, Quartyle, Quartylla, Quartyllah, Quartylle, Quintila, Quintilah, Quintile, Quintilla, Quintillah, Quintille, Quintyla, Quintylah, Quintyle, Quintylla, Quintyllah, Quintylle, Quyntila, Quyntilah, Quyntile, Quyntilla, Quyntillah, Quyntille, Quyntyla, Quyntylah, Quyntyle, Quyntylla, Quyntyllah, Quyntylle

Qubilah (Arabic) agreeable.
Quabila, Quabilah, Quabyla, Quabylah, Qubila, Qubyla, Qubylah

Queen (English) queen. See also Quinn.
Quean, Queena, Queenah, Quenna

Queenie (English) a form of Queen.
Queanee, Queaney, Queani, Queania, Queaniah, Queanie, Queany, Queanya, Queanyah, Queenation, Queenee, Queeneste, Queenet, Queeneta, Queenete, Queenett, Queenetta, Queenette, Queeney, Queeni, Queenia, Queeniah, Queenika, Queenique, Queeny, Queenya, Queenyah

Queisha (American) a short form of Quaneisha.
Qeysha, Qeyshia, Qeyshiah, Queishah, Queshia, Queshiah, Queshya, Queshyah, Queysha

Quelita (American) a combination of Queen + Lita.
Queleata, Queleatah, Queleeta, Queleetah, Queleta, Queletah, Quelitah, Quelyta, Quelytah

Quella (English) quiet, pacify.
Quela, Quele, Quellah, Quelle

Quenby (Scandinavian) feminine.
Queenbea, Queenbee, Queenbey, Queenbi, Queenbie, Quenbye

Quenisha (American) a combination of Queen + Aisha.
Queneesha, Quenesha, Quenishia, Quennisha, Quensha, Quonisha, Quonnisha

Quenna (English) a form of Queen.
Queana, Queanah, Quena, Quenell, Quenella, Quenelle, Quenessa, Quenesse, Queneta, Quenete, Quenetta, Quenette, Quennah

Querida (Spanish) dear; beloved.
Queridah, Queryda, Querydah

Questa (French) searcher.
Quest, Questah, Queste

Queta (Spanish) a short form of names ending in "queta" or "quetta."
Quetah, Quetta

Quiana, Quianna (American) combinations of the prefix Qu + Anna.
Quian, Quianah, Quianda, Quiane, Quiani, Quianita, Quiann, Quiannah, Quianne, Quionna, Quyana, Quyanah, Quyane, Quyann, Quyanna, Quyannah, Quyanne

Quieta (English) quiet.
Quietah, Quiete, Quietta, Quiettah, Quiette, Quyeta, Quyetah, Quyete, Quyetta, Quyettah, Quyette

Quilla (Incan) Mythology: Mama Quilla was the goddess of the moon.
Quila, Quilah, Quill, Quillah, Quille, Quyla, Quylah, Quyle, Quylla, Quyllah, Quylle

Quinby (Scandinavian) queen's estate.
Quinbea, Quinbee, Quinbey, Quinbi, Quinbie, Quynbea, Quynbee, Quynbey, Quynbi, Quynbia, Quynbie, Quynby

Quincey (Irish) a form of Quincy.
Quincee, Quinncee, Quinncey

Quincy (Irish) fifth.
Quinci, Quincia, Quincie, Quinnci, Quinncia, Quinncie, Quinncy, Quyncee, Quyncey, Quynci, Quyncia, Quyncie, Quyncy, Quynncee, Quynncey, Quynnci, Quynncie, Quynncy

Quinella (Latin) a form of Quintana.
Quinel, Quinela, Quinelah, Quinell, Quinellah, Quinelle, Quynel, Quynela, Quynelah, Quynele, Quynell, Quynella, Quynellah, Quynelle

Quinesha (American) a form of Quenisha.
Quineshia, Quinessa, Quinessia, Quinnesha, Quinneshia

Quinetta (Latin) a form of Quintana.
Quinette, Quinita, Quinnette

Quinisha (American) a form of Quenisha.
Quinisa, Quinishia, Quinnisha

Quinn (German, English) queen. See also Queen.
Quin, Quina, Quinah, Quinna, Quinnah, Quinne, Quiyn, Quyn, Quynn

Quinshawna (American) a combination of Quinn + Shawna.
Quinshea

Quintana (Latin) fifth. (English) queen's lawn. See also Quinella, Quinetta.
Quinta, Quintah, Quintanah, Quintane, Quintann, Quintanna, Quintannah, Quintanne, Quintara, Quintarah, Quintina, Quintona, Quintonah, Quintonice, Quynta, Quyntah, Quyntana, Quyntanah, Quyntanna, Quyntannah, Quyntanne, Quyntara, Quyntarah

Quintessa (Latin) essence. See also Tess.
Quintaysha, Quintesa, Quintesha, Quintessah, Quintesse, Quintessia, Quintice, Quinticia, Quintisha, Quintosha, Quyntessa, Quyntessah, Quyntesse

Quintina (Latin) a form of Quintana.
Quinntina, Quinntinah, Quinntine, Quintia, Quintiah, Quintila, Quintilla, Quintinah, Quintine, Quintyn, Quintyna, Quintynah, Quintyne, Quyntia, Quyntiah, Quyntila, Quyntilah, Quyntilla, Quyntillah, Quyntin, Quyntina, Quyntinah, Quyntine, Quyntyn, Quyntyna, Quyntynah, Quyntyne

Quintrell (American) a combination of Quinn + Trella.
Quintrela, Quintrella, Quintrelle

Quirita (Latin) citizen.
Quiritah, Quirite, Quiritta, Quirittah, Quiritte, Quiryta, Quirytah, Quiryte, Quirytta, Quiryttah, Quirytte, Quyryta, Quyrytah, Quyryte, Quyrytta, Quyryttah, Quyrytte

Quiterie (Latin, French) tranquil.
Quita, Quitah, Quiteree, Quiteri, Quiteria, Quiteriah, Quitery, Quyteree, Quyteri, Quyteria, Quyteriah, Quyterie, Quytery

Qwanisha (American) a form of Quaneisha.
Qwanechia, Qwanesha, Qwanessia, Qwantasha

R

Raanana (Hebrew) fresh; luxuriant.
Ranana, Rananah

Rabecca (Hebrew) a form of Rebecca.
Rabbeca, Rabbecah, Rabbecca, Rabeca,
Rabecka, Rabekah

Rabi (Arabic) breeze.
Raby

Rabia (Arabic) a form of Rabi.
Rabiah, Rabya, Rabyah

Rachael (Hebrew) a form of Rachel.
Rachaele, Rachaell

Rachal (Hebrew) a form of Rachel.
Rachall, Rachalle

Racheal (Hebrew) a form of Rachel.

Rachel (Hebrew) female sheep. Bible:
the second wife of Jacob. See also
Lahela, Rae, Rochelle.
Rachail, Rachela, Rachelann, Rahel, Raiche,
Raichel, Raichele, Raichell, Raichelle,
Raishel, Raishele, Ruchel, Ruchelle

Rachele, Rachell, Rachelle (French)
forms of Rachel. See also Shelley.
Rachella

Racquel (French) a form of Rachel.
Rackel, Racquele, Racquell, Racquella,
Racquelle

Radella (German) counselor.
Radela, Radelah, Radelia, Radeliah,
Radellah, Radelle, Radiliah, Radillia,
Radilliah, Radyla, Radylah, Radyllya,
Radyllyah

Radeyah (Arabic) content, satisfied.
Radeeyah, Radhiya, Radhiyah, Radiah,
Radiyah

Radhika (Indian) beloved. (Swahili)
agreeable.

Radinka (Slavic) full of life; happy, glad.
Radinkah, Radynka, Radynkah

Radmilla (Slavic) worker for the people.
Radmila, Radmilah, Radmile, Radmill,
Radmilla, Radmillah, Radmille, Radmyla,
Radmylah, Radmyle, Radmyll, Radmylla,
Radmyllah, Radmylle

Rae (English) doe. (Hebrew) a short form
of Rachel.
Raeh, Raeneice, Raeneisha, Raesha, Rai,
Raii, Ray, Raycene, Raye, Rayetta, Rayette,
Rayma, Rey

Raeann, Raeanne (American) combina-
tions of Rae + Ann. See also Rayan.
Raea, Raean, Raeane, Raiane, Raiann,
Raianne

Raeanna (American) a combination of
Rae + Anna.
Raeana, Raeanah, Raeannah, Raeona,
Raiana, Raianah, Raianna, Raiannah

Raechel, Raechelle (Hebrew) forms of
Rachel.
Raechael, Raechal, Raechele, Raechell,
Raechyl

Raeden (Japanese) Mythology: Raiden
was the god of thunder and lightning.
Raeda, Raedeen

Raegan (Irish) a form of Reagan.
Raegen, Raegene, Raegine, Raegyn

Raelene (American) a combination of
Rae + Lee.
Rael, Raela, Raelani, Raele, Raeleah,
Raelean, Raeleana, Raeleanah, Raeleane,
Raelee, Raeleen, Raeleena, Raeleenah,
Raeleene, Raeleia, Raeleigh, Raeleigha,
Raelein, Raelennia, Raelesha, Raelin,
Raelina, Raelinah, Raeline, Raelle, Railean,
Raileana, Raileanah, Raileane, Raileen,
Raileena, Raileenah, Raileene, Ralean,
Raleana, Raleanah, Raleane, Raleen,
Raleena, Raleenah, Raleene, Ralin,
Ralina, Ralinah, Raline

Raelyn, Raelynn (American) forms of Raelene.
Raelyna, Raelynah, Raelynda, Raelyne, Raelynne, Railyn, Railyna, Railynah, Railyne, Ralyn, Ralyna, Ralynah, Ralyne

Raena (German) a form of Raina.
Raeinna, Raen, Raenah, Raenee, Raeni, Raenia, Raenie, Raenna, Raeny, Raeonna, Raeyauna, Raeyn, Raeyonna

Raeven (English) a form of Raven.
Raevin, Raevion, Raevon, Raevonna, Raevyn, Raevynne, Raewyn, Raewynne

Rafa (Arabic) happy; prosperous.
Rafah, Raffa, Raffah

Rafaela (Hebrew) a form of Raphaela.
Rafaelah, Rafaelia, Rafaeliah, Rafaella, Rafaellah, Raffaela, Raffaelah, Raffaella, Raffaellah, Rafia, Rafiah, Rafya, Rafyah

Rafaelle (French) a form of Raphaelle.
Rafael, Rafaele, Rafaell, Raffaele, Raffaell, Raffaelle

Ragan, Ragen (Irish) forms of Reagan.
Ragean, Rageane, Rageen, Ragene, Rageni, Ragenna, Raggan

Ragine (English) a form of Regina.
Ragin, Ragina, Raginee

Ragnild (Scandinavian) battle counsel.
Ragna, Ragnah, Ragnel, Ragnela, Ragnele, Ragnell, Ragnella, Ragnelle, Ragnhild, Ragnilda, Ragnildah, Ragnyld, Ragnylda, Renilda, Renilde, Renyld, Renylda, Renylde

Raheem (Punjabi) compassionate God.
Raheema, Rahima

Rahel (German) a form of Rachel.
Rahela, Rahil

Ráidah (Arabic) leader.
Raeda, Raedah, Raida, Rayda, Raydah

Rain, Raine (Latin) short forms of Regina. A form of Raina, Rane.
Raene, Reyne

Raina (German) mighty. (English) a short form of Regina. See also Rayna.

Raheena, Rainah, Rainai, Rainea, Rainia, Rainiah, Rainna, Rainnah, Rainnia, Rainniah

Rainbow (English) rainbow.
Raenbo, Raenbow, Rainbeau, Rainbeaux, Rainbo, Rainebo, Rainebow, Raynbow, Reinbow, Reynbow

Rainee, Rainey, Raini, Rainy (Latin) familiar forms of Regina.
Rainie

Rainelle (English) a combination of Raina + Elle.
Rainel, Rainela, Rainelah, Rainele, Rainell, Rainella, Raynel, Raynela, Raynell, Raynella, Raynelle

Raisa (Russian) a form of Rose.
Raisah, Raissa, Raissah, Raiza, Raysa, Raysah, Rayssa, Rayssah, Rayza, Razia

Raizel (Yiddish) a form of Rose.
Raizela, Raizelah, Raizele, Rayzil, Rayzila, Rayzile, Rayzill, Rayzilla, Rayzille, Rayzyl, Rayzyla, Rayzylah, Rayzyle, Razil, Razila, Razile, Razill, Razilla, Razillah, Razille, Razyl, Razyla, Razylah, Razyle, Razyll, Razylla, Razyllah, Razylle, Reizel, Resel

Raja (Arabic) hopeful.
Raia, Rajaah, Rajae, Rajai

Rajah (Arabic) a form of Raja.

Rajani (Hindi) evening.
Rajanee, Rajaney, Rajanie, Rajany

Raku (Japanese) pleasure.

Raleigh, Raley (Irish) forms of Riley.
Ralea, Raleiah

Rama (Hebrew) lofty, exalted. (Hindi) godlike. Religion: an incarnation of the Hindu god Vishnu.
Ramah

Raman (Spanish) a form of Ramona.

Ramandeep (Sikh) covered by the light of the Lord's love.

Ramla (Swahili) fortuneteller.
Ramlah

Ramona (Spanish) mighty; wise protector. See also Mona.
Raemona, Raimona, Raimonah, Raimone, Ramonda, Raymona, Raymonah, Romona, Romonda

Ramosa (Latin) branch.
Ramosah, Ramose

Ramsey (English) ram's island.
Ramsha, Ramsi, Ramsie, Ramza

Ramya (Hindi) beautiful, elegant.
Ramia, Ramiah, Ramyah

Ran (Japanese) water lily. (Scandinavian) destroyer. Mythology: the Norse sea goddess who destroys.

Rana (Sanskrit) royal. (Arabic) gaze, look.
Rahna, Rahnah, Ranah, Ranna, Rannah

Ranait (Irish) graceful; prosperous.
Ranaita, Ranaitah, Ranaite, Ranayt, Ranayta, Ranaytah, Ranayte

Randa (Arabic) tree.
Randah

Randall (English) protected.
Randal, Randala, Randalah, Randale, Randalea, Randaleah, Randalee, Randalei, Randaleigh, Randaley, Randali, Randalie, Randaly, Randel, Randela, Randelah, Randele, Randell, Randella, Randelle, Randilee, Randilynn, Randlyn, Randyl

Randee, Randi, Randie, Randy (English) familiar forms of Miranda, Randall.
Rande, Randea, Randean, Randeana, Randeane, Randeen, Randena, Randene, Randey, Randii, Randin, Randina, Randine, Randyn, Randyna, Randyne

Rane (Scandinavian) queen.
Raen, Raene

Raneisha (American) a combination of Rae + Aisha.

Ranesha (American) a form of Raneisha.

Rangi (Maori) sky.
Rangee, Rangia, Rangiah, Rangie, Rangy

Rani (Sanskrit) queen. (Hebrew) joyful. A short form of Kerani.
Rahnee, Rahney, Rahni, Rahnie, Rahny, Ranee, Raney, Ranice, Ranie, Ranique, Rannee, Ranney, Ranni, Rannie, Ranny, Rany

Rania (Sanskrit, Hebrew) a form of Rani.
Raniah

Ranielle (American) a combination of Rani + Elle.
Rannielle, Rannyelle, Ranyelle

Ranisha (American) a form of Raneisha.

Ranita (Hebrew) song; joyful.
Ranata, Raneata, Raneatah, Raneate, Raneatt, Raneatta, Raneattah, Raneatte, Raneet, Raneeta, Raneetah, Raneete, Ranit, Ranitah, Ranite, Ranitta, Ranittah, Ranitte, Ranyta, Ranytah, Ranyte, Ranytta, Ranyttah, Ranytte, Ronita

Raniyah (Arabic) gazing.
Raniya

Ranya (Sanskrit, Hebrew) a form of Rani. (Arabic) a short form of Raniyah.
Ranyah

Rapa (Hawaiian) moonbeam.
Rapah

Raphaela (Hebrew) healed by God.
Raphaelah, Raphaella, Raphaellah

Raphaelle (French) a form of Raphaela.
Raphael, Raphaele, Raphaell

Raquel, Raquelle (French) forms of Rachel.
Rakel, Rakhil, Rakhila, Raqueal, Raquela, Raquele, Raquell, Raquella, Ricquel, Ricquelle, Rikell, Rikelle, Rockell

Rasha (Arabic) young gazelle.
Rahshea, Rahshia, Rahshiah, Rashae, Rashai, Rashea, Rashi, Rashia, Rashya, Rashyah

Rashanda (American) a form of Rashawna.
Rashunda

Rashawn (American) a short form of Rashawna.
Raseane, Rashane, Rashaun, Rashaune, Rashawne, Rashon

Rashawna (American) a combination of the prefix Ra + Shawna.
Raseana, Raseanah, Rashana, Rashanae, Rashanah, Rashani, Rashanna, Rashanta, Rashauna, Rashaunah, Rashaunda, Rashaundra, Rashawnah, Rashawnna, Rashona

Rashawnda (American) a form of Rashawna.

Rasheda (Swahili) a form of Rashida.
Rasheada, Rasheadah, Rashedah, Rasheeda, Rasheedah, Rasheeta, Rasheida

Rashel, Rashell, Rashelle (American) forms of Rachel.
Raeshelle, Raishell, Raishelle, Rashele, Rashella, Rayshel, Rayshele, Rayshell, Rayshelle

Rashida (Swahili, Turkish) righteous.
Rahshea, Rahsheda, Rahsheita, Rashdah, Rashidah, Rashidee, Rashidi, Rashidie, Rashyda, Rashydah

Rashieka (Arabic) descended from royalty.
Rasheeka, Rasheekah, Rasheika, Rasheka, Rashekah, Rashika, Rashikah, Rasika, Rasike, Rasiqua, Rasiquah, Rasyqua, Rasyquah, Rasyque

Rashonda (American) a form of Rashawna.

Rasia (Greek) rose.
Rasiah, Rasya, Rasyah

Ratana (Tai) crystal.
Ratania, Rataniah, Ratanya, Ratna, Ratnah, Rattan, Rattana, Rattane

Ratri (Hindi) night. Religion: the goddess of the night.
Ratree, Ratrey, Ratria, Ratriah, Ratrie, Ratry, Ratrya, Ratryah

Raula (French) wolf counselor.
Raolah, Raole, Raoula, Raulla, Raullah, Raulle

Raveen (English) a form of Raven.
Raveene, Raveenn

Raveena (English) a form of Raven.
Raveenah

Raven (English) blackbird.
Raivan, Raiven, Raivin, Raivyn, Ravan, Ravana, Ravanah, Ravanna, Ravannah, Ravena, Ravenah, Ravene, Ravenn, Ravenna, Ravennah, Ravenne, Raveon, Revena

Ravin, Ravon, Ravyn (English) forms of Raven.
Ravi, Ravina, Ravinah, Ravine, Ravinne, Ravion, Ravyna, Ravynah, Ravyne, Ravynn

Rawan (Gypsy) a form of Rawnie.

Rawnie (Gypsy) fine lady.
Rawna, Rawnah, Rawnee, Rawney, Rawni, Rawnia, Rawniah, Rawnii, Rawny, Rawnya, Rawnyah, Rhawna, Rhawnah, Rhawnee, Rhawney, Rhawni, Rhawnie, Rhawny, Rhawnya, Rhawnyah

Raya (Hebrew) friend.
Raia, Raiah, Raiya, Rayah

Rayan, Rayann, Rayanne (American) forms of Raeann.
Ray-Ann, Rayane, Reyan, Reyann, Reyanne

Rayanna (American) a form of Raeanna.
Rayana, Rayanah, Rayannah, Rayeanna, Reyana, Reyanna

Raychel, Raychelle (Hebrew) forms of Rachel.
Raychael, Raychela, Raychele, Raychell, Raychil

Rayelle (American) a form of Raylyn.
Rayel, Rayele

Raylee (American) a familiar form of Raylyn.
Rayleigh

Rayleen, Raylene (American) forms of Raylyn.
Raylean, Rayleana, Rayleanah, Rayleane, Rayleena, Rayleenah, Rayleene, Raylena, Rayline

Raylyn, Raylynn (American) combinations of Rae + Lyn.
Raylin, Raylina, Raylinah, Raylinn, Raylona, Raylyna, Raylynah, Raylyne, Raylynne

Raymonde (German) wise protector.
Raemond, Raemonda, Raemondah,
Raemonde, Raimond, Raimonda,
Raimondah, Raimonde, Rayma, Raymae,
Raymay, Raymie, Raymond, Raymonda,
Raymondah

Rayna (Scandinavian) mighty. (Yiddish)
pure, clean. (English) king's advisor.
(French) a familiar form of Lorraine.
See also Raina.
Raynah, Raynel, Raynell, Raynella,
Raynelle, Raynette, Rayney, Rayni, Raynia,
Rayniah, Raynie, Rayny, Raynya, Raynyah

Rayne (Scandinavian, Yiddish, French) a
form of Rane, Rayna.
Rayn

Raynisha (American) a form of Raneisha.

Rayonna (American) a form of Raeanna.
Rayona

Rayven (English) a form of Raven.
Rayvan, Rayvana, Rayvein, Rayvenne,
Rayveona, Rayvin, Rayvon, Rayvonia

Rayya (Arabic) thirsty no longer.

Razi (Aramaic) secretive.
Rayzil, Rayzilee, Raz, Razia, Raziah,
Raziela, Razilea, Razileah, Razilee,
Razilei, Razileigh, Raziley, Razili,
Razilia, Raziliah, Razilie, Razilla,
Razillah, Razille, Razyl, Razyla, Razylah,
Razylea, Razyleah, Razylee, Razylei,
Razyleigh, Razyley, Razyli, Razylia,
Razyliah, Razylie, Razyly

Raziya (Swahili) agreeable.
Raziyah

Rea (Greek) poppy flower.
Reah

Reagan (Irish) little ruler.
Raygan, Raygen, Raygene, Rayghan,
Raygin, Reagen, Reaghan, Reagin, Reagine,
Reagon, Reagyn, Reigan, Reigana, Reiganah,
Reigane, Reygan, Reygana, Reyganah,
Reygane

Reanna (German, English) a form of
Raina. (American) a form of Raeann.

Reana, Reanah, Reannah, Reeana Reiana,
Reianah, Reianna, Reiannah, Reyana,
Reyanah, Reyanna, Reyannah

Reanne (American) a form of Raeann,
Reanna.
Rean, Reane, Reann, Reannan, Reannen,
Reannon, Reian, Reiane, Reiann, Reianne,
Reyan, Reyane, Reyann, Reyanne

Reba (Hebrew) fourth-born child. A short
form of Rebecca. See also Reva, Riva.
Rabah, Reaba, Reabah, Rebah, Reeba,
Reebah, Reiba, Reibah, Reyba, Reybah,
Rheba, Rhebah, Rheiba, Rheibah, Rheyba,
Rheybah

Rebbecca, Rebeca, Rebeccah (Hebrew)
forms of Rebecca.
Rebbeca, Rebbecah, Rebecah

Rebecca (Hebrew) tied, bound. Bible: the
wife of Isaac. See also Becca, Becky.
Rebeccea, Rebecha, Rebecqua, Rebecquah,
Rebequa, Rebequah, Rebeque

Rebecka, Rebeckah (Hebrew) forms of
Rebecca.
Rebeccka, Rebecckah, Rebeckia, Rebecky

Rebekah, Rebekka, Rebekkah (Hebrew)
forms of Rebecca.
Rebeka, Rebekha, Rebekke

Rebi (Hebrew) a familiar form of
Rebecca.
Rebbie, Rebe, Rebie, Reby, Ree, Reebie

Reed (English) a form of Reid.
Raeed, Rheed

Reem (Arabic) a short form of Rima.

Reema, Reemah (Arabic) forms of Rima.
Reama, Reamah, Rema, Remah

Reena (Greek) peaceful. (English) a form
of Rina. (Hebrew) a form of Rinah.
Reen, Reenah, Reene, Reenia, Reeniah,
Reenie, Reeny, Reenya, Reenyah

Reet (Estonian) a form of Margaret.
Reat, Reata, Reatah, Reate, Reatha, Reeta,
Reetah, Reete, Reit, Reita, Reitah, Reite,
Reta, Retha, Reyt, Reyta, Reytah, Reyte

Regan, Reganne (Irish) forms of Reagan.
*Regana, Reganah, Regane, Regann,
Reganna, Regannah, Regen, Regin*

Reggie (English) a familiar form of
Regina.
Reggi, Reggy, Regi, Regia, Regiah, Regie

Reghan (Irish) a form of Reagan.

Regina (Latin) queen. (English) king's
advisor. Geography: the capital of
Saskatchewan. See also Gina.
*Raegina, Rega, Regeana, Regeanah, Regeena,
Regeenah, Regena, Regennia, Regiena,
Reginah, Reginia, Regis, Regyna, Regynah,
Reygina, Reyginah, Reygyna, Reygynah*

Regine (Latin) a form of Regina.
*Regeane, Regeene, Regin, Regyne, Reygin,
Reygine, Reygyn, Reygyne*

Rei (Japanese) polite, well behaved.

Reid (English) redhead.
Read, Reide, Reyd, Reyde, Ried

Reiko (Japanese) grateful.
Reyko

Reilly (Irish) a form of Riley.
Reilee, Reileigh, Reiley, Reili, Reilley, Reily

Reina (Spanish) a short form of Regina.
See also Reyna.
*Rein, Reinah, Reine, Reinie, Reinna,
Reiny, Reiona, Renia*

Rekha (Hindi) thin line.
*Reka, Rekah, Rekia, Rekiah, Rekiya,
Rekiyah*

Remedios (Spanish) remedy.

Remi (French) from Rheims, France.
*Raymi, Reims, Remee, Remey, Remia,
Remiah, Remie, Remmee, Remmi, Remmia,
Remmiah, Remmie*

Remington (English) raven estate.
Remmington

Remy (French) a form of Remi.
Remmey, Remmy

Ren (Japanese) arranger; water lily; lotus.

Rena (Hebrew) song; joy. A familiar form
of Irene, Regina, Renata, Sabrina, Serena.
Renah

Renae (French) a form of Renée.
*Renai, Renaia, Renaiah, Renay, Renaya,
Renaye, Rennae, Rennay, Rennaya,
Rennaye, Wrenae, Wrenai, Wrenay,
Wrennae, Wrennai, Wrennay*

Renata (French) a form of Renée.
*Ranata, Reinet, Reineta, Reinete, Reinett,
Reinetta, Reinette, Renada, Renatah,
Renate, Renatta, Reneata, Reneatah,
Rennie, Renyatta, Rinada, Rinata*

Rene (Greek) a short form of Irene,
Renée.
Reen, Reene, Renne

Renea (French) a form of Renée.
Reneah, Rennea, Renneah

Renee (French) a form of Renée.

Renée (French) born again.
Reenee, Reeney, Reneigh, Rennee, Rinee

Reneisha (American) a form of Raneisha.

Renelle (French) a form of Renée.
Renell

Renesha (American) a form of Raneisha.

Renisha (American) a form of Raneisha.

Renita (French) a form of Renata.
*Reneeta, Reneetae, Reneetah, Reneita,
Reneitah, Renetta, Renitah, Renitta,
Renittah, Renitte, Renitza, Renyta,
Renytah, Renyte*

Rennie (English) a familiar form of
Renata.
*Reenie, Reney, Reni, Renie, Renney, Renni,
Renny, Reny*

Reseda (Spanish) fragrant mignonette
blossom.
*Reseada, Reseadah, Reseeda, Reseedah,
Resedah, Resida, Residah, Resyda, Resydah,
Seda, Sedah*

Reshawna (American) a combination of
the prefix Re + Shawna.
*Resaunna, Reschauna, Reschaunah,
Reschaune, Reschawna, Reschawnah,
Reschawne, Rescheana, Rescheanah,
Rescheane, Reseana, Reseanah, Reshana,
Reshauna, Reshaunah, Reshaunda,*

Reshawnah, Reshawnda, Reshawnna,
Reshonda, Reshonn, Reshonta

Resi (German) a familiar form of Theresa.
Resee, Resey, Resia, Resie, Ressa, Resse,
Ressee, Ressi, Ressie, Ressy, Resy, Reza,
Rezee, Rezey, Rezi, Rezie, Rezka, Rezy,
Rezzee, Rezzey, Rezzi, Rezzie, Rezzy

Reta (African) shaken.
Reata, Reatah, Reate, Reatee, Reatey, Reati,
Reatie, Reatta, Reattah, Reaty, Reita, Reitah,
Reitta, Reittah, Retah, Retee, Retey, Retta,
Rettah, Reyta, Reytah, Reytta, Reyttah,
Rheata, Rheatah, Rheta, Rhetah, Rhetta,
Rhettah

Retha (Greek) a short form of Aretha.
Reatha, Reitha, Rethah, Rethia, Rethiah,
Rethya, Rethyah, Reti, Retie, Rety, Ritha

Reubena (Hebrew) behold a child.
Reubina, Reubinah, Reuvena, Reuvenah,
Rubena

Reva (Latin) revived. (Hebrew) rain;
one-fourth. A form of Reba, Riva.
Reava, Reavah, Ree, Reeva, Reevah, Revah,
Revia, Reviah, Revida, Revidah, Revya,
Revyah, Revyda, Revydah

Reveca, Reveka (Slavic) forms of Rebecca,
Rebekah.
Reve, Revecca, Reveccah, Revecka, Reveckah,
Revekah, Revekka

Rewuri (Australian) spring.
Rewuree, Rewurey, Rewurie, Rewury

Rexanne (American) queen.
Rexan, Rexana, Rexanah, Rexane,
Rexann, Rexanna, Rexannah, Rexanne

Reyhan (Turkish) sweet-smelling flower.
Reihan, Reihana, Reihanah, Reihane,
Reyhana, Reyhanah, Reyhane

Reyna (Greek) peaceful. (English) a form
of Reina.
Reyn, Reynah, Reyne, Reynee, Reyni,
Reynie, Reynna, Reyny

Reynalda (German) king's advisor.
Reinald, Reinalda, Reinaldah, Reinalde,
Reynaldah, Reynalde

Réz (Latin, Hungarian) copper-colored
hair.
Res, Rezz

Reza (Czech) a form of Theresa.
Rezah, Rezi, Rezie, Rezka, Rezza, Rezzah

Rhea (Greek) brook, stream. Mythology:
the mother of Zeus.
Rheá, Rhéa, Rheah, Rhealyn, Rhia

Rheanna (Greek) a form of Rhea.
Rheana, Rheanah, Rheannah, Rheeanna,
Rheeannah

Rheannon (Welsh) a form of Rhiannon.
Rheanan, Rheannan, Rheannin, Rheanon

Rhedyn (Welsh) fern.
Readan, Readen, Readin, Readon, Readyn,
Reedan, Reeden, Reedin, Reedon, Reedyn,
Rheadan, Rheaden, Rheadin, Rheadon,
Rheadyn, Rhedan, Rhedin, Rhedon,
Rheedan, Rheeden, Rheedin, Rheedon,
Rheedyn

Rhian (Welsh) a short form of Rhiannon.
Rheane, Rheann, Rheanne, Rheean,
Rheeane, Rheeann, Rheeanne, Rhiane,
Rhiann, Rhianne

Rhiana, Rhianna (Greek) forms of
Rheanna. (Welsh) forms of Rhian.
(Arabic) forms of Rihana.
Rhianah, Rhiannah, Rhiauna

Rhiannon (Welsh) witch; nymph; goddess.
Rhianen, Rhiannan, Rhiannen, Rhianon,
Rhianwen, Rhianyn, Rhinnon, Rhyanan,
Riannon, Rianon, Ryanan, Ryanen,
Ryanin, Ryanyn

Rhoda (Greek) from Rhodes, Greece.
Rhodah, Rhodeia, Rhodia, Rhodiah,
Rhodya, Rhodyah, Roda, Rodina

Rhodelia (Greek) rosy.
Rhodeliah, Rhodelya, Rhodelyah, Rodelia,
Rodeliah, Rodelya, Rodelyah

Rhody (Greek) rose.
Rhode, Rhodea, Rhodee, Rhodey, Rhodi,
Rhodie, Rhody, Rodi, Rodie

Rhona (Scottish) powerful, mighty.
(English) king's advisor.
Rhonae, Rhonnie

Rhonda (Welsh) grand.
Rhondah, Rhondene, Rhondia, Rhondiah, Rhondiesha, Rhondya, Rhondyah, Ronelle, Ronnette

Rhonwyn (Irish) a form of Bronwyn.
Rhonwena, Rhonwenah, Rhonwin, Rhonwina, Rhonwinah, Rhonwine, Rhonwinn, Rhonwinna, Rhonwinnah, Rhonwinne, Rhonwyna, Rhonwynah, Rhonwyne, Rhonwynn, Rhonwynna, Rhonwynnah, Rhonwynne, Ronwen, Ronwena, Ronwenah, Ronwene, Ronwin, Ronwina, Ronwinah, Ronwine, Ronwyn, Ronwyna, Ronwynah, Ronwyne, Ronwynn, Ronwynna, Ronwynnah, Ronwynne

Rhyan (Welsh) a form of Rhian.
Rhyane, Rhyann, Rhyanne

Rhyanna (Greek) a form of Rheanna.
Rhyana, Rhyanah, Rhyannah

Ria (Spanish) river.
Rhia, Rhiah, Rhya, Rhyah, Riah, Rya, Ryah

Rian, Riane, Rianne (Welsh) forms of Rhian.
Riann, Riayn, Rioann, Rioanne

Riana, Rianna (Irish) short forms of Briana. (Arabic) forms of Rihana.
Rianah, Riannah

Rica (Spanish) a short form of Erica, Frederica, Ricarda. See also Enrica, Sandrica, Terica, Ulrica.
Rhica, Rhicah, Rhicca, Rhiccah, Rhyca, Rhycah, Ricah, Ricca, Riccah, Ricka, Rickah, Rieca, Riecka, Rieka, Riqua, Riquah, Ryca, Rycah, Rycca, Ryccah, Rycka, Ryckah, Ryqua, Ryquah

Ricadonna (Italian) a combination of Ricarda + Donna.
Ricadona, Ricadonah, Ricadonnah, Riccadona, Riccadonah, Riccadonna, Riccadonnah, Rickadona, Rickadonah, Rickadonna, Rickadonnah, Rikadona, Rikadonah, Rikadonna, Rikadonnah, Rycadona, Rycadonah, Rycadonna, Rycadonnah, Ryckadona, Ryckadonah, Ryckadonna, Ryckadonnah, Rykadona, Rykadonah, Rykadonna, Rykadonnah

Ricarda (Spanish) rich and powerful ruler.
Riccarda, Riccardah, Richanda, Richarda, Richardah, Richardena, Richardina, Richena, Richenza, Richi, Rickarda, Rickardah, Rikarda, Rikardah, Ritcarda, Ritcharda, Rycadra, Rycardah, Rycharda, Rychardah, Ryckarda, Ryckardah, Rykarda, Rykardah

Ricci (American) a familiar form of Erica, Frederica, Ricarda. See also Ricki, Riki.
Riccy, Rici, Ricquie, Rique, Ryckee, Ryckey, Rycki, Ryckie, Rykee, Rykey, Ryki, Rykie, Ryky

Richa (Spanish) a form of Rica.

Richael (Irish) saint.
Ricael, Rickael, Rikael, Rycael, Ryckael, Rykael

Richelle (German, French) a form of Ricarda.
Richel, Richela, Richelah, Richele, Richell, Richella, Richellah, Richia, Rishel, Rishela, Rishelah, Rishele, Rishell, Rishella, Rishellah, Rishelle, Rychel, Rychela, Rychelah, Rychele, Rychell, Rychella, Rychellah, Rychelle, Ryshel, Ryshela, Ryshelah, Ryshele, Ryshell, Ryshella, Ryshellah, Ryshelle

Rickelle (American) a form of Raquel.
Rickel, Rickela, Rickell

Ricki, Rickie (American) familiar forms of Erica, Frederica, Ricarda. See also Ricci, Riki.
Rickee, Rickey, Rickilee, Ricky

Rickia (American) a form of Ricki.
Rickina, Rickita, Rikia, Rikita, Rikkia

Rickma (Hebrew) woven.
Rickmah, Ricma, Ricmah, Ryckma, Ryckmah, Rycma, Rycmah, Rykma, Rykmah

Ricquel (American) a form of Raquel.
Rickquel, Rickquell, Ricquelle, Rikell, Rikelle

Rida (Arabic) favored by God.
Ridah, Ryda, Rydah

Rihana (Arabic) sweet basil. See also Rhiana, Riana.

Rika (Swedish) ruler.
Rhika, Rhikah, Rhikka, Rhikkah, Rikah, Rikka, Rikkah, Ryka, Rykah, Rykka, Rykkah

Riki, Rikki (American) familiar forms of Erica, Frederica, Ricarda. See also Ricci, Ricki.
Rikee, Rikey, Rikie, Rikka, Rikke, Rikkee, Rikkey, Rikkie, Rikky, Riko, Riky

Rilee, Rileigh (Irish) forms of Riley.

Riley (Irish) valiant. See also Rylee.
Rielee, Rieley, Rielle, Rielly, Riely, Rilea, Rileah, Rilei, Rili, Rilie, Rily

Rilla (German) small brook.
Rhila, Rhilah, Rhilla, Rhillah, Rhyla, Rhylah, Rhylla, Rhyllah, Rila, Rilah, Rillah, Ryla, Rylah, Rylla, Ryllah

Rim (Arabic) a short form of Rima.

Rima (Arabic) white antelope.
Rheama, Rheamah, Rheema, Rheemah, Rheyma, Rheymah, Rhima, Rhimah, Rhime, Rhyma, Rhymah, Rhymia, Rimah, Ryma, Rymah

Rimona (Hebrew) pomegranate. See also Mona.
Reamona, Reamonah, Reamone, Reemona, Reemonah, Reemone, Remona, Remonah, Remone, Rheimona, Rheimonah, Rheimone, Rheymona, Rheymonah, Rheymone, Rhimona, Rhimonah, Rhimone, Rhymona, Rhymonah, Rhymone, Rimonah, Rimone, Rymona, Rymonah, Rymone

Rin (Japanese) park. Geography: a Japanese village.
Rini, Ryn, Rynn, Ryny

Rina (English) a short form of names ending in "rina." (Hebrew) a form of Rena, Rinah.
Rheena, Rheenah, Rinea, Riney, Rini, Rinie, Rinn, Rinna, Rinnah, Rinne, Rinnee, Rinney, Rinni, Rinnie, Rinny, Riny, Ryna, Ryne, Rynea, Rynee, Ryney, Ryni, Rynie, Ryny

Rinah (Hebrew) joyful.
Rynah

Rio (Spanish) river. Geography: Rio de Janeiro is a seaport in Brazil.
Ryo

Riona (Irish) saint.
Reaona, Reaonah, Reeona, Reeonah, Reona, Reonah, Rheaona, Rheaonah, Rheeona, Rheeonah, Rheiona, Rheionah, Rheona, Rheonah, Rheyona, Rheyonah, Rhiona, Rhionah, Rhyona, Rhyonah, Rionah, Ryona, Ryonah

Risa (Latin) laughter.
Reasa, Reasah, Reesa, Reesah, Reisa, Reisah, Resa, Resah, Risah, Rysa, Rysah

Risha (Hindi) Vrishabha is another name for the zodiac sign Taurus.
Rishah, Rishay, Rysha, Ryshah

Rishona (Hebrew) first.
Rishina, Rishon, Rishonah, Ryshona, Ryshonah

Rissa (Greek) a short form of Nerissa.
Rissah, Ryssa, Ryssah

Rita (Sanskrit) brave; honest. (Greek) a short form of Margarita.
Reda, Reeta, Reetah, Reetta, Reettah, Reida, Rheeta, Rheetah, Riet, Ritah, Ritamae, Ritamarie, Ritta, Rittah, Ryta, Rytah, Rytta, Ryttah

Ritsa (Greek) a familiar form of Alexandra.
Ritsah, Ritsi, Ritsie, Ritsy, Rytsa, Rytsah

Riva (French) river bank. (Hebrew) a short form of Rebecca. See also Reba, Reva.
Rivah, Rivalee, Rivi, Rivvy, Ryva, Ryvah

Rivalea (American) a combination of Riva + Lea.
Rivaleah, Rivalee, Rivalei, Rivaleigh, Rivaley, Rivali, Rivalia, Rivaliah, Rivaly, Rivalya, Rivalyah, Riverlea, Riverleah, Ryvalea, Ryvaleah, Ryvalee, Ryvalei, Ryvaleigh, Ryvali, Ryvalia, Ryvaliah, Ryvalie, Ryvaly, Ryvalya, Ryvalyah

River (Latin, French) stream, water.
Rivana, Rivanah, Rivane, Rivanna, Rivannah, Rivanne, Rivers, Riviane, Ryvana, Ryvanah, Ryvane, Ryvanna, Ryvannah, Ryvanne, Ryver

Rivka (Hebrew) a short form of Rebecca.
Rivca, Rivcah, Rivkah, Ryvka, Ryvkah

Riza (Greek) a form of Theresa.
*Riesa, Riesah, Rizah, Rizus, Rizza,
Rizzah, Ryza, Ryzah, Ryzza, Ryzzah*

Roanna (American) a form of Rosana.
*Ranna, Rhoanna, Rhoannah, Roan, Roana,
Roanae, Roanah, Roanda, Roane, Roann,
Roannae, Roannah, Roanne*

Robbi, Robbie (English) familiar forms
of Roberta.
Robby, Robbye, Robey, Robi, Robia, Roby

Robert (English) famous brilliance.

Roberta (English) a form of Robert. See
also Bobbette, Bobbi, Robin.
*Roba, Robertah, Robertena, Robertha,
Robertina, Robette, Robettia, Robettiah,
Roburta, Roburtah, Ryberta, Rybertah,
Ruperta*

Robin (English) robin. A form of Roberta.
*Rebin, Rebina, Rebinah, Rebine, Rebyn,
Rebyna, Rebynah, Rebyne, Robann,
Robban, Robbana, Robbanah, Robbane,
Robben, Robbena, Robbenah, Robbene,
Robbin, Robbina, Robbinah, Robbine,
Robbon, Robeen, Roben, Robena, Robenah,
Robenia, Robeniah, Robian, Robina,
Robinah, Robine, Robinia, Robiniah,
Robinn, Robon*

Robinette (English) a familiar form of
Robin.
*Robernetta, Robinatta, Robinet, Robinett,
Robinetta, Robinita, Robinta, Robynett,
Robynetta, Robynette*

Robyn, Robynn (English) forms of
Robin.
*Robbyn, Robbyna, Robbynah, Robbyne,
Robbynn, Robyna, Robyne, Robynne*

Rochel (Hebrew, French) a form of
Rochelle.

Rochelle (French) large stone. (Hebrew)
a form of Rachel. See also Shelley.
*Reshelle, Roch, Rocheal, Rochealle, Rochele,
Rochell, Rochella, Rochette, Rockelle, Rohcell,
Rohcelle, Roshel, Roshele, Roshell, Roshelle*

Rocio (Spanish) dewdrops.
Rocío, Rocyo

Roderica (German) famous ruler.
*Rodericka, Roderik, Roderika, Roderocah,
Roderyc, Roderyca, Roderycah, Roderyck,
Roderycka, Roderyka, Rodreicka, Rodricka,
Rodrika*

Rodnae (English) island clearing.
*Rodna, Rodnah, Rodnai, Rodnay, Rodneta,
Rodnete, Rodnett, Rodnetta, Rodnette,
Rodnicka*

Rodneisha (American) a combination of
Rodnae + Aisha.
*Rodesha, Rodisha, Rodishah, Rodnecia,
Rodneycia, Rodneysha*

Rodnesha (American) a form of
Rodneisha.
Rodneshia

Rodnisha (American) a form of
Rodneisha.

Rohana (Hindi) sandalwood. (American)
a combination of Rose + Hannah.
*Rochana, Rochanah, Rohan, Rohanah,
Rohane, Rohanna, Rohannah, Rohanne,
Rohena, Rohenah*

Rohini (Hindi) woman.
*Rohine, Rohiney, Rohinie, Rohiny, Rohynee,
Rohyney, Rohyni, Rohynie, Rohyny*

Roisin (Irish) a short form of Roisina.
Roisine, Roisyn, Roisyne, Roysyn, Roysyne

Roisina (Irish) rose.
*Roisinah, Roisyna, Roisynah, Roysyna,
Roysynah*

Rolanda (German) famous throughout
the land.
*Ralna, Rolandah, Rolande, Rolandia,
Rolandiah, Rolando, Rolandya, Rolandyah,
Rolaunda, Roleesha, Rolinda, Rollande*

Rolene (German) a form of Rolanda.
Rolaine, Rolena, Rolleen, Rollene

Rolonda (German) a form of Rolanda.

Roma (Latin) from Rome.
*Romah, Romai, Rome, Romeise, Romeka,
Romesha, Rometta, Romini, Romma,
Romola*

Romaine (French) from Rome.
Romain, Romaina, Romainah, Romana,
Romanah, Romanda, Romanel, Romanela,
Romanele, Romanella, Romanelle, Romania,
Romanique, Romany, Romayna, Romaynah,
Romayne, Romina, Rominah, Romine,
Romona, Romonia, Romyn, Romyna,
Romynah, Romyne

Romelda (German) Roman fighter.
Romeld, Romeldah, Romelde, Romilda,
Romildah, Romilde, Romildia, Romildiah,
Romylda, Romyldah, Romylde

Romia (Hebrew) praised.
Romiah, Romya, Romyah

Romola (Latin) a form of Roma.
Romel, Romela, Romelah, Romele, Romell,
Romella, Romellah, Romelle, Romellia,
Romelliah, Romila, Romilah, Romile,
Romilla, Romillah, Romille, Romillia,
Romolah, Romole, Romolla, Romollah,
Romolle, Romyla, Romylah, Romyle,
Romylla, Romyllah, Romylle

Romy (French) a familiar form of
Romaine. (English) a familiar form of
Rosemary.
Romee, Romey, Romi, Romie

Rona, Ronna (Scandinavian) short forms
of Ronalda.
Ronah, Ronalee, Ronnae, Ronnah, Ronnay,
Ronne, Ronsy

Ronaele (Greek) the name Eleanor
spelled backwards.

Ronalda (Scottish) powerful, mighty.
(English) king's advisor.
Rhonalda, Rhonaldah, Rhonaldia,
Rhonaldiah, Ronaldah, Ronaldia,
Ronaldiah, Ronaldya, Ronaldyah

Ronda (Welsh) a form of Rhonda.
Rondah, Rondai, Rondesia, Rondi, Rondie,
Ronelle, Ronnette

Rondelle (French) short poem.
Rhondelle, Rondel, Ronndelle

Roneisha (American) a combination of
Rhonda + Aisha.
Roneasha, Ronecia, Roneeka, Roneesha,
Roneice, Ronese, Ronessa, Ronesse,

Roneysha, Roniesha, Ronneisha, Ronnesa,
Ronniesha, Ronnysha, Ronysha

Ronelle (Welsh) a form of Rhonda,
Ronda.
Ranell, Ranelle, Ronel, Ronela, Ronelah,
Ronele, Ronell, Ronella, Ronielle, Ronnel,
Ronnela, Ronnele, Ronnell, Ronnella,
Ronnelle

Ronesha (American) a form of Roneisha.
Ronnesha

Roneshia (American) a form of Roneisha.
Ronesia, Ronessia, Ronneshia

Roni, Ronni, Ronnie, Ronny (American)
familiar forms of Veronica and names
beginning with "Ron."
Rone, Ronea, Ronee, Roney, Ronia,
Roniah, Ronie, Ronnee, Ronney, Rony,
Ronya, Ronyah, Ronye

Ronica, Ronika, Ronique (Latin) short
forms of Veronica.
Ronicah, Ronikah, Roniqua, Ronnica,
Ronnicah, Ronnika, Ronnikah

Ronisha, Ronnisha (American) forms of
Roneisha.
Ronice, Ronichia, Ronicia, Ronise, Ronnisa,
Ronnise, Ronnishia

Ronli (Hebrew) joyful.
Ronlea, Ronleah, Ronlee, Ronlei, Ronleigh,
Ronley, Ronlia, Ronliah, Ronlie, Ronly,
Ronnlea, Ronnleah, Ronnlee, Ronnlei,
Ronnleigh, Ronnley, Ronnlia, Ronnliah,
Ronnlie, Ronnly

Ronnette (Welsh) a familiar form of
Rhonda, Ronda.
Ronet, Roneta, Ronetah, Ronete, Ronett,
Ronetta, Ronettah, Ronette, Ronit, Ronita,
Ronnetta, Ronnit, Ronny

Rori, Rory (Irish) famous brilliance;
famous ruler.
Roarea, Roaree, Roarey, Roari, Roarie,
Roary, Rorea, Roree, Roria, Roriah, Rorie,
Rorya, Roryah

Ros (English) a short form of Rosalind,
Rosalyn. See also Roz.

Rosa (Italian, Spanish) a form of Rose.
History: Rosa Parks inspired the

Rosa *(cont.)*
American Civil Rights movement by refusing to give up her bus seat to a white man in Montgomery, Alabama. See also Charo, Roza.
Rosae, Rosah

Rosabel (French) beautiful rose.
Rosabela, Rosabelah, Rosabele, Rosabelia, Rosabell, Rosabella, Rosabellah, Rosabelle, Rosabellia, Rosabelliah, Rosebel, Rosebela, Rosebelah, Rosebele, Rosebell, Rosebella, Rosebellah, Rosebelle, Rosebellia, Rosebelliah, Rozabel, Rozabela, Rozabelah, Rozabele, Rozabell, Rozabella, Rozabellah, Rozabelle, Rozebel, Rozebela, Rozebelah, Rozebele, Rozebell, Rozebella, Rozebellah, Rozebelle

Rosalba (Latin) white rose.
Rosalbah, Roselba

Rosalee, Rosalie (English) forms of Rosalind.
Rosalea, Rosaleen, Rosalei, Rosaleigh, Rosalene, Rosali, Rosalle, Rosaly, Rosealee, Rosealie, Roselee, Roselei, Roseleigh, Roseley, Roseli, Roselie, Rosely, Rosilee, Rosli, Rozalee, Rozalei, Rozaleigh, Rozaley, Rozali, Rozalie, Rozaly, Rozele, Rozlee, Rozlei, Rozleigh, Rozley, Rozli, Rozlie, Rozly

Rosalia (English) a form of Rosalind.
Rosaleah, Rosaliah, Rosalla, Rosallah, Roselea, Roseleah, Roselia, Roseliah, Rozalea, Rozaleah, Rozália, Rozaliah, Rozlea, Rozleah, Rozlia, Rozliah

Rosalina (Spanish) a form of Rosalind.
Rosaleana, Rosaleanah, Rosaleena, Rosaleenah, Rosaleina, Rosaleinah, Rosalinah, Rosalyna, Rosalynah, Rozalaina, Rozalainah, Rozalana, Rozalanah, Rozalina, Rozalinah

Rosalind (Spanish) fair rose.
Rosalinde, Rosalynd, Rosalynde, Roselind, Rozalind, Rozalinde, Rozelynd, Rozelynde, Rozland

Rosalinda (Spanish) a form of Rosalind.
Rosalindah, Rosalynda, Rosalyndah, Roslynda, Roslyndah, Rozalinda, Rozalindah, Rozelynda, Rozelyndah

Rosalva (Latin) a form of Rosalba.

Rosalyn (Spanish) a form of Rosalind.
Rosalean, Rosaleane, Rosaleen, Rosaleene, Rosalein, Rosaleine, Rosalin, Rosaline, Rosalyne, Rosalynn, Rosalynne, Rosilyn, Rozalain, Rozalaine, Rozalan, Rozalane, Rozalin, Rozaline, Rozalyn

Rosamaria (English) a form of Rose Marie.
Rosamarie

Rosamond (German) famous guardian.
Rosamonda, Rosamondah, Rosamonde, Rosiemond, Rozamond, Rozamonda, Rozmond, Rozmonda, Rozmondah

Rosamund (Spanish) a form of Rosamond.
Rosamunda, Rosamundah, Rosamunde, Rosemund, Rosemunda, Rosemundah, Rosiemund, Rosiemunda, Rozmund, Rozmunda, Rozmundah

Rosana, Rosanna, Roseanna (English) combinations of Rose + Anna.
Rosanah, Rosania, Rosaniah, Rosannae, Rosannah, Rosannia, Rosanniah, Roseana, Roseanah, Roseania, Roseaniah, Roseannah, Roseannia, Roseanniah, Rosehanah, Rosehannah, Rosiana, Rosianah, Rosianna, Rosiannah, Rossana, Rossanna, Rosyana, Rosyanah, Rosyanna, Rosyannah, Rozana, Rozanah, Rozanna, Rozannah, Rozannia, Rozanniah, Rozannya, Rozeana, Rozeanah, Rozeanna, Rozeannah, Rozzanna, Rozzannah, Rozzannia, Rozzanniah, Rozzanya, Rozzanyah

Rosangelica (American) a combination of Rose + Angelica.
Rosangelika, Roseangelica, Roseangelika

Rosanne, Roseann, Roseanne (English) combinations of Rose + Ann.
Rosan, Rosane, Rosann, Rose Ann, Rose Anne, Rosean, Roseane, Rosian, Rosiane, Rosiann, Rosianne Rossann, Rossanne, Rosyan, Rosyane, Rosyann, Rosyanne, Rozan, Rozane, Rozann, Rozanne, Rozannie, Rozanny, Rozean, Rozeane, Rozeann, Rozeanne, Rozzann, Rozzanne

Rosario (Filipino, Spanish) rosary.
Rosaria, Rosariah, Rosarie, Rosary,
Rosarya, Rosaryah, Rozaria, Rozariah,
Rozarya, Rozaryah, Rozaryo

Rosaura (Filipino, Spanish) a form of
Rosario.
Rosarah

Rose (Latin) rose. See also Chalina, Raisa,
Raizel, Roza.
Rada, Rasia, Rasine, Rois, Róise, Rosea,
Roses, Rosina, Rosse, Roze, Rozelle

Rose Marie, Rosemarie (English)
combinations of Rose + Marie.
Rosemarea, Rosemaree, Rosemari,
Rosemaria, Rosemariah, Rozmari,
Rozmaria, Rozmariah, Rozmarie

Roselani (Hawaiian) heavenly rose.
Roselana, Roselanah, Roselanea, Roselanee,
Roselaney, Roselania, Roselaniah, Roselanie,
Roselany, Roselanya, Roslanea, Roslanee,
Roslaney, Roslani, Roslania, Roslaniah,
Roslanie, Roslany, Roslanya, Roslanyah

Roseline, Roselyn (Spanish) forms of
Rosalind.
Roselean, Roseleana, Roseleanah, Roseleane,
Roseleen, Roseleena, Roseleenah, Roseleene,
Roselein, Roseleina, Roseleinah, Roseleine,
Roselene, Roselin, Roselina, Roselinah,
Roselyna, Roselynah, Roselyne, Roselynn,
Roselynne, Rozelain, Rozelaina, Rozelainah,
Rozelaine, Rozelan, Rozelana, Rozelanah,
Rozelane, Rozelin, Rozelina, Rozelinah,
Rozeline, Rozelyn, Rozelyna, Rozelynah,
Rozelyne

Rosella (Latin) a form of Rose.
Rosela, Roselah, Rosellah, Rozela, Rozelah,
Rozella, Rozellah, Rozellia, Rozelliah

Rosemary (English) a combination of
Rose + Mary.
Rosemarey, Rosemarya, Rosemaryah,
Rozmary, Rozmarya, Rozmaryah

Rosemonde (French) a form of
Rosamond.
Rosemonda, Rosemondah, Rozmonde,
Rozmunde

Rosetta (Italian) a form of Rose.
Roset, Roseta, Rosetah, Rosete, Rosett,
Rosettah, Rosette, Rozet, Rozeta, Rozetah,
Rozete, Rozett, Rozetta, Rozettah, Rozette

Roshan (Sanskrit) shining light.
Roshaina, Roshainah, Roshaine, Roshana,
Roshanah, Roshane, Roshani, Roshania,
Roshaniah, Roshanie, Roshany, Roshanya,
Roshanyah

Roshawna (American) a combination of
Rose + Shawna.
Roseana, Roseanah, Roseane, Roshanda,
Roshann, Roshanna, Roshanta, Roshaun,
Roshauna, Roshaunah, Roshaunda,
Roshawn, Roshawnah, Roshawnda,
Roshawnna, Rosheen, Rosheena, Rosheene,
Roshona, Roshowna

Roshni (Indian) brighteners.

Roshonda (American) a form of
Roshawna.

Roshunda (American) a form of
Roshawna.

Rosie, Rosy (English) familiar forms of
Rosalind, Rosana, Rose.
Rosea, Roseah, Rosee, Rosey, Rosi, Rosia,
Rosiah, Rosse, Rosya, Rosyah, Rosye,
Rozsi, Rozy

Rosina (English) a familiar form of Rose.
Roseena, Roseenah, Roseene, Rosena,
Rosenah, Rosene, Rosinah, Rosine, Rosyna,
Rosynah, Rosyne, Roxina, Roxinah,
Roxine, Roxyna, Roxynah, Roxyne,
Rozeana, Rozeanah, Rozeane, Rozeena,
Rozeenah, Rozeene, Rozena, Rozenah,
Rozene, Rozina, Rozinah, Rozine,
Rozyna, Rozynah, Rozyne

Rosio (Spanish) a form of Rosie.

Rosita (Spanish) a familiar form of Rose.
Roseat, Roseata, Roseatah, Roseate, Roseet,
Roseeta, Roseetah, Roseete, Rosit, Rositah,
Rosite, Rositt, Rositta, Rosittah, Rositte,
Rosyt, Rosyta, Rosytah, Rosyte, Rozit,
Rozita, Rozitah, Rozite, Rozyt, Rozyta,
Rozytah, Rozyte, Rozytt, Rozytta,
Rozyttah, Rozytte

Roslyn (Scottish) a form of Rossalyn.
Roslain, Roslan, Roslana, Roslanah,
Roslane, Roslin, Roslina, Roslinah, Rosline,
Roslinia, Rosliniah, Roslyne, Roslynn,
Rosslyn, Rosslynn, Rozlain, Rozlayn,
Rozlayna, Rozlin, Rozlina, Rozlinah,
Rozline, Rozlyn, Rozlyna, Rozlynah,
Rozlyne, Rozlynn, Rozlynna, Rozlynnah,
Rozlynne

Rossalyn (Scottish) cape; promontory.
Rosalin, Rosaline, Rosalyne, Rossalin,
Rossaline, Rossalyne, Rosselyn, Rosylin,
Roszaliyn

Rowan (English) tree with red berries.
(Welsh) a form of Rowena.
Rhoan, Rhoane, Rhoann, Rhoanne, Rhoen,
Rhoin, Rhoina, Rhoinah, Rhoine, Rhoinn,
Rhoinna, Rhoinnah, Rhoinne, Rowana,
Rowanah, Rowane, Rowon, Rowona,
Rowonah, Rowone

Rowena (Welsh) fair-haired. (English)
famous friend. Literature: Ivanhoe's
love interest in Sir Walter Scott's novel
Ivanhoe.
Ranna, Row, Rowe, Roweana, Roweanah,
Roweena, Roweenah, Rowein, Roweina,
Rowen, Rowenah, Rowene, Rowin, Rowina,
Rowinah, Rowine, Rowyn, Rowyna,
Rowynah, Rowyne, Rowynn, Rowynna,
Rowynnah, Rowynne

Roxana, Roxanna (Persian) forms of
Roxann.
Rexana, Rexanah, Rexanna, Rexannah,
Rocsana, Roxanah, Roxannah, Roxannia,
Roxanniah, Roxannie, Roxanny

Roxane (Persian) a form of Roxann.

Roxann, Roxanne (Persian) sunrise.
Literature: Roxanne is the heroine of
Edmond Rostand's play *Cyrano de Bergerac.*
Rocxann, Roxan, Roxianne

Roxie, Roxy (Persian) familiar forms of
Roxann.
Roxi

Roya (English) a short form of Royanna.

Royale (English) royal.
Roial, Roiala, Roiale, Roiell, Roielle, Royal,
Royala, Royalene, Royalle, Royel, Royela,

Royele, Royell, Royella, Royelle, Roylee,
Roylene, Ryal, Ryale

Royanna (English) queenly, royal.
Roiana, Roianah, Roiane, Roianna,
Roiannah, Roianne, Royana, Royanah,
Royane, Royannah, Royanne

Roz (English) a short form of Rosalind,
Rosalyn. See also Ros.
Rozz, Rozzey, Rozzi, Rozzie, Rozzy

Roza (Slavic) a form of Rosa.
Rozah, Rozalia, Rozea, Rozeah, Rozelli,
Rozia, Rozsa, Rozsi, Rozyte, Rozza,
Rozzie

Rozelle (Latin) a form of Rose.
Rosel, Rosele, Rosell, Roselle, Rozel,
Rozele, Rozell

Rozene (Native American) rose blossom.
Rozeana, Rozeanah, Rozeane, Rozeena,
Rozeenah, Rozeene, Rozena, Rozenah,
Rozin, Rozina, Rozinah, Rozine, Rozyn,
Rozyna, Rozynah, Rozyne, Ruzena,
Ruzenah, Ruzene

Ruana (Spanish) poncho.
Ruan, Ruanah, Ruane, Ruann, Ruanna,
Ruannah, Ruanne, Ruon

Ruba (French) a form of Ruby.

Rubena (Hebrew) a form of Reubena.
Rubenah, Rubenia, Rubeniah, Rubina,
Rubinah, Rubine, Rubinia, Rubyn,
Rubyna, Rubynah

Rubi (French) a form of Ruby.
Rubbie, Rubia, Rubiah, Rubiann, Rubie

Ruby (French) precious stone.
Rubby, Rube, Rubea, Rubee, Rubetta,
Rubette, Rubey, Rubyann, Rubye

Ruchi (Hindi) one who wishes to please.
Ruchee, Ruchey, Ruchie, Ruchy

Rudee (German) a short form of Rudolfa.
Rudea, Rudeline, Rudey, Rudi, Rudia,
Rudiah, Rudie, Rudina, Rudy, Rudya,
Rudyah

Rudelle (American) a combination of
Rudee + Elle.
Rudel, Rudela, Rudele, Rudell, Rudella,
Rudellah

Rudolfa (German) famous wolf.
Rudolfea, Rudolfee, Rudolfia, Rudolfiah, Rudolphee, Rudolphey, Rudolphia, Rudolphiah

Rudra (Hindi) Religion: another name for the Hindu god Shiva.
Rudrah

Rue (German) famous. (French) street. (English) regretful; strong-scented herbs.
Roo, Ru, Ruey

Ruel (English) path.
Rual, Ruela, Ruelah, Ruele, Ruell, Ruella, Ruellah, Ruelle

Ruffina (Italian) redhead.
Rufeana, Rufeanah, Rufeane, Rufeena, Rufeenah, Rufeene, Rufeine, Rufina, Rufinah, Rufinia, Rufiniah, Rufynia, Rufyniah, Rufynya, Rufynyah, Ruphina, Ruphinah, Ruphinia, Ruphiniah, Ruphyna, Ruphynia, Ruphyniah, Ruphynya, Ruphynyah

Rui (Japanese) affectionate.

Rukan (Arabic) steady; confident.
Rukana, Rukanah, Rukane, Rukann, Rukanna, Rukannah, Rukanne

Rula (Latin, English) ruler.
Rulah, Rular, Rule, Ruler, Rulla, Rullah, Rulor

Rumer (English) gypsy.
Rouma, Roumah, Roumar, Ruma, Rumah, Rumar, Rumor

Runa (Norwegian) secret; flowing.
Runah, Rune, Runna, Runnah, Runne

Ruperta (Spanish) a form of Roberta.

Rupinder (Sanskrit) beautiful.

Ruri (Japanese) emerald.
Ruriko

Rusalka (Czech) wood nymph. (Russian) mermaid.
Rusalkah

Russhell (French) redhead; fox colored.
Rushel, Rushela, Rushelah, Rushele, Rushell, Rushella, Rushellah, Rushelle, Russellynn, Russhel, Russhela, Russhelah, Russhele, Russhella, Russhellah, Russhelle

Rusti (English) redhead.
Russet, Ruste, Rustee, Rustey, Rustie, Rusty

Ruth (Hebrew) friendship. Bible: daughter-in-law of Naomi.
Rooth, Routh, Rueth, Rute, Rutha, Ruthalma, Ruthe, Ruthella, Ruthetta, Ruthina, Ruthine, Ruthven

Ruthann (American) a combination of Ruth + Ann.
Ruthan, Ruthanna, Ruthannah, Ruthanne

Ruthie (Hebrew) a familiar form of Ruth.
Ruthey, Ruthi, Ruthy

Ruza (Czech) rose.
Ruz, Ruze, Ruzena, Ruzenah, Ruzenka, Ruzha, Ruzsa

Ryan, Ryann (Irish) little ruler.
Raiann, Raianne, Rye, Ryen, Ryenne

Ryane, Ryanne (Irish) forms of Ryan.

Ryanna (Irish) a form of Ryan.
Ryana, Ryanah, Ryannah

Ryba (Czech) fish.
Riba, Ribah, Rybah

Rylee (Irish) valiant. See also Riley.
Ryelee, Ryeley, Ryelie, Rylea, Ryleah, Rylei, Ryli, Rylina, Rylly, Ryly, Rylyn

Ryleigh, Ryley, Rylie (Irish) forms of Rylee.
Rylleigh, Ryllie

Ryo (Japanese) dragon.
Ryoko

S

Saarah (Arabic) princess.
Saara, Saarra, Saarrah

Saba (Arabic) morning. (Greek) a form of Sheba.
Sabaah, Sabah, Sabba, Sabbah

Sabi (Arabic) young girl.

Sabina (Latin) a form of Sabine. See also Bina.

Sabina *(cont.)*
Sabena, Sabenah, Sabiny, Saby, Sabyna, Savina, Sebina, Sebinah, Sebyna, Sebynah

Sabine (Latin) History: the Sabine were a tribe in ancient Italy.
Sabeen, Sabene, Sabienne, Sabin, Sabyne, Sebine, Sebyn, Sebyne

Sabiya (Arabic) morning; eastern wind.
Sabaya, Sabayah, Sabea, Sabia, Sabiah, Sabiyah, Sabya, Sabyah

Sable (English) sable; sleek.
Sabel, Sabela, Sabelah, Sabele, Sabella, Sabelle

Sabra (Hebrew) thorny cactus fruit. (Arabic) resting. History: a name for native-born Israelis, who were said to be hard on the outside and soft and sweet on the inside.
Sabara, Sabarah, Sabarra, Sabarrah, Sabera, Sabira, Sabrah, Sabre, Sebra

Sabreen (English) a short form of Sabreena.
Sabreane, Sabreene, Sabrene

Sabreena (English) a form of Sabrina.
Sabreana, Sabreanah, Sabreenah

Sabrena (English) a form of Sabrina.

Sabria (Hebrew, Arabic) a form of Sabra.
Sabrea, Sabreah, Sabree, Sabreea, Sabri, Sabriah, Sabriya

Sabrina (Latin) boundary line. (English) princess. (Hebrew) a familiar form of Sabra. See also Bree, Brina, Rena, Xabrina, Zabrina.
Sabrinah, Sabrinas, Sabrinia, Sabriniah, Sabrinna, Sebree, Subrina

Sabrine (Latin, Hebrew) a short form of Sabrina.
Sabrin

Sabryna (English) a form of Sabrina.
Sabrynah, Sabryne, Sabrynna

Sacha (Russian) a form of Sasha.
Sachah, Sache, Sachia

Sachi (Japanese) blessed; lucky.
Saatchi, Sachie, Sachiko

Sada (Japanese) chaste. (English) a form of Sadie.
Sadá, Sadah, Sadako, Sadda, Saddah

Sadaf (Indian) pearl. (Iranian) seashell.

Sade (Hebrew) a form of Chadee, Sarah, Shardae.
Sáde, Sadea, Saedea, Shadae, Shadai, Shaday

Sadé (Hebrew) a form of Sade.

Sadee (Hebrew) a form of Sade, Sadie.

Sadella (American) a combination of Sade + Ella.
Sadel, Sadela, Sadelah, Sadele, Sadell, Sadellah, Sadelle, Sydel, Sydell, Sydella, Sydelle

Sadhana (Hindi) devoted.
Sadhanah, Sadhanna, Sadhannah

Sadi (Hebrew) a form of Sadie. (Arabic) a short form of Sadiya.

Sadia (Arabic) a form of Sadiya.
Sadiah

Sadie (Hebrew) a familiar form of Sarah. See also Sada.
Saddie, Sadey, Sadiey, Sady, Sadye, Saedee, Saedi, Saedie, Saedy, Saide, Saidea, Saidee, Saidey, Saidi, Saidia, Saidie, Saidy, Seidy

Sadira (Persian) lotus tree. (Arabic) star.
Sadirah, Sadire, Sadra, Sadrah, Sadyra, Sadyrah, Sadyre

Sadiya (Arabic) lucky, fortunate.
Sadiyah, Sadiyyah, Sadya, Sadyah

Sadzi (Carrier) sunny disposition.
Sadzee, Sadzey, Sadzia, Sadziah, Sadzie, Sadzya, Sadzyah

Safa (Arabic) pure.
Safah, Saffa, Saffah

Saffi (Danish) wise.
Safee, Safey, Saffee, Saffey, Saffie, Saffy, Safi, Safie, Safy

Saffron (English) Botany: a plant with purple or white flowers whose orange stigmas are used as a spice.
Saffrona, Saffronah, Saffrone, Safron, Safrona, Safronah, Safrone, Safronna, Safronnah, Safronne

Safia (Arabic) a form of Safiya.
Safiah

Safiya (Arabic) pure; serene; best friend.
Safeia, Safeya, Safiyah

Sagara (Hindi) ocean.
Sagarah

Sage (English) wise. Botany: an herb used as a seasoning.
Saeg, Saege, Sagia, Sayg, Sayge

Sahar, Saher (Arabic) short forms of Sahara.
Saheer

Sahara (Arabic) desert; wilderness.
Saharah, Sahari, Saharra, Saharrah, Sahira

Sahra (Hebrew) a form of Sarah.
Sahrah

Sai (Japanese) talented.
Saiko, Say

Saida (Arabic) happy; fortunate. (Hebrew) a form of Sarah.
Saeda, Saedah, Said, Saidah, Saide, Saidea, Sayda, Saydah

Saige (English) a form of Sage.
Saig

Saira (Hebrew) a form of Sara.
Sairah, Sairi

Sakaë (Japanese) prosperous.
Sakai, Sakaie, Sakay

Sakari (Hindi) sweet.
Sakara, Sakarah, Sakaree, Sakari, Sakaria, Sakariah, Sakarie, Sakary, Sakarya, Sakaryah, Sakkara, Sakkarah

Saki (Japanese) cloak; rice wine.
Sakee, Sakia, Sakiah, Sakie, Saky, Sakya, Sakyah

Sakina (Indian) friend. (Muslim) tranquility, calmness.
Sakinah

Sakti (Hindi) energy, power.
Saktea, Saktee, Saktey, Saktia, Saktiah, Saktie, Sakty, Saktya, Saktyah

Sakuna (Native American) bird.
Sakunah

Sakura (Japanese) cherry blossom; wealthy; prosperous.
Sakurah

Sala (Hindi) sala tree. Religion: the sacred tree under which Buddha died.
Salah, Salla, Sallah

Salali (Cherokee) squirrel.
Salalea, Salaleah, Salalee, Salalei, Salaleigh, Salalia, Salaliah, Salalie, Salaly, Salalya, Salalyah

Salama (Arabic) peaceful. See also Zulima.
Salamah

Saleena (French) a form of Salina.
Saleen, Saleenah, Saleene, Salleen, Salleena, Salleenah, Salleene

Salem (Arabic) a form of Salím (see Boys' Names).
Saleem

Salena (French) a form of Salina.
Salana, Salanah, Salane, Salean, Saleana, Saleanah, Saleane, Salen, Salenah, Salene, Salenna, Sallene

Salette (English) a form of Sally.
Salet, Saleta, Saletah, Salete, Salett, Saletta, Salettah, Sallet, Salletta, Sallettah, Sallette

Salima (Arabic) safe and sound; healthy.
Saleema, Salema, Salim, Salimah, Salyma, Salymah

Salina (French) solemn, dignified. See also Xalina, Zalina.
Salin, Salinah, Salinda, Saline, Salinee, Sallin, Sallina, Sallinah, Salline, Sallyn, Sallyna, Sallynah, Sallyne, Sallynee, Salyn, Salyna, Salynah, Salyne

Salliann (English) a combination of Sally + Ann.
Saleann, Saleanna, Saleannah, Saleanne, Saleean, Saleeana, Saleeanah, Saleeane, Saleeann, Saleeanna, Saleeannah, Saleeanne, Salian, Saliana, Salianah, Saliane, Saliann, Salianna, Saliannah, Salianne, Salleeann, Salleeanna, Salleeannah, Salleeanne, Sallian, Salliana, Sallianah, Salliane, Sallianna, Salliannah, Sallianne, Sally-Ann, Sally-Anne, Sallyann, Sallyanna, Sallyannah, Sallyanne

Sallie (English) a form of Sally.
Sali, Salia, Saliah, Salie, Saliee, Salli, Sallia, Salliah

Sally (English) princess. History: Sally Ride, an American astronaut, became the first U.S. woman in space.
Sailee, Saileigh, Sailey, Saili, Sailia, Sailie, Saily, Sal, Salaid, Salea, Saleah, Salee, Salei, Saleigh, Salette, Saley, Sallea, Salleah, Sallee, Sallei, Salleigh, Salley, Sallya, Sallyah, Sallye, Saly, Salya, Salyah, Salye

Salma (Arabic) a form of Salima.

Salome (Hebrew) peaceful. History: Salome Alexandra was a ruler of ancient Judea. Bible: the niece of King Herod.
Salaome, Saloma, Salomah, Salomé, Salomea, Salomee, Salomei, Salomey, Salomi, Salomia, Salomiah, Salomyah, Salomyah

Salvadora (Spanish) savior.
Salvadorah

Salvia (Spanish) healthy; saved. (Latin) a form of Sage.
Sallvia, Sallviah, Salviah, Salviana, Salvianah, Salviane, Salvianna, Salviannah, Salvianne, Salvina, Salvinah, Salvine, Salvyna, Salvynah, Salvyne

Samah (Hebrew, Arabic) a form of Sami.
Sama

Samala (Hebrew) asked of God.
Samalah, Samale, Sammala, Sammalah

Samanatha (Aramaic, Hebrew) a form of Samantha.
Samanath

Samanfa (Hebrew) a form of Samantha.
Samanffa, Sammanfa, Sammanffa, Semenfa, Semenfah, Samenffa, Semenffah

Samanta (Hebrew) a form of Samantha.
Samantah, Smanta

Samantha (Aramaic) listener. (Hebrew) told by God. See also Xamantha, Zamantha.
Samana, Samanitha, Samanithia, Samanth, Samanthe, Samanthi, Samanthia,

Samanthiah, Semantha, Sementha, Simantha, Smantha

Samara (Latin) elm-tree seed.
Saimara, Samaira, Samar, Samarie, Samarra, Samary, Samera, Sammar, Sammara, Samora

Samarah (Latin) a form of Samara.

Samaria (Latin) a form of Samara.
Samari, Samariah, Samarrea, Sameria

Samatha (Hebrew) a form of Samantha.
Sammatha

Sameh (Hebrew) listener. (Arabic) forgiving.
Samaiya, Samaya

Sami (Arabic) praised. (Hebrew) a short form of Samantha, Samuela. See also Xami, Zami.
Samea, Samee, Samey, Samie, Samy, Samye

Samia (Arabic) exalted.
Samiha, Sammia, Sammiah, Sammya, Sammyah, Samya, Samyah

Samiah (Arabic) a form of Samia.

Samina (Hindi) happiness. (English) a form of Sami.
Saminah, Samyna, Samynah

Samira (Arabic) entertaining.
Samir, Samirah, Samire, Samiria, Samirra, Samyra, Samyrah, Samyre

Samiya (Arabic) a form of Samia.

Sammantha (Aramaic, Hebrew) a form of Samantha.
Sammanth, Sammanthia, Sammanthiah, Sammanthya, Sammanthyah

Sammi, Sammie, Sammy (Hebrew) familiar forms of Samantha, Samuel, Samuela. (Arabic) forms of Sami.
Samm, Samma, Sammah, Sammee, Sammey, Sammijo, Sammyjo

Samone (Hebrew) a form of Simone.
Samoan, Samoane, Samon, Samona, Samoné, Samonia

Samuel (Hebrew) heard God; asked of God. Bible: a famous Old Testament prophet and judge.

Samuela (Hebrew) a form of Samuel.
See also Xamuela, Zamuela.
Samelia, Sammila, Sammile

Samuelle (Hebrew) a form of Samuel.
Samella, Samiella, Samielle, Samilla,
Samille, Samuella

Sana (Arabic) mountaintop; splendid;
brilliant.
Sanaa, Sanáa, Sanaah, Sanah, Sane

Sancia (Spanish) holy, sacred.
Sanceska, Sancha, Sancharia, Sanche,
Sancheska, Sanchia, Sanchiah, Sanchie,
Sanchya, Sanchyah, Sanciah, Sancie,
Sanctia, Sancya, Sancyah, Santsia, Sanzia,
Sanziah, Sanzya, Sanzyah

Sandeep (Punjabi) enlightened.
Sandip

Sandi (Greek) a familiar form of Sandra.
See also Xandi, Zandi.
Sandea, Sandee, Sandia, Sandiah, Sandie,
Sandiey, Sandine, Sanndie

Sandra (Greek) defender of mankind. A
short form of Cassandra. History: Sandra
Day O'Connor was the first woman
appointed to the U.S. Supreme Court.
See also Xandra, Zandra.
Sahndra, Sandira, Sandrea, Sandria,
Sandrica, Sanndra

Sandrea (Greek) a form of Sandra.
Sandreah, Sandreea, Sandreia, Sandreiah,
Sandrell, Sandrella, Sandrellah, Sandrelle,
Sandria, Sandriah, Sanndria

Sandrica (Greek) a form of Sandra. See
also Rica.
Sandricah, Sandricka, Sandrickah, Sandrika,
Sandrikah, Sandryca, Sandrycah,
Sandrycka, Sandryckah, Sandryka,
Sandrykah

Sandrine (Greek) a form of Alexandra.
See also Xandrine, Zandrine.
Sandreana, Sandreanah, Sandreane,
Sandreen, Sandreena, Sandreenah,
Sandreene, Sandrene, Sandrenna,
Sandrennah, Sandrenne, Sandrianna,
Sandrina, Sandrinah, Sandryna,
Sandrynah, Sandryne

Sandy (Greek) a familiar form of
Cassandra, Sandra.
Sandey, Sandya, Sandye

Sanne (Hebrew, Dutch) lily.
Sanea, Saneh, Sanna, Sanneen, Sanneena

Santana (Spanish) saint.
Santa, Santah, Santania, Santaniah,
Santaniata, Santena, Santenah, Santenna,
Shantana, Shantanna

Santanna (Spanish) a form of Santana.
Santanne

Santina (Spanish) little saint. See also
Xantina, Zantina.
Santin, Santinah, Santine, Santinia,
Santyn, Santyna, Santynah, Santyne

Sanura (Swahili) kitten.
Sanora, Sanurah

Sanuye (Moquelumnan) red clouds at
sunset.

Sanya (Sanskrit) born on Saturday.
Saneiya, Sania, Sanyah, Sanyia

Sanyu (Luganda) happiness.

Sapata (Native American) dancing bear.
Sapatah

Saphire (Greek) a form of Sapphire.
Saphir, Saphyre

Sapphira (Hebrew) a form of Sapphire.
Saffira, Saffirah, Safira, Safirah, Safyra,
Safyrah, Sapheria, Saphira, Saphirah,
Saphyra, Sapir, Sapira, Sapphirah,
Sapphyra, Sapphyrah, Sapyr, Sapyra,
Sapyrah, Sephira

Sapphire (Greek) blue gemstone.
Saffir, Saffire, Safir, Safire, Safyr, Sapphir,
Sapphyr, Sapphyre

Sara, Sarra, Sarrah (Hebrew) forms of
Sarah.
Saralee

Sara Eve, Sarah Eve (American) combinations of Sarah + Eve.
Sara-Eve, Sarah-Eve

Sara Jane, Sarah Jane (American) combinations of Sarah + Jane.
Sara-Jane, Sarah-Jane

Sara Maude, Sarah Maud, Sarah Maude
(American) combinations of Sarah +
Maud.
Sara Maud, Sara-Maud, Sara-Maude,
Sarah-Maud, Sarah-Maude

Sarafina (Hebrew) a form of Serafina.

Sarah (Hebrew) princess. Bible: the wife
of Abraham and mother of Isaac. See
also Sadie, Saida, Sally, Saree, Sharai,
Xara, Zara, Zarita.
Sarae, Saraha, Sorcha

Sarah Ann, Sarah Anne (American)
combinations of Sarah + Ann.
Sara Ann, Sara Anne, Sara-Ann, Sara-Anne,
Sarah-Ann, Sarah-Anne, Sarahann,
Sarahanne, Sarann

Sarah Jeanne (American) a combination
of Sarah + Jeanne.
Sara Jeanne, Sara-Jeanne, Sarajeanne,
Sarah-Jeanne, Sarahjeanne

Sarah Marie (American) a combination
of Sarah + Marie.
Sara Marie, Sara-Marie, Saramarie,
Sarah-Marie, Sarahmarie

Sarahi (Hebrew) a form of Sarah.

Sarai, Saray (Hebrew) forms of Sarah.
Saraya

Saralyn (American) a combination of
Sarah + Lynn.
Saralena, Saraly, Saralynn

Saree (Arabic) noble. (Hebrew) a familiar
form of Sarah.
Sarry, Sary, Sarye

Sarena (Hebrew) a form of Sarina.
Saren, Sarenah, Sarene, Sarenna

Sarha (Hebrew) a form of Sarah.

Sari (Hebrew, Arabic) a form of Saree.
Sarie, Sarri, Sarrie

Saria, Sariah (Hebrew) forms of Sarah.
Sahria, Sahriah, Sahrya, Sahryah, Sarea,
Sareah, Sarria, Sarriah, Sarya, Saryah,
Sayria, Sayriah, Sayrya, Sayryah

Sarika (Hebrew) a familiar form of
Sarah. See also Xarika, Zarika.

Sareaka, Sareakah, Sareeka, Sareekah,
Sareka, Sarekah, Sarica, Saricah, Saricka,
Sarickah, Sarikah, Sarka, Saryca, Sarycah,
Sarycka, Saryckah, Saryka, Sarykah

Sarila (Turkish) waterfall.
Sarilah, Sarill, Sarilla, Sarillah, Sarille,
Saryl, Saryla, Sarylah, Saryle, Saryll,
Sarylla, Saryllah, Sarylle

Sarina (Hebrew) a familiar form of
Sarah. See also Xarina, Zarina.
Sarana, Saranah, Sarane, Saranna,
Sarannah, Saranne, Sareana, Sareanah,
Sareane, Sareen, Sareena, Sareenah, Sareene,
Sarin, Sarinah, Sarine, Sarinna, Sarinne,
Saryna, Sarynah, Saryne, Sarynna,
Sarynnah, Sarynne

Sarita (Hebrew) a familiar form of Sarah.
Sareata, Sareatah, Sareate, Sareatta,
Sareattah, Sareatte, Sareeta, Sareetah,
Sareete, Saret, Sareta, Saretah, Sarete, Sarett,
Saretta, Sarettah, Sarette, Sarit, Saritah,
Sarite, Saritia, Saritt, Saritta, Sarittah,
Saritte, Saryt, Saryta, Sarytah, Saryte,
Sarytt, Sarytta, Saryttah, Sarytte

Sarolta (Hungarian) a form of Sarah.
Saroltah

Sarotte (French) a form of Sarah.
Sarot, Sarota, Sarotah, Sarote, Sarott,
Sarotta, Sarottah

Sasa (Japanese) assistant. (Hungarian) a
form of Sarah, Sasha.
Sasah

Sasha (Russian) defender of mankind.
See also Zasha.
Sahsha, Sascha, Saschae, Sashae, Sashah,
Sashai, Sashana, Sashay, Sashea, Sashel,
Sashenka, Sashey, Sashi, Sashia, Sashiah,
Sashira, Sashsha, Sashya, Sashyah, Sasjara,
Sauscha, Sausha, Shasha, Shashi, Shashia

Sass (Irish) Saxon.
Sas, Sasi, Sasie, Sassi, Sassie, Sassoon,
Sassy, Sasy

Satara (American) a combination of
Sarah + Tara.
Satarah, Sataria, Satariah, Satarra, Satarrah,
Satarya, Sataryah, Sateria, Sateriah, Saterra,
Saterrah, Saterria, Saterriah, Saterya, Sateryah

Satin (French) smooth, shiny.
Satean, Sateana, Sateane, Sateen, Sateena,
Sateene, Satina, Satinah, Satinder, Satine,
Satyn, Satyna, Satynah, Satyne

Satinka (Native American) sacred dancer.
Satinkah

Sato (Japanese) sugar.
Satu

Saundra (English) a form of Sandra,
Sondra.
Saundee, Saundi, Saundie, Saundrea,
Saundree, Saundrey, Saundri, Saundria,
Saundriah, Saundrie, Saundry, Saundrya,
Saundryah

Saura (Hindi) sun worshiper.
Saurah

Savana, Savanah, Savanna (Spanish)
forms of Savannah.

Savannah (Spanish) treeless plain. See
also Zavannah.
Sahvana, Sahvanna, Sahvannah, Savan,
Savanha, Savania, Savann, Savannha,
Savannia, Savanniah, Savauna, Savona,
Savonna, Savonnah, Savonne, Sevan, Sevana,
Sevanah, Sevanh, Sevann, Sevanna,
Sevannah, Svannah

Savhanna (Spanish) a form of Savannah.
Savhana, Savhanah

Savina (Latin) a form of Sabina.
Savean, Saveana, Saveanah, Saveane,
Saveen, Saveena, Saveenah, Saveene,
Savinah, Savine, Savyna, Savynah, Savyne

Sawa (Japanese) swamp. (Moquelumnan)
stone.
Sawah

Sawyer (English) wood worker.
Sawyar, Sawyor

Sayde, Saydee (Hebrew) forms of Sadie.
Saydea, Saydi, Saydia, Saydie, Saydy, Saydye

Sayo (Japanese) born at night.
Saio, Sao

Sayra (Hebrew) a form of Sarah.
Sayrah, Sayre, Sayri

Scarlet (English) a form of Scarlett.
Scarleta, Scarlete

Scarlett (English) bright red. Literature:
Scarlett O'Hara is the heroine of
Margaret Mitchell's novel *Gone with the*
Wind.
Scarletta, Scarlette, Scarlit, Scarlitt, Scarlotte,
Scarlyt, Scarlyta, Scarlyte, Skarlette

Schyler (Dutch) sheltering.
Schiler, Schuyla, Schuyler, Schuylia, Schylar

Scotti (Scottish) from Scotland.
Scota, Scotea, Scoteah, Scotee, Scotey, Scoti,
Scotia, Scotiah, Scottea, Scotteah, Scottee,
Scottey, Scottia, Scottiah, Scottie, Scotty,
Scoty, Scotya, Scotyah

Scout (French) scout. Literature: Scout is
a protagonist in Harper Lee's *To Kill a*
Mockingbird.

Seaira, Seairra (Irish, Spanish) forms of
Sierra.

Sean (Hebrew, Irish) God is gracious.
Seaghan, Seain, Seaine, Séan, Seán, Seane,
Seann, Seayn, Seayne, Shaan, Shon, Siôn

Seana, Seanna (Irish) forms of Jane,
Sean. See also Shauna, Shawna.
Seaana, Seanah, Seannae, Seannah,
Seannalisa, Seanté

Searra (Irish, Spanish) a form of Sierra.
Seara, Searria

Sebastiane (Greek) venerable. (Latin)
revered. (French) a form of Sebastian
(see Boys' Names).
Sebastene, Sebastia, Sebastiana, Sebastianah,
Sebastiann, Sebastianna, Sebastiannah,
Sebastianne, Sebastien, Sebastienne,
Sebastyana, Sebastyann, Sebastyanna,
Sebastyanne, Sevastyana

Seble (Ethiopian) autumn.

Sebrina (English) a form of Sabrina.
Sebrena, Sebrenna, Sebria, Sebriana,
Sebrinah

Secilia (Latin) a form of Cecilia.
Saselia, Saseliah, Sasilia, Sasiliah, Secylia,
Secyliah, Secylya, Secylyah, Sesilia, Sesiliah,

Secilia *(cont.)*
Sesilya, Sesilyah, Sesylia, Sesyliah, Sesylya, Sesylyah, Sileas, Siselea, Siseleah

Secret (Latin) secret.

Secunda (Latin) second.
Seconda, Secondah, Secondea, Secondee, Secondia, Secondiah, Secondya, Secondyah

Seda (Armenian) forest voices.
Sedah

Sedna (Eskimo) well-fed. Mythology: the goddess of sea animals.
Sednah

Sedona (French) a form of Sidonie.

Seelia (English) a form of Sheila.

Seema (Greek) sprout. (Afghan) sky; profile.
Seama, Seamah, Seemah, Sima, Simah, Syma, Symah

Sefa (Swiss) a familiar form of Josefina.
Sefah, Seffa, Seffah

Seirra (Irish) a form of Sierra.
Seiara, Seiarra, Seira, Seirria

Sejal (Indian) river water.

Seki (Japanese) wonderful.
Seka, Sekah, Sekee, Sekey, Sekia, Sekiah, Sekie, Seky, Sekya, Sekyah

Sela, Selah (English) short forms of Selena.
Seeley, Sella, Sellah

Selam (Ethiopian) peaceful.
Selama, Selamah

Selda (German) a short form of Griselda. (Yiddish) a form of Zelda.
Seldah, Selde, Sellda, Selldah

Selena (Greek) a form of Selene. See also Celena, Zelena.
Saleena, Selana, Seleana, Seleanah, Seleena, Seleenah, Selen, Selenah, Séléné, Selenia, Selenna, Syleena, Sylena

Selene (Greek) moon. Mythology: Selene was the goddess of the moon.
Selean, Seleane, Seleen, Seleene, Seleni, Selenie, Seleny

Seleste (Latin) a form of Celeste.

Selestina (Latin) a form of Celestina.
Selesteana, Selesteanah, Selesteane, Selesteena, Selesteenah, Selesteene, Selestin, Selestina, Selestinah, Selestine, Selestyna, Selestynah, Selestyne

Selia (Latin) a short form of Cecilia.
Seel, Seelia, Seil, Seila, Selea, Seleah, Selee, Selei, Seleigh, Seley, Seli, Seliah, Selie, Sellia, Selliah, Sellya, Sellyah, Sely, Silia

Selima (Hebrew) peaceful.
Selema, Selemah, Selimah, Selyma, Selymah

Selin (Greek) a short form of Selina.
Selyn, Selyne, Selynne, Sillyn, Sylin, Sylyn, Sylyne

Selina (Greek) a form of Celina, Selena.
Selinah, Selinda, Seline, Selinia, Seliniah, Selinka, Sellina, Selyna, Selynah, Silina, Silinah, Siline, Sillina, Sillinah, Silline, Sillyna, Sillynah, Sillyne, Sylina, Sylinah, Syline, Sylyna, Sylynah

Selma (German) devine protector. (Irish) fair, just. (Scandinavian) divinely protected. (Arabic) secure. See also Zelma.
Sellma, Sellmah, Selmah

Sema (Turkish) heaven; divine omen.
Semah

Semaj (Turkish) a form of Sema.

Sena (Greek) a short form of Selena. (Spanish) a short form of Senalda.
Senda

Senalda (Spanish) sign.

Seneca (Iroquoian) a tribal name.
Senaka, Seneka, Senequa, Senequae, Senequai, Seneque

Senia (Greek) a form of Xenia.
Seniah, Senya, Senyah

September (Latin) born in the ninth month.

Septima (Latin) seventh.
Septime, Septym, Septyma, Septyme, Sevann, Sevanna, Sevanne, Sevena, Sevenah

Sequoia (Cherokee) giant redwood tree.
Seqoiyia, Seqouyia, Seqoya, Sequoi,
Sequoiah, Sequora, Sikoya

Sequoya, Sequoyah (Cherokee) forms
of Sequoia.

Sera, Serah (American) forms of Sarah.
Serra

Serafina (Hebrew) burning; ardent. Bible:
seraphim are an order of angels.
Seafina, Seaphina, Serafeena, Seraphe,
Serapheena, Seraphina, Seraphita,
Seraphyna, Seraphynah, Seraphyne, Serapia,
Serephyna, Serephynah, Serofina

Seraphyne (French) a form of Serafina.
Serafeen, Serafeene, Serafin, Serafine,
Serapheen, Serapheene, Seraphin, Seraphine,
Serephyn

Serena (Latin) peaceful. See also Rena,
Xerena, Zerena.
Sareana, Sareanah, Sareena, Sareenah,
Saryna, Seraina, Serana, Sereana, Sereanah,
Sereina, Serenah, Serenea, Serenia, Serenna,
Serreana, Serrena, Serrenna

Serene (French) a form of Serena.
Serean, Sereane, Sereen, Seren

Serenity (Latin) peaceful.
Serenidy, Serenitee, Serenitey, Sereniti,
Serenitie, Serenitiy, Serinity, Serrennity

Serica (Greek) silky smooth.
Sericah, Sericka, Serickah, Serika, Serikah,
Seryca, Serycah, Serycka, Seryckah, Seryka,
Serykah

Serilda (Greek) armed warrior woman.
Sarilda, Sarildah, Serildah, Serylda,
Seryldah

Serina (Latin) a form of Serena.
Sereena, Serin, Serinah, Serine, Serreena,
Serrin, Serrina, Seryn, Seryna, Serynah,
Seryne

Serita (Hebrew) a form of Sarita.
Seritah, Serite, Seritt, Seritta, Serittah,
Seritte, Seryt, Seryta, Serytah, Seryte, Serytt,
Serytta, Seryttah, Serytte

Sevilla (Spanish) from Seville, Spain.
Sevil, Sevila, Sevilah, Sevile, Sevill,
Sevillah, Seville, Sevyl, Sevyla, Sevylah,
Sevyle, Sevyll, Sevylla, Sevyllah, Sevylle

Shaba (Spanish) rose.
Shabah, Shabana, Shabanah, Shabina,
Shabinah, Shabine, Shabyna, Shabynah,
Shabyne

Shada (Native American) pelican.
Shadah, Shadee, Shadi, Shadie, Shaida,
Shaidah, Shayda, Shaydah

Shaday (American) a form of Sade.
Shadae, Shadai, Shadaia, Shadaya,
Shadayna, Shadei, Shadeziah, Shaiday

Shade (English) shade.
Shaed, Shaede, Shaid, Shaide, Shayd, Shayde

Shadia (Native American) a form of
Shada.
Shadea, Shadeana, Shadiah, Shadiya

Shadow (English) shadow.

Shadrika (American) a combination of
the prefix Sha + Rika.
Shadreeka, Shadreka, Shadrica, Shadricah,
Shadricka, Shadrieka, Shadrikah,
Shadriqua, Shadriquah, Shadrique,
Shadryca, Shadrycah, Shadrycka,
Shadryckah, Shadryka, Shadrykah,
Shadryqua, Shadryquah, Shadryque

Shae (Irish) a form of Shea.
Shaenel, Shaeya

Shae-Lynn, Shaelyn, Shaelynn (Irish)
forms of Shea. See also Shailyn.
Shael, Shaelaine, Shaelan, Shaelanie,
Shaelanna, Shaelean, Shaeleana, Shaeleanah,
Shaeleane, Shaeleen, Shaeleena, Shaeleenah,
Shaeleene, Shaelena, Shaelenah, Shaelene,
Shaelin, Shaelina, Shaelinah, Shaeline,
Shaelyna, Shaelynah, Shaelyne, Shaelynne

Shaela (Irish) a form of Sheila.
Shaeyla

Shaelee (Irish) a form of Shea.
Shaelea, Shaeleah, Shaelei, Shaeleigh, Shaeley,
Shaeli, Shaelia, Shaeliah, Shaelie, Shaely

Shaena (Irish) a form of Shaina.
Shaeina, Shaeine, Shaenah

Shafira (Swahili) distinguished.
Shaffira, Shafirah, Shafyra, Shafyrah

Shahar (Arabic) moonlit.
Shahara, Shaharah, Shaharia, Shahariah, Shaharya, Shaharyah

Shahina (Arabic) falcon.
Shahean, Shaheana, Shaheanah, Shaheane, Shaheen, Shaheena, Shaheenah, Shaheene, Shahi, Shahin, Shahinah, Shahine, Shahyna, Shahynah, Shahyne

Shahira (Arabic) famous.
Shahirah, Shahyra, Shahyrah

Shahla (Afghani) beautiful eyes.
Shahlah

Shai (Irish) a form of Shea.
Shaia, Shaiah

Shaianne (Cheyenne) a form of Cheyenne.
Shaeen, Shaeine, Shaian, Shaiana, Shaiandra, Shaiane, Shaiann, Shaianna

Shaila (Latin) a form of Sheila.
Shailah, Shailla

Shailee (Irish) a form of Shea.
Shailea, Shaileah, Shailei, Shaileigh, Shailey, Shaili, Shailia, Shailiah, Shailie, Shaily

Shailyn, Shailynn (Irish) forms of Shea. See also Shae-Lynn.
Shailean, Shaileana, Shaileanah, Shailean, Shaileen, Shaileena, Shaileenah, Shaileene, Shailin, Shailina, Shailinah, Shailine, Shailyna, Shailynah, Shailyne

Shaina (Yiddish) beautiful.
Schaina, Schainah, Schayna, Schaynah, Shainah, Shainna, Shajna, Shayndel, Sheina, Sheinah, Sheindel, Sheyna, Sheynah

Shajuana (American) a combination of the prefix Sha + Juanita. See also Shawana.
Shajana, Shajanah, Shajuan, Shajuanda, Shajuanita, Shajuanna, Shajuanne, Shajuanza

Shaka (Hindi) a form of Shakti. A short form of names beginning with "Shak." See also Chaka.
Shakah, Shakha

Shakala (Arabic) a form of Shakila.

Shakara, Shakarah (American) combinations of the prefix Sha + Kara.
Shacara, Shacarah, Shaccara, Shaccarah, Shakarya, Shakaryah, Shakkara, Shikara, Shykara, Shykarah

Shakari (American) a form of Shakara.
Shacari, Shacaria, Shakaria, Shakariah

Shakayla (Arabic) a form of Shakila.
Shakaela, Shakail, Shakaila

Shakeena (American) a combination of the prefix Sha + Keena.
Shakean, Shakeana, Shakeanah, Shakeane, Shakeen, Shakeena, Shakeenah, Shakeene, Shakein, Shakeina, Shakeinah, Shakeine, Shakeyn, Shakeyna, Shakeynah, Shakeyne, Shakin, Shakina, Shakinah, Shakine, Shakyn, Shakyna, Shakynah, Shakyne

Shakeita (American) a combination of the prefix Sha + Keita. See also Shaqueita.
Shakeata, Shakeatah, Shakeatia, Shakeatiah, Shakeeta, Shakeetah, Shakeetia, Shakeetiah, Shakeitah, Shakeitha, Shakeithia, Shaketa, Shaketah, Shaketha, Shakethia, Shaketia, Shaketiah, Shakeyta, Shakeytah, Shakyta, Shakytah, Shakytia, Shakytiah, Sheketa, Sheketah, Sheketia, Shekita, Shekitah, Shikita, Shikitha, Shikyta, Shikytah, Shykita, Shykitah, Shykitia, Shykyta, Shykytah, Shykytia, Shykytiah, Shykytya, Shykytyah

Shakela (Arabic) a form of Shakila.
Shakelah

Shakera, Shakerra (Arabic) forms of Shakira.
Shakerah

Shakeria, Shakerria (Arabic) forms of Shakira.
Chakeria, Shakeriah, Shakeriay, Shakerri, Shakerya, Shakeryia

Shakeya (American) a form of Shakia.

Shakia (American) a combination of the prefix Sha + Kia.
Shakeeia, Shakeeiah, Shakeeya, Shakeeyah, Shakeia, Shakeiah, Shakiah, Shakiya,

Shakiyah, Shakya, Shakyah, Shekeia,
Shekia, Shekiah, Shekya, Shekyah, Shikia

Shakiera (Arabic) a form of Shakira.
Shakierra

Shakila (Arabic) pretty.
Chakila, Shakeala, Shakealah, Shakeela,
Shakeelah, Shakeena, Shakilah, Shakyla,
Shakylah, Shekela, Shekila, Shekilla,
Shikeela, Shikila

Shakima (African) beautiful one.

Shakira (Arabic) thankful.
Shaakira, Shacora, Shaka, Shakeera,
Shakeerah, Shakeeria, Shakeira, Shakeirra,
Shakeyra, Shakir, Shakirah, Shakirat,
Shakirea, Shakora, Shakuria, Shekiera,
Shekira, Shikira, Shikirah, Shikyra, Shikyrah,
Shykira, Shykirah, Shykyra, Shykyrah

Shakirra (Arabic) a form of Shakira.

Shakita (American) a form of Shakeita.
Shakitah, Shakitra

Shakti (Hindi) energy, power. Religion: a
form of the Hindu goddess Devi.
Sakti, Shaktea, Shaktee, Shaktey, Shaktia,
Shaktiah, Shaktie, Shakty

Shakyra (Arabic) a form of Shakira.
Shakyrah, Shakyria

Shalana (American) a combination of
the prefix Sha + Lana.
Shalaana, Shalain, Shalaina, Shalainah,
Shalaine, Shalanah, Shalane, Shalann,
Shalanna, Shalannah, Shalanne, Shalaun,
Shalauna, Shalaunah, Shallan, Shallana,
Shallanah, Shelan, Shelana, Shelanah,
Shelanda, Shelane, Shelayna, Shelaynah,
Shelayne, Sholaina, Sholainah, Sholaine,
Sholana, Sholanah, Sholane, Sholayna,
Sholaynah, Sholayne

Shalanda (American) a form of Shalana.
Shaland

Shalayna (American) a form of Shalana.
Shalayn, Shalaynah, Shalayne, Shalaynna

Shaleah (American) a combination of
the prefix Sha + Leah.

Shalea, Shalei, Shaleigh, Shaley, Shali,
Shalia, Shaliah, Shalie, Shaly

Shalee (American) a form of Shaleah.
Shaleea

Shaleen, Shalene (American) short forms
of Shalena.
Shalean, Shaleane, Shaleene, Shalen,
Shalenne, Shaline

Shaleisha (American) a combination of
the prefix Sha + Aisha.
Shalesha, Shaleshah, Shalesia, Shalesiah,
Shalicia, Shaliciah, Shalisha, Shalishah,
Shalysha, Shalyshah

Shalena (American) a combination of
the prefix Sha + Lena. See also Chalina.
Shaleana, Shaleanah, Shaleena, Shaleenah,
Shálena, Shalenah, Shalené, Shalenna,
Shalennah, Shalina, Shalinah, Shalinda,
Shalinna, Shalyna, Shalynah, Shelena,
Shelenah

Shalini (American) a form of Shalena.

Shalisa (American) a combination of the
prefix Sha + Lisa.
Shalesa, Shalesah, Shalese, Shalessa, Shalice,
Shalicia, Shaliece, Shalisah, Shalise, Shalisha,
Shalishea, Shalisia, Shalisiah, Shalissa,
Shalissah, Shalisse, Shalyce, Shalys, Shalysa,
Shalysah, Shalyse, Shalyss, Shalyssa,
Shalyssah, Shalysse

Shalita (American) a combination of the
prefix Sha + Lita.
Shaleata, Shaleatah, Shaleeta, Shaleetah,
Shaleta, Shaletah, Shaletta, Shalettah,
Shalida, Shalidah, Shalitta, Shalittah,
Shalyta, Shalytah, Shalytta, Shalyttah

Shalon (American) a short form of
Shalona.
Shalone, Shalonne

Shalona (American) a combination of
the prefix Sha + Lona.
Shalonah, Shálonna, Shalonnah

Shalonda (American) a combination of
the prefix Sha + Ondine.
Shalondah, Shalonde, Shalondina,
Shalondine, Shalondra, Shalondria,
Shalondyna, Shalondyne

Shalyn, Shalynn, Shalynne (American) combinations of the prefix Sha + Lynn.
Shalin, Shalina, Shalinda, Shaline, Shalyna, Shalynda, Shalyne, Shalynna

Shamara (Arabic) ready for battle.
Shamar, Shamarah, Shamare, Shamarra, Shammara, Shamora, Shamorah, Shamori, Shamoria, Shamoriah, Shamorra, Shamorrah, Shamorria, Shamorriah, Shamorya, Shamoryah

Shamari (Arabic) a form of Shamara.
Shamaree, Shamarri

Shamaria (Arabic) a form of Shamara.
Shamarea, Shamariah, Shamarria, Shamarya, Shamaryah

Shameka (American) a combination of the prefix Sha + Meka.
Shameca, Shamecca, Shamecha, Shamecia, Shameika, Shameke, Shamekia, Shamekya, Shamekyah

Shamia (American) a combination of the prefix Sha + Mia.
Shamea, Shamiah, Shamyia, Shamyiah, Shamyne

Shamika (American) a combination of the prefix Sha + Mika.
Shameaka, Shameakah, Shameeca, Shameeka, Shamica, Shamicah, Shamicia, Shamicka, Shamickah, Shamieka, Shamikah, Shamikia, Shamyca, Shamycah, Shamycka, Shamyckah, Shamyka, Shamykah

Shamira (Hebrew) precious stone.
Shamir, Shamirah, Shamiran, Shamiria

Shamiya (American) a form of Shamia.
Shamiyah

Shamyra (Hebrew) a form of Shamira.
Shamyrah, Shamyria, Shamyriah, Shamyrya, Shamyryah

Shana (Hebrew) God is gracious. (Irish) a form of Jane.
Shaana, Shaanah, Shan, Shanah

Shanae, Shanea (Irish) forms of Shana.
Shanay

Shanaya (American) a form of Shania.
Shaneah

Shanda (American) a form of Chanda, Shana.
Shandae, Shandah, Shannda

Shandi (English) a familiar form of Shana.
Shandea, Shandee, Shandei, Shandeigh, Shandey, Shandice, Shandie

Shandra (American) a form of Shanda. See also Chandra.
Shandrah

Shandria (American) a form of Shandra.
Shandrea, Shandri, Shandriah, Shandrice, Shandrie, Shandry, Shandrya, Shandryah

Shandrika (American) a form of Shandria.
Shandreka

Shane (Irish) a form of Shana.
Schain, Schaine, Schayn, Schayne, Shaen, Shaene, Shain, Shaine, Shayn

Shanece (American) a form of Shanice.

Shanee (Irish) a familiar form of Shane. (Swahili) a form of Shany. See also Shanie.
Shanée

Shaneice (American) a form of Shanice.
Shanneice

Shaneika (American) a form of Shanika.
Shaneikah

Shaneisha (American) a combination of the prefix Sha + Aisha.
Shanesha, Shaneshia, Shanessa, Shaneysha, Shaneyshah, Shanisha, Shanishia, Shanishiah, Shanissha, Shanysha, Shanyshah

Shaneka (American) a form of Shanika.
Shaneaca, Shaneacah, Shaneacka, Shaneackah, Shaneaka, Shaneakah, Shaneca, Shanecka, Shaneeca, Shaneecah, Shaneecka, Shaneeckah, Shaneeka, Shaneekah, Shanekah, Shanekia, Shanekiah, Shaneyka, Shonneka

Shanel, Shanell, Shanelle, Shannel (American) forms of Chanel.
Schanel, Schanela, Schanelah, Schanele, Schanell, Schanelle, Shanela, Shanelah, Shanele, Shanella, Shanelly, Shannela,

Shannelah, Shannele, Shannell, Shannella, Shannellah, Shannelle, Shinelle, Shonel, Shonela, Shonelah, Shonele, Shonell, Shonella, Shonelle, Shynelle

Shanequa (American) a form of Shanika.
Shaneaqua, Shaneaquah, Shaneaque, Shaneequa, Shaneequah, Shaneeque, Shaneiqua, Shaneiquah, Shaneique, Shanequah, Shaneque

Shanese (American) a form of Shanice.
Shanesse

Shaneta (American) a combination of the prefix Sha + Neta.
Seanette, Shaneata, Shaneatah, Shaneate, Shaneeta, Shaneetah, Shanetah, Shanetha, Shanethia, Shanethis, Shanetta, Shanette, Shineta, Shonetta

Shani (Swahili) a form of Shany.
Shaenee, Shaeni, Shaenie, Shainee, Shaini, Shainie

Shania, Shaniah, Shaniya (American) forms of Shana.
Shaenea, Shaenia, Shaeniah, Shaenya, Shaenyah, Shainia, Shainiah, Shainya, Shainyah, Shanasia, Shannea, Shannia, Shanya, Shanyah, Shenia

Shanice (American) a form of Janice. See also Chanice.
Shaneace, Shanease, Shaneece, Shaneese, Shaneise, Shanicea, Shannice, Sheneice, Shenyce

Shanida (American) a combination of the prefix Sha + Ida.
Shaneeda, Shaneedah, Shannida, Shannidah, Shanyda, Shanydah

Shanie (Irish) a form of Shane. (Swahili) a form of Shany. See also Shanee.
Shanni, Shannie

Shaniece (American) a form of Shanice.

Shanika (American) a combination of the prefix Sha + Nika.
Shanica, Shanicah, Shanicca, Shanicka, Shanickah, Shanieka, Shanikah, Shanike, Shanikia, Shanikka, Shanikqua, Shanikwa, Shanyca, Shanycah, Shanycka, Shanyckah, Shanyka, Shanykah, Shineeca, Shonnika

Shaniqua, Shanique (American) forms of Shanika.
Shaniqa, Shaniquah, Shaniquia, Shaniquwa, Shaniqwa, Shanyqua, Shanyquah, Shanyque, Shinequa, Shiniqua

Shanise (American) a form of Shanice.
Shanisa, Shanisah, Shanisha, Shanisia, Shaniss, Shanissa, Shanissah, Shanisse, Shanysa, Shanysah, Shanyse, Shanyssa, Shanyssah, Shineese

Shanita (American) a combination of the prefix Sha + Nita.
Shanitah, Shanitha, Shanitra, Shanitt, Shanitta, Shanittah, Shanitte, Shanyt, Shanyta, Shanytah, Shanyte, Shanytt, Shanytta, Shanyttah, Shanytte, Shinita

Shanley (Irish) hero's child.
Shanlea, Shanleah, Shanlee, Shanlei, Shanleigh, Shanli, Shanlie, Shanly

Shanna, Shannah (Irish) forms of Shana, Shannon.
Shannea

Shannen, Shanon (Irish) forms of Shannon.
Shanen, Shanena, Shanene

Shannon (Irish) small and wise.
Shanadoah, Shanan, Shann, Shannan, Shanneen, Shannie, Shannin, Shannyn, Shanyn, Sheannon

Shanny (Swahili) a form of Shany.

Shanta (French) a form of Chantal.
Shantah

Shantae, Shanté (French) forms of Chantal.
Shantai, Shantay, Shantaya, Shantaye, Shantée

Shantal (American) a form of Shantel.
Shantale, Shantall, Shontal

Shantana (American) a form of Santana.
Shantaina, Shantainah, Shantan, Shantanae, Shantanah, Shantanell, Shantania, Shantaniah, Shantanickia, Shantanika, Shantanna, Shantanne, Shantanya, Shantanyah, Shantayna, Shantaynah, Shantena, Shantenah, Shantenna, Shentana, Shentanna

Shantara (American) a combination of the prefix Sha + Tara.
Shantarah, Shantaria, Shantariah, Shantarra, Shantarrah, Shantarria, Shantarriah, Shantarya, Shantaryah, Shantera, Shanterra, Shantira, Shantyra, Shantyrah, Shontara, Shuntara

Shante (French) a form of Chantal.
Shantea, Shantee, Shanteia

Shanteca (American) a combination of the prefix Sha + Teca.
Shantecca, Shantecka, Shanteka, Shantika, Shantikia, Shantikiah, Shantyca, Shantycka, Shantyckah, Shantyka, Shantykah

Shantel, Shantell, Shantelle (American) song. See also Shauntel.
Seantelle, Shanntell, Shanteal, Shanteil, Shantela, Shantelah, Shantele, Shantella, Shantellah, Shantyl, Shantyle, Shentel, Shentelle, Shontal, Shontalla, Shontalle

Shanteria, Shanterria (American) forms of Shantara.
Shanterica, Shanterrie, Shantieria, Shantirea, Shonteria

Shantesa (American) a combination of the prefix Sha + Tess.
Shantesah, Shantese, Shantessa, Shantessah, Shantesse, Shantice, Shantise, Shantisha, Shontecia, Shontessia

Shanti (American) a short form of Shantia.
Shantey, Shantie, Shanty

Shantia (American) a combination of the prefix Sha + Tia.
Shanteia, Shanteya, Shantiah, Shantida, Shantya, Shantyah, Shaunteya, Shauntia, Shauntya, Shauntyah

Shantille (American) a form of Chantilly.
Shanteil, Shantil, Shantilea, Shantileah, Shantilee, Shantiley, Shantili, Shantilie, Shantillea, Shantilleah, Shantillee, Shantillei, Shantilleigh, Shantilli, Shantillie, Shantilly, Shantyl, Shantyle, Shantylea, Shantyleah, Shantylee, Shantylei, Shantyleigh, Shantyley, Shantylli, Shantyllie, Shantylly, Shantyly

Shantina (American) a combination of the prefix Sha + Tina.

Shanteana, Shanteanah, Shanteena, Shanteenah, Shanteina, Shanteinah, Shanteyna, Shanteynah, Shantinah, Shantine, Shantyna, Shantynah, Shontina

Shantora (American) a combination of the prefix Sha + Tory.
Shantorah, Shantoree, Shantorey, Shantori, Shantorie, Shantory, Shantoya

Shantoria (American) a form of Shantora.
Shantorya, Shanttoria

Shantrell (American) a form of Shantel.

Shantrice (American) a combination of the prefix Sha + Trice. See also Chantrice.
Shanteace, Shantease, Shantrece, Shantrecia, Shantreece, Shantreese, Shantrese, Shantress, Shantrezia, Shantricia, Shantriece, Shantriese, Shantris, Shantrisa, Shantrisah, Shantrise, Shantrissa, Shantrisse, Shantryce, Shantryse, Shontrice

Shany (Swahili) marvelous, wonderful. See also Shani.
Shaeney, Shaeny, Shaenye, Shainey, Shainy, Shaney, Shannai, Shanya

Shanyce (American) a form of Shanice.
Shannyce

Shappa (Native American) red thunder.
Shapa, Shapah, Shappah

Shaquan (American) a short form of Shaquanda.

Shaquana, Shaquanna (American) forms of Shaquanda.
Shaquanah, Shaquannah

Shaquanda (American) a combination of the prefix Sha + Wanda.
Shaquand, Shaquandah, Shaquandra, Shaquandrah, Shaquandria, Shaquanera, Shaquani, Shaquania, Shaquanne, Shaquanta, Shaquantae, Shaquantay, Shaquante, Shaquantia, Shaquona, Shaquonda, Shaquondah, Shaquondra, Shaquondria

Shaquandey (American) a form of Shaquanda.

Shaqueita (American) a form of Shakeita.

Shaquetta (American) a form of Shakeita.
Shaqueta, Shaquetah, Shaquettah, Shaquette

Shaquia (American) a short form of Shakila.

Shaquila, Shaquilla (American) forms of Shakila.
Shaquilah, Shaquillah, Shaquillia, Shequela, Shequele, Shequila, Shquiyla

Shaquille (American) a form of Shakila.
Shaquail, Shaquil, Shaquile, Shaquill

Shaquira (American) a form of Shakira.
Shaquirah, Shaquire, Shaquirra, Shaqura, Shaqurah, Shaquri

Shaquita, Shaquitta (American) forms of Shakeita.
Shaquitah, Shequida, Shequidah, Shequita, Shequitah, Shequittia, Shequitya, Shequityah, Shequytya

Shara (Hebrew) a short form of Sharon.
Shaara, Sharah, Sharal, Sharala, Sharalee, Sharlyn, Sharlynn, Sharra, Sharrah

Sharai (Hebrew) princess. See also Sharon.
Sharae, Sharaé, Sharah, Sharaiah, Sharay, Sharaya, Sharayah, Sharrai, Sharray

Sharan (Hindi) protector.
Sharaine, Sharanda, Sharanjeet

Sharda (Punjabi, Yoruba, Arabic) a form of Shardae.

Shardae, Sharday (Punjabi) charity. (Yoruba) honored by royalty. (Arabic) runaway. A form of Chardae.
Shadae, Shar-Dae, Shar-Day, Shardah, Shardai, Sharde, Shardea, Shardee, Shardée, Shardei, Shardeia, Shardey, Shardi, Shardy

Sharee (English) a form of Shari.
Share, Sharea, Shareah, Sharree

Sharen, Sharron (English) forms of Sharon.
Sharene, Sharenn, Sharren, Sharrene, Sharrona

Shari (French) beloved, dearest. (Hungarian) a form of Sarah. See also Sharita, Sheree, Sherry.
Sharie, Sharri, Sharrie, Sharry, Shary

Shariah (French, Hungarian) a form of Shari.
Sharia, Sharria, Sharriah, Sharrya, Sharryah, Sharya, Sharyah

Shariann, Sharianne (English) combinations of Shari + Ann.
Sharian, Shariana, Sharianah, Sharianna, Shariannah

Sharice (French) a form of Cherice.
Shareace, Sharease, Shereece, Shareese, Sharese, Sharesse, Shariece, Sharis, Sharise, Sharish, Shariss, Sharisse, Sharyce, Sharyse

Sharik (African) child of God.
Sharica, Sharicka, Sharicke, Sharika, Sharike, Shariqua, Sharique, Sharyk, Sharyka, Sharyque

Sharina (English) a form of Sharon.
Shareana, Shareena, Sharena, Sharenah, Sharenna, Sharennah, Sharrena, Sharrina

Sharissa (American) a form of Sharice.
Sharesa, Sharessia, Sharisa, Sharisha, Shereeza, Shericia, Sherisa, Sherissa

Sharita (French) a familiar form of Shari. (American) a form of Charity. See also Sherita.
Shareeta, Sharrita

Sharla (French) a short form of Sharlene, Sharlotte.
Sharlah

Sharleen (French) a form of Sharlene.
Sharlee, Sharleena, Sharleenah, Sharleene

Sharlene (French) little and strong.
Scharlane, Scharlene, Shar, Sharlaina, Sharlaine, Sharlane, Sharlanna, Sharlean, Sharleana, Sharleanah, Sharleane, Sharlein, Sharleina, Sharleine, Sharlena, Sharleyn, Sharleyna, Sharleyne, Sharlin, Sharlina, Sharlinah, Sharline, Sharlyn, Sharlyna, Sharlynah, Sharlyne, Sharlynn, Sharlynne, Sherlean, Sherleen, Sherlene, Sherline

Sharlotte (American) a form of Charlotte.
Sharlet, Sharleta, Sharletah, Sharlete, Sharlett, Sharletta, Sharlettah, Sharlette, Sharlot, Sharlota, Sharlotah, Sharlote, Sharlott, Sharlotta, Sharlottah

Sharma (American) a short form of
Sharmaine.
Sharmae, Sharmah, Sharme

Sharmaine (American) a form of
Charmaine.
*Sharmain, Sharmaina, Sharman, Sharmane,
Sharmanta, Sharmayn, Sharmayna,
Sharmayne, Sharmeen, Sharmeena,
Sharmena, Sharmene, Sharmese, Sharmin,
Sharmina, Sharmine, Sharmon, Sharmona,
Sharmone, Sharmyn, Sharmyna, Sharmyne*

Sharna (Hebrew) a form of Sharon.
*Sharnae, Sharnah, Sharnai, Sharnay,
Sharne, Sharnea, Sharnee, Sharneta,
Sharnete, Sharnett, Sharnetta, Sharnette,
Sharney, Sharnie*

Sharnell (American) a form of Sharon.
Sharnelle

Sharnice (American) a form of Sharon.
*Sharnease, Sharneesa, Sharneese, Sharnesa,
Sharnese, Sharnisa, Sharnise, Sharnissa,
Sharnisse, Sharnyc, Sharnyce, Sharnys,
Sharnysa, Sharnysah, Sharnyse*

Sharolyn (American) a combination of
Sharon + Lynn.
*Sharolean, Sharoleana, Sharoleanah,
Sharoleane, Sharoleen, Sharoleena,
Sharoleenah, Sharoleene, Sharolin,
Sharolina, Sharolinah, Sharoline, Sharolyna,
Sharolynah, Sharolyne, Sharolynn,
Sharolynna, Sharolynnah, Sharolynne*

Sharon (Hebrew) desert plain. A form of
Sharai.
*Shaaron, Sharan, Sharean, Shareane,
Shareen, Shareene, Sharin, Sharine,
Sharone, Sharran, Sharrane, Sharrin,
Sharrinae, Sharrine, Sharryn, Sharryne,
Sharyn, Sharyon, Sheren, Sheron, Sherryn*

Sharonda (Hebrew) a form of Sharon.
Sharronda, Sheronda, Sherrhonda

Sharrona (Hebrew) a form of Sharon.
*Sharona, Sharonah, Sharone, Sharonia,
Sharonna, Sharony, Sharrana, Sharronne,
Sharryna, Shirona*

Shatara (Hindi) umbrella. (Arabic) good;
industrious. (American) a combination
of Sharon + Tara.

*Shatarah, Shatarea, Shatari, Shataria,
Shatariah, Shatarra, Shatarrah, Shataura,
Shateira, Shatherian, Shatierra, Shatiria,
Shatyra, Shatyrah, Sheatara*

Shateria (American) a form of Shatara.
Shateriah, Shaterri, Shaterria

Shaterra (American) a form of Shatara.
Shatera, Shaterah

Shatoria (American) a combination of
the prefix Sha + Tory.
*Shatora, Shatorah, Shatorea, Shatori,
Shatoriah, Shatorri, Shatorria, Shatory,
Shatorya, Shatoryah*

Shatoya (American) a form of Shatoria.

Shaun (Irish) a form of Sean. See also
Shawn.
*Schaun, Schaune, Shaughan, Shaughn,
Shaugn, Shaunahan, Shaune, Shaunn,
Shaunne*

Shauna (Hebrew, Irish) a form of Shana,
Shaun. See also Seana, Shawna, Shona.
*Schauna, Schaunah, Schaunee, Shaunah,
Shaunee, Shauneen, Shaunelle, Shaunette,
Shauni, Shaunie, Shaunika, Shaunisha,
Shaunnea, Shaunua, Sheann, Sheaon,
Sheaunna*

Shaunda (Irish) a form of Shauna. See
also Shanda, Shawnda, Shonda.
*Shaundal, Shaundala, Shaundra, Shaundrea,
Shaundree, Shaundria, Shaundrice*

Shaunice (Irish) a form of Shauna.
Shaunicy

Shaunna (Hebrew, Irish) a form of
Shauna.

Shaunta (Irish) a form of Shauna. See
also Shawnta, Shonta.
*Schaunta, Schauntah, Schaunte, Schauntea,
Schauntee, Schunta, Shauntah, Shaunte,
Shauntea, Shauntee, Shauntée, Shaunteena,
Shauntia, Shauntier, Shauntrel, Shauntrell,
Shauntrella, Sheanta*

Shauntae (Irish) a form of Shaunta.
Schauntae, Schauntay, Shauntay, Shauntei

Shauntel (American) song. See also
Shantel.

Shauntela, Shauntele, Shauntell, Shauntella, Shauntelle, Shauntrel, Shauntrell, Shauntrella, Shauntrelle

Shaunya (Hebrew, Irish) a form of Shauna.

Shavon, Shavonne (American) combinations of the prefix Sha + Yvonne. See also Siobhan.
Schavon, Schevon, Shavan, Shavaun, Shavone, Shavonia, Shavonn, Shavonni, Shavonnia, Shavonnie, Shavontae, Shavonte, Shavonté, Shavoun, Sheavon, Shivaun, Shivawn, Shivon, Shivonne, Shyvon, Shyvonne

Shavonda (American) a form of Shavon.
Shavondra

Shavonna (American) a form of Shavon.
Shavana, Shavanna, Shavona, Shavonah

Shawana, Shawanna (American) combinations of the prefix Sha + Wanda. See also Shajuana, Shawna.
Shawan, Shawanah, Shawanda, Shawannah, Shawanta, Shawante, Shiwani

Shawn (Irish) a form of Sean. See also Shaun.
Schawn, Schawne, Shawen, Shawne, Shawnee, Shawnn, Shawon

Shawna (Hebrew, Irish) a form of Shana, Shawn. See also Seana, Shauna, Shona.
Sawna, Schawna, Schawnah, Shaw, Shawnae, Shawnah, Shawnai, Shawnell, Shawnette, Shawnra, Sheona

Shawnda (Irish) a form of Shawna. See also Shanda, Shaunda, Shonda.
Shawndan, Shawndra, Shawndrea, Shawndree, Shawndreel, Shawndrell, Shawndria

Shawndelle (Irish) a form of Shawna.
Schaundel, Schaundela, Schaundele, Schaundell, Schaundella, Schaundelle, Schawndel, Schawndela, Schawndele, Schawndell, Schawndelle, Seandel, Seandela, Seandele, Seandell, Seandella, Seandelle, Shaundel, Shaundela, Shaundele, Shaundell, Shaundella, Shaundelle, Shawndal, Shawndala, Shawndel, Shawndela, Shawndele, Shawndella

Shawnee (Irish) a form of Shawna.
Schawne, Schawnea, Schawnee, Shawne, Shawneea, Shawneen, Shawneena, Shawney, Shawni, Shawnie

Shawnika (American) a combination of Shawna + Nika.
Shawnaka, Shawneika, Shawnequa, Shawnicka

Shawnna (Hebrew, Irish) a form of Shawna.

Shawnta (Irish) a form of Shawna. See also Shaunta, Shonta.
Shawntae, Shawntah, Shawntay, Shawnte, Shawnté, Shawntee, Shawnteria, Shawntia, Shawntina, Shawntish, Shawntrese, Shawntriece

Shawntel (American) song. See also Shantel, Shauntel.
Shawntela, Shawntelah, Shawntele, Shawntell, Shawntella, Shawntellah, Shawntelle, Shawntil, Shawntile, Shawntill, Shawntille

Shay, Shaye (Irish) forms of Shea.
Shayda, Shayha, Shayia, Shey, Sheye

Shaya (Irish) a form of Shay.
Shayah

Shayann, Shayanne (Irish) combinations of Shay + Ann.
Shay Ann, Shay-Ann, Shay Anne, Shay-Anne

Shayla, Shaylah (Irish) forms of Shay.
Shaylagh, Shaylain, Shaylan, Shaylea, Shayleah, Shaylla, Sheyla

Shaylee, Shayli, Shaylie (Irish) forms of Shea.
Shaylei, Shayleigh, Shayley, Shaylia, Shayliah, Shayly

Shayleen, Shaylene (Irish) forms of Shea.
Shaylean, Shayleana, Shayleanah, Shayleane, Shayleena, Shayleenah, Shayleene

Shaylen, Shaylin, Shaylyn, Shaylynn (Irish) forms of Shealyn.
Shaylina, Shaylinah, Shayline, Shaylinn, Shaylyna, Shaylynah, Shaylyne, Shaylynne

Shayna (Hebrew) beautiful.
*Shaynae, Shaynah, Shaynee, Shayney,
Shayni, Shaynia, Shaynie, Shaynna,
Shaynne, Shayny*

Shayne (Hebrew) a form of Shayna.
(Irish) a form of Shane.

Shea (Irish) fairy palace.
Shearra

Shealyn (Irish) a form of Shea. See also
Shaylen.
Shealy, Sheylyn

Sheba (Hebrew) a short form of
Bathsheba. Geography: an ancient
country of south Arabia.
*Sheaba, Sheabah, Shebah, Sheeba, Sheebah,
Sheiba, Sheibah, Sheyba, Sheybah*

Sheena (Hebrew) God is gracious. (Irish)
a form of Jane.
*Sheana, Sheanah, Sheanna, Sheenagh,
Sheenah, Sheenan, Sheeneal, Sheenna,
Sheina, Sheinah, Sheyna, Sheynah, Shiona*

Sheila (Latin) blind. (Irish) a form of
Cecelia. See also Cheyla, Zelizi.
*Sheela, Sheelagh, Sheelah, Sheilagh, Sheilah,
Sheileen, Sheiletta, Sheilia, Sheilla, Sheillah,
Sheillia, Sheilliah, Sheillynn, Sheilya, Shela,
Shelagh, Shelah, Shiela, Shielah*

**Shelbe, Shelbee, Shelbey, Shelbi,
Shelbie, Shellbie, Shellby** (English)
forms of Shelby.
Shelbbie, Shellbee, Shellbi

Shelby (English) ledge estate.
*Chelby, Schelby, Shel, Shelbea, Shelbye,
Shellbea, Shellbey*

Sheldon (English) farm on the ledge.
*Sheldina, Sheldine, Sheldrina, Sheldyn,
Shelton*

Shelee (English) a form of Shelley.
*Shelea, Sheleah, Shelee, Sheleen, Shelei,
Sheleigh, Shelena, Sheley, Sheli, Shelia,
Shelie, Shelina, Shelinda, Shelita, Shely*

Shelia (Latin, Irish) a form of Sheila.
Sheliah

Shelisa (American) a combination of
Shelley + Lisa.
*Sheleza, Shelica, Shelicia, Shelise, Shelisse,
Sheliza*

Shelley, Shellie, Shelly (English) meadow
on the ledge. (French) familiar forms of
Michelle. See also Chelley, Rochelle.
*Shell, Shella, Shellaine, Shellana, Shellany,
Shellea, Shelleah, Shellee, Shellei, Shelleigh,
Shellene, Shelli, Shellian, Shelliann, Shellina*

Shelsea (American) a form of Chelsea.
Shellsea, Shellsey, Shelsey, Shelsie, Shelsy

Shena (Irish) a form of Sheena.
*Shenada, Shenah, Shenda, Shene, Sheneda,
Shenee, Sheneena, Shenina, Shenita,
Shenna, Shennah, Shenoa*

Shenae (Irish) a form of Sheena.
Shenay, Shenea, Shennae

Shenandoa (Algonquin) beautiful star.
Shenandoah

Shenell, Shenelle (American) a form of
Shanel.
*Shenel, Shenela, Shenelah, Shenele, Shenella,
Shenellah, Shenelly*

Shenice, Shenise (American) forms of
Shanice.
Shenece, Sheniece

Shenika, Sheniqua (American) forms of
Shanika, Shena.
Sheenika, Shenequa, Shenica

Shera (Aramaic) light.
*Sheara, Shearah, Sheera, Sheerah, Sherae,
Sherah, Sheralla, Sheralle, Sheray, Sheraya*

Sheralee (American) a combination of
Shera + Lee.
Sheralea, Sheraleah, Sheraley

Sheree (French) beloved, dearest.
*Scherea, Scheree, Scherey, Scherie, Sheerea,
Sheeree, Shere, Sherea, Shereé, Sherey,
Sherrea, Sherree, Sherrey*

Shereen (French) a form of Sheree.
Shereena

Sherell, Sherelle, Sherrell (French)
forms of Cherelle, Sheryl.

Sherel, Sherela, Sherelah, Sherele, Sherella, Sheriel, Sherrel, Sherrelle, Shirelle

Sheri, Sherie, Sherri, Sherrie (French) forms of Sherry.
Sheria, Sheriah, Sherria, Sherriah

Sherian, Sheriann (American) combinations of Sheri + Ann.
Sherianne, Sherrina

Sherica (Punjabi, Arabic) a form of Sherika.
Shericah, Sherrica

Sherice (French) a form of Cherice.
Scherise, Sherece, Shereece, Sherees, Shereese, Sherese, Shericia, Sherise, Sherisse, Sherrish, Sherryse, Sheryce

Sheridan (Irish) wild.
Cherida, Cheriden, Sherida, Sheridane, Sherideen, Sheriden, Sheridian, Sheridin, Sheridon, Sheridyn, Sherridan, Sherridana, Sherridane, Sherridanne, Sherridon, Sherrydan, Sherrydana, Sherrydane, Sherrydin, Sherrydon, Sherrydyn, Sherydan, Sherydana, Sherydane

Sherika (Punjabi) relative. (Arabic) easterner.
Shereka, Sherekah, Shericka, Sherikah, Sheriqua, Sheriquah, Sherricka, Sherrika, Sheryca, Sherycah, Sherycka, Sheryckah, Sheryka, Sheryqua, Sheryquah

Sherilyn (American) a form of Sherylyn.
Sharilyn, Sherilin, Sherilina, Sherilinah, Sheriline, Sherilyna, Sherilynah, Sherilyne, Sherilynn, Sherilynna, Sherilynnah, Sherilynne

Sherissa (French) a form of Sherry, Sheryl.
Shereesa, Shereese, Shereeza, Shereeze, Sheresa, Shericia, Sherisa, Sherisah, Sherise, Sheriss, Sherissah, Sherisse, Sheriza, Sherizah, Sherize, Sherizza, Sherizzah, Sherizze, Sherrish, Sherys, Sherysa, Sherysah, Sheryse, Sheryss, Sheryssa, Sheryssah, Sherysse

Sherita (French) a form of Sherry, Sheryl. See also Sharita.
Shereata, Shereatah, Shereeta, Shereetah, Shereta, Sheretta, Sherette, Sheritah, Sherrita, Sheryta, Sherytah

Sherleen (French, English) a form of Sheryl, Shirley.
Sherileen, Sherlene, Sherlin, Sherlina, Sherline, Sherlyn, Sherlyne, Sherlynne

Sherley (English) a form of Shirley.
Sherlee, Sherli, Sherlie

Shermaine (American) a form of Sharmaine.

Sherron (Hebrew) a form of Sharon.
Sheron, Sherona, Sheronna, Sherronna, Sherronne

Sherry (French) beloved, dearest. A familiar form of Sheryl. See also Sheree.
Scheri, Scherie, Schery, Sheerey, Sheeri, Sheerie, Sheery, Sherey, Sherissa, Sherrey, Shery, Sherye, Sheryy

Sheryl (French) beloved. A familiar form of Shirley. See also Sherry.
Sharel, Sharil, Sharyl, Sharyll, Sheral, Sheriel, Sheril, Sherile, Sherill, Sherille, Sherily, Sherral, Sherril, Sherrill, Sherryl, Sheryle, Sheryll, Sherylle, Sherylly

Sherylyn (American) a combination of Sheryl + Lynn. See also Cherilyn.
Sharolin, Sharolyn, Sharyl-Lynn, Sheralin, Sheralina, Sheraline, Sheralyn, Sheralyna, Sheralyne, Sheralynn, Sheralynne, Sherralyn, Sherralynn, Sherrilyn, Sherrilynn, Sherrilynne, Sherrylyn, Sherylanne, Sherylin, Sherylina, Sherylinah, Sheryline, Sherylyna, Sherylynah, Sherylyne

Shevonne (American) a combination of the prefix She + Yvonne.
Shevaun, Shevon, Shevonda, Shevone

Sheyanne, Sheyenne (Cheyenne) forms of Cheyenne. See also Shyan.
Shayhan, Sheyan, Sheyane, Sheyann, Sheyanna, Sheyannah, Sheyen, Sheyene

Shi (Japanese) a short form of Shika.
She

Shian, Shiane, Shiann, Shianne (Cheyenne) forms of Cheyenne.
Shiante, Shiany, Shieann, Shieanne, Shiene, Shienn, Shienne

Shiana, Shianna (Cheyenne) forms of Cheyenne.

Shiana, Shianna *(cont.)*
Shianah, Shianda, Shiannah, Shieana, Shiena, Shienna

Shifra (Hebrew) beautiful.
Schifra, Shifrah, Shyfra, Shyfrah

Shika (Japanese) gentle deer.
Shikah

Shikha (Japanese) a form of Shika.

Shilah (Latin, Irish) a form of Sheila.
Shila, Shilea

Shilo (Hebrew) a form of Shiloh.

Shiloh (Hebrew) God's gift. Bible: a sanctuary for the Israelites where the Ark of the Covenant was kept.

Shilpa (Indian) well proportioned.
Shilpta

Shina (Japanese) virtuous, good; wealthy. (Chinese) a form of China.
Shinae, Shinay, Shine, Shinna

Shino (Japanese) bamboo stalk.

Shiquita (American) a form of Chiquita.
Shiquata, Shiquitta

Shira (Hebrew) song.
Shirah, Shiray, Shire, Shiree, Shiri, Shirit

Shirin (Persian) charming, sweet.

Shirlene (English) a form of Shirley.
Shirleen, Shirlena, Shirlina, Shirline, Shirlyn, Shirlynn

Shirley (English) bright meadow. See also Sheryl.
Shir, Shirl, Shirlee, Shirlie, Shirlly, Shirly, Shurlee, Shurley

Shivani (Hindi) life and death.
Shiva, Shivana, Shivanie, Shivanna

Shizu (Japanese) silent.
Shizue, Shizuka, Shizuko, Shizuyo

Shona (Irish) a form of Jane. A form of Shana, Shauna, Shawna.
Shiona, Shonagh, Shonah, Shonalee, Shone, Shonee, Shonette, Shoni, Shonie

Shonda (Irish) a form of Shona. See also Shanda, Shaunda, Shawnda.
Shondalette, Shondalyn, Shondel, Shondelle, Shondi, Shondia, Shondie, Shondra, Shondreka, Shounda

Shonna (Irish) a form of Shona.
Shonnah

Shonta (Irish) a form of Shona. See also Shaunta, Shawnta.
Shontá, Shontai, Shontalea, Shontasia, Shontedra, Shonteral, Shontol, Shontoy, Shontrail

Shontae (Irish) a form of Shonta.
Shontay, Shontaya, Shonté, Shountáe

Shontavia (Irish) a form of Shonta.
Shontaviea

Shonte (Irish) a form of Shonta.
Shontee, Shonti

Shontel, Shontell (American) forms of Shantel.
Shontela, Shontelah, Shontele, Shontella, Shontellah, Shontelle

Shontia (American) a form of Shantia.

Shoshana (Hebrew) a form of Susan.
Shosha, Shoshan, Shoshanah, Shoshane, Shoshanha, Shoshann, Shoshanna, Shoshannah, Shoshauna, Shoshaunah, Shoshawna, Shoshona, Shoshone, Shoshonee, Shoshoney, Shoshoni, Shoushan, Shushana, Sosha, Soshana

Shreya (Indian) better.

Shu (Chinese) kind, gentle.

Shug (American) a short form of Sugar.

Shula (Arabic) flaming, bright.
Shulah

Shulamith (Hebrew) peaceful. See also Sula.
Shulamit, Sulamith

Shunta (Irish) a form of Shonta.
Shuntae, Shunté, Shuntel, Shuntell, Shuntelle, Shuntia

Shura (Russian) a form of Alexandra.
Schura, Shurah, Shuree, Shureen, Shurelle, Shuritta, Shurka, Shurlana

Shy, Shye (Cheyenne) short forms of Shyan.

Shyan, Shyann, Shyanne, Shyenne (Cheyenne) forms of Cheyenne. See also Sheyanne.
Shyane, Shyene, Shynee

Shyanna (Cheyenne) a form of Cheyenne.
Shyana, Shyanah, Shyandra, Shyannah, Shyenna

Shyla (English) a form of Sheila.
Shya, Shyah, Shylah, Shylan, Shylana, Shylane, Shylayah, Shyle, Shyleah, Shylee, Shyley, Shyli, Shylia, Shylie, Shylyn

Shylo (Hebrew) a form of Shilo.
Shyloe, Shyloh, Shylon

Shyra (Hebrew) a form of Shira.
Shyrae, Shyrah, Shyrai, Shyrie, Shyro

Sianna (Irish) a form of Seana.
Sian, Siana, Sianae, Sianai, Sianey, Siannah, Sianne, Sianni, Sianny, Siany, Sina, Sion, Syon

Siara, Siarra (Irish) forms of Sierra.
Siarah, Siarrah

Sibeta (Moquelumnan) finding a fish under a rock.

Sibley (English) sibling; friendly. (Greek) a form of Sybil.
Sybley

Sidnee, Sidney, Sidnie (French) forms of Sydney.
Sidne, Sidnei, Sidneya, Sidni, Sidny, Sidnye

Sidonia (Hebrew) enticing.
Sydania, Syndonia

Sidonie (French) from Saint-Denis, France. See also Sydney.
Sidaine, Sidanni, Sidelle, Sidoine, Sidona, Sidonae, Sidonia, Sidony

Sidra (Latin) star child.
Sidrah, Sidras

Siena, Sienna (American) forms of Ciana.
Seini

Siera, Sierrah (Irish) forms of Sierra.
Sierah

Sierra (Irish) black. (Spanish) saw toothed. Geography: any rugged range of mountains that, when viewed from a distance, has a jagged profile. See also Ciara.
Seera, Sieara, Siearra, Sieria, Sierre, Sierrea, Sierriah

Sigfreda (German) victorious peace. See also Freda.
Sigfreida, Sigfrida, Sigfrieda, Sigfryda

Sigmunda (German) victorious protector.
Sigmonda

Signe (Latin) sign, signal. (Scandinavian) a short form of Sigourney.
Sig, Signa, Signy, Singna, Singne

Sigourney (English) victorious conquerer.
Sigournee, Sigourny

Sigrid (Scandinavian) victorious counselor.
Siegrid, Siegrida, Sigritt

Sihu (Native American) flower; bush.

Siko (African) crying baby.

Silvana (Latin) a form of Sylvana.
Silvaine, Silvanna, Silviane

Silver (English) a precious metal.

Silvia (Latin) a form of Sylvia.
Silivia, Silva, Silvya

Simcha (Hebrew) joyful.

Simona (Hebrew, French) a form of Simone.
Simmona, Simonetta, Simonia, Simonina

Simone (Hebrew) she heard. (French) a form of Simon (see Boys' Names). See also Ximena, Zimena.
Siminie, Simmi, Simmie, Simmone, Simoane, Simonette, Simonne, Somone

Simran (Sikh) absorbed in God.
Simren, Simrin, Simrun

Sina (Irish) a form of Seana.
Seena, Sinai, Sinaia, Sinan, Sinay

Sinclair (French) a form of Sinclaire.

Sinclaire (French) prayer.

Sindy (American) a form of Cindy.
Sinda, Sindal, Sindea, Sindeah, Sindee, Sindey, Sindi, Sindia, Sindie, Sinnedy, Synda, Syndal, Syndea, Syndeah, Syndee, Syndey, Syndi, Syndia, Syndie, Syndy

Sinead (Irish) a form of Jane.
Seonaid, Sine, Sinéad

Siobhan (Irish) a form of Joan. See also Shavon.
Shibahn, Shibani, Shibhan, Shioban, Shobana, Shobha, Shobhana, Siobahn, Siobhana, Siobhann, Siobhon, Siovaun, Siovhan

Sirena (Greek) enchanter. Mythology: Sirens were sea nymphs whose singing enchanted sailors and made them crash their ships into nearby rocks. See also Cyrena, Xirena, Zirina.
Sireena, Siren, Sirenah, Sirene, Sirine

Siri (Scandinavian) a short form of Sigrid.
Siree, Sirey, Siry

Sisika (Native American) songbird.

Sissy (American) a familiar form of Cecelia.
Sisi, Sisie, Sissey, Sissi, Sissie

Sita (Hindi) a form of Shakti.
Sitah, Sitha

Sitara (Sanskrit) morning star.
Sitarah, Sithara

Siti (Swahili) respected woman.

Sky, Skyy (Arabic, Dutch) forms of Skye.
Skky

Skye (Arabic) water giver. (Dutch) a short form of Skyler. Geography: an island in the Inner Hebrides, Scotland.
Ski, Skie, Skii

Skyla (Dutch) a form of Skyler.
Skya, Skylah

Skylar (Dutch) a form of Skyler.
Skyllar, Skyylar

Skyler (Dutch) sheltering.
Skila, Skilah, Skyela, Skyelar, Skyeler, Skyelur, Skylair, Skylee, Skylena, Skyli,

Skylia, Skylie, Skylin, Skylor, Skylyn, Skylynn, Skylyr, Skyra

Sloan (Irish) a form of Sloane.

Sloane (Irish) warrior.
Sloanne

Socorro (Spanish) helper.

Sofia (Greek) a form of Sophia. See also Zofia, Zsofia.
Sofeea, Sofeeia, Soficita, Sofija, Sofiya, Sofka, Sofya

Sofie (Greek) a form of Sofia.
Soffi, Sofi

Solada (Tai) listener.

Solana (Spanish) sunshine.
Solande, Solanna, Soleil, Solena, Soley, Solina, Solinda

Solange (French) dignified.

Soledad (Spanish) solitary.
Sole, Soleda

Solenne (French) solemn, dignified.
Solaine, Solene, Soléne, Solenna, Solina, Soline, Solonez, Souline, Soulle

Solita (Latin) alone.
Soleata, Soleatah, Soleeta, Soleetah, Soleete, Soleighta, Soleita, Soleitah, Solitah, Solite, Solitta, Solittah, Solitte, Solyta, Solytah, Solytta, Solyttah, Solytte

Soma (Hindi) lunar.

Somer (English, Arabic) a form of Sommer.

Sommer (English) summer; summoner. (Arabic) black. See also Summer.
Somara, Sommar, Sommara, Sommers

Sondra (Greek) defender of mankind.
Sondre, Sonndra, Sonndre

Sonia (Russian, Slavic) a form of Sonya.
Sonica, Sonida, Sonita, Sonna, Sonni, Sonnia, Sonnie, Sonny

Sonja (Scandinavian) a form of Sonya.
Sonjae, Sonjia

Sonya (Greek) wise. (Russian, Slavic) a form of Sophia.
Sonnya, Sonyae, Sunya

Sook (Korean) pure.

Sopheary (Cambodian) beautiful girl.

Sophia (Greek) wise. See also Sofia, Sonya, Zofia.

Sophie (Greek) a familiar form of Sophia. See also Zocha.
Sophey, Sophi, Sophy

Sophronia (Greek) wise; sensible.
Soffrona, Sofronia

Sora (Native American) chirping song-bird.

Soraya (Persian) princess.
Suraya

Sorrel (French) reddish brown. Botany: a plant whose leaves are used as salad greens.

Soso (Native American) tree squirrel dining on pine nuts; chubby-cheeked baby.

Souzan (Persian) burning fire.
Sousan, Souzanne

Spencer, Spenser (English) dispenser of provisions.

Speranza (Italian) a form of Esperanza.
Speranca

Spring (English) springtime.
Spryng

Stacee, Staci, Stacie (Greek) forms of Stacey.

Stacey, Stacy (Greek) resurrection. (Irish) a short form of Anastasia, Eustacia, Natasha.
Stacci, Stace, Staceyan, Staceyann, Staicy, Stasey, Stayce, Staycee, Stayci, Steacy

Stacia, Stasia (English) short forms of Anastasia.
Staysha

Star, Starr (English) star.
Staria, Starisha, Starleen, Starlet, Starlette, Starley, Starlight, Starre, Starri, Starria, Starrika, Starrsha, Starsha, Starshanna, Startish

Starla (English) a form of Star.
Starrla

Starleen (English) a form of Star.
Starleena, Starlena, Starlene

Starley (English) a familiar form of Star.
Starle, Starlee, Starly

Starling (English) bird.

Starlyn (English) a form of Star.
Starlin, Starlynn, Starrlen

Stasha (Greek, Russian) a form of Stasya.
Stashia

Stasya (Greek) a familiar form of Anastasia. (Russian) a form of Stacey.
Stasa, Stasja, Staska

Stefani, Stefanie, Stefany, Steffani, Steffanie, Steffany (Greek) forms of Stephanie.
Stafani, Stafanie, Staffany, Stefane, Stefanee, Stefaney, Stefanié, Stefanni, Stefannie, Stefanny, Stefenie, Steffane, Steffanee, Steffaney, Stefini, Stefinie, Stefoni

Stefania (Greek) a form of Stephanie.
Stefanija, Stefanya

Steffi (Greek) a familiar form of Stefani, Stephanie.
Stefa, Stefcia, Steffee, Steffie, Steffy, Stefi, Stefka, Stefy, Stepha, Stephi, Stephie, Stephy

Stella (Latin) star. (French) a familiar form of Estelle.
Steile, Stellina

Stepania (Russian) a form of Stephanie.
Stepa, Stepahny, Stepanida, Stepanie, Stepanyda, Stepfanie

Stephaine (Greek) a form of Stephanie.

Stephani, Stephannie, Stephany (Greek) forms of Stephanie.
Stephanni, Stephanye

Stephania (Greek) a form of Stephanie.
Stephanida

Stephanie (Greek) crowned. See also Estefani, Estephanie, Panya, Stevi, Zephania.
Stamatios, Stephaija, Stephana, Stephanas, Stephane, Stephanee, Stephaney, Stéphanie,

Stephanie (cont.)
Stephanine, Stephann, Stephianie, Stephinie, Stesha, Steshka, Stevanee

Stephene (Greek) a form of Stephanie.

Stephenie (Greek) a form of Stephanie.
Stephena, Stephenee, Stepheney, Stepheni, Stephenny, Stepheny

Stephine (Greek) a form of Stephanie.
Stephina, Stephyne

Stephney (Greek) a form of Stephanie.
Stephne, Stephni, Stephnie, Stephny

Sterling (English) valuable; silver penny.

Stevi, Stevie (Greek) familiar forms of Stephanie.
Steva, Stevana, Stevanee, Stevee, Stevena, Stevey, Stevy, Stevye

Stina (German) a short form of Christina.
Steena, Stena, Stine, Stinna

Stockard (English) stockyard.

Storm (English) storm.
Storme, Stormm

Stormi, Stormie (English) forms of Stormy.
Stormii

Stormy (English) impetuous by nature.
Stormee, Stormey

Suchin (Tai) beautiful thought.

Sue (Hebrew) a short form of Susan, Susana.

Sueann (American) a combination of Sue + Ann
Suann, Suanne, Sueanne

Sueanna (American) a combination of Sue + Anna.
Suanna, Suannah

Suela (Spanish) consolation.
Suelita

Sugar (American) sweet as sugar.

Sugi (Japanese) cedar tree.

Suke (Hawaiian) a form of Susan.

Sukey (Hawaiian) a familiar form of Susan.
Suka, Sukee, Suky

Sukhdeep (Sikh) light of peace and bliss.
Sukhdip

Suki (Japanese) loved one. (Moquelumnan) eagle-eyed.
Sukie

Sula (Icelandic) large sea bird. (Greek, Hebrew) a short form of Shulamith, Ursula.

Suletu (Moquelumnan) soaring bird.

Sulia (Latin) a form of Julia.
Suliana

Sullivan (Irish) black eyed.
Sullavan, Sullevan, Sully, Syllyvan

Sulwen (Welsh) bright as the sun.

Sumalee (Tai) beautiful flower.

Sumati (Hindi) unity.

Sumaya (American) a combination of Sue + Maya.
Sumayah, Sumayya, Sumayyah

Sumer (English) a form of Summer.

Sumi (Japanese) elegant, refined.
Sumiko

Summer (English) summertime. See also Sommer.
Summar, Summerann, Summerbreeze, Summerhaze, Summerine, Summerlee, Summerlin, Summerlyn, Summerlynn, Summers, Summyr, Sumrah, Sumyr

Sun (Korean) obedient.
Suncance, Sundee, Sundeep, Sundi, Sundip, Sundrenea, Sunta, Sunya

Sun-Hi (Korean) good; joyful.

Sunday (Latin) born on the first day of the week.

Sunee (Tai) good.

Suni (Zuni) native; member of our tribe.
Sunita, Sunitha, Suniti, Sunne, Sunnilei

Sunki (Hopi) swift.
Sunkia

Sunny (English) bright, cheerful.
Sunni, Sunnie

Sunshine (English) sunshine.
Sunshyn, Sunshyne

Surata (Pakistani) blessed joy.

Suri (Todas) pointy nose.
Suree, Surena, Surenia

Surya (Sanskrit) Mythology: a sun god.
Suria, Suriya, Surra

Susammi (French) a combination of
Susan + Aimee.
Suzami, Suzamie, Suzamy

Susan (Hebrew) lily. See also Shoshana,
Sukey, Zsa Zsa, Zusa.
*Sawsan, Siusan, Sosan, Sosana, Suesan,
Sueva, Suisan, Susen, Suson*

Susana, Susanna, Susannah (Hebrew)
forms of Susan. See also Xuxa, Zanna,
Zsuzsanna.
*Sonel, Sosana, Suesanna, Susanah, Susane,
Susanka*

Susanne (Hebrew) a form of Susan.
Susann

Suse (Hawaiian) a form of Susan.

Susette (French) a familiar form of
Susan, Susana.
Susetta

Susie (American) a familiar form of
Susan, Susana.
Susey, Susi, Sussi, Sussy, Susy

Suzan (English) a form of Susan.

Suzana, Suzanna, Suzannah (Hebrew)
forms of Susan.
Suzenna, Suzzanna

Suzanne (English) a form of Susan.
*Suszanne, Suzane, Suzann, Suzzane,
Suzzann, Suzzanne*

Suzette (French) a form of Susan.
Suzetta, Suzzette

Suzie (American) a familiar form of
Susan, Susana.
Suze, Suzi, Suzy, Suzzie

Suzu (Japanese) little bell.
Suzue, Suzuko

Suzuki (Japanese) bell tree.

Svetlana (Russian) bright light.
Sveta, Svetochka

SyÀ (Chinese) summer.

Sybella (English) a form of Sybil.
*Sebila, Sibbella, Sibella, Sibilla, Sibylla,
Sybila, Sybilla*

Sybil (Greek) prophet. Mythology: sibyls
were oracles who relayed the messages
of the gods. See also Cybele, Sibley.
*Sib, Sibbel, Sibbie, Sibbill, Sibby, Sibeal,
Sibel, Sibell, Sibelle, Sibyl, Sibylle, Sibylline,
Sybel, Sybelle, Sybille, Syble*

Sydne, Sydnee, Sydnei, Sydni, Sydnie
(French) forms of Sydney.

Sydney (French) from Saint-Denis,
France. See also Sidnee, Sidonie.
*Cidney, Cydney, Sy, Syd, Sydel, Sydelle,
Sydna, Sydnea, Sydny, Sydnye, Syndona,
Syndonah*

Syerra (Irish, Spanish) a form of Sierra.
Syera

Sying (Chinese) star.

Sylvana (Latin) forest.
*Sylva, Sylvaine, Sylvanah, Sylvania,
Sylvanna, Sylvina, Sylvinnia, Sylvonah,
Sylvonia, Sylvonna*

Sylvia (Latin) forest. Literature: Sylvia
Plath was a well-known American poet.
See also Silvia, Xylia.
Sylvette

Sylviann, Sylvianne (American) combinations of Sylvia + Ann.
Sylvian

Sylvie (Latin) a familiar form of Sylvia.
Silvi, Silvie, Silvy, Sylvi

Sylwia (Latin) a form of Sylvia.

Symantha (American) a form of
Samantha.

Symone (Hebrew) a form of Simone.
Symmeon, Symmone, Symona, Symoné,
Symonne

Symphony (Greek) symphony, harmonious sound.
Symfoni, Symphanée, Symphanie,
Symphany, Symphoni, Symphonie

Synthia (Greek) a form of Cynthia.
Sinthea, Sinthia, Sinthiah, Sinthya, Sinthyah,
Synthea, Synthiah, Synthya, Synthyah

Syreeta (Hindi) good traditions. (Arabic) companion.
Syretta, Syrrita

Syrena (Greek) a form of Sirena.
Syreana, Syreanah, Syreane, Syreen, Syreena,
Syreenah, Syreene, Syren, Syrenah, Syrenia,
Syreniah, Syrenna, Syrenya, Syrenyah,
Syrin, Syrina, Syrinah, Syrine, Syryn,
Syryna, Syrynah, Syryne

T

T'keyah (American) a form of Takia.

Tabatha, Tabbatha (Greek, Aramaic) forms of Tabitha.
Tabathe, Tabathia

Tabbitha (Greek, Aramaic) a form of Tabitha.

Tabby (English) a familiar form of Tabitha.
Tabbee, Tabbey, Tabbi, Tabbie

Tabea (Swahili) a form of Tabia.

Tabetha (Greek, Aramaic) a form of Tabitha.
Tabbetha

Tabia (Swahili) talented.
Tabya, Tabyah

Tabina (Arabic) follower of Muhammad.
Tabinah, Tabyna, Tabynah

Tabitha (Greek, Aramaic) gazelle.
Tabiatha, Tabita, Tabithia, Tabotha, Tabtha

Tabytha (Greek, Aramaic) a form of Tabitha.
Tabbytha

Tacey (English) a familiar form of Tacita.
Tace, Tacea, Tacee, Taci, Tacy, Tacye, Taicea,
Taicee, Taicey, Taici, Taicie, Taicy, Taycea,
Taycee, Taycey, Tayci, Taycie, Taycy

Taci (Zuni) washtub. (English) a form of Tacey.
Tacia, Taciana, Tacie

Tacita (Latin) silent.
Taceta, Tacetah, Tasita, Tasitah, Taycita,
Taycitah, Taycyta, Taycytah

Taddea (Greek) a form of Thaddea.
Taddeah, Tadea, Tadeah, Tadia, Tadiah,
Tadya, Tadyah

Tadita (Omaha) runner.
Tadeta, Tadetah, Taditah, Tadra, Tadyta,
Tadytah

Taelar, Taeler, Taelor (English) forms of Taylor.
Taellor, Taelore, Taelyr

Taesha (Latin) a form of Tisha. (American) a combination of the prefix Ta + Aisha.
Tadasha, Taeshayla, Taeshia, Taheisha,
Tahisha, Taiesha, Tayesha

Taffline (Welsh) beloved.
Taflina, Taflinah, Tafline, Taflyn, Taflyna,
Taflynah, Taflyne

Taffy (Welsh) a familiar form of Taffline.
Taafe, Taffea, Taffee, Taffey, Taffi, Taffia, Taffie,
Taffine, Taffye, Tafia, Tafisa, Tafoya, Tafy

Tafne (Egyptian) Mythology: the goddess of light.
Taffnee, Taffney, Taffni, Taffnie, Taffny, Tafna,
Tafnah, Tafnee

Tahira (Arabic) virginal, pure.
Taheera, Taheerah, Tahera, Tahere, Taheria,
Taherri, Tahiara, Tahirah, Tahireh, Tahyra,
Tahyrah

Tahiti (Polynesian) rising sun. Geography: an island in the southern Pacific Ocean.
Tahitea, Tahitee, Tahitey, Tahitia, Tahitie,
Tahity

Tahlia (Greek, Hebrew) a form of Talia.
Tahleah, Tahleia

Tai (Vietnamese) weather; prosperous; talented.

Taija (Hindi) a form of Taja.
Taiajára

Tailer, Tailor (English) forms of Taylor.
Tailar, Tailara, Taillor, Tailora, Tailore, Tailyr

Taima (Native American) clash of thunder.
Taimah, Taimi, Taimia, Taimy, Tayma, Taymah, Taymi, Taymie, Taymmi, Taymmie, Taymmy, Taymy

Taimani (Tongan) diamonds.
Taimanee, Taimaney, Taimania, Taimaniah, Taimanie, Taimany, Taimanya, Taimanyah

Taipa (Moquelumnan) flying quail.
Taipah, Taypa, Taypah

Taira (Aramaic, Irish, Arabic) a form of Tara.
Tairra

Tais (Greek) bound.
Taisa, Taisah, Tays, Taysa, Taysah

Taisha (American) a form of Taesha.
Taishae

Taite (English) cheerful.
Tait, Taita, Taitah, Tayt, Tayta, Tayte, Tayten

Taja (Hindi) crown.
Tajae, Tahai, Teja, Tejah, Tejal

Tajah (Hindi) a form of Taja.

Taka (Japanese) honored.
Takah

Takala (Hopi) corn tassel.

Takara (Japanese) treasure.
Takarah, Takaria, Takariah, Takarra, Takarrah, Takarya, Takaryah, Takra

Takayla (American) a combination of the prefix Ta + Kayla.
Takayler, Takeyli

Takeia (Arabic) a form of Takia.
Takeiah, Takeiya, Takeiyah

Takeisha (American) a combination of the prefix Ta + Keisha.

Takecia, Tekeesha, Tekeisha, Tekeshi, Tekeysia, Tekisha, Tikesha, Tikisha, Tokesia

Takenya (Hebrew) animal horn. (Moquelumnan) falcon. (American) a combination of the prefix Ta + Kenya.
Takenia, Takeniah, Takenja, Takenjah, Takenyah

Takeria (American) a form of Takira.
Takeara, Takearah, Takera, Takeri, Takerian, Takerra, Takerria, Takierria, Takoria, Taquera, Taquerah, Tekeria, Tekeriah

Takesha (American) a form of Takeisha.
Takeshia, Takesia

Takeya (Arabic) a form of Takia.
Takeyah

Taki (Japanese) waterfall.
Takee, Takey, Takie, Taky, Tiki

Takia (Arabic) worshiper.
Takhiya, Takiah, Takija, Takijah, Takkia, Takkiah, Takkya, Takkyah, Takya, Takyah, Takyia, Taqiya, Taqiyah, Taqiyya, Taquaia, Taquaya, Taquiia, Taquiiah, Tikia

Takila (American) a form of Tequila.
Takeila, Takela, Takelia, Takella, Takeyla, Takiela, Takilah, Takilla, Takilya, Takyla, Takylia, Tatakyla, Tehilla, Tekeila, Tekela, Tekelia, Tekilaa, Tekilia, Tekilla, Tekilyah, Tekla

Takira (American) a combination of the prefix Ta + Kira.
Takeera, Takeira, Takeirah, Takera, Takiara, Takiera, Takierah, Takierra, Takirah, Takiria, Takiriah, Takirra, Takora, Takyra, Takyrah, Takyrra, Taquira, Taquirah, Tekyra, Tekyria, Tekyriah, Tekyrya, Tikara, Tikarah, Tikira, Tikirah, Tikiria, Tikiriah, Tikirya, Tikiryah

Takisha (American) a form of Takeisha.
Takishea, Takishia

Takiya, Takiyah (Arabic) forms of Takia.

Tala (Native American) stalking wolf.
Talah

Talasi (Hopi) corn tassel.
Talasea, Talasee, Talasia, Talasiah, Talasy, Talasya, Talasyah

Talaya (American) a form of Talia.
Talayah, Talayia

Talea, Taleah (American) forms of Talia.
Taleana, Taleea, Taleéi, Taleia, Taleiya, Tylea,
Tyleah

Taleebin (Australian) young.
Taleabin, Taleabina, Taleabine, Taleabyn,
Taleabyna, Taleabyne, Taleebina, Taleebine,
Taleebyn, Taleebyna, Taleebyne

Taleisha (American) a combination of
Talia + Aisha.
Taileisha, Taleasha, Taleashia, Taleashiah,
Taleashya, Taleesha, Taleeshia, Taleeshiah,
Taleeshya, Taleise, Taleysha, Taleyshia,
Taleyshiah, Taleyshya, Taleyshyah, Talicia,
Taliesha, Talysha, Tilisha, Tyleasha, Tyleisha,
Tylicia, Tylisha, Tylishia

Talena (American) a combination of the
prefix Ta + Lena.
Talayna, Taleana, Taleanah, Taleane, Taleena,
Taleenah, Taleene, Talenah, Talene, Talihna,
Tallenia, Talná, Tilena, Tilene, Tylena

Talesha (American) a form of Taleisha.
Taleesha, Talesa, Talese, Taleshia, Talesia,
Tallese, Tallesia, Tylesha, Tyleshia, Tylesia

Talia (Greek) blooming. (Hebrew) dew
from heaven. (Latin, French) birthday. A
short form of Natalie. See also Thalia.
Taleya, Taleyah, Taliatha, Taliea, Talieya,
Tallia, Tylia

Taliah (Greek, Hebrew, Latin, French) a
form of Talia.
Talliah

Talina (American) a combination of Talia
+ Lina.
Talin, Talinah, Talinda, Taline, Tallyn, Talyn,
Talyna, Talynah, Talyne, Talynn, Tylina,
Tyline

Talisa, Talissa (English) forms of Tallis.
Talisah, Talisia, Talisiah, Talissah, Tallisa,
Tallisah, Tallysa, Tallysah, Talysa, Talysah,
Talysha, Talysia, Talysiah, Talyssa, Talyssah

Talisha (American) a form of Taleisha.
(English) a form of Talisa.
Talishia

Talitha (Arabic) young girl.
Taleetha, Taletha, Talethia, Taliatha, Talita,
Talith, Talithah, Talithe, Talithia, Talyth,
Talytha, Talythe, Telita, Tiletha

Taliyah (Greek) a form of Talia.
Taliya, Talliyah

Talley (French) a familiar form of Talia.
Talee, Talei, Taleigh, Taley, Tali, Talie, Talle,
Tallee, Tallei, Talleigh, Talli, Tallie, Tally, Taly,
Talye, Tylee

Tallis (French, English) forest.
Taleace, Talease, Taleece, Taleese, Taleice,
Taleise, Taleyce, Taleyse, Talice, Taliece, Taliese,
Talise, Taliss, Talisse, Talliss, Tallise, Tallys,
Tallyse, Talyce, Talys, Talyse, Talyss, Talysse

Tallulah (Choctaw) leaping water.
Tallou, Tallula, Talula

Talma (Native American) thunder.
Talmah

Talman (Hebrew) to injure, oppress.

Talon (French, English) claw, nail.
Taelon, Taelyn, Talen, Tallin, Tallon, Talyn

Talor (Hebrew) dew.
Talora, Talorah, Talore, Talorey, Talori, Taloria,
Taloriah, Talorie, Talory, Talorya, Taloryah,
Talorye

Talya (Greek) a form of Talia.
Tallya, Talyah, Talyia

Tam (Vietnamese) heart.

Tama (Japanese) jewel.
Tamaa, Tamah, Tamaiah, Tamala, Tema

Tamaira (American) a form of Tamara.
Tamairah

Tamaka (Japanese) bracelet.
Tamakah, Tamaki, Tamakia, Tamakiah,
Tamako, Tamaky, Tamakya, Tamakyah,
Timaka

Tamanna (Hindi) desire.
Tamana, Tamanah, Tamannah

Tamar (Russian) History: a twelfth-
century Georgian queen. (Hebrew) a
short form of Tamara.
Tamer, Tamor, Tamour

Tamara (Hebrew) palm tree. See also
Tammy.
Tamará, Tamarae, Tamaree, Tamarin,
Tamarla, Tamarria, Tamarrian, Tamarsha,
Tamary, Tamarya, Tamaryah, Tamma,
Tammara, Tamora, Tamoya, Tamura, Temara,
Temarian, Thamara, Tomara, Tymara

Tamarah, Tamarra (Hebrew) forms of
Tamara.
Tamarrah

Tamaria (Hebrew) a form of Tamara.
Tamari, Tamariah, Tamarie

Tamassa (Hebrew) a form of Thomasina.
Tamas, Tamasa, Tamasah, Tamasin, Tamasine,
Thamasa

Tameisha (American) a form of Tamesha.

Tameka (Aramaic) twin.
Tameca, Tamecah, Tamecka, Tameckah,
Tameeca, Tameecah, Tameeka, Tameekah,
Tamekah, Tamiecka, Tamieka, Temeka,
Tomeka, Trameika, Tymeka, Tymmeeka,
Tymmeka

Tamekia (Aramaic) a form of Tameka.
Tamecia, Tomekia

Tamela (American) a form of Tamila.
Tamelia

Tamera (Hebrew) a form of Tamara.
Tamer, Tamerai, Tameran, Tameria, Tamerra,
Tammera, Thamer, Timera

Tamesha (American) a combination of
the prefix Ta + Mesha.
Tameesha, Tameshah, Tamnesha, Tamysha,
Tamyshah, Temisha, Tomesha, Tomiese,
Tomise, Tomisha, Tramesha, Tramisha,
Tymesha

Tameshia (American) a form of Tamesha.
Tameeshia, Tameeshiah, Tameeshya,
Tameshkia, Tameshya, Tamishia, Tamishiah,
Tamyshia, Tamyshiah, Tamyshya, Tamyshyah

Tami, Tammi, Tammie (English) forms of
Tammy.
Tamie

Tamia (Hebrew, English) a form of Tammy.
Tameia, Tamiah

Tamika (Japanese) a form of Tamiko.
Tameika, Tamica, Tamicah, Tamicka,
Tamickah, Tamieka, Tamikah, Tamikia,
Tamikka, Tammika, Tamyca, Tamycah,
Tamycka, Tamyckah, Tamyka, Tamykah,
Timika, Timikia, Tomika, Tomyka, Tymika,
Tymmicka

Tamiko (Japanese) child of the people.
Tameeko, Tameko, Tamike, Tamiqua, Tamiyo,
Tammiko, Tamyko

Tamila (American) a combination of the
prefix Ta + Mila.
Tamala, Tamilah, Tamilla, Tamillah, Tamille,
Tamillia, Tamilya, Tamyla, Tamylah, Tamylla,
Tamyllah

Tamira (Hebrew) a form of Tamara.
Tamir, Tamirae, Tamirah, Tamiria, Tamirra

Tamisha (American) a form of Tamesha.
Tamishah

Tamiya (Hebrew, English) a form of
Tammy.

Tammy (English) twin. (Hebrew) a famil-
iar form of Tamara.
Tamee, Tamey, Tamijo, Tamilyn, Tamlyn,
Tammee, Tammey, Tamy, Tamya

Tamra (Hebrew) a short form of Tamara.
Tammra, Tammrah, Tamrah

Tamrika (American) a combination of
Tammy + Erika.
Tamricka, Tamrickah, Tamrikah, Tamriqua,
Tamriquah, Tamrique, Tamryca, Tamrycah,
Tamrycka, Tamryckah, Tamryka, Tamrykah,
Tamryqua, Tamryquah, Tamryque

Tamsin (English) a short form of
Thomasina.
Tamsen, Tamsina, Tamsinah, Tamsine,
Tamsyn, Tamsyna, Tamsynah, Tamsyne,
Tamzen, Tamzin, Tamzina, Tamzinah,
Tamzine, Tamzyn, Tamzyna, Tamzynah,
Tamzyne

Tamyra (Hebrew) a form of Tamara.
Tamyria, Tamyrra

Tana, Tanna (Slavic) short forms of Tanya.
Taina, Tanae, Tanaeah, Tanah, Tanalia,
Tanara, Tanavia, Tanaz, Tannah

Tanaya (Russian, Slavic) a form of Tanya.

Tandra (English) a form of Tandy.
Tandrea, Tandria

Tandy (English) team.
Tanda, Tandalaya, Tandea, Tandee, Tandey, Tandi, Tandia, Tandiah, Tandie, Tandis, Tandya, Tandyah, Tandye

Tanea (Russian, Slavic) a form of Tanya.
Taneah, Taneé, Taneeia, Taneia

Taneesha (American) a form of Tanesha.
Taneeshah

Taneisha (American) a form of Tanesha.
Tahniesha

Tanesha (American) combinations of the prefix Ta + Nesha.
Taineshia, Tanasha, Tanashah, Tanashia, Tanaysia, Taneasha, Taneshea, Taneshia, Taneshya, Tanesia, Tanesian, Tanessa, Tanessia, Tannesha, Tanneshia, Tanniecia, Tanniesha, Tantashea

Taneya (Russian, Slavic) a form of Tanya.
Taneeya, Taneeyah

Tangela (American) a combination of the prefix Ta + Angela.
Tangel, Tangelah, Tangele, Tangell, Tangella, Tangellah, Tangelle, Tanjel, Tanjela, Tanjelah, Tanjele, Tanjell, Tanjella, Tanjelle

Tangi, Tangie (American) short forms of Tangia.
Tanji, Tanjie, Tanjy

Tangia (American) a form of Tangela.
Tangiah, Tangya, Tangyah

Tani (Japanese) valley. (Slavic) stand of glory. A familiar form of Tania.
Tahnee, Tahney, Tahni, Tahnie, Tahny, Tanee, Taney, Tanie, Tany

Tania (Russian, Slavic) fairy queen.
Tahnia, Tahniah, Taneea, Taniah, Tanija, Tannia, Tanniah, Tarnia

Taniel (American) a combination of Tania + Danielle.
Taniela, Tanielah, Taniele, Taniell, Taniella, Taniellah, Tanielle, Tanyel, Tanyela, Tanyelah, Tanyele, Tanyell, Tanyella, Tanyellah, Tanyelle

Taniesha (American) a form of Tanesha.

Tanika, Taniqua (American) forms of Tania.
Taneek, Tanikka, Tanikqua, Tanique, Tannica, Tannika, Tianeka, Tianika

Tanis, Tannis (Slavic) forms of Tania, Tanya.
Tanas, Tanese, Taniese, Tanise, Tanisia, Tanisse, Tannese, Tanniece, Tanniese, Tannise, Tannisse, Tannus, Tannyce, Tannys, Tanys, Tiannis, Tonise, Tranice, Tranise, Tynice, Tyniece, Tyniese, Tynise

Tanisha (American) a combination of the prefix Ta + Nisha.
Tahniscia, Tahnisha, Tanasha, Tanashea, Tanicha, Tanish, Tanishah, Tanishia, Tanitia, Tannicia, Tannisha, Tanysha, Tanyshah

Tanissa (American) a combination of the prefix Tania + Nissa.
Tanesa, Tanisa, Tanisah, Tanissah, Tannesa, Tannisa, Tannisah, Tannissa, Tannissah, Tannysa, Tannysah, Tannyssa, Tannyssah, Tennessa, Tranissa

Tanita (American) a combination of the prefix Ta + Nita.
Taneeta, Taneetah, Taneta, Tanetta, Tanitah, Tanitra, Tanitta, Tanyta, Tanytah, Tanyte, Teneta, Tenetta, Tenita, Tenitta, Tyneta, Tynetta, Tynette, Tynita, Tynitra, Tynitta

Tanith (Phoenician) Mythology: Tanit is the goddess of love.
Tanitha, Tanithah, Tanithe, Tanyth, Tanytha, Tanythah, Tanythe

Taniya (Russian, Slavic) a form of Tania, Tanya.

Tanja (American) a short form of Tangela.
Tanjia

Tanner (English) leather worker, tanner.
Tannor

Tansy (Greek) immortal. (Latin) tenacious, persistent.
Tancy, Tansea, Tansee, Tansey, Tanshay, Tansi, Tansia, Tansiah, Tansie, Tansya, Tansyah, Tansye, Tanzey

Tanya (Russian, Slavic) fairy queen. See also Tania.
Tahnya, Tahnyah, Taniya, Tanniya, Tannya, Tannyah, Tanoya, Tany, Tanyah, Tanyia, Taunya, Thanya

Tao (Chinese, Vietnamese) peach.

Tara (Aramaic) throw; carry. (Irish) rocky hill. (Arabic) a measurement.
Taraea, Taráh, Tarai, Taralee, Tarali, Tarasa, Tarasha, Taraya, Tarha, Tayra, Tehra

Tarah, Tarra, Tarrah (Irish) forms of Tara.

Taralyn (American) a form of Teralyn.

Taran (Persian) a short form of Taraneh. (Irish) a form of Tara.

Taraneh (Persian) melody.
Tarana, Taranah, Tarane

Tarati (Maori) God's gift.
Taratea, Taratee, Taratey, Taratia, Taratiah, Taratie, Taraty, Taratya, Taratyah

Taree (Japanese) arching branch.
Tarea, Tarey, Tareya, Tari

Tari (Irish) a familiar form of Tara.
Taria, Tariah, Tarie, Tarila, Tarilyn, Tarita, Tary, Tarya, Tayah

Tarika (Hindi) star.
Tarikah, Taryka, Tarykah

Tarin, Tarryn, Taryn (Irish) forms of Tara.
Tareen, Tareena, Taren, Tarene, Tarina, Tarinah, Tarine, Taron, Tarren, Tarrena, Tarrin, Tarrina, Tarrinah, Tarrine, Tarron, Tarryna, Tarrynah, Tarryne, Taryna, Tarynah, Taryne, Tarynn, Tarynna, Tarynnah, Tarynne

Tarissa (American) a combination of Tara + Rissa.
Taris, Tarisa, Tarise, Tarisha

Tarne (Scandinavian) lake in the mountains. (Australian) salty water.
Tarnea, Tarnee, Tarney, Tarni, Tarnia, Tarnie, Tarny, Tarnya, Tarnyah

Tasarla (Gypsy) dawn.
Tasarlea, Tasarleah, Tasarlee, Tasarleigh, Tasarley, Tasarli, Tasarlia, Tasarliah, Tasarlie, Tasarly, Tasarlya, Tasarlyah, Tasarlye

Taseem (Indian) salute of praise.

Tasha (Greek) born on Christmas day. (Russian) a short form of Natasha. See also Tashi, Tosha.
Tacha, Tachiana, Tahsha, Tasenka, Tashe, Tasheka, Taska, Taysha, Thasha, Tiaisha, Tysha

Tashana (American) a combination of the prefix Ta + Shana.
Tashan, Tashanah, Tashanda, Tashaney, Tashani, Tashania, Tashaniah, Tashanie, Tashanika, Tashanna, Tashany, Tashanya, Tashanyah, Tashina, Tishana, Tishani, Tishanna, Tishanne, Toshanna, Toshanti, Tyshana

Tashara (American) a combination of the prefix Ta + Shara.
Tashar, Tasharah, Tasharia, Tasharna, Tasharra, Tashera, Tasherey, Tasheri, Tasherra, Tashira, Tashirah

Tashauna (American) a form of Tashawna.
Tashaugna, Tashaugnah, Tashaunah, Tashauni, Tashaunia, Tashauniah, Tashaunie, Tashaunna, Tashaunya, Tashaunyah, Toshauna

Tashawna (American) a combination of the prefix Ta + Shawna.
Taseana, Taseanah, Taseania, Taseanya, Tashawanna, Tashawn, Tashawnah, Tashawnda, Tashawnia, Tashawniah, Tashawnna, Tashawnnia, Tashawnya, Tashawnyah, Tashonda, Tashondra, Tiashauna, Tishawn, Tishunda, Tishunta, Toshawna, Tyshauna, Tyshawna

Tashay (Greek, Russian) a form of Tasha.
Tashae

Tasheena (American) a combination of the prefix Ta + Sheena.
Tasheana, Tasheeana, Tasheeni, Tasheona, Tashina, Tisheena, Tosheena, Tysheana, Tysheena, Tyshyna

Tashelle (American) a combination of the prefix Ta + Shelley.
Tachell, Tashel, Tashela, Tashelah, Tashele, Tashelia, Tasheliah, Tashelie, Tashell, Tashella, Tashellah, Tashellea, Tashelleah, Tashellee, Tashelleigh, Tashelley, Tashelli, Tashellia, Tashelliah, Tashellie, Tashelly, Tashellya,

Tashelle (cont.)
Tashellyah, Techell, Techelle, Teshell, Teshelle,
Tochell, Tochelle, Toshelle, Tychell, Tychelle,
Tyshell, Tyshelle

Tashena (American) a form of Tasheena.
Tashenna, Tashennia

Tashi (Hausa) a bird in flight. (Slavic) a
form of Tasha.
Tashe, Tashea, Tashee, Tashey, Tashie, Tashika,
Tashima, Tashy

Tashia (Slavic, Hausa) a form of Tashi.
Tashiah, Tashiya, Tashya, Tashyah

Tashiana (American) a form of Tashana.
Tashianna

Tasia (Slavic) a familiar form of Tasha.
Tachia, Tasiah, Tasija, Tasiya, Tassia, Tassiah,
Tassiana, Tasya, Tasyah

Tasmin (English) a short form of
Thomasina.
Tasma, Tasmyn, Tasmyna, Tasmynah,
Tasmyne, Tasmynn, Tasmynna, Tasmynnah,
Tasmynne, Tazmin, Tazmina, Tazminah,
Tazmine, Tazmyn, Tazmyna, Tazmynah,
Tazmyne

Tassie (English) a familiar form of Tasmin.
Tasee, Tasey, Tasi, Tasie, Tassee, Tassey, Tassi,
Tassy, Tazee, Tazey, Tazi, Tazie, Tazy,
Tazzee, Tazzey, Tazzi, Tazzie, Tazzy

Tassos (Greek) a form of Theresa.
Tasos

Tata (Russian) a familiar form of Tatiana.
Tatah, Tatia, Tatiah, Tatya, Tatyah

Tate (English) a short form of Tatum. A
form of Taite, Tata.

Tatiana (Slavic) fairy queen. See also
Tania, Tanya, Tiana.
Taitiann, Taitianna, Tatania, Tataniah,
Tatanya, Tatanyah, Tateana, Tateanna,
Tateonna, Tateyana, Tati, Tatia, Tatianah,
Tatiania, Tatianiah, Tatiayana, Tatie, Tatihana,
Tationna, Tatiyona, Tatiyonna, Tiatiana

Tatianna (Slavic) a form of Tatiana.
Tatiann, Tatiannah

Tatiyana (Slavic) a form of Tatiana.
Tatiyanna

Tatjana (Slavic) a form of Tatiana.

Tatum (English) cheerful.
Taitam, Taitem, Taitim, Taitom, Taitum,
Taitym, Tatam, Tatem, Tatim, Tatom, Tatumn,
Taytam, Taytem, Taytim, Taytom, Taytum,
Taytym

Tatyana, Tatyanna (Slavic) forms of
Tatiana.
Tatyanah, Tatyani, Tatyannah, Tatyanne,
Tatyona, Tatyonna

Taura (Latin) bull. Astrology: Taurus is a
sign of the zodiac.
Taurae, Taurah, Tauria, Tauriah, Taurina,
Taurya, Tauryah

Tauri (English) a form of Tory.
Taure, Taurie, Taury

Tavia (Latin) a short form of Octavia. See
also Tawia.
Taiva, Tauvia, Tava, Tavah, Taviah, Tavita,
Tavya, Tavyah

Tavie (Scottish) twin.
Tavee, Tavey, Tavi

Tawana, Tawanna (American) combina-
tions of the prefix Ta + Wanda.
Taiwana, Taiwanna, Taquana, Taquanna,
Tawan, Tawanda, Tawandah, Tawannah,
Tawannda, Tawanndah, Tawanne, Tequana,
Tequanna, Tequawna, Tewanna, Tewauna,
Tiquana, Tiwanna, Tiwena, Towanda,
Towanna, Tywania, Tywanna

Tawia (African) born after twins. (Polish)
a form of Tavia.
Tawiah, Tawya, Tawyah

Tawnee, Tawney, Tawni, Tawnie (English)
forms of Tawny.
Tawnnie

Tawny (Gypsy) little one. (English)
brownish yellow, tan.
Tahnee, Tany, Tauna, Tauné, Tauni, Taunisha,
Tawnesha, Tawnye, Tawnyell, Tiawna, Tiawni

Tawnya (American) a combination of
Tawny + Tonya.
Taunia, Tawna, Tawnea, Tawnia, Tawniah,
Tawnyah

Taya (English) a short form of Taylor.
Taia, Taiah, Tayah, Tayiah, Tayna, Tayra, Taysha, Taysia, Tayva, Tayvonne, Tiaya, Tiya, Tiyah, Tye

Tayana (English) a form of Taya.

Tayanita (Cherokee) beaver.
Taianita, Taianitah, Tayanitah, Tayanyta, Tayanytah

Taye (English) a short form of Taylor.
Tay

Tayla (English) a short form of Taylor.
Taila, Tailah, Tailea, Taileah, Tailee, Tailei, Taileigh, Tailey, Taili, Tailia, Tailiah, Tailie, Taylah, Taylea, Tayleah, Taylee, Taylei, Tayleigh, Tayley, Tayli, Taylia, Tayliah, Taylie, Tayly

Taylar, Tayler, Taylore, Taylour, Taylre
(English) forms of Taylor.
Taylara, Taylare, Tayllar, Tayller, Tayllore

Taylor (English) tailor.
Taiylor, Talar, Tayllor, Tayloir, Taylora, Taylorann, Taylorr, Taylur

Tazu (Japanese) stork; longevity.
Taz, Tazi, Tazoo

Teagan (Welsh) beautiful, attractive.
Taegan, Taegen, Taegin, Taegon, Taegun, Taegyn, Teage, Teagen, Teaghan, Teaghanne, Teaghen, Teaghin, Teaghon, Teaghun, Teaghyn, Teagin, Teagon, Teague, Teagun, Teagyn, Teegan, Teegen, Teeghan, Teegin, Teegon, Teegun, Teegyn, Teigan, Teigen, Teigin, Teigon, Teigun, Teigyn, Tejan, Teygan, Teygen, Teygin, Teygon, Teygun, Teygyn, Tiegan, Tigan, Tigen, Tigin, Tigon, Tigun, Tigyn, Tijan, Tijana, Tygan, Tygen, Tygin, Tygon, Tygun, Tygyn

Teah (Greek, Spanish) a form of Tia.
Téa

Teaira, Teairra (Latin) forms of Tiara.
Teair, Teairre, Teairria

Teal (English) river duck; blue green.
Teale, Teel, Teele, Teil

Teala (English) a form of Teal.
Tealah, Tealia, Tealisha, Teyla, Teylah

Teana, Teanna (American) combinations of the prefix Te + Anna. A form of Tiana.
Tean, Teanah, Teane, Teann, Teannah, Teanne, Teaunna, Teiana, Teianah, Teiane, Teiann, Teianna, Teiannah, Teianne, Teuana

Teara, Tearra (Latin) forms of Tiara.
Tearah, Téare, Teareya, Teari, Tearia, Teariea, Tearria

Teasha (Latin, American) a form of Taesha.
Teashia, Teashiah, Teashya, Teashyah

Teca (Hungarian) a form of Theresa.
Tecah, Techa, Tecka, Teckah, Teka, Tekah, Tica, Ticah, Tika, Tikah, Tyca, Tycah, Tyka, Tykah

Tecla (Greek) God's fame.
Tekla, Theckla

Teddi, Tedi (Greek) familiar forms of Theodora.
Tedde, Teddea, Teddee, Teddey, Teddia, Teddiah, Teddie, Teddy, Tediah, Tedie, Tedy

Tedra (Greek) a short form of Theodora.
Teddra, Teddrah, Teddreya, Tedera, Tedrah, Teedra, Teidra

Teela (English) a form of Teala.

Teena (Spanish, American) a form of Tina.
Teenah, Teenia, Teeniah, Teenya, Teenyah

Teesha (Latin) a form of Tisha.
Teeshia, Teeshiah

Tegan (Welsh) a form of Teagan.
Tega, Tegana, Tegane, Tegen, Teggan, Teghan, Tegin, Tegyn

Tehya (Hindi) a form of Taja.

Teia (Greek, Spanish) a form of Tia.
Teiah

Teila (English) a form of Teala.

Teira, Teirra (Latin) forms of Tiara.

Teisha (Latin, American) a form of Taesha.

Tekia (Arabic) a form of Takia.
Tekeiya, Tekeiyah, Tekeyia, Tekiah, Tekiya, Tekiyah

Telisha (American) a form of Taleisha.
Teleesha, Teleisia, Telesa, Telesha, Teleshia, Telesia, Telicia, Telisa, Telishia, Telisia, Telissa, Telisse, Tellisa, Tellisha, Telsa, Telysa

Temira (Hebrew) tall.
Temora, Timora

Tempany (Australian) a form of Tempest.
Tempanee, Tempaney, Tempani, Tempania, Tempaniah, Tempanie, Tempanya, Tempanyah

Tempest (French) stormy.
Tempesta, Tempestah, Tempeste, Tempist, Tempistt, Tempress, Tempteste

Tempestt (French) a form of Tempest.
Tempestta, Tempestte

Tenesha (American) a form of Tenisha.
Tenecia, Teneesha, Teneisha, Teneshia, Tenesia, Tenessa, Teneusa

Tenille, Tennille (American) combinations of the prefix Te + Nellie.
Teneal, Teneall, Tenealla, Tenealle, Teneil, Teneille, Teniel, Teniele, Tenielle, Tenil, Tenila, Tenilah, Tenile, Tenill, Tenilla, Tenillah, Tenneal, Tenneill, Tenneille, Tennia, Tennie, Tennielle, Tennil, Tennila, Tennilah, Tennile, Tennill, Tennilla, Tennillah, Tennyl, Tennyla, Tennylah, Tennyle, Tennyll, Tennylla, Tennyllah, Tennylle, Tenyl, Tenyla, Tenylah, Tenyle, Tenyll, Tenylla, Tenyllah, Tenylle, Tineal, Tiniel, Tonielle, Tonille

Tenise (Slavic) a form of Tanis.
Tenice, Tenyse

Tenisha (American) a combination of the prefix Te + Nisha.
Teniesha, Tenishia, Tenishka

Teodora (Czech) a form of Theodora.
Teadora, Teodory

Teona, Teonna (Greek) forms of Tiana.
Teon, Teoni, Teonia, Teonie, Teonney, Teonnia, Teonnie

Tequila (Spanish) a kind of liquor. See also Takila.
Taquela, Taquella, Taquila, Taquilla, Tequilia, Tiquila, Tiquilia

Tequilla (Spanish) a form of Tequila.

Tera, Terah, Terra, Terrah (Latin) earth. (Japanese) swift arrow. (American) forms of Tara.
Terai, Terrae

Teralyn (American) a combination of Teri + Lynn.
Teralin, Teralina, Teralinah, Teraline, Teralyna, Teralynah, Teralyne, Teralynn, Terralin, Terralina, Terralinah, Terraline, Terralyn, Terralyna, Terralynah, Terralyne

Teresa (Greek) a form of Theresa. See also Tressa.
Taresa, Taressa, Tarissa, Terasa, Tercza, Tereasa, Tereasah, Tereatha, Tereesa, Tereesah, Teresah, Teresea, Teresha, Teresia, Teresina, Tereson, Teretha, Tereza, Terezia, Terezie, Terezijya, Terezon, Terezsa, Terisa, Terisah, Terisha, Teriza, Terrasa, Terreasa, Terreasah, Terresa, Terresha, Terresia, Terrisa, Terrisah, Terrysa, Terrysah, Teruska, Teté, Tyresa, Tyresia

Terese (Greek) a form of Teresa.
Tarese, Taress, Taris, Tarise, Terease, Tereece, Terees, Tereese, Teress, Terez, Teris, Terise, Terreas, Terrease, Terrise, Terrys, Terryse

Teresina (Italian) a form of Teresa.
Terezinha, Terrosina, Theresina

Teresita (Spanish) a form of Teresa.

Teressa (Greek) a form of Teresa.
Terressa

Teri, Terri, Terrie, Terry (Greek) familiar forms of Theresa.
Tere, Teree, Tereey, Terie, Terree, Terrey, Terrye, Tery

Teria, Terria (Irish) forms of Tera. (Greek) forms of Teri.
Teriah, Terriah, Terrya, Terryah

Terica, Terrica, Terricka (American) combinations of Teri + Erica. See also Rica.
Tericka, Tyrica, Tyricka, Tyronica

Terika, Terrika (American) forms of Terica.
Tereka, Terreka, Tyrika, Tyrikka

Terrelle (German) thunder ruler.
Tarrell, Teral, Terall, Terel, Terela, Terele, Terell, Terella, Teriel, Terral, Terrall, Terrel,

Terrell, Terrella, Terriel, Terriell, Terrielle, Terrill, Terryelle, Terryl, Terryll, Terrylle, Teryl, Tyrell, Tyrelle

Terrene (Latin) smooth.
Tareena, Tarena, Teran, Teranee, Terean, Tereana, Tereane, Tereen, Tereena, Tereene, Terena, Terencia, Terene, Terenia, Terentia, Terentya, Terentyah, Terran, Terrean, Terreana, Terreane, Terreen, Terreena, Terreene, Terren, Terrena, Terron, Terrosina, Terun, Tyreen, Tyrene

Terriana, Terrianna (American) combinations of Teri + Anna.
Teriana, Terianna, Terriauna, Terrina, Terriyana, Terriyanna, Terryana, Terryauna, Tyrina

Terriann (American) a combination of Teri + Ann.
Terian, Teriann, Terianne, Teriyan, Terrian, Terrianne, Terryann

Terrin, Terryn, Teryn (Latin) forms of Terrene.
Terin, Terina, Terine, Terrina, Terrine, Terryna, Terryne, Teryna, Terynn

Terriona (American) a form of Terriana.
Terrionna

Terry-Lynn (American) a combination of Teri + Lynn.
Terelyn, Terelynn, Terri-Lynn, Terrilynn, Terrylynn

Tersea (Greek) a form of Teresa.
Tersa, Terza

Tertia (Latin) third.
Tercia, Tercina, Tercine, Terecena, Tersia, Tertiah, Tertya, Tertyah, Terza

Tesa (Greek) a form of Tessa.
Tesah

Tesha (Latin, American) a form of Taesha, Tisha.

Tesia, Tessia (Greek) forms of Tessa.

Tesla (American) a unit of magnetic flux density, named after its creator, Nikola Tesla, a Croatian-born physicist.

Tess (Greek) a short form of Quintessa, Theresa.
Tes, Tese

Tessa (Greek) reaper.
Tessah, Tezia

Tessie (Greek) a familiar form of Theresa.
Tesi, Tessey, Tessi, Tessy, Tezi

Tessla (American) a form of Tesla.

Tetsu (Japanese) strong as iron.
Tetsoo

Tetty (English) a familiar form of Elizabeth.

Tevy (Cambodian) angel.
Teva, Tevee, Tevey, Tevi, Tevie

Teya (English) a form of Taya. (Greek, Spanish) a form of Tia.

Teyana, Teyanna (American) forms of Teana.
Teyan, Teyanah, Teyane, Teyann, Teyannah, Teyanne, Teyuna

Teylor (English) a form of Taylor.
Teighlor, Teylar

Teyona (American) a form of Teana.

Thaddea (Greek) courageous. (Latin) praiser.
Taddea, Thada, Thadda, Thadia, Thadiah, Thadie, Thadina, Thadya, Thadyah, Thadyna, Thadyne

Thais (Greek) a form of Tais.
Thays

Thalassa (Greek) sea, ocean.
Thalassah

Thalia (Greek) a form of Talia. Mythology: the Muse of comedy.
Thaleia, Thaliah, Thalie, Thalya, Thalyah

Thamara (Hebrew) a form of Tamara.
Thama, Thamar, Thamarah, Thamare, Thamaria, Thamariah, Thamarra, Thamarya, Thamaryah

Thana (Arabic) happy occasion.
Thaina, Thainah, Thayna, Thaynah

Thandie (Zulu) beloved.
Thandee, Thandey, Thandi, Thandy

Thanh (Vietnamese) bright blue.
(Punjabi) good place.

Thania (Arabic) a form of Thana.
Thanie

Thao (Vietnamese) respectful of parents.

Thea (Greek) goddess. A short form of
Althea.
Theah, Theia, Theiah, Theo, Theya, Theyah

Theadora (Greek) a form of Theodora.

Thelma (Greek) willful.
Telma, Telmah, Thelmai, Thelmalina

Thema (African) queen.
Themah

Theodora (Greek) gift of God. See also
Dora, Dorothy, Feodora.
*Taedra, Tedra, Teodora, Theda, Thedorsha,
Thedrica, Theo, Theodore, Theodoria,
Theodorian, Theodosia, Theodra*

Theodosia (Greek) a form of Theodora.
*Teodosia, Teodosiah, Teodosya, Teodosyah,
Thedosia, Thedosiah, Thedosya, Thedosyah,
Theodosiah, Theodosya, Theodosyah*

Theone (Greek) gift of God.
*Theona, Theonah, Theondra, Theonee,
Theoni, Theonie*

Theophania (Greek) God's appearance.
See also Epiphany, Tiffany.
*Theophaniah, Theophanie, Theophano,
Theophanya, Theophanyah*

Theophila (Greek) loved by God.
*Teofila, Theofilia, Theofilie, Theophyla,
Theophylah, Theophylla, Theophyllah*

Theresa (Greek) reaper. See also Resi,
Reza, Riza, Tassos, Teca, Tracey, Zilya.
*Thereasa, Theresah, Theresia, Theresie,
Theresita, Theressa, Thereza, Therisa,
Therisah, Therissie, Therrisa, Therrisah,
Therrysa, Therrysah, Thersea, Therysa,
Therysah*

Therese (Greek) a form of Theresa.
*Thérése, Theresse, Therise, Therra, Therressa,
Therris, Therrise, Therrys, Therryse, Theryse*

Theta (Greek) Linguistics: a letter in the
Greek alphabet.

Thetis (Greek) disposed. Mythology: the
mother of Achilles.
*Thetisa, Thetisah, Thetise, Thetiss, Thetissa,
Thetisse, Thetys, Thetysa, Thetyse, Thetyss,
Thetyssa, Thetysse*

Thi (Vietnamese) poem.
Thia, Thy, Thya

Thirza (Hebrew) pleasant. See also Tirza.
*Thersa, Therza, Thirsa, Thirzah, Thursa,
Thurza, Thyrza, Thyrzah, Tirshka*

Thomasina (Hebrew) twin. See also
Tamassa, Tasmin.
*Thamasin, Thamasina, Thamasine,
Thomasa, Thomasah, Thomasia, Thomasin,
Thomasinah, Thomasine, Thomason,
Thomassine, Thomassyn, Thomassyna,
Thomassynah, Thomassyne, Thomasyn,
Thomasyna, Thomasynah, Thomasyne,
Thomazine, Thomencia, Thomethia,
Thomisha, Thomsina, Toma, Tomasa,
Tomasin, Tomasina, Tomasinah, Tomasine,
Tomasyn, Tomasyna, Tomasynah, Tomasyne,
Tomina, Tommina*

Thora (Scandinavian) thunder.
Thorah, Thorri

Thordis (Scandinavian) Thor's spirit.
*Thordia, Thordisa, Thordisah, Thordise,
Thordiss, Thordissa, Thordissah, Thordisse,
Thordys, Thordysa, Thordysah, Thordyse,
Thordyss, Thordyssa, Thordyssah, Thordysse*

Thrina (Greek) a form of Trina.
*Thrinah, Thrine, Thryn, Thryna, Thrynah,
Thryne*

Thu (Vietnamese) autumn; poem.

Thuy (Vietnamese) gentle.

Tia (Greek) princess. (Spanish) aunt.
*Teea, Teeah, Teeya, Ti, Tiah, Tialeigh,
Tiamarie, Tianda, Tiandria, Tiante, Tiia,
Tiye, Tya, Tyah, Tyja*

Tiaira (Latin) a form of Tiara.

Tiana, Tianna (Greek) princess. (Latin)
short forms of Tatiana. See also Tyana.

Tiahna, Tian, Tianah, Tiane, Tiann, Tiannah, Tianne, Tiannee, Tianni, Tiaon, Tiena

Tiani (Greek, Latin) a form of Tiana.
Tianea, Tianee

Tiara (Latin) crowned.
Teearia, Tiarah, Tiarea, Tiareah, Tiari, Tiaria, Tyara, Tyarah

Tiare (Latin) a form of Tiara.

Tiarra (Latin) a form of Tiara.
Tiairra, Tiarrah, Tyarra

Tiauna (Greek) a form of Tiana.
Tiaunah, Tiaunia, Tiaunna

Tiberia (Latin) Geography: the Tiber River in Italy.
Tib, Tibbie, Tibby, Tiberiah, Tyberia, Tyberiah, Tyberya, Tyberyah

Tichina (American) a combination of the prefix Ti + China.
Tichian, Tichin, Tichinia

Tida (Tai) daughter.
Tidah, Tyda, Tydah

Tieara (Latin) a form of Tiara.

Tiera, Tierra (Latin) forms of Tiara.
Tiéra, Tierah, Tierre, Tierrea, Tierria

Tierney (Irish) noble.
Tieranae, Tierani, Tieranie, Tieranni, Tierany, Tiernan, Tiernee, Tierni, Tiernie, Tierny, Tyernee, Tyerney, Tyerni, Tyernie, Tyerny

Tiesha (Latin) a form of Tisha.
Tieshia, Tieshiah

Tifani, Tiffaney, Tiffani, Tiffanie (Latin) forms of Tiffany.

Tifara (Hebrew) happy.
Tifarah, Tifarra, Tifarrah, Tyfara, Tyfarah, Tyfarra, Tyfarrah

Tiff (Latin) a short form of Tiffany.

Tiffany (Latin) trinity. (Greek) a short form of Theophania. See also Tyfany.
Taffanay, Taffany, Teffani, Tephanie, Tifanee, Tifaney, Tifanie, Tifany, Tiffanee, Tiffanny, Tiffayne, Tiffeney, Tiffeni, Tiffenie, Tiffennie, Tiffiani, Tiffianie, Tiffiany, Tiffynie, Triffany

Tiffini (Latin) a form of Tiffany.
Tiffine, Tiffiney, Tiffinie, Tiffiny

Tiffney (Latin) a form of Tiffany.
Tiffnay, Tiffni, Tiffny, Tifni

Tiffy (Latin) a familiar form of Tiffany.
Tiffey, Tiffi, Tiffie

Tigris (Irish) tiger. Geography: a river in southwest Asia that flows from Turkey, through Iraq, to the Euphrates River.
Tiger, Tigress, Tyger, Tygris, Tygriss, Tygrys, Tygryss

Tijuana (Spanish) Geography: a border town in Mexico.
Tajuana, Tajuanah, Tajuanna, Thejuana, Thejuanah, Tiajuana, Tiajuanah, Tiajuanna, Tiawanna, Tyawanna

Tikvah (Hebrew) hope.
Tikva

Tilda (German) a short form of Matilda.
Tildah, Tilde, Tildea, Tildeah, Tildee, Tildey, Tildi, Tildie, Tildy, Tylda, Tyldah, Tyldee, Tyldey, Tyldi, Tyldie, Tyldy

Tillie (German) a familiar form of Matilda.
Tilia, Tillea, Tilleah, Tillee, Tillei, Tilleigh, Tilley, Tilli, Tillia, Tilly, Tillye, Tily, Tylee, Tylei, Tyleigh, Tyley, Tyli, Tylie, Tyllea, Tyllee, Tyllei, Tylleigh, Tylley, Tylli, Tyllie, Tylly, Tyly

Timara (Hebrew) a form of Tamara.

Timber (English) wood.

Timeka (Aramaic) a form of Tameka.
Timeeka

Timesha (American) a form of Tamesha.
Timisha

Timi (English) a familiar form of Timothea.
Timee, Timey, Timie, Timmee, Timmey, Timmi, Timmie, Timmy, Timy, Tymee, Tymey, Tymi, Tymie, Tymmee, Tymmey, Tymmi, Tymmie, Tymmy, Tymy

Timia (English) a form of Timi.
Timea, Timmea, Tymea, Tymmea

Timothea (English) honoring God.
Timathea, Timithea, Timythea, Tymathea, Tymithea, Tymythea

Tina (Spanish, American) a short form of
Augustine, Martina, Christina, Valentina.
*Teina, Tena, Tenae, Tenah, Tiena, Tienah,
Tienna, Tiennah, Tinah, Tinai, Tine, Tinea,
Tinia, Tiniah, Tinna, Tinnia*

Tinble (English) sound bells make.
Tynbal, Tynble

Tinesha (American) a combination of the
prefix Ti + Niesha.
*Timnesha, Tinecia, Tineisha, Tinesa,
Tineshia, Tinessa, Tiniesha, Tinieshia, Tinsia*

Tinisha (American) a form of Tenisha.
Tinishia, Tinishya

Tiona, Tionna (American) forms of Tiana.
*Tionda, Tiondra, Tiondre, Tioné, Tionette,
Tioni, Tionia, Tionie, Tionja, Tionnah,
Tionne, Tionya*

Tiphanie (Latin) a form of Tiffany.
*Tiphane, Tiphanee, Tiphaney, Tiphani,
Tiphania, Tiphany*

Tiponya (Native American) great horned
owl.
*Tiponia, Tiponiah, Tiponyah, Typonia,
Typoniah, Typonya, Typonyah*

Tipper (Irish) water pourer. (Native
American) a short form of Tiponya.

Tippi (Greek) a familiar form of
Xanthippe.

Tira (Hindi) arrow.
Tirah, Tirea, Tirena

Tirranna (Australian) stream of water.
*Tirran, Tirrann, Tirrannah, Tirranne, Tyran,
Tyrana, Tyranah, Tyrane, Tyrann, Tyranna,
Tyrannah, Tyranne, Tyrran, Tyrrana,
Tyrranah, Tyrrane, Tyrrann, Tyrranna,
Tyrrannah, Tyrranne*

Tirtha (Hindi) ford.

Tirza (Hebrew) pleasant. See also Thirza.
Tierza, Tirsa, Tirzha, Tyrza, Tyrzah

Tirzah (Hebrew) a form of Tirza.

Tisa (Swahili) ninth-born.
Tisah, Tysa, Tyssa

Tish (Latin) a short form of Tisha.

Tisha (Latin) joy. A short form of Leticia.
*Teisha, Tish, Tishah, Tishal, Tishia, Tishiah,
Tysha, Tyshah, Tyshia, Tyshiah*

Tita (Greek) giant. (Spanish) a short form
of names ending in "tita." A form of
Titus (see Boys' Names).

Titania (Greek) giant. Mythology: the
Titans were a race of giants.
*Teata, Titaniah, Titanna, Titanya, Titanyah,
Tiziana, Tytan, Tytania, Tytaniah, Tytanya,
Tytanyah*

Titiana (Greek) a form of Titania.
*Titianay, Titiania, Titianna, Titiayana,
Titionia, Titiyana, Titiyanna, Tityana*

Tivona (Hebrew) nature lover.
*Tibona, Tivonah, Tivone, Tivoni, Tivonie,
Tivony, Tyvona, Tyvonah, Tyvone*

Tiwa (Zuni) onion.
Tiwah, Tywa, Tywah

Tiyana, Tiyanna (English) forms of
Tayana. (Greek) forms of Tiana.
Tiyan, Tiyani, Tiyania, Tiyonna

Tkeyah (American) a form of Takia.

Tobi (Hebrew) God is good.
*Toba, Tobe, Tobea, Tobee, Tobey, Tobia,
Tobiah, Tobie, Tobit, Toby, Tobya, Tobyah,
Tobyas, Tobye, Tove, Tovi, Tybi, Tybie, Tyby*

Tocarra (American) a combination of the
prefix To + Cara.
Tocara, Tocarah, Tocarrah, Toccara

Toinette (French) a short form of
Antoinette.
*Toinet, Toineta, Toinete, Toinett, Toinetta,
Tonetta, Tonette, Toniette, Toynet, Toyneta,
Toynete, Toynett, Toynetta, Toynette,
Tuanetta, Tuanette, Twanette*

Toki (Japanese) hopeful.
Tokee, Tokey, Toko, Tokoya, Tokyo

Tokoni (Tongan) helpful.
*Tokonee, Tokoney, Tokonia, Tokoniah,
Tokony, Tokonya, Tokonyah*

Tola (Polish) a form of Toinette.
Tolah, Tolla, Tollah, Tolsia

Tomi (Japanese) rich.
Tomea, Tomee, Tomey, Tomie, Tomiju, Tomy

Tommi, Tommie (Hebrew) short forms of Thomasina.
Tomme, Tommea, Tommee, Tommey, Tommia, Tommy

Tomo (Japanese) intelligent.
Tomoko

Toneisha (American) a combination of the prefix To + Niesha.
Toneisheia, Tonesia, Toniece, Toniesha, Tonneshia

Tonesha (American) a form of Toneisha.

Toni (Greek) flourishing. (Latin) praiseworthy.
Tonee, Toney, Tonneli, Tonni, Tony, Tonye

Tonia (Latin, Slavic) a form of Toni, Tonya.
Tonea, Toneea, Toniah, Toniea, Tonja, Tonje, Tonna, Tonnia, Tonniah, Tonnja

Tonie (Greek, Latin) a form of Toni.
Toniee, Tonnie

Tonisha (American) a form of Toneisha.
Tonisa, Tonise, Tonisia, Tonnisha

Tonneli (Swiss) a form of Toni.
Tonelea, Toneleah, Tonelee, Tonelei, Toneleigh, Toneley, Toneli, Tonelia, Toneliah, Tonelie, Tonely, Tonnelea, Tonneleah, Tonnelee, Tonnelei, Tonneleigh, Tonneley, Tonnelie, Tonnely

Tonya (Slavic) fairy queen.
Tonnya, Tonnyah, Tonyah, Tonyea, Tonyetta, Tonyia

Topaz (Latin) golden yellow gem.
Topaza, Topazah, Topazia, Topaziah, Topazz, Topazza, Topazzah, Topazzia, Topazziah

Topsy (English) on top. Literature: a slave in Harriet Beecher Stowe's novel *Uncle Tom's Cabin*.
Toppsy, Topsea, Topsee, Topsey, Topsi, Topsia, Topsie

Tora (Japanese) tiger.
Torah, Torra, Torrah

Toree, Torey, Torie, Torrey, Torri, Torrie (English) forms of Tori, Tory.
Tore, Torre, Torree

Tori (Japanese) bird. (English) a form of Tory.
Torei, Torrita

Toria (English) a form of Tori, Tory.
Torea, Toriah, Torreya, Torria, Torya, Toryah

Toriana (English) a form of Tori.
Torian, Torianah, Toriane, Toriann, Torianna, Toriannah, Torianne, Toriauna, Torin, Torina, Torine, Torinne, Torion, Torionna, Torionne, Toriyanna, Torrina, Toryan, Toryana, Toryanah, Toryane, Toryann, Toryanna, Toryannah, Toryanne

Torilyn (English) a combination of Tori + Lynn.
Torilynn, Torrilyn, Torrilynn

Tory (English) victorious. (Latin) a short form of Victoria.
Tauri, Torry, Torrye, Torye

Tosha (Punjabi) armaments. (Polish) a familiar form of Antonia. (Russian) a form of Tasha.
Toshea, Toshia, Toshiea, Toshke, Tosia, Toska

Toshi (Japanese) mirror image.
Toshee, Toshey, Toshie, Toshiko, Toshikyo, Toshy

Toski (Hopi) squashed bug.
Toskee, Toskey, Toskie, Tosky

Totsi (Hopi) moccasins.
Totsee, Totsey, Totsia, Totsie, Totsy, Totsya

Tottie (English) a familiar form of Charlotte.
Tota, Totee, Totey, Toti, Totie, Tottee, Tottey, Totti, Totty, Toty

Tova (Hebrew) a form of Tovah.

Tovah (Hebrew) good.
Tovia

Toya (Spanish) a form of Tory.
Toia, Toiah, Toyah, Toyanika, Toyanna, Toyea, Toylea, Toyleah, Toylenn, Toylin, Toylyn

Tracey, Tracy (Latin) warrior. (Greek) familiar forms of Theresa.

Tracey, Tracy *(cont.)*
*Trace, Tracea, Tracee, Tracell, Traice, Traicee,
Traicey, Traicy, Traisea, Traisee, Traisey, Traisy,
Trasea, Trasee, Trasey, Trasy, Traycea, Traycee,
Traycy, Traycya, Traysea, Traysee, Traysey,
Traysy, Treacy, Treesy*

Traci, Tracie (Latin) forms of Tracey.
*Tracia, Traciah, Tracilee, Tracilyn, Tracilynn,
Tracina, Traeci, Traici, Traicie, Traisi, Traisie,
Trasi, Trasia, Trasie, Trayci, Traycia, Traycie,
Traysi, Traysie*

Tralena (Latin) a combination of Tracey
+ Lena.
*Traleen, Tralene, Tralin, Tralinda, Tralyn,
Tralynn, Tralynne*

Tranesha (American) a combination of
the prefix Tra + Niesha.
*Traneice, Traneis, Traneise, Traneisha, Tranese,
Traneshia, Tranice, Traniece, Traniesha,
Tranisha, Tranishia*

Trang (Vietnamese) intelligent, knowledgeable; beautiful.

Trashawn (American) a combination of
the prefix Tra + Shawn.
*Trashan, Trashana, Trashauna, Trashon,
Trayshauna*

Trava (Czech) spring grasses.
Travah

Traviata (Italian) straying.
Traviatah, Travyata, Travyatah

Treasure (Latin) treasure, wealth; valuable.
*Treasa, Treasur, Treasura, Treasurah, Treasuré,
Treasury*

Trella (Spanish) a familiar form of Estelle.

Tresha (Greek) a form of Theresa.
Trescha, Trescia, Treshana, Treshia

Tressa (Greek) a short form of Theresa.
See also Teresa.
*Treaser, Tresa, Tresca, Trese, Treska, Tressia,
Tressie, Trez, Treza, Trisa*

Treva (Irish, Welsh) a short form of Trevina.

Trevina (Irish) prudent. (Welsh) home-
stead.
*Trevanna, Treveana, Treveanah, Treveane,
Treveena, Treveenah, Treveene, Trevena,*

*Trevenia, Treveon, Trevia, Treviana, Trevien,
Trevin, Trevinah, Trevine, Trevyn, Trevyna,
Trevynah, Trevyne*

Trevona (Irish) a form of Trevina.
*Trevion, Trevon, Trevonah, Trevone, Trevonia,
Trevonna, Trevonne, Trevonye*

Triana (Latin) third. (Greek) a form of
Trina.
*Tria, Trianah, Triane, Triann, Trianna,
Triannah, Trianne, Tryan, Tryana, Tryanah,
Tryane, Tryann, Tryanna, Tryannah, Tryanne*

Trice (Greek) a short form of Theresa.
Treece

Tricia (Latin) a form of Trisha.
Trica, Tricha, Trichelle, Tricina, Trickia

Trifena (Greek) delicate.
*Trifenah, Trifene, Trifenna, Trifennah,
Tryfena, Tryfenah, Tryfenna, Tryfennah,
Tryphena, Tryphenah*

Trilby (English) soft hat.
*Tribi, Trilbea, Trilbee, Trilbey, Trilbi, Trilbie,
Trillby, Trylbea, Trylbee, Trylbeey, Trylbi,
Trylbie, Trylby*

Trina (Greek) pure.
*Thrina, Treana, Treanah, Treena, Treenah,
Treina, Trenna, Trinah, Trind, Trinda, Trine,
Trinette, Trinia, Triniah, Trinica, Trinice,
Triniece, Trinika, Trinique, Trinisa, Tryna,
Trynah, Trynya, Trynyah*

Trini (Greek) a form of Trina.
*Treanee, Treaney, Treani, Treanie, Treany,
Treenee, Treeney, Treeni, Treenie, Trinia,
Trinie, Triny*

Trinity (Latin) triad. Religion: the Father,
the Son, and the Holy Spirit.
*Trinita, Trinite, Trinitee, Trinitey, Triniti,
Trinitie, Trinnette, Trinty, Trynitee, Tryniti,
Trynitie, Trynity*

Trish (Latin) a short form of Beatrice,
Trisha.
Trishell, Trishelle

Trisha (Latin) noblewoman. (Hindi)
thirsty. See also Tricia.
*Treasha, Trishann, Trishanna, Trishanne,
Trishara, Trishia, Trishna, Trissha, Trysha,
Tryshah*

Trissa (Latin) a familiar form of Patricia.
Trisa, Trisanne, Trisia, Trisina, Trissi, Trissie, Trissy, Tryssa

Trista (Latin) a short form of Tristan.
Tristah, Tristal, Tristess, Tristia, Trysta, Trystah, Trystia

Tristabelle (English) a combination of Tristan + Belle.
Tristabel, Tristabela, Tristabelah, Tristabele, Tristabell, Tristabella, Tristabellah, Trystabel, Trystabela, Trystabelah, Trystabele, Trystabell, Trystabella, Trystabellah, Trystabelle

Tristan (Latin) bold.
Tristana, Tristanah, Tristane, Tristann, Tristanni, Tristany

Tristen, Tristin, Triston, Tristyn (Latin) forms of Tristan.
Tristene, Tristine, Tristinye, Tristn, Tristony

Tristian (Irish) a short form of Tristianna.
Tristiane, Tristiann, Tristianne, Trystiane, Trystiann, Trystianne, Trystyane, Trystyann, Trystyanne

Tristianna (Irish) a combination of Tristan + Anna.
Tristiana, Tristianah, Tristiannah, Tristina, Trystian, Trystiana, Trystianah, Trystianna, Trystiannah, Trystyan, Trystyana, Trystyanah, Trystyanna, Trystyannah

Trixie (American) a familiar form of Beatrice.
Tris, Trissie, Trissina, Trix, Trixe, Trixee, Trixey, Trixi, Trixy, Tryxee, Tryxey, Tryxi, Tryxie, Tryxy

Troy (Irish) foot soldier. (French) curly haired. (English) water.
Troi, Troye, Troyton

Troya (Irish) a form of Troy.
Troia, Troiah, Troiana, Troianah, Troiane, Troiann, Troianna, Troianne, Troiya, Troyan, Troyana, Troyanah, Troyane, Troyann, Troyanna, Troyanne

Trudel (Dutch) a form of Trudy.
Trudela, Trudelah, Trudele, Trudell, Trudella, Trudellah, Trudelle

Trudy (German) a familiar form of Gertrude.
Truda, Trudah, Trude, Trudee, Trudessa, Trudey, Trudi, Trudia, Trudiah, Trudie, Trudya

Trycia (Latin) a form of Trisha.

Tryna (Greek) a form of Trina.
Tryane, Tryanna, Trynee

Tryne (Dutch) pure.
Trine

Trynel (Bavarian) a form of Katherine.
Treinel, Treinela, Treinele, Treinell, Treinella, Treinelle, Trynela, Trynelah, Trynele, Trynell, Trynella, Trynellah, Trynelle

Trystan, Trystyn (Latin) forms of Tristan.
Trystane, Trystann, Trystanne, Trysten, Trystin

Tsigana (Hungarian) a form of Zigana.
Tsigane, Tzigana, Tzigane

Tu (Chinese) jade.

Tuesday (English) born on the third day of the week.
Tuesdae, Tuesdai, Tuesdea, Tuesdee, Tuesdey, Tusdai

Tuhina (Hindi) snow.
Tuhinah, Tuhyna, Tuhynah

Tulip (French) tulip flower.
Tullip, Tullop, Tullyp, Tulyp

Tullia (Irish) peaceful, quiet.
Tulia, Tulliah, Tullya, Tullyah, Tulya, Tulyah

Tully (Irish) at peace with God.
Tulea, Tuleah, Tulee, Tulei, Tuleigh, Tuley, Tuli, Tulie, Tullea, Tulleah, Tullee, Tullei, Tulleigh, Tulley, Tulli, Tullie, Tuly

Tulsi (Hindi) basil, a sacred Hindi herb.
Tulsia, Tulsiah, Tulsy, Tulsya, Tulsyah

Turquoise (French) blue-green semi-precious stone.
Turkois, Turkoise, Turkoys, Turkoyse, Turquois

Tusa (Zuni) prairie dog.
Tusah

Tuyen (Vietnamese) angel.

Tuyet (Vietnamese) snow.

Twyla (English) woven of double thread.
Twila, Twilla

Ty (English) a short form of Tyler.
Ti, Tie, Tye

Tyana, Tyanna (Greek) forms of Tiana.
(American) combinations of Ty + Anna.
Tyanah, Tyannah, Tyannia

Tyann (Greek, American) a short form of
Tyana.
Tyan, Tyane, Tyanne

Tyasia (American) a form of Tyesha.
Tyasiah

Tyeesha (American) a form of Tyesha.

Tyeisha (American) a form of Tyesha.
Tyeishia

Tyesha (American) a combination of Ty
+ Aisha.
*Tyasha, Tyashia, Tyeyshia, Tyieshia, Tyisha,
Tyishea, Tyishia, Tyishya, Tyshia, Tyshya*

Tyeshia (American) a form of Tyesha.

Tyfany (American) a short form of
Tiffany.
*Tyfani, Tyfanny, Tyffanee, Tyffaney, Tyffani,
Tyffanie, Tyffanni, Tyffany, Tyffini, Typhanie,
Typhany*

Tyiesha (American) a form of Tyesha.
Tyieshia

Tykeisha (American) a form of Takeisha.
*Tykeesha, Tykeisa, Tykeishia, Tykesha,
Tykeshia, Tykeysha, Tykeza, Tykisha*

Tykera (American) a form of Takira.
*Tykeira, Tykeirah, Tykiera, Tykierra, Tykira,
Tykirah, Tykirra, Tykyra, Tykyrah*

Tykeria (American) a form of Tykera.
Tykereiah, Tykeriah, Tykerria, Tykiria

Tykia (American) a form of Takia.
Tykeia, Tykeiah, Tykiah, Tykya, Tykyah

Tylar, Tylor (English) forms of Tyler.

Tyler (English) tailor.
Tyller

Tyna (Czech) a short form of Kristina.
Tynae, Tynea, Tynia

Tyne (English) river.
Tine, Tyna, Tynelle, Tynessa, Tynetta

Tyneisha (American) a form of Tynesha.
Tyneicia, Tyneisia

Tynesha (American) a combination of Ty
+ Niesha.
Tynaise, Tynece, Tynesa, Tynessia, Tyniesha

Tyneshia (American) a form of Tynesha.

Tynisha (American) a form of Tynesha.
Tynisa, Tynise, Tynishi

Tyonna (American) a form of Tiana.
Tyona

Tyra (Scandinavian) battler. Mythology:
Tyr was the god of war. A form of
Thora. (Hindi) a form of Tira.
Thyra, Tyraa, Tyran, Tyria

Tyrah (Scandinavian, Hindi) a form of
Tyra.

Tyree (Scandinavian, Hindi) a form of
Tyra.

Tyshanna (American) a combination of
Ty + Shawna.
*Tyshana, Tyshanae, Tyshane, Tyshaun,
Tyshaunda, Tyshawn, Tyshawna, Tyshawnah,
Tyshawnda, Tyshawnna, Tysheann,
Tysheanna, Tyshonia, Tyshonna, Tyshonya*

Tytiana, Tytianna (Greek) forms of
Titania.
*Tytana, Tytanna, Tyteana, Tyteanna,
Tytianni, Tytionna, Tytiyana, Tytiyanna,
Tytyana, Tytyauna*

U

U (Korean) gentle.

Ualani (Hawaiian) rain from heaven.
*Ualana, Ualanah, Ualanea, Ualanee,
Ualaney, Ualania, Ualanie, Ualany*

Udele (English) prosperous.
Uda, Udah, Udella, Udelle, Yudelle

Ugolina (German) bright mind; bright
spirit.

Hugolina, Hugolinah, Hugoline, Hugolyna, Hugolynah, Hygolyne, Ugolin, Ugolinah, Ugoline, Ugolyna, Ugolynah, Ugolyne

Ujana (Breton) noble; exellent. (African) youth.
Jana, Janah, Ujanah, Uyana, Uyanah

Ula (Irish) sea jewel. (Scandinavian) wealthy. (Spanish) a short form of Eulalia.
Eula, Oola, Uli, Ulia

Ulalia (Greek) sweet; soft-spoken.
Ulaliah, Ulalya, Ulalyah

Ulani (Polynesian) cheerful.
Ulana, Ulanah, Ulane, Ulanee, Ulaney, Ulania, Ulanie, Ulany, Ulanya, Ulanyah

Ulima (Arabic) astute; wise.
Uleama, Uleamah, Uleema, Uleemah, Ulemah, Ulimah, Ullima, Ulyma, Ulymah

Ulla (German, Swedish) willful. (Latin) a short form of Ursula.
Ula, Ulah, Ullah, Ulli

Ulrica (German) wolf ruler; ruler of all. See also Rica.
Ulka, Ullrica, Ullricka, Ullrika, Ulricah, Ulricka, Ulrickah, Ulrika, Ulrikah, Ulrike, Ulrique, Ulryca, Ulrycah, Ulrycka, Ulryckah, Ulryka, Ulrykah, Ulryqua

Ultima (Latin) last, endmost, farthest.
Ultimah, Ultyma, Ultymah

Ululani (Hawaiian) heavenly inspiration.
Ululanee, Ululaney, Ululania, Ululanie, Ululany, Ululanya

Ulva (German) wolf.
Ulvah

Uma (Hindi) mother. Religion: another name for the Hindu goddess Devi.
Umah

Umay (Turkish) hopeful.
Umai

Umeko (Japanese) plum-blossom child; patient.
Ume, Umeyo

Umiko (Japanese) child of the sea.

Una (Latin) one; united. (Hopi) good memory. (Irish) a form of Agnes. See also Oona.
Unagh, Unah, Unna, Uny

Undine (Latin) little wave. Mythology: the undines were water spirits. See also Ondine.
Undeen, Undene, Undina, Undinah, Undyn, Undyna, Undynah, Undyne

Unice (English) a form of Eunice.

Unika (American) a form of Unique.
Unica, Unicka, Unik, Unikue

Uniqua (Latin) a form of Unique.
Unikqua

Unique (Latin) only one.
Uniqia, Uniquia

Unity (English) unity.
Uinita, Unita, Unite, Unitea, Unitee, Unitey, Unyta, Unytea, Unytee, Unytey, Unyti, Unytie, Unyty

Unn (Norwegian) she who is loved.

Unna (German) woman.
Unnah

Unnea (Scandinavian) linden tree.
Unea, Uneah, Unneah

Urania (Greek) heavenly. Mythology: the Muse of astronomy.
Uraina, Urainah, Urainia, Urainiah, Uranie, Uraniya, Uranya, Uranyah

Urbana (Latin) city dweller.
Urbanah, Urbanna, Urabannah

Uri (Hebrew) my light.
Uree, Urie, Ury

Uriana (Greek) heaven; the unknown.
Urianna, Uriannah, Urianne, Uryan, Uryana, Uryanah, Uryane, Uryann, Uryanna, Uryanne

Urika (Omaha) useful to everyone.
Ureka, Urica, Uricah, Uricka, Urickah, Urikah, Uriqua, Uryca, Urycah, Uryka, Urykah, Uryqua

Urit (Hebrew) bright.
Urice, Urita, Uritah, Uryt, Uryta, Urytah

Urith (German) worthy.
Uritha, Urithah, Urithe, Uryth, Urythah

Ursa (Greek) a short form of Ursula.
(Latin) a form of Orsa.
Ursah, Ursea, Ursey, Ursi, Ursie, Ursy

Ursula (Greek) little bear. See also Sula,
Ulla, Vorsila.
*Irsaline, Ursala, Ursel, Ursela, Ursella, Ursely,
Ursilla, Ursillane, Ursola, Ursule, Ursulina,
Ursuline, Ursulyna, Ursulyna, Ursylyn,
Urszula, Urszuli, Urzsulah, Urzula, Urzulah*

Usha (Hindi) sunrise.
Ushah

Ushi (Chinese) ox. Astrology: a sign of
the Chinese zodiac.
Ushee, Ushie, Ushy

Uta (German) rich. (Japanese) poem.
Utah, Utako

Utano (Japanese) field of songs.
Utan, Utana, Utanah

Utina (Native American) woman of my
country.
*Utahna, Uteana, Uteanah, Uteena, Uteenah,
Utinah, Utona, Utonna, Utyna, Utynah*

Uzza (Arabic) strong.
Uza, Uzah, Uzzah

Uzzia (Hebrew) God is my strength.
*Uzia, Uziah, Uzya, Uzyah, Uzziah,
Uzzya, Uzzyah*

V

Vachya (Hindi) talking.
Vachia, Vachiah, Vachyah

Vail (English) valley.
*Vaile, Vale, Valee, Valey, Vali, Valie, Valy, Vayl,
Vayle*

Vailea (Polynesian) talking water.
*Vaileah, Vailee, Vailei, Vaileigh, Vailey, Vaili,
Vailie, Vaily, Vailya, Vaylea, Vayleah, Vaylee,
Vaylei, Vayleigh, Vayley, Vayli, Vaylie, Vayly*

Val (Latin) a short form of Valentina,
Valerie.
Vall, Valle

Vala (German) singled out.
Valah, Valla, Vallah

Valarie (Latin) a form of Valerie.
*Valarae, Valaree, Valarey, Valari, Valaria,
Vallarie, Vallary*

Valborga (Swedish) mightly mountain.
Valborg, Valborgah

Valda (German) famous ruler.
Valdah, Valida, Velda

Valencia (Spanish) strong. Geography: a
region in eastern Spain.
*Valanca, Valancia, Valecia, Valence, Valenciah,
Valencya, Valencyah, Valenica, Valenzia*

Valene (Latin) a short form of Valentina.
*Valaina, Valainah, Valaine, Valean, Valeana,
Valeanah, Valeane, Valeda, Valeen, Valeena,
Valeenah, Valeene, Valen, Valena, Valenah,
Valeney, Valien, Valina, Valine, Vallan,
Vallana, Vallanah, Vallane, Vallen, Vallena,
Vallenah, Vallene, Vallina, Vallinah, Valline,
Vallyna, Vallynah, Vallyne, Valyn, Valynn*

Valentia (Italian) a form of Valentina.
Valentiah, Valentya, Valentyah

Valentina (Latin) strong. History:
Valentina Tereshkova, a Soviet cosmo-
naut, was the first woman in space. See
also Tina, Valene, Valli.
*Valantina, Valenteana, Valenteane, Valenteen,
Valenteena, Valenteene, Valentena, Valentia,
Valentijn, Valentin, Valentine, Valentyn,
Valentyna, Valentyne, Valtina*

Valera (Russian) a form of Valerie. See
also Lera.

Valeria (Latin) a form of Valerie.
*Valaria, Valariah, Valeriah, Valeriana,
Valeriane, Veleria*

Valerie (Latin) strong.
*Vairy, Valaree, Vale, Valeree, Valeri, Valeria,
Valérie, Valerye, Valka, Valleree, Valleri,
Vallerie, Vallirie, Valry, Valya, Velerie, Waleria*

Valery (Latin) a form of Valerie.
Valerye, Vallery

Valeska (Slavic) glorious ruler.
*Valesca, Valese, Valeshia, Valeshka, Valeskah,
Valezka, Valisha*

Valli (Latin) a familiar form of Valentina,
Valerie. Botany: a plant native to India.
*Valee, Valei, Valeigh, Valey, Vali, Valie, Vallee,
Vallei, Valleigh, Vallie, Vally, Valy*

Vallia (Spanish) strong protector.
*Valea, Valeah, Valia, Valiah, Vallea, Valleah,
Valliah, Vallya, Vallyah, Valya, Valyah*

Valma (Finnish) loyal defender.
Valmah, Valmai

Valonia (Latin) shadow valley.
*Valione, Valioney, Valioni, Valionia, Valioniah,
Valionie, Valiony, Valionya, Valionyah, Vallon,
Vallonia, Valloniah, Vallonya, Vallonyah,
Valona, Valoniah, Valonya, Valonyah,
Valyona, Valyonah, Valyonia, Valyoniah,
Valyony, Valyonya, Valyonyah*

Valora (Latin) a form of Valerie.
*Valorah, Valore, Valoria, Valoriah, Valorya,
Valoryah, Velora*

Valorie (Latin) a form of Valerie.
*Vallori, Vallory, Valoree, Valorey, Valori,
Valory, Valorye*

Van (Greek) a short form of Vanessa.

Vanda (German) a form of Wanda.
*Vandah, Vandana, Vandella, Vandetta, Vandi,
Vannda*

Vandani (Hindi) worthy, honorable.
Vandanee, Vandaney, Vandanie, Vandany

Vanesa, Vannesa, Vannessa (Greek)
forms of Vanessa.
*Vanesha, Vaneshah, Vaneshia, Vanesia,
Vanisa, Vannesha, Vannesse, Vannessee*

Vanessa (Greek) butterfly. Literature: a
name invented by Jonathan Swift as a
nickname for Esther Vanhomrigh. See
also Nessie.

*Vanassa, Vanesse, Vanessee, Vanessia,
Vanessica, Vanetta, Vaneza, Vaniece, Vaniessa,
Vanika, Vaniss, Vanissa, Vanisse, Vanissee,
Vanneza, Vannysa, Vannysah, Vannyssa,
Vanysa, Vanysah Vanyssa, Vanyssah, Varnessa*

Vanetta (English) a form of Vanessa.
*Vaneta, Vanetah, Vanete, Vanett, Vanettah,
Vanette, Vanita, Vanitah, Vanneta, Vannetta,
Vannita, Venetta*

Vani (Hindi) voice. (Italian) a form of Ann.
*Vanee, Vaney, Vanie, Vannee, Vanney, Vanni,
Vannie, Vanny, Vany*

Vania, Vanya (Russian) familiar forms of
Anna.
*Vanea, Vaneah, Vaniah, Vanija, Vanijah,
Vanina, Vaniya, Vanja, Vanka, Vannea,
Vanneah, Vannia, Vanniah, Vannya,
Vannyah, Vanyah*

Vanity (English) vain.
*Vanitee, Vanitey, Vaniti, Vanitie, Vanittee,
Vanittey, Vanitti, Vanittie, Vanitty, Vanyti,
Vanytie, Vanyty*

Vanna (Cambodian) golden. (Greek) a
short form of Vanessa.
*Vana, Vanae, Vanah, Vanelly, Vannah,
Vannalee, Vannaleigh, Vannie, Vanny*

Vanora (Welsh) white wave.
*Vannora, Vanorah, Vanorea, Vanoree, Vanorey,
Vanori, Vanoria, Vanoriah, Vanorie, Vanory,
Vanorya, Vanoryah*

Vantrice (American) a combination of
the prefix Van + Trice.
*Vantrece, Vantricia, Vantriciah, Vantricya,
Vantricyah, Vantrisa, Vantrise, Vantrisia,
Vantrisiah, Vantrissa, Vantrisya, Vantrisyah,
Vantrysia, Vantrysiah, Vantrysya, Vantrysyah*

Vara (Scandinavian) careful.
Varah, Varia, Variah

Varana (Hindi) river.
Varanah, Varanna, Varannah

Varda (Hebrew) rose.
*Vardia, Vardiah, Vardice, Vardina, Vardis,
Vardissa, Vardisse, Vardit, Vardita, Vardyce,
Vardys, Vardysa, Vardyse, Vardyta, Vardytah*

Vardina (Hebrew) a form of Varda.
Vardin, Vardinah, Vardine, Vardinia, Vardiniah, Vardyn, Vardyna, Vardynah, Vardyne

Varina (English) thorn.
Varinah, Varyna, Varynah, Varyne

Varvara (Slavic) a form of Barbara.
Varenka, Varinka, Varya, Varyusha, Vava, Vavka

Vashti (Persian) lovely. Bible: the wife of Ahasuerus, king of Persia.
Vashtee, Vashtie, Vashty

Vassy (Persian) beautiful.
Vasi, Vasie, Vassee, Vassey, Vassi, Vassie, Vasy

Veanna (American) a combination of the prefix Ve + Anna.
Veannah, Veeana, Veeanah, Veeann, Veeanna, Veeannah, Veeanne, Veena, Veenah, Veenaya, Veeona

Veda (Sanskrit) sacred lore; knowledge. Religion: the Vedas are the sacred writings of Hinduism.
Vedad, Vedah, Veida, Veleda

Vedette (Italian) sentry; scout. (French) movie star.
Vedet, Vedeta, Vedetah, Vedete, Vedett, Vedetta, Vedettah

Vedis (German) spirit from the forest.
Vediss, Vedissa, Vedisse, Vedys, Vedyss, Vedyssa, Vedysse

Vega (Arabic) falling star.
Vegah

Velda (German) a form of Valda.
Veldah

Velika (Slavic) great, wondrous.
Velikah, Velyka, Velykah

Velinda (American) a combination of the prefix Ve + Linda.
Velindah, Velynda, Velyndah

Velma (German) a familiar form of Vilhelmina.
Valma, Valmah, Vellma, Vellmah, Vilma, Vilmah, Vilna, Vylma, Vylmah

Velvet (English) velvety.
Velveta, Velvetah, Velvete, Velvett, Velvetta, Velvettah, Velvette, Velvit, Velvyt

Venecia (Italian) from Venice, Italy.
Vanecia, Vaneciah, Vanetia, Veneece, Veneise, Venesha, Venesher, Venicia, Veniece, Veniesa, Venise, Venisha, Venishia, Vennice, Vennise, Venyce, Vonizia, Vonizya, Vonysia, Vonysiah, Vonysya, Vonysyah

Venessa (Latin) a form of Vanessa.
Veneese, Venesa, Venese, Veneshia, Venesia, Venessah, Venesse, Venessia, Venisa, Venissa, Vennesa, Vennessa, Vennisa

Venetia (Italian) a form of Venecia.
Veneta, Venetiah, Venetta, Venette, Venetya, Venetyah, Venita, Venitia, Vinetia, Vinetiah, Vinita, Vinitah, Vonita, Vonitia, Vynita, Vynitah, Vynyta, Vynytah

Venezia (Italian) a form of Venecia.
Veniza, Venize

Venice (Italian) from Venice, Italy.

Venus (Latin) love. Mythology: the goddess of love and beauty.
Venis, Venusa, Venusina, Venussa, Venys, Vinny, Vynys

Vera (Latin) true. (Slavic) faith. A short form of Elvera, Veronica. See also Verena, Wera.
Vara, Veera, Veira, Verah, Verasha, Verra, Verrah, Vere, Verka, Verla, Viera, Vira, Vjera, Vyra, Vyrah

Veradis (Latin) truthful.
Veradissa, Veradisse, Veradys, Veradysa, Veradyss, Veradyssa

Verbena (Latin) sacred plants.
Verbeen, Verbeena, Verbeene, Verben, Verbene, Verbin, Verbina, Verbine, Verbyn, Verbyna, Verbyne

Verda (Latin) young, fresh.
Verdah, Verdea, Verdee, Verdey, Verdi, Verdie, Verdy, Virida

Verdad (Spanish) truthful.
Verdada

Verdianna (American) a combination of Verda + Anna.
Verdian, Verdiana, Verdiane, Verdiann, Verdianne, Verdyan, Verdyana, Verdyane, Verdyann, Verdyanna, Verdyanne, Virdian, Virdiana, Virdiane, Virdiann, Virdianna,

Virdianne, Vyrdian, Vyrdiana, Vyrdiane,
Vyrdiann, Vyrdianna, Vyrdianne, Vyrdyan,
Vyrdyana, Vyrdyane, Vyrdyann, Vyrdyanna,
Vyrdyanne

Verena (Latin) truthful. A familiar form
of Vera, Verna.
Varyn, Varyna, Varyne, Verean, Vereana,
Vereane, Vereen, Vereena, Vereene, Verenah,
Verene, Verin, Verina, Verine, Verinka,
Veroshka, Verunka, Verusya, Veryn, Veryna,
Veryne, Virna

Verenice (Latin) a form of Veronica.
Verenis, Verenise, Vereniz

Verity (Latin) truthful.
Verita, Veritah, Veritea, Veritee, Veritey, Veriti,
Veritie, Veryta, Verytah, Verytea, Verytee,
Verytey, Veryti, Verytie, Veryty

Verlene (Latin) a combination of
Veronica + Lena.
Verleen, Verlena, Verlin, Verlina, Verlinda,
Verline, Verlyn

Verna (Latin) springtime. (French) a
familiar form of Laverne. See also
Verena, Wera.
Verasha, Verla, Vernah, Verne, Verneta,
Vernetia, Vernetta, Vernette, Vernia, Vernita,
Viera, Virida, Virna, Virnah, Virnell, Vyrna,
Vyrnah

Vernice (Latin) a form of Bernice, Verna.
Vernese, Vernesha, Verneshia, Vernessa,
Vernica, Vernicca, Verniccah, Verniece,
Vernika, Vernique, Vernis, Vernise, Vernyca,
Vernycah, Vernycca, Vernyccah, Vyrnessa,
Vyrnessah, Vyrnesse

Vernisha (Latin) a form of Vernice.
Vernisheia, Vernissia

Veronic (Latin) a short form of Veronica.

Veronica (Latin) true image. See also
Ronica, Roni, Weronika.
Varonica, Varonicca, Varoniccah, Verhonica,
Verinica, Verohnica, Veron, Verona, Verone,
Véronic, Veronice, Veronne, Veronnica,
Veruszhka, Vironica, Vironicah, Vironicca,
Vironiccah, Vironiqua, Vron, Vronica,
Vronicah, Vyronica, Vyronicah, Vyronicca,
Vyroniccah

Veronika (Latin) a form of Veronica.
Varonika, Veronick, Véronick, Veronicka,
Veronik, Veronike, Veronka, Veronkia,
Veruka, Vironika, Vronika, Vyronika,
Vyronikah

Veronique, Véronique (French) forms of
Veronica.
Veranique, Veroniqua, Vironique, Vroniqua,
Vronique, Vyroniqua, Vyronique

Vespera (Latin) evening star.
Vesperah

Vesta (Latin) keeper of the house.
Mythology: the goddess of the home.
Vessy, Vest, Vestah, Vestea, Vestee, Vesteria,
Vestey

Veta (Slavic) a familiar form of Elizabeth.
Vetah

Vevila (Irish) melodious voice.
Vevilla, Vevillia, Vevilliah, Vevyla, Vevylah,
Vevyle, Vevylla, Vevyllah, Vevylle

Vevina (Irish) pleasant, sweet.
Vevinah, Vevine, Vevyna, Vevynah, Vevyne

Vi (Latin, French) a short form of Viola,
Violet.

Vianca (Spanish) a form of Bianca.
Vianeca, Vianica, Vianka, Vyaneca, Vyanica,
Vyanka

Vianey, Vianney (American) familiar
forms of Vianna.
Viany

Vianna (American) a combination of Vi
+ Anna.
Viana, Vianah, Viann, Viannah, Vianne,
Vyan, Vyana, Vyanah, Vyane, Vyanna,
Vyannah, Vyanne

Vica (Hungarian) a form of Eve.
Vicah, Vyca, Vycah

Vicka, Vika (Latin) familiar forms of
Victoria.
Vickah, Vikah, Vikka, Vikkah, Vikkia,
Vycka, Vyckah, Vyka, Vykah, Vykka,
Vykkah

Vicki, Vickie, Vicky (Latin) familiar forms
of Victoria. See also Vikki.

Vicki, Vickie, Vicky *(cont.)*
Vic, Viccey, Vicci, Viccy, Vicke, Vickee, Vickey, Vickia, Vickiana, Vickilyn, Vickkee, Vickkey, Vickki, Vickkie, Vickky, Vycke, Vyckee, Vyckey, Vycki, Vyckie, Vycky, Vykki, Vykkie, Vykky, Vyky

Victoria (Latin) victorious. See also Tory, Wicktoria, Wisia.
Victoriya, Victorria, Victorriah, Victorya, Vitoria, Vyctoria, Vyctoriah

Victorine (Latin) a form of Victoria.
Victoreana, Victoreane, Victoreene, Victoriana, Victorianna, Victorina, Victorinah, Victoryn, Victoryna, Victoryne, Viktorina, Viktorine, Vyctorina, Vyctorine, Vyctoryn, Vyctoryna, Vyctorynah, Vyctoryne, Vyktorin, Vyktorina, Vyktorinah, Vyktorine, Vyktoryn, Vyktoryna, Vyktorynah, Vyktoryne

Victory (Latin) victory.
Victoire, Victorie, Victorine, Vitorie

Vida (Sanskrit) a form of Veda. (Hebrew) a short form of Davida.
Veeda, Vidah, Vidamarie, Vyda, Vydah

Vidal (Latin) life.
Vital, Vydal, Vytal

Vidonia (Portuguese) branch of a vine.
Vedonia, Vidoniah, Vidonya, Vidonyah, Vydonia, Vydoniah, Vydonya, Vydonyah

Vienna (Latin) Geography: the capital of Austria.
Vena, Venah, Venia, Venna, Vennah, Vennia, Vienetta, Vienette, Vienne

Vigilia (Latin) wakeful, watching.
Vigiliah, Vijilia, Vijiliah, Vygilia, Vygiliah, Vygylia, Vyjilia

Vignette (French) small vine.
Vignet, Vigneta, Vignete, Vignett, Vignetta, Vygnet, Vygneta, Vygnete, Vygnett, Vygnetta, Vygnette

Vikki (Latin) a familiar form of Victoria. See also Vicki.
Vika, Viki, Vikie, Vikkee, Vikkey, Vikkie, Vikky, Viky

Viktoria (Latin) a form of Victoria.
Viktoriah, Viktorie, Viktorija, Viktorya, Viktoryah

Vila (Latin) from a house in the country.
Vilah, Villa, Villah, Vyla, Vylah, Vylla, Vyllah

Vilhelmina (German) a form of Wilhelmina.
Vilhalmine, Vilhelmine, Vylhelmina, Vylhelmine

Villette (French) small town.
Vietta, Vilet, Vileta, Viletah, Vilete, Vilett, Viletta, Vilette, Villet, Villeta, Villetah, Villete, Villett, Villetta, Villettah, Vylet, Vyleta, Vyletah, Vylete, Vylett, Vyletta, Vylettah, Vylette, Vyllet, Vylleta, Vylletah, Vyllete, Vyllette

Vilma (German) a short form of Vilhelmina.
Vilmah, Vylma, Vylmah

Vina (Hindi) Mythology: a musical instrument played by the Hindu goddess of wisdom. (Spanish) vineyard. (Hebrew) a short form of Davina. (English) a short form of Alvina. See also Lavina.
Veena, Veenah, Viña, Vinesha, Vinessa, Viniece, Vinique, Vinisha, Viñita, Vinna, Vinnah, Vinora, Vyna, Vynah, Vynna, Vynnah

Vincent (Latin) victor, conqueror.

Vincentia (Latin) a form of Vincent.
Vicenta, Vincensa, Vincensah, Vincensia, Vincensiah, Vincenta, Vincentah, Vincentena, Vincentina, Vincentine, Vincenza, Vincenzah, Vincenzia, Vincenziah, Vincy, Vinnie, Vyncenzia, Vyncenziah, Vyncenzya, Vyncenzyah

Vinia (Latin) wine.
Viniah, Vynia, Vyniah, Vynya, Vynyah

Viñita (Spanish) a form of Vina.
Viñeet, Viñeeta, Viñeete, Viñetta, Viñette, Viñitha, Viñta, Viñti, Viñtia, Vyñetta, Vyñette, Vyñita, Vyñyta, Vyñytta, Vyñytte

Viola (Latin) violet; stringed instrument in the violin family. Literature: the heroine of Shakespeare's play *Twelfth Night*.
Violah, Violaina, Violaine, Violainee, Violainey, Violaini, Violainia, Violanta, Violante, Viole, Violeine, Vyoila, Vyoilah,

Vyola, Vyolah, Vyolani, Vyolania, Vyolanie,
Vyolany, Vyolanya

Violet (French) Botany: a plant with
purplish blue flowers.
Violete, Violett, Violette, Vyolet, Vyolete,
Vyolett, Vyolette

Violeta, Violetta (French) forms of Violet.
Violatta, Violetah, Vyoleta, Vyoletah,
Vyoletta

Virgilia (Latin) rod bearer, staff bearer.
Virgilea, Virgileah, Virgilee, Virgileigh,
Virgili, Virgilie, Virgillia, Virgily, Virgilya,
Virjil, Virjilea, Virjileah, Virjilee, Virjileigh,
Virjiley, Virjili, Virjilie, Virjily, Vyrgilia,
Vylgiliah, Vyrgylya, Vyrgylyah

Virginia (Latin) pure, virginal. Literature:
Virginia Woolf was a well-known
British writer. See also Gina, Ginger,
Ginny, Jinny.
Verginia, Verginya, Virge, Virgeen, Virgeena,
Virgeenah, Virgeenia, Virgeeniah, Virgen,
Virgene, Virgenia, Virgenya, Virgie, Virgine,
Virginio, Virginnia, Virgy, Virjeana, Virjinea,
Virjineah, Virjinia, Virjiniah, Vyrginia,
Vyrginiah, Vyrgynia, Vyrgyniah, Vyrgynya,
Vyrgynyah

Virginie (French) a form of Virginia.
Virgeenee, Virginië, Virjinee

Viridiana (Latin) a form of Viridis.

Viridis (Latin) green.
Virdis, Virida, Viridia, Viridiss, Viridissa,
Viridys, Viridyss, Viridyssa, Vyridis, Vyridiss,
Vyridissa, Vyridys, Vyridyss, Vyridyssa

Virtue (Latin) virtuous.
Vertue, Virtu, Vyrtu, Vyrtue

Vita (Latin) life.
Veeta, Vitah, Vitaliana, Vitalina, Vitel,
Vitella, Vitia, Vitka, Vitke, Vitta, Vyta,
Vytah, Vytta, Vyttah

Vitoria, Vittoria (Spanish, Italian) forms
of Victoria.
Vitoriah, Vittoriah, Vittorya, Vittoryah,
Vytoria, Vytoriah, Vyttoria, Vyttoriah

Viv (Latin) a short form of Vivian.
Vive, Vyv

Viva (Latin) a short form of Aviva, Vivian.
Vica, Vivah, Vivan, Vivva, Vyva, Vyvah

Viveca (Scandinavian) a form of Vivian.
Vivecah, Vivecca, Vivecka, Viveka, Vivica,
Vivieca, Vyveca

Vivian (Latin) full of life.
Vevay, Vevey, Viv, Viva, Viveca, Vivi, Vivia,
Viviann, Vivina, Vivion, Vivyan, Vivyann,
Vivyanne, Vyvian, Vyvyan, Vyvyann,
Vyvyanne

Viviana, Vivianna (Latin) forms of Vivian.
Viviannah, Vivyana, Vyvyana, Vyvyanna

Viviane, Vivianne, Vivien (Latin) forms of
Vivian.
Vivee, Vivie, Vivienne

Voleta (Greek) veiled.
Volet, Voletah, Volett, Voletta, Volette, Volita,
Volitt, Volitta, Volitte, Volyta, Volytah, Volyte,
Volytt, Volytta, Volyttah, Volytte

Vondra (Czech) loving woman.
Vonda, Vondrah, Vondrea

Voneisha (American) a combination of
Yvonne + Aisha.
Voneishia, Vonesha, Voneshia

Vonna (French) a form of Yvonne.
Vona, Vonah, Vonia, Voniah, Vonnah,
Vonnia, Vonnya, Vonya

Vonny (French) a familiar form of Yvonne.
Vonney, Vonni, Vonnie, Vony

Vontricia (American) a combination of
Yvonne + Tricia.
Vontrece, Vontrese, Vontrice, Vontriece,
Vontrisha, Vontrishia, Vontrycia, Vontryciah,
Vontrycya, Vontrycyah

Vorsila (Greek) a form of Ursula.
Vorsilla, Vorsula, Vorsulah, Vorsulla, Vorsyla

Vulpine (English) like a fox.
Vulpina, Vulpinah, Vulpyna, Vulpynah,
Vulpyne

Vy (Latin, French) a form of Vi.
Vye

Vyoma (Hindi) sky.
Vioma, Viomah, Vyomah

Wadd (Arabic) beloved.
Wad

Wahalla (Scandinavian) immortal.
Valhalla, Walhalla

Waheeda (Arabic) one and only.

Wainani (Hawaiian) beautiful water.
Wainanee, Wainanie, Wainany

Wakana (Japanese) plant.
Wakanah

Wakanda (Dakota) magical power.
Wakandah, Wakenda

Wakeisha (American) a combination of
the prefix Wa + Keisha.
*Wakeishah, Wakeishia, Wakesha, Wakeshia,
Wakesia, Wakesiah, Wakeysha, Wakeyshah,
Wakeyshia, Wakeyshiah, Wakeyshya,
Wakeyshyah*

Walad (Arabic) newborn.
Waladah, Walida, Walidah, Walyda, Walydah

Walda (German) powerful; famous.
*Waldah, Waldina, Waldine, Walida, Wallda,
Walldah, Waldyna, Waldyne, Welda, Weldah,
Wellda, Welldah*

Waleria (Polish) a form of Valerie.
*Wala, Waleriah, Walerya, Waleryah,
Walleria, Walleriah, Wallerya, Walleryah*

Walker (English) cloth; walker.
Wallker

Wallis (English) from Wales.
*Walice, Walise, Wallie, Wallisa, Wallise,
Walliss, Wally, Wallys, Wallysa, Wallyse*

Wanda (German) wanderer. See also
Wendy.
*Vanda, Wahnda, Wandah, Wandely, Wandie,
Wandis, Wandja, Wandzia, Wannda,
Wanndah, Wonda, Wondah, Wonnda,
Wonndah*

Wandie (German) a familiar form of
Wanda.
Wandea, Wandee, Wandey, Wandi, Wandy

Waneta (Native American) charger. See
also Juanita.
*Waneata, Waneatah, Waneeta, Waneetah,
Waneita, Waneitah, Wanetah, Wanete,
Wanita, Wanitah, Wanite, Wanneata,
Wanneatah, Wanneeta, Wanneetah, Wanneita,
Wanneitah, Wanneta, Wannetah, Wannete,
Waunita, Wonita, Wonnita, Wonnitah,
Wonyta, Wonytah, Wonyte, Wynita*

Wanetta (English) pale face.
*Wanette, Wannetta, Wannette, Wonnitta,
Wonnitte, Wonytta, Wonyttah, Wonytte*

Wanika (Hawaiian) a form of Juanita.
*Waneeka, Wanicka, Wanikah, Wanyka,
Wanykah*

Warda (German) guardian.
*Wardah, Wardeh, Wardena, Wardenia,
Wardia, Wardine*

Washi (Japanese) eagle.
Washee, Washie, Washy

Wasila (English) healthy.
*Wasilah, Wasilla, Wasillah, Wasyla, Wasylah,
Wasylla, Wasyllah*

Wattan (Japanese) homeland.
Watan

Wauna (Moquelumnan) snow geese
honking.
Waunah, Waunakee

Wava (Slavic) a form of Barbara.
Wavah, Wavia, Waviah, Wavya, Wavyah

Waverly (English) quaking aspen-tree
meadow.
Waverley, Waverli, Wavierlee

Waynesha (American) a combination of
Waynette + Niesha.
Wayneesha, Wayneisha, Waynie, Waynisha

Waynette (English) wagon maker.
*Wainet, Waineta, Wainetah, Wainete,
Wainetta, Wainettah, Wainette, Waynel,
Waynelle, Waynet, Wayneta, Waynete,
Waynetta, Waynlyn*

Wednesday (Latin, English) born on the
fourth day of the week.

Weeko (Dakota) pretty girl.
Weiko, Weyko

Wehilani (Hawaiian) heavenly adornment.

Wenda (Welsh) a form of Wendy.
Wendah, Wendaine, Wendayne

Wendelle (English) wanderer.
*Wendalina, Wendalinah, Wendaline,
Wendall, Wendalla, Wendallah, Wendalle,
Wendalyn, Wendalyna, Wendalynah,
Wendalyne, Wendelin, Wendelina,
Wendelinah, Wendeline, Wendella,
Wendelline, Wendelly, Wendelyn, Wendelyna,
Wendelynah, Wendelyne*

Wendi (Welsh) a form of Wendy.
Wendia, Wendie

Wendy (Welsh) white; light skinned. A
familiar form of Gwendolyn, Wanda.
*Wende, Wendea, Wendee, Wendey, Wendya,
Wendye, Wuendy*

Wera (Polish) a form of Vera. See also
Verna.
Werah, Wiera, Wiercia, Wierka

Weronika (Polish) a form of Veronica.
*Weronica, Weronicah, Weronicka, Weronickah,
Weronikah, Weronike, Weronikra, Weroniqua,
Weronique, Weronyca, Weronycah,
Weronycka, Weronyckah, Weronyka,
Weronykah, Weronyqua, Weronyque*

Wesisa (Musoga) foolish.
Wesisah, Wesysa, Wesysah

Weslee (English) a form of Wesley.

Wesley (English) western meadow.
*Wesla, Weslah, Weslea, Wesleah, Weslei,
Wesleigh, Weslene, Wesli, Weslia, Weslie,
Wesly, Weslya, Weslyah, Weslyn*

Whaley (English) whale meadow.
*Whalea, Whaleah, Whalee, Whalei,
Whaleigh, Whali, Whalia, Whaliah, Whalie,
Whaly, Whalya*

Whisper (English, German) whisper.

Whitley (English) white field.
*Whitely, Whitlea, Whitleah, Whitlee, Whitlei,
Whitleigh, Whitli, Whitlia, Whitlie, Whitly,
Whitlya, Whittley, Whytlea, Whytleah,
Whytlee, Whytlei, Whytleigh, Whytley,
Whytli, Whytlia, Whytlie, Whytly, Whytlya*

Whitnee, Whitni, Whitnie, Whittney
(English) forms of Whitney.
Whittnee, Whittni, Whittnie

Whitney (English) white island.
*Whitani, Whiteney, Whitne, Whitné,
Whitnei, Whitneigh, Whitny, Whitnye,
Whittaney, Whittanie, Whittany, Whitteny,
Whittnay, Whytne, Whytnee, Whytney,
Whytni, Whytnie, Whytny, Witney*

Whoopi (English) happy; excited.
Whoopee, Whoopey, Whoopie, Whoopy

Wicktoria (Polish) a form of Victoria.
*Wicktoriah, Wicktorja, Wiktoria, Wiktoriah,
Wiktorja, Wycktoria, Wycktoriah, Wycktorja,
Wyktoria, Wyktoriah, Wyktorja*

Wila (Hawaiian) loyal, faithful.
Wilah, Wyla, Wylah

Wilda (German) untamed. (English)
willow.
Wildah, Willda, Wylda, Wyldah, Wylder

Wileen (English) a short form of
Wilhelmina.
*Wilean, Wileana, Wileane, Wileena,
Wileenah, Wileene, Wilene, Wilin, Wilina,
Wilinah, Wiline, Willeen, Willene, Wilyn,
Wilyna, Wilynah, Wilyne, Wylean,
Wyleana, Wyleanah, Wyleane, Wyleen,
Wyleena, Wyleenah, Wyleene, Wylin,
Wylina, Wylinah, Wyline, Wylyn, Wylyna,
Wylynah, Wylyne*

Wilhelmina (German) a form of Wilhelm
(see Boys' Names). See also Billie,
Guillerma, Helma, Minka, Minna,
Minnie.
*Vilhelmina, Wilhelmine, Willamina,
Willaminah, Willamine, Willemina,
Willeminah, Willemine, Williamina,
Williamine, Willmina, Willmine, Wimina,
Wimine, Wylhelmin, Wylhelmina,
Wylhelminah, Wylhelmine, Wylhelmyn,
Wylhelmyna, Wylhelmynah, Wylhelmyne,
Wyllhelmin, Wyllhelmina, Wyllhelminah,
Wyllhelmine, Wyllhelmyn, Wyllhelmyna,
Wyllhelmynah, Wyllhelmyne*

Wilikinia (Hawaiian) a form of Virginia.
Wilikiniah

Willa (German) a short form of Wilhelmina, William.
Wylla, Wyllah

Willabelle (American) a combination of Willa + Belle.
Wilabel, Wilabela, Wilabele, Willabel, Willabela, Willabele, Willabell, Willabella, Williabelle, Wylabel, Wylabela, Wylabele, Wylabell, Wylabella, Wylabelle, Wyllabel, Wyllabela, Wyllabele, Wyllabell, Wyllabella, Wyllabelle

Willette (English) a familiar form of Wilhelmina, Willa, William.
Wiletta, Wilette, Willetta, Williette

William (English) determined guardian.

Willie (English) a familiar form of Wilhelmina, William.
Wilea, Wileah, Wilee, Wilei, Wileigh, Wiley, Wili, Wilie, Willea, Willeah, Willee, Willei, Willeigh, Willi, Willina, Willisha, Willishia, Willy

Willow (English) willow tree.
Willo, Willough, Wyllo, Wyllow, Wylo, Wylow

Wilma (German) a short form of Wilhelmina.
Williemae, Wilmah, Wilmanie, Wilmayra, Wilmetta, Wilmette, Wilmina, Wilmyne, Wylma, Wylmah

Wilona (English) desired.
Willona, Willone, Wilonah, Wilone, Wylona, Wylonah, Wylone

Win (German) a short form of Winifred. See also Edwina, Wynne.
Winn, Winne

Winda (Swahili) hunter.

Windy (English) windy.
Windea, Windee, Windey, Windi, Windie, Wyndea, Wyndee, Wyndey, Wyndi, Wyndie, Wyndy

Winema (Moquelumnan) woman chief.
Winemah, Wynema, Wynemah

Wing (Chinese) glory.
Wing-Chiu, Wing-Kit

Winifred (German) peaceful friend. (Welsh) a form of Guinevere. See also Freddi, Una, Winnie.
Winafred, Winefred, Winefrid, Winefride, Winfreda, Winfrieda, Winiefrida, Winifrid, Winifryd, Winifryda, Winnafred, Winnafreda, Winnefred, Winniefred, Winnifred, Winnifreda, Winnifrid, Winnifrida, Wynafred, Wynafreda, Wynafrid, Wynafrida, Wynefred, Wynefreda, Wynefryd, Wynifred, Wynnifred

Winna (African) friend.
Wina, Winnah, Wyna, Wynah, Wynna, Wynnah

Winnie (English) a familiar form of Edwina, Gwyneth, Winifred, Winona, Wynne. History: Winnie Mandela kept the anti-aparteid movement alive in South Africa while her then-husband, Nelson Mandela, was imprisoned. Literature: the lovable bear in A. A. Milne's children's story *Winnie-the-Pooh*.
Winee, Winey, Wini, Winie, Winnee, Winney, Winni, Winny, Winy, Wynee, Wyney, Wyni, Wynie, Wynnee, Wynney, Wynni, Wynnie, Wynny, Wyny

Winola (German) charming friend.
Winolah, Wynola, Wynolah

Winona (Lakota) oldest daughter.
Wanona, Wanonah, Wenona, Wenonah, Winonah

Winter (English) winter.
Wintr

Wira (Polish) a form of Elvira.
Wirah, Wiria, Wirke, Wyra, Wyrah

Wisia (Polish) a form of Victoria.
Wicia, Wiciah, Wikta, Wisiah, Wysia, Wysiah, Wysya, Wysyah

Wren (English) wren, songbird.
Wrena, Wrenah, Wrene, Wrenee, Wrenie, Wrenn, Wrenna, Wrennah, Wrenny

Wyanet (Native American) legendary beauty.
Wianet, Wianeta, Wianete, Wianett, Wianetta, Wianette, Wianita, Wyaneta, Wyanete, Wyanett, Wyanetta, Wyanette, Wyanita, Wynette

Wynne (Welsh) white, light skinned. A short form of Blodwyn, Guinevere, Gwyneth. See also Win.
Wyn, Wyne, Wynn

Wynonna (Lakota) a form of Winona.
Wynnona, Wynona, Wynonah

Wynter (English) a form of Winter.
Wynteria

Wyoming (Native American) Geography: a western U.S. state.
Wy, Wye, Wyoh, Wyomia, Wyomya

Xabrina (Latin) a form of Sabrina.
Xabrinah, Xabrine, Xabryna, Xabrynah, Xabryne

Xalina (French) a form of Salina.
Xalean, Xaleana, Xaleanah, Xaleane, Xaleen, Xaleena, Xaleenah, Xaleene, Xalena, Xalenah, Xalinah, Xaline, Xalyna, Xalynah, Xalyne

Xamantha (Hebrew) a form of Samantha.
Xamanfa, Xamanfah, Xamanffa, Xamanffah, Xamanthah, Xamanthia, Xamanthiah, Xammantha, Xammanthia, Xammanthya

Xami (Hebrew) a form of Sami.
Xama, Xamah, Xamee, Xamey, Xamia, Xamiah, Xamie, Xamm, Xamma, Xammah, Xammi, Xammia, Xammiah, Xammie, Xammy, Xammya, Xammyah, Xamy, Xamya, Xamyah

Xamuela (Hebrew) a form of Samuela.
Xamuelah, Xamuele, Xamuell, Xamuella, Xamuellah, Xamuelle

Xana (Greek) a form of Xanthe.
Xanna, Xanne

Xandi (Greek) a form of Sandi.
Xandea, Xandee, Xandey, Xandia, Xandiah, Xandie, Xandy

Xandra (Greek) a form of Sandra. (Spanish) a short form of Alexandra.
Xander, Xandrah

Xandria (Greek, Spanish) a form of Xandra.
Xandrea, Xandreah, Xandreia, Xandreiah, Xandriah, Xandrya, Xandryah

Xandrine (Greek) a form of Sandrine.
Xandrean, Xandreana, Xandreanah, Xandreane, Xandreen, Xandreena, Xandreenah, Xandreene, Xandrina, Xandrinah, Xandryna, Xandrynah

Xanthe (Greek) yellow, blond. See also Zanthe.
Xantha, Xanthia, Xanthiah

Xanthippe (Greek) a form of Xanthe. History: Socrates's wife.
Xantippie, Zanthippe, Zantippie

Xantina (Spanish) a form of Santina.
Xantinah, Xantine, Xantyna, Xantynah, Xantyne

Xara (Hebrew) a form of Sarah.
Xarah, Xari, Xaria, Xariah, Xarie, Xarra, Xarrah, Xarri, Xarria, Xarriah, Xarrie, Xarry, Xary, Xarya, Xaryah

Xarika (Hebrew) a form of Sarika.
Xareaka, Xareakah, Xareeka, Xareekah, Xareka, Xarekah, Xarikah, Xarka, Xarkah

Xarina (Hebrew) a form of Sarina.
Xareana, Xareanah, Xareane, Xareena, Xareenah, Xareene, Xarena, Xarenah, Xarene, Xarinah, Xarine, Xarinna, Xarinnah, Xarinne, Xaryna, Xarynah, Xaryne, Xarynna, Xarynnah

Xavier (Arabic) bright. (Basque) owner of the new house.
Xabier, Xaiver, Xavaeir, Xaver, Xavery, Xavian, Xaviar, Xaviero, Xavior, Xavon, Xavyer, Xizavier, Xxavier, Xzavier

Xaviera (Basque, Arabic) a form of Xavier. See also Javiera, Zaviera.
Xavia, Xavierah, Xaviére, Xavyera, Xavyerah, Xavyere, Xiveria

Xela (Quiché) my mountain home.
Xelah, Xella, Xellah, Zela, Zelah, Zella, Zellah

Xena (Greek) a form of Xenia.
Xeena, Xenah, Xene, Xina, Xinah, Xyna, Xynah

Xenia (Greek) hospitable. See also Senia, Zena, Zina.
Xeenia, Xeeniah, Xenea, Xeniah, Xenya, Xenyah, Xinia

Xenosa (Greek) stanger.
Xenosah, Zenosa, Zenosah

Xerena (Latin) a form of Serena.
Xeren, Xerenah, Xerene

Xiang (Chinese) fragrant. See also Ziang.
Xeang, Xeeang, Xyang

Ximena (Spanish) a form of Simone.
Ximenah, Ximona, Ximonah, Ximone, Xymena, Xymenah, Xymona, Xymonah

Xiomara (Teutonic) glorious forest.
Xiomaris, Xiomayra

Xirena (Greek) a form of Sirena.
Xireena, Xireenah, Xirenah, Xirene, Xirina, Xirinah, Xyren, Xyrena, Xyrenah, Xyrene, Xyrina, Xyrinah, Xyrine, Xyryna, Xyrynah

Xiu Mei (Chinese) beautiful plum.

Xochilt (Aztec) a form of Xochitl.

Xochitl (Aztec) place of many flowers.
Xochil, Xochilth, Xochiti

Xuan (Vietnamese) spring.
Xuana, Zuan

Xuxa (Portuguese) a familiar form of Susanna.
Xuxah

Xyleena (Greek) forest dweller. See also Zylina.
Xilean, Xileana, Xileanah, Xileane, Xileen, Xileena, Xileenah, Xileene, Xilin, Xilina, Xilinah, Xiline, Xilyn, Xilyna, Xilynah, Xilyne, Xylean, Xyleana, Xyleanah, Xyleane, Xyleen, Xyleenah, Xyleene, Xylin, Xylina, Xylinah, Xyline, Xylona, Xylyn, Xylyna, Xylynah, Xylyne

Xylia (Greek) a form of Sylvia.
Xilia, Xiliah, Xylya, Xylyah

Xylona (Greek) a form of Xyleena.
Xilon, Xilona, Xilonah, Xilone, Xilonia, Xiloniah, Xylon, Xylonah, Xylone, Xylonia, Xyloniah, Xylonya, Xylonyah

Xylophia (Greek) forest lover.
Xilophia, Xilophiah, Xylophiah, Xylophila, Xylophilah, Zilophia, Zylophia

Yachne (Hebrew) hospitable.
Yachnee

Yadira (Hebrew) friend.
Yadirah, Yadirha, Yadyra

Yael (Hebrew) strength of God. See also Jael.
Yaela, Yaele, Yaeli, Yaell, Yaella, Yaelle, Yeala

Yaffa (Hebrew) beautiful. See also Jaffa.
Yafeal, Yaffah, Yaffit, Yafit

Yahaira (Hebrew) a form of Yakira.
Yahara, Yahayra, Yahira

Yajaira (Hebrew) a form of Yakira.
Yajara, Yajayra, Yajhaira

Yakira (Hebrew) precious; dear.
Yakirah, Yakyra, Yakyrah

Yalanda (Greek) a form of Yolanda.
Yalandah, Yalando, Yalonda, Ylana, Ylanda

Yalena (Greek, Russian) a form of Helen. See also Lena, Yelena.
Yalana, Yalanah, Yalane, Yaleana, Yaleanah, Yaleane, Yaleena, Yaleenah, Yaleene, Yalina, Yalinah, Yaline, Yalyna, Yalynah, Yalyne

Yaletha (American) a form of Oletha.
Yelitsa

Yamary (American) a combination of the prefix Ya + Mary.
Yamairee, Yamairey, Yamairi, Yamairie, Yamairy, Yamaree, Yamarey, Yamari, Yamaria, Yamarie, Yamaris, Yamarya, Yamaryah, Yamayra

Yamelia (American) a form of Amelia.
Yameily, Yameliah, Yamelya, Yamelyah, Yamelys, Yamilya, Yamilyah

Yamila (Arabic) a form of Jamila.
Yamela, Yamely, Yamil, Yamile, Yamiley, Yamill, Yamilla, Yamille, Yamyl, Yamyla, Yamyle, Yamyll, Yamylla, Yamylle

Yamilet (Arabic) a form of Jamila.

Yaminah (Arabic) right, proper.
Yamina, Yamini, Yamyna, Yamynah, Yemina, Yeminah, Yemini

Yaminta (Native American) mint, minty.
Yamintah, Yamynta, Yamyntah, Yiminta

Yamka (Hopi) blossom.

Yamuna (Hindi) sacred river.
Yamunah

Yana (Slavic) a form of Jana.
Yanae, Yanah, Yanay, Yanaye, Yanesi, Yaney, Yania, Yaniah, Yanina, Yanis, Yanisha, Yanitza, Yanna, Yannah, Yannia, Yanniah, Yannica, Yannina, Yannya, Yannyah, Yannyna

Yanaba (Navajo) brave.
Yanabah

Yaneli, Yanely (American) combinations of the prefix Ya + Nellie.
Yanela, Yanelis, Yaneliz, Yanelle, Yanelli, Yanelys

Yanet (American) a form of Janet.
Yanete, Yanette, Yannet, Yannette

Yaneth (American) a form of Janet.
Yanethe, Yanneth

Yáng (Chinese) sun.

Yani (Australian) peaceful. (Hebrew) a short form of Yannis.
Yanee, Yaney, Yanie, Yannee, Yanney, Yanni, Yannie, Yanny, Yany

Yannis (Hebrew) gift of God.
Yanis, Yannys, Yanys

Yara (Iranian) courage.

Yareli, Yarely (American) forms of Oralee.
Yaresly

Yarina (Slavic) a form of Irene.
Yarinah, Yarine, Yaryna, Yarynah, Yaryne

Yaritza (American) a combination of Yana + Ritsa.
Yaritsa, Yaritsah

Yarkona (Hebrew) green.
Yarkonah

Yarmilla (Slavic) market trader. See also Jarmilla.
Yarmila, Yarmilah, Yarmillah, Yarmille, Yarmyla, Yarmylah, Yarmylla, Yarmyllah, Yarmylle

Yasemin (Persian) a form of Yasmin.
Yasemeen

Yashira (Afghan) humble; takes it easy. (Arabic) wealthy.

Yasmeen, Yasmen (Persian) forms of Yasmin.
Yasmeene, Yasmene, Yasmenne, Yassmeen, Yassmen

Yasmin, Yasmine (Persian) jasmine flower.
Yashmine, Yasiman, Yasimine, Yasma, Yasmain, Yasmaine, Yasmeni, Yasmon, Yasmyn, Yasmyne, Yesmean, Yesmeen, Yesmin, Yesmine, Yesmyn

Yasmina (Persian) a form of Yasmin.
Yasmeena, Yasmeenah, Yasminah, Yasminda, Yasmyna, Yasmynah, Yesmina

Yasu (Japanese) resting, calm.
Yasuko, Yasuyo, Yazoo

Yazmin, Yazmine (Persian) forms of Yasmin.
Yazmeen, Yazmen, Yazmene, Yazmina, Yazminah, Yazmyn, Yazmyna, Yazmynah, Yazmyne, Yazzmien, Yazzmine, Yazzmyn, Yazzmyne

Yecenia (Arabic) a form of Yesenia.

Yedida (Hebrew) dear friend.
Yedidah, Yedyda, Yedydah

Yehudit (Hebrew) a form of Judith.
Yuta

Yei (Japanese) flourishing.

Yeira (Hebrew) light.
Yeirah, Yeyra, Yeyrah

Yekaterina (Russian) a form of Katherine.

Yelena (Russian) a form of Helen, Jelena. See also Lena, Yalena.
Yelain, Yelaina, Yelainah, Yelaine, Yelana, Yelanah, Yelane, Yeleana, Yeleanah, Yeleane, Yeleena, Yeleenah, Yeleene, Yelen, Yelenah, Yelenna, Yelenne, Yelina, Yelinah, Yeline,

Yelena *(cont.)*
Yellaina, Yellaine, Yellayna, Yellaynah, Yellena,
Yellenah, Yellene, Yelyna, Yelynah, Yelyne,
Yileana, Yileanah, Yileane, Yileena, Yileenah,
Yileene, Yilina, Yilinah, Yiline, Yilyna,
Yilynah, Yilyne, Ylena, Ylenia, Ylenna

Yelisabeta (Russian) a form of Elizabeth.
Yelizaveta

Yemena (Arabic) from Yemen.
Yemina, Yeminah, Yemyna, Yemynah

Yen (Chinese) yearning; desirous.
Yeni, Yenih, Yenny

Yenene (Native American) shaman.
Yenena, Yenenah, Yenina, Yeninah, Yenyna,
Yenynah, Yenyne

Yenifer (Welsh) a form of Jennifer.
Yenefer, Yennifer

Yeo (Korean) mild.
Yee

Yepa (Native American) snow girl.
Yepah, Yeppa, Yeppah

Yesenia (Arabic) flower.
Yasenya, Yeseniah, Yesenya, Yesenyah, Yesinia,
Yesnia

Yesica, Yessica (Hebrew) forms of Jessica.
Yesicah, Yesicka, Yesickah, Yesika, Yesikah,
Yesiko, Yessicah, Yessicka, Yessickah, Yessika,
Yessikah, Yesyka

Yessenia (Arabic) a form of Yesenia.
Yessena, Yessenah, Yesseniah, Yessenya,
Yessenyah, Yissenia

Yetta (English) a short form of Henrietta.
Yeta, Yette, Yitta, Yitty

Yeva (Ukrainian) a form of Eve.
Yevah

Yevgenia (Russian) a form of Eugenia.
Yevgena, Yevgeniah, Yevgenya, Yevgenyah,
Yevgina, Yevginah, Yevgyna

Yiesha (Arabic, Swahili) a form of Aisha.
Yiasha, Yieshah

Yín (Chinese) silver.

Ynez (Spanish) a form of Agnes. See also
Ines.
Ynes, Ynesita

Yoana, Yoanna (Hebrew) forms of Joana.

Yocelin, Yocelyn (Latin) forms of Jocelyn.
Yoceline, Yocelyne, Yuceli

Yohana (Hebrew) a form of Joana.
Yohanka, Yohanna, Yohannah

Yoi (Japanese) born in the evening.

Yoki (Hopi) bluebird.
Yokee, Yokie, Yoky

Yoko (Japanese) good girl.
Yo

Yolanda (Greek) violet flower. See also
Iolanthe, Jolanda, Olinda.
Yolaine, Yolana, Yoland, Yolande, Yolane,
Yolanna, Yolantha, Yolanthe, Yolette, Yorlanda,
Youlanda, Yulanda, Yulonda

Yolie (Greek) a familiar form of Yolanda.
Yola, Yolah, Yolee, Yoley, Yoli, Yoly

Yolonda (Greek) a form of Yolanda.

Yoluta (Native American) summer flower.
Yolutah

Yomara (American) a combination of
Yolanda + Tamara.
Yomaira, Yomarie, Yomira

Yon (Burmese) rabbit. (Korean) lotus
blossom.
Yona, Yonna

Yoné (Japanese) wealth; rice.

Yonie (Hebrew) a familiar form of Yonina.
Yonee, Yoney, Yoni, Yony

Yonina (Hebrew) a form of Jonina.
Yona, Yonah, Yoneena, Yoneene, Yoninah,
Yonine, Yonyna, Yonynah

Yonita (Hebrew) a form of Jonita.
Yonat, Yonati, Yonit, Yonitah, Yonyta, Yonytah

Yoomee (Coos) star.
Yoome

Yordana (Basque) descendant. See also
Jordana.
Yordanah, Yordanna, Yordannah

Yori (Japanese) reliable.
Yoriko, Yoriyo

Yoselin, Yoseline, Yoselyn (Latin) forms of Jocelyn.
Yosselin, Yosseline, Yosselyn

Yosepha (Hebrew) a form of Josephine.
Yosefa, Yosifa, Yosyfa, Yuseffa

Yoshi (Japanese) good; respectful.
Yoshee, Yoshey, Yoshie, Yoshiko, Yoshiyo, Yoshy

Yovela (Hebrew) joyful heart; rejoicer.
Yovelah, Yovella, Yovelle

Ysabel (Spanish) a form of Isabel.
Ysabela, Ysabelah, Ysabele, Ysabell, Ysabella, Ysabellah, Ysabelle, Ysbel, Ysbella, Ysibel, Ysibela, Ysibelah, Ysibele, Ysibell, Ysibella, Ysibellah, Ysibelle, Ysobel, Ysobela, Ysobele, Ysobell, Ysobella, Ysobelle, Ysybel, Ysybela, Ysybelah, Ysybele, Ysybell, Ysybella, Ysybellah, Ysybelle

Ysann, Ysanne (American) combinations of Ysabel + Ann.
Ysande, Ysanna, Ysannah

Yseult (German) ice rule. (Irish) fair; light skinned. (Welsh) a form of Isolde.
Yseulte, Ysolde, Ysolt

Yu (Chinese) universe.
Yue

Yuana (Spanish) a form of Juana.
Yuan, Yuanah, Yuanna, Yuannah

Yudelle (English) a form of Udele.
Yudela, Yudelah, Yudele, Yudelia, Yudeliah, Yudell, Yudella, Yudellah, Yudelya, Yudelyah

Yudita (Russian) a form of Judith.
Yudit, Yuditah, Yudith, Yuditt, Yuditta, Yudyta, Yudytah, Yudytta, Yudyttah

Yuki (Japanese) snow.
Yukee, Yukey, Yukie, Yukiko, Yukiyo, Yuky

Yulene (Basque) a form of Julia.
Yulean, Yuleana, Yuleanah, Yuleane, Yuleen, Yuleena, Yuleenah, Yuleene, Yulena, Yulenah

Yulia (Russian) a form of Julia.
Yula, Yulah, Yulenka, Yulinka, Yulka, Yulya, Yulyah

Yuliana (Spanish) a form of Juliana.
Yulenia, Yuliani

Yuri (Japanese) lily.
Yuree, Yuriko, Yuriyo, Yury

Yvanna (Slavic) a form of Ivana.
Yvan, Yvana, Yvanah, Yvania, Yvaniah, Yvannah, Yvannia, Yvannya, Yvannyah

Yvette (French) a familiar form of Yvonne. See also Evette, Ivette.
Yavette, Yevett, Yevetta, Yevette, Yvet, Yveta, Yvett, Yvetta

Yvonne (French) young archer. (Scandinavian) yew wood; bow wood. See also Evonne, Ivonne, Vonna, Vonny, Yvette.
Yavanda, Yavanna, Yavanne, Yavonda, Yavonna, Yavonne, Yveline, Yvon, Yvone, Yvonna, Yvonnah, Yvonnia, Yvonnie, Yvonny

Zabrina (American) a form of Sabrina.
Zabreana, Zabreanah, Zabreane, Zabreena, Zabreenah, Zabreenia, Zabreeniah, Zabrinah, Zabrine, Zabrinia, Zabriniah, Zabrinna, Zabrinnah, Zabrinnia, Zabrinniah, Zabryna, Zabrynah, Zabryne, Zabrynia, Zabryniah, Zabrynya, Zabrynyah

Zacharie (Hebrew) God remembered.
Zacara, Zacarah, Zacaree, Zacari, Zacaria, Zacariah, Zaccaree, Zaccari, Zacceaus, Zacchaea, Zachoia, Zackaria, Zackeisha, Zackeria, Zakaria, Zakariah, Zakelina, Zakeshia, Zakira, Zechari, Zecharie

Zachary (Hebrew) a form of Zacharie.
Zacarey, Zaccarey, Zackery, Zakary, Zakarya, Zakaryah, Zechary

Zada (Arabic) fortunate, prosperous.
Zayda, Zayeda

Zafina (Arabic) victorious.
Zafinah, Zafyna, Zafynah

Zafirah (Arabic) successful; victorious.
Zafira, Zafire, Zafyra, Zafyrah, Zafyre

Zahar (Hebrew) daybreak; dawn.
Zaher, Zahir, Zahyr

Zahara (Swahili) a form of Zahra.
Zaharra, Zahera, Zaherah, Zahira, Zahirah, Zahyra, Zahyrah, Zeeherah

Zahavah (Hebrew) golden.
Zachava, Zachavah, Zahavya, Zahavyah, Zechava, Zechavah, Zehava, Zehavah, Zehavi, Zehavia, Zehaviah, Zehavit, Zeheva, Zehuva

Zahra (Swahili) flower. (Arabic) white.
Sahra, Zahraa, Zahrah, Zahreh, Zahria, Zahriah

Zaida (Arabic) a form of Zada.

Zaidee (Arabic) rich.
Zaidea, Zaidey, Zaidi, Zaidie, Zaidy, Zaydea, Zaydee, Zaydi, Zaydie, Zaydy

Zaina (Spanish, English) a form of Zanna.
Zainah, Zainna

Zainab (Iranian) child of Ali.

Zainabu (Swahili) beautiful.

Zaira (Hebrew) a form of Zara.
Zairah, Zairea, Zirrea

Zaire (Hebrew) a short form of Zara.
Zair

Zakelina (Russian) a form of Zacharie.
Zacelina, Zacelinah, Zaceline, Zacelyn, Zacelyna, Zacelynah, Zacelyne, Zackelin, Zackelina, Zackelinah, Zackeline, Zackelyn, Zackelyna, Zackelynah, Zackelyne, Zakeleana, Zakeleanah, Zakeleane, Zakeleen, Zakeleena, Zakeleene, Zakelin, Zakelinah, Zakeline, Zakelyn, Zakelyna, Zakelynah, Zakelyne

Zakia (Swahili) smart. (Arabic) chaste.
Zakea, Zakeia, Zakiah

Zakira (Hebrew) a form of Zacharie.
Zaakira, Zakiera, Zakierra, Zakir, Zakirah, Zakiria, Zakiriya, Zykarah, Zykera, Zykeria, Zykerria, Zykira, Zykuria

Zakiya (Arabic) a form of Zakia.
Zakaya, Zakeya, Zakeyia, Zakiyaa, Zakiyah, Zakiyya, Zakiyyah, Zakkiyya,

Zakkiyyah, Zakkyyah, Zakya, Zakyah, Zakyya, Zakyyah

Zali (Polish) a form of Sara.
Zalea, Zaleah, Zalee, Zalei, Zaleigh, Zaley, Zalia, Zaliah, Zalie, Zaly, Zalya, Zalyah

Zalika (Swahili) born to royalty.
Salika, Zalik, Zalikah, Zalyka, Zalykah, Zuleika

Zalina (French) a form of Salina.
Zalean, Zaleana, Zaleanah, Zaleane, Zaleen, Zaleena, Zaleenah, Zaleene, Zalena, Zalenah, Zalene, Zalinah, Zaline, Zalyna, Zalynah, Zalyne

Zaltana (Native American) high mountain.
Zaltanah

Zamantha (Hebrew) a form of Samantha.
Zamanthia, Zamanthiah, Zammantha, Zammanthah, Zammanthia, Zammanthiah, Zammanthya, Zammanthyah

Zami (Hebrew) a form of Sami.
Zama, Zamah, Zamee, Zamey, Zamia, Zamiah, Zamie, Zamm, Zamma, Zammah, Zammi, Zammia, Zammiah, Zammie, Zammy, Zammya, Zammyah, Zamy, Zamya, Zamyah

Zamuela (Hebrew) a form of Samuela.
Zamuelah, Zamuele, Zamuell, Zamuella, Zamuellah, Zamuelle

Zana (Spanish, English) a form of Zanna.

Zandi (Greek) a form of Sandi.
Zandea, Zandee, Zandey, Zandia, Zandiah, Zandie, Zandy

Zandra (Greek) a form of Sandra.
Zahndra, Zandrah, Zandrie, Zandry, Zanndra, Zondra

Zandria (Greek) a form of Zandra.
Zandrea, Zandreah, Zandriah, Zandrya, Zandryah

Zandrine (Greek) a form of Sandrine.
Zandreen, Zandreena, Zandreenah, Zandreene, Zandreina, Zandreinah, Zandreine, Zandrina, Zandrinah, Zandryn, Zandryna, Zandrynah, Zandryne

Zaneta (Spanish) a form of Jane.
Saneta, Sanete, Sanetta, Zaneata, Zaneatah, Zaneeta, Zaneetah, Zanetah, Zanete, Zanett, Zanetta, Zanettah, Zanette, Zanita, Zanitah, Zanitra, Zanyta, Zanytah

Zanna (Spanish) a form of Jane. (English) a short form of Susanna.
Zanae, Zanah, Zanella, Zanette, Zannah, Zannette, Zannia, Zannie, Zannya, Zannyah

Zanthe (Greek) a form of Xanthe.
Zanth, Zantha, Zanthia, Zanthiah

Zantina (Spanish) a form of Santina.
Zantinah, Zantine, Zantyna, Zantynah, Zantyne

Zara, Zarah (Hebrew) forms of Sarah, Zora.
Zareh, Zarra, Zarrah

Zari (Hebrew) a form of Zara.
Zaree, Zareen, Zarie, Zarri, Zarrie, Zarry, Zary

Zaria (Hebrew) a form of Zara.
Zarea, Zareea, Zareena, Zareya, Zariah, Zariya, Zarria, Zarriah, Zarya, Zaryah

Zarifa (Arabic) successful.
Zarifah, Zaryfa, Zaryfah

Zarika (Hebrew) a form of Sarika.
Zareaka, Zareakah, Zareeka, Zareekah, Zareka, Zarekah, Zarikah, Zarka, Zarkah

Zarina (Hebrew) a form of Sarina.
Zareana, Zareanah, Zareane, Zareena, Zareenah, Zareene, Zarena, Zarenah, Zarene, Zarinah, Zarine, Zarinna, Zarinnah, Zarinne, Zaryna, Zarynah, Zaryne, Zarynna, Zarynnah

Zarita (Spanish) a form of Sarah.
Zareata, Zareatah, Zareate, Zareeta, Zareetah, Zareete, Zaritah, Zarite, Zaritta, Zarittah, Zaritte, Zaryt, Zaryta, Zarytah, Zaryte

Zasha (Russian) a form of Sasha.
Zascha, Zashenka, Zashka, Zasho

Zavannah (Spanish) a form of Savannah.
Zavana, Zavanah, Zavanna, Zevana, Zevanah, Zevanna, Zevannah

Zaviera (Spanish) a form of Xaviera.
Zavera, Zaverah, Zavierah, Zaviere, Zavira, Zavirah, Zavyera, Zavyerah

Zawati (Swahili) gift.
Zawatia, Zawatiah, Zawaty, Zawatya, Zawatyah

Zayit (Hebrew) olive.
Zayita

Zayna (Arabic) a form of Zaynah.

Zaynab (Iranian) a form of Zainab.

Zaynah (Arabic) beautiful.
Zayn

Zayra (Hebrew) a form of Zara.

Zaza (Hebrew) golden.
Zazah, Zazu

Zea (Latin) grain. See also Zia.
Sea, Zeah

Zefiryn (Polish) a form of Zephyr.
Zafirin, Zafirina, Zafirinah, Zefiryna, Zefirynah, Zefyrin, Zefyrina, Zefyrinah, Zefyryn, Zefyryna, Zefyrynah

Zeina (Greek, Ethiopian, Persian) a form of Zena.
Zein

Zeinab (Somali) good.

Zelda (Yiddish) gray haired. (German) a short form of Griselda. See also Selda.
Zeldah, Zelde, Zella, Zellda

Zelena (Greek) a form of Selena.
Zeleana, Zeleanah, Zeleena, Zeleenah, Zelenah, Zelina, Zelinah, Zelyna, Zelynah

Zelene (English) sunshine.
Zelean, Zeleane, Zeleen, Zeleene, Zelen, Zeline, Zelyn, Zelyne

Zelia (Spanish) sunshine.
Zele, Zeliah, Zelie, Zélie, Zelya, Zelyah

Zelizi (Basque) a form of Sheila.
Zelizia, Zeliziah, Zelzya, Zelzyah

Zelma (German) a form of Selma.
Zalmah

Zemirah (Hebrew) song of joy.
Senira, Senyra, Zemir, Zemira, Zemyr,
Zemyra, Zemyrah, Zimira, Zimirah,
Zymira, Zymirah, Zymyra, Zymyrah

Zena (Ethiopian) news. (Persian) woman.
(Greek) a form of Xenia. See also Zina.
Zanae, Zanah, Zeena, Zeenat, Zeenet,
Zenah, Zenana, Zenna, Zennah

Zenaida (Greek) white-winged dove.
Zenaidah, Zenayda, Zenochka

Zenaide (Greek) a form of Zenaida.
Zenaïde, Zenayde

Zenda (Persian) sacred; feminine.
Senda, Zendah

Zenia (Greek, Ethiopian, Persian) a form
of Zena.
Zeenia, Zeenya, Zenea, Zeniah, Zennia,
Zenya, Zenyah

Zenobia (Greek) sign, symbol. History: a
queen who ruled the city of Palmyra in
ancient Syria.
Senobe, Senobia, Senovia, Zeba, Zeeba,
Zenobiah, Zenobie, Zenobya, Zenobyah,
Zenovia

Zephania (Greek) a form of Stephanie.
Zepania, Zephanas, Zephaniah, Zephanya,
Zephanyah

Zephanie (Greek) a form of Stephanie.
Zephanee, Zephaney, Zephani, Zephany

Zephrine (English) breeze.
Sephrine, Zephrean, Zephreana,
Zephreanah, Zephreane, Zephreen,
Zephreena, Zephreenah, Zephreene,
Zephrin, Zephrina, Zephrinah, Zephryn,
Zephryna, Zephrynah, Zephryne, Zephyrine

Zephyr (Greek) west wind.
Zephra, Zephria, Zephyer

Zera (Hebrew) seeds.
Zerah, Zeriah

Zerdali (Turkish) wild apricot.
Zerdalia, Zerdaly, Zerdalya

Zerena (Latin) a form of Serena.
Zerenah, Zirena, Zirenah, Zyrena, Zyrenah

Zerlina (Latin, Spanish) beautiful dawn.
Music: a character in Mozart's opera
Don Giovanni.
Serlina, Serlyna, Serlyne, Zerla, Zerlean,
Zerleana, Zerleanah, Zerleane, Zerlee,
Zerleen, Zerleena, Zerleenah, Zerleene,
Zerlinah, Zerlinda, Zerline, Zerlyn,
Zerlyna, Zerlynah, Zerlyne

Zerrin (Turkish) golden.
Zerran, Zerren, Zerron, Zerryn

Zeta (English) rose. Linguistics: a letter in
the Greek alphabet.
Zetana

Zetta (Portuguese) rose.

Zhana (Slavic) forms of Jane.
Zhanae, Zhanay, Zhanaya, Zhanea,
Zhanee, Zhaney, Zhani, Zhaniah, Zhanna

Zhane (Slavic) a form of Jane.

Zhané (Slavic) a form of Jane.

Zhen (Chinese) chaste.
Zen, Zenn, Zhena

Zia (Latin) grain. (Arabic) light. See also
Zea.
Sia, Ziah, Zya, Zyah

Ziang (Chinese) a form of Xiang.
Zeang, Zeeang, Zyang

Zigana (Hungarian) gypsy girl. See also
Tsigana.
Ziganah, Zigane, Zygana, Zyganah

Zihna (Hopi) one who spins tops.
Zihnah, Zyhna, Zyhnah

Zilia (Greek) a form of Sylvia.
Ziliah, Zylia, Zyliah, Zylina, Zylyna

Zilla (Hebrew) shadow.
Sila, Zila, Zilah, Zillah, Zyla, Zylah,
Zylla, Zyllah

Zilpah (Hebrew) dignified. Bible: Jacob's
wife.
Silpah, Zilpha, Zylpa, Zylpah, Zylpha

Zilya (Russian) a form of Theresa.
Zilyah, Zylya, Zylyah

Zimena (Spanish) a form of Simone.
Zimenah, Zimene, Zimona, Zimonah,
Zimone, Zymena, Zymenah, Zymona,
Zymonah

Zimra (Hebrew) song of praise.
Zamira, Zamora, Zamyra, Zemira, Zemora,
Zemyra, Zimria, Zimrria, Zymria, Zymriah,
Zymrya, Zymryah

Zina (African) secret spirit. (English) hospitable. (Greek) a form of Zena.
Zeena, Zinah, Zine, Zyhna, Zyna, Zynah

Zinerva (Italian) fair, light-haired.
Zinervah, Zynerva, Zynervah

Zinnia (Latin) Botany: a plant with beautiful, rayed, colorful flowers.
Zeenia, Zinia, Ziniah, Zinniah, Zinny,
Zinnya, Zinya, Zynia, Zyniah, Zynyah

Zipporah (Hebrew) bird. Bible: Moses' wife.
Cipora, Sipora, Sippora, Zipora, Ziporah,
Zipporia, Ziproh, Zypora, Zyporah,
Zyppora, Zypporah

Zirina (Greek) a form of Sirena.
Zireena, Zireenah, Zirinah, Ziryna,
Zirynah, Zyreena, Zyreenah, Zyrina,
Zyrinah, Zyryna, Zyrynah

Zita (Spanish) rose. (Arabic) mistress. A short form of names ending in "sita" or "zita."
Zeeta, Zitah, Zyta, Zytah, Zytka

Ziva (Hebrew) bright; radiant.
Zeeva, Ziv, Zivanka, Zivi, Zivit, Zyva,
Zyvah

Zizi (Hungarian) a familiar form of Elizabeth.
Zsi Zsi, ZyZy

Zocha (Polish) a form of Sophie.
Zochah

Zoe (Greek) life.
Zoé, Zoë, Zoee, Zoelie, Zoeline, Zoelle,
Zowe, Zowey, Zowie

Zoey (Greek) a form of Zoe.
Zooey

Zofia (Slavic) a form of Sophia. See also Sofia.

Zofee, Zofey, Zofi, Zofiah, Zofie, Zofka,
Zofy, Zophee, Zophey, Zophi, Zophia,
Zophiah, Zophie, Zophya, Zophyah

Zohar (Hebrew) shining, brilliant.
Zohara, Zoharah, Zohera, Zoheret

Zohra (Hebrew) blossom.
Zohrah

Zohreh (Persian) happy.
Zahreh, Zohrah

Zoie (Greek) a form of Zoe.
Zoi, Zoye

Zoila (Italian) a form of Zola.

Zola (Italian) piece of earth.
Zoela, Zolah

Zona (Latin) belt, sash.
Zonah, Zonia

Zondra (Greek) a form of Zandra.
Zohndra, Zohndria, Zohndriah, Zohndrya,
Zohndryah, Zondrah, Zondria, Zondriah,
Zondrya, Zondryah

Zora (Slavic) aurora; dawn. See also Zara.
Sora, Zorah, Zorane, Zorna, Zorra, Zorrah,
Zory, Zorya

Zorina (Slavic) golden.
Sorina, Zorana, Zoranah, Zorean, Zoreana,
Zoreanah, Zoreane, Zoreen, Zoreena,
Zoreenah, Zoreene, Zori, Zorie, Zorin,
Zorinah, Zorine, Zoryna, Zorynah, Zoryne

Zoya (Slavic) a form of Zoe.
Zoia, Zoiah, Zoy, Zoyah, Zoyara,
Zoyechka, Zoyenka, Zoyya, Zoyyah

Zsa Zsa (Hungarian) a familiar form of Susan.
Zhazha

Zsofia (Hungarian) a form of Sofia.
Zsofi, Zsofiah, Zsofie, Zsofika, Zsofy,
Zsophee, Zsophey, Zsophi, Zsophia,
Zsophiah, Zsophie, Zsophy

Zsuzsanna (Hungarian) a form of Susanna.
Zsuska, Zsuzsa, Zsuzsi, Zsuzsika,
Zsuzska

Zudora (Sanskrit) laborer.
Zudorah

Zuleika (Arabic) brilliant.
Zeleeka, Zul, Zulay, Zulekha, Zuleyka

Zuleima (Arabic) a form of Zulima.

Zulema (Arabic) a form of Zulima.
Zulemah

Zuleyma (Arabic) a form of Zulima.
Zuleymah

Zulima (Arabic) a form of Salama.
*Zalama, Zalamah, Zulimah, Zulyma,
Zulymah*

Zurafa (Arabic) lovely.
Ziraf, Zirafa, Zuruf, Zurufa

Zuri (Basque) white; light skinned.
(Swahili) beautiful.
*Zuree, Zurey, Zuria, Zuriah, Zurie,
Zurisha, Zury, Zurya, Zuryah*

Zusa (Czech, Polish) a form of Susan.
*Zusah, Zuza, Zuzah, Zuzana, Zuzanka,
Zuzia, Zuzka, Zuzu*

Zuwena (Swahili) good.
Zwena

Zylina (Greek) a form of Xyleena.
*Zilin, Zilina, Zilinah, Ziline, Zilyna,
Zilynah, Zylin, Zylinah, Zyline, Zylyn,
Zylyna, Zylynah*

Zytka (Polish) rose.

Boys

A

'Aziz (Arabic) strong.
Azizz

Aakash (Hindi) a form of Akash.

Aamir (Hebrew, Punjabi, Arabic) a form of Amir.
Aamer

Aaran (Hebrew) a form of Aaron. (Scottish) a form of Arran.

Aaron (Hebrew) enlightened. (Arabic) messenger. Bible: the brother of Moses and the first high priest. See also Ron.
Aahron, Aaren, Aareon, Aarin, Aaronn, Aeron, Arek, Arren, Arrin, Arryn

Aaronjames (American) a combination of Aaron + James.
Aaron James, Aaron-James

Aarron, Aaryn (Hebrew, Arabic) forms of Aaron.
Aarronn, Aarynn

Aban (Persian) Mythology: a figure associated with water and the arts.

Abasi (Swahili) stern.
Abasee, Abasey, Abasie, Abasy

Abban (Latin) white.
Abben, Abbin, Abbine, Abbon

Abbas (Arabic) lion.

Abbey (Hebrew) a familiar form of Abe.
Abbee, Abbi, Abbie, Abby, Abee, Abey, Abi, Aby

Abbott (Hebrew) father; abbot.
Ab, Abad, Abba, Abbah, Abbán, Abbé, Abboid, Abbot, Abot, Abott

Abbud (Arabic) devoted.

Abdi (African) my servant.

Abdirahman (Arabic) a form of Abdulrahman.
Abdirehman

Abdul (Arabic) servant.
Abdal, Abdeel, Abdel, Abdoul, Abdual, Abdull, Abul

Abdulaziz (Arabic) servant of the Mighty.
Abdelazim, Abdelaziz, Abdulazaz, Abdulazeez

Abdullah (Arabic) servant of Allah.
Abdala, Abdalah, Abdalla, Abdallah, Abdela, Abduala, Abdualla, Abduallah, Abdula, Abdulah, Abdulahi, Abdulha, Abdulla

Abdullahi (Arabic) a form of Adullah.

Abdulmalik (Arabic) servant of the Master.

Abdulrahman (Arabic) servant of the Merciful.
Abdelrahim, Abdelrahman, Abdolrahem, Abdularahman, Abdurrahman, Abdurram

Abe (Hebrew) a short form of Abel, Abraham. (German) a short form of Abelard.
Ab, Abb, Abbe

Abel (Hebrew) breath. (Assyrian) meadow. (German) a short form of Abelard. Bible: Adam and Eve's second son.
Abele, Abell, Able, Adal, Avel

Abelard (German) noble; resolute.
Abalard, Abelarde, Abelhard, Abilard

Abelardo (Spanish) a form of Abelard.

Abernethy (Scottish) river's beginning.
Abernathie, Abernethi

Abi (Turkish) older brother.
Abbi, Abee

Abiah (Hebrew) God is my father.
Abia, Abiel, Abija, Abijah, Aviya, Aviyah, Avyya, Avyyah

Abidan (Hebrew) father of judgment.
Abiden, Abidin, Abidon, Abydan, Abyden, Abydin, Abydon, Abydyn

Abie (Hebrew) a familiar form of Abraham.
Abbie

Abiel (Hebrew) a form of Abiah.

Abir (Hebrew) strong.
Abyr

Abisha (Hebrew) gift of God.
Abijah, Abishai, Abishal, Abysha, Abyshah

Abner (Hebrew) father of light. Bible: the commander of Saul's army.
Ab, Avner, Ebner

Abraham (Hebrew) father of many nations. Bible: the first Hebrew patriarch. See also Avram, Bram, Ibrahim.
Abarran, Aberham, Abey, Abhiram, Abie, Abrahaim, Abrahame, Abrahamo, Abraheem, Abrahem, Abrahim, Abrahm, Abrao, Arram, Avram

Abrahan (Spanish) a form of Abraham.
Abrahán, Abrahin, Abrahon, Abrán

Abram (Hebrew) a short form of Abraham. See also Bram.
Abrama, Abramo, Abrams, Avram

Absalom (Hebrew) father of peace. Bible: the rebellious third son of King David. See also Avshalom, Axel.
Absalaam, Absalon, Abselon, Absolam, Absolom, Absolum

Acar (Turkish) bright.

Ace (Latin) unity.
Acer, Acey, Acie

Achilles (Greek) Mythology: a hero of the Trojan War. Literature: the hero of Homer's epic poem *Iliad*.
Achil, Achill, Achille, Achillea, Achilleus, Achillios, Achyl, Achyll, Achylle, Achylleus, Akilles

Ackerley (English) meadow of oak trees.
Accerlee, Accerleigh, Accerley, Ackerlea, Ackerlee, Ackerleigh, Ackerli, Ackerlie, Ackersley, Ackley, Akerlea, Akerlee, Akerleigh, Akerley, Akerli, Akerlie, Akerly

Ackley (English) a form of Ackerley.
Acklea, Acklee, Ackleigh, Ackli, Acklie, Ackly, Aklea, Aklee, Akleigh, Akley, Akli, Aklie, Akly

Acton (English) oak-tree settlement.
Actan, Acten, Actin, Actun, Actyn

Adahy (Cherokee) in the woods.
Adahi

Adair (Scottish) oak-tree ford.
Adaire, Adare, Adayr, Adayre, Addair, Addaire, Addar, Addare, Addayr, Addyre

Adalberto (Italian, Spanish, Portuguese) a form of Alberto.

Adam (Phoenician) man; mankind. (Hebrew) earth; man of the red earth. Bible: the first man created by God. See also Adamson, Addison, Damek, Keddy, Macadam.
Ad, Adama, Adamec, Adamo, Adão, Adas, Adem, Adham, Adhamh, Adim, Adné, Adok, Adom, Adomas, Adym, Edam, Edem, Edim, Edym

Adamec (Czech) a form of Adam.
Adamek, Adamik, Adamka, Adamko, Adamok

Adamson (Hebrew) son of Adam.
Adams, Adamsson, Addams, Addamson

Adan (Irish) a form of Aidan.
Adian, Adun

Adar (Syrian) ruler; prince. (Hebrew) noble; exalted.
Addar, Addare

Adarius (American) a combination of Adam + Darius.
Adareus, Adarias, Adarrius, Adarro, Adarruis, Adaruis, Adauris

Addam (Phoenician, Hebrew) a form of Adam.

Addison (English) son of Adam.
Addis, Addisen, Addisun, Addoson, Addyson

Addy (Hebrew) a familiar form of Adam, Adlai. (German) a familiar form of Adelard.
Addey, Addi, Addie, Ade, Adi

Ade (Yoruba) royal.

Adeel (Arabic) a form of Adil.
Adeele

Adel (German) a short form of Adelard.
Adal, Addel, Adél, Adell

Adelard (German) noble; courageous.
Adalar, Adalard, Adalarde, Adelar, Adelarde,
Adelhard

Adelric (German) noble ruler.
Adalric, Adelrich, Adelrick, Adelrik, Adelryc,
Adelryck, Adelryk

Aden (Arabic) Geography: a region in
southern Yemen. (Irish) a form of Aidan.

Adham (Arabic) black.

Adil (Arabic) just; wise.
Adill, Adyl, Adyll

Adin (Hebrew) pleasant.
Addin, Addyn, Adyn

Adir (Hebrew) majestic; noble.
Adeer

Adison (English) a form of Addison.
Adisson, Adyson

Aditya (Hindi) sun.

Adiv (Hebrew) pleasant; gentle.
Adeev, Adev

Adlai (Hebrew) my ornament.
Ad, Addlai, Addlay, Adlay

Adler (German) eagle.
Ad, Addlar, Addler, Adlar

Adli (Turkish) just; wise.
Adlea, Adlee, Adleigh, Adley, Adlie, Adly

Admon (Hebrew) peony.

Adnan (Arabic) pleasant.
Adnaan, Adnane

Adney (English) noble's island.
Adnee, Adni, Adnie, Adny

Adolf (German) noble wolf. History:
Adolf Hitler's German army was
defeated in World War II. See also Dolf.
Ad, Addof, Addoff, Adof

Adolfo (Spanish) a form of Adolf.
Addofo, Adolffo, Adolpho, Andolffo, Andolfo,
Andolpho

Adolph (German) a form of Adolf.
Adolphe

Adolphus (French) a form of Adolf.
Adolfius, Adolfus, Adolphius, Adulphus

Adom (Akan) help from God.

Adon (Hebrew) Lord. (Greek) a short
form of Adonis.

Adonis (Greek) highly attractive.
Mythology: the attractive youth loved
by Aphrodite.
Adonise, Adonnis, Adonys, Adonyse

Adri (Indo-Pakistani) rock.
Adree, Adrey, Adrie, Adry

Adrian (Greek) rich. (Latin) dark.
(Swedish) a short form of Hadrian.
Adarian, Ade, Adorjan, Adrain, Adreian,
Adreyan, Adriaan, Adriane, Adriann,
Adrianne, Adrianus, Adriean, Adrin,
Adrion, Adrionn, Adrionne, Adron,
Adryan, Adryn, Adryon

Adriano (Italian) a form of Adrian.
Adrianno

Adriel (Hebrew) member of God's flock.
Adrial, Adriall, Adriell, Adryel, Adryell

Adrien (French) a form of Adrian.
Adriene, Adrienne, Adryen

Adrik (Russian) a form of Adrian.
Adric

Adwin (Ghanaian) creative.
Adwyn

Aeneas (Greek) praised. (Scottish) a form
of Angus. Literature: the Trojan hero of
Vergil's epic poem *Aeneid*. See also Eneas.
Oneas

Afram (African) Geography: a river in
Ghana, Africa.

Afton (English) from Afton, England.
Affton, Aftan, Aften, Aftin, Aftyn

Agamemnon (Greek) resolute.
Mythology: the king of Mycenae who
led the Greeks in the Trojan War.

Agni (Hindi) Religion: the Hindu fire
god.

Agostino (Italian) a form of Augustine.
Agostine, Agosto, Agoston, Agostyne

Agrippa (Latin) born feet first. History: the commander of the Roman fleet that defeated Mark Antony and Cleopatra at Actium.
Agripa, Agripah, Agrippah, Agrypa, Agrypah, Agryppa, Agryppah

Agu (Ibo) leopard.

Agustin (Latin) a form of Augustine.
Aguistin, Agustein, Agusteyne, Agustis, Agusto, Agustus, Agustyn

Agustine (Latin) a form of Augustine.
Agusteen, Agustyne

Ahab (Hebrew) father's brother. Literature: the captain of the *Pequod* in Herman Melville's novel *Moby-Dick*.

Ahanu (Native American) laughter.

Aharon (Hebrew, Arabic) a form of Aaron.
Ahren

Ahdik (Native American) caribou; reindeer.
Ahdic, Ahdick, Ahdyc, Ahdyck, Ahdyk

Ahearn (Scottish) lord of the horses. (English) heron.
Ahearne, Aherin, Ahern, Aherne, Aheron, Aheryn, Hearn, Hearne

Ahir (Turkish) last.

Ahkeem (Hebrew) a form of Akeem.
Ahkiem, Ahkieme, Ahkyem, Ahkyeme

Ahmad (Arabic) most highly praised. See also Muhammad.
Achmad, Ahamad, Ahamada, Ahmaad, Ahmaud, Amad, Amahd

Ahmed (Swahili) praiseworthy.
Achmed, Ahamed, Amed

Ahsan (Arabic) charitable.

Aidan (Irish) fiery.
Aidun, Aydan, Aydin

Aiden (Irish) a form of Aidan.
Aidon, Aidwin, Aidwyn, Aidyn

Aiken (English) made of oak.
Aicken, Aikin, Ayken, Aykin

Aimery (French) a form of Emery.
Aime, Aimeree, Aimerey, Aimeri, Aimeric, Aimerie, Ameree, Amerey, Ameri, Americ, Amerie, Aymeree, Aymerey, Aymeri, Aymeric, Aymerie, Aymery

Aimon (French) house. (Irish) a form of Eamon.

Aindrea (Irish) a form of Andrew.
Aindreas, Ayndrea, Ayndreas

Ainsley (Scottish) my own meadow.
Ainslea, Ainslee, Ainslei, Ainsleigh, Ainsli, Ainslie, Ainsly, Ansley, Aynslea, Aynslee, Aynsley, Aynsli, Aynslie, Aynsly

Aizik (Russian) a form of Isaac.
Ayzik

Aj (Punjabi, American) a form of Ajay.

Ajala (Yoruba) potter.
Ajalah

Ajay (Punjabi) victorious; undefeatable. (American) a combination of the initials A. + J.
Aja, Ajae, Ajai, Ajaye, Ajaz, Ajé, Ajee, Ajit

Ajit (Sanskrit) unconquerable.
Ajeet, Ajith

Akar (Turkish) flowing stream.
Akara, Akare

Akash (Hindi) sky.
Akasha

Akbar (Arabic) great.
Akbara, Akbare

Akecheta (Sioux) warrior.
Akechetah

Akeem (Hebrew) a short form of Joachim.
Ackeem, Akeam, Akee, Akiem, Arkeem

Akemi (Japanese) dawn.
Akemee, Akemie, Akemy

Akhil (Arabic) a form of Akil.
Ahkeel

Akil (Arabic) intelligent. (Greek) a form of Achilles.
Akeel, Akeil, Akeyla, Akiel, Akila, Akilah, Akile, Akyl, Akyle

Akili (Greek) a form of Achilles. (Arabic) a form of Akil.

Akim (Hebrew) a short form of Joachim.
Achim, Achym, Ackim, Ackime, Ackym, Ackyme, Akima, Akym

Akins (Yoruba) brave.
Akin, Akyn, Akyns, Atkins, Atkyns

Akio (Japanese) bright.
Akiyo, Akyo

Akira (Japanese) intelligent.
Akihito, Akirah, Akyra, Akyrah

Akiva (Hebrew) a form of Jacob.
Akiba

Akmal (Arabic) perfect.
Ackmal

Akram (Arabic) most generous.

Aksel (Norwegian) father of peace.
Aksell

Akshat (Sanskrit) unable to be injured.

Akshay (American) a form of Akash.
Akshaj, Akshaya

Akule (Native American) he looks up.
Akul

Al (Irish) a short form of Alan, Albert, Alexander.

Alaa (Arabic) a short form of Aladdin.
Ala

Aladdin (Arabic) height of faith. Literature: the hero of a story in the *Arabian Nights*.
Alaaddin, Aladdan, Aladden, Aladdyn, Aladan, Aladean, Aladen, Aladin, Aladino, Aladyn

Alain (French) a form of Alan.
Alaen, Alaine, Alainn, Alayn, Alein, Aleine, Aleyn, Aleyne, Allain, Allayn, Allayne

Alaire (French) joyful.
Alair, Alayr, Alayre

Alam (Arabic) universe.
Alame

Alan (Irish) handsome; peaceful.
Ailan, Ailin, Alaan, Aland, Alande, Alando, Alane, Alani, Alann, Alano, Alanson, Alao, Alon, Alun, Alune, Alyn, Alyne

Alante, Allante, Allanté (Spanish) forms of Alan.

Alaric (German) ruler of all. See also Ulrich.
Alarich, Alarick, Alarico, Alarik, Alaryc, Alaryck, Alaryk, Aleric, Allaric, Allarick, Alric, Alrick, Alrik

Alastair (Scottish) a form of Alexander.
Alaisdair, Alaistair, Alaister, Alasdair, Alasteir, Alaster, Alastor, Aleister, Alester, Allaistar, Allastair, Allaster, Allastir, Allysdair, Alystair

Alban (Latin) from Alba, Italy.
Albain, Albany, Albean, Albein, Alby, Auban, Auben

Alberic (German) smart; wise ruler.
Alberich, Alberick, Alberyc, Alberyck, Alberyk

Albern (German) noble; courageous.
Alberne, Alburn, Alburne

Albert (German, French) noble and bright. See also Elbert, Ulbrecht.
Adelbert, Ailbert, Albertik, Albertus, Albrecht, Albret, Albyrt, Albyrte, Alvertos, Aubert

Alberto (Italian) a form of Albert.
Albertino, Berto

Albie, Alby (German, French) familiar forms of Albert.
Albee, Albey, Albi

Albin (Latin) a form of Alvin.
Alben, Albeno, Albinek, Albino, Albins, Albinson, Albun, Alby, Albyn, Auben

Albion (Latin) white cliffs. Geography: a reference to the white cliffs in Dover, England.
Albon, Albyon, Allbion, Allbyon

Alcandor (Greek) manly; strong.

Alcott (English) old cottage.
Alcot, Alkot, Alkott, Allcot, Allcott, Allkot, Allkott

Aldair (German, English) a form of Alder.
Aldahir, Aldayr

Alden (English) old; wise protector.
Aldan, Aldean, Aldin, Aldon, Aldyn

Alder (German, English) alder tree.
Aldar, Aldare, Aldyr

Alderidge (English) alder ridge.
*Alderige, Aldridge, Aldrige, Aldrydge,
Aldryge, Alldridge*

Aldis (English) old house. (German) a
form of Aldous.
Aldise, Aldiss, Aldys

Aldo (Italian) old; elder. (German) a short
form of Aldous.
Alda

Aldous (German) a form of Alden.
Aldis, Aldon, Aldos, Aldus, Elden

Aldred (English) old; wise counselor.
Alldred, Eldred

Aldrich (English) wise counselor. See also
Uldric.
*Aldric, Aldrick, Aldritch, Aldryc, Aldryck,
Aldryk, Alldric, Alldrich, Alldrick, Eldridge*

Aldwin (English) old friend.
*Aldwan, Aldwen, Aldwon, Aldwyn, Eldwin,
Eldwyn*

Alec, Aleck, Alek (Greek) short forms of
Alexander.
Aleik, Alekko, Aleko, Elek, Ellec, Elleck

Aleczander (Greek) a form of Alexander.
*Alecander, Aleckxander, Alecsandar,
Alecsander, Alecxander*

Alejandro, Alejándro (Spanish) forms of
Alexander.
Alejandra, Aléjo, Alexjandro

Aleksandar, Aleksander, Aleksandr,
(Greek) forms of Alexander.
Aleksandor, Aleksandras, Aleksandur

Aleksei (Russian) a short form of
Alexander.
Aleks, Aleksey, Aleksi, Aleksis, Aleksy

Alekzander (Greek) a form of Alexander.
Alekxander, Alekxzander

Alem (Arabic) wise.
Alym

Alen, Allan, Allen (Irish) forms of Alan.
*Allane, Allayne, Allene, Alley, Alleyn, Alleyne,
Allie, Allin, Alline, Allon, Allyn, Allyne*

Aleric (German) a form of Alaric.
*Alerick, Alerik, Alleric, Allerick, Alleryc,
Alleryck, Alleryk*

Aleron (Latin) winged.
Aleronn

Alessandro (Italian) a form of Alexander.
Alessand, Alessander, Alessandre, Allessandro

Alex, Alix (Greek) short forms of
Alexander.
*Alax, Alexx, Alixx, Allax, Allex, Allix,
Allixx, Allyx, Allyxx, Alyx, Elek*

Alexandar, Alexandr (Greek) forms of
Alexander.

Alexander (Greek) defender of mankind.
History: Alexander the Great was the
conqueror of the civilized world. See
also Alastair, Alistair, Iskander, Jando,
Leks, Lex, Lexus, Macallister, Oleksandr,
Olés, Sander, Sándor, Sandro, Sandy,
Sasha, Xan, Xander, Zander, Zindel.
Alekos, Alexandor, Alexxander

Alexandra (Greek) a form of Alexander.

Alexandre (French) a form of Alexander.

Alexandro (Greek) a form of Alexander.
Alexandru

Alexandros (Greek) a form of Alexander.
Alexandras

Alexei (Russian) a form of Aleksei.
(Greek) a short form of Alexander.
Alexey

Alexi, Alexy (Greek) short forms of
Alexander.
Alexe, Alexee, Alexie, Alexio, Alezio

Alexis (Greek) a short form of Alexander.
*Alexes, Alexey, Alexios, Alexius, Alexiz,
Alexsis, Alexsus, Alexus, Alexys*

Alexsander (Greek) a form of Alexander.

Alexzander (Greek) forms of Alexander.
Alexkzandr, Alexzandr, Alexzandyr

Alfie (English) a familiar form of Alfred.
Alfy

Alfonso, Alfonzo (Italian, Spanish) forms of Alphonse.
Affonso, Alfons, Alfonse, Alfonsus, Alfonza, Alfonzus

Alford (English) old river ford.
Allford

Alfred (English) elf counselor; wise counselor. See also Fred.
Ailfrid, Ailfryd, Alf, Alfeo, Alfredus, Alfrid, Alfried, Alfryd, Alured, Elfrid

Alfredo (Italian, Spanish) a form of Alfred.
Alfrido

Alger (German) noble spearman. (English) a short form of Algernon. See also Elger.
Aelfar, Algar, Algor, Allgar

Algernon (English) bearded, wearing a moustache.
Aelgernon, Algenon, Algin, Algon

Algie (English) a familiar form of Algernon.
Algee, Algia, Algy

Algis (German) spear.
Algiss

Ali (Arabic) greatest. (Swahili) exalted.
Aly

Alic (Greek) a short form of Alexander.
Alick, Aliek, Alik, Aliko, Alyc, Alyck, Alyk, Alyko, Ellic, Ellick

Alijah (Hebrew) a form of Elijah.

Alim (Arabic) scholar. (Arabic) a form of Alem.
Alym

Alisander (Greek) a form of Alexander.
Alisandre, Alisaunder, Alissander, Alissandre, Alsandair, Alsandare, Alsander

Alistair (English) a form of Alexander.
Alisdair, Alistaire, Alistar, Allistair, Allistar, Alstair, Alystair, Alystayr, Alystyre

Alixander (Greek) a form of Alexander.
Alixandre, Alixandru, Alixsander, Alixxander, Alixxzander, Alixzander, Alyxxander, Alyxxsander, Alyxxzander, Alyxzander

Allambee (Australian) quiet place.
Alambee, Alambey, Alambi, Alambie, Alamby, Allambey, Allambi, Allambie, Allamby

Allard (English) noble, brave.
Alard, Ellard

Allison (English) Alice's son.
Allisan, Allisen, Allisun, Allisyn, Allysan, Allysen, Allysin, Allyson, Allysun, Allysyn

Allister (English) a form of Alistair.
Alister, Allistir

Almeric (German) powerful ruler.
Almauric, Amaurick, Amaurik, Amauryc, Amauryck, Amauryk, Americk, Amerik, Ameryc, Ameryck, Ameryk

Almon (Hebrew) widower.
Alman, Almen, Almin, Almyn

Alois (German) a short form of Aloysius.
Alaois, Aloys

Aloisio (Spanish) a form of Louis.

Alok (Sanskrit) victorious cry.

Alon (Hebrew) oak.
Allon, Alonn

Alonso, Alonzo (Spanish) forms of Alphonse.
Alano, Alanzo, Allonzo, Alonz, Alonze

Alonza (Spanish) a form of Alphonse.
Allonza

Aloysius (German) a form of Louis.
Aloisius

Alphonse (German) noble and eager.
Alf, Alfons, Alphons, Alphonsa, Alphonsus, Alphonza, Alphonzus

Alphonso (Italian) a form of Alphonse.
Alphanso, Alphonzo, Fonso

Alpin (Irish) attractive.
Alpine, Alpyn, Alpyne

Alroy (Spanish) king.
Alroi

Alston (English) noble's settlement.
Allston, Alstan, Alsten, Alstin, Alstun, Alstyn

Altair (Greek) star. (Arabic) flying eagle.
Altayr, Altayre

Altman (German) old man.
Altmann, Altmen, Atman

Alton (English) old town.
Alten

Alva (Hebrew) sublime.
Alvah

Alvan (German) a form of Alvin.
Alvand, Alvun

Alvar (English) army of elves.
Alvara

Alvaro (Spanish) just; wise.

Alvern (Latin) spring.
Alverne, Elvern

Alvin (Latin) white; light skinned. (German) friend to all; noble friend; friend of elves. See also Albin, Elvin.
Aloin, Aluin, Alvan, Alven, Alvie, Alvon, Alvy, Alvyn, Alwin, Elwin

Alvino (Spanish) a form of Alvin.
Aluino

Alvis (Scandinavian) all-knowing.

Alwin (German) a form of Alvin.
Ailwyn, Alwan, Alwen, Alwon, Alwun, Alwyn, Alwynn, Aylwin

Amadeo (Italian) a form of Amadeus.

Amadeus (Latin) loves God. Music: Wolfgang Amadeus Mozart was a famous eighteenth-century Austrian composer.
Amad, Amadeaus, Amadée, Amadei, Amadis, Amadou, Amando, Amedeo, Amodaos

Amado (Spanish) a form of Amadeus.
Amadio

Amador (Spanish) a form of Amadeus.

Amal (Hebrew) worker. (Arabic) hopeful.
Amahl

Aman (Arabic) a short form of Amani.

Amanda (Latin) lovable.

Amandeep (Punjabi) light of peace.
Amandip, Amanjit, Amanjot

Amando (French) a form of Amadeus.
Amand, Amandio, Amaniel, Amato

Amani (Arabic) believer. (Yoruba) strength; builder.
Amanee

Amanpreet (Punjabi) a form of Amandeep.

Amar (Punjabi) immortal. (Arabic) builder.
Amare, Amario, Amaris, Amarjit, Amaro, Amarpreet

Amari (Punjabi, Arabic) a form of Amar.
Amaree, Amarri

Amato (French) loved.
Amat, Amatto

Ambar (Sanskrit) sky.

Amber (French) amber. (Sanskrit) a form of Ambar.

Ambroise (French) a form of Ambrose.
Ambrois

Ambrose (Greek) immortal.
Ambie, Ambrogio, Ambroisius, Ambros, Ambrosi, Ambrosio, Ambrosios, Ambrosius, Ambrossye, Ambrosye, Ambrotos, Ambroz, Ambrus, Amby

Ameen (Hebrew, Arabic, Hindi) a form of Amin.

Ameer (Hebrew) a form of Amir.
Ameir, Amere

Amer (Hebrew) a form of Amir.

Amerigo (Teutonic) industrious. History: Amerigo Vespucci was the Italian explorer for whom America is named.
Americo, Americus, Amerygo

Ames (French) friend.
Amess

Amicus (English, Latin) beloved friend.
Amic, Amick, Amicko, Amico, Amik, Amiko,
Amyc, Amyck, Amycko, Amyk, Amyko

Amiel (Hebrew) God of my people.
Amiell, Ammiel, Amyel, Amyell

Amin (Hebrew, Arabic) trustworthy;
honest. (Hindi) faithful.
Amen, Ammen, Ammin, Ammyn, Amyn,
Amynn

Amine (Hebrew, Arabic, Hindi) a form of
Amin.

Amir (Hebrew) proclaimed. (Punjabi)
wealthy; king's minister. (Arabic) prince.
Amire, Amiri, Amyr

Amish (Sanskrit) honest.

Amit (Punjabi) unfriendly. (Arabic) highly
praised.
Amita, Amitan

Ammar (Punjabi, Arabic) a form of Amar.
Ammer

Ammon (Egyptian) hidden. Mythology:
the ancient god associated with reproduction.
Amman

Amol (Hindi) priceless, valuable.
Amul

Amon (Hebrew) trustworthy; faithful.
Amun

Amory (German) a form of Emory.
Ameree, Amerey, Ameri, Amerie, Amery,
Ammeree, Ammerey, Ammeri, Ammerie,
Ammery, Ammoree, Ammorey, Ammori,
Ammorie, Ammory, Amor, Amoree, Amorey,
Amori, Amorie

Amos (Hebrew) burdened, troubled.
Bible: an Old Testament prophet.
Amose, Amous

Amram (Hebrew) mighty nation.
Amarien, Amran, Amren, Amryn

Amrit (Sanskrit) nectar. (Punjabi, Arabic)
a form of Amit.
Amreet, Amryt

Amritpal (Sikh) protector of the Lord's
nectar.

An (Chinese, Vietnamese) peaceful.
Ana

Anand (Hindi) blissful.
Ananda, Anant, Ananth

Anas (Greek) a short form of Anastasius.

Anastasios (Greek) a form of Anastasius.
Anastasio

Anastasius (Greek) resurrection.
Anastacio, Anastacios, Anastagio, Anastas,
Anastase, Anastasi, Anastatius, Anastice,
Anastisis, Anaztáz, Athanasius

Anatole (Greek) east.
Anatol, Anatoley, Anatoli, Anatolie,
Anatolijus, Anatolio, Anatolis, Anatoliy,
Anatoly, Anitoly, Antoly

Anchali (Taos) painter.
Anchalee, Anchaley, Anchalie, Anchaly

Anders (Swedish) a form of Andrew.
Andar, Ander

Anderson (Swedish) son of Andrew.
Andersen

Andoni (Greek) a form of Anthony.
Andonny

Andonios (Greek) a form of Anthony.
Andonis

Andor (Hungarian) a form of Andrew,
Anthony.

Andra (French) a form of Andrew.

Andrae (French) a form of Andrew.

András (Hungarian) a form of Andrew.
Andraes, Andri, Andris, Andrius, Andriy,
Aundras, Aundreas

Andre, André (French) forms of Andrew.
Andrecito, Andree, Andrie, Aundré

Andrea (Greek) a form of Andrew.
Andrean, Andreani,

Andreas (Greek) a form of Andrew.
Andries

Andrei, Andrey (Bulgarian, Romanian, Russian) forms of Andrew.
Andreian, Andrej, Andreyan, Andrie, Aundrei

Andres, Andrez (Spanish) forms of Andrew.
Andras, Andrés

Andrew (Greek) strong; manly; courageous. Bible: one of the Twelve Apostles. See also Bandi, Drew, Endre, Evangelos, Kendrew, Ondro.
Aindrea, Andery, Andonis, Andrews, Anker, Anndra, Antal, Audrew

Andrian (Greek) a form of Andrew.

Andros (Polish) sea. Mythology: the god of the sea.
Andris, Andrius, Andrus

Andru, Andrue (Greek) forms of Andrew.
Andrus

Andrzej (Polish) a form of Andrew.

Andy (Greek) a short form of Andrew.
Ande, Andee, Andey, Andi, Andie, Andino, Andis, Andje

Aneurin (Welsh) honorable; gold. See also Nye.
Aneirin

Anfernee (Greek) a form of Anthony.
Anferney, Anfernie, Anferny, Anfonee, Anfoney, Anfoni, Anfonie, Anfony, Anfranee, Anfrene, Anfrenee, Anpherne

Angel (Greek) angel. (Latin) messenger. See also Gotzon.
Ange, Angell, Angie, Angy, Anjel, Anjell

Angelo (Italian) a form of Angel.
Angeleo, Angelito, Angello, Angelos, Angelous, Angiolo, Anglo, Anjello, Anjelo

Angus (Scottish) exceptional; outstanding. Mythology: Angus Og was the Celtic god of youth, love, and beauty. See also Ennis, Gus.
Aonghas

Anh (Vietnamese) peace; safety.

Anibal (Phoenician) a form of Hannibal.

Anil (Hindi) wind god.
Aneal, Aneel, Anel, Aniel, Aniello, Anielo, Anyl, Anyll

Anish (Greek) a form of Annas.

Anka (Turkish) phoenix.

Anker (Danish) a form of Andrew.
Ankor, Ankur

Annan (Scottish) brook. (Swahili) fourth-born son.
Annen, Annin, Annon, Annun, Annyn

Annas (Greek) gift from God.
Anis, Anna, Annais

Anno (German) a familiar form of Johann.
Ano

Anoki (Native American) actor.
Anokee, Anokey, Anokie, Anoky

Anoop (Sikh) beauty.

Ansel (French) follower of a nobleman.
Ancell, Ansa, Anselino, Ansell, Ansellus, Anselyno, Ansyl

Anselm (German) divine protector. See also Elmo.
Anse, Anselme, Anselmi

Anselmo (Italian) a form of Anselm.

Ansis (Latvian) a form of Janis.

Ansley (Scottish) a form of Ainsley.
Anslea, Anslee, Ansleigh, Ansli, Anslie, Ansly, Ansy

Anson (German) divine. (English) Anne's son.
Ansan, Ansen, Ansin, Ansun, Ansyn

Antal (Hungarian) a form of Anthony.
Antek, Anti, Antos

Antares (Greek) giant, red star. Astronomy: the brightest star in the constellation Scorpio.
Antar, Antario, Antarious, Antarius, Antarr, Antarus

Antavas (Lithuanian) a form of Anthony.
Antaeus

Antavious (Lithuanian) a form of Antavas.
Antavius

Ante (Lithuanian) a short form of Antavas.
Antae, Anteo

Anthany (Latin, Greek) a form of Anthony.
Antanas, Antanee, Antanie, Antenee, Anthan, Antheny, Anthine, Anthney

Anthoney, Anthonie (Latin, Greek) forms of Anthony.
Anthone, Anthonee, Anthoni, Anthonia

Anthony (Latin) praiseworthy. (Greek) flourishing. See also Tony.
Anathony, Anothony, Anthawn, Anthey, Anthian, Anthino, Anthonio, Anthonu, Anthonysha, Anthoy, Anthyoine, Anthyonny

Antione (French) a form of Anthony.
Antion, Antionio, Antionne, Antiono

Antjuan (Spanish) a form of Anthony.
Antajuan, Anthjuan, Antuan, Antuane

Antoan (Vietnamese) safe, secure.

Antoine (French) a form of Anthony.
Anntoin, Anthoine, Antoiné, Antoinne, Atoine

Anton (Slavic) a form of Anthony.
Anthon, Antonn, Antons, Antos

Antone (Slavic) a form of Anthony.
Antonne

Antoni (Latin) a form of Anthony.
Antini

Antonia (Greek, Latin) a form of Anthony.

Antonino (Italian) a form of Anthony.

Antonio, Antonyo (Italian) forms of Anthony. See also Tino, Tonio.
Anthonio, Antinio, Antoinio, Antoino, Antonello, Antoneo, Antonin, Antonín, Antonnio, Antonyia, Antonyio,

Antonios (Italian) a form of Anthony.

Antonius (Italian) a form of Anthony.

Antony (Latin) a form of Anthony.
Antin, Antius, Antonee, Antoney, Antonie, Antonin, Antonyia, Antonyio

Antti (Finnish) manly.
Anthey, Anthi, Anthie, Anthy, Anti, Antty, Anty

Antwain, Antwane (Arabic) forms of Antwan.
Antwaina, Antwaine, Antwainn, Antwaion, Antwanne

Antwan, Antwaun, Antwoine, Antwon, Antwone (Arabic) forms of Anthony.
Antaw, Antawan, Antawn, Anthawn, Antowan, Antowaun, Antowine, Antown, Antowne, Antowyn, Antuwan, Antuwon, Antwann, Antwarn, Antwen, Antwian, Antwine, Antwion, Antwione, Antwoan, Antwonn, Antwonne, Antwoun, Antwuan, Antwun, Antwyné, Antwyon, Antwyone, Antyon, Antyonne, Antywon

Anwar (Arabic) luminous.
Anouar, Anour, Anwi

Apiatan (Kiowa) wooden lance.

Apolinar (Greek) a form of Apollo.
Apolinario

Apollo (Greek) manly. Mythology: the god of prophecy, healing, music, poetry, and light. See also Polo.
Apollos, Apolo, Apolonio, Appollo, Appolo, Appolonio

Aquila (Latin, Spanish) eagle.
Acquilla, Aquil, Aquilas, Aquileo, Aquiles, Aquilino, Aquill, Aquilla, Aquille, Aquillino, Aquyl, Aquyla, Aquyll, Aquylla

Ara (Syrian) a form of Aram.
Arra

Arafat (Arabic) mountain of recognition.

Araldo (Spanish) a form of Harold.
Aralodo, Aralt, Aroldo, Arry

Aram (Syrian) high, exalted.
Aramia, Arem, Arim, Arram, Arum, Arym

Aramis (French) Literature: one of the title characters in Alexandre Dumas's novel *The Three Musketeers.*
Airamis, Aramith, Aramys

Aran (Tai) forest. (Danish) a form of Aren. (Hebrew, Scottish) a form of Arran.
Arane

Arcadio (Spanish) a form of Archibald.

Archer (English) bowman.
Archar, Archor

Archibald (German) bold. See also Arkady.
Arch, Archaimbaud, Archambault,
Archibaldes, Archibaldo, Archibold,
Archybald, Archybalde, Archybaldes,
Archybauld, Archybaulde

Archie (German, English) a familiar form
of Archer, Archibald.
Arche, Archee, Archey, Archi, Archy

Ardal (Irish) a form of Arnold.
Ardale, Ardall

Ardell (Latin) eager; industrious.
Ardel

Arden (Latin) ardent; fiery.
Ard, Ardan, Ardene, Ardent, Ardian, Ardie,
Ardin, Ardint, Ardn, Arduino, Ardyn, Ardynt

Ardley (English) ardent meadow.
Ardlea, Ardlee, Ardleigh, Ardli, Ardlie, Ardly

Ardon (Hebrew) bronzed.
Ardun

Aren (Danish) eagle; ruler. (Hebrew,
Arabic) a form of Aaron.
Aaren

Aretino (Greek, Italian) victorious.
Aretin, Aretine, Artyn, Artyno

Argus (Danish) watchful, vigilant.
Agos, Arguss

Argyle (Irish) from Ireland.
Argile, Argiles, Argyles

Ari (Hebrew) a short form of Ariel.
(Greek) a short form of Aristotle.
Aree, Arey, Arieh, Arih, Arij, Ario, Arri,
Ary, Arye

Aria (Greek, Hebrew) a form of Ari.
Arias

Arian (Greek) a form of Arion.
Ariana, Ariane, Ariann, Arianne, Arrian

Aric, Arick, Arik (Scandinavian) forms of
Eric. (German) forms of Richard.
Aaric, Aarick, Aarik, Arec, Areck, Arich,
Ariek, Arrek, Arric, Arrick, Arrik, Aryc,
Aryck, Aryk

Arie (Greek, Hebrew) a form of Ari.
(Greek, Latin) a form of Aries.

Ariel (Hebrew) lion of God. Bible:
another name for Jerusalem. Literature:
the name of a sprite in the
Shakespearean play *The Tempest.*
Airal, Airel, Arel, Areli, Ariele, Ariell,
Arielle, Ariya, Ariyel, Arrial, Arriel, Aryel,
Aryell, Aryl, Aryll, Arylle

Aries (Latin) ram. Astrology: the first sign
of the zodiac.
Arees, Ares, Ariez, Aryes

Arif (Arabic) knowledgeable.
Areef, Aryf

Arin, Aryn (Hebrew, Arabic) forms of
Aaron. (Danish) forms of Aren.

Arion (Greek) enchanted. (Hebrew)
melodious.
Arien, Ario, Arione, Aryon

Aristides (Greek) son of the best.
Aris, Aristede, Aristedes, Aristeed, Aristide,
Aristides, Aristidis, Arystides, Arystydes

Aristotle (Greek) best; wise. History: a
third-century B.C. philosopher who
tutored Alexander the Great.
Aris, Aristito, Aristo, Aristokles, Aristotal,
Aristotel, Aristotelis, Aristotol, Aristott,
Aristotyl, Arystotle

Arjun (Hindi) white; milk colored.
Arjen, Arjin, Arju, Arjuna, Arjune

Arkady (Russian) a form of Archibald.
Arkadee, Arkadey, Arkadi, Arkadie, Arkadij,
Arkadiy

Arkin (Norwegian) son of the eternal
king.
Aricin, Arkeen, Arkyn

Arledge (English) lake with the hares.
Arlege, Arlidge, Arlledge, Arllege

Arlen (Irish) pledge.
Arlan, Arland, Arlend, Arlin, Arlinn, Arlon, Arlyn, Arlynn

Arley (English) a short form of Harley.
Arleigh, Arlie, Arly

Arlo (Spanish) barberry. (English) fortified hill. A form of Harlow. (German) a form of Charles.
Arlow

Armaan (Persian) a form of Arman.

Arman (Persian) desire, goal.
Armahn, Armaine, Armann

Armand (Latin, German) a form of Herman. See also Mandek.
Armad, Armanda, Armands, Armanno, Armaude, Armenta

Armando (Spanish) a form of Armand.
Armondo

Armani (Hungarian) sly. (Hebrew) a form of Armon.
Armanee, Armaney, Armanie, Armany, Armoni, Armonie, Armonio, Armonni, Armony

Armen, Armin (Hebrew) forms of Armon.
Armino

Armon (Hebrew) high fortress, stronghold.
Armonn, Armons, Armyn

Armond (Latin, German) a form of Armand.

Armstrong (English) strong arm. History: astronaut Neil Armstrong was the commander of Apollo 11 and the first person to walk on the moon.
Armstron, Armstronge

Arnaldo (Spanish) a form of Arnold.

Arnaud (French) a form of Arnold.
Arnaude, Arnauld, Arnault, Arnoll

Arne (German) a form of Arnold.
Arna, Arnay, Arnel, Arnele, Arnell, Arnelle

Arnette (English) little eagle.
Arnat, Arnatt, Arnet, Arnett, Arnetta, Arnot, Arnott

Arnie (German) a familiar form of Arnold.
Arnee, Arney, Arni, Arnny, Arny

Arno (German) a short form of Arnold. (Czech) a short form of Ernest.
Arnou, Arnoux

Arnold (German) eagle ruler.
Ardal, Arnald, Arndt, Arne, Arnhold, Arnol, Arnoldas, Arnolde, Arnoll, Arnolt, Arnot, Arnott, Arnoud, Arnyld

Arnoldo (Spanish) a form of Arnold.

Arnon (Hebrew) rushing river.
Arnan, Arnen, Arnin, Arnyn

Arnulfo (German) a form of Arnold.

Aron, Arron (Hebrew) forms of Aaron. (Danish) forms of Aren.
Aronek, Aronne, Aronos, Arrion

Aroon (Tai) dawn.
Aroone

Arran (Scottish) island dweller. Geography: an island off the west coast of Scotland. (Hebrew) a form of Aaron.
Aeran, Ahran, Aranne

Arrigo (Italian) a form of Harry.
Alrigo, Arrighetto

Arrio (Spanish) warlike.
Ario, Arrow, Arryo, Aryo

Arsenio (Greek) masculine; virile. History: Saint Arsenius was a teacher in the Roman Empire.
Arsen, Arsène, Arseneo, Arsenius, Arseny, Arsenyo, Arsinio, Arsinyo, Arsynio, Arsynyo

Arsha (Persian) venerable.
Arshah

Art (English) a short form of Arthur.
Arte

Artemio (Spanish) a form of Artemus.

Artemus (Greek) gift of Artemis. Mythology: Artemis was the goddess of the hunt and the moon.
Artemas, Artemis, Artimas, Artimis, Artimus

Arthur (Irish) noble; lofty hill. (Scottish) bear. (English) rock. (Icelandic) follower of Thor. See also Turi.
Artair, Artek, Arth, Arther, Arthor, Arthyr, Artor, Artus, Aurthar, Aurther, Aurthur

Artie (English) a familiar form of Arthur.
Artee, Artian, Arty, Atty

Artis (English) a form of Artie.

Artur (Italian) a form of Arthur.

Arturo (Italian) a form of Arthur.
Arthuro

Arun (Cambodian, Hindi) sun.
Aruns

Arundel (English) eagle valley.

Arve (Norwegian) heir, inheritor.
Arv

Arvel (Welsh) wept over.
Arval, Arvell, Arvelle, Arvil, Arvol, Arvyl

Arvid (Hebrew) wanderer. (Norwegian) eagle tree. See also Ravid.
Arv, Arvad, Arve, Arvie, Arvyd, Arvydas

Arvin (German) friend of the people; friend of the army.
Arv, Arvan, Arven, Arvie, Arvon, Arvy, Arvyn, Arwan, Arwen, Arwin, Arwon, Arwyn

Arvind (Hebrew, Norwegian) a form of Arvid. (German) a form of Arvin.
Arvinder

Arya (Hebrew) a form of Aria (see Girls' Names).

Aryan (Greek) a form of Arion.

Aryeh (Hebrew) lion.
Arye

Asa (Hebrew) physician, healer. (Yoruba) falcon.
Asaa, Asah, Ase

Asad (Arabic) a form of Asád. (Turkish) a form of Azad.

Asád (Arabic) lion.
Asaad, Asid, Assad

Asadel (Arabic) prosperous.
Asadour, Asadul, Asadyl, Asael

Ascot (English) eastern cottage; style of necktie. Geography: a village near London and the site of the Royal Ascot horseraces.
Ascott

Asgard (Scandinavian) court of the gods.

Ash (Hebrew) ash tree.

Ashanti (Swahili) from a tribe in West Africa.
Ashan, Ashani, Ashante, Ashantee, Ashaunte

Ashburn (English) from the ash-tree stream.
Ashbern, Ashberne, Ashbirn, Ashbirne, Ashborn, Ashborne, Ashbourn, Ashbourne, Ashburne, Ashbyrn, Ashbyrne

Ashby (Scandinavian) ash-tree farm. (Hebrew) a form of Ash.
Ashbee, Ashbey, Ashbi, Ashbie

Asher (Hebrew) happy; blessed.
Ashar, Ashir, Ashor, Ashyr

Ashford (English) ash-tree ford.
Ashforde

Ashley (English) ash-tree meadow.
Asheley, Ashelie, Ashely, Ashlan, Ashlea, Ashlee, Ashleigh, Ashlen, Ashli, Ashlie, Ashlin, Ashling, Ashlinn, Ashlone, Ashly, Ashlyn, Ashlynn, Aslan

Ashon (Swahili) seventh-born son.

Ashraf (Arabic) most honorable.

Ashten, Ashtin (English) forms of Ashton.

Ashton (English) ash-tree settlement.
Ashtan, Ashtian, Ashtion, Ashtonn, Ashtown, Ashtun, Ashtyn

Ashur (Swahili) Mythology: the principal Assyrian deity.

Ashwani (Hindi) first. Religion: the first of the twenty-seven galaxies revolving around the moon.
Ashwan

Ashwin (Hindi) star.
Ashwan, Ashwen, Ashwon, Ashwyn

Asiel (Hebrew) created by God.
Asyel

Asif (Arabic) forgiveness.

Asker (Turkish) soldier.

Aspen (English) aspen tree.

Astley (Greek) starry field.
Asterlea, Asterlee, Asterleigh, Asterley, Asterli, Asterlie, Asterly, Astlea, Astlee, Astleigh, Astli, Astlie, Astly

Aston (English) eastern town.
Astan, Asten, Astin, Astown, Astyn

Aswad (Arabic) dark skinned, black.
Aswald

Ata (Fante) twin.
Atah

Atek (Polish) a form of Tanek.

Athan (Greek) immortal.
Athen, Athens, Athin, Athon, Athons, Athyn, Athyns

Atherton (English) town by a spring.
Atharton, Atherton, Athorton

Athol (Scottish) from Ireland.
Affol, Athal, Athel, Athil, Atholton, Athyl

Atid (Tai) sun.
Atyd

Atif (Arabic) caring.
Ateef, Atef, Atyf

Atkins (English) from the home of the relatives.
Akin, Akins, Akyn, Akyns, Atkin, Atkyn, Atkyns

Atlas (Greek) lifted; carried. Mythology: Atlas was forced by Zeus to carry the heavens on his shoulders as a punishment for his share of the war of the Titans.

Atley (English) meadow.
Atlea, Atlee, Atleigh, Atli, Atlie, Atly, Attlea, Attlee, Attleigh, Attley, Attli, Attlie, Attly

Atticus (Latin) from Attica, a region outside Athens.

Attila (Gothic) little father. History: the Hun leader who invaded the Roman Empire.
Atalik, Atila, Atilio, Atilla, Atiya, Attal, Attilah, Attilio, Attyla, Attylah

Atwater (English) at the water's edge.
Attwater

Atwell (English) at the well.
Attwel, Atwel

Atwood (English) at the forest.
Attwood

Atworth (English) at the farmstead.
Attworth

Auberon (German) a form of Oberon.
Auberron, Aubrey

Aubrey (German) noble; bearlike. (French) a familiar form of Auberon. See also Avery.
Aubary, Aube, Aubery, Aubie, Aubré, Aubree, Aubreii, Aubri, Aubrie, Aubry, Aubury

Auburn (Latin) reddish brown.
Abern, Aberne, Abirn, Abirne, Aburn, Aburne, Abyrn, Abyrne, Aubern, Auberne, Aubin, Aubirn, Aubirne, Aubun, Auburne, Aubyrn, Aubyrne

Auden (English) old friend.
Audan, Audin, Audyn

Audie (German) noble; strong. (English) a familiar form of Edward.
Audee, Audey, Audi, Audiel, Audley, Audy

Audon (French) old; rich.
Audelon

Audrey (English) noble strength.
Audra, Audre, Audrea, Audri, Audrius, Audry

Audric (English) wise ruler.
Audrick, Audrik, Audryc, Audryck, Audryk

Audun (Scandinavian) deserted, desolate.

Augie (Latin) a familiar form of August.
Auggie, Augy

August (Latin) a short form of Augustine, Augustus.
Augie, Auguste, Augusto

Augustin (Latin) a form of Augustine.

Augustine (Latin) majestic. Religion: Saint Augustine was the first archbishop of Canterbury. See also Austin, Gus, Tino.

Augustine *(cont.)*
Augusteen, Augustein, Augusteyn, Augusteyne, Augustinas, Augustino, Augusto, Augustyn, Augustyne

Augustus (Latin) majestic; venerable. History: an honorary title given to the first Roman emperor, Octavius Caesar.
Agustas, Agustus, Agustys, Auguste

Aukai (Hawaiian) seafarer.
Aukay

Aundre (Greek) a form of Andre.
Aundrae, Aundray, Aundrea, Aundrey, Aundry

Aurek (Polish) golden haired.
Aurec

Aureliano (Latin) a form of Aurelius.

Aurelio (Latin) a short form of Aurelius.
Aurel, Aurele, Aureli, Aurellio

Aurelius (Latin) golden. History: Marcus Aurelius was a second-century A.D. philosopher and emperor of Rome.
Arelian, Areliano, Aurèle, Aurelien, Aurélien, Aurelyus, Aurey, Auriel, Aury

Aurick (German) protecting ruler.
Auric, Aurik, Auryc, Auryck, Auryk

Austen, Auston, Austyn (Latin) short forms of Augustine.
Austan, Austun, Austyne

Austin (Latin) a short form of Augustine.
Astin, Austine, Oistin, Ostin

Avel (Greek) breath.
Avell

Avent (French) born during Advent.
Advent, Aventin, Aventino, Aventyno

Averill (French) born in April.
Ave, Averal, Averall, Averel, Averell, Averiel, Averil, Averyl, Averyll, Avrel, Avrell, Avrill, Avryll

Avery (English) a form of Aubrey.
Avary, Aveary, Avere, Averee, Averey, Averi, Averie, Avrey, Avry

Avi (Hebrew) God is my father.
Avian, Avidan, Avidor, Avie, Aviel, Avion, Avy

Aviv (Hebrew) youth; springtime.
Avyv

Avner (Hebrew) a form of Abner.
Avneet, Avniel

Avraham (Hebrew) a form of Abraham.

Avram (Hebrew) a form of Abraham, Abram.
Arram, Avraam, Avrahom, Avrohom, Avrom, Avrum

Avshalom (Hebrew) father of peace. See also Absalom.
Avsalom

Awan (Native American) somebody.
Awen, Awin, Awon, Awun, Awyn

Axel (Latin) axe. (German) small oak tree; source of life. (Scandinavian) a form of Absalom.
Aksel, Ax, Axe, Axell, Axil, Axill, Axle, Axyl, Axyle

Axl (Latin, German, Scandinavian) a form of Axel.

Ayden (Irish) a form of Aidan. (Turkish) a form of Aydin.
Aydean, Aydon, Aydyn

Aydin (Turkish) intelligent.
Aydan, Aydon, Aydyn

Ayers (English) heir to a fortune.

Ayinde (Yoruba) we gave praise and he came.

Aylmer (English) a form of Elmer.
Aillmer, Ailmer, Allmer, Ayllmer

Aylwin (English) noble friends.
Ailwan, Ailwen, Ailwin, Ailwyn, Alwan, Alwen, Aylwan, Aylwen, Aylwon, Aylwyn

Ayman, Aymon (French) forms of Raymond.
Aiman, Aimen, Aimin, Aimon, Aimyn, Aymen, Aymin, Aymyn

Aymil (Greek) a form of Emil.
Aimil, Aimyl, Aymyl

Ayo (Yoruba) happiness.

Ayub (Arabic) penitent.

Azad (Turkish) free.
Azzad

Azeem (Arabic) a form of Azim.
Aseem, Azzeem

Azi (Nigerian) youth.
Azee, Azie, Azy

Azim (Arabic) defender.
Asim, Azeem, Azym

Azizi (Swahili) precious.

Azriel (Hebrew) God is my aid.

Azuriah (Hebrew) aided by God.
Azaria, Azariah, Azuria, Azurya, Azuruah

B

Baden (German) bather.
Badan, Bade, Badin, Badon, Badyn, Baedan, Baede, Baeden, Baedin, Baedon, Baedyn, Bayden, Baydon

Badrick (English) axe ruler.
Badric, Badrik, Badryc, Badryck, Badryk

Baez (Welsh) boar.

Bahir (Arabic) brilliant, dazzling.
Bahur

Bahram (Persian) ancient king.
Bairam

Bail (English) a form of Vail.
Bale, Balle, Bayl, Bayle

Bailey (French) bailiff, steward.
Bailea, Bailee, Baileigh, Baili, Bailie, Bailio, Baillea, Baillee, Bailleigh, Bailley, Bailli, Baillie, Bailly, Baily, Bailye, Baley

Bain (Irish) a short form of Bainbridge.
Baine, Bayn, Bayne, Baynn

Bainbridge (Irish) fair bridge.
Baenbridge, Baenebridge, Bainebridge, Baynbridge, Baynebridge

Baird (Irish) traveling minstrel, bard; poet.
Bairde, Bard, Bayrd, Bayrde

Bakari (Swahili) noble promise.
Bacari, Baccari, Bakarie, Bakary

Baker (English) baker. See also Baxter.
Bakir, Bakker, Bakory, Bakr

Bal (Sanskrit) child born with lots of hair.

Balasi (Basque) flat footed.

Balbo (Latin) stammerer.
Bailby, Balbi, Balbie, Balby, Ballbo

Baldemar (German) bold; famous.
Baldemer, Baldmar, Baldmare, Baumar, Baumer

Balder (Scandinavian) bald. Mythology: the Norse god of light, summer, purity, and innocence.
Baldier, Baldur, Baudier, Baulder

Baldomero (German) a form of Baldemar.

Baldric (German) brave ruler.
Baldrick, Baldrik, Baldryc, Baldryck, Baldryk, Baudric

Baldwin (German) bold friend.
Bald, Baldewin, Baldewyn, Baldovino, Balduin, Baldwinn, Baldwyn, Baldwynn, Balldwin, Baudoin, Baudoiun, Bealdwine

Balfour (Scottish) pastureland.
Balfor, Balfore

Balin (Hindi) mighty soldier.
Bali, Baline, Balyn, Balyne, Baylen, Baylin, Baylon, Valin

Ballard (German) brave; strong.
Balard, Balerd, Ballerd

Balraj (Hindi) strongest.

Baltazar (Greek) a form of Balthasar.
Baltasar

Balthasar (Greek) God save the king. Bible: one of the three wise men who bore gifts for the infant Jesus.
Badassare, Baldassare, Balthasaar, Balthazar, Balthazzar, Baltsaros, Belshazar, Belshazzar, Boldizsár

Banan (Irish) white.
Banen, Banin, Banon, Banun, Banyn

Bancroft (English) bean field.
Ban, Bancrofft, Bank, Bankroft, Banky

Bandi (Hungarian) a form of Andrew.
Bandee, Bandey, Bandie, Bandy

Bandit (German) outlaw, robber.
Badyt, Banditt, Bandytt

Bane (Hawaiian) a form of Bartholomew.
Baen, Baene, Ban

Banner (Scottish, English) flag bearer.
Banna, Bannar, Bannor, Banny

Banning (Irish) small and fair.
Baning, Bannie, Banny

Bao (Chinese) treasure.

Baptist (Greek) baptised.
Baptista, Baptiste, Baptysta, Battista

Baradine (Australian) small kangaroo.
Baradin, Baradyn, Baradyne

Barak (Hebrew) lightning bolt. Bible: the valiant warrior who helped Deborah.
Barrack, Barrak, Baruch

Baram (Hebrew) son of the people.
Barem, Barim, Barom, Barym

Baran (Russian) ram.
Baren, Barran, Barren

Barasa (Kikuyu) meeting place.
Barasah

Barclay (Scottish, English) birch-tree meadow.
Bar, Barclae, Barclaey, Barclai, Barclaie, Barcley, Barcklae, Barcklaey, Barcklai, Barcklaie, Barkclay, Barklay, Barklea, Barklee, Barkleigh, Barkley, Barkli, Barklie, Barkly, Barrclay, Berkeley

Bard (Irish) a form of Baird.
Bar, Barde, Bardia, Bardiya, Barr

Barden (English) barley valley.
Bairdan, Bairden, Bairdin, Bairdon, Bairdyn, Bardan, Bardon, Bardyn, Bayrdan, Bayrden, Bayrdin, Bayrdon, Bayrdyn

Bardolf (German) bright wolf.
Bardo, Bardolfe, Bardolph, Bardolphe, Bardou, Bardoul, Bardulf, Bardulph

Bardrick (Teutonic) axe ruler.
Bardric, Bardrik, Bardryck, Bardryk

Baris (Turkish) peaceful.
Barris, Barrys, Barys

Barker (English) lumberjack; advertiser at a carnival.
Barkker

Barlow (English) bare hillside.
Barloe, Barlowe, Barrlow, Barrlowe

Barnabas (Greek, Hebrew, Aramaic, Latin) son of the missionary. Bible: Christian apostle and companion of Paul on his first missionary journey.
Bane, Barna, Barnaba, Barnabe, Barnabus, Barnaby, Barnebas, Barnebus, Barney, Barnibas, Barnibus, Barnybas, Barnybus, Burnabas

Barnabe (French) a form of Barnabas.
Barnabé

Barnaby (English) a form of Barnabas.
Barnabee, Barnabey, Barnabi, Barnabie, Bernabé, Bernabee, Bernabey, Bernabi, Bernabie, Bernaby, Birnabee, Birnabey, Birnabi, Birnabie, Birnaby, Burnabee, Burnabey, Burnabi, Burnabie, Burnaby, Byrnabee, Byrnabey, Byrnabi, Byrnabie, Byrnaby

Barnard (French) a form of Bernard.
Barn, Barnard, Barnhard, Barnhardo, Barnhart

Barnes (English) bear; son of Barnett.

Barnett (English) nobleman; leader.
Barn, Barnet, Barnete, Barnette, Barney, Baronet, Baronett

Barney (English) a familiar form of Barnabas, Barnett.
Barnee, Barni, Barnie, Barny

Barnum (German) barn; storage place. (English) baron's home.
Barnham

Baron (German, English) nobleman, baron.
Baaron, Barin, Barion, Baronie, Baryn, Beron

Barret (German) a form of Barrett.
Barrat, Barrhet, Barrit, Berrit

Barrett (German) strong as a bear.
Bar, Baret, Barett, Barit, Baritt, Barretta,
Barrette, Barrhett, Barritt, Baryt, Barytt,
Berrett

Barric (English) grain farm.
Barrick, Barrik, Baryc, Baryck, Baryk, Beric,
Berric, Berrick, Berrik, Beryc, Beryck, Beryk

Barrington (English) fenced town.
Geography: a town in England.
Barington

Barron (German, English) a form of
Baron.
Barrin, Barrion, Barryn, Berron

Barry (Welsh) son of Harry. (Irish) spear,
marksman. (French) gate, fence.
Baree, Barey, Bari, Barie, Barree, Barrey,
Barri, Barrie, Bary

Bart (Hebrew) a short form of
Bartholomew, Barton.
Barrt, Barte, Bartel, Bartie, Barty

Bartel (German) a form of Bartholomew.
Barthel, Barthol, Bartholdy

Barthelemy (French) a form of
Bartholomew.
Barholomee, Barthelemi, Barthélemy,
Barthélmy, Bartholome, Bartholomy,
Bartolome, Bartolomé

Bartholomew (Hebrew) son of Talmaí.
Bible: one of the Twelve Apostles. See
also Jerney, Parlan, Parthalán.
Balta, Bartek, Barteleus, Bartelmes,
Barteo, Barth, Barthelemy, Bartho, Bartholo,
Bartholomaus, Bartholomeo, Bartholomeus,
Bartholomieu, Bartholomu, Bartimous,
Bartolomeo, Bartolomeô, Bartolommeo,
Bartome, Bartz

Bartlet (English) a form of Bartholomew.
Bartlett

Bartley (English) barley meadow.
Bartlea, Bartlee, Bartleigh, Bartli, Bartlie,
Bartly

Barto (Spanish) a form of Bartholomew.
Bardo, Bardol, Bartol, Bartoli, Bartolo, Bartos

Barton (English) barley town; Bart's town.
Barrton, Bartan, Barten, Bartin, Bartyn

Bartram (English) a form of Bertram.
Barthram

Baruch (Hebrew) blessed.
Boruch

Basam (Arabic) smiling.
Basem, Basim, Bassam, Bassem, Bassim

Basil (Greek, Latin) royal, kingly. Religion:
a saint and founder of monasteries.
Botany: an herb often used in cooking.
See also Vasilis, Wasili.
Bas, Basal, Base, Baseal, Basel, Basile,
Basilius, Basino, Basle, Bassel, Bazek,
Bazel, Bazil, Bazyli

Basile (French) a form of Basil.

Basilio (Greek, Latin) a form of Basil.
Basilios

Basir (Turkish) intelligent, discerning.
Bashar, Basheer, Bashir, Bashiyr, Basyr,
Bechir, Bhasheer

Bassett (English) little person.
Baset, Basett, Basit, Basset, Bassit

Bastien (German) a short form of
Sebastian.
Baste, Bastiaan, Bastian, Bastiane, Bastion,
Bastyan, Bastyane

Bat (English) a short form of
Bartholomew.
Bato

Baul (Gypsy) snail.

Bavol (Gypsy) wind; air.
Baval, Bavel, Bavil, Bavyl, Beval, Bevel,
Bevil, Bevol, Bevyl

Baxter (English) a form of Baker.
Bax, Baxie, Baxty, Baxy

Bay (Vietnamese) seventh son. (French)
chestnut brown color; evergreen tree.
(English) howler.
Bae, Bai, Baye

Bayard (English) reddish brown hair.
Baeyard, Baiardo, Baiyard, Bay, Bayardo,
Bayerd, Bayrd

Baylee, Bayley (French) forms of Bailey.
Baylea, Bayleigh, Bayli, Baylie, Bayly,
Beylea, Beylee, Beyleigh, Beyley, Beyli,
Beylie, Beyly

Bayron (German, English) a form of
Baron.

Beacan (Irish) small.
Beacán, Beacen, Becan, Becen, Becin, Becon,
Becyn

Beacher (English) beech trees.
Beach, Beachy, Beech, Beecher, Beechy

Beagan (Irish) small.
Beagen, Beagin, Beegan

Beale (French) a form of Beau.
Beal, Beall, Bealle, Beals, Beil, Beill, Beille,
Beyl, Beyll, Beylle

Beaman (English) beekeeper.
Beamann, Beamen, Beeman, Beemen,
Beman

Beamer (English) trumpet player.
Beemer

Beasley (English) field of peas.
Beaslea, Beaslee, Beasleigh, Beasli, Beaslie,
Beasly, Peaslee, Peasley

Beattie (Latin) blessed; happy; bringer
of joy.
Beatie, Beatti, Beatty, Beaty, Beeti, Beetie,
Beety

Beau (French) handsome.
Beale, Beaux, Bo

Beaufort (French) beautiful fort.
Bofort

Beaumont (French) beautiful mountain.
Bomont

Beauregard (French) handsome; beautiful; well regarded.
Beaureguard, Boregard, Boreguard

Beaver (English) beaver.
Beav, Beavo, Beever, Beve, Bevo

Bebe (Spanish) baby.

Beck (English, Scandinavian) brook.
Beckett

Bede (English) prayer. Religion: the
patron saint of lectors.

Bedir (Turkish) full moon.
Bedire, Bedyr, Bedyre

Bee (American) the letter B.

Bejay (American) a combination of Beau
+ Jay.
Beajae, Beajai, Beajay, Beejae, Beejai,
Beejay, Beejaye

Bela (Czech) white. (Hungarian) bright.
Béla, Belah, Belay

Belal (Czech, Hungarian) a form of Bela.
Belaal, Belall, Bellal

Belden (French, English) pretty valley.
Baliden, Balidin, Balidon, Balidyn, Beldan,
Beldin, Beldon, Beldyn, Belidan, Belldan,
Bellden, Belldin, Belldon, Belldyn

Belen (Greek) arrow.

Beli (Welsh) white.
Belee, Beley, Belie, Bely

Bell (French) handsome. (English) bell
ringer.
Bel

Bellamy (French) beautiful friend.
Belami, Belamie, Belamy, Bellamey, Bellamie

Bello (African) helper or promoter of
Islam.
Belo

Belmiro (Portuguese) good-looking;
attractive.
Belmirow, Belmyro, Belmyrow

Belveder (Italian) beautiful.
Belvedear, Belvedere, Belvidere, Belvydear,
Belvydere

Bem (Tiv) peace.
Behm

Ben (Hebrew) a short form of Benjamin.
Behn, Benio, Benn

Ben Zion (Hebrew) son of Zion.
Benzi

Ben-ami (Hebrew) son of my people.
Baram, Barami

Benedict (Latin) blessed. See also
Venedictos, Venya.
Benci, Bendict, Bendix, Bendrick, Benedictas,
Benedictus, Benediktas, Benedit, Benedyct

Benedicto (Spanish) a form of Benedict.

Benedikt (German, Slavic) a form of
Benedict.
Bendek, Bendic, Bendick, Bendik, Benedek,
Benedic, Benedick, Benedik, Benedix,
Benedyc, Benedyck, Benedyk

Bengt (Scandinavian) a form of Benedict.
Beng, Benke, Bent

Beniam (Ethiopian) a form of Benjamin.
Beneyam, Beniamin, Beniamino

Benito (Italian) a form of Benedict.
History: Benito Mussolini led Italy
during World War II.
Banyto, Bendetto, Benedetto, Benedo,
Bendino, Benino, Bennito, Benno, Beno,
Betto, Beto

Benjamen (Hebrew) a form of Benjamin.
Banjamen, Bengamen, Benejamen,
Benjermen, Benjjmen, Bennjamen

Benjamin (Hebrew) son of my right
hand. See also Peniamina, Veniamin.
Banjamin, Banjamyn, Behnjamin, Bejamin,
Benejaminas, Bengamin, Bengamon,
Bengamyn, Beniam, Beniamino, Benja,
Benjahmin, Benjaim, Benjam, Benjamain,
Benjamine, Benjaminn, Benjamino,
Benjamon, Benjamyn, Benjamynn,
Benjemin, Benjermain, Benjermin,
Benkamin, Bennjamin, Bennjamon,
Bennjamyn, Benyamin, Benyamino,
Binyamin, Mincho

Benjiman (Hebrew) a form of Benjamin.
Banjaman, Bemjiman, Bengaman,
Benjaman, Benjimen, Benjimin, Benjimon,
Benjmain, Bennjaman

Benjiro (Japanese) enjoys peace.

Benjy (Hebrew) a familiar form of
Benjamin.
Bengee, Bengey, Bengi, Bengie, Bengy,
Benjee, Benjey, Benji, Benjie, Bennjee,
Bennjey, Bennji, Bennjie, Bennjy

Bennett (Latin) little blessed one.
Benet, Benett, Benette, Benit, Benitt,
Bennet, Bennete, Bennette, Benyt, Benytt

Bennie, Benny (Hebrew) familiar forms
of Benjamin.
Bene, Benee, Beney, Beni, Benie, Benne,
Bennee, Benney, Benni, Beny

Beno (Hebrew) son. (Mwera) band
member.
Benno

Benoit (French) a form of Benedict.
Benoitt, Benott, Benoyt, Benoytt

Benoni (Hebrew) son of my sorrow.
Bible: Ben-oni was the son of Jacob
and Rachel.
Ben-Oni, Benonee, Benoney, Benonie,
Benony

Benson (Hebrew) son of Ben. A short
form of Ben Zion.
Bennsan, Bennsen, Bennsin, Bennson,
Bennsyn, Bensan, Bensen, Bensin, Benssen,
Bensson, Bensyn

Bentley (English) moor; coarse grass
meadow.
Bent, Bentlea, Bentlee, Bentleigh, Bentli,
Bentlie, Bently, Lee

Benton (English) Ben's town; town on
the moors.
Bent

Benzi (Hebrew) a familiar form of Ben
Zion.
Benzee, Benzey, Benzie, Benzy

Beppe (Italian) a form of Joseph.
Bepe, Beppy

Ber (English) boundary. (Yiddish) bear.

Beredei (Russian) a form of Hubert.
Berdry, Berdy, Beredej, Beredy

Berenger (French) courageous as a bear.
Berengir, Berynger

Berg (German) mountain.
Berdj, Berge, Bergh, Berje

Bergen (German, Scandinavian) hill
dweller.
Bergan, Bergin, Bergon, Bergyn, Birgin

Berger (French) shepherd.

Bergren (Scandinavian) mountain stream.
Berggren, Bergrin

Berk (Turkish) solid; rugged.
Berc, Berck, Berke

Berkeley, Berkley (English) forms of
Barclay.
*Berkelea, Berkelee, Berkeleigh, Berkeli,
Berkelie, Berkely, Berkie, Berklea, Berklee,
Berkleigh, Berkli, Berklie, Berkly, Berky,
Burkley*

Berl (German) a form of Burl.
*Bearl, Bearle, Berle, Berlea, Berlee, Berli,
Berlie, Birl, Birle*

Berlyn (German) boundary line. See also
Burl.
Berlin, Burlin, Burlyn

Bern (German) a short form of Bernard.
Berne

Bernabe (French) a form of Barnabas.

Bernal (German) strong as a bear.
*Bernald, Bernall, Bernalle, Bernhald,
Bernhold, Bernold, Burnal*

Bernard (German) brave as a bear. See
also Bjorn.
*Barnard, Bear, Bearnard, Benek, Ber,
Berend, Bern, Bernad, Bernadas, Bernardel,
Bernardin, Bernardus, Bernardyn, Bernarr,
Bernat, Bernek, Bernhal, Bernel, Bernerd,
Berngards, Bernhard, Bernhards, Bernhardt,
Bernhart, Burnard*

Bernardino (Spanish) a form of Bernard.
Barnardino

Bernardo (Spanish) a form of Bernard.
*Barnardo, Barnhardo, Bernaldo, Benardo,
Bernhardo, Berno, Burnardo, Nardo*

Bernie (German) a familiar form of
Bernard.
*Bernee, Berney, Berni, Berny, Birnee, Birney,
Birni, Birnie, Birny*

Bernstein (German) amber stone.
Bernsteen, Bernsteyn, Bernsteyne

Berry (English) berry; grape.
Berri, Berrie

Bersh (Gypsy) one year.
Besh

Bert (German, English) bright, shining.
A short form of Berthold, Berton,
Bertram, Bertrand, Egbert, Filbert.
Bertus, Birt, Byrt

Berthold (German) bright; illustrious;
brilliant ruler.
*Berthoud, Bertoide, Bertold, Bertoldi,
Bertolt, Burthold, Burtholde*

Bertie (English) a familiar form of Bert,
Egbert.
Berty, Birt, Birtie, Birty

Bertil (Scandinavian) bright; hero.
*Bertyl, Birtil, Birtyl, Burtil, Burtyl, Byrtil,
Byrtyl*

Bertín (Spanish) distinguished friend.
Bertyn, Burtin, Burtyn

Berto (Spanish) a short form of Alberto.
Burto

Bertoldi (Italian) a form of Berthold.
Bertolde, Bertuccio

Berton (English) bright settlement;
fortified town.
Bertan, Berten, Burtan, Burten

Bertram (German) bright; illustrious.
(English) bright raven. See also Bartram.
*Beltran, Beltrán, Beltrano, Bertrae, Bertraim,
Bertramus, Bertraum, Bertrem, Bertron*

Bertrand (German) bright shield.
Bertran, Bertrando, Bertranno, Burtrand

Berwick (English) barley farm.
Berwic, Berwik, Berwyc, Berwyck, Berwyk

Berwyn (Welsh) white head.
Berwin, Berwynn, Berwynne

Beval (English) like the wind.
Bevel, Bevil, Bevyl

Bevan (Welsh) son of Evan.
*Beavan, Beaven, Beavin, Bev, Beve, Beven,
Bevin, Bevo, Bevon, Bevyn*

Beverly (English) beaver meadow.
Beverlea, Beverlee, Beverleigh, Beverley,
Beverli, Beverlie

Bevis (French) from Beauvais, France;
bull.
Beavis, Beavys, Beauvais, Bevys, Beuves

Bhagwandas (Hindi) servant of God.

Bickford (English) axe-man's ford.
Bickforde, Bikford, Bycford, Byckford,
Bykford

Bienvenido (Filipino) welcome.

Bijan (Persian) ancient hero.
Bihjan, Bijann, Bijhan, Bijhon, Bijon,
Byjan

Bilal (Arabic) chosen.
Bila, Bilaal, Bilale, Bile, Bilel, Billaal, Billal

Bill (German) a short form of William.
Bil, Billee, Billijo, Billye, Byll, Will

Billie, Billy (German) familiar forms of
Bill, William.
Bilea, Bilee, Bileigh, Biley, Bili, Bilie, Bille,
Billea, Billee, Billey, Billi, Bily, Willie

Binah (Hebrew) understanding; wise.
Bina, Byna, Bynah

Bing (German) kettle-shaped hollow.
Byng

Binh (Vietnamese) peaceful.
Bin

Binkentios (Greek) a form of Vincent.

Binky (English) a familiar form of
Bancroft, Vincent.
Bink, Binki, Binkie

Birch (English) white; shining; birch tree.
Berch, Berche, Birche, Birk, Burch, Byrch,
Byrche

Birger (Norwegian) rescued.
Berger

Birin (Australian) cliff.
Biryn, Byrin, Byryn

Birkey (English) island with birch trees.
Berkee, Berkey, Berki, Berkie, Berky, Birk,
Birkee, Birki, Birkie, Birky

Birkitt (English) birch-tree coast.
Berket, Berkett, Berkette, Birk, Birket,
Birkett, Birkit, Burket, Burkett, Burkette,
Burkitt, Byrket, Byrkett

Birley (English) meadow with the cow
barn.
Berlea, Berlee, Berleigh, Berley, Berli, Berlie,
Berly, Birlea, Birlee, Birleigh, Birlie, Birly

Birney (English) island with a brook.
Birne, Birnee, Birni, Birnie, Birny, Burnee,
Burney, Burni, Burnie, Burny

Birtle (English) hill with birds.

Bishop (Greek) overseer. (English) bishop.
Bish, Bishup

Bjorn (Scandinavian) a form of Bernard.
Bjarne, Bjorne

Blackburn (Scottish) black brook.
Blackbern, Blackberne, Blackburne

Blade (English) knife, sword.
Bladen, Bladon, Bladyn, Blae, Blaed, Blaid,
Blaide, Blayd, Blayde

Bladimir (Russian) a form of Vladimir.
Bladimer

Blain (Irish, English) a form of Blaine.

Blaine (Irish) thin, lean. (English) river
source.
Blayne

Blair (Irish) plain, field. (Welsh) place.
Blaire, Blare, Blayr, Blayre

Blaise, Blaize (French) forms of Blaze.
Ballas, Balyse, Blais, Blaisot, Blase, Blasi,
Blasien, Blasius

Blake (English) attractive; dark.
Blaec, Blaek, Blaik, Blaike, Blakeman,
Blakey

Blakely (English) dark meadow.
Blakelea, Blakelee, Blakeleigh, Blakeley,
Blakeli, Blakelie, Blakelin, Blakelyn,
Blakeny, Blakley, Blakney

Blanco (Spanish) light skinned; white;
blond.
Blanko

Blane (Irish) a form of Blaine.
Blaney, Blanne

Blas (French) a form of Blaze.
Blass, Blaz

Blayke (English) a form of Blake.
Blayk

Blayne (Irish) a form of Blaine.
Blayn, Blayney

Blayze (French) a form of Blaze.
Blayse, Blayz, Blayze, Blayzz

Blaze (Latin) stammerer. (English) flame; trail mark made on a tree.
Balázs, Biaggio, Biagio, Blazen, Blazer

Bliss (English) blissful; joyful.
Blis, Blys, Blyss

Blondel (French) blond.
Blondell, Blundel, Blundell, Blundelle

Bly (Native American) high.
Bli, Bligh

Blythe (English) carefree; merry, joyful.
Blith, Blithe, Blyth

Bo (English) a form of Beau, Beauregard. (German) a form of Bogart.
Boe

Boaz (Hebrew) swift; strong.
Boas, Booz, Bos, Boz

Bob (English) a short form of Robert.
Bobb, Rob

Bobbie, Bobby (English) familiar forms of Bob, Robert.
Bobbee, Bobbey, Bobbi, Bobbye, Bobee, Bobey, Bobi, Bobie, Boby

Bobek (Czech) a form of Bob, Robert.

Boden (Scandinavian) sheltered. (French) messenger, herald.
Bodene, Bodin, Bodine, Bodyn, Bodyne, Boe

Bodhi (American) a form of Bodie.

Bodie (Scandinavian) a familiar form of Boden.
Boddie, Bode, Bodee, Bodey, Bodi, Boedee, Boedi, Boedy

Bodil (Norwegian) mighty ruler.
Bodyl

Bodua (Akan) animal's tail.
Boduah

Bogart (German) strong as a bow. (Irish, Welsh) bog, marshland.
Bogar, Bogey, Bogie, Bogy

Bohdan (Ukrainian) a form of Donald.
Bogdan, Bogdashka, Bogden, Bogdin, Bogdon, Bogdyn, Bohden, Bohdon

Bolton (English) from the manor farm.
Boltan, Bolten, Boltin, Boltyn

Bonaro (Italian, Spanish) friend.
Bona, Bonar, Bonnar

Bonaventure (Italian) good luck.
Bonaventura

Bond (English) tiller of the soil.
Bondie, Bondon, Bonds, Bondy

Boniface (Latin) do-gooder.
Bonifacio, Bonifacius, Bonifacy

Booker (English) bookmaker; book lover; Bible lover.
Bookie, Bookker, Books, Booky

Boone (Latin, French) good. History: Daniel Boone was an American pioneer.
Bon, Bone, Bonne, Boon, Boonie, Boony

Booth (English) hut. (Scandinavian) temporary dwelling.
Boot, Boote, Boothe, Bothe

Borak (Arabic) lightning. Mythology: the horse that carried Muhammed to seventh heaven.
Borac, Borack

Borden (French) cottage. (English) valley of the boar; boar's den.
Bord, Bordan, Bordie, Bordin, Bordon, Bordy, Bordyn

Borg (Scandinavian) castle.
Borge

Boris (Slavic) battler, warrior. Religion: the patron saint of Moscow, princes, and Russia.
Boriss, Borja, Borris, Borya, Boryenka, Borys

Borka (Russian) fighter.

Boseda (Tiv) born on Saturday.
Bosedah

Bosley (English) grove of trees.
Boslea, Boslee, Bosleigh, Bosli, Boslie, Bosly

Boswell (English) boar enclosure by the stream.
Boswel, Bozwel, Bozwell

Botan (Japanese) blossom, bud.
Boten, Botin, Boton, Botyn

Bourey (Cambodian) country.
Bouree

Bourne (Latin, French) boundary. (English) brook, stream.
Born, Borne, Bourn

Boutros (Arabic) a form of Peter.
Boutro

Bowen (Welsh) son of Owen.
Bow, Bowan, Bowe, Bowie, Bowin, Bowon, Bowyn, Bowynn

Bowie (Irish) yellow haired. History: James Bowie was an American-born Mexican colonist who died during the defense of the Alamo.
Bow, Bowee, Bowey, Bowi, Bowy

Boy (French) a short form of Boyce.

Boyce (French) woods, forest.
Boice, Boise, Boycey, Boycie, Boyse

Boyd (Scottish) yellow haired.
Boid, Boydan, Boyde, Boyden, Boydin, Boydon, Boydyn

Brad (English) a short form of Bradford, Bradley.
Bradd, Brade

Bradburn (English) broad stream.
Bradbern, Bradberne, Bradborn, Bradborne, Bradbourn, Bradbourne, Braddbourn, Braddbourne

Braden (English) broad valley.
Bradan, Bradden, Bradeon, Bradin, Bradine, Bradun, Bredan, Bredon

Bradey (Irish, English) a form of Brady.

Bradford (English) broad river crossing.
Braddford, Bradforde, Ford

Bradlee, Bradly (English) forms of Bradley.
Braddlea, Braddlee, Braddleigh, Braddli, Braddlie, Braddly, Bradlea, Bradleigh, Bradlie

Bradley (English) broad meadow.
Braddley, Bradlay, Bradlyn, Bradney

Bradon (English) broad hill.

Bradshaw (English) broad forest.
Braddshaw

Brady (Irish) spirited. (English) broad island.
Bradi, Bradie, Bradye, Braedee, Braedey, Braedi, Braedie, Braedy, Braidy

Bradyn (English) a form of Braden.
Bradynne, Braidyn, Braydyn, Breidyn

Braedan, Braeden, Braedyn (English) forms of Braden.
Braedin

Braedon (English) a form of Bradon.
Breadon

Bragi (Scandinavian) poet. Mythology: the god of poetry, eloquence, and song.
Brage

Braham (Hindi) creator.
Braheem, Braheim, Brahiem, Brahima, Brahm

Braiden (English) a form of Braden.
Braidan, Braidin

Braidon (English) a form of Bradon.

Brainard (English) bold raven; prince.
Brainerd, Braynard

Bram (Scottish) bramble, brushwood. (Hebrew) a short form of Abraham, Abram.
Brame, Bramm, Bramdon

Bramwell (English) bramble spring.
Brammel, Brammell, Bramwel, Bramwele, Bramwyll

Branch (Latin) paw; claw; tree branch.

Brand (English) firebrand; sword. A short form of Brandon.
Brandall, Brande, Brandel, Brandell, Brander, Brandley, Brann

Brandan (English) a form of Brandon.

Brandeis (Czech) dweller on a burned clearing.
Brandis

Branden (English) beacon valley.
Brandden, Brandene, Breandan

Brandin (English) a form of Branden.
Brandine

Brando (English) a form of Brand.
Brandol

Brandon (English) beacon hill.
Bran, Branddon, Brandone, Brandonn, Brandyn, Branndan, Branndon, Breandon, Brendon

Brandt (English) a form of Brant.

Brandy (Dutch) brandy. (English) a familiar form of Brand.
Branddy, Brandey, Brandi, Brandie

Brandyn (English) a form of Branden, Brandon.
Brandynn

Brannen, Brannon (Irish) forms of Brandon.
Branen, Brannan, Brannin, Branon

Bransen (English) a form of Branson.

Branson (English) son of Brandon, Brant. A form of Bronson.
Bransan, Bransin, Bransyn, Brantson

Brant (English) proud.
Brannt, Brante, Branton

Brantley, Brantly (English) forms of Brant.
Brantlee, Brantleigh, Brantlie, Brentlee, Brentley, Brently

Branton (English) Brant's town.

Brasil (Irish) brave; strong in conflict.
Brasill, Brasyl, Brasyll, Brazil, Brazill, Brazyl, Brazyll, Brazylle

Braulio (Italian) a form of Brawley.
Brauli, Brauliuo

Brawley (English) meadow on the hillside.
Brawlea, Brawlee, Brawleigh, Brawli, Brawlie, Brawly

Braxton (English) Brock's town.
Brax, Braxdon, Braxston, Braxtan, Braxten, Braxtin, Braxtyn, Braxxton

Brayan (Irish, Scottish) a form of Brian.
Brayn, Brayon

Brayden (English) a form of Braden.
Braydan, Braydin, Braydn, Breydan, Breyden

Braydon (English) a form of Bradon.
Braydoon, Breydon

Braylon (American) a combination of Braydon + Lynn.

Brayton (English) a form of Brighton. (Scottish) a form of Bret.
Braten, Braton

Breck (Irish) freckled.
Brec, Breckan, Brecken, Breckie, Breckin, Breckke, Breckyn, Breik, Brek, Brexton

Brede (Scandinavian) iceberg, glacier.
Bred

Brencis (Latvian) a form of Lawrence.
Brence, Brencys

Brendan (Irish) little raven. (English) sword.
Breandan, Breendan, Bren, Brenden, Brendis, Brendon, Brenn, Brenndan, Bryn

Brenden, Brendin (Irish) forms of Brendan.
Bren, Brendene, Brendine, Brennden, Brenndin

Brendon (English) a form of Brandon. (Irish, English) a form of Brendan.
Brenndon

Brendyn (Irish, English) a form of Brendan.
Brenndyn, Brenyan

Brenen, Brennan, Brennen, Brennon (English, Irish) forms of Brendan.

Bren, Brenan, Brenin, Brenn, Brenna, Brennann, Brennin, Brennun, Brennyn, Brenon

Brenner (English, Irish) a form of Brendan.
Brennor

Brent (English) a short form of Brenton.
Brendt, Brente, Brentson, Brentt

Brenten (English) a form of Brenton.
Brentten

Brentley (English) a form of Brantley.
Brentlee, Brently

Brenton (English) steep hill.
Brentan, Brentin, Brenttton, Brentun, Brentyn

Breon, Breyon (Irish, Scottish) forms of Brian.
Breyan

Bret, Brett (Scottish) from Great Britain. See also Britton.
Bhrett, Bretley, Bretlin, Brette

Breton, Bretton (Scottish) forms of Bret.
Bretan, Breten, Bretin, Brettan, Bretten, Brettun, Brettyn, Bretyn

Brewster (English) brewer.
Brew, Brewer, Brewstar, Brewstarr, Brewstir, Brewstor, Bruwster

Brian (Irish, Scottish) strong; virtuous; honorable. History: Brian Boru was an eleventh-century Irish king and national hero. See also Palaina.
Braiano, Briana, Briann, Brianna, Brianne, Briano, Briant, Briante, Briaun, Briayan, Brin, Briny

Briar (French) heather.
Brier, Brierly

Brice (Welsh) alert; ambitious. (English) son of Rice.
Bricen, Briceton, Brise, Brisen, Bryce

Brick (English) bridge.
Bric, Bricker, Bricklen, Brickman, Brik, Bryc, Bryck, Bryk

Bridgely (English) meadow near a bridge.
Bridgelea, Bridgelee, Bridgelei, Bridgeleigh, Bridgeley, Bridgeli, Bridgelie

Bridger (English) bridge builder.
Bridd, Bridgar, Bridge, Bridgir, Bridgor

Brien (Irish, Scottish) a form of Brian.
Brience, Brient

Brigham (English) covered bridge. (French) troops, brigade.
Brig, Brigg, Briggs, Bringham

Brighton (English) bright town.
Breighton, Bright, Brightin, Bryton

Brinley (English) tawny.
Brinlea, Brinlee, Brinlei, Brinleigh, Brinli, Brinlie, Brinly, Brynlea, Brynlee, Brynlei, Brynleigh, Brynley, Brynli, Brynlie, Brynly

Brion (Irish, Scottish) a form of Brian.
Brieon, Brione, Brionn, Brionne

Brishan (Gypsy) born during a rain.
Brishen, Brishin, Brishon, Bryshan, Bryshen, Bryshin, Bryshon, Bryshyn

Brit, Britt (Scottish) forms of Bret. See also Britton.
Brityce

Briton, Brittan, Britten (Scottish) forms of Britton.
Britain, Briten, Britian, Brittain, Brittian

Britton (Scottish) from Great Britain. See also Bret, Brit.
Britin, Brittin, Brittun, Brittyn

Broc (English) a form of Brock.

Brock (English) badger.
Brocke, Brockett, Brockie, Brockley, Brocky, Brok, Broque

Brockton (English) a form of Brock.

Brod (English) a short form of Broderick.
Brode

Broden (Irish) a form of Brody. (English) a form of Brod.

Broderick (Welsh) son of the famous ruler. (English) broad ridge. See also Roderick.
Brodaric, Brodarick, Brodarik, Brodderick, Brodderrick, Broderic, Broderik, Broderrick, Broderyc, Broderyck, Broderyk, Brodrick

Brodie (Irish) a form of Brody.
Broddie, Brodee, Brodi, Broedi

Brodrick (Welsh, English) a form of Broderick.
Broddrick, Brodric, Brodryck

Brody (Irish) ditch; canal builder.
Broddy, Brodey, Broedy

Brogan (Irish) a heavy work shoe.
Brogen, Broghan, Broghen

Bromley (English) brushwood meadow.
Bromlea, Bromlee, Bromleigh, Bromli, Bromlie, Bromly

Bron (Afrikaans) source.
Brone

Bronislaw (Polish) weapon of glory.
Bronislav, Bronyslav, Bronyslaw

Bronson (English) son of Brown.
Bransin, Bron, Bronnie, Bronnson, Bronny, Bronsan, Bronsen, Bronsin, Bronsonn, Bronsson, Bronsun, Bronsyn, Brunson

Brook (English) brook, stream.
Brooc, Brooker, Brookin, Brooklyn

Brooke (English) a form of Brook.

Brooks (English) son of Brook.
Brookes, Broox

Brown (English) brown; bear.
Browne

Bruce (French) brushwood thicket; woods.
Brooce, Broose, Brucey, Brucy, Brue, Bruis, Bruse

Bruno (German, Italian) brown haired; brown skinned.
Brunon, Bruns

Brutus (Latin) coarse, stupid. History: a Roman general who conspired to assassinate Julius Caesar.
Brootus, Brutas, Brutis, Brutiss, Brutos, Brutoss, Brutuss

Bryan (Irish) a form of Brian.
Brayan, Bryann, Bryen

Bryant (Irish) a form of Bryan.
Bryent

Bryar, Bryer (French) forms of Briar.
Bryor

Bryce (Welsh) a form of Brice.
Brycen, Bryceton, Bryse, Bryston

Bryden, Brydon (English) forms of Braden.
Brydan

Bryn (Welsh) mountain. (German, English) a form of Bryon.
Brin, Brinn, Bryne, Brynn, Brynne

Brynmor (Welsh) big mountain.
Brinmor, Brinmore, Brynmore

Bryon (German) cottage. (English) bear.
Bryeon, Bryone

Brysen (Welsh) a form of Bryson.

Bryson (Welsh) son of Brice.
Brysan, Brysun, Brysyn

Bryton (English) a form of Brighton.
Brayten, Breyton, Bryeton, Brytan, Bryten, Brytin, Brytten, Brytton

Bubba (German) a boy.
Babba, Babe, Bebba

Buck (German, English) male deer.
Buc, Buckie, Buckley, Buckner, Bucko, Bucky, Buk

Buckley (English) deer meadow.
Bucklea, Bucklee, Buckleigh, Buckli, Bucklie, Buckly, Buclea, Buclee, Bucleigh, Bucley, Bucli, Buclie, Bucly, Buklee, Bukleigh, Bukley, Bukli, Buklie, Bukly

Buckminster (English) preacher.

Bud (English) herald, messenger.
Budd

Buddy (American) a familiar form of Bud.
Budde, Buddee, Buddey, Buddi, Buddie, Budi, Budie, Budy

Buell (German) hill dweller. (English) bull.
Buel

Buford (English) ford near the castle.
Burford

Bundy (English) free.
Bundee, Bundey, Bundi, Bundie

Bunyan (Australian) home of pigeons.
Bunyen, Bunyin, Bunyon, Bunyyn

Burbank (English) from the castle on a slope.
Berbanc, Berbanck, Berbank, Burbanc, Burbanck

Burdan (English) birch valley.
Berdan, Berden, Berdin, Berdon, Berdyn, Birdan, Birden, Birdon, Birdyn, Burden, Burdin, Burdon, Burdun, Burdyn

Burdett (French) small shield.
Berdet, Berdett, Berdette, Burdet, Burdette

Burford (English) birch ford.
Berford, Berforde, Birford, Birforde, Burforde, Byrford, Byrforde

Burgess (English) town dweller; shopkeeper.
Bergess, Birgess, Burg, Burges, Burgh, Burgiss, Burr, Byrgess

Burian (Ukrainian) lives near weeds.
Berian, Beriane, Beryan, Beryane, Birian, Biriane, Biryan, Biryane, Buriane, Byrian, Byriane, Byryan, Byryane

Burke (German, French) fortress, castle.
Birk, Birke, Bourke, Burk, Byrk, Byrke

Burl (English) cup bearer; wine servant; knot in a tree. (German) a short form of Berlyn
Berl, Burle, Byrl, Byrle

Burleigh (English) meadow with knotted tree trunks.
Berleigh, Berley, Birlea, Birlee, Birleigh, Birley, Birli, Birlie, Birly, Burlea, Burlee, Burley, Burli, Burlie, Burly, Byrleigh, Byrlee

Burne (English) brook.
Beirne, Burn, Byrne

Burnell (French) small; brown haired.
Bernel, Bernell, Bernelle, Birnel, Birnell, Birnelle, Burnel, Burnele, Burnelle, Byrnel, Byrnell, Byrnelle

Burnett (English) burned nettle.
Bernet, Bernett, Birnet, Birnett, Burnet

Burney (English) island with a brook. A familiar form of Rayburn.
Burnee, Burni, Burnie, Burny, Byrnee, Byrney, Byrni, Byrnie, Byrny

Burr (Swedish) youth. (English) prickly plant.
Bur

Burril (Australian) wallaby.
Bural, Burel, Buril, Burol, Buryl, Burral, Burrel, Burril, Burrol, Burryl

Burris (English) town dweller.
Buris, Buriss, Byris, Buryss

Burt (English) a form of Bert. A short form of Burton.
Burrt, Burtt, Burty

Burton (English) fortified town.
Bertan, Berten, Bertin, Bertyn, Birtan, Birten, Birtin, Birton, Birtyn, Burtan, Burten, Burtin, Burtyn, Byrtan, Byrten, Byrtin, Byrton, Byrtyn

Busby (Scottish) village in the thicket; tall military hat made of fur.
Busbee, Busbey, Busbi, Busbie, Buzbi, Buzbie, Buzby, Buzz

Buster (American) hitter, puncher.
Bustar

Butch (American) a short form of Butcher.

Butcher (English) butcher.
Butch

Buzz (Scottish) a short form of Busby.
Buzzy

Byford (English) by the ford.
Biford, Biforde, Byforde

Byram (English) cattle yard.
Biram

Byran (French, English) a form of Byron.
Biran, Byrann

Byrd (English) birdlike.
Bird, Birdie, Byrdie

Byrne (English) a form of Burne.
Byrn, Byrnes

Byron (French) cottage. (English) barn.
Beyren, Beyron, Biren, Birin, Biron, Buiron, Byren, Byrom, Byrone

C

Cable (French, English) rope maker.
Cabell

Cadao (Vietnamese) folksong.

Cadby (English) warrior's settlement.
Cadbee, Cadbey, Cadbi, Cadbie

Caddock (Welsh) eager for war.
Cadock, Cadok

Cade (Welsh) a short form of Cadell.
Cady, Caid, Cayd

Cadell (Welsh) battler.
Cadel, Caidel, Caidell, Caydel, Caydel,
Cedell

Caden (American) a form of Kadin.
Cadan, Caddon, Cadian, Cadien, Cadin,
Cadon, Cadyn, Caeden, Caedon

Cadman (Irish) warrior.
Cadmen, Caedman, Caidman, Caydman

Cadmar (Irish) brave warrior.
Cadmer, Cadmir, Caedmar, Caidmar,
Caydmar

Cadmus (Greek) from the east.
Mythology: a Phoenician prince who
founded Thebes and introduced writing
to the Greeks.

Caelan (Scottish) a form of Nicholas.
Cael, Caelen, Caelin, Caellin, Caelon,
Caelyn, Cailan, Cailean, Cailen, Cailin,
Caillan, Callin, Cailon, Cailun, Cailyn,
Caylen, Cayley, Caylin, Caylon, Caylyn

Caesar (Latin) long-haired. History: a
title for Roman emperors. See also
Kaiser, Kesar, Sarito.
Caesarae, Caesare, Caesario, Caesarius,
Caeser, Caezar, Casar, Casare, Caseare,
Czar, Saecer, Saeser, Seasar

Caesear (Latin) a form of Caesar.

Cahil (Turkish) young, naive. See also
Kahil.
Cahill

Cai (Welsh) a form of Gaius.
Cae, Caio, Caius, Caw, Cay

Caiden (American) a form of Kadin.
Caid

Cain (Hebrew) spear; gatherer. Bible:
Adam and Eve's oldest son. See also
Kabil, Kane, Kayne.
Caen, Caene, Cayn, Cayne

Caine (Hebrew) a form of Cain.
Cainaen, Cainan, Cainen, Caineth

Cairn (Welsh) landmark made of a
mound of stones.
Cairne, Carn, Carne, Cayrn, Cayrne,
Cayrnes

Cairo (Arabic) Geography: the capital of
Egypt.
Cayro, Kairo

Cal (Latin) a short form of Calvert,
Calvin.

Calan (Scottish) a form of Caelan.
(Australian) a form of Callan.
Caleon, Calon, Calyn

Calder (Welsh, English) brook, stream.

Caldwell (English) cold well.
Caldwel, Kaldwel, Kaldwell

Cale (Hebrew) a short form of Caleb.
Cael, Caell, Cail, Caill, Calle, Cayl, Cayll

Caleb (Hebrew) dog; faithful. (Arabic)
bold, brave. Bible: one of the twelve spies
sent by Moses. See also Kaleb, Kayleb.
Caelab, Caeleb, Cailab, Calab, Calabe,
Callob, Calob, Calyb, Caylab, Cayleb,
Caylebb, Caylob

Calen, Calin (Scottish) forms of Caelan.
Calean

Caley (Irish) a familiar form of Calan,
Caleb.
Calea, Calee, Caleigh, Cali, Calie, Callea,
Callee, Calleigh, Calley, Calli, Callie, Cally,
Caly

Calhoun (Irish) narrow woods. (Scottish)
warrior.
Calhoon, Colhoun, Colhoune, Colquhoun,
Kalhoon, Kalhoun

Calib (Hebrew, Arabic) a form of Caleb.
Calieb, Caylib

Callahan (Irish) descendant of Ceallachen.
Calaghan, Calahan, Callaghan, Kallaghan, Kallahan

Callan (Australian) sparrow hawk.
(Scottish) a form of Caelan.
Callin, Callon, Callyn

Callen (Scottish) a form of Caelan.
(Australian, Scottish) a form of Callan.

Callis (Latin) chalice, goblet.
Calliss, Callys, Calyss, Kallis, Kalliss, Kallys, Kallyss

Callum (Irish) dove.
Callam, Callem, Callim, Callym, Kallum

Calum (Irish) a form of Callum.
Calam, Calem, Calim, Calym, Colum, Kalum

Calvert (English) calf herder.
Calbert, Calburt, Calvirt, Kalbert, Kalvert

Calvin (Latin) bald. See also Kalvin, Vinny.
Calv, Calvan, Calven, Calvien, Calvino, Calvon, Calvun, Calvyn

Cam (Gypsy) beloved. (Scottish) a short form of Cameron. (Latin, French, Scottish) a short form of Campbell.
Camm, Cammie, Cammy, Camy, Kam

Camaron (Scottish) a form of Cameron.
Camar, Camaran, Camaren, Camari

Camden (Scottish) winding valley.
Camdan, Camdin, Camdon, Camdyn, Kamden

Cameren (Scottish) a form of Cameron.

Cameron (Scottish) crooked nose. See also Kameron.
Cameran, Camerin, Cameroun, Camerron, Camerson, Camerun, Cameryn, Camiren, Camiron, Cammeron

Camille (French) young ceremonial attendant.
Camile

Camilo (Latin) child born to freedom; noble.
Camiel, Camillo, Camillus, Camilow, Kamilo

Campbell (Latin, French) beautiful field. (Scottish) crooked mouth.
Cambel, Cambell, Camp, Campy, Kampbell

Camren, Camrin, Camron, Camryn (Scottish) short forms of Cameron.
Cammrin, Cammron, Camran, Camreon, Camrynn

Canaan (French) a form of Cannon. History: an ancient region between the Jordan River and the Mediterranean.
Canan, Cannan, Caynan

Candide (Latin) pure; sincere.
Candid, Candida, Kandide

Candido (Latin) a form of Candide.
Candonino

Cannon (French) church official; large gun. See also Kannon.
Cannen, Cannin, Canning, Cannyn

Canon (French) a form of Cannon.
Canen, Canin, Canyn

Canute (Latin) white haired. (Scandinavian) knot. History: a Danish king who became king of England after 1016. See also Knute.
Cnut, Cnute

Canyon (Latin) canyon.
Cannyon, Cañon, Canyan, Canyen, Canyin, Kanyon

Cappi (Gypsy) good fortune.
Cappee, Cappey, Cappie, Cappy, Kappi

Car (Irish) a short form of Carney.
Kar

Carden (French) wool comber. (Irish) from the black fortress.
Cardan, Cardin, Cardon, Cardyn

Carey (Greek) pure. (Welsh) castle; rocky island. See also Karey.
Care, Caree, Cari, Carre, Carree, Carrey, Carrie, Cary

Carl (German, English) a short form of
Carlton. A form of Charles. See also
Carroll, Kale, Kalle, Karl, Karlen, Karol.
Carle, Carles, Carless, Carlis, Carll, Carlson

Carleton (English) a form of Carlton.
Karleton

Carlin (Irish) little champion.
*Carlan, Carlen, Carley, Carlie, Carling,
Carlino, Carlon, Carly*

Carlisle (English) Carl's island.
Karlisle

Carlito (Spanish) a familiar form of
Carlos.
Carlitos

Carlo (Italian) a form of Carl, Charles.
Carolo, Charlo, Karlo

Carlos (Spanish) a form of Carl, Charles.
Carlus, Carolos, Charlos, Karlos

Carlton (English) Carl's town.
*Carllton, Carlston, Carltonn, Carltton,
Karlton*

Carlyle (English) a form of Carlisle.
Carlysle, Karlyle

Carmel (Hebrew) vineyard, garden. See
also Carmine.
Carmeli, Carmiel, Karmel

Carmelo (Hebrew) a form of Carmel.
Carmello

Carmen (Latin, Italian) a form of
Carmine.
Carman, Carmon, Carmyn

Carmichael (Scottish) follower of
Michael.
Karmichael

Carmine (Latin) song; crimson. (Italian) a
form of Carmel.
Carmain, Carmaine, Carmyne, Karmine

Carnelius (Greek, Latin) a form of
Cornelius.
*Carnealius, Carneilius, Carnellius,
Carnilious*

Carnell (English) defender of the castle.
(French) a form of Cornell.
Carnel, Karnel, Karnell

Carney (Irish) victorious. (Scottish)
fighter. See also Kearney.
Car, Carnee, Carnie, Carny, Karney

Carr (Scandinavian) marsh. See also Kerr.
Karr

Carrick (Irish) rock.
*Carooq, Carric, Carricko, Carrik, Karric,
Karrick*

Carrington (Welsh) rocky town.

Carroll (Irish) champion. (German) a
form of Carl.
*Carel, Carell, Cariel, Cariell, Carol, Carole,
Carolo, Carols, Carollan, Carolus, Carrol,
Caryl*

Carsen (English) a form of Carson.

Carson (English) son of Carr.
Carsan, Carsin, Carsino, Carrson, Karson

Carsten (Greek) a form of Karsten.
Carston

Carter (English) cart driver.
Cart, Cartar, Cartor, Kartar, Karter, Kartor

Cartland (English) cart builder's island.
Cartlan, Kartlan, Kartland

Cartwright (English) cart builder.
Cartright

Carvell (French, English) village on the
marsh.
*Carvel, Carvelle, Carvellius, Karvel, Karvell,
Karvelle*

Carver (English) wood-carver; sculptor.
*Carvar, Carvir, Carvor, Karvar, Karver,
Karvir, Karvor*

Cary (Welsh) a form of Carey. (German,
Irish) a form of Carroll.
Carray, Carry

Case (Irish) a short form of Casey.
(English) a short form of Casimir.

Casey (Irish) brave.
*Casee, Casi, Casie, Cassee, Cassey, Cassi,
Cassie, Casy, Casye, Cayse, Caysey,
Cazzee, Cazzey, Cazzi, Cazzie, Cazzy*

Cash (Latin) vain. (Slavic) a short form of Casimir.
Cashe

Cashlin (Irish) little castle.
Cashlind, Cashlyn, Cashlynd, Kashlin, Kashlyn

Casimir (Slavic) peacemaker.
Cachi, Cas, Cashemere, Cashi, Cashmeire, Cashmere, Casimere, Casimire, Casimiro, Castimer, Cazimir, Cazimier, Kasimir, Kazio

Casper (Persian) treasurer. (German) imperial. See also Gaspar, Jasper, Kasper.
Caspar, Caspir

Cass (Irish, Persian) a short form of Casper, Cassidy.

Cassidy (Irish) clever; curly haired. See also Kazio.
Casidy, Cassady, Cassidee, Cassidey, Cassidi, Cassidie, Kassidy

Cassie (Irish) a familiar form of Cassidy.
Casi, Casie, Casio, Cassey, Cassi, Cassy, Casy, Cazi, Cazie, Cazy

Cassius (Latin, French) box; protective cover.
Casius, Cassia, Cassio, Cazzie, Cazzius, Kasius, Kassio, Kassius, Kazzius

Castle (Latin) castle.
Cassle, Castal, Castel

Castor (Greek) beaver. Astrology: one of the twins in the constellation Gemini. Mythology: one of the patron saints of mariners.
Castar, Caster, Castir, Caston, Kastar, Kaster, Kastor, Kastyr

Cater (English) caterer.

Cathal (Irish) strong; wise.
Cathel, Cathol, Kathal, Kathel, Kathol

Catherine (Greek) pure. (English) a form of Katherine (see Girls' Names).

Cathmor (Irish) great fighter.
Cathmore, Cathmoor, Cathmoore, Kathmor, Kathmore, Kathmoor, Kathmoore

Catlin (Irish) a form of Caitlin (see Girls' Names).

Cato (Latin) knowledgeable, wise.
Caton, Catón, Kato

Cavan (Irish) handsome. See also Kavan, Kevin.
Caven, Cavon, Cawoun

Cavell (French) small and active.
Cavel, Kavel, Kavell

Cavin (Irish) a form of Cavan.

Cawley (Scottish) ancient. (English) cow meadow.
Cawlea, Cawleah, Cawlee, Cawleigh, Cawli, Cawlie, Cawly, Kawlee, Kawleigh, Kawley, Kawli, Kawlie, Kawly

Cayden (American) a form of Caden.
Cayde, Caydin

Caylan (Scottish) a form of Caelan.
Caylans, Caylen, Caylon

Cazzie (American) a familiar form of Cassius.
Caz, Cazz, Cazzy

Ceasar (Latin) a form of Caesar.
Ceaser

Cecil (Latin) blind.
Cacelius, Cece, Cecile, Cecilius, Cecill, Cecilus, Cecyl, Siseal

Cecilio (Latin) a form of Cecil.
Celio, Cesilio

Cedar (Latin) a kind of evergreen conifer.

Cederic (English) a form of Cedric.
Cederick, Cederrick, Cedirick

Cedric (English) battle chieftain. See also Kedric, Rick.
Cad, Caddaric, Ced, Cedrec, Cédric, Cedryche, Sedric

Cedrick, Cedrik (English) forms of Cedric.
Ceddrick

Ceejay (American) a combination of the initials C. + J.
Cejay, C.J.

Celestine (Latin) celestial, heavenly.
Celestyn, Selestin, Selestine, Selestyn

Celestino (Latin) a form of Celestine.
Selestino

Celso (Italian, Spanish, Portuguese) tall.

Cemal (Arabic) attractive.

Cephas (Latin) small rock. Bible: the term used by Jesus to describe Peter.
Cepheus, Cephus

Cerdic (Welsh) beloved.
Caradoc, Caradog, Ceredig, Ceretic

Cerek (Polish) lordly. (Greek) a form of Cyril.
Cerik

Cesar (Spanish) a form of Caesar.
Casar, César, Cesare, Cesareo, Cesario, Cesaro, Ceseare, Ceser, Cesit, Cesor, Cessar

Cestmir (Czech) fortress.

Cezar (Slavic) a form of Caesar.
Cézar, Cezary, Cezek, Chezrae, Sezar

Chace (French) a form of Chase.
Chaice

Chad (English) warrior. A short form of Chadwick. Geography: a country in north-central Africa.
Ceadd, Chaad, Chaddi, Chaddie, Chaddy, Chade, Chadleigh, Chadler, Chadley, Chadlin, Chadlyn, Chadmen, Chado, Chadron, Chady

Chadd (English) a form of Chad.

Chadrick (German) mighty warrior.
Chaddrick, Chaderic, Chaderick, Chaderik, Chadrack, Chadric, Chadrik, Chadryc, Chadryck, Chadryk

Chadwick (English) warrior's town.
Chaddwick, Chadvic, Chadwic, Chadwik, Chadwyc, Chadwyck, Chadwyk

Chago (Spanish) a form of Jacob.
Chango, Chanti

Chaim (Hebrew) life. See also Hyman.
Chai, Chaimek, Chaym, Chayme, Haim, Khaim

Chaise (French) a form of Chase.
Chais, Chaisen, Chaison

Chal (Gypsy) boy; son.
Chalie, Chalin

Chalmers (Scottish) son of the lord.
Chalmer, Chalmr, Chamar, Chamarr

Cham (Vietnamese) hard worker.
Chams

Chan (Sanskrit) shining. (English) a form of Chauncey. (Spanish) a form of Juan.
Chann, Chano, Chayo

Chanan (Hebrew) cloud.
Chanen, Chanin, Channan, Channen, Channin, Channon, Channyn, Chanon, Chanyn

Chance (English) a short form of Chancellor, Chauncey.
Chanc, Chants, Chaynce

Chancellor (English) record keeper.
Chancellar, Chancellen, Chancelleor, Chanceller, Chansellor

Chancelor (English) a form of Chancellor.
Chancelar, Chancelen, Chanceleor, Chanceler, Chanselor, Chanslor

Chancey (English) a familiar form of Chancellor, Chauncey.
Chancee, Chancie, Chancy

Chander (Hindi) moon.
Chand, Chandan, Chandany, Chandara, Chandon

Chandler (English) candle maker.
Chandelar, Chandlan, Chandlar, Chandlier, Chandlor, Chandlyr

Chane (Swahili) dependable.
Chaen, Chaene, Chain, Chaine, Chayn, Chayne, Cheyn

Chaney (French) oak.
Chaynee, Cheaney, Cheney

Chankrisna (Cambodian) sweet smelling tree.

Channing (English) wise. (French) canon; church official.
Chane, Chanin, Chaning, Chann, Channin, Channyn, Chanyn

Chanse (English) a form of Chance.
Chans, Chansey, Chansy

Chante (French) singer.
Chant, Chantha, Chanthar, Chantra,
Chantry, Shantae

Chantz (English) a form of Chance.
Chanz, Chanze

Chapman (English) merchant.
Chap, Chapmann, Chapmen, Chapmin,
Chapmyn, Chappie, Chappy

Charles (German) farmer. (English)
strong and manly. See also Carl, Searlas,
Tearlach, Xarles.
Arlo, Chareles, Charels, Charl, Charle,
Charlen, Charlese, Charlot, Charlz,
Charlzell

Charleston (English) a form of Carlton.
Charlesten

Charley, Charlie, Charly (German,
English) familiar forms of Charles.
Charle, Charlea, Charlee, Charleigh, Charli

Charlton (English) a form of Carlton.
Charleton, Charlotin

Charro (Spanish) cowboy.
Charo

Chas (English) a familiar form of Charles.

Chase (French) hunter.
Chass, Chasse, Chastan, Chasten, Chastin,
Chastinn, Chaston, Chasyn, Chayse

Chasen, Chason (French) forms of
Chase.

Chaska (Sioux) first-born son.
Chaskah

Chatha (African) ending.

Chatham (English) warrior's home.
Chathem, Chathim, Chathom, Chathym

Chauncey (English) chancellor; church
official.
Chaunce, Chauncee, Chauncei, Chaunci,
Chauncie, Chauncecy, Chaunesy, Chaunszi

Chauncy (English) a form of Chauncey.

Chavez (Hispanic) a surname used as a
first name.

Chavaz, Chaves, Chaveze, Chavies,
Chavius, Chevez, Cheveze, Cheviez,
Chevious, Chevis, Chivez

Chavis (Hispanic) a form of Chavez.
Chivass

Chayanne (Cheyenne) a form of
Cheyenne.
Chayann, Shayan

Chayce, Chayse (French) forms of
Chase.
Chaysea, Chaysen, Chayson, Chaysten

Chayton (Lakota) falcon.
Chaiton

Chaz, Chazz (English) familiar forms of
Charles.
Chasz, Chaze, Chazwick, Chazy, Chez

Che, Ché (Spanish) familiar forms of
Jose. History: Ernesto "Che" Guevara
was a revolutionary who fought at Fidel
Castro's side in Cuba.
Chay

Checha (Spanish) a familiar form of
Jacob.

Cheche (Spanish) a familiar form of
Joseph.

Chee (Chinese, Nigerian) a form of Chi.

Chen (Chinese) great, tremendous.

Chencho (Spanish) a familiar form of
Lawrence.

Cheney (French) from the oak forest.
Chenee, Cheni, Chenie, Cheny

Chepe (Spanish) a familiar form of
Joseph.
Cepito

Cherokee (Cherokee) people of a differ-
ent speech.
Cherokey, Cheroki, Cherokie, Cheroky,
Cherrakee

Chesmu (Native American) gritty.
Chesmue

Chester (English) a short form of
Rochester.
Ches, Cheslav

Cheston (English) a form of Chester.

Chet (English) a short form of Chester.
Chett, Chette

Cheung (Chinese) good luck.

Chevalier (French) horseman, knight.
Chev, Chevalyer

Chevy (French) a familiar form of
Chevalier. Geography: Chevy Chase is
a town in Maryland. Culture: a short
form of Chevrolet, an American auto-
mobile company.
*Chev, Chevee, Chevey, Chevi, Chevie,
Chevvy, Chewy*

Cheyenne (Cheyenne) a tribal name.
Cheienne, Cheyeenne, Cheyene, Chyenne

Cheyne (French) a form of Chaney.
Cheyney

Chi (Chinese) younger generation.
(Nigerian) personal guardian angel.

Chick (English) a familiar form of Charles.
Chic, Chickie, Chicky

Chico (Spanish) boy.

Chik (Gypsy) earth.
Chic, Chyc, Chyk

Chike (Ibo) God's power.

Chiko (Japanese) arrow; pledge.
Chyko

Chilo (Spanish) a familiar form of
Francisco.
Chylo

Chilton (English) farm by the spring.
*Chil, Chill, Chillton, Chilt, Chiltown,
Chylt, Chylton*

Chim (Vietnamese) bird.
Chym

Chinua (Ibo) God's blessing.
*Chino, Chinou, Chinuah, Chynua,
Chynuah*

Chioke (Ibo) gift of God.
Chyoke

Chip (English) a familiar form of Charles.
Chipman, Chipp, Chyp, Chypp

Chipper (English) a form of Chip.

Chippia (Australian) duck.
*Chipia, Chipiah, Chippiah, Chippya,
Chipya, Chipyah, Chypia, Chypiah,
Chyppia, Chyppiah, Chyppya, Chyppyah,
Chypya, Chypyah*

Chiram (Hebrew) exalted; noble.
Chyram

Chris (Greek) a short form of Christian,
Christopher. See also Kris.
*Chriss, Christ, Chrys, Chryss, Cris, Criss,
Crist*

Christain (Greek) a form of Christian.
Christai, Christane, Christaun, Christein

Christan, Christen, Christin (Greek)
forms of Christian.
Christensen

Christapher (Greek) a form of
Christopher.

Christian (Greek) follower of Christ;
anointed. See also Cristian, Jaan, Kerstan,
Khristian, Kit, Krister, Kristian, Krystian.
*Chretien, Christa, Christé, Christiaan,
Christiana, Christiane, Christiann,
Christianna, Christianno, Christiano,
Christianos, Christino, Christion, Christon,
Christyan, Christyon, Chritian, Chrystian,
Crystek*

Christien (Greek) a form of Christian.
Christienne, Christinne, Chrystien

Christofer, Christoffer (Greek) forms of
Christopher.
*Christafer, Christaffer, Christaffur, Christafur,
Christefor, Christeffor, Christerfer, Christifer,
Christofher, Christoforo, Christofper,
Chrystofer*

Christoff (Russian) a form of
Christopher.
*Chrisof, Chrisstof, Chrisstoff, Christif,
Christof, Cristofe*

Christoper (Greek) a form of Christopher.
Christopehr

Christoph, Christophe (French) forms
of Christopher.
Chrisstoph, Chrisstophe

Christopher (Greek) Christ-bearer.
Religion: the patron saint of travelers.
See also Cristopher, Kester, Kit,
Kristopher, Risto, Stoffel, Tobal, Topher.
Chrisopherson, Christepher, Christerpher,
Christhoper, Christipher, Christobal,
Christoher, Christopherr, Christophor,
Christophr, Christophre, Christophyer,
Christophyr, Christorpher, Christovao,
Christpher, Christphere, Christphor,
Christpor, Christrpher, Chrystopher

Christophoros (Greek) a form of
Christopher.
Christoforos, Christophor, Christophorus,
Christphor

Christos (Greek) a form of Christopher.
See also Khristos.
Cristos

Chrysander (Greek) golden.
Chrisander, Chrisandor, Chrisandre,
Chrysandor, Chrysandre

Chucho (Hebrew) a familiar form of
Jesus.

Chuck (American) a familiar form of
Charles.
Chuckee, Chuckey, Chucki, Chuckie,
Chucky, Chuk, Chuki, Chukie, Chuky

Chui (Swahili) leopard.

Chul (Korean) firm.

Chuma (Ibo) having many beads, wealthy.
(Swahili) iron.

Chuminga (Spanish) a familiar form of
Dominic.
Chumin, Chumingah

Chumo (Spanish) a familiar form of
Thomas.

Chun (Chinese) spring.

Chung (Chinese) intelligent.
Chungo, Chuong

Churchill (English) church on the hill.
History: Sir Winston Churchill served as
British prime minister and won a Nobel
Prize for literature.
Churchil, Churchyl, Churchyll

Cian (Irish) ancient.
Céin, Cianán, Cyan, Kian

Ciaran (Irish) black; little.

Cicero (Latin) chickpea. History: a
famous Roman orator, philosopher, and
statesman.
Cicerón, Cicerone, Ciceroni, Cyro

Cid (Spanish) lord. History: title for
Rodrigo Díaz de Vivar, an eleventh-
century Spanish soldier and national hero.
Cidd, Cyd, Cydd

Ciqala (Dakota) little.

Cirilo, Cirrillo (Italian) forms of Cyril.
Cirilio Cirillo, Cyrilo, Cyryllo, Cyrylo

Ciro (Italian) a form of Cyril. (Persian) a
form of Cyrus. (Latin) a form of Cicero.

Cisco (Spanish) a short form of
Francisco.
Cisca, Cysco

Clancey (Irish) a form of Clancy.

Clancy (Irish) redheaded fighter.
Clance, Clancee, Clanci, Clancie, Claney,
Clanse, Clansee, Clansey, Clansi, Clansie,
Clansy

Clare (Latin) a short form of Clarence.
Clair, Clarey, Clary

Clarence (Latin) clear; victorious.
Clarance, Clare, Clarin, Clarince, Claronce,
Clarrance, Clarrence, Clarynce, Clearence

Clark (French) cleric; scholar.
Clarke, Clerc, Clerk

Claude (Latin, French) lame.
Claud, Claudan, Claudanus, Claudel,
Claudell, Claudey, Claudi, Claudian,
Claudianus, Claudie, Claudien, Claudin,
Claudis, Claudy

Claudio (Italian) a form of Claude.

Claudius (German, Dutch) a form of
Claude.
Claudios, Klaudius

Claus (German) a short form of
Nicholas. See also Klaus.
Claas, Claes, Clause

Clay (English) clay pit. A short form of
Clayborne, Clayton.
Clae, Clai, Klay

Clayborne (English) brook near the clay
pit.
*Claeborn, Claeborne, Claebourn,
Claebourne, Claeburn, Claeburne, Claibern,
Claiborn, Claiborne, Claibrone, Claiburn,
Claiburne, Claybon, Clayborn, Claybourn,
Claybourne, Clayburn, Clayburne, Clebourn*

Clayton (English) town built on clay.
*Claeton, Claiton, Clayten, Cleighton,
Cleyton, Clyton, Klayton*

Cleary (Irish) learned.
Clearey, Cleari, Clearie

Cleavon (English) cliff.
*Clavin, Clavion, Clavon, Clavone, Clayvon,
Claywon, Cleavan, Cleaven, Cleavin,
Cleavon, Cleavyn, Clevan, Cleven, Clevin,
Clévon, Clevonn, Clevyn, Clyvon*

Clem (Latin) a short form of Clement.
Cleme, Clemmy, Clim

Clemence (French) a form of Clement.
Clemens

Clement (Latin) merciful. Bible: a
coworker of Paul. See also Klement,
Menz.
Clément, Clementius, Clemmons

Clemente (Italian, Spanish) a form of
Clement.
Clemento, Clemenza

Cleo (Greek) a form of Clio (see Girls'
Names).

Cleon (Greek) famous.
Kleon

Cletus (Greek) illustrious. History: a
Roman pope and martyr.
Cleatus, Cledis, Cleotis, Clete, Cletis, Cleytus

Cleve (English) a short form of
Cleveland. A form of Clive.
Cleave, Cleeve, Clevey, Clevie

Cleveland (English) land of cliffs.
*Cleaveland, Cleavland, Clevelend,
Clevelynn*

Cliff (English) a short form of Clifford,
Clifton.
*Clif, Cliffe, Clift, Clyf, Clyfe, Clyff, Clyffe,
Clyph, Kliff*

Clifford (English) cliff at the river crossing.
Cliford, Clyfford, Clyford, Klifford

Clifton (English) cliff town.
Cliffton, Clift, Cliften, Clyffton, Clyfton

Clint (English) a short form of Clinton.
Clynt, Klint

Clinton (English) hill town.
*Clenten, Clindon, Clintan, Clinten,
Clintin, Clintion, Clintton, Clyndon,
Clynten, Clyntin, Clynton, Clynttan,
Klinton*

Clive (English) a form of Cliff.
*Cleiv, Cleive, Cliv, Clivans, Clivens, Clyv,
Clyve, Klyve*

Clovis (German) famous soldier. See also
Louis.
Clovys

Cluny (Irish) meadow.
Clunee, Cluney, Cluni, Clunie

Clyde (Welsh) warm. (Scottish)
Geography: a river in Scotland.
Clide, Cly, Clyd, Clywd, Klyde

Coady (English) a form of Cody.

Cobi, Coby (Hebrew) familiar forms of
Jacob.
*Cob, Cobby, Cobe, Cobee, Cobey, Cobia,
Cobie*

Coburn (English) meeting of streams.
*Cobern, Coberne, Cobirn, Cobirne, Cobourn,
Cobourne, Coburne, Cobyrn, Cobyrne*

Cochise (Apache) hardwood. History: a
famous Chiricahua Apache leader.
Cochyse

Coco (French) a familiar form of Jacques.
Coko, Koko

Codey, Codi, Codie (English) forms of
Cody.
Coadi, Coday, Codea, Code, Codee

Cody (English) cushion. History: William "Buffalo Bill" Cody was an American frontier scout who toured America and Europe with his Wild West show. See also Kodey.
Coddy, Codell, Codiak, Coedy

Coffie (Ewe) born on Friday.
Cofi, Cofie

Cola (Italian) a familiar form of Nicholas, Nicola.
Colah, Colas, Kola

Colar (French) a form of Nicholas.

Colbert (English) famous seafarer.
Calbert, Calburt, Colburt, Colvert, Culbert, Culvert

Colbey (English) a form of Colby.

Colby (English) dark; dark haired.
Colbee, Colbi, Colbie, Colbin, Colebee, Coleby, Collby

Cole (Latin) cabbage farmer. (English) a short form of Colbert, Coleman. (Greek) a short form of Nicholas.
Coal, Coale, Col, Colet, Colie, Kole

Coleman (Latin) cabbage farmer. (English) coal miner.
Colemann, Colm, Koleman

Colen, Colyn (Greek, Irish) forms of Colin.

Coley (Greek, Latin, English) a familiar form of Cole. (English) a form of Colley.

Colin (Irish) young cub. (Greek) a short form of Nicholas.
Cailean, Colan, Coleon, Colinn, Kolin

Collen (Scottish) a form of Collin.

Colley (English) black haired; swarthy.
Colea, Colee, Coleigh, Coley, Coli, Colie, Collea, Collee, Colleigh, Colli, Collie, Collis, Colly, Coly

Collier (English) miner.
Colier, Collayer, Collie, Collyer, Colyer

Collin (Scottish) a form of Colin, Collins.
Collan, Collian, Collon, Collyn

Collins (Greek) son of Colin. (Irish) holly.
Colins, Collis, Collyns, Colyns

Colman (Latin, English) a form of Coleman.
Colmann

Colson (Greek, English) son of Nicholas.
Colsan, Colsen, Colsin, Colsyn, Coulson

Colt (English) young horse; frisky. A short form of Colbert, Colter, Colton.
Colte, Kolt

Coltan, Colten, Coltin, Coltyn (English) forms of Colton.
Coltinn, Colttan, Coltyne

Colter (English) herd of colts.
Kolter

Colton (English) coal town.
Coltn, Coltrane, Coltton, Coltun, Kolton

Columba (Latin) dove.
Coim, Colum, Columb, Columbah, Columbas, Columbia, Columbias, Columbus

Colwyn (Welsh) Geography: a river in Wales.
Colwin, Colwinn, Colwyne, Colwynn, Colwynne

Coman (Arabic) noble. (Irish) bent.
Cománn, Comin, Comyn

Conall (Irish) high, mighty.
Conal, Conel, Conell, Conelle, Connal, Connall, Connolly

Conan (Irish) praised; exalted. (Scottish) wise.
Conant, Conary, Connen, Connon, Conon, Konan

Conary (Irish) a form of Conan.
Conaire

Conlan (Irish) hero.
Conlen, Conlin, Conlon, Conlyn

Conley (Irish) a form of Conlan.

Connar, Conner (Irish) forms of Connor.
Connary, Conneer, Connery, Konner

Connell (Irish) a form of Conall.
Connel, Connelle, Connelly

Connie (English, Irish) a familiar form of Conan, Conrad, Constantine, Conway.
Con, Conn, Conney, Conny

Connor (Scottish) wise. (Irish) a form of Conan.
Connoer, Connory, Connyr, Konner, Konnor

Conor (Irish) a form of Connor.
Conar, Coner, Conour, Konner

Conrad (German) brave counselor.
Coenraad, Conrade, Konrad

Conrado (Spanish) a form of Conrad.
Corrado, Currado

Conroy (Irish) wise.
Conroi, Conry, Roy

Constant (Latin) a short form of Constantine.
Constante

Constantine (Latin) firm, constant. History: Constantine the Great was the Roman emperor who adopted the Christian faith. See also Dinos, Konstantin, Stancio.
Considine, Constadine, Constandine, Constandios, Constanstine, Constant, Constantin, Constantinos, Constantinus, Constantios, Costa, Costandinos, Costantinos

Constantino (Latin) a form of Constantine.

Conway (Irish) hound of the plain.
Conwai, Conwy

Cook (English) cook.
Cooke, Cooki, Cookie, Cooky

Cooper (English) barrel maker. See also Keifer.
Coop, Couper, Kooper, Kuepper

Corban, Corben (Latin) forms of Corbin.

Corbett (Latin) raven.
Corbbitt, Corbet, Corbette, Corbit, Corbitt, Korbet, Korbett

Corbin (Latin) raven.
Corbon, Corbyn, Korbin

Corby (Latin) a familiar form of Corbett, Corbin.
Corbey, Corbie

Corcoran (Irish) ruddy.

Cord (French) a short form of Cordell, Cordero.

Cordarius (Spanish) a form of Cordero.
Cordarious, Cordarrius, Cordarus

Cordaro (Spanish) a form of Cordero.
Coradaro, Cordairo, Cordara, Cordarel, Cordarell, Cordarelle, Cordareo, Cordarin, Cordario, Cordarion, Cordarrel, Cordarrell, Cordarris, Cordarro, Cordarrol, Cordarryl, Cordaryal, Corddarro, Corrdarl

Cordel (French) a form of Cordell.
Cordele

Cordell (French) rope maker.
Cordae, Cordale, Corday, Cordeal, Cordeil, Cordelle, Cordie, Cordy, Kordell

Cordero (Spanish) little lamb.
Cordaro, Cordeal, Cordeara, Cordearo, Cordeiro, Cordelro, Corder, Cordera, Corderall, Corderias, Corderious, Corderral, Corderro, Corderryn, Corderun, Corderus, Cordiaro, Cordierre, Cordy, Corrderio, Corrderyo

Corey (Irish) hollow. See also Korey, Kory.
Core, Corea, Coree, Corian, Corio, Cory

Cori, Corie (Irish) forms of Corey.

Corin (Irish) a form of Corrin.
Coren, Corion, Coryn, Korin, Koryn

Corliss (English) cheerful; goodhearted.

Cormac (Irish) raven's son. History: a third-century king of Ireland who was a great lawmaker.
Cormack, Cormick

Cornelius (Greek) cornel tree. (Latin) horn colored. See also Kornel, Kornelius, Nelek.
Carnelius, Conny, Cornealous, Corneili, Corneilius, Corneille, Corneilus, Cornelias, Corneliaus, Cornelious, Cornelis, Corneliu, Cornellious, Cornellis, Cornellius, Cornellus, Cornelous, Corneluis, Cornelus, Corney, Cornie, Cornielius, Corniellus, Corny, Cournelius, Cournelyous, Nelius, Nellie

Cornell (French) a form of Cornelius.
Cornall, Corneil, Cornel, Cornelio, Corney, Cornie, Corny, Nellie

Cornwallis (English) from Cornwall.
Cornwalis

Corrado (Italian) a form of Conrad.
Carrado

Corrigan (Irish) spearman.
Carrigan, Carrigen, Corigan, Corogan,
Corrigon, Corrigun, Corrogun, Korrigan

Corrin (Irish) spear carrier.
Corrion, Corren, Corryn, Korrin, Korryn

Corry (Latin) a form of Corey.
Corree, Correy, Corria, Corrie, Corrye

Cort (German) bold. (Scandinavian) short.
(English) a short form of Courtney.
Corte, Cortie, Corty, Court, Kort

Cortez (Spanish) conqueror. History:
Hernando Cortés was a Spanish con-
quistador who conquered Aztec
Mexico.
Cartez, Cortes, Cortis, Cortize, Courtes,
Courtez, Curtez, Kortez

Cortland (English) a form of Courtland.

Cortney (English) a form of Courtney.
Cortnay, Cortne, Kortney

Corwin (English) heart's companion;
heart's delight.
Corwinn, Corwyn, Corwyne, Corwynn,
Corwynne, Korwin, Korwyn, Korwynn

Cory (Latin) a form of Corey. (French)
a familiar form of Cornell. (Greek) a
short form of Corydon.
Corye

Corydon (Greek) helmet, crest.
Coridan, Coriden, Coridon, Coridyn,
Corradino, Coryden, Corydin, Corydyn,
Coryell, Korydon

Cosgrove (Irish) victor, champion.

Cosme (Greek) a form of Cosmo.
Cosmé

Cosmo (Greek) orderly; harmonious;
universe.
Cos, Cosimo, Cosma, Cosmas, Cosmos,
Cozmo, Kosmo

Costa (Greek) a short form of
Constantine.
Costah, Costas, Costes

Coty (French) slope, hillside.
Cote, Cotee, Cotey, Coti, Cotie, Cottee,
Cottey, Cotti, Cottie, Cotty, Cotye

Coulter (English) a form of Colter.

Courtland (English) court's land.
Court, Courtlan, Courtlana, Courtlandt,
Courtlin, Courtlind, Courtlon, Courtlyn,
Kourtland

Courtney (English) court.
Court, Courten, Courtenay, Courteney,
Courtnay, Courtnee

Cowan (Irish) hillside hollow.
Coe, Coven, Covin, Cowen, Cowey, Cowie,
Cowin, Cowyn

Coy (English) woods.
Coi, Coye, Coyie, Coyt

Coyle (Irish) leader in battle.
Coil, Coile

Coyne (French) modest.
Coine, Coyan, Coyn

Craddock (Welsh) love.
Caradoc, Caradog, Craddoc, Craddoch,
Cradoc, Cradoch, Cradock

Craig (Irish, Scottish) crag; steep rock.
Craeg, Craege, Craegg, Crag, Craige, Craigen,
Craigery, Craigg, Craigh, Craigon, Crayg,
Crayge, Craygg, Creag, Creage, Creg,
Cregan, Cregg, Creig, Creigh, Creyg,
Creyge, Creygg, Criag, Crieg, Criege,
Criegg, Kraig

Cramer (English) full.
Crammer, Kramer, Krammer

Crandall (English) crane's valley.
Cran, Crandal, Crandel, Crandell, Crendal

Crane (English) crane.
Crain, Craine, Crayn, Crayne

Cranston (English) crane's town.
Crainston, Craynston

Crawford (English) ford where crows fly.
Craw, Crow, Crowford, Ford

Creed (Latin) belief.
Creeden, Creedin, Creedon, Creedyn

Creighton (English) town near the rocks.
(Welsh) a form of Crichton.
Craighton, Cray, Crayton, Creigh, Creight,
Creighto, Creightown, Crichtyn

Crepin (French) a form of Crispin.
Crepyn

Crevan (Irish) fox.
Creven, Crevin, Crevon, Crevyn

Crichton (Welsh) from the town on the
hill.
Crighton, Cryghton

Crisiant (Welsh) crystal.
Crisient, Crisyant, Crysiant, Crysyant,
Krisiant

Crispin (Latin) curly haired.
Crepin, Cris, Crispian, Crispien, Crispino,
Crispo, Crispyn, Cryspyn, Krispin

Cristian (Greek) a form of Christian.
Crétien, Cristean, Cristhian, Cristiano,
Cristien, Cristino, Cristle, Criston, Cristos,
Cristy, Cristyan, Crystek, Crystian

Cristo (Greek) a form of Cristopher.

Cristobal (Greek) a form of Christopher.
Cristóbal, Cristoval, Cristovao

Cristofer (Greek) a form of Christopher.

Cristoforo (Italian) a form of Christopher.
Christoforo, Christophoro, Cristofor

Cristopher (Greek) a form of Christopher.
Cristaph, Cristhofer, Cristifer, Cristoph,
Cristophe, Crystapher, Crysteffer, Crysteffor,
Crystifer

Crofton (Irish) town with cottages.
Krofton

Cromwell (English) crooked spring,
winding spring.
Cromwel, Cromwill, Cromwyl, Cromwyll

Crosby (Scandinavian) shrine of the cross.
Crosbee, Crosbey, Crosbi, Crosbie, Cross

Crosley (English) meadow of the cross.
Croslea, Croslee, Crosleigh, Crosli, Croslie,
Crosly, Cross

Crowther (English) fiddler.

Cruz (Portuguese, Spanish) cross.
Cruze, Cruzz, Kruz

Crystek (Polish) a form of Christian.

Crystian (Polish) a form of Christian.

Cuauhtemoc (Nahuatl) descending eagle.

Cuba (Spanish) tub. Geography: the
largest island country in the Carribean.

Cullan (Irish) a form of Cullen.

Cullen (Irish) handsome.
Culen, Cull, Cullin, Culyn

Culley (Irish) woods.
Culea, Culee, Culey, Culi, Culie, Cullea,
Cullee, Culleigh, Culli, Cullie, Cully, Culy

Culver (English) dove.
Colvar, Colver, Cull, Culvar

Cunningham (Irish) village of the milk
pail.

Curran (Irish) hero.
Curan, Curon, Curr, Curren, Currin, Curron

Currito (Spanish) a form of Curtis.
Curcio

Curry (Irish) a familiar form of Curran.
Currey, Curri, Currie

Curt (Latin) a short form of Courtney,
Curtis. See also Kurt.
Court

Curtis (Latin) enclosure. (French) courte-
ous. See also Kurtis.
Courtis, Courtys, Curio, Currito, Curtice,
Curtus, Curtys

Curtiss (Latin, French) a form of Curtis.
Curtyss

Cuthbert (English) brilliant.
Cuthberte, Cuthburt

Cutler (English) knife maker.
Cut, Cutlir, Cutlor, Cuttie, Cutty, Kutler

Cutter (English) tailor.

Cy (Persian) a short form of Cyrus.
Ci

Cyle (Irish) a form of Kyle.

Cynan (Welsh) chief.
*Cinan, Cinen, Cinin, Cinon, Cinyn,
Cynin, Cynon, Cynyn*

Cyprian (Latin) from the island of Cyprus.
*Ciprian, Cipriano, Ciprien, Cyprianus,
Cyprien, Cyprryan*

Cyrano (Greek) from Cyrene, an ancient
city in North Africa. Literature: *Cyrano
de Bergerac* is a play by Edmond Rostand
about a great guardsman and poet
whose large nose prevented him from
pursuing the woman he loved.
Cirano

Cyril (Greek) lordly. See also Kiril.
*Cerek, Cerel, Ceril, Ciril, Cirill, Cirille,
Cirrillo, Cyra, Cyrel, Cyrell, Cyrelle, Cyrill,
Cyrille, Cyrillus, Cyryl, Syrell, Syril*

Cyrus (Persian) sun. Historial: Cyrus the
Great was a king in ancient Persia. See
also Kir.
Cyress, Cyris, Cyriss, Cyruss, Syris, Syrus

D

D Andre (American) a form of Deandre.

D'andre (American) forms of Dandre,
Deandre.
D'andrea, D'Andre, D'andré,

D'angelo (American) a form of Dangelo,
Deangelo.
D'Angleo

D'ante (American) a form of Dante.
D'Ante, D'anté

D'anthony (American) a form of
Deanthony.
D'Anthony

D'arcy (American) a form of Darcy.
D'Aray, D'Arcy

D'juan, Djuan (American) forms of
Dajuan, Dejuan.
D'Juan

D'marco (American) a form of Damarco,
Demarco.
D'Marco

D'marcus (American) a form of
Damarcus, Demarcus.
D'Marcus

D'quan (American) a form of Daquan,
Dequan.
D'Quan

D'vonte (American) a form of Davonte,
Devonte.
D'Vonte, D'vonté

Da Quan, Da'quan (American) forms of
Daquan.

Da'shawn (American) a form of
Dashawn.
Da'shaun, Da'shon

Da'von (American) a form of Davon.

Dabi (Basque) a form of David.
Dabee, Dabey, Dabie, Daby

Dabir (Arabic) tutor.
Dabar, Daber, Dabor, Dabyr

Dacey (Latin) from Dacia, an area now in
Romania. (Irish) southerner.
*Dace, Dacee, Dache, Daci, Dacian, Dacias,
Dacie, Dacio, Dacy, Daice, Daicey, Daici,
Daicie, Daicy, Dayce, Daycee, Daycey,
Dayci, Daycie, Daycy*

Dacoda (Dakota) a form of Dakota.
Dacodah

Dacota, Dacotah (Dakota) forms of
Dakota.
Dac, Dack, Dackota, DaCota

Dada (Yoruba) curly haired.
Dadah, Dadi

Daegan (Irish) black haired.
*Daegen, Daegin, Daegon, Daegyn, Daigan,
Daigen, Daigin, Daigon, Daigyn, Daygan,
Daygen, Daygin, Daygon, Daygyn*

Daegel (English) from Daegel, England.
Daigel, Daygel

Daelen (English) a form of Dale.
*Daelan, Daelen, Daelin, Daelon, Daelyn,
Daelyne*

Daemon (Greek) a form of Damian.
(Greek, Latin) a form of Damon.
Daemen, Daemeon, Daemien, Daemin, Daemion, Daemiyn, Daemond, Daemyen

Daequan (American) a form of Daquan.
Daekwaun, Daekwon, Daequane, Daequon, Daequone, Daeqwan

Daeshawn (American) a combination of the prefix Da + Shawn.
Daesean, Daeshaun, Daeshon, Daeshun, Daisean, Daishaun, Daishawn, Daishon, Daishoun

Daevon (American) a form of Davon.
Daevion, Daevohn, Daevonne, Daevonte, Daevontey

Dafydd (Welsh) a form of David.
Dafid, Dafidd, Dafyd

Dag (Scandinavian) day; bright.
Daeg, Dagen, Dagny, Deegan

Dagan (Hebrew) corn; grain.
Dagen, Dageon, Dagin, Dagon, Dagyn

Dagwood (English) shining forest.

Dai (Japanese) big.
Dae, Dai, Daie, Daye

Daimian (Greek) a form of Damian.
Daemean, Daemian, Daiman, Daimean, Daimen, Daimien, Daimin, Daimiyn, Daimyan

Daimon (Greek, Latin) a form of Damon.
Daimeon, Daimeyon, Daimion, Daimone

Dain (Scandinavian) a form of Dana.
(English) a form of Dane.
Daine

Daiquan (American) a form of Daquan.
Daiqone, Daiqua, Daiquane, Daiquawn, Daiquon, Daiqwan, Daiqwon

Daivon (American) a form of Davon.
Daivain, Daivion, Daivonn, Daivonte, Daiwan

Dajon (American) a form of Dajuan.
Dajean, Dajiawn, Dajin, Dajion, Dajn, Dajohn, Dajonae

Dajuan (American) a combination of the prefix Da + Juan.
Da Jon, Da-Juan, Daejon, Daejuan, Dajwan, Dajwoun, Dakuan, Dakwan, Dawaun, Dawawn, Dawon, Dawoyan, Dijuan, Diuan, Dwaun

Dakarai (Shona) happy.
Dakairi, Dakar, Dakara, Dakaraia

Dakari (Shona) a form of Dakarai.
Dakarri

Dakoda (Dakota) a form of Dakota.
Dakodah, Dakodas

Dakota (Dakota) friend; partner; tribal name.
Dak, Dakcota, Dakkota, Dakoata, Dakotha, Dakotta, Dekota

Dakotah (Dakota) a form of Dakota.
Dakottah

Daksh (Hindi) efficient.
Dakshi

Dalal (Sanskrit) broker.

Dalan, Dalen, Dalon, Dalyn (English) forms of Dale.
Dailan, Dailen, Dalaan, Dalain, Dalane, Daleon, Dalian, Dalibor, Dalione

Dalbert (English) bright, shining. See also Delbert.
Dalbirt, Dalburt, Dalbyrt

Dale (English) dale, valley.
Dael, Dail, Daile, Dal, Daley, Dalibor, Daly, Dayl, Dayle

Daley (Irish) assembly. (English) a familiar form of Dale.
Daily, Daly, Dawley

Dalin (English) a form of Dallin.

Dallan, Dallen (English) forms of Dalan, Dallin.

Dallas (Scottish) valley of the water; resting place. Geography: a town in Scotland; a city in Texas.
Dal, Dalieass, Dall, Dalles, Dallus, Dallys, Dalys, Dellis

Dallin, Dallyn (English) pride's people.
Daelin, Dailin, Dalyn

Dallis (Scottish) a form of Dallas.

Dallon (English) a form of Dallan, Dalston.

Dalman (Australian) bountiful place.
*Dallman, Dallmen, Dallmin, Dallmon,
Dallmyn, Dalmen, Dalmin, Dalmon,
Dalmyn*

Dalphin (French) dolphin.
*Dalphine, Dalphyn, Dalphyne, Delphin,
Delphine, Delphyn, Delphyne, Dolphine,
Dolphyn*

Dalston (English) Daegel's place.
Dalis, Dallston

Dalton (English) town in the valley.
*Dal, Dalaton, Dalltan, Dallten, Dalltin,
Dallton, Dalltyn, Dalt, Daltan, Dalten,
Daltin, Daltyn, Delton*

Dalvin (English) a form of Delvin.
Dalven, Dalvon, Dalvyn

Dalziel (Scottish) small field.
Dalzil, Dalzyel, Dalzyl

Damain (Greek) a form of Damian.
Damaian, Damaine, Damaion

Daman, Damen, Damin (Greek, Latin)
forms of Damon.

Damani (Greek) a form of Damian.
Damanni

Damar (American) a short form of
Damarcus, Damario.
Damare, Damari, Damarre, Damauri

Damarco (American) a form of
Damarcus. (Italian) a form of Demarco.
Damarkco, Damarko, Damarrco

Damarcus (American) a combination of
the prefix Da + Marcus. A form of
Demarcus.
*Damacus, Damarcius, Damarcue,
Damarques, Damarquez, Damarquis*

Damario (Greek) gentle. (American) a
combination of the prefix Da + Mario.
*Damarea, Damareus, Damaria, Damarie,
Damarino, Damarion, Damarrea,
Damarrion, Damaryo*

Damarius (Greek, American) a form of
Damario.

*Damarious, Damaris, Damarrious,
Damarrius, Dameris, Damerius*

Damarkus (American) a form of
Damarcus.
Damarick, Damark, Damarkis

Damein (Greek) a form of Damian.

Dameion, Dameon (Greek) forms of
Damian.
Dameone

Damek (Slavic) a form of Adam.
Damick, Damicke, Damik, Damyk

Dametri (Greek) a form of Dametrius,
Demetrius.
Damitré, Damitri, Damitrie

Dametrius (Greek) a form of Demetrius.
*Dametries, Dametrious, Damitric,
Damitrious, Damitrius*

Damian (Greek) tamer; soother.
*Damaiaon, Damaien, Damaun, Damayon,
Dame, Damean, Damián, Damiane,
Damiann, Damiano, Damianos, Damiyan,
Damján, Damyan, Damyen, Damyin,
Damyyn, Daymian, Dema, Demyan*

Damien, Damion (Greek) forms of
Damian. Religion: Father Damien min-
istered to the leper colony on the
Hawaiian island Molokai.
*Daemien, Damie, Damienne, Damieon,
Damiion, Damine, Damionne, Damiyon,
Dammion, Damyen, Damyon*

Damon (Greek) constant, loyal. (Latin)
spirit, demon.
Damoni, Damonn, Damonni, Damyn

Damond (Greek, Latin) a form of Damon.

Damone (Greek, Latin) a form of Damon.

Damonta (Greek, Latin) a form of
Damon.
Damontis

Damonte (Greek, Latin) a form of
Damon.
Damontae, Damontez

Dan (Vietnamese) yes. (Hebrew) a short
form of Daniel.
Dahn, Danh, Dann, Danne

Dana (Scandinavian) from Denmark.
Daina, Danah, Dayna

Dandin (Hindi) holy man.
Dandan, Danden, Dandon, Dandyn

Dandre (French) a combination of the prefix De + Andre.
Dandrae, Dandras, Dandray, Dandrea, Dondrea

Dandré (French) a form of Dandre.

Dane (English) from Denmark. See also Halden.
Daen, Daene, Danie, Dhane

Danek (Polish) a form of Daniel.

Danforth (English) a form of Daniel.

Dang (Italian) a short form of Deangelo.

Dangelo (Italian) a form of Deangelo.

Danial (Hebrew) a form of Daniel.
Danal, Daneal, Danieal, Daniyal, Dannal, Dannial

Danick, Danik, Dannick (Slavic) familiar forms of Daniel.
Danek, Danieko, Danika, Danyck

Daniel (Hebrew) God is my judge. Bible: a Hebrew prophet. See also Danno, Kanaiela, Taniel.
Dacso, Dainel, Dan'l, Daneel, Daneil, Danel, Dániel, Daniël, Danielius, Daniell, Daniels, Danielson, Danukas, Dasco, Deniel, Doneal, Doniel, Donois, Nelo

Daniele, Danielle (Hebrew) forms of Daniel.
Danile, Danniele

Danilo (Slavic) a form of Daniel.
Danielo, Danil, Danila, Danilka, Danylo

Danior (Gypsy) born with teeth.
Danyor

Danish (English) from Denmark.

Danladi (Hausa) born on Sunday.
Danladee, Danladey, Danladie, Danlady

Dannie, Danny, Dany (Hebrew) familiar forms of Daniel.
Danee, Daney, Dani, Danie, Dannee, Danney, Danni, Dannye

Danniel (Hebrew) a form of Daniel.
Dannel, Dannil

Danno (Japanese) gathering in the meadow. (Hebrew) a familiar form of Daniel.
Dano

Dannon (American) a form of Danno.
Daenan, Daenen, Dainon, Danaan, Danen, Dannan, Dannen, Dannin, Dannyn, Danon, Danyn

Dano (Czech) a form of Daniel.
Danko

Dantae (Latin) a form of Dante.

Dante, Danté (Latin) lasting, enduring.
Danatay, Danaté, Dant, Dantay, Dantee, Dauntay, Dauntaye, Daunté, Dauntrae

Danton (American) a form of Deanthony.

Dantrell (American) a combination of Dante + Darell.
Dantrel, Dantrey, Dantril, Dantyrell

Danyel (Hebrew) a form of Daniel.
Daniyel, Danya, Danyal, Danyale, Danyele, Danyell, Danyiel, Danyil, Danyill, Danyl, Danyle, Danylets, Danyll, Danylo, Donyell

Danzel (Cornish) a form of Denzell.
Danzell

Daoud (Arabic) a form of Daniel, David.
Daudi, Daudy, Dauod, Dawud

Daquan (American) a combination of the prefix Da + Quan.
Daquandre, Daquandrey, Daquann, Daquantae, Daquante, Daquaun, Daquawn, Daquin, Daquwon, Daqwain, Daqwan, Daqwann, Daqwone

Daquane (American) a form of Daquan.
Daquain, Daquaine, Daqwane

Daquarius (American) a form of Daquan.

Daquon (American) a form of Daquan.
Daqon, Daquone, Daqwon

Dar (Hebrew) pearl.
Darr

Dara (Cambodian) stars.
Darah

Daran, Darin, Daron, Darrin, Darron, Darryn, Daryn (Irish, English) forms of Darren.
Daaron, Daeron, Dairon, Darann, Darawn, Darone, Daronn, Darran, Darroun, Darynn, Dayran, Dayrin, Dayron, Dearin, Dearon, Deran, Dharin, Dharon, Diron

Darby (Irish) free. (English) deer park.
Dar, Darb, Darbe, Darbee, Darbey, Darbi, Darbie, Derbe, Derbee, Derbey, Derbi, Derbie, Derby

Darcy (Irish) dark. (French) from Arcy, France.
Dar, Daray, Darce, Darcee, Darcel, Darcey, Darci, Darcie, Darcio, Darse, Darsee, Darsey, Darsi, Darsie, Darsy

Dareh (Persian) wealthy.
Dare

Darek, Darick, Darik, Darrick (German) forms of Derek.
Darec, Dareck, Daric, Darico, Darieck, Dariek, Darrec, Darrek, Darric, Darrik, Darryc, Darryck, Darryk, Daryk

Darell, Darrel (English) forms of Darrell.
Daral, Darall, Daralle, Dareal, Darel, Darelle, Darol

Daren (Hausa) born at night. (Irish, English) a form of Darren.
Daran, Dare, Dayren, Dheren

Dareon (Irish, English) a form of Darren.
Daryeon, Daryon

Darian, Darien, Darion, Darrian, Darrien, Darrion (Irish, English) forms of Darren.
Dairean, Dairion, Darrione, Darriun, Darriyun, Daryan, Derrion

Dariel (French) a form of Darrell.

Dario (Spanish) affluent.
Daryo

Darious, Darrious, Darrius (Greek) forms of Darius.
Darreus, Darrias, Darriuss, Darryus, Derrious, Derrius

Daris, Darris (Greek) short forms of Darius.
Darrus, Derris

Darius (Greek) wealthy.
Dairus, Darieus, Darioush, Dariuse, Dariush, Dariuss, Dariusz, Darrias, Darrios, Darrus, Darus, Daryos, Daryus

Darkon (English) dark.
Darkan, Darken, Darkin, Darkun, Darkyn

Darnel, Darnelle (English) forms of Darnell.
Darnele

Darnell (English) hidden place.
Dar, Darn, Darnall, Darneal, Darneil, Darnyell, Darnyll

Darrell (French) darling, beloved; grove of oak trees.
Dare, Darral, Darrall, Darril, Darrill, Darrol

Darren (Irish) great. (English) small; rocky hill.
Dare, Darran, Darrience, Darun, Dearron

Darryl, Daryl, Daryle (French) forms of Darrell.
Dahrll, Daril, Darl, Darly, Daroyl, Darryle, Darryll, Daryell, Daryll, Darylle, Derryl

Darshan (Sanskrit) philosophy; seeing clearly.
Darshaun, Darshen, Darshin, Darshon, Darshyn

Darton (English) deer town.
Dartan, Dartel, Darten, Dartin, Dartrel, Dartyn

Darvell (English) eagle town.
Darvel, Darvele, Darvelle, Darvil, Darvile, Darvill, Darville, Darvyl, Darvyle, Darvyll

Darvin (English) a form of Darwin.
Darvan, Darven, Darvon, Darvyn

Darwin (English) dear friend. History: Charles Darwin was the British naturalist who established the theory of evolution.
Darwen, Darwyn

Dasan (Pomo) leader of the bird clan.
Dasen, Dasin, Dason, Dassan, Dasyn

Dasean, Dashaun, Dashon (American) forms of Dashawn, Deshawn.

Dashawn (American) a combination of the prefix Da + Shawn.
Dashan, Dashane, Dashante, Dashaunte, Dashean, Dashonnie, Dashonte, Dashuan, Dashun, Dashwan

Dat (Vietnamese) accomplished.

Dauid (Swahili) a form of David.
Dawud

Daulton (English) a form of Dalton.

Davante, Davanté (American) forms of Davonte.
Davanta, Davantay, Davinte

Davaris (American) a combination of Dave + Darius.
Davario, Davarious, Davarius, Davarrius, Davarus

Davaughn (American) a combination of the prefix Da + Vaughn.

Dave (Hebrew) a short form of David, Davis.

Daven (Hebrew) a form of David. (Scandinavian) a form of Davin.

Daveon (American) a form of Davin.
Deaveon

Davey, Davy (Hebrew) familiar forms of David.
Davee, Davi, Davie

Davian, Davion (American) forms of Davin.
Davione, Davionne, Daviyon, Davyon

David (Hebrew) beloved. Bible: the second king of Israel. See also Dov, Havika, Kawika, Taaveti, Taffy, Taved, Tevel.
Dabi, Daevid, Daevyd, Dafydd, Dai, Daived, Daivid, Daivyd, Dauid, Dav, Daved, Daveed, Davidd, Davidde, Davide, Davidek, Davido, Davood, Davoud, Davyd, Davydas, Davydd, Davyde, Dayvid, Deved, Devid, Devidd, Devidde, Devyd, Devydd, Devydde, Devod, Devodd, Dodya

David Alexander (American) a combination of David + Alexander.
David-Alexander, Davidalexander

Davidson (Welsh) a form of Davis.
Davison, Davyson

Davin (Scandinavian) brilliant Finn.
Daevin, Davan, Davyn, Deavan, Deaven

Davis (Welsh) son of David.
Davies, Davys

Davon (American) a form of Davin.
Davone, Davonn, Davonne, Deavon, Deavone

Davonta (American) a form of Davonte.
Davontah

Davontae, Davontay, Davonté (American) forms of Davonte.
Davontai, Davontaye

Davonte (American) a combination of Davon + the suffix Te.
Davonnte, Davontea, Davontee, Davonti

Dawan (American) a form of Dajuan, Davin.
Dawann, Dawante, Dawaun, Dawin, Dawine, Dawon, Dawone, Dawoon, Dawyne, Dawyun

Dawid (Polish) a form of David.
Dawed, Dawud

Dawit (Ethiopian) a form of David.
Dawyt

Dawson (English) son of David.
Dawsan, Dawsen, Dawsin, Dawsyn, Dayson

Dax (French, English) water.

Daylan, Daylen, Daylin, Daylon (American) forms of Dalan, Dillon.
Daelon, Dailon, Daylun, Daylyn

Daymian (Greek) a form of Damian.
Daymayne, Daymeon, Daymiane, Daymien, Dayminn, Daymion, Daymn

Daymon (Greek, Latin) a form of Damon.
Dayman, Daymen, Daymin

Daymond (Greek, Latin) a form of Damon.

Dayne (Scandinavian) a form of Dane.
Dayn

Dayquan (American) a form of Daquan.
Dayquain, Dayquawane, Dayquin, Dayqwan

Dayshawn (American) a form of Dashawn.
Daysean, Daysen, Dayshaun, Dayshon, Dayson

Dayton (English) day town; bright, sunny town.
Daeton, Daiton, Daythan, Daython, Daytonn, Deyton

Daytona (English) a form of Dayton.
Daytonah

Dayvon (American) a form of Davin.
Dayven, Dayveon, Dayvin, Dayvion, Dayvonn

De (Chinese) virtuous.

De Andre, Deandré, Déandre (American) forms of Deandre.
De André, De Andrea, De Aundre, Déandrea

De Marcus, Démarcus (American) forms of Demarcus.

De Vante, Devanté, Dévante (American) forms of Devante.
De Vantae, De Vanté, Dévanté

Deacon (Greek) one who serves.
Deakin, Deicon, Deke, Deycon

Dean (French) leader. (English) valley. See also Dino.
Deane, Deen, Deene, Dene, Deyn, Deyne, Dyn, Dyne

Deandra (French) a form of Deandre.
Deaundera, Deaundra

Deandre (French) a combination of the prefix De + Andre.
Deandrae, Deandres, Deandrey, Deeandre, Deiandre, Deyandre, Dondre

Deandrea (French) a form of Deandre.

Deangelo (Italian) a combination of the prefix De + Angelo.
De Angelo, Danglo, Deaengelo, Deangelio, Deangello, Deangilio, Deangleo, Deanglo, Deangulo, Di'angelo, Diangelo, Diangello, Dyangello, Dyangelo

Déangelo (American) a form of Deangelo.

Deante, Deanté (Latin) forms of Dante, Deonte.
De Anté, Deanta, Deantai, Deantay, Deanteé, Deaunta

Deanthony (Italian) a combination of the prefix De + Anthony.
Dianthony

Déanthony (American) a form of Deanthony.

Dearborn (English) deer brook.
Dearborne, Dearbourn, Dearbourne, Dearburne, Deaurburn, Deerborn, Deerborne, Deerbourn, Deerbourne

Deaundre (French) a form of Deandre.
Deaundray, Deaundrey, Deaundry

Deaven (Hindi, Irish) a form of Deven.

Decarlos (Spanish) a combination of the prefix De + Carlos.
Dacarlo, Dacarlos, Decarlo, Dicarlo, Di'carlos

Decha (Tai) strong.
Dechah

Decimus (Latin) tenth.
Decymus

Declan (Irish) man of prayer. Religion: Saint Declan was a fifth-century Irish bishop.
Daclan, Deklan, Diclan, Dyclan

Dedric (German) a form of Dedrick.
Dederic, Dedryc, Detric

Dedrick (German) ruler of the people. See also Derek, Theodoric.
Deadric, Deadrick, Deadrik, Deddrick, Dederick, Dederik, Dedrek, Dedreko, Dedrix, Dedrrick, Dedryck, Dedryk, Deedrick, Detrik, Diedrich

Deems (English) judge's child.
Deam, Deim, Deym, Deyms

Deepak (Hindi) a form of Dipak.

Deion (Greek) a form of Deon, Dion.
Deione, Deionta, Deionte

Deiondre (American) a form of Deandre.
Deiondray, Deiondré

Deionte (American) a form of Deontae.
Deiontae, Deionté

Dejon, Déjon (American) forms of Dejuan.

Dejuan (American) a combination of the prefix De + Juan.
D'Won, Dejan, Dejuane, Dejun, Dijuan

Dekel (Hebrew, Arabic) palm tree, date tree.
Dekal, Dekil, Dekyl

Dekota (Dakota) a form of Dakota.
Decoda, Dekoda, Dekodda, Dekotes

Del (English) a short form of Delbert, Delvin, Delwin.

Delaney (Irish) descendant of the challenger.
Delaine, Delainey, Delaini, Delainie, Delainy, Delan, Delane, Delanny, Delany

Delano (French) nut tree. (Irish) dark.
Delanio, Delayno, Dellano

Delbert (English) bright as day. See also Dalbert.
Bert, Delbirt, Delburt, Delbyrt, Dilbert

Delfino (Latin) dolphin.
Delfin, Delfine, Delfyn, Delfyne, Delfyno, Delphino, Delphyno

Délì (Chinese) virtuous.

Dell (English) small valley. A short form of Udell.

Delling (Scandinavian) scintillating.

Delmar (Latin) sea.
Dalmar, Dalmer, Delmare, Delmario, Delmarr, Delmer, Delmor, Delmore

Delmon (French) mountain.
Delman, Delmen, Delmin, Delmyn

Delon (American) a form of Dillon.
Deloin, Delone, Deloni, Delonne

Delroy (French) belonging to the king. See also Elroy, Leroy.
Dalroi, Dalroy, Delray, Delree, Delroi

Delshawn (American) a combination of Del + Shawn.
Delsean, Delshon, Delsin, Delson

Delsin (Native American) he is so.
Delsan, Delsen, Delson, Delsyn

Delton (English) a form of Dalton.
Deltan, Delten, Deltin, Deltyn

Delvin (English) proud friend; friend from the valley.
Dalvyn, Delavan, Delvian, Delvyn

Delvon (English) a form of Delvin.

Delvonte (American) a form of Delvon.

Delwin (English) a form of Delvin.
Dalwin, Dalwyn, Dellwin, Dellwyn, Delwyn, Delwynn

Deman (Dutch) man.
Demann

Demarco (Italian) a combination of the prefix De + Marco.
Demarcco, Demarceo, Demarcio, Demarquo

Demarcus (American) a combination of the prefix De + Marcus.
Demarces, Demarcis, Demarcius, Demarcos, Demarcuse, Demarqus

Demarea (Italian) a form of Demario.
Demaree, Demareo, Demaria, Demariea

Demario (Italian) a combination of the prefix De + Mario.
Demari, Demariez, Demaris, Demarreio, Demarrio, Demaryo, Demerio, Demerrio

Demarion (Italian) a form of Demario.

Demarious (Italian) a form of Demario.
Demariuz

Demarius (American) a combination of the prefix De + Marius.

Demarko (Italian) a form of Demarco.
Demarkco, Demarkeo, Demarkes, Demarkis, Demarkos

Demarkus (Italian, American) a form of Demarco, Demarcus.

Demarquis (American) a combination of the prefix De + Marquis.
Demarques, Demarquez, Demarqui

Dembe (Luganda) peaceful.
Damba

Demetre, Demetri (Greek) short forms of Demetrius.
Demeter, Demetrea, Demetriel, Domotor

Demetric, Demetrick (Greek) forms of Demetrius.
Demeatric, Demetrics, Demetrik

Demetrice (Greek) a form of Demetrius.
Demeatrice

Demetrio (Greek) a form of Demetrius.

Demetrios (Greek) a form of Demetrius.

Demetrious (Greek) a form of Demetrius.

Demetris (Greek) a short form of Demetrius.
Demeatris, Demetres, Demetress, Demetricus, Demitrez, Demitries, Demitris

Demetrius (Greek) lover of the earth. Mythology: a follower of Demeter, the goddess of the harvest. See also Dimitri, Mimis, Mitsos.
Demeitrius, Demeterious, Demetreus, Demetrias, Demetriu, Demetrium, Demetrois, Demetrus, Demetryus, Demtrius, Demtrus, Dmetrius, Dymek, Dymetrias, Dymetrius, Dymetriys, Dymetryas, Dymetryus

Demetruis (Greek) a form of Demetrius.

Demichael (American) a combination of the prefix De + Michael.
Dumichael

Demitri (Greek) a short form of Demetrius.
Demitre, Demitrie

Demitrius (Greek) a form of Demetrius.
Demitirus, Demitrias, Demitriu, Demitrus,

Demon (Greek) demon.

Demond (Irish) a short form of Desmond.
Demonde, Demonds, Demone, Dumonde

Demondre (American) a form of Demond.

Demont (French) mountain.
Démont, Demontaz, Demontez

Demonta (American) a form of Demont.

Demontae, Demonte, Demonté (American) forms of Demont.
Demontay

Demontre (American) a form of Demont.

Demorris (American) a combination of the prefix De + Morris.
Demoris, DeMorris, Demorus

Demos (Greek) people.
Demas, Demous

Demothi (Native American) talks while walking.
Demoth

Dempsey (Irish) proud.
Demp, Demps, Dempsi, Dempsie, Dempsy

Dempster (English) one who judges.
Dempstar, Demster

Denham (English) village in the valley.
Denhem

Denholm (Scottish) Geography: a town in Scotland.

Denis, Deniz, Dennys (Greek) forms of Dennis.
Denas, Denes, Dénes, Denies, Denise, Denys, Dinis, Diniss, Dynis, Dyniss, Dynys, Dynyss

Denley (English) meadow; valley.
Denlea, Denlee, Denli, Denlie, Denly

Denman (English) man from the valley.
Denmen

Dennis (Greek) Mythology: a follower of Dionysus, the god of wine. See also Dion, Nicho.
Dannis, Dannys, Dennas, Dennes, Dennet, Dennez, Denya

Dennison (English) son of Dennis. See also Dyson, Tennyson.
Denison, Denisson, Dennyson, Denyson

Denny (Greek) a familiar form of Dennis.
Den, Deni, Denie, Denney, Denni, Dennie, Deny

Denton (English) happy home.
Dent, Denten, Dentin, Dentown

Denver (English) green valley. Geography: the capital of Colorado.
Denvor

Denzel, Denzil (Cornish) forms of Denzell.
Dennzil, Dennzyl, Denzial, Denziel, Denzill, Denzille, Denzyel, Denzyl, Denzyll, Denzylle

Denzell (Cornish) Geography: a location in Cornwall, England.
Dennzel, Denzal, Denzale, Denzall, Denzalle, Denzelle, Denzle, Denzsel

Deon (Greek) a form of Dennis. See also Dion.
Deone, Deonn, Deonno

Deondra (French) a form of Deandre.

Deondre, Deondré (French) forms of Deandre.
Deondrae, Deondray, Deondrea, Deondree, Deondrei, Deondrey

Deonta, Deontá (American) forms of Deontae.

Deontae (American) a combination of the prefix De + Dontae.
Deontai, Deontea, Deonteya, Deonteye, Deontia

Deontay, Deonte, Deonté, Déonte (American) forms of Deontae.
Deontaye, Deontée, Deontie

Deontrae, Deontray, Deontre (American) forms of Deontae.
Deontrais, Deontrea, Deontrey, Deontrez, Deontreze, Deontrus

Dequan (American) a combination of the prefix De + Quan.
Dequain, Dequane, Dequann, Dequaun, Dequawn, Dequian, Dequin, Dequine,

Dequinn, Dequion, Dequoin, Dequon, Deqwan, Deqwon, Deqwone

Déquan (American) a form of Dequan.

Dequante (American) a form of Dequan.
Dequantez, Dequantis

Dequavius (American) a form of Dequan.

Dereck, Deric, Derick, Derik, Derreck, Derrek, Derric, Derrick, Derrik, Deryck, Deryk (German) forms of Derek.
Derec, Derekk, Dericka, Derico, Deriek, Derikk, Derique, Derrec, Derreck, Derric, Derryc, Derryck, Derryk, Deryc, Deryke, Detrek, Dyrryc, Dyrryck, Dyrryk, Dyryc, Dyryck, Dyryck

Derek (German) a short form of Theodoric. See also Dedrick, Dirk.
Derak, Derecke, Derele, Derk, Derke, Deryek

Derian, Derion, Derrian, Derrion (Irish, English) forms of Darren.
Dereon, Derreon, Derrien, Deryan, Deryon

Derius, Derrius (Greek) forms of Darius
Deriues, Derrious, Derryus, Deryus

Dermot (Irish) free from envy. (English) free. (Hebrew) a short form of Jeremiah. See also Kermit.
Der, Dermod, Dermont, Dermott, Diarmid, Diarmuid

Deron (Hebrew) bird; freedom. (American) a combination of the prefix De + Ron.
Dereon, Deronn, Deronne, Derrin, Derronn, Derronne, Derryn, Deryn, Diron, Dyron

Deror (Hebrew) lover of freedom.
Derori, Derorie

Derrell (French) a form of Darrell.
Derel, Derele, Derell, Derelle, Derrel, Dérrell, Derriel, Derril, Derrill

Derren (Irish, English) a form of Darren.
Deren, Derran, Derraun, Derrin, Derryn, Deryn

Derron (Irish, English) a form of Darren. (Hebrew, American) a form of Deron.

Derry (Irish) redhead. Geography: a city in Northern Ireland.
Darrie, Darry, Deri, Derie, Derri, Derrie, Derrye, Dery

Derryl (French) a form of Darryl.
Deryl, Deryle, Deryll, Derylle

Derward (English) deer keeper.
Derwood, Dirward, Durward, Dyrward

Derwin (English) a form of Darwin.
Dervin, Dervon, Dervyn, Dervyne, Derwen, Derwyn, Derwyne, Derwynn, Durwin, Durwyn, Durwyne

Desean (American) a combination of the prefix De + Sean.
D'Sean, Dusean, Dysean

Désean (American) a form of Desean.

Deshane (American) a combination of the prefix De + Shane.
Deshan, Deshayne

Deshaun (American) a combination of the prefix De + Shaun.
Deshan, Deshane, Deshann, Deshaon, Deshaune, D'Shaun, D'shaun, Dushaun, Dyshaun

Déshaun (American) a form of Deshaun.

Deshawn (American) a combination of the prefix De + Shawn.
Deshauwn, Deshawan, Deshawon, D'Shawn, D'shawn, Dyshawn

Déshawn (American) a form of Deshawn.

Deshea (American) a combination of the prefix De + Shea.
Deshay

Déshì (Chinese) virtuous.

Deshon (American) a form of Deshawn.
Deshondre, Deshone, Deshonn, Deshonte, Dyshon, Dyshone, Dyshyn, Dyshyne

Deshun (American) a form of Deshon.
Deshunn

Desi (Latin) desiring. (Irish) a short form of Desmond.
Dezi

Desiderio (Spanish) desired.
Desideryo

Desmon (Irish) a form of Desmond.
Desimon, Desman, Desmane, Desmen, Desmine, Desmyn

Desmond (Irish) from south Munster.
Des, Desmand, Desmound, Desmund

Destin (French) destiny, fate.
Destan, Desten, Destine, Deston, Destun, Destyn

Destry (American) a form of Destin.
Destrey, Destrie

Detrick (German) a form of Dedrick.
Detrek, Detric, Detrich, Detrik, Detrix

Deuce (Latin) two; devil.

Devan, Devyn (Irish) forms of Devin.
Deavan, Deavyn, Devaan, Devain, Devane, Devann, Devean, Devun, Devyin, Devynn, Devynne, Diwan

Devanta (American) a form of Devante.

Devante (American) a combination of Devan + the suffix Te.
Devantae, Devantay, Devantée, Devantez, Devanty, Devaunte, Deventae, Deventay, Devente, Divante

Devaughn (American) a form of Devin.
Devaugh, Devaughntae, Devaughnte

Devaun (American) a form of Devaughn.

Devayne (American) a form of Dewayne.
Devain, Devaine, Devane, Devayn, Devein, Deveion

Deven (Hindi) for God. (Irish) a form of Devin.
Deiven, Devein, Devenn, Devven, Diven, Dyven

Deveon (American) a form of Devon.
Deveone

Deverell (English) riverbank.

Devin (Irish) poet.
Deavin, Deivin, Dev, Devinn, Devvin, Devy, Dyvon

Devine (Latin) divine. (Irish) ox.
Devyne, Dewine

Devion (American) a form of Devon.

Devlin (Irish) brave, fierce.
Dev, Devlan, Devland, Devlen, Devlon

Devlyn (Irish) a form of Devlin.

Devon, Dévon, Devonne (American)
forms of Davon. (Irish) forms of Devin.
*Deavon, Deivon, Devoen, Devohn,
Devonae, Devoni, Devonio, Devonn,
Devontaine, Devun, Devvon, Devvonne,
Dewon, Dewone, Divon, Diwon*

Devone (Irish, American) a form of
Devon.
Deivone, Deivonne

Devonta (American) a combination of
Devon + the suffix Ta.
*Deveonta, Devonnta, Devonntae, Devontai,
Devontay, Devontaye*

Devontá, Dévonta (American) forms of
Devonta.

Devontae, Devontay, Devonté
(American) forms of Devonte.

Devonte (American) a combination of
Devon + the suffix Te.
*Deveonte, Devionte, Devontea, Devontee,
Devonti, Devontia, Devontre*

Dewan (American) a form of Dejuan,
Dewayne.
Dewaun, Dewaune, Dewon

Dewayne (American) a combination of
the prefix De + Wayne. (Irish) a form
of Dwayne.
*Deuwayne, Devayne, Dewain, Dewaine,
Dewane, Dewayen, Dewean, Dewune*

Dewei (Chinese) highly virtuous.

Dewey (Welsh) prized.
Dew, Dewi, Dewie, Dewy

DeWitt (Flemish) blond.
Dewit, Dewitt, Dewyt, Dewytt, Wit

Dexter (Latin) dexterous, adroit. (English)
fabric dyer.
*Daxter, Decca, Deck, Decka, Dekka, Dex,
Dextar, Dextor, Dextrel, Dextron, Dextur*

Deyonte (American) a form of Deontae.

Dezmon (Irish) a form of Desmond.
Dezman, Dezmen, Dezmin

Dezmond (Irish) a form of Desmond.
Dezmand, Dezmund

Diamante, Diamonte (Spanish) forms of
Diamond.
*Diamanta, Diamont, Diamonta, Dimonta,
Dimontae, Dimonte*

Diamond (English) brilliant gem; bright
guardian.
*Diaman, Diamend, Diamenn, Diamund,
Dimond, Dymond*

Diandre (French) a form of Deandre.

Diante, Dianté (American) forms of
Deontae.
Diantae, Diantey

Dick (German) a short form of
Frederick, Richard.
*Dic, Dicken, Dickens, Dickie, Dickon,
Dicky, Dik*

Dickran (Armenian) History: an ancient
Armenian king.
Dicran, Dikran

Dickson (English) son of Dick.
Dickenson, Dickerson, Dikerson, Diksan

Didi (Hebrew) a familiar form of
Jedidiah, Yedidya.

Didier (French) desired, longed for.

Diedrich (German) a form of Dedrick,
Dietrich.
Didrich, Didrick, Didrik, Didyer, Diederick

Diego (Spanish) a form of Jacob, James.
Diaz

Dietbald (German) a form of Theobald.
Dietbalt, Dietbolt

Dieter (German) army of the people.
Deiter, Deyter

Dietrich (German) a form of Dedrick.
*Deitrich, Deitrick, Deke, Didric, Didrick,
Diedrich, Diedrick, Diedrik, Dierck, Dieter,
Dieterich, Dieterick, Dietric, Dietrick, Dietz,
Ditrik*

Digby (Irish) ditch town; dike town.
Digbe, Digbee, Digbey, Digbi, Digbie

Dijon (French) Geography: a city in
France. (American) a form of Dejon.

Dilan, Dillan, Dillen, Dillyn (Irish) forms
of Dillon.
Dilun, Dilyan

Dillian, Dillion (Irish) forms of Dillon.

Dillon (Irish) loyal, faithful. See also Dylan.
*Dil, Dill, Dillie, Dilly, Dillyn, Dilon,
Dilyn, Dilynn*

Dilwyn (Welsh) shady place.
Dillwin, Dillwyn, Dilwin

Dima (Russian) a familiar form of
Vladimir.
Dimah, Dimka, Dyma, Dymah

Dimitri (Russian) a short form of
Demetrius.
*Dimetra, Dimetri, Dimetric, Dimetrie,
Dimitr, Dimitric, Dimitrie, Dimitrij,
Dimitrik, Dimitris, Dimitry, Dimmy,
Dymetree, Dymetrey, Dymetri, Dymetrie,
Dymitr, Dymitry*

Dimitrios (Greek) a form of Demetrius.
Dhimitrios, Dimos, Dmitrios

Dimitrius (Greek) a form of Demetrius.
Dimetrius, Dimetrus, Dimitricus, Dmitrius

Dingbang (Chinese) protector of the
country.

Dinh (Vietnamese) calm, peaceful.
Din, Dyn, Dynh

Dino (German) little sword. (Italian) a
form of Dean.
Deano, Dyno

Dinos (Greek) a familiar form of
Constantine, Konstantin.
Dynos

Dinsmore (Irish) fortified hill.
*Dinmoar, Dinmoor, Dinmoore, Dinmor,
Dinmore, Dinnie, Dinny, Dinse, Dinsmoor,
Dinsmoore, Dynmoar, Dynmoor, Dynmoore,
Dynmor, Dynmore*

Diogenes (Greek) honest. History: an
ancient philosopher who searched with
a lantern in daylight for an honest man.
Diogenese

Dion (Greek) a short form of Dennis,
Dionysus.
Dio, Dionigi, Dionis, Dionn, Dyon, Dyone

Diondre (French) a form of Deandre.
Diondra, Diondrae, Diondrey

Dione, Dionne (American) forms of
Dion.

Dionicio (Spanish) a form of Dionysus.

Dionta (American) a form of Deontae.

Diontae, Diontay, Dionte, Dionté
(American) forms of Deontae.
Diontaye, Diontea

Dionysus (Greek) celebration.
Mythology: the god of wine.
*Dionesios, Dionisio, Dionisios, Dionusios,
Dionysios, Dionysius, Dyonisios, Dyonisus*

Dipak (Hindi) little lamp. Religion:
another name for the Hindu god Kama.

Diquan (American) a combination of the
prefix Di + Quan.
Diqawan, Diqawn, Diquane

Dirk (German) a short form of Derek,
Theodoric.
*Derc, Derk, Dirc, Dirck, Dirke, Durc, Durk,
Dyrc, Dyrck, Dyrk, Dyrrc, Dyrrck, Dyrrk*

Dixon (English) son of Dick.
*Dix, Dixan, Dixen, Dixin, Dixyn, Dyxan,
Dyxen, Dyxin, Dyxon, Dyxyn*

Dmitri, Dmitry (Russian) forms of
Dimitri.
Dmetriy, Dmitiri, Dmitrik, Dmitriy

Doane (English) low, rolling hills.
Doan

Dob (English) a familiar form of Robert.
Dobie

Dobry (Polish) good.
Dobri, Dobrie

Doherty (Irish) harmful.
Docherty, Dougherty, Douherty

Dolan (Irish) dark haired.
Dolin, Dollan, Dolyn

Dolf, Dolph (German) short forms of
Adolf, Adolph, Rudolf, Rudolph.
*Dolfe, Dolff, Dolffe, Dolfi, Dolphe, Dolphus,
Dulph, Dulphe*

Dom (Latin) a short form of Dominic.
Dome, Domm, Domó

Domanic (Latin) a form of Dominic.
Domanick

Domenic, Domenick (Latin) forms of
Dominic.
Domenik, Domenyc, Domenyck, Domenyk

Domenico (Italian) a form of Dominic.
*Demenico, Domicio, Dominico, Dominiko,
Menico*

Domingo (Spanish) born on Sunday. See
also Mingo.
Demingo, Domingos, Domyngo

Dominic (Latin) belonging to the Lord.
See also Chuminga.
*Deco, Dom, Domeka, Domini, Dominie,
Dominitric, Dominy, Domminic,
Domnenique, Domokos, Nick*

Dominick, Dominik (Latin) forms of
Dominic.
*Domiku, Domineck, Dominicke, Dominiek,
Dominnick, Dominyck, Dominyk,
Domminick, Dommonick, Domnick,
Donek, Dumin*

Dominique, Dominque (French) forms
of Dominic.
*Domeniq, Domeniqu, Domenique,
Domenque, Dominiqu, Dominiqueia,
Domnenique, Domnique, Domoniqu,
Domonique, Domunique*

Domokos (Hungarian) a form of
Dominic.
Dedo, Dome, Domek, Domok, Domonkos

Domonic, Domonick (Latin) forms of
Dominic.
Domonik

Don (Scottish) a short form of Donald.
See also Kona.
Donn

Donahue (Irish) dark warrior.
*Donahu, Donahugh, Donehue, Donohoe,
Donohu, Donohue, Donohugh*

Donal (Irish) a form of Donald.
Dónal, Donall, Donil

Donald (Scottish) world leader; proud
ruler. See also Bohdan, Tauno.
*Donalt, Donát, Donaugh, Doneld, Donild,
Donyld*

Donaldo (Spanish) a form of Donald.

Donatien (French) gift.
Donathan, Donathon, Donatyen

Donato (Italian) gift.
*Dodek, Donatello, Donati, Donatien,
Donatus, Doneto*

Donavan, Donavin, Donavon (Irish)
forms of Donovan.
Donaven, Donavyn

Dondre, Dondré (American) forms of
Deandre.
Dondra, Dondrae, Dondray, Dondrea

Donell (Irish) a form of Donnell.
*Doneal, Donel, Donele, Donelle, Doniel,
Donielle, Donyl*

Dong (Vietnamese) easterner.
Duong

Donivan (Irish) a form of Donovan.
Donnivan

Donkor (Akan) humble.

Donnell (Irish) brave; dark.
*Donnel, Donnele, Donnelle, Donniel,
Donnyl*

Donnelly (Irish) a form of Donnell.
Donelly, Donlee, Donley

Donnie, Donny (Irish) familiar forms of
Donald.
*Donee, Doney, Doni, Donie, Donnee,
Donney, Donni, Dony*

Donovan (Irish) dark warrior.
*Dohnovan, Donevan, Donevin, Donevon,
Donnovan, Donnoven, Donoven, Donovin,
Donvan, Donyvon*

Donovon (Irish) a form of Donovan.

Donta (American) a form of Dante.

Dontae, Dontay, Donte, Donté (Latin) forms of Dante.
Dontai, Dontao, Dontate, Dontaye, Dontea, Dontee

Dontarious, Dontarius (American) forms of Dontae.

Dontavious, Dontavius (American) forms of Dontae.

Dontavis (American) a form of Dontae.

Dontez (American) a form of Dontae.

Dontray, Dontre (American) forms of Dontrell.

Dontrell (American) a form of Dantrell.
Dontral, Dontrall, Dontreal, Dontrel, Dontrelle, Dontriel, Dontriell

Donyell (Irish) a form of Donnell.
Donyel

Donzell (Cornish) a form of Denzell.
Donzeil, Donzel, Donzelle, Donzello

Dooley (Irish) dark hero.
Doolea, Doolee, Dooleigh, Dooli, Doolie, Dooly

Dor (Hebrew) generation.

Doran (Greek, Hebrew) gift. (Irish) stranger; exile.
Dore, Doren, Dorin, Doron, Dorran, Dorren, Dorrin, Dorron, Dorryn, Doryn

Dorian (Greek) from Doris, Greece. See also Isidore.
Dore, Dorey, Dorie, Dorján, Dorrion, Dorryen, Dorryn, Dory

Dorien, Dorion, Dorrian (Greek) forms of Dorian.
Dorrien

Dorrell (Scottish) king's doorkeeper. See also Durell.
Dorrel, Dorrelle,

Dotan (Hebrew) law.
Dothan

Doug (Scottish) a short form of Dougal, Douglas.
Douge, Dougee, Dougey, Dougi, Dougie, Dougy, Dug, Dugee, Dugey, Dugi, Dugie, Dugy

Dougal (Scottish) dark stranger. See also Doyle.
Doogal, Doogall, Dougall, Dugal, Dugald, Dugall, Dughall

Douglas (Scottish) dark river, dark stream. See also Koukalaka.
Dougles, Dugaid, Dughlas

Douglass (Scottish) a form of Douglas.
Duglass

Dov (Yiddish) bear. (Hebrew) a familiar form of David.
Dove, Dovi, Dovidas, Dowid

Dovev (Hebrew) whisper.

Dovid (Hebrew, Yiddish) a form of Dov.

Dow (Irish) dark haired.

Doyle (Irish) a form of Dougal.
Doial, Doiale, Doiall, Doil, Doile, Doy, Doyal, Doyel, Doyele, Doyell, Doyelle

Drago (Italian) a form of Drake.

Drake (English) dragon; owner of the inn with the dragon trademark.
Draek, Draik, Draike, Drayk, Drayke

Draper (English) fabric maker.
Draeper, Draiper, Dray, Drayper, Draypr

Draven (American) a combination of the letter D + Raven.
Dravian, Dravin, Dravion, Dravon, Dravone, Dravyn, Drayven

Dre (American) a short form of Andre, Deandre.
Drae, Dray, Dré

Dreng (Norwegian) hired hand; brave.

Drequan (American) a combination of Drew + Quan.

Dréquan (American) a form of Drequan.

Dreshawn (American) a combination of Drew + Shawn.
Dreshaun, Dreshon, Dreshown

Drevon (American) a form of Draven.
Drevan, Drevaun, Dreven, Drevin, Drevion, Drevone

Drew (Welsh) wise. (English) a short form of Andrew.
Drewe

Drey (American) a form of Dre.

Driscoll (Irish) interpreter.
Driscol, Driscole, Dryscol, Dryscoll, Dryscolle

Dru, Drue (English) forms of Drew.
Druan, Drud, Drugi, Drui

Drummond (Scottish) druid's mountain.
Drummund, Drumond, Drumund

Drury (French) loving. Geography: Drury Lane is a street in London's theater district.
Druree, Drurey, Druri, Drurie

Dryden (English) dry valley.
Dridan, Driden, Dridin, Dridyn, Dry, Drydan, Drydin, Drydon, Drydyn

Duane (Irish) a form of Dwayne.
Deune, Duain, Duaine, Duana

Duarte (Portuguese) rich guard. See also Edward.
Duart

Dubham (Irish) black.
Dubhem, Dubhim, Dubhom, Dubhym

Dubric (English) dark ruler.
Dubrick, Dubrik, Dubryc, Dubryck, Dubryk

Duc (Vietnamese) moral.
Duoc

Duce (Latin) leader, commander.

Dudd (English) a short form of Dudley.
Dud, Dudde, Duddy

Dudley (English) common field.
Dudlea, Dudlee, Dudleigh, Dudli, Dudlie, Dudly

Duer (Scottish) heroic.

Duff (Scottish) dark.
Duf, Duffey, Duffie, Duffy

Dugan (Irish) dark.
Doogan, Doogen, Dougan, Dougen, Douggan, Douggen, Dugen, Duggan

Dujuan (American) a form of Dajuan, Dejuan.
Dujuane

Duke (French) leader; duke.
Duk, Dukey, Dukie, Duky

Dukker (Gypsy) fortuneteller.
Duker

Dulani (Nguni) cutting.
Dulanee, Dulaney, Dulanie, Dulany

Dumaka (Ibo) helping hand.

Duman (Turkish) misty, smoky.
Dumen, Dumin, Dumon, Dumyn

Duncan (Scottish) brown warrior. Literature: King Duncan was Macbeth's victim in Shakespeare's play *Macbeth*.
Doncan, Dunc, Dunkan

Dunham (Scottish) brown.
Dunhem

Dunixi (Basque) a form of Dionysus.

Dunley (English) hilly meadow.
Dunlea, Dunlee, Dunleigh, Dunli, Dunlie, Dunly

Dunlop (Scottish) muddy hill.
Dunlope

Dunmore (Scottish) fortress on the hill.
Dunmoar, Dunmoor, Dunmoore, Dunmor

Dunn (Scottish) a short form of Duncan.
Dun, Dune, Dunne

Dunstan (English) brownstone fortress.
Dun, Dunsten, Dunstin, Dunston, Dunstyn

Dunton (English) hill town.
Duntan, Dunten, Duntin, Duntyn

Dur (Hebrew) stacked up. (English) a short form of Durwin.

Duran (Latin) a form of Durant.

Durand (Latin) a form of Durant.

Durant (Latin) enduring.
Durance, Durand, Durante, Durontae, Durrant

Durell (Scottish, English) king's doorkeeper. See also Dorrell.
Durel, Durelle, Durial

Durko (Czech) a form of George.

Duron (Hebrew, American) a form of Deron.
Durron

Durrell (Scottish, English) a form of Durell.
Durrelle, Durreil

Durriken (Gypsy) fortuneteller.

Durril (Gypsy) gooseberry.
Duril, Durryl, Durryll, Duryl

Durward (English) gatekeeper.
Derward, Durwood, Ward

Durwin (English) a form of Darwin.

Dusan (Czech) lively, spirited. (Slavic) a form of Daniel.
Dusen, Dusin, Duson, Dusyn

Dushawn (American) a combination of the prefix Du + Shawn.
Dusean, Dushan, Dushane, Dushaun, Dushon, Dushun

Dustan, Dusten, Duston, Dustyn (German, English) forms of Dustin.

Dustin (German) valiant fighter. (English) brown rock quarry.
Dust, Dustain, Dustine, Dustion, Dustynn

Dusty (English) a familiar form of Dustin.
Dustee, Dustey, Dusti, Dustie

Dutch (Dutch) from the Netherlands; from Germany.

Duval (French) a combination of the prefix Du + Val.
Duvall, Duveuil, Duvyl

Duy (Vietnamese) a form of Duc.

Dwan (American) a form of Dajuan. (Irish) a form of Dwayne.

Dwaun (American) a form of Dajuan.
Dwaunn, Dwawn, Dwon, Dwuann

Dwayne (Irish) dark. See also Dewayne.
Dawayne, Dawyne, Duwain, Duwan, Duwane, Duwayn, Duwayne, Dwain, Dwaine, Dwane, Dwayn, Dwyane, Dywan, Dywane, Dywayne, Dywone

Dwight (English) a form of DeWitt.
Dwhite, Dwite, Dwyte

Dyami (Native American) soaring eagle.
Dyani

Dyer (English) fabric dyer.

Dyke (English) dike; ditch.
Dike

Dylan (Welsh) sea. See also Dillon.
Dylane, Dylann, Dylen, Dylian, Dyllen, Dyllian, Dyllyn, Dylyn

Dylin, Dyllan, Dyllon, Dylon (Welsh) forms of Dylan.
Dyllin, Dyllion

Dyre (Norwegian) dear heart.
Dire

Dyson (English) a short form of Dennison.
Dysen, Dysonn

Ea (Irish) a form of Hugh.
Eah

Eachan (Irish) horseman.
Eachen, Eachin, Eachon, Eachyn

Eagan (Irish) very mighty.

Eamon, Eamonn (Irish) forms of Edmond, Edmund.
Aimon, Eaman, Eamen, Eamin, Eamman, Eammen, Eammin, Eammon, Eammun, Eammyn, Eamun, Eamyn, Eiman, Eimen, Eimin, Eimon, Eimyn, Eyman, Eymen, Eymin, Eymon, Eymyn

Ean (English) a form of Ian.
Eaen, Eann, Eayon, Eon, Eonn, Eyan, Eyen, Eyon, Eyyn

Earl (Irish) pledge. (English) nobleman.
Airle, Earld, Earle, Earli, Earlie, Earlson, Early, Eorl, Erl, Erle

Earnest (English) a form of Ernest.
Earn, Earneste, Earnesto, Earnie, Eirnest, Eranest, Eyrnest

Easton (English) eastern town.
Eason, Eastan, Easten, Eastin, Eastton, Eastyn

Eaton (English) estate on the river.
Eatton, Eton, Eyton

Eb (Hebrew) a short form of Ebenezer.
Ebb, Ebbie, Ebby

Eben (Hebrew) rock.
Eban, Ebenn, Ebin, Ebyn

Ebenezer (Hebrew) foundation stone. Literature: Ebenezer Scrooge is a miserly character in Charles Dickens's *A Christmas Carol*.
Ebbaneza, Ebeneezer, Ebeneser, Ebenezar, Evanezer, Eveneser, Ibenezer

Eber (German) a short form of Eberhard.
Ebere

Eberhard (German) courageous as a boar. See also Everett.
Eberardo, Eberhardt, Evard, Everard, Everhardt, Everhart

Ebner (English) a form of Abner.
Ebnar, Ebnir, Ebnor, Ebnyr

Ebo (Fante) born on Tuesday.

Ebon (Hebrew) a form of Eben.

Ed (English) a short form of Edgar, Edsel, Edward.
Edd

Edan (Scottish) fire.
Eadan, Eadon, Edain, Edon, Edun

Edbert (English) wealthy; bright.
Ediberto

Eddie, Eddy (English) familiar forms of Edgar, Edsel, Edward.
Eddee, Eddi, Edi, Edie, Eddye, Edy

Edel (German) noble.
Adel, Edell, Edelmar, Edelweiss

Eden (Hebrew) delightful. Bible: the garden that was first home to Adam and Eve.
Eaden, Eadin, Eadyn, Edenson, Edyn, Eiden

Eder (Hebrew) flock.
Edar, Ederick, Edir, Edor, Edyr

Edgar (English) successful spearman. See also Garek, Gerik, Medgar.
Edek, Edgars, Edger, Edgir, Edgor

Edgard (English) a form of Edgar.

Edgardo (Spanish) a form of Edgar.

Edgerrin (American) a form of Edgar.

Edik (Slavic) a familiar form of Edward.
Edic, Edick

Edin (Hebrew) a form of Eden.

Edison (English) son of Edward.
Eddisen, Eddison, Eddisyn, Eddyson, Edisen, Edysen, Edyson

Edmond (English) a form of Edmund.
Edmen, Edmon, Edmonde, Edmondson, Edmynd, Esmond

Edmund (English) prosperous protector.
Eadmund, Edman, Edmand, Edmaund, Edmun, Edmunds

Edmundo (Spanish) a form of Edmund.
Edmando, Edmondo, Mundo

Edo (Czech) a form of Edward.

Edoardo (Italian) a form of Edward.

Edorta (Basque) a form of Edward.

Edouard (French) a form of Edward.
Édoard, Édouard

Edric (English) prosperous ruler.
Eddric, Eddrick, Eddrik, Eddryc, Eddryck, Eddryk, Ederic, Ederick, Ederik, Ederyc, Ederyck, Ederyk, Edrek, Edrice, Edrick, Edrico, Edrik, Edryc, Edryck, Edryk

Edsel (English) rich man's house.
Edsell

Edson (English) a short form of Edison.
Eddson, Edsen

Eduard (Spanish) a form of Edward.

Eduardo (Spanish) a form of Edward.

Edur (Basque) snow.
Edure

Edward (English) prosperous guardian.
See also Audie, Duarte, Ekewaka, Ned,
Ted, Teddy.
Edik, Edko, Edo, Edorta, Edus, Edvard,
Edvardo, Edwards, Edwy, Edzio, Etzio,
Ewart

Edwardo (Italian) a form of Edward.

Edwin (English) prosperous friend. See
also Ned, Ted.
Eadwin, Eadwinn, Edlin, Eduino, Edwan,
Edwen, Edwinn, Edwon, Edwyn, Edwynn

Efrain (Hebrew) fruitful.
Efraine, Efran, Efrane, Efrayin, Efrayn,
Efrayne, Efrian, Efrin, Efryn, Eifraine

Efrat (Hebrew) honored.

Efrem (Hebrew) a short form of Ephraim.
Efe, Efraim, Efrayim, Efrim, Efrum

Efren (Hebrew) a form of Efrain,
Ephraim.

Egan (Irish) ardent, fiery.
Egann, Egen, Egin, Egyn

Egbert (English) bright sword. See also
Bert, Bertie.
Egbirt, Egburt, Egbyrt

Egerton (English) Edgar's town.
Edgarton, Edgartown, Edgerton, Egeton

Egil (Norwegian) awe inspiring.
Egyl, Eigil, Eygel

Eginhard (German) power of the sword.
Eginhardt, Einhard, Einhardt, Egynhard,
Egynhardt, Enno

Egon (German) formidable.
Egun

Egor (Russian) a form of George. See
also Igor, Yegor.

Ehren (German) honorable.
Eren

Eian, Eion (Irish) forms of Ean, Ian.
Ein, Eine, Einn

Eikki (Finnish) ever powerful.
Eiki

Einar (Scandinavian) individualist.
Ejnar, Inar

Eitan (Hebrew) a form of Ethan.
Eita, Eithan, Eiton

Ejau (Ateso) we have received.

Ekewaka (Hawaiian) a form of Edward.

Ekon (Nigerian) strong.

Elam (Hebrew) highlands.
Elame

Elan (Hebrew) tree. (Native American)
friendly.
Elann

Elbert (English) a form of Albert.
Elberto, Elbirt, Elburt, Elbyrt

Elchanan (Hebrew) a form of John.
Elchan, Elchonon, Elhanan, Elhannan

Elden (English) a form of Alden, Aldous.
Eldan, Eldin, Eldun, Eldyn

Elder (English) dweller near the elder
trees.
Eldar, Eldir, Eldor, Eldyr

Eldon (English) holy hill. A form of
Elton.

Eldred (English) a form of Aldred.
Eldrid, Eldryd

Eldridge (English) a form of Aldrich.
El, Elderydg, Elderydge, Eldredge, Eldrege,
Eldrige, Elric, Elrick, Elrik

Eldwin (English) a form of Aldwin.
Eldwen, Eldwinn, Eldwyn, Eldwynn

Eleazar (Hebrew) God has helped. See
also Lazarus.
Elasar, Elasaro, Elazar, Elazaro, Eleasar,
Eléazar

Elek (Hungarian) a form of Alec, Alex.
Elec, Eleck, Elic, Elick, Elik, Elyc, Elyck,
Elyk

Elger (German) a form of Alger.
Elfar, Elgir, Elgor, Elgyr, Ellgar, Ellger

Elgin (English) noble; white.
Elgan, Elgen, Elgon, Elgyn

Eli (Hebrew) uplifted. A short form of Elijah, Elisha. Bible: the high priest who trained the prophet Samuel. See also Elliot.
Elay, Elier, Ellie

Elia (Zuni) a short form of Elijah.
Eliah, Eliya, Elya, Elyah

Elian (English) a form of Elijah. See also Trevelyan.
Elien, Elion, Elyan, Elyen, Elyin, Elyon, Elyn

Elias (Greek) a form of Elijah.
Elia, Eliasz, Elice, Eliyas, Ellias, Ellice, Ellis, Elyas, Elyes

Eliazar (Hebrew) a form of Eleazar.
Eliasar, Eliaser, Eliazer, Elizar, Elizardo

Elie (Hebrew) a form of Eli.

Eliezer (Hebrew) a form of Eleazar.
Elieser

Elihu (Hebrew) a short form of Eliyahu.
Elih, Eliu, Ellihu

Elijah (Hebrew) a form of Eliyahu. Bible: a Hebrew prophet. See also Eli, Elisha, Elliot, Ilias, Ilya.
El, Elija, Elijiah, Elijio, Elijuah, Elijuo, Eliya, Eliyah, Ellija, Ellijah, Ellyjah

Elijha (Hebrew) a form of Elijah.
Elisjsha

Elika (Hawaiian) a form of Eric.
Elyka

Elio (Zuni) a form of Elia. (English) a form of Elliot.

Eliot (English) a form of Elliot.
Eliott, Eliud, Eliut, Elyot, Elyott

Eliseo (Hebrew) a form of Elisha.
Elisee, Elisée, Elisei, Elisiah, Elisio

Elisha (Hebrew) God is my salvation. Bible: a Hebrew prophet, successor to Elijah. See also Eli, Elijah.
Elijsha, Elish, Elishah, Elisher, Elishia, Elishua, Elysha, Lisha

Eliyahu (Hebrew) the Lord is my God.
Eliyahou, Elihu

Elizabeth (Hebrew) consecrated to God.

Elkan (Hebrew) God is jealous.
Elkana, Elkanah, Elkin, Elkins, Elkyn, Elkyns

Elki (Moquelumnan) hanging over the top.
Elkie, Elky

Ellard (German) sacred; brave.
Allard, Elard, Ellerd

Ellery (English) from a surname derived from the name Hilary.
Elari, Elarie, Elery, Ellari, Ellarie, Ellary, Ellerey, Elleri, Ellerie

Elliot, Elliott (English) forms of Eli, Elijah.
Elliotte, Ellyot, Ellyott

Ellis (English) a form of Elias.
Elis, Ellys, Elys

Ellison (English) son of Ellis.
Elison, Ellson, Ellyson, Elson, Elyson

Ellsworth (English) nobleman's estate.
Ellswerth, Elsworth

Elman (German) like an elm tree.
Elmen

Elmer (English) noble; famous.
Aylmer, Elemér, Ellmer, Elmar, Elmir, Ulmer

Elmo (Greek) lovable, friendly. (Italian) guardian. (Latin) a familiar form of Anselm. (English) a form of Elmer.

Elmore (English) moor where the elm trees grow.
Ellmoar, Ellmoor, Ellmoore, Ellmor, Ellmore, Elmoar, Elmoor, Elmoore

Eloi (Hebrew) a form of Eli.

Elon (Spanish) a short form of Elonzo.

Elonzo (Spanish) a form of Alonso.
Elonso

Eloy (Latin) chosen. (Hebrew) a form of Eli.
Eloi

Elrad (Hebrew) God rules.
Ellrad, Elradd, Rad, Radd

Elroy (French) a form of Delroy, Leroy.
Elroi, Elroye

Elsdon (English) nobleman's hill.
Elsden, Elsdin, Elsdyn

Elston (English) noble's town.
Ellston

Elsu (Native American) swooping, soaring falcon.

Elsworth (English) noble's estate.
Ellsworth

Elton (English) old town.
Alton, Ellton, Eltan, Elten, Elthon, Eltin, Eltonia, Eltyn

Elvern (Latin) a form of Alvern.
Elver, Elverne, Elvirn, Elvirne

Elvin (English) a form of Alvin.
El, Elvyn, Elwen, Elwin, Elwyn, Elwynn

Elvio (Spanish) light skinned; blond.
Elvyo

Elvis (Scandinavian) wise.
El, Elviss, Elviz, Elvys, Elvyss

Elvy (English) elfin warrior.
Elvi, Elvie

Elwell (English) old well.
Elwel

Elwood (English) old forest. See also Wood, Woody.
Ellwood

Ely (Hebrew) a form of Eli. Geography: a region of England with extensive drained fens.
Elya, Elyie

Eman (Czech) a form of Emmanuel.
Emaney, Emani

Emanuel (Hebrew) a form of Emmanuel.
Emaniel, Emannual, Emannuel, Emanual, Emanueal, Emanuele, Emanuell, Emanuelle

Emerson (German, English) son of Emery.
Emmerson, Emreson

Emery (German) industrious leader.
Aimery, Emari, Emarri, Emeree, Emeri, Emerich, Emerie, Emerio, Emmeree, Emmeri, Emmerich, Emmerie, Emmery, Emrick, Inre, Imrich

Emil (Latin) flatterer. (German) industrious. See also Milko, Milo.

Aymil, Emiel, Emilek, Emill, Emils, Emilyan, Emyl, Emyll

Emile, Émile (French) forms of Emil.
Emiel, Emille, Emylle

Emiliano (Italian) a form of Emil.
Emilian, Emilion

Emilien (Latin) friendly; industrious.

Emilio (Italian, Spanish) a form of Emil.
Emielio, Emileo, Emilios, Emillio, Emilo

Emily (Latin, German) a form of Emil.

Emlyn (Welsh) waterfall.
Emelen, Emlen, Emlin

Emmanuel (Hebrew) God is with us. See also Immanuel, Maco, Mango, Manuel.
Emek, Emmahnuel, Emmanel, Emmaneuol, Emmanle, Emmanual, Emmanueal, Emmanuele, Emmanuell, Emmanuelle, Emmanuil

Emmet, Emmitt (German, English) forms of Emmett.
Emmit, Emmyt, Emmytt, Emyt, Emytt

Emmett (German) industrious; strong. (English) ant. History: Robert Emmett was an Irish patriot.
Em, Emet, Emett, Emitt, Emmette, Emmot, Emmott, Emmy

Emory (German) a form of Emery.
Emmo, Emmori, Emmorie, Emmory, Emorye

Emre (Turkish) brother.
Emra, Emrah, Emreson

Emrick (German) a form of Emery.
Emeric, Emerick, Emric, Emrik, Emrique, Emryc, Emryck, Emryk

Emry (Welsh) honorable.
Emree, Emrey, Emri, Emrie

Enan (Welsh) hammer.
Enen, Enin, Enon, Enyn

Enapay (Sioux) brave appearance; he appears.
Enapai

Endre (Hungarian) a form of Andrew.
Ender, Endres

Eneas (Greek) a form of Aeneas.
Eneias, Enné

Engelbert (German) bright as an angel.
See also Ingelbert.
*Bert, Engelburt, Englebert, Englebirt,
Engleburt, Englebyrt*

Enli (Dene) that dog over there.
Enly

Enmanuel (Hebrew) a form of
Emmanuel.

Ennis (Greek) mine. (Scottish) a form of
Angus.
Eni, Enis, Enni, Ennys, Enys

Enoc (Hebrew) a form of Enoch.

Enoch (Hebrew) dedicated, consecrated.
Bible: the father of Methuselah.
Enock, Enok

Enos (Hebrew) man.
Enosh

Enric, Enrick (Romanian) forms of
Henry.
Enrica, Enrik, Enryc, Enryck, Enryk

Enrico (Italian) a form of Henry.
Enzio, Rico

Enright (Irish) son of the attacker.
Enrit, Enrite, Enryght, Enryte

Enrikos (Greek) a form of Henry.

Enrique, Enrrique (Spanish) forms of
Henry. See also Quiqui.
Enrigué, Enriq, Enriqué, Enriquez

Enver (Turkish) bright; handsome.

Enyeto (Native American) walks like
a bear.
Enieto

Enzi (Swahili) powerful.
Enzie, Enzy

Enzo (Italian) a form of Enrico.

Eoin (Welsh) a form of Evan.

Ephraim (Hebrew) fruitful. Bible: the
second son of Joseph.
*Ephraen, Ephrain, Ephram, Ephrem,
Ephriam*

Erasmo (Greek) a form of Erasmus.

Erasmus (Greek) lovable.
Érasme, Rasmus

Erastus (Greek) beloved.
Éraste, Erastious, Ras, Rastus

Erbert (German) a short form of Herbert.
*Ebert, Erberto, Erbirt, Erbirto, Erburt,
Erburto, Erbyrt, Erbyrto*

Ercole (Italian) splendid gift.
Ercoal, Ercol

Erek, Erik (Scandinavian) forms of Eric.
Erike, Errik

Erhard (German) strong; resolute.
Erhardt, Erhart

Eriberto (Italian) a form of Herbert.
Erberto, Heriberto

Eric (Scandinavian) ruler of all. (English)
brave ruler. (German) a short form of
Frederick. History: Eric the Red was a
Norwegian explorer who founded
Greenland's first colony.
*Aric, Ehric, Éric, Erica, Ericc, Erico, Erric,
Rick*

Erich (Czech, German) a form of Eric.
Ehrich

Erick, Errick (English) forms of Eric.
Eryck

Erickson (English) son of Eric.
*Erickzon, Erics, Ericson, Ericsson, Eriks,
Erikson, Erikzzon, Eriqson*

Erikur (Icelandic) a form of Erek, Eric.

Erin (Irish) peaceful. History: an ancient
name for Ireland.
*Eran, Eren, Erine, Erinn, Erino, Errin,
Eryn, Erynn*

Eriq (American) a form of Eric.

Erland (English) nobleman's land.
Earlan, Earland, Erlan, Erlen, Erlend

Erling (English) nobleman's son.

Ermanno (Italian) a form of Herman.
Erman, Erminio

Ermano (Spanish) a form of Herman.
Ermin, Ermine, Ermon

Ernest (English) earnest, sincere. See also Arno.
Erneste, Ernestino, Ernestus, Ernist, Ernyst

Ernesto (Spanish) a form of Ernest.
Ernester, Ernestino, Neto

Ernie (English) a familiar form of Ernest.
Earnee, Earni, Earnie, Earny, Ernee, Erney, Erni, Erny

Erno (Hungarian) a form of Ernest.
Ernö

Ernst (German) a form of Ernest.
Erns

Erol (Turkish) strong, courageous.
Eroll

Eron, Erron (Irish) forms of Erin.
Erran, Erren, Errion

Eros (Greek) love, desire. Mythology: Eros was the god of love.

Errando (Basque) bold.

Errol (Latin) wanderer. (English) a form of Earl.
Erol, Erold, Erral, Errel, Erril, Erroll, Erryl, Erryll, Eryl, Eryll

Erroman (Basque) from Rome.
Eroman

Erskine (Scottish) high cliff. (English) from Ireland.
Ersin, Erskin, Erskyn, Erskyne, Kinny

Ervin, Erwin (English) sea friend. Forms of Irving, Irwin.
Earvan, Earven, Earvin, Earvon, Earvyn, Erv, Ervan, Erven, Ervon, Ervyn, Erwan, Erwinek, Erwinn, Erwyn, Erwynn

Ervine (English) a form of Irving.
Erv, Ervince, Erving, Ervins, Ervyne, Ervyng

Eryk (Scandinavian) a form of Eric.
Eryc

Esau (Hebrew) rough; hairy. Bible: Jacob's twin brother.
Esaw

Esben (Scandinavian) god.

Esbern (Danish) holy bear.
Esberne, Esbirn, Esbirne, Esburn, Esburne, Esburne, Esbyrn, Esbyrne

Esdras (Hebrew) a form of Ezra.

Esequiel (Hebrew) a form of Ezekiel.

Eshkol (Hebrew) grape clusters.

Esidore (Greek) a form of Isidore.
Easidor, Esidor, Ezador, Ezadore, Ezidor, Ezidore

Eskil (Norwegian) god vessel.
Eskyl

Esmond (English) rich protector.

Espen (Danish) bear of the gods.
Espan, Espin, Espon, Espyn

Essien (Ochi) sixth-born son.
Esien

Este (Italian) east.
Estes

Esteban, Estéban (Spanish) forms of Stephen.
Estabon, Esteben, Estefan, Estefano, Estefen, Estephan, Estephen

Estebe (Basque) a form of Stephen.

Estevan, Esteven (Spanish) forms of Stephen.
Estevon, Estiven, Estyvan, Estyven, Estyvin, Estyvon, Estyvyn

Estevao (Spanish) a form of Stephen.
Estevez

Estuardo (Spanish) a form of Edward.
Estvardo

Ethan (Hebrew) strong; firm.
Eathan, Eathen, Eathin, Eathon, Eathyn, Eeathen, Efan, Efen, Effan, Effen, Effin, Effon, Effyn, Efin, Efon, Efyn, Eithan, Eithen, Eithin, Eithon, Eithyn, Etan, Ethaen, Ethe, Ethian, Ethin, Ethon, Ethyn, Eythan, Eythen, Eythin, Eython, Eythyn

Ethen (Hebrew) a form of Ethan.

Etienne, Étienne (French) forms of Stephen.
Etian, Etien, Étienn, Ettien

Ettore (Italian) steadfast.
Etor, Etore

Etu (Native American) sunny.
Eetu

Euclid (Greek) intelligent. History: the founder of Euclidean geometry.
Euclyd

Eugen (German) a form of Eugene.

Eugene (Greek) born to nobility. See also Ewan, Gene, Gino, Iukini, Jenö, Yevgenyi, Zenda.
Eoghan, Eugeen, Eugeene, Eugen, Eugéne, Eugeni, Eugenius, Eujean, Eujeane, Eujeen, Eujein, Eujeyn

Eugenio (Spanish) a form of Eugene.
Eugenios

Eulises (Latin) a form of Ulysses.

Eustace (Greek) productive. (Latin) stable, calm. See also Stacey.
Eustacee, Eustache, Eustachio, Eustachius, Eustachy, Eustashe, Eustasius, Eustatius, Eustazio, Eustis, Eustiss

Evan (Irish) young warrior. (English) a form of John. See also Bevan, Owen.
Eavan, Ev, Evaine, Evann, Even, Evun, Ewen

Evander (Greek) benevolent ruler; preacher.
Evandar

Evangelos (Greek) a form of Andrew.
Evagelos, Evaggelos, Evangelo

Evans (Irish, English) a form of Evan.
Evens

Evelyn (English) hazelnut.
Evelin

Ever (English) boar. A short form of Everett, Everley, Everton. (German) a short form of Everardo.

Everardo (German) strong as a boar. A form of Eberhard.
Everado, Everard, Everhard, Everhardt, Everhart

Everett, Everette (English) forms of Eberhard.

Ev, Evered, Everet, Everhet, Everhett, Everit, Everitt, Everrett, Evert, Everyt, Everyte, Everytt, Evrett, Evryt, Evryte, Evrytt, Evrytte

Everley (English) boar meadow.
Everlea, Everlee, Everleigh, Everli, Everlie, Everly

Everton (English) boar town.

Evgeny (Russian) a form of Eugene. See also Zhek.
Evgeni, Evgenij, Evgenyi

Evin, Evon, Evyn (Irish) forms of Evan.
Evian, Evinn, Evins

Ewald (German) always powerful. (English) powerful lawman.

Ewan (Scottish) a form of Eugene, Evan. See also Keon.
Euan, Euann, Euen, Ewen, Ewhen, Ewin, Ewon, Ewyn

Ewert (English) ewe herder, shepherd.
Ewart, Ewirt

Ewing (English) friend of the law.
Ewin, Ewyng, Ewynn

Exavier (Basque) a form of Xavier.
Exaviar, Exavior, Ezavier

Eynstein (Norse) stone island.
Einstein, Einsteyn, Eynsteyn

Eyota (Native American) great.
Eiota, Eyotah

Ezekiel (Hebrew) strength of God. Bible: a Hebrew prophet. See also Haskel, Zeke.
Ezakeil, Ezéchiel, Ezeck, Ezeckiel, Ezeeckel, Ezekeial, Ezekeil, Ezekeyial, Ezekial, Ezekielle, Ezell, Eziakah, Eziechiele

Ezequiel (Hebrew) a form of Ezekiel.
Eziequel

Ezer (Hebrew) a form of Ezra.
Ezera, Ezerah

Ezra (Hebrew) helper; strong. Bible: a Jewish priest who led the Jews back to Jerusalem.
Esra, Esrah, Ezer, Ezrah, Ezri, Ezry

Ezven (Czech) a form of Eugene.
Esven, Esvin, Ezavin, Ezavine

F

Faas (Scandinavian) wise counselor.
Fas

Faber (German) a form of Fabian.
Fabar, Fabir, Fabor, Fabyr

Fabian (Latin) bean grower.
Fabain, Fabayan, Fabe, Fabean, Fabein, Fabek, Fabeon, Faber, Fabert, Fabi, Fabijan, Fabin, Fabion, Fabius, Fabiyan, Fabiyus, Fabyan, Fabyen, Fabyous, Faybian, Faybien

Fabiano (Italian) a form of Fabian.
Fabianno

Fabien (Latin) a form of Fabian.

Fabio (Latin) a form of Fabian. (Italian) a short form of Fabiano.
Fabbio

Fabrice (Italian) a form of Fabrizio.
Fabricio

Fabrizio (Italian) craftsman.
Fabrizius

Fabron (French) little blacksmith; apprentice.
Fabra, Fabre, Fabriano, Fabroni, Fabryn

Fadey (Ukrainian) a form of Thaddeus.
Faday, Faddei, Faddey, Faddi, Faddie, Faddy, Fade, Fadeyka, Fadie, Fady

Fadi (Arabic) redeemer.
Fadee, Fadhi

Fadil (Arabic) generous.
Fadal, Fadeel, Fadel, Fayl

Fagan (Irish) little fiery one.
Faegan, Faegen, Faegin, Faegon, Faegyn, Fagen, Fagin, Fagon, Fagyn, Faigan, Faigen, Faigin, Faigon, Faigyn, Faygan, Faygen, Faygin, Faygon, Faygyn

Fahd (Arabic) lynx.
Fahaad, Fahad

Fai (Chinese) beginning.

Fairfax (English) blond.
Fair, Fayrfax, Fax

Faisal (Arabic) decisive.
Faisel, Faisil, Faisl, Faiyaz, Faiz, Faizal, Faize, Faizel, Faizi, Fasel, Fasil, Faysal, Fayzal, Fayzel

Fakhir (Arabic) excellent.
Fahkry, Fakher

Fakih (Arabic) thinker; reader of the Koran.

Falco (Latin) falconer.
Falcko, Falckon, Falcon, Falconn, Falk, Falke, Falken, Faulco

Falito (Italian) a familiar form of Rafael, Raphael.

Falkner (English) trainer of falcons. See also Falco.
Falconer, Falconner, Falconnor, Faulconer, Faulconner, Faulconnor, Faulkner

Fane (English) joyful, glad.
Fain, Faine, Faines, Fanes, Faniel, Fayn, Fayne

Faraji (Swahili) consolation.
Farajy

Faraz (Arabic) a form of Faris.
Farhaz, Fariez

Farid (Arabic) unique.
Farad, Fared, Farod, Faryd

Faris (Arabic) horseman. (Irish) a form of Ferris.
Fares, Faress, Farice, Farrish, Fariss, Fariz, Farris, Farrys, Farys

Farlane (English) far lane.
Farlaen, Farlaene, Farlain, Farlaine, Farlayn, Farlayne

Farley (English) bull meadow; sheep meadow. See also Lee.
Fairlay, Fairlea, Fairlee, Fairleigh, Fairley, Fairlie, Far, Farlay, Farlea, Farlee, Farleigh, Farli, Farlie, Farly, Farrleigh, Farrley

Farnell (English) fern-covered hill.
Farnal, Farnall, Farnalle, Farnel, Farnelle, Fernal, Fernald, Fernall, Fernalle, Furnal, Furnald, Furnall, Furnalle, Furnel, Furnell, Furnelle, Fyrnel, Fyrnele, Fyrnell, Fyrnelle

Farnham (English) field of ferns.
Farnam, Farnem, Farnhem, Farnum, Fernham

Farnley (English) fern meadow.
Farnlea, Farnlee, Farnleigh, Farnli, Farnlie, Farnly, Fernlea, Fernlee, Fernleigh, Fernley, Fernli, Fernlie, Fernly

Faroh (Latin) a form of Pharaoh.
Faro, Farro, Farrow

Farold (English) mighty traveler.

Faron (English) a form of Faren (see Girls' Names).

Farquhar (Scottish) dear.
Fark, Farq, Farquar, Farquarson, Farque, Farquharson, Farquy, Farqy

Farr (English) traveler.
Faer, Far, Farran, Farren, Farrin, Farrington, Farron, Farrun, Farryn

Farrar (English) blacksmith.
Farar, Farer, Farrer

Farrell (Irish) heroic; courageous.
Faral, Farel, Faril, Farol, Faryl, Farral, Farrel, Farrill, Farryl, Farryll, Faryl, Ferol, Ferrel, Ferrell, Ferril, Ferryl

Farrow (English) piglet.
Farow

Farruco (Spanish) a form of Francis, Francisco.
Farruca, Farrucah, Farruka, Farruko, Faruca, Farucah, Faruco, Frascuelo

Faruq (Arabic) honest.
Farook, Farooq, Faroque, Farouk, Faruqh

Faste (Norwegian) firm.

Fath (Arabic) victor.

Fatin (Arabic) clever.
Fatine, Fatyn, Fatyne

Faust (Latin) lucky, fortunate. History: the sixteenth-century German necromancer who inspired many legends.
Fauste, Faustis, Faustise, Faustos, Faustus, Faustyce, Faustys

Faustino (Italian) a form of Faust.
Faustin, Faustine, Faustyn

Fausto (Italian) a form of Faust.

Favian (Latin) understanding.
Favain, Favien, Favio, Favion, Favyen, Favyon

Faxon (German) long-haired.
Faxan, Faxen, Faxin, Faxyn

Fazio (Italian) good worker.
Fazyo

Federico (Italian, Spanish) a form of Frederick.
Federic, Federigo, Federoquito

Feivel (Yiddish) God aids.
Feyvel

Feliciano (Italian) a form of Felix.
Felicio

Feliks (Russian) a form of Felix.

Felipe (Spanish) a form of Philip.
Feeleep, Felep, Felip, Felo

Felippo (Italian) a form of Philip.
Felipino, Lipp, Lippo, Pip, Pippo

Felix (Latin) fortunate; happy. See also Phelix, Pitin.
Fee, Felic, Félice, Felike, Feliks, Felo, Félix, Felizio, Filix, Filyx, Fylix, Fylyx

Felix Antoine (Latin, French) a combination of Felix + Antoine.
Felix-Antoine

Felix Olivier (Latin, French) a combination of Felix +Olivier.
Felix-Olivier

Felton (English) field town.
Feltan, Felten, Feltin, Feltun, Feltyn

Fenton (English) marshland farm.
Fen, Fennie, Fenny, Fentan, Fenten, Fentin, Fentun, Fentyn, Fintan, Finton

Feodor (Slavic) a form of Theodore.
Dorek, Feador, Feaodor, Feaodore, Fedar, Fedinka, Fedor, Fedore, Fedya, Feedor, Feeodor, Feeodore, Fidor, Fidore, Fiodor, Fiodore

Feoras (Greek) smooth rock.
Feora

Ferd (German) horse.
Ferda, Ferde, Ferdi, Ferdie, Ferdy

Ferdinand (German) daring, adventurous.
See also Hernando.
Ferdinan, Ferdinánd, Ferdinandus,
Ferdynand, Ferynand

Ferdinando (Italian) a form of Ferdinand.
Feranado, Ferdnando, Ferdynando, Ferrando,
Nando

Ferenc (Hungarian) a form of Francis.
Feri, Ferke, Ferko

Fergus (Irish) strong; manly.
Fearghas, Fearghus, Feargus, Ferghas,
Ferghus, Fergie, Ferguson, Fergusson, Firgus,
Firgusen, Firguson, Furgus, Furgusen,
Furguson, Fyrgus, Fyrgusen, Fyrgusun

Fermin (French, Spanish) firm, strong. See
also Firman.
Ferman, Firmin, Furmin, Furmyn, Fyrmen,
Fyrmin, Fyrmyn

Fernando (Spanish) a form of Ferdinand.
Ferando, Ferdo, Fernand, Fernandez,
Fernendo, Ferynando

Feroz (Persian) fortunate.
Firoz, Fyroz

Ferran (Arabic) baker.
Farran, Feran, Feren, Ferin, Feron, Ferren,
Ferrin, Ferron, Ferryn, Feryn

Ferrand (French) iron gray hair.
Farand, Farrand, Farrando, Farrant, Ferand,
Ferrant

Ferrell (Irish) a form of Farrell.
Ferel, Ferell, Ferrel, Ferrill, Ferryl

Ferris (Irish) a form of Peter.
Feris, Ferrice, Ferrise, Ferriss, Ferryce,
Ferryse, Ferryss

Festus (Latin) happy.
Festys

Fico (Spanish) a familiar form of Frederick.
Ficko, Fiko, Fyco, Fycko, Fyko

Fidel (Latin) faithful. History: Fidel Castro
was the Cuban revolutionary who

overthrew a dictatorship in 1959 and
established a communist regime in Cuba.
Fidele, Fidèle, Fidelio, Fidelis, Fidell, Fido,
Fydal, Fydel, Fydil, Fydyl

Field (English) a short form of Fielding.
Fields

Fielding (English) field; field worker.
Field

Fife (Scottish) from Fife, Scotland.
Fif, Fyf, Fyfe

Fifi (Fante) born on Friday.

Fil (Polish) a form of Phil.
Filipek

Filbert (English) brilliant. See also Bert,
Philbert.
Filberte, Filberti, Filberto, Filbirt, Filburt,
Filibert, Filibirt, Filiburt, Fillbert, Fillbirt,
Fylbert, Fylbirt, Fylburt, Fylibert, Fylibirt,
Fyliburt, Fyllbert, Fylbirt, Fyllbirt, Fyllbyrt

Filberte (French) a form of Filbert.
Filbirte, Filburte, Filiberte, Filibirte,
Filiburte, Fillberte, Fillbirte, Fylberte,
Fylbirte, Fylburte, Fyliberte, Fylibirte,
Fyliburte, Fyllberte, Fyllbirte, Fyllbyrte

Filiberto (Spanish) a form of Filbert.

Filip (Greek) a form of Philip.
Filippo

Fillipp (Russian) a form of Philip.
Filipe, Filipek, Filips, Fill, Fillip

Filmore (English) famous.
Fillmore, Filmer, Fyllmer, Fyllmore, Fylmer,
Fylmore, Philmore

Filya (Russian) a form of Philip.
Filyah, Fylya, Fylyah

Findlay (Irish) a form of Finlay.
Findlea, Findlee, Findleigh, Findley,
Fyndlay, Fyndlea, Fyndlee, Fyndleigh,
Fyndley, Fynndlay, Fynndlea, Fynndlee,
Fynndleigh, Fynndley

Fineas (Irish) a form of Phineas.
Finneas, Fyneas

Finian (Irish) light skinned; white. See
also Phinean.

Finian *(cont.)*
Finan, Fineen, Finien, Finnen, Finnian, Finyan, Fionan, Fionn, Fynia, Fynyan

Finlay (Irish) blond-haired soldier.
Findlay, Finlea, Finlee, Finleigh, Finley, Finnlea, Finnlee, Finnleigh, Finnley, Fynlay, Fynlea, Fynlee, Fynleigh, Fynley, Fynnlay, Fynnlea, Fynnlee, Fynnleigh, Fynnley

Finn (German) from Finland. (Irish) blond haired; light skinned. A short form of Finlay. (Norwegian) from the Lapland. See also Fynn.
Fin, Finnie, Finnis, Finny

Finnegan (Irish) light skinned; white.
Finegan, Fineghan, Finneghan, Fynegan, Fyneghan, Fynnegan, Fynneghan

Fintan (Irish) from Finn's town.
Finten, Fintin, Finton, Fintyn, Fyntan, Fynten, Fyntin, Fynton, Fyntyn

Fiorello (Italian) little flower.
Fiore, Fiorelleigh, Fiorelley, Fiorelli, Fiorellie, Fiorelly, Fyorellee, Fyorelleigh, Fyorelley, Fyorelli, Fyorellie, Fyorello, Fyorelly

Firas (Arabic) persistent.
Fira, Fyra, Fyras

Firman (French) firm; strong. See also Fermin.
Furman, Firmyn, Fyrman

Firth (English) woodland.
Fyrth

Fischel (Yiddish) a form of Phillip.
Fyschel

Fischer (English) a form of Fisher.

Fisher (English) fisherman.

Fiske (English) fisherman.
Fisk, Fysk, Fyske

Fitch (English) weasel, ermine.
Fitche, Fytch

Fitz (English) son.
Filz, Fits, Fyts, Fytz

Fitzgerald (English) son of Gerald.
Fitsgerald, Fitzgeraldo, Fytsgerald, Fytsgeraldo, Fytzgerald, Fytzgeraldo

Fitzhugh (English) son of Hugh.
Fitshu, Fitshue, Fitshugh, Fitzhu, Fitzhue, Fytshu, Fytzhue, Fytzhugh

Fitzpatrick (English) son of Patrick.
Fitspatric, Fitspatrik, Fitzpatric, Fitzpatrik, Fytspatric, Fytspatrick, Fytspatrik, Fytzpatric, Fytzpatrick, Fytzpatrik

Fitzroy (Irish) son of Roy.
Fitsroi, Fitsroy, Fitzroi, Fytsroi, Fytsroy, Fytzroi, Fytzroy

Flaminio (Spanish) Religion: Marcantonio Flaminio coauthored one of the most important texts of the Italian Reformation.

Flann (Irish) redhead.
Flainn, Flan, Flanan, Flanin, Flannan, Flannen, Flannery, Flannin, Flannon, Flanyn, Flanon, Flanyn

Flavian (Latin) blond, yellow haired.
Flavel, Flavelle, Flavien, Flavyan, Flawian, Flawiusz, Flawyan

Flavio (Italian) a form of Flavian.
Flabio, Flavias, Flavious, Flavius, Flavyo

Fleming (English) from Denmark; from Flanders.
Flemming, Flemmyng, Flemyng

Fletcher (English) arrow featherer, arrow maker.
Flecher, Fletch

Flint (English) stream; flint stone.
Flinte, Flynt, Flynte

Flip (Spanish) a short form of Felipe. (American) a short form of Philip.
Flipp, Flyp, Flypp

Florencio (Italian) a form of Florent.
Florenci, Florenzo, Florinio, Florino, Floryno

Florent (French) flowering.
Florentin, Florentine, Florentyn, Florentyne, Florentz, Florynt, Florynte

Florentino (Italian) a form of Florent.
Florentyno

Florian (Latin) flowering, blooming.
Florien, Florion, Florrian, Flory, Floryan, Floryant, Floryante

Floyd (English) a form of Lloyd.
Floid, Floyde

Flurry (English) flourishing, blooming.
Fluri, Flurie, Flurri, Flurrie, Flury

Flynn (Irish) son of the red-haired man.
Flin, Flinn, Flyn

Folke (German) a form of Volker.
Folker

Foluke (Yoruba) given to God.

Foma (Bulgarian, Russian) a form of
Thomas.
Fomah, Fomka

Fonso (German, Italian) a short form of
Alphonso.
Fonzo

Fontaine (French) fountain.
*Fontain, Fontayn, Fontayne, Fountain,
Fountaine, Fountayn, Fountayne*

Fonzie (German) a familiar form of
Alphonse.
*Fons, Fonsee, Fonsey, Fonsi, Fonsie, Fonsy,
Fonz, Fonzee, Fonzey, Fonzi, Fonzy*

Forbes (Irish) prosperous.
Forbe, Forbs

Ford (English) a short form of names
ending in "ford."
Forde

Fordel (Gypsy) forgiving.
*Fordal, Fordele, Fordell, Fordelle, Fordil,
Fordile*

Fordon (German) destroyer.
Fordan, Forden, Fordin, Fordyn

Forest (French) a form of Forrest.
Forestt, Foryst

Forester (English) forest guardian.
Forrestar, Forrester, Forrie, Forry, Foss

Forrest (French) forest; woodsman.
Forreste, Forrestt, Forrie

Fortino (Italian) fortunate, lucky.
Fortin, Fortine, Fortyn, Fortyne

Fortune (French) fortunate, lucky.
Fortun, Fortunato, Fortuné, Fortunio

Foster (Latin) a short form of Forester.
Forster

Fowler (English) trapper of wildfowl.

Fran (Latin) a short form of Francis.
Franh

Francesco (Italian) a form of Francis.

Franchot (French) a form of Francis.

Francis (Latin) free; from France.
Religion: Saint Francis of Assisi was the
founder of the Franciscan order. See also
Farruco, Ferenc.
*France, Frances, Franciskus, Francys, Frannie,
Franny, Franscis, Fransis, Franus, Frencis*

Francisco (Portuguese, Spanish) a form of
Francis. See also Chilo, Cisco, Farruco,
Paco, Pancho.
Fransysco, Frasco

Franco (Latin) a short form of Francis.
Franko

Francois, François (French) forms of
Francis.
Francoise

Frank (English) a short form of Francis,
Franklin. See also Palani, Pancho.
*Franc, Franck, Franek, Frang, Franio,
Franke, Franko*

Frankie, Franky (English) familiar forms
of Frank.
Francky, Franke, Frankey, Franki, Franqui

Franklin (English) free landowner.
*Francklen, Francklin, Francklyn, Francylen,
Frankin, Franklen, Franklinn, Franquelin*

Franklyn (English) a form of Franklin.
Franklynn

Frans (Swedish) a form of Francis.
Frants

Fransisco (Portuguese, Spanish) a form of
Francis.

Frantisek (Czech) a form of Francis.
Franta, Frantik, Frantyc, Frantyck, Frantyk

Frantz, Franz (German) forms of Francis.
Fransz, Franzen, Franzie, Franzin, Franzl,
Franzy

Fraser (French) strawberry. (English)
curly haired.
Frasier

Frayne (French) dweller at the ash tree.
(English) stranger.
Frain, Fraine, Frayn, Frean, Freane, Freen,
Freene, Frein, Freine, Freyn, Freyne

Frazer, Frazier (French, English) forms of
Fraser.
Fraizer, Fraze, Frazyer

Fred (German) a short form of Alfred,
Frederick, Manfred.
Fredd, Fredson

Freddie, Freddy, Fredi, Fredy (German)
familiar forms of Frederick.
Fredde, Freddi, Fredie

Freddrick, Fredrick (German) forms of
Frederick.
Feidrik, Fredric, Fredrich, Fredricka,
Fredricks, Fredrik

Frederic, Frederik (German) forms of
Frederick.
Frédéric, Frederich, Frédérik, Frederric,
Frederrik

Frederick (German) peaceful ruler. See
also Dick, Eric, Fico, Peleke, Rick.
Fredderick, Fredek, Fréderick, Frédérick,
Frederrick, Fredwick, Fredwyck

Frederico (Spanish) a form of Frederick.
Fredrico, Frederigo

Frederique (French) a form of Frederick.

Fredo (Spanish) a form of Fred.
Freddo

Freeborn (English) child of freedom.
Freborn, Free

Freeman (English) free.
Free, Freedman, Freemin, Freemon,
Friedman, Friedmann

Fremont (German) free; noble protector.
Fremonte

Frewin (English) free; noble friend.
Freewan, Freewen, Frewan, Frewen, Frewon,
Frewyn

Frey (English) lord. (Scandinavian)
Mythology: the Norse god who
dispenses peace and prosperity.
Frai, Fray, Frei

Frick (English) bold.
Fric, Frik, Friq, Frique, Fryc, Fryck, Fryk,
Fryq

Fridmund (German) peaceful guardian.
Frimond, Frymond, Frymund

Fridolf (English) peaceful wolf.
Freydolf, Freydolph, Freydolphe, Freydulf,
Freydulph, Freydulphe, Fridolph, Fridolphe,
Fridulf, Frydolph, Frydolphe, Frydulf

Friedrich (German) a form of Frederick.
Frideric, Friederick, Friderik, Fridrich, Friedel,
Friedrick, Fridrich, Fridrick, Friedrike,
Friedryk, Fryderic, Fryderick, Fryderyk,
Frydric, Frydrich, Frydrick, Frydrik

Frisco (Spanish) a short form of Francisco.

Fritz (German) a familiar form of
Frederick.
Fritson, Fritts, Fritzchen, Fritzl

Frode (Norwegian) wise.
Frod

Fulbright (German) very bright.
Fulbert, Fulbirt, Fulburt, Fulbyrt

Fuller (English) cloth thickener.
Fuler

Fulton (English) field near town.
Faulton, Folton

Funsoni (Nguni) requested.
Funsony

Fyfe (Scottish) a form of Fife.
Fyffe

Fynn (Ghanaian) Geography: another
name for the Offin River in Ghana. See
also Finn.
Fyn

Fyodor (Russian) a form of Theodore.
Fydor, Fydore, Fyodore

G

Gabby (American) a familiar form of Gabriel.
Gabbi, Gabbie, Gabi, Gabie, Gaby

Gabe (Hebrew) a short form of Gabriel.
Gab

Gabela (Swiss) a form of Gabriel.
Gabel, Gabelah, Gabell

Gabino (American) a form of Gabriel.
Gabin, Gabrino

Gábor (Hungarian) God is my strength.
Gabbo, Gabko, Gabo

Gabrial, Gabriele, Gabrielle (Hebrew)
forms of Gabriel.
*Gaberial, Gabrail, Gabreal, Gabriael,
Gabrieal*

Gabriel (Hebrew) devoted to God. Bible:
the angel of the Annunciation.
*Gabis, Gabrael, Gabraiel, Gabreil, Gabrel,
Gabrell, Gabriël, Gabrielius, Gabriell,
Gabrile, Gabris, Gebereal, Ghabriel, Riel*

Gabrielli (Italian) a form of Gabriel.
Gabriello

Gabryel (Hebrew) a form of Gabriel.
*Gabryalle, Gabryele, Gabryell, Gabryelle,
Gabys*

Gadi (Arabic) God is my fortune.
Gad, Gaddy, Gadie, Gadiel, Gady

Gael (Irish) Gaelic-speaking Celt. (Greek)
a form of Gale.

Gaetan (Italian) from Gaeta, a region in
southern Italy.
Gaetano, Gaetono

Gagan (Sikh) sky.

Gagandeep (Sikh) sky's light.

Gage (French) pledge.
Gager, Gayg, Gayge

Gaige (French) a form of Gage.
Gaig

Gair (Irish) small.
Gaer, Gayr, Gearr, Geir, Geirr

Gaius (Latin) rejoicer. See also Cai.

Gaje (French) a form of Gage.

Galbraith (Irish) Scotsman in Ireland.
Galbrait, Galbrayth, Galbreath

Gale (Greek) a short form of Galen.
Gail, Gaile, Gayl, Gayle

Galen (Greek) healer; calm. (Irish) little
and lively.
*Gaelan, Gaelen, Gaelin, Gaelyn, Gailen,
Galan, Galin, Galon, Galyn*

Galeno (Spanish) illuminated child.
(Greek, Irish) a form of Galen.

Gallagher (Irish) eager helper.

Galloway (Irish) Scotsman in Ireland.
*Gallowai, Gallwai, Gallway, Galwai,
Galway*

Galt (Norwegian) high ground.

Galton (English) owner of a rented estate.
Gallton, Galtan, Galten, Galtin, Galtyn

Galvin (Irish) sparrow.
*Gal, Gall, Gallven, Gallvin, Galvan,
Galven, Galvon, Galvyn*

Gamal (Arabic) camel. See also Jamal.
Gamall, Gamel, Gamil

Gamble (Scandinavian) old.
*Gambal, Gambel, Gambil, Gambol,
Gambyl*

Gamlyn (Scandinavian) small elder.
Gamlin

Gan (Chinese) daring, adventurous.
(Vietnamese) near.

Gannon (Irish) light skinned, white.
*Ganan, Ganen, Ganin, Gannan, Gannen,
Gannie, Ganny, Gannyn, Ganon, Ganyn*

Ganya (Zulu) clever.
Gania, Ganiah, Ganyah

Gar (English) a short form of Gareth,
Garnett, Garrett, Garvin.
Garr

Garcia (Spanish) mighty with a spear.
*Garcias, Garcya, Garcyah, Garcyas, Garsias,
Garsya, Garsyah, Garsyas*

Gardner (English) gardener.
*Gard, Gardener, Gardie, Gardiner, Gardnar,
Gardnor, Gardnyr, Gardy*

Garek (Polish) a form of Edgar.
Garak, Garok

Garen, Garin, Garren, Garrin (English)
forms of Garry.
*Garan, Garon, Garran, Garron, Garryn,
Garyn, Gerren, Gerron, Gerryn*

Garet, Garett, Garret (Irish) forms of
Garrett.
*Garhett, Garit, Garitt, Garrit, Garryt,
Garyt, Garytt, Gerret, Gerrot*

Gareth (Welsh) gentle. (Irish) a form of
Garrett.
*Garef, Gareff, Garif, Gariff, Garith,
Garreth, Garrith, Garyf, Garyff, Garyth*

Garfield (English) field of spears; battle-
field.
Garfyeld

Garion (English) a form of Garry.
Garrion, Garyon

Garland (French) wreath of flowers;
prize. (English) land of spears;
battleground.
*Garlan, Garlande, Garlen, Garllan,
Garlund, Garlyn*

Garman (English) spearman.
Garmann, Garmen, Garrman

Garner (French) army guard, sentry.
Garnar, Garnier, Garnit, Garnor, Garnyr

Garnet (Latin, English) a form of Garnett.

Garnett (Latin) pomegranate seed; garnet
stone. (English) armed with a spear.
Garnie

Garnock (Welsh) dweller by the alder
river.
Garnoc, Garnok

Garrad (English) a form of Garrett,
Gerard. See also Jared.

*Gared, Garrard, Garred, Garrid, Garrod,
Garrode, Garryd*

Garrett (Irish) brave spearman. See also
Jarrett.
*Garrette, Garritt, Garrytt, Gerrett, Gerritt,
Gerrott*

Garrick (English) oak spear.
*Gaerick, Garic, Garick, Garik, Garreck,
Garrek, Garric, Garrik, Garryc, Garryck,
Garryk, Garyc, Garyck, Garyk, Gerreck,
Gerrick*

Garrison (English) Garry's son. (French)
troops stationed at a fort; garrison.
*Garison, Garisson, Garris, Garryson,
Garyson*

Garroway (English) spear fighter.
Garraway

Garry (English) a form of Gary.
Garree, Garrey, Garri, Garrie

Garson (English) son of Gar.

Garth (Scandinavian) garden, gardener.
(Welsh) a short form of Gareth.
Garthe

Garvey (Irish) rough peace. (French) a
form of Gervaise.
*Garbhán, Garrvey, Garrvie, Garv, Garvan,
Garvi, Garvie, Garvy, Gervee*

Garvin (English) comrade in battle.
*Garvan, Garven, Garvyn, Garwan,
Garwen, Garwin, Garwon, Garwyn,
Garwynn, Gervon*

Garwood (English) evergreen forest. See
also Wood, Woody.
Garrwood

Gary (German) mighty spearman.
(English) a familiar form of Gerald.
See also Kali.
Gare, Garey, Gari, Garie

Gaspar (French) a form of Casper.
*Gáspár, Gasparas, Gaspard, Gaspare,
Gaspari, Gasparo, Gasper, Gazsi*

Gaston (French) from Gascony, France.
*Gascon, Gastan, Gastaun, Gasten, Gastin,
Gastyn*

Gauge (French) a form of Gage.

Gaute (Norwegian) great.
Gaut, Gauta

Gautier (French) a form of Walter.
Galtero, Gatier, Gatyer, Gaulterio, Gaultier,
Gaultiero, Gauthier

Gaven, Gavyn (Welsh) forms of Gavin.
Gavynn

Gavin (Welsh) white hawk.
Gav, Gavan, Gavinn, Gavn, Gavohn,
Gavon, Gavun

Gavino (Italian) a form of Gavin.

Gavriel (Hebrew) man of God.
Gav, Gavi, Gavrel, Gavryel, Gavryele,
Gavryell, Gavryelle, Gavy

Gavril (Russian) a form of Gavriel.
(Hebrew) a form of Gabriel.
Ganya, Gavrilla, Gavrilo, Gavryl, Gavryle,
Gavryll, Gavrylle

Gawain (Welsh) a form of Gavin.
Gauvain, Gawaine, Gawayn, Gawayne,
Gawen, Gwayne

Gaylen, Gaylon (Greek) forms of Galen.
Gaylin, Gaylinn, Gaylyn

Gaylord (French) merry lord; jailer.
Gaelor, Gaelord, Gailard, Gaillard, Gailor,
Gailord, Gallard, Gay, Gayelord, Gayler,
Gaylor

Gaynor (Irish) son of the fair-skinned
man.
Gaenor, Gainer, Gainor, Gay, Gayner,
Gaynnor

Geary (English) variable, changeable.
Gearee, Gearey, Geari, Gearie, Gery

Gedeon (Bulgarian, French) a form of
Gideon.

Geffrey (English) a form of Geoffrey. See
also Jeffrey.
Gefaree, Gefarey, Gefari, Gefarie, Gefary,
Geferi, Geferie, Gefery, Geffaree, Geffarey,
Geffari, Geffarie, Geffary, Gefferee, Gefferey,
Gefferi, Gefferie, Geffery, Geffree, Geffri,
Geffrie, Geffry

Gellert (Hungarian) a form of Gerald.

Gena (Russian) a short form of Yevgenyi.
Genya, Gine

Genaro (Latin) consecrated to God.
Genereo, Genero, Gennaro

Gene (Greek) a short form of Eugene.

Genek (Polish) a form of Gene.

Genesis (Greek) beginning, origin.

Geno (Italian) a form of John. A short
form of Genovese.
Genio, Jeno

Genovese (Italian) from Genoa, Italy.
Genovis

Gent (English) gentleman.
Gental, Gentel, Gentil, Gentle, Gentyl,
Gentyle

Gentry (English) a form of Gent.

Genty (Irish, English) snow.
Genti, Gentie

Geoff (English) a short form of Geoffrey.
Gef, Geff, Geof

Geoffery (English) a form of Geoffrey.
Geofery

Geoffrey (English) a form of Jeffrey. See
also Giotto, Godfrey, Gottfried, Jeff.
Geoffre, Geoffri, Geoffrie, Geoffroi, Geoffroy,
Geoffry, Geofrey, Geofri, Gofery

Geordan (Scottish) a form of Gordon.
Geordann, Geordian, Geordin, Geordon

Geordie (Scottish) a form of George.
Geordi, Geordy

Georg (Scandinavian) a form of George.

George (Greek) farmer. See also Durko,
Egor, Iorgos, Jerzy, Jiri, Joji, Jörg, Jorge,
Jorgen, Joris, Jorrín, Jur, Jurgis, Keoki,
Semer, Yegor, Yorgos, Yorick, Yoyi, Yrjo,
Yuri, Zhora.
Georgas, Georget, Gheorghe, Giorgos,
Goerge, Gordios, Gorje, Gorya, Grzegorz

Georges (French) a form of George.
Geórges

Georgio (Italian) a form of George.

Georgios (Greek) a form of George.
Georgious, Georgius

Georgy (Greek) a familiar form of George.
Georgi, Georgie, Georgii, Georgij, Georgiy

Geovani, Geovanni, Geovanny, Geovany (Italian) forms of Giovanni.
Geovan, Geovanne, Geovannee, Geovannhi

Geraint (English) old.
Geraynt

Gerald (German) mighty spearman. See also Fitzgerald, Jarel, Jarrell, Jerald, Jerry, Kharald.
Garald, Garold, Garolds, Gearalt, Gellert, Gérald, Geralde, Gerale, Gerold, Gerrald, Gerrell, Gerrild, Gerrin, Gerrold, Geryld, Giraldo, Giraud, Girauld

Geraldo (Italian, Spanish) a form of Gerald.

Gerard (English) brave spearman. See also Jerard, Jerry.
Garrat, Garratt, Gearard, Gerad, Gerar, Gérard, Geraro, Gerd, Gerrard, Girard

Gerardo (Spanish) a form of Gerard.
Gherardo

Géraud (French) a form of Gerard.
Geraud, Gerrad, Gerraud

Gerek (Polish) a form of Gerald, Gerard.

Geremia (Hebrew) exalted by God. (Italian) a form of Jeremiah.
Geremya

Geremiah (Italian) a form of Jeremiah.
Gerimiah, Geromiah

Geremy (English) a form of Jeremy.

Gerhard (German) a form of Gerard.
Garhard, Gerhardi, Gerhardt, Gerhart, Gerhort

Gerik (Polish) a form of Edgar.
Geric, Gerek, Gerick, Gérrick

Germain (French) from Germany. (English) sprout, bud. See also Jermaine.
Germane, Germano, Germayn, Germayne, Germin, Germon, Germyn

Germaine (French, English) a form of Germain.

German (French, English) a form of Germain.

Gerome (English) a form of Jerome.

Geronimo (Greek, Italian) a form of Jerome. History: a famous Apache chief.
Geronemo, Geronymo

Gerrit (Irish) a form of Garrett. (Dutch) a form of Gerald. (English) a form of Gerard.

Gerrod (English) a form of Garrad.
Gerred, Gerrid

Gerry (English) a familiar form of Gerald, Gerard. See also Jerry.
Geri, Gerre, Gerri, Gerrie, Gerryson

Gershom (Hebrew) exiled. (Yiddish) stranger in exile.
Gersham, Gersho, Gershon, Geurson, Gursham, Gurshan

Gerson (English) son of Gar. (Hebrew, Yiddish) a form of Gershom.
Gersan, Gershawn

Gert (German, Danish) fighter.

Gervaise (French) honorable. See also Jervis.
Garvais, Garvaise, Garvas, Garvase, Gerivas, Gervais, Gervas, Gervase, Gervasio, Gervaso, Gervasy, Gervayse, Gervis, Gerwazy

Gerwin (Welsh) fair love.
Gerwen, Gerwyn

Gethin (Welsh) dusky.
Geth, Gethyn

Gevork (Armenian) a form of George.

Ghazi (Arabic) conqueror.

Ghilchrist (Irish) servant of Christ. See also Gil.
Ghylchrist

Ghislain (French) pledge.

Gi (Korean) brave.

Gia (Vietnamese) family.
Giah, Gya, Gyah

Giacinto (Portuguese, Spanish) a form of Jacinto.
Giacintho, Gyacinto, Gyacynto

Giacomo (Italian) a form of Jacob.
Gaimo, Giacamo, Giaco, Giacobbe, Giacobo, Giacopo, Gyacomo

Gian (Italian) a form of Giovanni, John.
Ghian, Ghyan, Gianetto, Giann, Gianne, Giannes, Giannis, Giannos, Gyan

Giancarlo (Italian) a combination of Gian + Carlo.
Giancarlos, Gianncarlo, Gyancarlo

Gianfranco (Italian) a combination of Gian + Franco.

Gianluca (Italian) a combination of Gian + Luca.

Gianmarco (Italian) a combination of Gian + Marco.

Gianni (Italian) a form of Johnie.
Giani, Gionni

Gianpaolo (Italian) a combination of Gian + Paolo.
Gianpaulo

Gib (English) a short form of Gilbert.
Gibb, Gibbie, Gibby

Gibor (Hebrew) powerful.
Gibbor

Gibson (English) son of Gilbert.
Gibbon, Gibbons, Gibbs, Gibbson, Gilson

Gideon (Hebrew) tree cutter. Bible: the judge who defeated the Midianites.
Gedeon, Gideone, Gydeon, Hedeon

Gidon (Hebrew) a form of Gideon.

Gifford (English) bold giver.
Giff, Giffard, Gifferd, Giffie, Giffy, Gyfford, Gyford

Gig (English) horse-drawn carriage.

Gil (Greek) shield bearer. (Hebrew) happy. (English) a short form of Ghilchrist, Gilbert.

Gili, Gilie, Gill, Gilley, Gilli, Gillie, Gillis, Gilly, Gyl, Gyll

Gilad (Arabic) camel hump; from Giladi, Saudi Arabia.
Giladi, Giladie, Gilead, Gylad, Gylead

Gilamu (Basque) a form of William.
Gillen, Gylamu

Gilbert (English) brilliant pledge; trustworthy. See also Gil, Gillett.
Gib, Gilburt, Gilibeirt, Gilleabert, Gillbert, Gillburt, Giselbert, Giselberto, Giselbertus, Guilbert, Gylbert, Gylbirt, Gylburt, Gylbyrt

Gilberto (Spanish) a form of Gilbert.
Gilburto

Gilby (Scandinavian) hostage's estate. (Irish) blond boy.
Gilbee, Gilbey, Gilbi, Gilbie, Gillbee, Gillbey, Gillbi, Gillbie, Gillby, Gylbee, Gylbey, Gylbi, Gylbie, Gylby, Gyllbee, Gyllbey, Gyllbi, Gyllbie, Gyllby

Gilchrist (Irish) a form of Ghilchrist.
Gilcrist

Gilen (Basque, German) illustrious pledge.
Gilenn, Gylen

Giles (French) goatskin shield.
Gide, Gyles, Gylles

Gillean (Irish) Bible: Saint John's servant.
Gillan, Gillen, Gillian, Gillyan

Gilles (French) a form of Giles.

Gillespie (Irish) son of the bishop's servant.
Gillis, Gyllespie, Gyllespy

Gillett (French) young Gilbert.
Gelett, Gelette, Gilet, Gilett, Gilette, Gillette, Gillit, Gylet, Gylett, Gylit, Gylitt, Gylyt, Gylytt

Gilmer (English) famous hostage.
Gilmar, Gylmar, Gylmer

Gilmore (Irish) devoted to the Virgin Mary.
Gillmoor, Gillmoore, Gillmor, Gillmore, Gillmour, Gilmoor, Gilmoore, Gilmor, Gilmour, Gylmoor, Gylmoore, Gylmor, Gylmore

Gilon (Hebrew) circle.
Gylon

Gilroy (Irish) devoted to the king.
Gilderoi, Gilderoy, Gildray, Gildroi, Gildroy, Gillroi, Gillroy, Gyllroi, Gyllroy, Gylroi, Gylroy, Roy

Gino (Greek) a familiar form of Eugene. (Italian) a short form of names ending in "gene," "gino."
Ghino, Gyno

Giona (Italian) a form of Jonah.
Gionah, Gyona, Gyonah

Giordano (Italian) a form of Jordan.
Giordan, Giordana, Giordin, Guordan

Giorgio (Italian) a form of George.

Giorgos (Greek) a form of George.
Georgos, Giorgios

Giosia (Italian) a form of Joshua.
Giosiah, Giosya, Gyosia, Gyosya, Gyosyah

Giotto (Italian) a form of Geoffrey.

Giovani, Giovanny, Giovany (Italian) forms of Giovanni.
Giavani, Giovan, Giovane, Giovanie, Giovonny, Gyovani, Gyovanie, Gyovany

Giovanni (Italian) a form of John. See also Jeovanni, Jiovanni.
Giannino, Giovann, Giovannie, Giovanno, Giovon, Giovonathon, Giovonni, Giovonnia, Giovonnie, Givonni

Gipsy (English) wanderer.
Gipson, Gypsy

Girvin (Irish) small; tough.
Girvan, Girven, Girvon, Girvyn, Gyrvyn

Gitano (Spanish) gypsy.
Gytano

Giuliano (Italian) a form of Julius.
Giulano, Giulino, Giulliano

Giulio (Italian) a form of Julius.
Gyulio, Gyulyo

Giuseppe (Italian) a form of Joseph.
Giuseppi, Giuseppino, Giusseppe, Guiseppe, Guiseppi, Guiseppie, Guisseppe

Giustino (Italian) a form of Justin.
Giusto, Giustyno, Gyustino, Gyusto, Gyustyno

Givon (Hebrew) hill; heights.
Givan, Givawn, Given, Givyn

Gladwin (English) cheerful. See also Win.
Glad, Gladdie, Gladdy, Gladwen, Gladwenn, Gladwinn, Gladwyn, Gladwynn, Gladwynne

Glanville (English) village with oak trees.
Glannville, Glanvil, Glanvill, Glanvyl, Glanvyll, Glanvylle

Glasson (Scottish) from Glasgow, Scotland.
Glason, Glassan, Glassen, Glassin, Glassyn

Glen, Glenn (Irish) short forms of Glendon.
Glean, Gleann, Glennie, Glennis, Glennon, Glenny

Glendon (Scottish) fortress in the glen.
Glandan, Glandun, Glenden, Glendin, Glendyn, Glenndan, Glennden, Glenndin, Glenndon, Glenndyn, Glennton, Glenton, Glyndan, Glynden, Glyndin, Glyndon, Glyndyn, Glynndan, Glynnden, Glynndin, Glynndon, Glynndun, Glynndyn

Glendower (Welsh) from Glyndwr, Wales.

Glenrowan (Irish) valley with rowan trees.
Glennrowan, Glenrowen, Glenrowin, Glenrowyn, Glynnrowan, Glynnrowen, Glynnrowin, Glynnrowon, Glynnrowyn, Glynrowan, Glynrowen, Glynrowin, Glynrowon, Glynrowyn

Glenton (Scottish) valley town.
Glennton, Glynnton, Glynton

Glenville (Irish) village in the glen.
Glenvyl, Glenvyle, Glenvyll, Glenvylle, Glynnville, Glynville

Glyn, Glynn (Welsh) forms of Glen.
Glin, Glinn

Goddard (German) divinely firm.
Godard, Godart, Goddart, Godhardt, Godhart, Gothart, Gotthard, Gotthardt, Gotthart

Godfrey (Irish) God's peace. (German) a form of Jeffrey. See also Geoffrey, Gottfried.
Goddfree, Goddfrey, Godefroi, Godfree, Godfry, Godofredo, Godoired, Godrey, Goffredo, Gofraidh, Gofredo, Gorry

Godwin (English) friend of God. See also Win.
Godewyn, Godwen, Godwinn, Godwyn, Godwynn, Goodwin, Goodwyn, Goodwynn, Goodwynne

Goel (Hebrew) redeemer.

Golden (English) a form of Goldwin.

Goldwin (English) golden friend. See also Win.
Goldewin, Goldewinn, Goldewyn, Goldwinn, Goldwinne, Goldwyn, Goldwyne, Goldwynn, Goldwynne

Goliath (Hebrew) exiled. Bible: the giant Philistine whom David slew with a slingshot.
Golliath, Golyath

Gomda (Kiowa) wind.
Gomdah

Gomer (Hebrew) completed, finished. (English) famous battle.

Gomez (Spanish) man.
Gomaz

Gonza (Rutooro) love.
Gonzah

Gonzalo (Spanish) wolf.
Goncalve, Gonsalo, Gonsalve, Gonsalvo, Gonzales, Gonzalos, Gonzalous, Gonzelee, Gonzolo

Goran (Greek) a form of George.

Gordon (English) triangular-shaped hill.
Gord, Gordain, Gordan, Gorden, Gordin, Gordonn, Gordun, Gordyn

Gordy (English) a familiar form of Gordon.
Gordie

Gore (English) triangular-shaped land; wedge-shaped land.

Gorge (Latin) gorge. (Greek) a form of George.

Gorman (Irish) small; blue eyed.
Gormen

Goro (Japanese) fifth.

Gosheven (Native American) great leaper.

Gottfried (German) a form of Geoffrey, Godfrey.
Gotfrid, Gotfrids, Gottfrid

Gotzon (German) a form of Angel.

Govert (Dutch) heavenly peace.

Gower (Welsh) pure.

Gowon (Tiv) rainmaker.
Gowan, Gowen, Gowin, Gowyn

Gozol (Hebrew) soaring bird.
Gozal

Grady (Irish) noble; illustrious.
Gradea, Gradee, Gradey, Gradi, Gradie, Gradleigh, Graidee, Graidey, Graidi, Graidie, Graidy, Graydee, Graydey, Graydi, Graydie, Graydy

Graeme (Scottish) a form of Graham.
Graem, Graiam, Gram, Grame, Gramm, Grayeme

Graham (English) grand home.
Graeham, Graehame, Graehme, Grahame, Grahamme, Grahem, Graheme, Grahim, Grahime, Grahm, Grahme, Grahym, Graiham, Graihame, Grayham, Grayhame, Grayhim, Grayhym, Greyham, Greyhame, Greyhem, Greyheme

Granger (French) farmer.
Grainger, Grange, Graynger

Grant (English) a short form of Grantland.
Grand, Grandt, Grantham, Granthem

Grantland (English) great plains.
Granlan, Granland, Grantlan

Grantley (English) great meadow.
Grantlea, Grantlee, Grantleigh, Grantli, Grantlie, Grantly

Granville (French) large village.
Gran, Granvel, Granvil, Granvile, Granvill, Granvyl, Granvyll, Granvylle, Grenville, Greville

Gray (English) gray haired.
Grae, Grai, Graye, Greye

Grayden (English) gray haired.
Graden, Graedan, Graeden, Graedin, Graedyn, Graidan, Graiden, Graidin, Graidyn, Graydan, Graydin, Graydyn, Greyden, Greydin, Greydyn

Graydon (English) gray hill.
Gradon, Graedon, Graidon, Grayton, Greydon

Grayson (English) bailiff's son. See also Sonny.
Graeson, Graison, Graysen

Greeley (English) gray meadow.
Greelea, Greeleigh, Greeli, Greelie, Greely

Greenwood (English) green forest.
Green, Greener, Greenewood, Greenerwood

Greg, Gregg (Latin) short forms of Gregory.
Graig, Greig, Greigg, Gregson

Greggory (Latin) a form of Gregory.
Greggery, Greggori, Greggorie

Gregor (Scottish) a form of Gregory.
Gregoor, Grégor, Gregore

Gregorio (Italian, Portuguese) a form of Gregory.
Gregorios

Gregory (Latin) vigilant watchman. See also Jörn, Krikor.
Gergely, Gergo, Greagoir, Greagory, Greer, Gregary, Greger, Gregery, Grégoire, Gregorey, Gregori, Grégorie, Gregorius, Gregors, Gregos, Gregrey, Gregroy, Gregry, Greigoor, Greigor, Greigore, Greogry, Gries, Grisha, Grzegorz

Gresham (English) village in the pasture.

Grey (English) a form of Gray.

Greyson (English) a form of Grayson.
Greysen, Greysten, Greyston

Griffen (Latin) a form of Griffin.
Grifen

Griffin (Latin) hooked nose.
Griff, Griffie, Griffon, Griffy, Griffyn, Griffynn, Gryffin, Gryffyn, Gryphon

Griffith (Welsh) fierce chief; ruddy.
Griff, Griffeth, Griffie, Griffy, Gryffith

Grigor (Bulgarian) a form of Gregory.

Grigori (Bulgarian) a form of Gregory.
Grigoi, Grigore, Grigorij, Grigorios, Grigorov, Grigory

Grimshaw (English) dark woods.
Grymshaw

Grisha (Russian) a form of Gregory.
Grysha

Griswold (German, French) gray forest.
Gris, Griswald, Griswaldo, Griswoldo, Griz, Grizwald, Gryswald, Gryswaldo

Grosvener (French) big hunter.

Grover (English) grove.
Grove

Guadalupe (Arabic) river of black stones.
Guadalope

Gualberto (Spanish) a form of Walter.

Gualtiero (Italian) a form of Walter.
Gualterio

Guglielmo (Italian) a form of William.

Guido (Italian) a form of Guy.

Guilford (English) ford with yellow flowers.
Guildford

Guilherme (Portuguese) a form of William.

Guillaume (French) a form of William.
Guillaums, Guilleaume, Guilem, Guyllaume

Guillermo (Spanish) a form of William.
Guillerrmo

Guir (Irish) beige.

Gunnar (Scandinavian) a form of Gunther.

Gunner (English) soldier with a gun. (Scandinavian) a form of Gunther. *Guner*

Gunter (Scandinavian) a form of Gunther. *Guenter, Guntar, Guntero*

Gunther (Scandinavian) battle army; warrior. *Guenther, Gun, Gunthar, Günther*

Guotin (Chinese) polite; strong leader.

Gurdeep (Sikh) lamp of the guru.

Gurion (Hebrew) young lion. *Gur, Guri, Guriel, Guryon*

Gurjot (Sikh) light of the guru.

Gurpreet (Sikh) devoted to the guru; devoted to the Prophet. *Gurjeet, Gurmeet, Guruprit*

Gurveer (Sikh) guru's warrior.

Gurvir (Sikh) a form of Gurveer.

Gus (Scandinavian) a short form of Angus, Augustine, Gustave. *Guss, Gussie, Gussy, Gusti, Gustry, Gusty*

Gustaf (Swedish) a form of Gustave. *Gustaaf, Gustaff*

Gustave (Scandinavian) staff of the Goths. History: Gustavus Adolphus was a king of Sweden. See also Kosti, Tabo, Tavo. *Gustaof, Gustav, Gustáv, Gustava, Gustaves, Gustavius, Gustavs, Gustavus, Gustik, Gustus, Gusztav*

Gustavo (Italian, Spanish) a form of Gustave. *Gustabo*

Guthrie (German) war hero. (Irish) windy place. *Guthre, Guthree, Guthrey, Guthri, Guthry*

Gutierre (Spanish) a form of Walter.

Guy (Hebrew) valley. (German) warrior. (French) guide. See also Guido. *Guie, Guyon*

Guyapi (Native American) candid.

Guyllaume (French) a form of William.

Gwayne (Welsh) a form of Gawain. *Gwaine, Gwayn*

Gwidon (Polish) life. *Gwydon*

Gwilym (Welsh) a form of William. *Gwillym*

Gwyn (Welsh) fair; blessed. *Gwinn, Gwinne, Gwynn, Gwynne*

Gyasi (Akan) marvelous baby.

Gyorgy (Russian) a form of George. *Gyoergy, György, Gyuri, Gyurka*

Gyula (Hungarian) youth. *Gyala, Gyuszi*

Habib (Arabic) beloved. *Habyb*

Hackett (German, French) little wood cutter. *Hacket, Hackit, Hackitt, Hackyt, Hackytt*

Hackman (German, French) wood cutter. *Hackmen*

Hadar (Hebrew) glory.

Haddad (Arabic) blacksmith. *Hadad*

Hadden (English) heather-covered hill. *Haddan, Haddin, Haddon, Haddyn*

Haden (English) a form of Hadden. *Hadan, Hadin, Hadon, Hadun, Hadyn, Haeden*

Hadi (Arabic) guiding to the right. *Haddi, Hadee, Hady*

Hadley (English) heather-covered meadow. *Had, Hadlea, Hadlee, Hadleigh, Hadly, Leigh*

Hadrian (Latin, Swedish) dark.
Adrian, Hadrien, Hadrion, Hadryan, Hadryen, Hadryin, Hadryon, Hadryn

Hadwin (English) friend in a time of war.
Hadwen, Hadwinn, Hadwyn, Hadwynn, Hadwynne

Hagan (German) strong defense.
Haggan

Hagar (Hebrew) forsaken; stranger.
Hager, Hagir, Hagor, Hagyr

Hagen (Irish) young, youthful.
Hagin, Hagon, Hagun, Hagyn

Hagley (English) enclosed meadow.
Haglea, Haglee, Hagleigh, Hagli, Haglie, Hagly

Hagop (Armenian) a form of James.

Hagos (Ethiopian) happy.

Hahnee (Native American) beggar.

Hai (Vietnamese) sea.

Haidar (Arabic) lion.

Haiden (English) a form of Hayden.
Haidan, Haidin, Haidn, Haidon, Haidun, Haidyn

Haider (Arabic) a form of Haidar.

Haig (English) enclosed with hedges.
Hayg

Hailama (Hawaiian) famous brother.
Hailamah, Hailaman, Hairama, Hilama, Hilamah

Hailey (Irish) a form of Haley.
Haile, Hailea, Hailee, Haileigh, Haille, Haily, Halee

Haines (English) from the vine-covered cottage.
Hanes, Haynes

Haji (Swahili) born during the pilgrimage to Mecca.

Hakan (Native American) fiery.
Haken, Hakin, Hakon, Hakyn

Hakeem (Arabic) a form of Hakim.
Hakam, Hakem

Hakim (Arabic) wise. (Ethiopian) doctor.
Hackeem, Hackim, Hakiem, Hakym

Hakon (Scandinavian) of Nordic ancestry.
Haaken, Haakin, Haakon, Haeo, Hak, Hakan, Hakin, Hako, Hakyn

Hal (English) a short form of Halden, Hall, Harold.

Halbert (English) shining hero.
Bert, Halbirt, Halburt, Halbyrt

Halcyon (Greek) tranquil, peaceful; kingfisher. Mythology: the kingfisher bird was supposed to have the power to calm the wind and the waves while nesting near the sea.
Halcion

Halden (Scandinavian) half-Danish. See also Dane.
Hal, Haldan, Haldane, Haldin, Haldon, Haldyn, Halfdan, Halvdan

Hale (English) a short form of Haley. (Hawaiian) a form of Harry.
Hael, Haele, Hail, Hayl, Hayle, Heall

Halen (Swedish) hall.
Hailen, Hailin, Hailon, Hailyn, Hallen, Hallene, Haylen

Haley (Irish) ingenious.
Haleigh, Halley, Hayleigh, Hayley, Hayli

Halford (English) valley ford.
Haleford

Hali (Greek) sea.
Halea, Halee, Halie

Halian (Zuni) young.
Halyan

Halifax (English) holy field.
Halyfax

Halil (Turkish) dear friend.
Halill, Halyl

Halim (Arabic) mild, gentle.
Haleem, Halym

Hall (English) manor, hall.

Hallam (English) valley.
Halam

Hallan (English) dweller at the hall; dweller at the manor.

Hailan, Halan, Halin, Hallin, Hallon, Hallyn, Halon, Halyn, Haylan

Halley (English) meadow near the hall; holy.
Hallee, Halleigh, Halli, Hallie, Hally

Halliwell (English) holy well.
Haliwel, Haliwell, Hallewell, Halliwell, Hallywel, Hallywell, Halywel, Halywell, Hellewell, Helliwell

Hallward (English) hall guard.
Halward

Halsey (English) Hal's island.
Hallsea, Hallsey, Hallsy, Halsea, Halsy

Halstead (English) manor grounds.
Halsted

Halton (English) estate on the hill.
Haltan, Halten, Haltin, Haltyn

Halvor (Norwegian) rock; protector.
Hallvar, Hallvard, Halvar, Halvard

Ham (Hebrew) hot. Bible: one of Noah's sons.

Hamal (Arabic) lamb. Astronomy: a bright star in the constellation of Aries.
Hamel, Hamol

Hamar (Scandinavian) hammer.
Hamer, Hammar, Hammer

Hamed (Arabic) a form of Hamid.
Hamedo, Hameed, Hammed

Hamid (Arabic) praised. See also Muhammad.
Haamid, Hamaad, Hamadi, Hamd, Hamdrem, Hammad, Hammyd, Hammydd, Humayd

Hamidi (Kenyan) admired.
Hamidie, Hamidy

Hamill (English) scarred.
Hamel, Hamell, Hamil, Hammil, Hammill, Hamyl, Hamyll

Hamilton (English) proud estate.
Hamelton, Hamiltan, Hamilten, Hamiltun, Hamiltyn, Hamylton, Tony

Hamish (Scottish) a form of Jacob, James.
Hamysh

Hamisi (Swahili) born on Thursday.
Hamisie, Hamisy

Hamlet (German, French) little village; home. Literature: one of Shakespeare's tragic heroes.
Hamlit, Hamlot

Hamlin (German, French) loves his home.
Hamblin, Hamelen, Hamelin, Hamlan, Hamlen, Hamlon, Hamlyn, Lin

Hammet (English, Scandinavian) village.
Hammett, Hamnet, Hamnett

Hammond (English) village.
Hamond, Hammon, Hammund, Hamund

Hampton (English) Geography: a town in England.
Hamp, Hampden, Hamptan, Hampten, Hamptin, Hamptyn

Hamza (Arabic) powerful.
Hamze, Hamzia

Hamzah (Arabic) a form of Hamza.
Hamzeh

Hanale (Hawaiian) a form of Henry.
Haneke

Hanan (Hebrew) grace.
Hananel, Hananiah, Johanan

Hanbal (Arabic) pure. History: Ahmad Ibn Hanbal founded an Islamic school of thought.
Hanbel, Hanbil, Hanbyn

Handel (German, English) a form of John. Music: George Frideric Handel was a German composer whose works include *Messiah* and *Water Music*.
Handal, Handil, Handol, Handyl

Hanford (English) high ford.

Hanif (Arabic) true believer.
Haneef, Hanef, Hanyf

Hank (American) a familiar form of Henry.

Hanley (English) high meadow.
Handlea, Handlee, Handleigh, Handley, Handli, Handlie, Handly, Hanlea, Hanlee, Hanleigh, Hanly

Hanna, Hannah (German) forms of Johann.

Hannes (Finnish) a form of John.
Hanes, Hannus

Hannibal (Phoenician) grace of God. History: a famous Carthaginian general who fought the Romans.
Anibal, Hanibal, Hannybal, Hanybal

Hanno (German) a short form of Johann.
Hannon, Hannu, Hano, Hanon

Hans (Scandinavian) a form of John.
Hants, Hanz

Hansel (Scandinavian) a form of Hans.
Haensel, Hannsel, Hansal, Hansell, Hansil, Hansl, Hansol, Hansyl, Hanzel

Hansen (Scandinavian) son of Hans.
Hansan, Hansin, Hanssen, Hansun, Hansyn

Hansh (Hindi) god; godlike.

Hanson (Scandinavian) a form of Hansen.
Hansson

Hanus (Czech) a form of John.

Haoa (Hawaiian) a form of Howard.

Hara (Hindi) seizer. Religion: another name for the Hindu god Shiva.

Harald (Scandinavian) a form of Harold.
Haraldas, Haralds, Haralpos

Harb (Arabic) warrior.

Harbin (German, French) little bright warrior.
Harban, Harben, Harbon, Harbyn

Harcourt (French) fortified dwelling.
Court, Harcort

Hardeep (Punjabi) a form of Harpreet.

Harden (English) valley of the hares.
Hardan, Hardian, Hardin, Hardon, Hardun, Hardyn

Harding (English) brave; hardy.
Hardyng

Hardwin (English) brave friend.
Hardwen, Hardwenn, Hardinn, Hardwyn, Hardwynn

Hardy (German) bold, daring.
Harde, Hardee, Hardey, Hardi, Hardie

Harel (Hebrew) mountain of God.
Haral, Harell, Hariel, Harrel, Harrell, Haryel, Haryell

Harford (English) ford of the hares.
Hareford

Hargrove (English) grove of the hares.
Haregrove, Hargreave, Hargreaves

Hari (Hindi) tawny.
Harin

Haris (English) a form of Harris.
Hariss, Harys, Heris, Herys

Harith (Arabic) cultivator.
Haryth

Harjot (Sikh) light of God.
Harjeet, Harjit, Harjodh

Harkin (Irish) dark red.
Harkan, Harken, Harkon, Harkyn

Harlan (English) hare's land; army land.
Harlen, Harlenn, Harlin, Harlon, Harlyn, Harlynn

Harland (English) a form of Harlan.
Harlend

Harley (English) hare's meadow; army meadow.
Arley, Harle, Harlea, Harlee, Harleigh, Harly

Harlow (English) hare's hill; army hill. See also Arlo.
Harlo

Harman, Harmon (English) forms of Herman.
Harm, Harmann, Harmen, Harmin, Harmond, Harms, Harmyn

Harold (Scandinavian) army ruler. See also Jindra.
Araldo, Garald, Garold, Harald, Hareld, Harild, Haryld, Herald, Hereld, Herold, Heronim, Heryld

Haroon (Arabic) a form of Haroun.

Haroun (Arabic) lofty; exalted.
Haaroun, Haarun, Harin, Haron, Harron, Harrun, Harun

Harper (English) harp player.
Harp, Harpo

Harpreet (Punjabi) loves God, devoted to God.

Harrington (English) Harry's town.
Harringtown

Harris (English) a short form of Harrison.
Harrys, Herris, Herrys

Harrison (English) son of Harry.
Harison, Harreson, Harrisen, Harrisson, Harryson, Haryson

Harrod (Hebrew) hero; conqueror.
Harod

Harry (English) a familiar form of Harold, Henry. See also Arrigo, Hale, Parry.
Harray, Harrey, Harri, Harrie, Hary

Hart (English) a short form of Hartley.
Harte, Heart

Hartley (English) deer meadow.
Hartlea, Hartlee, Hartleigh, Hartly, Heartlea, Heartlee, Heartleigh, Heartley, Heartli, Heartlie, Heartly

Hartman (German) hard; strong.
Hartmen

Hartwell (English) deer well.
Hartwel, Hartwil, Hartwill, Hartwyl, Hartwyll, Harwel, Harwell, Harwil, Harwill

Hartwig (German) strong advisor.
Hartwyg

Hartwood (English) deer forest.
Harwood

Harvey (German) army warrior.
Harv, Harvee, Harvi, Harvie, Harvy, Herve

Harvir (Sikh) God's warrior.
Harvier

Hasaan, Hasan (Arabic) forms of Hassan.
Hasain, Hasaun, Hashaan, Hason

Hasad (Turkish) reaper, harvester.
Hassad

Hasani (Swahili) handsome.
Hasanni, Hassani, Hassian, Heseny, Husani

Hashim (Arabic) destroyer of evil.
Haashim, Hasham, Hasheem, Hashem, Hashym

Hasin (Hindi) laughing.
Haseen, Hasen, Hassin, Hassyn, Hasyn, Hesen

Haskel (Hebrew) a form of Ezekiel.
Haskell

Haslett (English) hazel-tree land.
Haslet, Haze, Hazel, Hazlet, Hazlett, Hazlitt

Hassan (Arabic) handsome.
Hassen, Hasson

Hassel (German, English) witches' corner.
Hasel, Hasell, Hassal, Hassall, Hassell, Hazael, Hazell

Hastin (Hindi) elephant.
Hastan, Hasten, Haston, Hastyn

Hastings (Latin) spear. (English) house council.
Hastie, Hasting, Hasty

Hatim (Arabic) judge.
Hateem, Hatem

Hauk (Norwegian) hawk.
Haukeye

Havelock (Norwegian) sea battler.
Haveloc, Haveloch, Havloche, Havlocke

Haven (Dutch, English) harbor, port; safe place.
Haeven, Havan, Havin, Havon, Havyn, Hevin, Hevon, Hovan

Havgan (Irish) white.
Havgen, Havgin, Havgon, Havgun, Havgyn

Havika (Hawaiian) a form of David.
Havyka

Hawk (English) hawk.
Hawke, Hawkin, Hawkins

Hawley (English) hedged meadow.
Hawlea, Hawlee, Hawleigh, Hawli, Hawlie,
Hawly

Hawthorne (English) hawthorn tree.
Hawthorn

Hayden (English) hedged valley.
Haydan, Haydenn, Haydin, Haydun,
Haydyn, Heydan, Heyden, Heydin, Heydn,
Heydon, Heydun, Heydyn

Haydn, Haydon (English) forms of
Hayden.

Hayes (English) hedged valley.
Hais, Haise, Haiz, Haize, Hays, Hayse, Hayz

Hayward (English) guardian of the
hedged area.
Haiward, Haward, Heiward, Heyvard,
Heyward

Haywood (English) hedged forest.
Heiwood, Heywood, Woody

Hazen (Hindi) a form of Hasin.

Hearn (Scottish, English) a short form
of Ahearn.
Hearne, Herin, Hern, Herne

Heath (English) heath.
Heaf, Heaff, Heathe, Heith

Heathcliff (English) cliff near the heath.
Literature: the hero of Emily Brontë's
novel *Wuthering Heights.*
Heafclif, Heafcliff, Heaffclif, Heaffcliff,
Heaffcliffe, Heaffclyffe, Heathclif, Heathcliffe,
Heathclyffe

Heaton (English) high place.
Heatan, Heaten, Heatin, Heatyn

Heber (Hebrew) ally, partner.
Hebar

Hector (Greek) steadfast. Mythology:
the greatest hero of the Trojan War in
Homer's epic poem *Iliad.*
Ector, Heckter, Hecktir, Hecktore, Hecktur,
Hectar, Hektar, Hekter, Hektir, Hektor,
Hektore, Hektur

Hedley (English) heather-filled meadow.
Headley, Headly, Heddlea, Heddlee,
Heddleigh, Heddley, Heddli, Heddlie,

Heddly, Hedlea, Hedlee, Hedleigh, Hedli,
Hedlie, Hedly

Hedwig (German) fighter.
Heddwig, Heddwyg, Hedwyg

Hedwyn (Welsh) friend of peace and
blessings. (English) a form of Hadwin.
Hedwen, Heddwin, Heddwyn, Hedwen,
Hedwin

Heinrich (German) a form of Henry.
Heiner, Heinreich, Heinric, Heinriche,
Heinrick, Heinrik, Heynric, Heynrich,
Heynrick, Heynrik, Hinric, Hinrich,
Hinrick, Hynric, Hynrich, Hynrick, Hynrik

Heinz (German) a familiar form of Henry.

Helaku (Native American) sunny day.

Helge (Russian) holy.
Helg

Helki (Moquelumnan) touching.

Helmer (German) warrior's wrath.

Helmut (German) courageous.
Hellmut, Helmuth

Heman (Hebrew) faithful.
Hemen

Henderson (Scottish, English) son of
Henry.
Hendrie, Hendries, Hendron, Henryson

Hendrick (Dutch) a form of Henry.
Hedric, Hedrick, Heindric, Heindrick,
Hendric, Hendricks, Hendrickson, Hendrik,
Hendriks, Hendrikus, Hendrix, Hendryc,
Hendryck, Hendrycks, Hendryx

Heniek (Polish) a form of Henry.
Henier

Henley (English) high meadow.
Henlea, Henlee, Henleigh, Henli, Henlie,
Henly

Henning (German) a form of Hendrick,
Henry.
Hennings

Henoch (Yiddish) initiator.
Enoch, Henock, Henok

Henri (French) a form of Henry.
Henrico, Henrri

Henrick (Dutch) a form of Henry.
Heinrick, Henerik, Henric, Henrich, Henrik,
Henryc, Henryck, Henryk

Henrique (Portuguese) a form of Henry.

Henry (German) ruler of the household.
See also Arrigo, Enric, Enrico, Enrikos,
Enrique, Hanale, Honok, Kiki.
Harro, Heike, Henery, Henraoi, Henrim,
Henrry, Heromin

Heraldo (Spanish) a form of Harold.
Haraldo, Haroldo, Haryldo, Heryldo,
Hiraldo, Hyraldo

Herb (German) a short form of Herbert.
Herbe, Herbee, Herbi, Herbie, Herby

Herbert (German) glorious soldier.
Bert, Erbert, Eriberto, Harbert, Hebert,
Hébert, Heberto, Herberte, Herbirt, Herburt,
Herbyrt, Hirbert, Hirbirt, Hirburt, Hirbyrt,
Hurbert, Hyrbert, Hyrbirt, Hyrburt, Hyrbyrt

Hercules (Latin) glorious gift.
Mythology: a Greek hero of fabulous
strength, renowned for his twelve labors.
Herakles, Herc, Hercule, Herculie

Heriberto (Spanish) a form of Herbert.
Heribert

Herman (Latin) noble. (German) soldier.
See also Armand, Ermanno, Ermano,
Mandek.
Hermaan, Hermann, Hermano, Hermie,
Herminio, Hermino, Hermon, Hermy,
Hermyn, Heromin

Hermes (Greek) messenger. Mythology:
the divine herald of Greek mythology.

Hernan (German) peacemaker.

Hernando (Spanish) a form of Ferdinand.
Hernandes, Hernandez

Herrick (German) war ruler.
Herick, Herik, Herrik, Herryc, Herryck,
Herryk

Herschel (Hebrew) a form of Hershel.
Herchel, Herschell, Hirschel, Hyrschel

Hersh (Hebrew) a short form of Hershel.
Hersch, Hirsch

Hershel (Hebrew) deer.
Hershal, Hershall, Hershell, Herzl, Hirshel,
Hyrshel

Hertz (Yiddish) my strife.
Herts, Herzel

Hervé (French) a form of Harvey.
Herv, Hervee, Hervey, Hervi, Hervie, Hervy

Hesperos (Greek) evening star.
Hespero

Hesutu (Moquelumnan) picking up a
yellow jacket's nest.

Hew (Welsh) a form of Hugh.
Hewe, Huw

Hewitt (German, French) little smart one.
Hewet, Hewett, Hewie, Hewit, Hewlett,
Hewlitt, Hughet, Hughett, Hughit, Hughitt,
Hughyt, Hughytt

Hewson (English) son of Hugh.
Hueson, Hughson

Hezekiah (Hebrew) God gives strength.
Hazikiah, Hezekia, Hezekyah, Hezikyah

Hiamovi (Cheyenne) high chief.
Hyamovi

Hiawatha (Iroquois) river maker. History:
the Onondagan leader credited with
organizing the Iroquois confederacy.

Hibah (Arabic) gift.
Hibah, Hyba, Hybah

Hideaki (Japanese) smart, clever.
Hideo, Hydeaki

Hieremias (Greek) God will uplift.

Hieronymos (Greek) a form of Jerome.
Art: Hieronymus Bosch was a fifteenth-
century Dutch painter.
Hierome, Hieronim, Hieronimo, Hieronimos,
Hieronymo, Hieronymus

Hieu (Vietnamese) respectful.
Hyew

Hilal (Arabic) new moon.
Hylal

Hilario (Spanish) a form of Hilary.

Hilary (Latin) cheerful. See also Ilari.
Hi, Hil, Hilair, Hilaire, Hilare, Hilarie,
Hilarion, Hilarius, Hilery, Hill, Hillary,
Hillery, Hilliary, Hillie, Hilly, Hylarie,
Hylary

Hildebrand (German) battle sword.
Hildebrando, Hildo

Hilderic (German) warrior; fortress.
Hilderich, Hilderiche, Hylderic, Hylderych,
Hylderyche

Hillel (Hebrew) greatly praised. Religion:
Rabbi Hillel originated the Talmud.
Hilel, Hylel, Hyllel

Hilliard (German) brave warrior.
Hiliard, Hillard, Hiller, Hillier, Hillierd,
Hillyard, Hillyer, Hillyerd, Hyliard, Hylliar

Hilmar (Swedish) famous noble.
Hillmar, Hilmer, Hylmar, Hylmer

Hilton (English) town on a hill.
Hillton, Hylton

Hinto (Dakota) blue.
Hynto

Hinun (Native American) spirit of the
storm.
Hynun

Hipolito (Spanish) a form of Hippolyte.

Hippolyte (Greek) horseman.
Hippolit, Hippolitos, Hippolytus, Ippolito

Hiram (Hebrew) noblest; exalted.
Hi, Hirom, Huram

Hiromasa (Japanese) fair, just.

Hiroshi (Japanese) generous.
Hyroshi

Hisoka (Japanese) secretive, reserved.
Hysoka

Hiu (Hawaiian) a form of Hugh.
Hyu

Ho (Chinese) good.

Hoang (Vietnamese) finished.

Hobart (German) Bart's hill. (German) a
form of Hubert.
Hobard, Hobarte, Hoebard, Hoebart

Hobert (German) Bert's hill.
Hobirt, Hoburt, Hobyrt

Hobie (German) a short form of Hobart,
Hobert.
Hobbie, Hobby, Hobey

Hobson (English) son of Robert.
Hobbs, Hobs, Hobsan, Hobsen, Hobsin,
Hobsyn

Hoc (Vietnamese) studious.
Hock, Hok

Hod (Hebrew) a short form of Hodgson.

Hodgson (English) son of Roger.
Hod

Hoffman (German) influential.
Hoffmen, Hofman, Hofmen

Hogan (Irish) youth.
Hogen, Hogin, Hogun, Hogyn

Holbrook (English) brook in the hollow.
Brook, Holbrooke

Holden (English) hollow in the valley.
Holdan, Holdin, Holdon, Holdun, Holdyn

Holic (Czech) barber.
Holick, Holik, Holyc, Holyck, Holyk

Holland (French) Geography: a former
province of the Netherlands.
Holand, Hollan

Holleb (Polish) dove.
Hollub, Holub

Hollis (English) grove of holly trees.
Hollie, Holliss, Holly, Hollys, Hollyss

Holmes (English) river islands.

Holt (English) forest.
Holtan, Holten, Holtin, Holton, Holtyn

Homar (Greek) a form of Homer.

Homer (Greek) hostage; pledge; security.
Literature: a renowned Greek epic poet.
Homere, Homère, Homeros, Homerus,
Omero

Homero (Spanish) a form of Homer.

Hondo (Shona) warrior.

Honesto (Filipino) honest.

Honi (Hebrew) gracious.
Choni, Honie, Hony

Honok (Polish) a form of Henry.

Honon (Moquelumnan) bear.

Honorato (Spanish) honorable.

Honoré (Latin) honored.
Honor, Honoratus, Honoray, Honorio, Honorius

Honovi (Native American) strong.

Honza (Czech) a form of John.

Hop (Chinese) agreeable.

Horace (Latin) keeper of the hours.
Literature: a famous Roman lyric poet and satirist.
Horaz

Horacio (Latin) a form of Horace.
Horazio, Orazio

Horatio (Latin) clan name. See also Orris.
Horatius, Oratio

Horst (German) dense grove; thicket.

Horton (English) garden estate.
Hort, Hortan, Horten, Hortin, Hortun, Hortyn, Orton

Hosa (Arapaho) young crow.
Hosah

Hosea (Hebrew) salvation. Bible: a Hebrew prophet.
Hose, Hoseia, Hoshea, Hosheah

Hotah (Lakota) white.
Hota

Hototo (Native American) whistler.
Hoto

Houghton (English) settlement on the headland.
Houghtan, Houghten, Houghtin, Huetan, Hueten, Huetin, Hueton, Hughtan, Hughten, Hughtin, Hughton

Houston (English) hill town. Geography: a city in Texas.
Houstan, Housten, Houstin, Houstun, Houstyn

Howard (English) watchman. See also Haoa.
Howerd, Ward

Howe (German) high.

Howell (Welsh) remarkable.
Hoell, Howal, Howall, Howel, Huell, Hywel, Hywell

Howi (Moquelumnan) turtledove.

Howie (English) a familiar form of Howard, Howland.
Howee, Howey, Howy

Howin (Chinese) loyal swallow.
Howyn

Howland (English) hilly land.
Howie, Howlan, Howlande, Howlen

Hoyt (Irish) mind; spirit.
Hoit, Hoyts

Hu (Chinese) tiger.

Hubbard (German) a form of Hubert.

Hubert (German) bright mind; bright spirit. See also Beredei, Uberto.
Bert, Hubbert, Huber, Hubertek, Hubertson, Hubirt, Huburt, Hubyrt, Hugibert, Huibert

Huberto (Spanish) a form of Hubert.

Hubie (English) a familiar form of Hubert.
Hube, Hubi

Hud (Arabic) Religion: a Muslim prophet.

Hudson (English) son of Hud.
Hudsan, Hudsen, Hudsin, Hudsyn

Huey (English) a familiar form of Hugh.
Hughee, Hughey, Hughi, Hughie, Hughy, Hui

Hugh (English) a short form of Hubert. See also Ea, Hewitt, Huxley, Maccoy, Ugo.
Fitzhugh, Hew, Hiu, Hue, Hughe, Hughes, Huw, Huwe

Hugo (Latin) a form of Hugh.
Huego, Ugo

Hugues (French) a form of Hugh.

Hulbert (German) brilliant grace.
Bert, Holbard, Holbert, Holberte, Holbirt,
Holburt, Holbyrt, Hulbard, Hulberte,
Hulbirt, Hulburd, Hulburt, Hulbyrt, Hull

Humbert (German) brilliant strength.
See also Umberto.
Hum, Humbirt, Humburt, Humbyrt

Humberto (Portuguese) a form of
Humbert.

Humphrey (German) peaceful strength.
See also Onofrio, Onufry.
Homfree, Homfrey, Homphree, Homphrey,
Homphry, Hum, Humfree, Humfredo,
Humfrey, Humfri, Humfrid, Humfrie,
Humfried, Humfry, Hump, Humph,
Humphery, Humphree, Humphry,
Humphrys, Hunfredo

Hung (Vietnamese) brave.

Hunt (English) a short form of names
beginning with "Hunt."
Hunta

Hunter (English) hunter.
Huntar, Huntur

Huntington (English) hunting estate.
Huntingdon

Huntley (English) hunter's meadow.
Huntlea, Huntlee, Huntleigh, Huntli,
Huntlie, Huntly

Hurley (Irish) sea tide.
Hurlea, Hurlee, Hurleigh, Hurli, Hurlie,
Hurly

Hurst (English) a form of Horst.
Hearst, Hirst, Hyrst

Husam (Arabic) sword.

Husamettin (Turkish) sharp sword.

Huslu (Native American) hairy bear.

Hussain, Hussien (Arabic) forms of
Hussein.
Hossain, Husain, Husani, Husayn, Husian,
Hussan, Hussin, Hussayn

Hussein (Arabic) little; handsome.
Hossein, Houssein, Houssin, Huissien,
Huossein, Husein, Husien

Huston (English) a form of Houston.
Hustin

Hutchinson (English) son of the hutch
dweller.
Hutcheson

Hute (Native American) star.

Hutton (English) house on the jutting
ledge.
Hut, Hutan, Huten, Hutin, Huton, Hutt,
Huttan, Hutten, Huttin, Huttun, Huttyn,
Hutun, Hutyn

Huxley (English) Hugh's meadow.
Hux, Huxlea, Huxlee, Huxleigh, Huxli,
Huxlie, Huxly, Lee

Huy (Vietnamese) glorious.

Hy (Vietnamese) hopeful. (English) a
short form of Hyman.

Hyacinthe (French) hyacinth.

Hyatt (English) high gate.
Hiat, Hiatt, Hiatte, Hyat, Hyatte

Hyde (English) cache; measure of land
equal to 120 acres; animal hide.

Hyder (English) tanner, preparer of animal
hides for tanning.

Hyman (English) a form of Chaim.
Haim, Hayim, Hayvim, Hayyim, Hy,
Hyam, Hymie

Hyrum (Hebrew) a form of Hiram
Hyram

Hyun-Ki (Korean) wise.

Hyun-Shik (Korean) clever.

I

Iago (Spanish, Welsh) a form of Jacob, James. Literature: the villain in Shakespeare's *Othello*.
Jago

Iain (Scottish) a form of Ian.

Iakobos (Greek) a form of Jacob.
Iakov, Iakovos, Iakovs

Iakona (Hawaiian) healer.
Iakonah

Ian (Scottish) a form of John. See also Ean, Eian.
Iane, Iann, Iin, Ion

Ianos (Czech) a form of John.
Iannis

Ib (Phoenician, Danish) oath of Baal.

Iban (Basque) a form of John.

Ibon (Basque) a form of Ivor.

Ibrahim (Hausa) my father is exalted. (Arabic) a form of Abraham.
Ibrahaim, Ibraham, Ibraheem, Ibrahem, Ibrahiem, Ibrahiim, Ibrahmim

Ibsen (German) archer's son. Literature: Henrik Ibsen was a nineteenth-century Norwegian poet and playwright whose works influenced the development of modern drama.
Ibsan, Ibsin, Ibson, Ibsyn

Ichabod (Hebrew) glory is gone. Literature: Ichabod Crane is the main character of Washington Irving's story "The Legend of Sleepy Hollow."

Ichiro (Japanese) born first.

Iden (English) pasture in the wood.
Idan, Idin, Idon, Idun, Idyn

Idi (Swahili) born during the Idd festival.

Idris (Welsh) eager lord. (Arabic) Religion: a Muslim prophet.
Idrease, Idrees, Idres, Idress, Idreus, Idriece, Idriss, Idrissa, Idriys, Idrys, Idryss

Iestyn (Welsh) a form of Justin.

Igashu (Native American) wanderer; seeker.
Igasho

Iggy (Latin) a familiar form of Ignatius.
Iggie

Ignacio (Italian) a form of Ignatius.
Ignazio

Ignatius (Latin) fiery, ardent. Religion: Saint Ignatius of Loyola founded the Jesuit order. See also Inigo, Neci.
Ignaas, Ignac, Ignác, Ignace, Ignacey, Ignacius, Ignas, Ignatas, Ignatios, Ignatious, Ignatus, Ignatys, Ignatz, Ignaz

Igor (Russian) a form of Inger, Ingvar. See also Egor, Yegor.
Igoryok

Ihsan (Turkish) compassionate.

Ike (Hebrew) a familiar form of Isaac. History: the nickname of the thirty-fourth U.S. president Dwight D. Eisenhower.
Ikee, Ikey, Ikke

Iker (Basque) visitation.

Ilan (Hebrew) tree. (Basque) youth.

Ilari (Basque) a form of Hilary.
Ilario, Ilaryo

Ilbert (German) distinguished fighter.
Ilbirt, Ilburt, Ilbyrt

Ilias (Greek) a form of Elijah.
Illias

Illan (Basque, Latin) youth.

Ilom (Ibo) my enemies are many.

Ilya (Russian) a form of Elijah.
Ilia, Ilie, Ilija, Iliya, Ilja, Illia, Illya, Ilyah

Ilyas (Greek) a form of Elijah.
Illyas, Ilyes

Imad (Arabic) supportive; mainstay.

Iman (Hebrew) a short form of Immanuel.

Imani (Hebrew) a short form of
Immanuel.
Imanni

Imbert (German) poet.
Imbirt, Imburt, Imbyrt

Immanuel (Hebrew) a form of
Emmanuel.
Imanol, Imanual, Imanuel, Imanuele,
Immanual, Immanuele, Immuneal

Imran (Arabic) host.
Imraan, Imren, Imrin, Imryn

Imre (Hungarian) a form of Emery.
Imri

Imrich (Czech) a form of Emery.
Imric, Imrick, Imrie, Imrus

Inay (Hindi) god; godlike.

Ince (Hungarian) innocent.

Incencio (Spanish) white.

Inder (Hindi) god; godlike.
Inderbir, Inderdeep, Inderjeet, Inderjit,
Inderpal, Inderpreet, Inderveer, Indervir,
Indra, Indrajit

Indiana (Hindi) from India.
Indi, Indy

Inek (Welsh) a form of Irvin.

Ing (Scandinavian) a short form of
Ingmar.
Inge

Ingelbert (German) a form of Engelbert.
Ingelberte, Ingelbirt, Ingelburt, Ingelburte,
Ingelbyrt, Inglebert, Ingleberte

Inger (Scandinavian) son's army.
Ingar

Inglis (Scottish) English.
Ingliss, Inglys, Inglyss

Ingmar (Scandinavian) famous son.
Ingamar, Ingamur, Ingemar

Ingram (English) angel.
Ingra, Ingraham, Ingrem, Ingrim, Ingrym

Ingvar (Scandinavian) Ing's soldier.
Ingevar

Inigo (Basque) a form of Ignatius.
Iñaki, Iniego, Iñigo

Iniko (Ibo) born during bad times.

Inir (Welsh) honorable.
Inyr

Innis (Irish) island.
Inis, Iniss, Innes, Inness, Inniss, Innys, Innyss

Innocenzio (Italian) innocent.
Innocenty, Innocentz, Innocenz, Innocenzyo,
Inocenci, Inocencio, Inocente, Inocenzio,
Inocenzyo, Inosente

Inteus (Native American) proud;
unashamed.

Ioakim (Russian) a form of Joachim.
Ioachime, Ioakimo, Iov

Ioan (Greek, Bulgarian, Romanian) a
form of John.
Ioane, Ioann, Ioannikios, Ionel

Ioannis (Greek, Bulgarian, Romanian) a
form of Ioan.
Ioannes

Iokepa (Hawaiian) a form of Joseph.
Keo

Iokia (Hawaiian) healed by God.
Iokiah, Iokya, Iokyah

Iolo (Welsh) the Lord is worthy.
Iorwerth

Ionakana (Hawaiian) a form of Jonathan.

Iorgos (Greek) a form of George.

Iosif (Greek, Russian) a form of Joseph.

Iosua (Romanian) a form of Joshua.

Ipyana (Nyakyusa) graceful.
Ipyanah

Ira (Hebrew) watchful.
Irah

Iram (English) bright.

Irfan (Arabic) thankfulness.

Irmin (German) strong.
Irman, Irmen, Irmun, Irmyn

Irumba (Rutooro) born after twins.

Irv (Irish, Welsh, English) a short form of Irvin, Irving.

Irvin (Irish, Welsh, English) a short form of Irving. See also Ervine.
Irven, Irvine, Irvinn, Irvon, Irvyn, Irvyne

Irving (Irish) handsome. (Welsh) white river. (English) sea friend. See also Ervin, Ervine.
Irvington, Irvyng

Irwin (English) a form of Irving. See also Ervin.
Irwing, Irwinn, Irwyn

Isa (Hebrew) a form of Isaiah. (Arabic) a form of Jesus.
Isaah, Isah

Isaac (Hebrew) he will laugh. Bible: the son of Abraham and Sarah. See also Itzak, Izak, Yitzchak.
Aizik, Icek, Ikey, Ikie, Isaack, Isaakios, Isacco, Isaic, Ishaq, Isiac, Isiacc, Issca

Isaak (Hebrew) a form of Isaac.
Isack, Isak, Isik, Issak

Isac, Isacc, Issac (Hebrew) forms of Isaac.
Issacc, Issaic, Issiac

Isai, Isaih (Hebrew) forms of Isaiah.

Isaiah (Hebrew) God is my salvation. Bible: a Hebrew prophet.
Essaiah, Isaia, Isaid, Isaish, Isaya, Isayah, Isia, Isiash, Issia, Izaiah, Izaiha, Izaya, Izayah, Izayaih, Izayiah, Izeyah, Izeyha

Isaias (Hebrew) a form of Isaiah.
Isaiahs, Isais, Izayus

Isam (Arabic) safeguard.

Isas (Japanese) meritorious.

Isekemu (Native American) slow-moving creek.

Isham (English) home of the iron one.

Ishan (Hindi) direction.
Ishaan, Ishaun

Ishaq (Arabic) a form of Isaac.
Ishaac, Ishak

Ishmael (Hebrew) God will hear. Literature: the narrator of Herman Melville's novel *Moby-Dick*.
Isamael, Isamail, Ishma, Ishmail, Ishmale, Ishmeal, Ishmeil, Ishmel, Ishmil

Isiah, Issiah (Hebrew) forms of Isaiah.
Issaiah, Issia

Isidore (Greek) gift of Isis. See also Dorian, Esidore, Ysidro.
Isador, Isadore, Isadorios, Isidor, Issy, Ixidor, Izador, Izadore, Izidor, Izidore, Izydor

Isidoro (Greek) a form of Isidore.
Isidoros

Isidro (Greek) a form of Isidore.

Iskander (Afghan) a form of Alexander.

Islam (Arabic) submission; the religion of Muhammad.

Ismael, Ismail (Arabic) forms of Ishmael.
Ismal, Ismale, Ismeil, Ismiel

Israel (Hebrew) prince of God; wrestled with God. History: the nation of Israel took its name from the name given Jacob after he wrestled with the angel of the Lord. See also Yisrael.
Iser, Israele, Israhel, Isrell, Isrrael, Isser, Izrael

Isreal (Hebrew) a form of Israel.
Isrieal

Issa (Swahili) God is our salvation.
Issah

Istu (Native American) sugar pine.

István (Hungarian) a form of Stephen.
Isti, Istvan, Pista

Ithel (Welsh) generous lord.
Ithell

Ittamar (Hebrew) island of palms.
Itamar

Itzak (Hebrew) a form of Isaac, Yitzchak.
Itzik

Iukini (Hawaiian) a form of Eugene.
Kini

Iustin (Bulgarian, Russian) a form of
Justin.

Ivan, Ivann (Russian) forms of John. See
also Vanya.
*Iván, Ivano, Ivas, Iven, Ivin, Ivon, Ivun,
Ivyn, Yvan, Yvann*

Ivanhoe (Hebrew) God's tiller. Literature:
Ivanhoe is a historical romance by Sir
Walter Scott.
Ivanho, Ivanhow

Ivar (Scandinavian) a form of Ivor. See
also Yves, Yvon.
Iv, Iva, Iver

Ives (English) young archer.
Ive, Iven, Ivey, Yves

Ivo (German) yew wood; bow wood.
Ivon, Ivonnie, Yvo

Ivor (Scandinavian) a form of Ivo.
Ibon, Ifor, Ivar, Ivry, Yvor

Ivory (Latin) made of ivory.
Ivoree, Ivorey, Ivori, Ivorie

Ivy (English) ivy tree.
Ivi, Ivie, Ivye

Iwan (Polish) a form of John.

Iyapo (Yoruba) many trials; many
obstacles.

Iye (Native American) smoke.

Izaac (Czech) a form of Izak.
Izaack, Izaak

Izak (Czech) a form of Isaac.
*Itzhak, Ixaka, Izac, Izaic, Izec, Izeke, Izick,
Izik, Izsak, Izsák, Izzak*

Izod (Irish) light haired.
Izad, Ized, Izid, Izud, Izyd

Izzy (Hebrew) a familiar form of Isaac,
Isidore, Israel.
*Isi, Isie, Issi, Issie, Issy, Izi, Izie, Izy, Izzi,
Izzie*

J (American) an initial used as a first name.

J. (American) a form of J.

J'quan (American) a form of Jaquan.

Ja (Korean) attractive, magnetic.

Ja'far (Sanskrit) little stream.
Jafari, Jaffar, Jaffer, Jafur

Ja'juan (American) a form of Jajuan.

Ja'marcus (American) a form of Jamarcus.

Ja'quan (American) a form of Jaquan.

Ja'von (American) a form of Javan.

Jaali (Swahili) powerful.
Jali

Jaan (Estonian) a form of Christian.
(Dutch, Slavic) a form of Jan.

Jaap (Dutch) a form of Jim.
Jape

Jabari (Swahili) fearless, brave.
*Jabahri, Jabarae, Jabare, Jabaree, Jabarei,
Jabarie, Jabarri, Jabarrie, Jabary, Jabbaree,
Jabbari, Jabiari, Jabier, Jabori, Jaborie*

Jabbar (Arabic) fixer.
Jabaar, Jabar, Jaber

Jabez (Hebrew) born in pain.
Jabe, Jabes, Jabesh

Jabin (Hebrew) God has created.
Jabain, Jabien, Jabon, Jabyn

Jabir (Arabic) consoler, comforter.
Jabiri, Jabori, Jabyr

Jabril (Arabic) a form of Jibril.
*Jabrail, Jabree, Jabreel, Jabrel, Jabrell, Jabrelle,
Jabri, Jabrial, Jabrie, Jabriel, Jabrielle, Jabrille*

Jabulani (Shona) happy.

Jacan (Hebrew) trouble.
Jachin

Jacari (American) a form of Jacorey.
Jacarey, Jacaris, Jacarius, Jacarre, Jacarri, Jacarrus, Jacarus, Jacary, Jacaure, Jacauri, Jaccar, Jaccari

Jaccob (Hebrew) a form of Jacob.

Jace (American) a combination of the initials J. + C. See also Jayce.
J.C., JC, Jacee, Jaci, Jacie, Jaece, Jaecee, Jaecey, Jaeci, Jaice, Jaicee, Jaicey, Jaici, Jaicie, Jaicy

Jacek (American) a form of Jace.

Jacen (Greek) a form of Jason.
Jaceon, Jacin, Jacon, Jacyn

Jacey (American) a form of Jace.

Jacinto (Portuguese, Spanish) hyacinth. See also Giacinto.
Jacindo, Jacint, Jacinta, Jacynto

Jack (American) a familiar form of Jacob, John. See also Keaka.
Jaac, Jaack, Jaak, Jac, Jacke, Jacko, Jackub, Jak, Jakk, Jax

Jackie, Jacky (American) familiar forms of Jack.
Jackey, Jacki

Jackson (English) son of Jack.
Jacksen, Jacksin, Jacson, Jakson

Jaco (Portuguese) a form of Jacob.

Jacob (Hebrew) supplanter, substitute. Bible: son of Isaac, brother of Esau. See also Akiva, Chago, Checha, Cobi, Diego, Giacomo, Hamish, Iago, Iakobos, Kiva, Kobi, Kuba, Tiago, Yakov, Yasha, Yoakim.
Jachob, Jaco, Jacobb, Jacub, Jaecob, Jaicob, Jalu, Jecis, Jeks, Jeska, Jocek, Jock, Jocob, Jocobb, Jokubas

Jacobe, Jacobi, Jacoby (Hebrew) forms of Jacob.
Jachobi, Jacobbe, Jacobee, Jacobey, Jacobie, Jacobii, Jacobis, Jocoby

Jacobo (Hebrew) a form of Jacob.
Jacobos

Jacobson (English) son of Jacob.
Jacobs, Jacobsen, Jacobsin, Jacobus

Jacolby (Hebrew) a form of Jacob.
Jacolbi, Jocolby

Jacorey (American) a combination of Jacob + Corey.
Jacori, Jacoria, Jacorie, Jacoris, Jacorius, Jacorrey, Jacorrien, Jacorry, Jacouri, Jacourie

Jacory (American) a form of Jacorey.

Jacquan (French) a form of Jacques.

Jacque (French) a form of Jacob.
Jackque, Jacquay, Jacqui

Jacquel (French) a form of Jacques.

Jacques (French) a form of Jacob, James. See also Coco.
Jackques, Jackquise, Jacot, Jacquees, Jacquese, Jacquess, Jacquet, Jacquett, Jacquis, Jacquise, Jarques, Jarquis

Jacquez, Jaquez (French) forms of Jacques.
Jaques, Jaquese, Jaqueus, Jaqueze, Jaquis, Jaquise, Jaquze

Jacy (Tupi-Guarani) moon. (American) a form of Jace.
Jaicy, Jaycee

Jad (Hebrew) a short form of Jadon. (American) a short form of Jadrien.
Jada, Jadd

Jadarius (American) a combination of the prefix Ja + Darius.

Jade (Spanish) jade, precious stone.
Jaed, Jaeid, Jaid, Jaide, Jayd

Jaden, Jadyn (Hebrew) forms of Jadon.
Jadee, Jadeen, Jadenn, Jadeon, Jadyne

Jadon (Hebrew) God has heard.
Jadan, Jadin, Jaiden

Jadrien (American) a combination of Jay + Adrien.
Jader, Jadrian, Jadryen, Jaedrian, Jaedrien, Jaidrian, Jaidrien, Jaidrion, Jaidryon, Jaydrian, Jaydrien, Jaydrion, Jaydryan

Jae (French, English) a form of Jay.

Jae-Hwa (Korean) rich, prosperous.

Jaeden, Jaedon (Hebrew) forms of Jadon.
Jaedan, Jaedin, Jaedyn

Jaegar (German) hunter.
Jaager, Jaeger, Jagur, Jaigar, Jaygar

Jael (Hebrew) mountain goat.
Jayl, Yael

Jaelen, Jaelin, Jaelon (American) forms
of Jalen.
Jaelan, Jaelaun, Jaelyn

jafar (Sanskrit) a form of Ja'far.

Jagdeep (Sikh) the lamp of the world.

Jagger (English) carter.
Gagger, Jagar, Jager, Jaggar

Jagmeet (Sikh) friend of the world.

Jago (English) a form of Jacob, James.
Jaego, Jaigo, Jaygo

Jaguar (Spanish) jaguar.
Jagguar

Jahi (Swahili) dignified.

Jahleel (Hindi) a form of Jalil.
Jahlal, Jahlee, Jahliel

Jahlil (Hindi) a form of Jalil.

Jahmal (Arabic) a form of Jamal.
*Jahmall, Jahmalle, Jahmeal, Jahmeel, Jahmeil,
Jahmel, Jahmelle, Jahmil, Jahmile, Jahmill,
Jahmille*

Jahmar (American) a form of Jamar.
Jahmare, Jahmari, Jahmarr, Jahmer

Jahvon (Hebrew) a form of Javan.
*Jahvan, Jahvaughn, Jahvine, Jahwaan,
Jahwon*

Jai (Tai) heart.
Jaie, Jaii

Jaiden (Hebrew) a form of Jadon.
Jaidan, Jaidin, Jaidon, Jaidyn

Jailen (American) a form of Jalen.
*Jailan, Jailani, Jaileen, Jailen, Jailon, Jailyn,
Jailynn*

Jaime (Spanish) a form of Jacob, James.
Jaimee, Jaimey, Jaimie, Jaimito, Jaimy

Jaiquan (American) a form of Jaquan.
Jaiqaun

Jair (Spanish) a form of Jairo.

Jairo (Spanish) God enlightens.
Jairay, Jaire, Jayrus

Jairus (American) a form of Jairo.

Jaison (Greek) a form of Jason.
*Jaisan, Jaisen, Jaishon, Jaishun, Jaisin,
Jaisun, Jaisyn*

Jaivon (Hebrew) a form of Javan.
Jaiven, Jaivion, Jaiwon

Jaja (Ibo) honored.
Jajah

Jajuan (American) a combination of the
prefix Ja + Juan.
*Ja Juan, Jaejuan, Jaijuan, Jauan, Jayjuan,
Jejuan*

Jakari (American) a form of Jacorey.
*Jakaire, Jakar, Jakaray, Jakarie, Jakarious,
Jakarius, Jakarre, Jakarri, Jakarus*

Jake (Hebrew) a short form of Jacob.
Jaik, Jakie, Jayck, Jayk, Jayke

Jakeb, Jakeob, Jakob, Jakub (Hebrew)
forms of Jacob.
*Jaekob, Jaikab, Jaikob, Jakab, Jakeub, Jakib,
Jakiv, Jakobe, Jakobi, Jakobus, Jakoby, Jakov,
Jakovian, Jakubek, Jekebs*

Jakeem (Arabic) uplifted.
Jakeam, Jakim, Jakym

Jakome (Basque) a form of James.
Jakom

Jal (Gypsy) wanderer.
Jall

Jalan, Jalin, Jalon, Jalyn (American)
forms of Jalen.
*Jalaan, Jalaen, Jalain, Jaland, Jalane, Jalani,
Jalanie, Jalann, Jalaun, Jalean, Jalian, Jaline,
Jallan, Jalone, Jaloni, Jalun, Jalynn, Jalynne*

Jaleel (Hindi) a form of Jalil.
Jaleell, Jaleil, Jalel

Jaleen (American) a form of Jalen.

Jalen (American) a combination of the
prefix Ja + Len.
Jalend, Jallen

Jalene (American) a form of Jalen.

Jalil (Hindi) revered.
Jalaal, Jalal

Jam (American) a short form of Jamal, Jamar.
Jama

Jamaal, Jamahl, Jamall, Jamaul (Arabic) forms of Jamal.
Jammaal

Jamaine (Arabic) a form of Germain.
Jamain, Jamayn, Jamayne

Jamal (Arabic) handsome. See also Gamal.
Jaimal, Jamael, Jamail, Jamaile, Jamala, Jamarl, Jammal, Jamual, Jaumal, Jomal, Jomall

Jamale (Arabic) a form of Jamal.
Jamalle

Jamar (American) a form of Jamal.
Jamaar, Jamaari, Jamaarie, Jamahrae, Jamair, Jamara, Jamaras, Jamaraus, Jamarr, Jamarre, Jamarrea, Jamarree, Jamarri, Jamarvis, Jamaur, Jammar, Jarmar, Jarmarr, Jaumar, Jemaar, Jemar, Jimar

Jamarcus (American) a combination of the prefix Ja + Marcus.
Jamarco, Jemarcus, Jimarcus, Jymarcus

Jamare (American) a form of Jamario.
Jamareh

Jamaree, Jamari (American) forms of Jamario.
Jamarea, Jamaria, Jamarie

Jamario (American) a combination of the prefix Ja + Mario.
Jamareo, Jamariel, Jamariya, Jamaryo, Jemario

Jamarious, Jamarius (American) forms of Jamario.

Jamaris (American) a form of Jamario.
Jemarus

Jamarkus (American) a combination of the prefix Ja + Markus.
Jamark

Jamarquis (American) a combination of the prefix Ja + Marquis.

Jamarkees, Jamarkeus, Jamarkis, Jamarqese, Jamarqueis, Jamarques, Jamarquez, Jamarquios, Jamarqus

Jameel (Arabic) a form of Jamal.
Jameal, Jamele, Jamyl, Jamyle, Jarmil

Jamel, Jamell (Arabic) forms of Jamal.
Jamelle, Jammel, Jamuel, Jamul, Jarmel, Jaumell, Je-Mell, Jimell

Jamen, Jamon (Hebrew) forms of Jamin.
Jaemon, Jaimon, Jamohn, Jamone, Jamoni

James (Hebrew) supplanter, substitute. (English) a form of Jacob. Bible: James the Great and James the Less were two of the Twelve Apostles. See also Diego, Hamish, Iago, Kimo, Santiago, Seamus, Seumas, Yago, Yasha.
Jaemes, Jaimes, Jamesie, Jamesy, Jamies, Jamse, Jamyes, Jemes

Jameson (English) son of James.
Jaemeson, Jaimeson, Jamerson, Jamesian, Jamesyn, Jaymeson

Jamey, Jamie (English) familiar forms of James.
Jaeme, Jaemee, Jaemey, Jaemi, Jaemie, Jaemy, Jaimee, Jaimey, Jaimie, Jame, Jamee, Jameyel, Jami, Jamia, Jamiah, Jamian, Jamiee, Jamme, Jammey, Jammie, Jammy, Jamy, Jamye

Jamez (Hebrew) a form of James.
Jameze, Jamze

Jamieson (English) a form of Jamison.
Jamiesen

Jamil (Arabic) a form of Jamal.
Jamiel, Jamiell, Jamielle, Jamile, Jamill, Jamille

Jamin (Hebrew) favored.
Jaman, Jamian, Jamien, Jamion, Jamionn, Jamun, Jamyn, Jarmin, Jarmon, Jaymin, Jaymon

Jamir (American) a form of Jamar.
Jamire, Jamiree

Jamison (English) son of James.
Jaemison, Jaemyson, Jaimison, Jaimyson, Jamis, Jamisen, Jamyson, Jaymison, Jaymyson

Jamond (American) a combination of James + Raymond.

Jamond *(cont.)*
Jaemond, Jaemund, Jaimond, Jaimund, Jamod, Jamont, Jamonta, Jamontae, Jamontay, Jamonte, Jamund, Jarmond, Jarmund, Jaymond, Jaymund

Jamor (American) a form of Jamal.
Jamoree, Jamori, Jamorie, Jamorius, Jamorrio, Jamorris, Jamory, Jamour

Jamsheed (Persian) from Persia.
Jamshaid, Jamshead, Jamshed

Jan (Dutch, Slavic) a form of John.
Jahn, Jana, Janae, Jann, Jano, Jenda, Jhan, Yan

Janco (Czech) a form of John.
Jancsi, Janke, Janko

Jando (Spanish) a form of Alexander.
Jandino

Janeil (American) a combination of the prefix Ja + Neil.
Janal, Janel, Janell, Janelle, Janiel, Janielle, Janile, Janille, Jarnail, Jarneil, Jarnell

Janek (Polish) a form of John.
Janak, Janik, Janika, Janka, Jankiel, Janko, Jhanick

Janis (Latvian) a form of John. See also Zanis.
Ansis, Jancis, Janyc, Janyce, Janys

Janne (Finnish) a form of John.
Jann, Jannes

János (Hungarian) a form of John.
Jancsi, Jani, Jankia, Jano

Jansen (Scandinavian) a form of Janson.
Janssen

Janson (Scandinavian) son of Jan.
Jansan, Janse, Jansin, Janssan, Janssin, Jansson, Jansun, Jansyn

Jantzen (Scandinavian) a form of Janson.
Janten, Jantsen, Jantson, Janzen

Janus (Latin) gate, passageway; born in January. Mythology: the Roman god of beginnings and endings.
Jannese, Jannus, Januario, Janusz

Japheth (Hebrew) handsome. (Arabic) abundant. Bible: a son of Noah. See also Yaphet.
Japeth, Japhet

Jaquan (American) a combination of the prefix Ja + Quan.
Jacquin, Jacquyn, Jaequan, Jaqaun, Jaquaan, Jaquain, Jaquane, Jaquann, Jaquanne, Jaquin, Jaquyn

Jaquarius (American) a combination of Jaquan + Darius.
Jaquari, Jaquarious, Jaquaris

Jaquavious, Jaquavius (American) forms of Jaquavis.
Jaquaveis, Jaquaveius, Jaquaveon, Jaquaveous, Jaquavias

Jaquavis (American) a form of Jaquan.
Jaquavas, Jaquavus

Jaquawn, Jaquon (American) forms of Jaquan.
Jaequon, Jaqawan, Jaqoun, Jaquinn, Jaqune, Jaquoin, Jaquone, Jaqwan, Jaqwon

Jarad, Jarid, Jarod, Jarrad, Jarred, Jarrid, Jarrod, Jarryd, Jaryd (Hebrew) forms of Jared.
Jaraad, Jarodd, Jaroid, Jarrayd

Jarah (Hebrew) sweet as honey.
Jara, Jarra, Jarrah, Jera, Jerah, Jerra, Jerrah

Jaran, Jaren, Jarin, Jarren, Jarron, Jaryn (Hebrew) forms of Jaron.
Jarian, Jarien, Jarion, Jarrain, Jarran, Jarrian, Jarrin, Jarryn, Jarynn, Jaryon

Jardan (French) garden. (Hebrew) a form of Jordan.
Jarden, Jardin, Jardon, Jardyn, Jardyne

Jareb (Hebrew) contending.
Jarib, Jaryb

Jared (Hebrew) a form of Jordan.
Ja'red, Jaraed, Jahred, Jaired, Jaredd, Jareid, Jerred

Jarek (Slavic) born in January.
Januarius, Janusz, Jarec, Jareck, Jaric, Jarick, Jarik, Jarrek, Jarric, Jarrick, Jaryc, Jaryck, Jaryk

Jarel, Jarell (Scandinavian) forms of Gerald.
Jaerel, Jaerell, Jaeril, Jaerill, Jaeryl, Jaeryll, Jairel, Jairell, Jarael, Jareil, Jarelle, Jariel, Jarryl, Jarryll, Jayryl, Jayryll, Jharell

Jaret, Jarett, Jarret (English) forms of Jarrett.

Jareth (American) a combination of Jared + Gareth.
Jaref, Jareff, Jarif, Jariff, Jarith, Jaryf, Jaryff, Jaryth, Jereth

Jarius, Jarrius (American) forms of Jairo.

Jarl (Scandinavian) earl, nobleman.
Jarlee, Jarleigh, Jarley, Jarli, Jarlie, Jarly

Jarlath (Latin) in control.
Jarlaf, Jarlen

Jarmal (Arabic) a form of Jamal.

Jarman (German) from Germany.
Jarmen, Jarmin, Jarmon, Jarmyn, Jerman, Jermen, Jermin, Jermon, Jermyn

Jarmarcus (American) a form of Jamarcus.

Jarom (Latin) a form of Jerome.
Jarome, Jarrom, Jarrome

Jaron (Hebrew) he will sing; he will cry out.
J'ron, Jaaron, Jaeron, Jairon, Jarone, Jayron, Jayrone, Jayronn, Je Ronn

Jaroslav (Czech) glory of spring.

Jarrell (English) a form of Gerald.
Jarrel, Jerall, Jerrell

Jarreth (American) a form of Jareth.
Jarref, Jarreff, Jarrif, Jarriff, Jarrith, Jarryf, Jarryff, Jarryth

Jarrett (English) a form of Garrett, Jared.
Jairet, Jairett, Jarat, Jarette, Jarhett, Jarit, Jarrat, Jarratt, Jarrette, Jarrit, Jarritt, Jarrot, Jarrote, Jarrott, Jarrotte, Jaryt, Jarytt

Jarvis (German) skilled with a spear.
Jaravis, Jarv, Jarvaris, Jarvas, Jarvaska, Jarvey, Jarvez, Jarvice, Jarvie, Jarvios, Jarvious, Jarvise, Jarvius, Jarvorice, Jarvoris, Jarvous, Jarvus, Jarvyc, Jarvyce, Jarvys, Jarvyse, Jervey

Jas (English) a familiar form of James. (Polish) a form of John.
Jasio

Jasdeep (Sikh) the lamp radiating God's glories.

Jase (Greek) a short form of Jason.

Jasen, Jasson (Greek) forms of Jason.
Jassen, Jassin, Jassyn

Jasha (Russian) a familiar form of Jacob, James.
Jascha

Jashawn (American) a combination of the prefix Ja + Shawn.
Jasean, Jashan, Jashaun, Jashion, Jashon

Jashua (Hebrew) a form of Joshua.

Jaskaran (Sikh) sings praises to the Lord.
Jaskaren, Jaskiran

Jaskarn (Sikh) a form of Jaskaran.

Jasmeet (Sikh) friend of the Lord. (Persian) a form of Jasmin.

Jasmin (Persian) jasmine flower.
Jasman, Jasmanie, Jasmine, Jasmon, Jasmond

Jason (Greek) healer. Mythology: the hero who led the Argonauts in search of the Golden Fleece.
Jaasan, Jaasen, Jaasin, Jaason, Jaasun, Jaasyn, Jaesan, Jaesen, Jaesin, Jaeson, Jaesun, Jaesyn, Jahsan, Jahsen, Jahson, Jasan, Jasaun, Jasin, Jasten, Jasun, Jasyn

Jaspal (Punjabi) living a virtuous lifestyle.
Jaspel

Jasper (French) brown, red, or yellow ornamental stone. (English) a form of Casper. See also Kasper.
Jaspar, Jazper, Jespar, Jesper

Jaspreet (Punjabi) virtuous.

Jathan (Greek) a form of Jason.
Jathon

Jatinra (Hindi) great Brahmin sage.
Jatinrah

Javan (Hebrew) Bible: son of Japheth.
Jaavan, Jaewan, Javyn, Jayvin, Jayvine

Javante (American) a form of Javan.
Javantae, Javantai, Javantée, Javanti

Javar (American) a form of Jarvis.

Javari (American) a form of Jarvis.
Javarri

Javarious, Javarius (American) forms of Javar.
Javarias, Javarreis, Javarrious, Javorious, Javorius, Javouris

Javaris (English) a form of Javar.
Javaor, Javaras, Javare, Javares, Javaries, Javario, Javarios, Javaro, Javaron, Javarous, Javarre, Javarris, Javarro, Javarros, Javarous, Javarte, Javarus, Javarys, Javoris

Javas (Sanskrit) quick, swift.
Jayvas, Jayvis

Javaughn (American) a form of Javan.
Jahvaughan, JaVaughn

Javen, Javin (Hebrew) forms of Javan.
Jaevin, Javine

Javeon (American) a form of Javan.

Javian, Javion (American) forms of Javan.
Javionne, Javien

Javier (Spanish) owner of a new house. See also Xavier.
Jabier, Javer, Javere, Javiar, Javyer

Javon (Hebrew) a form of Javan.
Jaavon, Jaevon, Jaewon, Jahvon, Javaon, Javohn, Javoni, Javonn, Javonni, Javonnie, Javoun

Javone (Hebrew) a form of Javan.
Javoney, Javonne

Javonta (American) a form of Javan.
Javona, Javonteh

Javontae, Javontay, Javonte, Javonté (American) forms of Javan.
Javonnte, Javontai, Javontaye, Javontee, Javontey

Jawad (Arabic) openhanded, generous.

Jawan, Jawaun, Jawon, Jawuan (American) forms of Jajuan.
Jawaan, Jawann, Jawn

Jawhar (Arabic) jewel; essence.

Jaxon, Jaxson (English) forms of Jackson.
Jaxen, Jaxsen, Jaxsun, Jaxun

Jay (French) blue jay. (English) a short form of James, Jason.
Jai, Jave, Jeays, Jeyes

Jayce (American) a combination of the initials J. + C. See also Jace.
J.C., JC, Jay Cee, Jayc, Jaycee, Jaycey, Jayci, Jaycie, Jaycy, Jecie

Jaycob (Hebrew) a form of Jacob.
Jaycobb, Jaycub, Jaykob, Jaykobb

Jayde (American) a combination of the initials J. + D.
J.D., JD, Jayd, Jaydee

Jayden (Hebrew) a form of Jadon. (American) a form of Jayde.

Jaydon (Hebrew) a form of Jadon.
Jaydan, Jaydin, Jaydn, Jaydyn

Jaye (French, English) a form of Jay.

Jaylan, Jaylin, Jayln, Jaylon, Jaylyn (American) forms of Jaylen.
Jaylaan, Jayleon, Jaylian, Jayline, Jaylynn, Jaylynne

Jayland (American) a form of Jaylen.
Jaylend, Jaylund, Jaylynd

Jaylee (American) a combination of Jay + Lee.
Jaelea, Jaelee, Jaeleigh, Jaeley, Jaeli, Jaelie, Jaely, Jailea, Jailee, Jaileigh, Jailey, Jaili, Jailie, Jaily, Jayla, Jayle, Jaylea, Jayleigh, Jayley, Jayli, Jaylie, Jayly

Jaylen (American) a combination of Jay + Len. A form of Jaylee.
Jayleen, Jaylun

Jayme (English) a form of Jamey.
Jaymee, Jaymey, Jaymi, Jaymie, Jaymy

Jaymes, Jaymz (English) forms of James.
Jaymis, Jayms

Jayquan (American) a combination of Jay + Quan.
Jaykwan, Jaykwon, Jayqon, Jayquawn, Jayqunn

Jayro (Spanish) a form of Jairo.

Jaysen, Jayson (Greek) forms of Jason.
Jaycent, Jaysan, Jaysin, Jaysn, Jayssen, Jaysson, Jaysun, Jaysyn

Jayshawn (American) a combination of Jay + Shawn. A form of Jaysen.
Jaysean, Jayshaun, Jayshon, Jayshun

Jayvon (American) a form of Javon.
Jayvion, Jayvohn, Jayvion, Jayvone, Jayvonn, Jayvontay, Jayvonte, Jaywan, Jaywaun, Jaywin

Jaz (American) a form of Jazz.

Jazz (American) jazz.
Jaze, Jazze, Jazzlee, Jazzman, Jazzmen, Jazzmin, Jazzmon, Jazztin, Jazzton, Jazzy

Jean (French) a form of John.
Jéan, Jeane, Jeannah, Jeannie, Jeannot, Jeano, Jeanot, Jeanty, Jeen, Jene

Jean Benoit (French) a combination of Jean + Benoit.

Jean Christoph (French) a combination of Jean + Christoph.

Jean Daniel (French) a combination of Jean + Daniel.

Jean David (French) a combination of Jean + David.

Jean Denis (French) a combination of Jean + Denis.

Jean Felix (French) a combination of Jean + Felix.

Jean Francois, Jean-Francois (French) combinations of Jean + Francois.

Jean Gabriel (French) a combination of Jean + Gabriel.

Jean Luc, Jean-Luc, Jeanluc (French) combinations of Jean + Luc.

Jean Marc, Jean-Marc (French) combinations of Jean + Marc.

Jean Michel (French) a combination of Jean + Michel.

Jean Nicholas (French) a combination of Jean + Nicholas.

Jean Pascal (French) a combination of Jean + Pascal.

Jean Philip, Jean Philippe, Jean-Philippe (French) combinations of Jean + Philip.

Jean Samuel (French) a combination of Jean + Samuel.

Jean Sebastien (French) a combination of Jean + Sebastien.

Jean Simon (French) a combination of Jean + Simon.

Jean-Claude (French) a combination of Jean + Claude.

Jean-Paul, Jeanpaul (French) combinations of Jean + Paul.

Jean-Pierre, Jeanpierre (French) a combination of Jean + Pierre.

Jeb (Hebrew) a short form of Jebediah.
Jebb, Jebi, Jeby

Jebediah (Hebrew) a form of Jedidiah.
Jebadia, Jebadiah, Jebadieh, Jebidia, Jebidiah, Jebidya, Jebydia, Jebydiah, Jebydya, Jebydyah

Jed (Hebrew) a short form of Jedidiah. (Arabic) hand.
Jedd, Jeddy, Jedi

Jediah (Hebrew) hand of God.
Jadaya, Jedaia, Jedaiah, Jedayah, Jedeiah, Jedi, Yedaya

Jedidiah (Hebrew) friend of God, beloved of God. See also Didi.
Jedadiah, Jeddediah, Jededia, Jedidia, Jedidiyah, Yedidya

Jedrek (Polish) strong; manly.
Jedrec, Jedreck, Jedric, Jedrick, Jedrik, Jedryc, Jedryck, Jedryk

Jeff (English) a short form of Jefferson, Jeffrey. A familiar form of Geoffrey.
Jef, Jefe, Jeffe, Jeffey, Jeffie, Jeffy, Jeph, Jhef

Jefferey, Jeffery (English) forms of Jeffrey.
Jefaree, Jefarey, Jefari, Jefarie, Jefary, Jeferee, Jeferey, Jeferi, Jeferie, Jefery, Jeffaree, Jeffarey, Jeffari, Jeffarie, Jeffary, Jeffeory, Jefferay, Jefferee, Jeffereoy, Jefferi, Jefferie, Jefferies, Jeffory

Jefferson (English) son of Jeff. History: Thomas Jefferson was the third U.S. president.
Gefferson, Jeferson, Jeffers

Jefford (English) Jeff's ford.
Jeford

Jeffrey (English) divinely peaceful. See also Geffrey, Geoffrey, Godfrey.
Jeffre, Jeffree, Jeffri, Jeffrie, Jeffries, Jefre, Jefri, Jeoffroi, Joffre, Joffrey

Jeffry (English) a form of Jeffrey.
Jefry

Jehan (French) a form of John.
Jehann

Jehu (Hebrew) God lives. Bible: a military commander and king of Israel.
Yehu

Jelani (Swahili) mighty.
Jel, Jelan, Jelanee, Jelaney, Jelanie, Jelany, Jelaun

Jem (English) a short form of James, Jeremiah.
Jemi, Jemie, Jemmi, Jemmie, Jemmy, Jemy

Jemal (Arabic) a form of Jamal.
Jemaal, Jemael, Jemale

Jemel (Arabic) a form of Jamal.
Jemeal, Jemehl, Jemehyl, Jemell, Jemelle, Jemello, Jemeyle, Jemile

Jemond (French) worldly.
Jemon, Jémond, Jemonde, Jemone, Jemun, Jemund

Jenkin (Flemish) little John.
Jenkins, Jenkyn, Jenkyns, Jennings

Jennifer (Welsh) white wave; white phantom. A form of Guinevere (see Girls' Names).

Jenö (Hungarian) a form of Eugene.
Jenoe

Jens (Danish) a form of John.
Jense, Jentz

Jensen (Scandinavian) a form of Janson.
Jensan, Jensin, Jenson, Jenssen, Jensyn

Jensi (Hungarian) born to nobility. (Danish) a familiar form of Jens.
Jenci, Jency, Jensee, Jensie, Jensy

Jeovanni (Italian) a form of Giovanni.
Jeovahny, Jeovan, Jeovani, Jeovanie, Jeovanny, Jeovany

Jequan (American) a combination of the prefix Je + Quan.
Jeqaun, Jequann, Jequon

Jerad, Jered, Jerid, Jerod, Jerrad, Jerred, Jerrid, Jerrod (Hebrew) forms of Jared.
Jeread, Jeredd, Jereed, Jerode, Jeroid, Jerryd, Jeryd

Jerahmy (Hebrew) a form of Jeremy.
Jerahmeel, Jerahmeil, Jerahmey

Jerald, Jerold, Jerrold (English) forms of Gerald.
Jeraldo, Jeroldo, Jerrald, Jerraldo, Jerroldo, Jerryld, Jeryld

Jerall (English) a form of Gerald.
Jerael, Jerai, Jerail, Jeraile, Jeral, Jerale, Jerall, Jerrail, Jerral, Jerrall

Jeramey, Jeramie, Jeramy (Hebrew) forms of Jeremy.
Jerame, Jeramee, Jerami, Jerammie

Jeramiah (Hebrew) a form of Jeremiah.

Jerard (French) a form of Gerard.
Jarard, Jarrard, Jeraude, Jerrard

Jerardo (Spanish) a form of Gerard.

Jere (Hebrew) a short form of Jeremiah, Jeremy.
Jeré, Jeree

Jerel, Jerell, Jerrell (English) forms of Gerald.
Jerelle, Jeriel, Jeril, Jerrail, Jerrel, Jerrelle, Jerrill, Jerrol, Jerroll, Jerryl, Jerryll, Jeryl, Jeryle

Jereme, Jeremey, Jeremi, Jeremie, Jérémie (English) forms of Jeremy.
Jarame, Jaremi, Jeremee, Jérémie, Jeremii

Jeremiah (Hebrew) God will uplift. Bible: a Hebrew prophet. See also Dermot, Yeremey, Yirmaya.
Geremiah, Jaramia, Jemeriah, Jemiah, Jeramiha, Jereias, Jeremaya, Jeremia, Jeremial, Jeremija, Jeremya, Jeremyah

Jeremias (Hebrew) a form of Jeremiah.
Jeremyas

Jeremy (English) a form of Jeremiah.

Jaremay, Jaremy, Jere, Jereamy, Jeremry, Jérémy, Jeremye, Jereomy, Jeriemy, Jerime, Jerimy, Jerremy

Jeriah (Hebrew) Jehovah has seen.
Jeria, Jerya, Jeryah

Jeric, Jerick (Arabic) short forms of Jericho. (American) forms of Jerrick.
Jerric

Jericho (Arabic) city of the moon. Bible: a city conquered by Joshua.
Jericko, Jeriko, Jerricko, Jerricoh, Jerriko, Jerrycko, Jerryko

Jerico (Arabic) a short form of Jericho.
Jerrico, Jerryco

Jerimiah (Hebrew) a form of Jeremiah.
Jerimiha, Jerimya

Jermain (French, English) a form of Jermaine.

Jermaine (French) a form of Germain. (English) sprout, bud.
Jarman, Jer-Mon, Jeremaine, Jeremane, Jerimane, Jerman, Jermane, Jermanie, Jermanne, Jermany, Jermayn, Jermayne, Jermiane, Jermine, Jermoney, Jhirmaine

Jermal (Arabic) a form of Jamal.
Jermaal, Jermael, Jermail, Jermall, Jermaul, Jermil, Jermol, Jermyll

Jermel, Jermell (Arabic) forms of Jamal.

Jermey (English) a form of Jeremy.
Jerme, Jermee, Jermere, Jermery, Jermie, Jermy, Jhermie

Jermiah (Hebrew) a form of Jeremiah.
Jermiha, Jermija, Jermiya

Jerney (Slavic) a form of Bartholomew.

Jerolin (Basque, Latin) holy.
Jerolyn

Jerome (Latin) holy. See also Geronimo, Hieronymos.
Gerome, Jere, Jeroen, Jerom, Jérome, Jérôme, Jeromo, Jerrome

Jeromy (Latin) a form of Jerome.
Jeromee, Jeromey, Jeromie, Jerromy

Jeron, Jerrin, Jerron (English) forms of Jerome.
J'ron, Jéron, Jerone, Jerrion, Jerrone

Jeronimo (Greek, Italian) a form of Jerome.

Jerret, Jerrett (Hebrew) forms of Jarrett.
Jeret, Jerett, Jeritt, Jerrete, Jerrette, Jerriot, Jerritt, Jerrot, Jerrott

Jerrick (American) a combination of Jerry + Derric.
Jaric, Jarrick, Jerik, Jerrik, Jerryc, Jerryck, Jerryk

Jerry (German) mighty spearman. (English) a familiar form of Gerald, Gerard. See also Gerry, Kele.
Jehri, Jere, Jeree, Jeri, Jerie, Jeris, Jerison, Jerree, Jerri, Jerrie, Jery

Jervis (English) a form of Gervaise, Jarvis.
Jervice, Jervise, Jervys

Jerzy (Polish) a form of George.
Jersey, Jerzey, Jerzi, Jurek

Jeshua (Hebrew) a form of Joshua.
Jeshuah

Jess (Hebrew) a short form of Jesse.

Jesse (Hebrew) wealthy. Bible: the father of David. See also Yishai.
Jescee, Jese, Jesee, Jesi, Jessé, Jezze, Jezzee

Jessee, Jessey, Jessi, Jessie, Jessy (Hebrew) forms of Jesse.
Jescey, Jesie, Jessye, Jessyie, Jesy, Jezzey, Jezzi, Jezzie, Jezzy

Jessica (Hebrew) a form of Jesse. Literature: a name perhaps invented by Shakespeare for a character in his play *The Merchant of Venice*.

Jestin (Welsh) a form of Justin.
Jessten, Jesten, Jeston, Jesstin, Jesston

Jesus (Hebrew) a form of Joshua. Bible: son of Mary and Joseph, believed by Christians to be the Son of God. See also Chucho, Isa, Yosu.
Jecho, Jessus, Jesu, Jezus, Josu

Jesús (Hispanic) a form of Jesus.

Jethro (Hebrew) abundant. Bible: the father-in-law of Moses. See also Yitro.
Jeth, Jethroe, Jetro, Jetrow, Jettro

Jett (English) hard, black mineral. (Hebrew) a short form of Jethro.
Jet, Jetson, Jette, Jetter, Jetty

Jevan (Hebrew) a form of Javan.
Jevaun, Jeven, Jevyn, Jevynn

Jevin (Hebrew) a form of Javan.

Jevon (Hebrew) a form of Javan.
Jevion, Jevohn, Jevone, Jevonn, Jevonne, Jevonnie

Jevonte (American) a form of Jevon.
Jevonta, Jevontae, Jevontaye, Jevonté

Jhon (Hebrew) a form of John.

Jhonathan (Hebrew) a form of Jonathan.

Jhonny (Hebrew) a form of Johnie.

Jiang (Chinese) fire.

Jibade (Yoruba) born close to royalty.
Jibad, Jybad, Jybade

Jibben (Gypsy) life.
Jibin

Jibril (Arabic) archangel of Allah.
Jibreel, Jibriel

Jihad (Arabic) struggle; holy war.

Jilt (Dutch) money.
Jylt

Jim (Hebrew, English) a short form of James. See also Jaap.
Jimbo, Jimm, Jym, Jymm

Jimbo (American) a familiar form of Jim.
Jimboo

Jimell (Arabic) a form of Jamel.
Jimel, Jimelle, Jimill, Jimmell, Jimmelle, Jimmiel, Jimmil, Jimmill, Jimmyl, Jimmyll, Jymel, Jymell, Jymil, Jymill, Jymmel, Jymmell, Jymmil, Jymmill, Jymmyl, Jymmyll, Jymyl, Jymyll

Jimi, Jimmie (English) forms of Jimmy.
Jimie, Jimmi

Jimiyu (Abaluhya) born in the dry season.

Jimmy (English) a familiar form of Jim.
Jimee, Jimey, Jimme, Jimmee, Jimmey, Jimmye, Jimmyjo, Jimy, Jyme, Jymee, Jymey, Jymi, Jymie, Jymme, Jymmee, Jymmey, Jymmi, Jymmie, Jymy

Jimmy Lee (American) a combination of Jimmy + Lee.

Jimoh (Swahili) born on Friday.
Jimo, Jymo, Jymoh

Jin (Chinese) gold.
Jinn, Jyn, Jynn

Jina (Swahili) name.

Jinan (Arabic) garden.
Jinen, Jinon, Jinyn

Jindra (Czech) a form of Harold.
Jindrah

Jing-Quo (Chinese) ruler of the country.

Jiovanni (Italian) a form of Giovanni.
Jio, Jiovani, Jiovanie, Jiovann, Jiovannie, Jiovanny, Jiovany, Jiovoni, Jivan, Jyovani, Jyovanie, Jyovany

Jirair (Armenian) strong; hard working.
Jyrair

Jiri (Czech) a form of George.
Jirka

Jiro (Japanese) second son.

Jivin (Hindi) life giver.
Jivan, Jivanta, Jiven, Jivon, Jivyn, Jyvan, Jyven, Jyvin, Jyvon, Jyvyn

Jo (Hebrew, Japanese) a form of Joe.

Joab (Hebrew) God is father. See also Yoav.
Joabe, Joaby

Joachim (Hebrew) God will establish. See also Akeem, Ioakim, Yehoyakem.
Joacheim, Joakim, Joaquim, Jokim, Jov

Joan (German) a form of Johann.

Joao, João (Portuguese) forms of John.
Joáo

Joaquim (Portuguese) a form of Joachim.

Joaquin, Joaquín (Spanish) forms of Joachim.
Jehoichin, Joaquyn, Joaquynn, Joquin, Juaquyn

Job (Hebrew) afflicted. Bible: a righteous man whose faith in God survived the test of many afflictions.
Jobe, Jobert

Joben (Japanese) enjoys cleanliness.
Joban, Jobin, Jobon, Jobyn

Jobo (Spanish) a familiar form of Joseph.

Joby (Hebrew) a familiar form of Job.
Jobee, Jobey, Jobi, Jobie

Jocelyn (Latin) joyous.

Jock (American) a familiar form of Jacob. A form of Jack.
Jocko, Joco, Jocoby, Jocolby

Jocquez (French) a form of Jacquez.
Jocques, Jocquis, Jocquise

Jocqui (French) a form of Jacque.
Jocque

Jodan (Hebrew) a combination of Jo + Dan.
Jodahn, Joden, Jodhan, Jodian, Jodin, Jodon, Jodonnis, Jodyn

Jody (Hebrew) a familiar form of Joseph.
Jodee, Jodey, Jodi, Jodie, Jodiha, Joedee, Joedey, Joedi, Joedie, Joedy

Joe (Hebrew) a short form of Joseph.
Jow

Joel (Hebrew) God is willing. Bible: an Old Testament Hebrew prophet.
Joël, Jôel, Joell, Joelle, Joely, Jole, Yoel

Joeseph, Joesph (Hebrew) forms of Joseph.

Joey (Hebrew) a familiar form of Joe, Joseph.

Johan (German) a form of Johann.

Johann (German) a form of John. See also Anno, Hanno, Yoan, Yohan.
Joahan, Johahn, Johanan, Johane, Johannan, Johaun, Johon

Johannes (German) a form of Johann.
Joannes, Johanes, Johannas, Johannus, Johansen, Johanson, Johonson

Johathan (Hebrew) a form of Jonathan.
Johanthan, Johatan, Johathe, Johathon

John (Hebrew) God is gracious. Bible: the name honoring John the Baptist and John the Evangelist. See also Elchanan, Evan, Geno, Gian, Giovanni, Handel, Hannes, Hans, Hanus, Honza, Ian, Ianos, Iban, Ioan, Ivan, Iwan, Keoni, Kwam, Ohannes, Sean, Ugutz, Yan, Yanka, Yanni, Yochanan, Yohance, Zane.
Jaenda, Janco, Jantje, Jen, Jian, Joen, Johne, Jone

John Paul, John-Paul, Johnpaul (American) combinations of John + Paul.

John-Michael, Johnmichael (American) combinations of John + Michael.

John-Robert (American) a combination of John + Robert.

Johnathan, Johnathen, Johnathon (Hebrew) forms of Jonathan. See also Yanton.
Johnatan, Johnathann, Johnathaon, Johnathyne, Johnaton, Johnatten, Johniathin, Johnothan

Johnie, Johnnie, Johnny, Johny (Hebrew) familiar forms of John. See also Gianni.
Johnee, Johney, Johni, Johnier, Johnney, Johnni

Johnpatrick (American) a combination of John + Patick.

Johnson (English) son of John.
Johnston, Jonson

Johntavius (American) a form of John.

Johnthan (Hebrew) a form of Jonathan.

Joji (Japanese) a form of George.

Jojo (Fante) born on Monday.

Jokim (Basque) a form of Joachim.
Jokeam, Jokeem, Jokin, Jokym

Jolon (Native American) valley of the dead oaks.
Jolyon

Jomar (American) a form of Jamar.
Jomari, Jomarie, Jomarri

Jomei (Japanese) spreads light.
Jomey

Jon (Hebrew) a form of John. A short
form of Jonathan.
J'on, Jonn

Jon-Michael (American) a combination
of Jon + Michael.

Jon-Pierre (American) a combination of
Jon + Pierre.

Jonah (Hebrew) dove. Bible: an Old
Testament prophet who was swallowed
by a large fish.
Giona, Jona, Yonah, Yunus

Jonas (Hebrew) he accomplishes.
(Lithuanian) a form of John.
*Jonahs, Jonass, Jonaus, Jonelis, Jonukas,
Jonus, Jonutis, Jonys, Joonas*

Jonatan (Hebrew) a form of Jonathan.
Jonatane, Jonate, Jonattan, Jonnattan

Jonathan (Hebrew) gift of God. Bible:
the son of King Saul who became a
loyal friend of David. See also Ionakana,
Yanton, Yonatan.
*Janathan, Jonatha, Jonathin, Jonathun,
Jonathyn, Jonethen, Jonnatha, Jonnathun*

Jonathen, Jonathon, Jonnathan
(Hebrew) forms of Jonathan.
*Joanathon, Jonaton, Jonnathon, Jonthon,
Jounathon, Yanaton*

Jones (Welsh) son of John.
Joenes, Joennes, Joenns, Johnsie, Joness, Jonesy

Jonny (Hebrew) a familiar form of John.
Jonhy, Joni, Jonnee, Jonni, Jonnie, Jony

Jonothan (Hebrew) a form of Jonathan.
Jonothon

Jontae (French) a combination of Jon +
the suffix Tae.
Johntae, Jontea, Jonteau

Jontavious (American) a form of Jon.

Jontay, Jonte (American) forms of Jontae.
Johntay, Johnte, Johntez, Jontai, Jonté, Jontez

Jonthan (Hebrew) a form of Jonathan.

Joop (Dutch) a familiar form of Joseph.
Jopie

Joost (Dutch) just.

Joquin (Spanish) a form of Joaquin.
*Jocquin, Jocquinn, Jocquyn, Jocquynn,
Joquan, Joquawn, Joqunn, Joquon*

Jora (Hebrew) teacher.
Jorah, Yora, Yorah

Joram (Hebrew) Jehovah is exalted.
Joran, Jorim

Jordan (Hebrew) descending. See also
Giordano, Yarden.
*Jardan, Jordaan, Jordae, Jordain, Jordaine,
Jordane, Jordani, Jordanio, Jordann, Jordanny,
Jordano, Jordany, Jordáo, Jordayne, Jordian,
Jordun, Jorrdan*

Jorden, Jordin, Jordon, Jordyn (Hebrew)
forms of Jordan.
Jeordon, Johordan, Jordenn

Jordi, Jordie, Jordy (Hebrew) familiar
forms of Jordan.

Jorell (American) he saves. Literature: a
name inspired by the fictional character
Jor-El, Superman's father.
*Jor-El, Jorel, Jorelle, Jorl, Jorrel, Jorrell,
Jorrelle*

Jorey, Jory (Hebrew) familiar forms of
Jordan.
Joar, Joary, Jori, Jorie, Jorrie

Jörg (German) a form of George.
Jeorg, Juergen, Jungen, Jürgen

Jorge, Jorje (Spanish) forms of George.

Jorgeluis (Spanish) a combination of
Jorge + Luis.

Jorgen (Danish) a form of George.
Joergen, Jorgan, Jörgen

Joris (Dutch) a form of George.

Jörn (German) a familiar form of
Gregory.

Jorrín (Spanish) a form of George.
Jorian

Jose, José, Josey (Spanish) forms of
Joseph. See also Che, Pepe.
Josean, Josecito, Josee, Joseito, Joselito

Josealfredo (Spanish) a combination of
Jose + Alfredo.

Joseantonio (Spanish) a combination of Jose + Antonio.

Josef (German, Portuguese, Czech, Scandinavian) a form of Joseph.
Joosef, Joseff, Josif, Jossif, Juzef, Juzuf

Joseguadalup (Spanish) a combination of Jose + Guadalupe.

Joseluis (Spanish) a combination of Jose + Luis.

Josemanuel (Spanish) a combination of Jose + Manuel.

Joseph (Hebrew) God will add, God will increase. Bible: in the Old Testament, the son of Jacob who came to rule Egypt; in the New Testament, the husband of Mary. See also Beppe, Cheche, Chepe, Giuseppe, Iokepa, Iosif, Osip, Pepa, Peppe, Pino, Sepp, Yeska, Yosef, Yousef, Youssel, Yusef, Yusif, Zeusef.
Jazeps, Jooseppi, Joseba, Josep, Josephat, Josephe, Josephie, Josephus, Josheph, Josip, Jóska, Joza, Joze, Jozeph, Jozhe, Jozio, Jozka, Jozsi, Jozzepi, Jupp, Jusepe, Juziu

Josh (Hebrew) a short form of Joshua.
Joshe

Josha (Hindi) satisfied.
Joshah

Joshawa (Hebrew) a form of Joshua.

Joshi (Swahili) galloping.
Joshee, Joshey, Joshie, Joshy

Joshua (Hebrew) God is my salvation. Bible: led the Israelites into the Promised Land. See also Giosia, Iosua, Jesus, Yehoshua.
Johsua, Johusa, Joshau, Joshaua, Joshauh, Joshawah, Joshia, Joshuaa, Joshuea, Joshuia, Joshula, Joshus, Joshusa, Joshuwa, Joshwa, Jousha, Jozshua, Jozsua, Jozua, Jushua

Joshuah (Hebrew) a form of Joshua.

Joshue (Hebrew) a form of Joshua.

Josiah (Hebrew) fire of the Lord. See also Yoshiyahu.
Joshiah, Josia, Josiahs, Josian, Josie, Josya, Josyah

Josias (Hebrew) a form of Josiah.

Joss (Chinese) luck; fate.
Jos, Josse, Jossy

Josue (Hebrew) a form of Joshua.
Joshu, Jossue, Josu, Josua, Josuha, Jozus

Jotham (Hebrew) may God complete. Bible: a king of Judah.
Jothem, Jothim, Jothom, Jothym

Jourdan (Hebrew) a form of Jordan.
Jourdain, Jourden, Jourdin, Jourdon, Jourdyn

Jovan (Latin) Jove-like, majestic. (Slavic) a form of John. Mythology: Jove, also known as Jupiter, was the supreme Roman deity.
Johvan, Johvon, Jovaan, Jovaann, Jovane, Jovanic, Jovann, Jovannis, Jovaughn, Jovaun, Joven, Jovenal, Jovenel, Jovi, Jovian, Jovin, Jovito, Jowan, Jowaun, Yovan, Yovani

Jovani, Jovanni, Jovanny, Jovany (Latin) forms of Jovan.
Jovanie, Jovannie, Jovoni, Jovonie, Jovonni, Jovony

Jovante (American) a combination of Jovan + the suffix Te.

Jovon (Latin) a form of Jovan.
Jovoan, Jovone, Jovonn, Jovonne

Jovonté (American) a combination of Jovon + the suffix Te.

Jozef (German, Portuguese, Czech, Scandinavian) a form of Josef.
Jozeff, József

Jr (Latin) a short form of Junior.
Jr.

Juan (Spanish) a form of John. See also Chan.
Juanch, Juanchito, Juane, Juann, Juaun

Juan Carlos, Juancarlos (Spanish) combinations of Juan + Carlos.

Juanantonio (Spanish) a combination of Juan + Antonio.

Juandaniel (Spanish) a combination of Juan + Daniel.

Juanito (Spanish) a form of Juan.

Juanjose (Spanish) a combination of Juan + Jose.

Juanmanuel (Spanish) a combination of Juan + Manuel.

Juaquin (Spanish) a form of Joaquin.
Juaqin, Juaqine, Juaquine

Jubal (Hebrew) ram's horn. Bible: a musician and a descendant of Cain.

Judah (Hebrew) praised. Bible: the fourth of Jacob's sons. See also Yehudi.
Juda, Judda, Juddah

Judas (Latin) a form of Judah. Bible: Judas Iscariot was the disciple who betrayed Jesus.
Juddas

Judd (Hebrew) a short form of Judah.
Jud

Jude (Latin) a short form of Judah, Judas. Bible: one of the Twelve Apostles, author of "The Epistle of Jude."

Judson (English) son of Judd.
Juddson

Juhana (Finnish) a form of John.
Juha, Juhanah, Juhanna, Juhannah, Juho

Jujuan (American) a form of Jajuan.

Juku (Estonian) a form of Richard.
Jukka

Jules (French) a form of Julius.
Joles, Julas, Jule

Julian, Jullian (Greek, Latin) forms of Julius.
Jolyon, Julean, Juliaan, Julianne, Julion, Julyan, Julyin, Julyon

Juliano (Spanish) a form of Julian.

Julien (Latin) a form of Julian.
Julen, Juliene, Julienn, Julienne, Jullien, Jullin, Julyen

Julio (Hispanic) a form of Julius.
Juleo, Juliyo, Julyo

Juliocesar (Hispanic) a combination of Julio + Cesar.

Julius (Greek, Latin) youthful, downy bearded. History: Julius Caesar was a great Roman dictator. See also Giuliano.
Julias, Julious, Juliusz, Jullius, Juluis

Jumaane (Swahili) born on Tuesday.
Jumane

Jumah (Arabic, Swahili) born on Friday, a holy day in the Islamic religion.
Jimoh, Juma

Jumoke (Yoruba) loved by everyone.
Jumok

Jun (Chinese) truthful. (Japanese) obedient; pure.
Joon, Junnie

Junior (Latin) young.
Junious, Junius, Junor, Junyor

Jupp (German) a form of Joseph.
Jup

Juquan (Spanish) a form of Juaquin.

Jur (Czech) a form of George.
Juraz, Jurek, Jurik, Jurko

Jurgis (Lithuanian) a form of George.
Jurgi, Juri

Juro (Japanese) best wishes; long life.

Jurrien (Dutch) God will uplift.
Jore, Jurian, Jurion, Jurre, Juryan, Juryen, Juryin, Juryon

Justan, Justen, Juston, Justyn (Latin) forms of Justin.
Jasten, Jaston, Justyne, Justynn

Justice (Latin) a form of Justis.
Justic, Justiz, Justyc, Justyce

Justin (Latin) just, righteous. See also Giustino, Iestyn, Iustin, Tutu, Ustin, Yustyn.
Jastin, Jobst, Jost, Jusa, Just, Justain, Justek, Justian, Justinas, Justinian, Justinius, Justinn, Justins, Justinus, Justn, Justo, Justton, Justukas, Justun

Justine (Latin) a form of Justin.

Justino (Spanish) a form of Justin.

Justis (French) just.
Justas, Justise, Justs, Justyse

Justus (French) a form of Justis.

Juvenal (Latin) young. Literature: a
Roman satirist.
Juventin, Juventyn, Juvon, Juvone

Juwan, Juwon (American) forms of
Jajuan.
*Juvon, Juvone, Juvaun, Juwaan, Juwain,
Juwane, Juwann, Juwaun, Juwonn, Juwuan,
Juwuane, Juwvan, Jwan, Jwon*

Ka'eo (Hawaiian) victorious.

Kabiito (Rutooro) born while foreigners
are visiting.
Kabito, Kabyto

Kabil (Turkish) a form of Cain.
Kabel, Kabyl

Kabir (Hindi) History: an Indian mystic
poet.
Kabar, Kabeer, Kabier, Kabyr, Khabir

Kabonero (Runyankore) sign.

Kabonesa (Rutooro) difficult birth.
Kabonesah

Kacey (Irish) a form of Casey. (American)
a combination of the initials K. + C.
See also Kasey, KC.
*Kace, Kacee, Kaci, Kaecee, Kaecey, Kaeci,
Kaecie, Kaecy, Kaicee, Kaicey, Kaici, Kaicie,
Kaicy, Kaycee*

Kacy (Irish, American) a form of Kacey.

Kadar (Arabic) powerful.
Kader, Kador

Kadarius (American) a combination of
Kade + Darius.
*Kadairious, Kadarious, Kadaris, Kadarrius,
Kadarus, Kaddarrius, Kaderious, Kaderius*

Kade (Scottish) wetlands. (American) a
combination of the initials K. + D.
Kadee, Kady, Kaed, Kayde, Kaydee

Kadeem (Arabic) servant.
Kadim, Kadym, Khadeem

Kaden (Arabic) a form of Kadin.
Caden, Kadeen, Kadein

Kadin (Arabic) friend, companion.
Kadan, Kadon, Kadyn

Kadir (Arabic) spring greening.
Kadeer, Kadyr

Kado (Japanese) gateway.

Kaeden (Arabic) a form of Kadin.
Kaedin, Kaedon, Kaedyn

Kaelan, Kaelen, Kaelin, Kaelon (Irish)
forms of Kellen.
Kael, Kaelyn

Kaeleb (Hebrew) a form of Kaleb.
Kaelib, Kaelob, Kaelyb, Kailab, Kaileb

Kaemon (Japanese) joyful; right-handed.
*Kaeman, Kaemen, Kaemin, Kaimon,
Kaymon*

Kaenan (Irish) a form of Keenan.
Kaenen, Kaenin, Kaenyn

Kafele (Nguni) worth dying for.

Kaga (Native American) writer.
Kagah

Kagan (Irish) a form of Keegan.
Kage, Kagen, Kaghen, Kaigan

Kahale (Hawaiian) home.
Kahail, Kahayl

Kahana (Hawaiian) priest.
Kahanah, Kahanna, Kahannah

Kahil (Turkish) young; inexperienced;
naive. See also Cahil.
Kaheel, Kaheil, Kahill, Kahyl, Kahyll

Kahlil (Arabic) a form of Khalíl.
*Kahleal, Kahlee, Kahleel, Kahleil, Kahli,
Kahliel, Kahlill*

Kaholo (Hawaiian) runner.

Kahraman (Turkish) hero.

Kai (Welsh) keeper of the keys. (Hawaiian)
sea. (German) a form of Kay. (Danish) a
form of Kaj.
Kae, Kaie, Kaii

Kaid (Scottish, American) a form of Kade.
Kaide

Kaiden (Arabic) a form of Kadin.
Kaidan

Kailen (Irish) a form of Kellen.
*Kail, Kailan, Kailey, Kailin, Kaillan,
Kailon, Kailyn*

Kaili (Hawaiian) Religion: a Hawaiian
god.
*Kaelea, Kaelee, Kaeleigh, Kaeley, Kaeli,
Kaelie, Kaely, Kailea, Kailee, Kaileigh,
Kailey, Kailie, Kailli, Kaily, Kaylea, Kaylee,
Kayleigh, Kayley, Kayli, Kaylie, Kayly*

Kain, Kaine (Welsh, Irish) forms of Kane.
Kainan, Kainen, Kainin, Kainon

Kainoa (Hawaiian) name.

Kaipo (Hawaiian) sweetheart.
Kaypo

Kairo (Arabic) a form of Cairo.
Kaire, Kairee, Kairi, Kayro

Kaiser (German) a form of Caesar.
Kaesar, Kaisar, Kaizer, Kayser

Kaiven (American) a form of Kevin.
Kaivan, Kaivon, Kaiwan

Kaj (Danish) earth.
Kaje

Kajuan (American) a combination of the
prefix Ka + Juan.

Kakar (Hindi) grass.

Kala (Hindi) black; phase. (Hawaiian) sun.
Kalah

Kalama (Hawaiian) torch.
Kalam, Kalamah

Kalameli (Tongan) caramel.
Kalamelie, Kalamely

Kalan (Hawaiian) a form of Kalani.
(Irish) a form of Kalen.
Kalane, Kallan

Kalani (Hawaiian) sky; chief.
Kalanee, Kalaney, Kalanie, Kalany

Kale (Arabic) a short form of Kahlil.
(Hawaiian) a familiar form of Carl.
Kael, Kaell, Kail, Kaill, Kaleu, Kayl

Kalea (Hawaiian) happy; joy.
Kaleah, Kalei, Kaleigh, Kaley

Kaleb, Kalib, Kalob (Hebrew) forms
of Caleb.
*Kaelab, Kailab, Kal, Kalab, Kalabe, Kalb,
Kaleob, Kalev, Kalieb, Kallb, Kalleb, Kaloeb,
Kalub, Kalyb, Kaylab, Kilab, Kylab*

Kaleel (Arabic) a form of Khalíl.
Kalel, Kalell

Kalen, Kalin (Arabic, Hawaiian) forms
of Kale. (Irish) forms of Kellen.
Kallin

Kalevi (Finnish) hero.
Kalevee, Kalevey, Kalevie, Kalevy

Kali (Arabic) a short form of Kalil.
(Hawaiian) a form of Gary.
Kalee, Kalie, Kaly

Kalil (Arabic) a form of Khalíl.
Kaliel, Kaliil

Kaliq (Arabic) a form of Khaliq.
Kalic, Kaliqu, Kalique

Kalkin (Hindi) tenth. Religion: Kalki is
the final incarnation of the Hindu god
Vishnu.
Kalki, Kalkyn

Kalle (Scandinavian) a form of Carl.
(Arabic, Hawaiian) a form of Kale.

Kallen, Kalon, Kalyn (Irish) forms of
Kellen.
*Kallan, Kallin, Kallion, Kallon, Kallun,
Kallyn, Kalone, Kalonn, Kalun, Kalyen,
Kalyne, Kalynn*

Kalmin (Scandinavian) manly, strong.
Kalman, Kalmen, Kalmon, Kalmyn

Kaloosh (Armenian) blessed event.

Kalvin (Latin) a form of Calvin.
*Kal, Kalv, Kalvan, Kalven, Kalvon, Kalvun,
Kalvyn, Vinny*

Kamaka (Hawaiian) face.
Kamakah

Kamakani (Hawaiian) wind.
Kamakanee, Kamakaney, Kamakanie, Kamakany

Kamal (Hindi) lotus. (Arabic) perfect, perfection.
Kamaal, Kamyl

Kamari (Swahili) a short form of Kamaria (see Girls' Names).

Kamau (Kikuyu) quiet warrior.

Kamden (Scottish) a form of Camden.
Kamdan, Kamdin, Kamdon, Kamdyn

Kamel (Hindi, Arabic) a form of Kamal.
Kameel

Kameron (Scottish) a form of Cameron.
Kam, Kamaren, Kamaron, Kameran, Kameren, Kamerin, Kamerion, Kamerron, Kamerun, Kameryn, Kamey, Kammeren, Kammeron, Kammy, Kamoryn

Kami (Hindi) loving.
Kamee, Kamey, Kamie, Kamy

Kamil (Arabic) a form of Kamal.
Kameel

Kamilo (Latin) a form of Camilo.
Kamillo, Kamillow, Kamyllo, Kamylo

Kampbell (Scottish) a form of Campbell.
Kambel, Kambell, Kamp

Kamran, Kamren, Kamron, Kamryn (Scottish) forms of Kameron.
Kammron, Kamrein, Kamrin, Kamrun

Kamuela (Hawaiian) a form of Samuel.
Kamuelah, Kamuele

Kamuhanda (Runyankore) born on the way to the hospital.

Kamukama (Runyankore) protected by God.

Kamuzu (Ngoni) medicine.

Kamya (Luganda) born after twin brothers.

Kana (Japanese) powerful; capable. (Hawaiian) Mythology: a demigod.
Kanah

Kanaan (Hindi) a form of Kannan.

Kanaiela (Hawaiian) a form of Daniel.
Kana, Kaneii

Kane (Welsh) beautiful. (Irish) tribute. (Japanese) golden. (Hawaiian) eastern sky. (English) a form of Keene. See also Cain.
Kaen, Kahan, Kaney

Kanen (Hindi) a form of Kannan.

Kange (Lakota) raven.
Kang, Kanga, Kangee, Kangi, Kangie, Kangy

Kaniel (Hebrew) stalk, reed.
Kan, Kani, Kaniell, Kannie, Kanny, Kannyel, Kanyel

Kannan (Hindi) Religion: another name for the Hindu god Krishna.
Kanan, Kanin, Kanine, Kannen

Kannon (Polynesian) free. (French) A form of Cannon.
Kanon

Kanoa (Hawaiian) free.
Kanoah

Kantu (Hindi) happy.

Kanu (Swahili) wildcat.

Kanya (Australian) rock. (Hindi) virgin.
Kania, Kaniah, Kanyah

Kanyon (Latin) a form of Canyon.

Kaori (Japanese) strong.
Kaoru

Kapali (Hawaiian) cliff.
Kapalee, Kapalie, Kapaly

Kapeni (Malawian) knife.
Kapenee, Kapenie, Kapeny

Kapila (Hindi) ancient prophet.
Kapil, Kapill, Kapilla, Kapyla, Kapylla

Kapono (Hawaiian) righteous.
Kapena

Kappi (Gypsy) a form of Cappi.
Kappee, Kappey, Kappie, Kappy

Karan, Karon (Greek) forms of Karen
(see Girls' Names).

Kardal (Arabic) mustard seed.
Karandal, Kardel, Kardell

Kare (Norwegian) enormous.

Kareem (Arabic) noble; distinguished.
*Karem, Kareme, Karreem, Karriem,
Karrym, Karym*

Karel (Czech) a form of Carl.
Karell, Karil, Karrell

Karey (Greek) a form of Carey.
*Karee, Kari, Karie, Karree, Karrey, Karri,
Karrie, Karry, Kary*

Karif (Arabic) born in autumn.
Kareef, Kariff

Kariisa (Runyankore) herdsman.

Karim (Arabic) a form of Kareem.

Karl (German) a form of Carl.
Kaarle, Kaarlo, Karcsi, Karlitis, Karlo, Kjell

Karlen (Latvian, Russian) a form of Carl.
*Karlan, Karlens, Karlik, Karlin, Karlis,
Karlon, Karlyn*

Karlos (Spanish) a form of Carlos.
Karlus

Karlton (English) a form of Carlton.

Karmel (Hebrew) a form of Carmel.
Karmeli, Karmelo, Karmiel, Karmilo

Karney (Irish) a form of Carney.
Karnee, Karni, Karnie, Karny

Karol (Czech, Polish) a form of Carl.
*Karal, Karalos, Karolek, Karolis, Károly,
Karrel, Karrol, Karroll*

Karr (Scandinavian) a form of Carr.

Karsen, Karson (English) forms of
Carson.
Karrson, Karsan, Karsin, Karsyn

Karsten (Greek) anointed.
*Carsten, Karstan, Karstein, Karstin,
Karston, Karstyn*

Karu (Hindi) cousin.
Karun

Karutunda (Runyankore) little.

Karwana (Rutooro) born during wartime.

Kaseem (Arabic) divided.
Kasceem, Kaseam, Kaseym, Kazeem

Kaseko (Rhodesian) mocked, ridiculed.

Kasem (Tai) happiness.
Kaseme

Kasen (Basque) protected with a helmet.
*Kasan, Kasean, Kasene, Kaseon, Kasin,
Kassen, Kasyn*

Kasey (Irish) a form of Casey.
*Kaese, Kaesee, Kaesey, Kaesi, Kaesie, Kaesy,
Kasay, Kase, Kasee, Kasi, Kasie, Kassee,
Kassey, Kassi, Kassie, Kassy, Kasy, Kazee,
Kazey, Kazzee, Kazzey, Kazzi, Kazzie,
Kazzy, Kazy*

Kashawn (American) a combination of
the prefix Ka + Shawn.
*Kashain, Kashan, Kashaun, Kashen,
Kashon*

Kasib (Arabic) fertile.
Kasyb

Kasim (Arabic) a form of Kaseem.
Kassim, Kasym

Kasimir (Arabic) peace. (Slavic) a form
of Casimir.
*Kashmir, Kasimyr, Kasymyr, Kazimier,
Kazimir, Kazmer, Kazmér, Kázmér*

Kasiya (Nguni) separate.
Kasiyah

Kason (Basque) a form of Kasen.

Kasper (Persian) treasurer. (German) a
form of Casper.
*Jasper, Kaspar, Kaspero, Kaspir, Kaspor,
Kaspyr*

Kass (German) blackbird.
Kaese, Kasch, Kase

Kasseem (Arabic) a form of Kaseem.
Kassem

Kassidy (Irish) a form of Cassidy.
Kassadee, Kassadey, Kassadi, Kassadie,
Kassady, Kassedee, Kassedey, Kassedi,
Kassedie, Kassedy, Kassidee, Kassidey,
Kassidi, Kassidie, Kassie, Kassy, Kassydee,
Kassydey, Kassydi, Kassydie, Kassydy

Kateb (Arabic) writer.

Kato (Runyankore) second of twins.

Katriel (Hebrew) crowned with God's
glory. (Arabic) peace.
Katryel

Katungi (Runyankore) rich.
Katungie, Katungy

Kaufman (German) merchant.
Kaufmann

Kauri (Polynesian) tree.
Kaeree, Kaurie, Kaury

Kavan (Irish) a form of Kevin. See also
Cavan.
Kavaugn, Kavyn

Kavanagh (Irish) Kavan's follower.
Cavanagh, Kavenagh, Kavenaugh

Kaveh (Persian) ancient hero.
Kavah

Kaven, Kavin, Kavon (Irish) forms of
Kavan.
Kaveon, Kavion, Kavone, Kaywon

Kavi (Hindi) poet.
Kavee, Kavey, Kavie, Kavy

Kawika (Hawaiian) a form of David.
Kawyka

Kay (Greek) rejoicing. (German) fortified
place. Literature: one of King Arthur's
knights of the Round Table.
Kaye, Kayson

Kayden (Arabic) a form of Kadin.
Kaydin, Kaydn, Kaydon

Kayin (Nigerian) celebrated. (Yoruba)
long-hoped-for child.
Kaiyan, Kaiyen, Kaiyin, Kaiyon, Kayan,
Kayen, Kayin, Kayon

Kaylan, Kaylen, Kaylin, Kaylon (Irish)
forms of Kellen.
Kaylyn, Kaylynn

Kayle (Hebrew) faithful dog. (Arabic) a
short form of Kahlil. (Arabic, Hawaiian)
a form of Kale.
Kaile, Kayl, Kayla

Kayleb (Hebrew) a form of Caleb.
Kaylib, Kaylob, Kaylub

Kayne (Hebrew) a form of Cain.
Kaynan, Kaynen, Kaynon

Kayode (Yoruba) he brought joy.

Kayonga (Runyankore) ash.

Kayvan, Kayvon (Irish) forms of Kavan.

Kazio (Polish) a form of Casimir,
Kasimir. See also Cassidy.

Kazuo (Japanese) man of peace.

KC (American) a combination of the
initials K. + C. See also Kacey.
K.C., Kcee, Kcey

Kc (American) a form of KC.

Keagan (Irish) a form of Keegan.
Keagean, Keagen, Keaghan, Keagyn

Keahi (Hawaiian) flames.

Keaka (Hawaiian) a form of Jack.

Kealoha (Hawaiian) fragrant.
Ke'ala, Kealohah

Kean (German, Irish, English) a form
of Keane.

Keanan (Irish) a form of Keenan.
Keanen, Keanna, Keannan, Keannen,
Keanon

Keandre (American) a combination of
the prefix Ke + Andre.
Keandra, Keandray, Keandré, Keandree,
Keandrell

Kéandre (American) a form of Keandre.

Keane (German) bold; sharp. (Irish)
handsome. (English) a form of Keene.

Keano (Irish) a form of Keanu.
Keanno, Keeno

Keanu (Irish) a form of Keenan.
*Keaneu, Keani, Keanie, Keanue, Keany,
Keenu, Kianu*

Kearn (Irish) a short form of Kearney.
Kearne

Kearney (Irish) a form of Carney.
Kearny

Keary (Irish) a form of Kerry.
Kearie

Keaton (English) where hawks fly.
*Keatan, Keaten, Keatin, Keatton, Keatun,
Keatyn, Keetan, Keeten, Keetin, Keeton,
Keetun, Keetyn, Keitan, Keiten, Keiton,
Keitun, Keityn*

Keaven (Irish) a form of Kevin.
Keavan, Keavin, Keavon, Keavun, Keavyn

Keawe (Hawaiian) strand.

Keb (Egyptian) earth. Mythology: an
ancient earth god, also known as Geb.
Kebb

Kedar (Hindi) mountain lord. (Arabic)
powerful. Religion: another name for
the Hindu god Shiva.
Kadar, Kedaar, Keder

Keddy (Scottish) a form of Adam.
Keddi, Keddie

Kedem (Hebrew) ancient.
Kedeam, Kedeem, Kedim, Kedym

Kedric, Kedrick (English) forms of
Cedric.
*Keddric, Keddrick, Keddrik, Keddryc,
Keddryck, Keddryk, Kederick, Kedrek,
Kedrik, Kedryc, Kedryck, Kedryk, Kiedric,
Kiedrick*

Keefe (Irish) handsome; loved.
*Keaf, Keafe, Keaff, Keaffe, Keef, Keeff, Keif,
Keife, Keiff, Keiffe, Keyf, Keyfe, Keyff,
Keyffe*

Keegan (Irish) little; fiery.
*Kaegan, Keagen, Keegen, Keeghan, Keegin,
Keegon, Keegun*

Keelan (Irish) little; slender. A form of
Kellen.
*Kealan, Kealen, Kealin, Kealon, Kealyn,
Keelen, Keelin, Keelon, Keelun, Keelyn*

Keeley (Irish) handsome.
*Kealee, Kealeigh, Kealey, Keali, Kealie,
Kealy, Keelea, Keelee, Keeleigh, Keeli,
Keelian, Keelie, Keelli, Keellie, Keelly, Keely*

Keenan (Irish) little Keene.
Kaenan, Keennan

Keene (German) bold; sharp. (English)
smart. See also Kane.
Kaene, Keen, Kein, Keine, Keyn, Keyne

Keenen, Keenon (Irish) forms of
Keenan.
Keenin, Keynen, Kienen

Kees (Dutch) a form of Kornelius.
*Keas, Kease, Keese, Keesee, Keis, Keys,
Keyes*

Keevon (Irish) a form of Kevin.
*Keevan, Keeven, Keevin, Keevun, Keevyn,
Keewan, Keewin*

Kegan (Irish) a form of Keegan.
*Kegen, Keghan, Keghen, Kegin, Kegon,
Kegun, Kegyn*

Kehind (Yoruba) second-born twin.
Kehinde, Kehynd

Keifer, Keiffer (German) forms of
Cooper.
Keefer, Keyfer, Keyffer

Keigan (Irish) a form of Keegan.
*Keigen, Keighan, Keighen, Keigin, Keigon,
Keigun, Keigyn, Keygan, Keygen, Keygin,
Keygon, Keygyn*

Keiji (Japanese) cautious ruler.
Keyjiy

Keilan (Irish) a form of Keelan.
*Keilen, Keilin, Keillene, Keillyn, Keilon,
Keilyn, Keilynn, Keylan, Keylen, Keylin,
Keylon, Keylyn*

Keiley (Irish) a form of Keeley.
*Keilea, Keilee, Keileigh, Keili, Keilie, Keily,
Keylea, Keylee, Keyleigh, Keyley, Keyli,
Keylie, Keyly*

Keion (Irish) a form of Keon.
Keionne

Keir (Irish) a short form of Kieran.
Keyr

Keiran (Irish) a form of Kieran.
Keiren, Keirin, Keiron

Keitaro (Japanese) blessed.
Keataro, Keita, Keytaro

Keith (Welsh) forest. (Scottish) battle place. See also Kika.
Keath, Keeth, Keithe, Keyth

Keithen (Welsh, Scottish) a form of Keith.
Keithan, Keitheon, Keithon

Keivan (Irish) a form of Kevin.
Keiven, Keivin, Keivn, Keivon, Keivone, Keivyn

Kejuan (American) a combination of the prefix Ke + Juan.

Kekapa (Hawaiian) tapa cloth.
Kekapah

Kekipi (Hawaiian) rebel.

Kekoa (Hawaiian) bold, courageous.
Kekoah

Kelan (Irish) a form of Keelan.

Kelby (German) farm by the spring. (English) a form of Kolby.
Keelby, Kelbee, Kelbey, Kelbi, Kelbie, Kellbee, Kellbey, Kellbi, Kellbie, Kellby

Kelcey (Scandinavian) a form of Kelsey.
Kelci, Kelcie, Kelcy, Kellci, Kellcie, Kellcy

Keldon (English) a form of Kelton.
Keldan, Kelden, Keldin

Kele (Hopi) sparrow hawk. (Hawaiian) a form of Jerry.
Kelle

Kelemen (Hungarian) gentle; kind.
Kelleman, Kellemen, Kellieman, Kelliemen, Kelliman, Kellimen, Kellyman, Kellymen, Kelyman, Kelymen

Kelevi (Finnish) hero.
Kelevee, Kelevey, Kelevie, Kelevy

Keli (Hawaiian) a form of Terry.
Kelee, Keleigh, Kelie, Kely

Keli'i (Hawaiian) chief.

Kelile (Ethiopian) protected.
Kelyle

Kell (Scandinavian) spring.
Kel

Kellan (Irish) a form of Kellen.
Keillan

Kellen (Irish) mighty warrior. A form of Kelly.
Kelden, Kelin, Kelle, Kellin, Kellyn, Kelyn, Kelynn

Keller (Irish) little companion.
Keler

Kelley (Irish) a form of Kelly.

Kelly (Irish) warrior.
Keallea, Keallee, Kealleigh, Kealley, Kealli, Keallie, Keally, Keilee, Keileigh, Keiley, Keili, Keilie, Keillea, Keillee, Keilleigh, Keilley, Keily, Kelle, Kellee, Kelli, Kellie, Kely, Keylee, Keyleigh, Keyley, Keyli, Keylie, Keyllee, Keylleigh, Keylley, Keilli, Keillie, Keilly, Keyly

Kelmen (Basque) merciful.
Kellman, Kellmen, Kelman, Kelmin

Kelsey (Scandinavian) island of ships.
Kelse, Kelsea, Kelsi, Kelsie, Kelso, Kelsy, Kesley, Kesly

Kelson (English) a form of Kelton.
Kelston

Kelton (English) keel town; port.
Keltan, Kelten, Keltin, Keltonn, Keltyn

Kelvin (Irish, English) narrow river. Geography: a river in Scotland.
Kelvan, Kelven, Kelvon, Kelvyn

Kelwin (English) friend from the ridge.
Kelwen, Kelwinn, Kelwyn, Kelwynn, Kelwynne

Kemal (Turkish) highest honor.
Kemel

Kemen (Basque) strong.
Keaman, Keamen, Keeman, Keemen, Keiman, Keimen, Keman, Keyman, Keymen

Kemp (English) fighter; champion.
Kempe

Kempton (English) military town.
Kemptan, Kempten, Kemptin, Kemptyn

Ken (Japanese) one's own kind. (Scottish) a short form of Kendall, Kendrick, Kenneth.
Kena, Kenn, Keno

Kenan (Irish) a form of Keenan.
Kenen, Kenin, Kenon, Kenyn

Kenard (Irish) a form of Kennard.
Kenerd

Kenaz (Hebrew) bright.

Kendal, Kendel, Kendell (English) forms of Kendall.
Kendali, Kendelle, Kendul, Kendyl

Kendale (English) a form of Kendall.

Kendall (English) valley of the river Kent.
Kendell, Kendyll, Kyndall

Kendarius (American) a combination of Ken + Darius.
Kendarious, Kendarrious, Kendarrius, Kenderious, Kenderius, Kenderyious

Kendrell (English) a form of Kendall.
Kendrall, Kendrel, Kendryll

Kendrew (Scottish) a form of Andrew.
Kandrew

Kendric (Irish, Scottish) a form of Kendrick.
Kendryc

Kendrick (Irish) son of Henry. (Scottish) royal chieftain.
Kenderrick, Kendrich, Kendricks, Kendrik, Kendrix, Kendryck, Kendryk, Kenedrick, Kenndrick, Keondric, Keondrick, Keondryc, Keondryck, Keondryk

Kenji (Japanese) intelligent second son.

Kenley (English) royal meadow.
Kenlea, Kenlee, Kenleigh, Kenli, Kenlie, Kennlea, Kennlee, Kennleigh, Kennley, Kennli, Kennlie, Kennly, Kenly

Kenn (Scottish) a form of Ken.

Kennan (Scottish) little Ken.
Kenna, Kennen, Kennin, Kennyn

Kennard (Irish) brave chieftain.
Kenner, Kennerd

Kennedy (Irish) helmeted chief. History: John F. Kennedy was the thirty-fifth U.S. president.
Kenedy, Kenidy, Kennadie, Kennady, Kennedey, Kennedi, Kennedie

Kenneth (Irish) handsome. (English) royal oath.
Keneth, Kenneith, Kennet, Kennethen, Kennett, Kennieth, Kennth, Kennyth, Kenyth

Kennith (Irish, English) a form of Kenneth.

Kennon (Scottish) a form of Kennan.

Kenny (Scottish) a familiar form of Kenneth.
Keni, Kenney, Kenni, Kennie, Kinnie

Kenric (English) a form of Kenrick.

Kenrick (English) bold ruler; royal ruler.
Kennric, Kennrick, Kennrik, Kennryc, Kennryck, Kennryk, Kenricks, Kenrik, Kenryc, Kenryck, Kenryk, Kenryks

Kent (Welsh) white; bright. (English) a short form of Kenton. Geography: a region in England.

Kentaro (Japanese) big boy.

Kenton (English) from Kent, England.
Kentan, Kenten, Kentin, Kentonn, Kentyn

Kentrell (English) king's estate.
Kenreal, Kentrel, Kentrelle

Kenward (English) brave; royal guardian.

Kenya (Hebrew) animal horn. (Russian) a form of Kenneth. Geography: a country in east-central Africa.
Kenia, Keniah, Kenja

Kenyan (Irish) a form of Kenyon.

Kenyatta (American) a form of Kenya.
*Kenyat, Kenyata, Kenyatae, Kenyatee,
Kenyatt, Kenyatter, Kenyatti, Kenyotta*

Kenyon (Irish) white haired, blond.
Kenyen, Kenyin, Kenynn, Keonyon

Kenzie (Scottish) wise leader. See also
Mackenzie.
Kensi, Kensie, Kensy, Kenzi, Kenzy

Keoki (Hawaiian) a form of George.

Keola (Hawaiian) life.

Keon (Irish) a form of Ewan.
Keaon, Keeon, Keone, Keonne, Kyon

Keondre (American) a form of Keandre.

Keoni (Hawaiian) a form of John.
Keonee, Keonie, Keony

Keonta (American) a form of Keon.

Keontae, Keonte, Keonté (American)
forms of Keon.
*Keonntay, Keontay, Keontaye, Keontez,
Keontia, Keontis, Keontrae, Keontre,
Keontrey, Keontrye*

Kerbasi (Basque) warrior.

Kerel (Afrikaans) young.
Kerell

Kerem (Turkish) noble; kind.
Kereem

Kerey (Gypsy) homeward bound.
Ker, Keree, Keri, Kerie, Kery

Kerman (Basque) from Germany.
Kermen, Kerrman, Kerrmen

Kermit (Irish) a form of Dermot.
*Kermey, Kermie, Kermitt, Kermy, Kermyt,
Kermytt*

Kern (Irish) a short form of Kieran.
*Keirn, Keirne, Kerne, Kerrn, Kerrne, Keyrn,
Keyrne*

Keron (Hebrew) a form of Keren (see
Girls' Names).

Kerr (Scandinavian) a form of Carr.
Karr

Kerrick (English) king's rule.
*Keric, Kerick, Kerik, Kerric, Kerrik, Kerryc,
Kerryck, Kerryk, Keryc, Keryck, Keryk*

Kerry (Irish) dark; dark haired.
Kerree, Kerrey, Kerri, Kerrie, Kery

Kers (Todas) Botany: an Indian plant.

Kersen (Indonesian) cherry.
Kersan, Kersin, Kerson, Kersyn

Kerstan (Dutch) a form of Christian.
Kersten, Kerstin, Kerston, Kerstyn

Kervin (Irish, English) a form of Kerwin.
Kervyn

Kerwin (Irish) little; dark. (English) friend
of the marshlands.
*Kerwan, Kerwane, Kerwain, Kerwaine,
Kerwinn, Kerwon, Kerwyn, Kerwynn,
Kerwynne, Kirwin, Kirwyn*

Kesar (Russian) a form of Caesar.
Kesare

Keshaun, Késhawn, Keshon (American)
forms of Keshawn.

Keshawn (American) a combination of
the prefix Ke + Shawn.
*Keeshaun, Keeshawn, Keeshon, Kesean,
Keshan, Keshane, Keshayne, Keshion,
Keshone*

Keshun (American) a form of Keshawn.

Kesin (Hindi) long-haired beggar.
Kesyn

Kesse (Ashanti, Fante) chubby baby.
*Kesse, Kessi, Kessie, Kessy, Kezi, Kezie,
Kezy, Kezzi, Kezzie, Kezzy*

Kester (English) a form of Christopher.

Kestrel (English) falcon.
Kes, Kestrell

Keung (Chinese) universe.

Kevan, Keven, Kevon, Kevyn (Irish)
forms of Kevin.
*Keve, Keveen, Kevone, Kevonne, Kevoyn,
Kevron, Keyvan, Keyven, Keyvon, Keyvyn,
Kiven, Kivon*

Kevin (Irish) handsome. See also Cavan.
Kaiven, Keaven, Keivan, Kev, Keverne,
Kevian, Kevien, Kévin, Kevinn, Kevins,
Kevis, Kevn, Kevun, Kevvy, Keyvin

Kevion (Irish) a form of Kevin.
Keveon

Kevontae, Kevonte (American) forms of
Kevin.

Kewan, Kewon (American) forms of
Kevin.
Kewane, Kewaun, Kewone, Kiwan, Kiwane

Key (English) key; protected.
Kei, Keye

Keyan, Keyon (Irish) forms of Keon.
Keyen, Keyin, Keyion

Keynan (Irish) a form of Keenan.
Keynin, Keynon, Keynyn

Keyonta (American) a form of Keon.

Keyshawn (American) a combination of
Key + Shawn.
Keyshan, Keyshaun, Keyshon, Keyshun

Keyton (English) a form of Keaton.
Keytan, Keyten, Keytin, Keytun, Keytyn

Khachig (Armenian) small cross.

Khachik (Armenian) a form of Khachig.

Khaim (Russian) a form of Chaim.

Khaldun (Arabic) forever.
Khaldoon, Khaldoun

Khaled, Khalid, Khallid (Arabic) forms
of Khälid.

Khaleel (Arabic) a form of Khalíl.

Khalfani (Swahili) born to lead.
Khalfan

Khälid (Arabic) eternal.
Khalyd

Khalil (Arabic) a form of Khalíl.

Khalíl (Arabic) friend.
Khahlil, Khailil, Khailyl, Khalee, Khaleil,
Khali, Khalial, Khaliel, Khalihl, Khalill,
Khaliyl

Khaliq (Arabic) creative.
Khaliqu, Khalique, Khalyq, Khalyqu,
Khalyque

Khamisi (Swahili) born on Thursday.
Kham, Khamisy, Khamysi, Khamysy

Khan (Turkish) prince.
Chan, Kahn, Khanh

Kharald (Russian) a form of Gerald.

Khayru (Arabic) benevolent.

Khiry (Arabic) a form of Khayru.
Khiri, Kiry

Khoury (Arabic) priest.
Khori, Khorie, Khory, Khouri, Khourie

Khristian (Greek) a form of Christian,
Kristian.
Khris, Khristan, Khristin, Khrystiyan,
Khriston, Khrystian

Khristopher (Greek) a form of
Kristopher.
Khristofer, Khristoffer, Khristoph,
Khristophar, Khristophe, Khrystopher

Khristos (Greek) a form of Christos.
Khrystos, Krystous

Ki (Korean) arisen.

Kian, Kion (Irish) forms of Keon.
Kione, Kionie, Kionne

Kibuuka (Luganda) brave warrior.
History: a Ganda warrior deity.
Kybuuka

Kidd (English) child; young goat.
Kid, Kyd

Kiefer, Kieffer (German) forms of
Keifer.
Kief, Kiefor, Kiffer, Kiiefer

Kiel (Irish) a form of Kyle.
Kiell

Kiele (Hawaiian) gardenia.
Kyele

Kienan (Irish) a form of Keenan.
Kienon

Kier (Irish) a short form of Kieran.
Kierr, Kierre

Kieran (Irish) little and dark; little Keir.
Keeran, Keeren, Keerin, Keeron, Kiaron, Kiarron, Kierian, Kierien, Kierin

Kieren, Kieron (Irish) forms of Kieran.
Kierron

Kiernan (Irish) a form of Kieran.
Kern, Kernan, Kiernen

Kiet (Tai) honor.
Kyet

Kifeda (Luo) only boy among girls.
Kyfeda

Kiho (Rutooro) born on a foggy day.
Kyho

Kijika (Native American) quiet walker.
Kijyka, Kyjika, Kyjyka

Kika (Hawaiian) a form of Keith.
Kikah, Kyka, Kykah

Kiki (Spanish) a form of Henry.

Kile (Irish) a form of Kyle.
Kilee, Kilei, Kileigh, Kilen, Kili, Kilie, Kily, Kiyl, Kiyle

Kiley (Irish) a form of Kyle.
Kylee, Kyley, Kylie

Killian (Irish) little Kelly.
Kilean, Kilian, Kiliane, Kilien, Killie, Killiean, Killien, Killienn, Killion, Killy, Kylia, Kylien, Kyllian, Kyllien

Kim (English) a short form of Kimball.
Kimie, Kimmy, Kym

Kimani (Shoshone) a form of Kimana (see Girls' Names).

Kimball (Greek) hollow vessel. (English) warrior chief.
Kimbal, Kimbel, Kimbele, Kimbell, Kimble, Kymbal, Kymbel, Kymbele, Kymbell

Kimo (Hawaiian) a form of James.

Kimokeo (Hawaiian) a form of Timothy.

Kin (Japanese) golden.
Kyn

Kincaid (Scottish) battle chief.
Kincade, Kincaide, Kincayd, Kincayde, Kinkaid, Kyncaid, Kyncayd, Kyncayde

Kindin (Basque) fifth.
Kindyn, Kyndin, Kyndyn

King (English) king. A short form of names beginning with "King."
Kyng

Kingsley (English) king's meadow.
Kings, Kingslea, Kingslee, Kingsleigh, Kingsli, Kingslie, Kingsly, Kingzlee, Kinslea, Kinslee, Kinsleigh, Kinsley, Kinsli, Kinslie, Kinsly, Kyngs, Kyngslea, Kyngslee, Kyngsleigh, Kyngsley, Kyngsli, Kyngslie, Kyngsly

Kingston (English) king's estate.
Kinston, Kyngston, Kynston

Kingswell (English) king's well.
Kingswel, Kyngswel, Kyngswell

Kini (Hawaiian) a short form of Iukini.

Kinnard (Irish) tall slope.
Kinard, Kynard, Kynnard

Kinsey (English) victorious royalty.
Kinsee, Kinsi, Kinsie, Kinze, Kinzie, Kynsee, Kynsey, Kynsi, Kynsie, Kynsy

Kinton (Hindi) crowned.
Kynton

Kioshi (Japanese) quiet.

Kip (English) a form of Kipp.
Kyp

Kipp (English) pointed hill.
Kippar, Kipper, Kippie, Kippy, Kypp

Kir (Bulgarian) a familiar form of Cyrus.

Kiral (Turkish) king; supreme leader.
Kyral

Kiran (Sanskrit) beam of light.
Kiren, Kirin, Kiron, Kirun, Kiryn

Kirby (Scandinavian) church village. (English) cottage by the water.
Kerbbee, Kerbbey, Kerbbi, Kerbbie, Kerbby, Kerbee, Kerbey, Kerbi, Kerbie, Kerby, Kirbee, Kirbey, Kirbie, Kirkby, Kyrbbee, Kyrbbey,

Kirby *(cont.)*
Kyrbbi, Kyrbbie, Kyrbby, Kyrbee, Kyrbey,
Kyrbi, Kyrbie, Kyrby

Kiri (Cambodian) mountain.
Kiry, Kyri, Kyry

Kiril (Slavic) a form of Cyril.
Kirill, Kiryl, Kiryll, Kyril, Kyrill, Kyrillos,
Kyryl, Kyryll

Kiritan (Hindi) wearing a crown.
Kiriten, Kiritin, Kiriton, Kirityn

Kirk (Scandinavian) church.
Kerc, Kerck, Kerk, Kirc, Kirck, Kurc, Kurck,
Kurk, Kyrc, Kyrck, Kyrk

Kirkland (English) church land.
Kerkland, Kirklind, Kirklynd, Kurkland,
Kyrkland

Kirkley (English) church meadow.
Kerklea, Kerklee, Kerkleigh, Kerkley, Kerkli,
Kerklie, Kerkly, Kirklea, Kirklee, Kirkleigh,
Kirkli, Kirklie, Kirkly, Kurklea, Kurklee,
Kurkleigh, Kurkley, Kurkli, Kurklie, Kurkly,
Kyrklea, Kyrklee, Kyrkleigh, Kyrkley,
Kyrkli, Kyrklie, Kyrkly

Kirklin (English) a form of Kirkland.
Kerklan, Kirklan, Kirklen, Kirkline,
Kirkloun, Kirklun, Kirklyn, Kirklynn,
Kurklan, Kyrklan

Kirkwell (English) church well; church
spring.
Kerkwel, Kerkwell, Kirkwel, Kurkwel,
Kurkwell, Kyrkwel, Kyrkwell

Kirkwood (English) church forest.
Kerkwood, Kurkwood, Kyrkwood

Kirt (Latin, German, French) a form of
Kurt.

Kirton (English) church town.
Kerston, Kirston, Kurston, Kyrston

Kishan (American) a form of Keshawn.
Kishaun, Kishawn, Kishen, Kishon,
Kyshon, Kyshun

Kistna (Hindi) sacred, holy. Geography: a
sacred river in India.
Kisstna, Kysstna, Kystna

Kistur (Gypsy) skillful rider.

Kit (Greek) a familiar form of Christian,
Christopher, Kristopher.
Kitt, Kitts

Kito (Swahili) jewel; precious child.
Kitto, Kyto, Kytto

Kitwana (Swahili) pledged to live.
Kitwanah

Kiva (Hebrew) a short form of Akiva,
Jacob.
Kiba, Kivah, Kivi, Kiwa, Kyva, Kyvah

Kiyoshi (Japanese) quiet; peaceful.

Kizza (Luganda) born after twins.
Kiza, Kizah, Kizzi, Kizzie, Kizzy, Kyza,
Kyzah, Kyzza, Kyzzah, Kyzzi, Kyzzie,
Kyzzy

Kjell (Swedish) a form of Karl.
Kjel

Klaus (German) a short form of
Nicholas. A form of Claus.
Klaas, Klaes, Klas, Klause

Klay (English) a form of Clay.

Klayton (English) a form of Clayton.

Kleef (Dutch) cliff.

Klement (Czech) a form of Clement.
Klema, Klemenis, Klemens, Klemet, Klemo,
Klim, Klimek, Kliment, Klimka

Kleng (Norwegian) claw.

Knight (English) armored knight.
Knightleigh, Knightly, Knyght

Knoton (Native American) a form of
Nodin.

Knowles (English) grassy slope.
Knolls, Nowles

Knox (English) hill.

Knute (Scandinavian) a form of Canute.
Kanut, Kanute, Knud, Knut

Kobi, Koby (Polish) familiar forms of
Jacob.
Kobby, Kobe, Kobee, Kobey, Kobia, Kobie

Kodey, Kodi, Kodie, Kody (English)
forms of Cody.
Kode, Kodee, Kodi, Kodye

Kofi (Twi) born on Friday.

Kohana (Lakota) swift.
Kohanah

Kohl (English) a form of Cole.
Kohle

Koi (Choctaw) panther. (Hawaiian) a form of Troy.

Kojo (Akan) born on Monday.

Koka (Hawaiian) Scotsman.
Kokah

Kokayi (Shona) gathered together.

Kolby (English) a form of Colby.
Koalby, Koelby, Kohlbe, Kohlby, Kolbe, Kolbey, Kolbi, Kolbie, Kolebe, Koleby, Kollby

Kole (English) a form of Cole.

Koleman (English) a form of Coleman.
Kolemann, Kolemen

Kolin, Kollin (English) forms of Colin.
Kolen, Kollen, Kollyn, Kolyn

Kolt (English) a short form of Koltan. A form of Colt.
Kolte

Koltan, Kolten, Koltin, Kolton, Koltyn (English) forms of Colton.
Koltn

Kolya (Russian) a familiar form of Nikolai, Nikolos.
Kola, Kolenka, Kolia, Koliah, Kolja

Kona (Hawaiian) a form of Don.
Konah, Konala

Konane (Hawaiian) bright moonlight.
Konan

Kondo (Swahili) war.

Kong (Chinese) glorious; sky.

Konner, Konnor (Irish) forms of Connar, Connor.
Kohner, Kohnor, Konar, Koner, Konor

Kono (Moquelumnan) squirrel eating a pine nut.

Konrad (German) a form of Conrad.
Khonrad, Koen, Koenraad, Kon, Konn, Konney, Konni, Konnie, Konny, Konrád, Konrade, Konrado, Kord, Kunz

Konstantin (German, Russian) a form of Constantine. See also Dinos.
Konstancji, Konstadine, Konstadino, Konstandinos, Konstantinas, Konstantine, Konstantio, Konstanty, Konstantyn, Konstantyne, Konstanz, Konstatino, Kostadino, Kostadinos, Kostandino, Kostandinos, Kostantin, Kostantino, Kostenka, Kostya, Kotsos

Konstantinos (Greek) a form of Constantine.

Kontar (Akan) only child.

Korb (German) basket.

Korbin (English) a form of Corbin.
Korban, Korben, Korbyn

Kordell (English) a form of Cordell.
Kordel

Korey, Kori, Korie (Irish) forms of Corey, Kory.
Korrey, Korri, Korrie

Kornel (Latin) a form of Cornelius, Kornelius.
Korneil, Kornél, Korneli, Kornelisz, Kornell, Krelis, Soma

Kornelius (Latin) a form of Cornelius. See also Kees, Kornel.
Karnelius, Korneilius, Korneliaus, Kornelious, Kornellius

Korrigan (Irish) a form of Corrigan.
Korigan, Korigan, Korrigon, Korrigun

Kort (German, Dutch) a form of Cort, Kurt. (German) a form of Konrad.
Kourt

Kortney (English) a form of Courtney.
Kortni, Kourtney

Korudon (Greek) helmeted one.

Kory (Irish) a form of Corey.
Kore, Koree, Korei, Korio, Korre, Korree, Korria, Korry, Korrye

Korydon (Greek) a form of Corydon.
Koridan, Koriden, Koridin, Koridon,
Koridyn, Korydan, Koryden, Korydin,
Korydyn

Kosey (African) lion.
Kosse, Kossee, Kossey

Kosmo (Greek) a form of Cosmo.
Kosmas, Kosmos, Kosmy, Kozmo

Kostas (Greek) a short form of
Konstantin.

Kosti (Finnish) a form of Gustave.

Kosumi (Moquelumnan) spear fisher.

Koty (English) a form of Cody.

Koukalaka (Hawaiian) a form of Douglas.

Kourtland (English) a form of Courtland.
Kortlan, Kortland, Kortlend, Kortlon,
Kourtlin

Kovit (Tai) expert.
Kovyt

Kraig (Irish, Scottish) a form of Craig.
Kraggie, Kraggy, Krayg, Kreg, Kreig, Kreigh

Kramer (English) a form of Cramer.
Krammer

Krikor (Armenian) a form of Gregory.

Kris (Greek) a form of Chris. A short
form of Kristian, Kristofer, Kristopher.
Kriss, Krys

Krischan, Krishan (German) forms of
Christian.
Krishaun, Krishawn, Krishon, Krishun

Krishna (Hindi) delightful, pleasurable.
Religion: the eighth and principal avatar
of the Hindu god Vishnu.
Kistna, Kistnah, Krisha, Krishnah,
Kryshanh, Kryshna

Krisiant (Welsh) a form of Crisiant.
Krisient, Krysient, Krysyent

Krispin (Latin) a form of Crispin.
Krispian, Krispino, Krispo, Kryspyn

Kristen, Kriston (Greek) forms of
Kristian.
Kristan, Kristin, Kristinn

Krister (Swedish) a form of Christian.
Krist, Kristar

Kristian (Greek) a form of Christian,
Khristian.
Kristek, Kristien, Kristine, Kristion

Kristjan (Estonian) a form of Christian,
Khristian.

Kristo (Greek) a short form of
Khristopher.
Khristo, Khrysto

Kristofer, Kristoffer (Swedish) forms of
Kristopher.
Kristafer, Kristef, Kristfer, Kristfor, Kristoforo,
Kristifer, Kristofo, Kristofor, Kristofyr,
Kristufer, Kristus

Kristoff (Greek) a short form of
Kristofer, Kristopher.
Khristof, Khristoff, Khrystof, Khrystoff,
Kristof, Kristóf, Krystof, Krystoff

Kristophe (French) a form of Kristopher.
Khristoph, Khrystoph, Kristoph, Krystoph

Kristopher (Greek) a form of
Christopher. See also Topher.
Krisstopher, Kristapher, Kristepher,
Kristophor, Krisus, Krystupas

Kruz (Spanish) a form of Cruz.
Kruise, Kruize, Kruse, Kruze, Kruzz

Krystian (Polish) a form of Christian.
Krys, Krystek, Krystien, Krystin

Krystopher (Greek) a form of
Christopher.
Krystofer

Krzysztof (Polish) a form of Kristoff.

Kuba (Czech) a form of Jacob.
Kubo, Kubus

Kueng (Chinese) universe.

Kugonza (Rutooro) love.

Kuiril (Basque) lord.

Kullen (Irish) a form of Cullen.

Kumar (Sanskrit) prince.

Kunle (Yoruba) home filled with honors.

Kuper (Yiddish) copper.
Kopper, Kupor, Kupper

Kurt (Latin, German, French) a short form of Kurtis. A form of Curt.
Kuno, Kurtt

Kurtis (Latin, French) a form of Curtis.
Kirtis, Kirtus, Kurtes, Kurtez, Kurtice, Kurties, Kurtiss, Kurtus, Kurtys, Kurtyss

Kuruk (Pawnee) bear.

Kuzih (Carrier) good speaker.

Kwabena (Akan) born on Tuesday.

Kwacha (Nguni) morning.

Kwako (Akan) born on Wednesday.
Kwaka, Kwakou, Kwaku

Kwam (Zuni) a form of John.

Kwame (Akan) born on Saturday.
Kwamen, Kwami, Kwamin

Kwamé (Akan) a form of Kwame.

Kwan (Korean) strong.
Kwane

Kwasi (Akan) born on Sunday. (Swahili) wealthy.
Kwasie, Kwazzi, Kwesi

Kwayera (Nguni) dawn.

Kwende (Nguni) let's go.

Ky, Kye (Irish, Yiddish) short forms of Kyle.

Kyele (Irish) a form of Kyle.

Kylan, Kylen (Irish) forms of Kyle.
Kyelen, Kyleen, Kylin, Kyline, Kylon, Kylun

Kylar, Kyler, Kylor (English) forms of Kyle.

Kyle (Irish) narrow piece of land; place where cattle graze. (Yiddish) crowned with laurels.
Cyle, Kilan, Kilen, Kyel, Kyll, Kyrell

Kylle (Irish) a form of Kyle.

Kynan (Welsh) chief.
Kinan

Kyndall (English) a form of Kendall.
Kyndal, Kyndel, Kyndell, Kyndle

Kyne (English) royal.

Kyran, Kyren, Kyron (Irish) forms of Kieran. (Sanskrit) forms of Kiran.
Kyrin, Kyrone, Kyrun, Kyryn

Kyree (Cambodian, Maori, Greek) a form of Kyrie (see Girls' Names).

Kyros (Greek) master.
Kiros

Kyven (American) a form of Kevin.
Kyvan, Kyvaun, Kyvon, Kywon, Kywynn

L

La'darius, Ladarrius (American) forms of Ladarius.
Ladarrias, Ladarries, Ladarrious

Laban (Hawaiian) white.
Laben, Labin, Labon, Labyn, Lebaan, Leban

Labaron (American) a combination of the prefix La + Baron.
Labaren, Labarren, Labarron, Labearon, Labron

Labib (Arabic) sensible; intelligent.
Labyb

Labrentsis (Russian) a form of Lawrence.
Labhras, Labhruinn, Labrencis

Lachlan (Scottish) land of lakes.
Lache, Lachlann, Lachlun, Lachlunn, Lachunn, Lakelan, Lakeland

Lacy (Greek, Latin) cheerful.

Ladarian (American) a combination of the prefix La + Darian.
Ladarien, Ladarin, Ladarion, Ladarren, Ladarrian, Ladarrien, Ladarrin, Ladarrion, Laderion, Laderrian, Laderrion

Ladarius (American) a combination of the prefix La + Darius.
Ladarious, Ladaris, Ladauris, Laderius, Laderrious, Laderris, Ladirus

Ladd (English) attendant.
Lad, Laddey, Laddie, Laddy

Laderrick (American) a combination of the prefix La + Derric.
Ladarrick, Ladereck, Laderic, Laderricks

Ladislav (Czech) a form of Walter.
Laco, Lada, Ladislao, Ladislas, Ladislaus, Ladyslas, Ladyslaus, Ladyslav

Lado (Fante) second-born son.

Lafayette (French) History: Marquis de Lafayette was a French soldier and politician who aided the American Revolution.
Lafaiete, Lafayett, Lafette, Laffyette

Laidley (English) path along the marshy meadow.
Laedlea, Laedlee, Laedleigh, Laedley, Laedli, Laedlie, Laedly, Laidlea, Laidlee, Laidleigh, Laidli, Laidlie, Laidly, Laydlea, Laydlee, Laydleigh, Laydley, Laydli, Laydlie, Laydly

Lain, Laine (English) forms of Lane.

Laird (Scottish) wealthy landowner.
Layrd

Lais (Arabic) lion.
Lays

Laith (Scandinavian, English) a form of Latham.
Lathe

Lajos (Hungarian) famous; holy.
Lajcsi, Laji, Lali

Lajuan (American) a combination of the prefix La + Juan.

Lake (English) lake.
Laek, Laik, Lakan, Lakane, Lakee, Laken, Lakin, Layk

Lakeith (American) a combination of the prefix La + Keith.

Lakota (Dakota) a tribal name.
Lakoda

Lal (Hindi) beloved.

Lamani (Tongan) lemon.
Lamanee, Lamaney, Lamanie, Lamany

Lamar (German) famous throughout the land. (French) sea, ocean.
Lamair, Lamaris, Lamarre, Larmar, Lemar

Lamarcus (American) a combination of the prefix La + Marcus.

Lamario (American) a form of Lamar.

Lamarr (German, French) a form of Lamar.

Lambert (German) bright land.
Bert, Lambard, Lamberto, Lamberts, Lambirt, Lambirto, Lamburt, Lamburto, Lambyrt, Lambyrto, Lampard, Landbert, Landberto, Landbirt, Landbirto, Landburt, Landburto, Landbyrt, Landbyrto, Landebirt, Landeburt, Landebyrt

Lami (Tongan) hidden.
Lamee, Lamey, Lamie, Lamy

Lamon (French) a form of Lamond.

Lamond (French) world.
Lammond, Lamonde, Lamondo, Lamondre, Lamund, Lemond, Lemund

Lamont (Scandinavian) lawyer.
Lamaunt, Lamonta, Lamontie, Lamonto, Lamount, Lemmont, Lemont, Lemonte

Lamonte (Scandinavian) a form of Lamont.

Lance (German) a short form of Lancelot.
Lancey, Lancy, Lanse, Lantz, Lanz, Launce

Lancelot (French) attendant. Literature: the knight who loved King Arthur's wife, Queen Guinevere.
Lancelott, Lancilot, Lancilott, Lancilotte, Lancilotto, Lancylot, Lancylott, Lancylotte, Launcelet, Launcelot, Launcelott, Launcelotte

Landan, Landen, Landin (English) forms of Landon.
Landenn

Lander (Basque) lion man. (English) landowner.
Landar, Landers, Landor, Landors, Launder, Launders

Lando (Portuguese, Spanish) a short form of Orlando, Rolando.
Londow

Landon (English) open, grassy meadow.
A form of Langdon.
Landyn, Landun

Landric (German) ruler of the land.
*Landrick, Landrik, Landryc, Landryck,
Landryk*

Landry (French, English) ruler.
Landre, Landré, Landri, Landrie, Landrue

Lane (English) narrow road.
Laney, Lani, Lanie, Layne

Lang (Scandinavian) tall man.
Laing, Lange

Langdon (English) long hill.
*Langdan, Langden, Langdin, Langdun,
Langdyn*

Langford (English) long ford.
Laingford, Lanford, Lankford

Langi (Tongan) heaven.
Langee, Langey, Langie, Langy

Langley (English) long meadow.
*Lainglea, Lainglee, Laingleigh, Laingley,
Laingli, Lainglie, Laingly, Langlea, Langlee,
Langleigh, Langli, Langlie, Langly*

Langston (English) long, narrow town.
Laingston, Langsden, Langsdon, Langstone

Langundo (Native American) peaceful.
Langund

Lani (Hawaiian) heaven.
Lanee, Laney, Lanie, Lany

Lanny (American) a familiar form of
Laurence, Lawrence.
Lannee, Lanney, Lanni, Lannie

Lanu (Moquelumnan) running around
the pole.

Lanz (Italian) a form of Lance.
Lanzo, Lonzo

Lao (Spanish) a short form of Stanislaus.

Lap (Vietnamese) independent.

Lapidos (Hebrew) torches.
Lapidoth

Laquan (American) a combination of the
prefix La + Quan.

*Laquain, Laquann, Laquanta, Laquantae,
Laquante, Laquawn, Laquawne, Laquin,
Laquinn, Laqun, Laquon, Laquone,
Laqwan, Laqwon*

Laquintin (American) a combination of
the prefix La + Quinten.
*Laquentin, Laquenton, Laquintas,
Laquinten, Laquintiss, Laquinton,
Laquyntan, Laquynten, Laquyntin,
Laquynton, Laquyntun, Laquyntyn*

Laramie (French) tears of love. Geography:
a town in Wyoming on the Overland
Trail.
Laramee, Laramey, Larami, Laramy, Laremy

Larenz (Italian, Spanish) a short form of
Larenzo.

Larenzo (Italian, Spanish) a form of
Lorenzo.
Larenza, Larinzo, Laurenzo

Larkin (Irish) rough; fierce.
Larkan, Larken, Larklin, Larklyn, Larkyn

Larnell (American) a combination of
Larry + Darnell.
Larnel

Laron (French) thief.
*La Ron, La Ruan, La'ron, Laran, Laraun,
Laren, Larin, Larone, Laronn, Larron,
Larun, Laryn*

Larrimore (French) armorer.
Larimore, Larmer, Larmor

Larry (Latin) a familiar form of
Lawrence.
Lari, Larie, Larri, Larrie, Lary

Lars (Scandinavian) a form of Lawrence.
*Laris, Larris, Larse, Larz, Laurans, Laurits,
Lavrans, Lorens*

Larson (Scandinavian) son of Lars.
Larsen, Larsson, Larzon

LaSalle (French) hall.
Lasal, Lasale, Lasalle, Lascell, Lascelles

Lash (Gypsy) a form of Louis.
Lashi, Lasho

Lashaun (American) a form of Lashawn.

Lashawn (American) a combination of the prefix La + Shawn.
Lasaun, Lasean, Lashajaun, Lashan, Lashane, Lashun

Lashon (American) a form of Lashawn.

Lashone (American) a form of Lashawn.
Lashonne

Lasse (Finnish) a form of Nicholas.
Lase

László (Hungarian) famous ruler.
Laci, Lacko, Laslo, Lazlo

Lateef (Arabic) gentle; pleasant.
Latif, Latyf, Letif, Letyf

Latham (Scandinavian) barn. (English) district.
Lathe, Lay

Lathan (American) a combination of the prefix La + Nathan.
Lathaniel, Lathen, Lathin, Lathyn, Leathan

Lathrop (English) barn, farmstead.
Lathe, Lathrope, Lay

Latimer (English) interpreter.
Lat, Latimor, Lattie, Latty, Latymer

Latravis (American) a combination of the prefix La + Travis.
Latavious, Latavius, Latraveus, Latraviaus, Latravious, Latravius, Latravys, Latrayvious, Latrayvous, Latrivis

Latrell (American) a combination of the prefix La + Kentrell.
Latreal, Latreil, Latrel, Latrelle, Letreal, Letrel, Letrell, Letrelle

Laudalino (Portuguese) praised.
Laudalin, Laudalyn, Laudalyno

Laughlin (Irish) servant of Saint Secundinus.
Lanty, Lauchlin, Laughlyn, Leachlain, Leachlainn

Laura (Latin) a form of Laurence.

Lauren (Latin) a form of Laurence.
Lauran

Laurence (Latin) crowned with laurel. A form of Lawrence. See also Rance, Raulas, Raulo, Renzo.
Larance, Larrance, Laurance, Laurans, Laureano, Laurencho, Laurentij, Laurentios, Laurentiu, Laurentius, Laurentz, Laurentzi, Laurenz, Laurin, Laurits, Lauritz, Laurnet, Laurus, Lurance

Laurencio (Spanish) a form of Laurence.
Lorencio

Laurens (Dutch) a form of Laurence.
Laurenz

Laurent (French) a form of Laurence.
Laurente

Laurie (English) a familiar form of Laurence.
Lauree, Laurey, Lauri, Laurri, Laurrie, Laurry, Laury, Lorry

Lauris (Swedish) a form of Laurence.

Lauro (Filipino) a form of Laurence.

LaValle (French) valley.
Lavail, Laval, Lavalei, Lavall, Lavalle

Lavan (Hebrew) white.
Lavane, Lavaughan, Laven, Lavin, Lavyn, Levan, Leven

Lavaughan (American) a form of Lavan.
Lavaughn, Levaughan, Levaughn

Lave (Italian) lava. (English) lord.
Laev, Laeve, Laiv, Laive, Layv, Layve

Lavell, Lavelle (French) forms of LaValle.
Lavel, Lavele, Levele, Levell, Levelle

Lavi (Hebrew) lion.
Lavee, Lavey, Lavie, Lavy

Lavon (American) a form of Lavan.
Lavion, Lavone, Lavonn, Lavonne, Lavont

Lavonte, Lavonté (American) forms of Lavon.

Lavrenti (Russian) a form of Lawrence.
Laiurenty, Larenti, Lavrentij, Lavrenty, Lavrusha, Lavrik, Lavro

Lawerence (Latin) a form of Lawrence.
Lawerance

Lawford (English) ford on the hill.

Lawler (Irish) soft-spoken.
Lawlor, Lollar, Loller

Lawley (English) low meadow on a hill.
Lawlea, Lawlee, Lawleigh, Lawli, Lawlie, Lawly

Lawrance (Latin) a form of Lawrence.

Lawrence (Latin) crowned with laurel. See also Brencis, Chencho.
Lanty, Larian, Larien, Larka, Larrance, Larrence, Larya, Law, Lawren, Lawron, Loreca, Lorenis, Lourenco, Lowrance, Lowrence

Lawry (English) a familiar form of Lawrence.
Lawree, Lawrey, Lawri, Lawrie, Lowree, Lowrey, Lowri, Lowrie, Lowry

Lawson (English) son of Lawrence.
Lawsen, Layson

Lawton (English) town on the hill.
Laughton, Law

Layne (English) a form of Lane.
Layn, Laynee, Layni, Laynie, Layny

Layton (English) a form of Leighton.
Laydon, Layten, Layth, Laythan, Laython

Lazar (Greek) a short form of Lazarus.
Lázár, Lazare

Lazaro (Italian) a form of Lazarus.
Lazarillo, Lazarito, Lazzaro

Lazarus (Greek) a form of Eleazar. Bible: Lazarus was raised from the dead by Jesus.
Lazarius, Lazaros, Lazorus

Le (Vietnamese) pearl.

Leander (Greek) lion-man; brave as a lion.
Ander

Leandre (French) a form of Leander.
Léandre

Leandro (Spanish) a form of Leander.
Leandra, Leandrew, Leandros

Leben (Yiddish) life.
Laben, Lebon

Lebna (Ethiopian) spirit; heart.

Ledarius (American) a combination of the prefix Le + Darius.
Ledarrious, Ledarrius, Lederious, Lederris

Lee (English) a short form of Farley, Leonard, and names containing "lee."
Leigh

Leggett (French) one who is sent; delegate.
Legat, Legate, Legette, Leggitt, Liggett, Lyggett

Lei (Chinese) thunder. (Hawaiian) a form of Ray.
Ley

Leib (Yiddish) roaring lion.
Leibel

Leif (Scandinavian) beloved.
Laif, Leaf, Leef, Leife, Leiff, Leyf, Lief

Leigh (English) a form of Lee.

Leighton (English) meadow farm.
Laeton, Laiton, Lay, Leeton, Leiton, Leyton

Leith (Scottish) broad river.

Lek (Tai) small.

Lekeke (Hawaiian) powerful ruler.

Leks (Estonian) a familiar form of Alexander.
Leksik, Lekso

Lel (Gypsy) taker.

Leland (English) meadowland; protected land.
Layland, Lealan, Lealand, Leelan, Leeland, Leighlan, Leighland, Lelan, Lelann, Lelend, Lelund, Leylan, Leyland

Lemar (French) a form of Lamar.
Lemario, Lemarr, Limar, Limarr, Lymar, Lymarr

Lemuel (Hebrew) devoted to God.
Lem, Lemmie, Lemmy

Len (Hopi) flute. (German) a short form of Leonard.
Lenn

Lenard (German) a form of Leonard.
Lennard

Lencho (Spanish) a form of Lawrence.
Lenci, Lenzy

Lennart (Swedish) a form of Leonard.
Lennerd

Lennie, Lenny (German) familiar forms
of Leonard. (American) forms of Lanny.
*Lenee, Leney, Leni, Lenie, Lennee, Lenney,
Lenni, Leny*

Lenno (Native American) man.
Leno

Lennon (Irish) small cloak; cape.
Lennan, Lennen, Lennin, Lennyn, Lenon

Lennor (Gypsy) spring; summer.
Lenor

Lennox (Scottish) with many elms.
Lennix, Lenox

Leo (Latin) lion. (German) a short form
of Leon, Leopold.
*Lavi, Leão, Leeo, Leio, Léo, Léocadie,
Leosko, Leos, Leosoko, Nardek*

Leobardo (Italian) a form of Leonard.

Leon (Greek, German) a short form of
Leonard, Napoleon.
*Leahon, Leaon, Léon, Leonas, Léonce,
Leoncio, Leondris, Leone, Leonek, Leonetti,
Leoni, Leonirez, Leonizio, Leonon, Leons,
Leontes, Leontios, Leontrae, Leyon, Lion,
Liutas, Lyon*

Leonard (German) brave as a lion.
*Leanard, Leanardas, Leanardus, Lena,
Lennart, Léonard, Leonardis, Leonart,
Leonerd, Leonhard, Leonidas, Leonnard,
Leontes, Lernard, Lienard, Linek, Lionard,
Lnard, Londard, Lonnard, Lonya, Lynnard,
Lyonard*

Leonardo (Italian) a form of Leonard.
Leonaldo, Lionardo, Lonnardo

Leondre (American) a form of Leon.

Leonel (English) little lion. See also
Lionel.
*Leaonal, Leaonall, Leaonel, Leaonell,
Leional, Leionall, Leionel, Leionell, Leonell*

Leonhard (German) a form of Leonard.
Leanhard, Leonhards, Lienhardt

Leonid (Russian) a form of Leonard.
Leonide, Lyonya

Leonidas (Greek) a form of Leonard.
Leonida, Leonides

Leopold (German) brave people.
*Leorad, Lipót, Lopolda, Luepold, Luitpold,
Poldi*

Leopoldo (Italian) a form of Leopold.

Leor (Hebrew) my light.
Leory, Lior

Lequinton (American) a combination of
the prefix Le + Quinten.
Lequentin, Lequenton, Lequinn

Lerenzo (Italian, Spanish) a form of
Lorenzo.
Leranzo, Lerinzo, Leronzo, Lerynzo

Leron (French) round, circle. (American)
a combination of the prefix Le + Ron.
*Le Ron, Leeron, Lerin, Lerone, Lerrin,
Leryn, Liron, Lyron*

Leroy (French) king. See also Delroy, Elroy.
*Learoi, Learoy, Leeroy, LeeRoy, Leighroi,
Leighroy, Leiroi, Leiroy, Lerai, LeRoi, Leroi,
LeRoy, Leyroi, Leyroy, Roy*

Les (Scottish, English) a short form of
Leslie, Lester.
Less, Lessie

Lesharo (Pawnee) chief.

Leshawn (American) a combination of
the prefix Le + Shawn.
*Lashan, Lesean, Leshaun, Leshon,
Leshonne, Leshun*

Leslie (Scottish) gray fortress.
*Leslea, Leslee, Leslei, Lesleigh, Lesley, Lesli,
Lesly, Lezlea, Lezlee, Lezlei, Lezleigh,
Lezley, Lezli, Lezlie, Lezly*

Lester (Latin) chosen camp. (English)
from Leicester, England.
Leicester

Lev (Hebrew) heart. (Russian) a form of
Leo. A short form of Leverett, Levi.
Leb, Leva, Levko

Levant (Latin) rising.
Lavant, Lavante, Levante

Leveni (Tongan) raven.
Levenee, Leveney, Levenie, Leveny

Leverett (French) young hare.
Leveret, Leverette, Leverit, Leveritt, Leveryt, Leverytt

Levi (Hebrew) joined in harmony. Bible: the third son of Jacob; Levites are the priestly tribe of the Israelites.
Leavi, Leevi, Leevie, Levey, Levie, Levitis, Levy, Lewi, Leyvi

Levin (Hebrew) a form of Levi.
Levine, Levion, Levyn, Levynn

Levon (American) a form of Lavon.
Leevon, Levone, Levonn, Levonne, Lyvon, Lyvonn, Lyvonne

Levonte (American) a form of Levon.

Lew (English) a short form of Lewis.

Lewin (English) beloved friend.
Lewan, Lewen, Lewon, Lewyn

Lewis (Welsh) a form of Llewellyn. (English) a form of Louis.
Lew, Lewes, Lewie, Lewy, Lewys

Lex (English) a short form of Alexander.
Lexi, Lexie, Lexin

Lexus (Greek) a short form of Alexander.
Lexis, Lexius, Lexxus

Leyati (Moquelumnan) shape of an abalone shell.
Leyatie, Leyaty

Lí (Chinese) strong.

Liam (Irish) a form of William.
Lliam, Lyam

Lian (Irish) guardian. (Chinese) graceful willow.
Lyan

Liang (Chinese) good, excellent.
Lyang

Liban (Hawaiian) a form of Laban.
Libaan, Lieban

Liberio (Portuguese) liberation.
Liberaratore, Libero, Liborio, Lyberio, Lyberyo

Lidio (Greek, Portuguese) ancient.

Liem (Irish) a form of Liam.

Ligongo (Yao) who is this?
Lygongo

Likeke (Hawaiian) a form of Richard.

Liko (Chinese) protected by Buddha. (Hawaiian) bud.
Like, Lyko

Lin (Burmese) bright. (English) a short form of Lyndon.
Linh, Linn, Linny

Linc (English) a short form of Lincoln.
Link, Lynk

Lincoln (English) settlement by the pool. History: Abraham Lincoln was the sixteenth U.S. president.
Lincon, Lincoyn, Lyncoln

Lindberg (German) mountain where linden grow.
Lindbergh, Lindbert, Lindburg, Lindy, Lyndberg, Lyndbergh, Lyndburg

Lindbert (German) a form of Lindberg.
Linbert, Linbirt, Linburt, Linbyrt, Lindbirt, Lindburt, Lynbert, Lynbirt, Lynburt, Lynbyrt, Lyndbert, Lyndbirt, Lyndburt, Lyndbyrt

Lindell (English) valley of the linden. See also Lyndal.
Lendall, Lendel, Lendell, Lindal, Lindall, Lindel

Linden, Lindon (English) forms of Lyndon.
Lindan, Lindin, Lindyn

Lindley (English) linden field.
Lindlea, Lindlee, Lindleigh, Lindli, Lindlie, Lindly, Lyndlea, Lyndlee, Lyndleigh, Lyndley, Lyndli, Lyndlie, Lyndly

Lindsay (English) a form of Lindsey.
Linsay, Lyndsay

Lindsey (English) linden island.
Lind, Lindsee, Lindsie, Lindsy, Lindzy, Linsey, Linzie, Linzy, Lyndsey, Lyndsie, Lynzie

Linford (English) linden ford.
Lynford

Linfred (German) peaceful, calm.
Linfrid, Linfryd, Lynfrid, Lynfryd

Linley (English) flax meadow.
*Linlea, Linlee, Linleigh, Linli, Linlie, Linly,
Lynlea, Lynlee, Lynleigh, Lynley, Lynli,
Lynlie, Lynly*

Lino (Portuguese) a short form of
Laudalino.

Linton (English) flax town.
Lintonn, Lynton, Lyntonn

Linu (Hindi) lily.
Lynu

Linus (Greek) flaxen haired.
*Linas, Linis, Liniss, Linous, Linux, Lynis,
Lyniss, Lynus*

Linwood (English) flax wood.

Lio (Hawaiian) a form of Leo.
Lyo

Lionel (French) lion cub. See also Leonel.
*Lional, Lionall, Lionell, Lionello, Lynel,
Lynell, Lyonel, Lyonal, Lyonall, Lyonell,
Lyonello*

Liron (Hebrew) my song.
Lyron

Lise (Moquelumnan) salmon's head
coming out of the water.
Lyse

Lisimba (Yao) lion.
*Lasimba, Lasimbah, Lisimbah, Lysimba,
Lysymba, Simba*

Lister (English) dyer.
Lyster

Litton (English) town on the hill.
Liton, Lyton, Lytten, Lytton

Liu (African) voice.

Liuz (Polish) light.
Lius, Lyus

Livingston (English) Leif's town.
Livingstone, Livinston, Livinstone

Liwanu (Moquelumnan) growling bear.
Lywanu

Llewellyn (Welsh) lionlike.
*Lewelan, Lewelen, Llewelin, Llewellen,
Llewelleyn, Llewellin, Llewelyn, Llywellyn,
Llywellynn, Llywelyn*

Lleyton (English) a form of Leighton.

Lloyd (Welsh) gray haired; holy. See also
Floyd.
Loy, Loyd, Loyde, Loydie

Lobo (Spanish) wolf.

Lochlain (Irish, Scottish) land of lakes.
*Loche, Lochee, Lochlan, Lochlann, Lochlen,
Lochlin, Lochlon, Lochlyn, Locklynn*

Locke (English) forest.
Loc, Lock, Lockwood

Loe (Hawaiian) a form of Roy.

Logan (Irish) meadow.
*Llogan, Loagan, Loagen, Loagon, Logann,
Loggan, Loghan, Login, Logon, Logn,
Logun, Logunn, Logyn*

Logen (Irish) a form of Logan.

Lok (Chinese) happy.

Lokela (Hawaiian) a form of Roger.
Lokelah

Lokni (Moquelumnan) raining through
the roof.

Lomán (Irish) bare. (Slavic) sensitive.
Lomen

Lombard (Latin) long bearded.
Bard, Barr, Lombarda, Lombardi, Lombardo

Lon (Irish) fierce. (Spanish) a short form
of Alonso, Leonard, Lonnie.
Lonn

Lonan (Zuni) cloud.
Lonen, Lonin, Lonon, Lonyn

Lonato (Native American) flint stone.

London (English) fortress of the moon.
Geography: the capital of the United
Kingdom.
Londen, Londyn, Lunden, Lundon

Long (Chinese) dragon. (Vietnamese) hair.

Lonnie, Lonny (German, Spanish) familiar forms of Alonso.
Loni, Lonie, Lonnell, Lonney, Lonni, Lonniel, Lony

Lono (Hawaiian) Mythology: the god of learning and intellect.

Lonzo (German, Spanish) a short form of Alonso.
Lonso

Lootah (Lakota) red.
Loota

Lopaka (Hawaiian) a form of Robert.

Loran (American) a form of Lauren.

Loránd (Hungarian) a form of Roland.

Lóránt (Hungarian) a form of Lawrence.
Lorant

Lorcan (Irish) little; fierce.
Lorcen, Lorcin, Lorcon, Lorcyn

Lord (English) noble title.

Loren, Lorin (Latin) short forms of Lawrence.
Lorren, Lorrin, Loryn

Lorenza (Italian, Spanish) a form of Lorenzo.
Larinza

Lorenzo (Italian, Spanish) a form of Lawrence.
Laurenzo, Laurinzo, Laurynzo, Lewrenzo, Lorantzo, Lorenc, Lorence, Lorenco, Lorencz, Lorenczo, Lorens, Lorenso, Lorentz, Lorentzo, Lorenz, Loretto, Lorinc, Lörinc, Lorinzo, Loritz, Lorrenzo, Lorrynzo, Lorynzo, Lourenza, Lourenzo, Lowrenzo, Zo

Loretto (Italian) a form of Lawrence.
Loreto

Lorimer (Latin) harness maker.
Lorrimer, Lorrymer, Lorymer

Loring (German) son of the famous warrior.
Lorring, Lorryng, Loryng

Loris (Dutch) clown.
Lorys

Loritz (Latin, Danish) laurel.
Lauritz, Laurytz, Lorytz

Lorne (Latin) a short form of Lawrence.
Lorn, Lornie, Lorny

Lorry (English) a form of Laurie. (Latin) a form of Lorimer.
Lori, Lorie, Lorri, Lorrie, Lory

Lot (Hebrew) hidden, covered. Bible: Lot fled from Sodom, but his wife glanced back upon its destruction and was transformed into a pillar of salt.
Lott

Lothar (German) a form of Luther.
Lotair, Lotaire, Lotarrio, Lothair, Lothaire, Lothario, Lotharrio, Lottario

Lou (German) a short form of Louis.

Loudon (German) low valley.
Lewdan, Lewden, Lewdin, Lewdon, Lewdyn, Loudan, Louden, Loudin, Loudyn, Lowdan, Lowden, Lowdin, Lowdon, Lowdyn

Louie (German) a familiar form of Louis.

Louis (German) famous warrior. See also Aloisio, Aloysius, Clovis, Luigi.
Loudovicus, Louies, Louise, Lucho, Lude, Ludek, Ludirk, Ludis, Ludko, Lughaidh, Lutek

Louis Alexander (French) a combination of Louis + Alexander.

Louis Charles (French) a combination of Louis + Charles.

Louis David (French) a combination of Louis + David.

Louis Mathieu (French) a combination of Louis + Mathieu.

Louis Philipp (French) a combination of Louis + Philip.

Louis Xavier (French) a combination of Louis + Xavier.

Lourdes (French) from Lourdes, France. Religion: a place where the Virgin Mary was said to have appeared.
Lordes

Louvain (English) Lou's vanity.
Geography: a city in Belgium.
Louvayn, Louvin

Lovell (English) a form of Lowell.
Louvell, Lovel, Lovelle, Lovey

Lowell (French) young wolf. (English)
beloved.
Lowe, Lowel, Lowelle

Loyal (English) faithful, loyal.
Loial, Loy, Loyall, Loye, Lyall, Lyell

Lubomir (Polish) lover of peace.
Lubomyr

Luboslaw (Polish) lover of glory.
Lubs, Lubz

Luc (French) a form of Luke.
Luce

Luca (Italian) a form of Lucius.
Lucah, Lucca, Luka

Lucas, Lucus (German, Irish, Danish,
Dutch) forms of Lucius.
*Lucais, Lucassie, Lucaus, Luccas, Luccus,
Luckas, Lucys*

Lucian (Latin) a form of Lucius.
*Liuz, Lucan, Lucanus, Lucianus, Lucias,
Lucjan, Lucyan, Lukianos, Lukyan, Luzian*

Luciano (Italian) a form of Lucian.
Lucino

Lucien (French) a form of Lucius.
Lucyen, Luzien

Lucio (Italian) a form of Lucius.
Luzio

Lucius (Latin) light; bringer of light.
*Lucanus, Luce, Lucious, Lucis, Lucyas,
Lucyus, Lusio, Luzius*

Lucky (American) fortunate. (Latin) a
familiar form of Luke.
*Luckee, Lucki, Luckie, Luckson, Lucson,
Luki, Lukie, Luky*

Ludlow (English) prince's hill.

Ludovic, Ludovick (German) forms of
Ludwig.
Ludovico

Ludwig (German) a form of Louis.
Music: Ludwig van Beethoven was a
famous nineteenth-century German
composer.
Ludvig, Ludvik, Ludwik, Lutz

Lui (Hawaiian) a form of Louis.

Luigi (Italian) a form of Louis.
Lui, Luiggi, Luigino, Luigy

Luis, Luiz (Spanish) forms of Louis.
Luise

Luisalberto (Spanish) a combination of
Luis + Alberto.

Luisangel (Spanish) a combination of
Luis + Angel.

Luisantonio (Spanish) a combination of
Luis + Antonio.

Luisenrique (Spanish) a combination of
Luis + Enrique.

Luka (Italian) a form of Luke.

Lukas, Lukasz, Lukus (Greek, Czech,
Swedish) forms of Luke.
*Loukas, Lukais, Lukash, Lukasha, Lukass,
Lukaus, Lukkas, Lukys*

Luke (Latin) a form of Lucius. Bible:
companion of Saint Paul and author of
the third Gospel of the New Testament.
*Luchok, Luck, Luk, Lúkács, Luken, Lukes,
Lukyan, Lusio*

Lukela (Hawaiian) a form of Russell.

Luken (Basque) bringer of light.
Lucan, Lucane, Lucano, Luk

Luki (Basque) famous warrior.

Lukman (Arabic) prophet.
Luqman

Lulani (Hawaiian) highest point in heaven.
Lulanee, Lulaney, Lulanie, Lulany

Lumo (Ewe) born facedown.

Lundy (Scottish) grove by the island.
Lundee, Lundey, Lundi, Lundie

Lunn (Irish) warlike.
Lonn, Lunni, Lunnie, Lunny

Lunt (Swedish) grove.
Lont

Lusila (Hindi) leader.
Lusyla

Lusio (Zuni) a form of Lucius.
Lusyo

Lutalo (Luganda) warrior.

Lutfi (Arabic) kind, friendly.

Luther (German) famous warrior.
History: Martin Luther was one of the
central figures of the Reformation.
Lothar, Lother, Lothur, Lutero, Luthor

Lutherum (Gypsy) slumber.

Luyu (Moquelumnan) head shaker.

Lyall, Lyell (Scottish) loyal.
Lyal, Lyel

Lyle (French) island.
Lisle, Ly, Lysle

Lyman (English) meadow.
*Leaman, Leamen, Leeman, Leemen, Leiman,
Leimen, Leyman, Liman, Limen, Limin,
Limon, Limyn, Lymen, Lymin, Lymon,
Lymyn*

Lynch (Irish) mariner.
Linch

Lyndal (English) valley of lime trees. See
also Lindell.
Lyndale, Lyndall, Lyndel, Lyndell

Lynden (English) a form of Lyndon.

Lyndon (English) linden hill. History:
Lyndon B. Johnson was the thirty-sixth
U.S. president.
Lyden, Lydon, Lyndan, Lyndin, Lyndyn

Lynn (English) waterfall; brook. A short
form of Lyndon. (Burmese, English) a
form of Lin.
Lyn, Lynell, Lynette, Lynnard, Lynoll

Lyron (Hebrew) a form of Leron, Liron.

Lysander (Greek) liberator.
Lyzander, Sander

M

Maalik (Punjabi) a form of Málik.
Maalek, Maaliek

Mac (Scottish) son.
Macs, Mak

Macabee (Hebrew) hammer.
Maccabee, Mackabee, Makabee

Macadam (Scottish) son of Adam.
*MacAdam, Mackadam, Makadam,
McAdam*

Macalla (Australian) full moon.
Macala, Macalah, Macallah

Macallister (Irish) son of Alistair.
*Macalaster, MacAlistair, MacAlister,
Macalister, Mackalistair, Mackalister,
Makalistair, Makalister, McAlister,
McAllister*

Macario (Spanish) a form of Makarios.
Macarios, Maccario, Maccarios, Macaryo

Macarthur (Irish) son of Arthur.
*MacArthur, Mackarthur, Makarthur,
McArthur*

Macaulay (Scottish) son of righteousness.
*Macaulea, Macaulee, Macaulei, Macauleigh,
Macauley, Macauli, Macaulie, Macaully,
Macauly, Maccauley, Mackaulea, Mackaulee,
Mackaulei, Mackauleigh, Mackauley,
Mackauli, Mackaulie, Mackauly, Macualay,
McCaulea, McCaulee, McCaulei,
McCauleigh, McCauley, McCauli,
McCaulie, McCauly*

Macbride (Scottish) son of a follower of
Saint Brigid.
*Macbryde, Mackbride, Mackbryde, Makbride,
Makbryde, Mcbride, McBride, McBryde*

Maccoy (Irish) son of Hugh, Coy.
*MacCoi, MacCoy, Mackoi, Mackoy, Makoi,
Makoy*

Maccrea (Irish) son of grace.
*MacCrae, MacCrai, MacCray, MacCrea,
Mackrea, Macrae, Macray, Makcrea, Makray,
Makrea, Mccrea, McCrea*

Macdonald (Scottish) son of Donald.
MacDonald, MackDonald, Mackdonald,
MakDonald, Makdonald, McDonald,
Mcdonald, Mcdonna, McDonnell, Mcdonnell

Macdougal (Scottish) son of Dougal.
MacDougal, MacDougall, Mackdougal,
MakDougal, Makdougal, MakDougall,
Makdougall, McDougal, Mcdougal,
McDougall

Mace (French) club. (English) a short
form of Macy, Mason.
Macean, Macer, Macey, Macie

Maceo (Spanish) a form of Mace.

Macfarlane (English) son of Farlane.
Macfarlan, Mackfarlan, Mackfarlane,
Macpharlan, Macpharlane, Makfarlan,
Makfarlane, Makpharlan, Makpharlane,
Mcfarlan, Mcfarlane, Mcpharlan, Mcpharlane

Macgregor (Scottish) son of Gregor.
Macgreggor

Macharios (Greek) blessed.
Macarius, Macharyos, Makarius

Machas (Polish) a form of Michael.

Mack (Scottish) a short form of names
beginning with "Mac" and "Mc."
Macke, Mackey, Mackie, Macks, Macky,
Mak

Mackenzie (Irish) son of Kenzie.
Mackensy, Mackenze, Mackenzee,
Mackenzey, Mackenzi, MacKenzie,
Mackenzly, Mackienzie, Mackinsey,
Mackinzie, Mickenzie

Mackenzy (Irish) a form of Mackenzie.

Mackinley (Irish) a form of Mackinnley.

Mackinnley (Irish) son of the learned
ruler.
Mackinlea, Mackinlee, Mackinlei,
Mackinleigh, Mackinli, Mackinlie,
Mackinly, MacKinnley, Mackinnly,
Mackynlea, Mackynlee, Mackynlei,
Mackynleigh, Mackynley, Mackynli,
Mackynlie, Mackynly, Makinlea, Makinlee,
Makinlei, Makinleigh, Makinley, Makinli,
Makinlie, Makinly, Makynlea, Makynlee,
Makynlei, Makynleigh, Makynley, Makynli,
Makynlie, Makynly

Macklain (Irish) a form of Maclean.
Macklaine, Macklane

Macklin (Scottish) a form of Mack.

Maclean (Irish) son of Leander.
Machlin, Macklain, MacKlean, Macklean,
MacLain, MacLean, Maclin, Maclyn,
Maklean, Makleen, McClean, McLaine,
McLean

Macmahon (Irish) son of Mahon.
Mackmahon, MacMahon, Makmahon,
McMahon

Macmurray (Irish) son of Murray.
Mackmuray, Mackmurray, Macmuray,
Macmurry, Makmuray, Makmurray,
McMurray, Mcmurry

Macnair (Scottish) son of the heir.
Macknair, Macknayr, Maknair, Maknayr,
McMayr, McNair

Maco (Hungarian) a form of Emmanuel.
Macko, Mako

Macon (German, English) maker.
Macan, Macen, Macin, Macun, Macyn

Macy (French) Matthew's estate.
Macey, Maci, Macie

Maddock (Welsh) generous.
Maddoc, Maddoch, Maddok, Madoc,
Madoch, Madock, Madog

Maddox (Welsh, English) benefactor's son.
Maddux, Madox

Madhar (Hindi) full of intoxication;
relating to spring.

Madison (English) son of Maude; good
son.
Maddie, Maddison, Maddy, Maddyson,
Madisen, Madisson, Madisyn, Madsen,
Madyson, Son, Sonny

Madon (Irish) charitable.
Madan, Maddan, Madden, Maddin,
Maddon, Maddyn, Maden, Madin, Madyn

Madongo (Luganda) uncircumcised.

Madu (Ibo) people.

Magar (Armenian) groom's attendant.
Magarious

Magee (Irish) son of Hugh.
MacGee, MacGhee, McGee

Magen (Hebrew) protector.

Magnar (Norwegian) strong; warrior.
Magne

Magnus (Latin) great.
Maghnus, Magnes, Magnuss, Manius

Magomu (Luganda) younger of twins.

Maguire (Irish) son of the beige one.
MacGuire, Macguyre, McGuire, McGwire

Mahammed (Arabic) a form of Muhammad.
Mahamad, Mahamed, Mahammad

Mahdi (Arabic) guided to the right path.
Mahde, Mahdee, Mahdy

Maher (Arabic, Hebrew) a form of Mahir.

Mahesa (Hindi) great lord. Religion: another name for the Hindu god Shiva.

Mahi'ai (Hawaiian) a form of George.

Mahir (Arabic, Hebrew) excellent; industrious.
Mair

Mahkah (Lakota) earth.
Maka, Makah

Mahmoud, Mahmúd (Arabic) forms of Muhammad.
*Mahamoud, Mahmed, Mahmmoud,
Mahmood, Mahmuod, Mahmut*

Mahomet (Arabic) a form of Muhammad.

Mahon (Irish) bear.

Mahpee (Lakota) sky.

Maidoc (Welsh) fortunate.
*Maedoc, Maedock, Maedok, Maidoc,
Maidock, Maidok, Maydoc, Maydock,
Maydok*

Maimun (Arabic) lucky.
Maimon, Maymon

Mairtin (Irish) a form of Martin.

Maison (French) house. A form of Mason.
Maisan, Maisen, Maisin, Maisun, Maisyn

Maitias (Irish) a form of Mathias.
Maithias

Maitiú (Irish) a form of Matthew.

Maitland (English) meadowland.
Maitlan, Maytlan, Maytland

Majed (Arabic) a form of Majid.

Majid (Arabic) great, glorious.
Majd, Majde, Majdi, Majdy, Majeed, Majyd

Major (Latin) greater; military rank.
Majar, Maje, Majer

Makaio (Hawaiian) a form of Matthew.
Makayo

Makalani (Mwera) writer.
*Makalanee, Makalaney, Makalanie,
Makalany*

Makani (Hawaiian) wind.
Makanie, Makany

Makarios (Greek) happy; blessed.
Makari, Makarie, Makaryos

Makenzie (Irish) a form of Mackenzie.
*Makensie, Makenzee, Makenzey, Makenzi,
Makenzy*

Makin (Arabic) strong.
Makeen, Makyn

Makis (Greek) a form of Michael.
Makys

Makoto (Japanese) sincere.

Maks (Hungarian) a form of Max.
Makszi

Maksim (Russian) a form of Maximilian.

Maksym (Polish) a form of Maximilian.
Makimus, Maksymilian

Makyah (Hopi) eagle hunter.
Makia, Makiah, Makyah

Mal (Irish) a short form of names beginning with "Mal."

Malachi (Hebrew) angel of God. Bible: the last canonical Hebrew prophet.

Malachi *(cont.)*
Maeleachlainn, Malachai, Malachia, Malachie, Malchija

Malachy (Irish) a form of Malachi.
Malechy

Malajitm (Sanskrit) garland of victory.

Malakai (Hebrew) a form of Malachi.
Malake, Malaki

Malcolm (Scottish) follower of Saint Columba who Christianized North Scotland. (Arabic) dove.
Malcalm, Malcohm, Malcolum, Malkolm

Malcom (Scottish) a form of Malcolm.
Malcome, Malcum, Malkom, Malkum

Malden (English) meeting place in a pasture.
Mal, Maldan, Maldin, Maldon, Maldun, Maldyn

Maleek, Maliek, Malique (Arabic) forms of Málik.

Malek, Malik (Arabic) forms of Málik.
Maleak, Maleik, Maleka, Maleke, Mallek

Maleko (Hawaiian) a form of Mark.

Málik (Punjabi) lord, master. (Arabic) a form of Malachi.
Mailik, Malak, Malic, Malick, Malicke, Maliik, Malike, Malikh, Maliq, Mallik, Malyc, Malyck, Malyk, Malyq

Malin (English) strong, little warrior.
Malen, Mallen, Mallin, Mallon, Mallyn, Malon, Malyn

Mallory (German) army counselor. (French) wild duck.
Lory, Mallery, Mallorey, Mallori, Mallorie, Malorey, Malori, Malorie, Malory

Maloney (Irish) church going.
Malone, Malonee, Maloni, Malonie, Malony

Malvern (Welsh) bare hill.
Malverne, Malvirn, Malvirne, Malvyrn, Malvyrne

Malvin (Irish, English) a form of Melvin.
Malvan, Malven, Malvinn, Malvon, Malvyn, Malvynn

Mamo (Hawaiian) yellow flower; yellow bird.

Man-Shik (Korean) deeply rooted.

Man-Young (Korean) ten thousand years of prosperity.

Manchu (Chinese) pure.

Manco (Peruvian) supreme leader. History: a sixteenth-century Incan king.

Mandala (Yao) flowers.
Manda, Mandela, Mandelah

Mandeep (Punjabi) mind full of light.
Mandieep

Mandek (Polish) a form of Herman.
Mandie

Mandel (German) almond.
Mandell

Mander (Gypsy) from me.
Mandar, Mandir, Mandor, Mandyr

Manford (English) small ford.
Manforde, Menford, Menforde

Manfred (English) man of peace. See also Fred.
Manfredo, Manfret, Manfrid, Manfried, Manfryd, Maniferd, Manifrid, Manifryd, Mannfred, Mannfryd, Manyfred, Manyfrid, Manyfryd

Manger (French) stable.
Mangar, Mangor

Mango (Spanish) a familiar form of Emmanuel, Manuel.

Manheim (German) servant's home.

Manipi (Native American) living marvel.

Manius (Scottish) a form of Magnus.
Manus, Manyus

Manjot (Indian) light of the mind.

Manley (English) hero's meadow.
Manlea, Manlee, Manleigh, Manli, Manlie, Manly

Mann (German) man.
Man, Manin

Manning (English) son of the hero.
Maning

Mannix (Irish) monk.
Mainchin, Mannox, Mannyx, Manox,
Manyx

Manny (German, Spanish) a familiar form
of Manuel.
Mani, Manni, Mannie, Many

Mano (Hawaiian) shark. (Spanish) a short
form of Manuel.
Manno, Manolo

Manoj (Sanskrit) cupid.

Manpreet (Punjabi) mind full of love.

Manrico (American) a combination of
Mann + Enrico.
Manricko, Manriko, Manrycko, Manryco,
Manryko

Mansa (Swahili) king. History: a
fourteenth-century king of Mali.
Mansah

Mansel (English) manse; house occupied
by a clergyman.
Mansell

Mansfield (English) field by the river;
hero's field.
Mansfyld

Mansür (Arabic) divinely aided.
Mansoor, Mansour

Manton (English) man's town; hero's town.
Mannton, Mantan, Manten, Mantin,
Mantyn

Manu (Hindi) lawmaker. History: the
reputed writer of the Hindi compendium
of sacred laws and customs. (Hawaiian)
bird. (Ghanaian) second-born son.

Manuel (Hebrew) a short form of
Emmanuel.
Mannuel, Mano, Manolón, Manual,
Manuale, Manue, Manuell, Manuelli,
Manuelo, Manuil, Manyuil, Minel

Manville (French) worker's village.
(English) hero's village.
Mandeville, Manvel, Manvil, Manvill,
Manvyl, Manvyle, Manvyll, Manvylle

Manzo (Japanese) third son.

Maona (Winnebago) creator, earth maker.

Mapira (Yao) millet.
Mapirah

Marat (Indian) life-death-birth-giving
cycle.

Marc (French) a form of Mark. (Latin) a
short form of Marcus.

Marc Alexander (French) a combination
of Marc + Alexander.

Marc Andre, Marc-Andre (French)
combinations of Marc + Andre.

Marc Antoine, Marc-Antoine (French)
combinations of Marc + Antoine.

Marc Etienne (French) a combination of
Marc + Etienne.

Marc Olivier, Marc-Olivier (French)
combinations of Marc + Olivier.

Marcanthony (American) a combination
of Marc + Anthony.

Marcel, Marcell (French) forms of
Marcellus.
Marcele, Marcelle, Marsale, Marsel, Marzel,
Marzell

Marcelino (Italian) a form of Marcellus.
Marceleno, Marcelin, Marcellin, Marcellino

Marcellis, Marcellous (Latin) forms of
Marcellus.
Marcelis

Marcello, Marcelo (Italian) forms of
Marcellus.
Marchello, Marsello, Marselo

Marcellus (Latin) a familiar form of
Marcus.
Marceau, Marceles, Marcelias, Marcelius,
Marcellas, Marcelleous, Marcelluas, Marcelus,
Marcely, Marciano, Marcilka, Marcsseau,
Marzellos, Marzellous, Marzellus

March (English) dweller by a boundary.

Marciano (Italian) a form of Martin.
Marci, Marcio

Marcilka (Hungarian) a form of Marcellus.
Marci, Marcilki

Marcin (Polish) a form of Martin.

Marco (Italian) a form of Marcus. History: Marco Polo was a thirteenth-century Venetian traveler who explored Asia.
Marcko, Marko

Marcoantonio (Italian) a combination of Marco + Antonio.

Marcos (Spanish) a form of Marcus.
Marckos, Marcous, Markose

Marcus (Latin) martial, warlike.
Marcas, Marcio, Marckus, Marcuss, Marcuus, Marcux, Markov

Marden (English) valley with a pool.
Mardan, Madrin, Mardon, Mardun, Mardyn

Marek (Slavic) a form of Marcus.

Maren (Basque) sea.
Maran, Maron

Mareo (Japanese) uncommon.

Marian (Polish) a form of Mark.
Maryan

Mariano (Italian) a form of Mark. A form of Marion.
Maryano

Marid (Arabic) rebellious.
Maryd

Marin (French) sailor.
Marine, Mariner, Marriner, Marryner, Maryn, Maryner

Marino (Italian) a form of Marin.
Marinos, Marinus, Mariono, Marynos, Marynus

Mario (Italian) a form of Marino.
Mareo, Marios, Marrio, Maryon

Marion (French) bitter; sea of bitterness.
Mareon, Maryon

Marius (Latin) a form of Marin.
Marious

Mark (Latin) a form of Marcus. Bible: author of the second Gospel in the New Testament. See also Maleko.
Marck, Marian, Marke, Markee, Markey, Markk, Markusha, Marx

Mark Anthony, Markanthony (Italian) combinations of Mark + Anthony.

Marke (Polish) a form of Mark.

Markel, Markell (Latin) forms of Mark.
Markelle, Markelo

Markes (Portuguese) a form of Marques.
Markess, Markest

Markese (French) a form of Marquis.
Markease, Markeece, Markees, Markeese, Markei, Markeice, Markeis, Markeise, Markes, Markice

Markez (French) a form of Marquis.
Markeze

Markham (English) homestead on the boundary.

Markis (French) a form of Marquis.
Markies, Markiese, Markise, Markiss, Markist

Marko (Latin) a form of Marco, Mark.
Markco

Markos (Spanish) a form of Marcos. (Latin) a form of Mark, Markus.

Markus (Latin) a form of Marcus.
Markas, Markcus, Markcuss, Markous, Márkus, Markys

Marland (English) lake land.
Mahland, Mahlend, Mahlind, Marlend, Marlind, Marlond, Marlynd

Marley (English) lake meadow.
Marlea, Marlee, Marleigh, Marli, Marlie, Marly, Marrley

Marlin (English) deep-sea fish.
Marlen, Marlion, Marlyn

Marlo (English) a form of Marlow.

Marlon (French) a form of Merlin.
Marlan

Marlow (English) hill by the lake.
Mar, Marlowe

Marmion (French) small.
Marmien, Marmyon

Marnin (Hebrew) singer; bringer of joy.
Marnyn

Maro (Japanese) myself.
Marow

Marquan (American) a combination of Mark + Quan.
Marquane, Marquante

Marque (American) a form of Mark.

Marquel, Marquell (American) forms of Marcellus.
Marqueal, Marquelis, Marquelle, Marquellis, Marquiel, Marquil, Marquiles, Marquill, Marquille, Marquillus, Marqwel, Marqwell

Marques (Portuguese) nobleman.
Markes, Markqes, Markques, Markqueus, Marquees, Marquess, Marquest

Marquese (Portuguese) a form of Marques.
Marqese, Markquese, Marqesse, Marquesse

Marquez (Portuguese) a form of Marques.
Marqez, Marqeze, Marqueze, Marquiez

Marquice (American) a form of Marquis.
Marquaice, Marquece

Marquies (American) a form of Marquis.

Marquis, Marquise (French) nobleman.
Marcquis, Marcuis, Markquis, Markquise, Markuis, Marqise, Marquee, Marqui, Marquie, Marquiss, Marquist, Marquiz, Marquize

Marquon (American) a combination of Mark + Quon.
Marquin, Marquinn, Marqwan, Marqwon, Marqwyn

Marqus (American) a form of Markus. (Portuguese) a form of Marques.

Marr (Spanish) divine. (Arabic) forbidden.

Mars (Latin) bold warrior. Mythology: the Roman god of war.

Marsalis (Italian) a form of Marcellus.
Marsalius, Marsallis, Marsellis, Marsellius, Marsellus

Marsden (English) marsh valley.
Marsdan, Marsdin, Marsdon, Marsdyn

Marsh (English) swamp land. (French) a short form of Marshall.

Marshal (French) a form of Marshall.
Marschal, Marshel

Marshall (French) caretaker of the horses; military title.
Marshell

Marshaun, Marshon (American) forms of Marshawn.

Marshawn (American) a combination of Mark + Shawn.
Marshaine, Marshauwn, Marshean, Marshun

Marston (English) town by the marsh.
Marstan, Marsten, Marstin, Marstyn

Martel (English) a form of Martell.
Martal, Martele

Martell (English) hammerer.
Martall, Martellis

Marten (Dutch) a form of Martin.
Maarten, Martein, Merten

Martese (Spanish) a form of Martez.

Martez (Spanish) a form of Martin.
Martaz, Martaze, Martes, Marteze, Marties, Martiese, Martiez, Martis, Martise, Martize

Marti (Spanish) a form of Martin.
Marte, Martee, Martie

Martial (French) a form of Mark.

Martice (Spanish) a form of Martez.
Martiece

Martin (Latin, French) a form of Martinus. History: Martin Luther King, Jr. led the Civil Rights movement and won the Nobel Peace Prize. See also Tynek.
Maartan, Maartin, Maarton, Maartyn, Mart, Martain, Martainn, Martan, Martijn, Martine, Martinien, Marto, Marton, Márton, Marts, Mattin, Mertin, Mertyn

Martinez (Spanish) a form of Martin.
Martines

Martinho (Portuguese) a form of Martin.

Martino (Italian) a form of Martin.
Martiniano

Martins (Latvian) a form of Martin.

Martinus (Latin) martial, warlike.
Martinas, Martinos, Martinous, Martynas,
Martynis, Martynos, Martynus, Martynys

Marty (Latin) a familiar form of Martin.
Martey

Martyn (Latin, French) a form of Martin.
Martyne

Marut (Hindi) Religion: the Hindu god
of the wind.

Marv (English) a short form of Marvin.
Marve, Marvi, Marvis

Marvel (Latin) marvel.

Marvell (Latin) a form of Marvel.

Marvin (English) lover of the sea.
Marvein, Marven, Marvion, Marvn,
Marvon, Marvyn, Marvyne, Murvan,
Murven, Murvin, Murvine, Murvon,
Murvyn, Murvyne, Murwin, Murwyn

Marwan (Arabic) history personage.
Marwen, Marwin, Marwon, Marwyn,
Marwynn, Marwynne

Marwood (English) forest pond.

Masaccio (Italian) twin.
Masaki

Masahiro (Japanese) broad-minded.
Masahyro

Masamba (Yao) leaves.
Masambah

Masao (Japanese) righteous.

Masato (Japanese) just.

Mashama (Shona) surprising.
Mashamah

Maska (Native American) powerful.
(Russian) mask.
Maskah

Maslin (French) little Thomas.
Maslan, Maslen, Masling, Maslon, Maslyn

Mason (French) stone worker.
Masan, Masen, Masin, Masson, Masun,
Masyn, Sonny

Masou (Native American) fire god.

Massey (English) twin.
Massi, Massie, Masy

Massimo (Italian) greatest.
Massymo

Masud (Arabic, Swahili) fortunate.
Masood, Masoud, Mhasood

Matai (Basque, Bulgarian) a form of
Matthew.
Máté, Matei

Matalino (Filipino) bright.

Mateo, Matteo (Spanish) forms of
Matthew.

Mateusz (Polish) a form of Matthew.
Matejs, Mateus

Mathe (German) a short form of
Matthew.

Mather (English) powerful army.

Matheu (German) a form of Matthew.
Matheau, Matheus, Mathu

Mathew (Hebrew) a form of Matthew.

Mathias, Matthias (German, Swedish)
forms of Matthew.
Mathi, Mathia, Matthia, Matthieus, Matus

Mathieu, Matthieu (French) forms of
Matthew.
Mathie, Mathieux, Mathiew, Matthiew,
Mattieu, Mattieux

Mathis (German, Swedish) a form of
Mathias.

Matias, Matías, Mattias (Spanish) forms
of Mathias.
Mattia

Mato (Native American) brave.

Matope (Rhodesian) our last child.
Matop

Matoskah (Lakota) white bear.

Mats (Swedish) a familiar form of Matthew.
Matts, Matz

Matson (Hebrew) son of Matt.
Matsen, Mattson

Matt (Hebrew) a short form of Matthew.
Mat

Matteen (Afghan) disciplined; polite.
Mateen, Matin, Matyn

Matteus (Scandinavian) a form of Matthew.
Matthaeus, Matthaios, Matthews

Mattew (Hebrew) a form of Matthew.

Mattheus (Scandinavian) a form of Matthew.

Matthew (Hebrew) gift of God. Bible: author of the first Gospel of the New Testament.
Maitiú, Makaio, Mata, Matai, Matek, Matfei, Mathe, Maztheson, Mathian, Mathieson, Matro, Matthaus, Matthäus, Mattmias

Mattison (Hebrew) a form of Matson.
Matison

Matty (Hebrew) a familiar form of Matthew.
Mattie

Matus (Czech) a form of Mathias.

Matvey (Russian) a form of Matthew.
Matviy, Matviyko, Matyash, Motka, Motya

Matyas (Polish) a form of Matthew.
Mátyás

Mauli (Hawaiian) a form of Maurice.

Maurice (Latin) dark skinned; moor; marshland. See also Seymour.
Maur, Maurance, Maureo, Mauri, Maurids, Mauriece, Maurikas, Maurin, Maurino, Maurise, Mauritius, Maurius, Maurrel, Maurtel, Mauryc, Mauryce, Maurycy, Maurys, Mauryse, Meurig, Meurisse, Morice, Moritz, Morrice

Mauricio (Spanish) a form of Maurice.
Mauriccio, Mauriceo, Maurico, Maurisio

Mauritz (German) a form of Maurice.
Maurits

Maurizio (Italian) a form of Maurice.

Mauro (Latin) a short form of Maurice.
Maur, Maurio

Maury (Latin) a familiar form of Maurice.
Maurey, Maurie

Maverick (American) independent.
Maveric, Maverik, Maveryc, Maveryck, Maveryk, Maveryke, Mavric, Mavrick, Mavrik, Mavryc, Mavryck, Mavryk

Mawuli (Ewe) there is a God.

Max, Maxx (Latin) short forms of Maximilian, Maxwell.
Maks, Maxe

Maxfield (English) Mack's field.
Macfield, Mackfield, Mackfyld, Makfield, Makfyld

Maxi (Czech, Hungarian, Spanish) a familiar form of Maximilian, Maximo.
Makszi, Maxie, Maxis

Maxim (Russian) a form of Maxime.
Maixim, Maxem

Maxime (French) most excellent.

Maximilian (Latin) greatest.
Maksimilian, Maksimillian, Maksymilian, Maxamilian, Maxamillion, Maxemilian, Maxemilion, Maximalian, Maximili, Maximilia, Maximilianos, Maximilianus, Maximillion, Maxmilian, Maxmillion, Maxon, Maxximillion, Maxymilian

Maximiliano (Italian) a form of Maximilian.
Massimiliano, Maximiano

Maximilien, Maximillian (Latin) forms of Maximilian.
Maximillan, Maximillano, Maximillien, Maxmillian, Maxximillian, Maxymillian

Maximino (Italian) a form of Maximilian.

Maximo, Máximo (Spanish) forms of Maximilian.
Maxi

Maximos (Greek) a form of Maximilian.
Maxymos, Maxymus

Maxwell (English) great spring.
Maxwel, Maxwill, Maxxwell

Maxy (English) a familiar form of Max, Maxwell.
Maxey

Maxyme (French) a form of Maxime.

Mayer (Latin) a form of Magnus, Major. (Hebrew) a form of Meir.
Mahyar, Maier, Mayar, Mayeer, Mayir, Mayor, Mayur

Mayes (English) field.
Maies, Mays

Mayhew (English) a form of Matthew. (Latin) a form of Maximilian.
Maehew, Maihew

Maynard (English) powerful; brave. See also Meinhard.
Mainard, May, Mayne, Maynhard, Ménard

Maynor (English) a form of Maynard.

Mayo (Irish) yew-tree plain. (English) a form of Mayes. Geography: a county in Ireland.
Maio

Mayon (Indian) person of black complexion. Religion: another name for the Indian god Mal.
Maion

Mayonga (Luganda) lake sailor.

Mayson (French) a form of Mason.

Mazi (Ibo) sir.
Mazzi

Mazin (Arabic) proper.
Mazan, Mazen, Mazinn, Mazon, Mazyn, Mazzin

Mbita (Swahili) born on a cold night.

Mbwana (Swahili) master.

Mccoy (Irish) a form of Maccoy.
McCoi, McCoy

McGeorge (Scottish) son of George.
MacGeorge

Mckade (Scottish) son of Kade.
Mccade

Mckay (Scottish) son of Kay.
Macai, Macay, Mackai, Mackay, Mackaye, MacKay, Makkai, Makkay, Makkaye, Mckae, Mckai, McKay

Mckenna (American) a form of Mackenzie.

Mckenzie, McKenzie (Irish) forms of Mackenzie.
Mccenzie, Mckennzie, Mckensey, Mckensie, Mckenson, Mckensson, Mckenzee, Mckenzi, Mckenzy, Mckinzie

Mckinley (Irish) a form of Mackinnley.
Mckinely, Mckinnely, Mckinnlee, Mckinnley, McKinnley

Mead (English) meadow.
Meade, Meed

Medgar (German) a form of Edgar.
Medger

Medric (English) flourishing meadow.
Medrick, Medrik, Medryc, Medryck, Medryk

Medwin (German) faithful friend.
Medwyn

Megan (Greek) pearl; great. (Irish) a form of Margaret (see Girls' Names).

Mehetabel (Hebrew) who God benefits.

Mehmet (Arabic) a form of Mahomet, Mohamet.
Mehemet

Mehrdad (Persian) gift of the sun.

Mehtar (Sanskrit) prince.
Mehta

Meinhard (German) strong, firm. See also Maynard.
Meinhardt, Meinke, Meino, Mendar, Meynhard

Meinrad (German) strong counsel.
Meynrad

Meir (Hebrew) one who brightens, shines; enlightener. History: Golda Meir was the prime minister of Israel.
Mayer, Meyer, Meyr, Muki, Myer

Meka (Hawaiian) eyes.
Mekah

Mel (English, Irish) a familiar form of Melvin.
Mell

Melbourne (English) mill stream.
Melborn, Melborne, Melburn, Melburne, Melby

Melchior (Hebrew) king.
Meilseoir, Melker, Melkior

Melchor (Hebrew) a form of Melchior.

Meldon (English) mill hill.
Meldan, Melden, Meldin, Meldyn

Meldrick (English) strong mill.
Meldric, Meldrik, Meldryc, Meldryck, Meldryk

Melino (Tongan) peace.
Melin, Melinos, Melyn, Melyno, Melynos

Melrone (Irish) servant of Saint Ruadhan.

Melvern (Native American) great chief.
Melverne, Melvirn, Melvirne, Melvyrn, Melvyrne

Melville (French) mill town. Literature: Herman Melville was a well-known nineteenth-century American writer.
Malvil, Malvill, Malville, Melvil, Melvill, Milville

Melvin (Irish) armored chief. (English) mill friend; council friend. See also Vinny.
Melvan, Melven, Melvine, Melvino, Melvon, Melvyn, Melwin, Melwyn, Melwynn

Menachem (Hebrew) comforter.
Menahem, Nachman

Menassah (Hebrew) cause to forget.
Manasseh, Menashe, Menashi, Menashia, Menashiah, Menashya

Mendel (English) repairman.
Mendal, Mendeley, Mendell, Mendie, Mendil, Mendy, Mendyl

Mengesha (Ethiopian) kingdom.

Menico (Spanish) a short form of Domenico.

Mensah (Ewe) third son.
Mensa

Menz (German) a short form of Clement.

Mercer (English) storekeeper.
Merce

Mered (Hebrew) revolter.

Meredith (Welsh) guardian from the sea.
Meredeth, Meredyth, Merideth, Meridith, Merry, Merydeth, Merydith, Merydyth

Merion (Welsh) from Merion, Wales.
Merrion

Merivale (English) pleasant valley.
Merival, Meryval, Meryvale

Merle (French) a short form of Merlin, Merrill.
Merl, Meryl, Murl, Murle

Merlin (English) falcon. Literature: the magician who served as counselor in King Arthur's court.
Merlen, Merlinn, Merlyn, Merlynn

Merrick (English) ruler of the sea.
Merek, Meric, Merick, Merik, Merric, Merrik, Merryc, Merryck, Merryk, Meryk, Meyrick, Myrucj

Merrill (Irish) bright sea. (French) famous.
Meril, Merill, Merrel, Merrell, Merril, Meryl, Meryll

Merritt (Latin, Irish) valuable; deserving.
Merit, Meritt, Merrett, Merrit, Merryt

Merton (English) sea town.
Mertan, Merten, Mertin, Mertyn, Murton

Merv (Irish) a short form of Mervin.
Merve

Merville (French) sea village.

Mervin (Irish) a form of Marvin.
Merv, Mervan, Merven, Mervine, Mervon, Mervyn, Mervyne, Mervynn, Merwin, Merwinn, Merwyn, Murvin, Murvyn, Myrvyn, Myrvynn, Myrwyn

Meshach (Hebrew) artist. Bible: one of Daniel's three friends who emerged unharmed from the fiery furnace of Babylon.

Mesut (Turkish) happy.

Metikla (Moquelumnan) reaching a hand underwater to catch a fish.

Mette (Greek, Danish) pearl.
Almeta, Mete

Meurig (Welsh) a form of Maurice.

Meyer (German) farmer. (Hebrew) a form of Meir.
Mayeer, Mayer, Meier, Myer

Mhina (Swahili) delightful.
Mhinah

Micael (Hebrew) a form of Michael.

Micah (Hebrew) a form of Michael. Bible: a Hebrew prophet.
Mic, Mica, Myca, Mycah

Micaiah (Hebrew) a form of Micah.
Michiah

Micha (Hebrew) a short form of Michael.
Micha, Michah

Michael (Hebrew) who is like God? See also Micah, Miguel, Mika, Miles.
Machael, Machas, Maikal, Makael, Makal, Makel, Makell, Makis, Meikil, Meikyl, Mekil, Mekyl, Mhichael, Micahel, Mical, Michaele, Michaell, Michalel, Michau, Michelet, Michiel, Micho, Michoel, Miekil, Miekyl, Mihail, Mihalje, Mihkel, Mikáele

Michaelangel (American) a form of Michael + Angel.

Michail (Russian) a form of Michael.
Mihas, Mikale

Michal (Polish) a form of Michael.
Michak, Michalek, Michall

Michale (Polish) a form of Michal.

Micheal (Irish) a form of Michael.

Michel (French) a form of Michael.
Michaud, Miche, Michee, Micheil, Michell, Michelle, Michon

Michelangelo (Italian) a combination of Michael + Angelo. Art: Michelangelo Buonarroti was one of the greatest Renaissance painters.
Michelange

Michele (Italian) a form of Michael.

Michio (Japanese) man with the strength of three thousand.

Mick (English) a short form of Michael, Mickey.
Myc, Myck

Mickael, Mickel (English) forms of Michael.
Mickaele, Mickal, Mickale, Mickeal, Mickell, Mickelle, Mickle, Myckael, Myckaele, Myckaell

Mickenzie (Irish) a form of Mackenzie.
Mickenze, Mickenzy, Mikenzie

Mickey (Irish) a familiar form of Michael.
Mickee, Micki, Mickie, Micky, Miki, Mikie, Miky, Mycke, Myckee, Myckey, Mycki, Myckie, Mycky, Mykee, Mykey, Myki, Mykie, Myky

Micu (Hungarian) a form of Nick.

Migel (Portuguese, Spanish) a form of Miguel.

Miguel (Portuguese, Spanish) a form of Michael.
Migeal, Migeel, Miguelly, Miguil, Myguel, Myguele, Myguell, Myguelle

Miguelangel (Spanish) a combination of Miguel + Angel.
Miguelangelo

Mihail (Greek, Bulgarian, Romanian) a form of Mikhail.
Mahail, Maichail, Mekhail, Micheil, Mihailo, Mihal, Mihalis

Mika (Ponca) raccoon. (Hebrew) a form of Micah. (Russian) a familiar form of Michael.
Miika, Myka, Mykah

Mikael (Swedish) a form of Michael.
Mikaeel, Mikaele, Mykael, Mykaele, Mykaell

Mikáele (Hawaiian) a form of Michael.
Mikele

Mikah (Hebrew) a form of Micah.
(Hebrew, Russian, Ponca) a form of
Mika.

Mikail (Greek, Russian) a form of Mikhail.

Mikal (Hebrew) a form of Michael.
Meikal, Mekal, Miekal, Mikahl, Mikale

Mikasi (Omaha) coyote.
Mykasi

Mike (Hebrew) a short form of Michael.
Myk, Myke

Mikeal (Irish) a form of Michael.

Mikel, Mikell (Basque) forms of Michael.
*Meikel, Mekel, Mekell, Miekel, Mikele,
Mikelle*

Mikelis (Latvian) a form of Michael.
Mikus, Milkins

Mikey (Hebrew) a short form of Michael.

Mikhael (Greek, Russian) a form of
Mikhail.

Mikhail (Greek, Russian) a form of
Michael.
*Mekhail, Mihály, Mikhale, Mikhalis,
Mikhalka, Mikhall, Mikhel, Mikhial,
Mikhos*

Miki (Japanese) tree.
Mikio

Mikkel (Norwegian) a form of Michael.
Mikkael, Mikle

Mikko (Finnish) a form of Michael.
*Mikk, Mikka, Mikkohl, Mikkol, Miko,
Mikol*

Mikolaj (Polish) a form of Nicholas.
Mikolai

Mikolas (Greek) a form of Nicholas.
Miklós

Miksa (Hungarian) a form of Max.
Miks, Myksa

Milan (Italian) northerner. Geography: a
city in northern Italy.
Milaan, Milano, Milen, Millan, Millen

Milap (Native American) giving.

Milborough (English) middle borough.
Milbrough, Mylborough, Mylbrough

Milburn (English) stream by the mill.
A form of Melbourne.
*Milborn, Milborne, Milbourn, Milbourne,
Milburne, Millborn, Millborne, Millbourn,
Millbourne, Millburn, Millburne*

Milek (Polish) a familiar form of Nicholas.
Mylek

Miles (Greek) millstone. (Latin) soldier.
(German) merciful. (English) a short
form of Michael.
Milas, Milles, Milson

Milford (English) mill by the ford.
Millford, Mylford, Myllford

Mililani (Hawaiian) heavenly caress.
Mililanee, Mililaney, Mililanie, Mililany

Milko (German) a familiar form of Emil.
(Czech) a form of Michael.
Milkins

Millard (Latin) caretaker of the mill.
Mill, Millward, Milward, Mylard, Myllard

Miller (English) miller; grain grinder.
*Mellar, Meller, Mellor, Milar, Miler, Millar,
Millen, Milor, Mylar, Myler, Myllar, Myller,
Mylor*

Mills (English) mills.
Mils, Mylls, Myls

Milo (German) a form of Miles. A familiar
form of Emil.
Millo, Mylo

Milos (Greek, Slavic) pleasant.
Mylos

Miloslav (Czech) lover of glory.
Myloslav

Milt (English) a short form of Milton.

Milton (English) mill town.
Millton, Miltie, Milty, Myllton, Mylton

Mimis (Greek) a familiar form of
Demetrius.

Min (Burmese) king.
Mina, Myn

Mincho (Spanish) a form of Benjamin.

Minel (Spanish) a form of Manuel.

Miner (English) miner.
Myner

Mingan (Native American) gray wolf.
Myngan

Mingo (Spanish) a short form of Domingo.

Minh (Vietnamese) bright.
Minhao, Minhduc, Minhkhan, Minhtong, Minhy, Mynh

Minkah (Akan) just, fair.
Minka, Mynka, Mynkah

Minor (Latin) junior; younger.

Minoru (Japanese) fruitful.

Mique (Spanish) a form of Mickey.

Miquel (Spanish) a form of Mique.
Mequel, Mequelin

Miracle (Latin) miracle.

Miron (Polish) peace.

Miroslav (Czech) peace; glory.
Mirek, Miroslaw, Miroslawy, Myroslav

Mirwais (Afghan) noble ruler.

Misael, Missael (Hebrew) forms of Michael.
Mischael, Mishael

Misha (Russian) a short form of Michail.
Misa, Mischa, Mishael, Mishal, Mishe, Mishenka, Mishka

Miska (Hungarian) a form of Michael.
Misi, Misik, Misko, Miso

Mister (English) mister.
Mistar, Mistur, Mystar, Myster, Mystur

Misu (Moquelumnan) rippling water.
Mysu

Mitch (English) a short form of Mitchell.
Mytch

Mitchel (English) a form of Mitchell.
Mitchael, Mitchal, Mitcheal, Mitchele, Mitchil, Mytchel

Mitchell (English) a form of Michael.
Mitchall, Mitchelle, Mitchem, Mytchell

Mitsos (Greek) a familiar form of Demetrius.

Modesto (Latin) modest.
Modesti, Modestie, Modesty

Moe (English) a short form of Moses.
Mo

Mogens (Dutch) powerful.
Mogen

Mohamad, Mohamed, Mohammad, Mohammed (Arabic) forms of Muhammad.
Mohamd, Mohameed, Mohamid, Mohammadi, Mohammd, Mohammid, Mohanad, Mohaned, Mohmad

Mohamet (Arabic) a form of Muhammad.

Mohamud (Arabic) a form of Muhammad.
Mohammud, Mohamoud

Mohan (Hindi) delightful.

Moise (Portuguese, Spanish) a form of Moises.

Moises (Portuguese, Spanish) a form of Moses.
Moices, Moisei, Moisés, Moisey, Moisis

Moishe (Yiddish) a form of Moses.

Mojag (Native American) crying baby.

Moki (Australian) cloudy.
Mokee, Mokey, Mokie, Moky

Molimo (Moquelumnan) bear going under shady trees.

Momuso (Moquelumnan) yellow jackets crowded in their nests for the winter.

Mona (Moquelumnan) gathering jimson-weed seed.
Monah

Monahan (Irish) monk.
Monaghan, Monoghan

Mongo (Yoruba) famous.

Monolo (Spanish) a familiar form of Manuel.

Monroe (Irish) from the mount on the river Roe.
Monro, Monrow, Munro, Munroe, Munrow

Montague (French) pointed mountain.
Montagne, Montagu

Montana (Spanish) mountain. Geography: a U.S. state.
Montaine, Montanah, Montanna

Montaro (Japanese) big boy.
Montero

Monte (French) a form of Montague. (Spanish) a short form of Montgomery.
Montae, Montaé, Montay, Montea, Montee, Monti, Montie, Montoya

Montel, Montell (American) forms of Montreal.
Montele, Montelle

Monterio (Japanese) a form of Montaro.
Montario

Montez (Spanish) dweller in the mountains.
Monteiz, Monteze, Montezz, Montise, Montisze, Montiz, Montize, Montyz, Montyze

Montgomery (English) rich man's mountain.
Montgomerie, Mountgomery

Montre (French) show.
Montra, Montrae, Montrai, Montray, Montrey

Montreal (French) royal mountain. Geography: a city in Quebec.
Montel, Monterial, Monterrell, Montrail, Montreall, Montrial

Montrel, Montrell (French) forms of Montreal.
Montral, Montrale, Montrall, Montrele, Montrelle

Montrez (French) a form of Montre.
Montraz, Montres, Montreze

Montsho (Tswana) black.

Monty (English) a familiar form of Montgomery.
Montey

Moore (French) dark; moor; marshland.
Moar, Moare, Moor, Mooro, More, Morre

Mordecai (Hebrew) martial, warlike. Bible: wise counselor to Queen Esther.
Mord, Mordie, Mordy

Mordechai (Hebrew) a form of Mordecai.
Mordachai

Mordred (Latin) painful. Literature: the bastard son of King Arthur.
Modred, Mordryd

Morel (French) an edible mushroom.
Morell, Morrel

Moreland (English) moor; marshland.
Moarlan, Moarland, Moorelan, Mooreland, Moorlan, Moorland, Morelan, Morlan, Morland

Morell (French) dark; from Morocco.
Morelle, Morelli, Morill, Morrell, Morrill, Murrel, Murrell

Morey (Greek) a familiar form of Moris. (Latin) a form of Morrie.
Moree, Morree, Morrey, Morry, Mory, Morye

Morgan (Scottish) sea warrior.
Morghan, Morgin, Morgon, Morgun, Morgunn, Morgwn, Morgyn, Morrgan

Morgen (Scottish) a form of Morgan.

Morio (Japanese) forest.
Moryo

Moris (Greek) son of the dark one. (English) a form of Morris.
Morey, Morisz, Moriz, Morys

Moritz (German) a form of Maurice, Morris.
Morisz

Morley (English) meadow by the moor.
Moorley, Moorly, Morlea, Morlee, Morleigh, Morli, Morlie, Morlon, Morly, Morlyn, Morrley

Morrie (Latin) a familiar form of
Maurice, Morse.
Morey, Mori, Morie, Morri

Morris (Latin) dark skinned; moor;
marshland. (English) a form of Maurice.
Moris, Moriss, Moritz, Morrese, Morrise,
Morriss, Morrys, Moss

Morse (English) son of Maurice.
Morresse, Morrison, Morrisson

Mort (French, English) a short form of
Mordecai, Morten, Mortimer, Morton.
Morte, Mortey, Mortie, Mortty, Morty

Morten (Norwegian) a form of Martin.
Mortan, Mortin, Mortyn

Mortimer (French) still water.
Mortymer

Morton (English) town near the moor.

Morven (Scottish) mariner.
Morvan, Morvien, Morvin

Mose (Hebrew) a short form of Moses.
Moyse

Moses (Hebrew) drawn out of the
water. (Egyptian) son, child. Bible: the
Hebrew lawgiver who brought the Ten
Commandments down from Mount
Sinai.
Mosese, Mosiah, Mosie, Mosses, Mosya,
Mosze, Moszek, Moyses, Moze, Mozes

Moshe (Hebrew, Polish) a form of Moses.
Mosheh

Mosi (Swahili) first-born.
Mosee, Mosey, Mosie, Mosy

Moss (Irish) a short form of Maurice,
Morris. (English) a short form of Moses.
Mos

Moswen (African) light in color.
Moswin, Moswyn

Motega (Native American) new arrow.
Motegah

Mouhamed (Arabic) a form of
Muhammad.
Mouhamad, Mouhamadou, Mouhammed,
Mouhamoin

Mousa (Arabic) a form of Moses.
Moussa

Mozart (Italian) breathless. Music:
Wolfgang Amadeus Mozart was a famous
eighteenth-century Austrian composer.
Mozar

Moze (Lithuanian) a form of Moses.
Mózes

Mpasa (Nguni) mat.
Mpasah

Mposi (Nyakyusa) blacksmith.

Mpoza (Luganda) tax collector.

Msrah (Akan) sixth-born.

Mtima (Nguni) heart.

Muata (Moquelumnan) yellow jackets in
their nest.
Mutah

Mugamba (Runyoro) talks too much.

Mugisa (Rutooro) lucky.
Mugisha, Mukisa

Muhammad (Arabic) praised. History: the
founder of the Islamic religion. See also
Ahmad, Hamid, Yasin.
Mahmúd, Muhamad, Muhamed, Muhamet,
Muhammadali,

Muhammed (Arabic) a form of
Muhammad.

Muhannad (Arabic) sword.
Muhanad

Muhsin (Arabic) beneficent; charitable.

Muhtadi (Arabic) rightly guided.

Muir (Scottish) moor; marshland.
Muire, Muyr, Muyre

Mujahid (Arabic) fighter in the way of
Allah.

Mukasa (Luganda) God's chief administrator.
Mukasah

Mukhtar (Arabic) chosen.
Mukhtaar

Mukul (Sanskrit) bud, blossom; soul.

Mulogo (Musoga) wizard.

Mun-Hee (Korean) literate; shiny.

Mundan (Rhodesian) garden.

Mundo (Spanish) a short form of Edmundo.

Mundy (Irish) from Reamonn.
Munde, Mundee, Mundey, Mundi, Mundie

Mungo (Scottish) amiable.

Munir (Arabic) brilliant; shining.
Munyr

Munny (Cambodian) wise.
Munee, Muney, Muni, Munie, Muny, Munnee, Munney, Munni, Munnie, Muny

Muraco (Native American) white moon.
Muracco

Murali (Hindi) flute. Religion: the instrument the Hindu god Krishna is usually depicted as playing.

Murat (Turkish) wish come true.

Murdock (Scottish) wealthy sailor.
Murdo, Murdoc, Murdoch, Murtagh

Murphy (Irish) sea warrior.
Murffee, Murffey, Murffi, Murffie, Murffy, Murfy, Murphee, Murphey, Murphi, Murphie

Murray (Scottish) sailor.
Moray, Murae, Murai, Muray, Murrae, Murrai, Murree, Murrey, Murri, Murrie, Murry

Murtagh (Irish) a form of Murdock.
Murtaugh

Musa (Swahili) child.

Musád (Arabic) untied camel.

Musoke (Rukonjo) born while a rainbow was in the sky.

Mustafa (Arabic) chosen; royal.
Mostafa, Mostafah, Mostaffa, Mostaffah, Moustafa, Mustafaa, Mustafah, Mustafe, Mustaffa, Mustafo, Mustoffa, Mustofo

Mustapha (Arabic) a form of Mustafa.
Mostapha, Moustapha

Muti (Arabic) obedient.

Mwaka (Luganda) born on New Year's Eve.

Mwamba (Nyakyusa) strong.

Mwanje (Luganda) leopard.

Mwinyi (Swahili) king.

Mwita (Swahili) summoner.

Mychael (American) a form of Michael.

Mychajlo (Latvian) a form of Michael.
Mykhaltso, Mykhas

Mychal (American) a form of Michael.
Mychall, Mychalo, Mycheal

Myer (English) a form of Meir.
Myers, Myur

Mykal, Mykel (American) forms of Michael.
Mykall, Mykell, Mykil, Mykill, Mykyl, Mykyle, Mykyll, Mykylle

Myles (Latin) soldier. (German) a form of Miles.
Myels, Mylez, Mylles, Mylz

Mylon (Italian) a form of Milan.
Mylan, Mylen, Mylyn, Mylynn

Mynor (Latin) a form of Minor.

Myo (Burmese) city.

Myriam (American) a form of Miriam (see Girls' Names).

Myron (Greek) fragrant ointment. (Polish) a form of Miron.
Mehran, Mehrayan, My, Myran, Myrone, Ron

Myung-Dae (Korean) right; great.

Mzuzi (Swahili) inventive.

N'namdi (Ibo) his father's name lives on.

Naaman (Hebrew) pleasant.
Naman

Nabeel (Arabic) a form of Nabil.

Nabiha (Arabic) intelligent.
Nabihah

Nabil (Arabic) noble.
Nabiel, Nabill, Nabyl, Nabyll

Nachman (Hebrew) a short form of
Menachem.
Nachum

Nada (Arabic) generous.
Nadah

Nadav (Hebrew) generous; noble.
Nadiv

Nader (Afghan, Arabic) a form of Nadir.

Nadidah (Arabic) equal to anyone else.

Nadim (Arabic) friend.
Nadeem, Nadym

Nadir (Afghan, Arabic) dear, rare.
Nadar, Nadyr

Nadisu (Hindi) beautiful river.
Nadysu

Naeem (Arabic) benevolent.
Naem, Naim, Naiym, Naym, Nieem

Naftali (Hebrew) wreath.
Naftalie

Nagid (Hebrew) ruler; prince.
Nagyd

Nahele (Hawaiian) forest.

Nahma (Native American) sturgeon.
Nahmah

Nahum (Hebrew) a form of Nachman.

Nailah (Arabic) successful.
Naila, Nayla, Naylah

Nairn (Scottish) river with alder trees.
Nairne, Nayrn, Nayrne

Najee (Arabic) a form of Naji.
Najae, Najée, Najei, Najiee

Naji (Arabic) safe.
Najie, Najih, Najy

Najíb (Arabic) born to nobility.
Najeeb, Najib, Najyb, Nejeeb, Nejib, Nejyb

Nakia (Arabic) pure.
*Nakai, Nakee, Nakeia, Naki, Nakiah,
Nakii*

Nakos (Arapaho) sage, wise.

Naldo (Spanish) a familiar form of
Reginald.

Nalren (Dene) thawed out.

Nam (Vietnamese) scrape off.

Namaka (Hawaiian) eyes.
Namakah

Namid (Ojibwa) star dancer.
Namyd

Namir (Hebrew) leopard.
Namer, Namyr

Nana (Hawaiian) spring.

Nandin (Hindi) Religion: a servant of
the Hindu god Shiva.
Nandan, Nandyn

Nando (German) a familiar form of
Ferdinand.
Nandor

Nangila (Abaluhya) born while parents
traveled.
Nangilah, Nangyla, Nangylah

Nangwaya (Mwera) don't mess with me.

Nansen (Swedish) son of Nancy.
Nansan, Nansin, Nanson, Nansyn

Nantai (Navajo) chief.
Nantay

Nantan (Apache) spokesman.
Nanten, Nantin, Nanton, Nantyn

Naoko (Japanese) straight, honest.

Napayshni (Lakota) he does not flee;
courageous.

Napier (Spanish) new city.
Napyer, Neper, Nepier, Nepyer

Napoleon (Greek) lion of the woodland.
(Italian) from Naples, Italy. History:
Napoleon Bonaparte was a famous
nineteenth-century French emperor.
*Leon, Nap, Napolean, Napoléon,
Napoleone, Nappie, Nappy*

Naquan (American) a combination of
the prefix Na + Quan.
Naqawn, Naquain, Naquen, Naquon

Narain (Hindi) protector. Religion: another name for the Hindu god Vishnu. *Narayan*

Narcisse (French) a form of Narcissus. *Narcis, Narciso, Narcisso, Narcyso, Narcyss, Narcysse, Narkis*

Narcissus (Greek) daffodil. Mythology: the youth who fell in love with his own reflection. *Narcisse, Narcyssus, Narkissos*

Nard (Persian) chess player.

Nardo (German) strong, hardy. (Spanish) a short form of Bernardo.

Narrie (Australian) bush fire. *Narree, Narrey, Narri, Narry*

Narve (Dutch) healthy, strong. *Narv*

Nashashuk (Fox, Sauk) loud thunder.

Nashoba (Choctaw) wolf.

Nasim (Persian) breeze; fresh air. *Naseem, Nassim, Nasym*

Nasir (Arabic) a form of Nasser. *Nassir*

Nasser (Arabic) victorious. *Naseer, Naser, Nasier, Nasr, Nassor, Nassyr*

Nat (English) a short form of Nathan, Nathaniel. *Natt, Natty*

Natal (Spanish) a form of Noël. *Natale, Natalie, Natalino, Natalio, Nataly*

Natan (Hebrew, Hungarian, Polish, Russian, Spanish) God has given. *Natain, Nataine, Natayn, Natayne, Naten*

Natanael (Hebrew) a form of Nathaniel. *Nataneal, Natanel, Nataniel, Nataniello*

Nate (Hebrew) a short form of Nathan, Nathaniel. *Nait, Naite, Nayt, Nayte*

Natesh (Hindi) destroyer. Religion: another name for the Hindu god Shiva.

Nathan (Hebrew) a short form of Nathaniel. Bible: a prophet during the reigns of David and Solomon. *Naethan, Naethin, Naethun, Naethyn, Naithan, Naithin, Naithon, Naithun, Naithyn, Nathann, Nathean, Nathian, Nathin, Nathun, Nathyn, Natthan, Naythan, Naythun, Naythyn, Nethan*

Nathanael (Hebrew) gift of God. Bible: one of the Twelve Apostles. Also known as Bartholomew. *Naethanael, Naethanial, Nafanael, Nafanail, Nafanyl, Nafanyle, Naithanael, Naithanyael, Naithanyal, Nathanae, Nathanal, Nathaneil, Nathanel, Nathaneol, Nathanual, Nathanyal Natthanial, Natthanyal, Nayfanial, Naythaneal, Naythanial, Nithanial, Nithanyal, Nothanial, Nothanyal*

Nathaneal, Nathanial, Nathaniel (Hebrew) forms of Nathanael. *Naithanyel, Nathanielle, Nathanil, Nathanile, Nathanuel, Nathanyel, Nathanyl, Natheal, Nathel, Nathinel, Natthaniel, Natthanielle, Natthaniuel, Natthanyel, Naythaniel, Naythanielle, Nethaniel, Nithaniel, Nithanyel, Nothaniel, Nothanielle, Nothanyel, Thaniel*

Nathanie (Hebrew) a familiar form of Nathaniel. *Nathania, Nathanni*

Nathen, Nathon (Hebrew) forms of Nathan. *Naethen, Naethon, Naithen, Naythen, Naython*

Nav (Gypsy) name.

Navarro (Spanish) plains. *Navara, Navaro, Navarra, Navarre*

Navdeep (Sikh) new light. *Navdip*

Naveen (Hindi) a form of Navin.

Navin (Hindi) new, novel. *Naven, Navyn*

Nawat (Native American) left-handed.

Nawkaw (Winnebago) wood.

Nayati (Native American) wrestler.
Nayaty

Nayland (English) island dweller.
Nailan, Nailand, Naylan

Nazareth (Hebrew) born in Nazareth,
Israel.
*Nazaire, Nazaret, Nazarie, Nazario,
Nazaryo, Nazerene, Nazerine*

Nazih (Arabic) pure, chaste.
*Nazeeh, Nazeem, Nazeer, Nazieh, Nazim,
Nazir, Nazyh, Nazz*

Ndale (Nguni) trick.

Neal, Neel (Irish) forms of Neil.
*Neale, Neall, Nealle, Nealon, Nealy,
Nealye, Neele, Neell, Neelle*

Neci (Latin) a familiar form of Ignatius.

Nectarios (Greek) saint. Religion: a saint
in the Greek Orthodox Church.

Ned (English) a familiar form of Edward,
Edwin.
Nedd, Neddie, Neddym, Nedrick

Neema (Swahili) born during prosperous
times.

Nehemiah (Hebrew) compassion of
Jehovah. Bible: a Jewish leader.
*Nahemia, Nahemiah, Nechemia, Nechemya,
Nehemia, Nehemias, Nehemie, Nehemyah,
Nehimiah, Nehmia, Nehmiah, Nemo,
Neyamia, Neyamiah, Neyamya, Neyamyah*

Nehru (Hindi) canal.

Neil (Irish) champion.
Neihl, Neile, Neill, Neille

Neka (Native American) wild goose.
Nekah

Nelek (Polish) a form of Cornelius.
Nelik

Nelius (Latin) a short form of Cornelius.

Nellie (English) a familiar form of
Cornelius, Cornell, Nelson.
Nell, Nelly

Nelo (Spanish) a form of Daniel.
Nello, Nilo

Nels (Scandinavian) a form of Neil,
Nelson.
Nelse

Nelson (English) son of Neil.
*Nealsan, Nealsen, Nealson, Nealsun,
Nealsyn, Neelsan, Neelsen, Neelsin,
Neelsun, Neelsyn, Neilsan, Neilsen,
Neilsin, Neilson, Neilsun, Neilsyn, Nellie,
Nels, Nelsen, Nelsin, Nelsun, Nelsyn,
Neylsan, Neylsen, Neylsin, Neylson,
Neylsun, Neylsyn, Nilsan, Nilsen, Nilsin,
Nilson, Nilsson, Nilsun, Nilsyn, Nylsan,
Nylsen, Nylsin, Nylson, Nylsun, Nylsyn*

Nemesio (Spanish) just.
Nemesyo, Nemi

Nemo (Greek) glen, glade. (Hebrew) a
short form of Nehemiah.
Nimo, Nymo

Nemuel (Hebrew) God's sea.
Nemuele, Nemuell, Nemuelle

Nen (Egyptian) ancient waters.

Neo (Greek) new. (African) gift.

Neptune (Latin) sea ruler. Mythology:
the Roman god of the sea.

Nero (Latin, Spanish) stern. History: a
cruel Roman emperor.
Niro, Nyro

Neron (Spanish) strong.
Nerone, Nerron

Nerville (French, Irish) village by the sea.
*Nervil, Nervile, Nervill, Nervyl, Nervyle,
Nervyll, Nervylle*

Nery (Hebrew, Arabic) a form of Nuri.
Neri

Nesbit (English) nose-shaped bend in a
river.
*Naisbit, Naisbitt, Naisbyt, Naisbytt, Nesbitt,
Nesbyt, Nesbytt, Nisbet, Nisbett, Nysbet,
Nysbett, Nysbit, Nysbitt, Nysbyt, Nysbytt*

Nestor (Greek) traveler; wise.
Nestar, Nester, Nestyr

Nethaniel (Hebrew) a form of
Nathaniel.

Netanel, Netania, Netaniah, Netaniel, Netanya, Nethanel, Nethanial, Nethaniel, Nethanuel, Nethanyal, Nethanyel

Neto (Spanish) a short form of Ernesto.

Nevada (Spanish) covered in snow. Geography: a U.S. state.
Navada, Nevadah, Nevade, Nevadia, Nevadya

Nevan (Irish) holy.
Nefan, Nefen, Nevean, Neven, Nevon, Nevun, Nivan, Niven, Nivon, Nyvan, Nyvven, Nyvon

Neville (French) new town.
Nev, Neval, Nevall, Nevel, Nevele, Nevell, Nevil, Nevile, Nevill, Nevyl, Nevyle, Nevyll, Nevylle

Nevin (Irish) worshiper of the saint. (English) middle; herb.
Nefin, Nev, Nevins, Nevyn, Nivyn, Nyvin, Nyvyn

Newbold (English) new tree.

Newell (English) new hall.
Newall, Newel, Newyle

Newland (English) new land.
Newlan

Newlin (Welsh) new lake.
Newlyn

Newman (English) newcomer.
Neiman, Neimann, Neimon, Neuman, Neumann, Newmann, Newmen, Numan, Numen

Newton (English) new town.
Nauton, Newt, Newtown

Ngai (Vietnamese) herb.

Nghia (Vietnamese) forever.

Ngozi (Ibo) blessing.

Ngu (Vietnamese) sleep.

Nguyen (Vietnamese) a form of Ngu.

Nhean (Cambodian) self-knowledge.

Niall (Irish) a form of Neil. History: Niall of the Nine Hostages was a famous Irish king.

Nial, Niale, Nialle, Niel, Niele, Niell, Nielle, Nyal, Nyale, Nyall, Nyalle, Nyeal, Nyeale, Nyeall, Nyealle

Nibal (Arabic) arrows.
Nibel, Nybal

Nibaw (Native American) standing tall.
Nybaw

Nicabar (Gypsy) stealthy.
Nycabar

Nicco, Nico (Greek) short forms of Nicholas.

Niccolo, Nicolo (Italian) forms of Nicholas.
Niccolò, Nicholo, Nicol, Nicolao, Nicoll, Nicollo

Nicho (Spanish) a form of Dennis.
Nycho

Nicholai (Norwegian, Russian) a form of Nicholas.

Nicholas (Greek) victorious people. Religion: Nicholas of Myra is a patron saint of children. See also Caelan, Claus, Cola, Colar, Cole, Colin, Colson, Klaus, Lasse, Mikolaj, Mikolas, Milek.
Niccolas, Nichalas, Nichelas, Nichele, Nichlas, Nichlos, Nichola, Nicholaas, Nicholaes, Nicholase, Nichole, Nicholias, Nicholl, Nichollas, Nicholus, Nioclás, Niocol, Nycholas

Nicholaus (Greek) a form of Nicholas.
Nichalaus, Nichalous, Nichaolas, Nichlaus, Nichloas, Nichlous, Nicholaos, Nicholous, Nicolaus

Nicholes, Nichols (English) son of Nicholas.
Nickoles, Nicolls

Nicholis (English) a form of Nicholes.

Nicholos (Greek) a form of Nicholas.

Nicholson (English) son of Nicholas.
Nickelson, Nickoleson, Nycholson, Nyckolson, Nykolson

Nick (English) a short form of Dominic, Nicholas. See also Micu.
Nic, Nicc, Nik, Nyck, Nyk

Nickalas, Nickalus (Greek) forms of Nicholas.
Nickalaus, Nickalis, Nickalos, Nickalous, Nickelas, Nickelous, Nickelus, Nickolau

Nicklaus, Nicklas (Greek) forms of Nicholas.
Nicklauss, Nicklos, Nicklous, Nicklus, Niclas, Niclasse, Niklaus

Nickolas, Nickolaus, Nickolis, Nickolus (Greek) forms of Nicholas.
Nickolaos, Nickolos, Nickolys, Nickoulas

Nicky (Greek) a familiar form of Nicholas.
Nickey, Nicki, Nickie

Nicodemus (Greek) conqueror of the people.
Nicodem, Nicodemius, Nikodem, Nikodema, Nikodemious, Nikodim

Nicola (Italian) a form of Nicholas. See also Cola.
Nickola, Nicolá, Nikolah

Nicolaas, Nicolas, Nicolaus (Italian) forms of Nicolas.
Nicolás, Nicoles, Nicolis, Nicolus

Nicolai (Norwegian, Russian) a form of Nicholas.
Nickolai, Nicolaj, Nicolau, Nicolay, Nicoly, Nikalai

Nicole (French) a form of Nicholas.

Niels (Danish) a form of Neil.
Niel, Nielsen, Nielson

Nien (Vietnamese) year.
Nyen

Nigan (Native American) ahead.
Nigen

Nigel (Latin) dark night.
Niegal, Niegel, Nigal, Nigale, Nigele, Nigell, Nigiel, Nigil, Nigle, Nijel, Nygal, Nygel, Nyigel, Nyjil

Nika (Yoruba) ferocious.
Nica, Nicah, Nicka, Nickah, Nikah, Nikka, Nyca, Nycah, Nycka, Nyckah, Nyka, Nykah

Nike (Greek) victorious.
Nikee, Nikey, Nikie, Nykee, Nykei, Nykey, Nykie

Nikhil (Indian) a form of Nicholas.

Niki, Nikki (Hungarian) familiar forms of Nicholas.
Nikia, Nikiah, Nikkie, Niky, Nyki, Nyky

Nikita (Russian) a form of Nicholas.
Nakita, Nakitah, Nykita, Nykitah, Nykyta, Nykytah

Nikiti (Native American) round and smooth like an abalone shell.
Nikity, Nikyti, Nityty, Nykiti, Nykity, Nykyty

Nikko, Niko (Hungarian) forms of Nicholas.
Nikoe, Nyko

Niklas (Latvian, Swedish) a form of Nicholas.
Niklaas, Niklaus

Nikola (Greek) a short form of Nicholas.
Nikolao, Nikolay, Nykola

Nikolai (Estonian, Russian) a form of Nicholas.
Kolya, Nikolais, Nikolaj, Nikolajs, Nikolay, Nikoli, Nikolia, Nikula

Nikolaos (Greek) a form of Nicholas.

Nikolas, Nikolaus (Greek) forms of Nicholas.
Nicanor, Nikalas, Nikalis, Nikalous, Nikalus, Nikholas, Nikolaas, Nikolis, Nikos, Nikulas, Nilos, Nykolas, Nykolus

Nikolos (Greek) a form of Nicholas. See also Kolya.
Niklos, Nikolaos, Nikolò, Nikolous, Nikolus

Nil (Russian) a form of Neil.
Nill, Nille, Nilya

Nila (Hindi) blue.
Nilah, Nyla, Nylah

Nile (Russian) a form of Nil.

Niles (English) son of Neil.
Nilese, Nilesh, Nyles, Nylles

Nilo (Finnish) a form of Neil.
Niilo

Nils (Swedish) a short form of Nicholas. (Danish) a form of Niels.

Nima (Hebrew) thread. (Arabic) blessing.

Nimrod (Hebrew) rebel. Bible: a great-grandson of Noah.
Nymrod

Nino (Spanish) a form of Niño.

Niño (Spanish) young child.
Neño, Nyño

Niran (Tai) eternal.
Niren, Nirin, Niron, Niryn, Nyran, Nyren, Nyrin, Nyron, Nyryn

Nishan (Armenian) cross, sign, mark.
Nishon, Nyshan

Nissan (Hebrew) sign, omen; miracle.
Nisan, Nissim, Nissin, Nisson, Nyssan

Nitis (Native American) friend.
Netis, Nytis, Nytys

Nixon (English) son of Nick.
Nixan, Nixen, Nixin, Nixson, Nixun, Nixyn, Nyxen, Nyxin, Nyxon, Nyxyx

Nizam (Arabic) leader.
Nyzam

Nkunda (Runyankore) loves those who hate him.
Nkundah

Noach (Hebrew) a form of Noah.

Noah (Hebrew) peaceful, restful. Bible: the patriarch who built the ark to survive the Flood.
Noach, Noak

Noam (Hebrew) sweet; friend.

Noble (Latin) born to nobility.
Nobe, Nobel, Nobie, Noby

Nodin (Native American) wind.
Knoton, Nodyn, Noton

Noe (Czech, French) a form of Noah.
Noé, Noi

Noé (Hebrew, Spanish) quiet, peaceful. See also Noah.

Noel (French) a form of Noël.

Noël (French) day of Christ's birth. See also Natal.
Noél, Noell, Nole, Noli, Nowel, Nowele, Nowell

Nohea (Hawaiian) handsome.
Noha, Nohe

Nokonyu (Native American) katydid's nose.
Noko, Nokoni

Nolan (Irish) famous; noble.
Noland, Nolande, Nolane, Nolin, Nollan, Nolon, Nolyn

Nolen (Irish) a form of Nolan.

Nollie (Latin, Scandinavian) a familiar form of Oliver.
Noll, Nolly

Noor (Sikh) divine light. (Aramaic) a form of Nura (see Girls' Names).

Norbert (Scandinavian) brilliant hero.
Bert, Norbie, Norburt, Norby, Norbyrt, Northbert, Northburt, Northbyrt

Norberto (Spanish) a form of Norbert.
Norburto, Norbyrto, Northberto, Northburto, Northbyrto

Norman (French) Norseman. History: a name for the Scandinavians who settled in northern France in the tenth century, and who later conquered England in 1066.
Norm, Normand, Normen, Normie, Normin, Normon, Normy, Normyn

Norris (French) northerner. (English) Norman's horse.
Norice, Norie, Noris, Norreys, Norrie, Norry, Norrys

Northcliff (English) northern cliff.
Northclif, Northcliffe, Northclyf, Northclyfe, Northclyff, Northclyffe

Northrop (English) north farm.
North, Northup

Norton (English) northern town.
Northton

Norville (French, English) northern town.
Norval, Norvel, Norvell, Norvil, Norvile,
Norvill, Norvylle

Norvin (English) northern friend.
Norvyn, Norwin, Norwinn, Norwyn,
Norwynn

Norward (English) protector of the
north.
Norwerd

Norwood (English) northern woods.
Northwood

Notaku (Moquelumnan) growing bear.

Nour (Aramaic) a short form of Nura
(see Girls' Names).

Nowles (English) a short form of
Knowles.
Nowl, Nowle

Nsoah (Akan) seventh-born.
Nsoa

Numa (Arabic) pleasant.
Numah

Numair (Arabic) panther.
Numayr

Nuncio (Italian) messenger.
Nunzi, Nunzio

Nuri (Hebrew, Arabic) my fire.
Noori, Nur, Nuris, Nurism, Nury

Nuriel (Hebrew, Arabic) fire of the Lord.
Nuria, Nuriah, Nuriya, Nuryel

Nuru (Swahili) born in daylight.

Nusair (Arabic) bird of prey.
Nusayr

Nwa (Nigerian) son.

Nwake (Nigerian) born on market day.

Nye (English) a familiar form of Aneurin,
Nigel.

Nyle (English) island. (Irish) a form of
Neil.
Nyal, Nyl, Nyll, Nylle

O'neil (Irish) son of Neil.
O'neal, O'neel, O'neele, O'neile, O'neill,
O'niel, O'niele, O'nil, O'nile, O'nyel,
O'nyele, O'nyl, O'nyle, Oneal, Oneil,
Onel, Oniel, Onil

O'shay, O'shea, Oshay, Oshea (Irish)
forms of O'Shea.

O'Shea (Irish) son of Shea.
O'Shane, Oshae, Oshai, Oshane, Oshaun,
Oshaye, Oshe, Osheon

Oakes (English) oak trees.
Oak, Oake, Oaks, Ochs

Oakley (English) oak-tree field.
Oak, Oakie, Oaklea, Oaklee, Oakleigh,
Oakli, Oaklie, Oakly, Oaky

Oalo (Spanish) a form of Paul.

Oba (Yoruba) king.
Obah

Obadele (Yoruba) king arrives at the
house.
Obadel

Obadiah (Hebrew) servant of God.
Obadia, Obadias, Obadya, Obadyah,
Obadyas, Obediah, Obedias, Obedya,
Obedyah, Obedyas, Ovadiach, Ovadiah,
Ovadya

Obed (English) a short form of Obadiah.
Obad

Oberon (German) noble; bearlike.
Literature: the king of the fairies in the
Shakespearean play *A Midsummer Night's*
Dream. See also Auberon, Aubrey.
Oberan, Oberen, Oberin, Oberron, Oberun,
Oberyn, Oeberon

Obert (German) wealthy; bright.
Obirt, Oburt, Obyrt

Obie (English) a familiar form of Obadiah.
Obbie, Obe, Obee, Obey, Obi, Oby

Ocan (Luo) hard times.

Ocean (Greek) a short form of Oceanus.
Oceane

Oceanus (Greek) Mythology: a Titan who rules over the outer sea encircling the earth.
Oceanis, Oceanos, Oceanous, Oceanys

Octavio (Latin) eighth. See also Tavey, Tavian.
Octave, Octavee, Octavey, Octavia, Octavian, Octaviano, Octavien, Octavo, Octavyo, Ottavio

Octavious, Octavius (Latin) forms of Octavio.
Octavaius, Octaveous, Octaveus, Octavias, Octaviaus, Octavous, Octavyos, Octavyous, Octavyus, Ottavios, Ottavious, Ottavius

Octavis (Latin) a form of Octavio.
Octavus

Odakota (Lakota) friendly.
Oda, Odakotah

Odd (Norwegian) point.
Oddvar

Ode (Benin) born along the road. (Irish, English) a short form of Odell.
Odee, Odey, Odi, Odie, Ody

Oded (Hebrew) encouraging.

Odell (Greek) ode, melody. (Irish) otter. (English) forested hill.
Dell, Odall, Odel, Odele

Odin (Scandinavian) ruler. Mythology: the Norse god of wisdom and war.
Oden, Odyn

Odion (Benin) first of twins.
Odyon

Odo (Norwegian) a form of Otto.
Audo, Oddo, Odoh

Odolf (German) prosperous wolf.
Odolfe, Odolff, Odolph, Odolphe, Odulf

Odom (Ghanaian) oak tree.

Odon (Hungarian) wealthy protector.

Odran (Irish) pale green.
Odhrán, Odren, Odrin, Odron, Odryn

Odwin (German) noble friend.
Odwinn, Odwyn, Odwynn

Odysseus (Greek) wrathful. Literature: the hero of Homer's epic poem *Odyssey*.
Odeseus

Ofer (Hebrew) young deer.
Opher

Og (Aramaic) king. Bible: the king of Basham.

Ogaleesha (Lakota) red shirt.

Ogbay (Ethiopian) don't take him from me.
Ogbae, Ogbai

Ogbonna (Ibo) image of his father.
Ogbonnah, Ogbonnia

Ogden (English) oak valley. Literature: Ogden Nash was a twentieth-century American writer of light verse.
Ogdan, Ogdin, Ogdon, Ogdyn

Ogilvie (Welsh) high.
Ogil, Ogyl, Ogylvie

Ogima (Ojibwa) chief.
Ogimah, Ogyma, Ogymah

Ogun (Nigerian) Mythology: the god of war.
Ogunkeye, Ogunsanwo, Ogunsheye

Ohanko (Native American) restless.

Ohannes (Turkish) a form of John.
Ohan, Ohane, Ohanes, Ohann, Ohanne

Ohanzee (Lakota) comforting shadow.
Ohanze

Ohin (African) chief.
Ohan, Ohyn

Ohitekah (Lakota) brave.
Ohiteka

Oisin (Irish) small deer.
Oisyn, Oysin, Oysyn

Oistin (Irish) a form of Austin.
Oistan, Oisten, Oistyn

OJ (American) a combination of the initials O. + J.
O.J., Ojay

Ojo (Yoruba) difficult delivery.

Okapi (Swahili) an African animal related to the giraffe but having a short neck.
Okapie, Okapy

Oke (Hawaiian) a form of Oscar.

Okechuku (Ibo) God's gift.

Okeke (Ibo) born on market day.
Okorie

Okie (American) from Oklahoma.
Okee, Okey, Oki, Oky

Oko (Ghanaian) older twin. (Yoruba) god of war.

Okorie (Ibo) a form of Okeke.

Okpara (Ibo) first son.
Okparah

Okuth (Luo) born in a rain shower.

Ola (Yoruba) wealthy, rich.
Olah, Olla, Ollah

Olaf (Scandinavian) ancestor. History: a patron saint and king of Norway.
Olaff, Olafur, Olaph, Ole, Olef, Olof, Oluf

Olajuwon (Yoruba) wealth and honor are God's gifts.
Olajawon, Olajawun, Olajowuan, Olajuan, Olajuanne, Olajuawon, Olajuwa, Olajuwan, Olajuwon, Olaujawon, Oljuwoun

Olamina (Yoruba) this is my wealth.
Olaminah, Olamyna, Olamynah

Olatunji (Yoruba) honor reawakens.

Olav (Scandinavian) a form of Olaf.
Ola, Olave, Olavus, Olov, Olyn

Ole (Scandinavian) a familiar form of Olaf, Olav.
Olay, Oleh, Olle

Oleg (Latvian, Russian) holy.

Oleksandr (Russian) a form of Alexander.
Olek, Olesandr, Olesko

Olen (Scandinavian) a form of Olaf. (Scandinavian, English) a form of Olin.

Olés (Polish) a familiar form of Alexander.

Olin (English) holly. (Scandinavian) a form of Olaf.
Olney, Olyn

Olindo (Italian) from Olinthos, Greece.
Olind, Olynd, Olyndo

Oliver (Latin) olive tree. (Scandinavian) kind; affectionate.
Nollie, Oilibhéar, Olivar, Ollivar, Olliver, Ollivor, Ollyvar, Ollyver, Ollyvir, Ollyvyr, Olvan, Olven, Olvin, Olyvar

Olivero, Oliveros (Italian, Spanish) forms of Oliver.
Oliveras, Oliverio, Oliverios, Olivieras, Oliviero

Olivier (French) a form of Oliver.
Olier

Oliwa (Hawaiian) a form of Oliver.
Olliva, Ollyva

Ollie (English) a familiar form of Oliver.
Olea, Olee, Oleigh, Oley, Oli, Olie, Olle, Ollee, Olleigh, Olley, Olli, Olly, Oly

Olo (Spanish) a short form of Orlando, Rolando.

Olric (German) a form of Ulric.
Oldrech, Oldrich, Olrick, Olrik, Olryc, Olryck, Olryk

Olubayo (Yoruba) highest joy.

Olufemi (Yoruba) wealth and honor favors me.

Olujimi (Yoruba) God gave me this.

Olushola (Yoruba) God has blessed me.

Omair (Arabic) a form of Omar.

Omar (Arabic) highest; follower of the Prophet. (Hebrew) reverent. See also Umar.
Omir, Omyr

Omari (Swahili) a form of Omar.
Omare, Omaree, Omarey, Omarie, Omary

Omarr (Arabic) a form of Omar.

Omer (Arabic) a form of Omar.
Omeer, Omero

Omolara (Benin) child born at the right time.
Omolarah

On (Burmese) coconut. (Chinese) peace.

Onan (Turkish) prosperous.
Onen, Onin, Onon, Onyn

Onani (African) quick look.
Onanee, Onanie, Onany

Onaona (Hawaiian) pleasant fragrance.
Onaonah

Ondro (Czech) a form of Andrew.
Ondra, Ondre, Ondrea, Ondrey

Onkar (Hindi) God in his entirety.

Onofrio (German) a form of Humphrey.
Oinfre, Onfre, Onfrio, Onofre, Onofredo

Onslow (English) enthusiast's hill.
Ounslow

Ontario (Native American) beautiful lake. Geography: a province and a lake in Canada.

Onufry (Polish) a form of Humphrey.

Onur (Turkish) honor.

Ophir (Hebrew) faithful. Bible: an Old Testament people and country.
Ophyr

Opio (Ateso) first of twin boys.
Opyo

Oral (Latin) verbal; speaker.

Oran (Irish) green.
Ora, Orane, Orran, Orron

Oratio (Latin) a form of Horatio.
Oratyo, Orazio, Orazyo

Orbán (Hungarian) born in the city.
Orben, Orbin, Orbon, Orbyn

Ordell (Latin) beginning.
Orde, Ordel, Ordele, Ordelle

Orel (Latin) listener. (Russian) eagle.
Oreel, Orele, Orell, Oriel, Oriele, Oriell, Orrel, Orrele, Orrell

Oren (Hebrew) pine tree. (Irish) light skinned, white.
Orono, Orren

Orestes (Greek) mountain man. Mythology: the son of the Greek leader Agamemnon.
Aresty, Orest, Oreste

Ori (Hebrew) my light.
Oree, Orey, Orie, Orri, Ory

Orien (Latin) visitor from the east.
Orian, Orie, Oris, Oron, Orono, Oryan, Oryen, Oryin

Orin (English) a form of Orrin.

Orion (Greek) son of fire. Mythology: a giant hunter who was killed by Artemis. See also Zorion.
Orryon, Oryon

Orji (Ibo) mighty tree.

Orlando (German) famous throughout the land. (Spanish) a form of Roland.
Lando, Olando, Orlan, Orland, Orlanda, Orlandas, Orlande, Orlandes, Orlandis, Orlandos, Orlandous, Orlandus, Orlo, Orlondo, Orlondon

Orleans (Latin) golden.
Orlean, Orlin

Orman (German) mariner, seaman. (Scandinavian) serpent, worm.
Ormand, Ormen

Ormond (English) bear mountain; spear protector.
Ormande, Ormon, Ormonde, Ormondo

Oro (Spanish) golden.

Orono (Latin) a form of Oren.
Oron, Orun

Orpheus (Greek) Mythology: a fabulous musician.
Orfeus

Orrick (English) old oak tree.
Oric, Orick, Orik, Orric, Orrik, Orryc, Orryck, Orryk, Oryc, Oryck, Oryk

Orrin (English) river.
Orryn, Oryn, Orynn

Orris (Latin) a form of Horatio.
Oris, Orriss, Orrys, Orryss

Orry (Latin) from the Orient.
Oarri, Oarrie, Orrey, Orri, Orrie, Ory

Orsino (Italian) a form of Orson.
Orscino, Orsine, Orsyne, Orsyno

Orson (Latin) bearlike. See also Urson.
Orsen, Orsin, Orsini, Orsino, Orsyn, Son, Sonny

Orton (English) shore town.
Ortan, Orten, Ortin, Ortyn

Ortzi (Basque) sky.
Ortzy

Orunjan (Yoruba) born under the mid-day sun.

Orval (English) a form of Orville.
Orvel

Orville (French) golden village. History: Orville Wright and his brother Wilbur were the first men to fly an airplane.
Orv, Orvell, Orvie, Orvil, Orvile, Orvill, Orvyl, Orvyle, Orvyll

Orvin (English) spear friend.
Orvan, Orven, Orvon, Orvyn, Orwin, Orwyn, Owynn

Osahar (Benin) God hears.

Osayaba (Benin) God forgives.

Osaze (Benin) whom God likes.
Osaz

Osbaldo (Spanish) a form of Oswald.
Osbalto

Osbert (English) divine; bright.
Osbirt, Osbyrt

Osborn (Scandinavian) divine bear. (English) warrior of God.
Osbern, Osbon, Osborne, Osbourn, Osbourne, Osburn, Osburne, Ozborn, Ozborne, Ozbourn, Ozbourne

Oscar (Scandinavian) divine spearman.
Oszkar

Osei (Fante) noble.
Osee, Osey, Osi, Osie, Osy

Osgood (English) divinely good.

Osip (Russian, Ukrainian) a form of Joseph, Yosef. See also Osya.

Oskar (Scandinavian) a form of Oscar.
Osker, Ozker

Osman (Turkish) ruler. (English) servant of God. A form of Osmond.
Osmanek, Osmen, Osmin, Osmon, Osmyn

Osmar (English) divine; wonderful.
Osmer, Osmir, Osmor, Osmyr

Osmond (English) divine protector.
Osmand, Osmonde, Osmondo, Osmont, Osmonte, Osmund, Osmunde, Osmundo, Osmunt, Osmunte

Osric (English) divine ruler.
Osrick, Osrig, Osrik, Osryc, Osryck, Osryg, Osryk

Ostin (Latin) a form of Austin.
Ostan, Osten, Oston, Ostun, Ostyn, Ostynn

Osvaldo (Spanish) a form of Oswald.
Osvald, Osvalda

Oswald (English) God's power; God's crest. See also Waldo.
Oswal, Oswall, Oswel, Osweld, Oswell, Oswold

Oswaldo (Spanish) a form of Oswald.
Osweldo

Oswin (English) divine friend.
Osvin, Oswinn, Oswyn, Oswynn

Osya (Russian) a familiar form of Osip.

Ota (Czech) prosperous.
Otah

Otadan (Native American) plentiful.

Otaktay (Lakota) kills many; strikes many.

Otek (Polish) a form of Otto.
Otik

Otello (Italian) a form of Othello.

Otem (Luo) born away from home.

Othello (Spanish) a form of Otto. Literature: the title character in the Shakespearean tragedy *Othello*.
Otello

Othman (German) wealthy.
Othmen, Ottoman

Otis (Greek) keen of hearing. (German) son of Otto.
Oates, Odis, Otes, Otess, Otez, Otise, Ottis, Ottys, Otys

Ottah (Nigerian) thin baby.
Otta

Ottar (Norwegian) point warrior; fright warrior.
Otar

Ottmar (Turkish) a form of Osman.
Otman, Otmen, Otomar, Otomars, Otthmor, Ottmar, Ottmen, Ottmer, Ottmor, Ottomar

Otto (German) rich.
Odo, Otek, Otello, Otfried, Otho, Othon, Otilio, Otman, Oto, Otoe, Otón, Otow, Otton, Ottone

Ottokar (German) happy warrior.
Otokar, Otokars, Ottocar

Otu (Native American) collecting seashells in a basket.
Ottu

Ouray (Ute) arrow. Astrology: born under the sign of Sagittarius.

Oved (Hebrew) worshiper, follower.
Ovid, Ovyd

Overton (English) high town.
Overtan, Overten, Overtin, Overtyn

Owen (Irish) born to nobility; young warrior. (Welsh) a form of Evan. See also Uaine, Ywain.
Owain, Owaine, Owan, Owayn, Owayne, Owens, Owin, Owine, Owon, Owone, Owyn, Owyne

Owney (Irish) elderly.
Onee, Oney, Oni, Onie, Ony, Ownee, Owni, Ownie, Owny

Oxford (English) place where oxen cross the river.
Ford, Oxforde

Oxley (English) ox meadow.
Oxlea, Oxlee, Oxleigh, Oxli, Oxlie, Oxly

Oxton (English) ox town.
Oxtan, Oxten, Oxtin, Oxtyn

Oya (Moquelumnan) speaking of the jacksnipe.
Oyah

Oystein (Norwegian) rock of happiness.
Ostein, Osten, Ostin, Øystein

Oz (Hebrew) a short form of Osborn, Oswald.
Ozz

Ozias (Hebrew) God's strength.
Ozia, Oziah, Ozya, Ozyah, Ozyas

Ozturk (Turkish) pure; genuine Turk.

Ozuru (Japanese) stork.
Ozuro, Ozuroo

Ozzie, Ozzy (English) familiar forms of Osborn, Oswald.
Osi, Osie, Ossi, Ossie, Ossy, Osy, Ozee, Ozi, Ozie, Ozy, Ozzi

P

Paavo (Finnish) a form of Paul.
Paav, Paaveli

Pablo (Spanish) a form of Paul.
Pable, Paublo

Pace (English) a form of Pascal.
Paice, Payce

Pacey (English) a form of Pace.

Pacifico (Filipino) peaceful.
Pacific, Pacifyc, Pacyfyc

Paco (Italian) pack. (Spanish) a familiar form of Francisco. (Native American) bald eagle. See also Quico.
Packo, Pacorro, Pako, Panchito, Paquito

Paddy (Irish) a familiar form of Padraic, Patrick.
Paddee, Paddey, Paddi, Paddie, Padi, Padie, Pady

Paden (English) a form of Patton.

Padget (English) a form of Page.
Padgett, Paget, Pagett, Paiget, Paigett, Payget, Paygett

Padraic (Irish) a form of Patrick.
Paddrick, Padhraig, Padrai, Pádraig, Padraigh, Padreic, Padriac, Padric, Padron, Padruig

Pagan (Latin) from the country.
Paegan, Paegen, Paegin, Paegon, Paegyn, Pagen, Pagin, Pagon, Pagun, Pagyn, Paigan, Paigen, Paigin, Paigon, Paigyn

Page (French) youthful assistant.
Paggio, Payg, Payge

Pagiel (Hebrew) worshiping God.
Paegel, Paegell, Pagiell, Paigel, Paigell, Paygel, Paygell

Paige (English) a form of Page.
Paeg, Paege, Paig

Painter (Latin) artist, painter.
Paintar, Paintor, Payntar, Paynter, Payntor

Pakelika (Hawaiian) a form of Patrick.

Paki (African) witness.

Pakile (Hawaiian) royal.
Pakil, Pakill, Pakyl, Pakyll

Pal (Swedish) a form of Paul.
Paal, Pall

Pál (Hungarian) a form of Paul.
Pali, Palika

Palaina (Hawaiian) a form of Brian.
Palainah

Palaki (Polynesian) black.
Palakee, Palakey, Palakie, Palaky

Palani (Hawaiian) a form of Frank.
Palanee, Palaney, Palanie, Palany

Palash (Hindi) flowery tree.

Palben (Basque) blond.

Palladin (Native American) fighter.
Pallaton, Palladyn, Palleten

Palmer (English) palm-bearing pilgrim.
Pallmer, Palmar

Palmiro (Latin) born on Palm Sunday.
Palmira, Palmirow, Palmyro

Palti (Hebrew) God liberates.
Palti-el

Panas (Russian) immortal.

Panayiotis (Greek) a form of Peter.
Panagiotis, Panajotis, Panayioti, Panayoti, Panayotis

Pancho (Spanish) a familiar form of Francisco, Frank.
Panchito

Panos (Greek) a form of Peter.
Pano

Paolo (Italian) a form of Paul.

Paquito (Spanish) a familiar form of Paco.

Paramesh (Hindi) greatest. Religion: another name for the Hindu god Shiva.

Pardeep (Sikh) mystic light.
Pardip

Paris (Greek) lover. Geography: the capital of France. Mythology: the prince of Troy who started the Trojan War by abducting Helen.
Paras, Paree, Pares, Parese, Parie, Parys

Parish (English) a form of Parrish.

Park (Chinese) cypress tree. (English) a short form of Parker.
Parc, Parke, Parkes, Parkey, Parks

Parker (English) park keeper.
Park

Parkin (English) little Peter.
Parkyn

Parlan (Scottish) a form of Bartholomew. See also Parthalán.
Parlen, Parlin, Parlon, Parlyn

Parnell (French) little Peter. History: Charles Stewart Parnell was a famous Irish politician.
Nell, Parle, Parnel, Parnele, Parnelle, Parrnell

Parr (English) cattle enclosure, barn.

Parris (Greek) a form of Paris.

Parrish (English) church district.
Parrie, Parrisch, Parrysh, Parysh

Parry (Welsh) son of Harry.
Paree, Parey, Pari, Parie, Parree, Parrey,
Parri, Parrie, Pary

Parth (Irish) a short form of Parthalán.
Partha, Parthey

Parthalán (Irish) plowman. See also
Bartholomew.

Parthenios (Greek) virgin. Religion: a
Greek Orthodox saint.

Pascal (French) born on Easter or
Passover.
Pascale, Pascall, Pascalle, Paschal, Paschalis,
Pascoe, Pascoli, Pascow

Pascual (Spanish) a form of Pascal.
Pascul

Pasha (Russian) a form of Paul.
Pashah, Pashka

Pasquale (Italian) a form of Pascal.
Pascuale, Pasqual, Pasquali, Pasquel

Pastor (Latin) spiritual leader.
Pastar, Paster, Pastir, Pastyr

Pat (Native American) fish. (English) a
short form of Patrick.
Pati, Patie, Patt, Patti, Pattie, Patty, Paty

Patakusu (Moquelumnan) ant biting a
person.

Patamon (Native American) raging.
Pataman, Patamen, Patamin, Patamyn

Patek (Polish) a form of Patrick.
Patick

Patric, Patrik, Patryk (Latin) forms of
Patrick.
Patryc, Patryck

Patrice (French) a form of Patrick.

Patricio (Spanish) a form of Patrick.
Patricius, Patrizio

Patrick (Latin) nobleman. Religion: the
patron saint of Ireland. See also
Fitzpatrick, Ticho.

Pakelika, Patrickk, Patrique, Patrizius, Pats,
Patsy, Pattrick

Patrin (Gypsy) leaf trail.

Patterson (Irish) son of Pat.
Paterson, Patteson

Pattin (Gypsy) leaf. (English) a form of
Patton.
Patin, Pattyn, Patyn

Patton (English) warrior's town.
Patan, Paten, Paton, Pattan, Patten, Pattun,
Patty, Peton

Patwin (Native American) man.
Patwyn

Patxi (Basque, Teutonic) free.

Paul (Latin) small. Bible: Saul, later
renamed Paul, was the first to bring the
teachings of Christ to the Gentiles.
Oalo, Pasko, Paulia, Paulis, Paull, Paulle,
Paulot, Pauls, Paulus, Pavlos

Pauli (Latin) a familiar form of Paul.
Pauley, Paulie, Pauly

Paulin (German, Polish) a form of Paul.

Paulino (Spanish) a form of Paul.

Paulinus (Lithuanian) a form of Paul.
Paulinas

Paulo (Portuguese, Swedish, Hawaiian) a
form of Paul.

Pavel (Russian) a form of Paul.
Paavel, Paval, Pavil, Pavils, Pavlik, Pavlo,
Pavol

Pavit (Hindi) pious, pure.
Pavitt, Pavyt, Pavytt

Pawel (Polish) a form of Paul.
Pawelek, Pawell, Pawl

Pax (Latin) peaceful.
Paxx

Paxton (Latin) peaceful town.
Packston, Paxon, Paxtan, Paxten, Paxtin,
Paxtun, Paxtyn

Payat (Native American) he is on his way.
Pay, Payatt

Payden (English) a form of Payton.
Paydon

Payne (Latin) from the country.
Paine, Pane, Payn, Paynn

Paytah (Lakota) fire.
Pay, Payta

Payton (English) a form of Patton.
Paiton, Pate, Peaton

Paz (Spanish) a form of Pax.

Pearce (English) a form of Pierce.
Pears, Pearse

Pearson (English) son of Peter. See also
Pierson.
Pearsson, Pehrson, Peirson

Peder (Scandinavian) a form of Peter.
Peadair, Peadar, Peader, Pedey

Pedro (Spanish) a form of Peter.
Pedrin, Pedrín, Petronio

Peerless (American) incomparable, without a peer.

Peers (English) a form of Peter.
Peerus

Peeter (Estonian) a form of Peter.
Peet

Peirce (English) a form of Peter.
Peirs

Pekelo (Hawaiian) a form of Peter.
Pekeio, Pekka

Peleke (Hawaiian) a form of Frederick.

Pelham (English) tannery town.
Pelhem, Pelhim, Pelhom, Pelhym

Pelí (Latin, Basque) happy.
Pelie, Pely

Pell (English) parchment.
Pall, Pel

Pello (Greek, Basque) stone.
Peru, Piarres

Pelton (English) town by a pool.
Peltan, Pelten, Peltin, Peltyn

Pembroke (Welsh) headland. (French)
wine dealer. (English) broken fence.
Pembrock, Pembrok, Pembrook

Pendle (English) hill.
Pendal, Pendel, Penndal, Penndel, Penndle

Peniamina (Hawaiian) a form of
Benjamin.
*Peni, Penmina, Penminah, Penmyna,
Penmynah*

Penley (English) enclosed meadow.
Penlea, Penlee, Penleigh, Penli, Penlie, Penly

Penn (Latin) pen, quill. (English) enclosure. (German) a short form of Penrod.
Pen, Penna

Penrod (German) famous commander.
Penn, Pennrod, Rod

Pepa (Czech) a familiar form of Joseph.
Pepek, Pepik

Pepe (Spanish) a familiar form of Jose.
*Pepee, Pepey, Pepi, Pepie, Pepillo, Pepito,
Pepy, Pequin, Pipo*

Pepin (German) determined; petitioner.
History: Pepin the Short was an eighth-
century king of the Franks.
Pepan, Pepen, Pepon, Peppie, Peppy, Pepyn

Peppe (Italian) a familiar form of Joseph.
Peppee, Peppey, Peppi, Peppie, Peppo, Peppy

Per (Swedish) a form of Peter.

Perben (Greek, Danish) stone.
Perban, Perbin, Perbon, Perbyn

Percival (French) pierce the valley.
Literature: a knight of the Round
Table who first appears in Chrétien
de Troyes's poem about the quest for
the Holy Grail.
*Parsafal, Parsefal, Parsifal, Parzival, Perc,
Perce, Perceval, Percevall, Percivale, Percivall,
Percyval, Peredur, Purcell*

Percy (French) a familiar form of Percival.
*Pearcey, Pearcy, Percee, Percey, Perci, Percie,
Piercey, Piercy*

Peregrine (Latin) traveler; pilgrim; falcon.
Pelgrim, Pellegrino, Peregrin, Peregryn,
Peregryne, Perergrin, Perergryn

Pericles (Greek) just leader. History: an
Athenian statesman.
Perycles

Perico (Spanish) a form of Peter.
Pequin, Perequin

Perine (Latin) a short form of Peregrine.
Perino, Perion

Perkin (English) little Peter.
Perka, Perkins, Perkyn, Perkyns

Pernell (French) a form of Parnell.
Perren, Perrnall

Perrin (Latin) a short form of Peregrine.
Perryn

Perry (English) a familiar form of
Peregrine, Peter.
Peree, Perey, Peri, Perie, Perree, Perrey, Perri,
Perrie, Perrye, Pery

Perth (Scottish) thorn-bush thicket.
Geography: a burgh in Scotland;
a city in Australia.
Pirth, Pyrth

Pervis (Latin) passage.
Pervez, Pervys

Pesach (Hebrew) spared. Religion:
another name for Passover.
Pesac, Pessach

Petar (Greek) a form of Peter.

Pete (English) a short form of Peter.
Peat, Peate, Peet, Peete, Peit, Peite, Petey,
Peti, Petie, Piet, Pit, Peyt, Pyete

Peter (Greek, Latin) small rock. Bible:
Simon, renamed Peter, was the leader of
the Twelve Apostles. See also Boutros,
Ferris, Takis.
Peater, Peiter, Péter, Peterke, Peterus, Piaras,
Piero, Piter, Piti, Pjeter, Pyeter

Peterson (English) son of Peter.
Peteris, Petersen

Petiri (Shona) where we are.
Petri, Petyri, Petyry

Peton (English) a form of Patton.
Peaten, Peatin, Peaton, Peatun, Peatyn,
Peighton, Peiton, Petan, Peten, Petin,
Petun, Petyn

Petr (Bulgarian) a form of Peter.
Pedr

Petras (Lithuanian) a form of Peter.
Petra, Petrelis

Petros (Greek) a form of Peter.
Petro

Petru (Romanian) a form of Peter.
Petrukas, Petruno, Petrus, Petruso

Petter (Norwegian) a form of Peter.

Peverell (French) piper.
Peverall, Peverel, Peveril, Peveryl

Peyo (Spanish) a form of Peter.

Peyton (English) a form of Patton,
Payton.
Peyt, Peyten, Peython, Peytonn

Pharaoh (Latin) ruler. History: a title for
the ancient kings of Egypt.
Faro, Faroh, Pharo, Pharoah, Pharoh

Phelan (Irish) wolf.
Felan, Pheland

Phelipe (Spanish) a form of Philip.
Phelippe

Phelix (Latin) a form of Felix.
Phelyx

Phelps (English) son of Phillip.
Felps, Phelp

Phil (Greek) a short form of Philip,
Phillip.
Fil, Phill

Philander (Greek) lover of mankind.
Filander, Fylander, Phylander

Philart (Greek) lover of virtue.
Filart, Filarte, Fylart, Fylarte, Phylarte,
Phylart, Phylarte

Philbert (English) a form of Filbert.
Philberte, Philberti, Philberto, Philbirt,
Philbirte, Philburt, Philburte, Philibert,
Philiberte, Philibirt, Philibirte, Philiburt,
Philiburte, Phillbert, Phillberte, Phillbirt,

Philbert (cont.)
*Phillbirte, Phillburt, Phillburte, Phillibert,
Philliberte, Phillibirt, Phillibirte, Philliburt,
Philliburte, Phylbert, Phylberte, Phylbirt,
Phylbirte, Phylburt, Phylburte, Phylibert,
Phyliberte, Phylibirt, Phylibirte, Phyliburt,
Phyliburte, Phyllbert, Phyllberte, Phyllbirt,
Phyllbirte, Phyllburt, Phyllburte, Phyllibert,
Phylliberte, Phyllibirt, Phyllibirte, Phylliburt,
Phylliburte*

Philemon (Greek) kiss.
*Phila, Philamin, Philamina, Philamine,
Philamyn, Phileman, Philémon, Philmon,
Philmyn, Philmyne, Phylmin, Phylmine,
Phylmon, Phylmyn*

Philip (Greek) lover of horses. Bible: one
of the Twelve Apostles. See also Felipe,
Felippo, Filip, Fillipp, Filya, Fischel, Flip.
*Philippo, Phillp, Philp, Phyleap, Phyleep,
Phylip, Phyleap, Phyleep, Phylip, Phylyp,
Pilib, Pippo*

Philipe, Philippe (French) forms of
Philip.
*Phillepe, Phillipe, Phillippe, Phillippee,
Phyllipe*

Philipp (German) a form of Philip.
Phillipp

Phillip (Greek) a form of Philip.
*Phillipp, Phillips, Phylleap, Phylleep, Phyllip,
Phyllyp*

Phillipos (Greek) a form of Phillip.
Philippos

Philly (American) a familiar form of
Philip, Phillip.
Phillie

Philo (Greek) love.
Filo, Fylo, Phylo

Phinean (Irish) a form of Finian.
Phinian, Phinyan, Phynian, Phynyan

Phineas (English) a form of Pinchas. See
also Fineas.
Phinehas, Phinny, Phyneas

Phirun (Cambodian) rain.

Phoenix (Latin) phoenix, a legendary bird.
Phenix, Pheonix, Phynix

Phuok (Vietnamese) good.
Phuoc

Pias (Gypsy) fun.

Pickford (English) ford at the peak.

Pickworth (English) wood cutter's estate.

Picton (English) town on the hill's peak.
*Pictan, Picten, Picktown, Picktun, Picktyn,
Piktan, Pikten, Piktin, Pikton, Piktown,
Piktun, Piktyn, Pyckton, Pyctin, Pycton,
Pyctyn, Pyktin, Pykton, Pyktyn*

Pier Alexander (French) a combination
of Pierre + Alexander.

Pier Luc, Pierre Luc, Pierre-Luc
(French) combinations of Pierre + Luc.
Piere Luc

Pier Olivier, Pierre Olivier (French)
combinations of Pierre + Olivier.

Pierce (English) a form of Peter.
Peerce, Peirce, Piercy

Piero (Italian) a form of Peter.
Pero, Pierro

Pierre (French) a form of Peter.
Peirre, Piere, Pierrot

Pierre Alexan (French) a combination of
Pierre + Alexander.

Pierre Andre (French) a combination of
Pierre + Andre.

Pierre Antoin (French) a combination of
Pierre + Antoine.

Pierre Etienn (French) a combination of
Pierre + Etienne.

Pierre Marc (French) a combination of
Pierre + Marc.

Pierre Yves (French) a combination of
Pierre + Yves.

Piers (English) a form of Peter. A form of
Peers.

Pierson (English) son of Peter. See also
Pearson.
Pierrson, Piersen, Piersson, Piersun, Pyerson

Pieter (Dutch) a form of Peter.
Pietr, Pietrek

Pietro (Italian) a form of Peter.

Pilar (Spanish) pillar.
Pillar, Pylar, Pyllar

Pili (Swahili) second born.
Pyli, Pyly

Pilipo (Hawaiian) a form of Philip.

Pillan (Native American) supreme essence.
Pilan, Pylan, Pyllan

Pin (Vietnamese) faithful boy.
Pyn

Pinchas (Hebrew) oracle. (Egyptian) dark skinned.
Phineas, Pincas, Pinchos, Pincus, Pinkas, Pinkus, Pynchas

Pinky (American) a familiar form of Pinchas.
Pink

Pino (Italian) a form of Joseph.

Piñon (Tupi-Guarani) Mythology: the hunter who became the constellation Orion.

Pio (Latin) pious.
Pyo

Piotr (Bulgarian) a form of Peter.
Piotrek

Pippin (German) father.
Pippyn

Piran (Irish) prayer. Religion: the patron saint of miners.
Peran, Pieran, Pieren, Pieryn, Pyran

Pirrin (Australian) cave.
Pirryn, Pyrrin, Pyrryn

Pirro (Greek, Spanish) flaming hair.
Piro, Pyro, Pyrro

Pista (Hungarian) a familiar form of István.
Pisti

Piti (Spanish) a form of Peter.

Pitin (Spanish) a form of Felix.
Pito

Pitney (English) island of the strong-willed man.
Pitnee, Pitni, Pitnie, Pitny, Pittney, Pytnee, Pytney, Pytni, Pytnie, Pytny

Pitt (English) pit, ditch.
Pit

Placido (Spanish) serene.
Placide, Placidio, Placidus, Placyd, Placydius, Placydo

Plato (Greek) broad shouldered. History: a famous Greek philosopher.
Platan, Platen, Platin, Platon, Platun, Platyn

Platt (French) flatland.
Platte

Plaxico (American) a form of Placido.

Po Sin (Chinese) grandfather elephant.

Pol (Swedish) a form of Paul.
Pól, Pola, Poll, Poul

Poldi (German) a familiar form of Leopold.
Poldo

Pollard (German) close-cropped head.
Polard, Polerd, Pollerd, Pollyrd

Pollock (English) a form of Pollux. Art: American artist Jackson Pollock was a leader of abstract expressionism.
Polick, Pollack, Pollick, Polloch, Pollok, Polock, Polok

Pollux (Greek) crown. Astronomy: one of the stars in the constellation Gemini.
Pollock, Polux

Polo (Tibetan) brave wanderer. (Greek) a short form of Apollo. Culture: a game played on horseback. History: Marco Polo was a thirteenth-century Venetian explorer who traveled throughout Asia.
Pollo

Pomeroy (French) apple orchard.
Pomaroy, Pomaroi, Pomeroi, Pommeray, Pommeroy

Ponce (Spanish) fifth. History: Juan Ponce de León of Spain searched for the Fountain of Youth in Florida.

Pony (Scottish) small horse.
Poni

Porfirio (Greek, Spanish) purple stone.
Porfiryo, Porfryio, Porfryo, Porphirios, Prophyrios

Porter (Latin) gatekeeper.
Port, Portie, Porty

Poshita (Sanskrit) cherished.

Poul (Danish) a form of Paul.
Poulos, Poulus

Pov (Gypsy) earth.

Powa (Native American) wealthy.
Powah

Powell (English) alert.
Powal, Powall, Powel, Powil, Powill, Powyl, Powyll

Prabhjot (Sikh) the light of God.

Pramad (Hindi) rejoicing.

Pravat (Tai) history.

Pravin (Hindi) capable.
Pravyn

Prem (Hindi) love.

Prentice (English) apprentice.
Prent, Prentis, Prentise, Prentiss, Prentyc, Prentyce, Prentys, Prentyse, Printes, Printiss

Prescott (English) priest's cottage. See also Scott.
Prescot, Prestcot, Prestcott

Presley (English) priest's meadow. Music: Elvis Presley was an influential American rock 'n' roll singer.
Preslea, Preslee, Presleigh, Presli, Preslie, Presly, Presslee, Pressley, Prestley, Priestley, Priestly

Preston (English) priest's estate.
Prestan, Presten, Prestin, Prestyn

Prewitt (French) brave little one.
Preuet, Prewet, Prewett, Prewit, Prewyt, Prewytt, Pruit, Pruitt, Pruyt, Pruytt

Price (Welsh) son of the ardent one.
Pryce

Pricha (Tai) clever.

Priest (English) holy man. A short form of Preston.

Primo (Italian) first; premier quality.
Preemo, Premo, Prymo

Prince (Latin) chief; prince.
Prence, Prins, Prinse, Prinz, Prinze, Prynce, Pryns, Prynse

Princeton (English) princely town.
Prenston, Princeston, Princton

Proctor (Latin) official, administrator.
Prockter, Proctar, Procter

Prokopios (Greek) declared leader.

Prosper (Latin) fortunate.
Prospero, Próspero

Pryor (Latin) head of the monastery; prior.
Prior, Pry

Pumeet (Sanskrit) pure.

Purdy (Hindi) recluse.

Purvis (French, English) providing food.
Pervis, Purves, Purvise, Purviss, Purvys, Purvyss

Putnam (English) dweller by the pond.
Putnem, Putnum

Pyotr (Russian) a form of Peter.
Petya, Pyatr

Q

Qabic (Arabic) able.
Quabic, Quabick, Quabik, Quabyc, Quabyck, Quabyk

Qabil (Arabic) able.
Qabill, Qabyl, Qabyll

Qadim (Arabic) ancient.
Quadym

Qadir (Arabic) powerful.
Qaadir, Qadeer, Quaadir, Quadeer, Quadir

Qamar (Arabic) moon.
Quamar, Quamir

Qasim (Arabic) divider.
Qasym, Quasim

Qimat (Hindi) valuable.
Qymat

Quaashie (Ewe) born on Sunday.
Quaashi, Quashi, Quashie

Quadarius (American) a combination of
Quan + Darius.
*Quadara, Quadarious, Quadaris,
Quandarious, Quandarius, Quandarrius,
Qudarius, Qudaruis*

Quade (Latin) fourth.
*Quadell, Quaden, Quadon, Quadre,
Quadrie, Quadrine, Quadrion, Quaid,
Quayd, Quayde, Qwade*

Quain (French) clever.
Quayn

Quamaine (American) a combination of
Quan + Jermaine.
*Quamain, Quaman, Quamane, Quamayne,
Quarmaine*

Quan (Comanche) a short form of
Quanah.

Quanah (Comanche) fragrant.

Quandre (American) a combination of
Quan + Andre.
Quandrae, Quandré

Quant (Greek) how much?
*Quanta, Quantae, Quantah, Quantai,
Quantas, Quantay, Quante, Quantea,
Quantey, Quantu*

Quantavious (American) a form of
Quantavius.

Quantavius (American) a combination of
Quan + Octavius.
*Quantavian, Quantavin, Quantavion,
Quantavis, Quantavous, Quatavious,
Quatavius*

Quantez (American) a form of Quant.

Quashawn (American) a combination of
Quan + Shawn.
*Quasean, Quashaan, Quashan, Quashaun,
Quashaunn, Quashon, Quashone, Quashun,
Queshan, Queshon, Qweshawn, Qyshawn*

Qudamah (Arabic) courage.
Qudam, Qudama

Quenby (Scandinavian) a form of
Quimby.
*Quenbee, Quenbey, Quenbi, Quenbie,
Quinbee, Quinby, Quynbee, Quynbey,
Quynbi, Quynbie, Quynby*

Quennell (French) small oak.
*Quenal, Quenall, Quenel, Quenell,
Quennal, Quennall, Quennel*

Quenten, Quenton (Latin) forms of
Quentin.
Quienten, Quienton

Quentin (Latin) fifth. (English) queen's
town.
*Qeuntin, Quantin, Queintin, Quent,
Quentan, Quentine, Quentyn, Quentynn,
Quientin, Quintan, Quyntan, Quyntyn,
Qwentan, Qwentin, Qwentyn, Qwyntan,
Qwyntyn*

Quest (Latin) quest.

Quico (Spanish) a familiar form of many
names.

Quigley (Irish) maternal side.
*Quiglea, Quiglee, Quigleigh, Quigli,
Quiglie, Quigly*

Quillan (Irish) cub.
*Quilan, Quilen, Quilin, Quill, Quille,
Quillen, Quillin, Quillyn, Quilyn*

Quillon (Latin) sword.
Quilon, Quyllon, Quylon

Quimby (Scandinavian) woman's estate.
*Quenby, Quembee, Quembey, Quemby,
Quymbee, Quymbey, Quymbi, Quymbie,
Quymby*

Quin (Irish) a form of Quinn.

Quincey (French) a form of Quincy.

Quincy (French) fifth son's estate.
Quenci, Quency, Quince, Quincee, Quinci,
Quinncy, Quinnsey, Quinnsy, Quinsey,
Quinzy, Quyncee, Quyncey, Quynnsey,
Quynnsy, Quynsy

Quindarius (American) a combination of
Quinn + Darius.
Quindarious, Quindarrius, Quinderious,
Quinderus, Quindrius

Quinlan (Irish) strong; well shaped.
Quindlen, Quinlen, Quinlin, Quinnlan,
Quinnlin, Quynlan, Quynlen, Quynlin,
Quynlon, Quynlyn

Quinn (Irish) a short form of Quincy,
Quinlan, Quinten.
Quyn, Quynn

Quintavious (American) a form of
Quintavius.

Quintavis (American) a form of
Quintavius.

Quintavius (American) a combination of
Quinn + Octavius.
Quintavus, Quintayvious

Quinten, Quintin, Quinton (Latin)
forms of Quentin.
Quinneton, Quinnten, Quinntin,
Quinnton, Quint, Quintan, Quintann,
Quintine, Quintion, Quintus, Quintyn,
Quiton, Qunton, Quynten, Quyntin,
Quynton, Qwenten, Qwentin, Qwenton,
Qwinton, Qwynten, Qwyntin, Qwynton

Quiqui (Spanish) a familiar form of
Enrique.
Quinto, Quiquin, Quyquy

Quitin (Latin) a short form of Quinten.
Quiten, Quito, Quiton

Quito (Spanish) a short form of Quinten.

Quoc (Vietnamese) nation.

Quon (Chinese) bright.

Ra'shawn, Rashaan, Rashaun, Rashon
(American) forms of Rashawn.
Rasaun, Rashann, Rashion, Rashone,
Rashonn, Rashuan, Rashun, Rhashaun

Raamah (Hebrew) thunder.
Raama, Rama, Ramah

Raanan (Hebrew) fresh; luxuriant.
Ranan

Rabi (Arabic) breeze. (Scottish) famous.
Rabbi, Rabby, Rabee, Rabeeh, Rabey,
Rabiah, Rabie, Rabih, Raby

Race (English) race.
Racee, Racel

Racham (Hebrew) compassionate.
Rachaman, Rachamim, Rachamin,
Rachamyn, Rachim, Rachman, Rachmiel,
Rachmyel, Rachum, Raham, Rahamim,
Rahamym

Rachel (Hebrew) sheep.

Rad (English) advisor. (Slavic) happy.
Raad, Radd, Raddie, Raddy, Rade, Radee,
Radell, Radey, Radi

Radbert (English) brilliant advisor.
Radbirt, Radburt, Radbyrt, Raddbert,
Raddbirt, Raddburt, Raddbyrt

Radburn (English) red brook; brook with
reeds.
Radbern, Radborn, Radborne, Radbourn,
Radbourne, Radburne, Radbyrn, Radbyrne

Radcliff (English) red cliff; cliff with reeds.
Radclif, Radcliffe, Radclith, Radclithe,
Radclyffe, Radclyth, Redclif, Redcliff,
Redcliffe, Redclyth

Radek (Czech) famous ruler.
Radec, Radeque

Radford (English) red ford; ford with
reeds.

Radley (English) red meadow; meadow
of reeds. See also Redley.
Radlea, Radlee, Radleigh, Radly

Radman (Slavic) joyful.
*Raddman, Radmen, Radmon, Reddman,
Redman*

Radnor (English) red shore; shore with
reeds.
Radnore, Rednor, Rednore

Radomil (Slavic) happy peace.
Radomyl

Radoslaw (Polish) happy glory.
Rado, Radoslav, Radzmir, Slawek

Radwan (Arabic) pleasant, delightful.
Radwen, Radwin, Radwon, Radwyn

Raekwon, Raequan (American) forms of
Raquan.
*Raekwan, Raequon, Raeqwon, Raikwan,
Raiquan, Raiquen, Raiqoun, Rakwane,
Rakwon*

Raeshawn (American) a form of
Rashawn.
Raesean, Raeshaun, Raeshon, Raeshun

Rafael (Spanish) a form of Raphael. See
also Falito.
*Rafaell, Rafaello, Rafaelo, Rafeal, Rafeé,
Rafello, Raffaell, Raffaello, Raffaelo, Raffeal,
Raffel, Raffiel, Rafiel*

Rafaele, Raffaele (Italian) forms of
Raphael.
Raffael

Rafaelle (French) a form of Raphael.
Rafelle

Rafal (Polish) a form of Raphael.
Rafel

Rafe (English) a short form of Rafferty,
Ralph.
Raff, Raffe

Rafer (Irish) a short form of Rafferty.
Raffer

Rafferty (Irish) rich, prosperous.
*Rafe, Rafer, Rafertee, Rafertey, Raferti,
Rafertie, Raferty, Raffarty*

Raffi (Hebrew, Arabic) a form of Rafi.
Raffee, Raffey, Raffie, Raffy

Rafi (Arabic) exalted. (Hebrew) a familiar
form of Raphael.
Rafee, Rafey, Rafie, Rafy

Rafiq (Arabic) friend.
*Raafiq, Rafeeq, Rafic, Rafique, Rafyq,
Rafyque*

Raghib (Arabic) desirous.
Raghyb, Raquib, Raquyb

Raghnall (Irish) wise power.
Raghnal, Ragnal, Ragnall

Ragnar (Norwegian) powerful army.
Ragner, Ragnir, Ragnor, Ragnyr, Ranieri

Rago (Hausa) ram.

Raheem (Punjabi) compassionate God.

Raheim (Punjabi) a form of Raheem.

Rahim (Arabic) merciful.
*Raaheim, Rahaeim, Raheam, Rahiem,
Rahiim, Rahime, Rahium*

Rahman (Arabic) compassionate.
*Rahmatt, Rahmen, Rahmet, Rahmin,
Rahmon, Rahmyn*

Rahsaan (American) a form of Rashean.

Rahul (Arabic) traveler.

Raíd (Arabic) leader.
Rayd

Raiden (Japanese) Mythology: the thun-
der god.
*Raedan, Raeden, Raedin, Raedon, Raedyn,
Raidan, Raidin, Raidon, Raidyn, Reidan,
Reiden, Reidin, Reidon, Reidyn*

Raimondo (Italian) a form of Raymond.
Raymondo, Reimundo

Raimund (German) a form of Raymond.
Rajmund

Raimundo (Portuguese, Spanish) a form
of Raymond.
Mundo, Raimon, Raimond, Raimonds

Raine (English) lord; wise.
Raen, Raene, Rain, Raines

Rainer (German) counselor.
*Rainar, Raineier, Rainey, Rainier, Rainieri,
Rayner, Reinar*

Rainey (German) a familiar form of Rainer.
Rainee, Rainie, Rainney, Rainy, Raynee, Rayney, Rayni, Raynie, Rayny, Reiny

Raini (Tupi-Guarani) Religion: the god who created the world.

Rainier (French) a form of Rainer.
Ranier, Raynier, Reignier, Reinier

Rainieri (Italian) a form of Rainer.
Rainierie

Raishawn (American) a form of Rashawn.
Raishon, Raishun

Raj (Hindi) a short form of Rajah.

Rajabu (Swahili) born in the seventh month of the Islamic calendar.

Rajah (Hindi) prince; chief.
Raja, Rajaah, Rajae, Rajahe, Raje, Rajeh, Raji

Rajak (Hindi) cleansing.

Rajan (Hindi) a form of Rajah.
Rajaahn, Rajain, Rajen, Rajin

Rakeem (Punjabi) a form of Raheem.
Rakeeme, Rakeim, Rakem

Rakim (Arabic) a form of Rahim.
Rakiim

Rakin (Arabic) respectable.
Rakeen, Rakyn

Raktim (Hindi) bright red.
Raktym

Raleigh (English) a form of Rawleigh.
Raelea, Raelee, Raeleigh, Raeley, Railea, Railee, Raileigh, Railey, Ralegh, Raylea, Raylee, Rayleigh, Rayley

Ralph (English) wolf counselor.
Radolphus, Radulf, Rafe, Ralf, Ralpheal, Ralphel

Ralphie (English) a familiar form of Ralph.
Ralphy

Ralston (English) Ralph's settlement.
Ralfston, Ralfstone, Ralfton, Ralftone, Ralphstone, Ralphton, Ralphtone, Ralstone, Ralstyn

Ram (Hindi) god; godlike. Religion: another name for the Hindu god Rama. (English) male sheep. A short form of Ramsey.
Ramie

Ramadan (Arabic) ninth month in the Islamic calendar.
Rama

Ramanan (Hindi) god; godlike.
Raman, Ramanjit, Ramanjot

Ramandeep (Hindi) a form of Ramanan.

Rambert (German) strong; brilliant.
Rambirt, Ramburt, Rambyrt

Rami (Hindi, English) a form of Ram. (Spanish) a short form of Ramiro.
Rame, Ramee, Ramey, Ramih

Ramiro (Portuguese, Spanish) supreme judge.
Ramario, Rameer, Rameir, Ramere, Rameriz, Ramero, Ramires, Ramirez, Ramos, Ramyro

Ramon, Ramón (Spanish) forms of Raymond.
Raman, Ramin, Ramyn, Remon, Remone, Romon, Romone

Ramond (Dutch) a form of Raymond.

Ramone (Dutch) a form of Raymond.
Raemon, Raemonn, Ramonte, Remone

Ramsden (English) valley of rams.
Ramsdan, Ramsdin, Ramsdon, Ramsdyn

Ramsey (English) ram's island.
Ramsay, Ramsee, Ramsi, Ramsie, Ramsy

Ramy (Hindi, English) a form of Ram.

Ramzi (American) a form of Ramsey.
Ramzee, Ramzey, Ramzy

Rance (American) a familiar form of Laurence. (English) a short form of Ransom.

Rancel, Rancell, Rances, Rancey, Rancie, Rancy, Ransel, Ransell

Rand (English) shield; warrior.

Randal, Randell (English) forms of Randall.
Randahl, Randale, Randel, Randl, Randle

Randall (English) a form of Randolph.
Randyll

Randeep (Sikh) battle lamp.

Randolph (English) shield wolf.
Randol, Randolf, Randolfe, Randolfo, Randolphe, Randolpho, Randolphus, Randulf, Randulfe, Randulph, Randulphe, Ranolph

Randy (English) a familiar form of Rand, Randall, Randolph.
Randdy, Randee, Randey, Randi, Randie, Ranndy

Ranen (Hebrew) joyful.
Ranan, Ranin, Ranon, Ranun, Ranyn

Ranger (French) forest keeper.
Rainger, Range, Raynger, Reinger, Reynger

Rangle (American) cowboy. See also Wrangle.
Ranglar, Rangler

Rangsey (Cambodian) seven kinds of colors.
Rangsea, Rangsee, Rangseigh, Rangsi, Rangsie, Rangsy

Rani (Hebrew) my song; my joy.
Ranee, Raney, Ranie, Rany, Roni

Ranieri (Italian) a form of Ragnar.
Raneir, Ranier, Rannier

Ranjan (Hindi) delighted; gladdened.

Rankin (English) small shield.
Randkin, Rankyn

Ransford (English) raven's ford.
Ransforde, Rensford, Rensforde

Ransley (English) raven's field.
Ranslea, Ranslee, Ransleigh, Ransli, Ranslie, Ransly, Renslee, Rensleigh, Rensley, Rensli, Renslie, Rensly

Ransom (Latin) redeemer. (English) son of the shield.
Randsom, Randsome, Ransome, Ranson

Raoul (French) a form of Ralph, Rudolph.
Raol, Reuel

Raphael (Hebrew) God has healed. Bible: one of the archangels. Art: a prominent painter of the Renaissance. See also Falito, Rafi.
Raphaél, Raphale, Raphaello, Raphel, Raphello, Raphiel, Rephael

Rapheal (Hebrew) a form of Raphael.
Rafel, Raphiel

Rapier (French) blade-sharp.
Rapyer

Raquan (American) a combination of the prefix Ra + Quan.
Raaquan, Rackwon, Racquan, Rahquan, Raquané, Raquon, Raquwan, Raquwn, Raquwon, Raqwan, Raqwann

Rashaad, Rashaud, Rashod (Arabic) forms of Rashad.
Rachaud, Rashaude, Rashoda, Rashodd, Rashoud, Rayshod, Reyshaad, Reyshod, Rhashod

Rashad (Arabic) wise counselor.
Raashad, Rachad, Rachard, Raeshad, Raishard, Rashaad, Rashadd, Rashade, Rashaud, Rasheed, Rashod, Reshad, Rhashad

Rashan (American) a form of Rashawn.

Rashard (American) a form of Richard.
Rasharrd

Rashawn (American) a combination of the prefix Ra + Shawn.
Rasaan, Raashawn, Raashen, Raeshawn, Rahshawn, Raishawn, Rasawn, Rashaughn, Rashaw, Rashun, Rashunn, Raushan, Raushawn, Rhashan, Rhashawn

Rashean (American) a combination of the prefix Ra + Sean.
Rahsean, Rahseen, Rasean, Rashane, Rashien, Rashiena

Rasheed (Arabic) a form of Rashad.
Rashead, Rashed, Rasheid, Rasheyd,
Rhasheed

Rasheen (American) a form of Rashean.

Rashid (Arabic) a form of Rashad.
Rasheyd, Rashied, Rashyd, Raushaid

Rashida (Swahili) righteous.
Rashidah, Rashieda

Rashidi (Swahili) wise counselor.

Rasmus (Greek, Danish) a short form of
Erasmus.

Raul (French) a form of Ralph.
Raúl

Raulas (Lithuanian) a form of Laurence.

Raulo (Lithuanian) a form of Laurence.

Raven (English) a short form of Ravenel.
Ravan, Ravean, Raveen, Ravin, Ravine,
Ravyn, Ravynn, Reven, Rhaven

Ravenel (English) raven.
Ravenell, Revenel

Ravi (Hindi) sun.
Ravee, Ravijot, Ravy

Ravid (Hebrew) a form of Arvid.
Ravyd

Raviv (Hebrew) rain, dew.
Ravyv

Ravon (English) a form of Raven.
Raveon, Ravion, Ravone, Ravonn,
Ravonne, Revon

Rawdon (English) rough hill.
Rawdan, Rawden, Rawdin, Rawdyn

Rawleigh (English) deer meadow.
Rawle, Rawlea, Rawlee, Rawley, Rawli,
Rawlie, Rawly

Rawlins (French) a form of Roland.
Rawlin, Rawling, Rawlings, Rawlinson,
Rawlyn, Rawlyng, Rawlyngs, Rawson

Ray (French) kingly, royal. (English) a
short form of Rayburn, Raymond. See
also Lei.
Rae, Rai, Raie, Raye

Rayan (Irish) a form of Ryan.
Rayaun

Rayburn (English) deer brook.
Burney, Raeborn, Raeborne, Raebourn,
Raebourne, Raeburn, Raeburne, Raibourn,
Raibourne, Raiburn, Raiburne, Raybourn,
Raybourne, Rayburne, Reibourn, Reibourne,
Reiburn, Reiburne, Reybourn, Reybourne,
Reyburn, Reyburne

Rayce (English) a form of Race.

Rayden (Japanese) a form of Raiden.
Raydun, Rayedon, Reydan, Reyden,
Reydin, Reydon, Reydyn

Rayfield (English) stream in the field.
Raefield, Raifield, Reifield, Reyfield

Rayford (English) stream ford.
Raeford, Raeforde, Raiford, Raiforde,
Reiford, Reiforde, Reyford, Reyforde

Rayhan (Arabic) favored by God.
Raehan, Raihan, Rayhaan

Rayi (Hebrew) my friend, my companion.

Raymon (English) a form of Raymond.
Raeman, Raemen, Raemin, Raemon,
Raemyn, Raiman, Raimen, Raimin,
Raimon, Raimyn, Rayman, Raymann,
Raymen, Raymin, Raymone, Raymun,
Raymyn, Reaman, Reamon, Reamonn,
Reamyn, Reymon, Reymun

Raymond (English) mighty; wise protec-
tor. See also Ayman.
Radmond, Raemond, Ramonde, Raymand,
Rayment, Raymont, Raymund, Raymunde,
Redmond, Reimond, Reimund

Raymundo (Spanish) a form of
Raymond. (Portuguese, Spanish)
a form of Raimundo.
Raemondo, Raimondo, Raymondo

Raynaldo (Spanish) a form of Reynold.
Raynal, Raynald, Raynold

Raynard (French) a form of Renard,
Reynard.
Raynarde

Rayne (English) a form of Raine.
Rayn, Rayno

Rayner (German) a form of Rainer.
Raynar, Reynar, Reyner, Reynir

Raynor (Scandinavian) a form of Ragnar.
Rainor, Reynor

Rayquan (American) a combination of
Ray + Quan.

Raysean, Rayshaun, Rayshon (American)
forms of Rayshawn.
Rayshonn

Rayshawn (American) a combination of
Ray + Shawn.
*Rayshaan, Rayshan, Raysheen, Rayshone,
Rayshun, Rayshunn*

Rayshod (American) a form of Rashad.
*Raeshod, Raishod, Raychard, Rayshad,
Rayshard, Rayshaud*

Rayvon (American) a form of Ravon.
*Rayvan, Rayvaun, Rayven, Rayvone,
Reyven, Reyvon*

Razi (Aramaic) my secret.
Raz, Razee, Razey, Razie, Raziq, Razy

Raziel (Aramaic) a form of Razi.

Read (English) a form of Reed, Reid.
Raed, Raede, Raeed, Reaad, Reade

Reading (English) son of the red
wanderer.
Redding, Reeding, Reiding

Reagan (Irish) little king. History:
Ronald Wilson Reagan was the fortieth
U.S. president.
*Raegan, Raegin, Raegon, Raegyn, Raigan,
Raigen, Raigin, Raigon, Raigyn, Raygan,
Raygen, Raygin, Raygon, Raygyn, Reagen,
Reaghan, Reegan, Reegen, Reegin, Reegon,
Reegyn, Reigan, Reigen, Reighan, Reigin,
Reign, Reigon, Reigyn, Reygan, Reygen,
Reygin, Reygon, Reygyn, Rheagan*

Real (Latin) real.

Rebel (American) rebel.
Reb, Rebell, Rebil, Rebill, Rebyl, Rebyll

Red (American) red, redhead.
Redd

Reda (Arabic) satisfied.
Redah, Rida, Ridah, Ridha

Redford (English) red river crossing.
Ford, Radford, Reaford, Red, Redd

Redley (English) red meadow; meadow
with reeds. See also Radley.
*Redlea, Redlee, Redleigh, Redli, Redlie,
Redly*

Redmond (German) protecting counselor.
(English) a form of Raymond.
*Radmond, Radmondo, Radmun, Radmund,
Radmundo, Reddin, Redmon, Redmondo,
Redmun, Redmund, Redmundo*

Redpath (English) red path.
Raddpath, Radpath, Reddpath

Reece (Welsh) enthusiastic; stream.
Reace, Rece, Reice, Reyce, Ryese

Reed (English) a form of Reid.
Raeed, Reyde, Rheed

Rees, Reese (Welsh) forms of Reece.
Rease, Reis, Reise, Reiss, Reyse, Riese, Riess

Reeve (English) steward.
*Reav, Reave, Reaves, Reeves, Reive, Reyve,
Rhyve*

Reg (English) a short form of Reginald.
Regg

Regan (Irish) a form of Reagan.
Regen, Regin, Regon, Regyn

Reggie (English) a familiar form of
Reginald.
Reggi, Reggy, Regi, Regie, Regy

Reginal (English) a form of Reginald.
Reginale, Reginel

Reginald (English) king's advisor. A form
of Reynold. See also Naldo.
*Regginald, Reginaldo, Reginalt, Reginauld,
Reginault, Reginold, Reginuld, Regnauld,
Ryginald, Ryginaldo*

Regis (Latin) regal.
Reggis, Regiss, Regys, Regyss

Rehema (Swahili) second-born.
Rehemah

Rei (Japanese) rule, law.

Reid (English) redhead.
Reide, Reyd, Reyde, Ried

Reidar (Norwegian) nest warrior.
  Reydar

Reilly (Irish) a form of Riley.
  Reilea, Reilee, Reileigh, Reiley, Reili, Reilie, Reillea, Reillee, Reilleigh, Reilley, Reilli, Reillie, Reily

Reinaldo (Spanish) a form of Reynold.
  Reinaldos

Reinhart (German) a form of Reynard. (English) a form of Reynold.
  Rainart, Rainert, Rainhard, Rainhardt, Rainhart, Reinart, Reinhard, Reinhardt, Renke, Reynart, Reynhard, Reynhardt

Reinhold (Swedish) a form of Ragnar. (English) a form of Reynold.
  Reinold

Reku (Finnish) a form of Richard.

Remi, Rémi (French) forms of Remy.
  Remie, Remmi, Remmie

Remington (English) raven estate.
  Rem, Reminton, Tony

Remus (Latin) speedy, quick. Mythology: Remus and his twin brother, Romulus, founded Rome.
  Remas, Remos

Remy (French) from Rheims, France.
  Ramey, Remee, Remey, Remmee, Remmey, Remmy

Renaldo (Spanish) a form of Reynold.
  Rainaldo, Ranaldo, Raynaldo, Reynoldo, Rinaldo, Rynaldo

Renard (French) a form of Reynard.
  Ranard, Reinard, Rennard

Renardo (Italian) a form of Reynard.

Renato (Italian) reborn.
  Renat, Renatis, Renatus, Renatys

Renaud (French) a form of Reynard, Reynold.
  Renauld, Renauldo, Renault, Renould

Rendor (Hungarian) policeman.
  Rendar, Render, Rendir, Rendyr

Rene (French) a form of René.

René (French) reborn.
  Renay, Renne

Renee (French) a form of René. (Irish, French) a form of Renny.

Renfred (English) lasting peace.
  Ranfred, Ranfrid, Ranfryd, Rinfred, Rinfryd, Ronfred, Ronfryd, Rynfred, Rynfryd

Renfrew (Welsh) raven woods.
  Ranfrew

Renjiro (Japanese) virtuous.
  Renjyro

Renny (Irish) small but strong. (French) a familiar form of René.
  Ren, Reney, Reni, Renie, Renn, Rennee, Renney, Renni, Rennie, Reny

Reno (American) gambler. Geography: a city in Nevada known for gambling.
  Renos, Rino, Ryno

Renshaw (English) raven woods.
  Ranshaw, Renishaw, Renshore

Renton (English) settlement of the roe deer.
  Rentown

Renzo (Latin) a familiar form of Laurence. (Italian) a short form of Lorenzo.
  Renz, Renzy, Renzzo

Reshad (American) a form of Rashad.
  Reshade, Reshard, Resharrd, Reshaud, Reshawd, Reshead, Reshod

Reshawn (American) a combination of the prefix Re + Shawn.
  Reshaun, Reshaw, Reshon, Reshun

Reshean (American) a combination of the prefix Re + Sean.
  Resean, Reshae, Reshane, Reshay, Reshayne, Reshea, Resheen, Reshey

Reuben (Hebrew) behold a son.
  Reuban, Reubin, Rheuben, Rhuben

Reuven (Hebrew) a form of Reuben.
  Reuvin, Rouvin, Ruvim

Rex (Latin) king.
  Rexx

Rexford (English) king's ford.
Rexforde

Rexton (English) king's town.

Rey (Spanish) a short form of Reynaldo, Reynard, Reynold. (French) a form of Roy.

Reyes (English) a form of Reece.
Reyce

Reyhan (Arabic) favored by God.
Reihan, Reyham

Reymond (English) a form of Raymond.
Reymon, Reymound, Reymund

Reymundo (Spanish) a form of Raymond.
Reimonde, Reimundo, Reymondo

Reynaldo (Spanish) a form of Reynold.
Reynaldos, Reynauldo

Reynard (French) wise; bold, courageous.
Raenard, Rainard, Reinhard, Reinhardt, Reinhart, Reiyard, Rennard, Reynardo, Reynaud

Reynold (English) king's advisor. See also Reginald.
Raenold, Rainault, Rainhold, Rainold, Ranald, Raynaldo, Raynold, Reinald, Reinwald, Renald, Renaldi, Renauld, Rennold, Renold, Reynald, Reynol, Reynolds, Rinaldo

Réz (Hungarian) copper; redhead.
Rezsö

Reza (German) a form of Resi (see Girls' Names).

Rezin (Hebrew) pleasant, delightful.
Rezan, Rezen, Rezi, Rezie, Rezon, Rezy, Rezyn

Rhett (Welsh) a form of Rhys. Literature: Rhett Butler was the hero of Margaret Mitchell's novel *Gone with the Wind*.
Rhet

Rhodes (Greek) where roses grow. Geography: an island of southeast Greece.
Rhoads, Rhodas, Rodas

Rhyan (Irish) a form of Ryan.
Rhian

Rhys (Welsh) a form of Reece.
Rhyce, Rhyse

Rian (Irish) little king. See also Ryan.
Rien, Rion, Riun, Riyn, Rhian, Rhien, Rhion, Rhiun, Rhiyn

Ric (Italian, Spanish) a short form of Rico. (German, English) a form of Rick.
Ricca

Ricardo, Riccardo (Portuguese, Spanish) forms of Richard.
Racardo, Recard, Recardo, Ricaldo, Ricard, Ricardoe, Ricardos, Riccard, Riccarrdo, Ricciardo, Richardo, Rickardo, Rikardo, Rychardo, Ryckardo, Rykardo

Ricco, Rico (Italian) short forms of Enrico. (Spanish) familiar forms of Richard.
Rycco, Ryco

Rice (English) rich, noble. (Welsh) a form of Reece.
Ryce

Rich (English) a short form of Richard.
Ritch, Rych

Richard (English) a form of Richart. See also Aric, Dick, Juku, Likeke.
Richar, Richards, Richardson, Richaud, Richer, Richerd, Richird, Richshard, Rickert, Rihardos, Rihards, Riocard, Riócard, Risa, Risardas, Rishard, Ristéard, Rostik, Rychard, Rychardt, Rychird, Rychyrd, Rysio, Ryszard

Richart (German) rich and powerful ruler.

Richie (English) a familiar form of Richard.
Richee, Richey, Richi, Richy, Rychee, Rychey, Rychi, Rychie, Rychy

Richman (English) powerful.
Richmen, Richmun, Rychman, Rychmen, Rychmon, Rychmun

Richmond (German) powerful protector.
Richmand, Richmando, Richmon, Richmondo, Richmondt, Richmound, Richmund, Richmundo, Rychmand, Rychmond, Rychmondo, Rychmont, Rychmund, Rychmundo, Rychmunt

Rick (German, English) a short form of Cedric, Frederick, Richard.
Ricke, Ricks, Rik, Riki, Ryc, Ryck, Ryk, Rykk

Rickard (Swedish) a form of Richard.
Ryckard

Ricker (English) powerful army.
Rickar, Rikar, Ryckar, Rykar

Rickey, Ricki, Rickie, Ricky (English) familiar forms of Richard, Rick.
Ricci, Rickee, Riczi

Rickward (English) mighty guardian.
Rickwerd, Rickwood, Ricward, Ryckward, Rycward

Rida (Arabic) favor.
Ridah, Ryda, Rydah

Riddock (Irish) smooth field.
Riddick, Riddoc, Riddok, Ridoc, Ridock, Ridok, Rydoc, Rydock, Rydok

Rider (English) horseman.
Ridder, Ridar, Ridder, Rydar

Ridge (English) ridge of a cliff.
Ridgy, Rig, Rydge

Ridgeley (English) meadow near the ridge.
Ridgeleigh, Ridglea, Ridglee, Ridgleigh, Ridgley, Ridgli, Ridglie, Ridgly, Rydglea, Rydglee, Rydgleigh, Rydgley, Rydgli, Rydglie, Rydgly

Ridgeway (English) path along the ridge.
Rydgeway

Ridley (English) meadow of reeds.
Rhidley, Riddley, Ridlea, Ridlee, Ridleigh, Ridli, Ridlie, Ridly

Riel (Spanish) a short form of Gabriel.
Reil, Reill, Riell, Rielle, Ryel, Ryell, Ryelle

Rigby (English) ruler's valley.
Rigbee, Rigbey, Rigbi, Rigbie, Rygbee, Rygbey, Rygbi, Rygbie, Rygby

Rigel (Arabic) foot. Astronomy: one of the stars in the constellation Orion.
Rygel

Rigg (English) ridge.
Rig, Riggs, Ryg, Rygg, Ryggs, Rygs

Rigo (Italian) a form of Rigg.

Rigoberto (German) splendid; wealthy.
Rigobert

Rikard (Scandinavian) a form of Richard.
Rikárd, Rykard

Riker (American) a form of Ryker.

Riki, Rikki (Estonian) forms of Rick.
Rikkey, Rikky, Riks, Riky

Riley (Irish) valiant.
Rhiley, Rhylee, Rhyley, Rieley, Rielly, Riely, Rilee, Rilley, Rily, Rilye

Rinaldo (Italian) a form of Reynold.
Rinald, Rinaldi

Ring (English) ring.
Ryng

Ringo (Japanese) apple. (English) a familiar form of Ring.
Ryngo

Rio (Spanish) river. Geography: Rio de Janeiro is a city in Brazil.

Riordan (Irish) bard, royal poet.
Rearden, Reardin, Reardon, Ryordan

Rip (Dutch) ripe; full grown. (English) a short form of Ripley.
Ripp, Ryp, Rypp

Ripley (English) meadow near the river.
Rip, Riplea, Riplee, Ripleigh, Ripli, Riplie, Riply, Ripplee, Rippleigh, Rippley, Rippli, Ripplie, Ripply, Ryplea, Ryplee, Rypleigh, Rypley, Rypli, Ryplie, Ryply, Rypplea, Rypplee, Ryppleigh, Ryppley, Ryppli, Rypplie, Rypply

Riqui (Spanish) a form of Rickey.

Rishad (American) a form of Rashad.
Rishaad

Rishawn (American) a combination of the prefix Ri + Shawn.
Rishan, Rishaun, Rishon, Rishone

Rishi (Hindi) sage. (English) a form of Richie.
Ryshi

Risley (English) meadow with shrubs. See also Wrisley.

Rislea, Rislee, Risleigh, Risli, Rislie, Risly, Ryslea, Ryslee, Rysleigh, Rysley, Rysli, Ryslie, Rysly

Risto (Finnish) a short form of Christopher.
Rysto

Riston (English) settlement near the shrubs. See also Wriston.
Ryston

Ritchard (English) a form of Richard.
Ritchardt, Ritcherd, Ritchyrd, Ritshard, Ritsherd

Ritchie (English) a form of Richie.
Ritchee, Ritchey, Ritchi, Ritchy

Rithisak (Cambodian) powerful.

Ritter (German) knight; chivalrous.
Rittar, Rittner, Ryttar, Rytter

River (English) river; riverbank.
Rivar, Rive, Rivers, Riviera, Rivor, Ryv, Ryver

Riyad (Arabic) gardens.
Riad, Riyaad, Riyadh, Riyaz, Riyod

Roald (Norwegian) famous ruler.

Roan (English) a short form of Rowan.
Rhoan, Roen

Roar (Norwegian) praised warrior.
Roary

Roarke (Irish) famous ruler.
Roark, Rork, Rorke, Rourk, Rourke, Ruark

Rob (English) a short form of Robert.
Rab, Robb, Robe

Robbie, Robby (English) familiar forms of Robert.
Rabbie, Raby, Rhobbie, Robbee, Robbey, Robbi, Robee, Robey, Robhy, Robi, Robie, Roby

Robert (English) famous brilliance. See also Bobek, Dob, Lopaka.
Bob, Bobby, Riobard, Riobart, Robars, Robart, Rober, Roberd, Robers, Roberte, Robirt, Robyrt, Roibeárd, Rosertas, Rudbert

Roberto (Italian, Portuguese, Spanish) a form of Robert.
Robertino, Ruberto

Roberts, Robertson (English) son of Robert.
Roberson, Robertas, Robirtson, Roburtson, Robyrtson

Robin (English) a short form of Robert.
Roban, Robban, Robben, Robbin, Robbon, Roben, Robinet, Robinn, Robon, Roibín

Robinson (English) a form of Roberts.
Robbins, Robbinson, Robens, Robenson, Robeson, Robins, Robson, Robynson

Robyn (English) a form of Robin.
Robbyn

Rocco (Italian) rock.
Rocca, Rocio, Rocko, Rokko, Roko

Roch (English) a form of Rock.

Rochester (English) rocky fortress.
Chester, Chet

Rock (English) a short form of Rockwell.
Roc, Rok

Rockford (English) rocky ford.

Rockland (English) rocky land.
Rocklan

Rockledge (English) rocky ledge.

Rockley (English) rocky field.
Rockle, Rocklea, Rocklee, Rockleigh, Rockli, Rocklie, Rockly

Rockwell (English) rocky spring. Art: Norman Rockwell was a well-known twentieth-century American illustrator.
Rockwel, Rocwel, Rocwell, Rokwel, Rokwell

Rocky (American) a familiar form of Rocco, Rock.
Rockee, Rockey, Rocki, Rockie, Rokee, Rokey, Roki, Rokie, Roky

Rod (English) a short form of Penrod, Roderick, Rodney.
Rodd

Rodas (Greek, Spanish) a form of Rhodes.

Roddy (English) a familiar form of Roderick.
Roddie, Rody

Roden (English) red valley. Art: Auguste
Rodin was an innovative French
sculptor.
*Rodan, Rodden, Rodin, Rodon, Rodyn,
Roedan, Roeddan, Roedden, Roeddin,
Roeddon, Roeddyn, Roeden, Roedin,
Roedon, Roedyn*

Roderich (German) a form of Roderick.

Roderick (German) famous ruler. See
also Broderick, Rodrik.
*Rhoderic, Rhoderick, Rhoderik, Rhoderyc,
Rhoderyck, Rhoderyk, Rodaric, Rodarick,
Rodarik, Rodderick, Roderic, Roderik,
Roderikus, Roderrick, Roderyc, Roderyck,
Roderyk, Rodgrick, Rodrugue, Roodney,
Rurik, Ruy*

Rodger (German) a form of Roger.
Rodge, Rodgir, Rodgy, Rodgyr

Rodman (German) famous man, hero.
Rodmann, Rodmond

Rodney (English) island clearing.
*Rhodney, Roddnee, Roddney, Roddni,
Roddnie, Roddny, Rodnee, Rodnei, Rodni,
Rodnie, Rodnne, Rodny*

Rodolfo (Spanish) a form of Rudolph,
Rudolpho.
Rodolpho, Rodulfo

Rodrick (German) a form of Rodrik.
*Roddrick, Rodric, Rodrich, Rodrique,
Rodryc, Rodryck*

Rodrigo (Italian, Spanish) a form of
Roderick.
Roderigo, Rodrigue

Rodriguez (Spanish) son of Rodrigo.
Roddrigues, Rodrigues

Rodrik (German) famous ruler. See also
Roderick.
Rodricki, Rodryk

Rodriquez (Spanish) a form of Rodriguez.
Rodrigquez, Rodriques, Rodriquiez

Roe (English) roe deer.
Row, Rowe

Rogan (Irish) redhead.
*Rogein, Rogen, Rogin, Rogon, Rogun,
Rogyn*

Rogelio (Spanish) famous warrior. A
form of Roger.
Rogelyo

Roger (German) famous spearman. See
also Lokela.
*Rog, Rogerick, Rogers, Rogier, Rogir, Rogyer,
Rüdiger*

Rogerio (Portuguese, Spanish) a form of
Roger.
Rogerios, Rogerius, Rogero, Rogiero

Rohan (Hindi) sandalwood.

Rohin (Hindi) upward path.
Rohyn

Rohit (Hindi) big and beautiful fish.
Rohyt

Roi (French) a form of Roy.

Roja (Spanish) red.
Rojay

Rojelio (Spanish) a form of Rogelio.

Roland (German) famous throughout the
land.
*Loránd, Roelan, Roeland, Rolan, Rolanda,
Rolek, Rowe*

Rolando (Portuguese, Spanish) a form of
Roland.
*Lando, Olo, Roldan, Roldán, Rollando,
Rolondo*

Rolf (German) a form of Ralph. A short
form of Rudolph.
Rolfe, Rolph, Rolphe

Rolland (German) a form of Roland.

Rolle (Swedish) a familiar form of
Roland, Rolf.

Rollie (English) a familiar form of
Roland.
Roley, Rolle, Rolli, Rolly

Rollin (English) a form of Roland.
Rolin, Rollins

Rollo (English) a familiar form of
Roland.
Rolla, Rolo

Rolon (Spanish) famous wolf.
Rollon

Romain (French) a form of Roman.
Romaine, Romane, Romanne, Romayn, Romayne, Romin, Romyn

Roman (Latin) from Rome, Italy. (Gypsy) gypsy; wanderer.
Roma, Romann, Romman

Romanos (Greek) a form of Roman.
Romano

Romany (Gypsy) a form of Roman.
Romanee, Romaney, Romani, Romanie

Romario (Italian) a form of Romeo, Romero.
Romar, Romarius, Romaro, Romarrio

Romel, Romell, Rommel (Latin) short forms of Romulus.
Romele

Romelo, Romello (Italian) forms of Romel.
Rommello

Romeo (Italian) pilgrim to Rome; Roman. Literature: the title character of the Shakespearean play *Romeo and Juliet*.
Roméo, Romio, Romyo

Romero (Latin) a form of Romeo.
Romeiro, Romer, Romere, Romerio, Romeris, Romeryo

Romney (Welsh) winding river.
Romni, Romnie, Romny, Romoney

Romulus (Latin) citizen of Rome. Mythology: Romulus and his twin brother, Remus, founded Rome.
Romolo, Romono, Romulo

Romy (Italian) a familiar form of Roman.
Romee, Romey, Romi, Romie, Rommie, Rommy

Ron (Hebrew) a short form of Aaron, Ronald.
Ronn

Ronald (Scottish) a form of Reginald. (English) a form of Reynold.
Ranald, Ronal, Ronnald, Ronnold, Rynald

Ronaldo (Portuguese) a form of Ronald.
Ronoldo, Rynaldo

Ronan (Irish) a form of Rónán.

Rónán (Irish) seal.
Renan, Ronat

Rondel (French) short poem.
Rondal, Rondale, Rondeal, Rondey, Rondie, Rondy

Rondell (French) a form of Rondel.
Rondall, Rondrell

Ronel, Ronell, Ronnell (American) forms of Rondel.
Ronal, Ronelle, Ronil, Ronnel, Ronyell, Ronyl

Roni (Hebrew) my song; my joy. (Scottish) a form of Ronnie.
Rani, Roneet, Roney, Ronit, Ronli

Ronnie, Ronny (Scottish) familiar forms of Ronald.
Ronee, Roney, Ronie, Ronnee, Ronni, Ronney

Ronson (Scottish) son of Ronald.
Ronaldson, Ronsen, Ronsin, Ronsun, Ronsyn

Ronté (American) a combination of Ron + the suffix Te.
Rontae, Rontay, Ronte, Rontez

Rony (Hebrew) a form of Roni. (Scottish) a form of Ronnie.

Rooney (Irish) redhead.
Roonee, Rooni, Roonie, Roony, Rowney

Roosevelt (Dutch) rose field. History: Theodore and Franklin D. Roosevelt were the twenty-sixth and thirty-second U.S. presidents, respectively.
Roosvelt, Rosevelt

Roper (English) rope maker.

Roque (Italian) a form of Rocco.

Rory (German) a familiar form of Roderick. (Irish) red king.
Roree, Rorey, Rori, Rorie, Rorrie, Rorry

Rosalio (Spanish) rose.
Rosalino

Rosario (Portuguese) rosary.
Rosaryo, Rozario, Rozaryo

Roscoe (Scandinavian) deer forest.
Rosco, Roscow

Roshad (American) a form of Rashad.
Roshard

Roshan (American) a form of Roshean.

Roshean (American) a combination of the prefix Ro + Sean.
Roshain, Roshane, Roshaun, Roshawn, Roshay, Rosheen, Roshene

Rosito (Filipino) rose.
Rosyto

Ross (Latin) rose. (Scottish) peninsula. (French) red. (English) a short form of Roswald.
Ros, Rosse, Rossell, Rossi, Rossie, Rossy

Rosswell (English) springtime of roses.
Rosswel, Rosvel, Roswel, Roswell

Rostislav (Czech) growing glory.
Rosta, Rostya

Roswald (English) field of roses.

Roth (German) redhead.

Rothwell (Scandinavian) red spring.
Rothwel

Rover (English) traveler.
Rovar, Rovir, Rovor

Rowan (English) tree with red berries.
Roan, Rowe, Rowen, Rowin, Rowney, Rowon, Rowyn

Rowdy (American) rowdy.

Rowell (English) roe-deer well.
Roewel, Roewell, Rowel

Rowland (English) rough land. (German) a form of Roland.
Rowlan, Rowlando, Rowlands, Rowlandson

Rowley (English) rough meadow.
Rowlea, Rowlee, Rowleigh, Rowli, Rowlie, Rowly

Rowson (English) son of the redhead.
Rawson

Roxbury (English) rook's town or fortress.
Roxburg, Roxburge, Roxburghe

Roy (French) king. A short form of Royal, Royce. See also Conroy, Delroy, Fitzroy, Leroy, Loe.
Roye, Ruy

Royal (French) kingly, royal.
Roial, Royale, Royall, Royell

Royce (English) son of Roy.
Roice, Roise, Royse, Royz

Royden (English) rye hill.
Roidan, Roiden, Roidin, Roidon, Roidyn, Royd, Roydan, Roydin, Roydon, Roydyn

Ruben, Rubin (Hebrew) forms of Reuben.
Ruban, Rube, Rubean, Rubens, Rubon, Rubyn

Rubert (Czech) a form of Robert.

Ruby (Hebrew) a familiar form of Reuben, Ruben.
Rube, Rubey

Ruda (Czech) a form of Rudolph.
Rude, Rudek

Rudd (English) a short form of Rudyard.

Rudi (Spanish) a familiar form of Rudolph. (English) a form of Rudy.
Ruedi

Rudo (Shona) love.

Rudolf (German) a form of Rudolph.
Rodolf, Rudolfe, Ruedolf

Rudolph (German) famous wolf. See also Dolf.
Rezsó, Rodolph, Rodolphe, Rudek, Rudolphus

Rudolpho (Italian) a form of Rudolph.
Ridolfo, Rudolfo

Rudy (English) a familiar form of Rudolph.
Roody, Ruddey, Ruddi, Ruddie, Ruddy, Rudey, Rudie

Rudyard (English) red enclosure.

Rueben (Hebrew) a form of Reuben.
Rueban, Ruebin

Ruff (French) redhead.
Ruf

Rufin (Polish) redhead.
Ruffin, Ruffyn, Rufyn

Rufino (Spanish) a form of Rufin, Rufus.

Ruford (English) red ford; ford with reeds.
Rufford

Rufus (Latin) redhead.
Rayfus, Ruefus, Rufe, Ruffis, Ruffus, Rufo, Rufous

Rugby (English) rook fortress. History: a famous British school after which the sport of Rugby was named.
Rugbee, Rugbey, Rugbi, Rugbie

Ruggerio (Italian) a form of Roger.
Rogero, Ruggero, Ruggiero

Ruhakana (Rukiga) argumentative.

Ruland (German) a form of Roland.
Rulan, Rulon, Rulondo

Rumford (English) wide river crossing.

Runako (Shona) handsome.

Rune (German, Swedish) secret.

Runrot (Tai) prosperous.

Rupert (German) a form of Robert.
Ruepert, Rueperth, Ruperth, Rupirt, Rupyrt

Ruperto (Italian) a form of Rupert.
Ruberto

Ruprecht (German) a form of Rupert.
Rupprecht

Rush (French) redhead. (English) a short form of Russell.
Rushi

Rushford (English) ford with rushes.
Rushforde

Rusk (Spanish) twisted bread.

Ruskin (French) redhead.
Ruskyn

Russ (French) a short form of Russell.

Russel (French) a form of Russell.
Rusal, Rusel, Russal, Russil, Russyl

Russell (French) redhead; fox colored. See also Lukela.

Roussell, Rusell, Russall, Russelle, Russill, Russyll

Rustin (French) a form of Rusty.
Ruston, Rustyn

Rusty (French) a familiar form of Russell.
Ruste, Rustee, Rusten, Rustey, Rusti, Rustie

Rutger (Scandinavian) a form of Roger.
Ruttger

Rutherford (English) cattle ford.
Rutherfurd, Ruverford

Rutland (Scandinavian) red land.
Rutlan

Rutledge (English) red ledge.

Rutley (English) red meadow.
Rutlea, Rutlee, Rutleigh, Rutli, Rutlie, Rutly

Ruy (Spanish) a short form of Roderick.
Rui

Ryan (Irish) little king. See also Rian.
Rhyne, Ryane, Ryian, Ryiann, Ryin, Ryuan, Ryun, Ryyan

Ryann, Ryen, Ryon (Irish) forms of Ryan.
Ryein, Ryien

Rycroft (English) rye field.
Ricroft, Ryecroft

Ryder (English) a form of Rider.
Rydder

Rye (English) a grain used in cereal and whiskey. A short form of Richard, Ryder. (Gypsy) gentleman.
Rie, Ry

Ryerson (English) son of Rider, Ryder.

Ryese (English) a form of Reece.
Reyse, Ryez, Ryse

Ryker (American) a surname used as a first name.
Ryk

Rylan (English) land where rye is grown.
Rilan, Rylean, Rylen, Rylin, Rylon, Rylyn, Rylynn

Ryland (English) a form of Rylan.
Riland, Ryeland, Rylund

Ryle (English) rye hill.
Riel, Riell, Ryal, Ryel, Ryele, Ryell, Ryelle

Rylee, Ryley, Rylie (Irish) forms of Riley.
Rillie, Ryeleigh, Ryleigh, Ryli, Ryely, Ryly

Ryman (English) rye seller.
Riman

Ryne (Irish) a form of Ryan.
Rine, Rynn

Ryo (Spanish) a form of Rio.

S

Sa'id (Arabic) happy.
Sa'ad, Sa'eed, Sa'ied, Saaid, Saed, Saeed, Sahid, Saide, Saied, Saiyed, Saiyeed, Sajid, Sajjid, Sayed, Sayeed, Sayid, Sayyid, Seyed

Saad (Arabic) fortunate, lucky.
Sad, Sadd

Sabastian (Greek) a form of Sebastian.
Sabastain, Sabastiano, Sabastin, Sabastion, Sabaston, Sabbastiun, Sabestian

Sabastien (French) a form of Sebastian.

Saber (French) sword.
Sabar, Sabir, Sabor, Sabre, Sabyr

Sabin (Basque) a form of Sabine (see Girls' Names).
Saban, Saben, Sabian, Sabien, Sabyn

Sabino (Basque) a form of Sabin.

Sabiti (Rutooro) born on Sunday.
Sabit, Sabyti

Sabola (Nguni) pepper.
Sabol, Sabolah

Sabrina (Latin) boundary line. (English) royal child. (Hebrew) a familiar form of Sabra (see Girls' Names).

Saburo (Japanese) third-born son.
Saburow

Sacha (Russian) a form of Sasha.
Sascha

Sachar (Russian) a form of Zachary.

Saddam (Arabic) powerful ruler.
Sadam

Sadiki (Swahili) faithful.
Saadiq, Sadeek, Sadek, Sadik, Sadiq, Sadique, Sadyki, Sadyky

Sadler (English) saddle maker.
Saddler

Sadoc (Hebrew) sacred.
Sadock, Sadok

Safari (Swahili) born while traveling.
Safa, Safarian

Safford (English) willow river crossing.
Saford

Sage (English) wise. Botany: an herb.
Sagen, Sager, Saig, Saje, Sayg, Sayge

Sahale (Native American) falcon.
Sael, Sahal, Sahel

Sahen (Hindi) above.
Sahan, Sahin, Sahon, Sahyn

Sahil (Native American) a form of Sahale.
Saheel, Sahel, Sahyl

Sahir (Hindi) friend.
Sahyr

Said (Arabic) a form of Sa'id.

Saige (English) a form of Sage.

Sajag (Hindi) watchful.

Saka (Swahili) hunter.
Sakah

Sakeri (Danish) a form of Zachary.
Sakarai, Sakaree, Sakarey, Sakari, Sakaria, Sakarie, Sakary

Sakima (Native American) king.
Sakimah, Sakyma, Sakymah

Sakuruta (Pawnee) coming sun.

Sal (Italian) a short form of Salvatore.
Sall

Saladin (Arabic) good; faithful.
Saladine, Saladyn, Saladyne

Salah (Arabic) righteousness. (Hindi) a form of Sala (see Girls' Names).

Salam (Arabic) lamb.
Salaam

Salamon (Spanish) a form of Solomon.
Salaman, Salamen, Salamun, Saloman,
Salomón

Salaun (French) a form of Solomon.

Saleem (Arabic) a form of Salím.

Saleh (Arabic) a form of Sálih.

Salem (Arabic) a form of Salím.

Salene (Swahili) good.
Salin, Saline, Salyn, Salyne

Sálih (Arabic) right, good.
Saleeh, Salehe

Salim (Swahili) peaceful.

Salím (Arabic) peaceful, safe.
Saliym, Salom, Salym

Salisbury (English) fort at the willow pool.
Salisberi, Salisberie, Salisberri, Salisberrie,
Salisberry, Salisbery, Salisburi, Salisburie,
Salisburri, Salisburrie, Salisburry, Salysberry,
Salysbery, Salysburry, Salysbury

Salmalin (Hindi) taloned.

Salman (Czech) a form of Salím, Solomon.
Salmaan, Salmaine, Salmin, Salmon,
Salmun, Salmyn

Salomon (French) a form of Solomon.
Saloman, Salomo, Salomone

Salton (English) manor town; willow town.
Saltan, Salten, Saltin, Saltyn

Salvador (Spanish) savior.
Salvadore

Salvatore (Italian) savior. See also Xavier.
Salbatore, Sallie, Sally, Salvator, Salvattore,
Salvidor, Sauveur

Sam (Hebrew) a short form of Samuel.
Samm, Sem, Shmuel

Samantha (Aramaic) listener. (Hebrew) told by God.

Sambo (American) a familiar form of Samuel.
Sambou

Sameer (Arabic) a form of Samír.

Sami, Samy (Hebrew) forms of Sammie.
Saamy, Samee, Sameeh, Sameh, Samey,
Samie, Samih, Sammi

Samir (Arabic) a form of Samír.

Samír (Arabic) entertaining companion.
Samyr

Samman (Arabic) grocer.
Saman, Samen, Samin, Sammen, Sammin,
Sammon, Sammun, Sammyn, Samon,
Samun, Samyn

Sammie, Sammy (Hebrew) familiar forms of Samuel.
Sammee, Sammey

Samo (Czech) a form of Samuel.
Samho, Samko, Samu

Sampson (Hebrew) a form of Samson.
Sampsan, Sampsen, Sampsin, Sampsun,
Sampsyn

Samson (Hebrew) like the sun. Bible: a judge and powerful warrior betrayed by Delilah.
Sansao, Sansim, Sansom, Sansome, Sansum,
Shymson

Samual (Hebrew) a form of Samuel.
Samuael, Samuail

Samuel (Hebrew) heard God; asked of God. Bible: a famous Old Testament prophet and judge. See also Kamuela, Zamiel, Zanvil.
Samael, Samaru, Samauel, Samaul, Samel,
Sameul, Samiel, Sammail, Sammel,
Sammuel, Samouel, Samuelis, Samuell,
Samuello, Samuil, Samuka, Samule, Samvel,
Sanko, Saumel, Simuel, Somhairle, Zamuel

Samuele (Italian) a form of Samuel.
Samulle

Samuru (Japanese) a form of Samuel.

Sanat (Hindi) ancient.

Sanborn (English) sandy brook.
Sanborne, Sanbourn, Sanbourne, Sanburn,
Sanburne, Sandborn, Sandborne, Sandbourn,
Sandbourne

Sanchez (Latin) a form of Sancho.
Sanchaz, Sancheze

Sancho (Latin) sanctified; sincere.
Literature: Sancho Panza was Don
Quixote's squire.
Sauncho

Sandeep (Punjabi) enlightened.
Sandip

Sander (English) a short form of
Alexander, Lysander.
Sandir, Sandyr, Saunder

Sanders (English) son of Sander.
Sanderson, Saunders, Saunderson

Sándor (Hungarian) a short form of
Alexander.
Sandar, Sandor, Sandur, Sanyi

Sandro (Greek, Italian) a short form of
Alexander.
Sandero, Sandor, Sandre, Saundro, Shandro

Sandy (English) a familiar form of
Alexander, Sanford.
Sande, Sandee, Sandey, Sandi, Sandie

Sanford (English) sandy river crossing.
Sandford, Sanforde

Sani (Hindi) the planet Saturn. (Navajo)
old.
Sanee, Saney, Sanie, Sany

Sanjay (American) a combination of
Sanford + Jay.
Sanjai, Sanjaya, Sanjaye, Sanje, Sanjey,
Sanjo, Sanjy, Sanjye

Sanjiv (Hindi) long-lived.
Sanjeev, Sanjyv

Sankar (Hindi) a form of Shankara,
another name for the Hindu god Shiva.

Sansón (Spanish) a form of Samson.
Sanson, Sansone, Sansun

Santana (Spanish) History: Antonio
López de Santa Anna was a Mexican
general and political leader.
Santanah, Santanio, Santanna, Santanyo

Santiago (Spanish) a form of James.
Santyago

Santino (Spanish) a form of Santonio.
Santion

Santo (Italian, Spanish) holy.

Santon (English) sandy town.
Santan, Santen, Santin, Santun, Santyn

Santonio (Spanish) Geography: a short
form of San Antonio, a city in Texas.
Santon, Santoni, Santonino, Santonyo

Santos (Spanish) saint.

Santosh (Hindi) satisfied.

Sanyu (Luganda) happy.

Saqr (Arabic) falcon.

Saquan (American) a combination of the
prefix Sa + Quan.
Saquané, Saquin, Saquon, Saqwan,
Saqwone

Sarad (Hindi) born in the autumn.
Saradd

Sarah (Hebrew) royal child.

Sargent (French) army officer.
Sargant, Sarge, Sarjant, Sergeant, Sergent,
Serjeant

Sargon (Persian) sun prince.
Sargan, Sargen, Sargin, Sargyn

Sarik (Hindi) bird.
Saarik

Sarito (Spanish) a form of Caesar.
Sarit

Sariyah (Arabic) clouds at night.
Sariya

Sarngin (Hindi) archer; protector.
Sarngyn

Sarojin (Hindi) like a lotus.
Sarojun, Sarojyn

Sasha (Russian) a short form of
Alexander.
Sash, Sausha

Sasson (Hebrew) joyful.
Sason

Satchel (French) small bag.
Satch

Satordi (French) Saturn.
Satordie, Satordy, Satori, Saturno

Saul (Hebrew) asked for, borrowed.
Bible: in the Old Testament, a king of
Israel and the father of Jonathan; in the
New Testament, Saint Paul's original
name was Saul.
Saül, Shaul

Saverio (Italian) a form of Xavier.

Saville (French) willow town.
*Savelle, Savil, Savile, Savill, Savyl, Savyle,
Savyll, Savylle, Seville, Siville*

Savion (American, Spanish) a form of
Savon.

Savon (American) a form of Savannah
(see Girls' Names).
*Savan, Savaughn, Saveion, Saveon, Savhon,
Saviahn, Savian, Savino, Savo, Savone,
Sayvon, Sayvone*

Saw (Burmese) early.

Sawyer (English) wood worker.
Sawer, Sawier, Sawyere, Soier

Sax (English) a short form of Saxon.
Saxe

Saxby (Scandinavian) Saxon farm.
Saxbee, Saxbey, Saxbi, Saxbie

Saxon (English) swordsman. History: the
Roman name for the Teutonic raiders
who ravaged the Roman British coasts.
*Sax, Saxan, Saxen, Saxin, Saxsin, Saxun,
Saxxon, Saxyn*

Saxton (English) Saxon town.
Saxtan, Saxten, Saxtin, Saxtyn

Sayer (Welsh) carpenter.
Say, Saye, Sayers, Sayr, Sayre, Sayres

Sayyid (Arabic) master.
Sayed, Sayid, Sayyad, Sayyed

Scanlon (Irish) little trapper.
Scanlan, Scanlen, Scanlin, Scanlyn

Schafer (German) shepherd.
Schaefer, Schaffer, Schiffer, Shaffar, Shäffer

Schmidt (German) blacksmith.
*Schmid, Schmit, Schmitt, Schmydt, Schmyt,
Schmytt*

Schneider (German) tailor.
Schnieder, Snider, Snyder

Schön (German) handsome.
Schoen, Schönn

Schuman (German) shoemaker.
*Schumann, Schumen, Schumenn, Shoeman,
Shoemann, Shoemen, Shoemenn, Shooman,
Shoomann, Shoomen, Shoomenn, Shueman,
Shuemann, Shuemen, Shuemenn, Shuman,
Shumann, Shumen, Shumenn, Shumyn,
Shumynn, Shyman, Shymann*

Schuyler (Dutch) sheltering.
Schuylar, Scoy, Scy

Schyler (Dutch) a form of Schuyler.
Schylar, Schylor, Schylre, Schylur

Scipion (Latin) staff; stick.
Scipio, Scipione, Scipyo, Scypion, Scypyo

Scoey (French) a short form of Scoville.
Scoee, Scoi, Scoie, Scowi, Scowie, Scowy, Scoy

Scorpio (Latin) dangerous, deadly.
Astronomy: a southern constellation
near Libra and Sagittarius. Astrology:
the eighth sign of the zodiac.
Scorpeo, Scorpyo

Scot (English) a form of Scott.

Scott (English) from Scotland. A familiar
form of Prescott.
Scotto, Skot, Skott

Scottie, Scotty (English) familiar forms
of Scott.
Scotie, Scottey, Scotti

Scoville (French) Scott's town.
*Scovil, Scovile, Scovill, Scovyl, Scovyle,
Scovyll, Scovylle*

Scribe (Latin) keeper of accounts; writer.
Scribner, Scryb, Scrybe

Scully (Irish) town crier.
*Scullea, Scullee, Sculleigh, Sculley, Sculli,
Scullie*

Seabert (English) shining sea.
Seabirt, Seabright, Seaburt, Seabyrt, Sebert,
Seebert, Seebirt, Seeburt, Seebyrt, Seibert,
Seibirt, Seiburt, Seibyrt, Seybert, Seybirt,
Seyburt, Seybyrt

Seabrook (English) brook near the sea.
Seabrooke, Seebrook, Seebrooke, Seibrook,
Seibrooke, Seybrook, Seybrooke

Seamus (Irish) a form of James.
Seamas, Seumas

Sean (Hebrew, Irish) a form of John.
Seaghan, Seain, Seaine, Séan, Seán, Seane,
Seann, Seayn, Seayne, Siôn

Seanan (Irish) wise.
Seanán, Seanen, Seannan, Seannen,
Seannon, Senan, Sinan, Sinon

Searlas (Irish, French) a form of Charles.
Séarlas, Searles, Searlus

Searle (English) armor.
Searl, Serl, Serle

Seasar (Latin) a form of Caesar.
Seasare, Seazar, Sesar, Sesear, Sezar

Seaton (English) town near the sea.
Seatan, Seaten, Seatin, Seatun, Seatyn,
Seeton, Setan, Seten, Setin, Seton, Setun,
Setyn

Sebastian (Greek) venerable. (Latin)
revered. See also Bastien.
Sebashtian, Sebastain, Sebastao, Sebastiane,
Sebastiao, Sebastin, Sebastine, Sebastyn,
Sebbie, Sebo, Sepasetiano

Sebastiano (Italian) a form of Sebastian.

Sebastien, Sébastien (French) forms of
Sebastian.
Sebaste, Sebasten, Sebastyen, Sebestyén

Sebastion (Greek) a form of Sebastian.

Secundus (Latin) second-born.
Secondas, Secondus, Secondys

Sedgely (English) sword meadow.
Sedgeley, Sedglea, Sedglee, Sedgleigh,
Sedgley, Sedgli, Sedglie, Sedgly

Sedgwick (English) sword grass.
Sedgwic, Sedgwik, Sedgwyc, Sedgwyck,
Sedgwyk

Sedric, Sedrick (Irish) forms of Cedric.
Seddrick, Sederick, Sedrik, Sedriq

Seeley (English) blessed.
Sealea, Sealee, Sealeigh, Sealey, Seali, Sealie,
Sealy, Seelea, Seelee, Seeleigh, Seeli, Seelie,
Seely, Seilea, Seilee, Seileigh, Seiley, Seili,
Seilie, Seily, Seylea, Seylee, Seyleigh, Seyley,
Seyli, Seylie, Seyly

Sef (Egyptian) yesterday. Mythology: one
of the two lions that make up the Akeru,
guardian of the gates of morning and
night.
Seff

Sefton (English) village of rushes.
Seftan, Seften, Seftin, Seftun, Seftyn

Sefu (Swahili) sword.

Seger (English) sea spear; sea warrior.
Seagar, Seager, Seegar, Seeger, Segar

Segun (Yoruba) conqueror.
Segan, Segen, Segin, Segon, Segyn

Segundo (Spanish) second.

Seibert (English) bright sea.
Sebert

Seif (Arabic) religion's sword.
Seyf

Seifert (German) a form of Siegfried.
Seifried

Sein (Basque) innocent.
Seyn

Sekaye (Shona) laughter.
Sekai, Sekay

Sekou (Guinean) learned.

Selby (English) village by the mansion.
Selbee, Selbey, Selbi, Selbie

Seldon (English) willow tree valley.
Seldan, Selden, Seldin, Seldun, Seldyn,
Sellden

Selig (German) a form of Seeley. See also
Zelig.
Seligg, Seligman, Seligmann, Selyg, Selygg

Selwyn (English) friend from the palace.
See also Wyn.
Selvin, Selwin, Selwinn, Selwynn, Selwynne

Semaj (Turkish) a form of Sema (see Girls' Names).

Semanda (Luganda) cow clan.
Semandah

Semer (Ethiopian) a form of George.
Semere, Semier

Semi (Polynesian) character.
Semee, Semey, Semie, Semy

Semon (Greek) a form of Simon.
Semion

Sempala (Luganda) born in prosperous times.
Sempalah

Sen (Japanese) wood fairy.
Senh

Sener (Turkish) bringer of joy.

Senior (French) lord.
Senyor

Sennett (French) elderly.
Senet, Senett, Senit, Senitt, Sennet, Sennit, Sennyt, Senyt

Senon (Spanish) living.
Senan, Senen, Senin, Senyn

Senwe (African) dry as a grain stalk.

Sepp (German) a form of Joseph.
Sep, Sepee, Sepey, Sepi, Sepie, Seppee, Seppey, Seppi, Seppie, Seppy, Sepy

Septimus (Latin) seventh.
Septimous

Serafin (Hebrew) a form of Seraphim.
Seraphin

Serafino (Portuguese) a form of Seraphim.
Seraphino

Seraphim (Hebrew) fiery, burning. Bible: the highest order of angels, known for their zeal and love.
Saraf, Saraph, Serafim, Seraphimus

Sereno (Latin) calm, tranquil.
Sereen, Serene, Serino, Seryno

Serge (Latin) attendant.
Seargeoh, Serg, Sergios, Sergius, Sergiusz, Serguel, Sirgio, Sirgios

Sergei, Sergey (Russian) forms of Serge.
Serghey, Sergi, Sergie, Sergo, Seryozha, Serzh

Sergio, Serjio (Italian) forms of Serge.
Serginio, Serigo

Servando (Spanish) to serve.
Servan, Servio

Seth (Hebrew) appointed. Bible: the third son of Adam.
Set, Sethan, Sethe, Shet

Setimba (Luganda) river dweller. Geography: a river in Uganda.
Setimbah

Seumas (Scottish) a form of James.
Seaumus

Severiano (Italian) a form of Séverin.

Séverin (French) severe.
Seve, Sevé, Severan, Severen, Severian, Severo, Severyn, Sevien, Sevrin

Severn (English) boundary.
Sevearn, Sevirn, Sevren, Sevrnn, Sevyrn

Sevilen (Turkish) beloved.
Sevilan, Sevilin, Sevilon, Sevilyn

Seward (English) sea guardian.
Seaward, Seawrd, Seeward, Seiward, Sewerd, Seyward, Siward

Sewati (Moquelumnan) curved bear claws.
Sewatee, Sewatey

Sewell (English) sea wall.
Seawal, Seawall, Seawel, Seawell, Seewal, Seewall, Seewel, Seewell, Seiwal, Seiwall, Seiwel, Seiwell, Sewal, Sewall, Sewel, Seywal, Seywall, Seywel, Seywell

Sexton (English) church offical; sexton.
Sextan, Sexten, Sextin, Sextyn

Sextus (Latin) sixth.
Sextis, Sextys, Sixtus

Seymour (French) prayer. Religion: name honoring Saint Maur. See also Maurice.
Seamoor, Seamoore, Seamor, Seamore, Seamour, Seamoure, See, Seemoor, Seemoore, Seemor, Seemore, Seemour, Seemoure,

Seymour *(cont.)*
Seimoor, Seimoore, Seimor, Seimore, Seimour,
Seymoor, Seymore, Seymoure

Shaan (Hebrew, Irish) a form of Sean.

Shabouh (Armenian) king, noble.
History: a fourth-century Persian king.

Shad (Punjabi) happy-go-lucky.
Shadd

Shade (English) shade.
Shaed, Shaede, Shaid, Shaide, Shayd,
Shayde

Shadi (Arabic) singer.
Shadde, Shaddi, Shaddy, Shadee, Shadeed,
Shadey, Shadie, Shydee, Shydi

Shadow (English) shadow.

Shadrach (Babylonian) god; godlike.
Bible: one of three companions who
emerged unharmed from the fiery
furnace of Babylon.
Shadrac, Shadrack, Shadrak

Shadrick (Babylonian) a form of
Shadrach.
Shadriq

Shadwell (English) shed by a well.
Shadwal, Shadwall, Shadwel, Shedwal,
Shedwall, Shedwel, Shedwell

Shady (Arabic) a form of Shadi.

Shae (Hebrew) a form of Shai. (Irish) a
form of Shea.

Shah (Persian) king. History: a title for
rulers of Iran.

Shaheem (American) a combination of
Shah + Raheem.
Shaheim, Shahiem, Shahm

Shaheed (Arabic) a form of Sa'id.
Shahed, Shahyd

Shahid (Arabic) a form of Sa'id.

Shai (Irish) a form of Shea. (Hebrew) a
short form of Yeshaya.
Shaie

Shaiming (Chinese) life; sunshine.
Shaimin, Shayming

Shain, Shaine (Irish) forms of Sean.

Shaka (Zulu) founder, first. History:
Shaka Zulu was the founder of the
Zulu empire.
Shakah

Shakeel (Arabic) a form of Shaquille.
Shakeil, Shakel, Shakell, Shakiel, Shakil,
Shakille, Shakyle

Shakir (Arabic) thankful.
Shaakir, Shakeer, Shakeir, Shakyr

Shakur (Arabic) a form of Shakir.
Shakuur

Shalom (Hebrew) peace.
Shalum, Shlomo, Sholem, Sholom

Shalya (Hindi) throne.

Shaman (Sanskrit) holy man, mystic,
medicine man.
Shaiman, Shaimen, Shamaine, Shamaun,
Shamen, Shamin, Shamine, Shammon,
Shamon, Shamone, Shayman, Shaymen

Shamar (Hebrew) a form of Shamir.
Shamaar, Shamare

Shamari (Hebrew) a form of Shamir.

Shamir (Hebrew) precious stone.
Shahmeer, Shahmir, Shameer, Shamyr

Shamus (American) slang for detective.
(Irish) a form of Seamus.
Shaimis, Shaimus, Shamas, Shames, Shamis,
Shamos, Shaymis, Shaymus, Shemus

Shan (Irish) a form of Shane.
Shann, Shanne

Shanahan (Irish) wise, clever.
Seanahan, Shaunahan, Shawnahan

Shandy (English) rambunctious.
Shande, Shandea, Shandey, Shandi, Shandie

Shane (Irish) a form of Sean.
Shaen, Shaene

Shangobunni (Yoruba) gift from Shango.

Shani (Hebrew) red. (Swahili) marvelous.
Shanee, Shaney, Shanie, Shany

Shanley (Irish) small; ancient.
Shaneley, Shanlea, Shanlee, Shanleigh,
Shanli, Shanlie, Shanly, Shannley

Shannon (Irish) small and wise.
Shanan, Shanen, Shanin, Shannan,
Shannen, Shannin, Shannone, Shannyn,
Shanon, Shanyn

Shant (French) a short form of Shantae.

Shantae (French) a form of Chante.
Shanta, Shantai, Shantay, Shante, Shantell,
Shantelle, Shanti, Shantia, Shantie,
Shanton, Shanty

Shap (English) a form of Shep.

Shaq (American) a short form of
Shaquan, Shaquille.

Shaquan (American) a combination of
the prefix Sha + Quan.
Shaqaun, Shaquand, Shaquane, Shaquann,
Shaquaunn, Shaquawn, Shaquen, Shaquian,
Shaquin, Shaqwan

Shaquell (American) a form of Shaquille.
Shaqueal, Shaqueil, Shaquel, Shaquelle,
Shaquiel, Shaquiell, Shaquielle

Shaquile (Arabic) a form of Shaquille.

Shaquill (Arabic) a form of Shaquille.

Shaquille (Arabic) handsome.
Shaquell, Shaquil, Shaqul, Shaquyl,
Shaquyle, Shaquyll, Shaquylle

Shaquon (American) a combination of
the prefix Sha + Quon.
Shaikwon, Shaqon, Shaquoin, Shaquoné

Sharad (Pakistani) autumn.
Sharid, Sharyd

Shareef (Arabic) a form of Sharíf.

Sharif (Arabic) a form of Sharíf.

Sharíf (Arabic) honest; noble.
Sharef, Shareff, Shareif, Sharief, Sharife,
Shariff, Shariyf, Sharrif, Sharyf, Sharyff,
Sharyif

Sharod (Pakistani) a form of Sharad.
Sharrod

Sharron (Hebrew) flat area, plain.
Sharan, Sharen, Sharin, Sharon, Sharone,
Sharonn, Sharonne, Sharran, Sharren,
Sharrin, Sharryn, Sharyn

Shattuck (English) little shad fish.
Shatuck

Shaun (Irish) a form of Sean.
Schaun, Schaune, Shaughan, Shaughn,
Shaugn, Shauna, Shaunahan, Shaune,
Shaunn, Shaunne

Shavar (Hebrew) comet.
Shaver, Shavir, Shavyr

Shavon (American) a combination of the
prefix Sha + Yvon.
Shauvan, Shauvon, Shavan, Shavaughn,
Shaven, Shavin, Shavone, Shawan,
Shawon, Shawun

Shaw (English) grove.
Shawe

Shawn (Irish) a form of Sean.
Schawn, Schawne, Shawen, Shawne,
Shawnee, Shawnn, Shawon

Shawnta (American) a combination of
Shawn + the suffix Ta.
Seanta, Seantah, Shaunta, Shawntae,
Shawntah, Shawntel, Shawnti

Shay, Shaye (Irish) forms of Shea.
Shaya, Shey

Shayan (Cheyenne) a form of Cheyenne.
Shayaan, Shayann, Shayon

Shayn, Shayne (Hebrew) forms of Sean.
Shaynne, Shean

Shea (Irish) courteous.
Sheah

Sheary (Irish) peaceful.
Shearee, Shearey, Sheari, Shearie

Shedrick (Babylonian) a form of
Shadrach.
Sheddrach, Shederick, Shedrach, Shedric,
Shedrik, Shedrique, Shedryc, Shedryck,
Shedryk

Sheehan (Irish) little; peaceful.
Shean, Sheehen

Sheffield (English) crooked field.
Field, Shef, Sheff, Sheffie, Sheffy, Sheffyeld, Shefield, Shefyeld

Shel (English) a short form of Shelby, Sheldon, Shelton.
Shell

Shelby (English) ledge estate. A form of Selby.
Shelbe, Shelbea, Shelbee, Shelbey, Shelbi, Shelbie, Shellby

Sheldon (English) farm on the ledge.
Sheldan, Shelden, Sheldin, Sheldun, Sheldyn

Shelley (English) a familiar form of Shelby, Sheldon, Shelton. Literature: Percy Bysshe Shelley was a nineteenth-century British poet.
Shell, Shellea, Shellee, Shelleigh, Shelli, Shellie, Shelly

Shelton (English) town on a ledge.
Sheltan, Shelten, Sheltin, Sheltyn

Shem (Hebrew) name; reputation. A form of Samson. (English) a short form of Samuel. Bible: Noah's oldest son.

Shen (Egyptian) sacred amulet. (Chinese) meditation.

Shep (English) a short form of Shepherd.
Shepp, Ship, Shipp

Shepherd (English) shepherd.
Shepard, Shephard, Sheppard, Shepperd

Shepley (English) sheep meadow.
Sheplea, Sheplee, Shepleigh, Shepli, Sheplie, Sheply, Shepply, Shipley

Sherborn (English) clear brook.
Sherborne, Sherbourn, Sherburn, Sherburne

Sheridan (Irish) wild.
Sheredan, Sheriden, Sheridon, Sheridyn, Sherridan, Sherydan, Sheryden, Sherydin, Sherydon, Sherydyn

Sherill (English) shire on a hill.
Sheril, Sherril, Sherrill, Sheryl, Sheryll

Sherlock (English) light haired. Literature: Sherlock Holmes is a famous British detective character, created by Sir Arthur Conan Doyle.
Sherloc, Sherloch, Sherloche, Sherlocke, Sherlok, Shurlock, Shurlocke

Sherman (English) sheep shearer; resident of a shire.
Scherman, Schermann, Sherm, Shermain, Shermaine, Shermann, Shermen, Shermie, Shermon, Shermy, Shirman, Shirmann, Shyrman, Shyrmann

Sherrod (English) clearer of the land.
Sherod, Sherrad, Sherrard, Sherrodd

Sherwin (English) swift runner, one who cuts the wind.
Sherveen, Shervin, Sherwan, Sherwind, Sherwinn, Sherwyn, Sherwynd, Sherwynn, Sherwynne, Win

Sherwood (English) bright forest.
Sharwood, Sherwoode, Shurwood, Woody

Shihab (Arabic) blaze.
Shyhab

Shìlín (Chinese) intellectual.
Shilan, Shilyn, Shylin, Shylyn

Shilo (Hebrew) a form of Shiloh.

Shiloh (Hebrew) God's gift.
Shi, Shile, Shiley, Shiloe, Shy, Shyle, Shylo, Shyloh

Shimon (Hebrew) a form of Simon.
Shymon

Shimshon (Hebrew) a form of Samson.
Shimson

Shing (Chinese) victory.
Shingae, Shingo, Shyng

Shipley (English) sheep meadow.
Shiplea, Shiplee, Shipleigh, Shipli, Shiplie, Shiply, Shyplea, Shyplee, Shypleigh, Shypley, Shypli, Shyplie, Shyply

Shipton (English) sheep village; ship village.
Shiptan, Shipten, Shiptin, Shiptun, Shiptyn, Shyptan, Shypten, Shyptin, Shypton, Shyptun, Shyptyn

Shiquan (American) a combination of the prefix Shi + Quan.
Shiquane, Shiquann, Shiquawn, Shiquoin, Shiqwan

Shiro (Japanese) fourth-born son.
Shirow, Shyro, Shyrow

Shiva (Hindi) life and death. Religion: the most common name for the Hindu god of destruction and reproduction.
Shiv, Shivah, Shivan, Shyva, Shyvah, Siva

Shlomo (Hebrew) a form of Solomon.
Shelmu, Shelomo, Shelomoh, Shlomi, Shlomot

Shmuel (Hebrew) a form of Samuel.
Schmuel, Shemuel, Shmiel

Shneur (Yiddish) senior.
Shneiur

Shomer (Hebrew) protector.
Shomar, Shomir, Shomor, Shomyr

Shon (German) a form of Schön. (American) a form of Sean.
Shoan, Shoen, Shondae, Shondale, Shondel, Shone, Shonn, Shonntay, Shontae, Shontarious, Shouan, Shoun

Shoni (Hebrew) changing.
Shonee, Shoney, Shonie, Shony

Shunnar (Arabic) pheasant.
Shunar

Si (Hebrew) a short form of Silas, Simon.

Sid (French) a short form of Sidney.
Sidd, Siddie, Siddy, Sidey, Syd, Sydd

Siddel (English) wide valley.
Siddell, Sidel, Sidell, Sydel, Sydell

Siddhartha (Hindi) History: Siddhartha Gautama was the original name of Buddha, the founder of Buddhism.
Sida, Siddartha, Siddhaarth, Siddhart, Siddharth, Sidh, Sidharth, Sidhartha, Sidhdharth, Sydartha, Syddhartha

Sidney (French) from Saint-Denis, France.
Cydney, Sidnee, Sidni, Sidnie, Sidny

Sidonio (Spanish) a form of Sidney.
Sidon

Sidwell (English) wide stream.
Siddwal, Siddwall, Siddwel, Siddwell, Sidwal, Sidwall, Sidwel, Syddwal, Syddwall, Syddwel, Syddwell, Sydwal, Sydwall, Sydwel, Sydwell

Siegfried (German) victorious peace. See also Zigfrid, Ziggy.
Siegfred, Sigfrid, Sigfried, Sigfroi, Sigfryd, Sigvard, Singefrid, Sygfred, Sygfreid, Sygfreyd, Sygfrid, Sygfried, Sygfryd

Sierra (Irish) black. (Spanish) saw-toothed.
Siera, Sierah, Sierrah, Syera, Syerah, Syerra, Syerrah

Siffre (French) a form of Siegfried.

Siffredo (Italian) a form of Siegfried.
Sifredo, Syffredo

Sig (German) a short form of Siegfried, Sigmund.

Siggy (German) a familiar form of Siegfried, Sigmund.

Sigifredo (German) a form of Siegfried.
Sigefredo, Sigefriedo, Sigfrido, Siguefredo

Sigismond (French) a form of Sigmund.
Sygismond, Sygismund, Sygysmon, Sygysmond, Sygysmun, Sygysmund

Sigismundo (Italian, Spanish) a form of Sigmund.
Sigismondo, Sygismondo, Sygismundo, Sygysmondo, Sygysmundo

Sigmund (German) victorious protector. See also Ziggy, Zsigmond, Zygmunt.
Saegmond, Saegmund, Siegmund, Sigismund, Sigismundus, Sigmond, Sigmundo, Sigsmond, Sygmond, Sygmondo, Sygmund, Sygmundo, Szygmond

Sigurd (German, Scandinavian) victorious guardian.
Sigord, Sjure, Sygurd, Syver

Sigwald (German) victorious leader.
Sigwaldo, Sygwald, Sygwaldo

Silas (Latin) a short form of Silvan.
Sias

Silburn (English) blessed.
Silborn, Silborne, Silbourn, Silbourne,
Silburn, Silburne, Sylborn, Sylborne,
Sylbourn, Sylbourne, Sylburn, Sylburne

Silvan (Latin) forest dweller.
Silvaon, Silvie, Sylvanus

Silvano (Italian) a form of Silvan.
Silvanos

Silvester (Latin) a form of Sylvester.
Silvestr, Silvy

Silvestre (Spanish) a form of Sylvester.

Silvestro (Italian) a form of Sylvester.

Silvino (Italian) a form of Silvan.

Silvio (Italian) a form of Silvan.
Sylvio

Simão (Portuguese) a form of Samuel.
Simao

Simba (Swahili) lion. (Yao) a short form
of Lisimba.
Sim, Simbah, Symba, Symbah

Simcha (Hebrew) joyful.
Simmy

Simeon (French) a form of Simon.
Seameon, Seemeon, Simion, Simione,
Simone, Symeon, Symyan

Simms (Hebrew) son of Simon.
Simm, Sims, Symms, Syms

Simmy (Hebrew) a familiar form of
Simcha, Simon.
Simmey, Simmi, Simmie, Symmy

Simon (Hebrew) he heard. Bible: one
of the Twelve Disciples. See also
Symington, Ximenes, Zimon.
Saimon, Samien, Seimein, Semein,
Seymeon, Seymon, Sim, Simen, Simmon,
Simmonds, Simmons, Simonas, Simone,
Simons, Siomon, Síomón, Siomonn, Simyon,
Symonn, Symonns

Simon Pierre (French) a combination of
Simon + Pierre.

Simpson (Hebrew) son of Simon.
Simonson, Simson, Simpsan, Simpsen,
Simpsin, Simpsyn, Sympsan, Sympsen,
Sympsin, Sympson, Sympsyn

Simran (Sikh) absorbed in God.

Sina (Irish) a form of Seana (see Girls'
Names).

Sinbad (German) prince; sparkling.
Sinbald, Synbad, Synbald

Sinclair (French) prayer. Religion: name
honoring Saint Clair.
Sinclaire, Sinclar, Sinclare, Synclair,
Synclaire, Synclar, Synclare, Synclayr

Singh (Hindi) lion.
Sing

Sinjin (English) a form of Sinjon.

Sinjon (English) saint, holy man.
Religion: name honoring Saint John.
Sinjun, Sjohn, Syngen, Synjen, Synjon

Sione (Tongan) God is gracious.
Sionee, Sioney, Sioni, Sionie, Soane, Sone

Sipatu (Moquelumnan) pulled out.
Sypatu

Sipho (Zulu) present.
Sypho

Sir (English) sir, sire.

Siraj (Arabic) lamp, light.
Syraj

Siseal (Irish) a form of Cecil.

Sisi (Fante) born on Sunday.
Sysi, Sysy

Sitric (Scandinavian) conqueror.
Sitrick, Sitrik, Sytric, Sytrick, Sytrik, Sytryc,
Sytryck, Sytryk

Siva (Hindi) a form of Shiva.
Siv

Sivan (Hebrew) ninth month of the
Jewish year.
Syvan

Siwatu (Swahili) born during a time of
conflict.
Siwazuri

Siwili (Native American) long fox's tail.
Siwilie, Siwily, Siwyli, Siwylie, Siwyly,
Sywili, Sywilie, Sywily, Sywyly

Skah (Lakota) white.
Skai

Skee (Scandinavian) projectile.
Ski, Skie

Skeeter (English) swift.
Skeat, Skeet, Skeets

Skelly (Irish) storyteller.
Shell, Skelea, Skelee, Skeleigh, Skeley, Skeli,
Skelie, Skellea, Skellee, Skelleigh, Skelley,
Skelli, Skellie, Skely

Skelton (Dutch) shell town.

Skerry (Scandinavian) stony island.
Skery

Skip (Scandinavian) a short form of
Skipper.
Skipp, Skyp, Skypp

Skipper (Scandinavian) shipmaster.

Skippie (Scandinavian) a familiar form of
Skipper.
Skipi, Skipie, Skippi, Skippy, Skipy, Skypi,
Skypie, Skyppi, Skyppie, Skyppy, Skypy

Skipton (English) ship town.
Skippton, Skyppton, Skypton

Skiriki (Pawnee) coyote.

Skule (Norwegian) hidden.
Skul, Skull

Sky, Skye (Dutch) short forms of Skylar.

Skylar, Skyler, Skylor (Dutch) forms of
Schuyler.
Skieler, Skilar, Skiler, Skkylar, Skuylar,
Skuyler, Skyelar, Skyeler, Skyelor, Skylaar,
Skylare, Skylarr, Skylayr, Skylee, Skyller,
Skyloer, Skylore, Skylour, Skylur, Skylyr

Slade (English) a short form of Sladen.
Slaid, Slaide, Slayd, Slayde

Sladen (English) child of the valley.
Sladan, Sladein, Sladon, Sladyn, Slaidan,
Slaiden, Slaidin, Slaidon, Slaidyn, Slaydan,
Slayden, Slaydin, Slaydon, Slaydyn

Slane (Czech) salty.
Slain, Slaine, Slan, Slayn, Slayne

Slater (English) roof slater.
Slaiter, Slader, Slate, Slayter

Slava (Russian) a short form of Stanislav,
Vladislav, Vyacheslav.
Slavah, Slavik

Slawek (Polish) a short form of
Radoslaw.

Slevin (Irish) mountaineer.
Slavan, Slaven, Slavin, Slavon, Slavyn,
Slawin, Slevan, Sleven, Slevon, Slevyn

Sloan (Irish) warrior.
Sloane, Slone

Smedley (English) flat meadow.
Smedlea, Smedlee, Smedleigh, Smedli,
Smedlie, Smedly

Smith (English) blacksmith.
Schmidt, Smid, Smidt, Smithe, Smithey,
Smithi, Smithie, Smithy, Smitt, Smitth,
Smitty, Smyth, Smythe

Snowden (English) snowy hill.
Snowdan, Snowdin, Snowdon, Snowdyn

Socrates (Greek) wise, learned. History: a
famous ancient Greek philosopher.
Socratis, Sokrates, Sokratis

Sofian (Arabic) devoted.
Sofyan

Sohail (Arabic) a form of Suhail.
Sohayl, Souhail

Sohrab (Persian) ancient hero.

Soja (Yoruba) soldier.
Sojah

Sol (Hebrew) a short form of Saul,
Solomon.
Soll

Solly (Hebrew) a familiar form of Saul,
Solomon. See also Zollie.
Sollie

Solomon (Hebrew) peaceful. Bible: a
king of Israel famous for his wisdom.
See also Zalman.

Solomon *(cont.)*
Salaun, Selim, Shelomah, Solamh, Solaman, Solmon, Soloman, Solomo, Solomonas, Solomyn

Solon (Greek) wise. History: a noted ancient Athenian lawmaker.
Solan, Solen, Solin, Solyn

Somerset (English) place of the summer settlers. Literature: William Somerset Maugham was a well-known British writer.
Sommerset, Sumerset, Summerset

Somerton (English) summer town.
Summerton

Somerville (English) summer village.
Somervil, Somervill, Somervyl, Somervyll, Somervylle, Sumervil, Sumervill, Sumerville, Sumervyl, Sumervyll, Sumervylle, Summervil, Summervill, Summerville, Summervyl, Summervyll, Summervylle

Son (Vietnamese) mountain. (Native American) star. (English) son, boy. A short form of Madison, Orson.

Songan (Native American) strong.
Song

Sonny (English) a familiar form of Grayson, Madison, Orson, Son.
Sonee, Soney, Soni, Sonie, Sonnee, Sonney, Sonni, Sonnie, Sony

Sono (Akan) elephant.

Soren (Danish) a form of Sören.

Sören (Danish) thunder; war.
Sorren

Sorley (Scandinavian) summer traveler; Viking.
Sorlea, Sorlee, Sorleigh, Sorli, Sorlie, Sorly

Soroush (Persian) happy.

Sorrel (French) reddish brown.
Sorel, Sorell, Soril, Sorill, Sorrell, Sorril, Sorrill, Soryl, Soryll

Soterios (Greek) savior.
Soteris, Sotero

Southwell (English) south well.
Southwal, Southwall, Southwel

Sovann (Cambodian) gold.
Sovan

Sowande (Yoruba) wise healer sought me out.
Sowand

Spalding (English) divided field.
Spaulding

Spangler (German) tinsmith.
Spengler

Spark (English) happy.
Sparke, Sparkee, Sparkey, Sparki, Sparkie, Sparky

Spear (English) spear carrier.
Speare, Spears, Speer, Speers, Speir, Speyr, Spiers

Speedy (English) quick; successful.
Speed, Speedee, Speedey, Speedi, Speedie

Spence (English) a short form of Spencer.
Spense

Spencer (English) dispenser of provisions.
Spencre

Spenser (English) a form of Spencer. Literature: Edmund Spenser was the British poet who wrote *The Faerie Queene*.
Spanser

Spike (English) ear of grain; long nail.
Spyke

Spiridone (Italian) a form of Spiro.
Spiridion, Spiridon, Spyridion, Spyridon, Spyridone

Spiro (Greek) round basket; breath.
Spyro, Spyros

Spoor (English) spur maker.
Spoors

Spreckley (English) twigs.
Sprecklea, Sprecklee, Spreckleigh, Spreckli, Sprecklie, Spreckly

Springsteen (English) stream by the rocks.
Springstein, Springsteyn, Spryngsteen, Spryngstein, Spryngsteyn

Sproule (English) energetic.
Sprowle

Spurgeon (English) shrub.

Spyros (Greek) a form of Spiro.
Spiros

Squire (English) knight's assistant; large landholder.
Squyre

Stacey, Stacy (English) familiar forms of Eustace.
Stace, Stacee, Staci, Stacie

Stafford (English) riverbank landing.
Staffard, Stafforde, Staford

Stamford (English) a form of Stanford.
Stemford

Stamos (Greek) a form of Stephen.
Stamatis, Stamatos

Stan (Latin, English) a short form of Stanley.
Stann

Stanbury (English) stone fortification.
Stanberi, Stanberie, Stanberri, Stanberrie, Stanberry, Stanbery, Stanburghe, Stanburi, Stanburie, Stanburri, Stanburrie, Stanburry, Stanbury, Stansbury

Stancil (English) beam.
Stancile, Stancyl, Stancyle

Stancio (Spanish) a form of Constantine.
Stancy

Stancliff (English) stony cliff.
Stanclif, Stanclife, Stancliffe, Stanclyf, Stanclyff

Standish (English) stony parkland. History: Miles Standish was a leader in colonial America.
Standysh

Stane (Slavic) a short form of Stanislaus.

Stanfield (English) stony field.
Stanfyld, Stansfield

Stanford (English) rocky ford.
Stamford, Standforde

Stanislaus (Latin) stand of glory. See also Lao, Tano.

Slavik, Stana, Standa, Stane, Stanislao, Stanislas, Stanislau, Stanislus, Stannes, Stano, Stanyslaus

Stanislav (Slavic) a form of Stanislaus. See also Slava.
Stanislaw

Stanley (English) stony meadow.
Stanely, Stanlea, Stanlee, Stanleigh, Stanli, Stanlie, Stanly

Stanmore (English) stony lake.
Stanmoar, Stanmoare, Stanmoor, Stanmoore, Stanmor

Stannard (English) hard as stone.
Stanard

Stanton (English) stony farm.
Stanten, Staunton

Stanway (English) stony road.
Stanwai, Stenwai, Stenway

Stanwick (English) stony village.
Stanwic, Stanwicke, Stanwik, Stanwyc, Stanwyck, Stanwyk

Stanwood (English) stony woods.
Stenwood

Starbuck (English) challenger of fate. Literature: a character in Herman Melville's novel *Moby-Dick*.
Starrbuck

Stark (German) strong, vigorous.
Starke, Stärke, Starkie

Starling (English) bird.
Starlin, Starlyn, Starlyng

Starr (English) star.
Star, Staret, Starlight, Starlon, Starwin

Stasik (Russian) a familiar form of Stanislaus.
Stas, Stash, Stashka, Stashko, Stasiek

Stasio (Polish) a form of Stanislaus.
Stas, Stasiek, Stasiu, Staska, Stasko

Stavros (Greek) a form of Stephen.
Stavro

Steadman (English) owner of a farmstead.
Steadmann, Steed

Stedman (English) a form of Steadman.
Stedmen

Steel (English) like steel.

Steele (English) a form of Steel.
Steale

Steen (German, Danish) stone.
Stean, Steane, Steene, Steenn

Steenie (Scottish) a form of Stephen.
*Steeni, Steeny, Steinee, Steiney, Steini,
Steinie, Steiny, Steynee, Steyney, Steyni,
Steynie, Steyny*

Steeve (Greek) a short form of Steeven.

Steeven (Greek) a form of Steven.
Steaven, Steavin, Steavon, Steevan, Steevn

Stefan (German, Polish, Swedish) a form
of Stephen.
*Steafan, Steaféan, Stefaan, Stefanson,
Stefaun, Stefawn*

Stefano (Italian) a form of Stephen.
Steffano

Stefanos (Greek) a form of Stephen.
Stefans, Stefos, Stephano, Stephanos

Stefen, Steffen (Norwegian) forms of
Stephen.
Steffin, Stefin

Steffan (Swedish) a form of Stefan.
Staffan

Steffon, Stefon (Polish) forms of
Stephon.
Staffon, Steffone, Stefone, Stefonne

Stein (German) a form of Steen.
Steine, Steyn, Steyne

Steinar (Norwegian) rock warrior.
*Steanar, Steaner, Steenar, Steener, Steiner,
Steynar, Steyner*

Stepan (Russian) a form of Stephen.
Stepa, Stepane, Stepanya, Stepka, Stipan

Steph (English) a short form of Stephen.

Stephan (Greek) a form of Stephen.
*Stepfan, Stephanas, Stephano, Stephanos,
Stephanus*

Stephane, Stéphane (French) forms of
Stephen.
Stefane, Stepháne, Stephanne

Stephanie (Greek) a form of Stephen.

Stephaun (Greek) a form of Stephen.

Stephen (Greek) crowned. See also
Esteban, Estebe, Estevan, Estevao,
Etienne, István, Szczepan, Tapani, Teb,
Teppo, Tiennot.
*Stenya, Stepanos, Stephanas, Stephens,
Stephfan, Stephin, Stepven*

Stephenson (English) son of Stephen.

Stephon (Greek) a form of Stephen.
*Stepfon, Stepfone, Stephfon, Stephion,
Stephonn, Stephonne*

Stephone (Greek) a form of Stephon.

Sterlin (English) a form of Sterling.
Sterlen, Styrlin, Styrlyn

Sterling (English) valuable; silver penny.
A form of Starling.
Styrling, Styrlyng

Stern (German) star.
Sturn

Sterne (English) austere.
Stearn, Stearne, Stearns, Sturne

Stetson (Danish) stepson.
Steston, Steton, Stetsen, Stetzon

Stevan (Greek) a form of Steven.
Stevano, Stevanoe, Stevaughn, Stevean

Steve (Greek) a short form of Stephen,
Steven.
Steave, Stevy

Steven (Greek) a form of Stephen.
Steiven, Stiven

Stevens (English) son of Steven.
Stevenson, Stevinson

Stevie (English) a familiar form of
Stephen, Steven.
Stevey, Stevy

Stevin, Stevon (Greek) forms of Steven.
Stevieon, Stevion, Stevyn

Stewart (English) a form of Stuart.
Steward, Stu

Stian (Norwegian) quick on his feet.

Stig (Swedish) mount.

Stiggur (Gypsy) gate.

Stillman (English) quiet.
Stillmann, Stillmon, Stilman, Styllman, Stylman

Sting (English) spike of grain.
Styng

Stirling (English) a form of Sterling.
Stirlin

Stockley (English) tree-stump meadow.
Stocklea, Stocklee, Stockleigh, Stockli, Stocklie, Stockly

Stockman (English) tree-stump remover.
Stockmen

Stockton (English) tree-stump town.

Stockwell (English) tree-stump well.
Stockwal, Stockwall, Stockwel

Stoddard (English) horse keeper.
Stodard

Stoffel (German) a short form of Christopher.

Stoker (English) furnace tender.
Stoke, Stokes, Stroker

Stone (English) stone.
Stoen, Stonee, Stoner

Stoney (English) a form of Stone.
Stoni, Stonie, Stoniy, Stony

Storm (English) tempest, storm.
Storme

Stormy (English) a form of Storm.
Stormee, Stormey, Stormi, Stormie, Stormmie

Storr (Norwegian) great.
Story

Stover (English) stove tender.

Stowe (English) hidden; packed away.
Stow

Strahan (Irish) minstrel.
Strachan

Stratford (English) bridge over the river. Literature: Stratford-upon-Avon was Shakespeare's birthplace.
Stradford, Strattford

Stratton (Scottish) river valley town.
Straten, Straton

Strephon (Greek) one who turns.

Strom (Greek) bed, mattress. (German) stream.

Strong (English) powerful.
Stronge

Stroud (English) thicket.

Struthers (Irish) brook.

Stu (English) a short form of Stewart, Stuart.
Stew

Stuart (English) caretaker, steward. History: a Scottish and English royal family.
Stuarrt

Studs (English) rounded nail heads; shirt ornaments; male horses used for breeding. History: Louis "Studs" Terkel is a famous American journalist.
Stud, Studd

Styles (English) stairs put over a wall to help cross it.
Stiles, Style, Stylz

Subhi (Arabic) early morning.

Suck Chin (Korean) unshakable rock.

Sudi (Swahili) lucky.
Su'ud

Sued (Arabic) master, chief.

Suede (Arabic) a form of Sued.

Suffield (English) southern field.
Sufield

Sugden (English) valley of sows.
Sugdan, Sugdin, Sugdon, Sugdyn

Suhail (Arabic) gentle.
Suhael, Sujal

Suhuba (Swahili) friend.
Suhubah

Sukhpreet (Sikh) one who values inner peace and joy.

Sukru (Turkish) grateful.
Sukroo

Sulaiman (Arabic) a form of Solomon.
Sulaman, Sulay, Sulaymaan, Sulayman, Suleiman, Suleman, Suleyman, Sulieman, Sulman, Sulomon, Sulyman

Sullivan (Irish) black eyed.
Sullavan, Sullevan, Syllyvan

Sully (French) stain, tarnish. (English) south meadow. (Irish) a familiar form of Sullivan.
Sullea, Sullee, Sulleigh, Sulley, Sulli, Sullie

Sultan (Swahili) ruler.
Sultaan, Sulten, Sultin, Sulton, Sultyn

Sum (Tai) appropriate.

Sumeet (English) a form of Summit.

Sumit (English) a form of Summit.

Summit (English) peak, top.
Sumet, Summet, Summitt, Summyt, Sumyt

Sumner (English) church officer; summoner.
Summner

Sundeep (Punjabi) light; enlightened.
Sundip

Sunny (English) sunny, sunshine.
Sun, Suni, Sunie, Sunni, Sunnie, Suny

Sunreep (Hindi) pure.
Sunrip

Surya (Sanskrit) sun.
Suria, Suriah, Suryah

Sutcliff (English) southern cliff.
Sutclif, Sutcliffe, Sutclyf, Sutclyff, Suttclif, Suttcliff

Sutherland (Scandinavian) southern land.
Southerland, Sutherlan

Sutton (English) southern town.
Suton

Sven (Scandinavian) youth.
Svein, Svend, Svenn, Swen, Swenson

Swaggart (English) one who sways and staggers.
Swaggert

Swain (English) herdsman; knight's attendant.
Swaine, Swane, Swanson, Swayn, Swayne

Swaley (English) winding stream.
Swail, Swailey, Swale, Swalea, Swalee, Swaleigh, Swales, Swali, Swalie, Swaly

Swannee (English) swan.
Swanee, Swaney, Swani, Swanie, Swanney, Swanni, Swannie, Swanny, Swany

Sweeney (Irish) small hero.
Sweanee, Sweaney, Sweani, Sweanie, Sweany, Sweenee, Sweeni, Sweenie, Sweeny

Swinbourne (English) stream used by swine.
Swinborn, Swinborne, Swinburn, Swinburne, Swinbyrn, Swynborn

Swindel (English) valley of the swine.
Swindell, Swyndel, Swyndell

Swinfen (English) swine's mud.
Swynfen

Swinford (English) swine's crossing.
Swynford

Swinton (English) swine town.
Swynton

Swithbert (English) strong and bright.
Swithbirt, Swithburt, Swithbyrt, Swythbert, Swythbirt, Swythburt, Swythbyrt

Swithin (German) strong.
Swithan, Swithen, Swithon, Swithun, Swithyn, Swythan, Swythen, Swythin, Swython, Swythun, Swythyn

Sy (Latin) a short form of Sylas, Symon.

Sydney (French) a form of Sidney.
Syd, Sydne, Sydnee, Sydni, Sydnie, Sydny, Syndey

Syed (Arabic) happy.
Syeed, Syid

Sying (Chinese) star.

Sylas (Latin) a form of Silas.
Syles, Sylus

Sylvain (French) a form of Silvan, Sylvester.
Silvain, Sylvian

Sylvan (Latin) a form of Silvan.
Silvanus

Sylvester (Latin) forest dweller.
Sly, Syl, Sylverster, Sylvestre

Symington (English) Simon's town, Simon's estate.
Simington

Symon (Greek) a form of Simon.
Syman, Symeon, Symion, Symms, Symone, Symonn, Symonns

Szczepan (Polish) a form of Stephen.

Szygfrid (Hungarian) a form of Siegfried.
Szigfrid

Szymon (Polish) a form of Simon.
Szimon

Taaveti (Finnish) a form of David.
Taavetie, Taavety, Taavi, Taavo, Taveti, Tavetie, Tavety

Tab (English) a short form of Tabner.
Tabb, Tabbie, Tabby, Tabi, Tabie, Taby

Tabari (Arabic) he remembers.
Tabahri, Tabares, Tabarious, Tabarius, Tabarus, Tabary, Tabur

Tabib (Turkish) physician.
Tabeeb, Tabyb

Tabner (German) shining, brilliant. (English) drummer. (German) spring.
Tab, Tabbener, Tabener

Tabo (Spanish) a short form of Gustave.

Tabor (Persian) drummer. (Hungarian) encampment.
Tabber, Taber, Taboras, Taibor, Tayber, Taybor, Taver

Tad (Welsh) father. (Greek, Latin) a short form of Thaddeus.
Tadd, Taddy, Tade, Tadek, Tadey

Tadan (Native American) plentiful.
Taden

Tadarius (American) a combination of the prefix Ta + Darius.
Tadar, Tadarious, Tadaris, Tadarrius

Tadashi (Japanese) faithful servant.
Tadashee, Tadashie, Tadashy

Taddeo (Italian) a form of Thaddeus.
Tadeo

Taddeus (Greek, Latin) a form of Thaddeus.
Taddeous, Taddius, Tadeas, Tades, Tadio, Tadious

Tadi (Omaha) wind.
Tadee, Tadey, Tadie, Tady

Tadleigh (English) poet from a meadow.
Tadlea, Tadlee, Tadley, Tadli, Tadlie, Tadly

Tadzi (Carrier) loon.
Tadzie, Tadzy

Tadzio (Polish, Spanish) a form of Thaddeus.
Taddeusz, Tadeusz

Taffy (Welsh) a form of David. (English) a familiar form of Taft.
Taffee, Taffey, Taffi, Taffie, Tafy

Taft (English) river.
Tafte, Tafton

Tage (Danish) day.
Tag, Taig, Taige, Tayg, Tayge

Taggart (Irish) son of the priest.
Tagart, Tagert, Taggert, Taggirt, Taggurt, Taggyrt, Tagirt, Tagurt, Tagyrt

Tahír (Arabic) innocent, pure.
Taheer, Taher, Tahyr

Tai (Vietnamese) weather; prosperous; talented.

Taima (Native American) born during a storm.
Taimah, Tayma, Taymah

Tain (Irish) stream. (Native American) new moon.
Taine, Tainn, Tayn, Tayne

Taishawn (American) a combination of Tai + Shawn.
Taisen, Taishaun, Taishon

Tait (Scandinavian) a form of Tate.
Taite, Taitt, Tayt, Tayte

Taiwan (Chinese) island; island dweller. Geography: a country off the coast of China.
Taewon, Tahwan, Taivon, Taiwain, Tawain, Tawan, Tawann, Tawaun, Tawon, Taywan

Taiwo (Yoruba) first-born of twins.
Taywo

Taj (Urdu) crown.
Taje, Tajee, Tajeh, Tajh, Taji

Tajo (Spanish) day.
Taio

Tajuan (American) a combination of the prefix Ta + Juan.
Taijuan, Taijun, Taijuon, Tájuan, Tajwan, Tayjuan

Takeo (Japanese) strong as bamboo.
Takeyo

Takis (Greek) a familiar form of Peter.
Takias, Takius

Takoda (Lakota) friend to everyone.
Takodah, Takota, Takotah

Tal (Hebrew) dew; rain. (Tswana) a form of Tale.
Talia, Tall, Talya

Talbert (German) bright valley.
Talberte, Talbirt, Talburt, Talburte, Talbyrt

Talbot (French) boot maker.
Talbott, Talibot, Talibott, Tallbot, Tallbott, Tallie, Tally, Talybot, Talybott

Talcott (English) cottage near the lake.
Talcot

Tale (Tswana) green.
Tael, Tail, Tayl

Talen (English) a form of Talon.
Tallen

Talib (Arabic) seeker.
Taleb, Talyb

Taliesin (Welsh) radiant brow.
Talisan, Taliesen, Talieson, Taliesyn, Tallas, Talyesin, Talyersyn, Tayliesin, Tayliesyn

Taliki (Hausa) fellow.

Talli (Delaware) legendary hero.
Talee, Taley, Tali, Tallee Talley, Tallie, Tally, Taly

Tallis (Persian) wise.
Talis, Tallys, Talys

Tallon (English, French) a form of Talon.

Talmadge (English) lake between two towns.
Talmage

Talmai (Aramaic) mound; furrow.
Talmay, Talmie, Telem

Talman (Aramaic) injured; oppressed.
Talmen, Talmin, Talmon, Talmyn

Talon (French, English) claw, nail.
Taelon, Taelyn, Talin, Tallin, Talyn

Talor (English) a form of Tal, Taylor.
Taelor, Taelur

Tam (Vietnamese) number eight. (Hebrew) honest. (English) a short form of Thomas.
Tamlane, Tamm

Taman (Slavic) dark, black.
Tama, Tamann, Tamen, Tamin, Tammen, Tamon, Tamone, Tamyn

Tamar (Hebrew) date; palm tree.
Tamarie, Tamario, Tamarr, Tamer, Tamor

Tamas (Hungarian) a form of Thomas.
Tamás, Tameas, Tammas

Tambo (Swahili) vigorous.
Tambow

Tamir (Arabic) tall as a palm tree.
Tameer, Tamirr, Tamyr, Tamyrr, Timir, Tymir, Tymyr

Tammany (Delaware) friendly.
Tamany

Tammy (English) a familiar form of
Thomas.
Tammie

Tamson (Scandinavian) son of Thomas.
*Tamsan, Tamsen, Tamsin, Tamson, Tamsun,
Tamsyn*

Tan (Burmese) million. (Vietnamese) new.
Than

Tandie (English) team.
Tandee, Tandey, Tandi, Tandy

Tane (Maori) husband.
Tain, Taine, Tainn, Tayn, Tayne, Taynn

Tanek (Greek) immortal. See also Atek.

Taneli (Finnish) God is my judge.
*Taneil, Tanel, Tanelie, Tanell, Tanella, Tanelle,
Tanely*

Taner (English) a form of Tanner.
Tanar, Tanery

Tanguy (French) warrior.
Tangui

Tani (Japanese) valley.
Tanee, Taney, Tanie, Tany

Taniel (Estonian) a form of Daniel.
Taniell, Tanyel, Tanyell

Tanis, Tannis (Slavic) forms of Tania,
Tanya (see Girls' Names).

Tanmay (Sanskrit) engrossed.

Tanner (English) leather worker; tanner.
Tann, Tannar, Tannery, Tannir, Tannor

Tannin (English) tan colored; dark.
Tanin, Tannen, Tannon, Tanyen, Tanyon

Tanny (English) a familiar form of Tanner.
Tana, Tannee, Tanney, Tanni, Tannie, Tany

Tano (Spanish) camp glory. (Ghanaian)
Geography: a river in Ghana. (Russian)
a short form of Stanislaus.
Tanno

Tanton (English) town by the still river.
Tantan, Tantin, Tantun, Tantyn

Tapan (Sanskrit) sun; summer.

Tapani (Finnish) a form of Stephen.
Tapamn, Tapanee, Tapaney, Tapanie, Tapany

Täpko (Kiowa) antelope.

Taquan (American) a combination of the
prefix Ta + Quan.
Taquann, Taquawn, Taquon, Taqwan

Tarak (Sanskrit) star; protector.

Taran (Sanskrit) heaven. (Sanskrit) a form
of Tarun.
Tarran

Taree (Australian) fig tree.
Tarey, Tari, Tarie, Tary

Tarek, Tarik, Tariq (Arabic) forms of
Táriq.
*Tareck, Tareek, Tareke, Taric, Tarick, Tariek,
Tarikh, Tarreq, Tarrick, Tarrik, Taryc, Taryck,
Taryk, Teryc, Teryck, Teryk*

Tarell, Tarrell (German) forms of Terrell.
Tarelle, Tarrel, Taryl

Taren, Tarren, Taryn (American) forms
of Taron.
Tarrin, Tarryn, Taryon

Tareton (English) a form of Tarleton.
*Taretan, Tareten, Taretin, Taretyn, Tartan,
Tarten, Tartin, Tarton, Tartyn*

Tarif (Arabic) uncommon.
Tareef, Taryf

Táriq (Arabic) conqueror. History: Tariq
bin Ziyad was the Muslim general who
conquered Spain.
Tareck, Tarique, Tarreq, Tereik

Tarleton (English) Thor's settlement.
*Tareton, Tarletan, Tarleten, Tarletin, Tarletyn,
Tarlton*

Taro (Japanese) first-born male.

Taron (American) a combination of Tad
+ Ron.
*Taeron, Tahron, Tarone, Tarrion, Tarron,
Tarrun*

Tarrance (Latin) a form of Terrence.
*Tarance, Tarence, Tarince, Tarrence, Tarrince,
Tarrynce, Tarynce*

Tarrant (Welsh) thunder.
*Tarant, Tarent, Tarrent, Terrant, Torant,
Torent, Torrant, Torrent*

Tarun (Sanskrit) young, youth.

Tarver (English) tower; hill; leader.
Terver

Tas (Gypsy) bird's nest.

Tashawn (American) a combination of the prefix Ta + Shawn.
Tashaan, Tashan, Tashaun, Tashon, Tashun

Tass (Hungarian) ancient mythology name.

Tasunke (Dakota) horse.

Tate (Scandinavian, English) cheerful. (Native American) long-winded talker.

Tatius (Latin) king, ruler. History: a Sabine king.
Tatianus, Tazio, Tytius, Tytyus

Tatum (English) cheerful.
Taitam, Taitem, Taitim, Taitom, Taitum, Taitym, Tatam, Tatem, Tatim, Tatom, Taytam, Taytem, Taytim, Taytom, Taytum, Taytym

Tau (Tswana) lion.

Tauno (Finnish) a form of Donald.

Taurean (Latin) strong; forceful. Astrology: born under the sign of Taurus.
Tauraun, Taurein, Taurin, Taurino, Taurion, Taurone, Tauryan, Tauryen, Tauryon

Taurus (Latin) Astrology: the second sign of the zodiac.
Taurice, Tauris

Tavares (Aramaic) a form of Tavor.
Tavaras, Tarvarres, Tavar, Tavaras, Tavarres, Taveress

Tavaris, Tavarus (Aramaic) forms of Tavor.
Tarvaris, Tavar, Tavari, Tavarian, Tavarous, Tavarri, Tavarris, Tavars, Tavarse, Tavarys, Tevaris, Tevarus, Tevarys, Teverus, Teverys

Tavarius (Aramaic) a form of Tavor.
Tavarious, Tevarius

Taved (Estonian) a form of David.
Tavad, Tavid, Tavod, Tavyd

Tavey (Latin) a familiar form of Octavio.
Tavy

Tavi (Aramaic) good.
Tavee, Tavie

Tavian (Latin) a form of Octavio.
Taveon, Taviann, Tavien, Tavieon, Tavio, Tavionne

Tavin, Tavon (American) forms of Tavian.
Tavonn, Tavonne, Tavonni

Tavion (Latin) a form of Tavian.

Tavis (Scottish) a form of Tavish.
Taviss, Tavys, Tavyss

Tavish (Scottish) a form of Thomas.
Tav, Tavysh

Tavo (Slavic) a short form of Gustave.

Tavor (Aramaic) misfortune.
Tarvoris, Tavores, Tavorious, Tavoris, Tavorise, Tavorres, Tavorris, Tavorrys, Tavorys, Tavuris, Tavurys

Tawno (Gypsy) little one.
Tawn

Tayib (Hindi) good; delicate.

Tayler (English) a form of Taylor.
Tailar, Tailer, Taylar, Tayller, Teyler

Taylor (English) tailor.
Taelor, Tailor, Talor, Tayllor, Taylour, Taylr, Teylor

Tayshawn (American) a combination of Taylor + Shawn.
Taysean, Tayshan, Tayshun, Tayson

Tayvon (American) a form of Tavian.
Tayvan, Tayvaughn, Tayven, Tayveon, Tayvin, Tayvohn, Taywon

Taz (Arabic) shallow ornamental cup.
Tazz

Tazio (Italian) a form of Tatius.

Teagan (Irish) a form of Teague.
Teagen, Teagun, Teegan

Teague (Irish) bard, poet.
Teag, Teage, Teak, Teeg, Teegue, Teig, Teige, Teigue, Tyg, Tygue

Teale (English) small freshwater duck.
Teal, Teel, Teele, Teil, Teile, Teyl, Teyle

Tearence (Latin) a form of Terrence.
Tearance, Tearnce, Tearrance

Tearlach (Scottish) a form of Charles.
*Tearlache, Tearloc, Tearloch, Tearloche,
Tearlock, Tearlok*

Tearle (English) stern, severe.
Tearl

Teasdale (English) river dweller.
Geography: a river in England.
Tedale

Teb (Spanish) a short form of Stephen.

Ted (English) a short form of Edward,
Edwin, Theodore.
Tedd, Tedek, Tedik, Tedson

Teddy (English) a familiar form of
Edward, Theodore.
*Teddee, Teddey, Teddi, Teddie, Tedee, Tedey,
Tedi, Tedie, Tedy*

Tedmund (English) protector of the land.
*Tedman, Tedmand, Tedmon, Tedmond,
Tedmondo, Tedmun*

Tedorik (Polish) a form of Theodore.
*Tedorek, Tedoric, Tedorick, Tedoryc, Tedoryck,
Tedoryk, Teodoor, Teodor, Teodorek*

Tedrick (American) a combination of
Ted + Rick.
*Teddrick, Tederick, Tedric, Tedrik, Tedryc,
Tedryck, Tedryk*

Teetonka (Lakota) big lodge.

Tefere (Ethiopian) seed.
Tefer

Tegan (Irish) a form of Teague.
Teghan, Teigan, Teigen, Tiegan

Tej (Sanskrit) light; lustrous.

Tejas (Sanskrit) sharp. (American) a form
of Tex.

Tekle (Ethiopian) plant.

Telek (Polish) a form of Telford.

Telem (Hebrew) mound; furrow.
Talmai, Tel, Tellem

Telford (French) iron cutter.
Telfer, Telfor, Telforde, Telfour, Tellford, Tellforde

Teller (English) storyteller.
Tell

Telly (Greek) a familiar form of Teller,
Theodore.
Telli, Tellie, Tely

Telmo (English) tiller, cultivator.

Telutci (Moquelumnan) bear making
dust as it runs.

Telvin (American) a combination of the
prefix Te + Melvin.
Tellvin, Telvan

Tem (Gypsy) country.

Teman (Hebrew) on the right side;
southward.
*Temani, Temanie, Temany, Temen, Temin,
Temon, Temyn*

Tembo (Swahili) elephant.
Tembeau

Tempest (French) storm.
Tempes, Tempess

Temple (Latin) sanctuary.

Templeton (English) town near the
temple.
Temp, Templeten, Templetown

Tennant (English) tenant, renter.
Tenant, Tennent

Tenner (Irish) Religion: a small form of
a rosary.

Tennessee (Cherokee) mighty warrior.
Geography: a southern U.S. state.
Tennesy, Tennysee

Tennyson (English) a form of Dennison.
Literature: Alfred, Lord Tennyson was a
nineteenth-century British poet.
*Tenney, Tenneyson, Tennie, Tennis, Tennison,
Tenny, Tenson, Tenyson*

Teo (Vietnamese) a form of Tom.
Tio, Tyo

Teobaldo (Italian, Spanish) a form of
Theobald.

Teodoro (Italian, Spanish) a form of
Theodore.
Teodore, Teodorico

Teon (Greek) a form of Teona (see Girls' Names).

Teppo (French) a familiar form of Stephen. (Finnish) a form of Tapani.

Tequan (American) a combination of the prefix Te + Quan.
Tequinn, Tequon

Teran, Terran, Terren, Terrin (Latin) short forms of Terrence.
Teren, Terin, Terone, Terrien, Terrone, Terryn, Teryn, Tiren

Terance, Terence, Terrance (Latin) forms of Terrence.
Terince, Terriance, Terrince, Terrynce, Terynce

Terel, Terell, Terelle, Terrelle (German) forms of Terrell.
Tereall

Teremun (Tiv) father's acceptance.

Terencio (Spanish) a form of Terrence.

Terez (Greek) a form of Teresa (see Girls' Names).

Teron (Latin) a form of Teran. (American) a form of Tyrone.

Terrell (German) thunder ruler.
Terrail, Terral, Terrale, Terrall, Terreal, Terryal, Terryel, Turrell

Terrence (Latin) smooth.

Terrick (American) a combination of the prefix Te + Derric.
Teric, Terick, Terik, Teriq, Terric, Terrik, Tirek, Tirik

Terrill (German) a form of Terrell.
Teriel, Teriell, Terril, Terryl, Terryll, Teryl, Teryll, Tyrill

Terrion (American) a form of Terron.
Tereon, Terion, Terione, Terrione, Terriyon, Terryon

Terris (Latin) son of Terry.
Teris, Terrys, Terys

Terron (American) a form of Tyrone.
Terone, Terrone, Terronn, Tiron

Terry (English) a familiar form of Terrence. See also Keli.

Tarry, Teree, Terey, Teri, Terie, Terree, Terrey, Terri, Terrie, Tery

Tertius (Latin) third.

Teshawn (American) a combination of the prefix Te + Shawn.
Tesean, Teshaun, Teshon

Tetley (English) Tate's meadow.
Tatlea, Tatlee, Tatleigh, Tetli, Tetlie, Tetly

Teva (Hebrew) nature.
Tevah

Tevan, Tevon, Tevyn (American) forms of Tevin.
Tevion, Tevohn, Tevone, Tevonne, Tevoun, Tevvan, Teyvon

Tevel (Yiddish) a form of David.
Tevell, Tevil, Tevill, Tevyl, Tevyll

Tevin (American) a combination of the prefix Te + Kevin.
Teavin, Teivon, Tevaughan, Tevaughn, Teven, Tevien, Tevinn, Tevvin

Tevis (Scottish) a form of Thomas.
Tevish, Teviss, Tevys, Tevyss

Tewdor (German) a form of Theodore.

Tex (American) from Texas.
Texx

Thabit (Arabic) firm, strong.
Thabyt

Thad (Greek, Latin) a short form of Thaddeus.
Thadd, Thade

Thaddeus (Greek) courageous. (Latin) praiser. Bible: one of the Twelve Apostles. See also Fadey.
Thaddaeus, Thaddaus, Thaddeau, Thaddeaus, Thaddeo, Thaddeos, Thaddeous, Thaddeys, Thaddiaus, Thaddis, Thaddius, Thadeaou, Thadeys, Thadia, Thadus

Thadeus (Greek, Latin) a form of Thaddeus.
Thadeas, Thadeaus, Thadeis, Thadeos, Thadeous, Thadieus, Thadios, Thadious, Thadius, Thadiys, Thadyas, Thadyos, Thadyus

Thady (Irish) praise.
Thadee, Thaddy, Thady

Thai (Vietnamese) many, multiple.

Thalmus (Greek) flowering.
Thalmas, Thalmis, Thalmos, Thalmous,
Thalmys

Thaman (Hindi) god; godlike.
Thamane, Thamen

Than (Burmese) million.
Tan

Thandie (Zulu) beloved.
Thandee, Thandey, Thandi, Thandiwe,
Thandy

Thane (English) attendant warrior.
Thain, Thaine, Thayn, Thayne

Thang (Vietnamese) victorious.

Thanh (Vietnamese) finished.

Thaniel (Hebrew) a short form of
Nathaniel.
Thaneal, Thaneel, Thaneil, Thaneyl,
Thaniell, Thanielle, Thanyel, Thanyell,
Thanyelle

Thanos (Greek) nobleman; bear-man.
Athanasios, Thanasis, Thanus

Thatcher (English) roof thatcher, repairer
of roofs.
Thacher, Thatch, Thaxter

Thaw (English) melting ice.

Thayer (French) nation's army.
Thay

Thebault (French) a form of Theobald.
Teobaud, Theòbault

Thel (English) upper story.

Thenga (Yao) bring him.
Thengah

Theo (English) a short form of Theodore.
Teo, Thio, Thyo

Theobald (German) people's prince. See
also Dietbald.
Tebaldo, Teobald, Teobaldo, Teobalt, Theballd,
Theobaldo, Theobalt, Thibault, Thyobald,

Thyobaldo, Thyobalt, Tibald, Tibalt, Tibold,
Tiebold, Tiebout, Toiboid, Tybald, Tybalt

Theodore (Greek) gift of God. See also
Feodor, Fyodor.
Téadóir, Teodomiro, Teodus, Teos, Theodor,
Theódor, Theodors, Theodorus, Theodosios,
Theodrekr, Tivadar, Tolek

Theodoric (German) ruler of the people.
See also Dedrick, Derek, Dirk.
Teodorico, Thedric, Thedrick, Thedrik,
Theodorick, Theodorik, Theodrick, Theodryk,
Theodryc, Theodryck, Theodryk

Theophilus (Greek) loved by God.
Teofil, Théophile, Theophlous, Theopolis

Theron (Greek) hunter.
Theran, Theren, Thereon, Therin, Therion,
Therrin, Therron, Theryn, Theryon

Theros (Greek) summer.
Theross

Thian (Vietnamese) smooth.

Thibault (French) a form of Theobald.
Thibaud, Thibaut, Tybault

Thien (Vietnamese) a form of Thian.

Thierry (French) a form of Theodoric.
Theirry, Theory

Thom (English) a short form of Thomas.
Thomy

Thoma (German) a form of Thomas.

Thomas (Greek, Aramaic) twin. Bible:
one of the Twelve Apostles. See also
Chuma, Foma, Maslin.
Thomason, Thomaz, Thommas, Thumas,
Tomcy

Thommy (Hebrew) a familiar form of
Thomas.
Thomee, Thomey, Thomi, Thomie, Thommee,
Thommey, Thommi, Thommie, Thomy

Thompson (English) son of Thomas.
Thomasin, Thomason, Thomeson, Thomison,
Thomsen, Thomson, Tompson, Tomson

Thor (Scandinavian) thunder. Mythology:
the Norse god of thunder.
Thore, Thorin, Thorr, Tor

Thorald (Scandinavian) Thor's follower.
Thorold, Torald

Thorbert (Scandinavian) Thor's brightness.
Thorbirt, Thorburt, Thorbyrt, Torbert, Torbirt, Torburt, Torbyrt

Thorbjorn (Scandinavian) Thor's bear.
Thorborn, Thorborne, Thorburn, Thorburne, Thurborn, Thurborne, Thurburn, Thurburne, Thorbyrn, Thorbyrne

Thorgood (English) Thor is good.

Thorleif (Scandinavian) Thor's beloved.
Thorleyf, Thorlief

Thorley (English) Thor's meadow.
Thorlea, Thorlee, Thorleigh, Thorli, Thorlie, Thorly, Torlee, Torleigh, Torley, Torli, Torlie, Torly

Thormond (English) Thor's protection.
Thormon, Thormondo, Thormun, Thormund, Thormundo

Thorndike (English) thorny embankment.
Thordike, Thordyke, Thorndyck, Thorndyke, Thorne, Thornedike, Thornedyke

Thorne (English) a short form of names beginning with "Thorn."
Thorn, Thornie, Thorny

Thornley (English) thorny meadow.
Thorley, Thorne, Thornlea, Thornlee, Thornleigh, Thornli, Thornlie, Thornly

Thornton (English) thorny town.
Thorne, Thornetan, Thorneten, Thornetin, Thorneton, Thornetyn, Thornetown, Thortan, Thorten, Thortin, Thorton, Thortyn

Thorpe (English) village.
Thorp

Thorwald (Scandinavian) Thor's forest.
Thorvald, Thorvaldo, Thorwaldo, Torvald

Thuc (Vietnamese) aware.

Thunder (English) thunder.

Thurlow (English) Thor's hill.
Thurlo

Thurman (English) Thor's servant.
Thirman, Thirmen, Thorman, Thurmen, Thurmun, Thurnman, Thurnmen

Thurmond (English) defended by Thor.
Thormond, Thurmondo, Thurmund, Thurmundo

Thurston (Scandinavian) Thor's stone.
Thirstan, Thirstein, Thirsten, Thirstin, Thirston, Thirstyn, Thorstan, Thorsteen, Thorstein, Thorsten, Thorstin, Thorstine, Thorston, Thorstyn, Thurstain, Thurstan, Thursteen, Thurstein, Thursten, Thurstin, Thurstine, Thurstyn, Torsten, Torston

Tiago (Spanish) a form of Jacob.

Tiba (Navajo) gray.
Tibah, Tibba, Tibbah, Tyba, Tybah, Tybba, Tybbah

Tibbot (Irish) bold.
Tibbott, Tibot, Tibott, Tibout, Tybbot, Tybot

Tiberio (Italian) from the Tiber River region.
Tiberias, Tiberious, Tiberiu, Tiberius, Tibius, Tyberious, Tyberius, Tyberrius

Tibor (Hungarian) holy place.
Tiburcio, Tybor

Tichawanna (Shona) we shall see.

Ticho (Spanish) a short form of Patrick.
Ticcho, Ticco, Tycco, Tycho, Tyco

Tieler (English) a form of Tyler.
Tielar, Tielor, Tielyr

Tien (Chinese) heaven.
Tyen

Tiennan (French) a form of Stephen.
Tyennan

Tiennot (French) a form of Stephen.
Tien

Tiernan (Irish) lord.
Tiarnach, Tiernan

Tierney (Irish) lordly.
Tyrney

Tige (English) a short form of Tiger.
Ti, Tig, Tyg, Tyge, Tygh

Tiger (American) tiger; powerful and energetic.
Tiga, Tige, Tigger, Tyger

Tighe (Irish) a form of Teague. (English) a short form of Tiger.

Tiimu (Moquelumnan) caterpillar coming out of the ground.
Timu, Tymu

Tiktu (Moquelumnan) bird digging up potatoes.

Tilden (English) tilled valley; tiller of the valley.
Tildan, Tildin, Tildon, Tildyn

Tilford (English) prosperous ford.
Tilforde, Tillford, Tillforde

Till (German) a short form of Theodoric.
Thilo, Til, Tillman, Tillmann, Tilman, Tilson, Tyl, Tyll

Tilton (English) prosperous town.
Tiltown, Tylton, Tyltown

Tim (Greek) a short form of Timothy.
Timm, Tym, Tymm

Timin (Arabic) born near the sea.
Timyn, Tymin, Tymyn

Timmie, Timmy (Greek) familiar forms of Timothy.
Timee, Timey, Timi, Timie, Timmee, Timmey, Timmi, Tymee, Tymey, Tymi, Tymie, Tymmee, Tymmey, Tymmi, Tymmie, Tymmy, Tymy

Timmothy (Greek) a form of Timothy.
Timmathy, Timmithy, Timmothee, Timmothey, Timmoty, Timmthy

Timo (Finnish) a form of Timothy.
Timio, Timmo, Tymmo, Tymo

Timofey (Russian) a form of Timothy.
Timofee, Timofei, Timofej, Timofeo

Timon (Greek) honorable.
Timan, Timen, Timin, Timyn

Timoteo (Italian, Portuguese, Spanish) a form of Timothy.
Timotao, Timotei

Timothe, Timothee (Greek) forms of Timothy.
Timothé, Timothée

Timothy (Greek) honoring God. See also Kimokeo.
Tadhg, Taidgh, Tiege, Tima, Timathee, Timathey, Timathy, Timithy, Timka, Timkin, Timok, Timontheo, Timonthy, Timót, Timote, Timoteus, Timotheo, Timotheos, Timotheus, Timothey, Timothie, Timthie, Tiomóid, Tomothy

Timur (Russian) conqueror. (Hebrew) a form of Tamar.
Timar, Timarr, Timer, Timor, Timour, Tymar, Tymarr, Tymer, Tymur

Tin (Vietnamese) thinker.
Tyn

Tino (Spanish) venerable, majestic. (Italian) small. A familiar form of Antonio. (Greek) a short form of Augustine.
Tion, Tyno

Tinsley (English) fortified field.
Tinslea, Tinslee, Tinsleigh, Tinsli, Tinslie, Tinsly, Tynslea, Tynslee, Tynsleigh, Tynsley, Tynsli, Tynslie, Tynsly

Tiquan (American) a combination of the prefix Ti + Quan.
Tiquawn, Tiquine, Tiquon, Tiquwan, Tiqwan

Tirrell (German) a form of Terrell.
Tirel, Tirrel

Tisha (Russian) a form of Timothy.

Tishawn (American) a combination of the prefix Ti + Shawn.
Tisean, Tishaan, Tishaun, Tishean, Tishon, Tishun

Tite (French) a form of Titus.
Tyte

Tito (Italian) a form of Titus.
Titos, Tyto

Titus (Greek) giant. (Latin) hero. A form of Tatius. History: a Roman emperor.
Titan, Titas, Titek, Titis

Tivon (Hebrew) nature lover.

TJ (American) a combination of the initials T. + J.
T.J., T Jae, Teejay, Tjayda

Tj (American) a form of TJ.

Toan (Vietnamese) complete; mathematics.

Tobal (Spanish) a short form of Christopher.
Tabalito

Tobar (Gypsy) road.
Tobbar

Tobi (Yoruba) great.
Tobbi

Tobias (Hebrew) God is good.
Tebes, Tobia, Tobiah, Tobiás, Tobiasz, Tobiath, Tobies, Tobyas

Tobin (Hebrew) a form of Tobias.
Toben, Tobian, Tobyn, Tovin

Tobit (Hebrew) son of Tobias.
Tobyt

Toby (Hebrew) a familiar form of Tobias.
Tobbee, Tobbey, Tobbie, Tobby, Tobe, Tobee, Tobey, Tobie, Tobye

Tod (English) a form of Todd.

Todd (English) fox.
Todde, Toddie, Toddy

Todor (Basque, Russian) a form of Theodore.
Teador, Tedor, Teodor, Todar, Todas, Todos

Toft (English) small farm.

Togar (Australian) smoke.
Tager, Togir, Togor, Togyr

Tohon (Native American) cougar.

Tokala (Dakota) fox.
Tokalah

Tokoni (Tongan) assistant, helper.
Tokonee, Tokonie, Tokony

Toland (English) owner of taxed land.
Tolan, Tolen, Tolin, Tolland, Tolon, Tolun, Tolyn

Tolbert (English) bright tax collector.
Tolberte, Tolbirt, Tolburt, Tolburte, Tolbyrt

Toller (English) tax collector.
Toler

Tolman (English) tax man.
Tollman, Tollmen, Tolmen

Tom (English) a short form of Thomas, Tomas.
Teo, Teom, Tome, Tomm

Toma (Romanian) a form of Thomas.
Tomah

Tomas (German) a form of Thomas.
Tomaisin, Tomaz, Tomcio, Tomek, Tomelis, Tomico, Tomik, Tomislau, Tommas, Tomo

Tomás (Irish, Spanish) a form of Thomas.
Tómas

Tomasso (Italian) a form of Thomas.
Tomaso, Tommaso

Tomasz (Polish) a form of Thomas.

Tombe (Kakwa) northerners.
Tomba

Tomer (Hebrew) tall.
Tomar, Tomir, Tomyr

Tomey, Tomy (Irish) familiar forms of Thomas.
Tome, Tomi, Tomie

Tomi (Japanese) rich. (Hungarian) a form of Thomas.
Tomee

Tomkin (English) little Tom.
Thomkin, Thomkyn, Tomkyn

Tomlin (English) little Tom.
Thomllin, Thomlyn, Tomlinson, Tomlyn

Tommie, Tommy (Hebrew) familiar forms of Thomas.
Tommee, Tommey, Tommi

Tonda (Czech) a form of Tony.
Tondah, Toneek, Tonek, Tonik

Toney, Toni, Tonny (Greek, Latin, English) forms of Tony.

Tong (Vietnamese) fragrant.

Toni (Greek, German, Slavic) a form of Tony.
Tonee, Tonie, Tonis, Tonnie

Tonio (Italian) a short form of Antonio. (Portuguese) a form of Tony.
Tono, Tonyo

Tony (Greek) flourishing. (Latin) praise-worthy. (English) a short form of Anthony. A familiar form of Remington.
Tonye

Tooantuh (Cherokee) spring frog.

Toomas (Estonian) a form of Thomas.
Toomis, Tuomas, Tuomo

Topher (Greek) a short form of Christopher, Kristopher.
Tofer, Tophor

Topo (Spanish) gopher.

Topper (English) hill.
Toper

Tor (Norwegian) thunder. (Tiv) royalty, king.
Tore, Torre

Toren, Torren (Irish) short forms of Torrence.
Torehn, Torreon, Torrin

Torey, Tori, Torrey, Torrie, Torry, Tory (English) familiar forms of Torr, Torrence.
Toree, Toreey, Torie, Torre, Torri

Torian (Irish) a form of Torin.
Toran, Torean, Toriano, Toriaun, Torien, Torion, Torrian, Torrien, Torryan

Torin (Irish) chief. (Latin, Irish) a form of Torrence.
Thorfin, Thorin, Thorstein, Thoryn, Torine, Torrine, Torryn, Torryne, Toryn

Torio (Japanese) tail of a bird.
Torrio, Torryo, Toryo

Torkel (Swedish) Thor's cauldron.

Tormey (Irish) thunder spirit.
Tormé, Tormee, Tormi, Tormie, Tormy

Tormod (Scottish) north.
Tormed, Tormon, Tormond, Tormondo, Tormun, Tormund, Tormundo

Torn (Irish) a short form of Torrence.
Toran, Torne

Torquil (Danish) Thor's kettle.
Torkel

Torr (English) tower.

Torrance (Irish) a form of Torrence.
Torance, Turance

Torrence (Irish) knolls. (Latin) a form of Terrence.
Tawrence, Toreence, Torence, Torenze, Torynce, Tuarence

Torrin (Irish, Latin, Irish) a form of Torin.

Torsten (Scandinavian) thunderstone.
Torstan, Torstin, Torston

Toru (Japanese) sea.

Toshi-Shita (Japanese) junior.

Tovi (Hebrew) good.
Tov, Tovee, Tovie, Tovy

Townley (English) town meadow.
Tonlea, Tonlee, Tonleigh, Tonley, Tonli, Tonlie, Tonly, Townlea, Townlee, Townleigh, Townli, Townlie, Townly

Townsend (English) town's end.
Town, Townes, Towney, Townie, Townsen, Townshend, Towny

Tra'von (American) a form of Travon.

Trace (Irish) a form of Tracy.
Trayce

Tracey (Irish) a form of Tracy.
Traci, Tracie, Treacey, Treaci, Treacie

Tracy (Greek) harvester. (Latin) coura-geous. (Irish) battler.
Tracee, Tracie, Treacy

Trader (English) well-trodden path; skilled worker.
Trade

Trae (English) a form of Trey.
Traey, Traie,

Traevon (American) a form of Trevon.

Trahern (Welsh) strong as iron.
Traherne, Trayhern, Trayherne

Trai (English) a form of Trey.

Tramaine (Scottish) a form of Tremaine.
*Tramain, Traman, Tramane, Tramayn,
Tramayne, Traymain, Traymon*

Traquan (American) a combination of
Travis + Quan.
*Traequan, Traqon, Traquon, Traqwan,
Traqwaun, Trayquan, Trayquane, Trayqwon*

Trashawn (American) a combination of
Travis + Shawn.
*Trasean, Trasen, Trashaun, Trashon, Trashone,
Trashun, Trayshaun, Trayshawn*

Traugott (German) God's truth.
Traugot

Travaris (French) a form of Travers.
*Travares, Travaress, Travarious, Travarius,
Travarous, Travarus, Travauris, Traveress,
Traverez, Traverus, Travoris, Travorus, Trevares,
Trevarious, Trevaris, Trevarius, Trevaros,
Trevarus, Trevores, Trevoris, Trevorus*

Travell (English) traveler.
*Travail, Travale, Travel, Traveler, Travelis,
Travelle, Travil, Travill, Traville, Travyl,
Travyll, Travylle*

Traven (American) a form of Trevon.
Travan, Trayven

Traveon (American) a form of Trevon.

Travers (French) crossroads.
Traver

Travion (American) a form of Trevon.
Travian, Travien, Travione, Travioun

Travis (English) a form of Travers.
*Travais, Travees, Traves, Traveus, Travious,
Traviss, Travius, Travous, Travus, Travys,
Travyss, Trayvis*

Travon (American) a form of Trevon.
Traivon, Travone, Travonn, Travonne

Travonte (American) a combination of
Travon + the suffix Te.

Tray (English) a form of Trey.
Traye

Trayton (English) town full of trees.
Traiton, Trayten

Trayvion (American) a form of Trayvon.
Trayveon

Trayvon (American) a combination of
Tray + Von.
Trayvin, Trayvone, Trayvonne, Trayvyon

Trayvond (American) a form of Trayvon.

Tre, Tré (American) forms of Trevon.
(English) forms of Trey.

Tre Von (American) a form of Trevon.

Trea (English) a form of Trey.

Treat (English) delight.
Treet, Treit, Treyt

Treavon (American) a form of Trevon.
Treavan, Treavin, Treavion

Treavor (Irish, Welsh) a form of Trevor.

Trebor (Irish, Welsh) a form of Trevor.

Tredway (English) well-worn road.
Treadway

Tremaine, Tremayne (Scottish) house
of stone.
*Tremain, Tremane, Treymaine, Tremayn,
Treymain, Treymayn, Treymayne, Trimaine*

Trent (Latin) torrent, rapid stream.
(French) thirty. Geography: a city in
northern Italy.
*Trant, Trante, Trente, Trentino, Trento,
Trentonio*

Trenten (Latin) a form of Trenton.

Trenton (Latin) town by the rapid stream.
Geography: the capital of New Jersey.
*Trendon, Trendun, Trentan, Trentin, Trentine,
Trentton, Trentyn, Trinten, Trintin, Trinton*

Trequan (American) a combination of
Trey + Quan.
*Trequanne, Trequaun, Trequian, Trequon,
Trequon, Treyquane*

Treshaun (American) a form of
Treshawn.

Treshawn (American) a combination of
Trey + Shawn.
*Treshon, Treshun, Treysean, Treyshawn,
Treyshon*

Treston (Welsh) a form of Tristan.
Trestan, Trestin, Trestton, Trestyn

Trev (Irish, Welsh) a short form of Trevor.

Trevar (Irish, Welsh) a form of Trevor.

Trevaughn (American) a combination of Trey + Vaughn.
Trevaughan, Trevaugn, Trevaun, Trevaune, Trevaunn, Treyvaughn

Trevell (English) a form of Travell.
Trevel, Trevelle, Trevil, Trevill, Treville, Trevyl, Trevyll, Trevylle

Trevelyan (English) Elian's homestead.
Trevelian

Treven, Trevin (American) forms of Trevon.
Trevien, Trevine, Trevinne, Trevyn, Treyvin

Treveon (American) a form of Trevon.
Treveyon, Treyveon

Trever (Irish, Welsh) a form of Trevor.

Trevion, Trévion (American) forms of Trevon.
Trevian, Trevione, Trevionne, Trevyon, Treyvion

Trevis (English) a form of Travis.
Trevais, Treves, Trevez, Treveze, Trevius, Trevus, Trevys, Trevyss

Trevon (American) a combination of Trey + Von.
Trevohn, Trevoine, Trevone, Trevonn

Trévon, Trevonne (American) forms of Trevon.
Trévan

Trevond (American) a form of Trevon.

Trevonte (American) a combination of Trevon + the suffix Te.

Trevor (Irish) prudent. (Welsh) homestead.
Travar, Traver, Travir, Travor, Trefor, Trevore, Trevour, Trevyr, Treyvor

Trey (English) three; third.
Trei, Treye

Treyton (English) a form of Trayton.
Treiton

Treyvon (American) a form of Trevon.
Treyvan, Treyven, Treyvenn, Treyvone, Treyvonn, Treyvun

Tri (English) a form of Trey.
Trie

Trigg (Scandinavian) trusty.
Trig

Trini (Latin) a short form of Trinity.
Triny, Tryny

Trinity (Latin) holy trinity.
Trenedy, Trinidy, Trinitee, Trinitey, Triniti, Trinitie, Trynyty

Trip, Tripp (English) traveler.
Tryp, Trypp

Tristan (Welsh) bold. Literature: a knight in the Arthurian legends who fell in love with his uncle's wife.
Tris, Trisan, Tristain, Tristann

Tristano (Italian) a form of Tristan.

Tristen, Tristin, Triston, Tristyn (Welsh) forms of Tristan.
Trisden, Trissten, Tristinn

Tristian (Welsh) a form of Tristan.

Tristram (Welsh) sorrowful. Literature: the title character in Laurence Sterne's eighteenth-century novel *Tristram Shandy*.
Tristam, Trystram, Trystran

Trot (English) trickling stream.

Trowbridge (English) bridge by the tree.
Throwbridge

Troy (Irish) foot soldier. (French) curly haired. (English) water. See also Koi.
Troi, Troye, Troyton

True (English) faithful, loyal.
Tru

Truesdale (English) faithful one's homestead.
Trudail, Trudale, Trudayl, Trudayle

Truitt (English) little and honest.
Truet, Truett, Truit, Truyt, Truytt

Truman (English) honest. History: Harry S. Truman was the thirty-third U.S. president.
Trueman, Trumain, Trumaine, Trumann

Trumble (English) strong; bold.
Trumbal, Trumball, Trumbel, Trumbell, Trumbul, Trumbull

Trung (Vietnamese) central; loyalty.

Trustin (English) trustworthy.
Trustan, Trusten, Truston

Trygve (Norwegian) brave victor.

Trystan, Trysten, Tryston (Welsh) forms of Tristan.
Tryistan, Trystann, Trystian, Trystin, Trystion, Trystn, Tristynne, Trystyn

Tsalani (Nguni) good-bye.

Tse (Ewe) younger of twins.

Tu (Vietnamese) tree.

Tuaco (Ghanaian) eleventh-born.

Tuan (Vietnamese) goes smoothly.
Tuane

Tuari (Laguna) young eagle.
Tuarie, Tuary

Tucker (English) fuller, tucker of cloth.
Tuck, Tuckar, Tuckie, Tucky, Tuckyr

Tudor (Welsh) a form of Theodore. History: an English ruling dynasty.
Todor, Tudore

Tug (Scandinavian) draw, pull.
Tugg

Tuketu (Moquelumnan) bear making dust as it runs.

Tukuli (Moquelumnan) caterpillar crawling down a tree.

Tulio (Italian, Spanish) lively.
Tullio

Tullis (Latin) title, rank.
Tullius, Tullos, Tully, Tullys

Tully (Irish) at peace with God. (Latin) a familiar form of Tullis.
Tulea, Tulee, Tuley, Tuli, Tulie, Tull, Tullea, Tullee, Tulley, Tulli, Tullie, Tuly

Tumaini (Mwera) hope.

Tumu (Moquelumnan) deer thinking about eating wild onions.

Tung (Vietnamese) stately, dignified. (Chinese) everyone.

Tungar (Sanskrit) high; lofty.

Tupi (Moquelumnan) pulled up.
Tupe, Tupee, Tupie, Tupy

Tupper (English) ram raiser.

Turi (Spanish) a short form of Arthur.
Ture

Turk (English) from Turkey.

Turlough (Irish) thunder shaped.
Thorlough, Torlough

Turner (Latin) lathe worker; wood worker.
Terner

Turpin (Scandinavian) Finn named after Thor.
Thorpin, Torpin

Tut (Arabic) strong and courageous. History: a short form of Tutankhamen, an Egyptian king.
Tutt

Tutu (Spanish) a familiar form of Justin.

Tuvya (Hebrew) a form of Tobias.
Tevya, Tuvia, Tuviah

Tuwile (Mwera) death is inevitable.

Tuxford (Scandinavian) shallow river crossing.
Tuxforde

Tuyen (Vietnamese) angel.

Twain (English) divided in two. Literature: Mark Twain (whose real name was Samuel Langhorne Clemens) was one of the most prominent nineteenth-century American writers.
Tawine, Twaine, Twan, Twane, Tway, Twayn, Twayne

Twia (Fante) born after twins.
Twiah

Twitchell (English) narrow passage.
Twitchel, Twytchel, Twytchell

Twyford (English) double river crossing.
Twiford, Twiforde, Twyforde

Txomin (Basque) like the Lord.

Ty (English) a short form of Tyler, Tyrone,
Tyrus.
Ti, Tie

Tybalt (Greek) people's prince.
Tibalt, Tybolt

Tyce (French) a form of Tyson.

Tye (English) a form of Ty.

Tyee (Native American) chief.

Tyger (English) a form of Tiger.
Tige, Tyg, Tygar, Tygger

Tyjuan (American) a form of Tajuan.

Tylar, Tylor (English) forms of Tyler.
Tilar, Tilor, Tyelar, Tylarr, Tylour

Tyler (English) tile maker.
*Tiler, Tyel, Tyeler, Tyelor, Tyhler, Tyle, Tylee,
Tylere, Tyller, Tylyr*

Tymon (Polish) a form of Timothy.
(Greek) a form of Timon.
*Tymain, Tymaine, Tyman, Tymane, Tymeik,
Tymek, Tymen, Tymin, Tymyn*

Tymothy (English) a form of Timothy.
*Tymithy, Tymmothee, Tymmothey, Tymmothi,
Tymmothie, Tymmothy, Tymoteusz,
Tymothee, Tymothi, Tymothie*

Tynan (Irish) dark.
Tinan, Tinane, Tynane

Tynek (Czech) a form of Martin.
Tynko

Tyquan (American) a combination of
Ty + Quan.
*Tykwan, Tykwane, Tykwon, Tyquaan,
Tyquane, Tyquann, Tyquine, Tyquinn,
Tyquon, Tyquone, Tyquwon, Tyqwan*

Tyran, Tyren, Tyrin, Tyron (American)
forms of Tyrone.
*Teiron, Tiron, Tirown, Tyraine, Tyrane,
Tyrinn, Tyrion, Tyrohn, Tyronn, Tyronna,
Tyroon, Tyroun, Tyrown, Tyrrin, Tyryn*

Tyre (Scottish) a form of Tyree.

Tyrece, Tyrese, Tyrice (American) forms
of Tyreese.
Tyreas, Tyresse

Tyree (Scottish) island dweller. Geography:
Tiree is an island off the west coast of
Scotland.
Tyra, Tyrae, Tyrai, Tyray, Tyrea, Tyrey, Tyry

Tyrée (Scottish) a form of Tyree.

Tyreek (American) a form of Tyrick.
Tyreik

Tyreese (American) a form of Terrence.
Tyrease, Tyreece, Tyreice, Tyres, Tyriece, Tyriese

Tyrek, Tyrik, Tyriq (American) forms of
Tyrick.
Tyreck, Tyreke

Tyrel, Tyrell, Tyrelle (American) forms of
Terrell.
Tyrrel, Tyrrell

Tyrez (American) a form of Tyreese.
Tyreze

Tyrick (American) a combination of
Ty + Rick.
Tyric, Tyriek, Tyrique

Tyrone (Greek) sovereign. (Irish) land of
Owen.
*Tayron, Tayrone, Teirone, Tirone, Tirowne,
Tyerone, Tyhrone, Tyroney, Tyronne, Tyrowne*

Tyrus (English) a form of Thor.
Tirus, Tiruss, Tyruss, Tyryss

Tysen (French) a form of Tyson.

Tyshaun, Tyshon (American) forms of
Tyshawn.

Tyshawn (American) a combination of Ty
+ Shawn.
*Tysean, Tyshan, Tyshauwn, Tyshian, Tyshinn,
Tyshion, Tyshone, Tyshonne, Tyshun,
Tyshunn, Tyshyn*

Tyson (French) son of Ty.
*Tison, Tiszon, Tycen, Tyesn, Tyeson, Tysie,
Tysin, Tysne, Tysone*

Tytus (Polish) a form of Titus.
Tytan

Tyus (Polish) a form of Tytus.

Tyvon (American) a combination of Ty + Von. (Hebrew) a form of Tivon.
Tyvan, Tyvin, Tyvinn, Tyvone, Tyvonne

Tywan, Tywon (Chinese) forms of Taiwan.
Tywain, Tywaine, Tywane, Tywann, Tywaun, Tywen, Tywone, Tywonne

Tzadok (Hebrew) righteous. See also Zadok.
Tzadik

Tzion (Hebrew) sign from God. See also Zion.

Tzuriel (Hebrew) God is my rock.
Tzuriya

Tzvi (Hebrew) deer. See also Zevi.
Tzevi

U

Uaine (Irish) a form of Owen.

Ualtar (Irish) a form of Walter.
Uailtar, Ualteir, Ualter

Ualusi (Tongan) walrus.
Ualusee, Ualusey, Ualusie, Ualusy

Ubadah (Arabic) serves God.
Ubada

Ubaid (Arabic) faithful.

Ubalde (French) a form of Ubaldus.
Ubald, Ubold

Ubaldo (Italian) a form of Ubaldus.
Uboldo

Ubaldus (Teutonic) peace of mind.
Ubaldas, Uboldas, Uboldus

Uberto (Italian) a form of Hubert.

Ucello (Italian) bird.
Uccelo, Uccello, Ucelo

Uche (Ibo) thought.

Uday (Sanskrit) to rise.
Udae, Udai

Udell (English) yew-tree valley. See also Dell, Yudell.
Eudel, Udale, Udall, Udalle, Udel, Udele, Udelle

Udit (Sanskrit) grown; shining.

Udo (Japanese) ginseng plant. (German) a short form of Udolf.

Udolf (English) prosperous wolf.
Udolfe, Udolff, Udolfo, Udolph, Udolphe

Ueli (Swiss) noble ruler.
Uelie, Uely

Uffo (German) wild bear.
Ufo

Ugo (Italian) a form of Hugh, Hugo.
Ugon

Ugutz (Basque) a form of John.

Uhila (Tongan) lightning.
Uhilah, Uhyla, Uhylah

Uilliam (Irish) a form of William.
Uileog, Uilleam, Ulick

Uinseann (Irish) a form of Vincent.

Uistean (Irish) intelligent.
Uisdean

Uja (Sanskrit) growing.

Uku (Hawaiian) flea, insect; skilled ukulele player.

Ulan (African) first-born twin.
Ulen, Ulin, Ulon, Ulyn

Ulbrecht (German) a form of Albert.
Ulbright, Ulbryght

Uldric (Lettish) a form of Aldrich.
Uldrick, Uldrics, Uldrik, Uldryc, Uldryck, Uldryk

Uleki (Hawaiian) wrathful.
Ulekee, Ulekie, Uleky

Ulf (German) wolf.
Ulph

Ulfer (German) warrior fierce as a wolf.
Ulpher

Ulfred (German) peaceful wolf.
Ulfrid, Ulfryd, Ulphrid, Ulphryd

Ulger (German) warring wolf.
Ulga, Ulgar

Ulices (Latin) a form of Ulysses.

Ulick (Scandinavian) bright, rewarding
mind.
Ulic, Ulik, Ulyc, Ulyck, Ulyk

Ulises, Ulisses (Latin) forms of Ulysses.
Ulishes, Ulisse

Ullivieri (Italian) olive tree.
Ulivieri

Ullock (German) sporting wolf.
*Uloc, Uloch, Uloche, Ulock, Ulok, Uloke,
Ulloc, Ulloch, Ulloche, Ullok, Ulloke*

Ulmer (English) famous wolf.
Ullmar, Ulmar, Ulmor, Ulmore

Ulmo (German) from Ulm, Germany.

Ulric (German) a form of Ulrich.
Ullric, Ullryc, Ulryc

Ulrich (German) wolf ruler; ruler of all.
See also Alaric, Olric.
*Uli, Ull, Ullrich, Ullrick, Ullrik, Ullrych,
Ullryck, Ullryk, Ulrech, Ulrick, Ulrico,
Ulrik, Ulrike, Ulrych, Ulryck, Ulryk, Ulu,
Ulz, Uwe*

Ultan (German) noble stone.
Ulten, Ultin, Ulton, Ultyn

Ultman (Hindi) god; godlike.

Ulyses (Latin) a form of Ulysses.
Ulysee, Ulysees

Ulysses (Latin) wrathful. A form of
Odysseus.
Eulises, Ulysse, Ulyssees, Ulyssius

Umang (Sanskrit) enthusiastic.
Umanga

Umar (Arabic) a form of Omar.
Umair, Umarr, Umayr, Umer

Umberto (Italian) a form of Humbert.
Umbirto, Umburto, Umbyrto

Umi (Yao) life.
Umee, Umie, Umy

Umit (Turkish) hope.

Unai (Basque) shepherd.
Una

Uner (Turkish) famous.

Unika (Lomwe) brighten.
Unikah

Unique (Latin) only, unique.
Uneek, Unek, Unikque, Uniqué, Unyque

Unity (English) unity.
Unitee, Unitey, Uniti, Unitie

Uno (Latin) one; first-born.
Unno

Unwin (English) nonfriend.
Unwinn, Unwyn

Upshaw (English) upper wooded area.

Upton (English) upper town.
Uptown

Upwood (English) upper forest.

Urban (Latin) city dweller; courteous.
Urbain, Urbaine, Urbanus, Urvan, Urvane

Urbane (English) a form of Urban.

Urbano (Italian) a form of Urban.

Uri (Hebrew) a short form of Uriah.
Urie

Uriah (Hebrew) my light. Bible: a soldier
and the husband of Bathsheba. See also
Yuri.
Uria, Urias, Urijah

Urian (Greek) heaven.
Urien, Urihaan, Uryan, Uryen

Uriel (Hebrew) God is my light.
Yuriel, Yuryel

Urson (French) a form of Orson.
Ursan, Ursen, Ursin, Ursine, Ursus, Ursyn

Urtzi (Basque) sky.

Urvil (Hindi) sea.
Ervil, Ervyl, Urvyl

Usama (Arabic) a form of Usamah.

Usamah (Arabic) like a lion.

Useni (Yao) tell me.
Usene, Usenet, Usenie, Useny

Usher (English) doorkeeper.
Usha

Usi (Yao) smoke.

Usman (Arabic) a form of Uthman.

Ustin (Russian) a form of Justin.
Ustan, Usten, Uston, Ustyn

Utatci (Moquelumnan) bear scratching itself.
Utatch

Uthman (Arabic) companion of the Prophet.
Uthmaan, Uthmen

Uttam (Sanskrit) best.

Uwe (German) a familiar form of Ulrich.

Uzair (Arabic) helpful.
Uzaire, Uzayr, Uzayre

Uzi (Hebrew) my strength.
Uzee, Uzey, Uzie, Uzy

Uziel (Hebrew) God is my strength; mighty force.
Uzia, Uzyel, Uzzia, Uzziah, Uzziel, Uzzyel

Uzoma (Nigerian) born during a journey.
Uzomah

Uzumati (Moquelumnan) grizzly bear.

V

Vachel (French) small cow.
Vache, Vachell, Vachelle

Vaclav (Czech) wreath of glory.
Vasek

Vadin (Hindi) speaker.
Vaden

Vail (English) valley. See also Bail.
Vael, Vaiel, Vaile, Vaill, Vale, Valle, Vayel, Vayl, Vayle

Vaina (Finnish) river's mouth.
Vainah, Vaino, Vayna, Vaynah, Vayno

Val (Latin) a short form of Valentin.
Vaal

Valborg (Swedish) mighty mountain.
Valbor

Valdemar (Swedish) famous ruler.
Valdimar, Valdymar, Vlademar

Valdus (German) powerful.
Valdis, Valdys

Valente (Italian) a form of Valentin.
Valenté

Valentin (Latin) strong; healthy.
Valentijn, Valentine, Valenton, Valenty, Valentyn, Valentyne

Valentino (Italian) a form of Valentin.
Valencio, Valentyno, Velentino

Valere (French) a form of Valerian.

Valerian (Latin) strong; healthy.
Valeriano, Valerio, Valerius, Valerya, Valeryan, Valeryn

Valerii (Russian) a form of Valerian.
Valera, Valerie, Valerij, Valerik, Valeriy, Valery

Valfrid (Swedish) strong peace.

Valgard (Scandinavian) foreign spear.
Valgarde, Valguard

Vali (Tongan) paint.
Valea, Valee, Valeigh, Valey, Valie, Valy

Valin (Hindi) a form of Balin.
Valan, Valen, Valon, Valyn

Vallis (French) from Wales.
Valis, Vallys, Valys

Valter (Lithuanian, Swedish) a form of Walter.
Valters, Valther, Valtr

Vamana (Sanskrit) praiseworthy.
Vamanah

Van, Vann (Dutch) short forms of Vandyke.
Vane, Vanno

Vance (English) thresher.
Vanse

Vanda (Lithuanian) a form of Walter.
Vandah, Venda

Vandan (Hindi) saved.
Vanden, Vandin, Vandon, Vandyn

Vander (Dutch) belongs.
Vandar, Vandir, Vandor, Vandyr, Vendar, Vender, Vendir, Vendor, Vendyr

Vandyke (Dutch) dyke.
Vandike

Vanya (Russian) a familiar form of Ivan.
Vanechka, Vanek, Vania, Vanja, Vanka, Vanusha, Vanyah, Wanya

Varad (Hungarian) from the fortress.
Vared, Varid, Varod, Varyd

Vardon (French) green knoll.
Vardaan, Vardan, Varden, Vardin, Vardon, Vardyn, Verdan, Verden, Verdin, Verdon, Verdun, Verdyn

Varen (Hindi) better.
Varan, Varin, Varon, Varyn

Varian (Latin) variable.
Varien, Varion, Varyan

Varick (German) protecting ruler.
Varak, Varek, Varic, Varik, Varyc, Varyck, Varyk, Warrick

Varil (Hindi) water.
Varal, Varel, Varol, Varyl

Vartan (Armenian) rose producer; rose giver.
Varten, Vartin, Varton, Vartyn

Varun (Hindi) rain god.
Varan, Varen, Varin, Varon, Varron, Varyn

Vasant (Sanskrit) spring.
Vasan, Vasanth

Vashawn (American) a combination of the prefix Va + Shawn.
Vashae, Vashan, Vashann, Vashaun, Vashawnn, Vashun

Vashon (American) a form of Vashawn.
Vishon

Vasilios (Italian) a form of Vasilis.
Vasileios, Vasilos, Vassilios

Vasilis (Greek) a form of Basil.
Vas, Vasaya, Vaselios, Vasil, Vasile, Vasileior, Vasilius, Vasilus, Vasily, Vasilys, Vasylis, Vasylko, Vasyltso, Vasylys, Vazul

Vasily (Russian) a form of Vasilis.
Vasilea, Vasilee, Vasileigh, Vasiley, Vasili, Vasilie, Vasilii, Vasilije, Vasilik, Vasiliy, Vassilea, Vassilee, Vassileigh, Vassiley, Vassili, Vassilie, Vassilij, Vassily, Vasya

Vasin (Hindi) ruler, lord.
Vasan, Vasen, Vason, Vasun, Vasyn

Vasu (Sanskrit) wealth.

Vasyl (German, Slavic) a form of William.
Vasos, Vassos

Vaughan (Welsh) a form of Vaughn.
Vaughen

Vaughn (Welsh) small.
Vaun, Vaune, Vawn, Vawne, Voughn

Veasna (Cambodian) lucky.
Veasnah

Ved (Sanskrit) sacred knowledge.

Vedie (Latin) sight.
Vedi, Vedy

Veer (Sanskrit) brave.
Vear, Veere

Vegard (Norwegian) sanctuary; protection.

Veiko (Finnish) brother.
Veyko

Veit (Swedish) wide.
Veyt

Velvel (Yiddish) wolf.

Vencel (Hungarian) a short form of Wenceslaus.
Vencal, Venci, Vencie, Vencil, Vencyl

Venedictos (Greek) a form of Benedict.
Venedict, Venediktos, Venedyct

Veniamin (Bulgarian) a form of Benjamin.
Venyamin, Verniamin

Venkat (Hindi) god; godlike. Religion: another name for the Hindu god Vishnu.

Venya (Russian) a familiar form of Benedict.
Venka

Verdun (French) fort on a hill. Geography: a city in France and in Quebec, Canada.
Virdun, Vyrdun

Vere (Latin, French) true.
Veir, Ver, Vir, Vyr

Vered (Hebrew) rose.
Verad, Verid, Verod, Veryd

Vergil (Latin) a form of Virgil. Literature: a Roman poet best known for his epic poem *Aenid*.
Verge, Vergel, Vergill, Vergille

Verlin (Latin) blooming.
Verlan, Verlain, Verlinn, Verlion, Verlon, Verlyn, Verlynn

Vermundo (Spanish) protective bear.
Vermond, Vermondo, Vermund

Vern (Latin) a short form of Vernon.
Verna, Vernal, Verne, Vernine, Vernis, Vernol, Virn, Virne, Vyrn, Vyrne

Vernados (German) courage of the bear.

Vernell (Latin) a form of Vernon.
Verneal, Vernel, Vernelle, Vernial

Verner (German) defending army.
Varner

Verney (French) alder grove.
Varney, Vernee, Verni, Vernie, Verny, Virnee, Virney, Virni, Virnie, Virny, Vurnee, Vurney, Vurni, Vurnie, Vurny, Vyrnee, Vyrney, Vyrni, Vyrnie, Vyrny

Vernon (Latin) springlike; youthful.
Varnan, Vernen, Vernin, Vernun, Vernyn

Verrill (German) masculine. (French) loyal.
Veral, Verall, Veril, Verill, Verral, Verrall, Verrell, Verroll, Veryl, Veryll

Veston (English) church town.
Vestan, Vesten, Vestin, Vestun, Vestyn

Vian (English) a short form of Vivian (see Girls' Names).

Vibert (American) a combination of Vic + Bert.
Viberte, Vybert, Vyberte

Vic (Latin) a short form of Victor.
Vick, Vicken, Vickenson, Vik, Vyc, Vyck, Vyk, Vykk

Vicar (Latin) priest, cleric.
Vickar, Vicker, Vickor, Vikar, Vycar, Vyckar, Vykar

Vicente (Spanish) a form of Vincent.
Vicent, Visente

Vicenzo (Italian) a form of Vincent.

Victoir (French) a form of Victor.

Victor (Latin) victor, conqueror. See also Wikoli, Wiktor, Witek.
Victa, Victer, Victorien, Victorin, Vitin, Vyctor

Victoriano (Spanish) a form of Victor.

Victorio (Spanish) a form of Victor.
Victorino

Victormanuel (Spanish) a combination of Victor + Manuel.

Vidal (Spanish) a form of Vitas.
Vida, Vidale, Vidall, Videll, Vydal, Vydall

Vidar (Norwegian) tree warrior.

Vidor (Hungarian) cheerful.
Vidore, Vidoor, Vydor

Vidur (Hindi) wise.

Vidya (Sanskrit) wise.
Vidyah, Vydya, Vydyah

Viet (Vietnamese) Vietnamese.

Viho (Cheyenne) chief.

Vijay (Hindi) victorious.

Vikas (Hindi) growing.
Vikash, Vikesh

Viking (Scandinavian) Viking; Scandinavian.
Vikin, Vykin, Vyking, Vykyn, Vykyng

Vikram (Hindi) valorous.
Vikrum

Vikrant (Hindi) powerful.
Vikran

Viktor (German, Hungarian, Russian) a form of Victor.
Viktoras, Viktors, Vyktor

Vilhelm (German) a form of William.
Vilhelms, Vilho, Vilis, Viljo, Villem

Vili (Hungarian) a short form of William.
Villy, Vilmos

Viliam (Czech) a form of William.
Vila, Vilek, Vilém, Viliami, Viliamu, Vilko, Vilous

Viljo (Finnish) a form of William.

Ville (Swedish) a short form of William.

Vimal (Hindi) pure.
Vylmal

Vin (Latin) a short form of Vincent.
Vinn

Vinay (Hindi) polite.
Vynah

Vince (English) a short form of Vincent.
Vence, Vinse, Vint, Vynce, Vynse

Vincens (German) a form of Vincent.
Vincents, Vincentz, Vincenz

Vincent (Latin) victor, conqueror. See also Binkentios, Binky, Wincent.
Uinseann, Vencent, Vicenzo, Vikent, Vikenti, Vikesha, Vincence, Vincentij, Vincentius, Vincenty, Vincien, Vincient, Vincint, Vinicent, Vinsent, Vinsint, Vinsynt, Vyncent, Vyncynt, Vyncynte, Vynsynt

Vincente (Spanish) a form of Vincent.
Vencente, Vinciente, Vinsynte, Vyncente

Vincenzo (Italian) a form of Vincent.
Vincencio, Vincenza, Vincenzio, Vinchenzo, Vinezio, Vinzenz

Vinci (Hungarian, Italian) a familiar form of Vincent.
Vinci, Vinco, Vincze

Vinny (English) a familiar form of Calvin, Melvin, Vincent.

Vinnee, Vinney, Vinni, Vinnie, Vynni, Vynnie, Vynny, Vyny

Vinod (Hindi) happy, joyful.
Vinodh, Vinood

Vinson (English) son of Vincent.
Vinnis, Vinsan, Vinsen, Vinsin, Vinsun, Vinsyn, Vyncen, Vyncyn, Vynsan, Vynsen, Vynsin, Vynson, Vynsun, Vynsyn

Vipul (Hindi) plentiful.

Viraj (Hindi) resplendent.

Virat (Hindi) very big.

Virgil (Latin) rod bearer, staff bearer.
Virge, Virgial, Virgie, Virgille, Virgilo, Vurgil, Vurgyl, Vyrge, Vyrgil, Vyrgyl

Virgilio (Spanish) a form of Virgil.
Virjilio

Virote (Tai) strong, powerful.

Vishal (Hindi) huge; great.
Vishaal

Vishnu (Hindi) protector.

Vitalis (Latin) life; alive.
Vital, Vitale, Vitaliss, Vitalys, Vitalyss, Vytal, Vytalis, Vytalys

Vitas (Latin) alive, vital.
Vitis, Vitus, Vytas, Vytus

Vito (Latin) a short form of Vittorio.
Veit, Vitin, Vitto, Vyto, Vytto

Vittorio (Italian) a form of Victor.
Vitor, Vitorio, Vittore, Vittorios

Vitya (Russian) a form of Victor.
Vitia, Vitja

Vivek (Hindi) wisdom.
Vivekinan

Vlad (Russian) a short form of Vladimir, Vladislav.
Vladd, Vladik, Vladko

Vladimir (Russian) famous prince. See also Dima, Waldemar, Walter.
Bladimir, Vimka, Vladamar, Vladamir, Vladimar, Vladimeer, Vladimer, Vladimere, Vladimire, Vladimyr, Vladjimir, Vladlen,

Vladimir *(cont.)*
Vladmir, Vladymar, Vladymer, Vladymir, Vladymyr, Volodimir, Volodya, Volya, Wladimir

Vladislav (Slavic) glorious ruler. See also Slava.
Vladya, Vladyslau, Vladyslav, Vlasislava, Wladislav

Vlas (Russian) a short form of Vladislav.

Vogel (German) bird.
Vogal, Vogil, Vogol, Vogyl

Volker (German) people's guard.
Folke

Volley (Latin) flying.
Volea, Volee, Voleigh, Voley, Voli, Volie, Vollea, Vollee, Volleigh, Volli, Vollie, Volly, Voly

Volney (German) national spirit.
Volnee, Volni, Volnie, Volny

Von (German) a short form of many German names. (Welsh) a form of Vaughn.
Vonn

Vova (Russian) a form of Walter.
Vovah, Vovka

Vuai (Swahili) savior.

Vyacheslav (Russian) a form of Vladislav. See also Slava.

W

Waban (Ojibwa) white.
Waben, Wabin, Wabon, Wabyn

Wade (English) ford; river crossing.
Wad, Wadi, Wadie, Waed, Waede, Waid, Waide, Whaid

Wadley (English) ford meadow.
Wadlea, Wadlee, Wadlei, Wadleigh, Wadli, Wadlie, Wadly

Wadsworth (English) village near the ford.
Waddsworth, Wadesworth

Wael (English) a form of Wales.

Wagner (German) wagoner, wagon maker. Music: Richard Wagner was a famous nineteenth-century German composer.
Waggoner, Wagnar, Wagnor, Wagoner

Wahid (Arabic) single; exclusively unequaled.
Waheed, Wahyd

Wahkan (Lakota) sacred.

Wahkoowah (Lakota) charging.

Wain (English) a short form of Wainwright. A form of Wayne.
Waine, Wane

Wainwright (English) wagon maker.
Wainright, Wainryght, Wayneright, Waynewright, Waynright, Waynryght

Waite (English) watchman.
Wait, Waitman, Waiton, Waits, Wayt, Wayte

Wake (English) awake, alert.
Waik, Waike, Wayk, Wayke

Wakefield (English) wet field.
Field, Waikfield, Waykfield

Wakely (English) wet meadow.
Wakelea, Wakelee, Wakelei, Wakeleigh, Wakeli, Wakelie, Wakely

Wakeman (English) watchman.

Wakiza (Native American) determined warrior.
Wakyza

Walby (English) house near a wall.
Walbee, Walbey, Walbi, Walbie

Walcott (English) cottage by the wall.
Walcot, Wallcot, Wallcott, Wolcott

Waldemar (German) powerful; famous. See also Valdemar, Vladimir.
Waldermar

Walden (English) wooded valley. Literature: Henry David Thoreau made Walden Pond famous with his book *Walden*.
Waldan, Waldin, Waldon, Waldyn, Welti

Waldo (German) a familiar form of Oswald, Waldemar, Walden.
Wald, Waldy

Waldron (English) ruler.
Waldran, Waldren, Waldrin, Waldryn

Waleed (Arabic) newborn.
Walead, Waled, Waleyd, Walyd

Walerian (Polish) strong; brave.
Waleryan

Wales (English) from Wales.
Wail, Whales

Walford (English) Welshman's ford.

Walfred (German) peaceful ruler.
Walfredd, Walfredo, Walfrid, Walfridd, Walfried, Walfryd, Walfrydd

Wali (Arabic) all-governing.

Walid (Arabic) a form of Waleed.

Walker (English) cloth walker; cloth cleaner.

Wallace (English) from Wales.
Wallas

Wallach (German) a form of Wallace.
Wallache, Walloch, Waloch

Waller (German) powerful. (English) wall maker.
Waler

Wallis (English) a form of Wallace.
Walice, Walise, Wallice, Wallise, Wallyce, Wallyse, Walyce, Walyse

Wally (English) a familiar form of Walter.
Walea, Walee, Waleigh, Waley, Wali, Walie, Wallea, Wallee, Walleigh, Walley, Walli, Wallie, Waly

Walmond (German) mighty ruler.

Walsh (English) a form of Wallace.
Walshi, Walshie, Walshy, Welch

Walt (English) a short form of Walter, Walton.
Waltey, Waltli, Walty

Walter (German) army ruler, general. (English) woodsman. See also Gautier, Gualberto, Gualtiero, Gutierre, Ladislav, Ualtar, Vladimir.
Valter, Vanda, Vova, Walder, Waltir, Waltli, Waltor, Waltyr, Wat, Wualter

Walther (German) a form of Walter.

Waltier (French) a form of Walter.
Waltyer

Walton (English) walled town.
Waltan, Walten, Waltin, Waltyn

Waltr (Czech) a form of Walter.

Walworth (English) fenced-in farm.
Wallworth, Wallsworth, Walsworth

Walwyn (English) Welsh friend.
Walwin, Walwinn, Walwynn, Walwynne, Welwyn

Wamblee (Lakota) eagle.
Wamblea, Wambleigh, Wambley, Wambli, Wamblie, Wambly

Wanbi (Australian) wild dingo.
Wanbee, Wanbey, Wanbie, Wanby

Wang (Chinese) hope; wish.

Wanikiya (Lakota) savior.
Wanikiyah

Wanya (Russian) a form of Vanya.
Wanyai

Wapi (Native American) lucky.
Wapie, Wapy

Warburton (English) fortified town.

Ward (English) watchman, guardian.
Warde

Wardell (English) watchman's hill.
Wardel

Warden (English) valley guardian.
Wardan, Wardin, Wardon, Wardun, Wardyn, Worden

Wardley (English) watchman's meadow.
Wardlea, Wardlee, Wardleigh, Wardli, Wardlie, Wardly

Ware (English) wary, cautious. (German) a form of Warren.
Warey

Warfield (English) field near the weir or fish trap.
Warfyeld

Warford (English) ford near the weir or fish trap.

Warick (English) town hero.
Waric, Warik, Warric, Warrick, Warrik,
Warryc, Warryck, Warryk, Waryc, Waryck,
Waryk

Warley (English) meadow near the weir
or fish trap.
Warlea, Warlee, Warlei, Warleigh, Warli,
Warlie, Warly

Warmond (English) true guardian.
Warmon, Warmondo, Warmun, Warmund,
Warmundo

Warner (German) armed defender.
(French) park keeper.
Warnor

Warren (German) general; warden; rabbit
hutch.
Waran, Waren, Waring, Warran, Warrenson,
Warrin, Warriner, Warron, Warrun, Warryn,
Worrin

Warton (English) town near the weir or
fish trap.
Wartan, Warten, Wartin, Wartyn

Warwick (English) buildings near the
weir or fish trap.
Warick, Warrick, Warwic, Warwik, Warwyc,
Warwyck, Warwyk

Waseem (Arabic) a form of Wasim.
Wasseem

Washburn (English) overflowing river.
Washbern, Washberne, Washbirn, Washbirne,
Washborn, Washborne, Washbourn,
Washbourne, Washburne, Washbyrn,
Washbyrne

Washington (English) town near water.
History: George Washington was the
first U.S. president.
Wash, Washingtan, Washingten, Washingtin,
Washingyn

Wasili (Russian) a form of Basil.
Wasily, Wassily, Wassyly, Wasyl, Wasyly

Wasim (Arabic) graceful; good-looking.
Wassim, Wasym

Watende (Nyakyusa) there will be
revenge.
Watend

Waterio (Spanish) a form of Walter.
Gualtiero

Watford (English) wattle ford; dam made
of twigs and sticks.
Wattford

Watkins (English) son of Walter.
Watkin, Watkyn, Watkyns, Wattkin,
Wattkins, Wattkyn, Wattkyns

Watson (English) son of Walter.
Wathson, Wattson, Whatson

Waverly (English) quaking aspen-tree
meadow.
Waverlea, Waverlee, Waverleigh, Waverley,
Waverli, Waverlie

Wayde (English) a form of Wade.
Wayd, Waydell

Wayland (English) a form of Waylon.
Waland, Wailand, Weiland, Weyland

Waylon (English) land by the road.
Walan, Wailan, Wailon, Wallen, Walon, Way,
Waylan, Waylen, Waylin, Waylyn, Whalan,
Whalen, Whalin, Whalon, Whalyn

Wayman (English) road man; traveler.
Waymon

Wayne (English) wagon maker. A short
form of Wainwright.
Wanye, Wayn, Waynell, Waynne, Whayne

Wazir (Arabic) minister.
Wazyr

Webb (English) weaver.
Web, Weeb

Weber (German) weaver.
Webber, Webner

Webley (English) weaver's meadow.
Webblea, Webblee, Webbleigh, Webbley,
Webbli, Webblie, Webbly, Weblea, Weblee,
Webleigh, Webli, Weblie, Webly

Webster (English) weaver.
Webstar

Weddel (English) valley near the ford.
Weddell, Wedel, Wedell

Wei-Quo (Chinese) ruler of the country.
Wei

Weiss (German) white.
Weis, Weise, Weisse, Weys, Weyse, Weyss, Weysse

Welborne (English) spring-fed stream.
Welbern, Welberne, Welbirn, Welbirne, Welborn, Welbourne, Welburn, Welburne, Welbyrn, Welbyrne, Wellbern, Wellberne, Wellbirn, Wellbirne, Wellborn, Wellborne, Wellbourn, Wellbourne, Wellburn, Wellbyrn, Wellbyrne

Welby (German) farm near the well.
Welbee, Welbey, Welbi, Welbie, Wellbey, Wellby

Weldon (English) hill near the well.
Weldan, Welden, Weldin, Weldyn

Welfel (Yiddish) a form of William.
Welvel

Welford (English) ford near the well.
Wellford

Wellington (English) rich man's town. History: the Duke of Wellington was the British general who defeated Napoleon at Waterloo.
Wellinton

Wells (English) springs.
Welles, Wels

Welsh (English) a form of Wallace, Walsh.
Welch

Welton (English) town near the well.
Welltan, Wellten, Welltin, Wellton, Welltyn, Weltan, Welten, Weltin, Weltyn

Wemilat (Native American) all give to him.

Wemilo (Native American) all speak to him.

Wen (Gypsy) born in winter.

Wenceslaus (Slavic) wreath of honor.
Vencel, Wenceslao, Wenceslas, Wiencyslaw

Wendel (German, English) a form of Wendell.

Wendell (German) wanderer. (English) good dale, good valley.

Wandale, Wendall, Wendil, Wendill, Wendle, Wendyl, Wendyll

Wene (Hawaiian) a form of Wayne.

Wenford (English) white ford.
Wynford

Wenlock (Welsh) monastery lake.
Wenloc, Wenloch, Wenlok

Wensley (English) clearing in a meadow.
Wenslea, Wenslee, Wensleigh, Wensli, Wenslie, Wensly

Wentworth (English) pale man's settlement.

Wenutu (Native American) clear sky.

Wenzel (Slavic) knowing. A form of Wenceslaus.
Wensel, Wensyl, Wenzell, Wenzil

Werner (English) a form of Warner.
Wernhar, Wernher

Wes (English) a short form of Wesley.
Wess

Wesh (Gypsy) woods.

Wesley (English) western meadow.
Weseley, Wesle, Weslea, Weslee, Wesleigh, Wesleyan, Wesli, Weslie, Wessley, Wezley

Wesly (English) a form of Wesley.

West (English) west. A short form of Weston.

Westbrook (English) western brook.
Brook, Wesbrook, Wesbrooke, Westbrooke

Westby (English) western farmstead.
Wesbee, Wesbey, Wesbi, Wesbie, Westbee, Westbey, Westbi, Westbie

Westcott (English) western cottage.
Wescot, Wescott, Westcot

Westin (English) a form of Weston.

Westley (English) a form of Wesley.
Westlee, Westleigh, Westly

Weston (English) western town.
Westan, Westen, Westyn

Wetherby (English) wether-sheep farm.
Weatherbey, Weatherbie, Weatherby, Wetherbey, Wetherbi, Wetherbie

Wetherell (English) wether-sheep corner.
Wetheral, Wetherall, Wetherel, Wetheril, Wetherill, Wetheryl, Wetheryll

Wetherly (English) wether-sheep meadow.
Wetherlea, Wetherlee, Wetherleigh, Wetherley, Wetherli, Wetherlie

Weylin (English) a form of Waylon.
Weilin, Weilyn, Weylan, Weylen, Weylon, Weylyn

Whalley (English) woods near a hill.
Whalea, Whalee, Whaleigh, Whaley, Whali, Whalie, Whallea, Whallee, Whalleigh, Whalli, Whallie, Whally, Whaly

Wharton (English) town on the bank of a lake.
Warton

Wheatley (English) wheat field.
Whatlea, Whatlee, Whatleigh, Whatley, Whatli, Whatlie, Whatly, Wheatlea, Wheatlee, Wheatleigh, Wheatli, Wheatlie, Wheatly

Wheaton (English) wheat town.
Wheatan, Wheaten, Wheatin, Wheatyn

Wheeler (English) wheel maker; wagon driver.
Wheelar

Whistler (English) whistler, piper.

Whit (English) a short form of Whitman, Whitney.
Whitt, Whyt, Whyte, Wit, Witt

Whitby (English) white house.
Whitbea, Whitbee, Whitbey, Whitbi, Whitbie

Whitcomb (English) white valley.
Whitcombe, Whitcumb, Whytcomb, Whytcombe

Whitelaw (English) small hill.
Whitlaw, Whytlaw

Whitey (English) white skinned; white haired.
Whitee, Whiti, Whitie, Whity

Whitfield (English) white field.
Whytfield

Whitford (English) white ford.
Whytford

Whitley (English) white meadow.
Whitlea, Whitlee, Whitleigh, Whitli, Whitlie, Whitly

Whitlock (English) white lock of hair.
Whitloc, Whitloch, Whitlok, Whytloc, Whytloch, Whytlock, Whytlok

Whitman (English) white-haired man.
Whit, Whitmen, Whytman, Whytmen

Whitmore (English) white moor.
Whitmoor, Whitmoore, Whittemoor, Whittemoore, Whittemore, Whytmoor, Whytmoore, Whytmore, Whyttmoor, Whyttmoore, Witmoor, Witmoore, Witmore, Wittemore, Wittmoor, Wittmoore, Wittmore, Wytmoor, Wytmoore, Wytmore, Wyttmoor, Wyttmoore, Wyttmore

Whitney (English) white island; white water.
Whittney, Whytnew, Whyttney, Widney, Widny

Whittaker (English) white field.
Whitacker, Whitaker, Whitmaker, Whytaker, Whyttaker

Wicasa (Dakota) man.
Wicasah

Wicent (Polish) a form of Vincent.
Wicek, Wicus

Wichado (Native American) willing.

Wickham (English) village enclosure.
Wick, Wikham, Wyckham, Wykham

Wickley (English) village meadow.
Wicklea, Wicklee, Wickleigh, Wickli, Wicklie, Wickly, Wilcley, Wycklea, Wycklee, Wyckleigh, Wyckley, Wyckli, Wycklie, Wyckly, Wyklea, Wyklee, Wykleigh, Wykley, Wykli, Wyklie, Wykly

Wid (English) wide.
Wido, Wyd, Wydo

Wies (German) renowned warrior.
Wiess, Wyes, Wyess

Wikoli (Hawaiian) a form of Victor.

Wiktor (Polish) a form of Victor.
Wyktor

Wil, Will (English) short forms of Wilfred, William.
Wilm, Wim, Wyl, Wyll

Wilanu (Moquelumnan) pouring water on flour.
Wylanu

Wilber (English) a form of Wilbur.

Wilbert (German) brilliant; resolute.
Wilberto, Wilbirt, Wilburt, Wilbyrt, Wylbert, Wylbirt, Wylburt, Wylbyrt

Wilbur (English) wall fortification; bright willows.
Wilburn, Wilburne, Willber, Willbur, Wilver, Wylber, Wylbir, Wylbur, Wylbyr, Wyllber, Wyllbir, Wyllbur

Wilder (English) wilderness, wild.
Wilde, Wylde, Wylder

Wildon (English) wooded hill.
Wildan, Wilden, Wildin, Wildyn, Willdan, Willden, Willdin, Willdon, Willdyn, Wyldan, Wylden, Wyldin, Wyldon, Wyldyn, Wylldan, Wyllden, Wylldin, Wylldon, Wylldyn

Wile (Hawaiian) a form of Willie.

Wiley (English) willow meadow; Will's meadow. See also Wylie.
Whiley, Wildy, Wilea, Wilee, Wileigh, Wili, Wilie, Willey, Wily

Wilford (English) willow-tree ford.
Wilferd, Willford, Wylford, Wyllford

Wilfred (German) determined peacemaker.
Wilferd, Wilfrid, Wilfride, Wilfried, Wilfryd, Willfred, Willfrid, Willfried, Willfryd

Wilfredo, Wilfrido (Spanish) forms of Wilfred.
Fredo, Wifredo, Willfredo

Wilhelm (German) determined guardian.
Wilhelmus, Wylhelm, Wyllhelm

Wiliama (Hawaiian) a form of William.
Pila

Wilkie (English) a familiar form of Wilkins.
Wikie, Wilke

Wilkins (English) William's kin.
Wilken, Wilkens, Wilkes, Wilkin, Wilks, Willkes, Willkins, Wylkin, Wylkins, Wylkyn, Wylkyns

Wilkinson (English) son of little William.
Wilkenson, Willkinson, Wylkenson, Wylkinson, Wylkynson

Willard (German) determined and brave.
Wilard, Williard, Wylard, Wyllard

Willem (German) a form of Wilhelm, William.
Willim

William (English) a form of Wilhelm. See also Gilamu, Guglielmo, Guilherme, Guillaume, Guillermo, Gwilym, Liam, Uilliam.
Bill, Billy, Vasyl, Vilhelm, Vili, Viliam, Viljo, Ville, Villiam, Wilek, Wiliam, Wiliame, Willaim, Willam, Willeam, Willil, Willium, Williw, Willyam, Wyliam, Wylliam, Wyllyam, Wylyam

Williams (German) son of William.
Wilams, Wiliamson, Willaims, Williamson, Wuliams, Wyliams, Wyliamson, Wylliams, Wylliamson, Wyllyams, Wylyams

Willie, Willy (German) familiar forms of William.
Wille, Willea, Willee, Willeigh, Willey, Willi, Willia, Wily, Wyllea, Wyllee, Wylleigh, Wylley, Wylli, Wyllie, Wylly

Willis (German) son of Willie.
Wilis, Willice, Williss, Willus, Wylis, Wyliss, Wyllis, Wylys, Wylyss

Willoughby (English) willow farm.
Willobee, Willobey, Willoughbey, Willoughbie, Willowbee, Willowbey, Willowbie, Willowby, Wyllowbee, Wyllowbey, Wyllowbi, Wyllowbie, Wyllowby, Wylobee, Wylobey, Wylobi, Wylobie, Wyloby

Wills (English) son of Will.

Wilmer (German) determined and famous.
Willimar, Willmer, Wilm, Wilmar, Wylmar, Wylmer

Wilmot (Teutonic) resolute spirit.
Willmont, Willmot, Wilm, Wilmont, Wilmott, Wylmot, Wylmott

Wilny (Native American) eagle singing while flying.
Wilni, Wilnie, Wylni, Wylnie, Wylny

Wilson (English) son of Will.
Willsan, Willsen, Willsin, Willson, Willsyn, Wilsan, Wilsen, Wilsin, Wilsyn, Wolson, Wyllsan, Wyllsen, Wyllsin, Wyllson, Wyllsyn, Wylsan, Wylsen, Wylsin, Wylson, Wylsyn

Wilstan (German) wolf stone.
Wilsten, Wilstin, Wilstyn, Wylstan, Wylsten, Wylstin, Wylstyn

Wilt (English) a short form of Wilton.

Wilton (English) farm by the spring.
Willtan, Willten, Willtin, Willton, Willtyn, Wiltan, Wilten, Wiltin, Wiltyn, Wylltan, Wyllten, Wylltin, Wyllton, Wylltyn, Wyltan, Wylten, Wyltin, Wylton, Wyltyn

Wilu (Moquelumnan) chicken hawk squawking.

Win (Cambodian) bright. (English) a short form of Winston and names ending in "win."
Winn, Winnie, Winny

Wincent (Polish) a form of Vincent.
Wicek, Wicenty, Wicus, Wince, Wincenty

Winchell (English) bend in the road; bend in the land.
Winchel, Wynchel, Wynchell

Windell (English) windy valley.
Windel, Wyndel, Wyndell

Windsor (English) riverbank with a winch. History: the surname of the British royal family.
Windsar, Windser, Wincer, Winsor, Wyndsar, Wyndser, Wyndsor

Winfield (English) friendly field.
Field, Winfrey, Winifield, Winnfield, Wynfield, Wynnfield

Winfred (English) a form of Winfield. (German) a form of Winfried.
Winfredd, Wynfred, Wynfredd

Winfried (German) friend of peace.
Winfrid, Winfryd, Wynfrid, Wynfryd

Wing (Chinese) glory.
Wing-Chiu, Wing-Kit

Wingate (English) winding gate.
Wyngate

Wingi (Native American) willing.
Wingee, Wingie, Wingy, Wyngi, Wyngie, Wyngy

Winslow (English) friend's hill.
Winslowe, Wynslow, Wynslowe

Winston (English) friendly town; victory town.
Winstan, Winsten, Winstin, Winstonn, Winstyn, Wynstan, Wynsten, Wynstin, Wynston, Wynstyn

Winter (English) born in winter.
Winterford, Winters, Wynter, Wynters

Winthrop (English) victory at the crossroads.
Wynthrop

Winton (English) a form of Winston.

Winward (English) friend's guardian; friend's forest.
Wynward

Wit (Polish) life. (English) a form of Whit. (Flemish) a short form of DeWitt.
Witt, Wittie, Witty, Wyt, Wytt

Witek (Polish) a form of Victor.
Wytek

Witha (Arabic) handsome.
Wytha

Witter (English) wise warrior.
Whiter, Whitter, Whyter, Whytter, Wytter

Witton (English) wise man's estate.
Whiton, Whyton, Wyton, Wytton

Wladislav (Polish) a form of Vladislav.
Wladislaw, Wladyslav, Wladyslaw

Wolcott (English) cottage in the woods.

Wolf (German, English) a short form of Wolfe, Wolfgang.
Wolff, Wolfie, Wolfy

Wolfe (English) wolf.
Woolf

Wolfgang (German) wolf quarrel. Music:
Wolfgang Amadeus Mozart was a
famous eighteenth-century Austrian
composer.
Wolfegang, Wolfgans

Wood (English) a short form of Elwood,
Garwood, Woodrow.

Woodfield (English) forest meadow.
Woodfyeld

Woodford (English) ford through the
forest.
Woodforde

Woodley (English) wooded meadow.
Woodlea, Woodlee, Woodleigh, Woodli,
Woodlie, Woodly

Woodrow (English) passage in the woods.
History: Thomas Woodrow Wilson was
the twenty-eighth U.S. president.
Woodman, Woodroe

Woodruff (English) forest ranger.
Woodruf

Woodson (English) son of Wood.
Woods, Woodsan, Woodsen, Woodsin,
Woodsyn

Woodville (English) town at the edge of
the woods.
Woodvil, Woodvill, Woodvyl, Woodvyll,
Woodvylle

Woodward (English) forest warden.
Woodard

Woody (American) a familiar form of
Elwood, Garwood, Wood, Woodrow.
Wooddy, Woodi, Woodie

Woolsey (English) victorious wolf.
Woolsee, Woolsi, Woolsie, Woolsy

Worcester (English) forest army camp.

Wordsworth (English) wolf-guardian's
farm. Literature: William Wordsworth
was a famous British poet.
Wordworth

Worie (Ibo) born on market day.

Worrell (English) lives at the manor of
the loyal one.
Worel, Worell, Woril, Worill, Worrel, Worril,
Worryl

Worth (English) a short form of
Wordsworth.
Worthey, Worthi, Worthie, Worthington,
Worthy

Worton (English) farm town.
Wortan, Worten, Wortin, Wortyn

Wouter (German) powerful warrior.

Wrangle (American) a form of Rangle.
Wrangla, Wrangler

Wray (Scandinavian) corner property.
(English) crooked.
Wrae, Wrai, Wreh

Wren (Welsh) chief, ruler. (English) wren.
Ren

Wright (English) a short form of
Wainwright.
Right, Wryght

Wrisley (English) a form of Risley.
Wrisee, Wrislie, Wrisly

Wriston (English) a form of Riston.
Wryston

Wuliton (Native American) will do well.
Wulitan, Wuliten, Wulitin, Wulityn

Wunand (Native American) God is good.
Wunan

Wuyi (Moquelumnan) turkey vulture
flying.

Wyatt (French) little warrior.
Whiat, Whyatt, Wiat, Wiatt, Wyat, Wyatte,
Wye, Wyeth, Wyett, Wyitt, Wytt

Wybert (English) battle bright.
Wibert, Wibirt, Wiburt, Wibyrt, Wybirt,
Wyburt, Wybyrt

Wyborn (Scandinavian) war bear.
Wibjorn, Wiborn, Wybjorn

Wyck (Scandinavian) village.
Wic, Wick, Wik, Wyc, Wyk

Wycliff (English) white cliff; village near the cliff.
Wiclif, Wicliff, Wicliffe, Wyckliffe, Wycliffe

Wylie (English) charming. See also Wiley.
Wye, Wylea, Wylee, Wyleigh, Wyley, Wyli, Wyllie, Wyly

Wyman (English) fighter, warrior.
Waiman, Waimen, Wayman, Waymen, Wiman, Wimen

Wymer (English) famous in battle.
Wimer

Wyn (Welsh) light skinned; white. (English) friend. A short form of Selwyn.
Wyne, Wynn, Wynne

Wyndham (Scottish) village near the winding road.
Windham, Winham, Wynndham

Wynono (Native American) first-born son.

Wynton (English) a form of Winston.
Wynten

Wythe (English) willow tree.
Withe, Wyth

Xabat (Basque) savior.

Xaiver (Basque) a form of Xavier.
Xajavier, Xzaiver

Xan (Greek) a short form of Alexander.
Xane

Xander (Greek) a short form of Alexander.
Xande, Xzander

Xanthippus (Greek) light-colored horse. See also Zanthippus.
Xanthyppus

Xanthus (Latin) golden haired. See also Zanthus.
Xanthius, Xanthos, Xanthyas

Xarles (Basque) a form of Charles.

Xaver (Spanish) a form of Xavier.
Xever, Zever

Xavier (Arabic) bright. (Basque) owner of the new house. See also Exavier, Javier, Salvatore, Saverio, Zavier.
Xabier, Xavaeir, Xaver, Xavery, Xavian, Xaviar, Xaviero, Xavior, Xavon, Xavyer, Xizavier, Xxavier

Xenophon (Greek) strange voice.
Xeno, Zennie, Zenophon

Xenos (Greek) stranger; guest.
Zenos

Xerxes (Persian) ruler. History: a king of Persia.
Xeres, Xerus, Zerk, Zerzes

Xeven (Slavic) lively.
Xyven

Ximenes (Spanish) a form of Simon.
Ximen, Ximene, Ximenez, Ximon, Ximun, Xymen, Xymenes, Xymon, Zimenes, Zymenes, Xymon

Xylon (Greek) forest.
Xilon, Zilon, Zylon

Xzavier (Basque) a form of Xavier.
Xzavaier, Xzaver, Xzavion, Xzavior, Xzvaier

Yabarak (Australian) sea.
Yabarac, Yabarack

Yadid (Hebrew) friend; beloved.
Yadyd, Yedid

Yadon (Hebrew) he will judge.
Yadean, Yadin, Yadun

Yael (Hebrew) a form of Jael.
Yaell

Yafeu (Ibo) bold.

Yagil (Hebrew) he will rejoice.
Yagel, Yagyl, Yogil, Yogyl

Yago (Spanish) a form of James.

Yahto (Lakota) blue.

Yahya (Arabic) living.

Yahye (Arabic) a form of Yahya.

Yair (Hebrew) he will enlighten.
Yahir, Yayr

Yakecen (Dene) sky song.

Yakez (Carrier) heaven.

Yakir (Hebrew) honored.
Yakire, Yakyr, Yakyre

Yakov (Russian) a form of Jacob.
Yaacob, Yaacov, Yaakov, Yachov, Yacoub, Yacov, Yakob, Yashko

Yale (German) productive. (English) old.
Yail, Yaill, Yayl, Yayll

Yamil (Arabic) a form of Yamila (see Girls' Names).

Yan, Yann (Russian) forms of John.

Yana (Native American) bear.

Yancey (Native American) a form of Yancy.
Yansey, Yantsey, Yauncey

Yancy (Native American) Englishman, Yankee.
Yance, Yanci, Yansy, Yauncy, Yency

Yang (Chinese) people of goat tongue.

Yanick, Yanik, Yannick (Russian) familiar forms of Yan.
Yanic, Yannic, Yannik, Yonic, Yonnik

Yanka (Russian) a familiar form of John.

Yanni (Greek) a form of John.
Ioannis, Yani, Yannakis, Yannis, Yanny, Yiannis

Yanton (Hebrew) a form of Johnathon, Jonathen.

Yao (Ewe) born on Thursday.

Yaphet (Hebrew) a form of Japheth.
Yapheth, Yefat, Yephat

Yarb (Gypsy) herb.

Yardan (Arabic) king.

Yarden (Hebrew) a form of Jordan.

Yardley (English) enclosed meadow.
Lee, Yard, Yardlea, Yardlee, Yardleigh, Yardli, Yardlie, Yardly

Yarom (Hebrew) he will raise up.
Yarum

Yaron (Hebrew) he will sing; he will cry out.
Jaron, Yairon

Yasashiku (Japanese) gentle; polite.

Yash (Hindi) victorious; glory.

Yasha (Russian) a form of Jacob, James.
Yascha, Yashka, Yashko

Yashwant (Hindi) glorious.

Yasin (Arabic) prophet.
Yasine, Yasseen, Yassin, Yassine, Yazen

Yasir (Afghan) humble; takes it easy. (Arabic) wealthy.
Yasar, Yaser, Yashar, Yasser

Yasuo (Japanese) restful.

Yates (English) gates.
Yaits, Yayts, Yeats

Yatin (Hindi) ascetic.

Yavin (Hebrew) he will understand.
Jabin

Yawo (Akan) born on Thursday.

Yazid (Arabic) his power will increase.
Yazeed, Yazide, Yazyd

Yechiel (Hebrew) God lives.

Yedidya (Hebrew) a form of Jedidiah. See also Didi.
Yadai, Yedidia, Yedidiah, Yido

Yegor (Russian) a form of George. See also Egor, Igor.
Ygor

Yehoshua (Hebrew) a form of Joshua.
Y'shua, Yeshua, Yeshuah, Yoshua, Yushua

Yehoyakem (Hebrew) a form of Joachim.
Yakim, Yehayakim, Yokim, Yoyakim

Yehuda, Yehudah (Hebrew) forms of
Yehudi.

Yehudi (Hebrew) a form of Judah.
Yechudi, Yechudit, Yehudie, Yehudit, Yehudy

Yelutci (Moquelumnan) bear walking
silently.

Yeoman (English) attendant; retainer.
Yeomen, Yoeman, Yoman, Youman

Yeremey (Russian) a form of Jeremiah.
Yarema, Yaremka, Yeremy, Yerik

Yervant (Armenian) king, ruler. History:
an Armenian king.

Yeshaya (Hebrew) gift. See also Shai.

Yeshurun (Hebrew) right way.

Yeska (Russian) a form of Joseph.
Yesya

Yestin (Welsh) just.
Yestan, Yesten, Yeston, Yestyn

Yevgeny (Russian) a form of Yevgenyi.

Yevgenyi (Russian) a form of Eugene.
Gena, Yevgeni, Yevgenij, Yevgeniy, Yevgeny

Yigal (Hebrew) he will redeem.
Yagel, Yigael

Yirmaya (Hebrew) a form of Jeremiah.
Yirmayahu

Yishai (Hebrew) a form of Jesse.

Yisrael (Hebrew) a form of Israel.
Yesarel, Ysrael

Yisroel (Hebrew) a form of Yisrael.

Yitro (Hebrew) a form of Jethro.

Yitzchak (Hebrew) a form of Isaac. See
also Itzak.
*Yitzaac, Yitzaack, Yitzaak, Yitzac, Yitzack,
Yitzak, Yitzchok, Yitzhak*

Yngve (Swedish) ancestor; lord, master.

Yo (Cambodian) honest.

Yoakim (Slavic) a form of Jacob.
Yoackim

Yoan, Yoann (German) forms of Johann.

Yoav (Hebrew) a form of Joab.

Yochanan (Hebrew) a form of John.
Yohanan

Yoel (Hebrew) a form of Joel.

Yogesh (Hindi) ascetic. Religion: another
name for the Hindu god Shiva.

Yogi (Sanskrit) union; person who prac-
tices yoga.
Yogee, Yogey, Yogie, Yogy

Yohan, Yohann (German) forms of
Johann.
*Yohane, Yohanes, Yohanne, Yohannes, Yohans,
Yohn*

Yohance (Hausa) a form of John.

Yonah (Hebrew) a form of Jonah.
Yona, Yonas

Yonatan (Hebrew) a form of Jonathan.
Yonathon, Yonaton, Yonattan

Yonathan (Hebrew) a form of Yonatan.

Yong (Chinese) courageous.
Yonge

Yong-Sun (Korean) dragon in the first
position; courageous.

Yoni (Greek) a form of Yanni.
Yonny, Yony

Yonis (Hebrew) a form of Yonus.

Yonus (Hebrew) dove.
Yonas, Yonnas, Yonos, Yonys

Yoofi (Akan) born on Friday.

Yooku (Fante) born on Wednesday.

Yoram (Hebrew) God is high.
Joram

Yorgos (Greek) a form of George.
Yiorgos, Yorgo

Yorick (English) farmer. (Scandinavian) a
form of George.
Yoric, Yorik, Yorrick, Yoryc, Yoryck, Yoryk

York (English) boar estate; yew-tree
estate.
Yorke, Yorker, Yorkie

Yorkoo (Fante) born on Thursday.

Yosef (Hebrew) a form of Joseph. See also Osip.
Yoceph, Yoosuf, Yoseff, Yoseph, Yosief, Yosif, Yosuf, Yosyf

Yóshi (Japanese) adopted son.
Yoshee, Yoshie, Yoshiki, Yoshiuki

Yoshiyahu (Hebrew) a form of Josiah.
Yoshia, Yoshiah, Yoshiya, Yoshiyah, Yosiah

Yoskolo (Moquelumnan) breaking off pine cones.

Yosu (Hebrew) a form of Jesus.

Yotimo (Moquelumnan) yellow jacket carrying food to its hive.

Yottoko (Native American) mud at the water's edge.

Young (English) young.
Yung

Young-Jae (Korean) pile of prosperity.

Young-Soo (Korean) keeping the prosperity.

Youri (Russian) a form of Yuri.

Youseef, Yousef (Yiddish) forms of Joseph.
Yousaf, Youseph, Yousif, Youssef, Yousseff, Yousuf

Youssel (Yiddish) a familiar form of Joseph.
Yussel

Yov (Russian) a short form of Yoakim.

Yovani (Slavic) a form of Jovan.
Yovan, Yovanni, Yovanny, Yovany, Yovni

Yoyi (Hebrew) a form of George.

Yrjo (Finnish) a form of George.

Ysidro (Greek) a short form of Isidore.

Yu (Chinese) universe.
Yue

Yudan (Hebrew) judgment.
Yuden, Yudin, Yudon, Yudyn

Yudell (English) a form of Udell.
Yudale, Yudel

Yuki (Japanese) snow.
Yukiko, Yukio

Yul (Mongolian) beyond the horizon.

Yule (English) born at Christmas.
Yull

Yuli (Basque) youthful.

Yuma (Native American) son of a chief.
Yumah

Yunus (Turkish) a form of Jonah.
Younis, Younys, Yunis, Yunys

Yurcel (Turkish) sublime.

Yuri (Russian, Ukrainian) a form of George. (Hebrew) a familiar form of Uriah.
Yehor, Yura, Yure, Yuria, Yuric, Yurii, Yurij, Yurik, Yurko, Yurri, Yury, Yurya, Yusha

Yusef, Yusuf (Arabic, Swahili) forms of Joseph.
Yussef, Yusuff

Yusif (Russian) a form of Joseph.
Yuseph, Yusof, Yussof, Yusup, Yuzef, Yuzep

Yustyn (Russian) a form of Justin.
Yusts

Yutu (Moquelumnan) coyote out hunting.

Yuuki (Japanese) a form of Yuki.

Yuval (Hebrew) rejoicing.

Yves (French) a form of Ivar, Ives.
Yvens, Yyves

Yvon (French) a form of Ivar, Yves.
Ivon, Yuvon, Yvan, Yven, Yvin, Yvonne, Yvyn

Ywain (Irish) a form of Owen.
Ywaine, Ywayn, Ywayne, Ywyn

Zabdi (Hebrew) a short form of Zabdiel.
Zabad, Zabdy, Zabi, Zavdi, Zebdy

Zabdiel (Hebrew) present, gift.
Zabdil, Zabdyl, Zavdiel, Zebdiel

Zac (Hebrew) a short form of Zachariah,
Zachary.
Zacc

Zacarias (Portuguese, Spanish) a form of
Zachariah.
*Zacaria, Zacariah, Zacarious, Zacarius,
Zaccaria, Zaccariah*

Zacary, Zaccary (Hebrew) forms of
Zachary.
*Zacaras, Zacari, Zacarie, Zaccari, Zaccary,
Zaccea, Zaccury, Zacery, Zacrye*

Zacchaeus (Hebrew) a form of
Zaccheus.

Zaccheus (Hebrew) innocent, pure.
Zacceus, Zacchious, Zachaios

Zach (Hebrew) a short form of
Zachariah, Zachary.

Zacharey, Zachari, Zacharie (Hebrew)
forms of Zachary.
*Zaccharie, Zachare, Zacharee, Zacheri,
Zachurie, Zecharie*

Zacharia (Hebrew) a form of Zachariah.
Zacharya

Zachariah (Hebrew) God remembered.
*Zacharyah, Zackeria, Zackoriah, Zaquero,
Zeggery, Zhachory*

Zacharias (German) a form of
Zachariah.
*Zacharais, Zachariaus, Zacharius, Zackarias,
Zakarias, Zakarius, Zecharias, Zekarias*

Zachary (Hebrew) a familiar form of
Zachariah. History: Zachary Taylor was
the twelfth U.S. president. See also
Sachar, Sakeri.
*Xachary, Zacchary, Zacha, Zachaery,
Zacharay, Zacharry, Zachaury, Zechary*

Zacheriah (Hebrew) a form of
Zachariah.
Zacheria, Zacherias, Zacherius, Zackeriah

Zachery (Hebrew) a form of Zachary.
*Zacchery, Zacheray, Zacherey, Zacherie,
Zechery*

Zachory (Hebrew) a form of Zachary.
Zachuery, Zachury

Zachrey, Zachry (Hebrew) forms of
Zachary.
*Zachre, Zachri, Zackree, Zackrey, Zackry,
Zakree, Zakri, Zakris, Zakry*

Zack (Hebrew) a short form of
Zachariah, Zachary.

Zackariah (Hebrew) a form of
Zachariah.

Zackary (Hebrew) a form of Zachary.
*Zackari, Zackare, Zackaree, Zackarie,
Zackhary, Zackie*

Zackery (Hebrew) a form of Zachary.
*Zackere, Zackeree, Zackerey, Zackeri,
Zackerie, Zackerry*

Zackory (Hebrew) a form of Zachary.
*Zackorie, Zacorey, Zacori, Zacory, Zacry,
Zakory*

Zadok (Hebrew) a short form of Tzadok.
*Zadak, Zaddik, Zadik, Zadoc, Zadock,
Zaydok*

Zadornin (Basque) Saturn.

Zafir (Arabic) victorious.
Zafar, Zafeer, Zafer, Zaffar

Zahid (Arabic) self-denying, ascetic.
Zaheed, Zahyd

Zahir (Arabic) shining, bright.
*Zahair, Zahar, Zaheer, Zahi, Zahyr, Zair,
Zayyir*

Zahur (Swahili) flower.

Zaid (Arabic) increase, growth.
Zaied, Zaiid, Zayd

Zaide (Hebrew) older.
Zayde

Zaim (Arabic) brigadier general.
Zaym

Zain (English) a form of Zane.
Zaine

Zaire (Arabic) a form of Zahir.
Geography: a country of central Africa.

Zak (Hebrew) a short form of Zachariah,
Zachary.
Zaks

Zakari, Zakary, Zakkary (Hebrew)
forms of Zachary.
Zakarai, Zakare, Zakaree, Zakarie,
Zakariye, Zake, Zakhar, Zakir, Zakkai,
Zakkari, Zakkyre, Zakqary

Zakaria, Zakariya (Hebrew) forms of
Zachariah.
Zakaraiya, Zakareeya, Zakareeyah,
Zakariah, Zakeria, Zakeriah

Zakariyya (Arabic) prophet. Religion: an
Islamic prophet.

Zakery (Hebrew) a form of Zachary.
Zakeri, Zakerie, Zakiry, Zakkery

Zaki (Arabic) bright; pure. (Hausa) lion.
Zakee, Zakie, Zakiy, Zakki, Zaky

Zakia (Swahili) intelligent.
Zakiyya

Zako (Hungarian) a form of Zachariah.
Zacko, Zaco

Zale (Greek) sea strength.
Zail, Zaile, Zayl, Zayle

Zalmai (Afghan) young.

Zalman (Yiddish) a form of Solomon.
Zalmen, Zalmin, Zalmon, Zalmyn,
Zaloman

Zalmir (Hebrew) songbird.
Zalmire, Zalmyr, Zelmir, Zelmire, Zelmyr,
Zelmyre

Zamiel (German) a form of Samuel.
Zamal, Zamuel

Zamir (Hebrew) song; bird.
Zameer, Zamer, Zamyr

Zan (Italian) clown.
Zann, Zanni, Zannie, Zanny, Zhan

Zander (Greek) a short form of
Alexander.
Zandar, Zandor, Zandore, Zandra, Zandrae,
Zandy, Zandyr

Zane (English) a form of John.
Zhane

Zanis (Latvian) a form of Janis.
Zannis, Zanys

Zanthippus (Greek) a form of
Xanthippus.
Zanthyppus

Zanthus (Latin) a form of Xanthus.
Zanthius, Zanthyus

Zanvil (Hebrew) a form of Samuel.
Zanwill

Zaquan (American) a combination of the
prefix Za + Quan.
Zaquain, Zaquon, Zaqwan

Zareb (African) protector.

Zared (Hebrew) ambush.
Zarad, Zarid, Zarod, Zaryd

Zarek (Polish) may God protect the king.
Zarec, Zareck, Zaric, Zarick, Zarik,
Zarrick, Zaryc, Zaryck, Zaryk, Zerek,
Zerick, Zerric, Zerrick

Zavier (Arabic) a form of Xavier.
Zavair, Zaverie, Zavery, Zavierre, Zavior,
Zavyer, Zavyr, Zayvius, Zxavian

Zayit (Hebrew) olive.

Zayne (English) a form of Zane.
Zayan, Zayin, Zayn

Zdenek (Czech) follower of Saint Denis.

Zeb (Hebrew) a short form of Zebediah,
Zebulon.
Zev

Zebadiah (Hebrew) a form of Zebediah.
Zebadia, Zebadya, Zebadyah

Zebedee (Hebrew) a familiar form of
Zebediah.
Zebadee, Zebede

Zebediah (Hebrew) God's gift.
Zebedia, Zebedya, Zebedyah, Zebidiah,
Zebidya, Zebidyah

Zebulon (Hebrew) exalted, honored;
lofty house.
Zabulan, Zebulan, Zebulen, Zebulin,
Zebulun, Zebulyn, Zevulon, Zevulun,
Zhebule

Zecharia, Zechariah (Hebrew) forms of
Zachariah.

Zecharia, Zechariah *(cont.)*
Zecharian, Zecheriah, Zechuriah, Zekariah, Zekarias, Zecharya, Zekeria, Zekeriah, Zekerya

Zed (Hebrew) a short form of Zedekiah.

Zedekiah (Hebrew) God is mighty and just.
Zedechiah, Zedekia, Zedekias, Zedekya, Zedekyah, Zedikiah

Zedidiah (Hebrew) a form of Zebediah.

Zeeman (Dutch) seaman.
Zeaman, Zeman, Zemen, Ziman, Zimen, Zyman, Zymen, Zymin, Zymyn

Zeév (Hebrew) wolf.
Zeévi, Zeff, Zif

Zeheb (Turkish) gold.

Zeke (Hebrew) a short form of Ezekiel, Zachariah, Zachary, Zechariah.
Zeak, Zeake, Zek

Zeki (Turkish) clever, intelligent.
Zekee, Zekey, Zekie, Zeky

Zelgai (Afghan) heart.

Zelig (Yiddish) a form of Selig.
Zeligman, Zelik, Zelyg

Zelimir (Slavic) wishes for peace.
Zelimyr, Zelymir, Zelymyr

Zemar (Afghan) lion.

Zen (Japanese) religious. Religion: a form of Buddhism.

Zenda (Czech) a form of Eugene.
Zendah

Zeno (Greek) cart; harness. History: a Greek philosopher.
Zenan, Zenas, Zenon, Zenos, Zenus, Zenys, Zino, Zinon

Zephaniah (Hebrew) treasured by God.
Zaph, Zaphania, Zenphan, Zenphen, Zenphone, Zenphyn, Zeph, Zephan

Zephyr (Greek) west wind.
Zeferino, Zeffrey, Zephery, Zephire, Zephram, Zephran, Zephrin, Zephyrus

Zerach (Hebrew) light.
Zerac, Zerack, Zerak

Zero (Arabic) empty, void.

Zeroun (Armenian) wise and respected.

Zeshan (American) a form of Zeshawn.
Zishan

Zeshawn (American) a combination of the prefix Ze + Shawn.
Zeshaun, Zeshon, Zishaan, Zshawn

Zesiro (Luganda) older of twins.

Zethan (Hebrew) shining.
Zethen, Zethin, Zethon, Zethyn

Zeus (Greek) living. Mythology: chief god of the Greek pantheon.
Zous, Zus

Zeusef (Portuguese) a form of Joseph.

Zev (Hebrew) a short form of Zebulon.

Zevi (Hebrew) a form of Tzvi.
Zhvie, Zhvy, Zvi

Zhek (Russian) a short form of Evgeny.
Zhenechka, Zhenka, Zhenya

Zhìxin (Chinese) ambitious.
Zhi, Zhi-yang, Zhìhuán, Zhipeng, Zhìyuan

Zhora (Russian) a form of George.
Zhorik, Zhorka, Zhorz, Zhurka

Zhuàng (Chinese) strong.

Zia (Hebrew) trembling; moving. (Arabic) light.
Ziah, Ziya, Ziyah, Zya, Zyah, Zyya, Zyyah

Zigfrid (Latvian, Russian) a form of Siegfried.
Zegfrido, Ziegfried, Zigfrids, Zygfred, Zygfreid, Zygfrid, Zygfried, Zygfryd

Ziggy (American) a familiar form of Siegfried, Sigmund.
Zigee, Zigey, Ziggee, Ziggey, Ziggi, Ziggie, Zigi, Zigie, Zigy, Zygi

Zigor (Basque) punishment.

Zikomo (Nguni) thank-you.
Zykomo

Zilaba (Luganda) born while sick.
Zilabamuzale

Zimon (Hebrew) a form of Simon.
*Ziman, Zimen, Zimene, Zimin, Zimyn,
Zyman, Zymen, Zymene, Zymin, Zymon,
Zymyn*

Zimra (Hebrew) song of praise.
*Zemora, Zimrat, Zimri, Zimria, Zimriah,
Zimriya*

Zimraan (Arabic) praise.
Zimran, Zymraan, Zymran

Zimri (Hebrew) valuable.
Zimry, Zymri, Zymry

Zinan (Japanese) second son.
Zynan

Zindel (Yiddish) a form of Alexander.
Xindel, Xyndel, Zindil, Zunde, Zyndel

Zion (Hebrew) sign, omen; excellent.
Bible: the name used to refer to Israel
and to the Jewish people.
*Tzion, Xion, Xyon, Zeeon, Zeon, Zione,
Zyon*

Ziskind (Yiddish) sweet child.

Ziv (Hebrew) shining brightly. (Slavic) a
short form of Ziven.
Zyv

Ziven (Slavic) vigorous, lively.
*Zev, Ziv, Zivan, Zivin, Zivka, Zivon,
Zivyn, Zyvan, Zyven, Zyvin, Zyvon,
Zyvyn*

Ziyad (Arabic) increase.
Zayd, Ziyaad

Zlatan (Czech) gold.
Zlatek, Zlatko

Zoe (Greek) life.

Zohar (Hebrew) bright light.
Zohair, Zohare

Zola (German) prince. (Italian) ball of
earth. Literature: Émile Zola was a
nineteenth-century French writer
and critic.
Zolah

Zollie, Zolly (Hebrew) forms of Solly.
Zoilo

Zoltán (Hungarian) life.
*Zolten, Zoltin, Zolton, Zoltun, Zoltyn,
Zsoltan*

Zonar (Latin) sound.
Zonair, Zonayr, Zoner

Zorba (Greek) live each day.

Zorion (Basque) a form of Orion.
*Zoran, Zoren, Zorian, Zoron, Zorrine,
Zorrion*

Zorya (Slavic) star; dawn.
Zoria, Zoriah, Zoryah

Zosime (French) a form of Zosimus.
Zosyme

Zosimus (Greek) full of life.
Zosime, Zosimos, Zosymos, Zosymus

Zotikos (Greek) saintly, holy. Religion: a
saint in the Eastern Orthodox Church.

Zotom (Kiowa) a biter.

Zsigmond (Hungarian) a form of
Sigmund.
*Zigimond, Zigimund, Zigmon, Zigmund,
Zsiga*

Zuberi (Swahili) strong.

Zubin (Hebrew) a short form of
Zebulon.
Zuban, Zubeen, Zuben, Zubon, Zubyn

Zuhayr (Arabic) brilliant, shining.
Zyhair, Zuheer

Zuka (Shona) sixpence.

Zuriel (Hebrew) God is my rock.
Zurial, Zuryal, Zuryel

Zygmunt (Polish) a form of Sigmund.
*Zygismon, Zygismond, Zygismondo,
Zygismun, Zygismund, Zygismundo,
Zygysmon, Zygysmond, Zygysmondo,
Zygysmun, Zygysmund, Zygysmundo*

Also from Meadowbrook Press

✦ *Pregnancy, Childbirth, and the Newborn*
More complete and up-to-date than any other pregnancy guide, this remarkable book is the "bible" for childbirth educators. Now revised with a greatly expanded treatment of pregnancy tests, complications, and infections; an expanded list of drugs and medications (plus advice for uses); and a brand-new chapter on creating a detailed birth plan.

✦ *Eating Expectantly*
Dietitian Bridget Swinney offers a practical and tasty approach to prenatal nutrition, combining nutrition guidelines for each trimester with 200 complete menus, 85 tasty recipes, plus cooking and shopping tips. Cited by *Child* magazine as one of the "10 best parenting books of 1993," *Eating Expectantly* is newly revised with the most current nutrition information.

✦ *365 Baby Care Tips*
If babies came with an owner's manual, *365 Baby Care Tips* would be it. Packed full of the information new parents need to know—from teething, diapers, and breast- and bottle-feeding to discipline, safety, and staying connected as a couple—*365 Baby Care Tips* is the easy, essential guide to caring for a new baby.

✦ *First-Year Baby Care*
This is one of the leading baby-care books to guide you through your baby's first year. It contains complete information on the basics of baby care, including bathing, diapering, medical facts, and feeding your baby. Includes step-by-step illustrated instructions to make finding information easy, newborn screening and immunization schedules, breastfeeding information for working mothers, expanded information on child care options, reference guides to common illnesses, and environmental and safety tips.

✦ *Feed Me! I'm Yours*
Parents love this easy-to-use, economical guide to making baby food at home. More than 200 recipes cover everything a parent needs to know about teething foods, nutritious snacks, and quick, pleasing lunches.

We offer many more titles written to delight, inform, and entertain.
To order books with a credit card or browse our full
selection of titles, visit our web site at:

www.meadowbrookpress.com

or call toll-free to place an order, request a free catalog, or ask a question:

1-800-338-2232

Meadowbrook Press • 5451 Smetana Drive • Minnetonka, MN • 55343

m